European Labour Law

European Labour Law

Fourteenth Edition

Roger Blanpain

This book was originally published as a monograph in the International Encyclopaedia of Laws/Labour Law and Industrial Relations.

General Editor: Roger Blanpain
Associate General Editor: Michele Colucci

Published by:
Kluwer Law International
PO Box 316
2400 AH Alphen aan den Rijn
The Netherlands
Website: www.kluwerlaw.com

Sold and distributed in North, Central and South America by:
Aspen Publishers, Inc.
7201 McKinney Circle
Frederick, MD 21704
United States of America
Email: customer.service@aspenpublishers.com

Sold and distributed in all other countries by:
Turpin Distribution Services Ltd.
Stratton Business Park
Pegasus Drive, Bigglulativeswade
Bedfordshire SG18 8TQ
United Kingdom
Email: kluwerlaw@turpin-distribution.com

DISCLAIMER: The material in this volume is in the nature of general comment only. It is not offered as advice on any particular matter and should not be taken as such. The editor and the contributing authors expressly disclaim all liability to any person with regard to anything done or omitted to be done, and with respect to the consequences of anything done or omitted to be done wholly or partly in reliance upon the whole or any part of the contents of this volume. No reader should act or refrain from acting on the basis of any matter contained in this volume without first obtaining professional advice regarding the particular facts and circumstances at issue. Any and all opinions expressed herein are those of the particular author and are not necessarily those of the editor or publisher of this volume.

Printed on acid-free paper.

ISBN 978-90-411-5178-0

This title is available on www.kluwerlawonline.com

© 2014, Kluwer Law International BV, The Netherlands

All rights reserved. No part of this publication may be reproduced, stored in a retrieval system, or transmitted in any form or by any means, electronic, mechanical, photocopying, recording, or otherwise, without written permission from the publisher.

Permission to use this content must be obtained from the copyright owner. Please apply to: Permissions Department, Wolters Kluwer Legal, 76 Ninth Avenue, 7th Floor, New York, NY 10011-5201, USA. Email: permissions@kluwerlaw.com

Printed and Bound by CPI Group (UK) Ltd, Croydon, CR0 4YY.

The Author

Prof. Dr Roger Blanpain is Professor Emeritus of the Faculty of Law of the Catholic University of Leuven, Belgium. He has been visiting professor at the Universities of Florida, Georgia (USA), Insead (France), Kentucky, Michigan State (USA), Paris (France), and Sophia (Japan).

At present he is a professor at the Faculty of Laws of the University of Tilburg, the Netherlands, where he teaches comparative and international labour law and globalisation. He has been member of the Flemish Royal Academy since 1992.

He has been Dean of the Leuven Faculty of Laws (1984–1988) and is Past President of the International Industrial Relations Association (1986–1989), a member of the Belgian Senate (1987–1989) and Honorary President of the International Society for Labour and Social Security Law. He is *doctor honoris causa* of the University of Szeged, Hungary (1997).

Professor Blanpain is General Editor of the *International Encyclopaedia of Laws* (more than 1,400 collaborators worldwide) and Editor-in-Chief of the *International Encyclopaedia for Labour Law and Industrial Relations*. He is also general editor of the *Bulletin for Comparative Labour Law* and the book *Comparative Labour Law and Industrial Relations* (10th edn. 2010).

The Author

Table of Contents

The Author	3
List of Abbreviations	37
Prologue	39
§1. LABOUR LAW	39
§2. GLOBALISATION	40
§3. SUPER–CAPITALISM	41
I. Global	41
II. Multinational Enterprises	41
A. Labour is a Cost	42
B. Research	42
C. Bonuses	43
D. Politics	43
E. Poor and Unemployed	43
§4. GLOCALISATION	43
§5. POVERTY AND LACK OF SOCIAL PROTECTION	44
I. Worldwide	44
II. The ILO: A Global Jobs Pact	45
III. The European Union	47
A. Youth Guarantee Schemes	49
B. Youth Employment Initiative	49
C. Helping Young People Find Employment across Borders	50
D. Apprenticeships	50
E. Social Partners	50
IV. Other European Union Actions	50
A. Context	53
B. Policy Expectations	54
C. ILO Means of Action	55
V. The Lisbon Strategy	56

Table of Contents

VI. Enlargement	58
VII. EU Population	59
§6. THE ROLE OF THE TRADE UNIONS	62
I. Freedom of Association and the Right to Collective Bargaining	62
A. Labour Relations are Power Relations	62
B. Freedom of Association and the Right to Collective Bargaining	63
II. Degree of Unionization	63
III. International Trade Union Action	65
A. International Trade Unions	65
B. Lack of International Solidarity	66
C. Transnational Company Agreements	66
§7. LABOUR LAW AND INDUSTRIAL RELATIONS AND HUMAN RESOURCES	67
I. National Systems vs. Regional and International Norms	67
§8. WHAT TO DO?	69
I. The European Union	69
II. Trade Unions	69
§9. SOCIAL PROTECTION	69
§10. FUNDAMENTAL SOCIAL RIGHTS	73
§11. A CONSTITUTION FOR EUROPE	78
I. The Convention (2003)	78
II. Implications for the Future Social and Employment Policy of the EU	78
III. Definitions and Objectives of the Union	79
IV. Role of the Social Partners	79
V. Fundamental Rights	79
VI. EU Policies and Functioning	80
VII. Employment and Social Policy Chapters	80
VIII. Vocational Training	81
§12. AGREEMENT BY MEMBER STATES (2004)	82
I. The Commission	82
II. Qualified Majority Voting	82
III. Charter of Fundamental Rights	83
IV. Enhanced Cooperation	83
§13. REFERENDA: REJECTION OF THE CONSTITUTION?	83
I. The Reform Treaty (2007)	83
§14. CONTENT OF THE MONOGRAPH	86

Table of Contents

General Introduction — 91

Chapter 1. The Institutional Framework — 91

§1. THE TREATIES — 91
    I. From a Community to a Union — 91
    II. The Functioning of the European Union — 93
        A. Objectives — 93
        B. Subsidiarity — 94
        C. Scrutiny by National Parliaments — 96
    III. Integration — 96

§2. THE INSTITUTIONS AND THEIR COMPETENCES — 97
    I. The European Parliament — 97
    II. The Council — 98
    III. The Commission — 100
    IV. The Court of Justice — 101

§3. OTHER ORGANS — 102
    I. The Economic and Social Committee — 102
    II. The European Social Fund — 103
        A. Tasks — 104
        B. Scope of Assistance — 104
        C. The Future of the ESF: 2014–2020 — 107
    III. European Centre for the Development of Vocational Training — 109
    IV. European Foundation for the Improvement of Living and Working Conditions — 109
    V. The Standing Committee on Employment — 110
    VI. The Employment Committee — 111
    VII. The European Agency for Safety and Health at Work — 112
    VIII. The Committee of the Regions — 114
    IX. Other Advisory Committees — 114
    X. Sectoral Joint Committees, Informal Groups and Sectoral Dialogue Committees — 114
        A. Creation of the Sectoral Social Dialogue Committees — 116
        B. Composition of the Sectoral Social Dialogue Committees — 117
        C. Operation of the Sectoral Social Dialogue Committees — 117
    XI. The Social Protection Committee — 119
    XII. The European Globalisation Adjustment Fund — 120
        A. Subject Matter and Scope — 120
        B. Intervention Criteria — 121
        C. Eligible Actions — 122
    XIII. The European Institute for Gender Equality — 122
        A. Objectives — 122
        B. Tasks — 123
        C. Composition of the Institute — 124

Table of Contents

XIV. The European Union Agency for Fundamental Rights	124
A. Objective	124
B. Scope	124
C. Tasks	124
D. Cooperation with Civil Society; Fundamental Rights Platform	125
E. Bodies of the Agency	125
XV. The Committee of Experts on Posting of Workers	126
A. Tasks	126
B. Membership – Appointment	127

§4. THE LEGISLATIVE PROCESS — 127
    I. Union Law — 127
    II. Secondary Law — 128
        A. Regulations — 129
        B. Directives — 129
        C. Decisions — 131
        D. Recommendations and Opinions — 131
        E. International Agreements — 131

§5. THE DECISION-MAKING PROCESS — 132
    A. First Reading — 133
    B. Second Reading — 133
    C. Conciliation — 133
    D. Third Reading — 134
    E. Special Provisions — 134

§6. RELATIONS WITH OTHER INTERNATIONAL ORGANISATIONS — 135
    I. General — 135
    II. The International Labour Organisation — 135
        A. EU–ILO Cooperation Striving for More Decent Work in ACP Countries — 145
        B. ILO and EU have a Shared Responsibility — 146
    III. The European Economic Area — 147

Chapter 2. The Social Partners — 148

§1. THE EMPLOYERS' ORGANISATIONS — 148
    I. BUSINESSEUROPE — 148
        A. Mission and Priorities — 151
            1. Mission — 151
            2. Priorities 2012–2013: Growing Out of the Crisis — 152
        B. Employment and Social Affairs — 152
            1. Employment and Flexicurity — 153
            2. Ageing — 153
            3. Social Affairs — 153
            4. Skills — 153
            5. Social Dialogue and Industrial Relations — 153

II. CEEP	153
III. UEAPME	154
A. Objectives	155
B. Strategy	156

§2. THE TRADE UNIONS — 156
    I. Members of the ETUC — 157
    II. Observer Organisations — 162
    III. European Trade Union Institute (ETUI) — 163
    IV. The Athens Manifesto — 163

§3. JOINT STATEMENT BY THE EUROPEAN SOCIAL PARTNERS ON THE EUROPE 2020 STRATEGY — 166

§4. ETUC POSITION ON EUROPE 2020 STRATEGY – AN ASSESSMENT — 171

Chapter 3. Competences of the EU Regarding Labour Law — 174

§1. INTRODUCTORY REMARKS — 174

§2. THE EU — 174
    I. The Hierarchy of Objectives: Non-inflationary Growth — 174
    II. Social Objectives — 176
    III. Fundamental Rights and Competences — 177
        A. Fundamental Rights — 177
            1. Mega-Principles — 177
            2. The European Convention for the Protection of Human Rights and Fundamental Freedoms — 177
            3. Fundamental Social Rights — 177
            4. Discrimination — 178
        B. Competences — 179
            1. The EU — 179
                a. Cooperation between Member States — 179
                b. Legislative Competence — 181
                    (1) Social Matters — 181
                        (a) Qualified majority voting — 182
                            (aa) Procedure — 182
                            (bb) Areas — 182
                        (b) Unanimous voting — 185
                            (aa) Procedure — 185
                            (bb) Areas — 185
                        (c) Excluded areas — 186
                            (aa) Pay — 187
                            (bb) Right of association — 187
                            (cc) Right to strike or to impose lock-outs — 187

Table of Contents

		(2) Approximation of Laws	187
	c.	Employment Policy	188
		(1) A Coordinated Strategy for Employment	188
		(2) The European Social Fund	190
	d.	Equal Pay, Opportunity and Treatment	190
	e.	Vocational Training	190
	f.	Paid Holiday Schemes	192
	g.	Economic and Social Cohesion	192
	h.	Reporting	192

IV. The Role of the Commission — 192
V. Involvement of the Social Partners — 193
   A. Consultation at Union Level — 193
      1. Procedure — 194
      2. Typology of the Results of the European Social Dialogue — 197
         a. Agreements Implemented in Accordance with Article 155(2) TFEU: Minimum Standards — 197
         b. Process-oriented Texts — 200
            (1) Frameworks of Action — 200
            (2) Guidelines and Codes of Conduct — 200
            (3) Policy Orientations — 201
         c. Joint Opinions and Tools: Exchange of Information — 203
            (1) Joint Opinions — 203
            (2) Declarations — 203
            (3) Tools — 204
         d. Procedural Texts — 205
         e. Drafting Checklist for New Generation Social Partner Texts — 205
         f. Sectoral Social Dialogue, 2010 — 206
      3. Social Partners — 207
   B. Implementation of Directives — 214
   C. Social Dialogue (Articles 154–155) — 216
   D. Community-wide Agreements (Article 155) — 216
      1. The Agreement of 31 October 1991 — 216
      2. The Maastricht Deal — 218
         a. Implementation in accordance with National Practice — 219
         b. Implementation by a Council Decision — 219
      3. The Communication of the Commission (1993) — 220
         a. Concluding an Agreement — 220
         b. The Implementation of the Agreements — 221
         c. The Council — 222
      4. The Collective Agreement on Parental Leave of 14 December 1995, revised 2009 — 223
      5. The Agreement on Part-time Work of 6 June 1997 — 224
      6. The Framework Agreement on Fixed-term Work of 18 March 1999 — 224
      7. The Voluntary Agreement on Telework of 16 July 2002 — 225

Table of Contents

	8. Framework Agreement on Work-related Stress of 8 October 2004	227
	9. The Framework Agreement on Harassment and Violence at Work (2007)	227
	a. Statement by Social Partners	228
	b. Aims of Agreement	228
	c. Implementation and Follow-up	229
	10. The Framework Agreement on Inclusive Labour Market (2010)	230
	a. Aims of Agreement	230
	b. Main Obstacles to an Inclusive Labour Market	230
	c. Potential Actions	231
	d. Key Recommendations	231
	11. Framework of Actions on Youth Employment (11 June 2013)	231
	E. The Judgment of the Court of First Instance of 17 June 1998	232
VI.	Evaluation: a Scenario for Social Dumping and a Dual Society	233
	A. Macroeconomic: Inflation and NAIRU	233
	B. Flexibility	234
	C. An Evaluation	235

Chapter 4. European Labour Law: Trailer or Locomotive?   237

§1. THE ECSC   237

§2. THE EC   237
   I. 1957–1974   238
   II. 1974–1989   239
   III. 1990 and Beyond: the Community Charter and the Social Action Programme – the Maastricht Agreement on Social Policy   241
      A. The Community Charter of Basic Social Rights   241
         1. Foundation   241
         2. Objectives   242
         3. Scope   242
         4. Content   243
            a. The Twelve Commandments   243
            b. Implementation   245
      B. The Action Programme   245
      C. The Maastricht Agreement on Social Policy (1991), the Green and the White Papers (1993)   246
   IV. The White Paper on Growth, Competitiveness and Employment (1993)   248
   V. The White Paper on European Social Policy (1994)   250
   VI. 1996 and Beyond: Unemployment   253
      A. The European Council in Essen (1994)   253
      B. The Confidence Pact for Employment (1996)   254
   VII. The Treaty of Amsterdam (1997) – Employment   254

Table of Contents

A. European Jobs Summit, Luxembourg, November 1997		258
1. Commission's Proposals		258
a. A New Culture of Entrepreneurship in the EU		258
b. A New Culture of Employability in the EU		259
c. A New Culture of Adaptability in the EU		260
d. A New Culture of Equal Opportunities in the EU		260
2. Social Partners		261
B. Jobs Summit: Conclusions Luxembourg		261

- VIII. The Treaty of Nice (December 2000): 'Socially not so nice' — 262
  - A. Charter of Fundamental Rights of the European Union (Nice, 7 December 2000), revised 2007 — 263
    - 1. Preamble — 263
    - 2. Content; List of Rights — 264
    - 3. Scope and Level of Protection — 265
      - a. Scope — 265
      - b. Level of Protection — 265
      - c. Prohibition of Abuse of Rights — 265
      - d. An Evaluation; Binding Effect — 266
      - e. Revised Charter 2007 — 266
  - B. Unanimity and Qualified Majority — 268
- IX. Employment Guidelines — 270
  - A. The Employment Guidelines 2003–2004 — 270
    - 1. Employment Guidelines — 270
    - 2. Active and Preventative Measures for Unemployed and Inactive People — 271
    - 3. Job Creation and Entrepreneurship — 271
    - 4. Addressing Change and Promoting Adaptability and Mobility in the Labour Market — 271
    - 5. Development of Human Capital and Lifelong Learning — 272
    - 6. Labour Supply and Active Ageing — 272
    - 7. Gender Equality — 272
    - 8. Integrating and Combating Discrimination against Disadvantaged People — 273
    - 9. Making Work Pay — 273
    - 10. Undeclared Work — 273
    - 11. Regional Employment Disparities — 273
    - 12. Implementation of Guidelines — 274
    - 13. Employment Recommendations — 274
  - B. The Employment Guidelines 2005–2008 — 275
    - 1. New Employment Guidelines for More and Better Jobs — 275
    - 2. The Employment Guidelines (2005–2008) — 276
    - 3. Guidelines for the Employment Policies of the Member States — 276
    - 4. Attract and Retain more People in Employment, Increase Labour Supply and Modernise Social Protection Systems — 278
    - 5. Improve Adaptability of Workers and Enterprises — 280

		6.	Increase Investment in Human Capital through Better Education and Skills	281
	C.	The Employment Guidelines 2008–2010		283
		1.	The Employment Guidelines 2008–2010 (Integrated Guidelines Nos. 17–24)	283
		2.	Attract and Retain More People in Employment, Increase Labour Supply and Modernise Social Protection Systems	285
		3.	Improve Adaptability of Workers and Enterprises	288
		4.	Increase Investment in Human Capital through Better Education and Skills	290
	D.	Overview of Targets and Benchmarks Set in the Framework of the European Employment Strategy		292
	E.	The Employment Guidelines 2010-2014 Lisbon Strategy 2020		292
		1.	Smart Growth	293
		2.	Sustainable Growth	293
		3.	Inclusive Growth	294
		4.	Participation by Women	294
		5.	Competitiveness in the Global Economy	294
		6.	National Reform Programmes	294
		7.	Europe 2020 Integrated Guidelines	295
X.	The Modernisation of Labour Law (2006)			301
	A.	Main issues		301
		1.	Flexicurity	301
		2.	Role of Social Dialogue	301
		3.	Non-standard Employment	301
		4.	Compliance with Employment Rights	302
		5.	Worker	302
		6.	Undeclared Work	302
		7.	Discussion at Employment Council	303
		8.	Reaction of Social Partners	303
	B.	Commentary		304
XI.	Flexicurity: More and Better Jobs through Flexibility and Security (2007): Main Issues			304
	A.	Flexicurity Pathways		306
XII.	Framework Agreement of Actions on Youth Employment (2013)			312
	A.	Challenges		313
	B.	Social Partners' Approach		314

§3. CONVERGENCE OR DIVERGENCE?   316

Part I. Individual Labour Law   323

Chapter 1. The Free Movement of Workers   324

§1. EQUAL TREATMENT   326

Table of Contents

    I. National Law: Eligibility for Employment   326
    II. Collective and Individual Agreements   335
    III. Work   337
    IV. Performance of Work   338
    V. Trade Union Freedom, Workers' Participation,
        Management of Public Bodies   348
    VI. Housing   349
    VII. Workers' Families   349

§2. SCOPE OF APPLICATION   350
    I. Workers   350
        A. In General   350
        B. Sports   354
            1. The *Meca* Case – the *Bosman* Case – the *Lethonen*
                Case – the *Kolpak* Case   354
                a. *Meca* Case   354
                b. *Bosman* Case   356
                    (1) Interpretation of Article 45 TFEU with regard
                          to the Transfer Rules   357
                          (a) Application of Article 45 to Rules Laid
                              Down by Sporting Associations   357
                          (b) Existence of an Obstacle to Freedom
                              of Movement for Workers   358
                          (c) Existence of Justifications   358
                    (2) Interpretation of Article 45 of the Treaty with
                          regard to the Nationality Clauses   359
                          (a) Existence of an Obstacle to Freedom
                              of Movement for Workers   359
                          (b) Existence of Justifications   360
                    (3) The Temporal Effects of this Judgment   360
                c. The *Lehtonen* Case   360
                d. The *Deliège* Case   363
                e. The *Kolpak* Case   365
                f. The *Balog* Case: Transfer and Competition Rules   366
                    (1) Facts   367
                    (2) Organisation of Football and Rules on Transfers   367
                    (3) Facts and Main Proceedings   367
                    (4) The Question Referred for a Preliminary Ruling   368
                    (5) Applicability of Article 101 TFEU   368
                    (6) Undertakings or Associations of Undertakings   369
                    (7) Agreements between Undertakings or Decisions
                        of Associations of Undertakings   369
                    (8) Relevant Market   369
                    (9) Restriction of Competition   370
                    (10) Necessity of the Transfer Regulations   370
                    (11) Appreciable Effect   371

				(12)	Effect on Trade between Member States	371

Table of Contents

			(12) Effect on Trade between Member States	371
			(13) Conclusion	372
		2.	Agreement between the European Commission, FIFA and UEFA (5 March 2001)	372
			a. The Declaration of Nice (December 2000)	372
			b. The Agreement of 5 March 2001, as Amended in 2005, between FIFA and the European Commission	374
			c. Consequences of the New System	375
			d. Incompatible with Fundamental Rights and EU Law	376
			e. Assessment of the New System	377
			f. Proposals	378
			g. Memorandum of Understanding (UEFA-FIFPRO) (2007)	379
		3.	The *Bernard* Case: Training Compensation	381
		4.	Specificity of Sports; the Lisbon Reform Treaty	385
			a. The Meaning of Specificity	385
			b. Specificity as seen by DRC and CAS	386
			(1) The *Mutu* Case	386
			(2) The *Matuzalem* Case	388
		5.	Commission Blows the Whistle over Inflated Football Transfer Fees and Lack of Level Playing Field	389
	C.	Others		391
II.	Exceptions			392
	A.	Employment in the Public Sector		392
	B.	Public Policy, Security and Public Health		394

§3. PROMOTION — 395
- I. Employment Services — 395
- II. Vocational Training — 397
- III. Recognition of Qualifications and Diplomas — 406
- IV. Blue Card: Admission and Mobility of Third Country Nationals of Highly Qualified Employment — 414
  - A. General Provisions — 415
    1. Subject Matter — 415
    2. Definitions — 416
    3. Scope — 416
  - B. Conditions of Admission — 417
    1. Criteria for Admission — 417
    2. Volumes of Admission — 418
  - C. EU Blue Card, Procedure and Transparency — 418
  - D. Rights — 418
    1. Labour Market Access — 418
    2. Equal Treatment — 418
    3. Transposition — 419
- V. Single Application Procedure for a Single Permit for Third-Country Nationals — 419

Table of Contents

A. General Provisions	419
1. Subject Matter	419
2. Definitions	420
3. Scope	420
B. Single Application Procedure and Single Permit	421
1. Single Application Procedure	421
2. Competent Authority	422
3. Single Permit	423
4. Residence Permits Issued for Purposes Other than Work	423
5. Procedural Guarantees	423
6. Access to Information	424
7. Fees	424
8. Rights on the Basis of the Single Permit	424
C. Right to Equal Treatment	424
D. Final Provisions	426
1. More Favourable Provisions	426
2. Information to the General Public	427
3. Reporting	427
4. Transposition	427
5. Entry into Force	427

§4. MINIMUM STANDARDS ON SANCTIONS AND MEASURES AGAINST EMPLOYERS OF ILLEGALLY STAYING THIRD-COUNTRY NATIONALS — 428

I. Subject Matter and Scope	428
II. Definitions	428
III. Prohibition of Illegal Employment	429
IV. Obligations on Employers	429
V. Financial Sanctions	430
VI. Back Payments to be Made by Employers	430
VII. Other Measures	431
VIII. Subcontracting	431
IX. Criminal Offence	432
X. Criminal Penalties	432
XI. Liability of Legal Persons	432
XII. Penalties for Legal Persons	433
XIII. Facilitation of Complaints	433
XIV. Inspections	433
XV. More Favourable Provisions	434
XVI. Transposition	434

Chapter 2. Freedom of Services — 435

§1. SCOPE OF APPLICATION — 435

I. Service	435
A. Material	435
B. Personal	436
II. For Remuneration	436

Table of Contents

  III. Temporary   436
  IV. Trans Border   437

§2. Prohibition of Restrictions and of Discrimination   437
  I. Restrictions   437
  II. Discrimination   438

§3. Justified Restrictions and Unequal Treatment   439
  I. Public Authority, Public Policy, Public Security or Public Health   439
   A. Public Authority   439
   B. Public Policy, Public Security or Public Health   439
  II. Restrictions on the Grounds of the Rule of Reason   440

§4. Protection of Workers   441
  I. Application of National Legislation and Collective Agreements: *Rush Portuguesa Lda*   441
   A. Facts   441
   B. The Court of Justice   442
    1. Equal Treatment   442
    2. Free Movement of Workers: No Work Permit   442
    3. Freedom of Services: Return to their Country of Origin   442
  II. Fine Tuning of the General Rule   443
   A. The *Vander Elst* Case   443
    1. Facts   443
    2. The Court   444
   B. The *Arblade* Case   447
    1. Facts   447
    2. Legislation and Collective Agreements of the Work Land   447
    3. The Court   450
   C. The *André Mazzoleni* Case   451
    1. Facts   451
    2. Minimum Remuneration   452
    3. General Principles   452
   D. *Finalarte Sociedade de Construção Civil Lda*   454
    1. Holiday Entitlement for Construction Workers in Germany   454
    2. The Main Proceedings and the Questions   456
    3. The Answers of the Court   457
   E. The *Portugaia Construções Lda* Case   462
    1. Facts   462
    2. The Answer of the Court   463
   F. *Commission v. Federal Republic of Germany*   465
   G. The *European Commission v. Federal Republic of Germany*   469
   H. The *European Commssion v. Spain*   471
   I. The *European Commission v. Austria*   471

Table of Contents

	J. *The Viking* and the *Laval* Cases: Freedom of Establishment and Services and Industrial Action	472
	1. The *Viking* Case	472
	2. The *Laval* Case	475
	3. Laval and *Viking*: Who Pays the Price?	481
	a. Fundamental Rights	481
	b. Social Justice	481
	c. A Compromise	482
	d. The Rule of Law: Limit on the Right to Strike	483
	e. *Viking*	484
	f. Jobs and Solidarity	484
	K. The *Rueffert* Case	484
	L. *Commission* v. *Germany*: Documents: Temporary Agencies	485
	M. *Palhota* Case: No Prior Declaration to Posting (Belgium)	486

§5. BOLKESTEIN: THE DRAFT DIRECTIVE ON SERVICES — 492

§6. THE DIRECTIVE ON SERVICES IN THE INTERNAL MARKET (2006) — 498
   I. Terms of the Directive — 498
   II. Reaction from European Social Partners — 499

Chapter 3. International Private Labour Law — 500

§1. THE COMPETENT JUDGE — 500
   I. Regulation 44/2001 (2000) — 500
   II. Regulation (EU) No. 1215/2012 (2012) — 505

§2. THE LAW APPLICABLE TO CONTRACTUAL OBLIGATIONS — 506
   I. Convention on Contractual Obligations (1980) — 507
   II. Regulation No. 593/2008 of 17 June 2008 on the Law Applicable to Contractual Obligations (Rome I) — 509
      A. Scope — 509
      B. Freedom of Choice — 509
      C. Individual Employment Contracts — 509
      D. Overriding Mandatory Provisions — 510
      E. Public Policy of the Forum — 510

§3. THE LAW APPLICABLE TO NON-CONTRACTUAL OBLIGATIONS: INDUSTRIAL ACTION — 511

§4. POSTING OF WORKERS: DIRECTIVE 96/71 OF 16 DECEMBER 1996 — 511
   I. Legal Base — 512
   II. Scope of Application — 512
   III. Terms and Conditions of Employment — 513
      A. Minimum Conditions — 513

Table of Contents

		B.	Other Conditions	515
		C.	Exceptions	517
	IV.	Cooperation and Transparency (Article 4)		517
	V.	Enforcement (Article 5)		518
		A.	Guarantee	518
		B.	Translation and Notification	522
		C.	EU Posting of Workers Certificate and Visa and Notification Procedure	523
			1. Prevention of Abusive Practices	523
			2. Compliance with Pay and Working Conditions	524
			3. Regular Workers	524
			4. Refusal of Residence Permits	524
		D.	Designate an ad hoc Agent	524
	VI.	Jurisdiction (Article 6)		525
	VII.	Implementation (Article 7) – Review (Article 8)		526
	VIII.	Commission Guidance on the Posting of Workers in the Framework of the Provision of Services		526
		A.	Guidance: Control Measures	526
			1. General Application Measures	526
			a. The Requirement to have a Representative Established on the Territory of the Host Member State	526
			b. The Requirement to Obtain Authorisation from the Competent Authorities of the Host Member State or to be Registered with Them, or any Other Equivalent Obligation	527
			c. Requirement to Make a Declaration	528
			d. The Requirement to Keep and Maintain Social Documents on the Territory of the Host Country and/or under the Conditions which Apply in its Territory	529
			2. Measures which Apply to Posted Workers who are Nationals of Third Countries	530
		B.	Cooperation on Information	531
			1. Access to Information	531
			2. Cooperation between Member States	532
		C.	Monitoring of Compliance with the Directive and Measures in the Event of Failure to Comply	532
		D.	Conclusions	534

Chapter 4. Individual Employment Contracts 537

§1. TEMPORARY WORK – PART-TIME – FIXED-TERM CONTRACTS – TELEWORK 537
    I. Directive: Health and Safety 537
        A. Scope 538
        B. Object: Equal Treatment 538
        C. Provision of Information to Workers 539

Table of Contents

	D.	Workers' Training	539
	E.	Use of Workers' Services and Medical Surveillance of Workers	539
	F.	Protection and Prevention Services	539
	G.	Temporary Employment: Responsibility	540
	H.	Reporting	540
II.	Part-time Work: the Collective Agreement of 6 June 1997		540
	A.	Developments	540
	B.	Purpose	541
	C.	Scope	541
	D.	Definitions	541
	E.	Principle of Non-discrimination	542
		1. *Wippel* Case	542
		2. *Bruno* Case	544
		a. Facts	544
		b. Questions	545
		c. Substance	545
		d. The Substantive Scope of the Framework Agreement	546
		e. The Temporal Scope of the Framework Agreement	550
		f. Question 1: Vertical-cyclical Part-time Working Arrangements	550
		g. Question 2: Significant Disincentive	553
		h. Question 3: Discrimination between Different Forms of Part-time Work	554
	F.	Opportunities for Part-time Work	555
	G.	Provisions on Implementation	557
III.	The Agreement on Fixed-term Contracts of 18 March 1999		558
	A.	Purpose of the Framework Agreement	559
	B.	Scope	559
	C.	Definitions	561
	D.	Principle of Non-discrimination	562
	E.	Measures to Prevent Abuse	566
	F.	Information and Employment Opportunities	574
	G.	Information and Consultation	574
	H.	Provisions on Implementation	575
IV.	Temporary Agency Work		576
	A.	General Provisions	576
		1. Aim	576
		2. Scope	576
		3. Definitions	577
		4. Review of Restrictions or Prohibitions	577
	B.	Employment and Working Conditions (Article 5)	578
		1. The Principle of Equal Treatment	578
		2. Access to Employment, Collective Facilities and Vocational Training (Article 6)	579
		a. Vacant Posts	579

Table of Contents

b. Freedom of Labour	579
c. Free of Charge	579
d. Access to the Amenities or Collective Facilities	580
3. Representation of Temporary Agency Workers	580
4. Information of Workers' Representatives	580
C. Implementation	580
V. Framework Agreement on Telework	581
A. General Considerations	581
B. Definition and Scope	582
C. Voluntary Character	582
D. Employment Conditions	583
E. Data Protection	583
F. Privacy	583
G. Equipment	583
H. Health and Safety	584
I. Organisation of Work	584
J. Training	585
K. Collective Rights Issues	585
L. Implementation and Follow-up	585
§2. CONDITIONS APPLICABLE TO THE CONTRACT OF EMPLOYMENT: INFORMATION	586
I. Scope	587
II. Obligation to Provide Information	587
A. In General	587
B. Expatriate Employees	589
C. Modifications	590
D. Term and Form of Information	590
III. Defence of Rights	590
IV. Implementation	591
§3. RECRUITMENT AND PLACEMENT: MONOPOLY OF THE PUBLIC EMPLOYMENT OFFICE?	591

Chapter 5. Child Care and the Protection of Young People at Work   596

§1. CHILD CARE	596
§2. PROTECTION OF YOUNG PEOPLE AT WORK (DIRECTIVE 94/33 EC OF 22 JUNE 1994)	597
I. Introductory Remarks	597
II. Purpose and Scope	598
A. Purpose	598
B. Scope	599
III. Definitions	599

Table of Contents

IV. Prohibition of Work by Children	600
V. Cultural or Similar Activities	600
VI. General Obligations on Employers	600
VII. Vulnerability of Young People – Prohibition of Work	601
VIII. Working Time	602
IX. Night Work	603
X. Rest Period	603
XI. Measures; Non-reducing Clause; Final Provisions	604

Chapter 6. Equal Treatment 605

§1. A GENERAL FRAMEWORK FOR EQUAL TREATMENT IN EMPLOYMENT AND OCCUPATION 607
    I. General Provisions 607
        A. Purpose 607
        B. Definitions and Concepts 609
        C. Scope 611
        D. Occupational Requirements 613
        E. Reasonable Accommodation for Disabled Persons 618
        F. Justification of Differences of Treatment on Grounds of Age 622
        G. Positive Action 638
        H. Minimum Requirements 638
    II. Remedies and Enforcement 639
        A. Defence of Rights 639
        B. Burden of Proof 640
        C. Victimisation 644
        D. Dissemination of Information 644
        E. Social Dialogue 644
        F. Dialogue with Non-governmental Organisations 644
    III. Final Provisions 645
        A. Compliance 645
        B. Sanctions 645
        C. Implementation 645
        D. Report 645

§2. EQUAL TREATMENT BETWEEN PERSONS IRRESPECTIVE OF RACIAL OR ETHNIC ORIGIN 646
    I. General Provisions 646
        A. Purpose 646
        B. Definitions and Concepts of Discrimination 646
        C. Scope 647
        D. Genuine and Determining Occupational Requirements 648
        E. Positive Action 648
        F. Minimum Requirements 648
    II. Remedies and Enforcement 648
        A. Defence of Rights 648

Table of Contents

    B. Burden of Proof and Victimisation and Dissemination of Information and Social Dialogue and Dialogue with Non-governmental Organisations   649
  III. Bodies for the Promotion of Equal Treatment   649
  IV. Final Provisions: Compliance and Sanctions and Implementation and Report   650

§3. EQUAL PAY FOR MEN AND WOMEN   650
  I. In General   650
  II. Man and Woman; Sexual Orientation   651

§4. DEFINITION   656
  I. Equality of Opportunity or of Outcome   657
  II. Direct and Indirect Discrimination   658
  III. Exceptions   668
    A. Nature of the Activity   668
    B. Protection of Women – Parental Leave   670
    C. Positive Discrimination   672

§5. OBJECT   675
  I. Equal Pay for Equal Work or Work of Equal Value   675
    A. Equal Work or Work of Equal Value   675
    B. Equal Pay   679
  II. Access to Employment, Promotion, Vocational Training   694
  III. Employment and Working Conditions   704
  IV. Social Security, Pensions   721
  V. Freedom of Association   721
  VI. Follow-up of the 1976 Directive; Promotion and Social Dialogue   722
    A. Enforcement   722
    B. Protection of Employees, including Representatives   723
    C. Promotion   723
    D. Social Dialogue   723
    E. Sanctions   724

§6. PROOF   724
  I. Aim   724
  II. Definitions   724
  III. Scope   725
  IV. Burden of Proof   725
  V. Information   727
  VI. Non-regression   727
  VII. Implementation   727

§7. DIRECT EFFECT   727

§8. AGE DIVERSITY GUIDELINES AGREED IN COMMERCE SECTOR   728

Table of Contents

§9. FRAMEWORK AGREEMENT OF ACTIONS ON GENDER EQUALITY	728
I. Addressing Gender Roles	729
II. Promoting Women in Decision-making	730
III. Supporting Work–Life Balance	730
IV. Tackling the Gender Pay Gap	730
V. Annexed Case Studies	731
VI. Actions and Follow-up	731
§10. DIRECTIVE 2006/54/EC ON THE IMPLEMENTATION OF THE PRINCIPLE OF EQUAL OPPORTUNITIES AND EQUAL TREATMENT OF MEN AND WOMEN	732
I. Purpose and Definitions	732
A. Purpose	732
B. Definitions	732
II. Equal Pay: Prohibition of Discrimination	733
III. Equal Treatment as Regards Access to Employment, Vocational Training and Promotion and Working Conditions	733
A. Prohibition of Discrimination	733
B. Return from Maternity Leave	734
C. Paternity and Adoption Leave	734
IV. Remedies and Enforcement	734
A. Defence of Rights	734
B. Compensation or Reparation	735
C. Burden of Proof	735
V. Promotion of Equal Treatment – Dialogue	735
A. Equality Bodies	735
B. Social Dialogue	736
C. Dialogue with Non-governmental Organisations	736
VI. Compliance	737
VII. Victimisation	737
VIII. Penalties	737
Chapter 7. Protection of Motherhood	738
Chapter 8. Working Time, Sunday Rest, Night Work and Parental Leave	749
§1. WORKING TIME	749
I. In General	749
II. Directive 2003/88/EC of 4 November 2003	750
A. Scope and Definitions	751
1. Purpose and Scope	751
2. Definitions	752
B. Minimum Rest Periods, Other Aspects of the Organisation of Working Time	758
1. Daily Rest	758

Table of Contents

		2. Breaks	758
		3. Weekly Rest Period	759
		4. Maximum Weekly Working Time	759
		5. Annual Leave	759
	C.	Night Work/Shift Work, Pattern of Work	767
		1. Length of Night Work	767
		2. Health Assessment and Transfer of Night Workers to Day Work	767
		3. Guarantees for Night-Time Working	768
		4. Notification of Regular Use of Night Workers	768
		5. Safety and Health Protection	768
		6. Pattern of Work	768
	D.	Miscellaneous Provisions	768
		1. More Specific Community Provisions	768
		2. More Favourable Provisions	769
		3. Reference Periods	769
	E.	Derogations and Exceptions	769
		1. Derogations	769
		2. Derogations by Collective Agreements	772
		3. Limitations to Derogations from Reference Periods	772
		4. Mobile Workers and Offshore Work	773
		5. Workers on Board Seagoing Fishing Vessels	773
		6. Miscellaneous Provisions	774
	F.	Final Provisions	775
		1. Level of Protection	775
		2. Reports	775
		3. Review of the Operation of Provisions with Regard to Workers on Board Seagoing Fishing Vessels	776
		4. Review of the Operation of Provisions with Regard to Workers Concerned with the Carriage of Passengers	776
		5. Entry into Force	776
III.	Working Time for Seafarers		776
	A. Scope		777
	B. Definitions		777
	C. Hours of Work		777
	D. Table		778
	E. Seafarers under 18 years		779
	F. Distress at Sea		779
	G. Records		779
	H. Manning Levels		779
	I. Persons under 16 Years		780
	J. Necessary Resources		780
	K. Health Certificate		780
	L. Watchkeepers and Night Work		782
	M. Safety and Health		782
	N. Annual Leave		782

Table of Contents

IV.	Working Time of Mobile Workers in Civil Aviation	782
	A. Scope	782
	B. Definitions	782
	C. Paid Annual Leave	783
	D. Health Assessment	783
	E. Safety and Health	783
	F. Working Time	784
	G. Days Free	784
	H. Review	784
	I. Implementation	785
V.	Working Time of Mobile Road Transport Workers	785
	A. Purpose	786
	B. Scope	786
	C. Definitions	786
	D. Maximum Weekly Working Time	788
	E. Breaks	788
	F. Rest Periods	789
	G. Night Work	789
	H. Derogations	789
	I. Information and Records	789
	J. Final Provisions	790
VI.	Certain Aspects of the Working Conditions of Mobile Workers Engaged in Interoperable Cross-border Services in the Railway Sector	790
	A. Scope	790
	B. Definitions	790
	C. Daily Rest at Home	791
	D. Daily Rest Away from Home	791
	E. Breaks	791
	1. Drivers	791
	2. Other On-board Staff	792
	F. Weekly Rest Period	792
	G. Driving Time	792
	H. Checks	792
	I. Non-regression Clause	792
	J. Follow-up to the Agreement	793
	K. Evaluation	793
	L. Review	793

§2.	SUNDAY REST	793
§3.	NIGHT WORK AND EQUAL TREATMENT	794
§4.	PARENTAL LEAVE	796
	I. Purpose and Scope	798
	A. Purpose	798
	B. Scope	798

Table of Contents

II. Parental Leave	798
III. Modalities of Application	799
IV. Adoption	800
V. Employment Rights and Non-discrimination	800
VI. Return to Work	801
VII. Time off from Work on Grounds of *Force Majeure*	802
VIII. Final Provisions	802

Chapter 9. Safety and Health — 804

§1. FIRST MEASURES — 804
    I. Euratom — 804
    II. EC: Transport — 804
    III. Other Actions — 805

§2. 1987: THE SINGLE EUROPEAN ACT AND ARTICLE 153 TFEU — 805
    I. Health and Safety in the Working Environment — 808
    II. Application — 810
        A. The Framework Directive of 12 June 1989 — 810
            1. Scope and Definitions — 810
            2. Employer's Obligations — 811
            3. Information, Consultation and Participation of Workers — 812
            4. Miscellaneous — 812
        B. The Individual Directives — 813

§3. FRAMEWORK AGREEMENT ON WORK-RELATED STRESS, 8 OCTOBER 2004 — 813
    I. Aim — 813
    II. Description of Work-related Stress — 813
    III. Identifying Problems of Work-related Stress — 814
    IV. Responsibilities of Employers and Workers — 814
    V. Preventing, Eliminating or Reducing Work-related Stress — 814
    VI. Implementation and Follow-up — 815

§4. FRAMEWORK AGREEMENT ON HARASSMENT AND VIOLENCE AT WORK (2007) — 817
    I. Aims — 818
    II. Content — 818
    III. Guidelines for Prevention of Third Party Violence and Harassment at Work (2010) — 819

§5. FRAMEWORK AGREEMENT ON PREVENTION FROM SHARP INJURIES IN THE HOSPITAL AND HEALTHCARE SECTOR (17 JULY 2009) — 820
    I. Purpose — 821
    II. Scope — 821
    III. Definitions — 821
    IV. Principles — 822

Table of Contents

    V. Risk Assessment — 823
    VI. Elimination, Prevention and Protection — 823
    VII. Information and Awareness-raising — 824
    VIII. Training — 824
    IX. Reporting — 825
    X. Response and Follow-up — 825
    XI. Implementation — 826

Chapter 10. Restructuring of Enterprises — 827

§1. COLLECTIVE REDUNDANCIES — 827
    I. Definitions and Scope — 828
    II. Information and Consultation of Workers' Representatives — 835
    III. The Role of the Government — 837

§2. TRANSFER OF UNDERTAKINGS, MERGERS AND DIVISIONS OF PUBLIC LIMITED LIABILITY COMPANIES — 843
    I. Transfer of Undertakings — 843
        A. Definitions and Scope — 843
        B. Acquired Rights — 870
            1. Individual Rights — 870
            2. Collective Agreements — 876
            3. Social Security — 877
            4. Protection against Dismissal — 880
            5. Workers' Representation — 883
        C. Information and Consultation — 884
    II. Mergers and Divisions of Public Limited Liability Companies — 885

§3. INSOLVENCY OF THE EMPLOYER — 886
    I. Definitions and Scope — 890
    II. Guaranteed Pay — 892
    III. Provisions Concerning Transnational Situations — 896
    IV. Social Security — 897
    V. Options for Member States — 898

Part II. Collective Labour Law — 901

Chapter 1. Collective Bargaining — 903

§1. THE SOCIAL DIALOGUE — 903

§2. EUROPEAN COLLECTIVE AGREEMENTS — 904
    I. Introductory Remarks — 904
        A. Broad and Narrow — 904

	B.	A Multifaceted Role	905
	C.	Agreement with a Double Content	905
		1. The Normative Part	905
		2. The Obligatory Part	906
	D.	Free Collective Bargaining: Pluralist Democracy	906
	E.	Subsidiarity	906
	F.	Abstention from an International (Legal) Framework	907
	G.	Specific Legislation	907
II.	Parties to the Agreement		908
	A.	The European Company Agreement	908
	B.	The European Industry Agreement	909
	C.	The European Multi-industry Agreement	909
	D.	The European Multi-regional Agreement	910
III.	The Competence to Conclude Collective Agreements		910
IV.	Articles 154 and 155 TFEU; Specific Legal Problems		910
	A.	Implementation in Accordance with National Practice	910
		1. Contracting Parties	910
		2. Content of the Agreement	911
		3. Form and Language	911
		4. Scope	911
		5. Binding Effect	912
		6. Interpretation	913
		7. Duration	913
	B.	Implementation by Council Decision	914
		1. Which Agreements?	914
		2. Content	914
		3. Scope	915
		4. Binding Effect	915
		5. Interpretation	915
		6. Master or Slave	916
		7. Collective Bargaining and Competition	916

Chapter 2. Workers' Participation — 918

§1. INFORMATION AND CONSULTATION — 918

§2. THE SOCIETAS EUROPAEA (SE) — 920
   I. More than 30 Years of Discussion — 920
   II. Models of Participation — 921
      A. Option 1: Maintain the Status quo — 923
      B. Option 2: Global Approach — 923
      C. Option 3: Immediate Action on the Proposals concerning the Statute for a European Company, a European Association, a European Co-operative society and a European Mutual Society — 924
   III. Board-level Participation Agreed at Aventis — 926
   IV. Nice Summit (7–10 December 2000): the Break-through — 926

Table of Contents

V. The Directive of 8 October 2001	927
A. Definitions	927
B. Formation of an SE	928
C. Structure of the SE	929
1. The Two-tier System	929
2. The One-tier System	929
D. Workers' Involvement	929
1. The Negotiating Procedure	930
a. Creation of an SNB	930
(1) Composition	930
(2) Arrangements for Involvement	931
(3) Rules for Decision-making	931
(4) Experts	931
(5) Opt-out	932
(6) Expenses	932
b. Content of the Agreement	932
c. Duration of Negotiations	933
d. Spirit of Cooperation	933
e. Legislation Applicable to the Negotiation Procedure	933
2. Standard Rules	933
a. Composition of the Body of Representatives of the Employees	934
b. Standard Rules for Information and Consultation	934
c. Standard Rules for Participation	936
d. The Application of Standard Rules	936
3. Miscellaneous Provisions	937
a. Reservation and Confidentiality	937
b. Operation of the RB and Procedure for the Information and Consultation of Employees	938
c. Protection of Employees' Representatives	938
d. Misuse of Procedures	939
e. Compliance with this Directive	939
f. Link between this Directive and other Provisions	939
(1) Some Preliminary Observations	940
(2) Geographical Distribution of European Companies	941
§3. INFORMATION AND CONSULTATION: THE DIRECTIVE ON EUROPEAN WORKS COUNCILS OR PROCEDURES	941
I. Introduction	941
II. General Remarks	943
A. Involvement of Employees	943
1. During the 1970s	944
2. During the 1980s	944
3. In the 1990s	946
a. 1994: Information and Consultation in Community-scale Undertakings	946
b. 1997: the Treaty of Amsterdam	947

Table of Contents

	4.	The Years 2000–2013	947
		a. Charter of Fundamental Rights of the European Union (2007)	947
		b. The Six Sisters	948
B.	The Directive of 6 May 2009		948
	1.	Review of the 1994 Directive	948
	2.	The 2000 Report of the Commission	948
	3.	The European Parliament and the Economic and Social Committee (2001–2007)	949
	4.	The European Social Partners	950
		a. The European Trade Union Confederation (ETUC) (1999)	950
		b. Union of Industrial and Employers' Confederations of Europe (UNICE)	951
		c. 'Lessons Learned'	952
		d. No Negotiations	954
	5.	The Commission Takes the Legal Initiative (2008)	955
		a. Status Questions	955
		(1) Insufficient Number of EWCs: Overview	955
		(2) Challenges and Objectives	957
		b. The Proposal for a Recast Directive of 2 July 2008 by the European Commission	958
		c. Advice of the European Social Partners	960
		d. The European Parliament	962
		(1) The Committee on Employment and Social Affairs	962
		(2) Plenary Session	964
C.	Summing up		965
	1.	Changes	965
	2.	Decision-making	965
	3.	Genesis	966
	4.	In Force?	966
III. Objective and Scope			966
A.	Objective		966
B.	Scope		967
	1.	Territorial	967
		a. The 28 EU Member States	967
		b. The European Economic Area (28 + 3)	967
		c. Companies with Headquarters outside the EEA	967
	2.	Personal: Which Companies?	968
		a. Numbers	968
		(1) Community-scale Undertaking	968
		(2) Group of Undertakings	969
		(a) Definition of 'controlling undertaking'	969
		(b) Community-scale group of undertakings	971
		b. Central Management	971
		c. Merchant Navy Crews	971

Table of Contents

IV. Definitions and Notions	972
A. Information and Consultation	972
1. Information	972
a. Notion	972
(1) Globalisation and Restructuring	972
(2) Effectiveness	972
(3) Definition	973
b. Scope: Transnational	973
2. Consultation	974
a. Notion	974
b. Scope: Transnational	975
B. Representation of Employees	975
V. Establishment of an EWC or a Procedure	975
A. The Obligation to Negotiate in a Spirit of Cooperation	977
B. Responsibility and Initiation of Negotiations	978
1. Responsibility of Central Management	978
2. Initiation of the Negotiation	978
3. One or More EWCs: Procedures	979
C. The Negotiation of the Agreement	979
1. Parties to the Agreement and the SNB	979
a. Composition of the SNB	980
b. Legal Personality of the SNB	981
c. Task of the Negotiating Parties	981
2. Experts and Costs	982
3. Role of the Trade Unions and of the Employers' Associations	983
D. Nature, Binding Effect, Form, Language and Interpretation of the Agreement	983
1. Nature and Binding Effect of the Agreement	983
2. Form and Language of the Agreement	984
3. Interpretation of the Agreement	985
E. Content of the Agreement	985
1. Scope	986
2. The Setting-up of an EWC	986
3. The Setting-up of a Procedure	989
VI. Prejudicial and Confidential Information: Ideological Guidance	990
VII. Role and Protection of Employees' Representatives	991
A. Role of Employees' Representatives	991
1. Representation of the Interest of the Employees	991
2. Information of National Representatives or Workforce	991
3. Training	991
B. Protection of Employees' Representatives	992
VIII. Compliance with the Directive – Links – Adaptation	993
A. Compliance with the Directive	993
B. Links	993
C. Adaptation	994

Table of Contents

IX. Subsidiary Requirements: a Mandatory EWC	995
A. Composition of the EWC	996
B. Competence	996
1. General Information (Annual)	997
2. *Ad Hoc* Information	997
C. Procedure	997
D. Role of Experts – Trade Unions – Employers' Associations	998
E. Expenses	998
F. Enforcement of the Subsidiary Requirements	998
G. Future Developments	999
X. Agreements in Force	999
A. Pre-existing Agreements	999
1. Timing, Form, Language and Format of the Agreement: Applicable Law	1000
a. Timing, Form and Language	1000
b. Nature, Binding Effect and Applicable Law	1000
2. Scope and Parties to the Agreement	1000
a. Scope	1000
b. Parties	1001
3. Content of the Agreement	1001
a. An EWC, a Procedure or Another Mechanism	1001
b. Competence: Information and Consultation	1002
c. Functioning	1002
d. Role of Experts	1002
e. Expenses	1003
4. Prejudicial and Confidential Information	1003
5. Status of the Employees' Representatives	1003
6. Duration of the Agreement	1004
B. Article 6 Agreements	1004
XI. Report of the Directive by the Commission	1004
XII. Transposition, Repeal, Entry into Force	1005
A. Transposition	1005
B. Repeal	1005
C. Entry into Force	1006
§4. A GENERAL FRAMEWORK FOR INFORMING AND CONSULTING RIGHTS OF EMPLOYEES IN THE EUROPEAN COMMUNITY	1006
I. Genesis of the Directive	1006
II. Object and Principles	1008
III. Definitions	1009
IV. Scope	1009
V. Practical Arrangements for Information and Consultation	1010
VI. Information and Consultation Deriving from an Agreement	1011
VII. Confidential Information	1011
VIII. Protection of Employees' Representatives	1012
IX. Protection of Rights	1012

Table of Contents

X. Link between this Directive and Other Community and National Provisions	1012
XI. Transitional Provisions	1013
XII. Transposition	1013
XIII. Review by the Commission	1013
XIV. Entry into Force	1013
XV. Some Concluding Remarks	1013
A. Renewed Interest	1013
B. Employee Involvement	1014
C. Influence on Decision-making?	1014
D. Employability	1015
E. The Three Sisters	1015
F. Coherence	1015
G. Spirit of Cooperation	1017
H. When?	1017
I. Summarising	1018
§5. THE EUROPEAN COOPERATIVE SOCIETY	1018
I. In General	1018
A. Background and Purpose	1018
B. Form of the SCE	1019
C. Formation of the SCE	1019
D. Structure of the SCE	1020
II. The Involvement of Employees	1021
A. In General	1021
B. Negotiating Procedure Applicable to SCEs Established by at Least Two Legal Entities or by Transformation	1021
1. The Special Negotiating Body	1021
2. The Agreement on Arrangements for the Involvement of Employees	1022
3. Standard Rules	1023
§6. TAKE-OVER BIDS AND CROSS-BORDER MERGERS	1024
I. Take-over Bids	1024
II. Definitions	1024
III. Cross-border Mergers	1025
§7. MERGERS OF PUBLIC LIMITED LIABILITY COMPANIES	1029

Epilogue: In Search of a European Social Model (ESM): a Dream   1031

Appendix 1. Community Charter on the Fundamental Social Rights of Workers (1989)   1037

Table of Contents

Appendix 2. Cooperation Agreement between UNICE and
              UEAPME of 12 November 1998   1044

Appendix 3. Charter of Fundamental Rights of the
              European Union (12 December 2007) (2007/C
              303/01)   1046

Selected Bibliography   1059

Alphabetical List of Cited Cases of the European
Court of Justice   1073

Index   1095

Table of Contents

List of Abbreviations

AETR	European Agreement concerning the Work of Crews of Vehicles Engaged in International Road Transport
Article	Article
CBI	Confederation of British Industry
CEEP	Centre Européen des Entreprises Publiques
COJ	Court of Justice
COPA	Comité des Organisations Agricoles
CSR	corporate social responsibility
EC	European Communities
ECB	European Central Bank
EEA	European Economic Area
EFTA	Economic Free Trade Association
ESC	Economic and Social Committee
ECSC	European Coal and Steel Community
ed.	Editor
EMF	European Metal Workers Federation
EMU	European Monetary Union
EP	European Parliament
ESF	European Social Fund
ESM	European Social Model
ETUC	European Trade Union Confederation
Euratom	European Atomic Energy Community
EWC	European Works Council
FIFpro	International Federation of Professional Football Players
FSR	Fundamental Social Right
GSP	Generalised System of Preferences
IELL	*International Encyclopaedia for Labour Law and Industrial Relations*
IGC	Intergovernmental Conference
ILO	International Labour Organisation
ITUC	International Trade Union Confederation (ITUC)
NGO	Non-governmental Organisation
OECD	Organisation for Economic Cooperation and Development
O.J.	Official Journal
RB	Representative Body

List of Abbreviations

SCE	European Corporative Society
SE	*Societas Europaea*
SEA	Single European Act
SNB	Social Negotiating Body
TEC	Treaty establishing the European Community
TEU	Treaty on European Union
TFEU	Treaty on the Functioning of the European
UEAPME	Union European Association of Craft, Small and Medium-Sized Enterprises
v.	versus
VAT	Value added tax
WCL	World Confederation of Labour
WTO	World Trade Organisation

Prologue

§1. LABOUR LAW

1. Labour law aims at monitoring economic developments. Its objective is to establish an appropriate balance in the relationship, interests, rights and obligations between the employer on the one hand and the employee on the other hand. Labour law should also contribute to the creation of jobs, which means active employment policies. Labour law should see to it that employees have 'decent jobs'.[1] It is an essential contribution to the welfare state.[2]

2. How to accomplish this is not evident, considering the objectives of a market economy. Indeed, a market economy wants to further the financial interest of enterprises. 'Corporate governance and shareholders' value' are the driving force in a competitive world. It is a manager's world. Within that framework the level of social protection of the employees, namely wages and conditions, has to be kept as low as possible; the shareholders have the last word.

3. For that reason, the economic actors, namely shareholders and managers, enjoy a 'managerial prerogative'. This means that they have the legal power to take the appropriate economic, technological and financial decisions, taking market developments into account.

4. Shareholders and managers also have power over the workforce, which they can command. Employees do indeed perform in subordination to their employers.

---

1. Decent work is the availability of employment in conditions of freedom, equity, security and human dignity. According to the International Labour Organisation ILO, decent work involves opportunities for work that is productive and delivers a fair income, security in the workplace and social protection for families, better prospects for personal development and social integration, freedom for people to express their concerns, organise and participate in the decisions that affect their lives and equality of opportunity and treatment for all women and men.
2. A welfare state is a 'concept of government in which the state plays a key role in the protection and promotion of the economic and social well-being of its citizens. It is based on the principles of equality of opportunity, equitable distribution of wealth, and public responsibility for those unable to avail themselves of the minimal provisions for a good life. The general term may cover a variety of forms of economic and social organization.'(Welfare state, *Britannica Online Encyclopedia*).

§2. GLOBALISATION

5. Another important factor is the evolution of the market economy. Our economies are becoming more globalised as well as localised.[3] There are no boundaries for the movement of capital, goods, services and technology.[4] These developments are enhanced through the increasing use of information technologies. Indeed, many companies have worldwide strategies. Also smaller enterprises, which operate locally, feel the pressures of international competition. Moreover, many SMEs are part of larger networks, in which services and goods are delivered across boundaries.

6. 'Despite considerable benefits for many workers, globalisation clearly has adverse consequences, such as growing job in security, concession bargaining, and increasing inequality, which will affect especially the more vulnerable sectors of the labour market.'[5] Since 2008 we have been confronted with a global financial meltdown, which is having a further impact on social protection. The current crisis is touching every country in the world, including the developing countries. One of the ways to combat the crisis is to have strong social policies.[6]

---

3. A. Turner, *Just Capital*, London, 2002; Bruce E. Kaufman, *The Global Evolution of Industrial Relations*, 2004, Geneva, 600 pp. 'Confronting Globalisation. The Quest for a Social Agenda', (ed. R. Blanpain), *Bulletin for Comparative Labour Relations*, no. 55, 2005, 218, Kluwer Law International, The Hague; Martin Wolf, *Why Globalisation Works*, Yale University Press, New Haven, 2005, 398 pp; Thomas L. Friedman, *Hot, Flat & Crowded* Penguin Books, 2009, London, 516pp; Robert B. Reich, *After-shock: The Next Economy and America's Future*, A. Knopf, New York, 2010, 173.
4. ILO, *Industrial Relations, Democracy and Social Stability. World Law Report*, 1997–1998, Geneva, 1998; R.D. Lansbury and Y.B. Park (eds.), 'The Impact of Globalisation on Employment Relations', *Bulletin of Comparative Labour Relations*, vol. 45, 2002, 151; R. Blanpain and B. Flodgren (eds.), 'Corporate and Employment Perspectives in a Global Environment', *Bulletin of Comparative labour Relations*, vol. 60, Kluwer Law International, 2006, 20pp.; R. Blanpain and L. Cutcher et al. (eds.), 'Globalisation and Employment Relations in Retail Banking', *Bulletin of Comparative labour Relations*, Kluwer Law International, vol. 63, forthcoming; Boaventura de Sousaz et al. (eds.) 'Law and Globalisation from Below: Towards a Cosmopolitan Legality', Cambridge University Press, 2005, 395pp; R. Blanpain et al., *The Global Workplace: International and Comparative Employment Law: Cases and Materials*, Cambridge, 2007, 647pp; R. Blanpain and F. Hendrickx, 'Labour Law between Change and Tradition'. *Liber Amicorum Antoine Jacobs, Bulletin of Comparative Labour Relations*, no. 78, Kluwer Law International, 2011, 198pp.
5. K. J. Vos, 'Globalization and Social Protection', *Bulletin for Comparative Labour Relations*, no. 70, 2009, 199 (ed. Roger Blanpain); Dani Rodrik, *The Globalization Paradox: Why Global Markets and Democracy can't Coexist*, Oxford University Press, Oxford, 2011, 346 pp.; Katherine V.W. Stone and Harry Arthurs (eds.), *Rethining Workplace Regulation: Beyond the Standard Contract of Employment*, New York, Russsel Sage Foundation, 2013, 421.
6. J. Stiglitz, 'The global crisis, social protection and jobs', *International Labour Review*, vol. 148, 2009, no. 2; R. Blanpain and William Bromwich et al., 'Rethinking Corporate Governance: From Shareholder Value to Stakeholder Value', *Bulletin of Comparative Labour Relations*, no. 77, Kluwer Law International, 359pp; R. Blanpain, 'Flexicurity in a Global Economy. We need both, also security', in T. Davulis and D. Petrylaité, *Labour markets of the 21st Century: Looking for Flexibility and Security*, 2011, Vilnius University, 19–29; S. Hayter, *The Role of Collective Bargaining in the Global Economy: Negotiating for Social Justice*, ILO, Geneva, 2011, 327pp; Joseph E. Stiglitz, *The Price of Inequality: How Today's Divided Society Endangers Our Future*, W. W. Norton & Company, 2012, 448pp.

Prologue

7. The relations between employees and employers, as well individual as collective labour relations, are part and parcel of the societies in which they evolve. This society is, for most countries, today and probably also tomorrow, a global one, with free flow of capital and investment and new information technologies. The market economy prevails. And *super-capitalism*[7] is in.[8]

Local actors, governments as well as trade unions and employers associations, are powerless; they pedal in empty air as the important financial and economic decisions are taken at international level, totally escaping the local grip. Even the European Union stands at the side line; as the EU is not competent for the 'core' social issues, like wages, freedom of association and the right to strike. The EU has neither a minimum wage nor a European social security system. The EU is a rather empty social box, a big boat with a very tiny motor. The consequence is clear: more rich and more poorer people as well between North and South, as within developed countries. A divided society.

§3. SUPER–CAPITALISM

I. Global

8. We live in a world of *global capitalism*. *Capital* moves freely, looking for maximum profit and if possible, zero taxes. Our economies are dominated by private *rating bureaus*, which classify countries on an economic scale (from AAA+ to B or C) and drive up interest rates for governments, who need to lend money on international markets in order to pay their debts and push them to savings, including diminishing social protection, as for example in Greece today.

II. Multinational Enterprises

9. A dominant role is played by *multinational enterprises*, which decide from far away headquarters where to invest, which technology to introduce, where to create jobs or close enterprises, as they may relocate them in other countries where investment conditions are more favourable. Multinationals view the world like a grocery store, looking for the best deal, playing one country off against the other.

> Wal-Mart Stores, Inc. is an American multinational retailer corporation that runs chains of large discount department stores and warehouse stores. The

---

7. Robert Reich, *Supercapitalism: The Transformation of Business, and Everyday Life*, New York, Alfred A. Knopf, 2007, 272pp.
8. According to Prof. Friedman of the Chicago school. 'Deregulation, privatization and social cutbacks ... Taxes should be low, rich and poor school should be taxed at the same flat rate. Corporations should be free to sell their products anywhere in the world. Prices, including the price of labour, should be determined by the market. There should be no minimum wage. Friedman wanted to privatize health care, education, retirement pensions. Workers' protection should be diminished. Friedman's vision coincides with the interests of large multinationals' (Naomi Klein, *The Shock Doctrine, The Rise of Disaster Capitalism*, Penguin Books, 2008, 55–57).

company is the world's third largest public corporation, according to the Fortune Global 500 list in 2012. It is also the biggest private employer in the world with over two million employees, and is the largest retailer in the world. Walmart remains a family-owned business, as the company is controlled by the Walton family who own a 48% stake in Walmart. It is also one of the world's most valuable companies.[9]

The top 500 multinationals control more than 50 per cent of the world wide gross product. 50 per cent of Flemish–Belgian industry is in the hands of multinationals. They represent 46 per cent of employment and 56 per cent of added economic value of the industry in Flanders.

10. We all bend the knee to multinational enterprises. Wherever they come from. We need investment and jobs. We are bound to be investment friendly. Flexible and cheap. Our wage costs are continuously compared with those of our surrounding countries. Multinationals pay taxes where it suits them best. Multinationals enterprises structure and restructure. They close. When Ford Motor Company (2012) decided to close its subsidiary in Genk, Belgium, 3,500 Ford jobs were lost and also 4,500 jobs of workers, employed by subcontractors of the US automobile giant. When General Motors (2010) closed its subsidiary in Antwerp Belgium, involving 2,500 employees, the Flemish Minister President Kris Peeters went to Detroit (US) to discuss with how top management to avoid the closure. He was received politely, got a cup of coffee and came home with empty hands.

A. Labour is a Cost

11. Where we might expect that enterprises are there in the first place to create jobs, we regret to have to see that the present capitalist system aims at liquidating jobs, because labour is a cost and costs need to be reduced as much as possible. When jobs are lost, shares go up. Also small subcontractors are out priced and get bankrupt. Many smaller employers of yesterday are unemployed today without unemployment compensation, in France no fewer than 220,000.

B. Research

12. Multinational enterprises equally control scientific research (for more than 70 per cent). They control new products and technologies and decide which technologies are transferred to their foreign subsidiaries. Universities are beggars for multinational funds in order to be able to engage into research. The contracts universities conclude with multinationals transfer the inventions, patent rights and the exploitation thereof into multinational hands.

---

9. Wikipedia, consulted 24 November 2012.

C. Bonuses

13. Sky-high bonuses of CEOs and bankers illustrate the casino capitalism we live in. Carlos Brito, the top CEO of the Brazilian-Belgian brewery AB-Inbev gave himself (2012) a bonus of not less than US$ 133 million. The minimum wage in Bulgaria is 123 euro a month. We read that the boss of Apple earns 60,000 times the salary of a Chinese worker, who assembles the Apple iPads in Foxconn.[10] 1 per cent of Americans take salaries and benefits amounting to 25 per cent of the US gross national product. In June 2012, Wall Street bankers awarded themselves a salary raise of 20 per cent.[11] Who pays, decides.

D. Politics

14. The example per excellence is the USA. The US presidential election (2012) costs $6 billion, the most expensive in history. Who pays? Also and especially companies. When Hilary Clinton ran for President four years ago, she was financially supported by the tobacco industry. Try to understand!!!! No wonder that President Bill Clinton, a democrat, deregulated the capital markets which finally led to casino-capitalism and the financial crisis which now ruins our economies.

Profits and bonuses go to the top. Capital takes an ever growing share. Labour loses. If the banks go broke, they are 'too big to fail' and governments have to step in: the tax payer pays. Bankers are also 'too big to jail' and continue as they did before.

E. Poor and Unemployed

15. We have more rich but many more poor. Also more unemployed. In two years the number of unemployed in the Eurozone increased by 2 million. In October 2012 close to 19 million people in the Eurozone were unemployed. In Greece 57 per cent of youngsters are out of a job.

§4. GLOCALISATION

16. Our economies are globalising as well as localising. One thing: employment in the globalised economy certain in the goods and services sector is decreasing. The labour factor is losing importance due to the enormous increase in productivity

---

10. Many of the people at 'Foxconn City' work six days a week, twelve hours a day, and they earn less than US$17 per day (Chris Rawson, 'Why Apple's products are "Designed in California" but "Assembled in China"', http://www.tuaw.com/2012/01/22/why-apples-products-are-designed-in-california-but-assembled/ (consulted 1 December 2012).
11. *De Tijd*, 6 June 2012.

as a consequence of automation, information technologies, re-engineering[12] and others. An important proportion of added economic value can be realised with fewer employees. Traded goods in agriculture and services also become cheaper and employment goes down. The ongoing restructurings are a consequence of this development.

17. As our (Western) societies become more wealthy and the population older the demand for personalised services increases exponentially and so consequently does employment in that sector. This is logical. In case of face-to-face services, like health and care for the elderly, catering, hairdressing and others, increases in productivity are either non-existent or very small. Moreover, services become more expensive. Unlike trade of goods, they cannot be stored: taking care of the sick and the elderly is *hic* and *nunc* and these services are provided when necessary. In Great Britain 31,000 people work in breweries to make beer while 600,000 are busy in pubs providing beer to customers.

Consequently, the proportion of personalised services in GNP increases, as well as its value and, just as important, so does employment in that sector. Personalised jobs are local jobs, as the sick and the elderly, who are in need of care, remain in one place and do not run away.

In short, our economy and or employment are as global as local; put together: glocal.

There is no doubt that 80 per cent or more of jobs are local. This contributes to a 24-hour economy whereby services are provided when consumers want them. Indeed, the customer is king. This requires a flexible labour market.

§5. POVERTY AND LACK OF SOCIAL PROTECTION

I. Worldwide

18. It is hard to understate the social challenges the world faces. In 2010, global GDP in real terms was ten times larger than in 1950– an increase of 260 per cent per capita. Yet despite the six decades of strong economic growth that followed the adoption of the Universal Declaration of Human Rights, access to adequate social protection benefits and services remains a privilege, afforded to relatively few people.

19. Current statistics speak eloquently of widespread poverty and deprivation. About 5.1 billion people, 75 per cent of the world population, are not covered by adequate social security (ILO) and 1.4 billion people live on less than US$ 1.25 a day (World Bank). Thirty-eight per cent of the global population, 2.6 billion people, do not have access to adequate sanitation and 884 million people lack access to adequate sources of drinking water (UN-HABITAT); 925 million suffer from

---

12. J. Champy, *Engineering the Corporation: Reinvent your Business in the Digital Age*, London, 2002, 232pp.

chronic hunger (FAO); nearly 9 million children under the age of five die every year from largely preventable diseases (UN ICEF /WHO); 150 million people suffer financial catastrophe annually and 100 million people are pushed below the poverty line when compelled to pay for health care (WHO).

20. While globalization has been a source of opportunities for those able to seize them, as the evidence above shows it has left many unprotected against new global challenges and transformations that are having deep repercussions at national and local levels. The persistence of such large numbers of excluded persons represents tremendous squandered human and economic potential. This is particularly important in a context of accelerated demographic ageing in countries with low coverage of pension and health systems.[13]

How to tackle those problems?

II. The ILO: A Global Jobs Pact

21. Our economies are indeed becoming more and more globalised. The question however is, for the benfit of whom?

In order to tackle the social problems which go along with globalisation, the International Labour Organisation established the World Commission on the Social Dimension of Globalisation. That commission had a look at the social impact of globalisation and developed a common agenda to make it work for all.[14]

The Commission's report acknowledges globalisation's potential for good – promoting open societies, open economies and a freer exchange of goods, knowledge and ideas. But the Commission also found deep-seated and persistent imbalances in the current workings of the global economy that are 'ethically unacceptable and politically unsustainable'.

Indeed, in an opinion piece, Juan Somavia, Director-General of the International Labour Office,[15] underlined that 'the globalisation debate is at an impasse. Trade negotiations are stalled. Jobs are disappearing. Financial instability continues. Meanwhile, politically sensitive issues such as migration and outsourcing are high on people's concerns, but low on the global problem-solving agenda.'

---

13. *Social Protection Floor: For a Fair and Inclusive Globalization*. Report of the Advisory Group chaired by Michelle Bachelet, ILO, Geneva, 2011, xxi.
14. *A Fair Globalisation: Creating Opportunities for All*, Geneva, 2004, 190pp. President Tarja Halonen of Finland and President Benjamin Mkapa of Tanzania chaired the commission, whose 26 members included a Nobel economics laureate, legislators, social and economic experts, and representatives of business, organised labour, academia and civil society.
15. 'For too many, globalisation isn't working', *The International Herald Tribune*, 27 February 2004 M. Naím, *Illicit: How Smugglers, Traffickers and Copycats are Hijacking the Global Economy*, Doubleday, New York, 2005, 340pp; J. Stiglitz, *Making Globalisation Work: The Next Steps to Global Justice*, Allen Lane, London, 2006, 358pp; S. Sciarra, 'Transnational and European Ways Forward for Collective bargaining' in *Liber Amicorum Ronnie Eklund*, Iustus Förlag, Upsala, 2010, 529–549; M. Weiss, 'Corporate Social responsibility: A Concept for the 21st Century', in T. Davulis and D. Petrylaité, *Labour Markets of the 21st Century: Looking for Flexibility and Security*, 2011, Vilnius University, 30-48.

22. Since the beginning of the financial crisis, the labour market situation in many countries has deteriorated dramatically with millions of workers losing their jobs. In fact, the overall impact of the crisis is still unfolding and the ILO expects unemployment to rise further. At the same time, businesses are under stress and the number of bankruptcies is growing. Vulnerable employment is also increasing, and more people are being pushed into poverty. What is also of concern is that the shortage of new employment opportunities is worsening: at least 300 million jobs need to be created globally over the next five years just to maintain a pre-crisis level of unemployment.[16]

The global crisis hit jobs hard. According to the OECD, between 2007 and 2010 the number of employed people fell by almost 5 million throughout OECD countries and the number of job seekers rose by over 16 million. It is now about two years since the trough of the recession, and unemployment rates remain at historical highs in many advanced economies despite signs of recovery in economic activity and labour demand.[17]

Experience suggests a considerable lag of four to five years on average in the recovery in labour markets after economic recovery. There is a risk of the global jobs crisis persisting for the next several years.

This is why the International Labour Conference adopted a global jobs pact aimed at placing employment creation and social protection at the centre of recovery policies. The aim of the pact is to make sure that both the extraordinary stimulus measures and other government policies better address the needs of people who need protection and work in order to accelerate combined economic and employment recovery. The pact was adopted at 98th Session of the International Labour Conference, Geneva, 2009.

23.

Recovering from the Crisis: A Global Jobs Pact

(1) The global economic crisis and its aftermath mean the world faces the prospect of a prolonged increase in unemployment, deepening poverty and inequality. Employment has usually only recovered several years after economic recovery. In some countries, the simple recovery of previous employment levels will not be enough to contribute effectively to strong economies, and to achieve decent work for women and men.

(2) Enterprises and employment are being lost. Addressing this situation must be part of any comprehensive response.

(3) The world must do better.

(4) There is a need for coordinated global policy options in order to strengthen national and international efforts centred around jobs, sustainable

---

16. R. Torres, 'Questions and answers on the global jobs crisis', www.ilo (July 2009).
17. Federico Cingano Alfonso Rosolia, 'Where are the jobs? Out there, somewhere. Perhaps?', ILO, 17 July 2011; Joseph E. Stiglitz, *Freefall. America, Free markets, and the sinking of the world economy*, New York, W.W. Norton & Company, 2010, 361 pp.

enterprises, quality public services, protecting people whilst safeguarding rights and promoting voice and participation.

(5) This will contribute to economic revitalization, fair globalization, prosperity and social justice.

(6) The world should look different after the crisis.

(7) Our response should contribute to a fair globalization, a greener economy and development that more effectively creates jobs and sustainable enterprises, respects workers' rights, promotes gender equality, protects vulnerable people, assists countries in the provision of quality public services and enables countries to achieve the Millennium Development Goals.

(8) Governments and workers' and employers' organizations commit to work together to contribute to the success of the Global Jobs Pact. The International Labour Organization's (ILO's) Decent Work Agenda forms the framework for this response.

24. Other points of the Jobs Pact concern:

– principles for promoting recovery and development;
– decent work responses:
– accelerating employment creation, jobs recovery and sustaining enterprises;
– building social protection systems and protecting people;
– strengthening respect for international labour standards;
– social dialogue: bargaining collectively, identifying priorities, stimulating action;
– the way forward: shaping a fair and sustainable globalisation;
– ILO action.

III. The European Union

25. Against the backdrop of persistent difficulties on the labour markets, marked by ever higher unemployment at EU level, and rising divergence across Member States, the number of people at risk of poverty or social exclusion in the EU now accounts for nearly one-fourth of the EU population.

26. Dragged down by falls in the levels of temporary and full-time employment, and despite some positive developments in part-time jobs, overall employment has continued to decline. Employment at EU level remains stubbornly weak. It has been trending down again since mid-2011. Over the year to the third quarter 2012, employment fell more steeply in the euro area (–0.7 per cent) than in the EU as a whole (-0.5 per cent, down 1.1 million). In the third quarter of this year, it fell again by 0.2 per cent. The steepest declines since last year were recorded in Greece (–8.9 per cent), Lithuania (–5.5 per cent), Spain and Portugal (both –4.1 per cent), hardly compensated by rises in Latvia (+3.4 per cent), Luxembourg, the UK, Malta and Estonia (+2.1 to +1.2 per cent). Most Member States – 19 out of the 24 for which

data are available – recorded an employment level below that of four years ago (EU: −2.4 per cent).

27. In this bleak context, the EU job-finding rate has declined further, from an already low level, while the risk of becoming unemployed has increased. The job-finding rate decreased to 12.1 per cent in the second quarter of 2012, from 12.5 per cent in the previous quarter, reaching a record low. Four years ago it stood at about 20 per cent. In addition, the risk for employed people of losing their job also increased slightly in the second quarter, with the job-loss rate at 3.5 per cent.

28. The number of unemployed in the EU has continued to rise over recent months, increasing by 3.5 million (or 15.7 per cent) since March 2011 and reaching a new high of more than 26 million (or 10.7 per cent of the active population), by November 2012. Unemployment trends remain less favourable in the euro area than in the EU as a whole. Moreover, divergence between EU Member States in terms of unemployment rates has continued to widen, with an all-time record gap of 22.1 percentage points (pps) now being observed between the Member State with the lowest rate of unemployment (Austria, 4.5 per cent) and that with the highest (Spain, 26.6 per cent).

29. Young people remain the first victims of the lack of jobs, with the youth unemployment rate reaching a new peak in November 2012, at 23.7 per cent, up by 1.5 pps over the year, a rise essentially driven by a dramatic decline for young people in temporary and full-time jobs. Most Member States have to cope with rising youth unemployment. As a consequence the EU employment rate for youth went down by 0.7 pp to 32.8 per cent over the year to the second quarter of 2012. Growing long-term unemployment and non-productive inactivity for youth pose serious risks for the young generation, which materialise particularly in the rising number of young people who are neither in employment nor in education and training (NEET), and which now account for nearly 13 per cent of the population aged 15 to 24.

30. On the positive side, overall inactivity rates kept falling in the EU over the year to the second quarter of 2012, in particular in those Member States with the highest rates. The decline in inactivity was mainly driven by continued rises in female participation, although inactivity also started to decline among men. Nevertheless, there are signs of increasing discouragement among the remaining population of inactive people, as employment prospects deteriorate. EU long-term unemployment continues its by now three-year upward trend. By the second quarter of 2012, the number of people who had been unemployed for more than a year.[18]

31. The euro area (EA17) seasonally adjusted unemployment rate was 12.1 per cent in March 2013, up from 12.0 per cent in February. The EU27 unemployment

---

18. Social Europe EU Employment and Social Situation, *Quarterly Review, December 2012*, 1-6.

rate was 10.9 per cent, stable compared with February. In both zones, rates have risen markedly compared with March 2012, when they were 11.0 per cent and 10.3 per cent respectively. These figures are published by Eurostat, the statistical office of the European Union.

Eurostat estimates that 26,521 million men and women in the EU27, of whom 19,211 million were in the euro area, were unemployed in March 2013. Compared with February 2013, the number of persons unemployed increased by 69,000 in the EU27 and by 62,000 in the euro area. Compared with March 2012, unemployment rose by 1.814 million in the EU27 and by 1.723 million in the euro area.

32. The EU leaders at the European Council meeting on 27–28 June in Brussels endorsed a comprehensive plan to combat youth unemployment; 23.5 per cent of Europeans under the age of 25 (approximately 7.5 million) across the EU are out of work. The plan includes speeding up the implementation of the Youth Employment Initiative and the Youth Guarantee scheme, as well as increasing youth mobility and the involvement of social partners.[19]

Young people are more than twice as likely to be unemployed as the adult population. The cost of failing to integrate some 14 million young people aged between 15 and 25 into the labour market is estimated to be equivalent to around 1.21 per cent of the EU's GDP.

A. Youth Guarantee Schemes

33. Under the Youth Guarantee, the Member States committed to ensure that within four months of becoming unemployed or leaving formal education all young people up to the age of 25 receive a high-quality offer of a job, an apprenticeship or a traineeship.

The EU will help the Member States to fund the Youth Guarantee schemes through the use of EU structural funds, notably the Youth Employment Initiative.

B. Youth Employment Initiative

34. The EU leaders agreed to front-load the billion that had been earmarked for the Initiative so that these funds are available in 2014–2016 euro, i.e. during the first two years of the next Multiannual Financial Framework (MFF), instead of being spread over its entire seven-year duration.

The leaders undertook to make the Youth Employment Initiative fully operational by January 2014.

---

19. 'EU leaders agree measures to fight youth unemployment', http://www.european-council.europa.eu/home-page/highlights/eu-leaders-agree-measures-to-fight-youth-unemployment?lang=en

The EU regions where youth unemployment rates are higher than 25 per cent will be the first to receive disbursements under the initiative. For this to happen, the beneficiary member states have to adopt plans to tackle youth unemployment, including through the implementation of the Youth Guarantee, before the end of the year. The other countries are encouraged to adopt such plans in 2014.

In addition, it has been agreed that the unspent MFF funds will be used primarily to support employment, especially for young people, but also in growth areas such as innovation and research.

C. Helping Young People Find Employment across Borders

35. Leaders agreed to strengthen existing initiatives, such as 'Your first EURES Job' and 'Erasmus +', which also fosters cross-border vocational training. The Member States would like it to be operational from January 2014. EURES currently provides access to over 1.4 million job vacancies and almost 31,000 registered employers across the EU.

In addition, Member States are encouraged to use part of their allocations from the European Social Fund to support cross-border mobility schemes.

D. Apprenticeships

36. The Member States agreed to launch the European Alliance for Apprenticeships in July, and the Quality Framework for Traineeships should be put in place in early 2014. The programmes are designed to link up the private sector, social partners and businesses to create high-quality apprenticeships.

E. Social Partners

37. Another measure to boost youth employment is the active involvement of social partners. The European Council welcomes the Framework of Actions on Youth Employment agreed by social partners in June 2013.

IV. Other European Union Actions

38. The informal Prague Employment Summit (May 2009) discussed concrete actions to help alleviate the employment and social consequences of the crisis. In the context of this discussion three priority areas which should receive particular attention were identified, both within the recovery packages of the Member States and within the initiatives launched at European level:

(1) maintaining employment, creating new jobs and promoting mobility;
(2) upgrading skills and matching labour market needs;
(3) increasing access to employment.

Prologue

39. Ten actions were suggested:

(1) keep as many people as possible in jobs, with temporary adjustment of working hours combined with retraining and supported by public funding (including from the European Social Fund);
(2) encourage entrepreneurship and job creation, e.g. by lowering non-wage labour costs and flexicurity;
(3) improve the efficiency of national employment services by providing intensive counselling, training and job search in the first weeks of unemployment, especially for the young unemployed;
(4) increase significantly the number of high quality apprenticeships and traineeships by the end of 2009;
(5) promote more inclusive labour markets by ensuring work incentives, effective active labour market policies and modernisation of social protection systems that also lead to a better integration of disadvantaged groups including the disabled, the low-skilled and migrants;
(6) upgrade skills at all levels with lifelong learning, in particular giving all school leavers the necessary skills to find a job;
(7) use labour mobility to match the supply and demand of labour to the best effect;
(8) identify job opportunities and skills requirements, and improve skills forecasting to get the training offer right;
(9) assist the unemployed and young people in starting their own businesses, e.g. by providing business support training and starting capital, or by lowering or eliminating taxation on start-ups;
(10) anticipate and manage restructuring through mutual learning and exchange of good practice.

40. Strengthening efforts to support employment, the European Summit of 18–19 June 2009 stated that the fight against unemployment remained a major priority. While action in this field was first and foremost a matter for the Member States, the European Union had an important role to play in providing and improving the common framework required to ensure that the measures taken were coordinated, mutually supporting and in line with single market rules. In this effort one needs to safeguard and further strengthen social protection, social cohesion and the rights of workers.

In the current situation, the summit underlined that 'flexicurity' was an important means to modernise and foster the adaptability of labour markets. Priority should be given to preparing labour markets for future recovery: creating a friendly environment for entrepreneurship and job creation, investing in a skilled, adaptable and motivated labour force and transforming Europe into a competitive, knowledge-based, inclusive, innovative and eco-efficient economy. Social protection systems and social inclusion policies play their role as automatic economic stabilisers and as effective mechanisms for cushioning the social impact of the downturn and for helping people back to the labour market. Particular attention must also be given to the most vulnerable and to new risks of exclusion.

41. The European Council of Luxembourg, 8 June 2009 adopted conclusions on flexicurity in times of crisis. The Council underlined that 'the basic principles behind the flexicurity approach are very much in line with the central elements of the EU strategy for growth and jobs' and with the increased need to strengthen the EU's competitiveness and social cohesion, and that the revised Lisbon strategy promotes an active response to the challenge of globalisation.

The Council indicated a set of measures which, as a balanced policy mix, could help Member States, and the social partners when and where relevant, to manage the impact of the global crisis through the application of flexicurity principles. These could include:

(1) maintaining employment, where at all possible, for example through helping companies operate alternatives to redundancy such as flexible working patterns and the temporary adjustment of working time, where applicable, and other forms of internal flexibility measures within companies;
(2) creation of a better entrepreneurial environment through a labour market which ensures at the same time the necessary flexibility and security;
(3) enhancing and improving activation measures;
(4) increased investment in human capital, especially retraining, skills upgrading and labour market needs-matching, including for persons working part-time or other flexible forms of employment and low-skilled workers;
(5) improving the effectiveness of the public employment services;
(6) adhering to the principle of gender mainstreaming in all responses to implementing flexicurity principles in order to tackle the crisis;
(7) facilitating the free movement of workers, in accordance with the Treaties and the Community *acquis*, and promoting mobility within the EU single market can contribute to tackling the persisting mismatch between existing skills and labour market needs, also during the economic downturn;
(8) implementing adequate responses with a view to adapting, if relevant, employment and labour market provisions in the framework of the flexicurity approach;
(9) integrating all flexicurity elements and pillars should focus on reducing segmentation and improving the functioning of the labour market;
(10) further attention to be paid to enhancing the quality of working life and to increasing productivity.

42. On 7 June 2011, the Commission adopted 27 sets of country-specific recommendations – plus one for the euro area as a whole – to help Member States gear up their economic and social policies to deliver on growth, jobs and public finances.[20]

Earlier this year [2012], Member States and the Commission agreed on ten key priorities to face the current crisis while paving the way for a more sustainable economy. As situations vary from one country to another, the Commission is today recommending targeted measures for each Member State. This should help each

---

20. Delivering on growth and jobs: Commission presents 2011 country-specific recommendations, June 2011.

country to focus on strategic levers in the next 12 to 18 months, and thus boost EU economy as a whole.

These sets of recommendations are part of the European Semester, whereby – for the first time this year [2012] – Member States and the Commission have been coordinating their economic and budgetary policies. Once priorities agreed at EU level, Member States presented their national programmes which the Commission has now fully assessed through these tailored, targeted and measurable recommendations.

Overall, Member States have sought to reflect the agreed EU priorities in their programmes and their macroeconomic assumptions are broadly realistic. However, national programmes often lack ambition and specificity. Many Member States need to be more ambitious on fiscal consolidation, while maintaining growth-enhancing measures (research and innovation, business environment, competition in the services sector). On labour markets, more efforts are needed to increase labour-force participation, combat structural unemployment, reduce youth unemployment and early school-leaving and ensure that wages reflect productivity.

43. The recommendations provide an EU input into national policy-making. Member States remain responsible for designing their economic policies and drawing up their national budgets. But there is today a broad recognition of our mutual interdependence in the EU in general and in the euro area in particular. That is why Member States have signed up to the common set of economic priorities for the EU, which Member States are committed to implementing at national level.

Each set of recommendations is based on an in-depth analysis of the economic situation in each Member State, set out in the Staff Working Papers also published today. Macroeconomic assumptions have been assessed against the Commission's own Spring Forecasts. National measures listed in the programmes have been scrutinised to see whether they provide an adequate response to the specific challenges faced.

44. In Oslo, Norway, on 8–11 April 2013, the ILO held its Ninth European Regional Meeting where the following Declaration was adopted: Restoring confidence in jobs and growth.[21]

A. *Context*

45. At the meeting, held in Lisbon in February 2009, Europe was in the middle of a severe economic crisis with rising unemployment, uncertainty and negative impacts on large numbers of workers and enterprises. This led to the adoption of the Global Jobs Pact in June 2009 which was subsequently endorsed by the G20 as part of their policy framework to confront the crisis.

Four years later, national realities are still differentiated. Some countries in the European and Central Asian (ECA) region are recovering from the crisis with stable or improving labour markets. However in significant parts of our region the crisis

---

21. www.ilo.org/wcmsp5/ ... /meetingdocument/wcms_210356.pdf (consulted 9 May 2013).

has deepened, with unemployment rising to alarming levels, particularly for young people, increasing job insecurity, growing inequalities, weakening of social protection, deteriorating and uncertain environment for enterprises and investment, while many governments are putting in place painful reforms and struggle with debt and monetary problems.

46. There is a need to create positive pathways in these countries to overcome negative economic, social and political consequences and restore trust. Social dialogue and collective bargaining serve as effective tools to mitigate the impact of the crisis, but in many countries they have been weakened.

Fiscal consolidation, structural reform and competitiveness, on the one hand, and stimulus packages, investment in the real economy, quality jobs, increased credit for enterprises, on the other, should not be competing paradigms. It is in our common interest to elaborate sustainable approaches in order to promote jobs, growth and social justice.

We consider that the measures contained in the 2009 Global Jobs Pact are relevant and should be effectively implemented. Confidence can be restored.

B. Policy Expectations

47. The ILO should:

- promote policies that foster decent work and job creation through:
  - employment-friendly macroeconomic policies and investment in the real economy;
  - an enabling environment for enterprises;
  - appropriate strategies to enhance competitiveness and sustainable development
while respecting fundamental principles and rights at work;
- promote strategies that improve job quality and close the gender wage gap;
- promote policies which build and maintain business confidence, enterprise sustainability, particularly of SMEs, in line with the 2007 ILC resolution on sustainable enterprises;
- promote policies that help jobseekers through efficient and effective active labour market programmes particularly targeting the needs of young and older workers and promoting women's participation;
- address the mismatches between the skills of workers and the needs of the labour market;
- promote the implementation of the ILC 2012 Call for Action on the youth employment crisis;
- promote strategies to enhance investment in research and development, including innovative technologies and the green economy;
- promote adequate and sustainable social protection systems;
- promote strong and responsible social partnership in order to have social dialogue at all levels which contributes to equitable distribution, social progress and stability based on productivity-oriented wage policies;

Prologue

– support the full realisation of the ILO 2008 Social Justice Declaration with particular attention to the fundamental principles and rights at work.

C. ILO Means of Action

48. The current situation demands an exceptional response from the ILO. The reform process at the ILO must enhance its abilities to take action.

We call upon the Office to:

- provide evidence-based, high-quality research, analysis and technical advice;
- provide assistance to constituents on specific challenges identified in respective countries of the region;
- assist in the implementation of fundamental labour standards and other relevant international labour standards;
- facilitate the exchange of experience, including through platforms for sharing good practices and through the organisation of seminars for mutual learning focused on concrete issues of concern;
- build capacity of governments and social partners to take up their responsibilities to reinforce their contribution, through enhanced social dialogue, collective bargaining and effective social partnership, to recovery and reforms;
- promote synergies and policy coherence with international and regional organizations and institutions – particularly the IMF, OECD, the World Bank, the EU and the Eurasian Economic Commission – on macroeconomic, labour market, employment, and social protection issues.

49. The impact of new technologies on the world of work cannot be overestimated.[22] A new economy is emerging, transforming the way enterprises are organised and products and services produced and delivered. Knowledge and information are 'the' sources of added value. The economy is spurred by an ongoing amount of new applications and services, which are rendered by the net economy. Start-ups are in and, more important, are attracting the best brains. This in turn compels companies to rely on creativity, knowledge and ability to acquire new knowledge of their core employees.[23]

50. It is self-evident that law, as the force regulating the labour of employees, needs to follow these economic and technological developments closely, if it wants to remain relevant and adequate. Workers need to be flexible and employable.

---

22. M. Colucci, 'The Impact of the Internet and New Technologies on the Workplace: A Legal Analysis from a Comparative Point of View', *Bulletin of Comparative Labour Relations*, vol. 43, 2002, 186.
23. ILO, *World Employment Report 2001. Life at Work in the Information Society*, Geneva, 2001, CD Rom, p. 4; R. Blanpain (ed.), 'European Framework Agreements and Telework: Law and Practice: A European and Comparative Study', *Bulletin of Comparative Labour Law*, Kluwer Law International, Alphen aan den Rijn, vol. 62, 2007, 283 pp; 'The World of Work in the XXIst Century', in *Flexicurity and the Lisbon Agenda: A Cross-Disciplinary Reflection*, ed. Frank Hendrickx, Intersentia, 2008, Social Europe Series, 1-32.

V. The Lisbon Strategy

51. EU Heads of State and Government agreed at the EU Spring Summit in Lisbon (March 2000) on the objective to create 'the most dynamic and competitive knowledge-based economy in the world, capable of sustainable economic growth with more and better jobs and greater social cohesion' by 2010, using a strategy with an economic, social and environmental dimension. The strategy contains specific targets in several areas, including overall employment levels, female employment rates, and the employment of older workers.

In November 2004, a report on the EU's 'Lisbon strategy', issued by a high-level group chaired by the former Dutch Prime Minister Wim Kok,[24] was discussed at the European Council meeting. The report stated that there had been disappointing progress in implementation. It urged all those involved to work together to make better progress.

The key areas where action is seen as urgent include:

– the 'knowledge society'. This includes increasing the attractiveness of Europe for researchers and scientists, making research and development a priority and promoting the use of information and communication technologies;
– the internal market. The internal market for the free movement of goods and capital should be completed and urgent action taken to create a single market for services;
– the business climate. The total administrative burden should be reduced, the quality of legislation improved, the start-up of businesses facilitated and a more supportive environment for business created; and
– the labour market. Strategies for lifelong learning and 'active ageing' should be developed.[25]

52. In 2009 the Commission proposed a European Council Recommendation on the implementation of the Lisbon Strategy Structural Reforms in the context of the European Economic Recovery Plan.[26]

In order to pursue the Lisbon strategy for growth and jobs in a coherent, integrated manner, these recommendations are adopted in a single instrument. This approach reflects the integrated structure of the NRPs and Implementation Reports, as well as the necessary consistency between the employment guidelines and the Article 99(2) broad economic policy guidelines, as underlined in Article 128(2).

53. In the context of the current economic downturn, the Commission has proposed a European Economy Recovery Plan, which the European Council in agreed December 2008. This plan provides for a coordinated budgetary stimulus, within the Stability and Growth Pact, to boost demand and restore confidence, taking account

---

24. *Facing the Challenge: The Lisbon Strategy for Growth and Employment.*
25. Andrea Broughton, IRS, 'Kok group issues report on Lisbon strategy' <www.eiro.eurofound.ie>, 2005.
26. Council Recommendation on the 2009 update of the broad guidelines for the economic policies of the Member States and the Community and on the implementation of Member States' employment policies (COM(2009) 34/2).

of Member States' starting positions and the efforts already undertaken in response to economic problems. The Recovery Plan foresees the budgetary stimulus being accompanied by an acceleration of structural reforms, grounded in the Lisbon Strategy, to stimulate the economy whilst boosting the Union's long-term growth potential, notably by promoting the transition towards a low-carbon, knowledge-intensive economy.

54. The Recovery Plan agreed by the European Council called on Member States to submit updated stability or convergence programmes, which the Commission has assessed, taking due account of the need to ensure the reversibility of the fiscal deterioration, improving budgetary policy-making, and ensuring long-term sustainability of public finances.

The country-specific recommendations should be updated, taking account of the principles of the Recovery Plan and progress made with their implementation since they were adopted. These reforms should be implemented swiftly. The Commission will provide assistance as part of the Lisbon partnership, monitor and regularly report on progress.

To fully implement the Lisbon strategy for growth and jobs, this recommendation should also contain specific recommendations to the Member States belonging to the euro area.

55. The bad news, however, remains that 5 million young people were unemployed in the EU in the first quarter of 2009. But the good news is that 72 per cent of people questioned in a recent survey think the EU plays a positive role in creating job opportunities and fighting unemployment, while 78 per cent think the EU improves access to education and training. The EU is also looking for additional ways to ease the burden of the economic and financial crisis. For example, the Commission has proposed to fund European Social Fund projects by up to 100 per cent and to raise the threshold above which approval from the Commission is required for environmental projects from 25 to 50 million euro. The Commission also provided a loan 1.5 billion euro to Romania to improve its balance of payments and accelerate the return to growth and jobs.

56. Following calls for the Lisbon strategy to be updated, the Europe 2020 strategy replaced the Lisbon strategy on 17 June 2010. The Europe 2020 strategy aims to create jobs, and encourage 'green' economic growth and create an inclusive society. The strategy's main targets include:

– raising the EU employment rate from 69 per cent to 75 per cent;
– reducing school drop-out rates to less than 10 per cent;
– reducing the number of Europeans living in poverty by 25 per cent (equivalent to 20 million people);
– reducing greenhouse gas emissions by 20 per cent compared to 1990 levels (or by 30 per cent if the conditions are right);
– 20 per cent of total energy consumption to be from renewable energy and increasing energy efficiency by 20 per cent;
– 3 per cent of the EU's GDP to be invested in research and development.

EU states' progress is monitored: states must outline how they intend to meet these targets in 'national reform programmes', which are submitted to the EU Commission, and the European Council evaluates states' progress at one summit each year.

VI. Enlargement

57. The EU has, since the beginning, been engaged in a process of ongoing enlargement.

The first six founding members were Belgium, France, Germany, Italy, Luxembourg and the Netherlands. The EU then had five enlargements:

- 1973: Denmark, Ireland and the United Kingdom;
- 1981: Greece;
- 1986: Portugal and Spain;
- 1995: Austria, Finland and Sweden.
- 1 May 2004, a total of ten new Member States joined the EU: Cyprus, the Czech Republic, Estonia, Hungary, Latvia, Lithuania, Malta, Poland, the Slovak Republic and Slovenia.
- Bulgaria and Romania joined the EU in 2007. This meant that the EU enlarged to 27 Member States.

58. Croatia applied for EU membership in 2003 and was in negotiations from 2005 until 2011.

On 9 December 2011 leaders from the EU and Croatia signed the accession treaty. Subject to its ratification by all EU countries and Croatia, then the country will have become the 28th EU member country on 1 July 2013.

Throughout the interim period until the accession, Croatia as an acceding country will have active observer status in the European institutions. The purpose is to allow Croatia to become familiar with the working methods of the EU institutions and to be involved in the decision-making process

59. The timing of accession of each country to the EU depends on the progress that it makes in preparing for membership, according to the criteria laid down by the European Council in Copenhagen in 1993. The Copenhagen criteria require:

- stability of institutions guaranteeing democracy, the rule of law, human rights and respect for and protection of minorities;
- the existence of a functioning market economy as well as the capacity to cope with competitive pressure and market forces within the Union;
- the ability to take on the obligations of membership, including adherence to the aims of political, economic and monetary union.

VII. EU Population

60. The population of the 28 EU countries now stands at more thant 500 million. The new Member States represent almost 20 per cent of the total population (82 million). This compares with 315 million for the USA, 127 million for Japan, 1.21 billion for India and 1.345 billion for China. Turkey has a population of some 76 million.

Table 1. Total EU Population at 1 January

	2002	2012
EU (27 countries)	484,635,119	503,663,601
Euro area (17 countries)	316,972,081	332,876,462
Euro area (16 countries)	315,610,839	331,536,800
Belgium	10,309,725	11,094,850
Bulgaria	7,891,095	7,327,224
Czech Republic	10,206,436	10,505,445
Denmark	5,368,354	5,580,516
Germany	82,440,309	81,843,743
Estonia	1,361,242	1,339,662
Ireland	3,899,702	4,582,769
Greece	10,968,708	11,290,067
Spain	40,964,244	46,196,276
France	61,424,036	65,327,724
Italy	56,993,742	60,820,696
Cyprus	705,539	862,011
Latvia	2,345,768	2,041,763
Lithuania	3,475,586	3,007,758
Luxembourg	444,050	524,853
Hungary	10,174,853	9,957,731
Malta	394,641	417,520
Netherlands	1,610,5285	16,730,348
Austria	8,063,640	8,443,018
Poland	38,242,197	38,538,447
Portugal	10,329,340	10,541,840
Romania	21,833,483	2,135,5849
Slovenia	1,994,026	2,055,496
Slovakia	537,8951	5,404,322
Finland	5,194,901	5,401,267
Sweden	8,909,128	9,482,855

United Kingdom	59,216,138	62,989,551
Iceland	286,575	319,575
Liechtenstein	33,525	36,475
Norway	4,524,066	4,985,870
Switzerland	7,255,653	7,954,662
Montenegro	617,085	621,240
Croatia	4,444,608	4,398,150
Former Yugoslav Republic of Macedonia, the	2,038,651	2,059,794
Turkey	68,838,069	74,724,269

Source: Eurostat; last update: 3 April; 2013 date of extraction: 15 April 2013.

Table 2. *EU Employment rate for persons aged 20-64(%)*

	1992	2002	2012
EU (27 countries)	na	667	685
Belgium	613	65	672
Bulgaria	na	558	63
Czech Republic	na	716	715
Denmark	757	777	754
Germany	689	688	767
Estonia	na	692	721
Ireland	57	707	637
Greece	587	625	553
Spain	536	627	593
France	656	687	693
Italy	na	594	61
Cyprus	na	751	702
Latvia	na	67	682
Lithuania	na	672	687
Luxembourg	648	682	714
Hungary	na	614	621
Malta	na	577	631
Netherlands	664	758	772
Austria	na	718	756
Poland	na	574	647
Portugal	711	736	665

Romania	na	633	638
Slovenia	na	69	683
Slovakia	na	636	651
Finland	697	726	74
Sweden	811	785	794
United Kingdom	705	745	742
Iceland	na	na	818
Norway	na	796	799
Switzerland	na	812	82
Croatia	na	584	553
Japan	762	731	na
Former Yugoslav Republic of Macedonia	na	na	482
Turkey	na	na	528
United States	736	75	na

Note: na = not available.
Source: Eurostat; Last update: 11 April; 2013 Date of extraction: 15 April 2013.

Table 3. *Unemployment rate of EU Member States(%)*

Geo\time	March 2012	February 2013
Euro area (changing composition)	11	12
Euro area (17 countries)	11	12
Euro area (16 countries)	11	12
EU (27 countries)	10.3	10.9
EU (15 countries)	10.4	11.1
Belgium	7.3	8.1
Bulgaria	12.2	12.5
Czech Republic	6.9	7.2
Denmark	7.6	7.4
Germany	5.5	5.4
Estonia	10.5	na
Ireland	15	14.2
Greece	22.3	na
Spain	24.2	26.3
France	10	10.8
Italy	10.4	11.6
Cyprus	10.7	14

Geo\time	March 2012	February 2013
Latvia	15.4	na
Lithuania	13.6	13,.1
Luxembourg	5	5.5
Hungary	11.1	na
Malta	6.3	6.6
Netherlands	5	6.2
Austria	4.2	4.8
Poland	10	10.6
Portugal	15.1	17.5
Romania	7.3	6.7
Slovenia	8.1	9.7
Slovakia	13.6	14.6
Finland	7.6	8.1
Sweden	7.6	8.2
United Kingdom	8.1	na
Iceland	6.9	51
Norway	3.1	na
Croatia	15.2	18.7
Turkey	8.1	na
United States	8.2	7.7
Japan	4.5	na

Note: na = not available
Source: Eurostat; last update: 11 April 2013; date of extraction: 15 April 2013.

§6. The Role of the Trade Unions

I. Freedom of Association and the Right to Collective Bargaining

A. Labour Relations are Power Relations

61. In this context it is good to repeat that 'Labour relations are power relations'. In a labour relations system the question of who makes the important decisions regarding investment, new technologies, wages and working conditions is resolved.

Prologue

In a capitalist system there are of necessity divergent interests between workers and employers, which need to be settled. In the modern welfare state it is accepted that the best way to resolve these differences is to let the involved parties make agreements and in order to come to an agreement to use pressure. In consequence, workers and employers have the right to associate, to establish trade unions and employer's associations in order to defend their interest and to do so using pressure, by taking collective action.

Employers have the managerial power to make decisions, the managerial prerogative, where to invest, disinvest, what kind of products to make and services to provide, to decide on working time, wages.

B. Freedom of Association and the Right to Collective Bargaining

62. Workers have the right to create trade unions in order to be able to conclude collective agreements, e.g. on wages and working conditions with an employer or an employers association, based on the right to strike. As we have said earlier, 'the right to collective bargaining, without the right to strike, amounts to collective begging'.

Freedom of association and collective bargaining are among the founding principles of the ILO and are laid down in the Conventions Nos. 87 and 98 on freedom of association and collective bargaining.

Conventions Nos. 87 and 98 are respectively ratified by 151 and 161 countries. Which is impressive....But quite a number of important countries like China, India and the United States have not ratified them, which comes close to 50 per cent of the world population. So here, progress is still possible. Especially as trade unions are losing ground in many countries.

II. Degree of Unionization

63. In many countries the degree of unionisation is rather low as shown in Table 3.

Table 3. Degree of Unionisation in selected countries (%)

Germany	20
Brazil, Japan and Mexico	18
Spain, Poland,	16
Chili	14
USA	12
France, India and Turkey	8
Peru	5
Certain Gulf states	0

Table 4. Trade union density in (%)

Country	Density	Country	Density	Country	Density
Western Europe		**Eastern Europe**		**Asia**	
Iceland (2006)	88	Moldova (2005)	80	China (2000)	90
Sweden (2007)	71	Macedonia (2006)	75	Tajikistan (2006)	90
Finland (2007)	70	Slovenia (2004)	45	Georgia (2005)	80
Denmark (2007)	69	Russia (2003)	45	Taiwan (2003)	38
Cyprus (2002)	68	Romania (2005)	30	Bangladesh (2001)	35
Malta (2005)	59	Slovakia (2004)	24	Kazakhstan (2002)	31
Norway (2007)	54	Czech Republic (2006)	21	Philippines (2002)	27
Belgium (2007)	53	Albania (2006)	20	Hong Kong SAR (2002)	22
Luxembourg (2007)	46	Hungary (2007)	17	Sri Lanka (no year)	20
Austria (2006)	40	Latvia (2006)	16	Singapore (2006)	19
Italy (2007)	33	Poland (2006)	16	Japan (2007)	18
Ireland (2007)	32	Bulgaria (2001)	16	Malaysia (2000)	18
Greece (2007)	30	Lithuania (2006)	14	Indonesia (2005)	14
United Kingdom (07)	28	Estonia (2005)	11	Rep. of Korea (2006)	10
Germany (2007)	20	**Centers and South America**		India (2001)	8
Netherland (2007)	20	Sunname (2006)	60	Thailand (2006)	3
Spain (2006)	16	Barbados (2002)	34	Pakistan (2002)	3
Portugal (2004)	19	Argentina (2002)	29	Cambodia (2006)	1
Switzerland (2006)	19	Bolivia (2006)	25	**Middle East and Africa**	
France (2007)	8	Brazil (2002)	18	Kenya (2006)	33
Australia and New Zealand		Uruguay (2000)	16	Namibia (2000)	32
New Zealand (2006)	22	Costa Rica (2002)	15	Israel (2006)	25
Australia (2007)	19	Chile (2006)	15	Botswana (2006)	20
North America		Honduras (2003)	14	Gambia (2006)	20
Canada (2007)	29	Puerto Rico (2002)	14	Tunisia (2004)	15
Mexico (2005)	18	Ecuador (2002)	12	Nigeria (2004)	10
USA (2007)	12	Venezuela (2002)	12	Turkey (2004)	8
		Panama (2005)	11	Morocco (2000)	5
		El Salvador (2003)	5	Tanzania (2002)	5
		Nicaragua (1998)	5	Oman (2007)	0
		Peru (2002)	5	Qatar (2004)	0
				Saudi Arabia (2000)	0
				United Arab Emirates (2004)	0

Source: From P. Hall-Jones, *Unionism and Economic Performance*, Internet article and statistics, consulted 24 November 2012.

Figure 1. Change in degree of unionisation (2003-2008) (%)

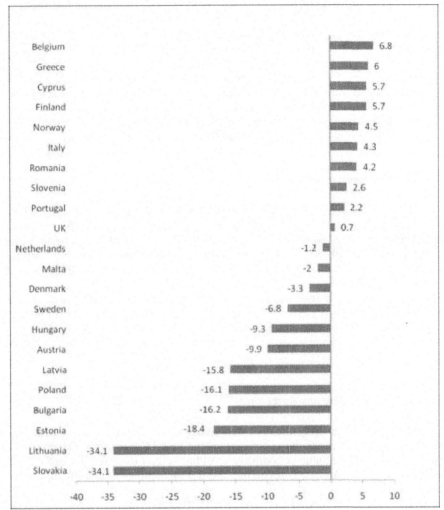

III. International Trade Union Action

A. *International Trade Unions*

64. The International Trade Union Confederation (ITUC) is the main international trade union organisation, representing the interests of working people worldwide. The ITUC was founded at its inaugural Congress in Vienna, Austria, on 1–3 November 2006. It groups together the former affiliates of the International Confederation of Free Trade Unions (ICFTU) and the World Confederation of Labour (WCL), along with trade union organisations which had no global affiliation. The

ICFTU and the WCL dissolved themselves on 31 October 2006, to pave the way for the creation of the ITUC.

65. In October 2011, the ITUC had 175,180,106 members in 309 affiliated organisations in 153 countries and territories.

> Global unions are international trade union organisations working together with a shared commitment to the ideals and principles of the trade union movement. They share a common determination to organize, to defend human rights and labour standards everywhere, and to promote the growth of trade unions for the benefit of all working men and women and their families.[27]

B. Lack of International Solidarity

66. One would expect that trade unions would, on the basis of strong international solidarity, give an answer to the challenges of globalisation. The European Trade Union Institute (Brussels) says 'whatever the case, there is no question that the organization of labour is currently in difficulties due, first of all, to a constant decline in trade union membership, but also to trade unions lack of willingness and possibly to mobilise resources to act transnationally'.[28]

There is no real trade union action at e.g. European or international level. When Ford Motor closed Ford Genk (2012) and jobs were saved in the German subsidiaries and more jobs created in the Spanish unit of Ford no European pressure was exerted on Ford to change its decision. The fact is that workers look for their own job.

C. Transnational Company Agreements[29]

67. This notwithstanding the fact that transnational company agreements are growing in numbers. Since the conclusion of the first TCA in 1988 (Danone), this new form of social dialogue at company level has spread over and, by early 2012, 224 TCAs have been signed, involving about 114 companies and 10 million of employees.[30]

The European Commission has defined a TCA as an

> agreement comprising reciprocal commitments the scope of which extends to the territory of several States and which has been concluded by one or more

---

27. Member organisations :BWI - - I IAEA - IFJ Industriall - ITF -ITUC - IUF - PSI - TUAC - UNI.
28. ETUI, *Transnational collective bargaining at company level. A new competent of European Industrial relations?* Brussels, 2012, p. 7.
29. Stefania Marassi, *A Comparative Analysis Between International Framework Agreements And European Framework Agreements*, Thesis Tilburg University, 2011, 115 pp.
30. European Commission, Commission Staff Working Document – Transnational company agreements: realising the potential of social dialogue, SWD (2012) 264 final, Brussels, 10 September 2012, p. 2 (hereinafter: European Commission 2012).

representatives of a company or a group of companies on the one hand, and one or more workers' organisations on the other hand, and which covers working and employment conditions and/or relations between employers and workers or their representative.[31]

68. Most of the companies which have concluded TCAs are headquartered in Europe (mainly in Germany, France, Sweden, the Netherlands and Italy), while, among countries outside Europe, enterprises headquartered in USA have signed more agreements than companies in Australia, Canada and South Africa.[32]

Regarding the sectors involved, a distinction has to be made between global agreements, which mainly deal with construction packaging, utilities and telecommunications and European agreements which cover especially the metal, financial, food and drinks sectors.[33]

The reasons for concluding these international company agreements are diverse. Some multinational enterprises want to promote their social profile with their employees and the public at large, much like they are proclaiming codes of conduct. Trade unions want to increase their influence on management decision making but barely succeed in obtaining the acceptance by multinationals to live up to the major 'core' ILO conventions, like prohibition of child and forced labour, freedom of association and the like. Moreover these agreements are not legally binding and there is almost no information on their effective follow up. The power relationship is clearly in favour of the multinational enterprises.

§7. LABOUR LAW AND INDUSTRIAL RELATIONS AND HUMAN RESOURCES

I. National Systems vs. Regional and International Norms

69. 'Today we live in a global economy, but not in a global society. The governance and rules are clearly lacking behind the economic developments'.[34] In a global economy, rules should relate to the trend of the market and at that level. This not forthcoming.

Multinational enterprises are, as said, global players. They have a potential global reach.

The decisions what and where to invest, not to invest, or to disinvest, are taken in headquarters and escape national government's sovereignty. MNEs invest according to market opportunities. However, employment law remains by and large national.

---

31. Commission of the European Communities, 'The role of transnational company agreements in the contexts of increasing transnational integrations' (Staff Working Document), SEC (2008) 2155, p. 6.
32. V. Telljohan, I. da Costa, T. Müller, U. Rehfeldt and R. Zimmer, 'European and International Framework Agreements Practical experiences and strategic approaches', Eurofound, Office for Official Publications of the European Communities, Luxembourg, 2009, p. 23; Available at: http://www.eurofound.europa.eu/pubdocs/2008/102/en/2/EF08102EN.pdf (accessed on 2 October 2012).
33. European Commission, *Mapping of transnational texts negotiated at corporate level*, EMPL F2 EP/bp 2008 (D) 14511, Brussels. 2 July 2008, para 5.
34. Tarja Halonen, 17, November 2003. (www.ilo.org).

Moreover, governments are competing with each other for FDI and trade of goods and services. Their countries must be investment friendly. Taxes on capital shift versus taxes to those, who are not footloose and stay: SMEs and labour/consumption. Governments remain local players, even when united in regional organisations like the EU or NAFTA.

National enterprises too are putting pressure on their respective governments to keep costs down and to liberalise the labour markets. Governments are bound to oblige and gradually flex labour conditions.

70. This goes along with the strategies of the IMF and the World Bank which preach and apply their Washington consensus: get the public deficit down, privatise and get rid of rigidities in the labour markets.

Labour legislation, collective bargaining included, indeed remains national and/ or are re-nationalised. There is no countervailing power, either regional or international to transnational economic decision-making.

This is even the case in the European Union, the most advanced regional organisation in the world. Indeed, the EU is not competent for issues like pay, freedom of association, strikes and lockout. Other important topics like social security, job security and workers participation are subject to the unanimity rule. From now on, unanimity will be even more difficult to reach than before as the European Union is composed of 28 Member States.

As a paradox, labour and employment law in the EU, which is, let's repeat it, the most advanced regional structure in the world, has, in a sense, become renationalised. This has been confirmed by the Treaties of Amsterdam (1997) and Nice (2000) as well as by the failure to agree on a new voting system;[35] and by the Reform Treaty (2009).

71. In other words, there is neither a global nor a regional appropriate and integrated legally binding reply to transnational economic decision making. The local decision makers, like we said earlier, are pedalling in empty air and bowing their heads for the multinational winds hoping that the transnational gods will be favourable to them. There is no equivalent and real countervailing power to international economic decision-making.

Even more than that, labour law becomes more and more soft[36] and HRM moves to the forefront.

72. There is no doubt, our labour markets are pushed by trends, which are making the old labour law look obsolete. From job security we move to flexibility, to flexicurity and to transsecurity. Globalisation is creating more wealth, but is not fair, as the divide between "the haves and the have nots" increases. The power of trade unions is fading away.

---

35. See: Roger Blanpain, *European Labour Law,* Kluwer Law International, 2007, 11th edn, 764 pp.
36. Blanpain Roger, 'The End of Labour Law' in The Global Labour Market: From Globalization to Flexicurity, in *Bulletin for Comparative Labour Relations,* no. 65, 2008, 3-12.

Our national labour law systems are at the same time competing with each other, in order to remain competitive and attract foreign investment. There is an on-going danger for social dumping between countries, even within the EU.

§8. WHAT TO DO?

I. The European Union

73. There is no real hope that the EU will in a near future have more competences in the social field. Member States will continue to compete each other by way of social dumping. Let's see further what the EU has realized on the social front, which is the subject of this monograph.

II. Trade Unions

74. Trade unions are more necessary than ever. Trade unions need first of all look to the future and not backwards, forever trying to block restructurations of companies and protect acquired rights. The market plays and changes are unavoidable. Also trade unions must accept changes, must adapt and see to it that workers are effectively socially protected by seeing to it that they are employable, have the needed skills to find new jobs.

The best example is undoubtedly Denmark where a system has been worked out between the social partners, where employees, in case of dismissals have:

– short terms of notice, but
– 80 per cent of the salary for a period of two years;
– immediate ongoing training by governmental and private agencies, outplacement included, so as to be qualified for a new job.

75. In Denmark, 25 per cent of employees changes jobs yearly; 75 per cent of people, aged 20–64 have a job, which matches the EU 2020 targets. The Danish labour market functions effectively, which is not the case in many other countries.

76. Secondly, trade unions need to work more together at international level. There is an absolute need for solidarity across borders. If not super-capitalism will continue to further undermine social protection, lead to divided societies and endanger our future.

§9. SOCIAL PROTECTION

77. This is the global framework in which labour law has to evolve. The question is, what kind of social protection is needed and feasible? At the same time the question arises of at what level social measures regarding wages, working time, dismissals, restructuring and other matters need to be taken. There are various levels at which decisions can be taken which affect the labour relations of employees. Here, one can distinguish between the level of the undertaking, of the state, regional (European) as well as international levels.

Should measures be taken at each of those levels? Should one consider establishing fundamental social rights to be respected worldwide? Is there a need for regional, such as European, rules, or should one limit legislation to national rules or measures at the level of the enterprise? In other words, is it necessary to have labour law, emanating from different sources, in order to adequately protect employees? The answer to that question is not self-evident, or purely academic. Which is the right level?

78. One should also take into account that the law is not only a question of justice, but also of power. And indeed, there is no doubt that the globalisation of the economy has had an enormous impact on the power relations between management and labour. Trade unions lost members and their impact on the marketplace has been diminished. They cannot act as a real force countervailing the power of management at European and international levels. Also the impact of the employers' organisations has been fading away. The players *par excellence* are the enterprises, in particular the multinationals.

These developments include the relations between governments and the economic actors whose relationship has also been dramatically affected. There is such a need for investment and jobs that everyone, political authorities included, is ready to yield to a great extent to the demands of the investors.

79. National labour law systems feel the heat of these developments and are under heavy pressure. There is indeed a growing demand by enterprises for less regulation and for more flexibility regarding wages and conditions. Enterprises need to be competitive. Some go as far as to proclaim that social protection has become superfluous, given the efficiency of the market; even that labour law is socially destructive and a job killer, because the cost of social protection reduces the competitiveness of companies and leads to job loss. National governments fear that a given level of social protection may discourage investors and lead to restructurings, including redundancies and job relocations.

80. One thing and another clearly indicates that a number of questions arise regarding the social Europe in which one wants to live. There is not only the question of which standards, more or less protective, are needed, but also whether these have to be elaborated at the European level and through which channels. Indeed, there are various options, which are not necessarily mutually exclusive.[37]

---

37. See further B. Hepple, 'New Approaches to International Labour Law', *Industrial Relations Journal*, vol. 26, no. 4, 1997, 353–366; M. Freedland, 'Developing the European Comparative Law of Personal Work Contracts', *Comparative Labor Law & Policy Journal*, vol. 28, no. 3, 2007, 487–500; M. Weiss, 'Convergence and/or Divergences in Labor Law Systems? An European perspective', *Comparative Labor Law & Policy Journal*, vol. 28, no. 3, 2007, 469–486; J. M. Servais, 'The Impact

Prologue　　　　　　　　　　　　　　　　　　　　　　　　　　　　　　**81–85**

81. One approach is that of ensuring that countries enforce their own domestic laws. The model one can refer to is the Labour Side Agreement of NAFTA, the North American Free Trade Agreement. In this arrangement, when one of the Member States of NAFTA believes that another is not following its own labour laws in one of the areas covered (safety, child labour, minimum wages) a complaint can be brought to a Commission, which may ultimately lead to judgment, by way of arbitration.

82. Another option is that of a more voluntary approach, by way of codes of conduct, guidelines or the acceptance of fundamental principles, which are monitored by way of reporting or other means of soft coercion. These codes can be established by international bodies, such as the ILO or the OECD, or can emanate from multinational enterprises themselves, wishing to project an appropriate social image towards their customers and thus obtain social respectability.

83. A third way is that of European integration. The EU follows the route of regional minimum standards, which are directly binding or oblige Member States to adapt their national legislation. Here, European collective bargaining also comes into the picture.

84. A number of important qualifications need to be made. There are first of all the rules of subsidiarity and proportionality, which are further examined. We can already state now that these principles have as a consequence that the EU will only be competent to regulate an issue when a problem cannot be settled appropriately at national level and that the European measure has to be limited to what is necessary. This means that legislative action must refrain from detail except when this is objectively justified.

85. Moreover, economic rationality prevails in Europe. Since the Treaties of Maastricht and Amsterdam, the shareholder has definitively come first. Social aspects have been reduced to a secondary place in the European edifice, as conceived in the Treaties of Maastricht (1991), of Amsterdam (1997) of Nice (2000) and of Lisbon (2009). Indeed, the objective of a non-inflationary economy in the framework of the EMU is the primary objective of the EU. The European Central Bank will guard price developments. In case of a danger of rising prices, the interest rate will be increased. This means that money becomes more expensive, and that SMEs in particular will have to reduce or cease their activities. This may contribute to higher unemployment. To continue to qualify for membership of EMU, Member States need to have a low degree of inflation, public expenses and deficits under control. This means that there is less and less money for infrastructure, education, culture, research and social policies, health and pensions included.

---

of Globalization on Employment and Social Inclusion Policies: Experiences and Proposals in Individual European Countries', *Bulletin of Comparative Labour Relations* (ed. R. Blanpain), 2009, no. 71, 3–32; G. Davidov and B. Langille (eds.), *The Idea of Labour Law*, Oxford University Press, 2011, 441 pp.

86. There is, however, no doubt that the TFEU sets very high goals for the EU:

- the promotion of employment;
- improved living and working conditions, so as to make possible their harmonisation while improvement is maintained;
- proper social protection;
- dialogue between management and labour;
- the development of human resources with a view to lasting high employment; and
- the combating of social exclusion (Article 151 TFEU).

87. With the Treaty of Amsterdam, the two-track social policy in the EU has come to an end, which has to be applauded. Indeed, the UK renounced its opt-out of the Agreement on Social Policy concluded at Maastricht in 1991. This agreement is now incorporated in the TFEU in a chapter called 'Social policy', which replaces the earlier Title VIII on Social Policy of the TEC. *De facto*, the Maastricht Agreement on Social Policy (1991) and the earlier Title III of the EC have been merged into one. There is also a new title which has been inserted in the TFEU, concerning employment (Title IX).

88. When one analyses the order of the various objectives which the EU pursues, one must recognise that European social policy, and especially employment strategy, is subordinated to the overall economic and monetary goals of the EU. This conclusion follows clearly from an analysis of the text of the TFEU, especially after the Amsterdam Treaty.

Indeed, at the top of the hierarchy of the various EU objectives lie the goals of non-inflationary growth and an economic policy in conformity with EMU, namely low inflation, public deficit under control and the like. These are the well-known Maastricht criteria.

89. This conclusion follows from the wording of the Title on Employment. Article 146 very clearly states:

> Member States, through their employment policies, shall contribute to the achievement of the objectives ... in a way consistent with the broad guidelines of the economic policies of the Member States and of the Community.

In other words, the employment strategy of the Member States has to be primarily non-inflationary.

Social policy, according to the Treaty of Amsterdam, will take account of the need to maintain the competitiveness of the Union economy (Article 151).

Let us repeat this conclusion, given its vital importance: social policy, including employment strategies, has to be non-inflationary and geared towards maintaining the competitiveness of the European economy.

The conclusions of the Dutch Presidency (ICG 1997) translated these choices as follows:

Restoring a sustained, high rate of non-inflationary growth is necessary to achieve a long lasting solution to the Community's unemployment problem and to make further headway towards sound public finances.

90. These political choices have as a consequence that, as we will demonstrate below, wage costs and employment remain national competencies over which the EU holds no normative power. This leads to social dumping, to unfair competition between Member States on the basis of wages and working conditions, and also social security contributions.

91. So much so that a full-fledged social Europe is farther away than ever and we need to continue to pursue our efforts for a more balanced European integration. Social and economic aspects, indeed, need to go hand in hand. An economic system which leads to social injustice carries the seed of its own downfall. Social misery and exclusion undermine democracy, which an efficient market economy needs more than anything else. We thus continue to opt for a more social Europe that would be competent in all social areas with full respect for the principles of subsidiarity and proportionality.

92. A more social Europe, providing for minimum conditions and setting rules for a social playing field, putting an end to social dumping and asymmetric developments, is a 'must'.

So this is a monograph for a social Europe. It is indeed clear that the individual must occupy a central place in the vast common European market, governed by the economic rules for free and creative enterprise. There is a need for socially inspired measures which monitor and guide economic development in such a way that justice and freedom foster well-being for all. The term 'social' means that Europe, in the framework of social and economic cohesion and genuine solidarity, guarantees fundamental human rights to employers, workers, the self-employed, handicapped persons and pensioners, in line with a humanistic and personalised vision, which should make Europe the shining light of the world.

We study the European labour law covering the 27 Member States of the EU. This law also applies to the EEA, which means also to Iceland, Liechtenstein and Norway.

§10. FUNDAMENTAL SOCIAL RIGHTS

93. Fundamental social rights can *in abstracto* be promulgated either by the International Labour Organisation (ILO), by the European institutions, by national states or by regions. It seems to me, however, that specific European measures are needed and indicated, for various reasons.

(a) The international standards laid down by the ILO are enormously important as worldwide rules of behaviour, but for evident reasons they need amending and adaptation in order to respond to Europe's social side and to the more advanced European level of development. European norms have still, of course, where possible and appropriate, to build further on the ILO conventions and recommendations.[38]

(b) National rules are not always sufficient: the national instruments stop at national borders. When issues and realities transcend national frontiers, such as the free movement of labour in the EU or the restructuring of enterprises, which affect workers in different countries and thus take on a European dimension, rules are needed at the appropriate level so that economy and justice go hand in hand and the standards, as well as the issues at stake, have a transnational or supranational character.

In short, Europe must have its own specific social policy and, consequently, its own full-fledged labour law.

94. This monograph deals with European law: Europe on the one hand and labour law on the other. Europe covers *in casu* the territory for which the EU is competent. Europe also needs a Union law. This concept is reasonably simple. However, the notion of labour law is more difficult. Although the expression 'labour law' is used in Article 156 of the TFEU, where the promotion of close cooperation between Member States in the social field is addressed, it is clear that an explicit and generally accepted definition of European labour law is at present non-existent. This is even more noticeable since 'provisions relating to the rights and interests of employed persons' are considered, in conformity with the European Single Act of 1986, to be of national – and not European – jurisdiction (Article 114(2) TFEU); indeed, measures relating to these rights and interests are subject to a unanimous decision by the Council so that each Member State enjoys a right of veto, as will be explained in much more detail later. However, since the Treaty of Amsterdam, a rather broad notion of labour law has prevailed within that framework. Indeed, Article 151 TFEU reads:

> The Union and the Member States, having in mind fundamental social rights such as those set out in the European Social Charter signed at Turin on 18

---

38. In this context a special mention has to be made of the Declaration on Fundamental Rights of Workers, of 18 June 1998, adopted by the General Assembly of the ILO. In this declaration the ILO
    (1) Recalls
        (a) that in freely joining the ILO, all Member States have endorsed the principles and rights set out in its Constitution and in the Declaration of Philadelphia, and have undertaken to work towards attaining the overall objectives of the Organisation to the best of their resources and fully in line with their specific circumstances;
        (b) that these principles and rights have been expressed and developed in the form of specific rights and obligations in Conventions recognised as fundamental both inside and outside the Organisation.
    (2) Declares that all Members, even if they have not ratified the Conventions in question, have an obligation arising from the very fact of membership in the Organisation, to respect, to promote and to realise, in good faith and in accordance with the Constitution, the principles concerning the fundamental rights which are the subject of those Conventions, namely:
        (a) freedom of association and the effective recognition of the right to collective bargaining;
        (b) the elimination of all forms of forced and compulsory labour;
        (c) the effective abolition of child labour; and
        (d) the elimination of discrimination in respect of employment and occupation.

October 1961 and in the 1989 Community Charter of the Fundamental Social Rights of Workers, shall have as their objectives the promotion of employment, improved living and working conditions, so as to make possible the harmonisation while the improvement is being maintained, proper social protection, dialogue between management and labour, the development of human resources with a view to lasting employment and the combating of exclusion. To this end the Union and the Member States shall implement measures which take account of the diverse forms of national practices, in particular in the field of contractual relations, and the need to maintain the competitiveness of the Union economy.

95. It is nevertheless possible to advance a European definition of labour law since the worker is the main focus on labour law and there is a European definition of a worker. This European definition was formulated by the Court during the settlement of disputes concerning the implementation of free movement for workers, and appears in Article 45 TFEU:

> Since freedom of movement for workers constitutes one of the fundamental principles of the Union, the term 'worker' in Article 45 TFEU may not be interpreted differently according to the law of each Member State but must have a Union meaning. Since it defines the scope of that fundamental freedom, the Union concept of a 'worker' must be interpreted broadly. That concept must be defined in accordance with objective criteria which distinguish the employment relationship by reference to the rights and duties of the persons concerned. *The essential feature of an employment relationship, however, is that for a certain period of time a person performs services for and under the direction of another person in return for which he receives remuneration.*[39]

96. In giving this interpretation, the European Court associates itself with the definition of the term 'worker', which is accepted in the Member States in general.[40] Labour law relates thus to employees, who work in subordination. Workers presuppose employers, namely those for which the services in subordination are rendered against pay. European labour law, consequently, like national labour law in the Member States, deals with the relations between employers and workers.

97. National labour law usually limits itself to regulating employment in the private sector. European labour law, however, also covers employment in the public sector. This is the case for the regulation of equal treatment of men and women

---

39. C.O.J., 3 July 1986, *Lawrie-Blum* v. *Land Baden-Württemberg*, no. 66/85, ECR, 1986, 2121. This does not diminish the fact that, for certain European instruments, reference is made to the national definitions. This is the case with the directive of 14 February 1997 concerning the transfer of enterprises (*Foreningen of Arbejdsledere i Danmark* v. *A/S Danmols Invenar*, no. 105/85, ECR, 1985, 2639).
40. 'Employed or Self-employed', Special Issue, *Bulletin of Comparative Labour Relations*, B. Brooks and C. Engels (Guest Editors), no. 24, 1992, p. 175; C. Engels, 'Subordinate Employees of Self-Employed Workers', in *Comparative Labour Law and Industrial Relations in Industrialized Market Economies* (ed. R. Blanpain), 2010, 11th and revised edn, 323–346.

regarding pay and working conditions or of the free movement of workers. The scope of European labour law has consequently to be defined accordingly, case by case.

European labour law, taking into account the fact that European rules, which relate to workers, deal with both individual (e.g. concerning the free movement of workers or the equal treatment of men and women) and collective labour relations (e.g. information and consultation of workers' representatives in the case of collective redundancies or workers' participation in the *Societas Europaea* (SE)), can be defined as 'the body of European legal rules that govern the individual and collective labour relations between employers and workers, namely those who perform work in subordination'.

98. The Maastricht Top of 9–10 December 1991 was an important event, also for those interested in what direction the Europe of the 12, as a social Community of some 150,000,000 managers and employees, would go. The debate in Maastricht was dominated by the battle between the United Kingdom and the European continental Member States concerning a more progressive profile for the European Community regarding social matters. The outcome was painful as well as historic. Painful in the sense that the United Kingdom opted out and went its own way, at least for the moment; historic as the 12 Member States, the United Kingdom included, not only agreed to confirm the *acquis communautaire* reached in the social field, but also, in a *Protocol on Social Policy*, that the other 11 Member States could equally do their own thing and launch more progressive social policies. Thus a new social European dimension came into being.

99. Obviously, mention has to be made of the Treaty of Amsterdam (16–17 June 1997), which contains no fewer than six sections. Above all, there was an inflation of protocols and declarations: 14 protocols and 46 declarations.

Quite a number of issues dealt with by the European Council relate directly to employment, industrial relations and labour law. As far as 'social Europe' is concerned, the playing field is clear. Some capital steps were taken with the introduction of a new Title and a new chapter in the Treaty of the European Community concerning employment (Title VIII) and social policy (Title XI, Chapter I), a general principle of non-discrimination, references to the Social Charter of the Council of Europe, etc.

The new Title XI incorporates the Social Agreement of Maastricht. This is quite important. The two track social Europe due to the British opt-out came to an end once the treaty was ratified. There is a possibility of doing something more at the European level in the social field.

100. The Treaty does not provide for new, directly enforceable individual or collective social rights. But it does give a legal basis for action by the appropriate institutions of the EU in certain areas, non-discrimination or employment policies, for example. So a dynamic process could be launched, if the political will is there and subsidiarity rules permit fully fledged European action.

The Treaty of Amsterdam entered into force on 1 May 1999.

Prologue

101. Special mention must be made of the following:

- fundamental rights, with reference to the European Convention for the Protection of Human Rights, the European Social Charter, issues like the principle of non-discrimination, disability, equality of men and women and protection of data;
- the Employment Title VIII: coordinating national strategies, as employment policies are clearly left to the competence of the Member States; – the Chapter on Social Policy, integrating the Maastricht Agreement on Social

Policy; and also providing for the possibility of positive discrimination;

- the environment: looking for a balance between the environment and high employment;
- culture and non-professional sport;
- a Protocol on the application of the principles of subsidiarity and proportionality, clearly indicating that regarding matters of mixed competence, the EU can only intervene when there is additional (European) value and only as far as necessary, leaving maximum authority to Member States and consequently to the Social Partners;
- the Presidency Conclusions regarding employment, competitiveness and growth.

In that framework mention has to be made of the Commission's Action Plan for the Single Market submitted to the Amsterdam Summit.

102. The European Top of Nice of December 2000 was downright disappointing as far as the increase of majority voting and the Charter of Fundamental Rights was concerned. Regarding majority voting almost nothing changed. The core of social policy issues remains the exclusive competence of Member States, while the Charter of Fundamental Rights was adopted by way of a Declaration.

Obviously, the Charter contains a lot of social rights. Some are fundamental; some are important but not fundamental. Here we can talk about an inflation of social rights as far as a Charter to be included in the European treaties is concerned. We think, for example, about rights like the right of access to placement services, to protection in the event of unjustified dismissal and about fair to just working conditions. These are important points indeed, but not the 'core rights' one is thinking about when discussing a Charter of Fundamental Rights. The 1998 ILO Declaration, on the other hand, concentrates on the real core social rights and the ILO solution seems to be more appropriate.

103. As far as the binding effect of the Charter is concerned, Nice was disappointing. The Presidency Conclusions of the Nice Top regarding the Charter read as follows:

> The European Council welcomes the joint proclamation, by the Council, the European Parliament and the Commission, of the Charter of Fundamental Rights, combining in a single text the civil, political, economic, social and societal rights hitherto laid down in a variety of international, European or

national sources. The European Council would like to see the Charter disseminated as widely as possible amongst the Union's citizens. In accordance with the Cologne conclusions, the question of the Charter's force will be considered later.

Later meant after enlargement and that some 27 Member States have to unanimously agree to give binding effect to the Charter.

§11. A CONSTITUTION FOR EUROPE

I. The Convention (2003)

104. The text of a Constitution for Europe was drawn up by a specially convened body – the European Convention – headed by the former French President, Valéry Giscard d'Estaing.

In the light of the fact that the European Union would admit ten new Member States in May 2004, thus enlarging its membership from 15 to 25 countries, a revision of the various EU Treaties was more than necessary. The aim of the revision was mainly to streamline the workings of the EU and also to simplify the Treaties and make the EU more accessible to its citizens. The Convention issued its final draft text in June 2003.

II. Implications for the Future Social and Employment Policy of the EU[41]

105. The draft Treaty establishing a Constitution for Europe, is divided into four parts, as follows:

– Part I, which sets out the definition and objectives of the Union. It also lays down the workings of the EU's institutions;
– Part II, which incorporates the Charter of Fundamental Rights of the European Union, which was approved by the Council, the European Parliament and the European Commission in 2000;
– Part III, which sets out the policies and functioning of the Union; and – Part IV, which contains a number of final provisions.

The new text comprises a single Treaty, replacing the previous grouping of the Union's policy and work under a range of different 'pillars'. Once in force, the new constitutional Treaty will repeal the Treaty on the European Union (TEU), the Treaty establishing the European Community (TEC) and the acts and treaties which have supplemented or amended them.

The draft new Treaty refers throughout to the European Union rather than the Community, giving it a single legal personality which, it is hoped, will enable it to

---

41. Andrea Broughton, IRS, 'Social policy provisions of draft EU constitutional Treaty examined', www.eiro.eurofound.ie.

take on a higher international profile. Other changes of terminology include a reference to 'European laws' rather than Regulations, 'European framework laws' rather than directives and the social partners, rather than 'management and labour'.

III. Definitions and Objectives of the Union

106. Part I sets out the key definitions and objectives of the Union, including its values. Most of these objectives and values are taken from the existing Treaties, although there is arguably more of an emphasis on non-discrimination in the new text. Thus, the values listed in Article I-2 include 'respect for human dignity, liberty, democracy, equality, the rule of law and respect for human rights'. It also makes reference to a society based on a range of values, including non-discrimination.

In Article I-3, the draft Treaty lists full employment as one of the objectives of the Union (the existing TEU refers to a high level of employment), along with combating social exclusion and discrimination, promoting equality between women and men and solidarity between generations.

Article I-4 lists the Union's fundamental freedoms and states that any discrimination on grounds of nationality shall be prohibited.

Article I-14 deals with the coordination of economic and employment policies, stating that the Union shall 'adopt measures to ensure coordination of the employment policies of the Member States, in particular by adopting guidelines for these policies'. This is a reference to the European employment strategy, which has been in existence since 1997.

IV. Role of the Social Partners

107. Specific reference is made to the role of the social partners in the European Union. Accordingly, Article I-47 states that: 'The European Union recognises and promotes the role of the social partners at Union level, taking into account the diversity of national systems; it shall facilitate dialogue between the social partners, respecting their autonomy.'

V. Fundamental Rights

108. Part II of the draft Treaty contains the Charter of Fundamental Rights of the European Union, which was originally drawn up in 2000 but not given legally binding status at that time. The incorporation of the Charter into the Treaty will give it legal status. The preamble notes that it is necessary to strengthen the protection of fundamental rights 'in the light of changes in society, social progress and scientific and technological developments by making those rights more visible in a Charter'.

The Charter sets out a range of rights, freedoms and principles for EU citizens. In the employment and industrial relations area, the key points include:

- freedom of assembly and association;
- freedom to choose an occupation and the right to engage in work;
- a right not to be discriminated against;
- a right to equality between men and women, including in the areas of employment, work and pay;
- a worker's right to information and consultation within an undertaking;
- the right of collective bargaining and action;
- the right of access to placement services;
- the right to protection in the event of unjustified dismissal;
- the right to fair and just working conditions;
- a ban on child labour; and
- protection of young people at work.

109. Title VII of the Charter, which deals with its interpretation and application, allows limitations on the exercise of its rights and freedoms if provided for by law and if they respect the essence of those rights and freedoms. These limitations may be made 'only if they are necessary and genuinely meet objectives of general interest recognised by the Union or the need to protect the rights and freedoms of others'. Further, it is stated that the fundamental rights in the Charter shall be interpreted in harmony with the constitutional traditions of Member States.

VI. EU Policies and Functioning

110. Part III of the proposed Treaty governs the policies and functioning of the Union. In its 'clauses of general application' (Title I), it states that in the activities referred to in this part of the Treaty, the Union shall aim to eliminate inequalities and to promote equality between men and women. It also states that the Union shall aim to combat discrimination based on sex, racial or ethnic origin, religion or belief, disability, age or sexual orientation.

Title II of this part of the draft Treaty is devoted to non-discrimination and citizenship, with the non-discrimination provisions currently set out in Article 13 of the TEC now contained in Article III-8.

VII. Employment and Social Policy Chapters

111. The draft Treaty's 'employment chapter' is contained in Title III, Chapter III, Articles III-97–102. There are no significant substantive changes to this chapter, compared with the current provisions.

The social policy provisions of the draft Treaty are contained in Articles III-103–112. It lists the social policy areas in which the Union is committed to supporting the actions of Member States as follows:

(a) improvement in particular of the working environment to protect workers' health and safety;
(b) working conditions;

(c) social security and social protection of workers;
(d) protection of workers where their employment contract is terminated;
(e) the information and consultation of workers;
(f) representation and collective defence of the interests of workers and employers, including co-determination (although not in the areas of pay, the right of association, the right to strike or the right to impose lock-outs);
(g) conditions of employment for third-country nationals legally residing in Union territory;
(h) the integration of persons excluded from the labour market;
(i) equality between men and women with regard to labour market opportunities and treatment at work;
(j) the combating of social exclusion; and
(k) the modernisation of social protection systems.

112. Under the provisions of the draft Treaty, legal instruments drawn up in these fields are subject to qualified majority voting in Council and co-decision with the EP, with the exception of laws in the areas covered by paragraphs (c), (d), (f) and

(g), which are subject to unanimity in the Council and consultation with the EP. However, the draft states that the Council may unanimously adopt a European decision (based on a proposal from the Commission) to apply what the Treaty terms the 'ordinary legislative procedure' (set out in Article III-302) – i.e. the co-decision procedure, subject to qualified majority voting in Council – in the case of the areas outlined in (d), (f) and (g) above.

113. One area where there is a straight switch from Council unanimity to qualified majority voting is the field of social security for migrant workers. The proposed new provisions are contained in Article III-21.

114. All of this effectively means that qualified majority voting is extended to one extra area – the field of social security for migrant workers. Further, if a unanimous Council decision is made allowing this, qualified majority voting may be extended to the areas of: protection of workers where their employment contract is terminated; the representation and collective defence of the interests of workers and employers, including co-determination; and conditions of employment for third-country nationals legally residing in Union territory.

VIII. Vocational Training

115. Articles III-182–183 deal with the issue of vocational training, containing no major substantive differences from the wording of these articles as set out in the TEC, with the exception of a specific reference to sport in the context of education, vocational training and youth.

§12. AGREEMENT BY MEMBER STATES (2004)[42]

116. EU heads of state and ministers reached on 17–18 June 2004 Agreement on the text of the Treaty establishing a Constitution for Europe (Constitutional Treaty). As before, the draft Treaty incorporates the Charter of Fundamental Rights of the European Union, which enshrines a number of labour and social rights for citizens.

In June 2004 agreement was on amendments to the Constitutional Treaty.

I. The Commission

117. Regarding the composition of the European Commission Member States agreed that the first Commission appointed under the provisions of the new Treaty would consist of one Commissioner from each Member State. After this, however, the Commission will consist of a number of members corresponding to two-thirds of the number of Member States. These members will be selected on the basis of a system of equal rotation between the Member States. Given that the Commission will thus, in future, no long always include nationals of all Member States.

II. Qualified Majority Voting

118. Agreement was reached on the following procedures:

– a qualified majority will be defined as at least 55 per cent of the members of the Council, comprising at least 15 Council members and representing Member States comprising at least 65 per cent of the population of the EU; – a blocking minority must include at least four Council members; and
– however, if the Council is not acting on a proposal from the Commission or from the EU's minister for foreign affairs, the qualified majority will be 72 per cent of the members of the Council, representing Member States comprising at least 65 per cent of the population of the EU.

An agreed decision on the implementation of this system states that if Council members representing at least three-quarters of the level of the EU population or at least three-quarters of the number of Member States that is necessary to form a blocking minority indicate their opposition to the Council on a particular proposal, the Council will discuss the issue and try to reach a satisfactory solution to address the concerns raised.

The current system of qualified majority voting, as set out in the Treaty of Nice, will apply until 31 October 2009. From 1 November 2009, the procedures outlined above would come into force.

---

42. Antoine Jacobs, *The European Constitution: How it was created; What it will change*, Wolf Legal Publishers, Nijmegen, 2005, 146 pp.

III. Charter of Fundamental Rights

119. The Charter, which sets out a range of basic labour, social and human rights for EU citizens, remains part of the Treaty as before, with its provisions unchanged.

IV. Enhanced Cooperation

120. Ministers agreed a change to the procedures governing 'enhanced cooperation' between an agreed number of Member States. This essentially gives a group of Member States an opportunity to progress more rapidly on a particular issue than the EU as a whole. These procedures have been amended to ensure that authorisation to proceed with enhanced cooperation will be subject to unanimous Council decision (Articles III 325 and 326). The Council may use qualified majority voting, if it decides unanimously to do so. Under this provision, a group of Member States may decide to progress proposals in most policy areas, including employment and social policy.[43]

§13. REFERENDA: REJECTION OF THE CONSTITUTION?

121. The new Constitution needs, self-evidently, to be ratified by the Member States. Indeed, all 27 EU members must ratify the constitution to bring it into force.

Some states have left this task to their Parliaments. Most Member States have so far ratified the constitution through their respective national parliaments. Others referred to referenda, which resounded in a yes vote in Spain and Luxembourg, but also in two loud nos, namely in the Netherlands and in France. Other Member States that had planned to hold referenda – including the UK, Denmark, Portugal, Poland and Ireland – shelved their plans after the decision of the European summit in June 2005 to put the ratification process on ice.

The Czech Republic, undecided until then, also announced that it would not hold a referendum.

A time of reflection was called for. This relates not only to the reasons for the 'yes' or the 'no', but also to whether a form of direct democracy, like a referendum, is indeed a suitable vehicle to solve complex societal questions in an appropriate and lasting way.[44]

I. The Reform Treaty (2007)

122. Following the rejection of the European Constitution by France and the Netherlands in 2005 and a two-year period of reflection, on 23 June 2007 the EU

---

43. Andrea Broughton, IRS, 'Agreement reached on Constitutional Treaty', www.eiro.eurofound.ie, 2004.
44. See Fareed Zakaria, *The Future of Freedom: Illiberal Democracy at Home and Abroad*, 2004, New York, Norton, 295 p.

leaders agreed on a detailed mandate for a new Intergovernmental Conference. The IGC opened on 23 July 2007, and completed its work on 18 October. The resulting Reform Treaty was signed in Lisbon on 18 December 2007.

The treaty would not apply until and unless it was ratified by each of the EU's 27 members. It was up to each country to choose the procedure for ratification, in line with its own national constitution.

The Treaty of Lisbon amends the current EU and EC treaties, without replacing them. It will provide the Union with the legal framework and tools necessary to meet future challenges and to respond to citizens' demands.

123.

(1) A more democratic and transparent Europe, with a strengthened role for the European Parliament and national parliaments, more opportunities for citizens to have their voices heard and a clearer sense of who does what at European and national level:
- a strengthened role for the European Parliament: the European Parliament, directly elected by EU citizens, will see important new powers emerge over EU legislation, the EU budget and international agreements. In particular, the increase of co-decision procedure in policy-making will ensure the European Parliament is placed on an equal footing with the Council, representing Member States, for the vast bulk of EU legislation;
- a greater involvement of national parliaments: national parliaments will have greater opportunities to be involved in the work of the EU, in particular thanks to a new mechanism to monitor that the Union only acts where results can be better attained at EU level (subsidiarity). Together with the strengthened role for the European Parliament, this will enhance democracy and increase legitimacy in the functioning of the Union;
- a stronger voice for citizens: thanks to the Citizens' Initiative, one million citizens from a number of Member States will have the possibility to call on the Commission to bring forward new policy proposals;
- who does what: the relationship between the Member States and the European Union will become clearer with the categorisation of competences;
- withdrawal from the Union: the Treaty of Lisbon explicitly recognises for the first time the possibility for a Member State to withdraw from the Union.

124.

(2) A more efficient Europe, with simplified working methods and voting rules, streamlined and modern institutions for an EU of 27 members and an improved ability to act in areas of major priority for today's Union:
- effective and efficient decision-making: qualified majority voting in the Council will be extended to new policy areas to make decision-making faster and more efficient. From 2014 on, the calculation of qualified majority will be based on the double majority of Member States and people, thus representing the dual legitimacy of the Union. A double majority will be

achieved when a decision is taken by 55 per cent of the Member States representing at least 65 per cent of the Union's population;
- a more stable and streamlined institutional framework: the Treaty of Lisbon creates the function of President of the European Council elected for two and a half years, introduces a direct link between the election of the Commission President and the results of the European elections, provides for new arrangements for the future composition of the European Parliament and for a smaller Commission, and includes clearer rules on enhanced cooperation and financial provisions;
- improving the life of Europeans: the Treaty of Lisbon improves the EU's ability to act in several policy areas of major priority for today's Union and its citizens. This is the case in particular for the policy areas of freedom, security and justice, such as combating terrorism or tackling crime. It also concerns to some extent other areas including energy policy, public health, civil protection, climate change, services of general interest, research, space, territorial cohesion, commercial policy, humanitarian aid, sport, tourism and administrative cooperation.

125.

(3) A Europe of rights and values, freedom, solidarity and security, promoting the Union's values, introducing the Charter of Fundamental Rights into European primary law, providing for new solidarity mechanisms and ensuring better protection of European citizens:
- democratic values: the Treaty of Lisbon details and reinforces the values and objectives on which the Union is built. These values aim to serve as a reference point for European citizens and to demonstrate what Europe has to offer its partners worldwide;
- citizens' rights and Charter of Fundamental Rights: the Treaty of Lisbon preserves existing rights while introducing new ones. In particular, it guarantees the freedoms and principles set out in the Charter of Fundamental Rights and gives its provisions a binding legal force. It concerns civil, political, economic and social rights;
- freedom of European citizens: the Treaty of Lisbon preserves and reinforces the 'four freedoms' and the political, economic and social freedom of European citizens;
- solidarity between Member States: the Treaty of Lisbon provides that the Union and its Member States act jointly in a spirit of solidarity if a Member State is the subject of a terrorist attack or the victim of a natural or man-made disaster. Solidarity in the area of energy is also emphasised;
- increased security for all: the Union will get an extended capacity to act on freedom, security and justice, which will bring direct benefits in terms of the Union's ability to fight crime and terrorism. New provisions on civil protection, humanitarian aid and public health also aim at boosting the Union's ability to respond to threats to the security of European citizens.

126.

(4) Europe as an actor on the global stage will be achieved by bringing together Europe's external policy tools, both when developing and deciding new policies. The Treaty of Lisbon will give Europe a clear voice in relations with its partners worldwide. It will harness Europe's economic, humanitarian, political and diplomatic strengths to promote European interests and values worldwide, while respecting the particular interests of the Member States in Foreign Affairs:
 – a new High Representative for the Union in Foreign Affairs and Security Policy, also Vice-President of the Commission, will increase the impact, the coherence and the visibility of the EU's external action;
 – a new European External Action Service will provide back up and support to the High Representative;
 – a single legal personality for the Union will strengthen the Union's negotiating power, making it more effective on the world stage and a more visible partner for third countries and international organisations;
 – progress in European Security and Defence Policy will preserve special decision-making arrangements but also pave the way towards reinforced cooperation amongst a smaller group of Member States.

Let us, however, underline that the social competences of the EU remained what they were. Here no progress was made.

The Treaty of Lisbon entered into force on 1 December 2009.

§14. CONTENT OF THE MONOGRAPH

127. This monograph contains a general introduction and two parts: one devoted to individual labour law (I) and a second that deals with collective labour law (II). The book ends with an epilogue, appendices, a short bibliography, an alphabetical list of cited cases from the European Court of Justice and an index.

In the general introduction, attention is paid to the institutional framework leading to European Union law (Chapter 1). Here, the three European Treaties (ECSC, Euratom and the EU) are examined, as well as the institutions of the Union (the EP, the Council, the Commission and the Court) and other organs, such as the ESC, the European Social Fund, certain advisory bodies, etc. Then follows the legislative process in the Union and the relationship of the EU to other international organisations, especially the ILO, the EEA and the Europa Agreements concluded with some Central and Eastern European States. Chapter 2 is devoted to the European social partners, especially Bussiness Europe, CEEP, UEAPME and the ETUC. Chapter 3 deals with the jurisdiction of the EU with regard to labour law matters. The section (Chapter 4) of the General Introduction examines the genesis and the development of European labour law. Special attention is paid to the relationship between the economic and social aspects of Union affairs and due regard is given to the solemn declaration of the basic social rights for workers (1989) and the social

Prologue

action programme, whose purpose is to implement that declaration. We self-evidently pay adequate attention to the remarkable progress, at least legally speaking, which was reached during the Maastricht Top of December 1991 where the already mentioned Protocol and Agreement on Social Policy were concluded, as well as to the Delors White Paper (December 1993), indicating measures to foster growth and combat unemployment and exclusion, the White Paper on European Social Policy (July 1994), the measures to combat unemployment as agreed upon by the Council at the European Top in Essen (December 1994), the Confidence Pact for Employment (1996) and self-evidently the IGC which started in 1996 and was finalised in 1997, the employment summit of Luxembourg (21–22 November 1997) and the employment guidelines. In this framework the question is raised of whether we need to include fundamental social rights in the Treaty of the European Union. The answer is 'yes'.

128. Following this order of ideas, speculation concerning and discussion of the question regarding the convergence or divergence of labour law systems in the Member States of the Union is of course a 'must'. This discussion concludes the General Introduction.

129. The first part is devoted to individual labour law. Here, important developments have taken place, especially due to the crucial role of the Court. We discuss the free movement of workers (Chapter 1) and freedom of services (Chapter 2), equal treatment (Chapter 6) and the restructuring of enterprises (Chapter 10) in relation to collective redundancies, the transfer of enterprises and the insolvency of the employer. A theme that made rather technical but nevertheless important headway is the health and safety of workers in the working environment (Chapter 9). Another far-reaching subject is the European Treaty of June 1980 relating to elements of international private labour law (Chapter 3). In other fields developments can be noted, and this is so in the area of working time (Chapter 8), the protection of motherhood (Chapter 7) and individual employment contracts (Chapter 4). Regarding the latter point some concrete measures were taken, namely regarding part-time employment, temporary work, fixed term contracts and the employer's obligation to inform employees of the conditions applicable to the contract of employment relationship.

130. The second part deals with collective labour law. Here the possibilities for European-wide collective agreements are evaluated against the background of European social realities (Chapter 1) in view of the Articles 154 and 155 of the TFEU. In Chapter 2 we examine workers' participation in the public limited liability company and the SE, as well as the very important directive on EWCs and transnational information and consultation procedures and the general framework directive on information and consultation.

The first chapter of Part II provides a general framework for the European collective agreements, which may be concluded in view of the Articles 154 and 155 of the EU. Indeed, the possible venue of European collective agreements leads to a number of complicated problems, also legal ones, which can only be tackled if one has a better insight into the complex and delicate set of relationships which constitute the collective bargaining process and which may eventually lead to collective agreements. Two of the more difficult points self-evidently concern the scope and the binding effect of those agreements. It is interesting to note that the social partners failed to agree on issues like the EWC and the shift of the burden of proof regarding equal treatment, but succeeded in concluding a first European collective agreement on Parental Leave on 14 December 1995, a second one on Part-time Work on 6 June 1997 and a third one on Fixed Term Contracts of 18 March 1999, all promulgated by a Council Directive.

Other issues, which were recently discussed in the framework of European collective bargaining, relate to telework and temporary work. Regarding telework stress a 'voluntary' agreement was concluded between the social partners, while on temporary work no agreement seemed possible, which led to a proposal for a directive by the European Commission. Framework Agreements were also reached on stress at work (2004), harassment and violence at work (2007) and on an inclusive market (2010). In this context mention should also be made of the agreements made in the framework of the sectoral social dialogue.

131. I would like to add a word about the language and terminology used. I am obviously writing in a foreign language, which, despite the best efforts of the best rewriter, remains an awkward exercise. The language and terminology used by the European Union do not simplify the task. A sentence such as 'the rights conferring immediate or prospective entitlement to old age benefits, including survivors' benefits, under supplementary company or inter-company pension schemes outside the national statutory social security schemes' may illustrate the point, certainly for non-native English speakers. Many European texts have been drafted in French and one is acutely aware of this fact when reading the translation. This is certainly the case for the smaller Union languages like Dutch, my mother tongue, which is practically never used as an original language for writing and formulating Union instruments. This deeply influences the language used in this book, because, for reasons of legal security, we wish to stick as closely as possible to the wording of Union law. Moreover, the terms used in the different Union languages to convey the same message do not always have the same meaning. A typical example can be found in the directive concerning the transfer of enterprises (1977). Here the terms *bedrijfstak*, company or intercompany, *professionnel ou interprofessionnel, betrieblichen oder überbetrieblichen, professionali o interprofessionali, fagliche eller fvaerfagliche*, should have the same meaning, *quod non*! Rightly the European Commission indicated that a Union instrument cannot be interpreted on the basis of one, isolated, linguistic version, but must be explained in accordance with the goals of the instrument and its direction in close relation with the versions in the other Union languages.[45]

---

45. *Commission* v. *Denmark*, 11 April 1990, No. C 100/90, ECR, 1991, 8. Action brought on 11 April 1990 by the Commission of the European Communities against the Kingdom of Denmark.

Prologue

132. The same problem was illustrated by the *Rockfon* case (Denmark),[46] where the meaning of the word 'establishment', used in the directive on collective redundancies (1975), was discussed. Indeed, the term 'establishment' is not defined in the directive. Rockfon maintained that it was not an establishment, since it had no management which could independently effect large-scale dismissals.

The Court observed that the term 'establishment' is a term of Community law and cannot be defined by reference to the laws of the Member States.

The various language versions of the directive use somewhat different terms to convey the concept in question:

the Danish version has *virksomhed*, the Dutch version *plaatselijke eenheid*, the English version *establishment*, the Finnish version *yritys*, the French version *établissement*, the German version *Betrieb*, the Greek version επιχειρηςη, the Italian version *stabilimento*, the Portuguese version *estabelecimento*, the Spanish version *centro de trabajo* and the Swedish version *arbetsplats*.

A comparison of the terms used show that they have different connotations signifying, according to the version in question, establishment, undertaking, work centre, local unit or place of work. As was held in *Bouchereau*, the different language versions of a Union text must be given a uniform interpretation and in case of divergence between the versions the provision in question must therefore be interpreted by reference to the purpose and general scheme of the rules of which it forms a part.[47]

133. The Summit of Edinburgh (11–12 December 1992) addressed the issue under the heading 'Simplification of and Easier Access to Community Legislation'. The Summit led to the following declaration:

Making new Community legislation clearer and simpler.
While the technical nature of most texts and the need to compromise among the various national positions often complicate the drafting process, practical steps should nevertheless be taken to improve the quality of Community legislation, such as the following:

(a) guidelines for the drafting of Community legislation should be agreed upon, containing criteria against which the quality of drafting of legislation would have to be checked;
(b) delegations of Member States should endeavour, at all levels of the Council proceedings, to check more thoroughly the quality of legislation;
(c) the Council Legal Service should be requested to review draft legislative Acts on a regular basis before they are adopted by the Council and make suggestions where necessary for appropriate redrafting in order to make such Acts as simple and clear as possible;
(d) the jurist-linguist group, which does the final legal editing of all legislation before it is adopted by the Council (with the participation of national

---

46. C.O.J., 7 December 1995, Case C-449/93, ECR, 1995, 4291.
47. *Regina* v. *Pierre Bouchereau*, 27 October 1977, C-30/77, ECR, 1977, 1999.

legal experts), should give suggestions for simplifying and clarifying the language of the texts without changing their substance.

In this context, one should note that the Treaty of Amsterdam (1997) contains a Chapter 10, under the heading 'Transparency'. The second paragraph of Article 1 of the TEU is amended, stating that 'decisions are taken as openly as possible and as close as possible to the citizen'. Article 15, TFEU states that 'any citizen of the Union ... shall have a right of access to .... documents of the Union's institutions, bodies, offices and agencies, whatever their medium, subject to the principles and the conditions to be defined in accordance with this paragraph'.

134. To conclude this prologue, a word of sincere thanks is more than due. For the writing of this book a great deal of material, especially of a legal and judicial nature, has been used. It is unnecessary to say that the mistakes and failures in this book are our own. The buck stops here.

Roger Blanpain
Leuven
15 July 2013

General Introduction

Chapter 1. The Institutional Framework

§1. THE TREATIES

I. From a Community to a Union

135. Since Amsterdam there have been no fewer than four treaties: the Treaty on the European Union (1997), the European Coal and Steel Community (1951), the European Economic Community and the European Atomic Energy Community (1957).

The three European Communities, namely the European Coal and Steel Community (1951), the European Economic Community and the European Atomic Energy Community (1957), were established by an equal number of treaties concluded among the Member States as independent bodies with a legal personality.[49]

The ECSC and Euratom aim at a rather limited sectoral integration. The EC, on the other hand, envisages much wider economic integration with a common market. This follows from Article 2 of the EC Treaty, which will be mentioned later.

136. The Treaty of Amsterdam marked a new stage in the process of creating an 'ever closer union among the peoples of Europe, where decisions are taken as closely as possible to the citizen'. The phrase 'ever closer union' replaces the words 'Union with a federal goal', which were part of the last draft of the Treaty by the Dutch Presidency at the occasion of the Maastricht Treaty and to which the British had fundamental objections. Indeed, for many British the word 'federalism' means bureaucratic centralism from Brussels, which they refuse.

The change in name of the new European construction, from a Community to a Union, gives, however, an important signal. A union constitutes a closer, a more intense relationship than a mere community: a community relates to people with the same characteristics or interests; a union means a far-reaching involvement, an intimate working together towards a common goal. It is like the difference between acquaintanceship and a (successful) marriage. Of course, we are still on our way and quite a number of further steps toward a real union have to be taken. It is a little

---

49. At Nice (December 2000) it was decided, 'desiring to settle certain questions relating to the expiry of the Treaty establishing the European Coal and Steel Community (ECSC) to confer ownership of the ECSC funds on the European Community. All assets and liabilities of the ECSC, as they exist on 23 July 2002, shall be transferred to the European Community on 24 July 2002.'

awkward that the most integrated part of the new European Union is the (European) Community.

The Maastricht and Amsterdam Treaties can be seen as very important events in post-war European history. Indeed, these Treaties have led to an Economic Monetary Union with a single European currency (euro) and to an independent Central Bank, German style.

These developments were confirmed by the Nice Treaty (December 2000) and the Lisbon Treaty (2009).

The EMU calls for strict economic discipline by the Member States, among other things regarding inflation and public debt (maximum 60 per cent of GNP).

137. The Union has the following objectives:

(1) The Union's aim is to promote peace, its values and the well-being of its peoples.
(2) The Union shall offer its citizens an area of freedom, security and justice without internal frontiers, in which the free movement of persons is ensured in conjunction with appropriate measures with respect to external border controls, asylum, immigration and the prevention and combating of crime.
(3) The Union shall establish an internal market. It shall work for the sustainable development of Europe based on balanced economic growth and price stability, a highly competitive social market economy, aiming at full employment and social progress, and a high level of protection and improvement of the quality of the environment. It shall promote scientific and technological advance.
   - It shall combat social exclusion and discrimination, and shall promote social justice and protection, equality between women and men, solidarity between generations and protection of the rights of the child.
   - It shall promote economic, social and territorial cohesion, and solidarity among Member States.
   - It shall respect its rich cultural and linguistic diversity, and shall ensure that Europe's cultural heritage is safeguarded and enhanced.
(4) The Union shall establish an economic and monetary union whose currency is the euro.
(5) In its relations with the wider world, the Union shall uphold and promote its values and interests and contribute to the protection of its citizens. It shall contribute to peace, security, the sustainable development of the Earth, solidarity and mutual respect among peoples, free and fair trade, eradication of poverty and the protection of human rights, in particular the rights of the child, as well as to the strict observance and the development of international law, including respect for the principles of the United Nations Charter.
(6) The Union shall pursue its objectives by appropriate means commensurate with the competences which are conferred upon it in the Treaties (Art. 3 TEU).

138. The objectives of the Union shall be achieved while respecting the principle of subsidiarity as defined in Article 5 of the TEU.

General Introduction, Ch. 1, The Institutional Framework

(1) The Union recognises the rights, freedoms and principles set out in the Charter of Fundamental Rights of the European Union of 7 December 2000, as adapted at Strasbourg, on 12 December 2007, which shall have the same legal value as the Treaties.

The provisions of the Charter shall not extend in any way the competences of the Union as defined in the Treaties.

The rights, freedoms and principles in the Charter shall be interpreted in accordance with the general provisions in Title VII of the Charter governing its interpretation and application and with due regard to the explanations referred to in the Charter, that set out the sources of those provisions.

(2) The Union shall accede to the European Convention for the Protection of Human Rights and Fundamental Freedoms. Such accession shall not affect the Union's competences as defined in the Treaties.

(3) Fundamental rights, as guaranteed by the European Convention for the Protection of Human Rights and Fundamental Freedoms and as they result from the constitutional traditions common to the Member States, shall constitute general principles of the Union's law (Art. 6 TEU).

II. The Functioning of the European Union

139. The Treaty establishing the European Economic Community was renamed as the European Union.

A. Objectives

140. The Lisbon Treaty 2009 sets out the objectives of the Union as follows.

The Lisbon Treaty clearly sets out the European Union's aims and values of peace, democracy, respect for human rights, justice, equality, rule of law and sustainability.

The Lisbon Treaty pledges that the European Union will:

- offer people an area of freedom, security and justice without internal frontiers;
- work for the sustainable development of Europe based on balanced economic growth and price stability, a highly competitive social market economy, aiming at full employment and social progress, with a high level of protection of the environment;
- combat social exclusion and discrimination and promote social justice and protection;
- promote economic, social and territorial cohesion, and solidarity among Member States;
- remain committed to economic and monetary union with the euro as its currency;
- uphold and promote the European Union's values in the wider world and contribute to peace, security, the sustainable development of the earth, solidarity and respect among peoples, free and fair trade, and the eradication of poverty;

- contribute to the protection of human rights, in particular the rights of the child, as well as the strict observance and development of international law, including respect for the principles of the United Nations Charter.

These are major goals. The Lisbon Treaty is designed to give the EU the tools to achieve them.

B. *Subsidiarity*

141. The EU's decisions must be taken as closely to the citizens as possible. Apart from those areas which fall under its exclusive competence, it does not take action unless this would be more effective than action taken at national, regional or local level. This principle is known as subsidiarity and it is reaffirmed in the Lisbon Treaty.

This principle is complemented by the proportionality principle whereby the EU must limit its action to that which is necessary to achieve the objectives set out in the Lisbon Treaty.

142. The question is twofold. First, at what level should decisions be taken: at EU level, at national level, or at more local levels: regional, at the level of a district or of a township or at sectoral, enterprise or plant level? Secondly, as far as labour law and industrial relations are concerned, the question is, who should take the decisions: the state, or any other governmental institution, public authorities therefore, or the social partners, namely management and labour, by way of collective agreements, in the framework of pluralistic societies, leaving room for autonomous norm-setting by the representatives of employers and employees in the area of labour and working conditions? Subsidiarity may also embrace unilateral decision-making by management, in the framework of 'managerial prerogatives' in the economic area, which constitute a recognised right in societies with free market economics.

Subsidiarity means first that one should not do at EU level what can be done equally well or better at some other level. It contains, as far as the competence of the EU is concerned, a restrictive meaning, both for the implied and the external powers of the EU. Thus, in order to constitute the appropriate level, the EU has to deliver 'better results' than at the other levels. As Article 5 states, the EU can only take action if and insofar as the objectives of the proposed action cannot be sufficiently achieved by the Member States. The better results will be achieved by reason of scale or effects of the proposed action. Scale refers undoubtedly to action which transcends national borders, like freedom of movement of workers, exchange of students, of migrant labour and the like, and should not be so difficult to determine.

143. The same reasoning applies, secondly, to the relations between the public authorities and the social partners. With equal results the autonomy of the social partners should prevail. This, however, presupposes that the social partners are really representative of the employers and the employees they are supposed to represent. This undoubtedly creates problems in countries where unions have less than, let us say, 20 per cent of workers organised, as is e.g. the case in France; the same applies *ceteris paribus* to the employers' associations. Self-evidently national criteria for 'representativeness' apply, as well as the ILO standards, especially for those EU Member States which have ratified Conventions Nos. 87 and 98 of the International Labour Organisation.

144. Once the level of action and (or) the competent actors are defined, the effect of the subsidiarity rule stops in the sense that subsidiarity does indeed not contain a principle following which recognised competences have to be interpreted restrictively. Once a competence is placed at the appropriate level it has to be interpreted on its own merits, as words mean what they mean.

It will not be easy to determine the appropriate level and the competent actors in a number of situations, especially in those areas where, pursuant to Article 153 TFEU, 'the Union shall support and complement the "activities" of the Member States', given the fundamental differences in approach to these matters in the various Member States. This is, in the framework of the social *acquis communautaire*, especially the case in the United Kingdom which adheres to legal noninterventionism, versus most continental European Member States like Belgium, Germany, France and others, which are legal interventionists.

145. Subsidiarity is both a legal and a political notion. It is for the political institutions of the Union, first of all the Commission, the European Parliament and the Council, to decide upon the scope and the application of the subsidiarity rule in gauging the objectives of proposed actions, their scale and their effects. It is questionable whether the European Court should intervene in this area by interpreting the meaning of subsidiarity, as defined in Article 5 of the EU Treaty, although this possibility cannot be excluded.

At the European summit in Edinburgh (11 and 12 December 1992), the European Council determined 'the overall approach to the application by the Council of the subsidiarity principle'.

146. According to the Council subsidiarity mainly covers three elements:

(1) *The principle of attribution of powers.* The principle that the Union can only act where given the power to do so – implying that national powers are the rule and the Union's the exception – has always been a basic feature of the Union legal order.
(2) *The principle of subsidiarity in the strict legal sense.* The principle that the Union should only take action where an objective can better be achieved at the level of the Union than at the level of the individual Member States is present in embryonic or implicit form in some provisions of the ECSC Treaty and the EEC Treaty. The principle holds for matters that do not fall within the exclusive powers of the Union.

(3) *The principle of proportionality or intensity.* The principle that the means to be employed by the Union should be proportional to the objective pursued applies to all Union action, whether outside or within exclusive powers.

C. *Scrutiny by National Parliaments*

147. The main difference resulting from the Lisbon Treaty concerns the new powers conferred on national parliaments as regards ensuring respect for the principle of subsidiarity. Under the second paragraph of Article 5(3) and Article 12(b) TEU, national parliaments ensure compliance with the principle of subsidiarity in accordance with the procedure set out in the Protocol on the application of the principles of subsidiarity and proportionality. According to this procedure, any national Parliament or any chamber of a national Parliament has eight weeks from the date of transmission of a draft legislative act to send to the Presidents of the European Parliament, the Council and the Commission a reasoned opinion stating why it considers that the draft in question does not comply with the principle of subsidiarity. Where reasoned opinions represent at least one third (one vote per chamber in a bicameral Parliamentary system and two votes in a unicameral system) of the votes allocated to the national Parliaments, the draft must be reviewed. This threshold is reduced to a quarter for legislation relating to police and judicial cooperation in criminal matters. If, under the ordinary legislative procedure, at least a simple majority of national Parliaments challenges the compliance of a proposal for a legislative act with the principle of subsidiarity and the Commission decides to maintain its proposal, the matter is referred to the (European Parliament and the Council), which shall issue a decision at first reading. If the legislator considers that the legislative proposal is not compatible with the principle of subsidiarity, it may reject it subject to a majority of 55 per cent of the members of the Council or a majority of the votes cast in the European Parliament.[50]

III. Integration

148. There is no doubt that the Union and the legal acts which emanate from constitute one integrated and cohesive body.

To give one example, Article 45 and following of the TFEU concerning free movement for workers are applicable to the other workers who are occupied in the atomic energy sector.

149. The 28 Member States of the European Communities are: Austria, Belgium, Bulgaria, Croatia, Czech Republic, Cyprus, Denmark, Estonia, France, Finland, Germany, Greece, Hungary, Ireland, Italy, Latvia, Lithuania, Luxembourg, Malta, the Netherlands, Poland, Portugal, Romania, Slovakia, Slovenia, Spain, Sweden and the United Kingdom.

---

50. Roberta Panizza, *The Principle of Subsidiarity*, Fact Sheets on the European Union, 2009.

General Introduction, Ch. 1, The Institutional Framework

§2. THE INSTITUTIONS AND THEIR COMPETENCES

150. The European Union has a number of common institutions, namely the European Parliament (EP), the Council, the Commission and the Court of Justice.

In addition, there is the already mentioned Committee of the Regions, which has a consultative competence (Article 307 TEU).

I. The European Parliament

151. The European Parliament shall be composed of representatives of the Union's citizens. They shall not exceed 750 in number, plus the President. Representation of citizens shall be degressively proportional, with a minimum threshold of 6 members per Member State. No Member State shall be allocated more than 96 seats.

152. The EP is a very special Parliament. First, there is in the European construction no real government which, like national governments, would need the confidence of Parliament. For the EP to exercise a certain control over the Commission and for it to censure the activities of the Commission, such a motion has to be carried by a two-thirds majority of the votes cast, representing a majority of the full Parliament. In fact, however, this procedure constitutes such a huge task that it has no real significance in practice. The legislative role of the EP is slowly expanding. Except where otherwise provided in the Treaty, the EP acts by an absolute majority of votes.

The Treaty of Amsterdam has strengthened the role of the EP through the codecision procedure, which has been extended to quite a number of areas, e.g. regarding:

– incentive measures concerning employment;
– the application of the principle of equal opportunities and equal treatment of men and women in matters of employment and occupation.

153. In quite a number of cases, the TEU and TFEU provide that the Council has to consult the EP. Thus, the very important Article 115 TFEU reads:

> the Council shall, acting unanimously on a proposal from the Commission, and after consulting the European Parliament and the Economic and Social Committee, issue directives for the approximation of such laws, regulations or administrative provisions of the Member States as directly affect the establishment or functioning of the common market.

This consultation is asked for on behalf of the Council. The advisory competence, however, relates to proposals emanating from the Commission, which may alter its proposal at any time, e.g. to take into account the resolutions of the EP, until and at such time as the Council comes to a decision. In this way the interplay between these three main actors is clearly demonstrated. Since the Maastricht Treaty of 1991, however, the EP may, acting by a majority of its members, request the Commission to submit any appropriate proposal on matters on which it considers that 'a Community act is required for the purpose of implementing the Treaties' (Article 225 TFEU). This gives a right of initiative to the EP.

154. Supervision by the EP in essence concerns the working of the Commission (not of the Council, although the Council answers written and oral questions from the members of the EP). Regarding the budget, however, the EP enjoys a codecision-making competence. The EP approves the budget.

155. The EP also has a decisive voice regarding the requests of European states to become Members of the Union. In this case the EP must give its assent (Article 49 TEU).

II. The Council

156. The Council of the European Union, established by Article 1 of the Merger Treaty of 1965, is undoubtedly the most important European institution, since the Council is the principal European legislator.

In conformity with Article 2 of that Treaty, the Council 'consists of representatives of Member States. Each government shall delegate to it one of its members.' Which member attends a given meeting depends on the agenda. If the Social Council meets, the Ministers competent for these affairs, e.g. the Ministers of Employment, will attend. The Social Council belongs to the so-called sectoral or specialised councils. If general points are on the agenda the Ministers of Foreign Affairs will meet in the General Council. The European Council is the Council of Heads of Governments and Prime Ministers, which meets three times a year together with the Ministers of Foreign Affairs.

157. The Council is an institution of the Union. This means that, although national interests are defended in the Council and the Ministers defend the point of view of their respective governments, Member States are bound to take all necessary measures to realise the objectives of the Union. This follows clearly from Article 4, 3 of the TEU:

> Pursuant to the principle of sincere cooperation, the Union and the Member States shall, in full mutual respect, assist each other in carrying out tasks which flow from the Treaties.
> The Member States shall take any appropriate measure, general or particular, to ensure fulfilment of the obligations arising out of the Treaties or resulting from the acts of the institutions of the Union.
> The Member States shall facilitate the achievement of the Union's tasks and refrain from any measure which could jeopardise the attainment of the Union's objectives.

158. The Council exercises only the powers which are conferred upon it by the Treaties; the Council thus does not enjoy a general competence, except in what will be discussed later on in relation to Article 352 TFEU.

159. As the most important tasks of the Council relating to labour law, we can mention:

- the organisation of the free movement for workers (Arts. 45–48 TFEU);
- the approximation of (labour) laws (Arts. 114–116 TFEU);
- the elaboration of a social policy (Arts. 151–161 TFEU);
- the implementation of decisions regarding the Social Fund (Arts. 164 TFEU);
- the development of quality education and vocational training (Arts. 165–166 TFEU);
- the promotion of a stronger economic and social cohesion (Arts. 174–178 TFEU);
- the implementation of the Social Charter (1989).

160. If action by the Union should prove necessary in order to attain one of the objectives of the Union and the Treaty does not provide the necessary powers, the Council can, acting unanimously on a proposal from the Commission and after consultation with the EP, take the appropriate measures.

161. The Council acts by absolute majority, qualified majority or unanimity. Absolute majority is the general rule.

162. In most cases, voting with a qualified majority is practised.

163. The Council shall act by a qualified majority except where the Treaties provide otherwise.

As from 1 November 2014, a qualified majority is defined as at least 55 per cent of the members of the Council, comprising at least 15 of them and representing Member States comprising at least 65 per cent of the population of the Union.

A blocking minority must include at least four Council members, failing which the qualified majority shall be deemed attained.

The other arrangements governing the qualified majority are laid down in Article 238(2) of the Treaty on the Functioning of the European Union.

The transitional provisions relating to the definition of the qualified majority which shall be applicable until 31 October 2014 and those which shall be applicable from 1 November 2014 to 31 March 2017 are laid down in the Protocol on transitional provisions (Art. 16 TEU).

164. The following are decided by qualified majority voting:

- free movement of workers (Art. 46 TFEU);
- workers' health and safety;
- working conditions;
- information and consultation of workers;

- equality between men and women (Arts. 153–157 TFEU);
- employment and incentive measures (Arts. 148–149 TFEU);
- the European Social Fund (Art. 164 TFEU);
- vocational training (Art. 166 TFEU);
- economic and social cohesion (Art. 178 TFEU).

165. The requirement of unanimity remains extremely important, however, for labour law matters in general.
Unanimity is required for decisions regarding:

- the rights and interests of employed persons (Art. 114 TFEU);
- economic and social cohesion (Art. 177 TFEU).

166. Unanimity is also required for:

- social security;
- the social protection of workers;
- protection of workers where their employment contract is terminated;
- representation and collective defence of the interests of workers and employers;
- conditions of employment for third-country nationals.

167. Excluded areas are:

- pay;
- the right of association;
- the right to strike;
- the right to impose lock-outs (Art. 153 TFEU).

III. The Commission

168. The Commission shall promote the general interest of the Union and take appropriate initiatives to that end. It shall ensure the application of the Treaties, and of measures adopted by the institutions pursuant to them. It shall oversee the application of Union law under the control of the Court of Justice of the European Union. It shall execute the budget and manage programmes. It shall exercise coordinating, executive and management functions, as laid down in the Treaties. With the exception of the common foreign and security policy, and other cases provided for in the Treaties, it shall ensure the Union's external representation. It shall initiate the Union's annual and multiannual programming with a view to achieving interinstitutional agreements.

Union legislative acts may only be adopted on the basis of a Commission proposal, except where the Treaties provide otherwise. Other acts shall be adopted on the basis of a Commission proposal where the Treaties so provide.

169. The Commission's term of office shall be five years.

The members of the Commission shall be chosen on the ground of their general competence and European commitment from persons whose independence is beyond doubt.

In carrying out its responsibilities, the Commission shall be completely independent. Without prejudice to Article 18(2), the members of the Commission shall neither seek nor take instructions from any Government or other institution, body, office or entity. They shall refrain from any action incompatible with their duties or the performance of their tasks.

170. The Commission appointed between the date of entry into force of the Treaty of Lisbon and 31 October 2014, shall consist of one national of each Member State, including its President and the High Representative of the Union for Foreign Affairs and Security Policy who shall be one of its Vice- Presidents.

As from 1 November 2014, the Commission shall consist of a number of members, including its President and the High Representative of the Union for Foreign Affairs and Security Policy, corresponding to two thirds of the number of Member States, unless the European Council, acting unanimously, decides to alter this number.

The members of the Commission shall be chosen from among the nationals of the Member States on the basis of a system of strictly equal rotation between the Member States, reflecting the demographic and geographical range of all the Member States.

IV. The Court of Justice

171. The Court 'shall ensure that in the interpretation and application of the Treaties the law is observed. Member States shall provide remedies' (Art. 19 TEU). Member States undertake not to submit a dispute concerning the interpretation or application of the Treaties to any method of settlement other than those provided for therein (Art. 344 TFEU).

The Court consists of one judge per Member State and is assisted by eight Advocates-General. It is the duty of the Advocate-General, acting with complete impartiality and independence, to make, in open court, reasoned submissions on cases which, in accordance with the Statute of the Court of Justice, require his involvement (Art. 252 TFEU):

> The Judges and Advocates-General are chosen from persons whose independence is beyond doubt and who possess the qualifications required for appointment to the highest judicial offices in their respective countries or who are jurisconsults of recognised competence; they are appointed by the common accord of the Governments of the Member States for a term of six years (Art. 253 TFEU).

172. The Court is competent to judge whether Member States live up to their duties under the Treaties (Arts. 258–259 TFEU) and to review the legality of the acts of the Council and of the Commission and whether they need to be declared void (Arts. 263–264 TFEU). The Court is likewise competent regarding preliminary rulings concerning the interpretation of Union law at the request of courts or judges of Member States (Art. 267 TFEU). This means, for example, that when a national judge is confronted in a case with Union law the meaning of which is not clear to him, he can ask the European Court one or more questions regarding the meaning of the Union law involved. The Court will eventually make a preliminary ruling which is binding for the national judge.

173. The judgments of the Court are made in last resort and are consequently not susceptible to appeal. They are enforceable in all Member States of the Union. Enforcement is governed by the rules of civil procedure in force in the state in whose territory it is carried out. The courts of the country concerned have jurisdiction over complaints that enforcement is being carried out in an irregular manner. In addition, natural and private persons also have access to the Court.

§3. OTHER ORGANS

174. Besides the four above-mentioned institutions, there is in the framework of the Union, even if one limits oneself to social affairs, an important number of other organs, with which representatives of employers and workers are associated. Some of these organs were explicitly established by the Treaties themselves, such as the ESC of the EU or the European Social Fund. Others were created in the course of time to assist the Council and/or the Commission in the execution of their tasks.

I. The Economic and Social Committee

175. The ESC consists of representatives of organisations of employers, of the employed, and of other parties representative of civil society, notably in socio-economic, civic, professional and cultural areas (Art. 300 TFEU). The members of the Committee are appointed by the Council for five years. Their appointments are renewable. They 'may not be bound by any mandatory instructions' and 'have to be completely independent in the performance of their duties, in the general interest of the Union' (Art. 300 TFEU). There are maximum 350 members. The members are divided in three groups: employers' and employee representatives and the so-called rest group (diverse interests).

The ESC is consulted by the Council or by the Commission where the Treaties so provide and may be consulted when these institutions consider it appropriate.

Since the Paris Summit of 1972, the Committee is entitled to give advice on its own initiative regarding Union matters.

II. The European Social Fund

176. The European Social Fund (ESF) is one of the EU's Structural Funds, set up to reduce differences in prosperity and living standards across EU Member States and regions, and therefore promoting economic and social cohesion.

The ESF is devoted to promoting employment in the EU. It helps Member States make Europe's workforce and companies better equipped to face new, global challenges. In short:

- funding is spread across the Member States and regions, in particular those where economic development is less advanced;
- it is a key element of the EU's strategy for growth and jobs targeted at improving the lives of EU citizens by giving them better skills and better job prospects.

177. The Fund was established by Article 162 of the TFEU:

> In order to improve employment opportunities for workers in the internal market and to contribute thereby to raising the standard of living, a European Social Fund is hereby established ... it shall aim to render the employment of workers easier and to increase their geographical and occupational mobility within the Union, and to facilitate their adaptation to industrial changes and to changes in production systems, in particular through vocational training and retraining.

178. The European Parliament and Council, acting in the framework of the ordinary legislative procedure and after consulting the Economic and Social Committee and the Committee of the Regions, adopts implementing decisions relating to the European Social Fund (Art. 164 TFEU).

Pursuant to Article 177 TFEU, the Council is obliged to define the tasks, priority objectives and the organisation of the Structural Funds, which may involve the grouping of the Funds (European Agricultural Guidance and Guarantee Fund, European Social Fund, European Regional Development Fund).

For the Fund these tasks are to:

> support measures to prevent and combat unemployment and to develop human resources and social integration into the labour market in order to promote a high level of employment, equality between men and women, sustainable development, and economic and social cohesion. In particular, the Fund shall contribute to the actions undertaken in pursuance of the European Employment Strategy and the Annual Guidelines on Employment.

A. Tasks

179.

(1) The Fund shall contribute to the priorities of the Union as regards strengthening economic and social cohesion by improving employment and job opportunities, encouraging a high level of employment and more and better jobs. It shall do so by supporting Member States' policies aiming to achieve full employment and quality and productivity at work, promote social inclusion, including the access of disadvantaged people to employment, and reduce national, regional and local employment disparities.

(1) In particular, the Fund shall support actions in line with measures taken by Member States on the basis of the guidelines adopted under the European Employment Strategy, as incorporated into the Integrated Guidelines for Growth and Jobs, and the accompanying recommendations.

(2) In carrying out these tasks, the Fund shall support the priorities of the Union as regards the need to reinforce social cohesion, strengthen productivity and competitiveness, and promote economic growth and sustainable development. In so doing, the Fund shall take into account the relevant priorities and objectives of the Union in the fields of education and training, increasing the participation of economically inactive people in the labour market, combating social exclusion – especially that of disadvantaged groups such as people with disabilities – and promoting equality between women and men and non-discrimination.

B. *Scope of Assistance*

180.

(1) Within the framework of convergence and regional competitiveness and employment objectives, the Fund shall support actions in Member States under the priorities listed below:
  (a) increasing adaptability of workers, enterprises and entrepreneurs with a view to improving the anticipation and positive management of economic change, in particular by promoting:
    (i) lifelong learning and increased investment in human resources by enterprises, especially SMEs, and workers, through the development and implementation of systems and strategies, including apprenticeships, which ensure improved access to training by, in particular, low-skilled and older workers, the development of qualifications and competences, the dissemination of information and communication technologies, e-learning, eco-friendly technologies and management skills, and the promotion of entrepreneurship and innovation and business start-ups;
    (ii) the design and dissemination of innovative and more productive forms of work organisation, including better health and safety at work, the identification of future occupational and skills requirements, and the development of specific employment, training and support services,

including outplacement, for workers in the context of company and sector restructuring;
(b) enhancing access to employment and the sustainable inclusion in the labour market of job seekers and inactive people, preventing unemployment, in particular long-term and youth unemployment, encouraging active ageing and longer working lives, and increasing participation in the labour market, in particular by promoting:
  (i) the modernisation and strengthening of labour market institutions, in particular employment services and other relevant initiatives in the context of the strategies of the European Union and the Member States for full employment;
  (ii) the implementation of active and preventive measures ensuring the early identification of needs with individual action plans and personalised support, such as tailored training, job search, outplacement and mobility, self-employment and business creation, including cooperative enterprises, incentives to encourage participation in the labour market, flexible measures to keep older workers in employment longer, and measures to reconcile work and private life, such as facilitating access to childcare and care for dependent persons;
  (iii) mainstreaming and specific action to improve access to employment, increase the sustainable participation and progress of women in employment and reduce gender-based segregation in the labour market, including by addressing the root causes, direct and indirect, of gender pay gaps;
  (iv) specific action to increase the participation of migrants in employment and thereby strengthen their social integration and to facilitate geographic and occupational mobility of workers and integration of cross-border labour markets, including through guidance, language training and validation of competences and acquired skills;
(c) reinforcing the social inclusion of disadvantaged people with a view to their sustainable integration in employment and combating all forms of discrimination in the labour market, in particular by promoting:
  (i) pathways to integration and re-entry into employment for disadvantaged people, such as people experiencing social exclusion, early school leavers, minorities, people with disabilities and people providing care for dependent persons, through employability measures, including in the field of the social economy, access to vocational education and training, and accompanying actions and relevant support, community and care services that improve employment opportunities;
  (ii) acceptance of diversity in the workplace and the combating of discrimination in accessing and progressing in the labour market, including through awareness-raising, the involvement of local communities and enterprises and the promotion of local employment initiatives;
(d) enhancing human capital, in particular by promoting:
  (i) the design and introduction of reforms in education and training systems in order to develop employability, the improvement of the labour market relevance of initial and vocational education and training and

the continual updating of the skills of training personnel with a view to innovation and a knowledge-based economy;
(ii) networking activities between higher education institutions, research and technological centres and enterprises.[51]
(e) promoting partnerships, pacts and initiatives through networking of relevant stakeholders, such as the social partners and non-governmental organisations, at the transnational, national, regional and local levels in order to mobilise for reforms in the field of employment and labour market inclusiveness.

(2) Within the framework of the Convergence objective, the Fund shall support actions in Member States under the priorities listed below:
(a) expanding and improving investment in human capital, in particular by promoting:
(i) the implementation of reforms in education and training systems, especially with a view to raising people's responsiveness to the needs of a knowledge-based society and lifelong learning;
(ii) increased participation in education and training throughout the lifecycle, including through actions aiming to achieve a reduction in early school leaving and in gender-based segregation of subjects and increased access to and quality of initial, vocational and tertiary education and training;
(iii) the development of human potential in research and innovation, notably through post-graduate studies and the training of researchers;
(b) strengthening institutional capacity and the efficiency of public administrations and public services at national, regional and local level and, where relevant, of the social partners and non-governmental organisations, with a view to reforms, better regulation and good governance especially in the

---

51. Regulation (EC) No. 1081/2006 of the European Parliament and of the Council of 5 July 2006 on the European Social Fund and repealing Regulation (EC) No. 1784/1999, O.J., 31 July 2006, L 210; Council Regulation (EC) No. 1083/2006 of 11 July 2006 laying down general provisions on the European Regional Development Fund, the European Social Fund and the Cohesion Fund and repealing Regulation (EC) No. 1260/1999, O.J., 31 July 2006, L 210; Council Regulation (EC) No. 1989/2006 of 21 December 2006 amending Annex III to Regulation (EC) No. 1083/ 2006 laying down general provisions on the European Regional Development Fund, the European Social Fund and the Cohesion Fund and repealing Regulation (EC) No. 1260/1999, O.J., 30 December 2006, L 411; Council Regulation (EC) No. 1341/2008 of 18 December 2008 amending Regulation (EC) No. 1083/2006 laying down general provisions on the European Regional Development Fund, the European Social Fund and the Cohesion Fund, in respect of certain revenue-generating projects O.J., 24 December 2008, L 348; Council Regulation (EC) No. 284/2009 of 7 April 2009 amending Regulation (EC) No. 1083/2006 laying down general provisions on the European Regional Development Fund, the European Social Fund and the Cohesion Fund concerning certain provisions relating to financial management O.J., 8 April 2009, L 94; Regulation (EC) No. 396/2009 of the European Parliament and of the Council of 6 May 2009 amending Regulation (EC) No. 1081/ 2006 on the European Social Fund to extend the types of costs eligible for a contribution from the ESF O.J., 21 May 2009, L 126; Commission Regulation (EC) No. 846/2009 of 1 September 2009 amending Regulation (EC) No. 1828/2006 setting out rules for the implementation of Council Regulation (EC) No. 1083/2006 laying down general provisions on the European Regional Development Fund, the European Social Fund and the Cohesion Fund and of Regulation (EC) No. 1080/2006 of the European Parliament and of the Council on the European Regional Development Fund, OJ, 23 September 2009, L 250.

economic, employment, education, social, environmental and judicial fields, in particular by promoting:
(i) mechanisms to improve good policy and programme design, monitoring and evaluation, including through studies, statistics and expert advice, support for interdepartmental coordination and dialogue between relevant public and private bodies;
(ii) capacity building in the delivery of policies and programmes in the relevant fields, including with regard to the enforcement of legislation, especially through continuous managerial and staff training and specific support to key services, inspectorates and socio-economic actors including social and environmental partners, relevant non-governmental organisations and representative professional organisations.

181. The Fund is administered by the Commission. The Commission is assisted in this task by a committee presided over by a member of the Commission and composed of representatives of governments, trade unions and employers' organisations (Article 163 TFEU).

Over the period 2007–2013 some EUR75 billion will be distributed to the EU Member States and regions to achieve its goals.

C. *The Future of the ESF: 2014–2020*

182. In October 2011, the Commission proposed new priorities and rules for the ESF over the next programming period 2014–2020. These will allow the Fund to continue providing concrete support to people who need help to find a job, or to progress in their current job.

The Commission proposal is part of an overall legislative package for the Union's future Cohesion Policy.

What are the proposed changes for the ESF?

183. The role of the European Social Fund is to increase employment opportunities, promote education and lifelong learning, enhance social inclusion, contribute to combating poverty, and improve the capacity of public administrations to serve citizens and job-seekers better. The new proposal reinforces the role of the ESF:

– There would be a minimum share of the budget allocated to each category of regions. It would be higher than before (at least 25 per cent for less-developed regions, 40 per cent for transition regions and 52 per cent for more-developed ones). This share of cohesion funding corresponds to at least €84 billion for the ESF budget, compared to the current €75 billion.
– Member States will have to concentrate ESF funding on a limited number of objectives and investment priorities in line with the Europe 2020 strategy, in order to reach a critical mass and increase its impact.
– A minimum share of 20 per cent of the ESF should be dedicated to social inclusion actions.

- There is greater emphasis on combating youth unemployment, promoting active and healthy ageing, and supporting the most disadvantaged groups and marginalised communities such as Roma. The Youth Employment Initiative would particularly support young people not in education, employment or training by integrating them into the labour market.
- More support will be provided for social innovation, i.e. testing and scaling up innovative solutions to address social needs – for example, improving social inclusion.
- Greater participation by social partners and civil society in implementing ESF activities, and in particular participation by non-governmental organisations (NGOs), will be encouraged through capacity-building, the promotion of community-led local development strategies and the simplification of the delivery system (see also: European Code of Conduct on Partnership). Simpler rules will govern the reimbursement of ESF projects, in particular for smaller beneficiaries who make up at least 50 percent of recipients of ESF funding – NGOs, small and medium-sized enterprises and others.
- Equipment linked to investments in social and human capital will become eligible for support from the ESF – for example, computers for schools.

184. The ESF could also be used to guarantee loans taken by Member State bodies to finance measures within its scope of intervention.

185. All EU regions will continue to receive support within three defined categories:

- less developed regions whose GDP per capita is below 75 per cent of the Union average, will continue to be the top priority for the policy;
- transition regions whose GDP per capita is between 75 per cent and 90 per cent of the EU27 average.
- more developed regions whose GDP per capita is above 90 per cent of the EU27 average.

186. The second category – covering 51 regions and more than 72 million people – eases the transition of regions which have become more competitive in recent years, but still need targeted support. As of 2014, 20 regions are forecast to move out of the current 'convergence' objective (less developed regions), reflecting the success of Cohesion Policy.

Partnership Contracts, agreed between the Commission and Member States, will set out the national commitments required to deliver Europe 2020 objectives. ESF investments will be fully aligned with Europe 2020 objectives and targets for employment, education and poverty reduction.

187. The Common Strategic Framework setting out the EU's top priorities will apply to all funds, including rural development and fisheries. Member States will be allowed to combine ERDF, ESF and Cohesion Fund financing in 'multi-fund' programmes to improve coordination on the ground and achieve integrated development.

New conditions will be introduced to ensure that EU funding contributes effectively to delivering Europe 2020 objectives. Some conditions will need to be in place before the funds are disbursed – for example, the proper functioning of public procurement systems.

188. Next steps: these proposals are now being examined by the Council and the European Parliament, with a view to adoption in 2013. This will allow a new generation of Cohesion Policy programmes to start in 2014.

III. European Centre for the Development of Vocational Training

189. The Centre (CEDEFOP) was established in 1975.[52] The aim of the Centre is to assist the Commission in encouraging the promotion and development of vocational training and in-service training at Community level. The Centre is located in Thessaloniki (Greece). It is administered by a management board comprising representatives from governments, the Commission and the social partners. The Centre assists the Commission through the organisation of scientific and technical documentation, information and research activities.

IV. European Foundation for the Improvement of Living and Working Conditions

190. The Foundation, established in 1975,[53] has the aim 'to contribute to the planning and establishment of better living and working conditions through action designed to increase the disseminate knowledge likely to assist this development'. Its priorities are the following:

---

52. Regulation No. 337/75 of 10 February 1975, O.J. L 39, 13 February 1975; as amended by Regulation No. 1946/93 of 30 June 1993, O.J. L 181, 23 July 1993, 13; Regulation No. 1131/94 of 16 May 1994, O.J. L 127, 19 May 1994; No. 251/95 of 6 February 1995, O.J. L 030, 9 February 1995, and No. 354/95 of 20 February 1995, O.J. L 041, 23 February 1995, Council Regulation (EC) No. 1655/2003 of 18 June 2003 amending Regulation (EEC) No. 337/75 establishing a European Centre for the Development of Vocational Training and repealing Regulation (EEC) No. 1416/76, O.J. L 245, 29 September 2003. Council Regulation (EC) No. 2051/2004 of 25 October 2004 amending Regulation (EEC) No. 337/75 establishing a European Centre for the Development of Vocational Training, O.J., 7 December 2004, L 355.
53. Regulation No. 1365/75 of 26 May 1975, O.J. L 139, 30 May 1975, as amended by Regulation No. 1947/73, 30 June 1993, O.J. L 181, 23 July 1993, 13; Council Regulation (EC) No. 1649/2003 of 18 June 2003, Council Regulation (EC) No. 1649/2003 of 18 June 2003, O.J. L 245, 29 September 2003. Council Regulation (EC) No. 1111/2005 of 24 June 2005 amending Regulation (EEC) No. 1365/75 on the creation of a European Foundation for the Improvement of Living and Working Conditions, O.J., 15 July 2005, L 184.

– people at work;
– the organisation of work and particularly job design;
– problems peculiar to categories of workers;
– long-term aspects of improvement of the environment;
– the distribution of human activities in space and in time.

191. The seat of the Foundation is located in Dublin. It is governed by an Administrative Board, composed of representatives of governments, the Commission and both sides of industry. A Committee of Experts helps the Foundation in an advisory capacity.

V. The Standing Committee on Employment

192. The Standing Committee was established in 1970.[54] It aimed at setting up permanent dialogue, concertation and consultation between the Council, the Commission and the social partners in order to facilitate the coordination of the labour market policies of the Member States. The Committee intervened before the competent Community institutions take decisions. The Committee offered a permanent possibility for confrontation of points of view from all partners involved in the shaping of social policies. It was, however, not a forum for negotiation. In practice, a lot of talk took place, but there was no real exchange of viewpoints nor were decisions reached.

193. In 1999, the Committee had a face-lift and won a higher profile[55] with the objective of involving the social partners at all stages of the coordinated employment strategy in order to make an important contribution to the implementation of the Employment Guidelines. The social partners' contribution to the coordinated employment strategy should be taken into account both at the level of the Employment Guidelines themselves and in examining their consistency with the Broad Economic Policy Guidelines, in order to provide for greater synergy and with a view to incorporating the objective of a high level of employment into the drawing up and implementation of the Community's policies.

The task of the Committee is to ensure that there is continuous dialogue, concertation and consultation between the Council, the Commission and the social partners in order to enable the social partners to contribute to the coordinated employment strategy and to facilitate coordination by the Member States of their policies in this field, taking into account the economic and social objectives of the Community as reflected in both the Employment Guidelines and the Broad Economic Policy Guidelines.

---

54. Decision No. 70/532 of 14 December 1970, as amended by Decision No. 75/62 of 20 January 1975, O.J. L 21, 28 January 1975.
55. Decision No. 1999/20 of 9 March 1999 on the reform of the Standing Committee on Employment and repealing Decision 70/532/EEC (O.J. L 072, 18 March 1999).

The members of the Council or their representatives, the Commission, and representatives of the social partners at European level take part in the work of the Committee.

There will be a maximum of 20 social partner representatives organised in two equal delegations, 10 from each side of industry.

The social partners' delegations shall cover the whole economy, being composed of European organisations representing either general interests or more specific interests of supervisory and professional staff and small and medium-sized businesses.

For this purpose, each delegation shall be made up of representatives of the organisations of social partners consulted by the Commission, falling within the following categories:

– general cross-industry organisations;
– cross-industry organisations representing certain categories of workers or undertakings, and
– sectoral organisations representing agriculture and trade.

The practical coordination of the workers' delegation is undertaken by the European Trade Union Confederation (ETUC), and that of the employers' delegation by BUSINESSEUROPE.

VI. The Employment Committee

194. The Lisbon Treaty provides for the establishment of an Employment Committee with advisory status to promote coordination between Member States on employment and labour market policies.

The tasks of the Committee shall be:

– to monitor the employment situation and employment policies in the Member States and the Community;
– to formulate opinions at the request of either the Council of the Commission or on its own initiative and help the Council regarding employment matters (reporting, guidelines and the like).

The Committee is composed of two members per Member State. The Committee has to consult with management and labour (Art. 150 TFEU).

The Committee was established by Council Decision No. 2000/98/EC of 24 January 2000.[56]

---

56. O.J. L 29/21, 4 February 2000.

VII. The European Agency for Safety and Health at Work

195. A European Agency for Safety and Health at Work was established by a regulation of 18 July 1994.[57] Bilbao (Spain) was designated as its seat.

The objective of the Agency is laid down as follows:

> In order to improve the working environment, as regards the protection of the safety and health of workers as provided for in the Treaty and successive Community strategies and action programmes concerning health and safety at the workplace, the aim of the Agency shall be to provide the Community bodies, the Member States, the social partners and those involved in the field with the technical, scientific and economic information of use in the field of safety and health at work.

For the purpose of achieving this aim the Agency's role shall be to:

(a) collect, analyse and disseminate technical, scientific and economic information in the Member States in order to pass it on to the Community bodies, Member States and interested parties; this collection shall take place to identify risks and good practices as well as existing national priorities and programmes and provide the necessary input to the priorities and programmes of the Community;
(b) collect and analyse technical, scientific and economic information on research into safety and health at work and on other research activities which involve aspects connected with safety and health at work and disseminate the results of the research and research activities;
(c) promote and support cooperation and exchange of information and experience among the Member States including information on training programmes;
(d) organise conferences and seminars and exchanges of experts from the Member States;
(e) supply Community bodies and Member States with the objective available technical, scientific and economic information they require to formulate and implement judicious and effective policies;
(f) establish, in cooperation with the Member States, and coordinate a network;
(g) collect and make available information on safety and health matters from and to third countries and international organisations (WHO, ILO, PAHO, IMO, etc.);
(h) provide technical, scientific and economic information on methods and tools for implementing preventive activities, identify good practices and promote preventive actions, paying particular attention to the specific problems of small and medium-sized enterprises. With regard to good practices, the Agency should in

---

57. No. 2062/94, O.J. L 216/1, 20 August 1994, amended by Regulation No. 1643/95 of 29 June 1995, O.J. L 156, 7 July 1995. Council Regulation (EC) No. 1654/2003 of 18 June 2003, O.J. L 245, 29 September 2003; Council Regulation (EC) No. 2051/2004 of 25 October 2004, O.J. L 355, 1 December 2004; Council Regulation (EC) No. 1112/2005 of 24 June 2005, O.J. L 184, 15 July 2005.

particular focus on practices which constitute practical tools to be used in drawing up an assessment of the risks to safety and health at work, and identifying the measures to be taken to tackle them;
(i) contribute to the development of Community strategies and action programmes relating to the protection of safety and health at work, without prejudice to the Commission's sphere of competence;
(j) the Agency shall ensure that the information disseminated is comprehensible to the end users. To achieve this objective, the Agency shall work closely with the national focal points referred to in Article 4(1), in accordance with the provisions of Article 4(2).

The Agency shall work as closely as possible with the existing institutions, foundations, specialist bodies and programmes at Community level in order to avoid any duplication. In particular, the Agency shall ensure appropriate cooperation with the European Foundation for the Improvement of Living and Working Conditions, without prejudice to its own aims.

196. By Council Decision of 22 July 2003 an Advisory Committee on Safety and Health at Work was set up:

(1) The Committee has the task of assisting the Commission in the preparation, implementation and evaluation of activities in the fields of safety and health at work.
 This task shall cover the public and the private sectors of the economy.
(2) Specifically, the Committee shall:
   (a) conduct, on the basis of the information available to it, exchanges of views and experience regarding existing or planned regulations;
   (b) help to devise a common approach to problems in the fields of safety and health at work and identify Community priorities as well as the measures necessary for implementing them;
   (c) draw the Commission's attention to areas in which there is an apparent need for new knowledge and for suitable training and research measures;
   (d) define, within the framework of Community action programmes:
      – the criteria and aims for preventing accidents at work and health hazards within the undertaking;
      – methods enabling undertakings and their employees to evaluate and to improve the level of protection;
   (e) contribute, alongside the European Agency for Safety and Health at Work, to keeping national administrations, trades unions and employers' organisations informed of Community measures in order to facilitate cooperation and to encourage any initiatives on their part to exchange experience and establish codes of practice;
   (f) give an opinion on plans for Community initiatives which affect safety and health at work;
   (g) give an opinion on the annual programme and the rotating four-year programme of the European Agency for Safety and Health at Work.

(3) In order to accomplish the above tasks, the Committee shall cooperate with the other Committees which are competent for safety and health at work, *inter alia* with the Senior Labour Inspectors Committee and the Scientific Committee for Occupational Exposure Limits to Chemical Agents, mainly by exchanging information.

VIII. The Committee of the Regions

197. The Committee of the Regions is a consultative body consisting of representatives of regional and local bodies. The Council appoints the members for a period of five years. Their term of office is renewable.

The Treaty of Lisbon introduces a number of areas for which the Committee must mandatorily be consulted on, among others:

– employment guidelines (Art. 148 TFEU);
– incentive measures regarding employment (Art. 149 TFEU);
– minimum requirements regarding social policy (Art. 153 TFEU);
– measures regarding public health (Art. 168 TFEU);
– measures regarding the environment (Art. 192 TFEU);
– implementing decisions regarding the European Social Fund (Art. 164 TFEU);
– measures regarding vocational training (Art. 166 TFEU).

IX. Other Advisory Committees

198. Quite a number of other consultative bodies in which representatives of business and labour are represented may be mentioned:

– the Advisory Committee on Safety, Hygiene and Health Protection at Work;
– the Advisory Committee on Equal Opportunities for Women and Men;
– the Advisory Committee on Vocational Training;
– the Advisory Committee on Free Movement of Workers.

X. Sectoral Joint Committees, Informal Groups and Sectoral Dialogue Committees

199. A number of joint and informal groups committees, composed of representatives of employers' and workers' organisations, have been set up and function at sectoral level, namely in the following sectors:

European Joint Committees and Working Groups (1996)

Joint Committees (JC)	Informal Working Parties
Agriculture (1963)	Hotel and catering (1984)
	Sugar (1984)

Road transport (1965)	Commerce and retail (1985)
	Insurance (1987)
Inland waterways (1967)	Banking (1990)
Rail transport (1972)	Furniture (1991)
	Footwear (1977)
Fishing (1974)	Construction (1991)
	Cleaning industry (1992)
Sea transport (1987)	Textiles and clothing (1992)
Civil aviation (1990)	Wood (1994)
Telecommunications (1990)	Private security (1994)
Postal services (1994)	

The most important task of these joint committees lies in the assistance of the Commission in formulating and executing social policies. They are, moreover, fora for dialogue, the exchange of information and the promotion of consultation between management and labour. They give advice to the Commission upon request or on their own initiative.

200. Overall, since 1998, a total of 40 sectoral social dialogue committees have been created, covering 145 million workers around the EU.

More than 500 texts have been produced as a result of sectoral social dialogue, including joint opinions and responses to consultations, autonomous agreements, and agreements that have been given legal force by means of a directive. The legally binding texts are as follows:

– Council Directive 2010/32/EU of 10 May 2010 implementing the framework agreement on prevention of sharps injuries in the hospital and healthcare sector, concluded by the European Hospital and Healthcare Employers' Association (HOSPEEM) and the European Federation of Public Service Unions (EPSU) in July 2009;
– Council Directive 2009/13/EC of 16 February 2009 implementing the agreement concluded by the European Community Shipowners' Associations (ECSA) and the European Transport Workers' Federation (ETF) on the Maritime Labour Convention, 2006, and amending Directive 1999/63/EC;
– Council Directive 1999/63/EC of 21 June 1999 concerning the agreement on the organisation of working time of seafarers, concluded by ECSA and the Federation of Transport Workers' Unions in the European Union (currently ETF);
– Council Directive 2005/47/EC of 18 July 2005 on the agreement between the Community of European Railways (CER) and ETF on certain aspects of the working conditions of mobile workers engaged in cross-border services;
– Council Directive 2000/79/EC of 27 November 2000 concerning the European Agreement on the Organisation of Working Time of Mobile Workers in Civil Aviation concluded by the Association of European Airlines (AEA), ETF, the European Cockpit Association (ECA), the European Regions Airline Association (ERA) and the International Air Carrier Association (IACA);

– An agreement has also been reached between 14 industrial sectors on workers' health protection through the good handling and use of crystalline silica and products containing it (signed on 25 April 2006).

The report notes that these texts have 'contributed to modernising industrial relations and to adopting new social standards'.[58]

201. However, directives are not always easy to come by.[59] The social partners in the hairdressing sector – Coiffure EU and UNI Europa Hair and Beauty concluded April 2012 a European framework agreement. The agreement aims to establish health and safety rules for hairdressers and was expected to form the basis of an EU directive, but it has been challenged by some Member States, amongst which the Dutch Government, who opposed any form of regulation in the sector. Stated UNI-Europe:

> We need to be very clear: we will defend our commitment for a stronger and healthier hairdressing sector against this unprecedented attack. [This] initiative is driven by the political will to undermine the EUs social dimension. It is using the current crisis as a pretext to dismantle achievements that have been at the very core of the EU's success and are so much needed in turning towards a new policy for growth, jobs and social inclusion. This attack by the Dutch government shows total disrespect for the work done by social partners.
> They stressed their view that the agreement would make the hair and beauty sector a better place in which to work, to the benefit of all hairdressers in salons and approximately 350 million potential clients in EU Member States. The social partners also stressed the importance of this sector, which has an estimated 400,000 salons and a workforce of over a million in the European Union.

remains to be seen in what the European Union is going to do.

A. Creation of the Sectoral Social Dialogue Committees

202. At sectoral level, the social dialogue underwent an important development in 1998, when the Commission decided on the establishment of sectoral dialogue committees promoting the dialogue between the social partners in the sectors at European level.[60] The Commission laid down precise provisions concerning the establishment, representativeness and operation of new sectoral committees, intended as central bodies for consultation, joint initiatives and negotiation.

---

58. Andrea Broughton, "Commission issues report on EU-level sectoral social dialogue", EIROonline, 19 October 2010.
59. Andrea Broughton, 'Unprecedented challenge to social dialogue in hairdressing sector' Euro-online, (consulted 10 May 2013).
60. Communication from the Commission 'Adapting and promoting the social dialogue at Community level' COM(1998) 322 final of 20 May 1998.

General Introduction, Ch. 1, The Institutional Framework

The sectoral social dialogue committees are established with due regard for the autonomy of the social partners. The social partner organisations must apply jointly to the European Commission in order to take part in a social dialogue at European level. The European organisations representing employers and workers must, when submitting this application, meet a number of criteria:

- relate to specific sectors or categories, and be organised at European level; – consist of organisations which are themselves an integral and recognised part of Member State's social partner structures, and have the capacity to negotiate agreements, and which are representative of several Member States;
- have adequate structures to ensure their effective participation in the work of the committees.

B. Composition of the Sectoral Social Dialogue Committees

203. The sectoral social dialogue committees consist of a maximum of 64 representatives of the social partners, comprising an equal number of employers' and workers' representatives. They are chaired either by a representative of the social partners or, at their request, by the representative of the Commission, who, in all cases, provides the secretariat for the committees.

C. Operation of the Sectoral Social Dialogue Committees

204. Each Committee adopts its own rules of procedure, and holds at least one plenary meeting per year, dealing with more specific questions at meetings of enlarged secretariats or restricted working parties. The task of preparing meetings, the agenda and following-up work is most frequently delegated to the respective secretariats of the social partners, together with the Commission.

Table 5. Sectors of activity and sectoral social dialogue committees[61]

Sectors	*Employees' organisations*	*Employers' organisations*	*Date of creation*
Agriculture	EFFAT	GEOPA/COPA	1999
Audiovisual	EURO-MEI, FIA, FIM, EFJ	UER/EBU, FIAPF, CEPI, AER, ACT	2004
Banking	UNI-Europa	FBE; ESBG; EACB	1999
Central government administrations	TUNED, EPSU, CESI	EUPAE	2011

---

61. Commission, *Recent Developments in the European Sectoral Social Dialogue* (2008).

Sectors	Employees' organisations	Employers' organisations	Date of creation
Chemical industry	EMCEF	ECEG	2004
Civil aviation	ETF; ECA	AEA; CANSO; ERA; ACI-EUROPE; IACA	2000
Cleaning industry	UNI-Europa	EFCI	1999
Commerce	UNI-Europa	Eurocommerce	1999
Construction	EFBWW	FIEC	1999
Contract catering	EEFAT	EFFCCO	2007
Education	ETUCE	EFEE	2010
Electricity	EPSU; EMCEF	Eurelectric	2000
Extractive industry	EMCEF	APEP; Euracoal; Euromines; IMA	2002
Food and drink industry	EFFAT	FoodDrinkEurope	2012
Footwear	ETUF:TCL	CEC	1999
Furniture	EFBWW	UEA	2001
Gas	EMCEF; EPSU	EUROGAS	2007
Horeca	EFFAT	Hotrec	1999
Hospitals and health care	EPSU	HOSPEEM	2006
Industrial cleaning	UNI	EFCI	1999
Inland waterways	ETF	EBU; ESO	1999
Insurance	UNI-Europa	CEA; BIPAR; ACME	1999
Live performance	EEA	Pearle	1999
Local and regional government	EPSU	CEMR	2004
Maritime transport	ETF	ECSA	1999
Metal	EMF	CEEMET	2010
Paper	EMCEF	CEPI	2010
Personal services-hairdressing	UNI-Europa	EU Coiffure	1999
Postal services	UNI-Europa	Posteurop	1999
Professional football	FIFpro	EPFL	2008
Private security	UNI-Europa	CoESS	1999
Railways	ETF	CER; EIM	1999
Road transport	ETF	IRU	1999
Sea fisheries	ETF	Europeche/Cogeca	1999
Shipbuilding	EMF	CESA	1999

General Introduction, Ch. 1, The Institutional Framework 205–206

Sectors	Employees' organisations	Employers' organisations	Date of creation
Steel	EMF	EUROFER	2006
Sugar	EFFAT	CEFS	1999
Tanning and leather	ETUF:TCL	Cotance	2001
Telecommunications	UNI-Europa	ETNO	1999
Temporary agency work	UNI-Europa	Eurociett	2000
Textile and clothing	ETUF:TCL	Euratex	1999
Woodworking	EFBWW	CEI-Bois	2000
	EMF	CLEPA	2006
	EFFAT	FERCO	2007
	EMF	EUROMETAUX	2007

205. The Commission is keen to focus the social dialogue more on the key themes or 'pillars' outlined in the current EU Employment Guidelines, such as equal opportunities, employability and adaptability. In particular under this last heading, strong calls are being made to the social partners to negotiate agreements to modernise the organisation of work in the tourism, private security and railways sectors; emphasis is being placed on training and the mutual recognition of vocational training standards; in commerce, one of the key themes continues to be the impact of the rise in electronic commerce; in the footwear sector, child labour continues to be one of the key issues; the cleaning industry is discussing the question of combating undeclared work in the sector and health and safety is on the list of topics to be discussed in the agriculture, fisheries and sugar sectors.

XI. The Social Protection Committee

206. In Nice (December 2000) it was decided that the Council, after consulting the European Parliament, would establish a Social Protection Committee with advisory status to promote cooperation on social protection policies between Member States and with the Commission.[62]

The tasks of the Committee are:

- to monitor the social situation and the development of social protection policies in the Member States and the Community;
- to promote exchanges of information, experience and good practice between Member States and with the Commission;

---

62. Council Decision of 4 October 2004 establishing a Social Protection Committee and repealing Decision 2000/436/EC (2004/689/EC), O.J. L 314, 13 October 2004.

– without prejudice to Article 240 TFEU, to prepare reports, formulate opinions or undertake other work within its fields of competence, at the request of either the Council or the Commission or on its own initiative.

The Committee shall work, as appropriate, in cooperation with other relevant bodies and committees dealing with social and economic policy matters, such as the Employment Committee and the Economic Policy Committee.

In fulfilling its mandate, the Committee shall establish appropriate contacts with the social partners and social non-governmental organisations, account being taken of their respective roles and responsibilities in the social protection sphere. The European Parliament shall also be informed regarding the activities of the Committee.

Each Member State and the Commission shall appoint two members of the Committee (Article 160 TFEU).

XII. The European Globalisation Adjustment Fund

207. In 2006 a European Globalisation Adjustment Fund (the EGF)[63] was established notwithstanding the positive effects of globalisation on growth, jobs and prosperity and the need to enhance European competitiveness further through structural change. Indeed, globalisation may also have negative consequences for the most vulnerable and least qualified workers in some sectors. It was therefore oppor- tune to establish a European Globalisation Adjustment Fund accessible to all Member States, through which the Community would show its solidarity towards workers affected by redundancies resulting from changes in world trade patterns.

The EGF should provide specific, one-off support to facilitate the re-integration into employment of workers in areas, sectors, territories, or labour market regions suffering the shock of serious economic disruption. The EGF should promote entrepreneurship, for example through micro-credits or for setting up cooperative projects.

A. Subject Matter and Scope

208. The EGF is established in order to enable the Community to provide support for workers made redundant as a result of major structural changes in world trade patterns due to globalisation where these redundancies have a significant adverse impact on the regional or local economy.

The aim is to facilitate reintegration into employment of workers affected by trade-related redundancies.

---

63. Regulation (EC) No. 1927/2006 of the European Parliament and of the Council of 20 December 2006 on establishing the European Globalisation Adjustment Fund, O.J., 30 December 2006, L 406, amended by Regulation (EC) No. 546/2009 of the European Parliament and of the Council of 18 June 2009, O.J., 29 June 2009, L 167/26.

B. Intervention Criteria

209. A financial contribution from the EGF shall be provided where major structural changes in world trade patterns lead to serious economic disruption, in particular a substantial increase of imports into the European Union, the rapid decline of the EU market share in a given sector or a delocalisation to third countries, which results in:

(a) at least 500 redundancies over a period of four months in an enterprise in a Member State, including workers made redundant in its suppliers or downstream producers; or
(b) at least 500 redundancies over a period of nine months, particularly in small or medium-sized enterprises, in a NACE 2 division in one region or two contiguous regions at NUTS II level;
(c) in small labour markets or in exceptional circumstances, where duly substantiated by the Member State concerned, an application for a contribution from the EGF may be considered admissible even if the intervention criteria laid down in points (a) or (b) are not entirely met, when redundancies have a serious impact on employment and the local economy. The Member State shall specify that its application does not entirely meet the intervention criteria set out in points (a) or (b). The aggregated amount of contributions in exceptional circumstances may not exceed 15 per cent of the annual maximum amount of the EGF.

210. For the purposes of calculating the number of redundancies provided for in points (a), (b) and (c) above, a redundancy shall be counted from:

– the date of the employer's individual notice to lay off or to terminate the contract of employment of the worker; – the date of the *de facto* termination of the contract of employment before its expiry; or,
– the date on which the employer, in conformity with the provisions of Article 3(1), of Council Directive 98/59/EC of 20 July 1998 on the approximation of the laws of the Member States relating to collective redundancies, notifies the competent public authority in writing of the projected collective redundancies; in this case, the applicant Member State(s) shall provide the Commission with additional information on the actual number of redundancies effected according to points (a), (b) or (c) above, and the estimated costs of the coordinated package of personalised services, prior to the completion of the assessment provided for in Article 10 of this Regulation.

For each enterprise in question the Member State(s) shall specify in the application how the redundancies are being counted.

C. Eligible Actions

211. A financial contribution under this regulation may be made for active labour market measures that form part of a coordinated package of personalised services designed to re-integrate redundant workers into the labour market, including:

(a) job-search assistance, occupational guidance, tailor-made training and re-training including ICT skills and certification of acquired experience, outplacement assistance and entrepreneurship promotion or aid for self-employment;
(b) special time-limited measures, such as job-search allowances, mobility allowances or allowances to individuals participating in lifelong learning and training activities; and
(c) measures to stimulate in particular disadvantaged or older workers, to remain in or return to the labour market.

The EGF will not finance passive social protection measures.

On the initiative of the Member State, the EGF may finance the preparatory, management, information and publicity, and control activities for its implementation.

XIII. The European Institute for Gender Equality

212. Given the fact that significant gender gaps continue to exist in most policy fields and that inequality between men and women is a multidimensional phenomenon has to be tackled by a comprehensive mix of policy measures and that enhanced efforts are needed to meet the Lisbon strategy targets a European Institute for Gender Equality was established in 2006.[64]

A. Objectives

213. The overall objectives of the Institute are to contribute to and strengthen the promotion of gender equality, including gender mainstreaming in all Community policies and the resulting national policies, and the fight against discrimination based on sex, and to raise EU citizens' awareness of gender equality by providing technical assistance to the Community institutions, in particular the Commission, and the authorities of the Member States.

---

64. Regulation (EC) No. 1922/2006 of the European Parliament and of the Council of 20 December 2006 on establishing a European Institute for Gender Equality, O.J., 30 December 2006, L 403.

B. Tasks

214.

(1) To meet these objectives the Institute will:
   (a) collect, analyse and disseminate relevant objective, comparable and reliable information as regards gender equality, including results from research and best practice communicated to it by Member States, Community institutions, research centres, national equality bodies, non-governmental organisations, social partners, relevant third countries and international organisations, and suggest areas for further research;
   (b) develop methods to improve the objectivity, comparability and reliability of data at European level by establishing criteria that will improve the consistency of information and take into account gender issues when collecting data;
   (c) develop, analyse, evaluate and disseminate methodological tools in order to support the integration of gender equality into all Community policies and the resulting national policies and to support gender mainstreaming in all Community institutions and bodies;
   (d) carry out surveys on the situation in Europe as regards gender equality;
   (e) set up and coordinate a European Network on Gender Equality, involving the centres, bodies, organisations and experts dealing with gender equality and gender mainstreaming in order to support and encourage research, optimise the use of available resources and foster the exchange and dissemination of information;
   (f) organise *ad hoc* meetings of experts to support the institute's research work, encourage the exchange of information among researchers and promote the inclusion of a gender perspective in their research;
   (g) in order to raise EU citizens' awareness of gender equality, organise, with relevant stakeholders, conferences, campaigns and meetings at European level, and present the findings and conclusions to the Commission;
   (h) disseminate information regarding positive examples of non-stereotypical roles for women and men in every walk of life, present its findings and initiatives designed to publicise and build on such success stories;
   (i) develop dialogue and cooperation with non-governmental and equal opportunities organisations, universities and experts, research centres, social partners and related bodies actively seeking to achieve equality at national and European level;
   (j) set up documentation resources accessible to the public;
   (k) make information on gender mainstreaming available to public and private organisations; and
   (l) provide information to the Community institutions on gender equality and gender mainstreaming in the accession and candidate countries.

C. *Composition of the Institute*

215. The Institute shall comprise:

(a) a Management Board;
(b) an Experts' Forum;
(c) a Director and his or her staff.

XIV. The European Union Agency for Fundamental Rights

216. The European Union Agency for Fundamental Rights[65] (the Agency) was established in 2007 and has its seat in Vienna.

A. *Objective*

217. The objective of the agency is to provide the relevant institutions, bodies, offices and agencies of the Community and its Member States when implementing Community law with assistance and expertise relating to fundamental rights in order to support them when they take measures or formulate courses of action within their respective spheres of competence to fully respect fundamental rights.

B. *Scope*

218. The Agency shall carry out its tasks for the purpose of meeting this objective within the competencies of the Community as laid down in the Treaty establishing the European Community and refer in carrying out its tasks to fundamental rights as defined in Article 6(3) of the Treaty on European Union.
    The Agency shall deal with fundamental-rights issues in the European Union and in its Member States when implementing Community law.

C. *Tasks*

219. The Agency shall:

(a) collect, record, analyse and disseminate relevant, objective, reliable and comparable information and data, including results from research and monitoring commun-icated to it by Member States, Union institutions as well as bodies, offices and agencies of the Community and the Union, research centres, national bodies, non-governmental organisations, third countries and international

---

65. Council Regulation (EC) No. 168/2007 of 15 February 2007 establishing a European Union Agency for Fundamental Rights, O.J., 22 February 2007, L 53.

organisations and in particular by the competent bodies of the Council of Europe;
(b) develop methods and standards to improve the comparability, objectivity and reliability of data at European level, in cooperation with the Commission and the Member States;
(c) carry out, cooperate with or encourage scientific research and surveys, preparatory studies and feasibility studies, including, where appropriate and compatible with its priorities and its annual work programme, at the request of the European Parliament, the Council or the Commission;
(d) formulate and publish conclusions and opinions on specific thematic topics, for the Union institutions and the Member States when implementing Community law, either on its own initiative or at the request of the European Parliament, the Council or the Commission;
(e) publish an annual report on fundamental-rights issues covered by the areas of the Agency's activity, also highlighting examples of good practice;
(f) publish thematic reports based on its analysis, research and surveys;
(g) publish an annual report on its activities; and
(h) develop a communication strategy and promote dialogue with civil society, in order to raise public awareness of fundamental rights and actively disseminate information about its work.

D. *Cooperation with Civil Society; Fundamental Rights Platform*

220. The Agency shall closely cooperate with non-governmental organisations and with institutions of civil society, active in the field of fundamental rights including the combating of racism and xenophobia at national, European or international level. To that end, the Agency shall establish a cooperation network (Fundamental Rights Platform), composed of non-governmental organisations dealing with human rights, trade unions and employer's organisations, relevant social and professional organisations, churches, religious, philosophical and non-confessional organisations, universities and other qualified experts of European and international bodies and organisations.

The Fundamental Rights Platform shall constitute a mechanism for the exchange of information and pooling of knowledge. It shall ensure close cooperation between the Agency and relevant stakeholders.

E. *Bodies of the Agency*

221. The Agency shall comprise:

(a) a Management Board;
(b) an Executive Board;
(c) a Scientific Committee; and
(d) a Director.

222. Mention should also be made of Regulation (EC) No. 1889/2006 of the European Parliament and of the Council of 20 December 2006 on establishing a financing instrument for the promotion of democracy and human rights worldwide.[66]

With this instrument the Community shall provide assistance, within the framework of the Community's policy on development cooperation, and economic, financial and technical cooperation with third countries, consistent with the European Union's foreign policy as a whole, contributing to the development and consolidation of democracy and the rule of law, and of respect for all human rights and fundamental freedoms.

Such assistance shall aim in particular at

(a) enhancing the respect for and observance of human rights and fundamental freedoms, as proclaimed in the Universal Declaration of Human Rights and other international and regional human rights instruments, and promoting and consolidating democracy and democratic reform in third countries, mainly through support for civil society organisations, providing support and solidarity to human rights defenders and victims of repression and abuse, and strengthening civil society active in the field of human rights and democracy promotion;
(b) supporting and strengthening the international and regional framework for the protection, promotion and monitoring of human rights, the promotion of democracy and the rule of law, and reinforcing an active role for civil society within these frameworks;
(c) building confidence in and enhancing the reliability of electoral processes, in particular through election observation missions, and through support for local civil society organisations involved in these processes.

XV. The Committee of Experts on Posting of Workers[67]

A. Tasks

223. The tasks of the Committee are to:

(1) support and assist the Member States in identifying and promoting the exchange of experience and good practice;
(2) promote the exchange of relevant information, including information on existing forms of (bilateral) administrative cooperation between the Member States and/ or social partners;
(3) examine any questions, difficulties and specific issues which might arise concerning the implementation and practical application of Directive 96/71/EC or the national implementing measures, as well as its enforcement in practice;

---

66. O.J., 29 December 2006, L 386.
67. Commission Decision of 19 December 2008 (2009/17/EC).

(4) examine any difficulties which might arise in the application of Article 3(10) of Directive 96/71/EC;
(5) monitor the progress achieved in improving both access to information and administrative cooperation, and in that context, inter alia, assess the different options for a suitable technical support for the information exchange needed to enhance administrative cooperation, including an electronic information exchange system;
(6) examine possibilities to increase effective compliance with, and enforcement of workers' rights and protection of their position, if necessary;
(7) engage in an in-depth examination of practical cross-border enforcement problems in order to solve existing problems, improve the practical application of existing legal instruments as well as to improve mutual assistance between Member States, if necessary.

B. *Membership – Appointment*

224. The Committee is composed of:

– two representatives per Member State;
– representatives of the two sides of industry at Community level, as well as representatives of the social partners in sectors with a high incidence of recourse to posted workers may attend meetings of the Committee as observers.

225. This group of observers comprises up to a maximum of 20 members composed as follows:

– five members representing employers' organisations at Community level;
– five members representing workers' organisations at Community level;
– a maximum of 10 representatives of the social partners (divided evenly between employers' and workers' organisations) in sectors with a high incidence of recourse to posted workers;
– representatives of the EEA/EFTA States, the EFTA Surveillance Authority, accession and candidate countries and Switzerland may equally attend meetings of the Committee as observers.

§4. THE LEGISLATIVE PROCESS

I. Union Law

226. Union law embraces the body of legal norms that prevail in the framework of the European Union. We distinguish between primary law on the one hand and secondary law on the other. Primary law consists of the legal norms that are contained in the Treaties and accessory documents such as the protocols and accession treaties. Secondary law concerns the legal norms that derive from the abovementioned documents and which are contained in the decisions taken by the European institutions pursuant to the powers that the Treaties have conferred upon them.

Also part of Union law are the norms that are made by the legal subjects of the Union themselves pursuant to the TFEU Treaty. Collective agreements are one example of norms that can be concluded in execution of Article 155 TFEU. 'Should management and labour so desire, the dialogue between them at Union level may lead to contractual relations, including agreements.'

Also part of Union law are the general principles common to the laws of the Member States. These are principles relating to equal treatment, respect for acquired rights and the like. It is also through this channel that fundamental human rights prevail in Community law.

In this context Article 6 of the EU Treaty is of the greatest importance. It reads:

(1) The Union recognises the rights, freedoms and principles set out in the Charter of Fundamental Rights of the European Union of 7 December 2000, as adapted at Strasbourg, on 12 December 2007, which shall have the same legal value as the Treaties.

    The provisions of the Charter shall not extend in any way the competences of the Union as defined in the Treaties.

    The rights, freedoms and principles in the Charter shall be interpreted in accordance with the general provisions in Title VII of the Charter governing its interpretation and application and with due regard to the explanations referred to in the Charter, that set out the sources of those provisions.

(2) The Union shall accede to the European Convention for the Protection of Human Rights and Fundamental Freedoms. Such accession shall not affect the Union's competences as defined in the Treaties.

(3) Fundamental rights, as guaranteed by the European Convention for the Protection of Human Rights and Fundamental Freedoms and as they result from the constitutional traditions common to the Member States, shall constitute general principles of the Union's law.

    Although respect for fundamental rights which form an integral part of those general principles of law is a condition of the legality of Union Acts, those rights cannot in themselves have the effect of extending the scope of the Treaty provisions beyond the competences of the Union.[68]

II. Secondary Law

227. In order to carry out this task, the Council and the Commission can, in accordance with the provisions of the Treaties, take five kinds of measure.

Three of them are legally binding, namely:

– the regulation;
– the directive;
– the decision.

---

68. C.O.J., 17 February 1998, *L.J. Grant/South West Trains Ltd*, C-249/96, ECR, 1998, 621.

General Introduction, Ch. 1, The Institutional Framework　　228–229

Not legally binding are:

- the recommendation and
- the opinion.

A. Regulations

228. The regulation 'shall have general application. It shall be binding in its entirety and directly applicable in all Member States' (Art. 288(2) TFEU). The regulation is clearly a generally binding norm, like an Act of Parliament. It is immediately and directly binding without any specific intervention of the national authorities. The regulation is also directly binding for citizens, who may invoke it before a national judge. Consequently, the regulation supersedes national law; and national law which is contrary to regulations is null and void and may not be applied. Regulations state the reasons on which they are based and refer to any proposals and opinions, which are required to be obtained pursuant to the Treaties (Art. 296 TFEU). Regulations are published in the Official Journal and enter into force on the date specified or, in the absence thereof, on the twentieth day following their publication (Art. 297(1) TFEU).

B. Directives

229. A directive is binding as to the result to be achieved, upon each Member State to which it is addressed, but leaves to the national authorities the choice of form and method (Art. 288(3) TFEU). A directive is thus, in comparison with a regulation, a much more flexible measure, which leaves it up to the national authorities to translate it into national law in the most appropriate way. It is only the result which counts. Compliance can be obtained by an Act of Parliament, but other ways are also possible. Thus, collective agreements are rendered obligatory by a governmental decree and may cover the private sector of the economy as a whole. The extension of collective agreements is possible in quite a number of Member States, namely, Belgium, France, Germany and the Netherlands, to give only a few examples. In Belgium, Directive No. 77/187 of 14 February 1977 regarding the transfer of enterprises was subject to a nation-wide collective agreement, No. 32*bis*, which was concluded in the National Labour Council in June 1985, and extended by Royal Decree. This extension has, according to Belgian law, the consequence that the normative part of the collective agreement becomes legally binding for all private employers and their employees and becomes a part of imperative law, which is penally sanctioned. In a case brought before it the Court decreed, in relation to an Italian affair, that where it is true that the Member States may leave the implementation of the social policy objectives pursued by a directive in the first instance to management and labour, this possibility does not, however, discharge them from the obligation of ensuring that all workers in the Union are afforded the full protection provided for in the directive. The state guarantee must cover all cases where effective protection is not ensured by other means. This is certainly the case when collective agreements only cover specific economic sectors and, owing to their contractual nature, create obligations only between members of the trade union in question and employers or undertakings bound by the agreements.[69]

The directive on European Works Councils of 22 September 1994 was partly transposed into the national laws of Belgium and Norway by way of collective agreement as is explained later. Whether that rather transnational directive could be transposed by way of a collective agreement, in lieu of an Act of Parliament, is a matter for discussion, to which we return later.

230. Directives state the reasons on which they are based and refer to the proposals or opinions that were required to be obtained (Art. 296 TFEU). In fact, directives are, for reasons that are self-evident, also published in the Official Journal. The directive indicates the date by which Member States must implement the measures necessary to comply with its provisions. The Member States must inform the Commission that they have done so. If a Member State does not comply in due time, the Commission may bring the matter before the Court. The Court can declare by judgment that, by failing to adopt within the prescribed time period the measures necessary to comply with a directive, a Member State has not fulfilled its obligations under the Treaty.

If the Court of Justice finds that a Member State has failed to fulfil an obligation under the Treaty, the state shall be required to take the necessary measures to comply with the judgment of the Court of Justice.

If the Commission considers that the Member State concerned has not taken such measures it shall, after giving that state the opportunity to submit its observations, issue a reasoned opinion specifying the points on which the Member State concerned has not complied with the judgment of the Court of Justice.

If the Member State concerned fails to take the necessary measures to comply with the Court's judgment within the time-limit laid down by the Commission, the latter may bring the case before the Court of Justice. In so doing it shall specify the amount of the lump-sum or penalty payment to be paid by the Member State concerned which it considers appropriate in the circumstances.

If the Court of Justice finds that the Member State concerned has not complied with its judgment it may impose a lump-sum or penalty payment on it (Art. 260 TFEU).

231. Directives that contain clear obligations have a direct, binding effect and can be invoked by a citizen against a Member State that does not sufficiently comply by adopting the necessary measures. In this case a citizen may invoke a directive before a national judge.

The Court decided in a landmark judgment that in case of failure of a Member State to transpose a directive, *in casu* relating to the protection of employees in the event of the insolvency of the employer, 'interested parties may not assert those rights against the State in proceedings before the national court in the absence of

---

69. C.O.J., 10 July 1986, *Commission v. Italy*, No. 235/84, ECR, 1986, 2291.

implementing measures adopted within the prescribed period'. A Member State is, however, obliged to make good the damage suffered by individuals as a result of the failure to implement the directive.[70]

C. Decisions

232. Like the regulation, a decision is binding in its entirety upon those to whom it is addressed (Article 297 TFEU). Decisions can be addressed to natural persons or to legal persons. A decision is not a general norm, but is directed to certain specific persons. Decisions, which are addressed to Member States, can have a binding effect on the individual, who can invoke the decision before the judge. Decisions are notified to those to whom they are addressed and take effect upon such notification. Some decisions are also published in the Official Journal, although this is not legally obligatory.

D. Recommendations and Opinions

233. Opinions and recommendations have no binding force (Article 288 TFEU). Likewise, resolutions and solemn declarations, like that of the Basic Social Rights of Workers, adopted on 8–9 December 1989 in Strasbourg by 11 Member States, are not legally binding. They only contain political engagements.

However, since recommendations cannot be regarded as having no legal effect at all, the national courts are bound to take them into consideration in order to decide disputes submitted to them, in particular where they cast light on the interpretation of national measures adopted in order to implement them or when they are designed to supplement binding Union decisions.[71]

E. International Agreements

234. Also part of Union law are the international agreements concluded by the Union; these agreements are binding on the institutions of the Union and on Member States (Art. 216 TFEU). Mention should also be made of international agreements that are concluded by the Member States at the occasion of a meeting of the Council. *De facto* these do not belong to Union law.

---

70. C.O.J., 19 November 1991, *A. Francovich and Others* v. *Italian Republic*, Nos. C-6/90 and C9/90; ECR, 1991, 5357. Sofia Moreira de Sousa and Wolfgang Heusel (eds.), *Enforcing Community Law from Francovich to Köler: Twelve Years of the State Liability Principle*, ERA, 2004, Cologne, 273pp.
71. C.O.J., 13 December 1989, *S. Grimaldi* v. *Fonds des Maladies Professionnelles*, No. 322/88, ECR, 1989, 4407.

§5. THE DECISION-MAKING PROCESS

235. The decision-making process leading to European legislation clearly demonstrates the underlying relations between the institutions involved, especially the Commission, the Council and the EP.

236. First, the position of the Commission should be repeated. The Commission enjoys the right of initiative: it has a monopoly in initiating Community legislation. In general, the Council may not make a decision without a proposal from the Commission. This right of initiative has, however, been eroded by the fact that the Coun cil can invite the Commission to make a proposal and the Commission usually does so. Since the Maastricht Treaty of 1991, however, the EP may, acting by a majority of its members, request the Commission to submit any appropriate proposal on matters on which it considers that 'a Union Act is required for the purpose of implementing this Treaty' (Art. 225 TFEU). This gives a right of initiative to the EP. It should be added that the Commission can always amend its proposal as long as the Council has not made a decision. This should allow the Commission to adapt its proposals to the resolutions or opinions from the EP or the ESC. Furthermore, where the Council, in pursuance of the Treaty, acts on a proposal from the Commission, unanimity is required for an Act constituting an amendment to that proposal (Art. 293 TFEU).

237. The Council, as indicated earlier, is not obliged to follow the opinion of either the Commission or the EP. If the Council does not follow the Commission, then decisions by the Council must be taken by unanimity.

238. The role of the EP has been enhanced considerably by the Treaty of Amsterdam (1997). In most cases the cooperation procedure was replaced by the codecision procedure (Art. 294 TFEU). That procedure has to be followed in case of:

– incentive measures regarding employment (Art. 149 TFEU);
– measures to ensure the application of the principle of equal opportunities and equal treatment of men and women (Art. 157 TFEU);
– the social measures meant in Art. 153 TFEU;
– free movement of workers (Art. 45 TFEU);
– approximation of laws (Art. 114 TFEU);
– education (Art. 165 TFEU);
– public health (Art. 168 TFEU);
– freedom of establishment (Art. 50 TFEU).

239. Codecision goes, according to Article 294 TFEU, as follows:

(2) The Commission shall submit a proposal to the European Parliament and the Council.

General Introduction, Ch. 1, The Institutional Framework

A. First Reading

240.

(3) The European Parliament shall adopt its position at first reading and communicate it to the Council.
(4) If the Council approves the European Parliament's position, the act concerned shall be adopted in the wording which corresponds to the position of the European Parliament.
(5) If the Council does not approve the European Parliament's position, it shall adopt its position at first reading and communicate it to the European Parliament.
(6) The Council shall inform the European Parliament fully of the reasons which led it to adopt its position at first reading. The Commission shall inform the European Parliament fully of its position.

B. Second Reading

241.

(7) If, within three months of such communication, the European Parliament:
  (a) approves the Council's position at first reading or has not taken a decision, the act concerned shall be deemed to have been adopted in the wording which corresponds to the position of the Council;
  (b) rejects, by a majority of its component members, the Council's position at first reading, the proposed act shall be deemed not to have been adopted;
  (c) proposes, by a majority of its component members, amendments to the Council's position at first reading, the text thus amended shall be forwarded to the Council and to the Commission, which shall deliver an opinion on those amendments.
(8) If, within three months of receiving the European Parliament's amendments, the Council, acting by a qualified majority:
  (a) approves all those amendments, the act in question shall be deemed to have been adopted;
(b) does not approve all the amendments, the President of the Council, in agreement with the President of the European Parliament, shall within six weeks convene a meeting of the Conciliation Committee.
(9) The Council shall act unanimously on the amendments on which the Commission has delivered a negative opinion.

C. Conciliation

242.

(10) The Conciliation Committee, which shall be composed of the members of the Council or their representatives and an equal number of members

representing the European Parliament, shall have the task of reaching agreement on a joint text, by a qualified majority of the members of the Council or their representatives and by a majority of the members representing the European Parliament within six weeks of its being convened, on the basis of the positions of the European Parliament and the Council at second reading.
(11) The Commission shall take part in the Conciliation Committee's proceedings and shall take all necessary initiatives with a view to reconciling the positions of the European Parliament and the Council.
(12) If, within six weeks of its being convened, the Conciliation Committee does not approve the joint text, the proposed act shall be deemed not to have been adopted.

D. Third Reading

243.

(13) If, within that period, the Conciliation Committee approves a joint text, the European Parliament, acting by a majority of the votes cast, and the Council, acting by a qualified majority, shall each have a period of six weeks from that approval in which to adopt the act in question in accordance with the joint text. If they fail to do so, the proposed act shall be deemed not to have been adopted.
(14) The periods of three months and six weeks referred to in this Article shall be extended by a maximum of one month and two weeks respectively at the initiative of the European Parliament or the Council.

E. Special Provisions

244.

(15) Where, in the cases provided for in the Treaties, a legislative act is submitted to the ordinary legislative procedure on the initiative of a group of Member States, on a recommendation by the European Central Bank, or at the request of the Court of Justice, paragraph 2, the second sentence of paragraph 6, and paragraph 9 shall not apply.

In such cases, the European Parliament and the Council shall communicate the proposed act to the Commission with their positions at first and second readings. The European Parliament or the Council may request the opinion of the Commission throughout the procedure, which the Commission may also deliver on its own initiative. It may also, if it deems it necessary, take part in the Conciliation Committee in accordance with paragraph 11.

245. It is convenient here to underline the role of Coreper (*Comité des représentants permanents*). This committee, composed of the Permanent Representatives of the Member States, prepares the meetings of the Council. *De facto*, Coreper is doing part of the Council's job by dealing with the proposals, opinions, amendments, etc., from the Commission. If agreement is reached within Coreper on a decision that must be taken by the Council, that point is placed in part A of the agenda of the Council and is automatically adopted. Coreper thus exercises significant influence. The Council itself negotiates the controversial issues that are eventually settled during (nightly) marathon sessions (Art. 240 TFEU).

§6. Relations with Other International Organisations

I. General

246. The relation of the EU to other international organisations is dealt with in Article 220 TFEU:

> The Union shall establish all appropriate forms of cooperation with the organs of the United Nations and its specialised agencies, the Council of Europe, the Organisation for Security and Cooperation in Europe and the Organisation for Economic Cooperation and Development.
>
> The Union shall also maintain such relations as are appropriate with other international organisations.
>
> The High Representative of the Union for Foreign Affairs and Security Policy and the Commission shall implement this Article.

Whether the Union is competent to contract legal obligations in regard to other international organisations depends on its competence regarding the issues at stake. This competence can follow explicitly from the Treaty or can be implicitly deduced from the internal competence conferred by the Treaties. The question then is whether conferred internal competence contains the possibility to contract international obligations. This is possible if the external competence is needed to exercise the internal competence fully. Subsequently, the question must be examined whether the conferred competence is exclusively an EU one or whether the competence is shared with the Member States. Finally, one must underline that within this framework one is talking not only about negotiation and the conclusion of international agreements but also about the competence to take part in the activities of other international organisations.

II. The International Labour Organisation

247. The question arises whether the EU as such has the competence to participate in the activities of the ILO, more specifically in the legislative activities of the ILO which lead to the adoption of international conventions and recommendations.

This problem cropped up again at the occasion of the discussion of the Night-work Convention (1990). This is not a simple matter, as the following illustrates.

248. First one has to examine whether the EU has the necessary external competence for the points under discussion and whether that competence is exclusive or not. In general, one can say that the Union, when Union law confers internal competence to Union institutions, is competent to contract international obligations that are necessary to achieve Union objectives.[72] This point is consequently to be examined case by case. The Union, to give an example, seems not to have external competence for 'the rights and interests of employed persons', which are, pursuant to Article 114(2) TFEU, dealt with by the unanimous vote of the Council. The Union, on the other hand, seems to have external competence regarding matters of safety and health of the workers on which, pursuant to Article 153 TFEU, a decision can be taken by qualified majority. That competence, however, is not exclusive to the Union, but is rather shared with the Member States. First, the Member States remain competent regarding health and safety, as Member States can maintain or introduce more stringent matters for the protection of working conditions. Moreover, Member States also remain competent to take measures regarding health and safety issues that are not dealt with by the Union. It is thus clearly a shared competence.

249. The Court of Justice delivered an opinion regarding the relationship with the ILO, on 19 March 1993.[73]

In its request, the Commission sought the Court's opinion on the compatibility with the EC Treaty of Convention No. 170 of the International Labour Organisation concerning safety in the use of chemicals at work and, in particular, on the Community's competence to conclude that Convention and the consequences which this would have for the Member States.

In its opinion the Court estimated that it was necessary to examine the question whether Convention No. 170 came within the Community's sphere of competence and, if so, whether the competence was exclusive in nature.

Convention No. 170 concerned safety in the use of chemicals at work. The field covered by Convention No. 170 falls within the 'social provisions' of the EC Treaty.

It appears from Article 153 of the Treaty that the Union enjoys an internal legislative competence in the area of social policy. Consequently, Convention No. 170, whose subject-matter coincides, moreover, with that of several directives adopted under Article 153, falls within the Union's areas of competence.

In order to determine whether that competence is exclusive it was relevant to note that the provisions of Convention No. 170 are not of such a kind as to affect rules adopted pursuant to Article 153.

However, any difficulties which might arise for the legislative function of the Union could not constitute the basis for exclusive Union competence. For the same reasons, exclusive competence could not be founded on the Union provisions adopted on the basis of Article 114 of the Treaty, such as, in particular, Council

---

72. H. Verschueren, *Internationale arbeidsmigratie. De toegang tot de arbeidsmarkt voor vreem-delingen naar Belgisch, internationaal en Europees Gemeenschapsrecht*, Bruges, 1990, Deel III, 2.1.
73. 2/91, ECR, 1993, Vol. 1, 1061.

Directive 80/1107/EC of 27 November 1980 on the protection of workers from the risks related to exposure to chemical, physical and biological agents at work and individual directives adopted pursuant to Article 8 of Directive 80/1107, all of which laid down minimum requirements.

250. A number of directives adopted in the areas covered by Part III of Convention No. 170 do, however, contain rules which were more than minimum requirements. This was the case, for instance, with regard to those on the classification, packaging and labelling of dangerous substances.

Those directives contain provisions which in certain respects constitute measures conferring on workers, in their conditions of work, more extensive protection than that accorded under the provisions contained in Part III of Convention No. 170.

The scope of Convention No. 170, however, is wider than that of the directives mentioned. The definition of chemicals, for instance, is broader than that of the products covered by the directives. In addition (and in contrast to the provisions contained in the directives), the Convention regulated the transport of chemicals.

While there is no contradiction between these provisions of the Convention and those of the directives mentioned, it must nevertheless be accepted that Part III of Convention No. 170 is concerned with an area which is already covered to a large extent by Community rules.

In those circumstances, it must be considered that the commitments arising from Part III of Convention No. 170, falling within the areas covered by the directives mentioned above, are of such a kind as to affect the Union rules laid down in those directives and that consequently Member States could not undertake such commitments outside the framework of the Union institutions.

In so far as it had been established that the substantive provisions of Convention No. 170 come within the Union sphere of competence, the Union is also competent to undertake commitments for putting those provisions into effect.

251. Article 3 requires that the most representative organisations of employers and workers should be consulted on the measures to be taken to give effect to the provisions of Convention No. 170.

As Union law stood, social policy and, in particular, cooperation between both sides of industry were matters which fell predominantly within the competence of the Member States.

This matter has not, however, been withdrawn entirely from the competence of the Union. According to Article 154 TFEU, the Commission is required to endeavour to develop the dialogue between management and labour at European level.

Consequently, the question of whether international commitments, whose purpose is consultation with representative organisations of employers and workers, fall within the competence of the Member States or of the Union cannot be separated from the objective pursued by such consultations.

252. Article 5 of Convention No. 170 requires that the competent authority was to have the power, if justified on safety and health grounds, to prohibit or restrict the use of certain hazardous chemicals, or to require advance notification and authorisation before such chemicals are used.

Even if the competent authority referred to in that article is an authority of one of the Member States, the Union might nevertheless assume the aforementioned obligation for external purposes. Just as, for internal purposes, the Union might provide, in an area covered by Union rules, that national authorities are to be given certain supervisory powers, it might also, for external purposes, undertake commitments designed to ensure compliance with substantive provisions which fall within its competence and imply the attribution of certain supervisory powers to national authorities.

253. In Ruling 1/7 of 14 November 1978, the Court pointed out that when it appears that the subject-matter of an agreement or contract falls in part within the competence of the Union and in part within that of the Member States, it is important to ensure that there is a close association between the institutions of the Union and the Member States both in the process of negotiation and conclusion and in the fulfilment of the obligations entered into. This duty of cooperation must also apply in the context of the TFEU since it results from the requirement of unity in the international representation of the Union.

In this case, cooperation between the Union and the Member States was all the more necessary in view of the fact that the former could not, as international law then stood, itself conclude an ILO convention and had to do so through the medium of the Member States.

It was therefore for the Union institutions and the Member States to take all the measures necessary so as to best ensure such cooperation both in the procedure of submission to the competent authority and ratification of Convention No. 170 and in the implementation of commitments resulting from that Convention.

In consequence the Court concluded that the ILO Convention No. 170 is a matter which falls within the joint competence of the Member States and the Union.

254. Subsequently one must consider the ILO procedures regarding the rights and obligations of regional groupings under the constitution of the ILO. *Grosso modo*, one can say that the EU as such can at present participate in the meetings set up by the ILO, is entitled to speak in the capacity of observer, but has neither the right to submit amendments, nor the right to vote. The centre of gravity consequently lies with the Member States. One must, however, distinguish different aspects.

255. The preparation of international labour standards is governed by Article 14(2) of the ILO Constitution and Articles 38 and 39 of the Standing Orders of the Conference. For countries that have ratified it, Article 5(1)(a) of Convention No. 144 is also relevant. The Constitution requires consultation of Member States. The question arises whether in certain circumstances the organs of a regional organisation can reply in place of or in addition to the Member States. On the occasion of the preparatory work for the Hours of Work and Rest Periods (Road Transport) Convention 1979 (No. 153), it appeared to the Office that there was nothing in the standing orders to prevent a group of governments from giving a body such as the Commission of the European Union the authority to reply on their joint behalf; the reply was treated for ILO purposes as a reply from the governments. Where the

Member States reply themselves, an additional reply from such a body can be taken into account in the reports to the Conference in the same manner as a reply from any other international organisation having by virtue of its functions an interest in the subject matter of the proposed international standards.

256. It is ILO constitutional practice for the most representative national organisations of employers and workers to be consulted in connection with the preparation of government replies. For states that are parties to Convention No. 144 such consultation is a legal obligation. However, nothing stands in the way for the Commission, when formulating its opinion, to seek the advice of the European social partners and pass that advice on to the ILO.[74]

257. The consideration and adoption of international labour standards is governed by Article 19(1) to (3) of the Constitution and Article 40 of the Standing Orders of the Conference. Under these provisions, the respective positions of the delegates of Member States belonging to a regional grouping and the representatives of any such grouping attending the Conference may be summarised as follows:

– both delegates and representatives are entitled to speak in committee and plenary sittings. There is nothing to prevent the delegates of a number of member governments from agreeing to have one spokesman, who could be one of these delegates or the representative of the regional grouping as such. Under ILO rules, no regional agreement may take away the right of the delegate of a Member State to speak in addition to the spokesman;
– the right to submit amendments to proposed texts is normally limited to delegates; however, on the occasion of consideration of Convention No. 153, it appeared to the Office that there was nothing in the Standing Orders to prevent a group of government delegates from authorising a representative of a regional body to hand in amendments on their joint behalf; such amendments were treated as submitted by the government delegates in question;
– only the delegates may vote. Article 4(1) of the Constitution seems to imply that their right to vote must be exercised individually.

258. Article 19(5)(b) and (c), (6)(b) and (7)(b)(i) and (ii) of the Constitution deals with the submission of Conventions and Recommendations to the competent authority. The competent authority is the one that has the power to legislate or to take action in order to implement the Convention on the Recommendation concerned. Convention No. 144 requires consultation of the most representative national organisations of employers and of workers on the proposals to be made to the competent authority in connection with the submission of Conventions and Recommendations. Where these proposals emanate from a body other than the governments of the Member States that are parties to that Convention, ways and means of

---

74. ILO, Governing Body, *The Relationship of Rights and Obligations under the Constitution of the ILO to Rights and Obligations under Treaties establishing regional Groupings*, 215th session. Fourth item on the agenda, February–March 1981.

satisfying that obligation will have to be found. Member States have a constitutional obligation to inform the Director-General of the measures taken to bring instruments before the competent authority, and of the action taken by that authority. It would seem to be possible for a group of Member States to authorise an organ of a regional grouping to inform the Director-General on their joint behalf. In any case, copies of such information must be communicated to the most representative organisations of employers and workers.

259. Ratification of international labour conventions is dealt with in Article 19(5)(d) of the ILO Constitution. The consistent interpretation of that provision has been that only ILO members may ratify such conventions. The responsibility for application and follow-up (making reports) of international labour standards also belongs to the Member States.

260. Finally, we must point out that the national organisations of workers and employers take the view that regional arrangements must not be such that they interfere with the performance by states of their obligations under the ILO Constitution.[75] This is easy to understand: the ILO is really tripartite and national delegations to the ILO Conference are equally tripartite, composed of representatives of the government and of both sides of industry. The same is not true at the European level. Within the framework of the European Union, the social partners have at most an advisory status and have often only a very marginal input.

261. The entering into force of the Single European Act and other developments in relations between the EU and the ILO made it necessary to update the understanding of their mutual relations, in particular with a view to strengtheningthe scope and procedures for cooperation and consultation in a spirit of reciprocity between the two institutions. This was done by an exchange of letters on 14 May 2001.

262. These read as follows (excerpts):

> The International Labour Organisation and the European Communities have a shared commitment to social and economic progress – to improving living and working conditions, and to promoting employment. Since the first agreement between the ILO and the Communities in 1958, the two organisations have progressively developed their cooperation to further these aims.
>
> The ILO and the European Communities, represented by the Commission, last exchanged letters in 1989. Since then, there have been profound changes in Europe while the global economy has been developing rapidly, and both the ILO and the European Communities have significantly reinforced and developed their capacity for responding to new challenges in the area of social and employment policy. It is therefore timely for us to bring our exchange of letters up to date. This new exchange of letters should thus serve, first, to identify

---

75. ILO, Governing Body, *Report of the Committee on Standing Orders and the Application of Conventions and Recommendations*, 215th session. Twelfth item on the agenda, 3–6 March 1981.

the areas in which new challenges have emerged for both our organisations, and second to establish on that basis the priority areas in which cooperation between the ILO and the Commission would be most beneficial.

Since 1989, social and employment issues have increasingly moved to the fore both at the European level and internationally – Globalisation has undoubtedly brought many benefits but it is widely felt that these are reaching too few. There has been growing public concern that the social aspects of globalisation have been neglected. It is also being recognised that new integrated approaches are called for at various levels, including by the institutions of the international community. The ILO has identified four strategic objectives as crucial to its mandate in the context of globalisation: fundamental principles and rights at work, the promotion of employment for women and men, the enhancement of social protection and the promotion of social dialogue. Together, these constitute the essence of 'Decent Work'. The process of European integration, for its part, has acquired a strong and dynamic social dimension. In this context, the promotion of quality is now at the heart of the EU's agenda for employment, social policy and industrial relations, as the driving force for a thriving economy, more and better jobs and an inclusive society. Moreover, the process of enlargement of the European Union will require the new Member States to adhere to the framework of the European social model.

263. With regard to labour standards and human rights, an area in which the Community and the ILO share a strong common interest, the importance of promoting respect for fundamental principles and rights at work alongside economic development and trade liberalisation is now more widely recognised than ever. In 1995, the World Summit for Social Development defined a social floor for the global economy in terms of the ILO Conventions covering four basic principles: freedom of association and collective bargaining, freedom from forced labour and discrimination and the abolition of child labour. In this context, the ILO has reinforced its role as the local point for international efforts to promote opportunities for women and men to obtain decent and productive work with the adoption of the Declaration of Fundamental Principles and Rights at Work. In the European Union, a reference to fundamental social rights is now included in the Treaty itself as is the possibility of concrete action by the Community against discrimination and social exclusion. Furthermore, the European Union has proclaimed a Charter of Fundamental Rights which will be another instrument in its efforts to promote economic and social progress. The Community is committed, moreover, to promoting core labour standards throughout its external relations policies and in its development cooperation.

With regard to the social dialogue, there have been significant developments in the EU since 1989. The social partners have been given new and enhanced responsibilities in the elaboration of social policy at the European level. This reinforces social dialogue at the EU level while pointing to a new way of moving ahead of social policy matters. These developments are particularly important in view of the forthcoming historic enlargement of the EU.

264. In respect of the promotion of employment, similarly, both the ILO and the European Community have significantly strengthened their efforts since the last exchange of letters. Indeed, creating greater employment opportunities for women and men has been declared one of the ILO's strategic objectives. The European Union, for its part, has developed an extensive employment strategy which seeks to maximise the employment potential of the European economy while respecting the principle of gender equality. It should further be noted that the ILO and the European Community now have common goals with respect to the promotion of social protection.

With regard to development cooperation, the challenges facing the ILO and the Communities have evolved considerably since the 1989 exchange of letters. It is a tribute not least to the advocacy of the ILO that the international system as a whole is increasingly integrating social considerations into programmes and strategies for economic development. This also serves to underscore the lasting importance of the 1995 World Summit for Social Development and its follow-up.

On the EU side, the Community aims, through its development cooperation policy in which equity is a guiding principle, to foster sustainable development and to help developing countries to eradicate poverty and to become integrated into the world economy. Indeed, the Community recently agreed that poverty reduction should be the central objective of its development efforts. The ILO's Decent Work agenda is also a development agenda based on growth, employment and jobs. Development cooperation is one means of action which the ILO uses to promote and realise its values while simultaneously responding to the developmental needs of its Member States.

265. Against this background, the Commission and the ILO agree that it would be of benefit to both organisations to develop their cooperation by focusing on the following priority areas: – the promotion of labour standards, notably with regard to the principles and rights set out in the 1998 ILO Declaration on Fundamental Principles and Rights at Work;

- the promotion of employment, notably through an exchange of information and experience on the European Employment Strategy and the ILO's efforts to create employment opportunities for women and men;
- social dialogue, not least with a view to the possible dissemination of the lessons from the European experience with social dialogue to other regions of the world;
- the social and employment policy aspects of enlargement of the EU, notably with regard to social dialogue;
- social protection through targeted collaboration on selected themes; and – development cooperation, notably with a view to strengthening the social dimension of development, while also collaborating at the operational level in the service of sustainable development.

In order to develop cooperation in these and in other areas of mutual interest, the Commission and the ILO confirm the usefulness of holding high-level meetings on an annual basis, alternately in Brussels and Geneva, which will review existing cooperation and plan joint activities for the following year.

General Introduction, Ch. 1, The Institutional Framework

The following provisions of the 1989 exchange of letters will continue to apply:

– The Community, represented by the Commission, will continue to be regularly invited to meetings of the ILO's International Labour Conference and of the Governing Body.
– The Commission will, in turn and as appropriate, invite representatives of the International Labour Office to meetings of the Commission at service level dealing with social and labour matters likely to be of interest to the International Labour Organisation.
– The President of the Commission and the Director-General of the ILO, or their representatives, will hold consultations on developments within their respective organisations which are likely to have implications for cooperation between the two parties.
– The appropriate form for the exchange of information or assistance in areas of shared interest can be agreed upon on a case by case basis (visit, preparation of a document, working group, financing of projects) by the programme managers concerned.

To facilitate cooperation through project financing, the ILO and the Commission will continue to hold discussions with a view to establishing standard financial and administrative modalities for ILO implementation of Commission-funded projects.

There is no doubt that by sharing our experience, engaging in joint reflection on new approaches to contemporary social issues and, where appropriate, pooling our expertise, we can both respond even more effectively to the need to promote employment opportunities and to maintain and improve living and working conditions worldwide.

266. The ILO and the European Commission held a high-level meeting on 14 February 2002 to discuss cooperation on a range of social issues. They will cooperate in areas such as the social aspects of globalisation, the alleviation of poverty, employment policy, health and safety, social protection and social dialogue.

The agenda of the meeting was divided into two parts. In the first, the social dimension of globalisation and cooperation between the EU and the ILO on the alleviation of poverty and on 'decent work' was discussed. The ILO stated that it was in the process of establishing a world commission on the social dimension of globalisation, which would involve other international organisations such as the World Trade Organisation (WTO) and the World Bank (WB). For its part, the European Commission stated that it is willing to cooperate with the ILO on poverty reduction programmes in developing countries, on technical cooperation programmes, on mainstreaming trade and core labour standards in development policy and on the management of migration and social protection in China. The Commission had issued two documents in this area in July 2001 – a Communication on the promotion of core labour standards and better social governance and a Green Paper on greater corporate social responsibility.

In addition, both the ILO and the Commission will 'reflect' on strengthening social dialogue and civil society in the framework of the stability pact for the Balkans.

The second part of the agenda covered:

– employment policy;
– health and safety at work;
– social protection (including migration issues); and
– social dialogue.

267. The Commission noted that the EU employment strategy has 'effectively influenced' the ILO's 'global employment agenda' and its 'global alliance for employment'. Cooperation between the two organisations in this area will include the development of 'quality in work' indicators and reports on employment, productivity and labour market performance.

In the area of health and safety, both organisations are preparing new strategies. They are also looking at cooperation in the areas of social protection, social exclusion and migration. In the area of social dialogue, the two organisations will concentrate on the development of the social dialogue in the context of EU enlargement, restructuring and the sectoral social dialogue in industries affected by globalisation.

The Commission and the ILO concluded by deciding to establish contact points which they hope will ensure an effective follow-up to their meeting. These contact points will report to an annual high-level meeting.[76]

268. The question arises what happens if a Member State has approved before its accession to the European Union an international convention, which happens to become contrary to EU legislation. This was the case with the Republic of Austria, which acceded to the European Union with effect from 1 January 1995 and had ratified Convention No. 45 of the ILO (employment of women on underground work in minds off all kinds) before that date.[77] Article 2 of that convention contains a general prohibition of the employment of women in underground work in mines. This is contrary to Directive 76/207 on equal treatment for men and women. Article 2(3) of Directive 76/207 does not allow women to be excluded from a certain type of employment solely on the ground that they ought to be given greater protection than men against risks which affect men and women in the same way and which are distinct from women's specific needs of protection, such as those expressly mentioned.

It follows from the third paragraph of Article 351 TFEU that the obligations arising from agreements concluded, by acceding States before the date of their accession, between one or more Member States on the one hand, and one or more third countries on the other, are not affected by the provisions of the TFEU.

---

76. 'European Commission and ILO cooperate on Social Issues', www.eiro.eurofound.ie.
77. According to Article 351 TFEU are the rights and obligations arising from agreements concluded before 1 January 1958 or, for acceding States, before the date of their accession, between one or more Member States on the one hand, and one or more third countries on the other, not to be affected by the provisions of this Treaty. To the extent that such agreements are not compatible with this Treaty, the Member State or States concerned shall take all appropriate steps to eliminate the incompatibilities established.

In those circumstances, while it is true that the Republic of Austria may, in principle, rely on the first paragraph of Article 351 TFEU to maintain in force the provisions of domestic law implementing the abovementioned obligations, the fact remains that the second paragraph of that article states that, to the extent that earlier agreements within the meaning of the first paragraph of the article are not compatible with the Treaty, the Member State or States concerned are to take all appropriate steps to eliminate the incompatibilities established.

In light of the conclusion reached by the Court, the obligations imposed on the Republic of Austria by Convention No. 45 of the ILO are incompatible with Articles 2 and 3 of Directive 76/207.

The appropriate steps for the elimination of such incompatibility referred to in the second paragraph of Article 351 TFEU include, *inter alia*, denunciation of the agreement in question.[78]

269. The EU regularly recommends Member States to ratify conventions of the International Labour Organisation, thus:

– 1999/130/EC: Commission Recommendation of 18 November 1998 on ratification of International Labour Organisation (ILO) Convention No. 180 concerning seafarers' hours of work and the manning of ships, and ratification of the 1996 Protocol to the 1976 Merchant Shipping (minimum standards) Convention (notified under document number C(1999) 372); – 2000/581/EC: Commission Recommendation of 15 September 2000 on the ratification of International Labour Organisation (ILO) Convention No. 182 of 17 June 1999 concerning the prohibition and immediate action for the elimination of the worst forms of child labour (notified under document number C(2000) 2674);
– 2005/367/: Council Decision of 14 April 2005 authorising Member States to ratify, in the interests of the European Community, the Seafarers' Identity Documents Convention of the International Labour Organisation (Convention No. 185);
– 2005/367/EC: Council Decision of 14 April 2005 authorising Member States to ratify, in the interests of the European Community, the Seafarers' Identity Documents Convention of the International Labour Organisation (Convention No. 185);
– 2007/431/EC: Council Decision of 7 June 2007 authorising Member States to ratify, in the interests of the European Community, the Maritime Labour Convention, 2006, of the International Labour Organisation.

A. *EU–ILO Cooperation Striving for More Decent Work in ACP Countries*

270. From 22 to 25 June 2009, the European Commission (EuropeAid) and the ILO organised a seminar on employment, social protection and decent work in ACP (African, Caribbean and Pacific) countries. The participants emphasised the significance of the Global Jobs Pact and also pointed out that in many cases the EU and the ILO share the same views on employment, employability, social protection and

---

78. C.O.J., 1 February 2005, *Commission v. Republic of Austria*, C-203/03, ECR, 2005, 935.

other issues related to decent work such as social dialogue and fundamental social rights. The European Commission and the ILO agreed to consult one another and work together more in the field in partner countries with a view to exchanging their respective expertise and initiatives, notably within the framework of the mid term review of the Country Strategy Papers.

271. The ILO Office and the European Commission services had their Ninth Annual High Level Meeting (HLM) on 20 May 2011 in Geneva. At the meeting the representatives from both institutions highlighted that mutual cooperation was intensifying, both in the EU and elsewhere. The joint agenda included the ongoing policy priorities of both institutions in the aftermath of the financial and economic crisis; social dialogue and international labour standards in times of crisis in the EU and elsewhere; and ILO–IMF–EU cooperation and collaboration in the G20. The HLM also resulted in convergent views on the role of social protection, including the UN social protection floor. This was important in the light of the upcoming key discussions on social protection at the June 2011 International Labour Conference. A session was devoted to ILO–EU cooperation in North African/Arab states. Other themes were collaboration on labour migration, development and trade issues.

B. ILO and EU have a Shared Responsibility

272. December 2012, for the tenth time in a row, the ILO and the European Commission held their annual high-level meeting defining the focus of their cooperation for the next year.

Over the past decade, the ILO and the EU have considerably intensified their cooperation, both within and outside the EU. The EU supports the promotion of decent work for all, the international labour standards and the wider Decent Work Agenda through its internal and external policies and actions such as development, policy dialogue and trade.

As an example, EU efforts have contributed to the ratification of core labour standards as well as other international labour conventions, both within EU Member States and outside the EU. In this regard, EU-ILO cooperation should continue promoting the application in practice of these standards.

273. Social dialogue is another area of close cooperation. 'ILO-EU cooperation can be instrumental for rebuilding social dialogue where it has been negatively affected by the crisis, such as in some EU countries', Guy Ryder, DG of the ILO said.

The ILO Director-General underlined the need and the opportunities for the ILO-EU partnership in the world of work today. 'The need comes from the consequences of the crisis', Guy Ryder said, adding that the ILO and the EU should cooperate as effectively as possible and orient their efforts towards a job rich recovery. He continued that the opportunities lie in the ILO and the EU's shared values

III. The European Economic Area

274. The Agreement on the European Economic Area (EEA), which entered into force on 1 January 1994, brings together the 28 EU Members and the three EFTA countries: Iceland, Liechtenstein and Norway – in a single internal market, referred to as the 'Internal Market'.[80]

275. The EEA Agreement provides for the inclusion of EU legislation that covers the four freedoms – the free movement of goods, services, persons and capital – throughout the 30 EEA States. In addition, the Agreement covers cooperation in other important areas such as research and development, education, social policy, the environment, consumer protection, tourism and culture, collectively known as 'flanking and horizontal' policies. The Agreement guarantees equal rights and obligations within the Internal Market for citizens and economic operators in the EEA.

---

79. Press release 6 December 2012.
80. Switzerland is not part of the EEA Agreement, but has a bilateral agreement with the EU.

Chapter 2. The Social Partners

§1. THE EMPLOYERS' ORGANISATIONS

I. BUSINESSEUROPE

276. At the European level, various employers' organisations are active. Besides BUSINESSEUROPE, which organises 41 central federations of industry from 35 countries and thus groups national confederations of employers' organisations, like the British CBI or the French MEDEF,[81] there are specific organisations for agriculture, namely COPA (*Comité des Organisations Agricoles*), for enterprises that are active in the public sector, namely CEEP (*Centre Européen des Entreprises Publiques*) UEAPME, which organises SMEs.

277. As the EU broadened and deepened, so BUSINESSEUROPE also grew. In 2011 there are now 41 members from 35 countries, including the European Union countries, the European Economic Area countries, and some Central and Eastern European countries. The current structure includes seven Main Committees, about 60 Working Groups, with a staff of 45 under the direction of the Secretary General and the organisation works under the leadership of the President.

278. The Council of Presidents, comprising the Presidents (i.e. the senior elected officials) of all the member federations, is the supreme governing body of the organisation, and determines BUSINESSEUROPE general strategy.

279. The Executive Bureau brings together representatives of federations from the five largest countries, the country holding the EU Presidency, and federations from five smaller countries on a rotating basis, and meets as necessary. The Bureau monitors the implementation of the annual programme, stimulating co-ordination with member federations; ensures that resources are adequate for the organisation's tasks; and responds quickly to urgent situations arising between the meetings of the main Committees.

280. The Executive Committee, composed of the Directors General (i.e. the senior employed officials) of all the member federations, translates the Council's strategy into activities and tasks for the organisation. Aided by the Executive Bureau, it ensures a balance between tasks and resources.

---

81. Z. Tyszkiewicz, 'Unice: the Voice of European Business and Industry in Brussels – A Programmatic Self-Presentation' in *Employers' Associations in Europe: Policy and Organisation*, D. Sadowski and O. Jacobi (eds), Baden, 1991, 92; Gary Rynhart and Jean Dujardin, 'Employers' Organisations', in R. Blanpain (ed.), *Comparative Labour Law and Industrial Relations in Industrialised Market Economies*, 10th and revised edition, The Hague, Kluwer Law International, 2010, 43–70; M. Behrens & F. Traxler, 'Employers's organisation in Europe', www.eiro.eurofound.ie, 2004; J. Dujardin, 'The International Organisation of Employers', in: Confronting Globalisation: the Quest for a Social Agenda, *Bulletin of Comparative Labour Relations*, Kluwer Law International, No. 55, 2005, 103–106.

General Introduction, Ch. 2, The Social Partners

281. Seven policy commitees (Economic and Financial Affairs; International Relations; Social Affairs; Industrial Affairs; Legal Affairs; Entrepreneurship & SMEs; and Internal Market), organise BUSINESSEUROPE practical work, and prepare BUSINESSEUROPE position papers on specific policy areas, through the Working Groups. The members of each Policy Committee are nominated by the member-federations, and chosen for their experience in the specific domain.

282. The Policy committees create and organise the 60 working groups, which are BUSINESSEUROPE great strength. In each domain a working group is established whenever there are developments which need debate, and to that group experts are nominated by the member-federations, often coming from companie in that country. The consensus papers that result from these debates can thus genuinely be claimed to represent business reaction throughout Europe to any given proposal.

283. Most member federations maintain an office in Brussels, and, among their other functions, the Heads of these bureaux are the Permanent Delegates to BUSINESSEUROPE. Convened once or twice a month by the Secretary-General, the Committee of Permanent Delegates provides a link between headquarters and the member federations.

284. The BUSINESSEUROPE headquarters, based in Brussels, has around 45 members of staff. It administers the whole organisation, coordinates the efforts of policy committees and working groups, prepares position papers, and communicates these positions to the EU institutions and other audiences both in Brussels and the member states. BUSINESSEUROPE executives are also involved in the Social Dialogue, consultative committees, management boards, conferences, exhibitions, and high-level delegations.

Federations – Members of BUSINESSEUROPE

Austria	IV	Industriellenvereinigung –
Belgium	(VBO-FEB)	Fédération des Entreprises de Belgique – Verbond van Belgische Ondernemingen
Bulgaria	(BIA)	Bulgarian Industrial Association
Montenegro	CG	Montenegrin Employers Federation
CH – Switzerland	Economiesuisse	Confederation of Swiss Employers
Croatia	HUP	Croatian Employers' Association (Hrvatska Udruga Poslodavaca)

Cyprus	OEB	Employers & Industrialists Federation Cyprus
Czech Republic	SPCR	Confederation of Industry of the Czech Republic
Denmark	DI	Confederation of Danish Industries
	DA	Danish Employers' Confederation
Estonia	ETTK	Estonian Employers' Confederation
Finland	EK	Confederation of Finnish Industries
France	MEDEF	Mouvement des Entreprises de France
Germany	BDI	Bundesverband der Deutschen Industrie
	BDA	Bundesvereinigung der Deutschen Arbeitgeberverbände
Great Britain	CBI	Confederation of British Industry
Greece	SEV	Fédération des Industries Grecques
Hungary	MGYOSZ	Confederation of Hungarian Employers and Industrialists
Iceland	FII	Federation of Icelandic Industries (Samtök idnadarins)
	IS	Confederation of Icelandic Employers
Ireland	IBEC	Irish Business and Employers Confederation
Italy	CONFINDUSTRIA	Confederazione Generale dell'Industria Italiana
Latvia	LDDK	Latvijas Darba Deveju Konfederacija Luxembourgeois
Lithuania	LPK	Lithuanian Confederation of Industrialists
Luxembourg	FEDIL	Fédération des Industriels
Malta	MFOI	Malta Federation of Industry
Montenegro	MEF	Montenegrin Employers Federation
Netherlands	VNO	Verbond van Nederlandse Ondernemingen

General Introduction, Ch. 2, The Social Partners

Norway	NCW	Nederlands Christelijk Werkgeversverbond
Poland	NHO	Confederation of Norwegian Business and Industry
Portugal	PKPP	Polish Confederation of Private Employers
	AIP	Associaçáo Industrial Portuguesa
Romania	CIP	Confederação da Indústria Portuguesa
	ACPR	Alianta Confederatiilor Patronale din Romania
San Marino	ANIS	Associazione Nazionale dell'Industria Sammarinese
Serbia	SAE	Serbian Association of Employers
Slovakia	RUZ	Republikova Unia Zamestnavatelov
Slovenia	ZDS	Združenje Delodajalcev Slovenije (Employers' Association of Slovenia)
Spain	CEOE	Confédération des Employeurs Espagnols
Sweden	SN	Svenskt Näringsliv (Confederation of Swedish Enterprise)
	SAF	Swedish Employers' Confederation
Turkey	TÜSIAD	Turkish Industrialists' and Businessmen's Association
	TISK	Turkish Confederation of

A. Mission and Priorities

1. Mission

285. BUSINESSEUROPE plays a crucial role in Europe as the main horizontal business organisation at EU level. Through its 41 member federations, BUSINESS–EUROPE represents more than 20 million companies from 35 countries. Its main task is to ensure that companies' interests are represented and defended *vis-à-vis* the European institutions with the principal aim of preserving

and strengtheningcorporate competitiveness. BUSINESSEUROPE is active in the European social dialogue to promote the smooth functioning of labour markets.

2. Priorities 2012–2013: Growing Out of the Crisis

286. In a policy document presented on 26 June 2012, BUSINESSEUROPE and all its members urge to take all the necessary decisions without further delay to restore confidence and put Europe back on track. In its five-point plan 'Growing out of the crisis' BUSINESSEUROPE presents concrete measures to:

- safeguard the euro: all possible means must be used to safeguard the euro;
- improve public finances and speed up structural reforms: only when businesses and households are sure that governments have fully committed to putting their public finances on a sustainable path, will they have the confidence to invest, recruit workers and increase consumption;
- promote private investment: Europe needs a stronger investment and competitiveness agenda to build prive-sector trust and confidence.;
- unleash the single market: the single market adds EUR 600 a year to our economy. Since 1992 it has helped create almost 3 million new jobs across the EU, and benefited the broader European Economic Area.;
- expand EU external trade: with almost 30 million EU jobs (more than 10 per cent of the EU workforce) dependent upon export markets outside the EU, Europe needs to build a strong presence in expanding global markets.

This strategy will allow Europe to double its long-term annual growth rate from 1.25 per cent to 2.5 per cent.

B. *Employment and Social Affairs*

287. For the EU to emerge from the economic crisis, preventing rising unemployment from becoming entrenched is a priority. In addition, the EU is facing an ageing workforce and increased international competition. Structural reforms are therefore needed to improve labour market flexibility, secure the availability of a skilled workforce – including through economic migration – and put in place modern social policies. The aim must be to have more people in work, working more productively. Flexicurity should be at the heart of the European employment strategy and the leading principle in the development of social policy. Employment, social and immigration policies must be adapted to the diversity of situations in the Member States.

288. BUSINESSEUROPE is actively engaged in the European social dialogue in order to find solutions reconciling economic and social needs of labour market players, and to devise concrete arrangements that benefit both companies and employees.

General Introduction, Ch. 2, The Social Partners

1. Employment and Flexicurity

289. As a result of the economic crisis, unemployment in the EU27 stands at just under 10.5 per cent as of June 2012. In order to improve employment prospects and increase the adaptability of workers, Member States must reform their labour markets based on the principles of flexicurity.

2. Ageing

290. BUSINESSEUROPE considers tackling demographic change one of the five key challenges facing European economies and societies. Demographic change means that the EU population is getting older and living for longer. In contrast, the number of working age people is shrinking. As a result, there will be less people in work to pay the contributions needed to provide income for a larger number of people, who will spend longer in retirement. Unless urgent measures are taken, this change will have a negative impact on pension provision and public finances.

3. Social Affairs

291. The economic crisis has shown that Member States have social systems that protect workers in difficult times. However, in order to safeguard the core of those systems, they need to be modernised.

4. Skills

292. As a result of the economic crisis, unemployment in the EU-27 stands at just under 10.5 per cent as of June 2012. In order to improve employment prospects and increase the adaptability of workers, Member States must reform their labour markets based on the principles of flexicurity.

5. Social Dialogue and Industrial Relations

293. Social partners are best placed to find solutions and to devise concrete arrangements reconciling economic and social needs of labour market players. Both at European and national level, priority should be given to actions by the social partners in their fields of competence.

II. CEEP

294. CEEP is the European Centre of Enterprises with Public Participation and of Enterprises of General Economic Interest.
CEEP is the European association representing:

– enterprises and employers' organisations with public participation and
– enterprises carrying out activities of general economic interest, whatever their legal ownership or status.

295. CEEP, and its Brussels office/General Secretariat, represents the interests of its members before the European institutions. It has excellent contacts with the departments of the EU Commission and other European institutions, such as the European Parliament and the Economic and Social Committee. Its status as a European Social Partner gives it access to contacts at the highest levels, including the members and President of the EU Commission. CEEP is consulted regularly by the Directorate-Generals of the European Commission on draft Regulations, Directives and other legislation of interest to its members, and is frequently asked to produce opinions. CEEP sends representatives and observers to a large number of committees and consultative bodies of the European institutions, and through its involvement is kept up to date with developments at European level which are of interest to its members. As a result, it is well informed at all times on the activities and plans of the European institutions, and is in a position to issue opinions and take other steps to ensure that the interests of its members are considered at an early stage.

CEEP works closely with other European industry associations. Although many of its members belong to these sector-specific umbrella organisations, CEEP provides them with an additional powerful lobbying instrument in Brussels by virtue of its role as a Social Partner and the European association representing all enterprises providing services of general interest.

CEEP moreover organises congresses, conferences and seminars on subjects of current interest for its members and on topics related to the development of the EU as a whole. Many of these events are organised in conjunction with the European Commission as well as with other social partners. CEEP also carries out research projects on behalf of the Commission along with its support.

III. UEAPME

296. UEAPME is the employer's organisation representing the interests of European crafts, trades and SMEs at EU level. UEAPME is a recognised European Social Partner and acts on behalf of crafts and SMEs in the European Social Dialogue and in discussions with the EU institutions. It is a non-profit seeking and non-partisan organisation.

As the European SME umbrella organisation, UEAPME incorporates 80 member organisations from 36 countries consisting of national cross-sector SME federations, European branch federations and other associate members, which support the SME family.

Across the whole of Europe UEAPME represents over 12 million enterprises with nearly 55 million employees across Europe.

297. UEAPME was originally formed as a result of the amalgamation of various European trade associations and organisations of medium-sized enterprises in 1979. The organisation has a number of committees spanning the major policy areas

of the EU, which meet to draw up its policy positions. The committees have set up a number of working groups to deal with topics of major importance to SMEs, such as the simplification of administrative burdens and the creation of businesses. The main stated objectives of UEAPME are to inform its members about developments in European policy; promote joint action on the part of national organisations at European level; and ensure that the interests and views of its members are understood and reflected by the EU institutions.

SMEs play an integral part in the European economy. UEAPME argues that SMEs employ more than 70 per cent of the working population in Europe. In addition, SMEs have created and maintained jobs at a higher rate than larger enterprises, which can be related to their faster and more flexible reaction to market fluctuations. Moreover, SMEs are given a key role in job-creation strategies under the current EU Employment Guidelines.

298. On 4 December 1998, the presidents of UNICE (now BUSINESS–EUROPE) and UEAPME agreed to strengthen collaboration by signing a cooperation agreement.

The agreement provides that employers' representatives will have the same rights in preparatory meetings of employers' organisations to discuss policy, but no representative has a veto over any negotiations. The agreement is said to be based upon the principle that the highest endeavours will be pursued to reach consensus on the issues or positions to be defended in the social dialogue, while at the same time respecting the autonomy of the two organisations. UNICE, as 'leader' for the employers' side, has pledged to consult UEAPME prior to expressing positions on behalf of employers in negotiations or other meetings of the European social dialogue. A reason for the cooperation agreement is that UEAPME has long claimed to be the legitimate representative of SMEs and has argued in the past that these interests were insufficiently represented by UNICE.[82]

A. *Objectives*

299. The main objectives of UEAPME, as the voice of of crafts, trades and SMEs in Europe include:

– monitoring the EU policy and legislative process and keeping its members informed on all matters of European Union policy of relevance to crafts, trades and SMEs;
– representing and promoting the interests, needs and opinions of its member organisations to the EU institutions and other international organisations;
– supporting its members academically, technically and legally on all areas of EU policy;
– supporting the idea of European integration and contributing to European co-operation.

---

82. Peter Foster, 'European employers' organisations forge closer links within social dialogue', www.eiro.eurofound.ie, 31 March 1999.

B. Strategy

300. As the recognised voice for the interests of crafts, trades and SMEs in Europe, UEAPME acts as an 'agenda setter' in the area of European SME policy. It has direct role in all EU policy that has an affect on SMEs. This is made possible through the maintenance of direct links and contact with the EU administration and strengthened by its status as a Social Partner.

UEAPME endeavours to ensure that the interests of crafts and SMEs are taken into account in all legislation that has an impact on them. Some of the key legislative areas in which UEAPME is active include: economic and fiscal policy, employment and social policy, environmental policy, enterprise policy, internal market, legal affairs, and R&D.

UEAPME analyses the role of SMEs in European economies and the challenges they face. On the basis of this analysis, UEAPME, with its members, identifies the ways in which SMEs can adapt to the challenges of the open and competitive EU economy.

§2. THE TRADE UNIONS

301. The most important European trade union is undoubtedly the ETUC. It has its headquarters in Brussels near most European institutions, which it tries to influence to the 5tmost. In the same building, one finds the International Trade Union Confederation (ITUC). The ETUC was created in 1973 and presently represents some 60 million members, who belong to 85 national trade unions from 36 countries.

The ETUC is a united, yet pluralist organisation which determines its policies through the deliberations of its Congress and its Executive Committee.

The Congress meets once every four years (the last was held in Athens in 2011) and is made up of delegates from affiliates in proportion to their membership. It elects the General Secretary and the two Deputy General Secretaries, as well as the President, whose role is to chair the ETUC's Congress, Executive and Steering Committees.

The Executive Committee meets four times a year with all affiliates being represented. If necessary, decisions can be taken by a qualified two-thirds majority vote. It is the Executive Committee which decides on the mandate and the composition of the delegations which negotiate with the European employers' organisations, in the European Social Dialogue, and which assesses the results.

The Steering Committee, a smaller body, is responsible for following up the decisions of the Executive Committee between its sessions. It meets eight times a year and is composed of 21 elected members from the Executive Committee.

The Secretariat runs the day-to-day activities of the ETUC and takes care of relations with the European institutions and the employers' organisations.

The General Secretary is the head and the spokesperson of the Confederation.

General Introduction, Ch. 2, The Social Partners

I. Members of the ETUC

302. ITUC International Trade Union Confederation

National Trade Union Confederations (83)

Andorra	USDA	Trade Union Andorra (Unió Sindical D'Andorra)
Austria	OGB	Austrian Trade Union Federation (Österreichischer Gewerkschaftsbund)
Belgium	ABVV/FGTB	General Labour Federation of Belgium (Algemeen Belgisch Vakverbond/Fédération Générale du Travail de Belgique)
	ACV/CSC	Confederation of Christian Trade Unions (Algemeen Christelijk Vakverbond/ Confédération des Syndicats Chrétiens)
	CGSLB	General Confederation of Liberal Trade Unions of Belgium (Centrale Générale des Syndicats Libéraux de Belgique)
Bulgaria	CITUB	Confederation of Independent Trade Unions of Bulgaria
	PODKREPA	Confederation of Labour
Croatia	SSSH/UATUC	Union of Autonomous Trade Unions of Croatia (Saveza Samotalnih Sindicata Hrvatske)
	NHS	Independent Trade Unions of Croatia (Nezavisni Hrvatski Sindicati)
Cyprus	SEK	Cyprus Workers' Confederation (Synomospondia Ergaton Kyprou)
	TURK-SEN	Turkish Workers' Trade Union Federation (Kibris Türk Isci Sendikalari Federasyonu)
	DEOK	The Democratic Labour Federation of Cyprus
Czech Republic	CMK OS	Czech Moravian Confederation of Trade Unions
Denmark	AC	Danish Confederation of Professional Associations (Akademikernes Centralorganisation)
	FTF	Salaried Employees' and Civil Servants' Confederation

		(Funktionærernes og Tjenestemændenes Fællesråd)
	LO-DK	Danish Confederation of Trade Unions (Landesorganisationen i Danmark)
Estonia	EAKL	Association of Estonian Trade Unions Eesti Ametiühingute Keskliit
	TALO	Estonian Employees' Unions' Association (Teenistujate Ametiliitude Organisatsioon)
Finland	AKAVA	Confederation of Unions for Academic Professionals in Finland
	SAK	Central Organisation of Finnish Trade Unions (Suomen Ammattiliittojen Keskusjärjestö)
	STTK	Finnish Confederation of Salaried Employees (Toimihenkilökeskusjärjestöry)
France	CFDT	French Democratic Confederation of Labour (Confédération Française Démocratique du Travail)
	CFTC	French Confederation of Christian Workers (Confédération Française des Travailleurs Chrétiens)
	CGT	General Confederation of Labour (Confédération Générale du Travail)
	FO	General Confederation of Labour – Workers' Power (Confédération Générale du Travail – Force Ouvrière)
	UNSA	National Union of Autonomous Trade Unions (Union Nationale des Syndicats Autonomes)
Germany	DGB	German Confederation of Trade Unions (Deutscher Gewerkschaftsbund Bundesvorstand)
Greece	ADEDY	Confederation of Greek Civil Servants' Trade Unions (Anotati Diikisis Enoseon Dimosion Ypallilon)
	GSEE	Greek General Confederation of Labour (Geniki Synomospondia Ergaton Ellados)
Hungary	ASzSz	Autonomous Trade Union Confederation
	LIGA	Democratic League of Independent Trade Unions

	MOSz	National Federation of Workers' Councils
	MSzOSz	National Confederation of Hungarian Trade Unions
	SZEF	Forum for the Co-operation of Trade Unions (Szakszervezetek Egyuttmukodesi Foruma)
	ÉSZT	Confederation of Unions of Professionals (Értelmiségi Szakszervezeti Tömörülés)
Iceland	ASI	Icelandic Confederation of Labour (Althydusamband Islands)
	BSRB	Confederation of State and Municipal Employees (Bandalag Starfsmanna Rikis of Baeja)
Ireland	ICTU	Irish Congress of Trade Unions
Italy	CGIL	Italian General Confederation of Labour (Confederazione Generale Italiana del Lavoro)
	CISL	Italian Confederation of Workers' Trade Unions (Confederazione Italiana Sindacati Lavoratori)
	UIL	Italian Union of Labour (Unione Italiana del Lavoro)
Latvia	LBAS	Union of Independent Trade Unions of Latvia (Latvijas Brivo Arodbiedrìbu Savieníba)
Liechtenstein	LANV	Liechtenstein Federation of Employees (Liechtensteinischer Arbeitnehmer Innenverband)
Lithuania	LDF	Lithuanian Labour Federation (Lietuvos Darbo Federacija)
	LPSK/LTUC	Lithuanian Trade Union Confederation (Lietuvos Profesiniu Sajungu Konfederacija)
	LPSS (LDS)	Lithuanian Trade Union 'Solidarumas' (Lietuvos Darbiniku Sajunga)
Luxembourg	CGT-L	General Confederation of Labour of Luxembourg (Confédération Générale du Travail de Luxembourg)
	LCGB	Luxembourg Christian Trade Union Confederation (Lëtzebuerger Chrëschtleche Gewerkschafts-Bond)
Malta	CMTU	Confederation of Malta Trade Unions
	FOR.U.M.	The Forum of Malte Unions

Monaco	GWU USM	General Workers' Union Union of Monaco Trade Unions (Union
(Principality)		Syndicale de Monaco)
Netherlands	CNV	National Federation of Christian Trade Unions (Christelijk Nationaal Vakverbond)
	FNV	Netherlands Trade Union Confederation (Federatie Nederlandse Vakbeweging)
	MHP	Trade Union Federation for Middle Classes and Higher Level Employees (Vakcentrale voor middengroepen en hoger personeel)
Norway	LO-N	Norwegian Confederation of Trade Unions (Landsorganisasjonen i Norge)
	YS	Confederation of Vocational Trade Unions (Yrkesorganisasjonenes Sentralforbund)
	UNIO	The Confederation of Unions for the Professionals
Poland	NSZZ Solidarnosc	Independent and Self-Governing Trade Union Union 'Solidarnosc' (Niezalezny Samorzadny Zwiazek Zawodowy 'Solidarnosc')
	OPZZ	All-Poland Alliance of Trade Unions (Ogólnopolskie Porozumienie Zwizków Zawodowych)
Portugal	CGTP-IN	General Confederation of Portuguese Workers (Confederação Geral dos Trabalhadores Portugueses)
	UGT-P	General Workers' Union – Portugal (União Geral de Trabalhadores)
Romania	BNS	The National Trade Unions Block
	CARTEL ALFA	National Trade Union Confederation – Cartel ALFA (Confederatia Natională Sindicală)
	CNSLR-Fratia	National Confederation of Free Trade Unions of Romania – FRATIA
	CSDR	Democratic Trade Union Confederation of Romania
San Marino	CSdl	San Marino Labour Confederation

	CDLS	(Confederazione Sammarinese del Lavoro) Democratic Confederation of San Marino workers (Confederazione Democratica lavoratori Sammarinese)
Slovakia	KOZ SR	Confederation of Trade Unions of the Slovak Republic
Slovenia	ZSSS	Slovenian Association of Free Trade Unions (Zveza Svobodnih Sindikatov Slovenije)
Spain	CC.OO	Trade Union Confederation of Workers' Commissions (Confederación Sindical de Comisiones Obreras)
	STV-ELA	Basque Workers' Union (Solidaridad de Trabajadores Vascos Eusko Langileen Alkartasuna)
	UGT-E	General Workers' Union – Spain (Union General de Trabajadores)
	USO	Workers' Union – Spain (Union Sindical Obrera)
Sweden	LO-S	Swedish Trade Union Confederation (Landsorganisationen i Sverige)
	SACO	Swedish Confederation of Professional Associations (Sveriges Akademikers Centralorganisation)
	TCO	Swedish Confederation of Professional Employees (Tjänstemännens Centralorganisation)
Switzerland	Travail Suisse	(Organisation faîtière des travailleurs. Dachorganisation der Arbeitnehmenden)
	SGB	Swiss Federation of Trade Unions (Schweizerischer Gewerkschaftsbund/Union Syndicale Suisse/Unione Sindacale Svizzera)
Turkey	DISK	Confederation of Progressive Trade Unions of Turkey (Türkiye Devrimci Isci Senikalari Konfederasyonu)
	HAK-IS	Confederation of Turkish Real Trade Unions (Türkiye Hak Isçi Sendikalari Konfederasyounu)

	KESK	Confederation of Public Employees' Trade Unions (Kamu Emekçileri Sendikalari Konfederasyonu Servants)
	TURK-IS	Confederation of Turkish Trade Unions (Türkiye Isci Sendikalari Konfederasyonu)
United Kingdom	TUC	Trades Union Congress

II. Observer Organisations

303.

- Bosnia and Herzegovina: CTUBiH Confederation of Trade Unions of Bosnia and Herzegovina;
- FYROM (Former Yugoslavic republic of Macedonia): SSM Federation of Trade Unions of Macedonia; KSS Confederation of Free Trade Unions;
- Serbia: NEZAVISNOST 'Independence' Trade Union Confederation (Ujedinjeni Granski Sindikati 'Nezavisnost'); CATUS Confederation of Autonomous Trade Unions of Serbia;
- Montenegro: UFTUM Union of Free Trade Unions of Montenegro; CTUM Confederation of Trade Unions of Montenegro;

304. European Trade Union Federations

- EAEA European Arts and Entertainment Alliance;
- EUROCOP European Confederation of Police;
- EFBWW/FETBB European Federation of Building and Woodworkers;
- EFFAT European Federation of Food, Agriculture and Tourism Trade Unions;
- EFJ/FEJ European Federation of Journalists;
- IndustriAll European Federation for Industry and Manufacturing workers;
- EPSU European Federation of Public Service Unions;
- ETF European Transport Workers' Federation;
- ETUCE/CSEE European Trade Union Committee for Education;
- UNI-EUROPA European Trade Union Federation for Services and Communication.[83]

---

83. J.P. Windmuller, S.K. Pursey and J. Baker, 'The International Trade Union Movement', in R. Blanpain (ed.), *Comparative Labour Law and Industrial Relations in Industrialised Market Economies*, 10th and revised edition, The Hague, Kluwer Law International, 2010.

III. European Trade Union Institute (ETUI)

305. The European Trade Union Institute is the independent research and training centre of the European Trade Union Confederation (ETUC) which itself affiliates European trade unions into a single European umbrella organisation. The ETUI places its expertise – acquired in particular in the context of its links with universities, academic and expert networks – in the service of workers' interests at European level and of the strengthening of the social dimension of the European Union.

The Institute is composed of three departments:

– research;
– education;
– working conditions, health and safety.

The ETUI conducts studies on socio-economic topics and industrial relations and monitors European policy developments of strategic importance for the world of labour. It creates, what is more, bridges between the academic sphere, the world of research and the trade union movement in order to encourage independent research on topics of decisive relevance to the world of labour.

306. The ETUI encourages training and learning activities. It provides the ETUC and its affiliates with programmes and exchanges that strengthen the European trade union identity.

The ETUI provides technical assistance in the field of health and safety with a view to achieving a high level of occupational health and safety protection for workers throughout Europe.

In the pursuit of its missions, a scientific council composed of twenty-two members, most of them academics, has been set up to contribute to the Institute's medium-term strategy.

The ETUI is a non-profit international association under Belgian law, employing a staff of some 70 persons from all over Europe. It receives financial support from the European Union.

IV. The Athens Manifesto

307. This was adopted by the XIIth ETUC Congress, Athens 16-19 May 2011. The central issue for European trade unions at present is that the financial crises affecting Greece, Ireland and Portugal and the more general policy of austerity governance in other Member States are exerting downward pressure on pay, public services, social security, pensions, and labour and living standards.

The ETUC is alarmed at the negative consequences so far of the bailouts of economies in distress organised by the EU and the International Monetary Fund. The austerity measures imposed, for example in Greece, Portugal and Ireland, have made the situation worse, and the countries concerned face a long period of continued recession, rising debt burdens, pressure on labour standards and labour rights and unemployment. There is a real risk of countries and their populations becoming even more strongly indebted, with huge dangers for Europe and its Member States.

308. The ETUC therefore urgently demands an important policy change in the EU's approach and for it to provide effective help to countries in difficulty.

The new Euro Plus pact applicable to the Eurozone and six other economies has far reaching implications particularly on pay since it includes recommendations to Member States on:

– comparisons of unit labour costs;
– hostility to wage indexation and more generally to centralised bargaining;
– linking pay to productivity, not including inflation;
– downward pressure on public sector pay and, in some cases, on minimum wages, also with consequences for the private sector;
– downward pressure on pension entitlements and early retirement schemes;
– promotion of strict budgetary and constitutional controls on public debt and expenditure.

309. The ETUC asserts that this approach is totally unacceptable to the trade unions of Europe and will campaign at all levels to uphold the following principles:

– wages are not the enemy of the economy but its motor, prompting growth and jobs;
– the autonomy of social partners in collective bargaining and wage negotiations must be respected while trade union organisations should better coordinate collective bargaining;
– the purchasing power of workers' wages and salaries must be improved, with increases being in line with inflation and productivity, while preserving existing wage indexation systems with the overall goal of a fair distribution of wealth;
– the process towards income inequality should be reversed;
– the fight against wage and fiscal dumping must be intensified, and the principle of equal pay for equal work applied;
– pension entitlements and systems should be protected and ensure decent living conditions; and
– rules on public debt should be adapted to economic realities and exceptional circumstances and not provoke recession and its social consequences through austerity measures.

In this context we are determined to

– combat the rising power of the far right and their narrow nationalist allies and to stand for a social Europe, and will be active, to that purpose, in the next European Parliamentary elections;
– fight unemployment, rising inequality, precarious work and austerity governance;
– mobilise for growth and sustainability;
– work for greater trade union strength and membership, and
– develop a joint response to an increasingly integrated European labour market.

General Introduction, Ch. 2, The Social Partners　　　　　　　　**310–310**

310. All this will be at the core of the ETUC's work in 2011–2014. The ETUC will:

(1) fight for a European New Deal for workers, against austerity governance, cuts in pay, social security and public services; and for a European economic governance that serves the interests of the European people and not the markets including qualitative growth, full employment, strengthening the European social model. Important examples are: a financial transaction tax, harmonisation of the corporate tax base, minimum taxation rates for companies, moves towards Eurobonds, and measures to protect investment for the future from blind austerity policies;
(2) demand and campaign that fundamental social rights take precedence over economic freedoms and consequently enshrine this principle in a Social Progress Protocol in European treaties, in a revised Posted Workers Directive and in internal market regulation known as 'Monti II';
(3) place more and better jobs at the top of the European agenda and at the heart of EU economic governance, and reflect it in the European social dialogue as well as in the evaluation of the 2020 strategy and Single Market Act;
(4) demand a coordinated attack on youth unemployment with guaranteed acces to education, training and jobs, investing in a good education system from early childhood to higher education;
(5) prioritise the improvement of working conditions of all European workers, the fight against undeclared work, corruption and the black economy and social and wage dumping, through legislation and within the social dialogue;
(6) develop joint initiatives with European employers for green jobs, growth and investment, sustainable industry policy, education and training;
(7) act so that all workers, whatever their form of work is, can lead a decent life and are protected through collective agreements and/or legislation, ensuring equal treatment, and that they can enjoy workers rights;
(8) demand effective and stringent regulation of financial markets and ratings agencies, an end to tax havens, a financial transaction tax, and a stop to excessive pay, golden handshakes and bonuses for executives;
(9) demand new systems of corporate governance to promote sustainability, long-termism, and fair pay levels for all – a system in which European Works Councils, trade unions and worker information, consultation and participation rights must play a fundamental role;
(10) actively contribute to managing a fair transition towards a low carbon economy, including through social dialogue; support research and innovation in new technologies and energy efficiency;
(11) support public services and fight against their dismantling due to austerity cuts and wholesale privatisation, ensuring their essential contribution to democratic development, sustainable growth, employment and social welfare;
(12) work actively for gender equality and fight against all forms of discrimination on the grounds of sex, race, religion, age, disability and sexual orientation. The EU as a whole must take a lead in finding solutions in relation to

external migration flows based on our commitment to equality, freedom, democracy and the rule of law enshrined in the Treaties;
(13) protect migrant workers by promoting mutual trade union membership recognition, and demand equal pay for equal work and work of equal value, based on the host country principle, and fighting against racism and xenophobia. Furthermore all migrant workers must have the right to be advised on their rights in the host country;
(14) improve health and safety standards, including by campaigning for working time regulation that protects health and ends opts outs, monitoring the agreements on stress, transposing ILO recommendations on AIDS, violence and harassment in the workplace, prioritising musculo-skeletal disorders, strengthening labour inspection, protecting personal data, implementing fully the REACH regulations on chemicals, increasing training, and devoting a day a year to celebrate and promote the work of health and safety representatives;
(15) assist in the EU enlargement by working with affiliates in Turkey and the Western Balkans;
(16) support fair and sustainable globalisation, including EU co-operation agreements (but not necessarily all bilateral trade agreements notably the one with Colombia), and work closely with the ITUC and TUAC;
(17) promote the European Social Model as a positive and sustainable model for world development, and campaign with the ITUC for trade union rights globally;
(18) support the Pan European Regional Council (PERC), and sub-regional activities in Europe, and also trade unions and social dialogue in the Euromed region; promote relations with trade unions organisations in Africa, North and Latin America and Asia;
(19) demand the right to strike on transnational issues and press the demand for a specific labour chamber in the European Court of Justice;
(20) maximise the use of the range of means available to the ETUC to improve the impact of the trade union agenda at European level, i.e. using campaigns and mobilisations, the EU institutions, employers and the social dialogue, allies in civil society, the Tripartite Social Summit, and EU external relations.

§3. JOINT STATEMENT BY THE EUROPEAN SOCIAL PARTNERS ON THE EUROPE 2020 STRATEGY

1. Introduction

311. The challenges that were there in 2000 when the Lisbon Strategy was set up remain the long-term challenges which our societies are facing now: these concern globalisation, ageing populations, the transition towards a low-carbon economy but also a more socially cohesive society based on equal opportunities as well as equal treatment. But the crisis has considerably heightened the urgency of tackling these challenges in a coherent and ambitious policy agenda for the European Union. Evidence is mounting that Europe is lagging behind in the global economic recovery. The main objective should be to put Europe on a sustained growth path, ensure a rapid return to more and better jobs, while ensuring fiscal sustainability. A sense of collective responsibility will be needed to achieve this objective, based on clear targets and greater accountability for Member States and EU institutions. It is also important that the right lessons from the economic and financial crisis are drawn, making sure that past mistakes are not being repeated. This implies reforming the global financial system, in order to foster greater stability and to get a financial sector that works for the economy and not the other way around. It implies facing the job crisis and restoring and improving growth dynamics to create more and better jobs. Improving competitiveness by having the European economy move up the ladder of innovation, technology and productivity is important. For this, it is crucial to mobilise the EU's human capital and the ingenuity of companies in an effective way. It is also important that Europe with its vast internal market becomes a greater engine of growth, with higher productivity and innovation gains and major investment in a greening of the economy. Social cohesion must also be seen as a precondition for a dynamic and sustainable economy. Promoting skills and entrepreneurship, revitalising the single market; developing an integrated EU industrial policy, supporting new means of financing for investment and taking on the fight against poverty and inequality will all be crucial factors for the EU's future success.

2. Policy priorities

2.1. Combining exit and entry strategies

312. The clear objective of macro economic policies should be to regain scope for action and be able to mobilise the necessary resources to sustain growthenhancing investments while ensuring the sustainability of public finances and social protection systems in order to maintain intergenerational solidarity and cohesion. This means to combine and sequence an exit strategy to cap public indebtedness with an entry strategy, investing in skills, technology and modern infrastructures. This can only be achieved through a reassignment of policy priorities leading to balanced reforms of public expenditure, tax systems and governance structures, while ensuring in the future sustainable levels of private indebtedness. In the context of the European Monetary Union, greater and broader surveillance of national economic policies between countries sharing the single currency will be a necessary condition for future growth and stability. Sustainability of public finances must go hand in hand with a renewed pledge to achieve excellence in education, training and research systems and allow for the effective deployment of new technologies and modern infrastructures to meet energy and climate challenges. This will require new sources of financing, using public funding and private saving as a lever. This should be done in particular by making greater and more targeted use of the European Investment Bank funding capacity, the EU budget and by developing true markets for infrastructure and innovation financing.

2.2. Promoting the knowledge triangle (education, research, innovation)

313. Europe must further strengthen its potential in terms of skilled workers, science, research and technology and thus its capacity to innovate as a key element of competitiveness. In any case, the knowledge triangle must remain at the heart of the EU2020 strategy. In this context the notion of innovation has to be widened to all kind of non-technological innovation including 'social innovation' in order to increase social capital which is important for both competitiveness and social cohesion. Insufficient investment in innovation and further education is exacerbating economic problems and affecting labour productivity. Looking ahead, our work patterns are changing. So are employers' needs for skills in the work force and the needs of workers to combine productive employment with family life and personal development. Europe must not only upgrade and update skills levels; it must also make sure that workers have the skills that are needed on the labour market and that these skills are fully used in high-quality jobs. Comprehensive lifelong learning strategies are required to ensure employability of workers. It is important to establish effective concepts for initial and further training, create jobs, not least for those who are excluded from the labour market due to, for example, shortcomings in their education, and to take effective steps to remove discrimination as far as access to and remaining in the labour market are concerned. Well educated workers and the capacity to innovate are key elements of competition and a prerequisite for prosperity. This is indispensable for the creation of productive and highly-skilled jobs.

2.3. Employment and social policies

314. Member States have acted to cushion the social and employment impact of the economic crisis. Nevertheless, unemployment rose to 23 million people in 2009 and youth unemployment has now reached over 21 per cent and many in a precarious situation. European employment rates are substantially lagging behind, with only two thirds of the work force currently in employment. The 70 per cent employment rate target of the Lisbon Strategy is further out of reach than before the crisis. This is a matter of immediate concern, as are the mediumand long-term challenges facing European labour markets. The EU 2020 should therefore strike the right balance between measures to address the employment impact of the crisis and reforms aimed at addressing Europe's mediumand long-term labour market challenges. An increase of employment that goes hand in hand with higher productivity should be the key objective. In concrete terms, an increase in EU growth rate to an average of at least 2 per cent should be the aim in coming years. A significantly higher growth rate, along with the creation of more and better jobs, is a precondition for achieving the EU employment rate of 75 per cent, and successfully addressing the labour market and financial implications of population ageing. From 2010, demographic ageing results in the decline in working-age population of over 3 million workers by 2020 and much more beyond. If the EU continues to ignore this trend, it will not only undermine its social protection systems, but also lose business opportunities and the related jobs and growth. To reach these objectives, modern labour markets are required. In view of creating more and better jobs, European Social Partners therefore call upon Member States to implement a right mix of policy measures addressing flexibility and security dimensions (labour law and contractual arrangements, effective and high-quality active labour market policies, lifelong learning policies, efficient and sustainable social protection systems, social dialogue) for workers and employers in a holistic and balanced way. In addition, European Social Partners call upon Member States to review, and if necessary adjust, the design of labour law, job protection systems and, together with social partners, collective bargaining practice with a view to:

– ensuring an optimal balance between flexibility and security for all employment relationships. Provide adequate security for workers under all forms of contracts in order to tackle segmented labour markets;
– developing complementary employment security measures promoting transitions into productive and rewarding jobs;
– enhancing legal certainty and transparency for both employers and workers with regard to the scope, coverage and the enforcement of labour law;
– implementing and respecting at national level the principles and rules of European social directives, including those deriving from a framework agreement among European social partners, as well as the basic principles of equal treatment and non-discrimination;
– promote stable employment relationships and sustainable labour market practices.

315. Flexicurity policies must be accompanied by sound macroeconomic policies, favourable business environment, adequate financial resources and the provision of good working conditions.

In particular, wage policies, autonomously set by social partners, should ensure that real wage developments are consistent with productivity trends, while non-wage labour costs are restrained where appropriate in order to support labour demand.

Unemployment and poverty traps must be addressed as well as disproportionate executive pay, making sure that remuneration policies are aligned with the longterm success of enterprises and sound management practices. Strengthened efforts are required to ensure a real and effective implementation of the various measures at the appropriate level. Member States should also involve social partners in the design of policy measures and develop their capacity where needed, for instance when integrating the various policy measures in national reform programmes. European social partners further call upon Member States to involve social partners in the design of policy measures and develop their capacity where needed; integrate the various policy measures in national reform programmes and strengthen efforts to ensure a real and effective implementation of the various measures at the appropriate level. For their part, social partners must actively contribute to the design and implementation of policy measures addressing the flexibility and security dimensions. Finally, striking the right balance between work and family life is an important factor to enhance gender equality and further increase female labour participation 2.4 A supportive public environment and access to high-quality, affordable and effective public services

316. The EU 2020 strategy should address public services' accessibility, quality and effectiveness; fostering their capacity to innovate and modernise. Effective public services provide an important infrastructure for business development and citizens' quality of life. Private companies, especially SMEs, depend to a large extent on the quality and affordability of public services such as transport and ICT infrastructures, education and training systems, employment and business support services. Accessibility, quality, efficiency and effectiveness must be enhanced, including by taking greater benefit from well balanced public-private partnerships and by modernising public administration systems. Efficient and sustainable social systems, providing income support and fostering labour market mobility and integration, are also a key prerequisite to citizen welfare and private business strength. In addition, efficient and effective regulations to ensure fair competition and a reliable legal framework are crucial in a social market economy. Improving the quality of regulation and strengthening its enforcement is thus an urgent priority. The European Small Business Act, including the commitment to the "Think Small First" Principles, needs to be applied.

3. Governance and procedures

317. Although Member States have the main responsibility for implementation of structural reforms, there needs to be an appropriate European framework enabling them to be implemented in a coordinated and consistent way. The absence of such a European framework was one of the main reasons why the Lisbon Strategy did not deliver. It is therefore necessary to review its lack of ownership and accountability in the attempts to coordinate structural reforms. In the new strategy, emphasis must be put on benchmarking in order to pin down structural weaknesses at national level, define clear quantitative targets and deadlines for achieving them. The Commission should closely monitor progress and exert its right of alert when Member States are not delivering on agreed commitments.

318. Integrated guidelines, which provide a basis for common reform priorities across member states, should be reduced in number and be more focused on the overall objectives of growth, competitiveness, more and better jobs and social cohesion. National reform programmes and country-specific recommendations must be tailored at addressing national structural weaknesses based on transparent analysis and evaluations. A pre-condition for the success of new governance mechanisms is a stronger involvement of the social partners at all levels (European, national, regional and local levels) in the design and in the monitoring of both European and national reforms strategies. Member States should strongly support a climate of trust and social dialogue between employers and worker organisations by respecting the autonomy of social partners, assisting and supporting social partners and associating them in decisions on how to spend capacity-building funds available notably under the European social fund. Finally, the next multiannual financial framework of the EU must reflect the EU 2020 objectives.

§4. ETUC POSITION ON EUROPE 2020 STRATEGY – AN ASSESSMENT[84]

319. The trade unions supported the Europe 2020 objectives themselves, as most of them are – if they are taken seriously and are pursued in the right way – traditional trade union objectives: full employment, quality jobs, the reduction of social inequalities and of poverty etc. However, Europe 2020 appears to be a highly complicated strategy. The complexity can be seen from the fact that it covers five targets, eight indicators and seven flagship initiatives. This therefore raises the question about its overall coherence and efficiency of its tools. Some ETUC affiliates even argue that the multitude of processes is undermining the role of the social partners.

Moreover, a year after the Europe 2020 strategy was adopted, it was put on an austerity regime and locked into the new economic governance architecture which prescribed hard indicators for fiscal consolidation. Sidelined Europe 2020 objectives were thus transformed into second tier goals which might be fulfilled in the new framework of austerity but which were no longer considered obligatory as fiscal ones. The question must be raised about the deadlock of Europe 2020 within the economic governance framework.

320. It is clear that, up until now, a majority of the 85 ETUC member organizations has not really been involved in the process which poses the question of its democratic legitimacy. The involvement of social partners at national and European level is not timely enough and often just a formality. The method of organizing big hearings does not allow the taking into account of specific social partners' input, neither on the implementation nor the National reform plans nor the other facets of the Europe 2020 strategy. Another discussion process is needed to enable proposals and initiatives from the social partners to be taken up – there is room for improvement. It is necessary to bridge the gap between ambitious rhetoric or the good intentions and the reality of not taking opinions sufficiently into consideration. The overall conclusion must be that the involvement of the social partners needs to be organized in a serious way.

321. When Europe 2020 was presented, the expectations were high but a first assessment shows that the actors involved have been unable to keep their promises. The majority of affiliates agree that the Europe 2020 strategy is not efficient, as the objectives are not really treated as binding, or as obligatory in the same way as other

---

84. Adopted at the Executive Committee meeting of 5-6 March 2013.

criteria (e.g. austerity, deficit criteria etc.). The instruments, in particular the flagship initiatives, are being considered as not very or only partly effective in achieving the objectives, some even consider the strategy as purely symbolic policymaking.

322. Looking more systematically at the different aspects of Europe 2020, neither the New Skills and Jobs, nor the initiative on Youth (despite both being promising and welcome proposals), nor the one on industrial policy have delivered the results which are necessary for achieving the objectives up until now. Even the Commission in its Progress Report admits that the commitments set out by the Member States are insufficient to meet the targets and that the results have not been the ones expected. Despite the Commission's finding that the commitments set out by the Member States in their National Reform Programmes (NRPs) are insufficient to meet most of the Europe 2020 targets, none was urged in the Country Specific Recommendations to be more ambitious with their national targets.

323. The ETUC's sceptical initial assessment of the inadequacy of the Europe 2020 framework for delivering on its promises (particularly in relation to employment and poverty) has, unfortunately, been shown to be correct. There is no clear majority of opinions however on what could and should be improved, except for the wrong economic policy. Most affiliates see the introduction of more binding instruments as a two-edged sword as these instruments could be used against a more social policy and in favour of even stricter economic governance. But on the other hand it is rather useful to have this strategy, as some affiliates argue, because it can be used to put forward an argument in favour of a more social policy.

324. In general, the European policy framework of austerity and fiscal consolidation is seen as an impediment to progress in achieving the Europe 2020 objectives. The austerity policy and economic governance procedures have increased unemployment, poverty, and economic and social divergence instead of convergence. Due to the supremacy of economic objectives and neoliberalism in general, to the encouragement of flexicurity, the majority of affiliates don't believe that the Europe 2020 strategy will, in the end, deliver its objectives.

325. It is indeed necessary to invest in active labour market programmes in order to achieve the full employment goal (75 per cent). Between 2008 and the end of 2012 the EU27 unemployment rate climbed from around 7 per cent to 10.7 per cent, equating to about 26 million unemployed people. Across the EU more than one in five young people is unemployed (22 per cent), with youth unemployment exceeding 50 per cent in some Member States. What is clear is that the surplus countries increase spending, while the deficit countries cut spending. In other words, there are cuts in active labour market policy in the countries where unemployment is the highest and the need the greatest.

Equally, to achieve the innovation goal (the 3 per cent goal was not achieved within the decade of the Lisbon strategy), or the climate change and energy goals, huge investment and an intelligent and sustainable industrial policy is needed.

326. In the same way, a great deal of investment is necessary to achieve the education and the anti-poverty goals. The current wage devaluation strategy advocated by the Troika in line with the austerity policy has proven to be the wrong tool. More than 115 million people are in danger of social exclusion in the EU27 because they are at an aggravated risk of poverty, are severely materially deprived or live in households with very low work intensity.

327. In fact, the new governance framework institutionalizes a structural bias towards the domination of economic over social governance; the Europe 2020 being subsumed into the European Semester. At best, the objectives are conceived as aiming at balancing or cushioning the social consequences of the austerity policy. The Europe 2020 objectives are taken into account in the Country Specific Recommendations, but they are not being respected in the same way that the deficit criteria are. It is necessary to put the former on the same footing as the latter in order to make them equally binding so that no Member State can treat them purely as suggestions. Current economic policies focus on the wrong instruments and supply-side measures, like fostering price-competitiveness and improving conditions for employers. This – in the eyes of many policy-makers – is supposed to foster growth and employment. From our point of view, promoting jobs and employment can currently be achieved by increasing demand. The supply-sided measures which are brought forward by the European Commission and others thus are counterproductive and rather lead to a decline in demand, economic growth and job creation.

328. The conclusion can be drawn that a radical policy change is necessary to stop the antisocial bias of European policy. If the social dimension is not put on the same footing as the economic objectives, the European project runs the risk of creating another unbalanced structure which will jeopardize the achievement of the social objectives. Therefore, the ETUC demands that:

– the Europe 2020 objectives are incorporated into the framework of an alternative and more balanced economic governance structure. Employment, education, innovation, poverty reduction and climate protection targets must be as binding as those of fiscal consolidation;
– the Commission and the European Parliament conduct an investigation into the relevance of the existing framework, namely its instruments, for achieving the objectives;
– the national and European social partners are fully involved in the Europe 2020 process – and that trade union suggestions are taken into account.

Chapter 3. Competences of the EU Regarding Labour Law

§1. Introductory Remarks

329. One can state quite categorically that the protection of workers as an explicit objective of the EU has been controversial from the very beginning and has been subordinate to the economic aims of the Union. The reasoning that the social caboose would be pulled by the economic locomotive has clearly prevailed.

The majority of the group of experts asked by the governments in 1955 to look into the question was of the opinion that there was no need for specific social clauses in the EC Treaty. It was only the French government which underlined that the difference in wages and working conditions among the Member States could influence competition in the Common Market. Consequently, the European Treaties contain few concrete competences allowing for a genuine social and labour law policy. The EU boat, in relation to social policy, is a small vessel with very short paddles. Once more, we repeat that the European institutions have only that power conferred upon them (explicitly or implicitly) by the Treaties. For other matters the national governments remain sovereign.

§2. The EU

I. The Hierarchy of Objectives: Non-inflationary Growth

330. The EU has set itself the high objectives, among others things:

(1) The Union's aim is to promote peace, its values and the well-being of its peoples.
(2) The Union shall offer its citizens an area of freedom, security and justice without internal frontiers, in which the free movement of persons is ensured in conjunction with appropriate measures with respect to external border controls, asylum, immigration and the prevention and combating of crime.
(3) The Union shall establish an internal market. It shall work for the sustainable development of Europe based on balanced economic growth and price stability, a highly competitive social market economy, aiming at full employment and social progress, and a high level of protection and improvement of the quality of the environment. It shall promote scientific and technological advance.

 It shall combat social exclusion and discrimination, and shall promote social justice and protection, equality between women and men, solidarity between generations and protection of the rights of the child.

 It shall promote economic, social and territorial cohesion, and solidarity among Member States.

 It shall respect its rich cultural and linguistic diversity, and shall ensure that Europe's cultural heritage is safeguarded and enhanced.
(4) The Union shall establish an economic and monetary union whose currency is the euro.

(5) In its relations with the wider world, the Union shall uphold and promote its values and interests and contribute to the protection of its citizens. It shall contribute to peace, security, the sustainable development of the Earth, solidarity and mutual respect among peoples, free and fair trade, eradication of poverty and the protection of human rights, in particular the rights of the child, as well as to the strict observance and the development of international law, including respect for the principles of the United Nations Charter.
(6) The Union shall pursue its objectives by appropriate means commensurate with the competences which are conferred upon it in the Treaties (Art. 3 TEU).

331. In order to evaluate the societal relevance and importance of Europe's renewed employment and social policy, the following points must be examined:

(1) what order the various objectives have within the hierarchy of the overall aims of the EU;
(2) whether the means which have been accorded to the EU to realise the social objectives are appropriate;
(3) what are the consequences of the given order and of the means retained to realise the social objectives in general, and their impact upon society as a whole and the well-being of the citizens, in particular;
(4) finally, it is necessary to evaluate the kind of 'social model' which is implicitly embedded in the European construction. We will compare this model with the experience of those countries where identical or equivalent socio-economic systems have been put into practice for various periods of time.[85]

332. When one analyses the order of the various objectives which the EU pursues, one has to recognise that European social policy, and especially employment strategy, is subordinated to the overall economic-monetary goals of the EU. This conclusion follows clearly from an analysis of the text of the TEC, especially of the Amsterdam Treaty.

Indeed, at the top of the hierarchy of the various EU objectives lies the goal of *non-inflationary growth and an economic policy, in conformity with the EMU,* namely low inflation, public deficit under control and the like. These are the wellknown Maastricht criteria.

This conclusion follows from the wording of the Title on Employment. Article 146 TFEU very clearly states:

> Member States, through their employment policies, shall contribute to the achievement of the objectives ... in a way consistent with the *broad guidelines of the economic policies of the Member States and of the Community* ...

In other words, the employment strategy of the Member States has to be noninflationary in the first place.

---

85. For this last point *see* R. Blanpain, *Institutional Changes and European Social Policies after the Treaty of Amsterdam*, Kluwer, The Hague, 1998, pp. 5–65.

Social policy, according to the TFEU, will take account of the need to maintain the competitiveness of the Community economy (Art. 151).

333. Let us repeat this conclusion, given its vital importance: social policy, including employment strategies, has to be non-inflationary and geared towards maintaining the competitiveness of the European economy.

The conclusion of the Dutch Presidency (IGC 1997) translated these choices as follows:

> Restoring a sustained, high rate of non-inflationary growth is necessary to achieve a long-lasting solution to the Community's unemployment problem and to make further headway towards sound public finances.
>
> These social objectives will ensue [*in the first place*][86] from the functioning of the common market, which will favour the harmonisation of the social systems, Article 151 TFEU declares.

Indeed, the means which would allow the EU to be proactive in realising its ambitious goals are meagre.

II. Social Objectives

334. Title X TFEU deals with social policy. The underlying philosophy appears quite clear when one reads Article 151 TFEU.

> The Union and the Member States, having in mind fundamental social rights such as those set out in the European Social Charter signed at Turin on 18 October 1961 and in the 1989 Community Charter of the Fundamental Social Rights of Workers, shall have as their objectives the promotion of employment, improved living and working conditions, so as to make possible the harmonisation while the improvement is being maintained, proper social protection, dialogue between management and labour, the development of human resources with a view to lasting employment and the combating of exclusion.
>
> To this end the Union and the Member States shall implement measures which take account of the diverse forms of national practices, in particular in the field of contractual relations, and the need to maintain the competitiveness of the Union's economy.
>
> They believe that such a development will ensue not only from the functioning of the common market, which will favour harmonisation of social systems, but also from the procedures provided for in this Treaty and from the approximation of provisions laid down by law, regulation or administrative action.

---

86. Added by the author.

III. Fundamental Rights and Competences

A. *Fundamental Rights*

1. Mega-Principles

335. The EU, according to Article 6 TEU, recognises the rights, freedoms and principles set out in the Charter of Fundamental Rights of the European Union which shall have the same legal value as the Treaties.

Fundamental rights, as guaranteed by the European Convention for the Protection of Human Rights and Fundamental Freedoms and as they result from the constitutional traditions common to the Member States, shall constitute the general principles of the Union's law.

2. The European Convention for the Protection of Human Rights and Fundamental Freedoms

336. Article 6(3) TEU provides that fundamental rights, as guaranteed by the European Convention and as they result from the constitutional traditions common to the Member States, shall constitute general principles of the Union's law. This is, as indicated earlier, the standing opinion of the Court of Justice and consequently does not contain much added value. Important is, however, the role of the Court in this matter. In practical terms this means that any action of the Council, the Commission and other Union institutions or directive might be examined from the point of view of the Human Rights Convention by the Court.

3. Fundamental Social Rights

337. The idea of including legally enforceable fundamental social rights in the Treaty was not retained at Amsterdam or in the Treaty of Nice or of Lisbon. Reference to such rights is, however, made in Article 151 TFEU in the following terms: 'The Union and the Member States having in mind fundamental social rights such as those set out in the European Charter signed at Turin on 18 October 1961 and the 1989 Community Charter of the Fundamental Social Rights of Workers.' No need to underline that this insertion is too weak to lead to legally binding obligations or rights. It is a pure declaration of intention, no more.

338. At the European Top of the European Council, which would be held in Nice, France (December 2000), the issue of fundamental social rights would be addressed. So, again, there was hope. When the European Council at Tampere (1999) met, Ministers decided to initiate the drafting of a charter of fundamental rights in the European Union. A joint body consisting of representatives of Member State governments, the Commission, the European Parliament and national parliaments would draft the charter. Other EU bodies, social groups and experts were to be invited to give their views to the joint body. There was a good chance that fun damental rights would be included in the European Treaty. It remained to be seen whether the Council would go beyond a mere declaration but lay down directly enforceable rights for the European citizens, employers and workers included. Legally enforceable fundamental standards would help to put 'social Europe' definitely on the map.

A Charter of Fundamental Rights was adopted at Nice (7 December 2000). A very large number of rights was retained, as will be explained later. As far as the binding effect of the Charter is concerned, Nice is, however, disappointing. The Presidency Conclusions of the Nice Top regarding the Charter read as follows:

> The European Council welcomes the joint proclamation, by the Council, the European Parliament and the Commission, of the Charter of Fundamental Rights, combining in a single text the civil, political, economic, social and societal rights hitherto laid down in a variety of international, European or national sources. The European Council would like to see the Charter disseminated as widely as possible amongst the Union's citizens. In accordance with the Cologne conclusions, the question of the Charter's force will be considered later.

On 12 December 2007, the EP, and the Commission adopted the Charter of Fundamental Rights of the European Union, which will replace the Charter of 2000 as from the date of entry into force of the Treaty of Lisbon.[87] Article 6, 1 TEU (Lisbon) indicates that the Charter shall have the same legal value as the Treaty.

4. Discrimination

339. Article 18 TFEU prohibits, within the scope of application of the Treaties, any discrimination on grounds of nationality. The Council may adopt rules designed to prohibit such discrimination

Moreover, Article 19 TFEU foresees the possibility to take appropriate action to combat discrimination based on sex, racial or ethnic origin, religion or belief, disability, age or sexual orientation.

A number of grounds leading to discrimination such as colour, national or social origin, culture or language, political opinion, marital status, family responsibilities and disability were not retained.[88]

Moreover, the Council does not enjoy a general competence to combat discrimination, as its possibilities are limited to the powers conferred by the Treaty upon the Union.[89]

---

87. 2007/C 303/01, O.J., 14 December 2007, C 303/1.
88. There is, however, the Declaration to the Final Act regarding persons with a disability: 'The Conference agrees that, in drawing up measures under Article 114 TFEU, the Institutions of the Community shall take account of the needs of persons with a disability.'
89. Article 19(2) TFEU.

B. Competences

340. The TFEU in order for the Union to realise the high social objectives, laid down in Articles 151–152, provides a number of competences, for the EU itself as well as for the social partners.

1. The EU

a. Cooperation between Member States

341. The Commission has been given the task of promoting close cooperation between Member States in the social field, in particular in matters relating to:

– employment;[90]
– labour law and working conditions;
– basic and advanced vocational training;
– social security;
– the prevention of occupational accidents and diseases;
– occupational hygiene;
– the right of association and collective bargaining between employers and workers (Article 156 TFEU).

342. This important task will be accomplished in close contact with Member States by making studies, delivering opinions and arranging consultations both on problems arising at national level and on those of concern to international organisations. In summary, Articles 151, 152 and 156 embrace broad objectives but do not contain sufficient measures.

343. A Spanish citizen, Fernando Roberto Gimenez Zaera, civil servant of His Majesty, wanted to gauge the effectiveness of both articles; he was prompted to do so by the rather unfriendly decision to suspend payment of his retirement pension provided for by the general social security scheme which Fernando, who is employed in the public service, received in respect of his previous employment in the private sector.[91] The decision was taken in application of a Spanish Act of 1983,

---

90. C.O.J., 9 July 1987, *Germany and Others* v. *Commission*, No. 281/285, ECR, 1987, 3203. The promotion of the integration into the workforce of workers from non-member countries must be held to be within the social field and within the meaning of Article 140, insofar as it is closely linked to employment. This also applies to their integration into society. With regard to the cultural integration of immigrant communities from non-member countries, whilst this may be linked, to an extent, with the effects of migration policy, it is aimed at immigrant communities in general without distinction between migrant workers and other foreigners, and its link with problems relating to employment and working conditions is therefore extremely tenuous.
91. C.O.J., 29 September 1987, *Giminez Zaera* v. *Instituto de la Seguridad Social y Tesoria General de la Seguridad Social*, No. 126/86, ECR, 1987, 3697.

which provided that the receipt of a retirement pension covered by the social security scheme was incompatible with the exercise of any remunerated function, profession or activity in any public administration. For Gimenez Zaera this was not 'the promotion of improved conditions and standard of living for workers' Article 151 had promised, on the contrary, and Fernando wanted to find out whether Article 151 was more than a mere scrap of wasted paper. More precisely, the referring Spanish judge, before whom Giminez Zaera had brought the case, wanted to know whether Articles 3 TEU, 151 and 156 TFEU were compatible with the decision to suspend the payment of a (private sector) retirement pension, while the employee was working and receiving pay from the public sector.

344. In formulating its answer to the Spanish judge, the Court took a deep breath and started from Article 3 TEU. The implementation of those aims is the essential object of the Treaty. With regard to the promotion, the Court concluded, of an accelerated raising of the standard of living, in particular, it should therefore be stated that this was one of the aims that inspired the creation of the EU and which, owing to its general terms and its systematic dependence on the establishment of the Common Market and the progressive approximation of economic policies, cannot impose legal obligations on Member States or confer rights on individuals.

345. The Court has consistently held that Article 151 is essentially in the nature of a programme. However, this does not mean that Article 151 is deprived of any legal effect. It constitutes an important aid, in particular for the interpretation of other provisions of the Treaty and of secondary Union legislation in the social field. The attainment of those objectives must nevertheless be the result of a social policy to be defined by the competent authorities.[92]

346. Article 156 does not encroach upon the Member States' power in the social field insofar as the latter is not covered by other provisions of the Treaty, such as, for example, the free movement of workers, the common agricultural policy or the common transport policy. It nevertheless provides that those powers must be exercised within the framework of cooperation between Member States which is to be organised by the Commission. In this connection, it must be emphasised that where an article of the TFEU – in this case Article 156 – confers a specific task on the Commission, it must be accepted, if that provision is not to be rendered wholly ineffective, that it confers on the Commission necessarily and *per se* the powers that are indispensable in order to carry out that task. Accordingly, the second paragraph of Article 156 must be interpreted as conferring on the Commission all the powers that are necessary to arrange the consultations. In order to perform the task of arranging consultations, the Commission must necessarily be able to require the Member States to notify essential information, in the first place to identify the problems and in the second place to pinpoint the possible guidelines for any future joint action on the part of the Member States; likewise it must be able to require them to

---

92. This was confirmed in: *Sloman Neptun Schiffarts AG v. Seebetriebsrat Bodo Ziesemer der Sloman Schiffarts AG*, No. C-72/91 and C-73/91, 17 March 1993, ECR, 1993, 887.

take part in the consultations. Since the Commission has a power of a purely procedural nature to initiate consultation, it cannot determine the result of that consultation and cannot prevent the Member States from implementing drafts, agreements and measures which it might consider not in conformity with Community policies and actions.[93]

347. In the meantime, we have not forgotten Fernando Roberto Gimenez Zaera. The outcome of the story is that national governments remain sovereign regarding social matters and the EU has no message to deliver as far as the cumulation of a private pension and public pay are concerned. Giminez Zaera was in the wrong place at the wrong time!

b. Legislative Competence

(1) Social Matters

348. The Title on 'Social policy' allows the Union to formulate regulations, directives or recommendations with either qualified majority or unanimity with a view of achieving the objectives of Article 156 TFEU in quite a number of fields, with the exclusion, however, of 'pay, the right of association, the right to strike or the right to impose lock-outs'. The 'provisions adopted pursuant to this article shall not prevent any Member State from maintaining or introducing more (stringent) protective measures compatible with the Treaty' (Article 153, 4)).

349. It seems to me that there is a delicate relationship between issues which can be dealt with by qualified majority and those for which unanimity is needed. It is e.g. possible that in the area of equal treatment between men and women, for which there is qualified majority, measures are put forward which would include an element of job protection, saying e.g. that a discriminated worker, who makes a complaint to the labour inspection, cannot be dismissed for the reason of doing so. The last point concerning job security belongs self-evidently to the group of issues to be dealt with on a basis of unanimity. Nevertheless, in accordance with the adage *accessorium sequitur principale*, the issue as a whole falling under the scope of equal treatment can be dealt with on the basis of qualified majority. One could draw an argument to arrive at an opposite conclusion from the wording of the last sentence of Article 155(2) (concerning the implementation of European collective agreements by way of a Council decision) where it reads 'that Council shall act by unanimously where the agreement in question contains one or more provisions relating to one of the areas for which unanimity is required pursuant to Article 153(2). This argument, however, is not decisive. Article 155(2) constitutes a deviation from a general principle of law. If the Member States had wanted to depart from that general principle also regarding Community legislation, pursuant to the Articles 151, 152, 153, 154 they should have done so *expressis verbis*.

---

93. C.O.J., 9 July 1987, *Germany and Others*, No. 281/285, ECR, 1993, 887.

(a) Qualified majority voting

(aa) Procedure

350. Article 153 provides that the Union shall, with a view to achieving the objectives of Article 151, support and complement Member States' activities in a number of fields, which we will enumerate later.

> To this end, the EP and the Council may adopt, by means of directives adopted by qualified majority, minimum requirements for gradual implementation, having regard to the conditions and technical rules obtaining in each of the Member States. Such directives shall avoid imposing administrative, financial and legal restraints in a way which would hold back the creation of small and medium-sized undertakings (Article 153(2)).

(bb) Areas

Health and safety

351. Directives with qualified majority can be taken in order to improve in particular the working environment to protect workers' health and safety. For the sense of the phrase 'working environment to protect workers' health and safety' we refer to what we said about Article 153 TFEU.[94]

Working conditions

352. 'Working conditions' is a notion with a rather broad content and relates to all the conditions under which work in subordination by an employee is performed for the benefit of an employer, such as:

- the different categories of workers: blue-collar, white collar, commercial travellers, seamen, student-workers … ;
- the individual labour contracts, including contracts for an indefinite period, fixed term contracts, temporary work, the trial clause as well as the form and the content of the contracts; also the ability to conclude a labour contract (for e.g. minors and migrant workers);
- rights and duties of the parties during the employment contract, thus the duties of the worker, like the execution of orders, the responsibility for damages etc. Equally the duties of the employer: the obligation to provide the employee with work in accordance with the individual agreement, the responsibility of the employer for the belongings of the worker, the ability to change the conditions of work … ;
- working time, including hours of work, part-time, overtime, night-, shift and Sunday work; as well as annual vacation and holidays;

---

94. *See* Part I, Chapter 7, §2, A.

General Introduction, Ch. 3, Competences of the EU

- incapacity to work in case of illness, of an accident at work, of military service, of an act of God. This includes the consequences as to the obligation to work and whether the execution of the (individual labour) contract is suspended or not in case of incapacity to work;
- protection of certain categories of workers, protection against discrimination in employment: this refers to young, elderly, handicapped and female workers, mothers, to measures to promote equal treatment regarding jobs, promotion and vocational training ... ;
- covenants of non-competition: this contract clause relates to the stipulation preventing the employee from engaging in a business or an employment contract competing with his employer also when the individual labour contract has been terminated or has come to an end;
- conditions regarding inventions by employees.

Information and consultation

353. The meaning of the word 'information' seems rather simple: it is the communication of knowledge. Disclosure of information to workers means that the employer provides information of which explanation may be sought and questions can be raised. The meaning of the word 'consultation' is, however, less clear and much more ambiguous. One may define consultation from a number of perspectives. In the British context consultation 'refers to subjects within the scope of managerial prerogative' while negotiation 'refers to matters within the power of joint regulation by management and trade unions'.[95] It thus refers to (a) the object of consultation, as well as (b) to the dimension of the influence of labour on management decision making. Others lay emphasis on (c) the nature of the exercise: consultation would then concern questions of common interests, whereas negotiation would relate to problems where management and labour have adversary relationships.[96] A. Marsh indicates that

> theoretically the distinction between consultation and negotiation depends on the proposition that consultation is non-competitive and integrative in nature, whereas negotiation is competitive and concerned with temporary and unsatisfying compromises, consultation therefore being equipped to resolve conflict and negotiation merely to contain it.[97]

Personally, we would like to define consultation from the point of view of influence by labour on management decision making. Consultation then means that advice is given to the employer, leaving the decision making of the employer intact. It implies that the employer retains the power to make decisions, after having listened to the views of the employee representatives. This advice does not require either unanimity or a majority, unless required, and can take place either at the request of the

---

95. IELL, *Great Britain*, 1992, paragraph 42.
96. See *La participation des travailleurs aux décisions dans l'entreprise*, geneva, ILO, 1981, 22 and ILO Recommendation No. 94 of 1952.
97. *Concise Encyclopaedia of Industrial Relations*, Oxford, 1979, p. 100.

employer or at the request of labour or may be mandatory by law. Consultation includes an exchange of views, even of proposals and counter proposals, in short, a discussion in depth.

Between consultation and negotiation, which are difficult to distinguish in practice, stands the expression used in quite a number of EU directives: 'consultation with a view to reaching agreement'.[98] It seems to me that this expression goes further than consultation in the strict sense, where the employer asks for the benefit of the ideas of the employees on the matter. Here more is required: the parties are also asked to try to reach an agreement, which actually means that one leaves the area of consultation and lands in fact in the area of negotiation.

354. The putting into effect of information and consultation rights involves a number of questions, which will have to be resolved by the Union legislator or by the social partners through a European collective agreement, although the last is not likely, as employers do not favour these developments.

The most important concern:

– the subject matter; what kind of information; topics of consultations; – the involved entity in the enterprise (plant or group) and access to decision-makers; – when information has to be given or consultations held;
– to whom information has to be given or who should be consulted; – the obligation of headquarters to help subsidiaries in providing required information and engage in meaningful consultation;
– the problems concerning confidentiality regarding the shared information, and the consultation process.[99]

355. The competence of the Union to deal with 'information and consultation' does, it seems to me, include the powers to establish mechanisms and structures through which and to which information can be given or through which consultation can be organised, e.g. the setting up of a European Works Council.

Equal Treatment

356. Another field which can be dealt with by qualified majority voting is the 'equality between men and women with regard to labour market opportunities and treatment at work'. This competence belongs self-evidently also to the *acquis communautaire* and we refer for its meaning to what we said about Article 157 TFEU and the relevant directives concerning equal treatment of men and women.[100]

Integration of excluded persons

357. This competence relates to the integration of persons excluded from the labour market, without prejudice to Article 166 TFEU. This article belongs to Title XII of the TFEU on Education, Vocational Training, Youth and Sport.

---

98. Directive of 1998 on Collective Redundancies or the 2001 Directive on Acquired Rights.
99. See R. Blanpain, *Comparative Labour Law and Industrial Relations*, 1st edn, 1982, pp. 208–219.
100. *See* Part I, Chapter 5.

(b) Unanimous voting

(aa) Procedure

358. According to Article 153(2) TFEU, the EP and the Council shall act unanimously on a proposal from the Commission, after consulting the ESC and the Committee of the Regions, in a number of areas, which are enumerated immediately hereafter.

(bb) Areas

Social security and social protection of workers

359. Unanimous voting is required in the field of social security and social protection of workers.

Job security

360. Unanimous voting is also required in the case of protection of workers where their employment contract is terminated. This relates to the different methods of terminating the employment relationship, e.g. by consent, by way of notice, immediate dismissal, through judicial dissolution and the like. It covers also the term of notice, the reason(s) for dismissals, reinstatement, special protection for shop stewards, members of works councils, supervisory boards, pregnant women workers and the like, all forms of compensation, redundancy payments and the like included. Job security covers, in our opinion, individual as well as collective dismissals.

Representation and collective defence including co-determination

361. Representation and collective defence of the interests of workers and employers, including co-determination, has to be read together with paragraph 5 of Article 153 TFEU. That paragraph indicates that the provisions of Article 153 TFEU do not apply to 'pay, the right of association, the right to strike and the right to impose lock-outs'.

362. Representation of workers relates to e.g. works councils, shop stewards, committees of health and safety, staff associations and the like as well as to representation through trade unions and at different levels: plant, enterprise, group of enterprises, multinational enterprises included, sectoral, national and European. Co-determination[101] also covers all forms of workers' participation, where an (elected) employee, a trade union representative, or someone whom the employees confide in (the so-called Dutch model) sits on the supervisory board or the management of a company. Needless to say, employers are mainly represented by employers' associations.

---

101. *See* Part II, Chapter 2, §3, II. 'In Britain used almost exclusively to describe the West German form of industrial democracy' (M. Terry and L. Dickens, *European Employment and Industrial Relations Glossary*, London, 1991, p. 48).

363. Collective defence of the interest of workers and employers involves, taking paragraph 5 of Article 153 and representation of employers and workers into account, mainly collective bargaining. This relates to the indication of the parties competent to conclude a collective agreement to the content and to the form of the agreement, to the level of bargaining, to the binding effect of the agreement, to the extension procedures and the like. One can also add the settlement of industrial disputes, by way of mediation, conciliation or arbitration.

Third-country nationals

364. This competence relates to conditions of employment for third-country nationals legally residing in Union territory. These nationals, when they are workers, do not enjoy among others the right of free movement in the Union and undoubtedly improvement in this field is called for.

Financial contributions for promotion of employment

365. A final competence, to be voted upon unanimously, concerns financial contributions for promotion of employment and job-creation, without prejudice to the provisions relating to the Social Fund.

(c) Excluded areas

366. The provisions of Article 153 do, as already mentioned, not apply to 'pay, the right of association, the right to strike or the right to impose lock-outs' (Article 153(5)) TFEU.

The rights of association, collective bargaining and to strike or to impose lock-outs are self-evidently completely interlinked and have no full-fledged and adequate meaning in themselves. Indeed, workers unite in order to be able to collectively defend their interests by way of collective bargaining on the basis of market strength, by the use of the ultimate weapon, the strike. The same is *ceteris paribus* true for the employers. For the ILO, freedom of association includes the right to strike.[102] As we have said earlier, 'collective bargaining without the right to strike amounts to collective begging'. It will therefore not be easy to clearly define each of these rights separately.

367. Pay, freedom of association, strike and lock-out remain thus purely national affairs. The different notions, the right of association, the right to strike and the right to impose lock-outs, have, however, a Union meaning in law. It will indeed in time be essential to know exactly what they signify in order to judge whether the European Union in dealing with a given issue acted within the limits of its powers or not. In the light of the fact that the Title on Social Policy aims at the construction of a social Europe, Article 153(5) TFEU must be seen as an exception to the general

---

102. W.B. Creighton, 'Freedom of Association' in *Comparative Labour Law and Industrial Relations in Industrialised Market Economies* (ed. R. Blanpain) 10th edn, Deventer, 2010.

rule and has thus to be interpreted restrictively. It is at the same time interesting to note that the High Contracting Parties in Maastricht put the right to strike and the right to impose lock-outs on an equal footing, which is e.g. not the case in a number of Member States, e.g. France and Italy.

(aa) Pay

368. For the notion of pay, we can, I assume, refer to what was said in relation to Article 157 TFEU, which deals with equal pay for male and female workers.[103] There are still important differences between the labour costs in various member countries. These differences, however, are matched by equivalent variations in the level of productivity in the countries concerned.

(bb) Right of association

369. The right of association contains the right to form and to join or not to join trade unions, staff associations or employers' associations, the right of those organisations to draw up their own constitutions and rules, to elect their representatives and to formulate their programmes. It includes the right to form and to join national federations and confederations of employers' associations and of trade unions, as well as European or international organisations. It also embraces the acquisition of legal personality and the right to own property, to conclude contracts and the like.

(cc) Right to strike or to impose lock-outs

370. The right to strike 'concerns the (collective) refusal by workers, usually but not always organised in a trade union, to continue working, in order to put pressure on employers or on the government'.[104] The lock-out is 'the employer practice of denying the possibility of work to employees in connection with an industrial dispute'.[105]

(2) Approximation of Laws

371. Article 115 TFEU provides the Union with broad powers and allows the Council, acting unanimously, 'to issue directives for the approximation of such laws, regulations or administrative provisions of the Member States as directly affect the establishment or functioning of the internal market'.

372. Article 114 TFEU has already served as the legal basis for very important directives in the social field, dealing with issues such as transfers of undertakings, collective dismissals and insolvencies.

373. An identical argument can be made with regard to the topics that the Lisbon Treaty excludes from the provisions of Article 153 TFEU.

---

103. *See* Part I, Chapter 4.
104. Terry and Dickens, *op. cit.*, p. 188.
105. *Ibid.*, p. 126.

Arguments are advanced that the introduction of the single currency will create a strong incentive among the Member States to start 'competing' in the area of minimum wages. The word 'social dumping' is often used in this context.

It is beyond doubt that any such form of competition, driving wages down, will have a direct impact on the functioning of the Internal Market. The establishment of a European minimum wage by way of directive with Article 114 TFEU as its legal basis would thus be perfectly acceptable from a legal perspective.

While there may not be sufficient political will to establish a European minimum wage, there are no legal impediments to its creation.

Similar arguments can be advanced for other issues mentioned in paragraph 5 of the new Article 153.

374. Differences in strike regulation and legislation, as well as government or court interventions in strike action, may directly influence the functioning of the Internal Market. Furthermore, certain forms of strike action have an even more direct impact on the functioning of the Internal Market.

Strike actions undertaken by the French truckers, paralysing traffic in France and having direct consequences on industrial production both inside and outside France, illustrate this point most directly. There is a direct effect on the functioning of the Internal Market, and thus from a legal perspective, Union action seems perfectly acceptable.

As in its old version, the new Article 153 foresees that the directives establishing minimum requirements or standards will avoid imposing such administrative, financial and legal constraints which could impede the creation and development of small and medium-sized undertakings. In a declaration to the Amsterdam Treaty, the Member States declared that the 'SME Sensitivity' requirement would not allow discrimination against the workers of the SMEs in a manner not warranted by the circumstances. According to the ECJ, the SME sensitivity requirement allows for specific economic measures to be taken for this kind of enterprise. It does not prevent the Union from taking mandatory measures, however.[106]

Union action seems to be perfectly acceptable.

c. Employment Policy

(1) A Coordinated Strategy for Employment

375. At the meeting in Amsterdam, the employment objective was formulated strongly. The Treaty of Lisbon contains a Title IX, dealing exclusively with employment.

Article 3(3) of the TEU reads:

---

106. ECJ, 12 November 1996, *Kingdom of Great Britain and Northern Ireland* v. *Council of the European Union*, Case No. C-84/94, ECR, 1996, 5755. *See also* ECJ, 30 November 1993, *P. KirshammerHack* v. *Nurham Sidal*, Case No. C-189/91, ECR, 1993, 6185.

The Union shall establish an internal market. It shall work for the sustainable development of Europe based on balanced economic growth and price stability, a highly competitive social market economy, *aiming at full employment* and social progress, and a high level of protection and improvement of the quality of the environment. It shall promote scientific and technological advance.

It shall combat social exclusion and discrimination, and shall promote social justice and protection, equality between women and men, solidarity between generations and protection of the rights of the child.

It shall promote economic, social and territorial cohesion, and solidarity among Member States.

It shall respect its rich cultural and linguistic diversity, and shall ensure that Europe's cultural heritage is safeguarded and enhanced.

376. The 'coordinated employment strategy' is further elaborated in the new Title on Employment and can be summarised as follows:

(1) It is the Member States, who are in the first place competent as regards employment policy. The role of the EU is merely supplementary and coordinating. This follows from the wording of Article 145 of the Title on Employment, which reads: Member States and the Union shall, in accordance with this Title, work towards developing a coordinated strategy for employment and particularly for promoting a skilled, trained and adaptable workforce and labour markets responsive to economic change with a view to achieving the objectives defined in Article 3 of the Treaty on European Union.
(2) Member States must coordinate their employment strategies at European level. This is set out in the Articles 145 and 146 of the Employment Title: Member States and the Union shall, according to this Title, work towards developing a coordinated strategy for employment.
(2) Article 146: Member States, having regard to the national practices related to the responsibilities of management and labour, shall regard promoting employment as a matter of common concern and shall coordinate their action in this respect within the Council, in accordance with the provisions of Article 148.
(3) The employment policy must be compatible with the broad guidelines of the economic policies of the EU, namely the EMU.[107]
(4) The Member States and the Union shall work towards developing a co-ordinated strategy:
(5) particularly for promoting a skilled, trained and adaptable workforce and labour markets responsive to economic change with a view to achieving the objectives defined in Article 3 of the Treaty on European Union (Art. 145).
(6) The European strategy shall consist of:
    – drawing up guidelines;
    – writing annual reports;
    – adopting incentive measures;

---

107. Member States, through their employment policies, shall contribute to the achievement of the objectives referred to in Article 145 in a way consistent with the broad guidelines of the economic policies of the Member States and of the Union adopted pursuant to Article 121.

- exchanging information and best practices;
- promoting innovative practices and recourse to pilot projects;
- making non-binding recommendations (Art. 148–149).

(7) National policies consist of:
- implementing the European guidelines;
- the drafting of annual reports to the Council (Art. 149).

(8) The measures that the Council can take 'shall not include harmonisation of the laws and regulations of the Member States' (Art. 149).

(9) An Employment Committee with advisory status will be established in order 'to promote coordination between Member States on employment and labour market policies' (Art. 150).

(2) The European Social Fund

377. The European Social Fund aims to improve employment opportunities for workers in the internal market and to contribute thereby to raising the standard of living; and to render the employment of workers easier and to increase their geographical and occupational mobility within the Union, and to facilitate their adaptation to industrial changes and to changes in production systems, in particular through vocational training and retraining (Art. 162 TFEU).[108]

d. Equal Pay, Opportunity and Treatment

378. According to Article 157 TFEU each Member State is obliged to ensure that the principle of equal pay for male and female workers for equal work or work of equal value is applied.

The EP and the Council take measures with qualified majority to ensure the application of the principle of equal opportunities and equal treatment of men and women in matters of employment and occupation, including the principle of equal pay for equal work or work of equal value.

The principle of equal treatment does not prevent any Member State from maintaining or adopting measures providing for specific advantages in order to make it easier for the under-represented sex to pursue a vocational activity or to prevent or compensate for disadvantage in professional careers.

e. Vocational Training

379. Title XII of the TFEU deals with education, vocational training, youth and sport. Pursuant to that Title, the Union shall contribute to the development of quality education by encouraging cooperation between Member States and, if necessary, by supporting and supplementing their action, while fully respecting the responsibility of the Member States for the content of teaching and the organisation of education systems and their cultural and linguistic diversity (Art. 165(1)).

---

108. See above: Chapter I, §3, II.

The Union action shall be aimed at:

- developing the European dimension in education, particularly through the teaching and dissemination of the languages of the Member States;
- encouraging mobility of students and teachers, *inter alia* by encouraging the academic recognition of diplomas and periods of study;
- promoting cooperation between educational establishments; – developing exchanges of information and experience on issues common to the education systems of the Member States;
- encouraging the development of youth exchanges and of exchanges of socio-educational instructors, and encouraging the participation of young people in democratic life in Europe;
- encouraging the development of distance education (Art. 165);
- developing the European dimension in sport, by promoting fairness and openness in sporting competitions and cooperation between bodies responsible for sports, and by protecting the physical and moral integrity of sportsmen and sportswomen, especially the youngest sportsmen and sportswomen.

The Union and the Member States shall foster cooperation with third countries and the competent international organisations in the field of education and sport, in particular the Council of Europe.

380. Regarding vocational training, the Union shall implement a vocational training policy which shall support and supplement the action of the Member States, while fully respecting the responsibility of the Member States for the content and organisation of vocational training (Art. 166(1)).

Union action shall aim to:

- facilitate adaptation to industrial changes, in particular through vocational training and retraining;
- improve initial and continuing vocational training in order to facilitate vocational integration and reintegration into the labour market;
- facilitate access to vocational training and encourage mobility of instructors and trainees and particularly young people;
- stimulate cooperation on training between educational or training establishments and firms;
- develop exchanges of information and experience on issues common to the training systems of the Member States.

The Union and the Member States shall foster cooperation with third countries and the competent international organisations in the sphere of vocational training. The Council, acting with qualified majority and after consulting the Economic and Social Committee and the Committee of the Regions, shall adopt measures to contribute to the achievement of the objectives, excluding any harmonisation of the laws and regulations of the Member States.' The Council, on a proposal from the Commission, shall adopt recommendations (Article 166(2–4)).

f. Paid Holiday Schemes

381. Member States shall endeavour to maintain the existing equivalence between paid holiday schemes (Art. 158 FTEU).

g. Economic and Social Cohesion

382. In order to promote its overall harmonious development, the Union will develop and pursue its actions leading to the strengthening of its economic and social cohesion. The aim is, in particular, to reduce disparities between the levels of development of the various regions and the backwardness of the least favoured regions or islands, including rural areas (Art. 174 TFEU).

The Community shall also support the achievement of these objectives by the action it takes through the structural funds:

– the European Agricultural Guidance and Guarantee Fund; – the European Social Fund;
– the European Regional Development Fund; and – the European Investment Bank (Art. 175 TFEU).

h. Reporting

383. The Commission shall draw up a report each year on progress in achieving the objectives of Article 151 TFEU, including the demographic situation in the Union. This report will be forwarded to the EP, the Council and the ESC (Article 159 TFEU).

IV. The Role of the Commission

384. The Title on Social Policy awards the Commission a very dynamic task, confirming its role of initiator and animator at European level. First, the Commission shall, with a view to achieving the objectives of Article 151 TFEU and without prejudice to other provisions of the TFEU, 'encourage cooperation' between the Member States and 'facilitate the coordination' of their action in all social policy fields under this Chapter (Art. 156).

Secondly, the Commission shall have the task of 'promoting the consultation' of management and labour at Union level and shall take any relevant measure to 'facilitate their dialogue' by ensuring balanced support for the parties (Art. 154(1)).

385. These last tasks are very important ones. Promotion of consultation is dealt with immediately hereafter. Facilitating the social dialogue relates not only to the interaction between the European Confederations like BUSINESSEUROPE, UEAPME, CEEP and the ETUC, but also to relations at European sectoral or enterprise level. Support may mean financial or logistic support to trade union meetings across boundaries, to the functioning of European works councils, to the organisation of management training e.g. in the conduct of a social dialogue at European level and the like. The support, Article 154(1) reads, certainly at the demand of BUSINESSEUROPE which was complaining about earlier unbalanced support, should be balanced and equally divided between management and labour.

V. Involvement of the Social Partners

386. The role of the social partners has been dramatically enhanced on the occasion of the Treaties of Maastricht and Amsterdam: from consultation with the European Union regarding the implementation of Union directives to collective bargaining at European level. In consequence the social partners are entitled to real involvement in the shaping of European labour law from the initial stages, as well as, for certain countries where this is legally possible,[109] in the implementation of Council directives. At the same time a stronger legal basis has been laid for European-wide collective bargaining and mechanisms were introduced ensuring a binding effect of European collective agreements *erga omnes*. Nonetheless, especially regarding these agreements quite a number of extremely complex problems of a legal nature arise, for the solution of which ultimately further Union legislation may be needed.

A. Consultation at Union Level

387. The Commission has the task of promoting the consultation of management and labour at Community level (Article 154(1), TFEU). To this end, before submitting proposals in the social field, the Commission must consult management and labour on the possible direction of Union action (Article 154(2), TFEU). This means that the social partners are involved *ab initio*, before the decision is taken to do something or not. If, after such consultation, the Commission considers Union action advisable, it shall consult management and labour on the envisaged proposal. Management and labour shall forward to the Commission an opinion, or where appropriate, a recommendation (Article 154(3)) TFEU. Management and labour can thus formulate either their own opinion or a joint recommendation, which the Commission self-evidently is free to incorporate or not.

To our mind, this consultation constitutes an essential element of the European legislative process and a possible ground for the annulment of a Union decision by the Court of Justice if that part of the legislative procedure has not been properly respected.

---

109. These are countries where there exists a so-called extension procedure by which through a (governmental) measure the collective agreements are made binding on all employers and employees which fall within the territorial and professional scope of the agreement, whether they are a member of one of the contracting parties or not.

1. Procedure

388. In this context the Communication (1993)[110] of the Commission describes the Agreement as containing two stages:

– *Stage 1*: Article 154(2) TFEU specifies that 'before submitting proposals in the social policy field, the Commission shall consult management and labour on the possible direction of Union action'.
– *Stage 2*: if, after such consultation, the Commission considers Union action advisable, it shall consult management and labour on the content of the envisaged proposal. Management and labour shall forward to the Commission an opinion or, where appropriate, a recommendation (Article 154(3) TFEU).

In the light of the experience already acquired, the Commission proposes to proceed as follows:

– the first consultation of the social partners would take place on receipt of the letter from the Commission. The requested consultation may be by letter or, if the social partners so desire, by the convening of an *ad hoc* meeting. The consultation period should not exceed six weeks;
– the Commission will decide its position in the light of comments received during the first round of consultations, and will decide whether to proceed to the second phase;
– the second consultation phase will be initiated with the receipt of the second letter sent by the Commission, setting out the content of the planned proposal together with indication of the possible legal basis.

On the occasion of this second consultation, the social partners should deliver to the Commission in writing and, where the social partners so wish, through an *ad hoc* meeting, an opinion setting out the points of agreement and disagreement in their respective positions on the draft text. Where appropriate, they should deliver a recommendation setting out their joint positions on the draft text. The duration of this second phase shall also not exceed 6 weeks.

389. The new consultative procedures will not be a complete substitute for the old, especially where these involve the use of well established tripartite consultative committees. In particular, the following committees would be the mechanism for consultation of the social partners, including where appropriate consultation under the terms of Article 154 TFEU: the Advisory Committee on Safety, Hygiene and Health Protection at Work, the Advisory Committee on the Free Movement of Workers, the Advisory Committee for Social Security for Migrant Workers, the European Social Fund, the Advisory Committee for Vocational Training and the

---

110. Commission Communication: Adapting and promoting the Social Dialogue at Community Level, 20 May 1998, COM(98) 322.

Advisory Committee for Equal Opportunities for Women and Men.[111] The two procedures may, on occasion, therefore operate in a parallel way depending on the subject matter of the specific proposal. The Commission will ensure, however, that duplication is avoided and that there is the maximum of transparency at all stages of the different procedures.

390. In a Communication of 26 June 2002[112] the Commission states that 'for implementation and monitoring of the agreements negotiated by the social partners, two options are available:

– The Commission presents a proposal for a Council Decision in areas covered by Article 153 TFEU. This takes place at the joint request of the signatory parties following examination by the Commission of the following: sufficiently representative contracting parties, lawfulness of all clauses of the agreement under Union law, and compliance with the provisions concerning small and medium-sized enterprises. The social partners' agreement is then presented to the European Parliament for its opinion and transmitted to the Council for its decision. In that case, which is a procedure for extending agreements negotiated and concluded by the social partners, the Council is required to take a decision on the social partners' text without changing the substance. Implementation of the Council decision is monitored in accordance with the nature of the instrument used (directive, regulation or decision). However, the Commission believes that the social partners who triggered the regulatory text hold special responsibility for its implementation.

  The Member States should associate the social partners in the transposal at national level of Community texts having formed the subject of a negotiated agreement. The Commission will systematically consult the social partners who have signed agreements on implementation reports, as was the case with parental leave and part-time work.
– The European agreement is brought into effect in accordance with the social partners' and Member States' own procedures and practices. This option was chosen, for example, by the negotiators on the improvement of paid employment in agriculture and on telework at cross-industry level. In that case, the Commission calls on the social partners to strengthen substantially the procedures for on-the-spot monitoring and to prepare regular reports on implementation of the agreements signed. These reports should outline progress on the content of the implementation of agreements and their coverage. Such structured reporting is particularly necessary where the agreement negotiated by the social partners follows Commission consultation under Article 154 TFEU of the Treaty. The Commission can review with the social partners the technical and logistic facilities required for such monitoring, either by using existing budgetary tools or by introducing new mechanisms. Looking ahead and in the medium term, the development of the

---

111. Communication (COM(93)) 600 final of 14 December 1993.
112. Communication from the Commission – *The European social dialogue, a force for innovation and change*, COM/2002/341 final.

European social dialogue raises the question of European collective agreements as sources of law.

391. The sectoral level is according to the Commission a very important area for development both on general issues such as employment, industrial change and a new organisation of work and on upcoming specific demands on the labour market. The development of negotiations at sectoral level is therefore a key issue.

In order to improve the input of the sectoral dialogue in quantitative and qualitative terms it seemed necessary to replace the existing structures and encourage a more effective dialogue. The operating procedures will be streamlined: one high-level plenary meeting each year, a restricted social partner delegation, reimbursement for maximum 15 participants from each side. The competent DG will provide secretarial services and chair the meetings in its role as facilitator in the absence of a joint request from the social partners that a member of one of the delegations chair. Each sector will be firmly supported through a partnership between the competent DG and the other relevant DGs, including improved technical backup for the preparation and follow-up to meetings.

392. According to the Commission Decision of 20 May 1998, the Sectoral Dialogue Committees are established in those sectors where the social partners make a joint request to take part in a dialogue at European level, and where the organisations representing both sides of industry fulfil the following criteria:

(1) relate to specific sectors or categories and be organised at European level;
(2) consist of organisations, which are themselves an integral and recognised part of Member States' social partner structures and with the capacity to negotiate agreements, and which are representative of several Member States;
(3) have adequate structures to ensure their effective participation in the work of the Committees (Article 1).

The Committees are consulted on developments at Union level having social implications for their respective sectors and to develop and promote the social dialogue. There is a maximum of 40 members, with equal representation from both sides (Article 2).

The Commission invites the representatives on a proposal from the social partners (Article 3).

The Committees shall meet at least once a year (Article 5). If the Commission has informed a Committee that a matter discussed relates to a matter of a confidential nature, members of the Committee shall be bound not to disclose any information acquired at the meetings of the Committee or its Secretariat (Article 6).

393. Regarding the autonomous agreements, the Commission (2004)[113] fully recognises the negotiating autonomy of the social partners on the topics falling within their competence.

---

113. Communication from the Commission, 'Partnership for change in an enlarged Europe – Enhancing the contribution of European social dialogue', Brussels, 12 August 2004, COM(2004) 557 final.

However in the specific case of autonomous agreements implemented in accordance with Article 155(2) TFEU, the Commission has a particular role to play if the agreement was the result of an Article 154 TFEU consultation, *inter alia* because the social partners' decision to negotiate an agreement temporarily suspends the legislative process at Union level initiated by the Commission in this domain.

While respecting the principle of the autonomy of the social partners, the Commission will publish autonomous agreements and inform the European Parliament and the Council of Ministers, after undertaking an ex-ante assessment as it does for Article 155(2) agreements to be implemented by Council decision.

Upon the expiry of the implementation and monitoring period, while giving precedence to the monitoring undertaken by the social partners themselves, the Commission will undertake its own monitoring of the agreement, to assess the extent to which the agreement has contributed to the achievement of the Union's objectives.

Should the Commission decide that the agreement does not succeed in meeting the Union's objectives, it will consider the possibility of putting forward, if necessary, a proposal for a legislative act. The Commission may also exercise its right of initiative at any point, including during the implementation period, should it conclude that either management or labour are delaying the pursuit of Union objectives.

While recognising the broad scope of the social partners' competences, in line with the previous concerns of the Commission, where fundamental rights or important political options are at stake, or in situations where the rules must be applied in a uniform fashion in all Member States and coverage must be complete, preference should be given to implementation by Council decision. Autonomous agreements are also not appropriate for the revision of previously existing directives adopted by the Council and European Parliament through the normal legislative procedure.

2. Typology of the Results of the European Social Dialogue

394. With a view to assisting understanding of the various social dialogue instruments and helping the social partners to improve transparency, the following typology identifies four broad categories, each of which has sub-categories: agreements implemented in accordance with Article 155(2) TFEU; process-oriented texts; joint opinions and tools; and procedural texts. The social partners are encouraged to draw on this typology when drafting their texts in the future.

The new generation texts, which the social partners seek to follow-up themselves, fall within the first two categories, namely autonomous agreements and process-oriented texts.

It should be pointed out that the loose use of terminology makes it difficult to categorise some of the texts and some overlap categories.

a. Agreements Implemented in Accordance with Article 155(2) TFEU: Minimum Standards

395. The texts in this category establish minimum standards and entail the implementation of certain commitments by a given deadline. Article 155(2) makes it clear that two main types of agreement fall within this category, the main difference relating to the method of implementation foreseen.

Agreements implemented in accordance with Article 155(2): minimum standards

Type of agreement	Examples
Agreements implemented by Council decision	
Implemented by Council decision-monitored by the Commission	– Framework agreement on parental leave, 1995
	– Framework agreement on part-time work, 1997
	– Framework agreement on fixed-term work, 1999
	– European agreement on the organisation of working time of seafarers, 1998
	– European agreement on the organisation of working time of mobile workers in civil aviation, 2000
	– European agreement on certain aspects of the working conditions of mobile workers assigned to interoperable cross-border services, 2004
Autonomous agreements implemented by the procedures and practices specific to management and labour and the Member States	
Implementation and monitoring by the social partners	– Framework agreement on telework, 2002
	– Framework agreement on work-related stress, 2004
	– Agreement on the European licence for drivers carrying out a cross- border interoperability service, 2004
	– Framework Agreement on Harassment and Violence at Work 2007)
	– Framework Agreement on Inclusive Labour Market (2010)

396. The first kind of agreement consists of those which are implemented at the joint request of the signatory parties by a Council decision (in practice so far by Council directives) on a proposal from the Commission. This category includes the three cross-industry framework agreements on parental leave, part-time work and fixed-term contracts, as well as the maritime transport and civil aviation sector agreements on working time, and the railway sector agreement on the working conditions of mobile workers assigned to cross-border interoperable services. The three cross-industry framework agreements were negotiated as a result of a Commission consultation under Article 154, whereas the sectoral agreements make use of the space left to the social partners by a directive[114] to adapt the Union provisions to the specific needs of the sector.

The responsibility for ensuring that agreements implemented by Council decision are transposed and implemented lies with the Member States, even in cases where the provisions are implemented through collective bargaining by the social partners. Responsibility for monitoring these agreements lies with the Commission, although the social partners are systematically consulted on the implementation reports.[115]

397. With regard to the second type of agreement – those implemented in accordance with the procedures and practices specific to management and labour and the Member States – it is the social partners themselves who are responsible for implementing and monitoring these agreements. The *Framework agreement on telework* of July 2002 is the first cross-industry example of this type of agreement and was the result of an Article 154 TFEU consultation. In May 2004 the cross-industry social partners concluded their second agreement of this type on the topic of workrelated stress, which was also the result of an Article 154 TFEU consultation.

Another Framework Agreement concerning Harassment and Violence at Work was concluded on 26 April 2007 as well as a Framework Agreement on Inclusive Labour Market on 25 March 2010.

Effective implementation and monitoring is important in the case of agreements of this kind, particularly if they have been negotiated subsequent to a Commission consultation under Article 154 TFEU. Article 155(2) TFEU states that the Union level agreements '*shall* be implemented' (emphasis added), which implies that there is an obligation to implement these agreements and for the signatory parties to exercise influence on their members in order to implement the European agreement.

---

114. In this instance Directive 93/104/EC concerning certain aspects of the organisation of working time (O.J. L 307, 13 December 1993).
115. The ETUC's European Trade Union Institute (ETUI) has produced its own implementation reports on the parental leave, part-time and fixed-term work agreements through its NETLEX network of national legal experts. The agreement on working time in civil aviation and the agreement on working conditions in the railway sector indicate that the social partners will undertake evaluations of the implementation of these agreements.

b. Process-oriented Texts

398. This category consists of a variety of joint texts which are implemented in a more incremental and process-oriented way than agreements. In these texts the European social partners make recommendations of various kinds to their members for follow-up, and they should involve regular evaluation of the progress made towards achieving their objectives in order to ensure they have a real impact. The implementation of some aspects of these texts may require cooperation with national public authorities.

Texts of this kind can be useful in areas in which legislation at European level may not be the most appropriate solution, often because of the complex and diverse array of measures already in place in Member States, but in which the social partners may nevertheless have an interest in working together. They can also assist the exchange of good practice and mutual learning. Such texts sometimes help to prepare the ground for future Union legislation.

There are three main types of instrument falling within this category. The ETUC's European Trade Union Institute (ETUI) has produced its own implementation reports on the parental leave, part-time and fixed-term work agreements through its NETLEX network of national legal experts. The agreement on working time in civil aviation and the agreement on working conditions in the railway sector indicate that the social partners will undertake evaluations of the implementation of these agreements.

(1) Frameworks of Action

399. Frameworks of action consist of the identification of certain policy priorities towards which the national social partners undertake to work. These priorities serve as benchmarks and the social partners report annually on the action taken to follow-up these texts.

(2) Guidelines and Codes of Conduct

400. Guidelines and codes of conduct make recommendations and/or provide guidelines to national affiliates concerning the establishment of standards or principles. In some cases these are intended to serve as principles or minimum European standards to be implemented at national or company level. In other cases they seek to promote higher standards than those provided for in existing legislation. This category also includes codes of conduct intended to promote the implementation in companies' supply chains of existing internationally agreed standards in the area of labour law established by international conventions. The content of some of these codes of conduct goes beyond the core ILO conventions.

General Introduction, Ch. 3, Competences of the EU 401–401

(3) Policy Orientations

401. This sub-category refers to texts in which the social partners pursue a proactive approach to promoting certain policies among their members. The texts explain how these will be promoted (e.g. collection and exchange of good practice, awareness-raising activities) and how the social partners undertake to assess the follow-up given and its impact.

Process-oriented texts	
Type of text	Examples[116]
Frameworks of action – working towards common priorities	
Follow-up and annual reporting by the social partners	Framework of actions on the lifelong development of competencies and qualifications, 2002
Guidelines, codes of conduct – establishing standards or principles	
Regular follow-up and reporting by the social partners Establishing new European standards or principles:	
	– Recommendation framework agreement on the improvement of paid employment in agriculture, 1997
	– Agreement on promoting employment in the postal sector in Europe, 1998
	– Guidelines on telework in telecommunications, 2001
	– European agreement on guidelines on telework in commerce, 2001
	– Code of conduct – Guidelines for European hairdressers, 2001[117]
	– Voluntary guidelines supporting age diversity in commerce, 2002
	– Joint declaration on lifelong learning in the banking sector, 2002
	– European agreement on vocational training in agriculture, 2002[117]
	– Code of conduct on CSR in the European sugar industry, 2003

---

116. Some of these texts do not include detailed provisions on follow-up and reporting, but have been included because they consist of recommendations to the members of the signatory organisations.
117. Although these texts are referred to as 'agreements', they have been included in this category as their provisions appear to consist mainly of recommendations to their members and do not include a date by which implementation of the various objectives must be accomplished.

- Code of conduct and ethics for the private security sector, 2003
- Electricity sector joint declaration on telework, 2003
- Local & regional government joint statement on telework, 2004
- Statement on promoting employment and integration of disabled people in the commerce and distribution sector, 2004
- Guidelines for customer contact centres (telecommunications), 2004
- Joint recommendation on the prevention of occupational stress, Construction, 2006
- Rules of procedure, Personal services, 2006
- Joint position against undeclared work, Private security, 2006

Promoting and enforcing existing internationally agreed standards:
- Code of conduct on child labour in the footwear sector, 1996
- Code of conduct for the European textile/clothing sector, 1997
- Agreement on Fundamental Rights and Principles at Work, in the commerce sector, 1999
- Code of conduct in the leather and tanning sector, 2000
- Code of conduct in the footwear sector, 2000
- Code of Conduct – A Charter for the social partners in the European woodworking industry, 2002
- Work programme 2006 Joint position on the European Globalisation Adjustment Fund
- Third implementation report on corporate social responsibility – code of conduct of the European Sugar Industry, 2006

Policy orientations – the proactive promotion of policies	
Regular follow-up and reporting by the social partners	– Joint recommendation on apprenticeship in the sugar sector, 1998 – Electricity sector joint declaration on equal opportunities/diversity, 2003 – Orientations for reference in managing change and its social consequences, 2003 (cross-industry social partners) – Joint Statement on Corporate Social Responsibility in commerce, 2003 – Common recommendations of the European social partners for the cleaning industry, 2004 – 2006/2007 Work Programme Joint statement on the development of social dialogue in local and regional government, Local and regional government, 2006

c. Joint Opinions and Tools: Exchange of Information

402. This category consists of social partner texts and tools which contribute to exchanging information, either upwards from the social partners to the European institutions and/or national public authorities, or downwards, by explaining the implications of EU policies to national members. The instruments in this category do not entail any implementation, monitoring or follow-up provisions.

(1) Joint Opinions

403. This category includes the majority of social partner texts adopted over the years such as their joint opinions and joint statements, which are generally intended to provide input to the European institutions and/or national public authorities. These include texts which respond to a Union consultation (green and white papers, consultation documents, Communications), which adopt a joint position with regard to a given Union policy, which explicitly ask the Commission to adopt a particular stance, or which ask the Commission to undertake studies or other actions.

(2) Declarations

404. This category refers to texts which are essentially declarations – usually directed at the social partners themselves – outlining future work and activities which the social partners intend to undertake (e.g. the organisation of seminars, roundtables, etc.).

(3) Tools

405. This category refers to the tools developed by the social partners, such as guides and manuals providing practical advice to employees and companies on subjects such as vocational training, health and safety and public procurement, often with the assistance of Union grants. These can make a very practical contribution at the grass-roots level, for example by helping to explain the implications of EU legislation on certain topics, or helping to exchange knowledge of good practice.

Joint opinions and tools	
Type of instrument	Examples[118]
Declarations	Joint opinions
– Joint declaration on the social partners of the cleaning industry and EU enlargement, 2000	– Position on training and continuing training (mines), 2003
– Joint statement and final report on the study on life-long learning in electricity sector, 2003	– Joint declaration on the European the harmonisation of legislation governing the private security sector, 2001
Tools	– Joint declaration on the objectives of the European directive on private agency work (temporary work sector), 2001
– Selecting best value – A guide for organisations awarding contracts for cleaning services (cleaning industry)	– Joint opinion of the European social partners in aviation, 2001
	– Joint position against undeclared work, Private security, 2006
– Training Kit of Basic Office Cleaning Techniques (cleaning industry)	
– European Vocational Training Manual for Basic Guarding (private security)	
– Brochure on tutoring in the construction industry, 2004	
– Website of the postal sector social dialogue committee, 2003	

---

118. This list is not exhaustive and only provides a few examples.

> – Joint declaration on strengthening
> social dialogue and reinforcing the
> capacities of national social partner
> organisations in the new Member
> States in the performing arts sector,
> Live performance, 2006

d. Procedural Texts

406. This final category consists of texts which seek to lay down the rules for the bipartite dialogue between the parties. This includes the cross-industry social partners' Agreement of 31 October 1991, which made proposals for the revision of the policy-making procedures in the EC Treaty in the social policy field. These proposals were incorporated virtually verbatim into the Treaty on European Union by the Intergovernmental Conference of 1991. This category also includes the social partner texts which determine the rules of procedure for the sectoral social dialogue committees.

e. Drafting Checklist for New Generation Social Partner Texts

407.
– clearly indicate to whom they or the various provisions are addressed, e.g. the Commission, other European Union institutions, national public authorities, social partners;
– indicate the status and purpose of the text clearly;
– where applicable, indicate the deadline by which the provisions should be implemented;
– indicate clearly how the text will be implemented and promoted at national level, including whether or not it should be implemented in a binding fashion in all cases;
– indicate clearly through which structures the monitoring/reporting will be undertaken, and the purpose of the reports at different stages;
– indicate when and/or at which intervals monitoring/reporting will take place;
– specify the procedures to be followed for dispute settlement (e.g. disagreements over the interpretation of the meaning of the text);
– be dated;
– be signed;
– agreements should include an annex listing the members of the signatory parties at whom the text is directed;
– indicate which language(s) is/are the original.

f. Sectoral Social Dialogue, 2010

408.

Table 6. Examples of significant tools and outcomes from the European sectoral social dialogue committees (2006–2010)

Agriculture
Framework agreement on the reduction of workers' exposure to the risk of work-related musculo-skeletal disorders (2006)
Civil aviation
Guidelines for consultation arrangements for functional airspace blocks (2007)
Commerce
Toolkit on preventing third-party violence in commerce (2009)
Construction
Recommendations on self-employment and bogus self-employment (2010)
Common 'posting database' (2008)
Catering
Common statement on obesity (2007)
Electricity
Toolkit for socially responsible restructuring with a best practice guide (2008)
Gas
Toolkit on demographic change, age management and competencies (2009)
Hospitals
Code of conduct and follow-up on ethical cross-border recruitment and retention (2008)
Cleaning industry
Manual on ergonomics in cleaning operations (2007)
Insurance
Joint statement on demographical challenges (2010)
Local and regional governments
Guidelines to drawing up gender equality action plans (2007)
Personal services
Agreement on the implementation of European hairdressing certificates (2009)
Private security
European educational toolkit for three private security activities/profiles: 1. Mobile patrolling, 2. Alarm response centres, 3. Airport security (2006)
Railways
The concept of employability in the railway sector — Recommendations (2007)

Joint recommendations for better representation and integration of women in the railway sector (2007)

Sea fisheries

Handbook on prevention of accidents at sea and the safety of fishermen (2007)

Sugar

Fifth implementation report (2007) on the code of conduct on corporate social responsibility

Leather/tanning industry

Social and environmental reporting standard (2008)

Telecoms

Diversity at work: review of good practices (2007)

Textile and clothing

Recommendations: how to secure better anticipation and management of industrial change and sectoral restructuring (2008).

Source: Commission Staff Working Document on the functioning and potential of European Social Dialogue, Brussels, 22 July 2010 SEC(2010) 964 final.

3. Social Partners

409. One of the important questions to be solved concerns self-evidently the problem which organisations qualify to be consulted.

This very delicate question is in the Communication (1993) dealt with as follows:

> As a matter of general principle the Commission believes that organisations should be consulted within the terms of Article 154 TFEU in so far as they meet the following criteria.

The organisations should:

– be cross-industry or relate to specific sectors or categories and be organised at European level;
– consist of organisations which are themselves an integral and recognised part of Member State social partner structures and with the capacity to negotiate agreements, and which are representative of all Member States, as far as possible;
– have adequate structures to ensure their effective participation in the consultation process.

At the same time, the Commission recognises that there is a substantial body of experience behind the social dialogue established between BUSINESSEUROPE, UEAPME, CEEP and ETUC. It has also taken note of their joint position regarding the implementation of the new procedures introduced by the Agreement.

There are a number of organisations which meet the criteria set out and which are thus potential candidates for involvement in the consultation process. The Commission does not wish to take a restrictive view of this issue, but is at the same time conscious of the practical problems posed by a multiplicity of potential actors. Only the organisations themselves are in a position to develop their own dialogue and negotiating structures. The Commission will endeavour to promote the development of new linking structures between all the social partners so as to help rationalise and improve the process. Special attention will be paid here to the due representation of small and medium-sized undertakings.

This raises the question of whether or not it is necessary in the first phase to create some form of consultation body or 'umbrella liaison' committee for the purposes of the procedure foreseen under Article 154 TFEU. Having carefully considered the matter, the Commission considers that at this initial stage this is not the best way forward, though this question will undoubtedly need to be re-examined in the light of experience as the process develops.

410. The situation regarding consultation of the social partners on social policy matters is now as follows:

- The Commission will continue its policy of wide-ranging consultation to ensure that its policy relates as closely as possible to economic and social realities. Such consultation will cover all European or, where appropriate, national organisations which might be affected by the Union's social policy.
- Within the framework of Article 154 TFEU it will undertake formal consultations with the European social partners' organisations.
- The Commission feels that these specific consultation procedures should apply to all social policy proposals, whatever legal basis is eventually decided on. The Commission also reserves the right to engage in specific consultations on any other horizontal or sectoral-based relations (including agreements) within the social partners' sphere of competence.

411. List of European social-partner organisations consulted under Article 154 TFEU:[119]

1. General cross-industry organisations
   - BUSINESSEUROPE
   - European Centre of Enterprises with Public Participation and of Enterprises of General
   - Economic Interest (CEEP)
   - European Trade Union Confederation (ETUC)
2. Cross-industry organisations representing certain categories of workers or undertakings
   - EUROCADRES (Council of European Professional and Managerial Staff)
   - European Association of Craft and Small and Medium-Sized Enterprises (UEAPME)

---

119. Last update: February 2013.

General Introduction, Ch. 3, Competences of the EU 411–411

- European Confederation of Executives and Managerial Staff (CEC)
3. Specific organisations
   - Eurochambres
4. Sectoral organisations representing employers
   - Airports Council International (ACI EUROPE)
   - Airport Services Association (ASA Europe)
   - Association of Commercial Television in Europe (ACT)
   - Association of European Airlines (AEA)
   - Association of European Professional Football Leagues (EPFL)
   - Association of European Public Postal Operators (PostEurop)
   - Association of European Radios (AER)
   - Association of Mutual Insurers and Insurance Cooperatives in Europe (AMICE)
   - Association of National Organisations of Fishing Enterprises in the EU (EUROPECHE)
   - Civil Air Navigation Services Organisation (CANSO)
   - Community of European Railway and Infrastructure Companies (CER)
   - Confederation of European Paper Industries (CEPI)
   - Confederation of European Security Services (CoESS)
   - Confederation of National Associations of Tanners and Dressers of the European Community (COTANCE)
   - Council of European Employers of the Metal, Engineering and Technology-Based Industries (CEEMET)
   - Council of European Municipalities and Regions (CEMR)
   - Employers' Group of the Committee of Agricultural Organisations in the European Union (GEOPA-COPA)
   - European Aggregates Association (UEPG)
   - European Apparel and Textile Organisation (EURATEX)
   - European Association for Coal and Lignite (Euracoal)
   - European Association of Co-operative Banks (EACB)
   - European Association of Employers' Organisations in Hairdressing (Coiffure EU)
   - European Association of Mining Industries (Euromines)
   - European Association of Potash Producers (APEP)
   - European Banking Federation (EBF)
   - European Barge Union (EBU)
   - European Broadcasting Union (EBU)
   - European Chemical Employers Group (ECEG)
   - European Club Association (ECA)
   - European Committee of Sugar Manufacturers (CEFS)
   - European Community Shipowners Association (ECSA)
   - European Confederation of Iron and Steel Industries (Eurofer)
   - European Confederation of Private Employment Agencies (Eurociett)
   - European Confederation of the Footwear Industry (CEC)
   - European Confederation of Woodworking Industries (CEI–Bois)
   - European Construction Industry Federation (FIEC)
   - European Coordination of Independent Producers (CEPI)

- European Federation of Cleaning Industries (EFCI)
- European Federation of Contract Catering Organisations (FERCO)
- European Federation of Education Employers (EFEE)
- European Federation of National Insurance Associations (Insurance Europe)
- European Furniture Industries Confederation (EFIC)
- European Furniture Manufacturers Federation (UEA)
- European Hospital and Healthcare Employers' Association (HOSPEEM)
- European Industrial Minerals Association (IMA)
- European Public Administration Employers (EUPAE)
- European Rail Infrastructure Managers (EIM)
- European Regions Airline Association (ERA)
- European Savings Banks Group (ESBG)
- European Ships and Maritime Equipment Association (SEA Europe)
- European Skippers Organisation (ESO)
- European Telecommunications Network Operators' Association (ETNO)
- European Union of the Natural Gas Industry (EUROGAS)
- Europe's Food and Drink Industry Organisation (FoodDrinkEurope)
- Hotels, Restaurants and Cafés in Europe (HOTREC)
- International Air Carrier Association (IACA)
- International Federation of Film Producers Associations (FIAPF)
- International Federation of Insurance Intermediaries (BIPAR)
- International Road Transport Union (IRU)
- Performing Arts Employers Associations League Europe (PEARLE*)
- Retail, Wholesale and International Trade Representation to the EU (EuroCommerce)
- Union of the Electricity Industry (EURELECTRIC)

5. Sectoral European trade union organisations
   - European Arts and Entertainment Alliance (EAEA)
   - European Cockpit Association (ECA)
   - European Confederation of Independent Trade Unions (CESI)
   - European Federation of Building and Woodworkers (EFBWW)
   - European Federation of Journalists (EFJ)
   - European Federation of Public Service Unions (EPSU)
   - European Federation of Trade Unions in the Food, Agriculture and Tourism Sectors and Allied Branches (EFFAT)
   - European Trade Union Committee for Education (ETUCE)
   - European Transport Workers' Federation (ETF)
   - industriAll European Trade Union (industriAll)
   - International Federation of Actors (FIA)
   - International Federation of Musicians (FIM)
   - International Federation of Professional Footballers' Associations – Division Europe (FIFPro)
   - Union Network International – Europe (UNI Europa)
   - Union Network International – Media and Entertainment International – Europe (EURO MEI)

The list will be adapted as new sectoral social dialogue committees are set up and/or in the light of the study of representativeness

Last update: February 2013

412. The Communication (1993) by the Commission has been widely criticised, in the EP as well as in the ESC.[120] Both institutions are of the opinion that the list of representative organisations has to be reviewed. The ESC feels that a representative organisation should satisfy the following four criteria:

(1) a European representative organisation must be widely spread over the EU. This means that it must have member organisations at the appropriate relevant negotiation level in at least three-quarters of the EU Member States and be seeking to be represented in the others;
(2) the European organisation must have a mandate from its member organisations to negotiate at European level;
(3) all the organisations affiliated to the European organisation, either in their own name or through their member organisations, must be entitled to negotiate in the Member States and must be able to implement conventions concluded at European level in accordance with national practices and usage;
(4) the European organisation must be made up of organisations that are considered in their Member States as representative.

413. Alongside this form of representativeness there is another matter to consider. If the social partners offer an agreement to the Commission and request that it be submitted to the Council for a decision, has the agreement concluded been reached by organisations which represent a sufficient quantity of employers and employees, on the understanding that the social partners have autonomy in their choice of negotiating partners? This question should not be answered using criteria based on figures. What is essential when answering this question is that every representative organisation which fulfils the criteria set out above should be admitted to the talks if it so wishes, at the appropriate relevant negotiation level.

This criticism has been repeated at the occasion of the conclusion of the European Collective Agreements on Parental Leave of 14 December 1995 and of 6 June 1997 on part-time working. Also organisations like UEAPME (the European Union of Crafts and SMEs) or CESI repeated their objections concerning the representative nature of the social partners in negotiations in the framework of the social dialogue. UEAPME indicated that in the absence of a solution, a legal conflict with the Commission seemed inevitable. On 6 September 1996, UEAPME, which claims to represent 6 million SMEs, employing 27,000,000 workers, introduced a claim with the Court of First Instance to annul the Directive of 3 June 1996, which rendered

---

120. Opinion of the ESC on the 'Commission communication concerning the development of the social dialogue at Community level', O.J. C 89/28, 19 March 1997.

binding the Collective Agreement on Parental Leave, as UEAPME considers that it should have been a party to the negotiations.[121]

414. The Commission's position remained unchanged. In a written question[122] regarding the fact in the EU Member States, SMEs account for more than 60 per cent of jobs in the private sector, that the organisation representing such undertakings should take part in the talks, given its important expertise in connection with private sector jobs, and that employers' associations from a number of countries are currently involved in Europe-wide efforts to set up a joint umbrella organisation, the Commission was asked how to ensure that the current tripartite talks become official quadripartite talks, so that the interests of SMEs, the undertakings which actually create jobs, are better represented.

The Commission answered as follows:

> In a recent Communication, the Commission points out that the social dialogue is a key element of the European social model.[123] The economic and political integration of Europe, as well as its social stability, would have been unthinkable without the involvement and active support of the social partners. This Communication presents all the aspects of the social dialogue, the issues it deals with and the way it operates, and raises questions concerning the effectiveness of certain of its aspects, the transparency and profile of its results, and the problem of representativeness.
>
> The social dialogue covers different situations and practices. The Agreement on Social Policy annexed to the EC Treaty makes a very clear distinction between the consultation of the social partners, on the one hand, and the dialogue between them, which may lead to negotiations and the conclusion of agreements at Community level, on the other.
>
> The Commission regularly informs a large number of trade union and employers' organisations of the main lines and content of its social initiatives. In a Communication of 14 December 1993 it gave a list of organisations to be consulted formally under Article 154 TFEU, which includes organisations representing small and medium-sized enterprises (SMEs).
>
> As regards negotiations proper, the Commission sees a need to ensure that the principle of the independence of employers' and workers' organisations is preserved, which means that they must recognise each other as partners authorised to negotiate at European level. It follows that the Commission does not have the power to impose the participation of a particular trade union or employers' organisation at the negotiating table.

---

121. The claim was based on Article 190 TFEU which allows to challenge the legality of acts of the Council by individuals or organisations which have an interest. *See further UEAPME v. Council*, C-135/196, ECR, 1998, 2235.
122. E-0447/97 by Kirsi Piha, O.J. C 319/87, 18 October 1997. *See also* EP: 'Resolution on the Commission communication concerning the development of the social dialogue at Community level', O.J. C 286/338, 22 September 1997. (The EP asks to be granted a power of co-decision within the framework of the legislative procedure, in the form of rejection or approval.)
123. COM(96) 448.

The Commission would remind that the development of the dialogue and the negotiating structures is the exclusive responsibility of the social partners. It encourages the partners to promote a dialogue which is as open and representative as possible by showing openness and flexibility in order to ensure appropriate participation in the negotiations. The Commission is ready to support all positive measures adopted by the partners in this area.

415. Indeed, the notion of 'social partner', as used in Article 154 TFEU, is a legal concept the European Court of Justice may have to interpret. It is self-evident that the meaning which is given to the notion of social partner has to be appropriate in view of the tasks which have been given to the social partners in the relevant Community texts. Indeed, the notion has not been defined in the EC texts.

It follows, however, as well from the texts as from the missions which have been given to the social partners, that there are two levels on which they have to act, namely:

(a) The level of the Member States regarding
 – implementation of directives by the social partners (Article 153(3) TFEU);
 – implementation of agreements, concluded at Union level (Article 155(2) TFEU.
(b) At Union level regarding
 – consultation of management and labour at Union level (Article 154(1) TFEU);
 – the dialogue between management and labour at European level which could lead to relations based on agreements (Article 155 TFEU).

416. Both levels are self-evidently intimately intertwined. Indeed, they concern first the establishment of European legislation, which then has to be transposed into national rule-setting, and secondly European collective agreements, which may, according to national procedures and practices, be implemented at national level. In other words, the notion social partners needs to take both levels into account and not only a single one.

Self-evidently, the criteria which have been elaborated by the International Labour Organisation in its case law concerning the 87 and 98 Conventions on trade union freedom and collective bargaining have to be taken into account, as all the EU Member States are members of the ILO and the above-mentioned Conventions have been ratified by most if not all of them. Trade union freedom, moreover, is retained as such in the Constitution of the ILO.

According to the ILO, employers' associations and trade unions need to be representative. Repeatedly, the ILO's Committee on Freedom of Association has underlined that the determination of the most representative trade union organisation has to be made in an *objective* and *independent* manner, so as to avoid any opportunity for partiality or abuse. Precise and objective criteria for the determination of the representativity should exist in the legislation and such a determination should not be left to governments.

B. Implementation of Directives

417. According to Article 153(3) TFEU a Member State may entrust management and labour, at their joint request, with the implementation of directives adopted pursuant to Article 153.

In this case, the Member State 'must ensure that, no later than the date on which a directive must be transposed, management and labour have introduced the necessary measures by agreement, the Member State being required to take any measure enabling it at any time to be in a position to guarantee the results imposed by that directive' (Art. 153(3) TFEU).

418. For practical purposes this means that directives can be transposed into national law by way of collective bargaining between management and labour at national, inter-industry, level. It presupposes that such collective agreements can have, through one mechanism or another, an effect *erga omnes*, namely become legally binding upon all employers and workers who are meant to be covered by the collective agreement. It also means that the binding effect of the collective agreement should be such that private parties (employer-employees) cannot deviate from them; and also that there is a mechanism through which the directive continues to have effect, even when contracting parties to the collective agreement would have denounced the collective agreement until a new act implementing the directive has been enacted.

419. Article 153(3) TFEU does in fact not add anything new. Implementation of directives by way of collective bargaining was already a current and by the EC accepted practice in such countries as Belgium, where collective agreements, concluded at national inter-industry level, can be extended to the private sector as a whole by a Royal Decree, which means government involvement. These extended agreements are penally sanctioned and have, once announced, at least for the individual normative part of the agreement, a prolonged binding effect, as the individual obligations between employer and employee, under the collective agreement, are legally supposed to have been incorporated in the individual agreements of workers covered by the (extended) collective agreement.

In Belgium, this has been, as said, standing practice. Directives such as those on collective redundancies (1975–1998), on acquired rights in case of transfer of enterprises (1977–2001) and on information and consultation (EWCs 1994), have been transposed into Belgian law, totally or partially, by way of extended collective agreements. It has been a way for the Belgian social partners to demonstrate, with subdued acquiescence by the Belgian Parliament, their social autonomy. It is in this context interesting to note that the Ghent Labour Court of Appeal (Belgium)[124] accepted that an extended collective agreement transposing a directive of which the objective has a binding effect, *in casu* the transfer of enterprises directive of 1977, can change imperatively binding civil law, in this case concerning the transfer of obligations.

---

124. 11 October 1989, *Journal des Tribunaux de Travail*, 1989, 489.

In Belgium, governmental intervention may, however, be needed in order to fully implement the directives, as even extended collective agreements do not necessarily cover public companies, which effect the functioning of the Common Market.

420. This is to say that only some of the industrial relations systems in the Member States of the Union qualify, unless dramatic changes would occur in those countries, *quod non*, to have their collective bargaining systems act as a conveyer belt of directives into national law. Belgium, Germany, France, the Netherlands, to give some examples, may, under certain conditions, be in that league as they have extension procedures in one form or another.

421. Regarding this matter the Communication (1993) of the Commission reads as follows:

> Article 153(3) TFEU states that a signatory Member State 'may entrust management and labour, at their joint request, with the implementation of directives adopted pursuant to paragraph 2'. However, in this case, the Member State 'shall ensure that, no later than the date on which a directive or a decision must be transposed or implemented, management and labour have introduced the necessary measures by agreement, the Member State concerned being required to take any necessary measure enabling it at any time to be in a position to guarantee the results imposed by that directive or that decision'.

This provision establishes, in the context of the Agreement, the general principle that directives may be implemented by collective agreement. This principle has been recognised in the case law of the Court of Justice.[125] It is also in line with the implementation requirements of the International Labour Organisation[126] and the Council of Europe.[127]

Article 153(3) TFEU does not require the Member States to introduce any particular or special procedures or that any explicit formal terms of reference be given to the social partners; nor is there any need for them to submit a joint request prior to negotiations between them on an agreement for implementation of the directive. The actual conclusion of an agreement and its forwarding to the competent authority of the Member State should be regarded as a tacit joint request within the meaning of the first paragraph of Article 153(3) TFEU.

422. The Communication continues:

> According to Article 153(3) TFEU the Member State concerned remains responsible for ensuring that, no later than the date on which a directive must be transposed an agreement is made the social partners have introduced the necessary measures by agreement and for taking 'any necessary measure enabling it at any time to be in a position to guarantee the results imposed by

---

125. Case 91/81 (1982) ECR 2133; Case 193/83 (1985) ECR 427.
126. ILO Conventions Nos. 100, 101, 106, 111, 171, 172, etc.
127. Article 35(1) of the European Social Charter.

that directive or that decision'. This wording is a slightly amended version of corresponding provisions in certain directives.[128]

C. Social Dialogue (Articles 154–155)

423. The social dialogue, in the sense of meetings and exchange of views between management and labour at Union level, which may eventually lead to contractual relations, including collective agreements, has become an outspoken and expressly foreseen priority of the European Union. The Commission, it is stated in Article 154(1) TFEU, 'shall take any relevant measure to facilitate their dialogue by ensuring balanced support for the parties.' This language and approach underline the voluntarism of the industrial relation system the founding fathers wanted to develop at Union level. This tendency is reinforced by the possibility to conclude European collective agreements and by giving the social partners the right of the firstborn to create European law as will be described in the following paragraphs.

D. Community-wide Agreements (Article 155)

1. The Agreement of 31 October 1991

424. On the occasion of the Maastricht summit sufficient legitimacy was finally given to European collective bargaining. This was made possible by a historic agreement between UNICE, CEEP and the ETUC, concluded in Brussels on 31 October 1991, which paved the way for Maastricht – just in time for the summit. That agreement was elaborated with the dynamic support and under the competent guidance of the Commission and especially of the then Director-General of DG V, Mr. J. Degimbe.[129]

425. An agreement was possible due to different factors, in particular to the divergent interests of the parties involved, namely of the Commission, of the employers' association and of the trade unions.

The Commission had indeed to conclude that the Union approach to social policy, through the Community Social Charter of 1989 and the Action Programme, had not been successful and was looking for other ways to provide the Community with a fair social face.

The social partners, employers as well as trade union representatives, had to face the fact that their input in the Community legislative process, also due to the well-known democratic deficit, was rather minimal.

---

128. Article 2(1) of Council Directive 92/56/EEC of 24 June 1992; Article 9(1) of Council Directive 91/533/EEC of 14 October 1991.
129. R. Delarue, 'Europees collectief overleg: tussen euforie en eurofobie'. *De Gids op Maatschappelijk Gebied*, 1991, pp. 1083–1094.

The employers were moreover in a sense afraid of Union legislation, especially labour law directives which might impose undue restrictive obligations on business; at the same time UNICE's representatives got a little bit tired of formulating polite no's to proposals in the social field.

Trade unions, on the other hand, were eagerly looking forward to play a more effective role at a European level in the furthering of the interests of their members and the workers, as the ETUC's Luxemburg Congress had clearly indicated.

Mr. Z.J.A. Tyskiewicz, the then Secretary General of UNICE, explains as follows:[130]

> Why did UNICE accept the idea of European-level negotiations? Why did we go down that road? Why in a Europe where collective bargaining tends to move away from the centre as far down as the plant level are we recentralising bargaining and bringing it up to the European level? The reason is that the employers were convinced that Maastricht would result in much wider powers for the Commission and the Council in the social field: a great extension of qualified majority voting, and therefore a greater number of legislative acts in the social field. Experience so far in EC social legislation is that the legislator is getting it wrong.
>
> The legislator is being too detailed, too prescriptive, is trying to fix everything from Brussels. We became convinced that the only way to stop him or her would be by negotiating some of these issues ourselves. We felt we would be better custodians of subsidiarity than the legislator. We were also quite convinced the unions would be too. The reason is that our members and theirs will be breathing down our necks because they do not want to lose national sovereignty. Naturally they do not want the European level organisations treading on their territory. That is very healthy. They will allow us to go along only with broad framework type agreements, rather than the prescriptive and detailed type of legislation that we are getting from the Commission.
>
> That was our reason for agreeing to negotiate. The unions' reason was different. Of course they can get more out of the European legislator than they can out of European employers. But for them it was very important to consolidate their role at European level because in many cases they are losing power and influence at national level and this was a way of regaining a part of that power at European level. Although their motivation and ours was not the same, we reached the same destination point.

426. *De facto* quite an evolution took place as well in the ETUC as in UNICE. Until the 7th Congress (1991) the ETUC was mainly a coordinating body of the 44 associated national confederations. The 15 sectoral committees were not integrated in the decision-making structure. The British TUC and the Scandinavian unions wanted to continue this way. Others, like the Belgian unions, wanted to go a step further and build a supranational structure. This was done at the Luxemburg Congress of May 1991. The sectoral committees became integrated in the ETUC, the financial means of the European union increased and the decision-making structure

---

130. 'Social Policy after Maastricht. The point of view of the employers', November 1992 (mimeo).

strengthened. Without those changes the Agreement of 31 October 1991 would for mere organisational purposes practically not have been possible.

In the beginning UNICE was opposed to European bargaining. Its official credo was that aside from some specific fields like health and safety, free movement of labour, vocational training and the like, labour matters were to be dealt with at a national level. Within UNICE, however, the mentality slowly changed as some European labour law seemed to be unavoidable in the long run. Better to join. The British CBI was, however, resolutely opposed to eventual European bargaining: consultation yes, negotiation no. The British employers feared that European agreements might lead to mandatory national negotiations in Britain. Needless to say the Conservative government was not too happy either. Other confederations, like the Greek and the Portuguese ones, also had doubts. The majority however, led by the Belgians, the French and the Italians, was of the opinion that UNICE should play a constructive role. It was that group that finally won.

The social partners, the ETUC included, will have to further supra-nationalise their decision-making structure. It is impossible to continue to work on a basis of unanimous decision-making: also here majority decisions are called for.

427. These divergent interests paved the way for an agreement whereby the Commission and the social partners (gladly) accepted to increase the role of the Commission and the consultative role of the partners, to promote their dialogue and to give management and labour the right for a first try to elaborate European social minimum standards by way of agreements, thus getting in a sense preeminence over the EP, which is not involved in that part of the legislative process. Only if the social partners would not succeed and/or their proposal not be implemented by a Council decision, would the legislative process resume its normal course. One of the great technical difficulties was self-evidently the question of how to arrive at a procedure whereby those collective agreements would become binding *erga omnes*, namely for all concerned employers and employees, throughout the Community.

This Brussels agreement between the social partners of 31 October 1991 paved, as said, the way for the acceptance at the Maastricht summit of Articles 3(4) and 4 which contain the legal basis for collective bargaining at European level. This does however not take away that, as already indicated above, enormous complex legal problems remain to be solved as the collective agreements themselves are a complex institution, even more so at a European level.

2. The Maastricht Deal

428. The Maastricht Agreement concerning the Community's future social policy on the basis of a reinforced dialogue between the social partners reads as follows:

> if at the occasion of consultations between the Commission and the Social Partners on the possible direction of Community action or advisable Community action, the partners express the feeling that they would like to deal themselves with the involved problem, they can express to the Commission their

wish to do so and initiate the procedure provided for in Article 4. The duration of the procedure shall not exceed *nine months*, unless the management and labour concerned and the Commission decide jointly to extend it (Articles 3(3–4)).

429. Article 155 TFEU which integrated the Maastricht Agreement, thus lays down the groundwork for European collective agreements. 'Should management and labour so desire,' it reads, 'the dialogue between them at Union level may lead to contractual relations including agreements.'

Two ways are foreseen to implement these agreements concluded at Union level: they shall be implemented either:

(1) in accordance with the procedures and practices specific to management and labour and the Member States; or
(2) in matters covered by Article 153 TFEU, at the joint request of the signatory parties, by a Council decision on a proposal from the Commission. The EP shall be informed (Article 155(2) TFEU).

a. Implementation in accordance with National Practice

430. Implementing European agreements between the social partners in accordance with national practice does not imply any obligation on the Member States to apply the agreements directly or to work out rules for their transposition, nor any obligation to amend national legislation in force to facilitate their implementation. This means that the European agreements will have to be implemented in the Member States through the collective bargaining system which is prevalent in each country. It signifies also clearly that the Member States at this stage do not want to change the national systems of bargaining in any way.

This way of doing things engages self-evidently a number of intricate problems to which we will come back later in section IV of this General Introduction.

b. Implementation by a Council Decision

431. The Council can, at the joint request of the signatory parties and on a proposal from the Commission, implement an agreement by a decision, whether this is a regulation, a directive or even, theoretically at least, a recommendation. The Council shall act by qualified majority, except where the agreement in question contains one or more provisions relating to one of the areas referred to in Article 153(2) TFEU, in which case it will act unanimously (Article 155(2) TFEU). Quite a number of problems arise here too, which we will discuss in section IV. In order to do so the 'Union agreements' have to be put in a more general perspective and some explanatory remarks are due.

3. The Communication of the Commission (1993)

a. Concluding an Agreement

432. According to the Communication (1993):

> the social partners consulted by the Commission on the content of a proposal for Community action may deliver an opinion or, where appropriate, a recommendation to the Commission. Alternatively, they may also, as stated in Article 154 TFEU, 'inform the Commission of their wish to initiate the process provided for in Article 155 TFEU'. Should they decide on this latter course of action, they may embark, independently, upon a process of negotiation which could lead to the establishment of a direct agreement between the parties. The negotiation process may take up to nine months and may be extended with the agreement of the Commission.
>
> The question of whether an agreement between social partners representing certain occupational categories or sectors constitutes a sufficient basis for the Commission to suspend its legislative action will have to be examined on a case-by-case basis with particular regard to the nature and scope of the proposal and the potential impact of any agreement between the social partners concerned on the issue which the proposals seek to address.
>
> In their independent negotiations, the social partners are in no way required to restrict themselves to the content of the proposal in preparation within the Commission or merely to making amendments to it, bearing in mind, however, that Union action can clearly not go beyond the areas covered by the Commission's proposal. The social partners concerned will be those who agree to negotiate with each other. Such agreement is entirely in the hands of the different organisations. However, the Commission takes the view that the provisions regarding small and medium-sized undertakings referred to in Article 153(2) TFEU should be borne in mind by organisations which are signatory to an agreement.
>
> The negotiations may not exceed nine months, unless the social partners concerned and the Commission decide jointly to extend them. The Agreement between the Eleven has associated the Commission in this decision on extension and empowered it to assess the two parties' chances of arriving at an agreement within the period set. This will prevent any prolongation of fruitless negotiations which would ultimately block the Commission's ability to regulate. In making such an assessment, the Commission will respect fully the social partners' independence.

433. The Communication continues:

> At or before the end of this nine-month period, therefore, the social partners have to submit to the Commission a report taking stock of the negotiations. This report may inform the Commission that:

(a) they concluded an agreement and jointly request the Commission to propose that the Council adopt a decision on implementation, or
(b) having concluded an agreement between themselves, they prefer to implement it in accordance with the procedures and practices specific to management and labour and to the Member States, or
(c) they envisage pursuing the negotiations beyond the nine months and accordingly request the Commission to decide with them upon a new deadline, or
(d) they are unable to reach an agreement. Where point d) applies, the Commission will look into the possibility of proposing, in the light of the work already done, a legislative instrument in the field in question and will forward the result of its deliberations to the Council. The Economic and Social Committee and the European Parliament will also be consulted in accordance with the procedures laid down in the Treaty.

At any event, and without prejudicing the principle of the autonomy of the social partners (a principle which underlies Articles 154 and 155 TFEU), the Commission feels that the European Parliament must be fully informed at all stages of any consultation or negotiation procedure involving the social partners.

434. Consultation of the Member States will take place as in the past. As regards the situation in the EFTA countries, the point has already been made that the Protocol forms parts of the *acquis communautaire* like any other provision of the EU Treaty. Thus, a decision taken on the basis of Article 155 TFEU may be extended to the EFTA countries too. In practice, the social partners' organisations normally cover the EFTA countries, so that they are *de facto* integrated at all stages of the consultation procedure, with negotiation being a matter for the social partners.

b. The Implementation of the Agreements

435. Agreements concluded at Union level are to be implemented:

(a) either in accordance with the procedures and practices specific to management and labour and the Member States; this provision is subject to the following declaration:
(b) The High Contracting Parties declare that the first of the arrangements for application of the agreements between management and labour at Union level – referred to in Article 155(2) – will consist in developing, by collective bargaining according to the rules of each Member State, the content of the agreements, and that consequently this arrangement implies no obligation on the Member States to apply the agreements directly or to work out rules for their transposition, nor any obligation to amend national legislation in force to facilitate their implementation.
(c) or, in matters covered by Article 154 TFEU, at the joint request of the signatory parties, by a Council decision on a proposal from the Commission;

(d) the Council is to act by qualified majority, except where the agreement in question contains one or more provisions relating to one of the areas referred to in Article 154(3) TFEU, in which case it is to act unanimously.

In the event of negotiations resulting in an agreement that the social partners decide to implement via the voluntary route, the terms of this agreement will bind their members and will affect only them and only in accordance with the practices and procedures specific to them in their respective Member States.

c. The Council

436. The Commission's view is that implementing an agreement concluded at Union level by means of a Council decision on a proposal from the Commission at the joint request of the social partners, leads to the adoption of a decision on the agreement as concluded.

> By virtue of its role as guardian of the Treaties, the Commission will prepare proposals for decisions to the Council following consideration of the representative status of the contracting parties, their mandate and the "legality" of each clause in the collective agreement in relation to Union law, and the provisions regarding small and medium-sized undertakings set out in Article 153(2) TFEU. At all events, the Commission intends to provide an explanatory memorandum on any proposal presented to the Council in this area, giving its comments and assessment of the agreement concluded by the social partners.
>
> Where it considers that it should not present a proposal for a decision to implement an agreement to the Council, the Commission will immediately inform the signatory parties of the reasons for its decision.

437. The Communication of 1993 states:

> Under Article 155(2) TFEU, the Commission is not legally required to consult the European Parliament on requests made to it by the social partners concerning implementation of an agreement by means of a Council decision. However, the Commission has to inform Parliament and to send it the text of the agreement, together with its proposal for a decision and the explanatory memorandum, so that Parliament may, should it consider it advisable, deliver its opinion to the Commission and to the Council.
>
> The Council decision must be limited to making binding the provisions of the agreement concluded between the social partners, so the text of the agreement would not form part of the decision, but would be annexed thereto.
>
> If the Council decides, in accordance with the procedures set out in the last subparagraph of Article 155(2) TFEU, not to implement the agreement as concluded by the social partners, the Commission will withdraw its proposal for a decision and will examine, in the light of the work done, whether a legislative instrument in the area in question would be appropriate.

4. The Collective Agreement on Parental Leave of 14 December 1995, revised 2009[131]

438. The foundations and steps leading to the conclusion of this agreement and its implementation by way of a directive were as follows:

– management and labour may, as said, request jointly that agreements at Community level be implemented by a Council decision on a proposal from the Commission; – paragraph 16 of the Community Charter of the Fundamental Social Rights of
Workers on equal treatment for men and women provides, *inter alia*, that 'measures should also be developed enabling men and women to reconcile their occupational and family obligations';
– the Council, despite the existence of a broad consensus, had not been able to act on the proposal for a directive on parental leave for family reasons, as amended on 15 November 1984;
– the Commission, in accordance with Article 154(2) TFEU, consulted management and labour on the possible direction of Community action with regard to reconciling working and family life;
– the Commission, considering after such consultation that Community action was desirable, once again consulted management and labour on the substance of the envisaged proposal in accordance with Article 154(3) TFEU;
– the general cross-industry organisations (UNICE, CEEP and the ETUC) informed the Commission in their joint letter of 5 July 1995 of their desire to initiate the procedure provided for by Article 155 TFEU;
– the said cross-industry organisations concluded on their own, on 14 December 1995, a framework agreement on parental leave and they have forwarded to the Commission their joint request to implement this framework agreement by a Council Decision on a proposal from the Commission in accordance with Article 155(2) TFEU;
– the Commission then drafted its proposal for a Directive, taking into account the representative status of the signatory parties, their mandate and the legality of the clauses of the framework agreement and compliance with the relevant provisions concerning small and medium-sized undertakings;
– the Commission, in accordance with its Communication of 14 December 1993 concerning the implementation of the Protocol on social policy, informed the European Parliament by sending it the text of the framework agreement, accompanied by its proposal for a Directive and the explanatory memorandum; – the Commission also informed the Economic and Social Committee by sending it the text of the framework agreement, accompanied by its proposal for a Directive and the explanatory memorandum;
– The Council implemented the Agreement on Parental Leave by way of a Directive of 3 June 1996.

---

131. This Framework Agreement was revised by the Social Partners by agreement of 18 June 2009.

5. The Agreement on Part-time Work of 6 June 1997

439. Negotiations between the social partners started on 21 October 1996, when the Commission decided to involve the social partners on this issue as the adoption of a Directive on 'atypical work' did not seem possible.

The agreement does not cover all atypical workers which the ETUC would have liked (e.g. also temporary workers, contracts of a short duration, seasonal work, homework, telework), but only part-time work.

The purpose of the agreement is two-fold:

(a) to provide for the removal of discrimination against part-time workers and to improve the quality of part-time work; and
(b) to facilitate the development of part-time work on a voluntary basis and to contribute to the flexible organisation of working time in a manner which takes into account the needs of employers and workers.

The agreement was implemented by Council Directive 97/81 EC of 15 December 1997.[132]

6. The Framework Agreement on Fixed-term Work of 18 March 1999

440. As the Council of Social Ministers had been unable to reach a decision on the proposal for a Directive on certain employment relationships with regard to distortions of competition, or on the proposal for a Directive on certain employment relationships with regard to working conditions, the Commission once again consulted management and labour on the substance of the envisaged proposal. The general cross-industry organisations UNICE, CEEP and the ETUC informed the Commission of their desire to initiate the procedure leading to a collective agreement. On 18 March 1999, they concluded a framework agreement on fixed-term work.

With the agreement, management and labour wish to give particular attention to fixed-term work, while at the same time indicating that it is their intention to consider the need for a similar agreement relating to temporary agency work.

The signatory parties set out the general principles and minimum requirements for fixed-term employment contracts and employment relationships with the aim to improve the quality of fixed-term work by ensuring the application of the principle of non-discrimination and establishing a framework to prevent abuse arising from the use of successive fixed-term employment contracts or relationships.

The agreement was implemented by Directive 1999/70/EC of 28 June 1999.[133]

---

132. Concerning the Framework Agreement on part-time work concluded by UNICE, CEEP and the ETUC, O.J. L 14/9, 20 January 1998.
133. Council Directive 1999/70/EC of 28 June 1999 concerning the framework agreement on fixed-term work concluded by ETUC, UNICE and CEEP, O.J. L 175, 10 July 1999.

General Introduction, Ch. 3, Competences of the EU

7. The Voluntary Agreement on Telework of 16 July 2002

441. A new strategy between the social partners in the area of the social dialogue was embarked upon, at the initiative of UNICE, namely by the conclusion of a voluntary agreement on telework.

The agreement reads in its preamble as follows.

> In the context of the European employment strategy, the European Council invited the social partners to negotiate agreements modernising the organisation of work, including flexible working arrangements, with the aim of making undertakings productive and competitive and achieving the necessary balance between flexibility and security.

442. The European Commission, in its second stage consultation of social partners on modernising and improving employment relations, invited the social partners to start negotiations on telework. On 20 September 2001, the ETUC (and the liaison committee EUROCADRES/CEC), UNICE/UEAPME and CEEP announced their intention to start negotiations aimed at an agreement to be implemented by the members of the signatory parties in the Member States and in the countries of the European Economic Area. Through them, they wished to contribute to preparing the transition to a knowledge-based economy and society as agreed by the European Council in Lisbon.

443. This voluntary agreement aims at establishing a general framework at the European level to be implemented by the members of the signatory parties in accordance with the national procedures and practices specific to management and labour. The signatory parties also invite their member organisations in candidate countries to implement this agreement.

Implementation of this agreement does not constitute valid grounds to reduce the general level of protection afforded to workers in the field of this agreement. When implementing this agreement, the members of the signatory parties avoid unnecessary burdens on SMEs.

This agreement does not prejudice the right of social partners to conclude, at the appropriate level, including European level, agreements adapting and/or complementing this agreement in a manner, which will take note of the specific needs of the social partners concerned.'

444. The implementation and follow up read as follows:

> In the context of Article 155 TFEU, this European framework agreement shall be implemented by the members of UNICE/UEAPME, CEEP and ETUC (and the liaison committee EUROCADRES/CEC) in accordance with the procedures and practices specific to management and labour in the Member States.
>
> This implementation will be carried out within three years after the date of signature of this agreement.
>
> Member organisations will report on the implementation of this agreement to an *ad hoc* group set up by the signatory parties, under the responsibility of

the social dialogue committee. This *ad hoc* group will prepare a joint report on the actions of implementation taken. This report will be prepared within four years after the date of signature of this agreement.

In case of questions on the content of this agreement, member organisations involved can separately or jointly refer to the signatory parties.

The signatory parties shall review the agreement five years after the date of signature if requested by one of the signatory parties.

445. This agreement raises many questions as well of a legal as of a political nature.

Legal questions are first, what is a voluntary agreement? Indeed, all agreements are voluntary. It probably means in this context that the agreement is not legally binding, so that it has only 'moral consequences' for the parties involved and is not enforceable before the courts. In this case the agreement would constitute a sort of voluntary code of conduct. No legal action would be possible against a signatory party or a member in case a member would not implement the agreement.

The second question is whether the signatory parties can oblige their constituent members to implement the agreement. This will depend on the mandate the signatory parties have from their members. This does not seem to be the case, so that also here no legal obligations can be ascertained.

Regarding the interpretation of the agreement, member organisations can refer to the signatory parties.

The conclusion is self-evident. The agreement imposes no legal obligation whatsoever and depends completely on the good will of the member organisations, which may implement the agreement at their will.

446. Moreover, many difficulties arise. Implementation will take place according to national practice. For countries, where nation-wide collective bargaining is prevalent and extension procedures are available this might be no problem. In those countries, workers may enjoy the rights which are contained in the European Agreement on Telework. For other countries, where those mechanisms do not exist, like the UK, national collective bargaining may provide only a very partial answer and codes of conduct may be another way of implementing the agreement.

So much to say that this presents very soft law for which the European Court will not have to intervene as there is no legally binding European rule subject to interpretation. Nor is there a role for European Parliament in this scenario.

So much to say that a European Regulation on European collective bargaining is necessary, unless this new road of 'voluntarism' is one of the ways to modernise European labour law, namely by way of non-enforceable agreements. This is, however, to my mind, too soft and undermines further the already weak European social model. The ETUC was right to question this development; but the European Commission hailed the agreement as a landmark deal. 'Not only will this initiative benefit both workers and businesses, but it is the first European agreement to be implemented by the social partners themselves.'

8. Framework Agreement on Work-related Stress of 8 October 2004[134]

447. This agreement is, like the one on telework, a voluntary agreement. It will be implemented in accordance with the procedures and practices specific to individual countries rather than by an EU Directive, aims to establish a framework within which employers and employee representatives can work together to prevent, identify and combat stress at work.

The signatories were: for trade unions, the European Trade Union Confederation (ETUC) and the Council of European Professional and Managerial Staff (EUROCADRES)/European Confederation of Executives and Managerial Staff (CEC) liaison committee; and for employers the Union of Industrial and Employers' Confederations of Europe (UNICE), the European Association of Craft, Small and Medium-Sized Enterprises (UEAPME) and the European Centre of Enterprises with Public Participation and of Enterprises of General Economic Interest (CEEP).

This accord has been signed in the context of the social partners' 2003–2005 work programme. The talks began on 18 September 2003. An agreement was formally signed on 8 October 2004.

The signatory parties to the stress agreement want it to be implemented in accordance with procedures and practices in individual countries rather than by a Council decision and give a deadline of three years for implementation (8 October 2007).

The member organisations of the signatory parties will be obliged to report to the EU-level Social Dialogue Committee on the implementation of the accord. The Social Dialogue Committee will, during the three years that follow the signature of the agreement, prepare an annual table summarising its implementation and prepare a full report during the fourth year following signature.

Any questions on the content of the agreement can be referred jointly or separately by member organisations to the signatory parties, which will reply either jointly or separately. Unnecessary burdens on small and medium-sized enterprises should be avoided when implementing the agreement. The accord also states that its implementation does not constitute valid grounds to reduce the general level of protection afforded to workers in the areas covered by the agreement.

Any time after five years from signature, the signatory parties will, if one of them requests this, evaluate and review the agreement. The accord does not prejudice the right of the social partners to conclude, at the appropriate level, agreements adapting or complementing this agreement.

9. The Framework Agreement on Harassment and Violence at Work (2007)

448. On 26 April 2007, the new Framework Agreement on harassment and violence at work was signed by the general secretaries of the European social partner organisations: the European Trade Union Confederation (ETUC); the Confederation of European Business (BUSINESSEUROPE); the European Association of Craft, Small and Medium-Sized Enterprises (UEAPME); and the European Centre

---

134. Andrea Broughton, IRS, 'Social partners sign work-related stress agreement', www.eiro.eurofound.ie, 2004.

of Enterprises with Public Participation and of Enterprises of General Economic Interest (CEEP). This is the sixth framework agreement to be signed by the social partners since the beginning of European social dialogue 20 years ago. It is also the third voluntary and autonomous agreement to be concluded, following the agreements on telework in 2002 and work-related stress in 2004.

Negotiations on the agreement began in the wake of an official European Commission consultation of the social partners in January 2005, as required by the EC Treaty prior to presenting social legislation. The successful completion of the agreement came about after 10 months of negotiations. The decision-making bodies of the European social partner organisations approved the final text of the agreement in December 2006. It was the task of the national social partners in all EU Member States to adopt the agreement within a three-year period, according to their own procedures and practices.

a. Statement by Social Partners

449. In a joint press release issued on the same day the agreement was signed, the social partners unequivocally condemn harassment and violence 'in all their forms' and recognise that harassment and violence can potentially affect any workplace and any worker, 'even if in practice some groups and sectors can be more at risk'. The parties also describe the successful conclusion of their negotiations as a major achievement for the European Social Dialogue Work Programme 2006–2008.

With the signature of the agreement, the parties aim to increase awareness and understanding on the issues of harassment and violence at work, and to provide employers and employees with an action-oriented framework to identify and manage problems of this kind. The fundamental objective of the agreement is to prevent, identify and manage problems related to harassment and violence at the workplace.

b. Aims of Agreement

450. Under the terms of the agreement, the social partners are required to ensure the following objectives:

– enterprises should have a clear statement outlining that harassment and violence at the workplace will not be tolerated and specifying the procedure to be followed if problems arise;
– responsibility for determining, reviewing and monitoring the appropriate measures rests with the employer, in consultation with workers and/or their representatives; – provisions are put in place to deal with cases of violence by third parties, where appropriate.

c. Implementation and Follow-up

451. In the context of Article 155 TFEU, this autonomous European framework agreement commits the members of BUSINESSEUROPE, UEAPME, CEEP and ETUC (and the liaison committee EUROCADRES/CEC) to implement it in accordance with the procedures and practices specific to management and labour in the Member States and in the countries of the European Economic Area.

The signatory parties also invite their member organisations in candidate countries to implement this agreement.

The implementation of this agreement will be carried out within three years after the date of signature of this agreement.

Member organisations will report on the implementation of this agreement to the Social Dialogue Committee. During the first three years after the date of signature of this agreement, the Social Dialogue Committee will prepare and adopt a yearly table summarising the on-going implementation of the agreement. A full report on the implementation actions taken will be prepared by the Social Dialogue Committee and adopted by the European social partners during the fourth year.

452. The signatory parties shall evaluate and review the agreement any time after the five years following the date of signature, if requested by one of them.

In case of questions on the content of this agreement, member organisations involved can jointly or separately refer to the signatory parties, who will jointly or separately reply.

When implementing this agreement, the members of the signatory parties avoid unnecessary burdens on SMEs.

Implementation of this agreement does not constitute valid grounds to reduce the general level of protection afforded to workers in the field of this agreement.

453. This agreement does not prejudice the right of social partners to conclude, at the appropriate level, including the European level, agreements adapting and/or complementing this agreement in a manner which will take note of the specific needs of the social partners concerned.

The agreement comes in the context of increasing recognition of the psychological health problems at work that are caused or worsened by harassment and violence, including bullying. According to the Fourth European Working Conditions Survey, carried out by the European Foundation for the Improvement of Living and Working Conditions in 2005 and published in 2007, one in 20 workers had been exposed to bullying and/or harassment in the workplace during the previous 12-month period. A similar proportion had reported being the victim of violence, although such action was more likely to have been perpetrated by people outside the workplace, such as customers or clients, than by colleagues. Some groups of workers are considered to be at greater risk than others, in particular women, white-collar workers and those working in large companies.[135]

---

135. Sonia McKay, 'Social partners sign agreement to combat harassment and violence at work' Working Lives Research Institute, EIRO.

10. The Framework Agreement on Inclusive Labour Market (2010)[136]

454. On 25 March 2010, the EU-level cross-sector social partners concluded a new agreement on achieving an inclusive labour market. The agreement sets out the main challenges and develops a range of actions that the social partners can take to help disadvantaged people to enter, remain and develop in the labour market. The member organisations of the signatory parties have three years to implement the agreement, and an implementation report will be drawn up in 2014.

The parties involved included the European Trade Union Confederation (ETUC), the European Centre of Enterprises with Public Participation and of Enterprises of General Economic Interest (Centre européen des entreprises à participation publique et des entreprises d'intérêt économique général, CEEP), the employer organisation BUSINESSEUROPE and the European Association of Craft, Small and Medium-sized Enterprises (Union Européenne de l'artisanat et des petites et moyennes enterprises, UEAPME).

a. Aims of Agreement

455. The agreement sets out to provide a general framework, focusing on what can be done to enhance labour market inclusion. It has three main aims, namely to:

– consider access, return, retention and development, with a view to achieving full integration of individuals in the labour market;
– increase awareness, understanding and knowledge of employers, workers and their representatives of the benefits of inclusive labour markets;
– provide workers, employers and their representatives with an 'action-oriented' framework to identify obstacles to inclusive labour markets and solutions to overcome them.

b. Main Obstacles to an Inclusive Labour Market

456. The agreement identifies a non-exhaustive list of potential barriers to an inclusive labour market, all of which have the potential to affect the full integration of individuals into the labour market. These potential obstacles are:

– the availability of information about jobseekers and about the jobs that are available;
– recruitment-related obstacles such as recruitment methods that do not attract a wide diversity of applicants;
– training-related obstacles – for example, investment in or access to learning opportunities is identified as important, as is recognition of individual skills, competences and professional experience, and the match between the offer of training and the needs of the labour market;

---

136. Andrea Broughton, "EU social partners reach agreement on inclusive labour market" *EIROnline*, 1 July 2010.

– the responsibilities and attitudes of employers, workers, their representatives and jobseekers;
– working life issues such as working conditions and work organisation, worklife balance policies and career development prospects.

c. Potential Actions

457. The agreement lists the relevant actions that the social partners could take, as follows:

– organising awareness-raising campaigns and action plans to improve the image of economic sectors or occupations;
– organising awareness-raising campaigns and tools to promote the diversity of the workforce;
– disseminating information about the availability of jobs and training schemes;
– cooperating with the third sector – that is, charities and voluntary, not for profit or non-governmental organisations – to support those who have particular difficulties in relation to the labour market;
– cooperating with education and training systems to better match the needs of the individual and those of the labour market;
– implementing specific and effective recruitment methods and induction policies and ensuring the right working conditions;
– introducing jointly agreed individual competence development plans for workers; – improving transparency and transferability for workers and for companies;
– promoting more and better apprenticeship and traineeship contracts.

d. Key Recommendations

458. The annex to the agreement contains a list of recommendations to public authorities and other actors, urging them to design and implement comprehensive policies to promote inclusive labour markets, in the following areas:

– the extent and quality of specific transitional measures for people who encounter difficulties in the labour market;
– the effectiveness of employment and career advice services;
– education and training;
– the adequacy of investment in territorial development;
– access to transport, care, housing and education;
– starting, sustaining and expanding businesses;
– tax and benefit systems

11. Framework of Actions on Youth Employment (11 June 2013)

459. On 11 June 2013, ETUC, BUSINESSEUROPE, UEAPME and CEEP presented their Framework of Actions on Youth Employment, resulting from social dialogue negotiations.

With youth unemployment rates currently at 24.4 per cent in the euro area and 23.5 per cent in the EU27, urgent and determined action is needed. Europe cannot afford such a waste of talent.

This Framework of Actions is the first priority of the European Social Dialogue Work Programme for 2012–2014. With it, the European social partners aim to promote solutions to reduce youth unemployment. They call on national social partners, public authorities and other stakeholders to act together and achieve concrete progress in favour of youth employment.

460. A multi-pronged approach is needed to foster dynamic, open and mobile labour markets for young people with measures and appropriate resources focusing on the creation of more and better jobs, high quality learning outcomes, and better match between skills supply and demand, including through the spread of work-based learning across Europe.

461. This Framework of Actions is based on existing and new practices linked to the four priorities identified: learning, transition, employment and entrepreneurship. The European social partners aim to promote the most effective initiatives identified across Europe that could be used as inspiration for designing solutions by national social partners in their respective contexts. Recommendations to other relevant actors such as the EU institutions and Member States are also included.

National social partners will report on their activities annually over the next three years.

E. The Judgment of the Court of First Instance of 17 June 1998[137]

462. UEAPME did introduce a request to annul Directive 96/34 EC of 3 June 1996, which has implemented the European collective agreement of 6 November 1995 concerning parental leave. In this way UEAPME wanted to obtain its recognition as a full-fledged European social partner. UEAPME is of the opinion that it has the right, as the representative of the SMEs in Europe, to participate in the negotiating and conclusion of European wide collective agreements.

The Court, however, refuted UEAPME's claim on the following grounds: according to the standing European law, no one of the social partners has a right to participate in the negotiations. Moreover, UNICE also has SMEs among its members. So, the Court concluded, these enterprises are adequately represented.

It will surprise no one that we deeply regret this judgment. First, from a democratic point of view. Indeed, one expects from the social partners that they replace in a sense the democratically elected EP in this legislative process. How then can the Court refuse UEAPME at the table of negotiations, since it organises the larger part of the SMEs? Also from the point of view of employment, the Court's decision has to be rejected. Indeed, everyone recognises that it is the SMEs which are the job creators *par excellence*, and yet they are kept at arm's length.

It is, however, especially in the area of fundamental social rights that this judgment is totally inadequate. The right to collectively bargain is a fundamental right, belonging to the core of fundamental rights laid down by the ILO. The already men

---

137. *UEAPME* v. *Council*, T-135/96, ECR, 1998, 2235.

tioned Conventions 87 and 98 deal explicitly with freedom of association and collective bargaining. All EU Member States, as well as the national social partners, belong to the ILO. The ILO Conventions, moreover, are a part of the general principles of law the Court has to respect and apply. In other words, when the criteria for representativeness are not clearly spelled out at European level, the Court has to look for inspiration in the ILO Conventions. The ILO has repeatedly said that the criteria of representativity need to be objective, precise and known beforehand. The Court should have directed the Commission to establish these criteria and to respect them.

Pending legal procedures introduced by UEAPME concerning the directives implementing framework agreements have, however, been put to an end according to a Cooperation agreement concluded between UNICE and UEAPME, 12 November 1998.[138]

The Framework Agreement on Parental Leave (revised) of 18 June 2009 was also signed by BUSINESSEUROPE, CEEP, ETUC as by UEAPME.

VI. Evaluation: a Scenario for Social Dumping and a Dual Society

A. *Macroeconomic: Inflation and NAIRU*

463. The EMU intends to maintain a non-inflationary economy. Such an economy presupposes a certain degree of unemployment. So it is that a certain level of increasing unemployment is 'the instrument' to contain inflationary tendencies.

The EMU approach translates a certain economic vision, represented by the Chicago school, favouring supply-side economics, which has gradually conquered the world since the beginning of the 1970s, first the UK and the USA, then Western Europe and later Latin-America, Africa, Asia and since the beginning of the 1990s, Central and Eastern Europe.

Supply-side economics are not – in contrast to the economy policy inspired by Keynes – centred on demand and full employment, but directed at the control of inflation. This theory accepts a so-called national degree of unemployment, which is, so the argument goes, mainly the consequence of structural rigidities on the labour market.

When inflation is threatening to accelerate, the (independent) Central Bank will intervene and eventually raise the interest rate. This has a negative effect on employment.

The idea is that the economy will become overheated when unemployment is too low. The leading economic school is of the opinion that accelerating inflation is unavoidable unless a certain number of workers are unemployed.

The minimum employment needed to check inflation is called NAIRU, which stands for 'non-accelerating inflation rate of unemployment'. The minimum is not a standard, but differs from period to period and from country to country.

---

138. *See* Appendix 2.

464. The use of unemployment as a weapon to contain inflation is a blunt instrument and leads to lasting and great damage. Some enterprises close down, machines become idle and investment decreases. Bankruptcies are on the increase. Long-term unemployed workers become unemployable and are no longer fit to work.

Moreover, the acceleration of inflation can have many different causes. Price rises can be a consequence of the increased payments for public services, like transport, or of the increase of taxes on wine or on tobacco or of certain services, like medical services, which are also determined by the government, or have to do with the rising price of petroleum, which is imported.

In short, enterprises and workers are often the innocent victims of antiinflationary policies, when in fact they are not responsible at all for the eventual acceleration of inflation, as the price of the goods/services they produce may have diminished and inflation goes up for reasons which have nothing to do with their behaviour on the labour markets.

When financial credit becomes more expensive, 'cross-sectionally, small companies that do not have significant buffer-stock cash holdings are most likely to trim their investment... around the periods of tight money'. Nevertheless, it is argued that employment will be especially created by SMEs.

B. Flexibility

465. Microeconomic supply-side economics are intended to free enterprises from certain regulatory constraints by providing enterprises with more flexibility, so as to promote economic growth and consequently create more jobs. Protective labour measures, such as a minimum wage, working time restrictions, dismissals and others, are looked upon as hindrances to growth and should be done away with.

Labour costs especially have to go down. The worker has to be paid according to, and in relation to, the economic value that he adds in the process.

It is up to the Member States and their national social partners to see that the necessary flexibility is introduced. In any case, they have no other choice as market forces will oblige them to do so anyway.

466. The fact that social policy in the EU remains mainly a national affair means that social dumping – the deliberate attraction of investment on the basis of lower wage costs and lower working conditions – is not only accepted, but globally and on a European scale intentionally organised as the way to enforce more flexibility. The market will play in full: the more expensive operators will have to give up, unless they succeed in becoming cheaper, which means reducing the cost of their operations.

In a global, market-driven economy, services and goods have to become continuously better and cheaper. This means that enterprises will invest in those countries where costs are the lowest. There are, certainly, other factors which come into play when companies decide to invest, but labour costs may be an important one. Consequently, European nations competing with each other will also do their utmost to reduce labour costs because everyone else is doing it. So the trend is downwards, and is the direction that social harmonisation in Europe will go in.

It is similar to a theatre. When spectators on the first row stand up in order to see the stage better, the others have to get up in order to see something and then the benefit the first standing spectators had is done away with. So it is with the downward spiral of wages and labour conditions. Labour costs must be reduced; others do the same, and again the former countries are no longer competitive. So, they downsize their costs even more; this means more restructuring, relocations, more machines to replace workers, more dismissals. It is clear that national social systems cannot stand on their own and must yield in the face of a fierce globalised market economy. They have to give way to the lowest social denominator.

C. An Evaluation

467. The European employment strategy can be summarised in three main points.

The first is the goal of achieving and maintaining a non-accelerating inflation role of employment (NAIRU).

The second is a generalised flexibility of wages and labour conditions, which introduces job insecurity in the lives of many workers as a strategic element to contain inflation.

And the third point is the organisation of an ongoing competitive battle, which will be waged between the national social and fiscal systems of the Member States in and outside the EU. A country with high wage costs or which spends more on social policies than others will become less competitive. This means a kind of institutionalised social dumping between the EU Member States themselves and outside the EU.

Europe has no 'core' social competencies, which could bring about a real European social policy, including a proper employment strategy, which would involve wages, working conditions – e.g. job security – and social security, being based on fundamental social rights, European minimum standards.

Such a policy will only be possible when the EU has the competence to make decisions, including those about 'core' matters and fiscal affairs, with a qualified majority.

What things are about now is a harmonisation downwards and not 'while the improvement is being maintained', as Article 151 TFEU rather naively promises.

Obviously, inflation has to be kept under control, as well as public finances. But is it conceivable that Europe is not empowered to take appropriate social measures to combat unemployment and establish minimum standards? That a European collective agreement concerning pay would have no proper European legal status? That a European minimum wage will never be possible and that even the idea of a European social security system could always be countered by the veto of one Member State?

In short, the TFEU beyond Lisbon is much more than a choice or a preference for a free market economy, with which most will agree. It is a definite and final choice for a certain type of ultra liberal (conservative) policy which precludes almost forever a proper European social policy, employment included. As the Treaty of Lisbon has been ratified, this political choice has indeed become quasi-eternal And it will go on, as the political will to give the EU more social competences is lacking.

Chapter 4. European Labour Law: Trailer or Locomotive?

468. The previous section leaves no doubt regarding the answer to our title. However, this does not take away from the fact that certain important social steps were taken. Let us first take a look at the accomplishments of the ECSC, as an example of social progress in two sectors of industry, and thereupon examine the EC record.

§1. THE ECSC

469. The ECSC[139] constituted a first attempt toward a common policy, not only at economic, but also at social and regional levels, encroaching in an important way upon the far-reaching restructurings that have been carried out in the coal and steel sectors over the years. Between 1960 and 1980, coal production decreased in the Community from about 450 million tons to 21 million tons. One million jobs were lost. Between 1984 and 1988, 40,000 jobs disappeared every year. In Belgium the number of workers fell by 68 per cent. The steel sector was also harshly hit. In 10 years during the 1970s, out of 800,000 jobs, 300,000 were lost. Jobs continue to go.

Article 56 of the ECSC Treaty offers the Community the possibility of promoting the creation of new and economically sound activities capable of reabsorbing redundant workers into productive employment by way of granting subventions. Pursuant to this article, non-repayable restructuring loans permitted the creation of new jobs in other sectors of industry. In the steel sector, important vocational retraining programmes were set up. One should also mention the housing programme for coal and steel workers, whereby[140] houses (with cheap rent facilities) were built.

470. The Treaty establishing the ECSC, which was concluded for a period of 50 years, having entered into force on 23 July 1952 expired on 23 July 2002.

In 1960, there were 1,073,000 jobs in steel and 1,538,000 in coal. In 2002 there were 271,000 jobs left in steel and 94,000 in coal. The ECSC monitored that transition in very effective and socially responsible way. Its competences are transferred to the European Union.

§2. THE EC

471. As far as social development in the EC is concerned, we shall distinguish between three periods: the first, 1957 to 1974, was characterised by a rather cautious approach; the second, 1974 to 1990, was at first a golden period for labour law until 1980, at which time it witnessed an abrupt breakdown. The third period, which started in 1990, has been marked for the adoption of the Community Charter for basic social rights for workers.

---

139. EC, *A Social Europe*, 4th edn., Brussels, 1990, pp. 49–51.
140. European Commission, *Social Policy of the Community*, Brussels, 1996.

472–473 General Introduction, Ch. 4, European Labour Law: Locomotive?

I. 1957–1974

472. During this first period, the economic credo of the EC was clearly adhered to. Nevertheless, some steps were taken regarding social security for workers within the framework of free movement for workers and by the launching of the European Social Fund. A new climate, however, came about through the adoption of 'preliminary guidelines for a Community social policy programme',[141] drafted by the Commission in 1971, which led to the important declaration of Heads of State and Prime Ministers at the occasion of the 1972 Paris Summit that: 'they attach as much importance to vigorous action in the social field as to the achievement of the monetary and economic union'.[142]

473. Little by little the way was paved toward the Social Action Programme, which was adopted by the Council in a resolution of 21 January 1974.[143] The Council underlined the necessity to take measures toward realising the following priorities:

– *attainment of full and better employment in the Community*
  (1) the establishment of appropriate consultation between Member States on their employment policies and the promotion of better cooperation by national employment services;
  (2) the establishment of an action programme for migrant workers who are nationals of Member States or third countries;
  (3) the implementation of a common vocational training policy and the setting up of a European Vocational Training Centre;
  (4) the undertaking of action to achieve equality between men and women with regard to access to employment and vocational training and advancement with regard to working conditions, including pay.
– *the improvement of living and working conditions so as to make their harmonisation possible while maintaining their improvement*
  (5) the establishment of appropriate consultation among Member States on their social protection policies;
  (6) the establishment of an initial action programme, relating in particular to health and safety at work, the health of workers and improved organisation of tasks, beginning in those economic sectors where working conditions appear to be the most difficult;
  (7) the implementation, in cooperation with the Member States, of specific measures to combat poverty by drafting pilot schemes.
– *increased involvement of management and labour in the economic and social decisions of the Community and of workers in the life of undertakings*

---

141. 'Preliminary Guidelines for a Community Social Programme', *Bulletin of Comparative Labour Relations*, no. 3, 1972, pp. 81–149 (out of print).
142. Ph. Van Praag, 'Trends and Achievements in the Field of Social Policy in the European Communities', *Bulletin of Comparative Labour Relations*, no. 4, 1973, p. 150 (out of print).
143. Social Action Programme. Resolution of the Council of 21 January 1974, *Bulletin of Comparative Labour Relations*, no. 5, 1974, pp. 135–187 (out of print).

(1) the progressive involvement of workers or their representatives in the life of undertakings in the Community;
(2) the promotion of the involvement of management and labour in the economic and social decisions of the Community.

It is beyond doubt that the action programme was only partly implemented when the 1976 deadline expired. A partial success cannot, however, be denied.

II. 1974–1989

474. This period can be divided into two parts: the first from 1974 to 1980 and the second from 1980 to approximately 1989, which has been marked by the movement toward deregulation, headed by Mrs. Thatcher.

475. The first part of this period has been labelled by some as 'the golden period of harmonisation'.[144] Various labour law directives were adopted, namely:

– 1975: the directives relating to equal pay on the one hand and to collective redundancies on the other; – 1976: the directive concerning equal treatment of men and women with regard to working conditions;
– 1977: the directive concerning the transfer of enterprises and acquired rights for workers;
– 1978: the directive relating to equality between men and women with regard to social security;
– 1980: the directive relating to the insolvability of the employer.

The 1970s also saw the beginning of the publication of a series of directives concerning health and safety.

476. New winds started to blow in the 1980s. Deregulation and in particular flexibility became the holy slogans in the battle against the economic and social crisis, against sluggish economic growth and massive unemployment and toward the successful conquering of domestic and foreign markets. The vision of Mrs. Thatcher and of employers prevailed: more regulations led to greater unemployment and produced counter-productive effects for the workers. Many proposals for directives failed to obtain approval in the Council: the notorious Vredeling proposals regarding the information and consultation of workers in undertakings with a complex structure (1980–1983); the proposal on part-time work (1982); the proposal concerning temporary work (1982–1984); as well as the proposed recommendation in relation to the reduction and reorganisation of working time. The revised proposal of 1972 concerning the Fifth Directive which related to limited liability companies and forms of workers' participation (1983) was likewise unsuccessful, while the proposal regarding the SE, already initiated in 1970, was a dead duck. No wonder

---

144. F. Blanquet, *1992: l'Europe: vers l'harmonisation des législations sociales*, 1987, working paper (*l'âge d'or de l'harmonisation*).

then that the new social action programme of 22 June 1984 was less ambitious.[145] It addressed five points:

- unemployment, especially of young people;
- the introduction of new technologies;
- industrial safety;
- the cost of social security and its influence on the competitiveness of undertakings and on the living standards of workers;
- a more intense dialogue between the employers' and workers' representatives at a European level.

Much attention was also paid to safety at work and many directives toward that goal were adopted: the protection of workers from risks related to exposure to chemical, physical and biological agents at work (1980); the major accidents hazards of certain industrial activities (1982); the protection of workers against metallic lead (1982), asbestos (1983) and noise at work (1986).

477. Nonetheless, it is the Single European Act of 1986, aiming at the establishment of the internal market, in particular, that attracted most of the attention in the second half of the 1980s. The White Paper of 1985 concerning the internal market does not contain a single word on the harmonisation of labour law. On top of that, the Single Act confirmed, as indicated earlier, the national sovereignty of Member States over 'rights and interests of employed persons' which requires, in the case of Community decisions, unanimous voting by the Council. In so doing it gives each Member State the right to veto those proposals from the Commission which regard labour law. Under these circumstances, it was difficult to maintain that social policies were as important as economic and monetary matters. Undoubtedly, Article 137 TEC allows qualified majority voting concerning health and safety for workers. This gave birth to the framework directive of 12 June 1989 concerning measures to encourage the safety and health of workers at work. This directive contains a number of minimum requirements and general principles relating to the prevention of industrial risks, vocational training, information, consultation and participation of workers, and should be looked upon as the basis for a number of specific directives relating to the workplace, machinery, personal protective equipment and display screen equipment.

478. A new article, Article 158 TEC, insists on the necessity of economic and social cohesion in the Community, meaning that the differences between regions should be done away with through a dynamic action of the structural funds (the social fund, the regional fund and the agricultural fund) in favour of less-developed regions. Here important decisions have already been taken. From 1993 on, the funds will dispose of no less than 15 billion ECU yearly. Five objectives guiding future structural policies were retained:

---

145. O.J. C 175/1, 1984.

- aid will be granted to regions with a gross national product per inhabitant of less than 75 per cent of the European average;
- aid will be granted to regions that are undergoing industrial deterioration with the aim to contribute to the restructuring of enterprises, to combat unemployment and to create new jobs in new economic sectors;
- the long-standing fight against unemployment will be continued;
- the insertion of young people into the work process will be promoted;
- structural problems, especially in the agricultural sector, will be fought.

479. These measures notwithstanding, the criticism remained that the White Paper of 1985 concerning the 1992 internal market was one-sided, liberal (conservative) and purely economic and that there was a social vacuum. Voices were raised to plead again for a social dimension of the internal market. These voices were heard and the Commission created an interdepartmental working party, whose mission was to draft a report concerning the social dimension of the Common Market. This was published as a separate number of 'Social Europe' in 1988. The European Council also intervened; at the 1989 Madrid Summit, the 1972 catch phrase that as much importance must be given to the social dimension as to economic and monetary policies was repeated.

These developments, under the dynamic leadership of the President of the Commission, the French socialist Jacques Delors, led to a Community Charter of Basic Social Rights for Workers, which was solemnly approved and promulgated at the occasion of the meeting of Heads of State and Prime Ministers, with the exception of Great Britain, in Strasbourg on 9 December 1989, exactly 200 years after the 1789 French Universal Declaration of Human Rights. The idea is that future social policies in general and those regarding labour law in particular will be inspired by this Community Charter in the years to come.

III. 1990 and Beyond: the Community Charter and the Social Action Programme – the Maastricht Agreement on Social Policy

A. The Community Charter of Basic Social Rights

1. Foundation

480. The basic social rights for workers are founded upon the firm will to promote the standard of living on the one hand and social consensus on the other. The Charter is based in the first place on Article 136 TEC of the EC Treaty under the terms of which the Member States have agreed on the need to promote improved living and working conditions for workers so as to make their harmonisation possible while maintaining their improvement. The preamble to the Charter indicates that one of the priority objectives in the economic and social field is to promote employment; to this end the completion of the internal market presents major opportunities for growth and for job creation. Social consensus contributes to the strengthening of the competitiveness of undertakings, of the economy as a whole and of the creation of employment; thus it is an essential condition for ensuring sustained economic development.

2. Objectives

481. The Charter should, drawing upon the Conventions of the ILO and the European Social Charter of the Council of Europe, guarantee social improvements especially regarding:

– the freedom of movement;
– living and working conditions;
– health and safety in the workplace;
– social protection;
– education and training;
– equal treatment combating every form of social exclusion and discrimination, including discrimination on grounds of sex, race, colour, opinion and religion;
– equal treatment of migrant workers and nationals of third countries.

3. Scope

482. With regard to the scope of the Charter, different points must be made. First, the solemn declaration has only political consequences and no legally binding effect. It was an expression of the political will of the eleven governments which supported the Charter, nothing more, nothing less. Departing from the fact that the Charter is not legally binding, one can ask whether the Court could describe the stipulations of the Charter as being 'general principles of Community law'. The answer is no. After all, for the Court to conform to a consistent opinion, there must be a treaty signed by all Member States, and this is not the case here, because the British opted out. In summary, one can say that the Charter is not an instrument of Community law, nor is it a treaty signed by all Member States in relation to which Community law could be examined by the Court for its compatibility with the principles contained in the Charter.[146] The Charter must still be implemented by policy decisions made by the Community institutions. The decisions that the Community intends to take are contained in the Action Programme put forward by the Commission on 29 November 1989.

483. It should be underlined that the preamble leaves no doubt that the implementation of the Charter cannot lead to an extension of the competences of the Community, as they are conferred on the institutions by the Treaties. Of equal importance is the principle of subsidiarity: responsibility for the initiatives to be taken with regard to the implementation of basic social rights, which must be

---

146. L. Betten, 'EG Handvest van sociale grondrechten een hol vat?', *Sociaal Maandblad Arbeid*, 1990, p. 127.

applied according to the principle of subsidiarity, lies, according to the circumstances, with the Member States or their constituent parts or with the European Community. The implementation may take the form of laws, collective agreements or existing practices, and requires, where appropriate, the active involvement of both sides of industry at the various levels concerned. In summary, the respective roles of the Community, national governments and the social partners are to be respected. Finally, we read in the preamble that the Charter tries to consolidate what has already been achieved at a social level through the actions of Member States, the social partners and the Community and that the solemn declaration of basic social rights at the Community level must not, when implemented, provide grounds for any retrogression compared with the situation currently existing in each Member State. Let it be added that the Charter not only addresses employees, but also self-employed workers and on certain points European citizens in general.

4. Content

484. The Charter consists of a preamble, which we have just analysed, and two titles: the first title contains the basic social rights for workers; the second deals with the implementation of the Charter.

a. The Twelve Commandments

485. Title I contains 12 headings, which are further detailed in 26 points. These headings relate to:

- the right to freedom of movement;
- employment and remuneration;
- the improvement of living and working conditions;
- the right to social protection;
- the right to freedom of association and collective bargaining;
- the right to vocational training;
- the right of men and women to equal treatment;
- the right of workers to information, consultation and participation;
- the right to health protection and safety at the workplace;
- the protection of children and adolescents;
- the protection of elderly persons; and
- the protection of disabled persons.

486. This enumeration clearly shows that most of the social rights contained in the Charter are already provided for by other Conventions or EC instruments and consequently do not contain much added social value. The right of free movement for workers is already foreseen in Articles 39 to 42 of the EC Treaty. Vocational training is dealt with in Article 150 of the EC Treaty; equal treatment is widely covered by the existing directives, with the exception of the provision that measures should also be developed enabling men and women to reconcile their occupational and family obligations (point 16). Health protection and safety at the workplace is already dealt with in Article 137 of the EC Treaty.

487. Other headings do, however, contain new elements. Under the heading employment and remuneration, the following rights are guaranteed: freedom of occupation (point 4); an equitable wage, sufficient to enable a decent standard of living, also in the case of atypical employment contracts as for instance when wages are withheld, seized or transferred (point 5), as well as access to public placement services free of charge (point 6). The improvement of living and working conditions must result from an approximation of these conditions, while improvement is being maintained in regard particularly to the duration and organisation of working time and forms of employment other than open-ended contracts, such as fixed term contracts, part-time, temporary work and seasonal work. The improvement must cover, where necessary, the development of certain aspects of employment regulations such as procedures for collective redundancies and those regarding bankruptcies (point 7). A right to a weekly rest and to annual paid leave is likewise guaranteed (point 8). The conditions of employment must be stipulated in laws, a collective agreement or a contract of employment (point 9). *Social protection* embraces an adequate level of social security benefits, sufficient resources and social assistance (point 10).

488. Under freedom of association and collective bargaining, trade union (both positive and negative) freedom is guaranteed (point 11), as well as the right to negotiate and conclude collective agreements, not only at a European level in particular but also at inter-occupational and sectoral levels (point 12). The right to strike is explicitly recognised as well as the necessity to encourage the settlement of industrial disputes through the establishment and utilisation of conciliation, mediation and arbitration procedures (point 13). Internal legal order will determine under which conditions and to what extent such rights apply to the armed forces, the police and the civil service (point 14).

489. Information, consultation and participation of workers must be especially developed in companies or groups of companies having establishments or companies in more than one Member State. Such information, consultation and participation must be implemented in due time and particularly when technological changes are introduced; in the case of restructuring or mergers of undertakings, of collective redundancies and when transborder workers in particular are affected by employment policies pursued by the undertaking where they are employed (points 17–18). In view of the protection of children and adolescents, the employment age must not be lower than 15 years (point 20); these workers must receive equitable remuneration (point 21); measures should be taken to guarantee specific development, vocational training and access to employment; yet at the same time the duration of work must be limited (no overtime) and night work prohibited in the case of workers under 18 years of age (point 22), while vocational training should take place during working hours (point 23). Elderly persons are entitled at the time of retirement to enjoy resources affording a decent standard of living (point 24), as well as medical and social assistance specifically suited to their needs (point 25). Finally, all disabled persons must be entitled to additional concrete measures aimed at improving their social and professional integration. These measures must concern vocational training, ergonomics, accessibility, mobility, means of transport and housing (point 26).

In most cases it is provided that measures must be taken 'in accordance with arrangements applying in each country', 'in accordance with national law', 'in accordance with national practices', 'under the conditions laid down by national legislation and practice', or (once) 'the internal legal order'. Another expression used is: 'taking account of the practices in force in the various Member Countries', namely, regarding 'information, consultation and participation of workers'. These different formulations are absolutely not accidental and co-determine who is competent to enact the measures: the EC, the Member States or their constituent parts, the social partners or the individual natural or legal person.

b. Implementation

490. Title II (points 27–30) deals with the implementation of the Charter. It is more particularly the responsibility of the Member States, in accordance with national practices, notably by means of legislative measures or collective agreement (which is, however, the job of the social partners), to guarantee the fundamental social rights and to implement the social measures indispensable to the smooth operation of the internal market as part of a strategy of economic and social cohesion. Thus, and this is important, it is the Member States that are in the front line to implement the Charter. Then comes the Commission. The European Council invites the Commission to submit initiatives that fall within its powers, as provided for in the Treaties, with a view to adopting legal instruments for an effective implementation. During the last three months of every year, the Commission shall establish a report on the application of the Charter by the Member States and by the EC. The report shall be forwarded to the European Council, the EP and the ESC.

B. *The Action Programme*

491. The Commission communicated its Action Programme relating to the implementation of the Community Charter of Basic Social Rights for Workers on 29 November 1989.[147] The action programme contains a number of measures which, according to the Commission, need to be developed in order to implement the most urgent aspects of the principles of the Charter. In accordance with the already referred to principle of subsidiarity whereby the Community acts when the set objectives can be reached more effectively at its level than at that of the Member States, the Commission's proposals relate to only part of the issues raised in certain articles of the Charter. The Commission indeed takes the view that responsibility for the initiatives to be taken, as regards the implementation of social

---

147. COM(89) 568 final.

rights, lies with the Member States, their constituent parts or the two sides of industry as well as, within the limits of its powers, the European Community.

In most cases, the Commission has indicated the nature of the proposals to be presented: proposals for a directive, regulation, decision, recommendation or communication or again opinions within the meaning of Article 140 of the EC Treaty. The first set of proposals, representing the most urgent priorities, were put forward in the Commission's 1990 programme. A second set were included in the 1991 work programme. Further proposals were presented in 1992. The Commission asked the Council to undertake to adopt a decision concerning the Commission proposals within a period of 18 months, but in any case within two years at the outside, after transmission of the proposals to the EP, the ESC and the two sides of industry. The overall outcome has not been unsuccessful, as we will see later, when the different proposals and or directives are examined.

C. *The Maastricht Agreement on Social Policy (1991), the Green and the White Papers (1993)*

492. The Maastricht Agreement which was incorporated in the Treaty of Amsterdam (1997) entered into force on 1 November 1993. So it is too early to evaluate its implementation. One can, however, already note that on the social front, not much has happened since Maastricht approved – *grosso modo* – the Agreement of 31 October 1991, concluded by the social partners. The Commission has started the consultation procedure on information and consultation of employees, after the failure to agree on the proposal for an EWC in the framework of the 12.

At the end of 1993, Commissioner Flynn presented his Green Paper on 'European Social Policy. Options for the Future'.

According to the Green Paper, European social policy is entering into a critical phase. This is due to three main factors:

(i) the present social action programme is reaching its natural end. The Commission has presented all of the 47 proposals involved and, while some of the most important proposals are still pending before the Council, the majority have been adopted;
(ii) the entry into force of the Treaty on European Union has opened up new possibilities for Community action in the social field, particularly by giving a stronger role to the social partners; and
(iii) the changing socio-economic situation, reflected notably in the serious levels of unemployment, is requiring a new look at the link between economic and social policies, both at national and Community level. The Commission considers that this situation requires the launching of a wide-ranging debate about the future direction of social policy, before it proceeds to put forward specific proposals.

493. To prepare this Green Paper, the Commission issued a public appeal for contributions and comments.

The intention was to stimulate a wide-ranging debate within all Member States about the future lines of social policy in the European Union. The Commission will follow these discussions carefully and seek to draw from them the major themes of the future White Paper. This Green Paper does not deal with the procedural implications of the new Maastricht provisions as these will be the subject of a separate Communication.

Of course, this process will be taking place at a moment when the attention of the Community is focused on the whole issue of how to reconcile economic and social objectives in the face of rising unemployment and growing concern about Europe's ability to remain competitive into the 21st century.

There is much debate in all Member States about how to tackle employment, much of which is now recognised as being structural in character. The issues under discussion include the need for greater labour market adaptability, the suggestion that wage differentials should be widened and that wages should vary more in function of economic conditions, and questions about whether social benefits should be reduced or targeted so as to provide greater incentives to seek work. This is linked to the problems which all Member States are having in funding the growing demand on social protection systems and the search for greater efficiency in the operation of these as one means of making savings.

At the same time, there exists a growing degree of public concern that, contrary to the objective of ensuring that economic and social progress should go hand in hand as clearly stated in both the Treaties of Rome and Maastricht, the net impact of the integration process could be a levelling down of social standards. This is reflected in the fear that the creation of a single market could open the way to a form of social dumping, that is the gaining of unfair competitive advantage within the Community through unacceptably low social standards. But there is also a concern that, somehow, the imperative of action at European level can become a pretext for changes in social standards at national level.

In this context, this Green Paper, and the process of debate which it is designed to trigger, will be interactive with the discussions around the White Paper on growth, competitiveness and employment, adopted at the European Council on 10 December 1993.

494. The premise at the heart of this Green Paper is that the next phase in the development of European social policy cannot be based on the idea that social progress must go into retreat in order for economic competitiveness to recover. On the contrary, as has been stated on many occasions by the European Council, the Community is fully committed to ensuring that economic and social progress go hand in hand. Indeed, much of Europe's influence and power has come precisely from its capacity to combine wealth creation with enhanced benefits and freedoms for its people.

495. In current conditions this will not be easy, the Green Paper admits. But Europe's continuing contribution to the search for a model of sustainable development which combines economic dynamism with social progress can only be made if the issues are openly debated and a consensus arrived at. The rich diversity of the cultures and social systems within the European Union is a competitive advantage in a fast changing world. All societies are in the same process of learning. But diversity may deteriorate into disorder if the common goals, which embody the distinctive values of European society and are set out in the Treaty on European Union, are not defended by the efforts of Member States and by people themselves.

496. Part I of the Green Paper sets out what the Community has already achieved in the social sphere. Part II looks at the social challenges now facing us all. It examines the risks of declining social cohesion in Europe and the threats to important common goals such as social protection, solidarity and high levels of employment. A new medium-term strategy is needed which will draw together economic and social policies in partnership rather than in conflict with each other. Only in this way will sustainable growth, social solidarity and public confidence be restored. It is acknowledged that European production systems need to be based on the new technologies. There can be no social progress without wealth creation. But it should also be recognised that the consequent structural changes will have considerable impact on other important areas, such as employment intensity, working and living conditions, the quality of life and the development of industrial relations. Part III discusses the possible responses of the Union to these challenges, both in terms of what Member States want and of what the Community is trying to achieve. Part IV provides a brief conclusion. Part V brings together the questions raised in different parts of the Green Paper. These will be the focus of the debate to follow.

Europe is at a turning point, the Green Paper concludes. Decisions taken in the coming period will set the direction of social policy for many years to come. Now is the time for all sections of opinion to make their views known.

IV. The White Paper on Growth, Competitiveness and Employment (1993)

497. At the Brussels Summit, 10 and 11 December 1993, the European Council focused on the examination of the economic situation and measures to combat unemployment in the light of the White Paper on the medium-term strategy for growth, competitiveness and employment, prepared by the Commission. It adopted a shortand medium-term action plan whose implementation it will itself monitor: based on specific measures at the levels of the Union and of the Member States directed at, in the short term, reversing the trend and then, by the end of the century, significantly reducing the number of unemployed.

The action plan consists of:

– a general framework for the policies to be pursued at Member State level to promote employment;
– specific accompanying measures to be conducted at Community level;
– a monitoring procedure.

498. The primary purpose of the action plan is to reinforce the competitiveness of the European economy. The economy must respond to new requirements. It must also adapt to a world undergoing unprecedented change in production systems, organisation of work and modes of consumption. The action plan rests on four prerequisites:

(i) a healthy economy;
(ii) an open economy;
(iii) an economy geared to solidarity:
(iv) The necessary adjustments must not call into question the model of our society, which is founded on economic and social progress, a high level of social protection and continuous improvement in the quality of life. Solidarity must first be shown between those with jobs and those without; one expression of such solidarity is to allocate part of productivity gains on a priority basis to investment and job creation, in particular through a policy of wage moderation. In addition, solidarity must contribute, by means of a comprehensive policy covering both prevention and reintegration, to the fight against social exclusion. Solidarity must also be shown between regions in the context of economic and social cohesion;
(v) a more decentralised economy, given the growing importance of the local level; the economy needs to be geared to the possibilities offered by the new technologies and to mobilise to a greater extent than hitherto the job-creation potential available within small and medium-sized enterprises.

Because of the institutional, legislative and contractual peculiarities of each Member State, the Community's action must focus on defining objectives, while leaving Member States free to choose the means appropriate to their situation within a general framework defined in common. Member States should pay particular attention to the following measures:

– improving education and training systems. Continuing training is, in particular, to be facilitated so as to ensure ongoing adjustment of skills to the needs of competitiveness and to combating unemployment;
– improving flexibility within enterprises and on the labour market by removing excessive rigidities resulting from regulation as well as through greater mobility;
– examination, at enterprise level, of economically sound formulas for the re-organisation of work; such measures must not be directed towards a general redistribution of work, but towards internal adjustments compatible with improved productivity;
– targeted reductions in the indirect cost of labour (statutory contributions), and particularly of less-skilled work, in order to achieve a better balance between the costs of the various factors of production; fiscal measures possibly relating, *inter alia*, to the environment could be one of the means of offsetting a drop in social contributions, within a general context of stabilising all statutory contributions and reducing the tax burden;
– better use of public funds set aside for combating unemployment by means of a more active policy of information, motivation and guidance of job-seekers through specialised agencies, whether public or private;
– specific measures concerning young people who leave the education system without adequate training;

– developing employment in connection with meeting new requirements linked to the quality of life and protection of the environment.

499. The common framework thus defined will serve as a reference for Member States' policies. These policies will be periodically reviewed within the Council in order to analyse the results and learn from experience how future action should be conducted.

Specific action at Community level consists of:

(1) full use of the single market;
(2) trans-European networks in transport and energy;
(3) infrastructures in the sphere of information;
(4) funding of the energy, transport and environment networks and infrastructures in the sphere of information;
(5) research (framework programme for 1994–1998) (especially in information technology) and lastly;
(6) the social dialogue.

500. The success of the action plan presupposes the commitment of all those involved to preserving social cohesion; this will be easier to achieve if a dialogue is established at all appropriate levels on the objectives to be pursued and the means to be employed. In this connection the European Council invites the Commission to continue its efforts to lead the social dialogue and to make full use, subject to the provisions of the Protocol on Social Policy, of the new possibilities and calls upon both sides of industry to respond constructively.

Each year, beginning in December 1994, the European Council will take stock of the results of the action plan and will at the same time take any measure it deems necessary to achieve the objectives it has set itself.

The European Council's discussions will among others be based on:

– a summary report from the Commission, accompanied by any new suggestions; in this context the European Council in particular requests the Commission to study the question of new sources of jobs;
– a report from the Council on the lessons to be drawn from national employment policies.

V. The White Paper on European Social Policy (1994)

501. On 27 July 1994 the Commission adopted a White Paper on European Social Policy. The White Paper sets out the Commission's approach to the next phase of social policy development (1995–1999) and follows the wide ranging debate which was initiated by the Green Paper on Social Policy – 'Options for the Union'. In all, more than 500 reactions have been received from a wide variety of sources. The Commission's White Paper on Growth, Competitiveness and Employment also provided a valuable complementary focus in the debate about the need to create more jobs and at the same time preserve the basis of social protection which the people of Europe have come to prize.

The White Paper makes a number of proposals which are intended to form the basis for discussing on a new social action programme – to be agreed by the next Commission in 1995.

The White Paper stresses that European social policy must serve the interests of the Union as a whole and of all its people, both those in employment and those who are not: the Union's social policy cannot be secondary to economic development or to the functioning of the internal market. Europe needs to look for new ways to reconcile the twin objectives of economic growth and social progress.

502. Key features of the social policy White Paper are:

(1) *The need for a new mix between economic and social policies.* The paper emphasises the need to take a broader view of social policy particularly in the current climate of major socio-economic upheaval. Social policy should not simply be focused on the labour market and labour law, but on integrating all people into the economy and society as a whole, particularly by widening access to paid employment.
(2) *Jobs – top priority.* The central message of the paper is that the pursuit of better, stable jobs is both a central objective of the Union and the means of addressing more effectively many of the Union's widest social objectives. The White Paper contributed to the process already mapped out by the White Paper on 'Growth, Competitiveness and Employment' leading to the adoption of a new action plan at the Essen Summit in December 1994.

The White Paper stresses two other important issues in relation to employment:

– there is a separate chapter on the specific issue of skills and the need for a massive effort of investment in training particularly through the European Social Fund;
– a series of actions aimed at promoting the development of a real European labour market.

(3) *Developing and consolidating the legislative base.* The White Paper does not propose a lengthy new legislative agenda. However, it focuses on two main themes:
   (i) compelling the existing legislative programme:
   (ii) Progress made over the last eighteen months with the adoption of the Directives on Working Time and Young People and the adoption of a common position on the Directive on Information and Consultation means that the existing legislative corpus covers the main preoccupations addressed in the

previous action programme. The White Paper stresses the Commission's determination to see progress made between now and the end of the year on the pending Directives concerning:
- the posting of workers
- non-standard work.
(iii) If progress cannot be made, the Commission will reopen discussions with the social partners on the issues addressed in these proposals.
(iv) application of European law
(v) The White Paper stresses the Commission's determination to pursue vigorously the implementation of existing legislation. For example, in the field of Health and Safety, only one Member State has transposed all the adopted Directives.
(4) *Strengthening cooperation and action.* The White Paper sets out specific proposals and suggestions for future action across a whole range of related themes. Some of the key elements are:
- establishment of a high level panel to review the operation of the single market with regard to the free movement of people;
- a new action programme on equal opportunities between men and women announced for next year;
- renewed emphasis on the role of the social dialogue between management and labour at European level as well as on increased cooperation with voluntary and other non-governmental bodies.

503. The White Paper also calls for a longer term perspective with regard to the develop-ment of social policy. In particular it suggested that the following matters should be seriously considered at the next Intergovernmental Conference, due to be held in 1996:

- the need to ensure that European social policy is once again founded on one legal framework. This is vital if the integrity of the law and the principle of the equal treatment of all are to be respected;
- the fact that the Treaties as they stand do not give the Commission any explicit competence to combat racial discrimination. If the revision of the Treaty gives the Union competence in this field, consideration will be given to legislation combating all kinds of discrimination including those on the grounds of race, religion, age and disability;
- whether the time is now ripe for the Union to move towards a Citizens' Charter of Social Rights, taking forward the Community Charter of the Fundamental Social Rights of Workers and defining the social rights of all citizens of the Union.

VI. 1996 and Beyond: Unemployment

A. The European Council in Essen (1994)[148]

504. In line with the strategy of the (1993) White Paper to consolidate growth, improve the competitiveness of the European economy and the need to create more jobs, the European Council in Essen (9–10 December 1994) decided to take measures in the following five key areas:

(1) Improving employment opportunities for the labour force by promoting investment in vocational training. To that end a key role falls to the acquisition of vocational qualifications, particularly by young people. As many people as possible must receive initial and further training which enables them through lifelong learning to adapt to changes brought about by technological progress, in order to reduce the risk of losing their employment.
(2) Increasing the employment-intensiveness of growth, in particular by:
    - more flexible organisation of work in a way which fulfils both the wishes of employees and the requirements of competition;
    - a wage policy which encourages job-creating investments and in the present situation requires moderate wage agreements below increases in productivity, and finally;
    - the promotion of initiatives, particularly at regional and local level, that create jobs which take account of new requirements, e.g. in the environmental and social-services spheres.
(3) Reducing non-wage labour costs extensively enough to ensure that there is a noticeable effect on decisions concerning the taking on of employees and in particular of unqualified employees. The problem of non-wage labour costs can only be resolved through a joint effort by the economic sector, trade unions and the political sphere.
(4) Improving the effectiveness of labour-market policy: the effectiveness of employment policy must be increased by avoiding practices which are detrimental to readiness to work, and by moving from a passive to an active labour-market policy. The individual incentive to continue seeking employment on the general labour market must remain. Particular account must be taken of this, when working out income-support measures.
(4) The need for and efficiency of the instruments of labour-market policy must be assessed at regular intervals.
(5) Improving measures to help groups which are particularly hard hit by unemployment: particular efforts are necessary to help young people, especially school leavers, who have virtually no qualifications, by offering them either employment or training.
(5) The fight against long-term unemployment must be a major aspect of labour market policy. Varying labour market policy measures are necessary according to the very varied groups and requirements of the long-term unemployed.

---

148. *See* R. Blanpain, 'Work in the XXIst Century', in *Comparative Labour Law and Industrial Relations*, 7th ed. (ed. R. Blanpain and C. Engels), Kluwer, The Hague, 2001.

(5) Special attention should be paid to the difficult situation of unemployed women and older employees.

505. The European Council urged the Member States to transpose these recommendations in their individual policies into a multi-annual programme having regard to the specific features of their economic and social situation. It requests the Labour and Social Affairs and Economic and Financial Affairs Councils and the Commission to keep close track of employment trends, monitor the relevant policies of the Member States and report annually to the European Council on further progress on the employment market starting in December 1995.

Thus, each year the European Council will take stock of the results of the action plan and will at the same time take any measure it deems necessary to achieve the objectives it has set itself.

The European Council's discussions will be based on:

- summary reports from the Commission, accompanied by any new suggestions; in this context, the European Council, in particular, requests the Commission to study the question of new sources of jobs;
- reports from the Council on the lessons to be drawn from national employment policies.

B. The Confidence Pact for Employment (1996)

506. In the meantime, the President of the European Commission has bravely fought to engage all European and national actors in a European Confidence Pact for Employment (1996). However, much more than grandiose statements has not been obtained. National governments have no money to invest in European (information) infrastructures, however necessary they may be. The European Union indeed fails to put its ambitious plans into deeds. Employment conditions continue to deteriorate.

VII. The Treaty of Amsterdam (1997) – Employment

507. The Treaty of Amsterdam contains some capital improvements with the introduction of new Titles concerning employment (Title VIII) and social policy (Title XI, Chapter 1), a general principle of non-discrimination, and references to the Social Charter of the Council of Europe.

The new Chapter on Social Provisions incorporates the Social Agreement of Maastricht, which is quite important. Once the Treaty of Amsterdam ratified, the two-track social Europe, brought about by the British opt-out, has come to an end. There will be the possibility to do something more at the European level in the social field.

The Treaty does not provide for new, directly enforceable individual or collective social rights. But it does give a legal basis for action by the appropriate institutions of the EU in certain areas, such as regarding non-discrimination or employment policies. Thus, a dynamic process can be launched, if the political will is there and subsidiarity rules, allowing fully fledged European action.

508. The following topics merit special mention:

– fundamental rights, with reference to the European Convention for the Protection of Human Rights, the European Social Charter, issues like the principle of non-discrimination, disability, equality of men and women and protection of data;
– the Employment Title: coordinating national strategies, since employment policies are clearly left to the competence of the Member States;
– the Chapter on Social Policy, integrating the Maastricht Agreement on Social Policy; and also providing for the possibility of positive discrimination;
– environment: looking for a balance between environment and high employment;
– culture and non-professional sport;
– a Protocol on the application of the principles of subsidiarity and proportionality, clearly indicating that regarding matters of mixed competence, the EU can only intervene when there is additional (European) value and only as far as necessary, leaving maximum authority to Member States and consequently to the Social Partners;
– the Presidency Conclusions regarding employment, competitiveness and growth.

In that framework mention has to be made of the Commission's Action Plan for the Single Market submitted to the Amsterdam Summit. Below are some of the more important conclusions:

(1) In order to maintain momentum in fostering economic growth and fighting unemployment, an extraordinary meeting of the European Council under the Luxembourg Presidency will review progress in the implementation of, among others, the initiatives concerning job creating potentials for small and medium-sized enterprises, a new Competitiveness Advisory Group, the study of good practices on employment policies of the Member States, and the initiatives of the EIB in creating employment opportunities, as referred to in the European Council Resolution on Growth and Employment. The European Council invites the Commission and the Council, in cooperation with the EIB, to prepare a progress report to this European Council.

(2) The Council reiterates the need for a positive and coherent approach to job creation, encompassing a stable macroeconomics framework, completion of the Single Market, active employment policies and the modernisation of labour markets to bring Member States further towards the goal of full employment.

(3) The European Council welcomed the interim joint report on employment prepared by ECOFIN, the Labour and Social Affairs Council and the Commission and the progress report on the Confidence Pact on Action for Employment in Europe, presented by the President of the Commission.

(4) Restoring a sustained, high rate of non-inflationary growth is necessary to achieve a long-lasting solution to the Community's unemployment problem

and to make further headway towards sound public finances. Structural deficiencies continue to restrain both growth and the degree to which growth can be translated into additional employment.
(5) The European Council attaches paramount importance to creating conditions in the Member States that would promote a skilled and adaptable workforce and flexible labour markets responsive to economic change. This requires active intervention by the Member States in the labour market to help people develop their employability. Such action is important if the European Union is to remain globally competitive, and in order to tackle the scourge of unemployment.
(6) A reduction in the overall tax burden is desirable in most Member States, in particular the tax burden on labour. Also, a restrictive restructuring of public expenditure is called for to encourage investment in human capital, research and development, innovation and the infrastructure essential to competitiveness.
(7) Furthermore, the employment relevance of training and lifelong learning should be strengthened, tax and social welfare systems should be further reviewed in order to enhance employment opportunities, and more active labour market policy measures should be implemented. Efficiency and equity gains are to be improved by using social transfers in a more active way and by transforming benefit systems into proactive systems which improve the employability of workers.
(8) The European Council notes with satisfaction the work done on indicators that will allow bench-marking of the measures and policies pursued by the Member States under their multi-annual employment programmes. The European Council invites the Employment and Labour Market Committee and the Economic Policy Committee to discuss these issues with a view to enabling Member States to identify particularly good performance and effective practices and to take them into account in the formulation of their policies.
(9) Efforts made by social partners on wage moderation were acknowledged and should be pursued. Furthermore, wage agreements should take more account of differences in qualifications and between regions in order to facilitate job creation.
(10) The European Council strongly welcomes the agreement concluded by the Social Partners on part-time working and calls on them to bear in mind in their discussions the need to strike a balance between labour market adaptability and social security, in order to enhance employability.
(11) The European Council notes with satisfaction the overwhelmingly positive reaction of Member States to its invitation made in Florence to select regions or cities which could act as candidates for pilot projects on territorial and local employment pacts. As a result, around 90 such pacts have been established that will be launched at a conference in Brussels in November this year.
(12) The European Council reaffirms the importance it attaches to a well functioning internal market as an essential element of the overall strategy to promote competitiveness, economic growth and employment throughout

the Union. It welcomes the Commission's 'Action Plan for the Single Market'[149] and endorses its overall objective. The four strategic targets in the Action Plan should form the basis for a renewed political effort to remove remaining obstacles so as to ensure that the full potential benefit of the Single Market is realised.

509. The fact that an Employment Title was introduced by the Treaty of Amsterdam underlines the fact that unemployment was considered to be the number one social enemy.

The Title is part of an ongoing effort by governments and social partners, laid down at the Council meeting in Essen and stated in the 'Recommendation on the broad guidelines of the economic policies of the Member States and of the Community' of 2 July 1997. The guidelines are not a binding set of rules, but references for national governments. They aim to promote sustainable, non-inflationary growth and a high level of employment through sound public finances; a macro-economic policy mix conducive to growth, employment and convergence; price and exchange-rate stability; better functioning of product and service markets; and fostering employment and labour market reforms. The Council wants Member States to intensify their efforts to implement the Essen strategy.

The recommendation calls for:

– more efforts to eliminate labour market rigidities and ensure more efficient operation while 'ensuring both equity and efficiency in the social protection system'.
– The occupational and regional mobility of labour should be improved and the efficiency of employment services enhanced to 'reduce bottlenecks which could lead to an early end to the growth process':

---

149. The Action Plan follows the Commission's report on the Impact and Effectiveness of the Single Market. It sets priorities to give a clear and strategic vision of what is now needed.
   Four Strategic Targets have been set. They are of equal importance and must be pursued in parallel.
   (1) *Making the rules more effective*: The Single Market is based on confidence. Proper enforcement of common rules is the only way to achieve this goal. Simplification of rules at Community and national level is also essential to reduce the burden on business and create more jobs.
   (2) *Dealing with key market distortions*: There is general agreement that tax barriers and anticompetitive behaviour constitutes distortions that need to be tackled.
   (3) *Removing sectoral obstacles to market integration*: The Single Market will only deliver its full potential if barriers that remain – and of course, any new ones that emerge – are removed. This may require legislative action to fill gaps in the Single Market framework, but it also calls for a significant change in national administrations' attitudes towards the Single Market.
   (4) *Delivering a Single Market for the benefit of all citizens*: The Single Market generates employment, increases personal freedom and benefits consumers, while ensuring high levels of both health and safety and environmental protection. But further steps are needed, including steps to enhance the social dimension of the Single Market. And to enjoy their Single Market's rights to the full, citizens must be aware of them and be able to obtain speedy redress.
   Within each of these Strategic Targets, the Commission has identified a limited number of important specific actions aimed at improving the functioning of the Single Market by 1 January 1999 (E.C., *Forum. Special Jobs Summit*, Brussels, 1997, p. 11).

- the whole educational system – including vocational training – should be adapted both to the needs of markets and to 'the improvement of human capital'. Priority should be given to improving the employability of unemployed people, especially low-skilled, inexperienced labour, and to reducing skill mismatches on the labour market.
- Attention should also be given to improving the employment prospects of young people and women:
- higher employment growth should be fostered through 'the maintenance of appropriate wage trends and in some cases by wages that better reflect productivity differentials'. Where possible, non-wage labour costs should be cut to encourage employment, and attention should be given to incentives to employ disadvantaged groups. Adaptation of working time and work organisation 'in the mutual interest of firms and workforces' will also encourage employment; and
- local and regional initiatives in the field of new labour-intensive services should be encouraged.[150]

510. On 29 November 1996, the social partners, CEEP, ETUC and UNICE, adopted a joint statement calling for a coordinated strategy on employment at EU level.

All these efforts, however, did not seem to succeed in solving the unemployment problem. The European monetary strategy, coupled with an increasing insistence on more flexibility of the labour markets, seems to be insufficient to cope with the massive problem of millions of unemployed.

A. *European Jobs Summit, Luxembourg, November 1997*

1. Commission's Proposals

511. The extraordinary Council meeting in Luxembourg on Employment, 20–21 November 1997, was preceded by a document of the Commission containing various proposals.[151]

The European Commission, in drafting European Employment Guidelines, suggested that an integrated strategy must be built on four priorities or pillars: entrepreneurship, employability, adaptability and equal opportunities.

a. A New Culture of Entrepreneurship in the EU

512. The idea is to engender a new climate and spirit to stimulate the creation of more jobs and better jobs. We must make it easier to start up and run businesses by providing a clear, stable and predictable set of rules. Member States should review and simplify the administrative burdens on small and medium-size enterprises.

---

150. *European Industrial Relations Review*, September 1996, no. 272:2.
151. *Forum special. Jobs summit*, 1997.

- reduce significantly the overhead costs for enterprises of hiring an additional worker;
- adapt existing regulations to facilitate easier transition to self-employment.

Obstacles, especially those within existing social security regimes, for people moving from employment to self-employment and setting up microenterprises need to be tackled;
- develop the markets for venture capital, thereby mobilising Europe's wealth behind entrepreneurs and innovators. Member States should examine the specific needs of small and medium enterprises as regards financing, principally in the form of equity or guarantee capital;
- establish a pan-European secondary market for trading in less important stocks and shares, particularly designed for small and medium enterprises (secondary capital market) by the year 2000;
- make the taxation system more employment friendly. In order to encourage enterprises to create new jobs, Member States must reverse the average longterm trend towards higher taxes and charges on labour (which have increased from 35 per cent in 1980 to over 42 per cent in 1995);
- set a target for reducing the tax burden on labour, while maintaining budget neutrality, with a view to achieving substantial progress by the year 2000.

b. A New Culture of Employability in the EU

513. The idea is to tackle the skills gap, by modernising education and training systems, and by strengthening their link to the workplace, so that all workers, especially jobseekers, are equipped to take new employment opportunities. Currently, over 20 per cent of young people in the Union leave education and training without recognised qualifications. Only 10 per cent of those adults who are formally unemployed are getting any training at all. It means that jobs are often vacant because no one with adequate skills can be recruited. To improve the employability of people we must:

- Tackle long-term and youth unemployment.
   Member States should seek early identification of individual needs and early action to ensure that every unemployed adult is offered a new start – in the form of a job, training, retraining, work placement or other employability measure – before reaching twelve months of unemployment. Every unemployed young person is given such a new start before reaching six months of unemployment.
- Ease the transition from school to work. Employment prospects are poor for the 10 per cent of young people who drop out of the school system early and many of the 45 per cent who do not complete upper secondary education. Member States must seek to reduce the numbers dropping out of the education system early by 50 per cent within five years and progressively reduce the share who do not complete upper secondary level.
   Improve the apprenticeship systems and increase participation in apprenticeship training in line with the best performing Member States.

– Move from passive to active measures. Benefit and training systems should ensure that they actively support employability and provide clear incentives for the unemployed to seek and take up work or training opportunities. Each Member State should set a target for the number of people to be transferred from passive income support to active workers.
– Develop a partnership approach. Both enterprises and the social partners should be involved in joint efforts to invest Europe's wealth in its future by offering the necessary work experience/training positions. The Social Partners are urged to decide on a framework agreement as soon as possible on how to open workplaces across Europe for training, work practice, traineeships and other forms of employability measures and to agree on the terms and conditions.

Continue the impressive contribution which has been made over the past five years to the wage moderation which has contributed so much to the improved economic outlook and the improved prospects for new job creation.

c. A New Culture of Adaptability in the EU

514. The idea behind this pillar is to equip enterprises and the workforce to embrace new technologies and new market conditions.

To promote and encourage adaptability we must:

– Modernise work organisation. Social partners and Member States should rethink existing working patterns. It is suggested that social partners negotiate, at the appropriate levels, agreements on work organisation and flexible working arrangements, including reductions in working time. Member States should put in place a framework for more adaptable forms of contracts. Those in non-standard work should be given greater security and occupational status. Those who opt to work reduced hours should not be penalised in terms of career progression or in terms of maintaining social security protection.
– Support adaptability in enterprises. In order to renew skill levels within enterprises, Member States should remove fiscal and other obstacles for the promotion of investment in human resources and offer tax incentives for the development of in-house training. Incentives to workers to avail of training opportunities should also be encouraged.

Re-focus their state aid policies on upgrading the labour force, the creation of sustainable jobs and efficiently functioning labour markets.

d. A New Culture of Equal Opportunities in the EU

515. The idea is to modernise societies so that men and women can work on equal terms, with equal responsibilities, to develop the full growth capacity of our economies. To strengthen equal opportunities we must:

– Tackle gender gaps. Member States should translate their commitment to equality of opportunity and breaking down gender segregation, and make consistent efforts to reduce the gap in unemployment rates between women and men by actively supporting the increased employment of women.
– Reconcile work and family life. Policies on career breaks, parental leave and part-time work are of particular importance to women, as are adequate provision of good quality care for children and other dependants. Member States should seek to raise levels of care provision, using the standards of the best performing Member States as a benchmark.
– Facilitate return to work. Specific attention should be given to women considering a return to the paid workforce after an absence. They may face problems of poor employability due to outdated skills and may have difficulty in accessing training opportunities if they have not been registered as 'jobseekers'. Moreover, negative taxation and benefit systems may reduce financial incentives to seek work. Member States should address these and other obstacles.

These four pillars represent the European Commission's view of the priorities for action. They represent priorities for a Europe in transition. These guidelines refer to Member States' employment policy, not to new initiatives at European level. The guidelines represent a challenge to traditional thinking by declaring long-term objectives.

Europe can change its employment situation by working together to ensure that employers and employees are equipped to engage fully in the new, more diverse, skill and process driven European economy.

2. Social Partners

516. The social partners (CEEP, UNICE, ETUC) were fully involved in the preparation of the summit meeting and were regularly consulted. They broadly subscribed to the strategy and the four pillars put forward by the Commission. The employers obviously were reluctant to accept specific employment targets. Needless to say that the social partners remained miles away from each other regarding reorganisation of working time, especially the 35-hour week and the issue of information and consultation at national level, as suggested by the Commission.

B. Jobs Summit: Conclusions Luxembourg

517. The European Council decided that the relevant provisions of the new Title on employment in the Treaty of Amsterdam are to be put into effect immediately. This decision makes it possible in practice to implement the provisions on coordination of Member States' employment policies in advance, as of 1998. Such coordination will be based on common lines of approach for both objectives and means, the 'employment guidelines', drawing directly on the experience built up in the multilateral surveillance of economic policies, with success observed in the case of convergence. The idea is, while respecting the differences between the two areas and between the situations of individual Member States, to create for employment, as for economic policy, the same resolve to converge jointly towards set, verifiable, regularly updated targets.

The implementation of the 'guidelines' may vary according to their nature, their impact on Member States and the parties to whom they are addressed. They must respect the principle of subsidiarity and Member States' responsibilities with regard to employment and must be compatible with the broad economic policy guidelines.

After being adopted by the Council on the basis of a proposal from the Commission, the 'guidelines' will have to be incorporated into national employment action plans drawn up by the Member States in a multi-annual perspective. This is how they will be given practical effect, in the form of national objectives which are quantified wherever possible and appropriate, followed by their transposition into national regulatory, administrative or other measures. The differing situations of the Member States in relation to the problems addressed by the 'guidelines' will result in differing solutions and emphases, in line with individual situations. Member States will set themselves deadlines for achieving the desired result in the light, *inter alia*, of the administrative and financial resources which can be drawn upon. However, it is crucial for the coherence and effectiveness of the approach as a whole that all Member States make use of the 'guidelines' in analysing their own situation and framing their policy and that they establish their attitude to each of them in their national employment action plan.

In a similar way to the multilateral surveillance principle applied in the economic convergence process, Member States will each year send the Council and the Commission their national employment action plan, together with a report on the manner of its implementation. On that basis, the Council will hold an annual review of the way in which Member States have put the 'guidelines' into practice in their national policies and will submit a report to the European Council, which will establish the approach required in laying down the 'guidelines' for the following year.

Regular contact with the Council will properly pave the way for the six-monthly meeting of the social partners with a *troika* at the level of Heads of State or Government and the Commission before the European Council meeting. In the course of such contacts between the Council and the social partners, a detailed exchange of views will in particular be held on the implementation of the 1989 Community Charter of the Fundamental Social Rights of Workers.

VIII. The Treaty of Nice (December 2000): 'Socially not so nice'

518. At the European Top of the European Council, which would be held in Nice, France (December 2000), the issues of more majority voting and fundamental social rights would be addressed. So, again, there was hope. The IGC (2000), which was engaged in preparing the enlargement of the European Union, would also address the issue of expanding the majority vote. Everyone realised, one would imagine, that maintaining unanimity when the Union expands to possibly 27–30 Member States means paralysing the decision-making. So there was hope that more labour issues would fall within the reach of majority voting.

Moreover, when the European Council met at the Tampere Council (1999), Ministers decided to initiate the drafting of a charter of fundamental rights in the European Union. A joint body consisting of representatives of Member State governments, the Commission, the European Parliament and national parliaments would draft the charter. Other EU bodies, social groups and experts were to be invited to give their views to the joint body. There was a good chance that fundamental rights would be included in the European Treaty. It remained to be seen whether the Council would go beyond a mere declaration but lay down directly enforceable rights for the European citizens, employers and workers included. Legally enforceable fundamental standards would help to put 'social Europe' definitely on the map.

Again, our hopes faded like the morning haze before a rising sun.

A. *Charter of Fundamental Rights of the European Union (Nice, 7 December 2000)[152], revised 2007[153]*

1. Preamble

519. The Preamble sounds great. It reads as follows:

> The peoples of Europe, in creating an ever closer union among them, are resolved to share a peaceful future based on common values.
>
> Conscious of its spiritual and moral heritage, the Union is founded on the indivisible, universal values of human dignity, freedom, equality and solidarity; it is based on the principles of democracy and the rule of law. It places the individual at the heart of its activities, by establishing the citizenship of the Union and by creating an area of freedom, security and justice.
>
> The Union contributes to the preservation and to the development of these common values while respecting the diversity of the cultures and traditions of the peoples of Europe as well as the national identities of the Member States and the organisation of their public authorities at national, regional and local levels; it seeks to promote balanced and sustainable development and ensures free movement of persons, goods, services and capital, and the freedom of establishment.
>
> To this end, it is necessary to strengthen the protection of fundamental rights in the light of changes in society, social progress and scientific and technological developments by making those rights more visible in a Charter.

---

152. For the full text *see* Appendix 3.
153. On 12 December 2007, the EP, and the Commission adopted the Charter of Fundamental Rights of the European Union, which will replace the Charter of 2000 as from the date of entry into force of the Treaty of Lisbon.

This Charter reaffirms, with due regard for the powers and tasks of the Community and the Union and the principle of subsidiarity, the rights as they result, in particular, from the constitutional traditions and international obligations common to the Member States, the Treaty on European Union, the Community Treaties, the European Convention for the Protection of Human Rights and Fundamental Freedoms, the Social Charters adopted by the Community and by the Council of Europe and the case law of the Court of Justice of the European Communities and of the European Court of Human Rights.

Enjoyment of these rights entails responsibilities and duties with regard to other persons, to the human community and to future generations. The Union therefore recognises the rights, freedoms and principles set out hereafter.

520. On 12 December 2007, the EP, and the Commission adopted the Charter of Fundamental Rights of the European union, which will replace the Charter of 2000 as from the date of entry into force of the Treaty of Lisbon. Article 6, 1 TEU (Lisbon) indicates that the Charter has the same legal value as the Treaty.

2. Content; List of Rights

521. The Charter contains the following social rights:

- prohibition of slavery and forced labour;
- respect for private and family life;
- protection of personal data;
- freedom of thought, conscience and religion;
- freedom of expression and information;
- freedom of assembly and of association;
- right to education;
- freedom to choose an occupation and right to engage in work;
- freedom to conduct a business;
- non-discrimination;
- equality between men and women;
- workers' right to information and consultation within the undertaking;
- right of collective bargaining and action;
- right of access to placement services;
- protection in the event of unjustified dismissal;
- fair and just working conditions;
- prohibition of child labour and protection of young people at work;
- family and professional life;
- social security and social assistance;
- freedom of movement and of residence.

3 Scope and Level of Protection

a. Scope

522. The provisions of this Charter are addressed to the institutions and bodies of the Union with due regard for the principle of subsidiarity and to the Member States only when they are implementing Union law.

They shall therefore respect the rights, observe the principles and promote the application thereof in accordance with their respective powers.

This Charter does not establish any new power or task for the Community or the Union, or modify powers and tasks defined by the Treaties.

Any limitation on the exercise of the rights and freedoms recognised by this Charter must be provided for by law and respect the essence of those rights and freedoms. Subject to the principle of proportionality, limitations may be made only if they are necessary and genuinely meet objectives of general interest recognised by the Union or the need to protect the rights and freedoms of others.

Rights recognised by this Charter, which are based on the Community Treaties, or the Treaty on European Union shall be exercised under the conditions and within the limits defined by those Treaties.

Insofar as this Charter contains rights, which correspond to rights guaranteed by the Convention for the Protection of Human Rights and Fundamental Freedoms, the meaning and scope of those rights shall be the same as those laid down by the said Convention. This provision shall not prevent Union law providing more extensive protection.

b. Level of Protection

523. Nothing in this Charter shall be interpreted as restricting or adversely affecting human rights and fundamental freedoms as recognised, in their respective fields of application, by Union law and international law and by international agreements to which the Union, the Community or all the Member States are party, including the European Convention for the Protection of Human Rights and Fundamental Freedoms, and by the Member States' constitutions.

c. Prohibition of Abuse of Rights

524. Nothing in this Charter shall be interpreted as implying any right to engage in any activity or to perform any act aimed at the destruction of any of the rights and freedoms recognised in this Charter or at their limitation to a greater extent than is provided for herein.

d. An Evaluation; Binding Effect

525. Obviously, the Charter contains a lot of social rights. Some are fundamental; some are important but not fundamental. Here we can talk about an inflation of social rights as far as a Charter to be included in the European treaties is concerned. We think for example about rights like the right of access to placement services, to protection in the event of unjustified dismissal and fair and just working conditions. These are important points indeed, but not the 'core rights' one is thinking about when discussing a Charter of Fundamental Rights. The 1998 ILO Declaration, on the contrary, is concentrating on the real core social rights and the ILO solution seems more appropriate.

As far as the binding effect of the Charter is concerned Nice was disappointing. The Presidency Conclusions of the Nice Top regarding the Charter read as follows:

> The European Council welcomes the joint proclamation, by the Council, the European Parliament and the Commission, of the Charter of Fundamental Rights, combining in a single text the civil, political, economic, social and societal rights hitherto laid down in a variety of international, European or national sources. The European Council would like to see the Charter disseminated as widely as possible amongst the Union's citizens. In accordance with the Cologne conclusions, the question of the Charter's force will be considered later.

e. Revised Charter 2007

526. As indicated earlier, on 12 December 2007, the EP, and the Commission adopted the Charter of Fundamental Rights of the European Union, which replaces the Charter of 2000 as from December 2009. Article 6, 1 TEU (Lisbon) indicates that the Charter shall have the same legal value as the Treaty.

527. In the *BECTU* Case (C-173/99), the Advocate-General made reference (8 February 2001) to the Nice Declaration. The facts were as follows.

BECTU is a union in the broadcasting, film, theatre, cinema, and related sectors; it has about 30,000 members who are sound recordists, cameramen, special effects technicians, projectionists, editors, researchers, hairdressers, make-up artistes amongst others.

The British legislation which implements the European working time directive of 1993 provides that entitlement to leave is conditional upon the person concerned having been continuously employed for 13 weeks by the same employer. Furthermore, it may not be replaced by a payment in lieu except where the employment is terminated.

The workers represented by BECTU are only employed on short-term contracts which are often less than 13 weeks. As a result, they do not become entitled to the right to annual leave under British law.

According to the Advocate-General, the right to paid annual leave is a fundamental social right; this is stated in various international instruments and is enshrined in the Charter of Fundamental Rights of the European Union of 7 December 2000. The

Advocate-General underlines that the purpose of the Charter, where its provisions allow, is a substantive point of reference for all those involved in the Community context.

528. More specifically, the Advocate-General declared:

> As early as 1948, the Universal Declaration of Human Rights recognised the right to rest, including reasonable limitations on working time and periodic holidays with pay (Article 24). Subsequently, both the European Social Charter approved in 1961 by the Council of Europe (Article 2(3)), and the United Nations Charter of 1966 on economic, social and cultural rights (Article 7(d)), specifically upheld the right to paid leave as a manifestation of the right to fair and equitable working conditions.
>
> In the Community context, it will be remembered that the Heads of State or Government enshrined that same right in paragraph 8 of the Community Charter of the Fundamental Social Rights of Workers adopted by the European Council in Strasbourg in 1989 which is referred to in the fourth recital in the preamble to the Working Time Directive itself.
>
> The instruments to which I have so far referred collectively and in general terms are certainly distinct from each other in certain respects. As has been seen, their substantive content is not the same in all cases, nor is their legislative scope, since in some cases they are international conventions, in others solemn declarations; and of course the persons to whom they apply differ. However, it is significant that in all those instruments the right to a period of paid leave is unequivocally included among workers' fundamental rights.
>
> Even more significant, it seems to me, is the fact that that right is now solemnly upheld in the Charter of Fundamental Rights of the European Union, published on 7 December 2000 by the European Parliament, the Council and the Commission after approval by the Heads of State and Government of the Member States, often on the basis of an express and specific mandate from the national parliaments. Article 31(2) of the Charter declares that: 'Every worker has the right to limitation of maximum working hours, to daily and weekly rest periods and to an annual period of paid leave.' And that statement, as expressly declared by the Presidium of the Convention which drew up the Charter, is inspired precisely by Article 2 of the European Social Charter and by paragraph 8 of the Community Charter of Workers' Rights, and also took due account of Directive 93/104/EC concerning certain aspects of the organisation of working time.
>
> Admittedly, like some of the instruments cited above, the Charter of Fundamental Rights of the European Union has not been recognised as having genuine legislative scope in the strict sense. In other words, formally, it is not in itself binding. However, without wishing to participate here in the wideranging debate now going on as to the effects which, in other forms and by other means, the Charter may nevertheless produce, the fact remains that it includes statements which appear in large measure to reaffirm rights which are enshrined in other instruments. In its preamble, it is moreover stated that 'this Charter reaffirms, with due regard for the powers and tasks of the Community

and the Union and the principle of subsidiarity' the rights as they result, in particular, from the constitutional traditions and international obligations common to the Member States, the Treaty on European Union, the Community Treaties, the European Convention for the Protection of Human Rights and Fundamental Freedoms, the Social Charters adopted by the Community and by the Council of Europe and the case law of the Court of Justice of the European Communities and of the European Court of Human Rights.

I think therefore that, in proceedings concerned with the nature and scope of a fundamental right, the relevant statements of the Charter cannot be ignored; in particular, we cannot ignore its clear purpose of serving, where its provisions so allow, as a substantive point of reference for all those involved – Member States, institutions, natural and legal persons – in the Community context. Accordingly, I consider that the Charter provides us with the most reliable and definitive confirmation of the fact that the right to paid annual leave constitutes a fundamental right.

The Advocate-General added that the right to annual leave does not only concern the individual worker but corresponds to a general social interest for the health and safety of workers; therefore it is an automatic and unconditional right which does not fall within the derogations allowed for in the directive in other circumstances.

The Court of Justice declared consequently that 'the entitlement of every worker to paid annual leave must be regarded as a particularly important principle of Community social law from which there can be no derogations'.[154]

529. In other words, the Charter constitutes fundamental rights 'as they result from the constitutional traditions common to the Member States, as general principles of Community law' (Article 6(3) TEU). This is, of course, of the greatest importance.

B. *Unanimity and Qualified Majority*

530. Here nothing changes. On the contrary, Article 153 of the Treaty looks as follows:

(1) With a view to achieving the objectives of Article 151, the Union shall support and complement the activities of the Member States in the following fields:
   (a) improvement in particular of the working environment to protect workers' health and safety;
   (b) working conditions;
   (c) social security and social protection of workers;
   (d) protection of workers where their employment contract is terminated;
   (e) the information and consultation of workers;

---

154. 26 June 2001, ECR, 2001, 4881.

(f) representation and collective defence of the interests of workers and employers, including co-determination, subject to paragraph 5;
(g) conditions of employment for third-country nationals legally residing in Community territory;
(h) the integration of persons excluded from the labour market, without prejudice to Article 166;
(i) equality between men and women with regard to labour market opportunities and treatment at work;
(j) the combating of social exclusion;
(k) the modernisation of social protection systems without prejudice to point (c).

(2) To this end, the EP and the Council:
(a) may adopt measures designed to encourage cooperation between Member States through initiatives aimed at improving knowledge, developing exchanges of information and best practices, promoting innovative approaches and evaluating experiences, excluding any harmonisation of the laws and regulations of the Member States;
(b) may adopt, in the fields referred to in paragraph 1(a) to (i), by means of directives, minimum requirements for gradual implementation, having regard to the conditions and technical rules obtaining in each of the Member States. Such directives shall avoid imposing administrative, financial and legal constraints in a way which would hold back the creation and development of small and medium-sized undertakings.

The EP and the Council shall act in accordance with the ordinary legislative procedure after consulting the Economic and Social Committee and the Committee of the Regions.

In the fields referred to in paragraph 1(c), (d), (f) and (g), the Council shall act unanimously, in accordance with a special legislative procedure, after consulting the EP and the said Committees.

The Council, acting unanimously on a proposal from the Commission, after consulting the EP, may decide to render the ordinary legislative procedure applicable to paragraph 1 (d), (f) and (g).

(3) A Member State may entrust management and labour, at their joint request, with the implementation of directives adopted pursuant to paragraph 2, or, where appropriate, with the implementation of a Council decision adopted in accordance with Article 155.

(3) In this case, it shall ensure, that, no later thanthe date on which a directive or a decision must be transposed or implemented, management and labour have introduced the necessary measures by agreement, the Member State concerned being required to take any necessary measure enabling it at any time to be in a position to guarantee the results imposed by that directive or that decision.

(4) The provisions adopted pursuant to this Article:
– shall not affect the right of Member States to define the fundamental principles of their social security systems and must not significantly affect the 'financial equilibrium' thereof,

– shall not prevent any Member State from maintaining or introducing more stringent protective measures compatible with the Treaties.
(5) The provisions of this Article shall not apply to pay, the right of association, the right to strike or the right to impose lock-outs.

IX. Employment Guidelines

531. The Council adopted employment guidelines for 1998, 1999, 2000, 2001, 2002, 2003–2004, 2005–2008, 2008–2010 and 2010–2014.

The Member States incorporate the guidelines into National Actions Plans (NAPs) and report to the Commission on their implementation.

A. The Employment Guidelines 2003–2004[155]

532. These 2003 guidelines[156] and recommendations were drawn up within the context of the European employment strategy (EES), which has been in place since 1997. Following a review of the EES undertaken in 2002 after five years of operation and proposals for its streamlining, made by the Commission in a Communication in September 2002, the timing and the content has changed. Notably, the employment guidelines have been revised so as to ensure a stronger link with EU economic policy coordination (through streamlined timetables); lay down fewer guidelines with a broader perspective; provide a medium-term time horizon in order to achieve an increased emphasis on results and outcomes; and strengthen the involvement of the social partners, local authorities and other stakeholders.

1. Employment Guidelines

533. The 2003 employment guidelines to the Member States set out three main objectives:

– full employment;
– improving quality and productivity at work; and
– strengthening social cohesion and inclusion.

The guidelines focus on ten policy priorities, rather than grouping a range of guidelines into four pillars, as has previously been the practice. These ten priorities are set out below.

---

155. Andrea Broughton (IRS), '2003 employment guidelines and recommendations adopted', www.eiro.eurofound.ie, 2003.
156. Decision 2003/578/EC of July 2003.

2. Active and Preventative Measures for Unemployed and Inactive People

534. Member States are urged to develop and implement active and preventative measures in order to prevent inflow into long-term unemployment. These include the concrete targets of:

- ensuring that every unemployed person is offered a 'new start' within 12 months of being unemployed (six months in the case of young people). This can take the form of training, retraining, work practice, a job or some other employability measure; and
- by 2010, ensuring that 25 per cent of long-term unemployed people participate in an active measure, with the aim of all countries achieving the average performance of the three most advanced Member States.

Member States are also urged to modernise and strengthen their labour market institutions, in particular employment services, and to evaluate and review the effectiveness and efficiency of labour market programmes.

3. Job Creation and Entrepreneurship

535. Member States are urged to encourage the creation of more and better jobs by fostering entrepreneurship, innovation, investment capacity and a favourable business climate. The focus should be particularly on exploiting the job creation potential of new enterprises, the service sector and research and development.

In particular, Member States are urged to simplify and reduce administrative and regulatory burdens for business start-ups and small and medium-sized enterprises (SMEs), making it simpler to hire new staff and improving access to capital for start-ups, SMEs and companies with a high growth and employment potential. Member States are also urged to promote education and training in entrepreneurial and management skills.

4. Addressing Change and Promoting Adaptability and Mobility in the Labour Market

536. The guidelines ask Member States to facilitate the adaptability of workers and firms to change, 'taking account of the need for both flexibility and security and emphasising the key role of the social partners'. They also ask Member States to: review and reform 'overly restrictive' elements of employment legislation; develop social dialogue; foster corporate social responsibility; promote diversity of contractual and working arrangements, particular in order to favour career progression and a balance between work and private life and between flexibility and security; and promote access to training. Member States are also asked to promote: better working conditions; the design and dissemination of innovative and sustainable forms of work organisation; and the anticipation and positive management of economic change and restructuring.

Member States are urged to address labour shortages and bottlenecks by means of a range of measures such as promoting occupational mobility and removing obstacles to geographic mobility, improving the recognition and transparency of qualifications and competencies and the transferability of social security and pensions rights. It is hoped that, by 2005, jobseekers in the EU should be able to consult all vacancies advertised through Member States' employment services.

5. Development of Human Capital and Lifelong Learning

537. Member States are asked to implement lifelong learning strategies in order to equip individuals with the skills required in today's workforce, to permit career development and to reduce skills mismatches and labour market bottlenecks.

The following targets should be achieved by 2010:

- at least 85 per cent of 22-year-olds in the EU should have completed upper secondary education; and
- the EU average level of participation in lifelong learning should be at least 12.5 per cent of the adult working-age population (25–64-year-olds).

6. Labour Supply and Active Ageing

538. Member States are urged to increase labour market participation by using the potential of all groups in the population, using a comprehensive approach. They are also asked to promote 'active ageing', notably by fostering working conditions which are conducive to job retention. This could include measures such as access to continuing training and innovative and flexible forms of work organisation. Further, incentives for early exit from the labour market should be eliminated, largely by reforming early retirement systems, giving people incentives to remain active in the labour market and encouraging employers to recruit older workers.

By 2010, it is hoped that there will be a five-year increase in the average EU exit age from the labour market – this was estimated to be 59.9 years in 2001. The guidelines emphasise the important role of the social partners in this regard.

7. Gender Equality

539. Member States are asked to encourage female labour market participation and achieve a substantial reduction in gender gaps in employment rates, unemployment rates and pay by 2010. The gender pay gap should be reduced using measures such as addressing sectoral and occupational segregation, education and training, job classifications and pay systems, awareness-raising and transparency.

Reconciling work and private life is identified as an important aspect of gender equality. Concrete targets, to be achieved by 2010, are to provide childcare to at least 90 per cent of children between three years old and the mandatory school age and to at least 33 per cent of children under three years of age.

8. Integrating and Combating Discrimination against Disadvantaged People

540. People at a disadvantage in the labour market include early school-leavers, low-skilled workers, people with disabilities, immigrants and people from ethnic minorities. Member States are urged to develop their employability, increase job opportunities for them and prevent discrimination against them. Concrete targets to be achieved by 2010 are as follows:

- an EU average of no more than a ten per cent early school-leaver rate; – a significant reduction in the 'unemployment gaps' for people at a disadvantage, according to nationally-set targets and definitions; and
- a significant reduction in the 'unemployment gaps' between non-EU and EU nationals, according to nationally-set targets.

9. Making Work Pay

541. Member States are exhorted to develop policies which will make work attractive and thus encourage people to seek and remain in work. Tax and benefit systems should be reviewed and, where appropriate, reformed, in order to encourage more people into work, particularly women, low-skilled workers, older workers, people with disabilities and 'those furthest from the labour market'.

By 2010, Member States should aim to have policies in place which achieve a significant reduction in high marginal effective tax rates and, where this is appropriate, in the tax burden on low-paid workers, although this should reflect national circumstances.

10. Undeclared Work

542. Undeclared work is an area where the Commission hopes to see significant improvement in the coming years. The guidelines state that Member States should aim to eliminate undeclared work using measures such as: the simplification of the business environment, removing disincentives to declaring work; providing incentives to declare work, by means of adjustments to the tax and benefits system; and improving law enforcement and the application of sanctions.

11. Regional Employment Disparities

543. Member States should work towards reducing regional employment and unemployment disparities. In particular, they should promote favourable conditions for private sector activity and investment in the poorer regions and ensure that public support in these regions is focused on investment in human and knowledge capital and an adequate infrastructure. Further, the potential of the EU cohesion and structural funds and of the European Investment Bank should be 'fully exploited'.

12. Implementation of Guidelines

544. The 2003 employment guidelines include a section on 'good governance and partnership' in their implementation. Member States are to ensure the effective implementation of the guidelines, including at the regional and local level, and should involve parliamentary bodies, social partners and other relevant actors. Good governance and partnership are seen as important issues for the implementation of the EES, 'while fully respecting national traditions and practices'.

With regard to the social partners, they should be invited at national level – 'in accordance with their national traditions and practices' – to ensure the effective implementation of the guidelines and to report on their most significant contributions in all areas under their responsibility, in particular concerning: the management of change and adaptability; 'synergy' between flexibility and security; 'human capital development'; gender equality; making work pay; active ageing; and health and safety at work. The European-level social partners at intersectoral and sectoral level are invited to contribute to the implementation of the employment guidelines and to support efforts undertaken by the national social partners at all levels. As announced in their joint work programme for 2003–5, the European intersectoral social partners will report annually on their contribution to the implementation of the guidelines. Furthermore, the European sectoral social partners are invited to report on their respective actions.

13. Employment Recommendations

545. The 2003 recommendations give each Member State guidance on policy and the implementation of the employment guidelines, in the following 12 policy fields:

– unemployment prevention and activation;
– job creation in regions;
– change and adaptability;
– lifelong learning;
– labour supply and active ageing;
– gender equality;
– people at a disadvantage;
– making work pay;
– undeclared work;
– job mobility;
– social partnership; and
– delivery services.

All Member States have at least three recommendations addressed to them, and 57 recommendations have been issued in total. More than half of the Member States have received recommendations in the field of labour supply and active ageing, gender equality, lifelong learning and unemployment prevention and activation, including development and modernisation of employment services.

The 2003 guidelines were maintained for 2004.[157]

B. The Employment Guidelines 2005–2008

546. 12th July 2005, the European Council adopted a set of integrated guidelines for the EU Member States' employment and economic policies, which it described as a 'three-year blueprint for growth and jobs'. This 'integrated guidelines package' seeks to lay down a comprehensive strategy of macroeconomic, microeconomic and employment policies to redress Europe's weak growth performance and insufficient job creation.[158]

The integrated guidelines stress that Member States and the EU should take every opportunity to involve regional and local governments, social partners and civil society in their implementation. On this basis, Member States will draw up three-year 'national reform programmes' (rather than one-year programmes) and they will report on these programmes each autumn, in a single 'national Lisbon report'. The Commission considers that this 'simplified mechanism of reports' will allow Member States to focus 'more fully' on implementation. The Commission will then analyse and summarise these reports in an 'EU annual progress report' in January each year. Subject to the findings of the annual report, the Commission may propose amendments to the integrated guidelines.

1. New Employment Guidelines for More and Better Jobs

547. The Commission states that progress on achieving the Lisbon employment objectives is insufficient. It is projecting a slow reduction in the unemployment rate, to 8.7 per cent in 2006. The estimated overall employment rate for the EU 25 countries is 62.9 per cent in 2003, significantly below the Lisbon strategy target of 70 per cent by 2010. Progress towards the Lisbon strategy's female employment rate target of 60 per cent by 2010 is slow, with the rate standing at 56.1 per cent for the EU 25 countries.

The largest gap between the actual employment rate and the target rate is evident among older workers, which, at just over 40.2 per cent, is well below the target rate of 50 per cent for 2010. At the same time, progress in improving 'quality' in work has been mixed and the economic slowdown has raised the profile of social inclusion problems. Long-term unemployment has increased again after several years of decline, and it is not expected to fall again in the near future.

---

157. Decision 2004/740/EC of 4 October 2004, O.J. L 326.
158. Beatrice Harper, IRS, 'Commission adopts 2005–8 integrated guidelines package', www.eiro.eurofound.ie, 2005; Council Decision of 19 June 2007 on guidelines for the employment policies of the Member States.

2. The Employment Guidelines (2005–2008)[159]

548.

> (Integrated Guidelines Nos. 17–24)
> – Guideline No. 17: Implement employment policies aiming at achieving full employment, improving quality and productivity at work, and strengthening social and territorial cohesion;
> – Guideline No. 18: Promote a lifecycle approach to work;
> – Guideline No. 19: Ensure inclusive labour markets, enhance work attractiveness, and make work pay for job-seekers, including disadvantaged people, and the inactive;
> – Guideline No. 20: Improve matching of labour market needs;
> – Guideline No. 21: Promote flexibility combined with employment security and reduce labour market segmentation, having due regard to the role of the social partners;
> – Guideline No. 22: Ensure employment-friendly labour cost developments and wage-setting mechanisms;
> – Guideline No. 23: Expand and improve investment in human capital;
> – Guideline No. 24: Adapt education and training systems in response to new competence requirements.

3. Guidelines for the Employment Policies of the Member States

549. Member States, in cooperation with the social partners, shall conduct their policies with a view to implementing the objectives and priorities for action specified below. Reflecting the Lisbon strategy, the Member States' policies shall foster in a balanced manner:

– Full employment: Achieving full employment, and reducing unemployment and inactivity, by increasing the demand for and supply of labour, is vital to sustain economic growth and reinforce social cohesion.
– Improving quality and productivity at work: Efforts to raise employment rates go hand in hand with improving the attractiveness of jobs, quality at work and labour productivity growth, and reducing the share of working poor. Synergies between quality at work, productivity and employment should be fully exploited.
– Strengthening social and territorial cohesion: Determined action is needed to strengthen social inclusion, prevent exclusion from the labour market and support integration in employment of people at a disadvantage, and to reduce regional disparities in terms of employment, unemployment and labour productivity, especially in regions lagging behind.

---
159. Council Decision of 12 July 2005 on Guidelines for the employment policies of the Member States, O.J., 6 August 2005, L 205/21.

Equal opportunities and combating discrimination are essential for progress. Gender mainstreaming and the promotion of gender equality should be ensured in all action taken. As part of a new intergenerational approach, particular attention should be paid to the situation of young people, implementing the European Youth Pact, and to promoting access to employment throughout working life. Particular attention must also be paid to significantly reducing employment gaps for people at a disadvantage, including disabled people, as well as between third-country nationals and EU citizens, in line with any national targets.

In taking action, Member States should ensure good governance of employment policies. They should establish a broad partnership for change by involving parliamentary bodies and stakeholders, including those at regional and local levels. European and national social partners should play a central role. A number of targets and benchmarks which have been set at EU level in the framework of the European Employment Strategy in the context of the 2003 guidelines are included at the end of this Annex and should continue to be followed up with indicators and scoreboards. Member States are also encouraged to define their own commitments and targets, for which they should take these into account, as well as the 2004 recommendations agreed at EU level.

Good governance also requires greater efficiency in the allocation of administrative and financial resources. In agreement with the Commission, Member States should target the resources of the Structural Funds, in particular the European Social Fund, on the implementation of the European Employment Strategy and report on the action taken. Particular attention should be paid to strengthening institutional and administrative capacity in the Member States.

Guideline No. 17: Implement employment policies aiming at achieving full employment, improving quality and productivity at work, and strengthening social and territorial cohesion.
Policies should contribute to achieving an average employment rate for the European Union (EU) of 70 per cent overall, of at least 60 per cent for womenand of 50 per cent for older workers (55 to 64) by 2010, and to reduce unemployment and inactivity. Member States should consider setting national employment rate targets

---

550. In addressing these objectives, action should concentrate on the following priorities:

(1) attract and retain more people in employment, increase labour supply and modernise social protection systems;
(2) improve adaptability of workers and enterprises;
(3) increase investment in human capital through better education and skills.

4. Attract and Retain more People in Employment, Increase Labour Supply and Modernise Social Protection Systems

551. Raising employment levels is the most effective means of generating economic growth and promoting socially inclusive economies whilst ensuring a safety net for those unable to work. Promoting an increased labour supply in all groups, a new lifecycle approach to work and modernising social protection systems to ensure their adequacy, financial sustainability and responsiveness to changing needs in society are all the more necessary because of the expected decline in the working-age population. Special attention should be paid to tackling the persistent employment gaps between women and men, and the low employment rates of older workers and young people, as part of new intergenerational approach. Action is also required to tackle youth unemployment which is on average double the overall unemployment rate. The right conditions must be put in place to facilitate progress in employment, whether it is first time entry, a move back to employment after a break or the wish to prolong working lives. The quality of jobs, including pay and benefits, working conditions, employment security, access to lifelong learning and career prospects, is crucial, as are support and incentives stemming from social protection systems.

> **Guideline No. 18**: Promote a lifecycle approach to work through:
>
> – a renewed endeavour to build employment pathways for young people and reduce youth unemployment, as called for in the European Youth Pact;
> – resolute action to increase female participation and reduce gender gaps in employment, unemployment and pay;
> – better reconciliation of work and private life and the provision of accessible and affordable childcare facilities and care for other dependants;
> – support for active ageing, including appropriate working conditions, improved (occupational) health status and adequate incentives to work and discouragement of early retirement;
> – modern social protection systems, including pensions and healthcare, ensuring their social adequacy, financial sustainability and responsiveness to changing needs, so as to support participation and better retention in employment and longer working lives.
>
> *See also* integrated guideline 'To safeguard economic and fiscal sustainability as a basis for increased employment' (No. 2).

552. Facilitating access to employment for job seekers, preventing unemployment and ensuring that those who become unemployed remain closely attached to the labour market and increase their employability are essential to increase participation and combat social exclusion. This requires breaking down barriers to the labour market by assisting with effective job searching, facilitating access to training and other active labour market measures and ensuring that work pays, as well as removing unemployment, poverty and inactivity traps. Special attention should be paid to promoting the inclusion of disadvantaged people, including low-skilled workers, in the labour market, including through the expansion of social services and the social economy, as well as the development of new sources of jobs in response to collective needs. Combating discrimination, promoting access to employment for disabled people and integrating immigrants and minorities are particularly essential.

Guideline No. 19: Ensure inclusive labour markets, enhance work attractiveness, and make work pay for job-seekers, including disadvantaged people, and the inactive through:

– active and preventive labour market measures including early identification of needs, job search assistance, guidance and training as part of personalised action plans, provision of necessary social services to support the inclusion of those furthest away from the labour market and contribute to the eradication of poverty; – continual review of the incentives and disincentives resulting from the tax and benefit systems, including the management and conditionality of benefits and a significant reduction of high marginal effective tax rates, notably for those with low incomes, whilst ensuring adequate levels of social protection;
– development of new sources of jobs in services for individuals and businesses, notably at local level.

553. To allow more people to find better employment, it is also necessary to strengthen the labour market infrastructure at national and EU level, including through the EURES network, so as to better anticipate and resolve possible mismatches. In this context, mobility of workers within the EU is key and should be fully ensured within the context of the Treaties. Full consideration must also be given on the national labour markets to the additional labour supply resulting from immigration of third-country nationals.

Guideline No. 20: Improve matching of labour market needs through:

– the modernisation and strengthening of labour market institutions, notably employment services, also with a view to ensuring greater transparency of employment and training opportunities at national and European level;
– removing obstacles to mobility for workers across Europe within the framework of the Treaties;

- better anticipation of skill needs, labour market shortages and bottlenecks;
- appropriate management of economic migration.

5. Improve Adaptability of Workers and Enterprises

554. Europe needs to improve its capacity to anticipate, trigger and absorb economic and social change. This requires employment-friendly labour costs, modern forms of work organisation and well-functioning labour markets allowing more flexibility combined with employment security to meet the needs of companies and workers. This should also contribute to preventing the emergence of segmented labour markets and reducing undeclared work.

In today's increasingly global economy with market opening and the continual introduction of new technologies, both enterprises and workers are confronted with the need, and indeed the opportunity, to adapt. While this process of structural changes is overall beneficial to growth and employment, it also brings about transformations which are disruptive to some workers and enterprises. Enterprises must become more flexible to respond to sudden changes in demand for their goods and services, adapt to new technologies and be in a position to innovate constantly in order to remain competitive. They must also respond to the increasing demand for job quality which is related to workers' personal preferences and family changes, and they will have to cope with an ageing workforce and fewer young recruits. For workers, working life is becoming more complex as working patterns become more diverse and irregular and an increasing number of transitions need to be managed successfully throughout the lifecycle. With rapidly changing economies and attendant restructuring, they must cope with new ways of working, including enhanced exploitation of Information and Communication Technologies (ICT) and changes in their working status, and be prepared for lifelong learning. Geographical mobility is also needed to access job opportunitiesmore widely and in the EU at large.

Guideline No. 21: Promote flexibility combined with employment security and reduce labour market segmentation, having due regard to the role of the social partners, through:

- the adaptation of employment legislation, reviewing where necessary the different contractual and working time arrangements;
- addressing the issue of undeclared work; – better anticipation and positive management of change, including economic restructuring, notably changes linked to trade opening, so as to minimise their social costs and facilitate adaptation;
- the promotion and dissemination of innovative and adaptable forms of work organisation, with a view to improving quality and productivity at work, including health and safety;

> – support for transitions in occupational status, including training, self-employment, business creation and geographic mobility.
>
> *See also* integrated guideline 'To promote greater coherence between macro-economic, structural and employment policies' (No. 5).

555. To maximise job creation, preserve competitiveness and contribute to the general economic framework, overall wage developments should be in line with productivity growth over the economic cycle and should reflect the labour market situation. Efforts to reduce non-wage labour costs and to review the tax wedge may also be needed to facilitate job creation, especially for low-wage employment.

> **Guideline No. 22**: Ensure employment-friendly labour cost developments and wage-setting mechanisms by:
>
> – encouraging social partners within their own areas of responsibility to set the right framework for wage bargaining in order to reflect productivity and labour market challenges at all relevant levels and to avoid gender pay gaps;
> – reviewing the impact on employment of non-wage labour costs and where appropriate adjust their structure and level, especially to reduce the tax burden on the low-paid.
>
> *See also* integrated guideline 'To ensure that wage developments contribute to macroeconomic stability and growth' (No. 4).

6. Increase Investment in Human Capital through Better Education and Skills

556. Europe needs to invest more in human capital. Too many people fail to enter or to remain in the labour market because of a lack of skills, or due to skills mismatches. To enhance access to employment for all ages, raise productivity levels and quality at work, the EU needs higher and more effective investment in human capital and lifelong learning for the benefit of individuals, enterprises, the economy and society.

Knowledge-based and service-based economies require different skills from traditional industries; skills which also constantly need updating in the face of technological change and innovation.

Workers, if they are to remain and progress in work, need to accumulate and renew skills regularly. The productivity of enterprises is dependent on building and maintaining a workforce that can adapt to change. Governments need to ensure that educational attainment levels are improved and that young people are equipped with the necessary key competences, in line with the European Youth Pact. All stakeholders should be mobilised to develop and foster a true culture of lifelong learning from the earliest age. To achieve a substantial increase in public and private investment in human resources per capita and guarantee the quality and efficiency of these investments, it is important to ensure fair and transparent sharing of costs and responsibilities between all actors. Member States should make better use of the Structural Funds and the European Investment Bank for investment in education and training. To achieve these aims, Member States commit themselves to establishing comprehensive lifelong learning strategies by 2006 and implementing the Education and Training 2010 Work Programme.

Guideline No. 23: Expand and improve investment in human capital through:

– inclusive education and training policies and action to facilitate significantly access to initial vocational, secondary and higher education, including apprenticeships and entrepreneurship training;
– significantly reducing the number of early school leavers;
– efficient lifelong learning strategies open to all in schools, businesses, public-authorities and households according to European agreements, including appropriate incentives and cost-sharing mechanisms, with a view to enhancing participation in continuous and workplace training throughout the life-cycle, especially for the low-skilled and older workers.

See also integrated guideline 'To increase and improve investment in R&D, in particular by private business' (No. 7).

---

557. Setting ambitious objectives and increasing the level of investment by all actors is not enough. To ensure that supply meets demand in practice, lifelong learning systems must be affordable, accessible and responsive to changing needs. Adaptation and capacity-building of education and training systems is necessary to improve their labour market relevance, their responsiveness to the needs of the knowledge-based economy and society and their efficiency. ICT can be used to improve access to learning and better tailor it to the needs of employers and employees. Greater mobility for both work and learning purposes is also needed to access job opportunities more widely in the EU at large. The remaining obstacles to mobility within the European labour market should be lifted, in particular those relating to the recognition and transparency of qualifications and competences. It will be important to make use of the agreed European instruments and references to support reforms of national education and training systems, as is laid down in the Education and Training 2010 Work Programme.

Guideline No. 24: Adapt education and training systems in response to new competence requirements by:

– raising and ensuring the attractiveness, openness and quality standards of education and training, broadening the supply of education and training

> opportunities and ensuring flexible learning pathways and enlarging possibilities for mobility for students and trainees;
> – easing and diversifying access for all to education and training and to knowledge by means of working time organisation, family support services, vocational guidance and, if appropriate, new forms of cost sharing;
> – responding to new occupational needs, key competences and future skill requirements by improving the definition and transparency of qualifications, their effective recognition and the validation of non-formal and informal learning.

C. The Employment Guidelines 2008–2010

558. The reform of the Lisbon Strategy in 2005 has placed the emphasis on growth and jobs. The examination of the Member States' National Reform Programmes shows that Member States should continue to make every effort to address the priority areas of:

– attracting and retaining more people in employment, increasing labour supply and modernising social protection systems,
– improving adaptability of workers and enterprises, and
– increasing investment in human capital through better education and skills.

Special attention should be paid to the agreed targets and benchmarks. The Employment Guidelines are valid for three years, while in the intermediate years until the end of 2010 their updating should remain strictly limited.

1. The Employment Guidelines 2008–2010 (Integrated Guidelines Nos. 17–24)

559. The Employment Guidelines form part of the Integrated Guidelines for 2008–2010, which are based on three pillars: macroeconomic policies, microeconomic reforms and employment policies. Those pillars, together, contribute towards achieving the objectives of sustainable growth and employment and strengthening social cohesion.

Member States, in cooperation with the social partners and where appropriate other stakeholders, shall conduct their policies with a view to implementing the objectives and priorities for action specified below so that more and better jobs and a better educated and skilled labour force support an inclusive labour market. Reflecting the Lisbon strategy and taking into account the common social objectives, the Member States' policies shall foster in a balanced manner:

– full employment: Achieving full employment, and reducing unemployment and inactivity, by increasing the demand for and supply of labour, is vital to sustain economic growth and reinforce social cohesion. An integrated flexicurity

approach is essential to achieve these goals. Flexicurity policies address simultaneously the flexibility of labour markets, work organisation and labour relations, reconciliation of work and private life, and employment security and social protection,
– improving quality and productivity at work: Efforts to raise employment rates go hand in hand with improving the attractiveness of jobs, quality at work, labour productivity growth; substantially reducing segmentation, gender inequality and in-work poverty. Synergies between quality at work, productivity and employment should be fully exploited,
– strengthening economic, social and territorial cohesion: Determined action is needed to strengthen and reinforce social inclusion, fight poverty – especially child poverty–, prevent exclusion from the labour market, support integration in employment of people at a disadvantage, and to reduce regional disparities in terms of employment, unemployment and labour productivity, especially in regions lagging behind. Strengthened interaction is needed with the Open Method of Coordination in Social Protection and Social Inclusion.

560. Equal opportunities and combating discrimination are essential for progress. Gender mainstreaming and the promotion of gender equality should be ensured in all action taken. Particular attention must also be paid to significantly reducing all gender-related gaps in the labour market in line with the European Pact for Gender Equality. As part of a new intergenerational approach, particular attention should be paid to the situation of young people, implementing the European Youth Pact, and to promoting access to employment throughout working life, including for older workers. Particular attention must also be paid to significantly reducing employment gaps for people at a disadvantage, including disabled people, as well as between third-country nationals and EU citizens, in line with any national targets. This will assist Member States in addressing the demographic challenge.

Member States should aim towards active inclusion of all through promotion of labour force participation and fight poverty and exclusion of marginalised groups.

In taking action, Member States should ensure good governance of employment and social policies and ensure that the positive developments in the fields of economics, labour and social affairs are mutually reinforcing. They should establish a broad partnership for change by fully involving parliamentary bodies and stakeholders, including those at regional and local levels and civil society organizations. European and national social partners should play a central role. The targets and benchmarks which have been set at EU level in the framework of the European Employment Strategy in the context of the 2003 guidelines should continue to be followed up with indicators and scoreboards. Member States are also encouraged to define their own commitments and targets, which should be taken into account, along with the country-specific recommendations agreed at EU level. In addition, Member States are encouraged to monitor the social impact of reforms.

Good governance also requires greater efficiency in the allocation of administrative and financial resources. In agreement with the Commission, Member States should target the resources of the Structural Funds, in particular the European Social Fund, on the implementation of the European Employment Strategy and report on the action taken. Particular attention should be paid to strengthening institutional and administrative capacity in the Member States.

> **Guideline 17**: Implement employment policies aiming at achieving full employment, improving quality and productivity at work, and strengthening social and territorial cohesion.
>
> Policies should contribute to achieving an average employment rate for the European Union (EU) of 70 per cent overall, of at least 60 per cent for women and of 50 per cent for older workers (55 to 64) by 2010, and to reduce unemployment and inactivity. Member States should consider setting national employment rate targets.

561. In addressing these objectives, action should concentrate on the following priorities:

– attract and retain more people in employment, increase labour supply and modernise social protection systems,
– improve adaptability of workers and enterprises,
– increase investment in human capital through better education and skills.

2. Attract and Retain More People in Employment, Increase Labour Supply and Modernise Social Protection Systems

562. Raising employment levels is the most effective means of generating economic growth and promoting socially inclusive economies whilst ensuring a safety net for those unable to work. Promoting labour supply, a lifecycle approach to work and modernising social protection systems to ensure their adequacy, financial sustainability and responsiveness to changing needs in society are all the more necessary because of the expected decline in the working-age population. Special attention should be paid to substantially reducing the persistent employment gaps between women and men, and the gender pay gap. Further increasing the employment rates of older workers and young people, as part of a new intergenerational approach, and promoting active inclusion of those most excluded from the labour market is also important. Intensified action is also required to improve the situation of young people in the labour market, especially for the low skilled, and to significantly reduce youth unemployment, which is on average double the overall unemployment rate.

The right conditions must be put in place to facilitate progress in employment, whether it is first-time entry, a move back to employment after a break or the wish to prolong working lives. The quality of jobs, including pay and benefits, working conditions, access to lifelong learning and career prospects, are crucial, as are support and incentives stemming from social protection systems. To enhance a lifecycle approach to work and to promote reconciliation between work and family life, policies regarding childcare provision are necessary. Securing coverage of at least 90 per cent of children between 3 years old and the mandatory school age and at least 33 per cent of children under 3 years of age by 2010 is a useful benchmark at national level, but specific efforts are also needed to tackle regional disparities within countries. The increase in the average employment rate of parents, especially single parents, who are usually exposed to higher poverty risk, requires measures to support families. In particular, Member States should take account of the special needs of single parents and families with many children. Furthermore, by 2010 the effective average exit age from the labour market at EU level should increase by 5 years compared to 2001.

Member States should also enact measures for improved (occupational) health status with the goal of reducing sickness burdens, increasing labour productivity and prolonging working life. The implementation of the European Youth Pact, the Pact for Gender Equality; and the European Alliance for Families should also be a contribution to a lifecycle approach to work, in particular by facilitating the transition from education to the labour market. Young people with fewer opportunities should be given equal chances for social and professional integration through individually tailored measures.

Guideline 18: promote a lifecycle approach to work through:

- a renewed endeavour to build employment pathways for young people and reduce youth unemployment, as called for in the European Youth Pact,
- resolute action to increase female participation and reduce gender gaps in employment, unemployment and pay,
- better reconciliation of work and private life and the provision of accessible and affordable childcare facilities and care for other dependants,
- support for active ageing, including appropriate working conditions, improved (occupational) health status and adequate incentives to work and discouragement of early retirement,
- modern social protection systems, including pensions and healthcare, ensuring their social adequacy, financial sustainability and responsiveness to changing needs, so as to support participation and better retention in employment and longer working lives.

See also integrated guideline 'To safeguard economic and fiscal sustainability as a basis for increased employment' (no. 2).

---

563. Active inclusion policies can increase labour supply and strengthen society's cohesiveness and are a powerful means of promoting the social and labour market integration of the most disadvantaged.

Every unemployed person should be offered a job, apprenticeship, additional training or other employability measure; in the case of young persons who have left school within no more than 4 months by 2010 and in the case of adults within no more than 12 months. Policies aiming at offering active labour market measures to the long-term unemployed should be pursued, taking into consideration the participation rate benchmark of 25 per cent in 2010. Activation should be in the form of training, retraining, work practice, a job or other employability measure, combined where appropriate with on-going job search assistance. Facilitating access to employment for job seekers, preventing unemployment and ensuring that those who become unemployed remain closely connected to the labour market and employable are essential to increase participation, and combat social exclusion. Attaining these objectives requires removing barriers to the labour market by assisting with effective job-searching, facilitating access to training and other active labour market measures. Ensuring affordable access to basic social services, adequate levels of minimum resources to all, combined with the principle of fair remuneration in order to make work pay are equally important. This approach should, at the same time, ensure that work pays for all workers, as well as remove unemployment, poverty and inactivity traps.

Special attention should be paid to promoting the inclusion of disadvantaged people, including low-skilled workers, in the labour market, inter alia, through the expansion of social services and the social economy, as well as the development of new sources of jobs in response to collective needs. Combating discrimination, promoting access to employment for disabled people and integrating immigrants and minorities are particularly essential.

Guideline 19: ensure inclusive labour markets, enhance work attractiveness, and make work pay for job-seekers, including disadvantaged people, and the inactive through:

- active and preventive labour market measures including early identification of needs, job search assistance, guidance and training as part of personalised action plans, provision of necessary social services to support the inclusion of those furthest away from the labour market and contribute to the eradication of poverty,
- continual review of the incentives and disincentives resulting from the tax and benefit systems, including the management and conditionality of benefits and a significant reduction of high marginal effective tax rates, notably for those with low incomes, whilst ensuring adequate levels of social protection,
- development of new sources of jobs in services for individuals and businesses, notably at local level.

---

564. To allow more people to find better employment, it is also necessary to strengthen the labour market infrastructure at national and EU level, including through the EURES network, so as to better anticipate and resolve possible mismatches. Better transitions between jobs and into employment are essential and policies to enhance mobility and matching on the labour market should be promoted. Job-seekers throughout the EU should be able to consult all job vacancies advertised through Member States' employment services. Mobility of workers within the EU should be fully ensured within the context of the Treaties. Full consideration must also be given on the national labour markets to the additional labour supply resulting from immigration of third-country nationals.

> **Guideline 20**: improve matching of labour market needs through:
>
> – the modernisation and strengthening of labour market institutions, notably employment services, also with a view to ensuring greater transparency of employment and training opportunities at national and European level,
> – removing obstacles to mobility for workers across Europe within the framework of the Treaties,
> – better anticipation of skill needs, labour market shortages and bottlenecks,
> – appropriate management of economic migration,

3. Improve Adaptability of Workers and Enterprises

565. Europe needs to improve its capacity to anticipate, trigger and absorb economic and social change. This requires employment-friendly labour costs, modern forms of work organisation, promoting 'good work' and well-functioning labour markets allowing more flexibility combined with employment security to meet the needs of companies and workers. This should also contribute to preventing the emergence of segmented labour markets and reducing undeclared work (*see also* Guidelines 18, 19, 20 and 23).

In today's increasingly global economy with market opening and the continual introduction of new technologies, both enterprises and workers are confronted with the need, and indeed the opportunity, to adapt. While this process of structural change is overall beneficial to growth and employment, it also brings about transformations which are disruptive to some workers and enterprises. Enterprises must become more flexible to respond to sudden changes in demand, adapt to new technologies and innovate constantly, in order to remain competitive.

They must also respond to the increasing demand for job quality related to workers' personal preferences and family changes, and they will have to cope with an ageing workforce and fewer young recruits. For workers, working life is becoming more complex as working patterns become more diverse and irregular and an increasing number of transitions need to be managed successfully throughout the lifecycle. With rapidly changing economies, workers must be furnished with lifelong learning opportunities, in order to cope with new ways of working, including enhanced exploitation of Information and Communication Technologies (ICT). Changes in working status with associated risks of temporary losses of income should be better accommodated through the provision of appropriate modernised social protection.

To successfully meet these challenges an integrated flexicurity approach is needed. Flexicurity involves the deliberate combination of flexible and reliable contractual arrangements, comprehensive lifelong learning strategies, effective active labour market policies and modern, adequate and sustainable social protection systems.

Member States should implement their own flexicurity pathways, based on the common principles adopted by the Council. These principles serve as a useful basis for reforms, framing national policy options and specific national arrangements in the field of flexicurity. There is no single pathway and no single principle is more important than another.

Guideline 21: promote flexibility combined with employment security and reduce labourmarket segmentation, having due regard to the role of the social partners, through:

- the adaptation of employment legislation, reviewing where necessary the different contractual and working time arrangements,
- addressing the issue of undeclared work,
- better anticipation and positive management of change, including economic restructuring, notably changes linked to trade opening, so as to minimise their social costs and facilitate adaptation,
- the promotion and dissemination of innovative and adaptable forms of work organisation, with a view to improving quality and productivity at work, including health and safety,
- support for transitions in occupational status, including training, self-employment, business creation and geographic mobility.

See also integrated guideline 'To promote greater coherence between macroeconomic, structural and employment policies' (no. 5).

---

566. To maximise job creation, preserve competitiveness and contribute to the general economic framework, overall wage developments should be in line with productivity growth over the economic cycle and should reflect the labour market situation. The gender pay gap should be substantially reduced. Particular attention should be given to explaining and addressing the reasons for the low wage levels in professions and sectors which tend to be dominated by women. Efforts to reduce non-wage labour costs and to review the tax wedge may also be needed to facilitate job creation, especially for low-wage employment.

Guideline 22: Ensure employment-friendly labour cost developments and wage-setting mechanisms by:

- encouraging social partners within their own areas of responsibility to set the right framework for wage bargaining in order to reflect productivity and labour

> market challenges at all relevant levels and to avoid gender pay gaps, – reviewing the impact on employment of non-wage labour costs and where appropriate adjust their structure and level, especially to reduce the tax burden on the low-paid.
>
> *See also* integrated guideline 'To ensure that wage developments contribute to macroeconomic stability and growth' (no. 4).

4. Increase Investment in Human Capital through Better Education and Skills

567. Europe needs to invest more and more effectively in human capital. Too many people fail to enter, progress or remain in the labour market because of a lack of skills, or due to skills mismatches. To enhance access to employment for men and women of all ages, raise productivity levels, innovation and quality at work, the EU needs higher and more effective investment in human capital and lifelong learning.

Knowledge-based and service-based economies require different skills from traditional industries; skills which also constantly need updating in the face of technological change and innovation. Workers, if they are to remain and progress in work and be prepared for transition and changing labour markets, need to accumulate and renew skills regularly. The productivity of enterprises is dependent on building and maintaining a workforce that can adapt to change. Governments need to ensure that educational attainment levels are improved and that young people are equipped with the necessary key competences, in line with the European Youth Pact. In order to improve labourmarket prospects for youth, the EU should aim for an average rate of no more than 10 per cent early school leavers; and for at least 85 per cent of 22-year-olds to have completed upper secondary education by 2010. Policies should also aim at increasing the EU average level of participation in lifelong learning to at least 12.5 per cent of the adult working-age population (25 to 64 age group). All stakeholders should be mobilised to develop and foster a true culture of lifelong learning from the earliest age. To achieve a substantial increase in public and private investment in human resources per capita and guarantee the quality and efficiency of these investments, it is important to ensure fair and transparent sharing of costs and responsibilities between all actors. Member States should make better use of the Structural Funds and the European Investment Bank for investment in education and training. To achieve these aims, Member States must implement the coherent and comprehensive lifelong learning strategies to which they have committed themselves.

> **Guideline 23**: Expand and improve investment in human capital through:
>
> – inclusive education and training policies and action to facilitate significantly access to initial vocational, secondary and higher education, including apprenticeships and entrepreneurship training,

- significantly reducing the number of early school leavers,
- efficient lifelong learning strategies open to all in schools, businesses, public authorities and households according to European agreements, including appropriate incentives and cost-sharing mechanisms, with a view to enhancing participation in continuous and workplace training throughout the life-cycle, especially for the low-skilled and older workers.

See also integrated guideline 'To increase and improve investment in R & D, in particular by private business' (no. 7).

568. Setting ambitious objectives and increasing levels of investment by all actors is not enough. To ensure that supply meets demand in practice, lifelong learning systems must be affordable, accessible and responsive to changing needs. Adaptation and capacity-building of education and training systems and measures to improve the evidence base of education and training policies are necessary to improve their labour market relevance, their responsiveness to the needs of the knowledge-based economy and society and their efficiency, excellence and equity. An easily accessible, widespread and integrated system of lifelong career orientation should increase both individuals' access to education and training and the relevance to skills needs of education and training offered. ICT can be used to improve access to learning and to tailor it better to the needs of employers and employees.

Greater mobility for both work and learning purposes is also needed to access job opportunities more widely in the EU at large. The remaining obstacles to mobility within the European labour market should be lifted, in particular those relating to the recognition and transparency and use of learning outcomes and qualifications, notably by implementing the European Qualifications Framework by relating national qualification systems to that Framework by 2010 and, where appropriate, by developing national qualification frameworks. It will be important to make use of the agreed European instruments and references to support reforms of national education and training systems, as laid down in the Education and Training 2010 Work Programme.

Guideline 24: adapt education and training systems in response to new competence requirements by:

- raising and ensuring the attractiveness, openness and quality standards of education and training, broadening the supply of education and training opportunities and ensuring flexible learning pathways and enlarging possibilities for mobility for students and trainees,
- easing and diversifying access for all to education and training and to knowledge by means of working time organisation, family support services, vocational guidance and, if appropriate, new forms of cost sharing,

– responding to new occupational needs, key competences and future skill requirements by improving the definition and transparency of qualifications, their effective recognition and the validation of non-formal and informal learning.

D. Overview of Targets and Benchmarks Set in the Framework of the European Employment Strategy

569. The following targets and benchmarks have been agreed in the context of the European Employment Strategy:

– that every unemployed person is offered a job, apprenticeship, additional training or other employability measure; in the case of young persons who have left school within no more than 4 months by 2010 and in the case of adults within no more than 12 months;
– that 25 per cent of long-term unemployment should participate by 2010 in an active measure in the form of training, retraining, work practice, or other employability measure, with the aim of achieving the average of the three most advanced Member States;
– that jobseekers throughout the EU are able to consult all job vacancies advertised through Member States' employment services;
– an increase by five years, at EU level, of the effective average exit age from the labour market by 2010 compared to 2001;
– the provision of childcare by 2010 to at least 90 per cent of children between 3 years old and the mandatory school age and at least 33 per cent of children under 3 years of age;
– an EU average rate of no more than 10 per cent early school leavers; – at least 85 per cent of 22-year olds in the EU should have completed upper secondary education by 2010;
– EU average level of participation in lifelong learning should be at least 12.5 per cent of the adult working-age population (25 to 64 age group).[160]

E. The Employment Guidelines 2010-2014[161] Lisbon Strategy 2020

570. The Guidelines 2010–2014 are inspired by the Lisbon Strategy 2020. The Commission proposed to set up a new strategy for the next decade, known as 'the Europe 2020 Strategy', to enable the Union to emerge stronger from the crisis, and to turn its economy towards smart, sustainable and inclusive growth, accompanied

---

160. Council Decision of 15 July 2008 on guidelines for the employment policies of the Member States (2008/618/EC).
161. Council Decision of 21 October 2010 on guidelines for the employment policies of the Member-States (2010/707/EU).

by high level employment, productivity and social cohesion. Five headline targets, listed under the relevant guidelines, constitute shared objectives which guide the action of the Member States, taking into account their relative starting positions and national circumstances, and which also guide the action of the Union. The Member States should, furthermore, make every effort to meet the national targets and to remove the bottlenecks that constrain growth.

571. As part of comprehensive 'exit strategies' for the economic crisis, Member States should carry out ambitious reforms to ensure macroeconomic stability, the promotion of more and better jobs and the sustainability of public finance, improve competitiveness and productivity, reduce macroeconomic imbalances and enhance labour market performance. The withdrawal of the fiscal stimulus should be implemented and coordinated within the framework of the Stability and Growth Pact.

1. Smart Growth

572. Within the Europe 2020 strategy, Member States and the Union should implement reforms aimed at 'smart growth', i.e. growth driven by knowledge and innovation. Reforms should aim at improving the quality of education and ensuring access for all, as well as strengthening research, business performance and further improving the regulatory framework in order to promote innovation and knowledge transfer throughout the Union. Reforms should encourage entrepreneurship, the development of small and medium-sized enterprises (SMEs) and help to turn creative ideas into innovative products, services and processes that can create growth, quality and sustainable jobs, territorial, economic and social cohesion, and address more efficiently European and global societal challenges. Making the most of information and communication technologies is essential in this context.

2. Sustainable Growth

573. The policies of the Union and of Member States, including their reform programmes, should aim at 'sustainable growth'. Sustainable growth means building an energy and resource-efficient, sustainable and competitive economy, a fair distribution of the cost and benefits and exploiting Europe's leadership in the race to develop new processes and technologies, including green technologies. Member States and the Union should implement the necessary reforms to reduce greenhouse gas emissions and use resources efficiently, which will also help to prevent environmental degradation and biodiversity loss. They should also improve the business environment, stimulate the creation of green jobs and help enterprises to modernise their industrial base.

3. Inclusive Growth

574. The policies of the Union and Member States' reform programmes should also aim at 'inclusive growth'. Inclusive growth means building a cohesive society in which people are empowered to anticipate and manage change and consequently to actively participate in society and the economy. Member States' reforms should therefore ensure access and opportunities for all throughout their lifecycle, thus reducing poverty and social exclusion through removing barriers to labour market participation, especially for women, older workers, young people, people with disabilities and legal migrants. They should also make sure that the benefits of economic growth reach all citizens and all regions and foster employment-enhancing growth, based on decent work. Ensuring the effective functioning of the labour markets through investing in successful transitions, education and training systems, appropriate skills development, raising job quality, and fighting segmentation, structural unemployment, youth unemployment, and inactivity while ensuring adequate, sustainable social protection and active inclusion to prevent and reduce poverty, with particular attention to combating in-work poverty and reducing poverty amongst the groups most at risk from social exclusion, including children and young people, while at the same time adhering to agreed fiscal consolidation, should therefore be at the heart of Member States' reform programmes.

4. Participation by Women

575. Increased labour market participation by women is a precondition for boosting growth and for tackling the demographic challenges. A visible gender equality perspective, integrated into all relevant policy areas, is therefore crucial for the implementation of all aspects of the guidelines in the Member States. Conditions should be created to support the supply of adequate, affordable, high-quality childcare services for pre-school age children. The principle of equal pay for male and female workers for equal work or work of equal value should be applied.

5. Competitiveness in the Global Economy

576. The Union's and Member States' structural reforms can effectively contribute to growth and jobs if they enhance the Union's competitiveness in the global economy, open up new opportunities for Europe's exporters and provide competitive access to vital imports. Reforms should therefore take into account their external competitiveness implications to foster European growth and participation in open and fair markets worldwide.

6. National Reform Programmes

577. When designing and implementing their National Reform Programmes taking account of these guidelines, Member States should ensure effective governance

General Introduction, Ch. 4, European Labour Law: Locomotive?

of employment policy. While these guidelines are addressed to Member States, the Europe 2020 strategy should, as appropriate, be implemented, monitored and evaluated in partnership with all national, regional and local authorities, closely associating parliaments, as well as social partners and representatives of civil society, who shall contribute to the elaboration of National Reform Programmes, to their implementation and to the overall communication on the strategy.

7. Europe 2020 Integrated Guidelines

578. The Europe 2020 strategy is underpinned by a smaller set of guidelines, replacing the previous set of 24 and addressing employment and broad economic policy issues in a coherent manner. The guidelines for the employment policies of the Member States are intrinsically linked with the guidelines for the economic policies of the Member States and of the Union, Together, they form the 'Europe 2020 integrated guidelines'.

Even though they must be drawn up each year, these guidelines should remain stable until 2014 to ensure a focus on implementation.

579.

Guideline 7: Increasing labour market participation of women and men, reducing structural unemployment and promoting job quality

Activation is key to increasing labour market participation. Member States should integrate the flexicurity principles endorsed by the European Council into their labour market policies and apply them, making appropriate use of European Social Fund and other EU funds support, with a view to increasing labour market participation and combating segmentation, inactivity and gender inequality, whilst reducing structural unemployment. Measures to enhance flexibility and security should be both balanced and mutually reinforcing. Member States should therefore introduce a combination of flexible and reliable contractual arrangements, active labour market policies, effective lifelong learning, policies to promote labour mobility, and adequate social security systems to secure labour market transitions accompanied by clear rights and responsibilities for the unemployed to actively seek work. Together with the social partners, adequate attention should also be paid to internal flexicurity at the work place.

Member States should step up social dialogue and tackle labour market segmentation with measures addressing precarious employment, underemployment and undeclared work. Professional mobility should be rewarded. The quality of jobs and employment conditions should be addressed. Member States should combat in-work poverty and promote occupational health and safety. Adequate social security should also be ensured for those on fixed-term contracts and the self-employed. Employment services play an important role in activation and matching and they should therefore be strengthened with personalised services and active and preventive labour market measures at an early stage. Such services and measures should be open to all, including young people, those threatened by unemployment, and those furthest away from the labour market.

Policies to make work pay remain important. In order to increase competitiveness and raise participation levels, particularly for the low-skilled, and in line with economic policy guideline 2, Member States should encourage the right framework conditions for wage bargaining and labour cost development consistent with price stability and productivity trends. Member States should review tax and benefit systems, and public services capacity to provide the support needed, in order to increase labour force participation and stimulate labour demand. They should promote active ageing, gender equality including equal pay, and the integration in the labour market of young people, people with disabilities, legal migrants and other vulnerable groups. Work-life balance policies with the provision of affordable care and innovation in the manner in which work is organised should be geared to raising employment rates, particularly among young people, older workers and women. Member States should also remove barriers to labour market entry for newcomers, promote selfemployment, entrepreneurship and job creation in all areas including green employment and care and promote social innovation.

The EU headline target, on the basis of which Member States will set their national targets, taking into account their relative starting positions and national circumstances, is to aim to raise the employment rate for women and men aged 20-64 to 75 per cent by 2020, including through the greater participation of young people, older workers and low-skilled workers and the better integration of legal migrants.

580.

> **Guideline 8:** Developing a skilled workforce responding to labour market needs and promoting lifelong learning
>
> Member States should promote productivity and employability through an adequate supply of knowledge and skills to match current and future demand in the labour market. Quality initial education and attractive vocational training must be complemented with effective incentives for lifelong learning for those who are in and those who are not in employment, thus ensuring every adult the chance to retrain or to move one step up in their qualification and overcome gender stereotypes, as well as by opportunities for second-chance learning and by targeted migration and integration policies. Member States should develop systems for recognising acquired competencies, and should remove barriers to occupational and geographical mobility of workers, promote the acquisition of transversal competences to support creativity, innovation and entrepreneurship. In particular, efforts should focus on supporting those with low and obsolete skills, increasing the employability of older workers, enhancing training, skills and experience of highly skilled workers, including researchers and women in scientific, mathematical and technological fields.
>
> In cooperation with social partners and firms, Member States should improve access to training, strengthen education and career guidance. These improvements should be combined with the provision of systematic information on new job openings and opportunities, the promotion of entrepreneurship and enhanced anticipation of skill needs. Investment in human resource development, up-skilling and participation in lifelong learning schemes should be promoted through joint financial contributions from governments, individuals and employers. To support young people and in particular those not in employment, education or training, Member States, in cooperation with the social partners, should enact schemes to help those people find initial employment, job experience, or further education and training opportunities, including apprenticeships, and should intervene rapidly when young people become unemployed. Regular monitoring of the performance of up-skilling and anticipation policies should help identify areas for improvement and increase the responsiveness of education and training systems to current and emerging labour market needs, such as the low-carbon and resource-efficient economy. The ESF and other EU funds should be mobilised, where appropriate, by Member States to support these objectives. Policies stimulating labour demand could complement investments in human capital.

581.

> **Guideline 9:** Improving the quality and performance of education and training systems at all levels and increasing participation in tertiary or equivalent education
>
> In order to ensure access to quality education and training for all and to improve educational outcomes, Member States should invest efficiently in education and training systems notably to raise the skill level of the EU's workforce, allowing it to meet the rapidly changing needs of modern labour markets and society at large. In line with the lifelong learning principles, action should cover all sectors (from early childhood education and schools through to higher education, vocational education and training, as well as adult learning) taking into account also learning in informal and non-formal contexts. Reforms should aim to ensure the acquisition of the key competencies that every individual needs for success in a knowledge-based economy, notably in terms of employability in line with the priorities mentioned in guideline 4 . International mobility for learners and teachers should be encouraged. Steps should also be taken to ensure that learning mobility for young people and teachers becomes the norm. Member States should improve the openness and relevance of education and training systems, particularly by implementing national qualification frameworks enabling flexible learning pathways, and by developing partnerships between the worlds of education/training and work. The teaching profession should be made more attractive and attention should be paid to the initial education and the continuous professional development of teachers. Higher education should become more open to non-traditional learners and participation in tertiary or equivalent ducation should be increased. With a view to reducing the number of young people not in employment, education, or training, Member States should take all necessary steps to prevent early school leaving.
>
> The EU headline target, on the basis of which Member States will set their national targets, taking into account their relative starting positions and national circumstances, will aim to reduce drop out rates to less than 10 per cent, and increase the share of 30-34 year-olds having completed tertiary or equivalent education to at least 40 per cent.

582.

> **Guideline 10:** Promoting social inclusion and combating poverty
> The extension of employment opportunities is an essential aspect of Member States' integrated strategies to prevent and reduce poverty and to promote full participation in society and economy. Appropriate use of the European Social Fund and other EU funds should be made to that end. Efforts should concentrate on ensuring equal opportunities, including through access for all to high quality, affordable, and sustainable services, in particular in the social field. Public services (including online services, in line with guideline 4) play an important role in this respect. Member States should put in place effective anti-discrimination measures. Empowering people and promoting labour market participation for those furthest away from the labour market while preventing in-work poverty will help fight social exclusion. This would require enhancing social protection systems, lifelong learning and comprehensive active inclusion policies to create opportunities at different stages of people's lives and shield them from the risk of exclusion, with special attention to women. Social protection systems, including pensions and access to healthcare, should be modernised and fully deployed to ensure adequate income support and services — thus providing social cohesion – whilst remaining financially sustainable and encouraging participation in society and in the labour market.
> Benefit systems should focus on ensuring income security during transitions and reducing poverty, in particular among groups most at risk from social exclusion, such as one-parent families, minorities including the Roma, people with disabilities, children and young people, elderly women and men, legal migrants and the homeless. Member States should also actively promote the social economy and social innovation in support of the most vulnerable. All measures should also aim at promoting gender equality.
> The EU headline target, on the basis of which Member States will set their national targets, taking into account their relative starting conditions and national circumstances, will aim at promoting social inclusion, in particular through the reduction of poverty by aiming to lift at least 20 million people out of the risk of poverty and exclusion.[162]

583. According to Council Decision to 2013/208/EU of 22 April 2013,[163] the guidelines for the employment policies of the Member States, as set out in the Annex to Decision 2010/707/EU, are maintained for 2013 and shall be taken into account by the Member States in their employment policies.

---

162. The population is defined as the number of persons who are at risk of poverty and exclusion according to three indicators (at risk of poverty; material deprivation; jobless household), leaving Member States free to set their national targets on the basis of the most appropriate indicators, taking into account their national circumstances and priorities.
163. *O.J.* 22 April 2013, L118.

584. The Council explains as follows:

The Europe 2020 strategy proposed by the Commission enables the Union to turn its economy towards smart, sustainable and inclusive growth, accompanied by high level employment, productivity and social cohesion. On 13 July 2010, the Council adopted its Recommendation on broad guidelines for the economic policies of the Member States and of the Union [3]. Furthermore, on 21 October 2010, the Council adopted its Decision 2010/707/EU on guidelines for the employment policies of the Member States "employment guidelines". Those sets of guidelines form the integrated guidelines for implementing the Europe 2020 strategy. Five headline targets, listed under the relevant integrated guidelines, constitute shared objectives which guide the action of the Member States, taking into account their relative starting positions and national circumstances as well as the positions and circumstances of the Union. The European Employment Strategy plays the leading role in the implementation of the employment and labour market objectives of the Europe 2020 strategy.

585. The integrated guidelines are in line with the conclusions of the European Council of 17 June 2010. They give precise guidance to the Member States on defining their national reform programmes and on implementing reforms. The employment guidelines should form the basis for any country-specific recommendations that the Council may address to the Member States under Article 148(4) of the TFEU, in parallel with the country-specific recommendations addressed to the Member States under Article 121(2) of the TFEU. The employment guidelines should also form the basis for the establishment of the Joint Employment Report sent annually by the Council and the Commission to the European Council.

586. The examination of the Member States' draft national reform programmes, contained in the Joint Employment Report adopted by the Council on 28 February 2013, shows that Member States should continue to make every effort to address the following priorities: increasing labour market participation and reducing structural unemployment, developing a skilled workforce responding to labour market needs and promoting job quality and lifelong learning, improving the performance of education and training systems at all levels and increasing participation in tertiary education, promoting social inclusion and combating poverty.

587. The employment guidelines adopted in 2010 should remain stable until 2014 to ensure a focus on their implementation. Until the end of 2014, any updating of the employment guidelines should remain strictly limited. In 2011 and 2012, the employment guidelines were maintained. They should be maintained for 2013.

Member States should explore the use of the European Social Fund when implementing the employment guidelines.

X. The Modernisation of Labour Law (2006)[164]

588. On 22 November 2006, the European Commission presented the Green Paper Modernising labour law to meet the challenges of the 21st century,[165] which had been announced in the Social Agenda 2005–2010 and in the Communication on Restructuring and Employment. At the presentation of the Green Paper, the Commission also launched a public consultation on the need to review current labour law systems, addressed to Member States, social partners and other stakeholders.

A. Main Issues

1. Flexicurity

589. The Green Paper examines the role of a modernisation of labour law in advancing a 'flexicurity' agenda of increased labour flexibility combined with adequate employment security. It discusses developments in labour markets, technologies and work organisation, and the increasing emergence of a wide variety of non-standard employment contracts, regardless of whether they are explicitly covered by EU and national legislation.

2. Role of Social Dialogue

590. The Green Paper assesses the role of social dialogue at Member State and EU level in modernising labour law. Improving the quality of work and safeguarding working conditions is a matter for national legislation, while at EU level the social *acquis* (EU body of law) supports and complements the actions of the Member States. Social dialogue at national, sectoral and company level demonstrates how workplace rules can be adapted to changing economic realities and be applied to new categories of workers, such as temporary agency workers. The Green Paper points to a new role for collective agreements, which no longer merely supplement working conditions already defined by law but serve as important tools in adjusting legal principles to specific economic or sectoral circumstances.

3. Non-standard Employment

591. The primary focus of the Green Paper is on individual labour law. It outlines the key priorities for a meaningful labour law reform, its contributions to flexibility, employment security, preventing segmentation of the labour market, and improving the regulations affecting small and medium-sized enterprises (SMEs). The proportion of non-standard employment contracts and self-employment has

---

164. Anni Weiler, AWWW GmbH ArbeitsWelt – Working World, 'Commission presents Green Paper on modernising labour law', EIRO, 2007.
165. COM(2006) 708 final.

increased from 36 per cent in 2001 to almost 40 per cent of the EU25 workforce in 2005. Moreover, the document highlights a strong gender and intergenerational dimension as women, older and also younger workers are disproportionately represented in non-standard employment.

The boundaries between labour and commercial law have become less clear with the emergence of diverse forms of non-standard work. The Green Paper discusses illegal practices of 'disguised employment', which is understood as a misclassification of self-employment in the context of unclear legal definitions of the status of self-employment. The paper distinguishes 'disguised employment' from the concept of 'economically dependent work', which covers situations falling between the two established concepts of subordinate employment and independent self-employment (*see* EIRO study on economically dependent workers).

4. Compliance with Employment Rights

592. Other issues concern the responsibility of the various parties in multiple employment relationships to comply with employment rights. These problems relate in particular to temporary agency work and to work involving extended chains of subcontracting. Several Member States have sought to address the problems of workers in such situations by making principal contractors responsible for the obligations of their subcontractors.

5. Worker

593. In the context of mobility of workers, the definition of the term 'worker' is discussed. Most EU labour law legislation leaves the definition of 'worker' to the Member States. However, the variations in the definitions used in different directives question the consistent application of EU labour law. Difficulties have emerged particularly in the implementation of Directive 96/71/EC concerning the posting of workers in the framework of the provision of services and of Council Directive 2001/23/EC on the approximation of the laws of the Member States relating to the safeguarding of employees' rights in the event of transfers of undertakings, businesses or parts of undertakings or businesses. These complications are also of concern in the case of 'frontier workers', who live in one Member State and work in another, and in the context of the transnational operation of businesses and services.

6. Undeclared Work

594. Undeclared work is seen as a particularly worrying and enduring feature of today's labour markets, often associated with cross-border labour movement. It is considered to be the main factor contributing to 'social dumping' and to be responsible for both the exploitation of workers and the distortion of competition. The Green Paper emphasises that the problem was identified by the European social partners as an integral part of the balance between flexibility and security, and is a key issue for action in their work programme for 2006–2008.

7. Discussion at Employment Council

595. On 1 December 2006, the Employment Council held a preliminary exchange of views on the Green Paper. The council emphasised the need to consider specific features of national labour markets while preserving minimum standards at European level. Several issues received particular attention, namely the:

– importance of a meaningful social dialogue;
– prevention of market fragmentation, reduction of workers' rights and lack of job security;
– need to deal with the situation of the economically dependent worker;
– effective enforcement of labour law, including combating undeclared work;
– better reconciliation of work and family life, and initiatives to remove disincentives to the participation of women in the labour market;
– need to combat all forms of discrimination in the labour market.

8. Reaction of Social Partners

596. BUSINESSEUROPE and UEAPME emphasised that the competence to modernise labour law rests primarily with national actors. BUSINESSEUROPE strongly opposes suggestions of an EU-wide definition of 'worker' and rejects the focus on preservation of existing employment. In its view, modernising labour law must be part of the flexicurity debate based on a sound analysis and should encompass both flexibility and security. UEAPME considers that the Green Paper presents a balanced analysis of the key policy challenges ahead and is based on a reasonable approach towards new forms of work. UEAPME welcomes the fact that SME-related questions are addressed and that the document examines the ways in which labour law affects small businesses. The wording on self-employment, for example, recognises the importance of encouraging entrepreneurship.

597. CEEP restated that the questions posed in the Green Paper go in the right direction but the instrument and procedures used are not appropriate. CEEP recognises that a developed framework of flexicurity requires intervention from different actors including the state, social security institutions, and education and training providers. However, in the opinion of CEEP, 80 per cent of the questions addressed fall within the direct remit of the social partners, who should therefore have been properly and separately consulted.

598. The ETUC underlines that all relevant stakeholders at EU level need to engage in an urgent debate on how to adapt labour law and social policy to align with the modern world of work, while providing for fair and decent working conditions and labour standards for all workers. ETUC recalls that the European Commission consulted the European social partners six years ago on the need to review systems of labour law and emphasises that in the meantime several Member States have made labour law reforms leading to a two-tier labour market with growing insecurity for the most vulnerable group of workers. As the Green Paper only addresses some relevant issues, ETUC states that it will make proposals on working time, temporary agency work, European Works Councils, information and consultation and restructuring.

B. Commentary

599. According to Anni Weiler:

> the Green Paper highlights the importance of defining the term 'worker' in the application of EU labour law but remains undecided on the role of the Member States and the EU in modernising these laws. The almost exclusive focus on non-standard employment is puzzling as standard employment relationships are also affected by organisational, technological or legal developments. Moreover, the lack of a precise definition of part-time work is problematic. A reduction of normal working hours does not necessarily lead to a precarious form of employment contract. On the other hand, marginal employment hardly features in the analysis.
>
> The analysis is inconsistent in its attempt to quantify non-standard employment. For example, it provides statistical data on fixed-term, part-time and temporary agency contracts, as well as self-employment. However, in the further description and in the consultation questions, some of these forms of nonstandard employment are not mentioned again. Conversely, other atypical forms of work such as disguised employment, economically dependent work or undeclared work are not included in the statistical analysis.
>
> The Green Paper has introduced new categories in the debate on flexicurity such as 'extended chains of subcontracting' as an additional form of 'multiple employment relationship'. More research seems to be required to understand the impact of such developments.
>
> The Green paper altogether shows the European Commission has no clear vision on which way to go in order to adequately protect the interests of the workers in a globalised economy. One wonders what the follow up will be.

XI. Flexicurity: More and Better Jobs through Flexibility and Security (2007): Main Issues

600. The European Commission proposes, in its Communication of 27 June 2007, the establishment of common principles of flexicurity to promote more and better jobs by combining flexibility and security for workers and companies. Flexicurity strategies can help modernise European labour markets and better address the

opportunities and challenges of globalisation, and include flexible and reliable contractual arrangements, active labour market policies, comprehensive lifelong learning strategies and modern social protection systems that provide adequate income support during periods of unemployment. The Commission also sets out a number of typical pathways to help Member States draw up their own national strategies for flexicurity and learn from each other's experiences and best practices. In line with the EU's Lisbon Strategy for Growth and Jobs, the common principles of flexicurity aim to ensure that more Europeans get the most out of today's fast-changing global economy.

601. Europe needs to find new ways of making its labour markets more flexible while providing employment security at the same time. Flexicurity is a comprehensive approach to labour market policy which combines sufficient flexibility in contractual arrangements – to allow firms and employees to cope with change – with the provision of security for workers to stay in their jobs or be able to find a new one quickly with the assurance of an adequate income between jobs. The Communication highlights that it can be positive for both workers and companies. Flexibility is about making sure workers can move easily into a job, and between jobs; it covers external and internal flexibility within the same company. Security is not just for workers but for businesses too: improving workers' skills also provides additional security and benefits for an employer. Flexibility and security can be mutually reinforcing.

602. The Communication identifies the main flexicurity policy areas (flexicurity components) and sets out proposals for eight common flexicurity principles. These principles are reference points that Member States should agree on. They include:

(1) reinforcing the implementation of the EU's strategy for Jobs and Growth and strengthening the European social models;
(2) striking a balance between rights and responsibilities;
(3) adapting flexicurity to different circumstances, needs and challenges of the Member States;
(4) reducing the gap between those in non-standard, sometimes precarious contractual arrangements on the one hand (so-called 'outsiders'), and those in permanent, full-time jobs on the other (the 'insiders');
(5) developing internal and external flexibility, by helping employees move up the career ladder (internal) as well as across the job market (external);
(6) supporting gender equality and promoting equal opportunities for all;
(7) producing balanced policy packages to promote a climate of trust between social partners, public authorities and other stakeholders;
(8) ensuring a fair distribution of the costs and benefits of flexicurity policies, and contribution to sound and financially sustainable budgetary policies.

603–604   General Introduction, Ch. 4, European Labour Law: Locomotive?

A. Flexicurity Pathways

Pathway 1: tackling contractual segmentation

This typical pathway is of interest to countries where the key challenge is segmented labour markets, with insiders and outsiders. This pathway would aim to distribute flexibility and security more evenly over the workforce. It would provide entry ports into employment for newcomers and it would promote their progress into better contractual arrangements.

603. In these countries, open-ended contracts have been seen as the main access route to protection by labour laws and collective agreements. Training opportunities and social security provisions also tend to depend on having an open ended contract. Due to attempts to increase labour market flexibility, a high incidence of fixed-term contracts, on-call contracts, agency work, etcetera, has developed. Often workers are on repeated fixed term contracts for a long time before obtaining an open ended contract. Rather than as stepping stones, these contracts risk working as traps. In these countries, security tends to rely on job protection rather than social benefits. As a consequence, unemployment benefits are rather low and social assistance systems are weakly developed. Benefit administrations and public employment services, in their present situation, are in need of institutional reinforcement to offer sound management and effective active labour market policies to the unemployed.

Benefits for citizens and society would accrue if effective stepping stones are created enabling workers to enter and progress on the labour market and achieve upward mobility.

604. Within contractual arrangements, this pathway would aim to improve the position of workers on fixed term contracts, agency work, on-call work, etc. It would ensure that adequate protection is offered to these workers, for example equal pay and a minimum number of working hours for on-call workers. Secondary employment conditions, such as coverage by occupational pension funds and access to training, would also apply to these workers. Legislation and collective agreements would limit consecutive use of non-standard contracts and promote timely progress into better contracts.

A complementary approach would be to redesign the open ended contract. In this option, workers would have an open ended contract from the very beginning of the employment relationship with their employer and would no longer, as is now often the case, start with a series of fixed term or agency contracts. The open ended contract would be redesigned to include a progressive build-up of job protection. It would start with a basic level of job protection, and protection would build up progressively with job tenure, until 'full' protection is achieved. This 'tenure track approach' would guarantee automatic progress into better contractual conditions; the risk of getting 'stuck' in less protected contracts would thus be reduced.

Redesigning rules for economic dismissals would be envisaged for open ended contracts, addressing bureaucracy, length of procedures, improving transparency of outcomes, and making the process more reliable.

605. On lifelong learning, employers and public authorities should work together to improve training facilities for temporary workers. At present, these categories often do not receive training opportunities because the employer is not sure how long he or she will keep theworker. Training funds and training institutes at branch or regional level would be installed to ensure that everybody can benefit from training. Incentives for workers and enterprises, including financial contributions and tax credits, would be strengthened to enhance participation.

606. Active labour market policies would start with strengthening public employment services in terms of staff and skills. Cooperation with market partners, such as temporary work agencies, would be considered. Active labour market policies would be designed to support not only (long-term) unemployed but also those who are experiencing frequent intervals of unemployment.

Social security systems would ensure the possibility for temporary workers to accumulate rights and would improve portability of entitlements across firm or branch borders. They would be remodelled towards providing higher benefits during shorter spells of unemployment. The introduction of a social assistance system would be considered to increase citizens' mobility and make them less dependent on informal family support.

Trust between social partners would be further strengthened by creating opportunities for them to make the benefits of change visible to their constituencies.

607. As to sequencing and financing, priority would be given to addressing segmentation, which entails limited direct costs. Measures under lifelong learning and active labour market policies are of the highest importance but may take time to deliver. They also require public and private investments. Improving social security, especially setting up social assistance, may require additional or redeployed public expenditure that must go hand in hand with monitoring and conditionality of benefits in order to ensure that such spending is cost effective. In parallel, redesigning economic dismissal rules would be feasible with putting these conditions in place.

Pathway 2: developing flexicurity within the enterprise and offering transition security.

This typical pathway is of interest to countries with relatively low job-flows. It would increase investments in employability to allow workers within enterprises to continuously update their capabilities and thus be better prepared for future changes in production methods, organisation of work. This pathway would also look beyond the actual job and the actual employer, by putting in place systems that provide safe and successful job to job transitions in the case of company restructurings and redundancy.

608. The countries which are addressed by this pathway are dominated by larger enterprises, offering high levels of job protection. Workers are strongly attached to their enterprise and labour market dynamism is rather low. In recent years, this tradition has come under strain because company restructurings and outsourcing are becoming more frequent. Social security systems in these countries are largely well developed and benefits are adequate. Combining good benefits with strong incentives for accepting jobs remains a challenge. Spending on active labour market policies has often increased strongly, but programmes are not always effective, especially when it comes to offering roads back into employment for long term unemployed.

Benefits for citizens and society would accrue from enhanced mobility of workers between enterprises. Workers will be more inclined to take risks associated with job transfers if benefits are adequate during transition periods and if prospects for new and better jobs are real.

609. Contractual arrangements would be made to meet the following requirements: (a) a preventative approach, with continuous investment in lifelong learning (see below), improved working time flexibility and arrangements to combine work and care responsibilities; (b) early intervention, meaning that the search for a new job is not delayed until the worker has been made redundant, but starts immediately when it becomes clear that this is likely, and (c) joint action by all concerned. Employers, social partners, public employment services and temporary work agencies would work together to organise transitions and prevent redundant workers becoming (long-term) unemployed. If these conditions are met, dismissal procedures can be made considerably lighter, less costly and less time consuming.

610. Enterprises would be expected to forcefully step up their investments in lifelong learning and employability of their workforce. This would be done in a way that takes into account the diversity of enterprises and their size. Skills development programmes would offer personal training and career programmes to each employee. Such programmes would be seen as part of the employment contract, constituting a mutual obligation to do everything possible to meet the agreed skills requirements. Employability would also be made an issue of negotiation at enterprise or branch level. Collective agreements would set skills requirements for each relevant profession, provide training facilities needed to achieve these skills, and set time frames for workers to meet the requirements. In branches dominated by SMEs, cooperation at branch level would be helpful in creating effective human capital development policies.

Active labour market policies, operated by public employment services, would contribute to successful job-to-job transitions (*see above*). Apart from this, public employment services would focus on the long-term unemployed. They would offer them programmes which would be made more responsive to the demands of the labour market and personalised coaching of jobseekers.

Social security systems would focus on ensuring conditionality of benefits and effective monitoring of job search efforts. Benefit levels, although generally adequate, may need to be raised during the first periods of unemployment, in order to improve the situation of workers in transition.

Although institutional social dialogue is well-developed, trust between the social partners is in urgent need of reinforcement, especially at national level. Wherever possible, decentralised levels would be implicated in the negotiations.

As to sequencing and financing, priority would be given to measures and investments by enterprises and branches, to further develop internal flexicurity and transition security. This would go hand in hand with refocusing dismissal procedures towards early intervention and transition. Improved active labour market policies would require better spending rather than more spending.

Pathway 3: tackling skills and opportunity gaps among the workforce

This typical pathway is of interest to countries where the key challenge is large skills and opportunity gaps among the population. It would promote opportunities of low-skilled people to enter into employment and develop their skills in order to obtain a sustainable position at the labour market.

611. In these countries, employment rates tend to be high, but not all groups are equally on board. Upward mobility needs to be promoted. Contractual arrangements tend to be sufficiently flexible, but may in some cases need to provide more protection to weaker groups on the labour market. Skills gaps and opportunity gaps may lead to segmentation in sectors and workplaces as well as in outcomes on the labour market. There are risks that specific groups (women, single mothers, migrants, the disabled, youth and older workers) are being excluded from the labour market. This may result in high shares of people on permanent benefits and could increase poverty rates. Active labour market policies provide strong incentives towards job acceptance, but efforts may be needed to ensure progress in terms of job quality and skills levels.

Benefits for citizens and society would accrue from offering improved chances of social mobility to the low skilled by preparing people to progress into different professions with new opportunities.

612. Contractual arrangements would allow low-skilled workers to enter employment at conditions which are favourable to potential employers, but would also allow them to progress into more stable contractual arrangements when their skills improve and the working relationship acquires a more permanent character.

Lifelong learning policies would address opportunity gaps among the workforce, starting at the initial education system. Early school leaving would be fought and general qualification levels of school leavers would be improved. Illiteracy and innumeracy problems among the adult population would be addressed. Workforce training would be targeted especially at the low skilled. Combinations of work and training and mobility between training systems would be promoted. Informal learning would be recognised and validated and low-threshold, easy access language and computer training inside and outside the workplace would be organised. Taking into account their diversity and size, enterprises would develop comprehensive skills strategies, allowing all their staff to train and acquire new skills. Public authorities may improve incentives to enterprises to invest in their workforce, using tax incentives or other instruments. But they would also increase incentives to workers, for example by putting in place a system of individual training accounts. Such accounts would allow workers to spend a certain amount of (working) time and money on their personal development, in cooperation with their employers.

613. Active labour market policies would distinguish clearly between those jobseekers that are sufficiently skilled, and those who need to strengthen their skills. For the first group, emphasis can be on individual job search support. For the second group, however, active labour market policies would focus on providing adequate training to support upward mobility and sustainable, rather than quick, reintegration.

Social security systems would offer incentives to low-skilled benefit recipients and monitor the conditionality of such benefits in order to ensure that taking up work pays, if necessary by providing supplementary benefits or gradual phasing out of benefits. Thus, they would contribute to avoiding problems of the working poor. They would also contribute to reducing non-wage labour costs of low-skilled workers.

Where the role of social partnership is not strongly developed, social dialogue could be revitalised by bringing new issues into the discussion, such as R&D, innovation, and education and skills.

As to sequencing and financing, improvements in initial education would be implemented as a priority, but they will take time to deliver. Improved workplace training would require private investments, supported by public incentives. Effective active labour market policies and policies in the social security field to increase the attractiveness of recruiting the lowskilled have to be enhanced.

Pathway 4: improving opportunities for benefit recipients and informally employed workers

This typical pathway is of interest to countries which have experienced substantive economic restructuring in the recent past, resulting in high numbers of people on long-term benefits with difficult perspectives of returning to the labour market. It would aim at improving opportunities for benefit recipients and shifting from informal to formal employment through development of effective active labour market policies and lifelong learning systems combined with an adequate level of unemployment benefits.

614. In these countries, traditional, often industrial, enterprises were forced to lay off large numbers of people. Unemployed workers receive benefits that are often designed as 'labour market exit benefits' rather than 'transition into new employment'. Investments in active labour market policies are limited and chances of finding new employment are low. Benefit administrations and public employment services need institutional reinforcement to provide effective active labour market policies. New economic activity is developing, mostly in services. For benefit recipients, it is difficult to seize the employment opportunities associated with this new economic development. New jobs often have low levels of protection, while some measures that apply to old jobs may be too restrictive. Gender gaps persist. Many people are taking recourse to the informal economy. Weak vocational training systems make difficult for low skilled workers and young people without work experience to adjust to the requirements of the labour market.

Benefits for citizens and society would accrue from creating new opportunities for the unemployed and from bringing informal economic activity into the formal economy.

615. Within contractual arrangements, it would be ensured that workers employed in emerging sectors of the economy, many of whom work on fixed term or on call basis, are offered adequate levels of protection. Regularising informal work could be made more attractive by improving informal workers' rights and providing access to professional training. Higher regularised employment would lead to increased tax revenues and social contributions. Transitions to formal employment would also require further reforms of labour taxation, business registration requirements as well as strengthening of labour inspectorates and financial institutions combating informal work. Workers on open ended contracts would benefit from increased investments in their training and early action in case of threatened redundancy. If these conditions are in place, there is less need to apply strict rules with respect to economic dismissals.

616. Lifelong learning, education and vocational training systems would be developed in close cooperation with enterprises, geared towards labour market needs. Company investments in lifelong learning would be stimulated. An obligation for employers to invest in their employees could be a key issue in collective bargaining. Developing lifelong learning and vocational training systems would require close partnership between private companies and public authorities. Better linking the allocation of resources with education outcomes is needed for these systems to be cost-effective.

The administrative capacity of public employment services would be a priority. This requires improvement in terms of staff numbers, skills, decision-making process and work organisation. Cooperation between benefits administrations and public employment services would be strengthened in order to provide effective active labour market policies. Active labour market policies would concentrate on long term unemployed and disabled workers and workers threatened with dismissals. They would provide tailor-made assistance, including programmes more responsive to the needs of the labour market, to successful re-employment of job seekers. Public–private partnership of all stakeholders (public authorities at all levels, education and training providers, social partners, companies, NGOs, private employment agencies) could contribute to effectiveness of active labour market policies.

617. On social security systems, unemployment benefits would be brought at an adequate level, to enable job search without workers taking up informal jobs. At the same time work incentives and the conditionality of benefits, both, for workers and employers, need to be improved. They would encourage on one hand people on benefits who can work to look for jobs and on the other hand employers to create new jobs. Conditions for the integration of the disabled into labour markets would be facilitated. Portability of social security entitlements would be improved.

618. The capacity of the social partners would be reinforced, e.g. by extending rights to negotiate key elements of working conditions including working time.

619–622   General Introduction, Ch. 4, European Labour Law: Locomotive?

Governments would promote the creation of comprehensive employer and employee organisations and their merging into larger bodies. Both bipartite and tripartite social dialogue could be strengthened. Social dialogue could also be developed at branch and regional level.

619. As to sequencing and financing, priority would be given to bringing informal work into the formal system. Institutional reinforcement of public employment services and improvements in social security would thus become more affordable. Investments in lifelong learning would require joint efforts of public authorities and enterprises. Redesigning dismissal procedures would be feasible in parallel with improving active labour market policies, lifelong learning and social security.

XII. Framework Agreement of Actions on Youth Employment (2013)

620. Youth unemployment is one of Europe's most pressing problems. In the current economic and financial crisis the lack of job opportunities has affected young people more than any other group in society; this is reflected in high and increasing youth unemployment rates and levels of precariousness.

In Europe, more than 5.68 million young people are unemployed. The average rate of youth unemployment (23.4 per cent) is more than double the overall unemployment rate (10.7 per cent). Even before the crisis the youth unemployment rate was particularly high (17 per cent compared with an average rate of 7 per cent in 2008).

Those with jobs are strongly represented in temporary and part-time work with 42 per cent on temporary contracts and 32 per cent in part-time contracts, especially young women.

621. This shows that there are structural reasons including lack of job opportunities, in particular in some regions, making it difficult for young people to fully integrate into labour markets. The crisis has exacerbated this youth unemployment challenge in many countries especially for disadvantaged groups. More than half of young men and women on the labour markets are now unemployed in some countries. Urgent action is required to provide more and better jobs for the young and avoid scarring effects both to young people and European economies and societies as a whole.

When they enter into the labour market, many young people lack work experience. Therefore, in order to achieve a quick introduction of new recruits into labour market, it is necessary to address this issue. In addition, insufficient basic skills, lack of focus on learning outcomes in education and training, as well as a negative perception of initial vocational education and training (IVET) can lead to difficult integration into the labour market.

622. Contracts of indefinite duration are the majority form of employment relationships. For some young people, temporary contracts could provide a helpful stepping stone into the labour market. However, supporting young people to develop their career from there is important so as to limit as much as possible the proportion of young people who may well find themselves stuck without longer-term prospects. Social partners should support them in doing this and ensure the adequate protections apply to these contracts.

Longer and unpredictable transitions to the labour markets can have a negative impact on young people's confidence in the future and daily lives, notably in terms of access to a regular income, risk of poverty, possibility of forming a family, and health. Moreover, without a job and adequate social protection, more young people are dependent on their families for a longer time and are more likely to slip into poverty.

623. According to Eurofound, the cost of 7.5 million young people (15-29) who are not in education, employment or training (NEETs) is more than €153 billion a year, or 1.2 per cent of EU GDP. We risk missing a great deal of the potential of the young generation of Europeans. If this risk materialises, European economies would be losing a part of the young to social exclusion. This would also undermine Europe's competitiveness and innovation potential for the next decades.

Active labour market policies are part of the solution, but reducing youth unemployment is not possible without a strong commitment to education, growth and recovery. Adequate financial resources should be allocated at the appropriate level taking into account fiscal discipline and the objectives of the Europe 2020 strategy.

Employability is a valuable way for young people to invest in their future. Measures and targeted incentives should be put in place to stimulate employment and achieve a better match between young people's aspirations and available vacancies.

A. Challenges

624. The crisis together with the on-going process of economic transformation coincides with profound demographic, cultural and social changes throughout Europe.

Youth unemployment is a key European concern that needs to be addressed. Two main objectives are to create the right conditions to foster employment opportunities for young people and to ease their transitions between education and work.

European social partners aim to address three inter-related challenges:

1. Create more and better jobs and attractive career opportunities for young people;
2. Strengthen the quality and relevance of education and training at all levels to address skills mismatches;
3. Optimise the role of industry, in particular SMEs, and of high-performing public services in Europe as a driver of sustainable and inclusive growth.

625. More specific challenges include the following:

– Creating more and better jobs and the right framework conditions for smoother transitions into employment: With more than 26 million people unemployed, the

main challenge remains the stimulation of a job-rich growth pattern and the creation of jobs. In this context, social partners together with institutions should engage at European, national and local levels to foster economic growth, productivity and competitiveness in order to improve the quality and increase the number of jobs. This will make it possible for young people to fully integrate into the labour market.
- Promoting the attractiveness of vocational education and training (VET) and ensuring its quality: This will contribute to improving the learning environment and providing young people with relevant skills and competences.
- Promoting the acquisition of transversal and specific competences and skills: The evolution towards process-oriented and interdisciplinary work organisation increasingly requires transversal and technical competences, problem-solving and communication skills, and teamwork. Transversal and specific competences and skills should be promoted on a lifelong learning basis including in the work place.
- Dealing with the increasing need for highly skilled workers: Together with medium-skill, high-skill jobs are very likely to be on the rise in the coming decades (CEDEFOP forecasts 2020). Preventing young people from dropping out from school and training and incentivising them to achieve medium and high educational attainments, be it through higher vocational education and training or university pathways, will contribute to reinforcing the EU's competitive edge through higher added value and quality production and services. Higher educational attainments will also contribute to their personal and social development.
- Improving the matching between skills supply and demand: Closing this gap will help fill the current 2 million job vacancies in European labour markets. In some regions in particular, even qualified young people face difficulties integrating in labour markets due to a lack of jobs or skills mismatches. This requires increasing collaboration between educational institutions and social partners so that young people acquire the right skills. Closing the skills gap will also require better information to young workers on possible attractive career prospects of sectors/areas they may not have considered. This will increase the chances for employers to find the right candidates and for employees to choose the career they aspire to.

B. Social Partners' Approach

626. The European social partners reject the inevitability of a lost generation. That is why they have included this Framework of Actions as the first priority of the Work Programme for 2012–2014. They agreed to 'focus on the link between education, young people's expectations and labour market needs, while taking account of young people's transition from school into the labour market, in an effort to increase employment rates in general'.

In this respect, European social partners fully support the objective of article 3 of the TEU of working for a highly competitive social market economy and article 9 of the TFEU of promoting 'a high level of employment, the guarantee of adequate social protection, the fight against social exclusion, and a high level of education, training and protection of human health.'

With this Framework of Actions, we call on national social partners, public authorities and other stakeholders to act together to achieve concrete progress in favour of youth employment. A multi-pronged approach is needed with measures and appropriate resources to secure high quality learning outcomes, promote vocational education and training, and create jobs.

627. The European social partners are thus committed to putting forward practical solutions to address youth unemployment taking into account the specific situation of each country, in order to contribute to growth, employment and social cohesion.

This Framework of Actions is based on existing and new practices. European social partners aim to promote the most effective initiatives identified across Europe that could be used as inspiration for designing solutions by national social partners in their respective contexts. One also includes recommendations to other relevant actors such as the EU institutions and Member States.

628.

BUSINESSEUROPE, UEAPME, CEEP and ETUC:

– are convinced that investing and creating more and better jobs is the way forward to improve the situation of young people on labour markets;
– consider that much can be achieved by high-performing education and training systems to deliver the right skills for young people, while taking into account their expectations, and the efficiency and resilience of labour markets;
– stress the importance of measures and means aiming to stimulate sustainable and inclusive growth and job creation in Europe;
– want to contribute to setting the right incentives and framework conditions to make the hiring of young people a more attractive option for employers, particularly through collective bargaining between social partners;
– aim to promote adaptability of both enterprises and workers, and opportunities to workers through more dynamic careers;
– recall that inclusive, open and efficient labour markets are fundamental for improving young people's access and sustainable integration in employment;
– affirm the joint responsibility of social partners at all levels in policy development through constructive autonomous social dialogue, in line with the diversity of national industrial relation systems;
– acknowledge the broader dimension of the challenge, which calls for close cooperation with public authorities, as well as education, training institutions;
– consider that current and future measures taken must comply with the aims of intergenerational solidarity, stress the shared responsibility of employers, public authorities and individuals to invest in skills development.

§3. Convergence or Divergence?

629. The question is asked whether the accomplishment of a real internal market will bring the different national systems of labour law and of industrial relations closer together, and eventually make them more harmonised or even uniform. One could indeed be of the opinion that the fact that our different national systems within that one large market will be confronted with the same challenges, such as ever-growing (international) economic competition, the continuous introduction of new technologies, with the new worker – more educated, more creative and more participatory (the knowledge worker) –, with the same urbanisation of our societies, with similar environmental problems, will have a convergent influence. The fact is that similar problems tend to be solved by the same solutions. One could also advance the argument that the labour law rules of the game – like many other rules for that matter – should be the same in order so that fair competition between countries does not have an adverse effect. The fact that it is easier to dismiss a worker in Great Britain than in the Netherlands disturbs the market. Investors may be attracted by cheaper conditions in those countries where there are the fewest 'social constraints'. Thus, in order to combat eventual competition falsification we need at least to harmonise or, if possible, make uniform labour law rules. It then becomes a duty for the European authorities to see to it that the rules of the game are the same for all or at least equivalent. A convergent movement, i.e. getting closer together, would first be brought about by the natural functioning of the invisible hand, the market, and subsequently through a pointed policy of the authorities.

630. One could also argue that the existent divergence between the national systems of labour law and of industrial relations will continue and even persist further and that governments should not intervene in that process, but let them take their natural (or national?) course. This attitude is based first in the enormous variety of solutions that currently characterise the labour law systems of the 27 Member States and which will probably persist. Before answering the question 'divergence or convergence?', let us look into this diversity, which is greater than is usually realised. It is said with reason that this diversity is not accidental, but rather the result of our own proper social, cultural, political, historical and societal developments, which must be respected in their individuality. Some examples may suffice to illustrate the point.

631. A first distinction regarding labour between the Member States is undoubtedly the fact that some systems are very formal while others are very informal. One of the most formal systems of the EU countries is undoubtedly the German system, in which most matters are dealt with by law, in which judges intervene with authority and efficiency and where every German seems to be a born lawyer, believing in the rule of law and approaching societal problems from the legal angle. Workers' participation, to give one example, is meticulously detailed and the legal rules are lived up to in practice; in Germany a strike is not only legally but also *de facto* governed by the peace obligation between the social partners and so on. In other words, the German system is legally predictable and probably a little bit boring. In Belgium, on the other hand, one might say that law and strikes have almost nothing to do with each other. Strikes in Belgium are a matter of pure power relations in the field.

Germany is at one end of the spectrum, Italy is at the other: the formal elements in Italy are less important. Informality carries the day. Labour relations develop in relation to individual and collective emotions, which themselves are carried by the moods of the time, thus making Italy a paradise of immense creativity, and bringing a lot of – not always pleasant – surprises, such as was the case in the Coba wildcat strikes. It is only in Italy that the notion *stato di agitazione* as an element of industrial warfare is known.

632. A second distinction can be found in the organisation of workers, more precisely the degree of unionisation, trade union structures and trade union ideology. The degree of unionisation differs enormously from country to country. Belgium and Denmark score rather high: some 50 per cent or more of workers are organised (there are no really controlled and certified figures available); France and Spain are at a much lower level with less than 10 per cent of the workforce organised. Lately, the number of trade union members has diminished dramatically in certain countries. In a space of 10 years, the French unions lost 50 per cent of their membership. At present only 2 per cent of French young people between the ages of 18 and 24 are members of a union. Other countries lie between the two extremes.

One can find the same diversity in the trade union structures: on the one hand, Germany has a streamlined trade union organisation per sector of industry, on the other, Great Britain still has craft unions, which are organised in certain sectors on the basis of craft or trade; then there are the demarcation lines between the trade unions themselves running along different patterns in the Member States, whereby, for example, workers organised by the French metal workers' union are members of the Belgian textile organisation.

The same is true for the trade union ideology: one distinguishes between unions from the North, which are more or less integrated in the neo-capitalist system, and the more contesting organisations from the South; while British unions are characterised by their adversarial approach with, as it is called, some touches of 'new realism' shown by certain organisations which are convinced that they can only adequately defend the interests of their members when they accept the reality of the market economy and the profit motive. Diametrically opposed to this is the still communist French Confédération Générale du Travail, which has the greatest number of members in France, and which for that reason was for a long time denied membership of the ETUC.

633. A third example of diversity can be found in the structure and the role of the employers' associations. Some organisations are more centralised than others, pursuant to the proper character of their own labour relations system. The *Deutsche Arbeitgebersbund* is more centralised in its organisation and decision-making structure than, say, the British Confederation of Industries. Another point: all employers' organisations self-evidently engage in wide-ranging political lobbying, giving advice to their members on tax and related matters, exports, etc. There is nevertheless an important difference depending on the question whether the employers' organisations also engage in collective bargaining and are parties to a collective agreement or not. Thus, we cite the Belgian Federation of Enterprises which has a clear profile as the employers' negotiator for the Belgian private sector as a whole. It is clear that the British organisation does not play such a role. This is again a very important point of diversity between the Member States regarding industrial relations.

634. Still another, and probably the most important distinction can be found in the difference in legal culture between Great Britain on the one hand and continental Europe (minus Scandinavia) on the other. It is indeed a fact that 'it is not in the tradition of Her Majesty's Government to regulate conditions of work by Acts of Parliament'. Working conditions in Great Britain are not regulated by Acts. This is a job for the social partners. And if the government feels that one of the partners has too much power, there may be legal intervention, such as Mrs. Thatcher instigated, to curb trade union power and in so doing increase the power of the employers to make their points more easily accepted at the bargaining table, if there is bargaining at all. This could be looked upon as one pointed form of legal interventionism. This characteristic of the British legal system is of the utmost importance for Community developments regarding labour law. Indeed, Mrs. Thatcher was consistent with herself when she underlined in her famous speech in Bruges in 1988 that she was not going to accept labour law rules from Brussels, where she had prevented them successfully in London. That is why she refused to sign the Social Charter and why John Major did not accept the Maastricht Agreement on Social Policy. Tony Blair and New Labour continued that tradition. The European continent, on the other hand, is generally more legally interventionist: our labour law codes are more than full of texts, even in a period of so-called deregulation.

635. An equally striking difference concerns the legally binding effect of collective agreements.[166] It is unthinkable for continental lawyers that a collective agreement in Great Britain is not legally binding and constitutes only a 'gentlemen's agreement', that it cannot lead to legal obligations because 'parties do not have the intention to create such obligations'. A collective agreement is only binding in law if the parties expressly declare this in their agreement. In continental Europe, on the contrary, there is, in accordance with the Roman adage *pacta sunt servanda*, a clear legal binding effect of the obligations created by the agreement. Just as important is the possibility in certain Member States to give the collective agreement a general binding effect by which the normative part of the collective agreement, which is, say, concluded at sectoral level, becomes legally binding for all employers and all workers of that sector, whether they are members of the contracting parties or not. If the agreement is concluded at inter-industry level all employers and all workers of the private sector may fall within the scope of the legally binding agreement. Such a procedure by which agreements can be extended exists in Belgium, France, Germany and the Netherlands, to give a few examples. The impact of this extension procedure on a national system of industrial relations is enormous. One example may suffice. In Great Britain where extension of agreements is not a given practice,

---

166. *See*: Thomas Blanke and Edgar Rose (eds), 'Collective bargaining and Wages in Comparative Perspective. Germany, France, The Netherlands, Sweden and the United Kingdom', *Bulletin of Comparative Labour Relations*, no. 56, 2005, 176 pp.

Ford Motor Co. conducts negotiations with its employees on its own, without being for that matter a very active member of the employers' association. In Belgium, on the contrary, where extension of agreements is standard practice, Ford Motor Co. is a very active member of Agoria, the employers' organisation of the metal working trades. The reason is self-evident: Ford wants maximum influence over the outcome of the collective agreement that will be negotiated by Agoria, an agreement which Ford would be involved in, even if it were not a member of the organisation. In summary, the extension of agreements leads to stronger employers' associations and more centralised labour relations and therefore has a basic influence over labour law and industrial relations.

636. The role of governments in industrial relations, particularly in the area of income policies, is another topical example. In certain Member States, governments play the role of third parties in the industrial relations scene, sometimes that of the most important actor, and do not hesitate to intervene in wage policies when it becomes necessary to protect the competitiveness of the undertakings. Over the last few years, such interventions have taken place in Belgium, France, Greece and Spain, not to mention other countries. In Germany, such an intervention is unheard of and almost constitutionally impossible. In Germany, the holy principle of 'tariff' autonomy of the social partners prevails, meaning that the government cannot interfere directly in the setting of wages, as this belongs to the autonomy and prerogative of the social partners. The most the German government can do is bring the parties together within the framework of what is called 'concerted action' in order to give, on the basis of an experts' report on the economic situation in Germany, some guidelines concerning pay, which one hopes the social partners will respect. This situation in Germany is easily understandable when one realises that it is the outcome of a reaction against Nazi Germany, where a dictatorship controlled almost every aspect of life; in the Federal Republic the power of the government has been confined within the framework of a pluralistic democracy in favour of the social partners. This is just another large difference between the systems of the Member States.

637. One could go on for ever citing examples regarding workers' participation, the way strikes are allowed and regulated and so on. Diversity is the general rule. In other words, there is no European system of industrial relations. The systems are mainly national and will remain so for a long time to come. Therefore one has to give a very nuanced answer to the question: convergence or divergence of labour law in Europe? First, it is clear that diversity will continue, not only because this lies in the nature of things: Germans are not Italians and vice versa and it is best that it stays this way. As important is the fact that the national systems constitute a delicate balance between social factors and actors, which has come about over the years and evolves in its own rhythm and tempo. Harmonisation over the boundaries jeopardises those balances and has a strong chance of being rejected. This is certainly the case in relation to everything in labour relations to do with power, namely collective bargaining, workers' participation, strikes, lock-outs, etc. It is no accident that the European proposals concerning the workers' participation European Company Statute (SE) was on the table for more than 30 years before being adopted. These proposals encroach too much upon the existing balance of power. Moreover, collective labour relations are bedevilled by ideology and mask societal options: pro-market or pro-government intervention. Moreover, quite a number of voices quickly point out that our labour relations should become more decentralised and that problems regarding e.g. working time, except for very general framework (national or sectoral) agreements, must be dealt with at the level of the undertaking, thus taking into account that it is the enterprises that have to do battle on the markets and that the great diversity in goods and services prevalent today make simple, uniform formulae that are valid for all enterprises and situations totally inadequate.

On the other hand, it is likewise clear that the market comes into play and that it will push the national systems together from the point of view of cost, while a certain harmonisation 'while improvement is being maintained' (Article 151 TFEU) is also indicated. European measures, for that matter, can perfectly respect the diversity between the Member States. But here one should also be cautious. Lower unit labour costs and longer working hours may constitute, for example for Portugal, a winning card in the attraction of foreign investment and thus jobs, which would disappear if one started to equalise wages over the boundaries and make working time more uniform.

638. In a nutshell, one can say that there will be a convergence of systems and a certain harmonisation of labour law as far as the result and the cost of the systems are concerned: the market will come into play and lead, together with the common challenges that confront all Member States, to an unavoidable convergence which, supported by political and trade union pressure, will bring the systems closer to each other. This convergence will, however, go hand in hand with a continuous divergence as far as the content of labour relations and labour law is concerned: the way people are hired and fired, the way strikes are organised and so on. These will mainly be determined at a national level. Summing up: convergence of costs versus divergence of content. The danger is that convergence of costs goes together with an ongoing process of social dumping.[167] There is asymmetry between an economic monetary Europe and a social Europe, which remains mainly national. Competing on labour costs in a free market without a social counter balance leads to social dumping and diminishing working conditions.

639. Consequently it becomes self-evident that the establishment of the internal market calls more now than ever for an intensive comparison of legal systems. We not only need to know each other's systems better than before; the harmonisation process presupposes that one starts with an examination of the national systems, of what they have in common and how they differ from each other in order, if necessary, to develop Union law which has most of its roots in national practices and experiences. It was with this preoccupation in mind, and one that supersedes the EU anyway, that in 1975 we started the publication of an *International Encyclopaedia*

---

167. The granting of benefits to undertakings (reduction of social security contributions) that are most exposed to international competition, in order to promote job creation, is an advantage constituting State aid caught by Article 107 TFEU. It is therefore incompatible with the common market (Belgium, *Maribel* case, Decision of the Commission, 4 December 1996).

of Labour Law and Industrial Relations, which consists at present of some 75 international and national monographs, and that in 1991 the *International Encyclopaedia of Laws* was launched. The IEL will also contain international and national monographs of about 60 countries in diverse fields of law such as, civil procedure, commercial and economic law, constitutional law, contracts, corporations and partnerships, criminal law, cyber law, energy law, environmental law, insurance law, tort law, intergovernmental organisations, medical law, social security law, family and succession law, intellectual property, private international law, property and trust, sports law, tort law and transport law. In 2007, migration, media and religious law were added.[168] The *International Encyclopaedia of Laws* is more than an academic dream of 1400 scholars and practitioners from some 110 countries and international organisations. Indeed, The Encyclopaedia is now on line, in easy reach of everybody, world-wide. We live in a global society with global information needs. We are happy to make a contribution, especially now that IELaws are on line, in easy reach of all.

---

168. http://www.ielaws.com

Part I. Individual Labour Law

640. Individual labour law consists of the body of rules that relate to the individual relations between the employer and the worker. Consecutively we deal with:

– free movement of workers;
– freedom of services;
– international private labour law;
– individual employment contracts;
– child care and the protection of young people at work;
– the equal treatment of men and women;
– protection of motherhood;
– working time, Sunday rest, night work and parental leave;
– health and safety at the workplace;
– restructuring of enterprises: collective redundancies, transfer of enterprises and the insolvency of the employer.

Chapter 1. The Free Movement of Workers

641. The free movement of persons in general and for workers in particular is one of the cornerstones of the EU. Pursuant to Article 3 TFEU, the activities of the Union include: an internal market comprising 'an area without internal frontiers in which the free movement of goods, persons, services and capital is ensured in accordance with the provisions of the Treaties' (Article 26 (2) TFEU)) (the so-called four fundamental freedoms). The right of citizens of the Union and their family members to move and reside freely within the territory of the Member States is further regulated by Directive 2004/38/EC of 29 April 2004.[169]

642. The provisions of Union law governing the free movement of workers do not apply to purely internal situations of a Member State.[170] A national of a Member State who has never exercised the right of freedom of movement within the Union cannot rely on Article 45 TFEU in circumstances wholly within the domestic sphere of that Member State.[171]

643. Freedom of movement constitutes a fundamental right of workers and their families. It is, however, not an autonomous, but a purposeful right within the framework of the economic objectives of the Union; this right is only conferred for reasons of the performing of an economic activity. It is a contribution to the economic needs of the Member States.

> Mobility of labour is looked upon as one of the means by which the worker is guaranteed the possibility of improving his living and working conditions and promoting his social advancement, while helping to satisfy the requirements of the economies of the Member States.[172]

---

169. On amending Regulation (EEC) No. 1612/68 and repealing Directives 64/221/EEC, 68/360/ EEC, 72/194/EEC, 73/148/EEC, 75/34/EEC, 75/35/EEC, 90/364/EEC, 90/365/EEC and 93/96/ EEC, O.J., 30 April 2004, L 158.
    Articles 10 and 11 of Regulation (EEC) No. 1612/68 and Directives 64/221/EEC, 68/360/ EEC, 72/194/EEC, 73/148/EEC, 75/34/EEC, 75/35/EEC, 90/364/EEC, 90/365/EEC and 93/96/ EEC shall be repealed with effect from two years from the date of entry into force of this Directives (Article 38). Member States shall bring into force the laws, regulations and administrative provisions necessary to comply with this Directive two years from the date of entry into force of this Directive (Article 40). This is 30 April 2006. The Directive entered into force on 30 April 2004 (Article 41).
170. C.O.J., 18 October 1990, *Massam Dzodzi* v. *Belgian State*, Joined Cases Nos. 297/88 and 197/ 89, ECR, 1990, 3763.
171. C.O.J., 28 January 1992, *Volker Steen* v. *Deutsche Bundespost*, C-332/90, ECR, 1992, 341; 16 June 1994, *Volker Steen* v. *Deutsche Bundespost*, C-132/93, ECR, 1994, 2715; 16 January 1997, *Unità Socio-Sanitaria Locale Nr. 47 di Biella (USSL)* v. *Instituto nazionale per l'assicurazione contro gli infortuno sul lavoro (INAIL)*, C-134/95, ECR, 1997, 195. *Land Nordrhein/Westfalen* v. *Kari Uecker and Vera Jacquet*, C-64/96 and C-65/96, ECR, 1997, 3171.
172. Considering Regulation No. 492/2011 of 5 April 2011 on freedom of movement for workers within the Union.

Part I, Ch. 1, The Free Movement of Workers

It should be underlined that Article 45 concerning the free movement of workers has a direct effect on the legal orders of the Member States and confers on individuals rights which national courts must protect.[173] Article 45, however, does not aim to restrict the power of the Member States to lay down restrictions within their own territory on the freedom of movement of all persons subject to their jurisdiction in the implementation of domestic criminal law.[174]

In order to be truly effective, the right of workers to be engaged and employed without discrimination necessarily entails as a corollary the employer's entitlement to engage them in accordance with the rules governing freedom of movement for workers. The rule of equal treatment can be relied upon as well by a worker as by an employer.[175]

644. Free movement of workers entails the right to work in another Member State under the same conditions as national workers; it includes the right to move freely within the territory of Member States for this purpose and the right to stay in a Member State. The expression 'free movement for workers' was first used in the EC Treaty. In the case of the ECSC, one could not really talk of free movement for workers. It has indeed characteristic for the now defunct ECSC rules that access to the labour market was restricted to specific sectors of the economy and to specific groups of workers within those sectors who have special qualifications. It was also restricted in time and regarding the possibility to search freely for work. Free movement was only possible in the ECSC when there was an offer of employment actually made.[176] Pursuant to Articles 2G and 96 of the Euratom Treaty there is in the sector of atomic energy free movement for skilled workers. In this study we limit ourselves, for obvious reasons, to the free movement for workers in the EU.

645. Freedom of movement for workers, which is a fundamental aspect of the freedom of movement for persons and of the internal market, allows the nationals of any Member State to work in another Member State under the same conditions as nationals of that State.[177]

646. On 1 January 2007 Bulgaria and Romania joined the EU. A transitional period of up to seven years after accession prevails and certain conditions may be applied that restrict the free movement of workers to and between these Member States from 1 January 2007 until 31 December 2013.

---

173. C.O.J., 14 July 1974, *G. Dona* v. *M. Mantero*, No. 13/76, ECR, 1976, 1333.
174. C.O.J., 28 March 1979, *Regina* v. *V.A. Saunders*, No. 175/78, ECR, 1979, 1129.
175. C.O.J., 7 May 1998, *Clean Car Autoservice GesmbH* v. *Landeshauptmann von Wien*, C-350/96, ECR, 1998, 2512.
176. H. Verschueren, *Grensoverschrijdende arbeid*, Brugge, 2000, 180 pp.
177. Freedom of movement for workers after enlargement, Scadplus, www.europa.eu.int/scadplus/leg/en/cha/c10524.htm.

§1. EQUAL TREATMENT

647. Freedom of movement entails the abolition of any discrimination based on nationality between workers of the Member States as regards employment, remuneration and other conditions of work and employment (Article 45 TFEU); it also implies the right to stay in a Member State for the purpose of employment in accordance with the provisions governing the employment of nationals (Article 45(3)(c) TFEU). These provisions regarding equal treatment are a specification of the more general principle of equality, which is laid down in Article 18 TFEU and following which:

> within the scope of application of the Treaties, and without prejudice to any special provisions contained therein, any discrimination on grounds of nationality shall be prohibited.[178]

648. Equal treatment regarding free movement for workers is further elaborated in Regulation No. 492/2011 of 5 April 2011 on freedom of movement for workers within the Union.[179] The regulation is to be interpreted in the light of the requirement that family life be respected, as referred to in Article 8 of the Convention for the Protection of Human Rights and Fundamental Freedoms. Compliance with that requirement constitutes one of the fundamental rights recognised, as the Court has consistently held, in Union law. The Court judged rightly that equal treatment:

> plays an important role in the integration of a migrant worker and his family into the host country, and thus in achieving the objective of free movement of workers.[180]

I. National Law: Eligibility for Employment

649. According to Regulation 492/2011:

> Any national of a Member State shall, irrespective of his place of residence, have the right to take up an activity as an employed person, and to pursue such activity, within the territory of another Member State. He shall, in particular, have the right to take up available employment in the territory of another Member State with the same priority as nationals of that State (Aticle 1).
>
> A national of a Member State who seeks employment in the territory of another Member State shall receive the same assistance there as that afforded by the employment offices in that State to their own nationals seeking employment (Article 5).

---

178. The EP and the Council, may adopt rules designed to prohibit such discrimination (Article 18 TFEU).
179. C.O.J., 18 May 1989, *Commission v. Germany*, 18 May 1989, No. 249/86, ECR, 1989, 1263.
180. 11 July 1985, *Ministère Public v. R.H.M. Mutsch*, No. 137/84, ECR, 1985, 2681.

The engagement and recruitment of a national of one Member State for a post in another Member State shall not depend on medical, vocational or other criteria which are discriminatory on grounds of nationality by comparision with those applied to nationals of the other Member State who wish to pursue the same activity.

A national who holds an offer in his name from an employer in a Member State other than that of which he is a national may have to undergo a vocational test, if the employer expressly requests this when making his offer of employment (Article 6).

A requirement that nationals of the other Member States must reside in the state concerned in order to be appointed managers of undertakings exercising a trade constitutes indirect discrimination based on nationality. It would be otherwise only if the imposition of such a residence requirement were based on objective considerations independent of the nationality of the employees concerned and proportionate to a legitimate aim pursued by the national law. A requirement to ensure that the manager can be served with notice of the fines which may be imposed upon him and that they can be enforced against him is inappropriate. First, a manager residing in the state but at a considerable distance from the place at which the undertaking exercises its trade should normally find it more difficult to act effectively in the business than a person whose place of residence, even if in another Member State, is at no great distance from that at which the undertaking exercises its trade. Secondly, other less restrictive measures, such as serving notice of fines at the registered office of the undertaking employing the manager and ensuring that they will be paid by requiring a guarantee to be provided beforehand, would make it possible to ensure that the manager can be served with notice of any such fines imposed upon him and that they can be enforced against him. Finally, even such measures as those just indicated are not justified by the aims in question of the service of notice of fines imposed on a manager resident in another Member State and their enforcement against him are guaranteed by an international convention concluded between the Member State in which the undertaking exercises its trade and that in which the manager resides.[181]

650. One can of course require that the worker concerned has the linguistic knowledge required by reason of the nature of the post to be fulfilled (Article 3(1)). This requirement is, however, as an exception to the general rule of free movement for workers, to be interpreted restrictively. The post of full-time teacher, whatever the subject taught, is one of those posts. In order to foster one of its national languages, a Member State may therefore rely on that provision when laying down the requirement that any candidate for such a post should possess a sufficient knowledge of the language concerned. This must be interpreted as not precluding national provisions making access to a post subject to the requirement that candidates should have a sufficient knowledge of one of the official languages of a Member State, provided that the conditions in which that requirement is declared satisfied are not more

---

181. C.O.J., 7 May 1998, *Clean Car Autoservice GesmbH* v. *Landeshauptmann von Wien*, C-350/96, ECR, 1998, 2521.

favourable to persons who have pursued their linguistic studies in the Member State concerned than to persons who possess diplomas recognised as equivalent by that State but who pursued the same studies in another Member State.[182]

Article 45(2) TFEU precludes the legislation of a Member State from limiting to one year, with the possibility of renewal, the duration of contracts of employment for foreign language assistants at a university where no such limitation existed in principle in relation to other teachers;[183] as well as the application of national law according to which posts for foreign-language assistants must or may be the subject of employment contracts of limited duration, whereas, for other teaching staff performing special duties, recourse to such contracts must be individually justified by an objective reason.[184]

651. Mr. Angonese, an Italian national whose mother tongue is German and who is resident in the province of Bolzano, went to study in Austria between 1993 and 1997. In August 1997, he applied to take part in a competition for a post with a private banking undertaking in Bolzano, the Cassa di Risparmio.

One of the conditions for entry to the competition was possession of a type-B certificate of bilingualism (in Italian and German) ('the Certificate'), which used to be required in the province of Bolzano for access to the former *carriera di concetto* (managerial career) in the public service.

The Certificate is issued by the public authorities of the province of Bolzano after an examination which is held only in that province. It is usual for residents of the province of Bolzano to obtain the Certificate as a matter of course for employment purposes. Obtaining the Certificate is viewed as an almost compulsory step as part of normal training.

Although Mr. Angonese was not in possession of the Certificate, he was perfectly bilingual. With a view to gaining admission to the competition, he had submitted a certificate showing completion of his studies as a draftsman and certificates attesting to his studies of languages (English, Slovene and Polish) at the Faculty of Philosophy at Vienna University and had stated that his professional experience included practising as a draftsman and translating from Polish into Italian.

On 4 September 1997, the Cassa di Risparmio informed Mr.Angonese that he could not be admitted to the competition because he had not produced the Certificate. The requirement for the Certificate imposed by the Cassa di Risparmio was founded on the National Collective Agreement for Savings Banks of 19 December 1994.

Mr. Angonese complained that he had been discriminated against; the Court accepted his complaint. It stated that under Article 45 TFEU freedom of movement for workers within the Community entails the abolition of any discrimination based on nationality between workers of the Member States as regards employment, remuneration and other conditions of work and employment. It should be noted, the

---

182. C.O.J., 28 November 1989, *A. Groener v. Minister for Education and the City of Dublin Vocational Educational Committee*, No. 379/87, ECR, 1989, 3967.
183. C.O.J., *Allué P. and Others v. Università degli Studi di Venzia and Others*, 2 August 1993, No. C-259/91, C-331/991 and C-332/91, ECR, 1993, 4309.
184. C.O.J., *Spotti M.C. v. Freistant Bayern*, 20 October 1993, C-272/92, ECR, 1993, 457.

Court said, at the outset that the principle of non-discrimination set out in Article 45 is drafted in general terms and is not specifically addressed to the Member States.

Consequently, the prohibition of discrimination on grounds of nationality laid down in Article 45 of the Treaty must be regarded as applying to private persons as well.

A requirement, such as the one at issue in the main proceedings, making the right to take part in a recruitment competition conditional upon possession of a language diploma that may be obtained in only one province of a Member State and not allowing any other equivalent evidence could be justified only if it were based on objective factors unrelated to the nationality of the persons concerned and if it were in proportion to the aim legitimately pursued.

652. The Court has ruled that the principle of non-discrimination precludes any requirement that the linguistic knowledge in question must have been acquired within the national territory (*see* Case C-379/87 *Groener* v. *Minister for Education and the City of Dublin Vocational Educational Committee* [1989] ECR 3967, paragraph 23).

So, even though requiring an applicant for a post to have a certain level of linguistic knowledge may be legitimate and possession of a diploma such as the Certificate may constitute a criterion for assessing that knowledge, the fact that it is impossible to submit proof of the required linguistic knowledge by any other means, in particular by equivalent qualifications obtained in other Member States, must be considered disproportionate in relation to the aim in view. It follows that, where an employer makes a person's admission to a recruitment competition subject to a requirement to provide evidence of his linguistic knowledge exclusively by means of one particular diploma, such as the Certificate, issued only in one particular province of a Member State, that requirement constitutes discrimination on grounds of nationality contrary to Article 45 TFEU.[185]

653. An important judgment of the Court of Justice[186] relates to a Flemish decree (1973) in Belgium, which requires a.o. that the employment contract be drafted in Dutch. Translations are permitted. The idea was to preserve and promote the Dutch language, which is one of the three official languages in Belgium and protect it against the Francophonisation or Anglofonisation of the employment relations in Flanders, given the fact that more than 50 per cent of the workforce is employed by multinationals. This decree was also applied to EU nationals working in Flanders in the framework of the free movement of labour. The Court rules that this requirement is contrary to the freedom movement of workers.

Indeed, in Belgium, a decree of the Flemish Community requires the use of Dutch, inter alia, for the drafting of employment contracts concluded between employees and employers, where the employer's established place of business is in the Dutch-language region. Non-compliance with that linguistic obligation results

---

185. C.O.J., 6 June 2000, *Roman Angonese* v. *Cassa di Risparmio di Bolzano SpA*, Case C-281/98, ECR, 2000, 4139.
186. C.O.J., 16 April 2013, *Anton Las* v. *PSA Antwerp NV*, C-202/11, www.curia. eu.

in the nullity of the employment contract, but without prejudice to the employee or to the rights of third parties.

654. Mr Anton Las, a Netherlands national resident in the Netherlands, was hired in 2004 as a Chief Financial Officer by PSA Antwerp, a company established in Antwerp (Belgium) but belonging to a multinational group whose registered office is in Singapore. The employment contract, drafted in English, stipulated that Mr Las was to carry out his work in Belgium.

In 2009, by a letter drafted in English, Mr Las was dismissed by PSA Antwerp, who paid him a severance allowance calculated on the basis of his employment contract. Mr Las brought an action before the Labour Court, Belgium claiming that the provisions of the employment contract were null and void because they infringed the provisions of the Flemish Decree on Use of Languages. He sought, *inter alia*, a higher severance allowance, in accordance with Belgian employment law.

The Belgian court asked the Court of Justice whether the Flemish Decree on Use of Languages infringes freedom of movement for workers within the EU, in that it imposes an obligation on all undertakings established in the Dutch-language region, when hiring a worker for a cross-border post, to draft all documents relating to the employment relationship in Dutch, failing which the contract is to be declared null and void by the national courts of their own motion.

655. In its judgment, the Court points out, first, that the employment contract at issue falls within the scope of freedom of movement for workers, since it was concluded between a Dutch national, resident in the Netherlands, and a company established in Belgian territory. In addition, the principle of freedom of movement may be relied on not only by workers, but also by employers. The Court points out that the provisions relating to freedom of movement for workers are intended to facilitate the pursuit of occupational activities of all kinds throughout the EU, and preclude measures which might place EU nationals at a disadvantage when they wish to pursue an economic activity in the territory of another Member State.

The Court notes that only the Dutch text is authentic in the drafting of cross-border employment contracts concluded by employers whose established place of business is located in the Dutch-speaking region of Belgium. Consequently, such legislation, which is liable to have a dissuasive effect on non-Dutch-speaking employees and employers from other Member States, constitutes a restriction on freedom of movement for workers.

The Court states that such a restriction is justified only if it pursues an objective in the public interest, is appropriate to ensuring the attainment of that objective, and is strictly proportionate.

In response to the justifications advanced by the Belgian Government, the Court points out that EU law does not preclude the adoption of a policy for the protection and promotion of one or more official languages of a Member State. The EU must respect its rich cultural and linguistic diversity. It must also respect the national identity of its Member States, which includes protection of the official language or languages of those States.

656. The Court also examines the objectives raised by Belgium concerning the protection of employees, which consists of enabling them to examine employment documents in their own language and to enjoy the effective protection of their representative bodies and national authorities, and the efficacy of the checks and supervision of the Employment Inspectorate.

The Court accepts that those objectives are among the overriding reasons in the general interest capable of justifying a restriction on freedom of movement for workers.

However, it is apparent from the contested decree that the penalty for breach of the obligation to draft in Dutch an employment contract concluded between a worker and an employer whose established place of business is located in the Dutch-speaking region of the Kingdom of Belgium is the nullity of that contract, which must be declared by the national courts of their own motion provided that that decision does not adversely affect the worker and is without prejudice to the rights of third parties.

657. Yet parties to a cross-border employment contract do not necessarily have knowledge of Dutch. In such a situation, the establishment of free and informed consent between the parties requires those parties to be able to draft their contract in a language other than the official language of that Member State. Moreover, the Court continues, legislation which would also permit the drafting of an authentic version in a language known to all the parties concerned would be less prejudicial to freedom of movement for workers while being appropriate for securing the objectives pursued by that legislation. Therefore, according to the Court, the contested decree goes beyond what is strictly necessary to attain the objectives invoked and cannot be regarded as proportionate.

In those circumstances, the Court holds that the contested decree which requires all employers whose established place of business is located in Flanders to draft all cross-border employment contracts exclusively in Dutch is in breach of EU law.

658. The judgment of the Court relates only to free movement of workers in the EU. There must be a transborder working relationship, related to the EU.

This means that the Flemish decree retains its full legitamicy regarding Belgians working in Flanders as well as to foreigners, non nationals of a EU Member State, e.g. an American or a Chinese.

659. The judgment raises a lot of difficulties as the foreign EU worker is entitled to have an employment contract in a language he understands. There are in the EU not less than 23 official languages and 60 recognised regional languages. Does this mean that a Polish worker in France or Germany is entitled to an employment contract in Polish? What about the work rules? The collective agreements, the other social documents the worker is entitled to like his wage document? Should they also be in the language of the worker? In certain enterprises there may be workers from 30 to 40 nationalities active. Should the employer operate in 20 or more languages? The future will show that this judgment has created more problems than solved. For indeed, the Flemish decree has de facto not hindered the free movement of workers as the facts over more than 40 years that the Decree applies clearly show.

660. The reservation of appointments to fill temporary teaching vacancies in universities for tenured teachers and established researchers, and the exclusion from consideration of foreign language assistants, is, however, acceptable.[187]

661. The exclusion to take into account the previous employment of a musician in the Nice municipal orchestra (France) for the purposes of granting a seniority increment and of grading him on the salary scale of the Thessalonika orchestra (Greece), on the sole ground that the previous employment was not performed in Greek public service, is in breach of Article 45 TFEU.[188]

662. A number of cases relate to the *recognition of diplomas*. Thus the *Burbaud* case.[189] In 1981, Ms. Burbaud, who was at that time a Portuguese national, obtained a degree in law from the University of Lisbon (Portugal). In 1983, she was awarded the qualification of hospital administrator by the National School of Public Health, Lisbon ('the NSPH'). From 1983 to 1989 she worked as a hospital administrator in the Portuguese public service. She later completed a French doctorate in law, in the course of leave for training purposes, and acquired French nationality.

On 2 July 1993, Ms. Burbaud applied to the French Minister responsible for health for admission to the hospital managers' corps of the French public service, relying on the qualifications that she had obtained in Portugal.

By decision of 20 August 1993, the Minister rejected her application, essentially on the ground that to be admitted to that corps it was first necessary to pass the entrance examination of the *École nationale de la santé publique* (National School of Public Health; 'the ENSP') in Rennes (France).

Ms. Burbaud brought an action before the *Tribunal administratif de Lille* (Administrative Court, Lille) (France) for annulment of that decision. By judgment of 8 July 1997, that court dismissed her application. Ms. Burbaud appealed against that judgment to the national court which has made this reference, seeking to have the judgment set aside and the decision of 20 August 1993 annulled.

In those circumstances, the *Cour administrative d'appel de Douai* decided to stay proceedings and refer the following questions to the Court for a preliminary ruling:

(1) Is a training course in a practical training school for public servants, such as the ENSP, leading to permanent appointment to the public service, to be treated in the same way as a diploma within the meaning of Council Directive 89/48/EEC of 21 December 1988 and, if so, how was the equivalence of the diplomas from the National School of Public Health, Lisbon, and the National School of Public Health, Rennes, to be assessed?
(2) If the answer to the first question is in the affirmative, may the competent authority make admission to the public service of public servants from another Member State who rely on an equivalent diploma subject to conditions, and in

---

187. C.O.J., 20 November 1997, *David Petrie e.a.* v. *Università degli studi di Verona and Camilla Bettoni*, C-90/96, ECR, 1997, 6527.
188. C.O.J., 12 March 1998, *Commissie* v. *Hellenese Republiek*, C-187/96, ECR, 1998, 1095.
189. C.O.J., 9 September 2003, *Isabel Burbaud* v. *Ministère de l'Emploi et de la Solidarité* Case C285/01, ECR, 2003, 8219.

particular subject to passing the School's entrance examination, even for those who have sat a similar competition in their country of origin?

663. The Court refuted the French Government's argument that public service employment which is governed by special public service rules, such as the position of manager in the hospital public service which is at issue here, does not come within the scope of the Directive since such employment cannot be regarded as a 'profession' within the meaning of Article 2 of the Directive.

The Directive does not allow for such a broad exemption from its field of application. It follows from the legal basis of the Directive, from the 12th recital in its preamble, and from the second paragraph of Article 2 of the Directive that employment in the public service falls in principle within the scope of the Directive, except where it is covered by Article 45(4) TFEU or by a separate directive establishing arrangements for the mutual recognition of diplomas by Member States.

As the French Government accepts, employment as a manager in the hospital public service is not covered by the exemption set out in Article 45(4) TFEU. Such employment does not involve direct or indirect participation in the exercise of public authority or in duties whose object is the protection of the general interests of the State or of other public authorities. Moreover, there is no separate directive, within the meaning of the second paragraph of Article 2 of the Directive, which is applicable to such employment.

664. Furthermore, the Court has already held that public bodies are required to comply with the provisions of the Directive.

In addition, the fact that under national law a particular post in the public service is governed by special public service rules is not relevant for the purposes of determining whether that post is a regulated profession within the meaning of the Directive.

The definition of a regulated profession is a matter of Union law whereas the national legal classifications of worker, employee and public servant or, moreover, of employment governed by public law or by private law can be varied freely by national legislatures and cannot therefore provide an appropriate criterion for interpretation.

665. The Court ruled:

(1) Confirmation of passing the final examination of the *École nationale de la santé publique*, which leads to permanent appointment to the French hospital public service, must be regarded as a 'diploma' within the meaning of Council Directive 89/48/EEC of 21 December 1988 on a general system for the recognition of higher-education diplomas awarded on completion of professional education and training of at least three years' duration. It is for the national court to determine, for the purposes of applying point (a) of the first paragraph of Article 3 of that directive, whether a qualification obtained in another Member State by a national of a Member State wishing to pursue a regulated profession in the

host Member State can be regarded as a diploma within the meaning of that provision and, if so, to determine the extent to which the training courses whose successful completion leads to the award of those diplomas are similar with regard to both their duration and the matters covered. If it is apparent from that court's examination that both qualifications constitute diplomas within the meaning of that directive and that those diplomas are awarded on the completion of equivalent education or training, the directive precludes the authorities of the host Member State from making access by that national of a Member State to the profession of manager in the hospital public service subject to the condition that he complete the training given by the *École nationale de la santé publique* and pass the final examination at the end of that training.

(2) Where a national of a Member State holds a diploma obtained in one Member State which is equivalent to the diploma required in another Member State in order to take up employment in the hospital public service, Community law precludes the authorities of the second Member State from making that national's access to the employment in question subject to his passing a competition such as the entrance examination of the *École nationale de la santé publique*.

Failing to take into account professional experience acquired by Community nationals in the civil service of another Member State, for the purposes of the participation of those nationals in competitions for the recruitment of teaching staff in Italian State schools, the Italian Republic has failed to fulfil its obligations under Article 45 TFEU and Article 3 of Regulation (EU) No. 492/2011 of 5 April 2011 on freedom of movement for workers within the Union.[190]

666. It follows from the whole of that case-law that the refusal to recognise the professional experience and seniority gained in the exercise of a comparable activity within the public administration of another Member State by Union nationals employed subsequently in the Italian civil service, on the ground that those nationals would not have sat an open competition prior to working in the public sector of that other state, cannot be allowed, since not all Member States recruit for all public sector posts by open competition alone. Discrimination can be avoided only if account is taken of comparable periods of employment in another Member State's public sector by a person recruited in accordance with local requirements.[191]

It is contrary to Article 45(2) TFEU that, when a fixed-term contract of employment as an exchange assistant is replaced by a contract of employment for an indefinite period as a linguistic associate, a person should be refused recognition of the rights acquired since the date of her first recruitment, with consequences with regard to remuneration, the account to be taken of seniority and the payment, by the employer, of contributions to a social security scheme, inasmuch as a national

---

190. C.O.J., 12 May 2005, *Commission of the European Communities v. Italian Republic*, C-278/03, ECR, 2005, 3747.
191. C.O.J., *Commission of the European Communities v. Italian Republic*, C-371/04, 26 October 2006, ECR, 2006, 10257.

worker placed in a comparable situation would have been entitled to such recognition.[192]

II. Collective and Individual Agreements

667. Pursuant to Article 7(4) of Regulation No. 492/2011, any clause of a collective agreement or any other collective regulation concerning eligibility for employment, remuneration and other conditions of work or dismissal is null and void insofar as it lays down or authorises discriminatory conditions in respect to workers who are nationals of other Member States. The same applies to individual employment contracts.

Consequently, the Court ruled that a clause in a collective agreement applicable to the public service of a Member State which provides for promotion on grounds of seniority for employees of that service after eight years' employment in a salary group determined by that agreement without taking any account of previous periods of comparable employment completed in the public service of a Member State is contrary to Article 45 TFEU and Article 7(1) and (4) of Regulation No. 492/2011. The national court must therefore apply the same rules to the members of the group disadvantaged by that discrimination as those applicable to the other workers.[193]

668. Article 45 TFEU and Article 7(1) and (4) of Regulation (EU) No. 492/ 2011 preclude a national rule (collective agreement) concerning the account to be taken of previous periods of service for the purposes of determining the pay of contractual teachers and teaching assistants, where the requirements which apply to periods spent in the other Member States are stricter than those applicable to periods spent in comparable institutions of the Member State concerned.

Where a Member State is obliged to take into account, in calculating the pay of contractual teachers and teaching assistants, periods of employment in certain comparable institutions in other Member States, such periods must be taken into account without any temporal limitation.[194]

669. Non-competition agreements and freedom of movement were raised in a Parliamentary Question,[195] which read as follows:

> The purpose of an agreement prohibiting competition between an employer and an employee is to protect the employer's knowledge and know-how relating to product development, research and similar matters from competitors and to ensure that the interests of employer and employee are respected, in a more impartial manner.

---

192. 15 May 2008, *Nancy Delay v. Università degli studi di Firenze*, C-276/07, ECR, 2008, 3635.
193. C.O.J., 15 January 1998, *Kalliope Schöning-Kougebetopoulo v. Freie und Hansestad Hamburg*, C-15/96, ECR, 1998, 47.
194. C.O.J., 30 November 2000, *Österrreisschicher Gewerkschaftsbund, Gewerkschaft öffentlicher Dienst v. Republik österrreich*, C-195/98, ECR, 2000, 10497.
195. Written Question E-1637/02, by Riitta Myller (PSE) to the Commission (10 June 2002), O.J. C 92 E, 17 April 2003.

However, such agreements are now widely used for work in respect of which there is no need to protect the employee's position, his duties or information required for the employing firm's activities. They are often valid for a long period and often contain severe penalty clauses to ensure compliance. The agreements also often impose unreasonable demands and conflict with the Community law principle of proportionality.

Agreements prohibiting competition restrict the employee's right to move into the service of another employer, and hinder freedom of movement, since the employee is unable to found his own firm in the same area. They thus impede in a general way the free movement of workers and services from one Member State to another. National legislation on the admissibility of such agreements varies considerably within the EU. The restrictions imposed by agreements prohibiting competition therefore mean that workers in the Member States have differing attitudes towards moving between Member States for job application purposes and to work. This leads to inequalities between workers from different Member States.

What measures does the Commission propose to take to harmonise the provisions of agreements prohibiting competition and to correct the above-mentioned undesirable state of affairs?

670. Commissioner Monti answered on behalf of the Commission (11 July 2002):

There is no European legislation dealing specifically with non-competition clauses between employer and employee after the end of their contract. The Commission has no plans to make proposals for legislation in this respect.

The vast majority of the clauses referred to by the Honourable Member cover employers and employees within a Member State. In that case the Union rules on the free movement of workers and services do not apply. These clauses concern primarily contract law issues which are governed by Member States' law. However, it is obvious that any restrictions, for example those resulting from the differences in national legislation, may have cross-border consequences. The issue of whether a particular clause is compatible with the Union rules on free movement of workers under Article 45 TFEU and/or the freedom to provide services under Article 56 TFEU should be examined on a case-by-case basis.

671. As regards free movement of workers, it is important that a balance exists, on the one hand, between the fundamental rights of a worker to work and to exercise his right to free movement and, on the other hand, the right of the employer to protect his legitimate interests against competitors. When such a balance exists and the clause is proportionate to its aim and does not unnecessarily limit the right of the worker to free movement, the clause seems not to be contrary to the provisions of free movement for workers within the Community. In this respect, reference should be made to the case law of the European Court of Justice in the *Bosman* case,[196] in which the Court held that measures which constitute obstacles to the free movement of workers would not be contrary to Union law if they pursued a legitimate aim compatible with the TFEU and were justified by pressing reasons of public interests and, moreover, were in line with the principle of proportionality.

672. A particular clause which has a disproportionate effect on a person's ability to seek employment may well amount to a barrier to the provision of services under Article 56 TFEU as well (e.g. in the case where a company which operates in the high-tech sector needs to recruit a highly qualified person to be able to provide its services). Any rules that may hinder or make less attractive the exercise of a fundamental freedom guaranteed by the TFEU, such as the freedom to provide services must, according to the established case law of the Court of Justice, fulfil certain requirements.[197] There are four such requirements: they must be applied in a non-discriminatory manner; they must be justified by imperative requirements in the general interest; they must be suitable for securing the attainment of the objective which they pursue; and they must not go beyond what is necessary in order to attain it.

It is for the national authorities to apply the said criteria in individual cases and the question of the compatibility or otherwise of an agreement with the said criteria is a matter for the national courts to assess in the light of Union rules and principles on free movement of workers and services.

III. Work

673. Activities are subject to Union law regarding equal treatment within the framework of the EU only insofar as they constitute an economic activity within the meaning of the Treaty.[198] The rule of non-discrimination applied in judging all legal relationships, by reason either of the place where they are entered into or the place where they take effect, can be located within the territory of the Union.[199] It follows that activities temporarily carried on outside the territory of the Union are not sufficient to exclude the application of that principle, as long as the employment relationship retains a sufficiently close link with that territory.[200] In the absence of any distinction, in Article 45 TFEU:

---

196. Case C-415/93, *Bosman*, ECR, 1995, 4921.
197. *See*, for example, Case C-55/94, *Gebhard*, ECR, 1995, 4165.
198. C.O.J., 12 December 1974, *B.N.O. Walrave, L.N.J. Koch v. Association Union Cycliste Internationale*, No. 36/74, ECR, 1974, 1405.
199. *Idem.*
200. C.O.J., 12 July 1984, *Sàrl Prodest v. Caisse Primaire d'assurance maladie de Paris*, No. 237/ 83, ECR, 1984, 3153. The case concerned the question whether a Belgian temporary worker sent by a French undertaking to Nigeria remained covered by the French social security system. The answer was yes.

it is of interest whether a worker is engaged as a workman, a clerk of an official or even whether the terms on which he is employed come under public or private law. So the public sector as well as the private sector is involved. The exception contained in Article45(4) regarding employment in the public service is to be interpreted as meaning that this exception to the free movement concerns only access to a post forming part of the public service. Once the worker is employed in the public sector the equality principle prevails in full. The nature of the legal relationship between the employee and the employing administration is of no consequence in this respect.[201]

674. The free movement of workers self-evidently concerns persons in employment, namely employment in subordination. Articles 18, 45 (free movement of workers) and 49 (right of establishment for self-employed persons) TFEU have in common the prohibition, in their respective spheres of application, of any discrimination on the grounds of nationality.[202]

675. Equal treatment for workers entails the right to take up an activity as an employed person, to exchange applications for and offers of employment, and to conclude and perform contracts of employment (Articles 1–2 of the regulation).[203]

Medical, vocational and other criteria should not be discriminatory, although a vocational test is not excluded (Article 6). The employment offices should provide the same assistance to nationals of other Member States as to their own nationals (Article 5).

IV. Performance of Work

676. According to Article 7 of the Regulation:

(1) A worker who is a national of a Member State may not, in the territory of another Member State, be treated differently from national workers by reason of his nationality in respect of any conditions of employment and work, in particular as regards remuneration, dismissal, and, should he become unemployed, reinstatement or re-employment.
(2) He shall enjoy the same social and tax advantages as national workers.
(3) He shall also, by virtue of the same right and under the same conditions as national workers, have access to training in vocational schools and retraining centres.

---

201. C.O.J., 12 February 1974, *Giovanni Maria Sotgiu v. Deutsche Bundespost*, No. 152/73; *see also: Commission v. Italian Republic*, 16 June 1987, No. 225/85, ECR, 1987, 2625.
202. *Walrave/Koch* case, *op. cit.*
203. Union law does not prevent a Member State from requiring as a condition for permitting a vessel to participate under its catch quorum that 75 per cent of the crew should be nationals of the EC Member States: it does prevent the requirement that 75 per cent of the crew should have their domicile in the harbour of the Stare concerned (C.O.J., 14 December 1989, *The Queen v. Ministry of Agriculture, Fisheries and Food ex Parre Agegore Ltd.*, No. C-3/87, ECR, 1989, 4459. See also C.O.J., 19 January 1988, *Pesca Vaknria Limited v. Minister for Fisheries and Forestry, Ireland and the Attorney General*, C-223/86, ECR, 1988, 83).

Part I, Ch. 1, The Free Movement of Workers 676–676

(4) Any clause of a collective or individual agreement or of any other collective regulation concerning eligibility for employment, remuneration and other conditions of work or dismissal shall be null and void in so far as it lays down or authorises discriminatory conditions in respect of workers who are nationals of the other Member States'.[204] Equality of treatment of workers shall be ensured 'in fact and by law'.[205]

Inasmuch as the object of the provisions of the Treaty and of secondary law is to regulate the situation of individuals and to ensure their protection, it is also for national courts to examine whether individual decisions are compatible with the relevant provisions of Union law.[206]

The right to equal treatment with regard to social and tax advantages (Article 7, §2 of the regulation) operates only for the benefit of workers and does not apply to nationals of Member States who move in search of employment. Those who move in search of employment qualify for equal treatment only as regards access to employment.[207] There is a basis in Union law for the view that the rights guaranteed to migrant workers do not necessarily depend on the actual or continuing existence of the employment relationship. Persons who have previously pursued an effective and genuine activity as an employed person in the host Member State but who are no longer employed are nevertheless considered to be workers under certain provisions of Union law.[208]

Likewise, no discrimination may take place regarding working conditions on the basis of nationality Article 7, 1–3 of the Regulation No. 492/2011 namely regarding:

– remuneration, dismissal and, if the worker becomes unemployed, reinstatement or re-employment;
– social and tax advantages;

---

204. O.J. L141, 27 May 2011.
205. Taking into consideration, as a criterion for the grant of a separation allowance, the fact that a worker has his residence in the territory of another Member State may, according to the circumstances, constitute discrimination forbidden by Article 7(1) and (4) of Regulation No. 492/2011 (C.O.J., 12 February 1974, *Sotgia v. Deutsche Bundespost*, No. 152/73, ECR, 1974, 153). 'Where a public body of a Member State, in recruiting staff for posts which do not fall within the scope of Article 45(4) TFEU, provides for account to be taken of candidates' previous employment in the public service, that body may not, in relation to Community nationals, make a distinction according to whether such employment was in the public service of that particular State or in the public service of another Member State' (C.O.J., 23 February 1994, *Scholz I. v. Opera Universitaria di Cagliari and Others*, No. C-419/92, ECR, 1994, 505).
206. C.O.J., 28 October 1974, *Rutilli v. Minister of the Interior*, No. 35/75, ECR, 1975, 1205.
207. C.O.J., 18 June 1987, *Centre public d'aide sociale de Courcelles v. M.C. Lebon*, C-316/85, ECR, 1987, 2811.
208. C.O.J., 21 June 1988, *Sylvie Lair v. Universität Hannover*, C-39/86, ECR, 1988, 3161. The case concerned a national of a Member Stare who had taken up employment in another Member State and there, after giving up her employment, commenced a course of higher education leading to a professional qualification. The question was whether Union law entitles that national to claim a training grant on the same basis as a national from the host Member State. The Court said yes, provided there is a link between the previous occupational activity and the studies in question.

– training in vocational schools[209] and retraining centres.

677. The notion 'social advantage' receives a rather extensive interpretation by the Court. The Court judged that:

> in view of the equality of treatment which the provision seeks to achieve, the substantive area of application must be delineated so as to include all social and tax advantages, whether or not attached to the contract of employment[210]

and that the concept of social advantage encompasses 'not only the benefits accorded by virtue of a right but also those granted on a discretionary basis.'[211]

> As the Court has repeatedly held, the purpose of Article 7, 2 of Regulation No. 492/2011 is to achieve equal treatment, and therefore the concept social advantage, extended by that provision to workers who are nationals of other Member States, must include all advantages which, whether or not linked to a contract of employment, are generally granted to national workers primarily because of their objective status as workers or by virtue of the mere fact of their residence on the national territory and the extension of which to workers who are nationals of other Member Countries therefore seems suitable to facilitate their mobility within the Union.[212]

678. One must recognise that the Court, in its interpretation of the concept social advantages as working conditions, has gone beyond the widest meaning of the concepts. This is not a criticism from an ideological point of view, but a mere legal ascertainment. It does not seem necessary, in order to obtain the Union objectives, to qualify the right to live together with a non-married partner as a social advantage of a worker. It might have sufficed to invoke the right of equal treatment under Article 18 TFEU.

679. The Court of Justice seems to accept the following as 'social advantages':

– measures with a view to allowing the rehabilitation of the handicapped, insofar as such measures concern workers themselves;[213] – the suspension of the

---

209. It should be noted that in order for an educational institution to be regarded as a vocational school for the purposes of that provision, the fact that some vocational training is provided is not sufficient. The concepts of a vocational school is a more limited one and refers exclusively to institutions which provide only instruction either alternating with or closely linked to an occupational activity, particularly during apprenticeship. This is not true of universities (*idem*).
210. 30 September 1975, *A. Christie v. Société Nationale des Chemins de Fer Français*, C-32/75, ECR, 1975, 1085.
211. 14 January 1982, *F. Reina and L. Reina v. Landeskredithank Baden-Wurttemberg*, C-65/81, ECR, 1982, 33.
212. 17 April 1986, *State of the Netherlands v. A. F. Reed*, C-59/85, ECR, 1986, 1283.
213. 11 April 1973, *Michel v. Fonds national de reclassemems des handicapés*, No. 76/72, ECR, 1973, 457.

execution of the employment contract in order to fulfil the obligations of military service, also when the military service is performed in another Member State;[214]
- a separation allowance;[215]
- a special protection against dismissal;[216]
- fare reduction cards issued by a national railway authority to large families;[217] – allowances for a handicapped adult of another Member State who has never worked in the State, but who resides there and is dependent upon his father who is employed there as a worker.[218]

680. The Court ruled that the advantages that this regulation extends to workers who are nationals of other Member States, are all those which, whether or not linked to a contract of employment, are generally granted to national workers primarily because of their objective status as workers or by virtue of the mere fact of their residence on the national territory. Therefore, a benefit to certain categories of national workers, who have rendered services in wartime to their own country and whose essential objective is to give those nationals an advantage by reason of the hardships suffered for their country, does not fulfil the essential characteristics of the 'social advantages' referred to in Article 7, 2.

681. The Court ruled likewise that the Union does not exceed the limits of its jurisdiction because the exercise of its jurisdiction affects measures adopted in the field of demographic policy for which the EU is not competent. Moreover, the concept of 'social advantage' encompasses interest-free loans granted at childbirth by a credit institution incorporated under public law, on the basis and guidelines and with the financial assistance from the State, to families with a low income with a view to stimulating the birthrate.[219]

682. Other social advantages are:

- guaranteed income for old persons;[220] a minimum income[221] and a special old-age allowance guaranteeing a minimum income;[222]

---

214. 15 October 1969, *S. Ugliola* v. *WurttemBergische Milchverwertung Sudmilch* A.G., C-15/69, ECR, 1969, 363.
215. *Sotgiu, op. cit.*
216. In the case of an industrial accident resulting in a loss of earning capacity of more than 50 per cent (13 December 1972, *P. Marsman* v. *M. Rasskamp*, C-44/72, ECR, 1972, 1243).
217. C.O.J., 30 September 1975, *Anita Cristini* v. *Société National des Chemins de Fer Français*, C-32/75, *op. cit.*
218. 16 December 1976, *V. Inzirillo* v. *Caisse d'Allocations Familiales de l'Arrorrdissement de Lyon*, C-63/16, ECR, 1976, 2057. See also C.O.J., 27 May 1993, *Hugo Schmid* v. *Belgian State*, C310/91, ECR, 1993, 3011.
219. *Reina* Case, *op. cit.*
220. *C. Castelli* v. *Office National des Pensions pour Travailleurs Salariés*, C-261/83, ECR, 1984, 3199.
221. Courcelles Case, *op. cit.*; see also C.O.J., 20 June 2002, *Commission* v. *Luxembourg*, C-299/01, ECR, 2002, 5899.
222. 9 July 1987, *M. Frascogna* v. *Caisse de dépots et consignarions*, C-256/86, ECR, 1987, 3431.

- the right to a worker to use his own language in proceedings before the courts of the Member State in which the worker resides, under the same conditions as national workers;[223]
- job security and the lack of career structure which makes it impossible for the workers to move to higher grades and has an impact on their pay and retirement pensions;[224]
- the assistance for maintenance and training with a view to the pursuit of university studies leading to a professional qualification;[225]
- a fellowship in the framework of a cultural agreement;[226]
- study funding granted by a Member State to the children of workers;
- childbirth and maternity allowances;[227] – tide-over allowances;[228]
- a funeral payment;[229]
- reimbursement of travel expenses in respect of the domestic stretch of the journey;[230] – loyalty bonus.[231]

683. Not only benefits fall within that category. In *Peter de Vos* v. *Stadt Bielefeld*,[232] the question arose of the qualification of advantages accorded at the occasion of the military service. Peter de Vos was a senior doctor at the city of Bielefeld.

A collective labour agreement (1966) applicable to employees of the Federal Republic of Germany and the *Länder* and to employees of municipal authorities and undertakings ('the CLA'), envisages supplementary old-age and survivors' insurance with the Pension Institution of the Federal Republic and the *Länder* ('the VBL'). The employer pays monthly contributions to that body for the person insured.

The plaintiff performed military service in the Belgian army from 29 March 1993 to 1 March 1994. During that period, the defendant did not contribute to the VBL on behalf of the plaintiff. The VBL therefore suspended the plaintiff's membership from 28 March 1993 to 2 March 1994.

In the action brought before the Labour Court of Bielefeld, the plaintiff claimed that the defendant was required to pay contributions to the VBL during the period of his military service in the Belgian army, by virtue of Article 45 TFEU and 7 of Regulation No. 492/2011.

---

223. *Mutsch* Case, *op. cit.*
224. *Commission* v. *Italy*, C-225/85, *op. cit.*
225. *Lair* Case, *op. cit.*, see also C.O.J., 15 March 1989, G.B.C. *Echternach and A. Moritz* v. *Dutch Minister of Education and Sciences*, C-389 *and* 390/87, ECR, 1989, 723.
226. C.O.J., 27 September 1988, *A. Matteuci* v. *Communauté Française de Belgique*, C-235/87, ECR, 1988, 5589.
227. C.O.J., 19 March 1993, *Commission of the European Communities* v. *Grand Duchy of Luxembourg*, C-111/91, ECR, 1993, 817.
228. C.O.J., 12 September 1996, *Commission* v. *Belgium*, C-278/98, ECR, 1996, 4307.
229. C.O.J., 23 May 1996, *John O'Flynn* v. *Adjudication Officer*, C-237/94, ECR, 1996, 2617.
230. C.O.J., 17 March 2005, *Karl Robert Kranemann* v. *Land Nordrhein-Westfalen*, C-109/04, ECR, 2005, 2421.
231. See C.O.J., 30 September 2003, *Gerhard Köbler* v. *Republik Österreich*, C-224/01, ECR, 2003, 10239.
232. C.O.J., 14 March 1996, *Peter de Vos* v. *Stadt Bielefeld*, C-315/94, ECR, 1996, 1417.

The obligation on the part of the employer to contribute is, however, not linked to the employment contract. It should therefore be held, so ruled the Court of Justice, 'that the continued payment of supplementary old-age and survivors' pension insurance contributions, as provided for by the German legislation, is not made by virtue *of a* statutory or contractual obligation incumbent on the employer as conditions of employment and work within the meaning of Article 7(1), but is an advantage granted by the State itself to those called upon as partial compensation for the consequences of their obligation to perform military service.

Such an advantage cannot therefore, the Court concluded, be considered to be granted to national workers because of their objective status as workers or by virtue of the mere fact of their residence on the national territory and it thus does not have the essential characteristics of social advantages referred to in Article 7(2) of Regulation No. 492/2011.

One wonders about the outcome of this case and is a little puzzled about the conclusion of the Court that the obligation on the part of the employer is not linked to the employment contract when one sees that the advantage is provided for by a collective labour agreement, negotiated for the benefit of employees.

684. Another case relates to child-raising allowance.[233] Ms Geven was a Netherlands national. When her son was born in December 1997, she was living in the Netherlands with her husband, who worked in that Member State. After the statutory maternity protection period, during the first year of her son's life, she worked in Germany with a weekly working time varying between 3 and 14 hours and weekly earnings of between DEM 40.00 and DEM 168.87.

Her application for child-raising allowance for the first year of her son's life was refused by the *Land* of North Rhine-Westphalia, by decision of 5 June 1998, in the version of the decision of 27 January 2000 on her objection. The grounds for the refusal were that Ms Geven did not have her permanent or ordinary residence in Germany and was not in a contractual employment relationship of at least 15 hours a week.

685. The *Bundessozialgericht* referred the following question to the Court for a preliminary ruling:

> Does it follow from Union law (in particular from Article 7(2) of Regulation (EU) No. 492/2011 ...) that the Federal Republic of Germany is precluded from excluding a national of another Member State who lives in that State and is in minor employment (between 3 and 14 hours a week) in Germany from receiving German child-raising allowance because she does not have her permanent or ordinary residence in Germany?

---

233. C.O.J., 18 July 2007, *Wendy Geven* v. *Land Nordrhein-Westfalen*, C-213/05, not yet published; *see also* C.O.J., 18 July 2007, *Gertraud Hartmann* v. *Freistaat Bayern*, C-212/05, www.curia.

686. The Court answered as follows:

Article 7(2) of Regulation No. 492/2011 provides that a migrant worker is to enjoy the same social and tax advantages in the host Member State as national workers.

The reference to 'social advantages' in that provision cannot be interpreted restrictively. According to settled case-law, 'social advantages' are to be understood as all advantages which, whether or not linked to a contract of employment, are generally granted to national workers because of their objective status as workers or by virtue of the mere fact of their residence on the national territory, and whose extension to workers who are nationals of other Member States therefore seems likely to facilitate their mobility within the European Community.

The Court has already held that German child-raising allowance constitutes a social advantage within the meaning of Article 7(2).

As the Court has already held, while a person in minor employment of the kind referred to in the national court's question has the status of worker within the meaning of Article 45 TFEU, social policy is, in the current state of Union law, a matter for the Member States, who have a wide discretion in exercising their powers in that respect. However, that wide discretion cannot have the effect of undermining the rights granted to individuals by the provisions of the TFEU in which their fundamental freedoms are enshrined.

The aim of the German legislature is, in a situation such as that at issue in the main proceedings, to grant a child-raising allowance to persons who have a sufficiently close connection with German society, without reserving that allowance exclusively to persons who reside in Germany.

In exercising its powers, that legislature could reasonably consider that the exclusion from the allowance in question of non-resident workers who carry on an occupation in the Member State concerned that does not exceed the threshold of minor employment as defined in national law constitutes a measure that is appropriate and proportionate, having regard to the objective mentioned in the preceding paragraph.

In the light of the above considerations, the answer to the national court's question must be that Article 7(2) does not preclude the exclusion, by the national legislation of a Member State, of a national of another Member State who resides in that State and is in minor employment (between 3 and 14 hours a week) in the former State from receiving a social advantage with the characteristics of German child-raising allowance on the ground that he does not have his permanent or ordinary residence in the former State.

687. In a Dutch case the Court ruled[234] that making funding for studies abroad subject to a residence requirement gives rise to inequality of treatment between Netherlands workers and migrant workers.

---

234. C.O.J., 14 June 2012, *European Commission v. Kingdom of the Netherlands*, C-542/09, www.curia.eu.

Part I, Ch. 1, The Free Movement of Workers 688–692

688. The Netherlands Law on the Financing of Studies defines who can receive funding to study in the Netherlands and abroad. For higher education in the Netherlands, funding for studies is available to students who are between 18 and 29 years old and have Netherlands nationality or the nationality of any other Member State of the European Union. To receive funding for higher education pursued outside the Netherlands, students must be eligible for funding for higher education in the Netherlands and must additionally have resided lawfully in the Netherlands for at least three out of the six years preceding enrolment at an educational establishment abroad. This condition, known as the '3 out of 6 years' requirement, applies irrespective of the student's nationality.

689. The Court notes that, under the TFEU, freedom of movement for workers is to entail the abolition of any discrimination based on nationality between workers of the Member States as regards employment, remuneration and other conditions of work and employment. Moreover, it is apparent from Regulation No. 1612/68 that a worker who is a national of a Member State is to enjoy, in the territory of another Member State, the same social and tax advantages as national workers. That applies equally to migrant workers residing in a host Member State and frontier workers employed in that Member State while residing in another.

690. The Court points out that assistance granted for maintenance and education in order to pursue university studies evidenced by a professional qualification constitutes a social advantage for the purposes of Regulation No. 1612/68. For the migrant worker, study finance granted by a Member State to the children of workers constitutes a social advantage for the purposes of that regulation, where the worker continues to support the child.

In that respect, the Court notes that the principle of equal treatment prohibits not only direct discrimination on grounds of nationality but also all indirect forms of discrimination which, through the application of other criteria of differentiation, lead in fact to the same result. That is the position, in particular, in the case of a measure which requires a specified period of residence, in that it primarily operates to the detriment of migrant workers and frontier workers who are nationals of other Member States, in so far as non-residents are usually non-nationals.

691. The Court therefore finds that the '3 out of 6 years' residence requirement creates inequality in treatment as between Netherlands workers and migrant workers residing in the Netherlands or employed there as frontier workers. Such an inequality constitutes unlawful indirect discrimination, unless it is objectively justified.

692. In that regard, the Court rejects the argument of the Netherlands that the residence requirement is necessary in order to avoid an unreasonable financial burden which could have consequences for the very existence of the assistance scheme. The Court points out that the objective of avoiding an unreasonable financial burden cannot be regarded as an overriding reason relating to the public interest, capable of justifying the unequal treatment between Netherlands workers and workers from other Member States.

The Court notes that the objective of encouraging student mobility is in the public interest and constitutes an overriding reason relating to the public interest, capable of justifying a restriction of the principle of non-discrimination on grounds of nationality. The Court points out, however, that legislation which is liable to restrict a fundamental freedom guaranteed by the Treaty, such as freedom of movement for workers, can be justified only if it is appropriate for attaining the legitimate objective pursued and does not go beyond what is necessary in order to attain that objective.

693. While stating that the Luxembourg legislation which excludes the children of frontier workers from entitlement to financial aid for higher education studies pursues a legitimate objective, the European Court[235] holds that the current system goes beyond what is necessary to attain that objective. The objective of increasing the number of persons in the Luxembourg population with a higher education degree may be attained using less restrictive measures. The Court rules as follows:

694. EU law requires Member States to grant migrant workers the same social and tax advantages as national workers. Luxembourg grants financial aid, in the form of a grant and a loan, in order to promote higher education studies by students in its territory or in the territory of any other State. That aid is granted to students holding Luxembourg nationality or the nationality of another Member State, who are resident in Luxembourg when they are about to embark on higher education studies. Thus, the children of cross-border workers, who usually reside in a country bordering upon Luxembourg, are not entitled to the aid.

695. A number of children of cross-border workers to whom financial aid had been denied are contesting the lawfulness of their exclusion from the category of beneficiaries of the aid before the Luxembourg courts. The tribunal administratif (Luxembourg), before which those disputes have been brought, asks the Court of Justice whether the Luxembourg legislation relating to the grant of that aid is compatible with the principle of the freedom of movement of workers.

696. In its judgment the Court recalls that aid granted in order to finance the university studies of the child of a migrant worker constitutes, for that worker, a social advantage which must be granted to him under the same conditions as those applying to national workers. The Court makes clear in that regard that that equal treatment must not be limited to migrant workers residing in a host Member State but must extend to cross-border workers who, while employed as a worker in that Member State, reside in another Member State.

---

235. C.O.J., 20 June 2013, *Elodie Giersch and Others* v. *État du Grand-Duché de Luxembourg*, C-20/12, www. curia.eu.

In addition, where the social advantage is granted directly to the child of a migrant worker, that child may himself or herself rely on the principle of equal treatment.

Second, the Court holds that the condition of residence required by Luxembourg legislation amounts to indirect discrimination on grounds of nationality in so far as it is liable to operate mainly to the detriment of nationals of other Member States, as non-residents are in the majority of cases foreign nationals. In that context, the Court states that such discrimination cannot be justified by budgetary considerations, since the application and the scope of the principle of non-discrimination on grounds of nationality cannot depend on the state of the public finances of the Member States.

697. The Court nevertheless considers that the condition of residence is appropriate for attaining the objective pursued by Luxembourg of promoting higher education studies and of significantly increasing the proportion of Luxembourg residents who hold a higher education degree. Students who are resident in Luxembourg when they are about to embark on their higher education studies may be more likely than non-resident students to settle in Luxembourg and become integrated in the Luxembourg labour market after completing their studies, even if those studies were undertaken abroad.

However, the Court holds that the system of financial aid in question is too exclusive in nature. By imposing a prior condition of residence by the student in Luxembourg territory, the law favours an element which is not necessarily the sole representative element of the actual degree of attachment of the person concerned to Luxembourg.

698. Thus, it is possible that a non-resident student may also have an attachment to the Grand Duchy sufficient to make it reasonably probable that he or she will return to settle in Luxembourg and make himself or herself available to the labour market of that Member State.

That is the case where that student resides alone or with his or her parents in a Member State which borders upon the Grand Duchy of Luxembourg and where, for a significant period of time, his or her parents have worked in Luxembourg and live near to that Member State.

699. The Court points out in that regard that less restrictive measures are available which make it possible to attain the objective sought by the Luxembourg legislature. For example, where the aid granted consists in a loan, a system of financing which made the grant of that loan, or even the outstanding balance thereof, or its non-reimbursement, conditional on the student who receives it returning to Luxembourg after his or her studies abroad in order to work and reside there, would be better adapted to the special situation of the children of cross-border workers. In addition, in order to avoid 'study grant forum shopping' and to ensure that the cross-border worker parent of the student has a sufficient link with Luxembourg society, the financial aid could be made conditional on that parent having worked in Luxembourg for a certain minimum period of time.

Finally, the risk of duplication with equivalent financial aid paid in the Member State in which the student resides, with or without his parents, could be avoided by taking that aid into account in the grant of the aid paid by Luxembourg.

In those circumstances, the Court replies that the contested Luxembourg legislation goes beyond what is necessary to attain the objective pursued by the legislature. Therefore, that legislation is contrary to the principle of the freedom of movement for workers.

V. Trade Union Freedom, Workers' Participation, Management of Public Bodies

700. Equal treatment in the framework of free movement of labour also encompasses *collective labour relations*, namely the right of employees to become a member of a trade union, including the right to vote and to be eligible for the administration or management posts of a trade union. Likewise, the worker has the right of eligibility for workers' representative bodies in the undertaking. The worker who is a national of another Member State may, however, be excluded from taking part in the management of bodies governed by public law and from holding an office governed by public law (Article 8).

Concerning the question whether certain jobs in the Belgian Railroads could be reserved for Belgians only and answering a point made by the Belgian Government, the Court ruled relating to the meaning of Article 8 of the regulation:

> indeed as the Belgian Government itself admits, Article 8 of Regulation No. 492/2011 is not intended to debar workers from other Member States from certain posts, but simply permits them to be debarred in some circumstances from certain activities which involve their participation in the exercise of powers conferred by public law, such as – to use the examples given by the Belgian Government itself-those involving the presence of trade-union representatives on the board of administration of many bodies governed by public law with powers in the economic sphere.[236]

Freedom of movement prohibits national legislation from denying foreign workers the right to vote in elections for members of a professional institute (in case of occupational guild) for which they are required to be affiliated and to which they must pay contributions, and which is responsible for defending the interests of the affiliated workers and exercises a consultative role with regard to legislation.[237]

---

236. C.O.J., 17 December 1980, *Commission v. Belgium*, C-149/79, ECR, 1980, 3881.
237. C.O.J., 4 July 1991, *ASTI Association de Soutien aux Travailleurs Immigrés v. Chambre des Employés Privés*, C-213/90, ECR, 1991, 3507.

Part I, Ch. 1, The Free Movement of Workers 701–702

VI. Housing

701. Equal treatment furthermore encompasses all the rights and benefits accorded to national workers in matters of housing, including ownership of the housing he needs.[238] A worker from another Member State may, with the same rights as nationals, put his name down on the housing lists in the region in which he is employed, where such lists exist; he enjoys the resulting benefits and priorities. If his family has remained in the country from which he came, they are considered for this purpose as residing in the said region where national workers benefit from a similar presumption (Article 9).

VII. Workers' Families

702. Finally, again in view of promoting the social integration of the Union migrant worker and his family Regulation No. 492/2011 provides that the children of a migrant worker are admitted to the host State's general educational, apprenticeship and vocational training courses under the same conditions as the nationals of that State, if such children are residing in its territory (Article 10). Although the national authorities retain full jurisdiction regarding education and the determination of the conditions referred to in Article 10, these conditions must however be applied without discrimination between the children of national workers and those of workers who are nationals of another Member State and who reside in the territory.[239]

In the case of *Carmina Di Leo (an Italian national, and a child of a Community worker)* v. *Land Berlin*, the question was raised whether the German authorities could refuse her the benefit of educational or training grants for studies completed outside the territory of Germany provided by the German law on individual inducement to enter training, on the ground that Miss Di Leo was registered as a medical student at the University of Sienna in Italy and that the nationals of a Member State of the EU are excluded from the benefit of the aid when the training is given in a State of which they are nationals. The Court ruled that according to Article 10, when a Member State offered its nationals the possibility of receiving a grant for education or training given abroad, the child of a Union worker had to be able to receive the same benefit if it decided to pursue its studies outside the host Member State. That interpretation could not be invalidated by the fact that the prospective recipient of the education or training decided to follow courses in the Member State of which that person was a national. Neither the residence notice laid down in Article 10 nor the objective pursued by the Regulation justified such a restriction which, moreover would give rise to another form of discrimination against children of Union workers in comparison with nationals of the host Member State. Therefore children of Union workers are to be treated as nationals for the purpose of awarding educational or training grams, not only when the education or training takes place

---

238. *See also* C.O.J., 30 May 1989, *Commission* v. *Hellas*, C-305/87, ECR, 1989, 1461.
239. C.O.J., 3 July 1974, *Donato Cassagrande* v. *Landeshaupstad Munchen*, C-91/74, ECR, 1976, 773.

in the host State but also when it is provided in a State of which those children are nationals.[240]

703. This right of the children to training encompasses any form of education, including courses provided at a university,[241] and the guidance, training and vocational rehabilitation of the handicapped.[242] Article 10 refers not only to rules relating to admission; aid for maintenance and training with the view to following (middle and higher) education constitutes a social advantage in the sense of Article 2, §7 of the regulation to which migrant workers are entitled under the same conditions as national workers. The regulation aims again at the social integration of the Union foreign worker and his family in the host Member State.[243]

Since study funding granted by a Member State to the children of workers constitutes, for a migrant worker, a social advantage within the meaning of Article 7(2) of Regulation (EC) No. 492/2011 when the worker continues to provide for the maintenance of the child, no further requirements may be imposed such as conditions relating to residence.[244]

§2. SCOPE OF APPLICATION

I. Workers

A. *In General*

704. The Court has ruled consistently that the notion 'worker' in Article 45 TFEU has a Union meaning in law. The term 'worker' and 'an activity as an employed person' may not be defined by reference to the national laws of the Member States. If that were the case, the Union rules on free movement for workers would be frustrated, as the meanings of those terms could be fixed and modified unilaterally, without any control by the Union institutions, by national laws which would thus be able to exclude at will certain categories of persons from the benefit of the Treaty.

705. It is appropriate therefore, in order to determine their meaning, to have recourse to the generally recognised principles of interpretation, beginning with the ordinary meaning to be attributed to those terms in their context and in light of the objectives of the Treaty.[245] In this respect, it must be stressed that the terms 'worker' and 'activity as an employed person' define the field of application of one of the fundamental freedoms guaranteed by the Treaty and, as such, may not be interpreted restrictively.

---

240. 13 November 1990, *Carmina Di Leo v. Land Berlin*, C-308/89, ECR, 1990, 4185.
241. *Echternach* Case, *op. cit.*
242. S. *Michel v. Fonds national de reclassement social des handicapés*, C-76/72, o.c.
243. *Idem.*
244. C.O.J., 26 February 1992, *M.J.E. Bernini v. Netherlands Ministry of Education and Science*, No. C-3/90, ECR, 1992, 1071.
245. *Idem.*

Nevertheless, a person who has worked only as a self-employed person before becoming unemployed cannot be classified as a 'worker' within the meaning of Article 45 TFEU, not even when the person concerned previously worked as an employed person.[246]

706. The concept of 'worker' must, the Court rightly ruled, be defined in accordance with objective criteria which distinguish the employment relationship by reference to the rights and duties of the persons concerned. The essential feature of an employment relation, however, is the fact that for a certain period of time a person performs services for and under the direction of another person in return for which he receives remuneration.[247] The Court therefore retained three criteria: (1) performance of services (2) in subordination for (3) remuneration.

707. This was confirmed in the *Karl Robert Kranemann* case,[248] where the question was dealt with whether a trainee lawyer, who is undergoing part of his preparatory legal training in a Member State other than that of which he is a national, is covered by Article 45 TFEU.

The Court stated 'according to settled case law, the concept of 'worker' within the meaning of Article 45 TFEU has a specific Union meaning and must not be interpreted narrowly. Any person who pursues activities which are real and genuine, to the exclusion of activities on such a small scale has to be regarded as purely marginal and ancillary must be regarded as a 'worker'. The essential feature of an employment relationship is, according to that case law, that for a certain period of time a person performs services for and under the direction of another person in return for which he receives remuneration.[249]

As regards those undergoing a traineeship, the Court has held that the fact that the traineeship may be regarded as practical preparation directly related to the actual pursuit of the occupation in point is not a bar to the application of Article 45 of the Treaty if the training period is completed under the conditions of genuine and effective activity as an employed person.[250]

As the Court held,[251] the practical legal training required in Germany constitutes a period of training and a necessary prerequisite of access to employment in the judicial service or the higher civil service.

As regards the activities carried out by trainee lawyers, according to the order for reference such trainees are required to apply in practice the legal knowledge acquired during their course of study and thus make a contribution, under the guidance of the employer providing them with training, to that employer's activities and

---

246. C.O.J., 4 October 1991, *D. Maxwell Middleburgh v. Chief Adjudication Officer*, No. C-15/90, ECR, 1991, 4655.
247. *Lawrie-Blum* case, *op. cit.*
248. C.O.J., 17 March 2005, *Karl Robert Kranemann v. Land Nordrhein-Westfalen*, C-109/04, ECR, 2005, 2421.
249. *See, in particular*, Case 66/85 *Lawrie-Blum*, 1986, ECR, 2121, paragraphs 16 and 17, Case C3/90 *Bernini*, 1992, ECR, 1071, paragraph 14, and Case C-456/02, *Trojani*, 7 September 2004, paragraph 15, ECR, 2004, 7573.
250. *Lawrie-Blum*, cited above, paragraph 19, and *Bernini*, cited above, paragraph 15.
251. In Case C-79/99 *Schnorbus*, 2000, ECR, 10997, paragraph 28.

trainees receive payment in the form of a maintenance allowance for the duration of their training.

... such an employment relationship cannot fall outside the scope of Article 45 TFEU merely because the allowance paid to trainees constitutes only assistance allowing them to meet their minimum needs and, for trainees undergoing practical training outside the public sector, the payment of such an allowance by the State could not be considered to be made in return for services rendered by the trainee.

According to settled case law neither the origin of the funds from which the remuneration is paid nor the limited amount of the remuneration can have any consequence in regard to whether or not the person is a worker for the purposes of Union law.[252]

708. Given that trainee lawyers carry out genuine and effective activity as an employed person they must be considered to be workers within the meaning of Article 45 TFEU.

The application of Article 45 cannot be excluded on the basis of the exception laid down in Article 45(4) in respect of 'employment in the public service'. As regards a trainee who is undergoing part of his training, as here, outside the public sector, suffice it to note that the concept of 'employment in the public service' does not encompass employment by a private natural or legal person, whatever the duties of the employee.[253]

Nor can the case of a trainee lawyer who has left his Member State of origin to undergo part of his training in another Member State be excluded from the scope of the Treaty as a situation purely internal to a Member State.

In the light of the foregoing, it must be considered that a trainee lawyer who is a national of a Member State and undergoes part of his practical training in another Member State under conditions of genuine and effective activity as an employed person is a worker within the meaning of Article 45 TFEU.

709. Performance of services means the pursuit of effective and genuine activities, part-time included, with the exclusion of activities of such a small scale as to be regarded as purely marginal and ancillary. It follows both from the statement of the principle of freedom of movement for workers and from the place occupied by the rules related to that principle that they only guarantee the free movement for workers who pursue or are desirous of pursuing an economic activity.[254] A worker employed under an *oproepcontract* (on call contract) under which the person concerned performed 60 hours of work is a worker within the meaning of Article 45 TFEU.[255] The motives that may have prompted a worker to seek employment in another Member State are of no account in regard to his right to enter and reside in the territory of the latter, provided that he pursues or wishes to pursue an effective

---

252. *See* Case 53/81 *Levin*, 1982, ECR, 1035, paragraph 16; Case 344/87 *Bettray*, 1989, ECR, 1621, paragraph 16; and *Trojani*, paragraph 16.
253. Case C-283/99 *Commission* v. *Italy*, 2001, ECR, 4363, paragraph 25.
254. *Levin* case, *op. cit.*
255. C.O.J., 26 February 1992, V.J.M. *Raulin* v. *Netherlands Ministry of Education and Science*, No. C-357/89, ECR, 1992, 1027.

Part I, Ch. 1, The Free Movement of Workers 709–709

and genuine activity.[256] The fact that teachers' preparatory service, like apprenticeships in other occupations, may be regarded as practical preparation directly related to the actual pursuit of the occupation in point is not a bar to the application of Article 45 TFEU if the service is performed under the conditions of an activity as an employed person.[257] Equally a national of a Member State who has worked in another Member State within the framework of a course of vocational training must be regarded as a worker within the meaning of Article 45 TFEU, at least if he has provided services for which he has received payment and provided his activities were effective and genuine.[258]

The duration of the activities pursued by the person concerned is a factor which may be taken into account by the national court when assessing whether they are effective and genuine or whether they are so limited as to be merely marginal and ancillary.[259] In assessing whether a person is a worker, account should be taken of all the occupational activities which the person concerned has pursued within the host Member State, but not the activities which he has pursued elsewhere within the Union.[260]

A migrant worker who voluntarily leaves his employment in order to take up, after a certain lapse of time, a course of full-time study in the country of which he is a national retains his status as a worker provided that there is a link between the previous occupational activity and the studies in question.[261] However, a migrant worker who leaves his employment and begins a course of full-time study unconnected with the previous occupational activities will not retain his status as a migrant worker for the purposes of Article 45 TFEU, except if he becomes involuntarily unemployed.[262]

A researcher preparing a doctoral thesis on the basis of a grant contract concluded with the Max-Planck-Gesellschaft zur Förderung der Wissenschaften eV, must be regarded as a worker within the meaning of Article 45 TFEU only if his activities are performed for a certain period of time under the direction of an institute forming part of that association and if, in return for those activities, he receives remuneration.

A private-law association, such as the Max-Planck-Gesellschaft zur Förderung der Wissenschaften eV, must observe the principle of non-discrimination in relation to workers.

If the applicant in the main proceedings is justified in relying on damage caused by the discrimination to which he has been subject, it is for the referring court to assess, in

---

256. *Levin* case, *op. cit.*
257. *Lawrie-Blum* case, *op. cit.*
258. C.O.J., 26 February 1992, *M.J.E. Bernini v. Netherlands Ministry of Education and Science*, No. C-3/90, ECR, 1992, 1071.
259. C.O.J., 26 February 1992, *V.J.M. Raulin v. Netherlands Ministry of Education and Science*, No. C-357/89, ECR, 1992, 1027.
260. *Idem.*
261. C.O.J., 26 February 1992, *M.J.E. Bernini v. Netherlands Ministry of Education and Science*, No. C-3/90, ECR, 1992, 1071.
262. C.O.J., 26 February 1992, *V.J.M. Raulin v. Netherlands Ministry of Education and Science*, No. C-357/89, ECR, 1992, 1027.

the light of the national legislation applicable in relation to non-contractual liability, the nature of the compensation which he would be entitled to claim.[263]

710. The fact that a person is related by marriage to the director and sole shareholder of the company for which he pursues an effective and genuine activity does not preclude that person from being classified as a 'worker' within the meaning of Article 45 and of Regulation (EEC) No. 492/2011, so long as he pursues his activity in the context of a relationship of subordination.[264]

B. Sports

1. The *Meca* Case – the *Bosman* Case – the *Lethonen* Case – the *Kolpak* Case

a. *Meca* Case

711. The job has to have an economic nature within the meaning of the TFEU. Consequently, the Court ruled that the practice of sport is subject to Union law only insofar as it constitutes an economic activity.[265]

> This applies to the activities of professional or semi-professional football players, who are in the nature of gainful employment or remunerated service.

It follows logically that:

> where such players are nationals of a Member State they benefit in all the other Member States from the provisions of Union law concerning freedom of movement of persons and of provision of services. However, those provisions do not prevent the adoption of rules or of a practice excluding foreign players from participation in certain matches for reasons which are not of an economic nature, which relate to the particular nature and context of such matches and are thus of sporting interest only, such as, for example, matches between national teams from different countries.[266]

712. The competence of the EU concerning sports was fully addressed in the *David Meca* case.[267] This case concerns the appeal brought by Mr Meca-Medina and Mr Majcen against the judgment of the Court of First Instance of the European Communities of 30 September 2004. The applicants were two professional athletes who competed in long distance swimming, the aquatic equivalent of the marathon.

---

263. C.O.J. 17 July 2008, *Andrea Raccanelli* v. *Max-Planck-Gesellschaft zur Förderung der Wissenschaften eV*, C-94/07, OJ, C-223, 30 August 2008.
264. C.O.J., 8 June 1999, *C.P.M. Meeusen and Hoofddirectie van de Informatie Beheer Groep*, Case C-337/97, ECR, 1999, 3289.
265. *Walrave/Koch* case, *op. cit.*
266. C.O.J., 14 July 1976, *G. Dona* v. *M. Mantero*, No. 13/76, ECR, 1976, 1333.
267. C.O.J., 18 July 2006, *David Meca-Medina & Igor Majcen* v. *Commission of the European Communities*, C-519/04, ECR, 2006, 6991.

Part I, Ch. 1, The Free Movement of Workers

In an anti-doping test during the World Cup (1999) in that discipline at Salvador de Bahia (Brazil), where they had finished first and second respectively, the applicants tested positive for nandrolone. FINA's doping panel suspended the applicants for a period of four years.

In their complaint, the appellants challenged the compatibility of certain regulations adopted by the IOC and implemented by the *Fédération internationale de natation amateur*, and certain practices relating to doping control, with the Community rules on competition (Articles 101, 102 TFEU) and freedom to provide services (Article 56 TFEU).

713. The Court stated as follows:

> It is to be remembered that, having regard to the objectives of the Community, sport is subject to Union law in so far as it constitutes an economic activity within the meaning of the Treaty.
>
> Thus, where a sporting activity takes the form of gainful employment or the provision of services for remuneration, which is true of the activities of semi-professional or professional.
>
> These Union provisions on freedom of movement for persons and freedom to provide services not only apply to the action of public authorities but extend also to rules of any other nature aimed at regulating gainful employment and the provision of services in a collective manner.
>
> The Court has, however, held that the prohibitions enacted by those provisions of the Treaty do not affect rules concerning questions which are of purely sporting interest and, as such, have nothing to do with economic activity.
>
> With regard to the difficulty of severing the economic aspects from the sporting aspects of a sport, the Court has held that the provisions of Union law concerning freedom of movement for persons and freedom to provide services do not preclude rules or practices justified on non economic grounds which relate to the particular nature and context of certain sporting events. It has stressed, however, that such a restriction on the scope of the provisions in question must remain limited to its proper objective. It cannot, therefore, be relied upon to exclude the whole of a sporting activity from the scope of the Treaty.
>
> In light of all of these considerations, it is apparent that the mere fact that a rule is purely sporting in nature does not have the effect of removing from the scope of the Treaty the person engaging in the activity governed by that rule or the body which has laid it down.
>
> If the sporting activity in question falls within the scope of the Treaty, the conditions for engaging in it are then subject to all the obligations which result from the various provisions of the Treaty. It follows that the rules which govern that activity must satisfy the requirements of those provisions, which, in particular, seek to ensure freedom of movement for workers, freedom of establishment, freedom to provide services, or competition.
>
> Thus, where engagement in the sporting activity must be assessed in the light of the Treaty provisions relating to freedom of movement for workers or freedom to provide services, it will be necessary to determine whether the rules

which govern that activity satisfy the requirements of Articles 45 and 56 TFEU, that is to say do not constitute restrictions prohibited by those articles.

Likewise, where engagement in the activity must be assessed in the light of the Treaty provisions relating to competition, it will be necessary to determine, given the specific requirements of Articles 101, 102 TFEU, whether the rules which govern that activity emanate from an undertaking, whether the latter restricts competition or abuses its dominant position, and whether that restriction or that abuse affects trade between Member States.

Therefore, even if those rules do not constitute restrictions on freedom of movement because they concern questions of purely sporting interest and, as such, have nothing to do with economic activity that fact means neither that the sporting activity in question necessarily falls outside the scope of Articles 101, 102 TFEU nor that the rules do not satisfy the specific requirements of those articles.

714. However, the Court of First Instance held that the fact that purely sporting rules may have nothing to do with economic activity, with the result that they do not fall within the scope of Articles 45 TFEU and 56 TFEU, means, also, that they have nothing to do with the economic relationships of competition, with the result that they also do not fall within the scope of Articles 101, 102 TFEU.

In holding that rules could thus be excluded straightaway from the scope of those articles solely on the ground that they were regarded as purely sporting with regard to the application of Articles 45 TFEU and 56 TFEU, without any need to determine first whether the rules fulfilled the specific requirements of Articles 101, 102 TFEU, the Court of First Instance made an error of law.

715. Union law is also applicable to football trainers.[268] There is no need to underline that the free movement of professional soccer players is *de facto* not respected given the restrictions imposed upon players for reasons of nationality on one hand and the systems of blockade which operate in the case of a transfer of players from one club to another, at international as well as national level, on the other hand. FIFA and UEFA, which have set up international cartels to monopolise professional soccer on a worldwide basis, are violating Union law relating to competition in general and to Articles 101, 102 TFEU in particular.

b. *Bosman* Case

716. This was more than confirmed in the *Bosman* case,[269] where the Court of Justice did justice, which was more than overdue in sports, especially regarding the transfer system in which sportsmen, especially soccer players, were – and still are outside the EU – treated like cattle which can be sold and bought. The Court reaffirmed that free movement of workers applies to professional sports and that it

---

268. C.O.J., 15 October 1987, *Unectef* v. *G. Heylens*, No. 222/86, ECR, 1987, 4097.
269. C.O.J., 15 December 1995, *Union Royale Belge des Sociétés de Football Association ASBL and Others* v. *Jean-Marc Bosman and Others*, Case C-415/93, ECR, 1995, 4921.

Part I, Ch. 1, The Free Movement of Workers

constitutes a fundamental right. Transfer systems designed to block players and nationality clauses limiting EU players to be lined up are contrary to Article 39 (Art. 45 TFEU). This landmark decision is a marvellous example of the contribution of European law to human rights and human dignity. Let us consider the facts, the arguments and the Court's ruling.

Mr. Bosman, a professional footballer of Belgian nationality, was employed from 1988 by RC Liège, a Belgian first division club, under a contract expiring on 30 June 1990, which assured him an average monthly salary of BEF 120,000, including bonuses. On 21 April 1990, RC Liège offered Mr. Bosman a new contract for one season, reducing his pay to BEF 30,000, the minimum permitted by the URBSFA (Belgian Soccer Federation) federal rules. Mr. Bosman refused to sign and was put on the transfer list. The compensation fee for training was set, in accordance with the said rules, at BEF 11,743,000.

Since no club showed an interest in a compulsory transfer, Mr. Bosman contacted US Dunkerque, a club in the French second division, which led to his being signed.

On 27 July 1990, a contract was also concluded between RC Liège and US Dunkerque for the temporary transfer of Mr. Bosman for one year, against payment by US Dunkerque to RC Liège of a compensation fee of BEF 1,200,000 payable on receipt by the Fédération Française de Football (FFF) of the transfer certificate issued by URBSFA.

However, RC Liège did not ask URBSFA to send the said certificate to FFF. As a result, neither contract took effect. On 31 July 1990, RC Liège also suspended Mr. Bosman, thereby preventing him from playing for the entire season.

(1) Interpretation of Article 45 TFEU with regard to the Transfer Rules

The first question was to ascertain whether Article 45 precludes the application of rules laid down by sporting associations, under which a professional footballer who is a national of one Member State may not, on the expiry of his contract with a club, be employed by a club of another Member State unless the latter club has paid to the former a transfer, training or development fee.

(a) Application of Article 45 to Rules Laid Down by Sporting Associations

717. It is to be remembered that, having regard to the objectives of the Union, sport is subject to Union law only in so far as it constitutes an economic activity within the meaning of the Treaty. This applies to the activities of professional or semi-professional footballers, where they are in gainful employment or provide a remunerated service.

It is not necessary, for the purposes of the application of the Union provisions on freedom of movement for workers, for the employer to be an undertaking; all that is required is the existence of, or the intention to create, an employment relationship.

Furthermore, application of Article 45 is not precluded by the fact that the transfer rules govern the business relationships between clubs rather than the employment relationships between clubs and players.

The argument based on points of alleged similarity between a sport and culture cannot be accepted, since the question relates to the scope of the freedom of movement of workers, which is a fundamental freedom in the Union system.

As regards the arguments based on the principle of freedom of association, it must be recognised that this principle, enshrined in Article 11 of the European Convention for the Protection of Human Rights and Fundamental Freedoms and resulting from the constitutional traditions common to the Member States, is one of the fundamental rights which, as the Court has consistently held and as is reaffirmed in the preamble to the Single European Act and in Article F(2) of the Treaty on European Union, are protected in the Union legal order.

However, the rules laid down by sporting associations to which the national court refers cannot be seen as necessary to ensure enjoyment of that freedom by those associations, by the clubs or by their players, nor can they be seen as an inevitable result thereof.

Finally, the principle of subsidiarity, as interpreted to the effect that intervention by public authorities, and particularly Union authorities, in the area in question must be confined to what is strictly necessary, cannot lead to a situation in which the freedom of private associations to adopt sporting rules restricts the exercise of rights conferred on individuals by the Treaty.

(b) Existence of an Obstacle to Freedom of Movement for Workers

718. It is true that the transfer rules in issue in the main proceedings apply also to transfers of players between clubs belonging to different national associations within the same Member State and that similar rules govern transfers between clubs belonging to the same national association.

However, those rules are likely to restrict the freedom of movement of players who wish to pursue their activity in another Member State by preventing or deterring them from leaving the clubs to which they belong even after the expiry of their contracts of employment with those clubs.

Since they provide that a professional footballer may not pursue his activity with a new club established in another Member State unless it has paid his former club a transfer fee agreed upon between the two clubs or determined in accordance with the regulations of the sporting associations, the said rules constitute an obstacle to the freedom of movement for workers.

Consequently, the transfer rules constitute an obstacle to freedom of movement for workers prohibited in principle by Article 45 of the Treaty. It could only be otherwise if those rules pursued a legitimate aim compatible with the Treaty and were justified by pressing reasons of public interest. But even if that were so, application of those rules would still have to be such as to ensure achievement of the aim in question and not go beyond what is necessary for that purpose.

(c) Existence of Justifications

719. First, it was argued that the transfer rules are justified by the need to maintain a financial and competitive balance between clubs and to support the search for talent and the training of young players.

In view of the considerable social importance of sporting activities and in particular football in the Union, the aims of maintaining a balance between clubs by preserving a certain degree of equality and uncertainty as to results and of encouraging the recruitment and training of young players must be accepted as legitimate.

As regards the first of those aims, Mr. Bosman has rightly pointed out that the application of the transfer rules is not an adequate means of maintaining a financial and competitive balance in the world of football. Those rules neither preclude the richest clubs from securing the services of the best players nor prevent the availability of financial resources from being a decisive factor in competitive sport, thus considerably altering the balance between clubs.

As regards the second aim, it must be accepted that the prospect of receiving transfer, development or training fees is indeed likely to encourage football clubs to seek new talent and train young players.

However, because it is impossible to predict the sporting future of young players with any certainty and because only a limited number of such players go on to play professionally, those fees are by nature contingent and uncertain and are in any event unrelated to the actual cost borne by clubs of training both future professional players and those who will never play professionally. The prospect of receiving such fees cannot, therefore, be either a decisive factor in encouraging recruitment and training of young players or an adequate means of financing such activities, particularly in the case of smaller clubs.

It has also been argued that the transfer rules are necessary to safeguard the worldwide organisation of football.

However, the present proceedings concern application of those rules within the Union and not the relations between the national associations of the Member States and those of non-member countries.

(2) Interpretation of Article 45 of the Treaty with regard to the Nationality Clauses

720. By its second question, the national court seeks in substance to ascertain whether Article 45 of the Treaty precludes the application of rules laid down by sporting associations, under which, in matches in competitions which they organise, football clubs may field only a limited number of professional players who are nationals of other Member States.

(a) Existence of an Obstacle to Freedom of Movement for Workers

721. Article 45(2) expressly provides that freedom of movement for workers entails the abolition of any discrimination based on nationality between workers of the Member States as regards employment, remuneration and conditions of work and employment.

That principle precludes the application of clauses contained in the regulations of sporting associations which restrict the right of nationals of other Member States to take part, as professional players, in football matches.

(b) Existence of Justifications

722. It was argued that the nationality clauses are justified on non-economic grounds, concerning only the sport as such.

Here, the nationality clauses do not concern specific matches between teams representing their countries but apply to all official matches between clubs and thus to the essence of the activity of professional players.

In those circumstances, the nationality clauses cannot be deemed to be in accordance with Article 45, otherwise it would be deprived of its practical effect and the fundamental right of free access to employment which the Treaty confers individually on each worker in the Union would be rendered nugatory.

None of the arguments submitted detracts from that conclusion.

(3) The Temporal Effects of this Judgment

723. In the present case, the specific features of the rules laid down by the sporting associations for transfers of players between clubs of different Member States, together with the fact that the same or similar rules applied to transfers both between clubs belonging to the same national association and between clubs belonging to different national associations within the same Member State, may have caused uncertainty as to whether those rules were compatible with Union law.

In such circumstances, overriding considerations of legal certainty militate against calling in question legal situations whose effects have already been exhausted. An exception must, however, be made in favour of persons who may have taken timely steps to safeguard their rights.

These arguments induced the Court to decide that:

> Article 45 precludes the application of rules laid down by sporting associations, under which a professional footballer who is a national of one Member State may not, on the expiry of his contract with a club, be employed by a club of another Member State unless the latter club has paid to the former club a transfer, training or development fee.
>
> Article 45 precludes the application of rules laid down by sporting associations under which, in matches in competitions which they organise, football clubs may field only a limited number of professional players who are nationals of other Member States.
>
> The direct effect of Article 45 cannot be relied upon in support of claims relating to a fee in respect of transfer, training or development which has already been paid on, or is still payable under an obligation which arose before, the date of this judgment, except by those who have brought court proceedings or raised an equivalent claim under the applicable national law before that date.

c. The *Lehtonen* Case

724. Another important question was raised in proceedings between Mr. Lehtonen and Castors Canada Dry Namur-Braine ASBL (hereinafter 'Castors Braine')

and Fédération Royale Belge des Sociétés de Basketball ASBL (herein-after 'the FRBSB') and Ligue Belge – Belgische Liga ASBL (hereinafter 'the BLB') concerning the right of Castors Braine to field Mr. Lehtonen in matches in the first division of the Belgian national basketball championship.

Rules on the organisation of basketball and on transfer periods are as follows. Basketball is organised at world level by the International Basketball Federation (FIBA). The Belgian federation is the FRBSB, which governs both amateur and professional basketball. The BLB, which consisted on 1 January 1996 of 11 of the 12 basketball clubs in the first division of the Belgian national championship, has the objective of promoting basketball at the highest level and representing top-grade Belgian basketball at national level, in particular in the FRBSB.

In Belgium the national men's first division basketball championship is divided into two stages: a first stage in which all clubs take part, and a second stage which includes only the best-placed clubs (play-off matches to decide the national title) and the clubs at the bottom of the league table (play-off matches to decide which clubs will stay in the first division).

The FIBA rules governing international transfers of players apply in their entirety to all the national federations (Rule 1(b)). For national transfers, the national federations are recommended to take the international rules as guidance and draw up their own rules on transfers of players in the spirit of the FIBA rules (Rule 1(c)). Those rules define a foreign player as a player who does not possess the nationality of the State of the national federation which has issued his licence (Rule 2(a)). A licence is the necessary authorisation given by a national federation to a player to allow him to play basketball for a club which is a member of that federation.

The FIBA rules prescribe generally that, for national championships, clubs are not allowed, after the deadline fixed for the zone in question as defined by FIBA, to include in their teams players who have already played in another country in the same zone during that season. For the European zone the deadline for the registration of foreign players is 28 February. After that date it is still possible for players from other zones to be transferred.

The FIBA rules that when a national federation receives an application for a licence for a player who has previously been licensed in a federation of another country, it must, before issuing him with a licence, obtain a letter of release from that federation.

According to the FRBSB rules, a distinction must be drawn between affiliation, which binds the player to the national federation, registration, which is the link between the player and a particular club, and qualification, which is the necessary condition for a player to be able to take part in official competitions. A transfer is defined as the operation by which an affiliated player obtains a change of registration.

The FRBSB rules concern transfers between Belgian clubs of players affiliated to the FRBSB, which may take place during a defined period in each year, which in 1995 ran from 15 April to 15 May and in 1996 from 1 to 31 May of the year preceding the championship in which the club in question takes part. No player may be registered with more than one Belgian club in any one season.

In the version applicable at the material time, the FRBSB rules stated: 'Players who are not registered with the club or who are suspended may not be fielded. This prohibition also applies to friendly matches and tournaments.'

725. Mr. Lehtonen is a basketball player of Finnish nationality. During the 1995/1996 season he played in a team which took part in the Finnish championship, and after that was over he was engaged by Castors Braine, a club affiliated to the FRBSB, to take part in the final stage of the 1995/1996 Belgian championship. To that end the parties on 3 April 1996 concluded a contract of employment for a remunerated sportsman, under which Mr. Lehtonen was to receive BEF 50,000 net per month as fixed remuneration and an additional BEF 15,000 for each match won by the club.

That engagement had been registered with the FRBSB on 30 March 1996, the player's letter of release having been issued on 29 March 1996 by the federation of origin. On 5 April 1996 the FRBSB informed Castors Braine that if FIBA did not issue the licence the club might be penalised and that if it fielded Mr. Lehtonen it would do so at its own risk.

Despite that warning Castors Braine fielded Mr. Lehtonen in the match of 6 April 1996 against Belgacom Quaregnon. The match was won by Castors Braine. On 11 April 1996, following a complaint by Belgacom Quaregnon, the competition department of the FRBSB penalised Castors Braine by awarding to the other club by 20-0 the match in which Mr. Lehtonen had taken part in breach of the FIBA rules on transfers of players within the European zone. In the following match, against Pepinster, Castors Braine included Mr. Lehtonen on the team sheet but in the end did not field him. The club was again penalised by the award of the match to the other club. As it ran the risk of being penalised again each time it included Mr. Lehtonen on the team sheet, or even of being relegated to the lower division in the event of a third default, Castors Braine dispensed with the services of Mr. Lehtonen for the play-off matches.

On 16 April 1996 Mr. Lehtonen and Castors Braine brought proceedings against the FRBSB in the *Tribunal de Première Instance*, Brussels, sitting to hear applications for interim relief. They sought essentially for the FRBSB to be ordered to lift the penalty imposed on Castors Braine for the match of 6 April 1996 against Belgacom Quaregnon, and to be prohibited from imposing any penalty whatever on the club preventing it from fielding Mr. Lehtonen in the 1995/1996 Belgian championship, on pain of a monetary penalty of BEF 100,000 per day of delay in complying with the order.

726. The Court rules as follows. In the light of the above, the national court's question must be understood as essentially asking whether Articles 6 and 48 of the Treaty preclude the application of rules laid down in a Member State by sporting associations which prohibit a basketball club from fielding players from other Member States in matches in the national championship, where the transfer has taken place after a specified date.

The existence of an obstacle to freedom of movement for workers having thus been established, it must be ascertained whether that obstacle may be objectively justified.

Part I, Ch. 1, The Free Movement of Workers

The FRBSB, the BLB and all the governments which submitted observations to the Court submit that the rules on transfer periods are justified on non-economic grounds concerning only sport as such.

On this point, it must be acknowledged that the setting of deadlines for transfers of players may meet the objective of ensuring the regularity of sporting competitions.

Late transfers might be liable to change substantially the sporting strength of one or other team in the course of the championship, thus calling into question the comparability of results between the teams taking part in that championship, and consequently the proper functioning of the championship as a whole.

The risk of that happening is especially clear in the case of a sporting competition which follows the rules of the Belgian first division national basketball championship. The teams taking part in the play-offs for the title or for relegation could benefit from late transfers to strengthen their squads for the final stage of the championship, or even for a single decisive match.

However, measures taken by sports federations with a view to ensuring the proper functioning of competitions may not go beyond what is necessary for achieving the aim pursued.

It appears from the rules on transfer periods that players from a federation outside the European zone are subject to a deadline of 31 March rather than 28 February, which applies only to players from federations in the European zone, which includes the federations of the Member States.

d. The *Deliège* Case

727. Another sports case relates to Ms. Deliège, a Belgian judoka, who has practised judo at a very high level since 1983.

Judo, a martial art, is organised at world level by the International Judo Federation. At European level, the membership of the European Judo Union comprises the various national federations. The Belgian federations are responsible for the selection of athletes with a view to participation in international tournaments. Ms. Deliège maintained that the Belgian federations had improperly frustrated her career development by not allowing her to take part in important competitions. She considered that she engaged in an economic activity, a matter involving a freedom guaranteed by Union law.

The Belgian court sought a ruling from the Court of Justice of the European Union as to the compatibility of the rules laid down by the sports authorities with the freedom to provide services, as regards in particular the requirement that professional sportsmen (or semi-professionals or persons aspiring to achieve that status) be authorised or selected by their national federation in order to be able to take part in an international competition.

The Court pointed out first of all that, by virtue of its judgment in *Bosman*, rules for the organisation of sports must comply with Union law in so far as sport constitutes an economic activity within the meaning of the Treaty.

That case law is consonant with the Amsterdam Treaty, which takes account of the particular characteristics of amateur sport, namely situations in which sport does not constitute an economic activity.

The mere circumstance that the placings achieved by athletes in those competitions were taken into account in determining which countries may enter representatives in the Olympic Games cannot justify treating those competitions as events between national teams which, under the case law of the Court, might fall outside the scope of Union law.

Moreover, the fact that a sports association or federation classifies its members as 'amateur' athletes does not in itself mean that those members do not engage in economic activities.

728. The Court therefore ruled that sports activities, and in particular a high-ranking athlete's participation in an international competition, are capable of involving the provision of a number of separate, but closely related, services. Thus, athletes taking part in a sports event which the public may attend, which television broadcasters may retransmit and which may be of interest to advertisers and sponsors, provide the basis for services of an economic nature.

Accordingly, it is for the national court to determine, on the basis of those criteria of interpretation, whether Ms. Deliège's sporting activities constitute an economic activity and the provision of services.

The Court then considered whether the selection rules at issue might constitute a restriction on the freedom to provide services. It observed that, in contrast to the rules applicable to the *Bosman* case, the selection rules at issue in the main proceedings do not determine the conditions governing access to the labour market by professional sportsmen and do not contain nationality clauses limiting the number of nationals of other Member States who may participate in a competition.

Although selection rules inevitably have the effect of limiting the number of participants in a tournament, such a limitation is inherent in the conduct of an international high-level sports event, which necessarily involves certain selection rules or criteria being adopted. Such rules may not therefore in themselves be regarded as constituting a restriction on the freedom to provide services. Moreover, those selection rules apply both to competitions organised within the Union and to those taking place outside it and involve both nationals of Member States and those of non-member countries.

The national federations, which reflect the arrangements adopted in most sporting disciplines, are therefore entitled to lay down appropriate rules and to make selections.[270]

At first sight, such a rule must be regarded as going beyond what is necessary to achieve the aim pursued. It does not appear from the material in the case-file that a transfer between 28 February and 31 March of a player from a federation in the European zone jeopardises the regularity of the championship more than a transfer in that period of a player from a federation not in that zone.

---

270. C.O.J., 11 April 2000, *Christelle Deliège* v. *Ligue Francophone de Judo et Disciplines ASBL and Others*, Joined Cases C-51/96 and C-191/97, ECR, 2000, 2549.

However, it is for the national court to ascertain the extent to which objective reasons, concerning only sport as such or relating to differences between the position of players from a federation in the European zone and that of players from a federation not in that zone, justify such different treatment.

In the light of all the foregoing, the answer to the national court's question, as reformulated, must be that Article 45 of the Treaty precludes the application of rules laid down in a Member State by sporting associations which prohibit a basketball club from fielding players from other Member States in matches in the national championship, where they have been transferred after a specified date, if that date is earlier than the date which applies to transfers of players from certain non-member countries, unless objective reasons concerning only sport as such or relating to differences between the position of players from a federation in the European zone and that of players from a federation not in that zone justify such different treatment.[271]

e. The *Kolpak* Case

729. Mr. Kolpak,[272] who is a Slovak national, entered in March 1997 into a fixed-term employment contract expiring on 30 June 2000 and subsequently, in February 2000, entered into a new fixed-term contract expiring on 30 June 2003 for the post of goalkeeper in the German handball team TSV Östringen eV Handball, a club which plays in the German Second Division. Mr. Kolpak receives a monthly salary. He is resident in Germany and holds a valid residence permit.

The (German Handball federation) DHB, which organises league and cup matches at federal level, issued to him, under Rule 15 of the (federal regulations governing competitive games) SpO, a player's licence marked with the letter A on the ground of his Slovak nationality.

Mr. Kolpak, who had requested that he be issued with a player's licence which did not feature the specific reference to nationals of non-member countries, brought an action before the *Landgericht* (Regional Court) Dortmund (Germany) challenging that decision of the DHB. He argued that the Slovak Republic is one of the non-member countries nationals of which are entitled to participate without restriction in competitions under the same conditions as German and Union players by reason of the prohibition of discrimination resulting from the combined provisions of the TFEU and the Association Agreement with Slovakia.

The *Landgericht* ordered the DHB to issue Mr. Kolpak with a player's licence not marked with an A on the ground that, under Rule 15 of the SpO, Mr. Kolpak was not to be treated in the same way as a player who was a national of a non-member country. The DHB appealed against that decision to the Oberlandesgericht Hamm.

---

271. C.O.J., 13 April 2000, *Jyri Lehtonen and Castors Canada Dry Namur-Braine ASBL v. Fédération royale belge des sociétés de basket-ball ASBL (FRBSB)*, Case C-176/96, ECR, 2000, 2681.
272. C.O.J., 8 May 2003, *Deutscher Handballbund eV v. Maros Kolpak*, C-438/00, ECR, 2003, 4135.

730. Article 38(1) of the Association Agreement, which features in Title IV, Chapter I, entitled 'Movement of workers', provides:
Subject to the conditions and modalities applicable in each Member State:

– treatment accorded to workers of Slovak Republic nationality legally employed in the territory of a Member State shall be free from any discrimination based on nationality, as regards working conditions, remuneration or dismissal, as compared to its own nationals, – the legally resident spouse and children of a worker legally employed in the territory of a Member State, with the exception of seasonal workers and of workers coming under bilateral agreements within the meaning of Article 42, unless otherwise provided by such agreements, shall have access to the labour market of that Member State, during the period of that worker's authorised stay of employment.'

The *Oberlandesgericht* accordingly asks whether Rule 15(1)(b) of the SpO is contrary to Article 38 of the Association Agreement. If that were so, and if the latter provision were to have direct effect in regard to individuals, Mr. Kolpak would be entitled to be issued with an unrestricted licence.

In the opinion of the *Oberlandesgericht*, the DHB breaches the prohibition in Article 38 of the Association Agreement with Slovakia through its refusal to issue Mr. Kolpak with an unrestricted licence on the ground of his nationality.

In that regard, the *Oberlandesgericht Hamm* observes that Mr. Kolpak's contract, which is governed by Rule 15 of the SpO, is an employment contract, as that player undertakes thereby, in return for a fixed monthly salary, to provide sporting services, as an employee, in connection with training and matches organised by his club and that this constitutes his main professional activity.

The Court answered as follows:

731. The first indent of Article 38(1) of the Europe Agreement establishing an association between the European Communities and their Member States, of the one part, and the Slovak Republic, of the other part, signed in Luxembourg on 4 October 1993 and approved on behalf of the Communities by Decision 94/909/ECSC, EEC, Euratom of the Council and the Commission of 19 December 1994, must be construed as *precluding the application to a professional sportsman of Slovak nationality, who is lawfully employed by a club established in a Member State, of a rule drawn up by a sports federation in that State under which clubs are authorised to field, during league or cup matches, only a limited number of players from non-member countries that are not parties to the Agreement on the European Economic Area.*

f. The *Balog* Case:[273] Transfer and Competition Rules

732. The *Balog* case was never judged by Court of Justice. The sport organisations, out of fear for another disaster in the Court, backed out and negotiated a deal

---

273. Opinion of Advocate General Stix-Hackl, *Tibor Balog* v. *Royal Charleroi Sporting Club ASBL (RCSC)*, C-264/98, 29 March 2001, IELL, Case Law.

Part I, Ch. 1, The Free Movement of Workers 733–735

with the player, who was bought out. Nevertheless, the opinion of the Advocate General speaks for itself and shows clearly that transfer systems are also in contradiction with the EU competition rules. We discuss the main points.

(1) Facts

733. The *Balog* case concerns the relationship between professional sport and competition law, and specifically the significance of the rule against cartels for the transfer rules in football.

Unlike previous sports cases, however, the question referred for a preliminary ruling relates exclusively to the prohibition of cartels and the transfer of third-country nationals, third countries meaning States which are neither Member States nor contracting parties to the EEA Agreement.

(2) Organisation of Football and Rules on Transfers

734. Football is organised by a series of federations and associations which may be thought of as forming a pyramid. At international level the responsible body is FIFA (*Fédération Internationale de Football Association*), an association governed by Swiss law, which functions as a sort of umbrella association. At European level UEFA (*Union des Associations Européennes de Football*) operates, whose members include in particular the national associations of the Member States and the EEA Contracting States. The individual clubs form national associations, in Belgium URBSFA (*Union Royale Belge des Sociétés de Football Association*). These organisations govern both professional and amateur football.

(3) Facts and Main Proceedings

735. Mr. Tibor Balog, a Hungarian national born on 1 March 1966, was employed from 1993 as a professional football player by Royal Charleroi Sporting Club (RCSC); his last contract expired on 30 June 1997. On 21 April 1997 RCSC sent him the draft of a new contract for one season, which he turned down. Mr. Balog submits that he approached various football clubs abroad, in particular in France and Norway, with a view to being transferred, but the clubs did not pursue negotiations because RCSC, in accordance with Article IV/85 of the URBSFA regulations, demanded a transfer compensation of several million Belgian francs. He then contacted managers, whose approaches for the purpose of a transfer were likewise unsuccessful for the same reasons. In December 1997 Mr. Balog was engaged by an Israeli club. No compensation was sought from that club, since the transfer was limited to the 1997/98 season and he was to return to RCSC after its expiry. On 1 April 1998 the representative of Mr. Balog called on RCSC to acknowledge in particular that RCSC could not demand any transfer compensation or fee from a possible future employer. On 6 April 1998 RCSC refused to do so. On 16 April 1998 it sent Mr. Balog a new offer of a contract, which was not accepted. On 23 April

1998 Mr. Balog brought proceedings for interim relief in the Tribunal de première instance de Charleroi.

Mr. Balog sought an order requiring RCSC to refrain from any conduct, in particular the assertion of a claim for a 'transfer fee', with the intent or effect of directly or indirectly exercising pressure on or obstructing his freedom of contract or that of any club interested in employing him as a professional footballer. Secondly, Mr. Balog sought an order requiring RCSC to pay him a monthly amount of BEF 45,000 until an enforceable decision of the court on the substance of the case, unless he were able in the meantime to find employment with a gross remuneration at least equivalent thereto. In the alternative, he asked the court to make the interim order sought and refer a question to the Court of Justice for a preliminary ruling, with the proceedings being stayed.

(4) The Question Referred for a Preliminary Ruling

736. Is it compatible with Article 101 of the Treaty of Rome and/or with Article 53 of the Agreement on the European Economic Area for a football club established in the territory of a Member State of the European Union to claim, on the basis of the rules and circulars of the national and international federations (URBSFA, UEFA, FIFA), payment of a "transfer sum" on the occasion of the engagement of one of its former players, a professional footballer of nonCommunity nationality who has reached the end of his contract, by a new employer established in the same Member State, in another Member State of the European Union or the European Economic Area, or in a non-member country?

737. It is apparent from the question referred that it relates only to certain aspects in connection with transfers. First, it relates only to transfers of players on expiry of a contract, not to the legal position for a transfer before a contract expires. Further, it does not concern possible prohibitions of transfers of players below a specified age limit or during the season. Nor has the Court been asked questions on related problems such as the maximum length of a contract and the right of a player to terminate a contract unilaterally.

(5) Applicability of Article 101 TFEU

738. Under Article 101 TFEU all agreements between undertakings, decisions by associations of undertakings and concerted practices which may affect trade between Member States and which have as their object or effect the prevention, restriction, or distortion of competition within the common market are incompatible with the common market and prohibited.

The transfer regulations at issue must therefore be examined below by reference to the individual elements of Article 101(1) TFEU. It does not appear appropriate to look at the transfer regulations separately according to different transfer directions, or only in relation to nationals of third countries, even though the question referred is confined to them. Against such an approach is the fact that all the transfer rules

Part I, Ch. 1, The Free Movement of Workers 739–741

at issue are not only connected with each other but also form part of a complex transfer system. Since parts of a system are, according to the Court's case law, to be treated as a whole, or as the aspects not addressed expressly in the question referred ought to be taken into account as concomitant circumstances, the transfer regulations will basically, apart from certain aspects, not be examined below by means of such a differentiated approach.

(6) Undertakings or Associations of Undertakings

739. It must first be considered whether the associations are to be categorised as associations of undertakings and the individual clubs as undertakings within the meaning of Article 101 TFEU. The first point to look at here is whether the clubs or associations in question carry on an economic activity.

The conclusion must therefore be that institutions such as professional clubs can – at least for the application of the Union competition rules – be regarded as undertakings. FIFA, and also UEFA, and the national associations may, depending on the factual situation, be classified either as undertakings themselves or as associations of undertakings or groupings of associations of undertakings.

It makes no difference to that assessment that amateur clubs also belong to the national associations, in so far as the associations are at least formed by economically active clubs.

(7) Agreements between Undertakings or Decisions of Associations of Undertakings

740. The next point to consider is whether the transfer regulations are based on agreements between undertakings or decisions of associations of undertakings.

The transfer regulations at issue of the associations are in this respect altogether an expression of the free will of the relevant associations and are not imposed by the State. That in several Member States certain legal consequences may in certain circumstances be attached to the regulations adopted by international associations or the relevant national association need not be considered further here.

As for regulations of sporting associations which are to be attributed to the State, it should be pointed out that such measures too may be covered by Union law, in particular if they prescribe, facilitate or magnify the effect of anticompetitive conduct. Such regulations of sports associations would then have to be examined in the light of Article 101 TFEU. But even in such cases the undertakings could be liable for their conduct if, for instance, they made use of their residual discretion in a manner contrary to Union law.

(8) Relevant Market

741. The relevant market for the transfer regulations is therefore the market which is formed by the supply of and demand for players, hence the acquisition market, as the French and Italian Governments have correctly indicated. However, that does not exclude the possibility of possible interferences with competition having an effect on the downstream markets.

On the geographically relevant market in this case, it needs only to be said that it covers the territory of all the associations in which the transfer regulations which are the subject-matter of the case are applied.

(9) Restriction of Competition

742. The transfer system at issue deprives the purchasing clubs of opportunities which they could have in the absence of the interferences.

The transfer system, in particular the rules on transfer payments, thus prevent clubs from developing their economic activity on the downstream markets. The clubs are prevented from raising the quality of their sporting performance and thereby also making that performance more exploitable. That affects especially small, economically weaker clubs. They are scarcely in a position to engage better qualified, that is, more expensive players. At the same time the system strengthens the position of economically strong clubs, because they can obtain the better players for themselves.

Furthermore, the transfer system at issue affects the players as well. The clubs clearly react to the high transfer fees by depressing the level of pay of the employees concerned, that is, the players. Players probably receive from their new club and employer smaller real remuneration than corresponds to their marginal product. Paying smaller remuneration can yield the clubs a special return. The transfer system thus works to the detriment of third parties, namely the players, in this respect. They would obviously earn more without the transfer system. In addition, on expiry of his contract a club might offer a player poorer conditions because the club has the power of refusing consent to a transfer. That would particularly affect players to whom another club offers the possibility of a more favourable contract.

The rise in players' wages following the changes to the transfer regulations after the *Bosman* judgment clearly demonstrates the negative effects of transfer regulations on competition.

(10) Necessity of the Transfer Regulations

743. The question to be examined below is to what extent the transfer regulations at issue are essential for the functioning of professional football. If that is the case, the restrictions of competition associated with them would be permissible under the Court's case law as 'ancillary restrictions'.

The question of the necessity of payments on the occasion of the transfer of a player depends essentially on the size of the payment and hence on the basis of calculation. Objective criteria are thus needed, which ought to be based primarily on the costs of training. The contribution of the player concerned to the economic success of the club should also be taken into account, however.

Part I, Ch. 1, The Free Movement of Workers 744–745

Other possible objective factors are the remaining length of the contract, the salary paid hitherto, the age and the level of play of the professional footballer concerned. Further, it would be possible for the transfer fee to be shared by all the clubs which the player in question played for, which might include amateur clubs. A formula for sharing would have to be determined.

It must be considered in principle whether the system could not be recast in such a way that transfer fees are payable only on the first transfer away from the club which trained the player. Another alternative would be the setting up of a fund system. This could be based on a solidarity fund. The fund might have *inter alia* the function of reimbursing the training costs in the place of the new club. It could be financed essentially from receipts from the sale of tickets and the exploitation of transmission rights. The receipts could be shared out according to a specified formula between the clubs and the association to which the fund might be affiliated. This solution would correspond essentially to the 'nursery system'. In such a system young players develop in smaller clubs – training places – that is, they are recruited and trained by them. This is financed by strong teams as buyers of the players, with the transfer fee being paid not to the former club only as in the transfer system at issue, but to the 'system'.

In order to bring the regulations on transfers of players into conformity with the competition rules, methods other than the transfer system are also available, however. Thus provisions on a transfer to a new club might be laid down at contractual level, whether in the individual contracts of players with their (former) clubs or in the form of a collective agreement.

(11) Appreciable Effect

744. The present case has the particular feature that the main emphasis of the regulations at issue which interfere with competition lies essentially in a system which applies worldwide. FIFA comprises all the over 200 national associations, to which the individual football clubs of the countries concerned in turn belong. All sources of supply are thus in principle brought into the transfer system, although there are some national differences. The circumstance that as a consequence of the *Bosman* judgment certain transfers were excluded from the system at issue does not change the appreciable effect of the interferences, since the alternative possibilities for clubs which wish to recruit players nevertheless remain restricted.

On the basis of all the above considerations, it must therefore be concluded that the transfer regulations at issue have the effect of interfering with competition in the relevant market.

(12) Effect on Trade between Member States

745. There is an effect on trade between Member States not only when transfers actually take place between Member States, but presumably also where the economic activities of the clubs and associations on the downstream markets are the object of trade between the Member States. In this connection the Commission mentions some telling examples which demonstrate the international interlacement, even going beyond the Member States, such as the participation of clubs in international contests, the supporters who travel abroad, the awarding of transmission rights to foreigners and cooperation with foreign sponsors.

That the transfer regulations at issue are capable of affecting trade may also be deduced from the fact that by their nature they obstruct the exercise of fundamental freedoms.

Even if it is assumed that the transfer regulations merely maintain trade flows, that may also be an interference, if further penetration of the market is thereby prevented.

(13) Conclusion

746. On the basis of the above considerations, I propose that the Court give the following answer to the national court's question:

> It is not compatible with Article 101(1) TFEU and/or Article 53 of the Agreement on the European Economic Area for a football club established in a Member State of the European Union to demand payment of a "transfer sum", as provided for by the regulations and circulars of the national and international associations (URBSFA, UEFA, FIFA) in the versions in force at the material time, on the engagement of one of its former employees, a professional footballer of non-Union nationality who has reached the end of his contract, by a new employer who is established in the same Member State, in another Member State of the European Union or of the European Economic Area, or in a third country.

2. Agreement between the European Commission, FIFA and UEFA (5 March 2001)

a. The Declaration of Nice (December 2000)[274]

747. Since *Bosman*, the European Commission and also the European Summit have been following a different track. The autonomy of sport must be recognised, even though that means derogating from EU law. The sports element takes precedence, with Union law becoming the exception. So-called sporting reasons justify setting aside Union law. The specific nature of sport wins over Union law.

All this is clear from the Declaration of Nice, manipulated by sports lobbying and political sway.

---

274. R. Blanpain, *The Status of Sportsmen and Sportswomen under international European and Belgian national and regional law*, Larcier, 2003.

After the Nice summit (December 2000), the European Council adopted a 'Declaration on the specific characteristics of sport and its social function in Europe, which should be taken into consideration when implementing Community policies'.

Not only is the very fact of the adoption of the Declaration on Sport important, but it is also important in terms of its content. The Nice Declaration has indeed provided a clear political signal for sport, along with its social and educational values, to be taken more into account in national and Community policies.

748. In this Declaration the European Council first stressed that sports organisations and Member States have an essential responsibility in the running of sports matters. Nevertheless, although sport does not feature among the areas for which the Community has been allocated direct responsibilities under the Treaty, the Community must take due account of the social, educational and cultural functions of sport that explain its uniqueness, in order to respect and promote the ethics and solidarity needed if sport is to preserve its role in society. Moreover, the horizontal provisions of the Treaty apply in full to sport as an economic activity.

After clearly stressing the principle of subsidiarity, the Declaration focused on the following themes:

– support for sporting activity at all levels;
– the central role of sports federations in organising competitions, establishing sporting rules and awarding titles;
– ensuring training policies for young sportsmen and sportswomen;
– safeguarding the health and education of young sportsmen and sportswomen;
– strict regulation of commercial transactions involving minors;
– ensuring fair competition, having regard to the economic conditions governing the various participating structures;
– transfer rules in professional sport;
– solidarity between the various levels of sporting activity.

749. The significance of this Declaration lies in the level at which it was adopted and consequently in its political weight. In terms of content, however, it pretends to be in line with the approach previously followed by the Commission and the Parliament and enshrined by the Court of Justice.

All the Union institutions have therefore acknowledged that sport is set apart from other activities by certain characteristics and specific needs. Following on from Amsterdam, the Council has taken the same line. This was the whole purpose of the Nice Declaration.

In short, sport is something special and unique. This must be taken into account in applying EU law. The rule of subsidiarity must operate, which means that regulating sport is primarily a task for the sports organisations themselves: they are autonomous.

What is more, at least according to the European Commission, the *Bosman* judgment disrupted the economic balance between clubs and players and put the training of young athletes by clubs under pressure. Certain clubs with training centres for professional players saw some of their best sporting prospects leave, without themselves receiving any compensation for the resources they had invested in these youngsters' training.

In short, the *Bosman* judgment *delenda est*. From this point of view the two federations FIFA and UEFA and the European Commission were to set about negotiating, with the players' union FIFPro as a marginal partner, on the sidelines.

Mention has already been made several times of intervention from European government leaders, who also put pressure on the Commission.

b. The Agreement of 5 March 2001, as Amended in 2005, between FIFA and the European Commission

750. The resultant agreement contained an undertaking from the FIFA president to amend FIFA's 1997 regulations on player transfers on the basis of the following general principles:

– in cases of the transfer of players aged under 23 a training compensation fee should be paid in order to encourage and reward the provision of training by clubs, notably small clubs;
– creation of a solidarity mechanism that would enable a significant proportion of revenues to be redistributed to the training clubs concerned, including amateur clubs;
– international transfers of players aged under 18 to be allowed only subject to certain objective conditions; the football authorities will establish a code of conduct to guarantee these young players both sports training and academic education; – limitation of transfer periods to one per season plus a further mid-season window restricted to exceptional cases, with a limit of one transfer per year per player per season;
– establishment of a minimum and maximum duration of contracts from one year to five years;
– protected contracts for the first three years for players aged up to 28 and the first two years for players aged over 28;
– in order to promote the regularity and proper functioning of competitions, unilateral breaches of the contract of employment are possible only at the end of the season; – in cases where a contract is breached unilaterally, whether by a player or a club, financial compensation is payable;
– in cases of unilateral breach without just cause or without sporting just cause during the protected period, proportional sanctions can be imposed on players, clubs or players' agents;
– creation of an efficient, quick and objective arbitration body with members chosen in equal numbers by players and clubs and with an independent chairman;
– voluntary arbitration which in no way precludes recourse by players to the ordinary courts.

Part I, Ch. 1, The Free Movement of Workers

c. Consequences of the New System

751. These are self-evident.

– Players whose contract simply expires are very much the exception. Contracts are concluded for a lengthy term: five years or more, and sometimes (under pressure) extended. The possibility for a player to break the contract unilaterally is in fact an empty one, because of the sporting and/or financial sanctions that he would incur. It has to be remembered here that, on average, a player's career lasts for only eight years. For all practical purposes the player is, just as before, tied to his employing club for the whole of his playing life. Only if his employer agrees is he able to enter into a new relationship as a footballer.
– Selling players during the course of the contract is becoming the general rule.

Prices will still be sky-high. They have little or nothing to do with the level of players' pay but are related to the worth and talents of the footballer as an individual. – This means that the new system promotes human trafficking, as – shamefully – the trade in black 'pearls' in Belgium illustrates only too well.

– A system of this kind has a destabilising effect because big money can be made by organising transfers. Although a player is tied (indissolubly) to his club for a minimum of two years or three years, the club is under no obligation whatever in the matter other than to field him in at least 10 per cent of its official matches – and that can be in C-team matches. The club can sell the player after just one year by *de facto* forcing him to agree if necessary. In short, the stability of teams, which is purportedly a prime consideration, is undermined by the fact that transfers are an easy way of making big money. The system has a counter-productive effect. More transfers mean more money but correspondingly less stability.
– The training compensation fee bears no resemblance to the 'objectively calculated and fair transfer payments, i.e. sums that are related to the resources invested in the training of the athlete concerned' previously recommended, quite rightly, by the European Commission.

752. Training compensation amounts are being inflated by, among other things, the player factor of 10 by which the annual training costs have to be multiplied.

It becomes entirely unworkable when for non-EU/EEA the costs used in the calculation may be those applicable to the acquiring club.

These sums will soar so high that they will become an obstacle to the free transfer of players and make transfers possible only for top players. The amount of training compensation payable is the same in the case of a merely average professional player as in that of the very best.

Furthermore, a look at a sample case calculated by the FIFA task force shows that the smaller clubs receive only peanuts – some 5–6 per cent of the sums involved will go to the training clubs. The large clubs will make off with by far the largest slice of the solidarity cake. This is confirmed by the figures cited earlier on the matter by the European Commission.[275] The same is true of the 5 per cent solidarity contribution. The lion's share goes to the big clubs.

The much-vaunted solidarity is, in short, marginal and benefits only a few of the amateur clubs. Solidarity is a fallacy, false colours used to dress up human trafficking.

In other words, the new system restricts freedom, promotes human trafficking, does not foster solidarity at all and has a destabilising effect. Footballers are modern-day slaves, gladiators of sport. The fact that a few of them earn a great deal of money is no excuse.

d. Incompatible with Fundamental Rights and EU Law

753. It is clear that, first and foremost, freedom of labour and freedom of movement have yet again been dealt a serious blow. All player freedom has gone out of the window. A professional footballer is, in practice, tied to his club for the whole of his playing career.

Human trafficking is flourishing on a large scale. The principle that man is not a commodity is being grossly violated.

It can safely be said that the *Bosman* judgment is dead and buried and that the political lobbying waged by the federations has been more than successful in re-introducing the old system of masters who can sell their servants.

The result is that the football labour market is badly disrupted and that players are either not available or can be paid for by only a few large clubs. Smaller clubs, in so far as they are permitted to recruit professional players under the relevant statutes, are quite unable to afford better players. This situation represents an infringement of competition law.

The new system is in fact invalid and unacceptable in that it conflicts with both public-order principles and mandatory law:

(1) human trafficking, incompatible with *inter alia* Article 5(3) of the Charter of Fundamental Rights of the European Union;
(2) freedom of labour, as enshrined in Article 23 of the Belgian Constitution;
(3) incompatible with the United Nations Convention on the Rights of the Child (1989);
(4) free movement of workers, as established in Article 45 TFEU;
(5) competition law, as established in Article 101 TFEU.

754. The system is consequently contrary to EU law, as established in the *Bosman* judgment and the subsequent *Lehtonen* and *Deliège* judgments: more specifically, to Articles 45 and 101 TFEU. Sport is subject to EU law in so far as it constitutes an economic activity. Exceptions to this are possible provided they are inherent in the organisation of sport itself, and rules on selection and transfer periods certainly fall under this latter heading.

---

275. *See* Part I, §4, IV.

Part I, Ch. 1, The Free Movement of Workers

It is, however, quite a different matter when access to the profession is made more difficult or impossible, which is the case with training compensation.

e. Assessment of the New System

755. Training compensation fees and contractual minimum periods of employment (forced labour) are neither necessary nor inherently bound up with the organisation of sport itself.
The solidarity argument will not wash, because the amateur clubs see little or none of this money, as was pointed out by the European Court of Justice in its *Bosman* judgment and bears repeating here:

> Because it is impossible to predict the sporting future of young players with any certainty and because only a limited number of such players go on to play professionally, those fees are by nature contingent and uncertain and are in any event unrelated to the actual cost borne by clubs for training both future professional players and those who will never play professionally. The prospect of receiving such fees cannot, therefore, be either a decisive factor in encouraging recruitment and training of young players or an adequate means of financing such activities, particularly in the case of smaller clubs (paragraph 109).

All this is certainly also true of the 'new-style' training compensation. Also, the stated goal of solidarity is in any case not one that is easy to achieve. Training compensation is too contingent for that. Many smaller clubs will get nothing out of it financially.

756. What is more, insiders know only too well that the money for training young players is used *de facto* for the professional-player section in clubs.
The possible restriction of players' freedom is a fact because the large sums for training that are associated with transfers will inevitably have a negative influence on employment opportunities, certainly for average-ranking players. The so-called training costs of an entire generation of players are passed on to a single player. This is certainly the case with non-EU/EEA transfers, where the costs are those applicable in the new club. These high fees will inevitably influence a player's freedom since clubs will think twice about paying such sums before hiring a player.
Furthermore, training compensation has nothing to do with the training costs of the individual player concerned but is related to the artificial costs entailed in successfully producing one professional player. In short, the infringement of the freedom of labour and free movement of workers, which are fundamental rights for every employee, is not justified by a wholly fictitious and fraudulent solidarity mechanism.

757. The fact of being tied to a club for two years or three years also constitutes an unjustified restriction on the freedom of labour and free movement of workers. The system as laid down today by FIFA means that, in effect, a player is tied to the

club for the whole of his playing life and – except in the case of a handful of top-ranking stars – becomes a mere puppet in the hands of the club. If any player is not meekly submissive the club is free to relegate him to the 'C'-squad, with all the attendant repercussions on, for example, his earnings. Players are pressurised into extending their contracts and then sold for the highest price, which bears no relation to the player's wages or the training costs.

The normal compensation payable under general labour legislation in the event of breach of contract, coupled with a ban on playing during the season concerned, should be sufficient to guarantee the stability of a team. That is the situation for every business enterprise, and sport is no exception in this respect.

The system encourages human trafficking, particularly the importing of players from low-wage countries such as Africa, in which players fall into the clutches of sharks who sell them here and, if things go wrong, dump them.

As stated earlier, Article 101 TFEU is also liable to be pushed aside since the professional-footballer labour market cannot function normally. Players do not enjoy the normal freedom of contract. Clubs can choose not to hire players because they are not freely available or because they are too expensive. The monopoly situation that prevails in football leads to an abuse of power to the disadvantage of players in their capacity as employees.

f. Proposals

758. Consequently, the FIFA regulations on transfers should be strenuously rejected. It is a disgrace to society that footballers, who have a brief and highly risk-prone career and should in fact enjoy special social protection, are reduced to being pariahs.

The European Commission should do its homework over again. There is no disputing the fact that the social function of sport is very important. There is a need for autonomy and subsidiarity and also for solidarity, and special heed has to be paid to the training of young sportsmen and sportswomen.

Nevertheless, as Advocate General Lenz commented in point 226 *et seq.* of his Opinion in the *Bosman* case, those objectives can be attained by alternative means which do not constitute a hindrance to the free movement of workers.

If there is truly a wish to organise solidarity within the football family as a whole the training compensation fee should be dropped, because it does not really serve the purpose. To create a real sense of solidarity between all members of the football family, solidarity funds should be created at national, European and international level into which a significant proportion of their revenues from TV rights, advertising, gambling and lotteries, merchandising, gate receipts and so on should be paid in by the highest divisions and then distributed to the lower-division clubs according to the number of effectively playing members they have.

The rules binding players contractually to a club for two years or three years should be abolished. The normal contractual rules of labour law are sufficient. The transfer fee payable during the course of the contract should be linked to the player's pay and amount at most to one year's pay.

That would lead us to a system under which players can transfer freely at the end of their contract, would remove the pressure on them to extend fixed-term contracts and would mean that transfer during the course of the contract involves moderate sums of money – which would put an end to human trafficking in sport.

Such a system would reduce the role of agents to realistic proportions. Shady dealing in 'black pearls' would be phased out. There would no longer be any opportunities in football for wide boys.

g. Memorandum of Understanding (UEFA-FIFPRO)[276] (2007)

759. A Memorandum of Understanding between the *Union des Associations Européennes de Football* (UEFA) and the *Fédération Internationale des Associations de Footballeurs Professionnels* (FIFPro) 'FIFPRO Division Europe' was concluded on 11 October 2007. The parties recognise each other as partners in the football family and agree to cooperate and dialogue on the major issues in football. This way the adversarial attitude between both parties, which came to a peak with the *Bosman* case, has come to and end.

The parties share similar values and concerns. These include:

– the key values such as solidarity, equality and fraternity which have underpinned the development and growth of both the sporting movement and the trade union movement;
– an equitable redistribution of wealth;
– collective rather than individual exploitation of resources;
– a commitment to democrary;
– the need to treat all members equally, regardless of wealth or size (members for FIFPro being national player unions and their individual members; members for UEFA being national associations and their affiliated regional associations, leagues, clubs, players and other members);
– the importance of the link that binds all levels of football; – the need to preserve the values of sport in the face of growing corporate control, influence and commercialisation which can cause serious damage to the parties, their members and their values; and
– the protection and development of a large and healthy professional football sector in Europe.

760. More specifically, the parties recognise:

– the specificity of the career of a professional footballer;
– the specificity of sport, the autonomy of federations and the fact that football is best-served by the existing football family structures (although the balance of representativeness of key stakeholders within those structures can be developed further);

---

276. For the text of the Memorandum *see*: http://www.uefa.com/uefa/keytopics/kind64/ newsid601346.html.

- that national team football provides net benefits to players, clubs, leagues and associations alike, and is an essential complement and balance to club football;
- that strong national championships and competitions are vital for a large professional football sector to exist;
- that the continuing participation of all players and clubs in the main national leagues and UEFA club competitions is essential to support the existence of a large and healthy professional football sector in Europe;
- the need for a correct balance between labour legislation and the specific characteristics of football as a sport (which might also be achieved through collective bargaining agreements); and
- that disputes should be resolved within football and the importance of balanced representation in dispute resolution.

Seek solutions to the major issues in football by all those involved (players, clubs, leagues, federations, confederations and FIFA) within legitimate structures, favouring consultation and resolving disputes within a football framework and making use of methods of social dialogue such as collective agreements.

The balance between national and international legislation, particularly with regard to the right to work, and taking into account the specific characteristics of football as well as the autonomy of the governing bodies of the sport.

The parties agree to conduct all relations in a spirit of good faith, trust, transparency, democracy, responsibility and professionalism.

The Agreement is also composed of two Annexes. Annex 1 contains the *European Professional Football Player Contract Minimum Requirements* and Annex 2 the list of topics which both UEFA and FIFPro Division Europe agree as forming part of the 'specificity of sport'.

Earlier a Memorandum of understanding was concluded between FIFA and FIFPRO (2 November 2006). This includes an agreement on the status and the transfer of the players, characterised by following principles:

- training compensation for young players;
- maintenance of contractual stability in football.

761. On these issues there was complete agreement between soccer federations and the trade union.

Of specific importance are:

(1) The solidarity mechanism

> If a player moves during the course of a contract, after reaching the age of 23 or after his second transfer (whichever comes first), a proportion (5%) of any compensation paid to the previous club will be distributed to the club(s) involved in the training and education of the player. This distribution will be made in proportion to the number of years the player has been registered with the relevant clubs between the age of 12 and 23.

Part I, Ch. 1, The Free Movement of Workers

(2) The dispute resolution, disciplinary and arbitration system

Without prejudice to the right of any player or club to seek redress before a civil court, a dispute resolution and arbitration system shall be established, which shall consist of the following elements:

– Conciliation facilities offered by FIFA, through which a low cost, speedy, confidential and informal resolution of any dispute will be explored with the parties by an independent mediator. If no such solution is found within one month, either party can bring the case before FIFA's Dispute Resolution Chamber.
– Dispute Resolution Chamber, with members chosen in equal numbers of players and clubs and with an independent chairman, instituted within FIFA's Player Status Committee, establishing breach of contract, applying sport sanctions and disciplinary measures as a deterrent to unethical behaviour (e.g. to sanction a club which has procured a breach of contract), determining financial compensation, etc. In addition, the Dispute Resolution Chamber can review disputes concerning training compensation fees and shall have discretion to adjust the training fee if it is clearly disproportionate in the individual circumstances. Rulings of the Chamber can be appealed by either party to the Football Arbitration Tribunal.
– Football Arbitration Tribunal, with members chosen in equal numbers by players and clubs and with an independent chairman, according to the principles of the New York Convention of 1958.

For the avoidance of doubt, the Dispute Resolution and Arbitration System will take account of all relevant arrangements, laws and/or collective bargaining agreements, which exist at national level, as well as the specificity of sport as recognised in the relevant Declaration appended to Presidency conclusions of the European Council at Nice in December 2000.

In this way Fifpro, UEFA and FIFA have agreed that disputes should be resolved within football, without recourse to the ordinary courts, which can of course not be excluded. Hopefully the football family will amend existing rules which are contrary to fundamental principles of law by way of negotiation. Otherwise the possibility of a new *Bosman* case cannot be excluded.

3. The *Bernard* Case:[277] Training Compensation

762. In 1997, Olivier Bernard signed a *joueur espoir* contract with the French football club Olympique Lyonnais, with effect from 1 July that year, for three seasons. Before that contract was due to expire, Olympique Lyonnais offered him a professional contract for one year from 1 July 2000. Mr Bernard (apparently dissatisfied with the salary proposed) did not accept the offer but, in August 2000,

---

277. *Olympique Lyonnais* v. *Olivier Bernard and Newcastle United*, Opinion of Advocate General Sharpston, 16 July 2009, Case C-325/08, www.curia.eu.

signed a professional contract with the English club Newcastle United.

On learning of that contract, Olympique Lyonnais sued Mr Bernard before the Conseil de prud'hommes (Employment Tribunal) in Lyon, seeking an award of damages jointly against him and Newcastle United. The amount claimed was €53,357.16 – equivalent, according to the order for reference, to the remuneration which Mr Bernard would have received over one year if he had signed the contract offered by Olympique Lyonnais.

The case went up to the the Cour de Cassation, which refers to the ruling in *Bosman*, that Article 45 TFEU 'precludes the application of rules laid down by sporting associations, under which a professional footballer who is a national of one Member State may not, on the expiry of his contract with a club, be employed by a club of another Member State unless the latter club has paid to the former club a transfer, training or development fee', and considers that the case raises a serious difficulty in interpreting that article.

It therefore seeks a preliminary ruling on the following questions:

(1) Does the principle of freedom of movement for workers laid down in [Article 45 TFEU] preclude a provision of national law pursuant to which a "joueur espoir" who at the end of his training period signs a professional player's contract with a club of another Member State of the European Union may be ordered to pay damages?
(2) If so, does the need to encourage the recruitment and training of young professional players constitute a legitimate objective or an overriding reason in the general interest capable of justifying such a restriction?

The Advocate-General was of the opinion that only a measure which compensates clubs in a manner commensurate with their actual training costs is appropriate and proportionate in that way.

If, as appears to be the case, training of professional footballers is normally at the clubs' expense, then a system of compensation between clubs, not involving the players themselves, seems appropriate. And I would stress that, if the player himself were to bear any liability to pay training compensation, the amount should be calculated only on the basis of the individual cost of training him, regardless of overall training costs. If it is necessary to train n players in order to produce one who will be successful professionally, then the cost to the training club (and the saving to the new club) is the cost of training those n players. It seems appropriate and proportionate for compensation between clubs to be based on that cost. For the individual player, however, only the individual cost seems relevant.

To sum up, the need to encourage the recruitment and training of young professional football players is capable of justifying a requirement to pay training compensation where an obligation to remain with the training club for a specified (and not over-lengthy) period after completion of training is not respected. However, that will be so only if the amount concerned is based on the actual training costs incurred

Part I, Ch. 1, The Free Movement of Workers 763–765

by the training club and/or saved by the new club and, to the extent that the compensation is to be paid by the player himself, limited to the outstanding cost of the individual training.

The Advocate-General did not want to give an opinion on the actual FIFA rules concerning training compensation as those rules did not apply to the case, as the case dates from 2000 and the rules from 2001.

Nevertheless the Advocate-General was of the opinion that:

(1) A rule of national law pursuant to which a trainee football player who at the end of his training period signs a professional player's contract with a club of another Member State may be ordered to pay damages is, in principle, precluded by the principle of freedom of movement for workers embodied in Article 45 TFEU.
(2) Such a rule may none the less be justified by the need to encourage the recruitment and training of young professional football players, provided

> that the amount concerned is based on the actual training costs incurred by the training club and/or saved by the new club and, to the extent that the compensation is to be paid by the player himself, limited to any outstanding cost of the individual training.

763. It was to be hoped that the Court, before pronouncing itself will consider that neither the player nor a trade union of players intervened in the debate and will have a good look at the FIFA rules on training as they, as already indicated, infringe on the freedom of movement of workers. The FIFA rules indeed amount to a system of trade in humans. This is also clearly demonstrated by the case law of the CAS In Lausanne.

764. Our hope was in vain. The Court ruled on 16 March 2010 that football clubs may seek compensation for the training of young players whom they have trained where those players wish to sign their first professional contract with a club in another Member State. The amount of that compensation is to be determined by taking account of the costs borne by the clubs in training both future professional players and those who will never play professionally.

765. As said earlier, the Professional Football Charter of the Fédération française de football contains rules applicable to the employment of football players in France. According to the Charter, *joueurs espoir*, are football players between the ages of 16 and 22 employed as trainees by a professional club under a fixed-term contract. At the end of his training, the Charter obliges a *joueur espoir* to sign his first professional contract with the club that trained him, if the club requires him to do so.

In 1997, Olivier Bernard signed a *joueur espoir* contract with Olympique Lyonnais for three seasons. Before that contract was due to expire, Olympique Lyonnais offered him a professional contract for one year. Mr Bernard refused to sign that contract and signed a professional contract with Newcastle United FC, an English football club.

Olympique Lyonnais sued Mr Bernard, seeking an award of damages against him and Newcastle United of €53,357.16, equivalent to the salary which Mr Bernard would have received over one year if he had signed the contract offered by Olympique Lyonnais.

766. The *Cour de cassation*, before which a final appeal was brought, asked the Court of Justice whether the principle of freedom of movement for workers permitted the clubs which provided the training to prevent or discourage their *joueurs espoir* from signing a professional contract with a football club in another Member State inasmuch as the signature of such a contract might give rise to an order to pay damages.

767. The Court states first that Mr Bernard's gainful employment constitutes an economic activity and, as such, is subject to European Union law. The Court notes that the Charter has the status of a national collective agreement aimed at regulating gainful employment and, as such, also falls within the scope of European Union law.

768. The Court then holds that the rules at issue, according to which a 'joueur espoir', at the end of his training period, is required, under pain of being sued for damages, to sign a professional contract with the club which trained him, is likely to discourage that player from exercising his right of free movement. Consequently, those rules are a restriction on freedom of movement for workers.

769. However, as the Court has already held in the *Bosman* case, in view of the considerable social importance of sporting activities, and in particular football in the European Union, the objective of encouraging the recruitment and training of young players must be accepted as legitimate.

In considering whether a system which restricts the freedom of movement of such players is suitable to ensure that the said objective is attained and does not go beyond what is necessary to attain it, account must be taken of the specific characteristics of sport in general, and football in particular, and of their social and educational function.

In the Court's view, the prospect of receiving training fees is likely to encourage football clubs to seek new talent and train young players.

770. The Court states that a scheme providing for the payment of compensation for training where a young player, at the end of his training, signs a professional contract with a club other than the one which trained him can, in principle, be justified by the objective of encouraging the recruitment and training of young players. However, such a scheme must be capable of actually attaining that objective and be proportionate to it, taking due account of the costs borne by the clubs in training both future professional players and those who will never play professionally.

It follows that the principle of freedom of movement for workers does not preclude a scheme which, in order to attain the objective of encouraging the recruitment and training of young players, guarantees compensation to the club which provided the training if, at the end of his training period, a young player signs a professional contract with a club in another Member State, provided that the scheme is suitable to ensure the attainment of that objective and does not go beyond what is necessary to attain it.[278]

771. It is doubtful that the present FIFA system (training solidarity payments) corresponds to the requirements of the Bernard ruling, namely 'does not go beyond what is necessary to attain it'. The present system is part of an overall scheme of worldwide human trafficking, which seems to enjoy the support of the EU as well of a number of leading politicians, which prefer the glamour of sports TV above the respect of fundamental human rights.

4. Specificity of Sports; the Lisbon Reform Treaty

a. The Meaning of Specificity

772. Sports organisations, the International Olympic Committee and FIFA and UEFA included, have a used all their influence and obtained a clause in the EU Reform Treaty on the specificity of sports. The Treaty on the Functioning of the EU reads:

Article 6
The Union shall have competence to carry out actions to support, coordinate or supplement the actions of the Member States. The areas of such action shall, at European level, be:
(e) ... sport. Article 165

(1) 1 ... . The Union shall contribute to the promotion of European sporting issues, while taking account of the specific nature of sport, its structures based on voluntary activity and its social and educational function.
(2) Union action shall be aimed at: – ...
– developing the European dimension in sport, by promoting fairness and openness in sporting competitions and cooperation between bodies responsible for sports, and by protecting the physical and moral integrity of sportsmen and sportswomen, especially the youngest sportsmen and sportswomen.

---

278. With regard to the French scheme at issue in the main proceedings, the Court notes that it is characterised by the payment to the club which provided the training, not of compensation for training, but of damages, to which the player concerned would be liable for breach of his contractual obligations and the amount of which was unrelated to the real training costs incurred by the club. The damages in question were not calculated in relation to the training costs incurred by the club providing that training but in relation to the total loss suffered by the club. Therefore, the Court held the French scheme went beyond what is necessary to encourage recruitment and training of young players and to fund those activities.

(3) The Union and the Member States shall foster cooperation with third countries and the competent international organisations in the field of education and sport, in particular the Council of Europe.

773. This reference to Sport in the Treaty immediately leads to two fundamental remarks.

First, the EU's legal competence with respect to sport is one of support and coordination. This basically means that the union has no power to harmonise the organisation of sport in Europe. It should remain respectful of the States' primary competence in this domain and the autonomy of the sporting world.

Secondly, the particular reference to sport as included in the Reform treaty means that sporting activities will no longer be exempted from European or national law. This is especially the case in relation to the issues of free movement and non-discrimination'.[279]

In determining whether a certain sporting rule is compatible with EU law, an assessment can only be made on a case by case basis, as confirmed by the Court of Justice in the *Meca-Medina* case. Namely, whether the effects of sport rule are proportionate to the legitimate genuine sporting interest pursued. In other words, 'the proportionality test requires that each case is assessed on its own merits according to its own particular features or characteristics'.[280]

b. Specificity as seen by DRC and CAS

774. The FIFA rules on the Dispute Resolution Chamber and the Court of Arbitration in Lausanne have as a consequence that most sporting football disputes end up in the Court of Arbitration and very few before the civil courts. This answers the desire of the UEFA and FIFA to escape the application of European law. It is not by chance that the place of arbitration is Lausanne. Arbitration in Switzerland makes it impossible to escape the Community legal order.[281]

The DRC and CAs' interpretation of the specificity of sports confirms the fact that soccer is a war for money: In their view the FIFA rules have to be applied in case of a soccer dispute, which leads to the disregards of fundamental principles of EU and labour law. A couple of CAS cases may illustrate these points.

(1) The *Mutu* Case

775. In the *Mutu* case, CAS confirmed the decision of FIFA's DRC. Mutu, a Roumanian player, was sold from an Italian Club to Chelsea for the amount of 22,000,000 euro and signed a contract for the duration of five years (2003–2008).

---

279. M. Colucci, 'Sport in the EU Treaty: In the Name of Spercificity and Autonomy', in 'The Future of Sports law in the European Union. Beyond the EU Reform treaty and the White Paper', in *Bulletin of Comparative Labour Relations*, no. 66 (Ed. Roger Blanpain), 2008, 23.
280. R. Siekmann, 'is Sport "Special" in EU Law and Policy?', *op. cit.*, 49.
281. Wathelet M. 'Sport Governance and the EU Legal order: Present and Future', *o.c.*, 67.

The player was subject to a drug test, which was positive and the Club terminated his contract (2004). The club asked also compensation. The case came before the DRC. In this respect, the DRC

> stated that the basis of the specificity of sport and the list of objective criteria contained in art. 22 of the FIFA Regulations,[282] the DRC had established, inter alia, guidelines for the calculation of compensation payable for unjustified breach of contract by a player. In particular, as a general rule, the compensation payable to the former club shall be the result of an addition of the amount of the fees and expenses paid or incurred by the former club, amortised over the term of the contract, plus the amount of the remuneration due to the player under the contract that was breached until the ordinary expiry of the former contract. Moreover, in case of breach of contract during the protected period, thus under circumstances like in the case at hand, this amount needs being increased accordingly subject to particular circumstances. By means of this formula for the calculation of the compensation, the DRC aims, on the one hand, at taking into account objective criteria such as the amount of the fees and expenses paid or incurred by the former club, the remuneration due to the player under the existing contract and the time remaining on the existing contract. On the other hand, the possibility to increase the relevant amount of compensation accordingly subject to particular circumstances allows the DRC to take into consideration the specificity of sport and other criteria that are not explicitly listed in art. 22 of the Regulations on a case-by-case basis. Obviously, in case it deems it necessary, the DRC is always free to deviate from these guidelines.

776. The CAS confirmed the decision of the DRC. The player, Mr Adrian Mutu, was ordered to pay to Chelsea Football Club Limited the[283] (extraordinary) amount of 17,173,990 euro plus interest of 5 per cent p.a. starting on 12 September 2008 until the effective date of payment. If he does not pay, he will not be allowed to play for another club.

---

282. Article 22: Unless specifically provided for in the contract, and without prejudice to the provisions on training compensation, compensation for breach of contract (whether by the player or the club), shall be calculated with due respect to the national law applicable, the specificity of sport, and all objective criteria which may be relevant to thecase, such as:
   (1) Remuneration and other benefits under the existing contract and/or the new contract,
   (2) Length of time remaining on the existing contract (up to a maximum of 5 years),
   (3) Amount of any fee or expense paid or incurred by the former club, amortised over the length of the contract, …
283. CAS 2008/A/1644 *Adrian Mutu* v. *Chelsea Football Club Limited*, Arbitral Award, 31 July 2009. FIFpro website (11 June 2009).

(2) The *Matuzalem* Case

777. Take the case of the Brazilian player Matuzalem Frencellino da Silva, 29 years old. He played in 2003–2005 for the Italian club Brescia Calcio Spa. In 2004, he was sold at a Russian Club FC Shakhtar Donetsk for the sum of 8 million euro. To this has to be added the 'fees' of the agents, to whom Donetsk paid not less than €3,750,000. On top of that there were the so-called 'solidarity compensations' of €221,000 to the Brazilian club where Matuzalem played as a boy. Totalling €11,971,092. Matuzalem concluded a contract for the duration of five years. If the player would like to leave the club earlier he should have to pay Donetsk a compensation of 25 million euro. He received a wage of about 100,000 euro a month, plus an apartment and a car.

In 2007, Matuzalem wanted to end the contract, for family reasons. He tried to save his marriage, as his wife could not stand living in Donetsk anymore. The club did seemingly not understand. In the meantime Donetsk got an offer from the Italian Club Palermo of 7,000,000 US dollars. Donetsk refused this offer. Matuzalem concludes a new agreement with the Spanish club Real Zaragossa. In 2008 Zoragoza lends Mautuzalem out to the Italian Club Lozio Spa, Roma. This agreement contains an option clause whereby Roma can obtain the property of the player in 2009 for a sum of €14,000,000. Still in 2008, a contract is concluded with Zaragossa for a period of three years. If the player would break the contract before its end, he would pay to Zaragossa a compensation of €35,000,000.

Try to understand. The Russian club attacks and demands from Matuzalem compensation of €25 million. On 19 May 2009 the Court of Arbitration for Sport (CAS), with its seat in Lausanne, takes its decision. Mutuzalem and Zaragossa are condemned to jointly pay €11,858,934 – increased with 5 per cent interest to pay to the Russian club. The CAS applies the transfer rules of FIFA, the International Football League. Those rules have been accepted by the European Commission and also by FIFPro. In total the player has to pay a compensation of 13 million euro. Says FIFPro: 'The Matuzalem case is not unfavourable for players'.[284]

Soccer players are in the grip of commerce in which they are the pawns. They are bought and sold like cattle. This amounts to human trafficking. At all levels. Contracts are concluded at young ages, like 16 years old for five years and the traffic starts. There is an ongoing traffic in youngsters from Africa and South America, which are dumped it they do not succeed on the soccer market.

FifPro should stick to its principles where it states that it takes 'an exceptionally critical attitude to any form of transfer system for professional players'. It should review its mutual agreement with UEFA and its presence in RDC and the CAS, as players are not treated in a fair way, as the *Matuzalem* case shows. FIFA has to adapt its rules and practices.

778. It is obvious that the EU, especially the European Commission, has to take another look at what is happening the world of football. It is time to have a criticial review of:

---

284. FIFpro website (11 June 2009).

- the training compensation;
- the solidarity contribution;
- the transfer fees;
- the trade in humans, especially from Africa and Brazil.

5. Commission Blows the Whistle over Inflated Football Transfer Fees and Lack of Level Playing Field[285]

779. The following is the result of a critical study undertaken on behalf of the European Commission. Football clubs spend around €3 billion a year on player transfers, but very little of this money trickles down to smaller clubs or the amateur game. The number of transfers in European football more than tripled in the period 1995–2011, while the amounts spent by clubs on transfer fees increased seven-fold. But most of the big spending is concentrated on a small number of clubs which have the largest revenues or are backed by very wealthy investors. The situation is only increasing the imbalances that exist between the haves and have-nots, as less than 2 per cent of transfer fees filter down to smaller clubs and amateur sport which are essential for developing new talent. The level of redistribution of money in the game, which should compensate for the costs of training and educating young players, is insufficient to allow smaller clubs to develop and to break the strangle-hold that the biggest clubs continue to have on the sport's competitions.

780. 'The European Commission fully recognises the right of sports authorities to set rules for transfers, but our study shows that the rules as they are do not ensure a fair balance in football or anything approaching a level playing field in League or Cup competitions. We need a transfer system which contributes to the development of all clubs and young players,' said Androulla Vassiliou, European Commissioner responsible for sport.

Transfer rules are set by the sport governing bodies – for example, FIFA for football and FIBA for basketball. FIFA's online Transfer Matching System (TMS), which is used by 4 600 clubs worldwide, has increased transparency in international transfer operations but more needs to be done at national level. The report finds that the current system continues to mostly benefit the wealthiest clubs, superstar players and their agents.

781. It recommends that FIFA and national football associations' rules should ensure stronger controls over financial transactions and for the introduction of a 'fair-play levy' on transfer fees, beyond an amount to be agreed by the sport's governing bodies and clubs, to encourage a better redistribution of funds from rich to less wealthy clubs.

The study also suggests a limit on the number of players per club, a review of the issue of 'third-party ownership', where a player is effectively leased to a club by an agent, and an end to contractual practices which inflate transfer fees, such as where a club extends the protected period during which players cannot be transferred without its consent. The report also calls for full implementation of UEFA's Financial Fair Play rule and stronger 'solidarity mechanisms' to enhance youth development

---

285. 7 February 2013

and the protection of minors. The authors of the study urge sports bodies to improve their cooperation with law enforcement authorities to combat money laundering and corruption.

782. The labour market in football is extremely segmented, with a 'primary market' consisting of a small number of superstar players and a secondary market made up of professional or semi-pro players who do not earn big money and often face difficulties in developing their careers, especially after their playing days come to an end.
In order to improve fair and balanced competition through better and increased redistribution between clubs, the study proposes to:

(i) establish a 'fair play levy' on transfer fees beyond a certain amount in order to encourage better redistribution of funds from rich to less wealthy clubs. The aim of the levy would be to restore some competitive balance. The threshold, the rate of the levy and its scope should be determined by international football governing bodies in consultation with clubs;
(ii) better publicise the movement of players to ensure that the relevant solidarity compensation is paid to clubs and that the latter are aware of their rights;
(iii) establish a limit on the number of players per club;
(iv) regulate the loan transfer mechanism;
(v) address the issue of 'third-party ownership' of players' rights by adopting rules which protect the integrity and freedom of players as well as fairness of sport competition. The rules should not disproportionally hinder financial investment in sport and should be compatible with EU rules on free movement of capital;
(vi) support the implementation of Financial Fair Play rules to encourage clubs not to spend more than their revenues;
(vii) address teams' instability in basketball.

783. To limit inflated fees, the study recommends that:

(i) clubs are prevented from extending the 'protected period' during which a player needs consent to be transferred because this effectively forces up transfer fees (contracts are normally protected for three years up to the age of 28 and two years thereafter);
(ii) 'buy-out' clauses in players' contracts should be proportionate.

784. FIFPro identified notably three areas where the Commission should take initiatives: the issue of training compensation, which had increased too much recently and did not respect the standards set by the European Court of Justice in the Olivier Bernard ruling; the issue of contract stability, whereby the current situation was in FIFPro's views not in compliance with EU law, with FIFPro calling for discussions to find a balanced solution within the EU Social Dialogue Committee; and the fact that arbitration organs such as the Court of Arbitration for Sport (CAS) did not apply EU law, stressing that players were deprived of the possibility of relying on EU law principles in arbitration.

C. Others

785. According to the Court of Justice, the following activities have an economic character: the membership of a religious community, provided that for effective and genuine activities there is a certain counterpart; the apprenticeship of a teacher, when lessons are given to the school's pupils and thus provide a service of some economic value to the school.[286] Activities are not considered economic if they constitute employment in the framework of therapy – because here the social element supersedes the economic one, again showing that in the EU the economic prevails over the social.[287]

786. Freedom of movement also applies to activities in the public sector (as well as to public international organisations)[288] and to activities in the private sector that take place on the territory of the EU, or even outside the Union, provided there are enough close links, as indicated above.

787. The decision of the Court in the *Rush Portuguese* case concerning free movement of workers is remarkable. The Court recognised the right of undertakings which are performing activities in another Member State, on the basis of the free movement of services, to perform them with their own workers, even if those workers themselves – as was the case with Portuguese workers until 1992 – do not benefit from the right of free movement on the basis of Article 45 TFEU.[289] This could mean that workers from third countries, non-member states, who are already present and employed in a given Member State might, through the channel of rendering of services under Articles 56-57 TFEU, be employed in other Member States.

788. Work in subordination means to perform services for and under the direction and supervision of another person. In *Lawrie-Blum*, the Court ruled that:

> in the present case, it is clear that during the entire period of preparatory service the trainee teacher is under the direction and supervision of the school to which he is assigned. It is the school that determines the services to be performed by him and his working hours and it is the school's instructions that he must carry out and that he must observe.

789. To this needs to be added that the migrant worker should be a national of a Member State (Article 1, Regulation No. 1612/68). Each Member State determines who are and who are not its nationals. The Union has, however, the jurisdiction to indicate the consequences of the nationality in relation to the free movement of workers. Moreover there must be intra-Union movement. Union law regarding

---

286. *Lawrie-Blum* case, op. cit.
287. C.O.J., 31 May 1989, *J. Bettray* v. *Staatssecretaris van Justitie*, No. 344/87, ECR, 1989, 1621.
288. *Echternach* case, op. cit.
289. C.O.J., 27 March 1990, *Rush Portuguesa LDA* v. *Office National d'Immigration*, No. 113/89, ECR, 1990, 1417. See also C.O.J., 9 August 1994, *R. van der Elst* v. *Office des Migrations Internationales*, C-43/93, ECR, 1994, 3803.

free movement for workers is not applicable on a purely domestic relation within a Member State, as in the case of workers who have never taken advantage of free movement within the Union.[290]

790. Finally, there must be remuneration. This income may be lower than what, in the host state, is considered as the minimum required for subsistence, whether that person supplements the income from his activity as an employed person with other income so as to arrive at that minimum or is satisfied with the means of support that is lower than the said minimum, provided that he pursues an activity as an employed person that is effective and genuine;[291] the fact that he claims financial assistance out of the public funds of the latter in order to supplement the income he receives from those activities does not exclude him from the provisions of Union law relating to freedom of movement for workers.[292]

II. Exceptions

A. Employment in the Public Sector

791. Pursuant to Article 45(4) TFEU, the provisions of free movement for workers do not apply to employment in the public sector. This provision has given rise to a great deal of controversy. The Court is, for evident reasons, of the opinion that the term 'employment in the public sector' requires uniform interpretation and application throughout the Union. It should indeed be recalled, as the Court has constantly emphasised in its case law, that recourse to the provisions of the domestic legal system to restrict the scope of the provisions of Union law would have the effect of impairing the unity and efficacy of that law and consequently cannot be accepted.[293] Moreover, it must be borne in mind that, as a derogation from the fundamental principle that workers in the Union should enjoy freedom of movement and not suffer discrimination, Article 45(4) TFEU must be construed in such a way that it limits its scope to what is strictly necessary for safeguarding the interests which that provision allows the Member States to protect.[294] The Court comes to the conclusion that 'employment in the public sector' must be understood as meaning those posts which involve direct or indirect participation in the exercise of powers conferred by public law in the discharge of functions whose purpose is to safeguard the general interests of the state or of other public authorities. In order to carry out these functions, a special relationship of allegiance to the state on the part of persons occupying them and the reciprocity of rights and duties which form the

---

290. *See* C.O.J., 28 January 1992, *Volker Steen v. Deutsche Bundespost*, C-332/90, ECR, 1992, I-341.
291. *Levin* case, *op. cit.*
292. C.O.J., 3 June 1986, *R.H. Kempf v. Staatssecretaris van Justitie*, No. 139/85, ECR, 1986, 1741.
293. C.O.J., 17 December 1980, *Commission v. Belgium*, No. 149/79, ECR, 1980, 3881.
294. *Lawrie-Blum* Case, *op. cit.*

foundation of the bond of nationality is needed.[295] Thus the Court retains the content of the function and not the legal qualification of the employment relationship as a criterion:

> in the absence of any distinction in the provision Article 45(4) TFEU it is of no interest whether a worker is engaged as a blue-collar worker (*ouvrier*), a white-collar worker (*employé*) or an official (*fonctionnaire*) or even whether the terms on which he is employed come under public or private law.

Finally, it should be indicated that Article 45(4) TFEU only relates to the access to public employment. It cannot justify discriminatory measures with regard to remuneration or other conditions of employment once they have been admitted to the public sector.[296]

792. The following jobs are not considered to be public functions: post office workers;[297] trainee locomotive drivers, loaders, plate-layers, shunters and signallers with the national railways and unskilled workers with the local railways as well as posts for hospital nurses, children's nurses, nightwatchmen, plumbers, carpenters, electricians, garden hands, architects and supervisors with a municipality;[298] permanent employment as a nurse in a public hospital;[299] a trainee teacher;[300] a researcher;[301] a foreign-language teacher at a university[302] and a secondary school teacher.[303] The same goes for posts in the public sectors of research, teaching, health, transport, ports and telecommunications, and in the water, gas and electricity distribution services.[304] On the other hand, duties of managing or advising the state on scientific questions could be described as employment in the public sector within the meaning of Article 45(4) TFEU.[305] Finally, one should note that a Member State may reserve the promotion to certain public functions that involve participation in the exercise of power to its own nationals.[306]

Article 106(1) TFEU, in conjunction with Articles 31, 39 and 98, pre-cludes rules of a Member State which confer on an undertaking established in that State the exclusive right to organise dock work and requires it for that purpose to have

---

295. *Idem.*
296. *Sotgiu* Case, *op. cit.*
297. *Sotgiu* Case, *op. cit.*
298. *Commission v. Belgium*, No. 149/79, ECR, 1982, 1845.
299. C.O.J., 3 June 1986, *Commission v. France*, No. 307/84, ECR, 1986, 1725.
300. *Lawrie-Blum* case, *op. cit.*
301. C.O.J., 16 June 1987, *Commission v. Italy*, No. 225/85, ECR, 1987, 2625.
302. C.O.J., 30 May 1989, *P. Allué and C.M. Coonan v. Università degli Studi di Venezia*, No. 33/88, ECR, 1989, 1591.
303. 27 November 1991, *A. Bleis v. Ministère de l'Education Nationale*, No. C-4/91, ECR, 1991, 5627.
304. C.O.J., 2 July 1996, *Commission v. Luxemburg*, Case C-473/93, ECR, 1996, 3207; see also C.O.J., 2 July 1996, *Commission v. Belgium* (distribution of water, gas and electricity), Case C-173/94; 2 July 1996, *Commission v. Hellas*, Case C-290/94, ECR, 1996, 3285.
305. *Commission v. Italy*, No. 225/85, ECR, 1987, 2625.
306. *Commission v. Belgium*, No. 149/79, ECR, 1982, 1845.

recourse to a dock-work company whose workforce is composed exclusively of nationals.[307]

The concept of employment in the public service does not encompass employment by a private natural or legal person, whatever the duties of the employee. Thus, it is undeniable that sworn private security guards do not form part of the public service.[308]

Article 45(4) TFEU allows a Member State to reserve for its nationals the posts of master and chief mate of merchant ships flying its flag only if the rights under powers conferred by public law on masters and chief mates of such ships are actually exercised on a regular basis and do not represent a very minor part of their activities.[309]

B. Public Policy, Security and Public Health

793. Pursuant to Article 45(3) TFEU, free movement for workers entails the right:

(a) to accept offers of employment actually made;
(b) to move freely within the territory of Member States for this purpose;
(c) to stay in a Member State for the purpose of employment in accordance with the provisions governing the employment of nationals of that state laid down by law, regulation or administrative action;
(d) to remain in the territory of a Member State after having been employed in that state, subject to conditions which shall be embodied in implementing regulations to be drawn up by the Commission.

These rights are, however, subject to limitations justified on grounds of public policy, public security or public health. These limitations were more precisely defined in Directive No. 64/221 of 25 February 1964,[310] which aims at protecting the nationals of other Member States against possible abuse of these limitations regarding the free movement of workers.

794. Taken as a whole, these limitations, placed on the powers of Member States in respect of the control of aliens, are a specific manifestation of the more general principle enshrined in Articles 8, 9, 10 and 11 of the Convention for the Protection of Human Rights and Fundamental Freedoms, signed in Rome on 4 November 1950 and ratified by all the Member States, and in Article 2 of Protocol No. 4 of the same

---

307. C.O.J., 10 December 1991, *Merci Convenzionali Porto di Genova* v. *Siderurgica Gabrielli SpA*, No. C-179/90, ECR, 1991, 5889.
308. C.O.J., 25 May 2001, *Commission of the European Communities* v. *Italian Republic*, Case C-283/99, ECR, 2001, 4363.
309. C.O.J., 30 September 2003, *Colegio de Oficiales de la Marina Mercante Española* v. *Administración del Estado*, Case C-405/01, ECR, 2003, 10391.
310. Directive on the coordination of special measures concerning the movement and residence of foreign nationals that are justified on the grounds of public policy, public security or public health, O.J. L 56, 4 April 1964, 250–857.

Convention, signed in Strasbourg on 16 September 1963. These provide in identical terms that no restrictions in the interests of national security or public safety shall be placed on the rights secured by the above quoted Articles other than such as are necessary for the protection of those interests in a democratic society.[311] There are moreover procedural safeguards:

> any person enjoying the protection of the provisions of Directive No. 64/221 must be entitled to a double safeguard comprising notification to him of the grounds on which any restrictive measure has been adopted in his case and the availability of a right of appeal.[312]

795. Neither Article 45 TFEU nor the provisions of secondary legislation which implement the freedom of movement for workers preclude a Member State from imposing, in relation to a migrant worker who is a national of another Member State, administrative police measures limiting that worker's right of residence to a part of the national territory, provided:

– that such action is justified by reasons of public order or public security based on his individual conduct;
– that, by reason of their seriousness, those reasons could otherwise give rise only to a measure prohibiting him from residing in, or banishing him from, the whole of the national territory; and
– that the conduct which the Member State concerned wishes to prevent gives rise, in the case of its own nationals, to punitive measures or other genuine and effective measures designed to combat it.[313]

§3. PROMOTION

I. Employment Services

796. Free movement for workers in a single market demands the development of a direct cooperation between the central and regional employment services. This cooperation was established by Regulation No. 492/2011 of April 2011 regarding the clearing of vacancies and applications for employment and the resulting placing of workers in employment along with the exchange of information and the making of studies of employment and unemployment with the view to securing freedom of movement for workers within the Union (Articles 11–12).

797. The Regulation provides as follows:

---

311. C.O.J., 28 October 1975, *Roland Rutilly* v. *Minister for the Interior*, No. 36/75, ECR, 1975, 1219.
312. *Idem.*
313. C.O.J., 26 November 2002, *Ministre de l'Intérieur* v. *Aitor Oteiza Olazabal*, C-100/01, ECR, 2002, 10981. Reasons were, intimidation and terror (ETA).

Cooperation between the Member States and with the Commission

Article 11

(1) The Member States or the Commission shall instigate or together undertake any study of employment or unemployment which they consider necessary for freedom of movement for workers within the Union.
The central employment services of the Member States shall cooperate closely with each other and with the Commission with a view to acting jointly as regards the clearing of vacancies and applications for employment within the Union and the resultant placing of workers in employment.
(2) To this end the Member States shall designate specialist services which shall be entrusted with organising work in the fields referred to in the second subparagraph of paragraph 1 and cooperating with each other and with the departments of the Commission.
The Member States shall notify the Commission of any change in the designation of such services and the Commission shall publish details thereof for information in the *Official Journal of the European Union*.

Article 12

(1) The Member States shall send to the Commission information on problems arising in connection with the freedom of movement and employment of workers and particulars of the state and development of employment.
(2) The Commission, taking the utmost account of the opinion of the Technical Committee referred to in Article 29 ('the Technical Committee'), shall determine the manner in which the information referred to in paragraph 1 of this Article is to be drawn up.
(3) In accordance with the procedure laid down by the Commission taking the utmost account of the opinion of the Technical Committee, the specialist service of each Member State shall send to the specialist services of the other Member States and to the European Coordination Office referred to in Article 18 such information concerning living and working conditions and the state of the labour market as is likely to be of guidance to workers from the other Member States. Such information shall be brought up to date regularly.

The specialist services of the other Member States shall ensure that wide publicity is given to such information, in particular by circulating it among the appropriate employment services and by all suitable means of communication for informing the workers concerned.

Machinery for vacancy clearance

Article 13

(1) The specialist service of each Member State shall regularly send to the specialist services of the other Member States and to the European Coordination Office referred to in Article 18:

(a) details of vacancies which could be filled by nationals of other Member States;
(b) details of vacancies addressed to third countries;
(c) details of applications for employment by those who have formally expressed a wish to work in another Member State;
(d) information, by region and by branch of activity, on applicants who have declared themselves actually willing to accept employment in another country. The specialist service of each Member State shall forward this information to the appropriate employment services and agencies as soon as possible.
(2) The details of vacancies and applications referred to in paragraph 1 shall be circulated according to a uniform system to be established by the European Coordination Office referred to in Article 18 in collaboration with the Technical Committee.

This system may be adapted if necessary.

798. The regulation also contains measures for controlling the balance of the labour market. On the basis of a report from the Commission, drawn up from the information supplied by the Member States, the latter and the Commission shall at least once a year analyse jointly the results of Union arrangements regarding vacancies and applications.

The Commission and the Member States will also examine the possibilities of giving priority to nationals of Member States when filling employment vacancies in order to achieve a balance between vacancies and applications for employment within the Union (Article 17, 2).

Regulation No. 942/2011 established a European Coordination Office with the task of promoting vacancy clearance at Union level (Article 18), as well as an Advisory Committee responsible for studies and advice (Articles 21–28) and a Technical Committee charged with the mission to assist the Commission (Articles 29–34).

II. Vocational Training

799. The Commission has the task of promoting close cooperation between Member States regarding basic and advanced vocational training (Article 156 TFEU).

Article 166 TFEU, underlining the principle of subsidiarity, reads as follows:

(1) The Union shall implement a vocational training policy which shall support and supplement the action of the Member States, while fully respecting the responsibility of the Member States for the content and organisation of vocational training.
(2) Union action shall aim to: – facilitate adaptation to industrial changes, in particular through vocational training and retraining;
   – improve initial and continuing vocational training in order to facilitate vocational integration and reintegration into the labour market;

- facilitate access to vocational training and encourage mobility of instructors and trainees and particularly young people;
- stimulate cooperation on training between educational or training establishments and firms;
- develop exchanges of information and experience on issues common to the training systems of the Member States.
(3) The Union and the Member States shall foster cooperation with third countries and the competent international organisations in the sphere of vocational training.

To implement these goals, the European Centre for the Development of Vocational Training was established in 1975. Mention should be made of Article 47 TFEU which provides for the exchange of young workers between Member States within the framework of a joint programme, as well as of Council Recommendation of 30 June 1993 on access to continuing vocational training.[314]

800. By a decision of 2 April 1963, the Council laid down the general principles for implementing a common vocational training policy (No. 63/266).[315] These general principles must enable every person to receive adequate training with due regard to freedom of choice of occupation, place of training and place of work. The common vocational training policy should enable every person to acquire the technical knowledge and skills necessary to pursue a given occupation and to reach the highest possible level of training, whilst encouraging, particularly in regard to young persons, intellectual and physical advancement, civic education and physical development. The general guidelines laid down by the Council in 1971 state that:

> in view of the constantly changing needs of the economy, the aim of vocational training should be to offer the opportunity of basic and advanced training and a continuity of in-service training designed, from a general and vocational point of view, to enable the individual to develop his personality and to take up a career.

This led the Court to rule in the *Gravier* case:

> that any form of education which prepares for a qualification of a particular profession, trade or employment or which provides the necessary training and skills for such a profession, trade or employment, is vocational training whatever the age and the level of training of the pupils or students, even if the training programme includes an element of general education.[316]

801. With regard to the issue whether university studies prepare for a qualification for a particular profession, trade or employment or provide the necessary training and skills for these, it must be emphasised that this is the case not only where

---

314. O.J. No. 181, 23 July 1993, 37.
315. O.J. No. 63, 20 April 1963, 1338/63.
316. C.O.J., 13 February 1985, *Françoise Gravier v. City of Liège*, No. 293/83, ECR, 1985, 593.

the final academic examination directly provides the required qualification for a particular profession, trade or employment, but also insofar as the studies in question provide specific training and skills, even if no legislative or administrative provisions make acquisition of that knowledge a prerequisite for that purpose. In general, therefore, university studies fulfil these criteria. The only exceptions are certain courses of study which, because of their particular nature, are intended for persons wishing to improve their general knowledge rather than prepare themselves for an occupation.[317]

802. The meaning of the term 'vocational training' is somewhat restricted by Article 53 TFEU. This article relates to the directives for the mutual recognition of diplomas, certificates and other evidence of formal qualifications. Consequently, these directives, even when they relate to vocational training, are not covered by Article 166 TFEU.[318]

803. In the above-mentioned *Gravier* case,[319] the Court was of the opinion that the common vocational policy referred to in Article 166 TFEU is gradually being established and that it constitutes an indispensable element of the free movement of persons. Access to vocational training is in particular likely to promote free movement of persons throughout the Union by enabling them to obtain a qualification in the Member State where they intend to work and to complete their training and develop their particular talents in the Member State whose vocational training programmes include the special subject desired. It follows from all the foregoing that the conditions of access to vocational training fall within the scope of the Treaty and that the imposition on students who are nationals of other Member States of a charge, a registration fee or the so-called 'minerval' as a condition of access to vocational training, where the same fee is not imposed on students who are nationals of the host Member State, constitutes discrimination on grounds of nationality contrary to Article 18 TFEU.

Article 18 TFEU therefore applies to financial aid granted by a Member State to its own nationals in order to allow them to follow a course of vocational training in so far as that aid is intended to cover the costs of access to the courses.

A national of a Member State who has been admitted to a course of vocational training in another Member State derives from Union law a right of residence in the second Member State for the purpose of following that course and for the duration thereof. That right may be exercised regardless of whether the host Member State has issued a residence permit. The right of residence in question may nevertheless be made subject to certain conditions to which the prohibition of discrimination with regard to access to vocational training does not apply.[320]

---

317. C.O.J., 2 February 1988, *Vincent Blaizot v. Université de Liège*, No. 24/86, ECR, 1988, 379.
318. C.O.J., 30 May 1989, *Commission v. Council*, No. 242/87, IELL, *Case Law*, No. 135*bis*, ECR, 1989, 1925.
319. *Gravier* case, *op. cit.*; see also C.O.J., 3 May 1994, *Commission v. Belgium*, No. C-47/93, ECR, 1994, 1593.
320. C.O.J., 26 February 1992, *V.J.M. Raulin v. Netherlands Ministry of Education and Science*, No. C-357/89, ECR, 1992, 1027.

804. In a Dutch case[321], the Court ruled that making funding for studies abroad subject to a residence requirement gives rise to inequality of treatment between Netherlands workers and migrant workers

805. The Netherlands Law on the Financing of Studies defines who can receive funding to study in the Netherlands and abroad. For higher education in the Netherlands, funding for studies is available to students who are between 18 and 29 years old and have Netherlands nationality or the nationality of any other Member State of the European Union. To receive funding for higher education pursued outside the Netherlands, students must be eligible for funding for higher education in the Netherlands and must additionally have resided lawfully in the Netherlands for at least three out of the six years preceding enrolment at an educational establishment abroad. This condition, known as the '*3 out of 6 years*' requirement, applies irrespective of the student's nationality.

806. The Court notes that, under the TFEU, freedom of movement for workers is to entail the abolition of any discrimination based on nationality between workers of the Member States as regards employment, remuneration and other conditions of work and employment. Moreover, it is apparent from Regulation No 1612/68 that a worker who is a national of a Member State is to enjoy, in the territory of another Member State, the same social and tax advantages as national workers. That applies equally to migrant workers residing in a host Member State and frontier workers employed in that Member State while residing in another.

807. The Court points out that assistance granted for maintenance and education in order to pursue university studies evidenced by a professional qualification constitutes a social advantage for the purposes of Regulation No 1612/68. For the migrant worker, study finance granted by a Member State to the children of workers constitutes a social advantage for the purposes of that regulation, where the worker continues to support the child.

In that respect, the Court notes that the principle of equal treatment prohibits not only direct discrimination on grounds of nationality but also all indirect forms of discrimination which, through the application of other criteria of differentiation, lead in fact to the same result. That is the position, in particular, in the case of a measure which requires a specified period of residence, in that it primarily operates to the detriment of migrant workers and frontier workers who are nationals of other Member States, in so far as non-residents are usually non-nationals.

808. The Court therefore finds that the '*3 out of 6 years*' residence requirement creates inequality in treatment as between Netherlands workers and migrant workers residing in the Netherlands or employed there as frontier workers. Such an inequality constitutes unlawful indirect discrimination, unless it is objectively justified.

---

321. C.O.J., 14 June 2012, *European Commission v. Kingdom of the Netherlands*, C-542/09), www.curia.eu.

In that regard, the Court rejects the argument of the Netherlands that the residence requirement is necessary in order to avoid an unreasonable financial burden which could have consequences for the very existence of the assistance scheme. The Court points out that the objective of avoiding an unreasonable financial burden cannot be regarded as an overriding reason relating to the public interest, capable of justifying the unequal treatment between Netherlands workers and workers from other Member States.

809. The Netherlands also claim that, given that the national legislation at issue is intended to encourage students to pursue studies outside the Netherlands, the requirement ensures that the portable funding is available solely to those students who, without it, would pursue their education in the Netherlands. By contrast, the first instinct of students who do not reside in the Netherlands would be to study in the Member State in which they are resident and, accordingly, mobility would not be encouraged.

The Court notes that the objective of encouraging student mobility is in the public interest and constitutes an overriding reason relating to the public interest, capable of justifying a restriction of the principle of non-discrimination on grounds of nationality. The Court points out, however, that legislation which is liable to restrict a fundamental freedom guaranteed by the Treaty, such as freedom of movement for workers, can be justified only if it is appropriate for attaining the legitimate objective pursued and does not go beyond what is necessary in order to attain that objective.

810. In that context, the Netherlands claim that the legislation at issue has the merit of encouraging student mobility and point to the enrichment which studies outside the Netherlands bring, not only to the students, but also to Netherlands society and its employment market. Accordingly, the Netherlands expects that students who receive funding under that scheme will return to the Netherlands after completing their studies in order to reside and work there.

811. The Court acknowledges that those aspects tend to reflect the situation of most students and that the residence requirement is therefore appropriate for attaining the objective of promoting student mobility. Nevertheless, the Netherlands should at least have shown why they opted for the '3 out of 6 years' rule, prioritising length of residence to the exclusion of all other representative elements. By requiring specific periods of residence in the territory of the Member State concerned, the '3 out of 6 years' rule accords most importance to an element which is not necessarily the sole element representative of the actual degree of attachment between the concerned party and that Member State. In consequence, the Court holds that the Netherlands has failed to establish that the residence requirement does not go beyond what is necessary to attain the objective sought by that legislation.

812. Whilst it is true that the conditions for access to vocational training, including university studies in general, fall within the scope of the TFEU for the purposes of Article 18 thereof, assistance given by a Member State to its nationals when they undertake such studies nevertheless falls outside the Treaty, at the present stage of development of Union law, except to the extent to which such assistance is intended to cover registration and other fees, in particular tuition fees, charged for access to education.[322]

Article 18 TFEU, the Court furthermore states, precludes a Member State from requiring a student who is a national of another Member State and who enjoys, under Union law, a right of residence in the host Member State, to possess a residence permit in order to be entitled to benefit under the system of funding study costs.[323]

813. Access to education has retained the increased attention of the European Court.

The first case concerned Mr. Bidar,[324] a French national, entered the territory of the United Kingdom (1998), accompanying his mother who was to undergo medical treatment there. It is common ground that in the United Kingdom he lived with his grandmother, as her dependant, and pursued and completed his secondary education without ever having recourse to social assistance.

In September 2001 he started a course in economics at University College London.

While Mr. Bidar received assistance with respect to tuition fees, his application for financial assistance to cover his maintenance costs, in the form of a student loan, was refused on the ground that he was not settled in the United Kingdom.

Mr. Bidar submitted that, by making the grant of a student loan to a national of a Member State conditional on his being settled in the United Kingdom, the Student Support Regulations introduced discrimination prohibited under Article 18 TFEU. He submitted, in the alternative, that, even if it were accepted that the provision of a grant falls outside the scope of the Treaty, that is not the case with an application for assistance in the form of a subsidised loan.

In that context, the national court wished to know whether assistance granted to students to cover their maintenance costs is within the scope of application of the Treaty within the meaning of the first paragraph of Article 18 TFEU, which states that, without prejudice to any special provisions contained in the Treaty, any discrimination on grounds of nationality is prohibited within that scope of application.

The Court reasoned as follows:

> To assess the scope of application of the Treaty within the meaning of Article 18 TFEU, that article must be read in conjunction with the provisions of the Treaty on citizenship of the Union. Citizenship of the Union is destined to be the fundamental status of nationals of the Member States, enabling those who

---

322. C.O.J., 21 June 1988, *Sylvie Lair* v. *Universität Hannover*, No. 39/86, ECR, 1988, 3161.
323. C.O.J., 26 February 1992, *V.J.M. Raulin* v. *Netherlands Ministry of Education and Science*, No. C-357/89, ECR, 1992, 1027.
324. 15 March 2005, *The Queen (on the application of Dany Bidar)*, v. *London Borough of Ealing, Secretary of State for Education and Skills*, C-209/03, www.curia.eu.

find themselves in the same situation to receive the same treatment in law irrespective of their nationality, subject to such exceptions as are expressly provided for.[325]

814. According to settled case law, a citizen of the European Union lawfully resident in the territory of the host Member State can rely on Article 18 TFEU in all situations which fall within the scope *ratione materiae* of Union law.[326]

Those situations include those involving the exercise of the fundamental freedoms guaranteed by the Treaty and those involving the exercise of the right to move and reside within the territory of the Member States, as conferred by Article 21 TFEU.[327]

Moreover, there is nothing in the text of the Treaty to suggest that students who are citizens of the Union, when they move to another Member State to study there, lose the rights which the Treaty confers on citizens of the Union.[328]

815. As is apparent from an earlier case,[329] a national of a Member State who goes to another Member State and pursues secondary education there exercises the freedom to move guaranteed by Article 21 TFEU.

Furthermore, a national of a Member State who, like the claimant in the main proceedings, lives in another Member State where he pursues and completes his secondary education, without it being objected that he does not have sufficient resources or sickness insurance, enjoys a right of residence on the basis of Article 21 TFEU and Directive 90/364 of 28 June 1990 on the right of residence.

With regard to social assistance benefits, the Court[330] ruled that a citizen of the Union who is not economically active may rely on the first paragraph of Article 18 TFEU where he has been lawfully resident in the host Member State for a certain time or possesses a residence permit.

816. It is true that the Court held[331] that 'at the present stage of development of Community law assistance given to students for maintenance and for training falls in principle outside the scope of the TFEU for the purposes of Article 18 TFEU'. In those judgments the Court considered that such assistance was, on the one hand, a matter of education policy, which was not as such included in the spheres entrusted to the Union institutions, and, on the other, a matter of social policy, which fell within the competence of the Member States in so far as it was not covered by specific provisions of the TFEU.

However, since judgment was given in *Lair* and *Brown*, the Treaty on European Union has introduced citizenship of the Union into the TFEU.

---

325. Case C-184/99, *Grzelczyk*, 2001, ECR, 6193, paragraphs 30 and 31, and Case C-148/02 *Garcia Avello*, 2003, ECR, 11613, paragraphs 22 and 23.
326. Case C-85/96, *Martinez Sala*, 1998, ECR, 2691, paragraph 63, and *Grzelczyk*, paragraph 32.
327. See, Case C-274/96, *Bickel and Franz*, 1998, ECR, 7637, paragraphs 15 and 16, *Grzelczyk*, paragraph 33, and *Garcia Avello*, paragraph 24.
328. *Grzelczyk*, paragraph 35.
329. Case C-224/98, *D'Hoop*, 2002, ECR, 6191, paragraphs 29 to 34.
330. Held in Case C-456/02, *Trojani*, paragraph 43, *op. cit.*
331. In *Laira* and *Brown*, paragraphs 15 and 18, *op. cit.*

Thus Article 165(1) TFEU gives the Union the task of contributing to the development of quality education by encouraging cooperation between Member States and, if necessary, by supporting and supplementing their action, while fully respecting the responsibility of those States for the content of teaching and the organisation of education systems and their cultural and linguistic diversity.

Under paragraphs 2 and 4 of that article, the Council may adopt incentive measures, excluding any harmonisation of the laws and regulations of the Member States, and recommendations aimed in particular at encouraging the mobility of students and teachers.

817. In view of those developments since the judgments in *Lair* and *Brown*, it must be considered that the situation of a citizen of the Union who is lawfully resident in another Member State falls within the scope of application of the Treaty within the meaning of the first paragraph of Article 18 TFEU for the purposes of obtaining assistance for students, whether in the form of a subsidised loan or a grant, intended to cover his maintenance costs.

818. That development of Union law is confirmed by Article 24 of Directive 2004/38, which states in paragraph 1 that all Union citizens residing in the territory of another Member State on the basis of that directive are to enjoy equal treatment 'within the scope of the Treaty'. In that the Union legislature, in paragraph 2 of that article, defined the content of paragraph 1 in more detail, by providing that a Member State may in the case of persons other than workers, self-employed persons, persons who retain such status and members of their families restrict the grant of maintenance aid in the form of grants or loans in respect of students who have not acquired a right of permanent residence, it took the view that the grant of such aid is a matter which, in accordance with Article 24(1), now falls within the scope of the Treaty.

819. The Court decided as follows:

> Assistance, whether in the form of *subsidised loans or of grants*, provided to students lawfully resident in the host Member State to cover their maintenance costs falls within the scope of application of the TFEU for the purposes of the prohibition of discrimination laid down in the first paragraph of Article 18 TFEU.
>
> The first paragraph of Article 18 TFEU must be interpreted as precluding national legislation which grants students the right to assistance covering their maintenance costs only if they are settled in the host Member State, while precluding a national of another Member State from obtaining the status of settled person as a student even if that national is lawfully resident and has received a substantial part of his secondary education in the host Member State and has consequently established a genuine link with the society of that State.

820. Also the *conditions of access to university education* falls under Union law. The Court had to evaluate paragraph 36 of the Austrian Law (UniStG), which lays down the conditions governing access to higher or university education in Austria.

In that connection, it provides that, in addition to satisfying the general requirements for access to higher or university studies, holders of general university entrance qualifications awarded in other Member States must prove that they meet the specific requirements governing access to the chosen course, which are laid down by the State which issued those qualifications and give entitlement to direct admission to those studies.

821. These were considered to be discriminatory. Therefore the Court declared:

> that, by failing to take the necessary measures to ensure that holders of secondary education diplomas awarded in other Member States can gain access to higher and university education organised by it under the same conditions as holders of secondary education diplomas awarded in Austria, the Republic of Austria has failed to fulfil its obligations under Articles 18, 165 and 166 TFEU.[332]

In an earlier case, Belgium was condemned by the European Court for discrimination against holders of diplomas from other Member States.

822. The Commission noted that it follows from the *Gravier* case that the conditions of access to vocational training fall within the scope of the Treaty. It also follows from the case law of the Court that the term 'vocational training' must be construed very widely. Moreover, under Article 165 TFEU all levels and types of education are henceforth covered by the Treaty.

The Commission claimed that nationals of other Member States, who hold diplomas and qualifications awarded on successful completion of secondary studies in other Member States who wish to gain access to higher education in Belgium (medical studies, dental and veterinary science, and agricultural engineering) must take and pass an aptitude test if they are not able to prove, by way of additional requirement, that they qualify for admission in their own country of origin to a university with no entry examination or other condition of access.

It maintained that the additional requirement for access to higher education in the French Community, in so far as it applies exclusively to holders of diplomas awarded in another Member State, is liable to have a greater effect on nationals of those other Member States than on Belgian nationals.

The Commission was of the opinion that that additional requirement, which takes the form of a so-called *maturité* examination, which only holders of diplomas awarded in another Member State must take, constitutes a condition of access to higher and university education within the meaning of the aforementioned case law.

The Commission claimed that that system creates twofold discrimination, against holders of diplomas awarded in other Member States, and against nationals of other Member States on the basis of the education system within which they were awarded their diploma on completion of secondary studies.

---

332. C.O.J., 7 July 2005, *Commission v. Republic of Austria*, C-147/03, ECR, 2005, 5969.

823. As the Court has already held in paragraph 25 of *Gravier* the conditions of access to vocational training fall within the scope of the Treaty.[333]

Article 165(2) TFEU, second indent, expressly provides that Union action is to be aimed at encouraging mobility of students and teachers, *inter alia* by encouraging the academic recognition of diplomas and periods of study. Further, Article 166(2) TFEU, third indent, provides that Union action is to aim to facilitate access to vocational training and encourage mobility of instructors and trainees and particularly young people.

In respect of access to vocational training, the Treaty does not lay down any special provisions that require, in the light of the first paragraph of Article 18 TFEU, to be examined first.

The first paragraph of Article 18 TFEU therefore applies to the conditions set by the Member States for access to higher education.

It is clear from the Court's case law that the principle of equal treatment, of which the prohibition on any discrimination on grounds of nationality in the first paragraph of Article 18 TFEU is a specific instance, prohibits not only overt discrimination by reason of nationality but also all covert forms of discrimination which, by the application of other criteria of differentiation, lead in fact to the same result.[334]

In the present case, the legislation in question places holders of secondary education diplomas awarded in a Member State other then Belgium at a disadvantage, since they cannot gain access to higher education organised by the French Community under the same conditions as holders of the CESS or the equivalent Luxembourg diploma. The criterion of differentiation applied works primarily to the detriment of nationals of other Member States.

The Kingdom of Belgium does not put forward any argument capable of justifying that criterion.

It must therefore be held that, by failing to take the measures necessary to ensure that holders of secondary education diplomas awarded in other Member States can gain access to higher education organised by the French Community under the same conditions as holders of the CESS, the Kingdom of Belgium has failed to fulfil its obligations under Article 18 TFEU, read in conjunction with Articles 165 TFEU and 166 TFEU.[335]

III. Recognition of Qualifications and Diplomas

824. It is self-evident that, given the ever-increasing education of Europeans and advanced training, there can only be full-fledged free movement for workers once

---

[333]. *See also* Case 24/86, *Blaizot*, 1988, ECR, 379, paragraph 11; Case 42/87, *Commission v. Belgium*, 1988, ECR, 5445, paragraph 7; and Case C-295/90, *Parliament v. Council*, 1992, ECR, 4193, paragraph 15.

[334]. *See, inter alia,* Case C-3/88, *Commission v. Italy*, 1989, ECR, 4035, paragraph 8, and Case C388/01, *Commission v. Italy*, 2003, ECR, 721, paragraph 13.

[335]. 1 July 2004, *Commission v. Kingdom of Belgium*, C-65/03, ECR, 2004, 6427.

Part I, Ch. 1, The Free Movement of Workers 825–826

diplomas obtained in one Member State are valid in the other Member States.[336] With this aim in view, the Council adopted a number of directives concerning the mutual recognition of diplomas, certificates and other evidence of formal qualifications (Article 53 TFEU). Notwithstanding the fact that 53 TFEU relates to self-employed persons only, one must ascertain that some of those directives, such as those concerning medical doctors, pharmacists and others, contain a clause making those directives also applicable to the workers and their dependants as stated in Regulation No. 492/2011.

825. It soon became clear, however, that it is impossible to make individual directives for each profession, a training programme of its own included, and that more general measures are indicated. Such a general measure is Council Decision No. 85/368 of 16 July 1985 on the comparability of vocational training qualifications between the Member States of the European Union.[337] The Commission establishes this comparability in close cooperation with the Member States and the organisations of workers and employers at Community level. To that end:

– the relevant occupations or groups of occupations are selected on a proposal from the Member States or the competent employer or worker organisations at Community level; – mutually agreed job descriptions for the occupations are drawn up;
– the vocational training qualifications recognised in the various Member States are matched with the job descriptions.

Finally, tables incorporating information are established on the level of vocational training, the vocational titles and the corresponding vocational training qualifications, the organisations and institutions responsible for dispensing vocational training and the organisations competent to issue or to validate diplomas, certificates or other documents certifying that vocational training has been acquired (Article 3).

826. Of capital importance is Directive No. 89/48 of 21 December 1988 on a general system for the recognition of higher-education diplomas awarded on

---

336. However, Article 45 TFEU does not preclude a Member State from prohibiting one of its own nationals who holds an academic title acquired through postgraduate studies and awarded in another Member State from using that title in its territory without obtaining administrative authorisation for that purpose. The authorisation procedure must be intended solely to verify whether the academic title acquired through postgraduate studies was duly awarded, must be easily accessible and is not subject to the payment of excessive administrative charges. Furthermore, the decision that is taken must be open to judicial review, the person concerned must be able to ascertain the grounds for that decision and the penalties prescribed for non-observance of the authorisation procedure may not be disproportionate to the seriousness of the offence. See C.O.J., 31 March 1993, *Dieter Kraus v. Land Baden Württemberg*, No. C-19/92, ECR, 1993, 1663.
337. O.J. L 199/29, 31 July 1985.

completion of professional education and training of at least three years' duration.[338] This directive applies to any national of a Member State wishing to pursue a regulated profession in a host Member State in a self-employed capacity or as an employed person (Article 2(1)). The directive does not apply to a national of a Member State in a situation which is confined in all respects within that one Member State.[339] In a nutshell, the directive provides that the holder of a diploma of a post-secondary course of at least three years' duration can take up or pursue that profession in any Member State. The same applies if the applicant has pursued the profession in question full-time for two years during the previous ten years in another Member State which does not regulate that profession (Articles 1 and 3).[340] Notwithstanding this, the host Member State may under certain conditions require the applicant to provide evidence of professional experience or to complete an adaptation period not exceeding three years or to take an aptitude test (Article 4). The host state may allow the applicant to undergo there, on the basis of equivalence, that part of his professional education and training that is required and which he has not undergone in his Member State of origin (Article 5). The directive contains further rules concerning the eventual proof of good character, whether the applicants have been declared bankrupt or not as well as concerning the suspension or prohibition of the pursuit of the profession (Article 6); it also regulates the use of professional titles of the host state corresponding to that profession (Article 7). Finally, attention must be drawn to the *Heylens* case in which the Court ruled that:

> where in a Member State access to an occupation [in this case football trainer] as an employed person is dependent upon the possession of a national certificate or a foreign diploma recognised as equivalent, the principle of free movement of workers laid down in Article 45 TFEU requires that it must be possible for a decision refusing to recognise the equivalence of a diploma granted to a worker who is a national of another Member State by the Member State to be made the subject of judicial proceedings in which its legality under Union law can be reviewed, and for the person concerned to ascertain the reasons for the decision.[341]

---

338. O.J. L 19/16, 24 January 1989. A profession cannot be described as regulated when there are in the host Member State no laws, regulations or administrative provisions governing the taking up or pursuit of that profession or of one of its modes of pursuit, even though the only education and training leading to it consists of at least four and a half years of higher-education studies on completion of which a diploma is awarded and, consequently, only persons possessing that higher-education diploma as a rule seek employment in and pursue that profession (C.O.J., 1 February 1996, *Georgios Aranitis* v. *Land Berlin*, Case C-164/94, ECR, 1996, 135).
339. C.O.J., 2 July 1998, *Anestis Kapasakalis, Dimitris Skiathitis, Antonis Kougiankas*, Joined Cases C-225/95, C-226/95 and C-227/95, ECR, 1998, 4239.
340. 'When the holder of a diploma awarded in one Member State applies for permission to take up a regulated profession in another Member State, the competent authorities of that Member State are not precluded by Council Directive 89/48/EEC of 21 December 1988 from partly allowing that application, if the holder of the diploma so requests, by limiting the scope of the permission to those activities which that diploma allows to be taken up in the Member State in which it was obtained' (*Colegio de Ingenieros de Caminos, Canales y Puertos* v. *Administración del Estado*, C-330/03, 19 January 2006, ECR, 2006, 807).
341. 15 October 1987, No. 226/86, ECR, 1988, 4309.

827. In the *Toki* case,[342] the Court rules that professional activities subject to rules issued by a private organisation recognised by a Member State are to be regarded as activities not regulated by that Member State. Recognition, in another Member State, of qualifications relating to those activities must be based on continuous and regular professional experience, covering a range of activities characteristic of the profession

The directive for the recognition of higher education diplomas[343] provides for two mechanisms of recognition of higher education diplomas, according to whether the applicant holds a diploma issued in a Member State which regulates that profession, or whether the applicant has pursued the profession in question full-time for two years in another Member State which does not regulate that profession.

While in Greece the profession of environmental engineer is regulated by the State, it is not in the United Kingdom. The pursuit there of that profession is regulated to a certain extent by the Engineering Council (a private organisation expressly referred to in Directive 89/48). Membership of that organisation is not obligatory in order to pursue the engineering profession.

828. Ms Christina Toki, a Greek national, obtained Bachelor of Engineering and Master of Science degrees in environmental engineering at the end of the 1990s in the United Kingdom. From 1999 to 2002 she worked for the University of Portsmouth, in the Department of Civil Engineering. Her activities included research work, assisting the work of students and assessing the effectiveness of a pioneering method of waste processing in collaboration with a private undertaking which specialised in that field.

She then applied for recognition in Greece of her right to pursue there the profession of environmental engineer, on the basis of the qualifications and experience acquired in the United Kingdom. Her application was rejected in 2005 by the Council for the Recognition of the Equivalence of Higher Education Diplomas, because she was not a full member of the Engineering Council and consequently did not hold the title of Chartered Engineer.

MS Toki brought an action against that decision (Greece), and that court seeks from the Court of Justice clarification of the conditions established by the general system for the recognition of higher education diplomas where a profession is regulated by a private organisation such as the Engineering Council and where the applicant for recognition is not a full member of such an organisation.

829. The Court notes, first, that the Greek legislation transposing the directive has the effect of excluding the application of the mechanism of recognition based on professional experience where the person has acquired his/her education and training in a Member State in which the pursuit of that profession is regulated not by the Member State itself but by private organisations recognised by that Member State.

---

342. C.O.J., 5 April 2011, C-424/09, www.curia.
343. Council Directive 89/48/EEC of 21 December 1988 on a general system for the recognition of higher education diplomas awarded on completion of professional education and training of at least three years' duration (OJ 1989 L 19, p. 16).

In respect of the professions concerned, the Court holds that solely the mechanism of recognition which requires full-time pursuit of the profession for at least two years is applicable. That mechanism of recognition is applicable irrespective of whether the person concerned is, or is not, a member, of the organisation concerned.

830. The Court then states the three requisite conditions governing whether professional experience should be taken into account.

First, the professional experience must consist of full-time work for at least two years during the previous ten years. That test enables the host Member State to have the benefit of safeguards comparable to those in place where the profession is regulated by the Member State of origin. The organisational and regulatory framework, or whether the institution where the profession was pursued was profit making, are not relevant factors. Whether the profession was pursued in a self employed capacity or as an employed person is also not relevant.

Second, the work must have consisted of the continuous and regular pursuit of a range of professional activities which characterise the profession concerned in the Member State of origin. That work need not encompass all activities characteristic of the profession. The question of which professional activities are characteristic of a specific profession is a question of fact which must be resolved by the competent authorities of the host Member State, subject to review by the national courts and tribunals. If the profession is not a regulated profession in the Member State of origin, reference should be made to the professional activities normally pursued by the members of that profession in that Member State.

Third, the profession, as it is normally pursued in the Member State of origin, must be equivalent, in respect of the activities which it covers, to the profession which the person has sought authorisation to pursue in the host Member State. The directive covers professions which, in the Member State of origin and the host Member State, are identical or analogous or, in some cases, simply equivalent in terms of the activities they cover.

831. The Court considers that the activities pursued by Ms Toki, such as research work or assisting the work of students, do not constitute actual pursuit of the profession of environmental engineer: they do not therefore constitute professional experience which should be taken into account for the recognition in Greece of the British qualifications. On the other hand, the work of assessment carried out in collaboration with a private company which specialised in technology relating to liquid waste processing might constitute actual pursuit of the profession concerned. If it were to be established that Ms Toki actually pursued the profession of environmental engineer in the United Kingdom, it would then be necessary to determine whether that profession constitutes the same profession as that which she has sought to pursue in Greece. It is for the competent authorities of the host Member State to verify those matters of fact.

Part I, Ch. 1, The Free Movement of Workers

832. In an earlier instance, in the *Vandoura* case[344] the Court had ruled that:

> A national authority responsible for recognition of professional qualifications acquired in another Member State is bound, pursuant to Articles 45 TFEU and 49 TFEU, to take into account, when setting any supplementary requirements to compensate for substantial differences between the education and training undertaken by an applicant and the education and training required in the host Member State, all practical experience which, in whole or in part, covers those differences.

Before imposing supplementary requirements to cover differences between the education and training provided in the Member State of origin and that provided in an applicant's host Member State, the competent national authorities must therefore assess whether the knowledge acquired by an applicant, including knowledge acquired in the host Member State, in the course of practical experience can be taken into account for the purpose of proving possession of the knowledge required by the latter.

It is true that the experience acquired in the course of the pursuit of the regulated profession in question in the Member State of origin will, in most cases, be the most relevant to that assessment, which wholly justifies the express imposition of the obligation, in the second subparagraph of Article 4(1)(b) of Directive 89/48, on the competent authorities in a host Member State, to take such experience into consideration.

833. However, in so far as all practical experience in the pursuit of related activities can increase an applicant's knowledge, it is incumbent on the competent national authorities to take into consideration all practical experience of use in the pursuit of the profession to which access is sought. The precise value to attach to such experience will be for the competent national authority to determine in the light of the specific functions carried out, knowledge acquired and applied in pursuit of those functions, responsibilities assumed and the level of independence accorded to the person concerned.

In that regard, in most cases, pursuit of activities relating to a regulated profession under the control and responsibility of a duly qualified professional in the host Member State, whilst not in itself amounting to pursuit of the regulated profession in question in that Member State, confers on the person concerned relevant knowledge of considerable value. Whilst, as the European Commission submits, lawful and non-lawful experience cannot be considered to be of equal worth, nonetheless, contrary to the fears expressed by the Greek Government during the hearing, the pursuit of a professional activity supervised in that way should not be regarded as unlawful since the person concerned is not himself pursuing the regulated profession in such circumstances.

---

344. C.O.J., 2 December 2010, *Vassiliki Stylianou Vandorou v. Ipourgos Ethnikis Pedias kai Thriskevmaton*, (C-422/09), www.curia.

It should be added that the obligation to take into account all the applicant's relevant experience does not cease to exist as a result of the adoption of directives on mutual recognition of diplomas.

834. The Council Directive 89/48 limits itself to the recognition of higher education diplomas awarded on completion of professional education and training of at least three years' duration. Other forms of professional education fall outside the scope of Directive No. 89/48. In order to also cover these, a new directive was passed, Directive No. 92/51, on a second general system for the recognition of professional education and training to supplement Directive 89/48.[345] This complementary general system is based on the same principles and contains the same rules as the initial general system. This complementary system covers levels of education and training not covered by the initial general system, namely that corresponding to other post-secondary education and training courses, and that corresponding to long or short secondary courses, possibly complemented by professional training or experience.

Since the complementary system covers occupations the pursuit of which is dependent on the possession of professional or vocational education and training qualifications of secondary level and generally requires manual skills, the complementary system must also provide for the recognition of such qualifications even when they have been acquired solely through professional experience in a Member State which does not regulate such professions. The Directive 92/51 contains several systems of recognition, namely the system where a host Member State requires possession of a diploma (Articles 3 and 4);[346] the system where a host Member State requires possession of a diploma and the applicant is the holder of a certificate or has received corresponding education and training (Article 5); and the system of recognition where a host Member State requires possession of a certificate (Articles 6 and 7). Articles 8 and 9 of the Directive 92/51 deal with special systems for the recognition of other qualifications.

Mention should also be made of the Resolution of 3 December 1992 concerning transparency of qualifications[347] and the Joint Opinion of the Social Partners of 3 July 1992 on vocational qualifications and certification and of Directive 1999/42/EC of 7 June 1999 establishing a mechanism for the recognition of qualifications in respect of the professional activities covered by the Directives on liberalisation and

---

345. O.J. L 209/25, 24 July 1992; amended by Directive 2001/19 EC of 14 May 2001 (O.J. 31 July 2001, L 206).
346. 'Where national measures transposing the directive are not adopted within the period prescribed in Article 17 of Directive 92/51, a national of a Member State may rely on Article 3(a) of that directive in order to obtain, in the host Member State, authorisation to pursue a regulated profession such as that of occupational therapist. That possibility may not be made subject to recognition of the qualifications of the person concerned by the competent national authorities. The compensatory measures referred to in Article 4(1) of Directive 92/51 may be imposed on the person concerned only in so far as they are provided for by the national legislation in force at the time of processing the application in question' (*Maria Aslanidou* v. *Ypourgos Ygeias & Pronoias*, 14 July 2005, C-142/04, ECR, 2005, 7181). *See also Harold Price* v. *Conseil des ventes volontaires de meubles aux enchères publiques*, C-149/05, 7 September 2006, ECR, 2006, 7691.
347. O.J. C 49/1, 19 February 1993.

transitional measures and supplementing the general systems for the recognition of qualifications.[348]

835. As the relevant directives have been amended on several occasions, and their provisions should be reorganised and rationalised by standardising the principles applicable, it was necessary to replace Council Directives 89/48/EEC and 92/51/EEC[349] by combining them in a single text, namely: Directive 2005/36/EC of the European Parliament and of the Council of 7 September 2005 on the recognition of professional qualifications.[350]

Purpose

836. This Directive establishes rules according to which a Member State which makes access to or pursuit of a regulated profession in its territory contingent upon possession of specific professional qualifications (the host Member State) shall recognise professional qualifications obtained in one or more other Member States (the home Member State) and which allow the holder of the said qualifications to pursue the same profession there, for access to and pursuit of that profession.

Scope

837. This Directive shall apply to all nationals of a Member State wishing to pursue a regulated profession in a Member State, including those belonging to the liberal professions, other than that in which they obtained their professional qualifications, on either a self-employed or employed basis.

Each Member State may permit Member State nationals in possession of evidence of professional qualifications not obtained in a Member State to pursue a regulated profession on its territory in accordance with its rules. In the case of professions covered by Title III,[351] Chapter III,[352] this initial recognition shall respect the minimum training conditions laid down in that Chapter.

Where, for a given regulated profession, other specific arrangements directly related to the recognition of professional qualifications are established in a separate instrument of Community law, the corresponding provisions of this Directive shall not apply.

---

348. O.J., 31 July 1999.
349. As well as Directive 1999/42/EC of the European Parliament and of the Council on the general system for the recognition of professional qualifications, and Council Directives 77/452/EEC, 77/453/EEC, 78/686/EEC, 78/687/EEC, 78/1026/EEC, 78/1027/EEC, 80/154/EEC, 80/155/ EEC, 85/384/EEC, 85/432/EEC, 85/433/EEC and 93/16/EEC concerning the professions of nurse responsible for general care, dental practitioner, veterinary surgeon, midwife, architect, pharmacist and doctor.
350. O.J., 30 September 2005, L 255.
351. Freedom of establishment.
352. Recognition of professional experience.

Contact points

838. Each Member State shall designate a contact point whose remit shall be:

(a) to provide the citizens and contact points of the other Member States with such information as is necessary concerning the recognition of professional qualifications provided for in this Directive, such as information on the national legislation governing the professions and the pursuit of those professions, including social legislation, and, where appropriate, the rules of ethics;
(b) to assist citizens in realising the rights conferred on them by this Directive, in cooperation, where appropriate, with the other contact points and the competent authorities in the host Member State.

Implementation

839. The directive was to be implemented by 20 October 2007. In the *Rubino* case,[353] the Court ruled that the fact that access to a profession is reserved to candidates who have been successful in a procedure to select a predefined number of persons on the basis of a comparative assessment of the candidates rather than by application of absolute criteria, which confers a qualification the validity of which is strictly limited in time, does not mean that that profession constitutes a regulated profession within the meaning of Article 3(1)(a) of Directive 2005/36/EC on the recognition of professional qualifications.

Article 3(1)(a) of Directive 2005/36 contains the following definition:

(a) 'regulated profession': a professional activity or group of professional activities, access to which, the pursuit of which, or one of the modes of pursuit of which is subject, directly or indirectly, by virtue of legislative, regulatory or administrative provisions to the possession of specific professional qualifications; in particular, the use of a professional title limited by legislative, regulatory or administrative provisions to holders of a given professional qualification shall constitute a mode of pursuit ... ".

Nevertheless, Article 45 TFEU requires qualifications obtained in other Member States to be accorded their proper value and to be duly taken into account in such a procedure.

IV. Blue Card: Admission and Mobility of Third Country Nationals of Highly Qualified Employment

840. The Council Directive 2009/50/EC of 25 May 2009 on the conditions of entry and residence of third-country nationals for the purposes of highly qualified

---

353. C.O.J, 17 December 2009, *Angelo Rubino v. Ministero Dell'Università e della Ricerca*, C-586/ 08, www.curia.eu.

Part I, Ch. 1, The Free Movement of Workers 841–841

employment[354] is intended to contribute to achieving the objectives of the Lisbon strategy and addressing labour shortages by fostering the admission and mobility – for the purposes of highly qualified employment – of third-country nationals for stays of more than three months, in order to make the Union more attractive to such workers from around the world and sustain its competitiveness and economic growth.

To reach these goals, it is necessary to facilitate the admission of highly qualified workers and their families by establishing a fast-track admission procedure and by granting them equal social and economic rights as nationals of the host Member State in a number of areas. It is also necessary to take into account the priorities, labour market needs and reception capacities of the Member States. This Directive is without prejudice to the competence of the Member States to maintain or to introduce new national residence permits for any purpose of employment. The third-country nationals concerned should have the possibility to apply for an EU Blue Card or for a national residence permit. Moreover, this Directive does not affect the possibility for an EU Blue Card holder to enjoy additional rights and benefits which may be provided by national law, and which are compatible with this Directive.

This Directive is without prejudice to the right of the Member States to determine the volumes of admission of third-country nationals entering their territory for the purposes of highly qualified employment. This should include also third-country nationals who seek to remain on the territory of a Member State in order to exercise a paid economic activity and who are legally resident in that Member State under other schemes, such as students having just completed their studies or researchers.

Moreover, regarding volumes of admission, Member States retain the possibility not to grant residence permits for employment in general or for certain professions, economic sectors or regions.

A. General Provisions

1. Subject Matter

841. The purpose of this Directive is to determine:

(a) the conditions of entry and residence for more than three months in the territory of the Member States of third-country nationals for the purpose of highly qualified employment as EU Blue Card holders, and of their family members;
(b) the conditions for entry and residence of third-country nationals and of their family members under point (a) in Member States other than the first Member State.

---

354. O.J., 18 June 2009, L 155.

2. Definitions

842. For the purposes of this Directive:

(a) 'third-country national' means any person who is not a citizen of the Union;
(b) 'highly qualified employment' means the employment of a person who:
    – in the Member State concerned, is protected as an employee under national employment law and/or in accordance with national practice, irrespective of the legal relationship, for the purpose of exercising genuine and effective work for, or under the direction of, someone else,
    – is paid; and,
    – has the required adequate and specific competence, as proven by higher professional qualifications,
(c) 'EU Blue Card' means the authorisation bearing the term 'EU Blue Card' entitling its holder to reside and work in the territory of a Member State under the terms of this Directive;
(d) 'first Member State' means the Member State which first grants a thirdcountry national an 'EU Blue Card';
(e) 'second Member State' means any Member State other than the first Member State;
(f) 'family members' means third-country nationals as defined in Article 4(1) of Directive 2003/86/EC;
(g) 'higher professional qualifications' means qualifications attested by evidence of higher education qualifications or, by way of derogation, when provided for by national law, attested by at least five years of professional experience of a level comparable to higher education qualifications and which is relevant in the profession or sector specified in the work contract or binding job offer;
(h) 'higher education qualification' means any diploma, certificate or other evidence of formal qualifications issued by a competent authority attesting the successful completion of a post-secondary higher education programme, namely a set of courses provided by an educational establishment recognised as a higher education institution by the State in which it is situated. For the purposes of this Directive, a higher education qualification shall be taken into account, on condition that the studies needed to acquire it lasted at least three years;
(i) 'professional experience' means the actual and lawful pursuit of the profession concerned;
(j) 'regulated profession' means a regulated profession as defined in Article 3(1)(a) of Directive 2005/36/EC.

3. Scope

843. This Directive applies to third-country nationals who apply to be admitted to the territory of a Member State for the purpose of highly qualified employment under the terms of this Directive.

Part I, Ch. 1, The Free Movement of Workers

B. Conditions of Admission

1. Criteria for Admission

844. A third-country national who applies for an EU Blue Card under the terms of this Directive shall:

(a) present a valid work contract or, as provided for in national law, a binding job offer for highly qualified employment, of at least one year in the Member State concerned;
(b) present a document attesting fulfilment of the conditions set out under national law for the exercise by Union citizens of the regulated profession specified in the work contract or binding job offer as provided for in national law;
(c) for unregulated professions, present the documents attesting the relevant higher professional qualifications in the occupation or sector specified in the work contract or in the binding job offer as provided for in national law;
(d) present a valid travel document, as determined by national law, an application for a visa or a visa, if required, and evidence of a valid residence permit or of a national long-term visa, if appropriate. Member States may require the period of validity of the travel document to cover at least the initial duration of the residence permit;
(e) present evidence of having or, if provided for by national law, having applied for a sickness insurance for all the risks normally covered for nationals of the Member State concerned for periods where no such insurance coverage and corresponding entitlement to benefits are provided in connection with, or resulting from, the work contract;
(f) not be considered to pose a threat to public policy, public security or public health.
(2) Member States may require the applicant to provide his address in the territory of the Member State concerned.
(3) In addition to the conditions laid down in paragraph 1, the gross annual salary resulting from the monthly or annual salary specified in the work contract or binding job offer shall not be inferior to a relevant salary threshold defined and published for that purpose by the Member States, which shall be at least 1,5 times the average gross annual salary in the Member State concerned.
(4) When implementing paragraph 3, Member States may require that all conditions in the applicable laws, collective agreements or practices in the relevant occupational branches for highly qualified employment are met.
(5) By way of derogation to paragraph 3, and for employment in professions which are in particular need of third-country national workers and which belong to the major groups 1 and 2 of ISCO, the salary threshold may be at least 1,2 times the average gross annual salary in the Member State concerned. In this case, the Member State concerned shall communicate each year to the Commission the list of the professions for which a derogation has been decided.
(6) This Article shall be without prejudice to the applicable collective agreements or practices in the relevant occupational branches for highly qualified employment.

2. Volumes of Admission

845. This Directive does not affect the right of a Member State to determine the volume of admission of third-country nationals entering its territory for the purposes of highly qualified employment.

C. EU Blue Card, Procedure and Transparency

846. A third-country national who has applied and fulfils the requirements and for whom the competent authorities have taken a positive decision shall be issued with an EU Blue Card.

The Member State concerned shall grant the third-country national every facility to obtain the requisite visas.

Member States shall set a standard period of validity of the EU Blue Card, which shall be comprised between one and four years. If the work contract covers a period less than this period, the EU Blue Card shall be issued or renewed for the duration of the work contract plus three months.

During the period of its validity, the EU Blue Card shall entitle its holder to enter, re-enter and stay in the territory of the Member State issuing the EU Blue Card.

D. Rights

1. Labour Market Access

847. For the first two years of legal employment in the Member State concerned as an EU Blue Card holder, access to the labour market for the person concerned shall be restricted to the exercise of paid employment activities. After these first two years, Member States may grant the persons concerned equal treatment with nationals as regards access to highly qualified employment.

2. Equal Treatment

848.

(1) EU Blue Card holders shall enjoy equal treatment with nationals of the Member State issuing the Blue Card, as regards:
   (a) working conditions, including pay and dismissal, as well as health and safety requirements at the workplace;
   (b) freedom of association and affiliation and membership of an organisation representing workers or employers or of any organisation whose members are engaged in a specific occupation, including the benefits conferred by such organisations, without prejudice to the national provisions on public policy and public security;

(c) education and vocational training;
(d) recognition of diplomas, certificates and other professional qualifications in accordance with the relevant national procedures;
(e) provisions in national law regarding the branches of social security;
(f) without prejudice to existing bilateral agreements, payment of income-related acquired statutory pensions in respect of old age, at the rate applied by virtue of the law of the debtor Member State(s) when moving to a third country;
(g) access to goods and services and the supply of goods and services made available to the public, including procedures for obtaining housing, as well as information and counselling services afforded by employment offices;
(h) free access to the entire territory of the Member State concerned, within the limits provided for by national law.

3. Transposition

849. Member States shall bring into force the laws, regulations and administrative provisions necessary to comply with this Directive by 19 June 2011.

V. Single Application Procedure for a Single Permit for Third-Country Nationals

850. Directive 2011/98/EU of 13 December 2011 relates to a single application procedure for a single permit for third-country nationals to reside and work in the territory of a Member State and on a common set of rights for third-country workers legally residing in a Member State

A. General Provisions

1. Subject Matter

851. This Directive lays down:

(a) a single application procedure for issuing a single permit for third-country nationals to reside for the purpose of work in the territory of a Member State, in order to simplify the procedures for their admission and to facilitate the control of their status; and
(b) a common set of rights to third-country workers legally residing in a Member State, irrespective of the purposes for which they were initially admitted to the territory of that Member State, based on equal treatment with nationals of that Member State.

2. This Directive is without prejudice to the Member States' powers concerning the admission of third-country nationals to their labour markets.

2. Definitions

852. For the purposes of this Directive, the following definitions apply:

(a) 'third-country national' means a person who is not a citizen of the Union within the meaning of Article 20(1) TFEU;
(b) 'third-country worker' means a third-country national who has been admitted to the territory of a Member State and who is legally residing and is allowed to work in the context of a paid relationship in that Member State in accordance with national law or practice;
(c) 'single permit' means a residence permit issued by the authorities of a Member State allowing a third-country national to reside legally in its territory for the purpose of work;
(d) 'single application procedure' means any procedure leading, on the basis of a single application made by a third-country national, or by his or her employer, for the authorisation of residence and work in the territory of a Member State, to a decision ruling on that application for the single permit.

3. Scope

853. 1. This Directive shall apply to:

(a) third-country nationals who apply to reside in a Member State for the purpose of work;
(b) third-country nationals who have been admitted to a Member State for purposes other than work in accordance with Union or national law, who are allowed to work and who hold a residence permit in accordance with Regulation (EC) No 1030/2002; and
(c) third-country nationals who have been admitted to a Member State for the purpose of work in accordance with Union or national law.

This Directive shall not apply to third-country nationals:

(a) who are family members of citizens of the Union who have exercised, or are exercising, their right to free movement within the Union in accordance with Directive 2004/38/EC of the European Parliament and of the Council of 29 April 2004 on the right of citizens of the Union and their family members to move and reside freely within the territory of the Member States [17];
(b) who, together with their family members, and irrespective of their nationality, enjoy rights of free movement equivalent to those of citizens of the Union under

agreements either between the Union and the Member States or between the Union and third countries;
(c) who are posted for as long as they are posted;
(d) who have applied for admission or have been admitted to the territory of a Member State to work as intra-corporate transferees;
(e) who have applied for admission or have been admitted to the territory of a Member State as seasonal workers or au pairs;
(f) who are authorised to reside in a Member State on the basis of temporary protection, or who have applied for authorisation to reside there on that basis and are awaiting a decision on their status;
(g) who are beneficiaries of international protection under Council Directive 2004/83/EC of 29 April 2004 on minimum standards for the qualification and status of third-country nationals or stateless persons as refugees or as persons who otherwise need international protection and the content of the protection granted [18] or who have applied for international protection under that Directive and whose application has not been the subject of a final decision;
(h) who are beneficiaries of protection in accordance with national law, international obligations or the practice of a Member State or have applied for protection in accordance with national law, international obligations or the practice of a Member State and whose application has not been the subject of a final decision;
(i) who are long-term residents in accordance with Directive 2003/109/EC;
(j) whose removal has been suspended on the basis of fact or law;
(k) who have applied for admission or who have been admitted to the territory of a Member State as self-employed workers;
(l) who have applied for admission or have been admitted as seafarers for employment or work in any capacity on board of a ship registered in or sailing under the flag of a Member State.

854. Member States may decide that Chapter II does not apply to third-country nationals who have been either authorised to work in the territory of a Member State for a period not exceeding six months or who have been admitted to a Member State for the purpose of study.

Chapter II shall not apply to third-country nationals who are allowed to work on the basis of a visa.

B. *Single Application Procedure and Single Permit*

1. Single Application Procedure

855.

1. An application to issue, amend or renew a single permit shall be submitted by way of a single application procedure. Member States shall determine whether applications for a single permit are to be made by the third-country national or by the third-country national's employer. Member States may also decide to

allow an application from either of the two. If the application is to be submitted by the third-country national, Member States shall allow the application to be introduced from a third country or, if provided for by national law, in the territory of the Member State in which the third-country national is legally present.
2. Member States shall examine an application made under paragraph 1 and shall adopt a decision to issue, amend or renew the single permit if the applicant fulfils the requirements specified by Union or national law. A decision to issue, amend or renew the single permit shall constitute a single administrative act combining a residence permit and a work permit.
3. The single application procedure shall be without prejudice to the visa procedure which may be required for initial entry.
   4. Member States shall issue a single permit, where the conditions provided for are met, to third-country nationals who apply for admission and to third-country nationals already admitted who apply to renew or modify their residence permit after the entry into force of the national implementing provisions.

2. Competent Authority

856.

1. Member States shall designate the authority competent to receive the application and to issue the single permit.
2. The competent authority shall adopt a decision on the complete application as soon as possible and in any event within four months of the date on which the application was lodged.
   The time limit referred to in the first subparagraph may be extended in exceptional circumstances, linked to the complexity of the examination of the application.
   Where no decision is taken within the time limit provided for in this paragraph, any consequences shall be determined by national law.
3. The competent authority shall notify the decision to the applicant in writing in accordance with the notification procedures laid down in the relevant national law.
4. If the information or documents in support of the application are incomplete according to the criteria specified in national law, the competent authority shall notify the applicant in writing of the additional information or documents required, setting a reasonable deadline to provide them. The time limit referred to in paragraph 2 shall be suspended until the competent authority or other relevant authorities have received the additional information required. If the additional information or documents is not provided within the deadline set, the competent authority may reject the application.

3. Single Permit

857.

1. Member States shall issue a single permit using the uniform format as laid down in Regulation (EC) No 1030/2002 and shall indicate the information relating to the permission to work in accordance with point (a)7.5-9 of the Annex thereto.
   Member States may indicate additional information related to the employment relationship of the third-country national (such as the name and address of the employer, place of work, type of work, working hours, remuneration) in paper format, or store such data in electronic format as referred to in Article 4 of Regulation (EC) No 1030/2002 and in point (a)16 of the Annex thereto.
2. When issuing the single permit Member States shall not issue additional permits as proof of authorisation to access the labour market.

4. Residence Permits Issued for Purposes Other than Work

858.

1. When issuing residence permits in accordance with Regulation (EC) No 1030/2002 Member States shall indicate the information relating to the permission to work irrespective of the type of the permit.
   Member States may indicate additional information related to the employment relationship of the third-country national (such as the name and address of the employer, place of work, type of work, working hours, remuneration) in paper format, or store such data in electronic format as referred to in Article 4 of Regulation (EC) No 1030/2002 and point (a)16 of the Annex thereto.
2. When issuing residence permits in accordance with Regulation (EC) No 1030/2002, Member States shall not issue additional permits as proof of authorisation to access the labour market.

5. Procedural Guarantees

859.

1. Reasons shall be given in the written notification of a decision rejecting an application to issue, amend or renew a single permit, or a decision withdrawing a single permit on the basis of criteria provided for by Union or national law.
2. A decision rejecting the application to issue, amend or renew or withdrawing a single permit shall be open to legal challenge in the Member State concerned, in accordance with national law. The written notification referred to in paragraph 1 shall specify the court or administrative authority where the person concerned may lodge an appeal and the time limit therefor.

3. An application may be considered as inadmissible on the grounds of volume of admission of third-country nationals coming for employment and, on that basis, need not to be processed.

6. Access to Information

860. Member States shall provide, upon request, adequate information to the third-country national and the future employer on the documents required to make a complete application.

7. Fees

861. Member States may require applicants to pay fees, where appropriate, for handling applications in accordance with this Directive. The level of such fees shall be proportionate and may be based on the services actually provided for the processing of applications and the issuance of permits.

8. Rights on the Basis of the Single Permit

862. Where a single permit has been issued in accordance with national law, it shall authorise, during its period of validity, its holder at least to:

(a) enter and reside in the territory of the Member State issuing the single permit, provided that the holder meets all admission requirements in accordance with national law;
(b) have free access to the entire territory of the Member State issuing the single permit within the limits provided for by national law;
(c) exercise the specific employment activity authorised under the single permit in accordance with national law;
(d) be informed about the holder's own rights linked to the permit conferred by this Directive and/or by national law.

C. *Right to Equal Treatment*

863.

1. Third-country workers as referred to in points (b) and (c) of Article 3(1) shall enjoy equal treatment with nationals of the Member State where they reside with regard to:

Part I, Ch. 1, The Free Movement of Workers

(a) working conditions, including pay and dismissal as well as health and safety at the workplace;
(b) freedom of association and affiliation and membership of an organisation representing workers or employers or of any organisation whose members are engaged in a specific occupation, including the benefits conferred by such organisations, without prejudice to the national provisions on public policy and public security;
(c) education and vocational training;
(d) recognition of diplomas, certificates and other professional qualifications in accordance with the relevant national procedures;
(e) branches of social security, as defined in Regulation (EC) No 883/2004;
(f) tax benefits, in so far as the worker is deemed to be resident for tax purposes in the Member State concerned;
(g) access to goods and services and the supply of goods and services made available to the public including procedures for obtaining housing as provided by national law, without prejudice to the freedom of contract in accordance with Union and national law;
(h) advice services afforded by employment offices.

864.

2. Member States may restrict equal treatment:

(a) under point (c) of paragraph 1 by:
  (i) limiting its application to those third-country workers who are in employment or who have been employed and who are registered as unemployed;
  (ii) excluding those third-country workers who have been admitted to their territory in conformity with Directive 2004/114/EC;
  (iii) excluding study and maintenance grants and loans or other grants and loans;
  (iv) laying down specific prerequisites including language proficiency and the payment of tuition fees, in accordance with national law, with respect to access to university and post-secondary education and to vocational training which is not directly linked to the specific employment activity;
(b) by limiting the rights conferred on third-country workers under point (e) of paragraph 1, but shall not restrict such rights for third-country workers who are in employment or who have been employed for a minimum period of six months and who are registered as unemployed.

In addition, Member States may decide that point (e) of paragraph 1 with regard to family benefits shall not apply to third-country nationals who have been authorised to work in the territory of a Member State for a period not exceeding six months, to third-country nationals who have been admitted for the purpose of study, or to third-country nationals who are allowed to work on the basis of a visa.

(c) under point (f) of paragraph 1 with respect to tax benefits by limiting its application to cases where the registered or usual place of residence of the family members of the third-country worker for whom he/she claims benefits, lies in the territory of the Member State concerned.
(d) under point (g) of paragraph 1 by:
  (i) limiting its application to those third-country workers who are in employment;
  (ii) restricting access to housing;

865.

3. The right to equal treatment laid down in paragraph 1 shall be without prejudice to the right of the Member State to withdraw or to refuse to renew the residence permit issued under this Directive, the residence permit issued for purposes other than work, or any other authorisation to work in a Member State.
4. Third-country workers moving to a third country, or their survivors who reside in a third country and who derive rights from those workers, shall receive, in relation to old age, invalidity and death, statutory pensions based on those workers' previous employment and acquired in accordance with the legislation referred to in Article 3 of Regulation (EC) No 883/2004, under the same conditions and at the same rates as the nationals of the Member States concerned when they move to a third country.

D. *Final Provisions*

1. More Favourable Provisions

866.

1. This Directive shall apply without prejudice to more favourable provisions of:
  (a) Union law, including bilateral and multilateral agreements between the Union, or the Union and its Member States, on the one hand and one or more third countries on the other; and
  (b) bilateral or multilateral agreements between one or more Member States and one or more third countries.
2. This Directive shall be without prejudice to the right of Member States to adopt or maintain provisions that are more favourable to the persons to whom it applies.

2. Information to the General Public

867. Each Member State shall make available to the general public a regularly updated set of information concerning the conditions of third-country nationals' admission to and residence in its territory in order to work there.

3. Reporting

868.

1. Periodically, and for the first time by 25 December 2016, the Commission shall present a report to the European Parliament and the Council on the application of this Directive in the Member States and shall propose amendments it deems necessary.
2. Annually, and for the first time by 25 December 2014, Member States shall communicate to the Commission statistics on the volumes of third-country nationals who have been granted a single permit during the previous calendar year, in accordance with Regulation (EC) No 862/2007 of the European Parliament and of the Council of 11 July 2007 on Community statistics on migration and international protection [19].

4. Transposition

869.

1. Member States shall bring into force the laws, regulations and administrative provisions necessary to comply with this Directive by 25 December 2013. They shall forthwith communicate to the Commission the text of those provisions.
   When Member States adopt those measures, they shall contain a reference to this Directive or shall be accompanied by such a reference on the occasion of their official publication. The methods of making such reference shall be laid down by Member States.
2. Member States shall communicate to the Commission the text of the main provisions of national law which they adopt in the field covered by this Directive.

5. Entry into Force

870. This Directive shall enter into force on the day following its publication in the Official Journal of the European Union.

§4. Minimum Standards on Sanctions and Measures Against Employers of Illegally Staying Third-Country Nationals

871. Directive 2009/52/EC of 18 June 2009 providing for minimum standards on sanctions and measures against employers of illegally staying third-country nationals[355] provides for the strengthening of the cooperation among Member States in the fight against illegal immigration and in particular that measures against illegal employment should be intensified at Member State and EU level.

A key pull factor for illegal immigration into the EU is the possibility of obtaining work in the EU without the required legal status. Action against illegal immigration and illegal stay should therefore include measures to counter that pull factor.

The centrepiece of such measures should be a general prohibition on the employment of third-country nationals who do not have the right to be resident in the EU, accompanied by sanctions against employers who infringe that prohibition.

I. Subject Matter and Scope

872. This directive prohibits the employment of illegally staying third-country nationals in order to fight illegal immigration. To this end, it lays down minimum common standards on sanctions and measures to be applied in the Member States against employers who infringe that prohibition.

II. Definitions

873. For the specific purposes of this Directive, the following definitions apply:

(a) 'third-country national' means any person who is not a citizen of the Union and who is not a person enjoying the Community right of free movement;
(b) 'illegally staying third-country national' means a third-country national present on the territory of a Member State, who does not fulfil, or no longer fulfils, the conditions for stay or residence in that Member State;
(c) 'employment' means the exercise of activities covering whatever form of labour or work regulated under national law or in accordance with established practice for or under the direction and/or supervision of an employer;
(d) 'illegal employment' means the employment of an illegally staying third-country national;
(e) 'employer' means any natural person or any legal entity, including temporary work agencies, for or under the direction and/or supervision of whom the employment is undertaken;

---

355. O.J., 30 June 2009, L 168.

- (f) 'subcontractor' means any natural person or any legal entity, to whom the execution of all or part of the obligations of a prior contract is assigned;
- (g) 'legal person' means any legal entity having such status under applicable national law, except for States or public bodies exercising State authority and for public international organisations;
- (h) 'temporary work agency' means any natural or legal person who, in compliance with national law, concludes contracts of employment or employment relationships with temporary agency workers in order to assign them to user undertakings to work there temporarily under their supervision and direction;
- (i) 'particularly exploitative working conditions' means working conditions, including those resulting from gender based or other discrimination, where there is a striking disproportion compared with the terms of employment of legally employed workers which, for example, affects workers' health and safety, and which offends against human dignity;
- (j) 'remuneration of illegally staying third-country national' means the wage or salary and any other consideration, whether in cash or in kind, which a worker receives directly or indirectly in respect of his employment from his employer and which is equivalent to that which would have been enjoyed by comparable workers in a legal employment relationship.

III. Prohibition of Illegal Employment

874. Member States shall prohibit the employment of illegally staying third-country nationals. Infringements of this prohibition shall be subject to the sanctions and measures laid down in this Directive.

IV. Obligations on Employers

875. Member States shall oblige employers to:

- (a) require that a third-country national before taking up the employment holds and presents to the employer a valid residence permit or other authorisation for his or her stay;
- (b) keep for at least the duration of the employment a copy or record of the residence permit or other authorisation for stay available for possible inspection by the competent authorities of the Member States;
- (c) notify the competent authorities designated by Member States of the start of employment of third-country nationals within a period laid down by each Member State.

V. Financial Sanctions

876.

(1) Member States shall take the necessary measures to ensure that infringements of the prohibition are subject to effective, proportionate and dissuasive sanctions against the employer.
(2) Sanctions in respect of infringements of the prohibition shall include:
    (a) financial sanctions which shall increase in amount according to the number of illegally employed third-country nationals; and
    (b) payments of the costs of return of illegally employed third-country nationals in those cases where return procedures are carried out. Member States may instead decide to reflect at least the average costs of return in the financial sanctions.
(3) Member States may provide for reduced financial sanctions where the employer is a natural person who employs an illegally staying third-country national for his or her private purposes and where no particularly exploitative working conditions are involved.

VI. Back Payments to be Made by Employers

877.

(1) In respect of each infringement of the prohibition, Member States shall ensure that the employer shall be liable to pay:
    (a) any outstanding remuneration to the illegally employed third-country national. The agreed level of remuneration shall be presumed to have been at least as high as the wage provided for by the applicable laws on minimum wages, by collective agreements or in accordance with established practice in the relevant occupational branches, unless either the employer or the employee can prove otherwise, while respecting, where appropriate, the mandatory national provisions on wages;
    (b) an amount equal to any taxes and social security contributions that the employer would have paid had the third-country national been legally employed, including penalty payments for delays and relevant administrative fines;
    (c) where appropriate, any cost arising from sending back payments to the country to which the third-country national has returned or has been returned.
(2) In order to ensure the availability of effective procedures Member States shall enact mechanisms to ensure that illegally employed third-country nationals:
    (a) may introduce a claim, subject to a limitation period defined in national law, against their employer and eventually enforce a judgment against the employer for any outstanding remuneration, including in cases in which they have, or have been, returned; or

Part I, Ch. 1, The Free Movement of Workers

(3) when provided for by national legislation, may call on the competent authority of the Member State to start procedures to recover outstanding remuneration without the need for them to introduce a claim in that case.
(3) Illegally employed third-country nationals shall be systematically and objectively informed about their rights under this paragraph and under Article 13 before the enforcement of any return decision.
(4) Member States shall provide that an employment relationship of at least three months duration be presumed unless, among others, the employer or the employee can prove otherwise.
(5) Member States shall ensure that the necessary mechanisms are in place to ensure that illegally employed third-country nationals are able to receive any back payment of remuneration which is recovered as part of the claims, including in cases in which they have, or have been, returned.

VII. Other Measures

878. Member States shall take the necessary measures to ensure that employers shall also, if appropriate, be subject to the following measures:

(a) exclusion from entitlement to some or all public benefits, aid or subsidies, including EU funding managed by Member States, for up to five years;
(b) exclusion from participation in a public contract for up to five years;
(c) recovery of some or all public benefits, aid, or subsidies, including EU funding managed by Member States, granted to the employer for up to 12 months preceding the detection of illegal employment;
(d) temporary or permanent closure of the establishments that have been used to commit the infringement, or temporary or permanent withdrawal of a licence to conduct the business activity in question, if justified by the gravity of the infringement.

VIII. Subcontracting

879.

(1) Where the employer is a subcontractor and without prejudice to the provisions of national law concerning the rights of contribution or recourse or to the provisions of national law in the field of social security, Member States shall ensure that the contractor of which the employer is a direct subcontractor may, in addition to or in place of the employer, be liable to pay:
   (a) any financial sanction imposed; and
   (b) any back payments due.
(2) Where the employer is a subcontractor, Member States shall ensure that the main contractor and any intermediate subcontractor, where they knew that the employing subcontractor employed illegally staying third-country nationals,

may be liable to make the payments in addition to or in place of the employing subcontractor or the contractor of which the employer is a direct subcontractor.

IX. Criminal Offence

880.

(1) Member States shall ensure that the infringement of the prohibition referred to in Article 3 constitutes a criminal offence when committed intentionally, in each of the following circumstances as defined by national law:
   (a) the infringement continues or is persistently repeated;
   (b) the infringement is in respect of the simultaneous employment of a significant number of illegally staying third-country nationals;
   (c) the infringement is accompanied by particularly exploitative working conditions;
   (d) the infringement is committed by an employer who uses work or services exacted from an illegally staying third-country national with the knowledge that he or she is a victim of trafficking in human beings;
   (e) the infringement relates to the illegal employment of a minor.
(2) Member States shall ensure that inciting, aiding and abetting the intentional conduct is punishable as a criminal offence.

X. Criminal Penalties

881.

(1) Member States shall take the necessary measures to ensure that natural persons who commit a criminal offence are punishable by effective, proportionate and dissuasive criminal penalties.
(2) Unless prohibited by general principles of law, the criminal penalties provided for in this Article may be applied under national law without prejudice to other sanctions or measures of a non-criminal nature, and they may be accompanied by the publication of the judicial decision relevant to the case.

XI. Liability of Legal Persons

882.

(1) Member States shall ensure that legal persons may be held liable for the offence where such an offence has been committed for their benefit by any person who has a leading position within the legal person, acting either individually or as part of an organ of the legal person, on the basis of:
   (a) a power of representation of the legal person;

Part I, Ch. 1, The Free Movement of Workers

(b) an authority to take decisions on behalf of the legal person; or
(c) an authority to exercise control within the legal person.
(2) Member States shall also ensure that a legal person may be held liable where the lack of supervision or control has made possible the commission of the criminal offence for the benefit of that legal person by a person under its authority.
(3) Liability of a legal person shall not exclude criminal proceedings against natural persons who are perpetrators, inciters or accessories in the offence referred to in.

XII. Penalties for Legal Persons

883. Member States shall take the necessary measures to ensure that a legal person held liable is punishable by effective, proportionate and dissuasive penalties, which may include measures such as those referred to in VI.

Member States may decide that a list of employers who are legal persons and who have been held liable for the criminal offence is made public.

XIII. Facilitation of Complaints

884.

(1) Member States shall ensure that there are effective mechanisms through which third-country nationals in illegal employment may lodge complaints against their employers, directly or through third parties designated by Member States such as trade unions or other associations or a competent authority of the Member State when provided for by national legislation.
(2) Member States shall ensure that third parties which have, in accordance with the criteria laid down in their national law, a legitimate interest in ensuring compliance with this Directive, may engage either on behalf of or in support of an illegally employed third-country national, with his or her approval, in any administrative or civil proceedings provided for with the objective of implementing this Directive.

XIV. Inspections

885.

(1) Member States shall ensure that effective and adequate inspections are carried out on their territory to control employment of illegally staying third-country nationals. Such inspections shall be based primarily on a risk assessment to be drawn up by the competent authorities in the Member States.
(2) With a view to increasing the effectiveness of inspections, Member States shall, on the basis of a risk assessment, regularly identify the sectors of activity in

which the employment of illegally staying third-country nationals is concentrated on their territory.

In respect of each of those sectors, Member States shall, before 1 July of each year, communicate to the Commission the inspections, both in absolute numbers and as a percentage of the employers for each sector, carried out in the previous year as well as their results.

XV. More Favourable Provisions

886. This Directive shall be without prejudice to the right of Member States to adopt or maintain provisions that are more favourable to third-country nationals to whom it applies in relation with Articles 6 and 13, provided that such provisions are compatible with this Directive.

XVI. Transposition

887. Member States shall bring into force the laws, regulations and administrative provisions necessary to comply with this Directive by 20 July 2011.

Chapter 2. Freedom of Services

888. Freedom of services is since 1957 one of the pillars of the European Common Market, next to free movement of capital, goods and persons, free movement of workers included (Article 56 TFEU).

§1. SCOPE OF APPLICATION

889. Services relate, according to Articles 56, 57 TFEU, to services of an economic nature, normally provided for remuneration, which are temporary and trans border. Let's have a look at each of these elements.

I. Service

A. Material

890. A service is a task in the broad sense of the word. 'services' shall in particular include:

(a) activities of an industrial character;
(b) activities of a commercial character;
(c) activities of craftsmen;
(d) activities of the professions (Article 57).

Meant are, by way of example, the giving of a lecture, of a concert, the building of a house, harvesting, help as a nurse in a hospital, in short, every task, which a person can perform for the benefit of another person.

Also services like: managerial tasks, consultancy, certification and tests, facility management, advertising, selection of personnel and the like.

Equally: legal or tax advice, services in the real estate as an intermediary, the organisation of fairs, the renting of cars, the activities of a travel agency, of security services etc.

Also services in the health sector, home care, like help to elderly persons, in tourism, audiovisual services, sport centres and amusements parks fall within the scope of application.

Services in the sense of Article 56 TFEU are those in so far as they are not governed by the provisions relating to freedom of movement for goods, capital and persons (Article 57 TFEU).[356]

---

356. The sending of a television message is a service, but the materials, sound carriers and films as well as other materials used to send the message are goods and subject to the rules concerning the free movement of goods (Lenaerts, K. and Van Nuffel, P. *Europees recht in hoofdlijnen*, third edn, Maklu, Antwerp, 2003, 235).

B. Personal

891. A service can be performed by a natural person, either as a self-employed or as an employee of a service-provider or by a legal person, either by a company (profit) or an association (non-profit) or by a factual grouping, without legal personality.

The service can be provided for the benefit of another person, be it a natural person or a legal person or a factual grouping.

II. For Remuneration

892. Services are those, normally provided for remuneration (Article 57). Concerned are services of an economic nature, as well services in the private as in the public sector.

Free services fall not in the scope of application, as normally a remuneration is necessary. Sporadic free is consequently not a problem. It is important that payment is done with private money. Activities, which are financed by government money, do not qualify. Thus is education in schools, financed by the government, not a service. A service in a hospital, which is paid by a sickness fund and thus on the basis of private contributions qualifies.

III. Temporary

893. Only services that are temporary qualify for the rules concerning freedom of services (Article 57 TFEU). Through this temporary character, freedom of services distinguishes itself from freedom of establishment. The latter means that one establishes its headquarters or a permanent establishment in a Member State in order to deliver or receive services in a permanent way.

The notion temporary is not necessarily the same as a fixed period. In the *Gebhard*[357] case (a lawyer) the Court of Justice ruled:

1. A national of a Member State who pursues a professional activity on a stable and continuous basis in another Member State where he holds himself out from an established professional base to, amongst others, nationals of that State comes under the chapter relating to the right of establishment and not the chapter relating to services.
2. As appears from the third paragraph of Article 57 of the Treaty, the rules on freedom to provide services cover: – at least where the provider moves in order to provide his services; – the situation in which a person moves from one Member State to another, not for the purposes of establishment there, but in order to pursue his activity there on a temporary basis.The temporary nature of the activities in question has to be determined in the light of its duration, regularity,

---

357. C.O.J., 30 November 1995, *Reinhard Gebhard* v. *Consiglio dell'Ordine degli Avvocati e Procuratori di Milano*, Case C-55/94, ECR, 1995, 4165.

periodicity and continuity. This does not mean that the provider of services within the meaning of the Treaty may not equip himself with some form of infrastructure in the host Member State (including an office, chambers or consulting rooms) in so far as such infrastructure is necessary for the purposes of performing the services in question.

The temporary nature of the activities in question has to be determined not only in the light of its duration, but also on the basis of its regularity, periodicity and continuity.

What this *in concreto* means is not clear at all. Follows that the distinction between freedom of services on the one hand and freedom of establishment on the other hand remains diffuse and problematic.

IV. Trans Border

894. According to Article 56 TFEU, meant are services, which transcend national borders. The recipient of the service is located in another Member State than the one from which the service is delivered. Beneficiaries are indeed nationals of Member States who are established in a State of the Union other than that of the person for whom the services are intended.

Meant are, as indicated above, natural persons as well as legal persons and factual groupings, which operate as providers or receivers of services.

Activities, which are in all their relevant aspects performed in one Member State do not fall under the heading of freedom of services, as there is no trans border element involved.

§2. PROHIBITION OF RESTRICTIONS AND OF DISCRIMINATION

895. According to Article 56 TFEU, restrictions on freedom to provide services within the Union shall be prohibited in respect of nationals of Member States who are established in a State of the Union other than that of the person for whom the services are intended.

These commandments are clear: 1) no restrictions on freedom to provide services and 2) equal treatment, namely no discrimination on the basis of nationality. These stipulations have direct binding effect. All national rules, which are contrary to them, are *de jure* null and void. They are considered not to exist.

I. Restrictions

896. The prohibition of restrictions is to be interpreted in an extensive way. According to the European Court:[358]

---

358. 25 July 1991, *Manfred Säger* v. *Dennemeyer & Co. Ltd.*, Case C-76/90, ECR, 1991, 4221.

Article 56 TFEU requires not only the elimination of all discrimination against a person providing services on the grounds of his nationality, but also the abolition of any restriction, even if it applies without distinction to national providers of services and to those of other Member States, when it is liable to prohibit or otherwise impede the activities of a provider of services established in another Member State where he lawfully provides similar services. In particular, a Member State may not make the provision of services in its territory subject to compliance with all the conditions required for establishment and thereby deprive of all practical effectiveness the provisions of the Treaty whose object is, precisely, to guarantee the freedom to provide services.

Such is indeed an extensive interpretation:

> It is settled case law that Article 56 TFEU requires not only the elimination of all discrimination on grounds of nationality against providers of services who are established in another Member State, but also the abolition of any restriction, even if it applies without distinction to national providers of services and to those of other Member States, which is liable to prohibit, impede or render less attractive the activities of a provider of services established in another Member State in which he lawfully provides similar services.[359]

II. Discrimination

897. As well direct as indirect discrimination are forbidden. Discrimination is every unjustified unequal treatment, based on prohibited grounds.

Discrimination has to be distinguished from differentiation: an unequal treatment on the basis of grounds, which are acceptable from the societal point of view, as the reward for the best student, a golden medal at the occasion of the Olympic Games and so on.

For a more precise definition of the notion discrimination we can refer to the abundant case law of the European Court, which is adequately summarised in Council Directive 2000/78/EC of 27 November 2000 establishing a general framework for equal treatment in employment and occupation.[360]

898.

(1) For the purposes of this Directive, the 'principle of equal treatment' shall mean that there shall be no direct or indirect discrimination whatsoever on any of the forbidden grounds.

---

359. 24 January 2002, *Portugaia Construções Ld^a*, Case C-164/99, ECR, 2002, 787 and the references to case law.
360. O.J. L 303, 2 December 2000.

(2) There is:
- (a) *direct discrimination* when one person is treated less favourably than another is, has been or would be treated in a comparable situation, on any of the forbidden grounds
- (b) *indirect discrimination* when an apparently neutral provision, criterion or practice would put persons having a particular religion or belief, a particular disability, a particular age, or a particular sexual orientation at a particular disadvantage compared with other persons unless:
    - (i) that provision, criterion or practice is objectively justified by a legitimate aim and the means of achieving that aim are appropriate and necessary, or
- (c) ... *Harassment* shall be deemed to be a form of discrimination within the meaning of paragraph 1, when unwanted conduct related to any of the grounds referred to in Article 1 takes place with the purpose or effect of violating the dignity of a person and of creating an intimidating, hostile, degrading, humiliating or offensive environment. In this context, the concept of harassment may be defined in accordance with the national laws and practice of the Member States (Article 2).

§3. JUSTIFIED RESTRICTIONS AND UNEQUAL TREATMENT

899. The TFEU accepts certain restrictions to the freedom of services and also case law has recognised restrictions on the basis of the rule of reason, which amounts to justified unequal treatment.

I. Public Authority, Public Policy, Public Security or Public Health

A. Public Authority

900. According to Article 62 TFEU, which refers to Article 51 TFEU, 'shall the provisions concerning freedom of services not apply, so far as any given Member State is concerned, to activities which in that State are connected, even occasionally, with the exercise of official authority'. This applies to activities, which imply a direct and specific participation to the exercise of official authority in a given Member Sate, like the task of a Cabinet Officer, a member of parliament, a judge and the like.

B. Public Policy, Public Security or Public Health

901. According to Articles 52 and 62 TFEU 'shall the provisions concerning freedom of services and measures taken in pursuance thereof not prejudice the applicability of provisions laid down by law, regulation or administrative action providing for special treatment for foreign nationals on grounds of public policy, public security or public health.

This relates to basically the same restrictions as those, which prevail regarding free movement of workers, according to Article 45(3) TFEU. We therefore refer to what we said above.[361]

II. Restrictions on the Grounds of the Rule of Reason

902. Restrictions of the freedom of services are, according to the case law of the Court of Justice, justified when they respond to a number of conditions:

– applied without discrimination;
– justified by imperative reasons relating to the public interest;
– objectively necessary in order to ensure compliance with professional rules;
– not exceed what is necessary to attain those objectives'.

The Court of Justice ruled:

> Having regard to the particular characteristics of certain provisions of services, specific requirements imposed on the provider, which result from the application of rules governing those types of activities, cannot be regarded as incompatible with the Treaty. However, as a fundamental principle of the Treaty, the freedom to provide services may be limited only by rules which are justified by imperative reasons relating to the public interest and which apply to all persons or undertakings pursuing an activity in the State of destination, in so far as that interest is not protected by the rules to which the person providing the services is subject in the Member State in which he is established. In particular, those requirements must be objectively necessary in order to ensure compliance with professional rules and to guarantee the protection of the recipient of services and they must not exceed what is necessary to attain those objectives.[362]

903. This case law has been repeatedly confirmed:

> Even if there is no harmonisation in the field, the freedom to provide services, as one of the fundamental principles of the Treaty, may be restricted only by rules justified by overriding requirements relating to the public interest and applicable to all persons and undertakings operating in the territory of the State where the service is provided, in so far as that interest is not safeguarded by the rules to which the provider of such a service is subject in the Member State where he is established.
>
> The application of national rules to providers of services established in other Member States must be appropriate for securing the attainment of the objective

---

361. Part I. Chapter I, §2, III.
362. 25 July 1991, *Manfred Säger* v. *Dennemeyer & Co. Ltd.*, Case C-76/90, ECR, 1991, 4221.

Part I, Ch. 2, Freedom of Services

which they pursue and must not go beyond what is necessary in order to attain it.[363]

It is appropriate to consider the compatibility of the requirements at issue here with Article 56 TFEU in the light of those principles.[364]

Protection of workers belong to the overriding requirements relating to the public interest, which justify restrictions on the free movement of services. Let us see how the European Court has applied this principle.

§4. PROTECTION OF WORKERS[365]

I. Application of National Legislation and Collective Agreements: *Rush Portuguesa Lda*[366]

904. Union law does not preclude Member States from extending their legislation, or collective labour agreements entered into by both sides of industry, to any person who is employed, even temporarily, within their territory, no matter in which country the employer is established; nor does Union law prohibit Member States from enforcing those rules by appropriate means. This issue was raised in the *Rush Portuguesa Lda* case.

A. Facts

905. This case concerned *Rush Portuguesa Lda*, an undertaking established in Portugal specializing in construction and public works, and the Office national d'immigration. Rush Portuguesa entered into a subcontract with a French undertaking for the carrying out of works for the construction of a railway line in the west of France. For that purpose it brought its Portuguese employees from Portugal. This was the period that Portugal, which had only become a Member State of the EU, was in a transitional period as far as free movement of workers was concerned.

By virtue of the French Labour Code, only the *Office national d'immigration* may recruit in France nationals of third countries.

After establishing that Rush Portuguesa had not complied with the requirements of the Labour Code relating to the activities of employed persons, carried on in France by nationals of non-member countries, the Director of the *Office national d'immigration* notified Rush Portuguesa of a decision by which he required payment of a special contribution, which an employer employing foreign workers in breach of the provisions of the Labour Code is liable to pay.

---

363. Criminal proceedings against 23 November 1999 *Jean-Claude Arblade and Arblade & Fils SARL*, C-369/96 and *Bernard Leloup, Serge Leloup and Sofrage SARL*, C-376/96, ECR, 1999, 8453.
364. C.O.J., 21 October 2004, *Commission of the European Communities* v. *Grand Duchy of Luxemburg*, C-445/03, www.curia.eu.
365. See also Part I. Chapter 3, §3 on the posting of workers.
366. C.O.J., 27 March 1990, *Rush Portuguesa Lda* v. *Office national d'immigration*, C-113/89, ECR, 1990, 1417.

B. The Court of Justice

1. Equal Treatment

906. The Court observed first of all that the freedom to provide services laid down in Article 56 TFEU entails, according to Article 57 TFEU, that the person providing a service may, in order to do so, temporarily pursue his activity in the State where the service is provided 'under the same conditions as are imposed by that State on its own nationals'.

2. Free Movement of Workers: No Work Permit

907. The Treaty therefore precludes a Member State from prohibiting a person providing services established in another Member State from moving freely on its territory with all his staff and preclude that Member State from making the movement of staff in question subject to restrictions such as a condition as to engagement in situ or an obligation to obtain a work permit. To impose such conditions on the person providing services established in another Member State discriminates against that person in relation to his competitors established in the host country who are able to use their own staff without restrictions, and moreover affects his ability to provide the service.

3. Freedom of Services: Return to their Country of Origin

908. In contrast with free movement of workers, there is a temporary movement of workers who are sent to another Member State to carry out construction work or public works as part of a provision of services by their employer. In fact, such workers return to their country of origin after the completion of their work without at any time gaining access to the labour market of the host Member State.

Finally, the Court concluded, it should be stated, in response to the concern expressed in this connection by the French Government, that Union law does not preclude Member States from extending their legislation, or collective labour agreements entered into by both sides of industry, to any person who is employed, even temporarily, within their territory, no matter in which country the employer is established; nor does Union law prohibit Member States from enforcing those rules by appropriate means.

The Court has already taken such a point of view in 1982 in the *Seco* case, regarding minimum wages.[367]

909. As a general rule prevails that a Member State can extend its legislation, collective labour agreements included, to workers from another Member State who work within the framework of the freedom of services work in that Member State.

---

367. C.O.J., 9 August 1994, *Raymond Vander Elst v. Office des Migrations Internationales*, C-43/93, ECR, 1994, 3803.

II. Fine Tuning of the General Rule

910. The general approach by the Court that a Member State has the right to impose its own legislation and collective agreements to workers from another Member State, who perform in that Member State, had of course to be fine tuned.

It is indeed self evident that national legislation can not be imposed when the interests of the worker, in so far as that interest is not safeguarded by the rules to which the provider of such a service, is subject in the Member State where he is established.

A. *The Vander Elst Case*

911. This issue was raised in proceedings between Mr. Vander Elst, an employer of Belgian nationality established in Belgium, and the *Office des Migrations Internationales* (International Migration Office, hereinafter 'OMI'), a French body attached to the Ministry of Employment and responsible *inter alia* for the recruitment of foreign workers in France. The question was whether the requirement of work permits was justified.

1. Facts

912. Mr. Vander Elst operates a specialist demolition business in Brussels. In addition to Belgian nationals, the business has for several years continuously employed Moroccan nationals, who are legally resident in Belgium, hold Belgian work permits, are covered by the Belgian social security scheme and are paid in Belgium.

In 1989, the Vander Elst business carried out demolition work involving the recovery of materials on a building in Reims called 'Château Lanson'. The work took one month. In order to carry out the work, Mr. Vander Elst put a team of eight persons on site, who were regular employees and of whom four were Belgian and four Moroccan. For the latter, he had previously obtained short-stay visas, valid for one month, from the French Consulate in Brussels.

French employment inspectors found that the Moroccan workers employed by Mr. Vander Elst and working on the site did not have work permits issued by the French authorities. According to the inspectors, a short-stay visa was not sufficient to enable them to take up paid employment in France.

The French Labour Code provides that all aliens wishing to take up paid employment in France must submit 'an employment contract countersigned by the administrative authorities or a work permit and a medical certificate', in addition to the documents and corresponding visas. The penalty for failure to comply with those provisions, is payment of a special contribution to the OMI, the amount of which may not be less than 500 times the guaranteed minimum hourly.

The French employment inspectors considered that Mr. Vander Elst had infringed the French Labour Code by employing in France nationals of non-member countries who had no corresponding work permits, without informing the OMI. On the basis of the report drawn up by the inspectors, the OMI accordingly demanded a special contribution.

Mr. Vander Elst lodged an administrative appeal. In support of his action, he claimed in particular that the contested provisions of the French Labour Code constituted a barrier to the freedom to provide services, which was incompatible with Article 56 *et seq.* TFEU.

2. The Court

913. The Court ruled as follows.

Work permits and obligation to pay a fee considerable financial burden

First, the Court says that the requirement in France that undertakings should obtain work permits in order to employ nationals of non-member countries is coupled with the obligation to pay a fee which, like the heavy administrative fine imposed for non-compliance with that obligation, may entail a considerable financial burden for employers.

Right to Enter the Territory

914. Furthermore, it should be borne in mind that the nationals of Member States of the Union have the right to enter the territory of the other Member States in the exercise of the various freedoms recognised by the Treaty and in particular the freedom to provide services which, according to settled case law, is enjoyed both by providers and by recipients of services.

The Abolition of any Restriction and Equal Treatment

915. Article 56 TFEU therefore requires not only the elimination, against a person providing services who is established in another Member State, of all discrimination on the ground of his nationality but also the abolition of any restriction, even if it applies without distinction to national providers of services and to those of other Member States, when it is liable to prohibit or otherwise impede the activities of a provider of services established in another Member State where he lawfully provides similar services.

Administrative Licence Constitutes a Restriction

916. Similarly, the Court has already held that national legislation which makes the provision of certain services on national territory by an undertaking established in another Member State subject to the issue of an administrative licence constitutes a restriction on the freedom to provide services within the meaning of Article 56 TFEU. Furthermore, it is apparent that legislation of a Member State which requires undertakings established in another Member State to pay fees in order to be able to employ in its own territory workers in respect of whom they are already liable for the same periods of employment to pay similar fees in the State in which they are established proves financially to be more onerous for those employers, who in fact have to bear a heavier burden than those established within the national territory.

Reasons in the General Interest

917. Finally, as one of the fundamental principles of the Treaty, freedom to provide services may be restricted only by rules which are justified by overriding reasons in the general interest and are applied to all persons and undertakings operating in the territory of the State where the service is provided.

Practical Effectiveness

918. In any event, as the Court has emphasised on several occasions, a Member State may not make the provision of services in its territory subject to compliance with all the conditions required for establishment and thereby deprive of all practical effectiveness the provisions whose object is to guarantee the freedom to provide services.

Moroccan Workers Lawfully Resident in Belgium

919. In the circumstances, it is important to note, first, that the Moroccan workers employed by Mr. Vander Elst were lawfully resident in Belgium, the State in which their employer was established and where they had been issued with work permits.

Short-stay Visas: Valid Documents

920. Secondly, it is apparent from the documents and hearings before the Court that the short-stay visas held by the persons concerned, issued by the French Consulate at their request, constituted valid documents permitting them to remain in France for as long as was necessary to carry out the work. Consequently, the national legislation applicable in the host State concerning the immigration and residence of aliens had been complied with.

Return to their Country of Origin: Work Permit Contrary to the Freedom of Servives

921. Finally, as regards the work permits which are the focus of the main proceedings, they are required in order for a national of a non-member country to be employed by an undertaking established in France, whatever the nationality of the employer, because a short-stay visa is not equivalent to a permit.

Such a system is intended to regulate access to the French labour market for workers from non-member countries.

Workers employed by an undertaking established in one Member State who are temporarily sent to another Member State to provide services do not in any way seek access to the labour market in that second State, if they return to their country of origin or residence after completion of their work. Those conditions were fulfilled in the present case.

In those circumstances, the requirements at issue go beyond what may be laid down as a precondition for the provision of services. Accordingly, those requirements are contrary to Articles 56 and 57 TFEU.

Minimum Wages

922. As is clear from the case law of the Court, Union law does not preclude Member States from extending their legislation, or collective labour agreements entered into by both sides of industry relating to minimum wages, to any person who is employed, even temporarily, within their territory, no matter in which country the employer is established; nor does Union law prohibit Member States from enforcing those rules by appropriate means.

The Application of the Belgian System Excludes any Substantial Risk of Exploitation

923. It is also important to note that, in this case, the Moroccan workers possess valid employment contracts governed by Belgian law and all discrimination based on nationality between Union workers and those of Moroccan nationality, as regards working conditions or remuneration, and also in the field of social security, was to be eliminated.

As the Advocate General has rightly observed, irrespective of the possibility of applying national rules of public policy governing the various aspects of the employment relationship to workers sent temporarily to France, the application of the Belgian system in any event excludes any substantial risk of workers being exploited or of competition between undertakings being distorted.

Decision: No Work Permit, nor Fine

924. The answer to the questions referred to the Court must therefore be that Articles 56 and 57 TFEU are to be interpreted as precluding a Member State from requiring undertakings which are established in another Member State and enter the first Member State in order to provide services, and which lawfully and habitually employ nationals of non-member countries, to obtain work permits for those workers from a national immigration authority and to pay the attendant costs, with the imposition of an administrative fine as the penalty for infringement.

Part I, Ch. 2, Freedom of Services

B. *The Arblade Case*

925. Another example of the fine tuning of the general principle that the legislation and collective agreements of the work land are the general rule is the *Arblade* Case,[368] a typical Belgian-Franco case.

1. Facts

926. Arblade and Leloup carried out works in connection with the construction of a complex of silos, with a capacity of 40,000 tonnes, for the storage of white crystallised sugar on the site belonging to Sucrerie Tirlemontoise at Wanze in Belgium.

To that end, Arblade deployed a total of 17 workers on that site. In the course of checks carried out on the site the representatives of the Belgian Social Law Inspectorate requested Arblade and Leloup to produce various social documents provided for under the Belgian legislation.

Arblade and Leloup considered that they were not obliged to produce the documents requested. They maintained, first, that they had complied with all the French legislation and, second, that the Belgian legislation and rules in issue were contrary to Articles 56 and 57 TFEU. Leloup did produce the staff register kept pursuant to French law.

2. Legislation and Collective Agreements of the Work Land

Country of Origin or Work Land?

927. Arblade and Leloup were prosecuted in Belgium for non-compliance with the obligations imposed by the Belgian legislation as the civilly liable party for failure to comply with various social obligations provided for by Belgian legislation, an offence punishable by penalties under Belgian public-order legislation.

The National Legislation

928. The obligations concerning the drawing-up, keeping and retention of social and labour documents, minimum remuneration in the construction industry and the systems of *timbres-intempéries* (bad weather stamps) and *timbres-fidélité* (loyalty stamps), and the monitoring of compliance with those obligations, are imposed by the following legislation:

– the Law of 8 April 1965 introducing labour regulations;
– the Law of 16 November 1972 concerning the Labour Inspectorate;
– Royal Decree No. 5 of 23 October 1978 concerning the keeping of social documents;

---

368. *Op. cit.*

- the Royal Decree of 8 August 1980 concerning the keeping of social documents;
- the Collective Labour Agreement of 28 April 1988, concluded under the *aegis* of the Construction Sector Joint Committee, concerning the award of *timbresfidélité* and *timbres-intempéries* ('the CLA of 28 April 1988') and rendered compulsory by the Royal Decree of 15 June 1988);
- the Royal Decree of 8 March 1990 concerning the keeping of individual records for workers and
- the Collective Labour Agreement of 28 March 1991 concluded under the aegis of the Construction Sector Joint Committee, concerning working conditions ('the CLA of 28 March 1991') and rendered compulsory by the Royal Decree of 22 June 1992.

Various Aspects of that Legislation are Relevant for the Purposes of the Present Judgment

929. First, a system has been organised for monitoring compliance with the legislation relating to the keeping of social documents, hygiene and medical care in the workplace, employment protection, labour rules and employment relationships, safety in the workplace, social security and social assistance. Employers are under an obligation not to hinder such surveillance (Royal Decree No. 5 of 23 October 1978 and the Law of 16 November 1972).

Second, in view of the compulsory effect given to the CLA of 28 March 1991 by royal decree, construction undertakings carrying out work in Belgium are required, whether or not they are established in that State, to pay their workers the minimum remuneration fixed by that agreement.

Third, under the CLA of 28 April 1988, which has been given compulsory effect by royal decree, such undertakings are required to pay, in relation to their workers, contributions to the *timbres-intempéries and timbres-fidélité schemes*.

In that connection, the employer is required to issue to each worker an 'individual record' (Article 4(3) of Royal Decree No. 5 of 23 October 1978). That record, which may be provisional or definitive, must contain the information listed in the Royal Decree of 8 March 1990. It must be validated by the Construction Workers' Subsistence Protection Fund, which will do so only if the employer has paid, in particular, all the contributions due in respect of *timbres-intempéries* and *timbres-fidélité*, together with the sum of BEF 250 for each record submitted.

930. Fourth, the employer is required to draw up work rules binding on him *vis-à-vis* his workers and to keep a copy of those regulations in each place where he employs workers (Law of 8 April 1965).

Fifth, the employer is required to keep a 'staff register' in respect of all his workers (Article 3(1) of the Royal Decree of 8 August 1980); this must contain various items of compulsory information (Articles 4 to 7 of that decree).

In addition, an employer who employs workers in more than one workplace must keep a 'special staff register' in each of those places apart from the place in which he keeps the 'staff register' (Article 10 of the Royal Decree of 8

August 1980). In certain circumstances, employers who employ workers to carry out construction works are exempt from the obligation to keep the special register in each workplace, provided that they maintain, in respect of each employee working there, an 'individual document' containing the same information as that contained in the special register (Article 11 of that decree).

The employer is also required to draw up, in relation to each worker, an 'individual account' (Article 3(2) of the Royal Decree of 8 August 1980). That document must contain various items of compulsory information concerning, in particular, the worker's remuneration (Articles 13 to 21 of the Royal Decree of 8 August 1980).

931. Sixth, the staff register and the individual accounts must be kept either at one of the workplaces, or at the address in Belgium at which the employer is registered in the records of a body responsible for the collection of social security contributions, or at the place of residence or registered office of the employer in Belgium, or, in the absence thereof, at the place of residence in Belgium of a natural person who, as the employer's agent or servant, keeps the staff register and the individual accounts. In addition, the employer is required to give advance notice, by registered letter, to the Chief District Inspector of the Social Law Inspectorate of the Ministry of Employment and Labour for the district in which those documents are to be kept (Articles 8, 9 and 18 of the Royal Decree of 8 August 1980).

An employer established in another Member State, who employs workers in Belgium is required in any event to appoint an agent or servant to keep the relevant documents either at one of the workplaces or at his place of residence in Belgium.

932. Seventh, the employer is required to retain, for a period of five years, the social documents comprising the staff register and the individual accounts, in the form of originals or copies thereof, either at the address in Belgium at which he is registered in the records of a body responsible for the collection of social security contributions, or at the seat of the approved employers' social secretariat to which he is affiliated, or at the place of residence or registered office of the employer in Belgium, or, in the absence thereof, at the place of residence in Belgium of a natural person who, as the employer's agent or servant, keeps the staff register and the individual accounts.

However, if the employer ceases to employ workers in Belgium, he is required to keep those documents at his place of residence or registered office in Belgium or, failing that, at the place of residence of a natural person in Belgium. The employer is required to give advance notice to the Chief District Inspector of the Social Law Inspectorate of the Ministry of Employment and Labour for the district in which the documents are to be kept (Articles 22 to 25 of the Royal Decree of 8 August 1980).

The abovementioned obligations concerning the retention of social documents become applicable only where an employer established in another Member State ceases to employ workers in Belgium.

933. Eighth, criminal penalties for infringement of the aforesaid provisions are laid down.

Lastly, all legislation providing for the protection of workers constitutes public-order legislation within the meaning of the first paragraph of Article 3 of the Belgian Civil Code, to which all persons within the territory of Belgium are therefore subject.

3. The Court

934. The Court answered as follows:

(1) Articles 56 and 57 TFEU do not preclude the imposition by a Member State on an undertaking established in another Member State, and temporarily carrying out work in the first State, of an obligation to pay the workers deployed by it the minimum remuneration fixed by the collective labour agreement applicable in the first Member State, provided that the provisions in question are sufficiently precise and accessible that they do not render it impossible or excessively difficult in practice for such an employer to determine the obligations with which he is required to comply.
(2) These articles preclude the imposition by a Member State on an undertaking established in another Member State, and temporarily carrying out work in the first State, of an obligation – even if laid down in public-order legislation – to pay, in respect of each worker deployed, employers' contributions to schemes such as the Belgian *timbres-intempéries and timbres-fidélité schemes*, and to issue to each of such workers an individual record, where the undertaking in question is already subject, in the Member State in which it is established, to obligations which are essentially comparable, as regards their objective of safeguarding the interests of workers, and which relate to the same workers and the same periods of activity.
(3) Articles 56 and 57 TFEU preclude the imposition by a Member State on an undertaking established in another Member State, and temporarily carrying out work in the first State, of an obligation – even if laid down in public-order legislation – to draw up social or labour documents such as work rules, a special staff register and an individual account for each worker in the form prescribed by the rules of the first State, where the social protection of workers which may justify those requirements is already safeguarded by the production of social and labour documents kept by the undertaking in question in accordance with the rules applying in the Member State in which it is established.
(3) That is the position where, as regards the keeping of social and labour documents, the undertaking is already subject, in the Member State in which it is established, to obligations which are comparable, as regards their objective of safeguarding the interests of workers, to those imposed by the legislation of the host Member State, and which relate to the same workers and the same periods of activity.

Part I, Ch. 2, Freedom of Services

(4) Articles 56 and 57 TFEU do not preclude the imposition by a Member State on an undertaking established in another Member State, and temporarily carrying out work in the first State, of an obligation to keep social and labour documents available, throughout the period of activity within the territory of the first Member State, on site or in an accessible and clearly identified place within the territory of that State, where such a measure is necessary in order to enable it effectively to monitor compliance with legislation of that State which is justified by the need to safeguard the social protection of workers.

(5) These articles preclude the imposition by a Member State on an undertaking established in another Member State, and temporarily carrying out work in the first State, of an obligation – even if laid down in public-order legislation – to retain, for a period of five years after the undertaking in question has ceased to employ workers in the first Member State, social documents such as a staff register and individual accounts, at the address within that Member State of a natural person who holds those documents as an agent or servant.

Concluding:

935. The question is whether the legislation of the work land are necessary and proportionate in relation to the objective, namely the protection of workers.

The Court rules, after consideration:

– payment of the minimum remuneration: yes; – payment of contributions to the *timbres-intempéries* and *timbres-fidélité* schemes: no;
– the drawing-up of individual records: no; – the keeping of social documents: yes;
– the retention of social documents during a period of five years: no.

C. The André Mazzoleni Case[369]

1. Facts

936. ISA, which is established in Mont-Saint-Martin, France, employed 13 workers as security officers at a shopping mall in Belgium.

Some of those workers were employed full-time in Belgium, while others were employed there for only some of the time and also worked in France.

In the course of a check, the Belgian Social Law Inspectorate requested Mr. Mazzoleni to produce various documents required by Belgian legislation, in particular pay slips.

---

369. C.O.J., 15 March 2001, Criminal proceedings against André Mazzoleni and Inter Surveillance Assistance SARL C-165/98, ECR, 2001, 2189.

Proceedings were brought against Mr. Mazzoleni and ISA before the *Tribunal Correctionnel* for failure to fulfil the obligation to pay a wage which was not below the minimum hourly rate of pay fixed by the CLA. Mr. Guillaume and four more of the 13 workers concerned claimed civil damages.

2. Minimum Remuneration

937. The question is seeking essentially to ascertain whether an undertaking established in a frontier region, some of whose employees may be required to perform, on a part-time basis and for brief periods, a part of their services in the adjacent territory of a Member State other than that in which the undertaking is established, is required to comply with the host Member State's national rules on minimum wages where the workers enjoy comparable overall protection in the Member State of establishment although the minimum wage there is lower.

3. General Principles

Justified by Overriding Requirements Relating to the Public Interest

938. The Court answered as follows:

the freedom to provide services, as one of the fundamental principles of the Treaty, may be restricted only by rules justified by overriding requirements relating to the public interest and applicable to all persons and undertakings operating in the territory of the State where the service is provided, in so far as that interest is not safeguarded by the rules to which the provider of such a service is subject in the Member State where he is established.

Appropriate and not go Beyond What is Necessary

939. The application of the national rules of a Member State to providers of services established in other Member States must be appropriate for securing the attainment of the objective which they pursue and must not go beyond what is necessary in order to attain it.

The overriding reasons relating to the public interest which have been recognised by the Court include the protection of workers.

As regards more specifically national provisions relating to minimum wages, such as those at issue in the main proceedings, it is clear from the case law of the Court that Union law does not preclude Member States from extending their legislation, or collective labour agreements entered into by both sides of industry, relating to minimum wages, to any person who is employed, even temporarily, within their territory, regardless of the country in which the employer is established. It follows that the provisions of a Member State's legislation or collective labour agreements which guarantee minimum wages may

Part I, Ch. 2, Freedom of Services

in principle be applied to employers providing services within the territory of that State, regardless of the country in which the employer is established.

Minimum Remuneration

940. It follows that Union law does not preclude a Member State from requiring an undertaking established in another Member State which provides services in the territory of the first State to pay its workers the minimum remuneration fixed by the national rules of that State.

However, there may be circumstances in which the application of such rules would be neither necessary nor proportionate to the objective pursued, namely the protection of the workers concerned.

If such be the circumstances, even if it be accepted that the rules of the host Member State imposing a minimum wage have the legitimate objective of protecting workers, the national authorities of that State must, before applying them to a service provider established in an adjacent region of another Member State, consider whether the application of those rules is necessary and proportionate for the purpose of protecting the workers concerned.

Equivalent Position

941. The host Member State's objective of ensuring the same level of welfare protection for the employees of such service providers as that applicable in its territory to workers in the same sector may be regarded as attained if all the workers concerned enjoy an equivalent position overall in relation to remuneration, taxation and social security contributions in the host Member State and in the Member State of establishment.

Additional, Disproportionate Administrative Burden – Cohesion of the Collective Labour Agreements

942. Furthermore, application of the host Member State's national rules on minimum wages to service providers established in a frontier region of a Member State other than the host Member State may result, first, in an additional, disproportionate administrative burden including, in certain cases, the calculation, hour-by-hour, of the appropriate remuneration for each employee according to whether he has, in the course of his work, crossed the frontier of another Member State and, second, in the payment of different levels of wages to employees who are all attached to the same operational base and carry out identical work. That last consequence might, in its turn, result in tension between employees and even threaten the cohesion of the collective labour agreements that are applicable in the Member State of establishment.

Necessary and Proportionate

943. It is therefore incumbent on the competent authorities of the host Member State, for the purpose of determining whether application of its rules

imposing a minimum wage is necessary and proportionate, to evaluate all the relevant factors.

That evaluation means that they must take account, in particular, of the duration of the provision of services, of their predictability, and of whether the employees have actually been sent to work in the host Member State or continue to be attached to the operational base of their employer in the Member State in which it is established.

Equivalent

944. In order to ensure that the protection enjoyed by employees in the Member State of establishment is equivalent, they must, in particular, take account of factors related to the amount of remuneration and the work-period to which it relates, as well as the level of social security contributions and the impact of taxation.

Accordingly, the answer to the second question must be that Articles 56 and 57 TFEU do not preclude a Member State from requiring an undertaking established in another Member State which provides services in the territory of the first State to pay its workers the minimum remuneration fixed by the national rules of that State. The application of such rules might, however, prove to be disproportionate where the workers involved are employees of an undertaking established in a frontier region who are required to carry out, on a part-time basis and for brief periods, a part of their work in the territory of one, or even several, Member States other than that in which the undertaking is established. It is consequently for the competent authorities of the host Member State to establish whether, and if so to what extent, application of national rules imposing a minimum wage on such an undertaking is necessary and proportionate in order to ensure the protection of the workers concerned.

D. Finalarte Sociedade de Construção Civil Lda[370]

1. Holiday Entitlement for Construction Workers in Germany

945. This case concerns employers established in a Member State other than the Federal Republic of Germany who posted workers to Germany, and who received demands from the fund to pay contributions and to provide information for the calculation of those contributions pursuant to the *Verfahrenstarifvertrag* (Collective Agreement on the social fund scheme, 'the VTV').

The scheme of paid leave for workers in the construction industry is governed, in Germany, by the *Mindesturlaubsgesetz für Arbeitnehmer – Bundesurlaubsgesetz*

---

370. C.O.J., 25 October 2001, *Finalarte Sociedade de Construção Civil Lda* (C-49/98), *Portugaia Construções Lda* (C-70/98) and *Engil Sociedade de Construção Civil SA* (C-71/98) v. *Urlaubsund Lohnausgleichskasse der Bauwirtschaft and Urlaubsund Lohnausgleichskasse der Bauwirtschaft* v. *Amilcar Oliveira Rocha* (C-50/98), *Tudor Stone Ltd.* (C-52/98), *TecnambTecnologia do Ambiente Lda* (C-53/98), *Turiprata Construções Civil Lda* (C-54/98), *Duarte dos Santos Sousa* (C-68/98) and *Santos & Kewitz Construções Lda* (C-69/98), ECR, 2001, 7831.

(Law on minimum holiday entitlement for workers) and by the *Bundesrahmentarifvertrag für das Baugewerbe* (Collective framework agreement for the construction industry, the 'BRTV-Bau').

It is implemented by means of a system of funds for paid leave governed, in all essential respects, by the VTV. The State Secretary, Federal Ministry of Labour and Social Affairs, extended the scope of the VTV and the BRTV-Bau to the whole of the construction industry.

In the construction industry workers change employers frequently. For that reason, the BRTV-Bau provides that the various employment relationships entered into by the worker during the reference year are to be treated as if they were a single employment relationship. This fiction enables the worker to accumulate holiday entitlement acquired with different employers in the course of the reference year and to claim that full entitlement from his current employer, irrespective of the duration of the employment relationship with that employer.

The ordinary consequence of that system would be to impose a heavy financial burden on the current employer because he is required to pay the worker holiday pay even for holiday acquired with other employers. The fund was established in order to overcome this drawback and to ensure an equitable distribution of the financial burden between the employers concerned.

To this end, employers established in Germany pay contributions to the fund amounting to 14.45 per cent of their total gross wages. In return the employers are entitled, *inter alia*, to full or partial reimbursement of the benefits paid to workers in respect of holiday pay and additional holiday allowance.

Every month employers must disclose certain information to the fund to enable it to ascertain their total monthly gross wages and to calculate the amount of contributions due.

The Posting of Workers

946. The *Arbeitnehmerentsendegesetz* (Law on the posting of workers) of 26 February 1996 (BGBl. I, p. 227, the 'AEntG') applies the provisions of the collective agreements concerning entitlement to paid leave in the construction industry, with effect from 1 March 1996, and, subject to certain conditions, to employment relationships between undertakings whose registered office is situated outside Germany and workers they send to carry out construction work on sites in Germany.

Employers established outside Germany are thereby required to contribute to the holiday pay funds scheme.

Differences for the Employers Established Abroad

947. None the less there are differences between the scheme applying to employers established in Germany and that applying to other employers. First, in contrast to the scheme for employers established in Germany, the employer established abroad is not entitled to claim reimbursement from the fund. It is always the posted worker himself who is entitled under the VTV to receive holiday pay from the fund.

Second, employers established outside Germany must disclose more information to the fund than those established in Germany.

Third, 'business' is given a different meaning depending on whether the employer is established in Germany or not.

By contrast, it appears from paragraph 7 of the BRTV-Bau that, to ascertain whether an employer established in Germany is subject to the collective agreements of the construction industry, a construction site or even the workers deployed exclusively on a construction site are not regarded as a business. It is the organisational entity from which workers are posted to a construction site that constitutes the business.

2. The Main Proceedings and the Questions

948. Of the employers who are parties to the main proceedings, eight are established in Portugal and one in the United Kingdom. During 1997 they each posted workers to Germany to carry out construction work.

The fund requires that these employers contribute to the scheme to finance the holiday entitlement of construction workers.

In order to prepare the collection of contributions due, as laid down by those provisions, it requests these employers to provide certain information set out in the VTV.

949.

Following Questions were Submitted to the Court for a preliminary ruling:

(1) On a proper construction of Articles 54, 66 and 75 TFEU, are those provisions infringed by a provision of national law – the first sentence of paragraph 1(3) of the AEntG – which extends the application of provisions of collective agreements which have been declared generally binding concerning the collection of contributions and the grant of benefits in connection with workers' holiday entitlements by joint bodies of parties to collective agreements, and thus the provisions of those agreements concerning the scheme to be complied with in that regard, to employers established abroad and their workers who have been posted to the area within which those collective agreements apply?

(2) On a proper construction of Articles 54, 56 and 75 TFEU, are those provisions infringed by the second sentence of paragraph 1(1) and the first sentence of paragraph 1(3) of the AEntG which result in the application of provisions of collective agreements declared to be generally binding which:
  (a) provide for leave which exceeds the minimum length of annual leave laid down by Council Directive 93/104/EC of 23 November 1993 concerning certain aspects of the organisation of working time; and/or

Part I, Ch. 2, Freedom of Services

    (b) allow employers established in Germany to claim the reimbursement of expenditure on holiday pay and holiday allowances from joint bodies of the parties to the collective agreements whereas, in the case of employers established abroad, they do not provide for such a claim but instead for a direct claim by the posted workers against the joint bodies of the parties to the collective agreements; and/or

    (c) in connection with the social fund scheme to be complied with under those collective agreements, impose on employers established abroad obligations to provide the joint bodies of the parties to the collective agreements with more information than that required from employers established in Germany?

(3) On a proper construction of Articles 54, 56 and 75 TFEU, are those provisions infringed by paragraph 1(4) of the AEntG under which – for the purposes of classifying businesses as covered by a collective agreement which has been declared generally binding and which, under the first sentence of Paragraph 1(3) of that Law, also applies to employers established abroad and their workers who have been posted to the area within which that collective agreement applies – all workers posted to Germany, but only those workers, are treated as a business, while a different definition of a business applies to employers established in Germany which in certain cases results in different businesses falling within the scope of the generally binding collective agreement?

(4) Is Article 3(1)(b) of Directive 96/71/EC of the European Parliament and of the Council of 16 December 1996 concerning the posting of workers in the framework of the provision of services to be interpreted as in any event, having regard to the correct interpretation of Articles 54, 56 and 75 TFEU, neither requiring nor permitting the rules at issue in Questions 1, 2 and 3?

3. The Answers of the Court

No Access to the Labour Market

950. The Court has held that workers employed by a business established in one Member State who are temporarily sent to another Member State to provide services do not, in any way, seek access to the labour market in that second State if they return to their country of origin or residence after completion of their work.

The Abolition of any Restriction-equal Treatment

951. According to settled case law, Article 56 TFEU requires not only the elimination of any discrimination on grounds of nationality against providers of services who are established in another Member State but also the abolition of any restriction, even if it applies without distinction to national providers of services and to those of other Member States, which is liable to prohibit,

impede or render less advantageous the activities of a provider of services established in another Member State where he lawfully provides similar services.

Practical Effect

952. In particular, a Member State may not make the provision of services in its territory subject to compliance with all the conditions required for establishment and thereby deprive the provisions of the Treaty whose object is, precisely, to guarantee the freedom to provide services, of all practical effect.

In that regard, the application of the host Member State's national rules to providers of services is liable to prohibit, impede or render less attractive the provision of services to the extent that it involves expense and additional administrative and economic burdens.

Overriding Requirements Relating to the Public Interest

953. The freedom to provide services, as one of the fundamental principles of the Treaty, may be restricted only by rules justified by overriding requirements relating to the public interest and applicable to all persons and businesses operating in the territory of the State where the service is provided, in so far as that interest is not safeguarded by the rules to which the provider of such a service is subject in the Member State where he is established.

Be Appropriate

954. The application of the national rules of a Member State to providers of services established in other Member States must be appropriate for securing the attainment of the objective which those rules pursue, and must not go beyond what is necessary in order to attain it.

Protection of Workers

955. Overriding reasons relating to the public interest already recognised by the Court include the protection of workers.

Necessary, Effectively and Appropriate

956. Such a restriction of the freedom to provide services is justifiable only if it is necessary in order to pursue, effectively and by appropriate means, an objective in the public interest.

Unfair Competition

957. In this respect, the national court points out that it appears from the explanatory memorandum of the AEntG that the declared aim of that law is to protect German businesses in the construction industry from the increasing

Part I, Ch. 2, Freedom of Services

pressure of competition in the European internal market, and thus from foreign providers of services. The national court adds that, from the start of discussions on the draft of that law, it had been pointed out on numerous occasions that such a law would, above all, combat the allegedly unfair practice of European businesses engaged in low-pay competition.

Cannot be Justified by Economic Aims

958. According to settled case law, measures restricting the freedom to provide services cannot be justified by economic aims, such as the protection of national businesses.

Significantly Adds to Their Social Protection

959. In this respect, it is necessary to check whether those rules confer a genuine benefit on the workers concerned, which significantly adds to their social protection. In this context, the stated intention of the legislature may lead to a more careful assessment of the alleged benefits conferred on workers by the measures it has adopted.

It is for the national court to consider whether such potential benefits confer real additional protection on posted workers. That assessment must take account, first, of the protection as to paid leave that workers already enjoy under the law of the Member State where their employer is established, since the rules at issue in the main proceedings cannot be regarded as conferring real additional protection on posted workers if the latter enjoy the same protection, or essentially similar protection, under the legislation of the Member State where their employer is established.[371]

---

371. An action against the Federal Republic of Germany was brought before the Court of Justice of the European Communities on 29 November 2004 by the Commission of the European Communities, The applicant claims that the Court should:
    (1) declare that, by providing that
        (a) foreign undertakings are obliged to pay contributions to the German holiday pay fund for their posted workers, even if they enjoy an essentially similar level of protection under the law of the State where their employer is established;
        (b) foreign undertakings are obliged to have the employment contract (or the documents required, pursuant to Directive 91/533/EEC, under the law of the State where the employee is resident), pay slips, time sheets, proof of payment of wages, and all other documents required by the German authorities, translated into German;
        (c) foreign employment agencies are obliged not only to give prior notification each time a worker is posted to a user of the worker's services in Germany, but also each time a worker starts a new job on a building site at the request of the user of his services; the Federal Republic of Germany has failed to fulfil its obligations under Article 56 TFEU.
            Pleas in Law and Main Arguments
            The Commission contends that furthermore certain provisions of the AEntG which transposed Directive 96/71/EC on the posting of workers into national law do not comply with certain provisions of that directive.
            Rules relating to the obligation of employers established in a Member State other than Germany to pay contributions to the German holiday pay fund
            In the Commission's view, the obligation to pay contributions to the German holiday pay fund constitutes an inadmissible restriction on the freedom to provide services,

It is important to check that, when workers have returned to the Member State where their employer is established, the workers concerned are genuinely able to assert their entitlement to holiday pay from the fund, having regard, in particular, to the formalities to be observed, the language to be used and the procedure for payment.

Balance

960. A balance should be made between the administrative and economic burdens that the rules impose on providers of services against the increased social protection that they confer on workers compared with that guaranteed by the law of the Member State where their employer is established.

Similar Level of Protection and Proportionate

961. The TFEU does not preclude a Member State from imposing national rules guaranteeing entitlement to paid leave for posted workers, on a business established in another Member State which provides services in the first Member State by posting workers for that purpose, on the two-fold condition that: (i) the workers do not enjoy an essentially similar level of protection under the law of the Member State where their employer is established, so that the application of the national rules of the first Member State confers a genuine benefit on the workers concerned, which significantly adds to their social protection, and (ii) the application of those rules by the first Member State is proportionate to the public interest objective pursued.

---

within the meaning of Article 56 TFEU, where employers who post their workers grant them the same paid holiday entitlement as that laid down by the German rules contained in the collective agreements and, under the legal system in the State from which they are posted, such workers enjoy the same or similar protection with respect to holiday pay as is guaranteed in Germany.

Rules relating to the obligation of employers established in a Member State other than Germany to translate documents.
In the Commission's view, the requirement for documents to be translated is appropriate to meeting Germany's monitoring needs. However, having regard to the cooperation on information provided for by Article 4 of the Directive on the posting of workers, the obligation to translate all documents is no longer necessary and is therefore too far-reaching.

Rules relating to the obligation of employment agencies established in a Member State other than Germany to notify the competent authorities of the change before each transfer of a posted worker from one building site to another one.
Even if the obligation of employment agencies established outside Germany to notify each change has been slightly amended, the Commission is of the view that there is still unequal treatment, as, in the case of employment agencies established in Germany, the obligation to notify each change falls on the user of the worker's services, while in the case of employment agencies established outside Germany that obligation falls in principle on the supplier of labour and can be transferred to the user of the worker's services only by means of a contractual agreement. This unequal treatment constitutes an inadmissible restriction on the freedom to provide services within the meaning of Article 56 TFEU (Case C-490/04).

Part I, Ch. 2, Freedom of Services

Longer Period of Paid Leave

962. The Treaty does not preclude the extension of the rules of a Member State which provide for a longer period of paid leave than that provided for by Directive 93/104 to workers posted to that Member State by providers of services established in other Member States during the period of the posting.

Claim Reimbursement from the Fund

963. Articles 56 and 57 TFEU do not preclude national rules from allowing businesses established in the Federal Republic of Germany to claim reimbursement of expenditure on holiday pay and holiday allowances from the fund, whereas it does not provide for such a claim in the case of businesses established in other Member States, but instead provides for a direct claim by the posted workers against the fund, in so far as that is justified by objective differences between businesses established in the Federal Republic of Germany and those established in other Member States.

Provide more Information to the Fund than Employers Established in Germany

964. In this respect, it should be accepted that rules designed to provide effective protection of workers in the construction industry, in particular as regards their entitlement to paid holiday, does require that certain information be supplied. More specifically, such a requirement may be the only appropriate measure of control having regard to the objective pursued by those rules.

Nevertheless, an obligation of the kind imposed by the rules at issue in the main proceedings, to disclose certain information to the authorities of the host Member State, gives rise to additional expense and administrative and economic burdens for businesses established in another Member State.

The fact that businesses established outside the Federal Republic of Germany are given additional burdens in terms of the information to be disclosed therefore, a fortiori, constitutes a restriction on the freedom to provide services within the meaning of Article 56 TFEU.

Such a restriction may be justified only if it is necessary in order to safeguard, effectively and by appropriate means, the overriding public interest of the social protection of workers.

Furthermore, the fact that businesses established outside the Federal Republic of Germany are not subject to the same obligations to provide information may be attributed to objective differences between those businesses and businesses established in Germany.

Control

965. By contrast, the duty to disclose specific documents to the Member State cannot be justified if that State can perform the necessary checks on the

basis of the documents required by the rules of the Member State of establishment.

It is for the national court to determine the type of information that the German authorities may reasonably require of providers of services established outside the Federal Republic of Germany, having regard to the principle of proportionality. For this purpose, the national court should consider whether the objective differences between the position of businesses established in Germany and that of businesses established outside Germany objectively require the additional information required of the latter.

Part of Activities

966. The Treaty precludes the application of a Member State's scheme for paid leave to all businesses established in other Member States providing services to the construction industry in the first Member State where businesses established in the first Member State, only part of whose activities are carried out in that industry, are not all subject to that scheme in respect of their workers engaged in that industry.

E. *The* Portugaia Construções Lda *Case*[372]

1. Facts

967. Portugaia is a company established in Portugal. Between March and July 1997, it carried out structural building work in *Tauberbischofsheim*. In order to carry out that work, it posted a number of its workers to that building site.

In March and May 1997, the *Arbeitsamt* (Employment Office) in *Tauberbischofsheim* carried out an investigation into the employment conditions on that building site. On the basis of the documentation submitted by Portugaia, it concluded that Portugaia was paying the workers who had been the object of the inspection a wage lower than the minimum wage payable under the collective agreement. It accordingly ordered payment of the sum outstanding, that is to say the difference between the hourly wage payable and that actually paid, multiplied by the total number of hours worked, making a total sum of DEM 138,018.52.

Preliminary Question

968. Is an interpretation of Directive 96/71/EC of the European Parliament and of the Council of 16 December 1996 concerning the posting of workers in the framework of the provision of services … or, if that directive is not applicable, an interpretation of Article 66 *et seq.* TFEU, under which overriding requirements of public interest capable of justifying a restriction on the freedom to provide services in cases involving the posting of employees can lie

---

372. C.O.J., 24 January 2002, *Portugaia Construções Ld^a*, C-164/99, ECR, 2002, 787.

Part I, Ch. 2, Freedom of Services 969–973

not only in the social protection of the employees posted but also in the protection of the national construction industry and the reduction in national unemployment for the purpose of preventing social tension, consistent with Community law?

2. The Answer of the Court

Principle: no Discrimination nor Restriction

969. It is settled case law that Article 56 of the Treaty requires not only the elimination of all discrimination on grounds of nationality against providers of services who are established in another Member State, but also the abolition of any restriction, even if it applies without distinction to national providers of services and to those of other Member States, which is liable to prohibit, impede or render less attractive the activities of a provider of services established in another Member State in which he lawfully provides similar services.

Practical Effectiveness

970. In particular, a Member State may not make the provision of services in its territory subject to compliance with all the conditions required for establishment, thereby depriving of all practical effectiveness the provisions of the Treaty whose object is, precisely, to guarantee the freedom to provide services.

Expenses and Additional Administrative and Economic Burdens

971. In that regard, the application of the host Member State's domestic legislation to service providers is liable to prohibit, impede or render less attractive the provision of services by persons or undertakings established in other Member States to the extent that it involves expenses and additional administrative and economic burdens.

Overriding Requirements Relating to the Public Interest

972. However, it clear from settled case law that, where such domestic legislation is applicable to all persons and undertakings operating in the territory of the Member State in which the service is provided, it may be justified where it meets overriding requirements relating to the public interest in so far as that interest is not safeguarded by the rules to which the provider of such a service is subject in the Member State in which he is established and in so far as it is appropriate for securing the attainment of the objective which it pursues and does not go beyond what is necessary in order to attain it.

The Protection of Workers

973. Overriding reasons relating to the public interest which have been recognised by the Court include the protection of workers.

Minimum Remuneration

974. As regards, more specifically, national provisions relating to minimum wages, such as those at issue in the main proceedings, it is clear from the case law of the Court that in principle Community law does not preclude a Member State from requiring an undertaking established in another Member State which provides services in the territory of the first State to pay its workers the minimum remuneration laid down by the national rules of that State.

In other words, it may be acknowledged that, in principle, the application by the host Member State of its minimum-wage legislation to providers of services established in another Member State pursues an objective of public interest, namely the protection of employees.

Exceptions

975. However, there may be circumstances in which the application of such rules would not be in conformity with Articles 56 and 57 of the Treaty.

Protection of Domestic Businesses

976. It is therefore for the national authorities or, as the case may be, the courts of the host Member State, before applying the minimum-wage legislation to service providers established in another Member State, to determine whether that legislation does indeed pursue an objective of public interest and by appropriate means.

In the present case, the national court points out that, according to the stated grounds of the AEntG, the purpose of that Law is to protect the domestic construction industry and to reduce unemployment in order to avoid social tensions.

However, according to settled case law, measures forming a restriction on the freedom to provide services cannot be justified by economic aims, such as the protection of domestic businesses.

Whilst the intention of the legislature, as apparent from the statement of the grounds on which a Law was adopted, may be an indication of the aim of that Law, that declared intention is not conclusive.

Objectively

977. It is, however, for the national court to determine whether, viewed objectively, the rules in question in the main proceedings promote the protection of posted workers.

Genuine Benefit

978. As the Court has already held, it is necessary to determine whether those rules confer a genuine benefit on the workers concerned, which significantly augments their social protection. In this context, the stated intention of

the legislature may lead to a more careful assessment of the alleged benefits conferred on workers by the measures which it has adopted.

It follows from the foregoing considerations that the answer to be given to the first question must be that, in assessing whether the application by the host Member State to service providers established in another Member State of domestic legislation laying down a minimum wage is compatible with Articles 56 and 57 of the Treaty, it is for the national authorities or, as the case may be, the national courts to determine whether, considered objectively, that legislation provides for the protection of posted workers. In that regard, although the declared intention of the legislature cannot be conclusive, it may nevertheless constitute an indication as to the objective pursued by the legislation.

Pay Wages Lower than the Minimum Wage

979. By its second question, the national court asks essentially whether the fact that a domestic employer may, in concluding a collective agreement specific to one undertaking, pay wages lower than the minimum wage laid down by a collective agreement declared to be generally binding, whilst an employer established in another Member State cannot do so, constitutes an unjustified restriction on the freedom to provide services.

As regards the substance of the matter, the fact that, unlike an employer from the host Member State, an employer established in another Member State has no possibility of avoiding the obligation to pay the minimum wage laid down by the collective agreement governing the economic sector concerned creates unequal treatment contrary to Article 56 of the Treaty. It must be emphasised in this regard that no ground of justification provided for by the Treaty has been invoked.

The reply to be given to that question must therefore be that the fact that, in concluding a collective agreement specific to one undertaking, a domestic employer can pay wages lower than the minimum wage laid down in a collective agreement declared to be generally applicable, whilst an employer established in another Member State cannot do so, constitutes an unjustified restriction on the freedom to provide services.

F. Commission v. Federal Republic of Germany[373]

980. In this case the Federal Republic of Germany was condemned because it does not respect the freedom of services by imposing that construction undertakings established in other Member States

(a) may not provide transfrontier services on the German market as part of a consortium unless they have their seat or at least an establishment in Germany

---

373. C.O.J., 25 October 2001, *Commission v. Federal Republic of Germany*, Case C-493/99, ECR, 2001, 8163.

employing their own staff and have concluded a company-wide collective agreement for those staff;
(b) may not contract out workers from another country to other construction undertakings unless they have their seat or at least an establishment in Germany employing their own staff and, as members of a German employers' association, are covered by framework and social-welfare collective agreements;
(c) may not establish in Germany a subsidiary recognised as a construction undertaking if its staff is entrusted solely with work on administration, marketing, planning, supervision and/or wages and salaries, but, in order to be so recognised, such an establishment must employ on the German labour market workers who spend more than 50 per cent of firm's total working time on building sites.

981. The Court of Justice ruled as follows:

Obstacle

982. Since contracting out workers constitutes a provision of services within the meaning of the Treaty, it is not disputed that the requirement to have an establishment in the territory of the Member State in which services are to be provided, laid down by the legislation at issue, constitutes an obstacle to exercise of the freedom to provide services.

Requirement of a Permanent Establishment

983. The requirement of a permanent establishment is the very negation of the fundamental freedom to provide services in that it results in depriving Article 56 of the Treaty of all effectiveness, a provision whose very purpose is to abolish restrictions on the freedom to provide services of persons who are not established in the State in which their services are to be provided. If such a requirement is to be accepted, it must therefore be shown that it constitutes a condition indispensable for attaining the objective pursued.

The Social Protection of Workers

984. It is true that the social protection of workers in the construction industry is one of the overriding reasons of public interest capable of justifying a restriction on the freedom to provide services. It is also true that, according to the case law of the Court, overriding reasons of public interest which justify the substantive provisions of a Member State's legislation may also justify measures necessary to check compliance with it.

Considerations of a Purely Administrative Nature

985. However, the Court has always emphasised that considerations of a purely administrative nature cannot make lawful a restriction of the freedom to provide services.

Part I, Ch. 2, Freedom of Services 986–989

Comparable Obligations

986. The Court has thus held that the Member State in which services are provided may not require an undertaking to keep documents specific to that State if that undertaking is already subject, in the Member State in which it is established, to obligations comparable, as regards their objective of safeguarding the interests of workers, in respect of the same workers and the same periods of activity, to those laid down by the legislation of the first Member State.

Beyond What is Necessary

987. It must be concluded that the requirement to have an establishment in the Member State in which the services are to be provided, such as that under the legislation in question, goes beyond what is necessary to attain the objective of providing social protection for workers in the building industry.

It has not been shown that such a requirement, imposed without distinction on any undertaking wanting to contract out workers to a consortium or to other undertakings in the building industry is in itself necessary to achieve the aim of providing social protection for workers in the building industry.

50 per cent of Working Time

988. The Commission contends, that in German law, only undertakings in which more than 50 per cent of working time is spent by workers on building sites may be regarded as construction undertakings. That condition makes it unattractive for construction undertakings established in other Member States to set up branches in the Federal Republic of Germany where those undertakings might wish to assign to their German branch only administrative or technical staff or sales staff responsible for advertising or launching projects. Since such a branch will not be considered to be a construction undertaking and cannot therefore benefit from the provisions of the legislation, it will not, in the event of a successful bid, be able to carry out the works required by transferring workers from other branches or from the parent company where these are established in Member States other than the Federal Republic of Germany.

On the other hand, according to the Commission, German branches of German construction undertakings are always treated as undertakings belonging to this sector, even if they do not strictly fulfil the rule requiring 50 per cent of working time to be spent on building sites. It means in substance, that undertakings, which in association with other construction undertakings, carry out, exclusively or principally, management, sales, planning or accounting tasks or perform laboratory analyses for members of that association are also to be regarded as construction undertakings.

Judgment

989. It is not in dispute that, in German law, a German branch of a construction undertaking established in a Member State other than the Federal

Republic of Germany is not regarded as belonging to that sector unless more than 50 per cent of total staff working time is spent by workers on construction sites.

This condition impedes the freedom of establishment for those undertakings through the creation of branches.

For one thing, that condition complicates access to the German market for those construction undertakings in that it makes treatment of their German branches as construction undertakings depend on fulfilment of criteria which those branches have difficulty in fulfilling.

For another thing, that condition is likely to be less onerous for undertakings from the Federal Republic of Germany than for undertakings from other Member States in so far as there is less need for German undertakings to assign administrative, technical and sales staff to their German branches because such tasks can be performed by the staff employed at the undertaking's seat in Germany.

990. The Court judged as follows:

(1) A Member State fails to fulfil its obligations under Article 56 of the Treaty where it provides in its legislation that construction undertakings established in other Member States may not provide transfrontier services on the national market as part of a consortium unless they have their seat or at least an establishment on its national territory employing their own staff and have concluded a company-wide collective agreement for those staff. Such an establishment requirement constitutes an obstacle to exercise of the freedom to provide services and goes beyond what is necessary to attain the objective of providing social protection for workers in the building industry.
(2) A Member State fails to fulfil its obligations under Article 56 of the Treaty where it provides in its legislation that construction undertakings established in other Member States may not contract out workers from another country to other construction undertakings unless they have their seat or at least an establishment in its national territory employing their own staff and, as members of a national employers' association, are covered by framework and social-welfare collective agreements. Such an establishment requirement constitutes an obstacle to exercise of the freedom to provide services and goes beyond what is necessary to attain the objective of providing social protection for workers in the building industry.
(3) A Member State fails to fulfil its obligations under the Treaty where it provides in its legislation that construction undertakings established in other Member States may not establish in its national territory a branch recognised as a construction undertaking if its staff is entrusted solely with work on administration, marketing, planning, supervision and/or wages and salaries, but in order to be so recognised, such an establishment must employ on the national labour market workers who spend more than 50 per cent of the firm's total working time on building sites.

(4) On the one hand, that condition complicates access to the national market for those construction undertakings in that it makes treatment of the branches established on its national territory as construction undertakings depend on fulfilment of criteria which those branches have difficulty in fulfilling. On the other hand, that condition is likely to be less onerous for undertakings from the first Member State than for undertakings from other Member States in so far as there is less need for the former undertakings to assign administrative, technical and sales staff to their national branches because such tasks can be performed by the staff employed at the undertaking's seat on national territory.

G. The European Commission v. Federal Republic of Germany[374]

991. In this case the Court ruled that the work regime applied by Germany to nationals of non-member states posted by service providers established in other Member States was contrary to the freedom to provide services. A simple prior declaration by the undertaking intending to post workers who are nationals of non-member states would be a less restrictive measure than the requirement of at least a year's prior employment by that undertaking. It would enable abuse and circumvention of the freedom to provide services to be prevented.

992. The posting of employed persons who are nationals of a non-member state is governed in Germany by the Law on Aliens. That law provides that foreigners intending to reside for more than three months on German territory and to pursue paid employment there must be in possession of a specific residence visa. Thus, undertakings wishing to provide services in Germany must ensure that their workers from non-member states obtain a visa from the German diplomatic representation in the Member State where the undertaking is established. As regards the detailed rules for the issue of that visa, a circular lays down that the German diplomatic representation is to satisfy itself, in advance, that, among other criteria, the worker has been employed for at least a year by the undertaking which intends to effect the posting.

Since it considered that the practice based on the checking of certain criteria, in advance of the posting, and restriction of posting to workers employed for at least a year by the provider, established in another Member State, amount to obstacles to the freedom to provide services, the Commission brought this action for failure to fulfil obligations against Germany before the Court of Justice of the European Communities.

---

374. C.O.J., 19 January 2006, *Commission of the European Communities* v. *Germany*, C-244/04, ECR, 2006, 885.

The Prior Nature of the Check

993. The Court of Justice finds, first of all, that such a prior check may make it more difficult, or even impossible, to exercise the freedom to provide services through posted workers who are nationals of non-member States.

It considers next whether such a prior check can be justified by a public interest objective and whether that check is necessary to pursue, effectively and by appropriate means, that objective. Germany relied on grounds relating to the prevention of abuse of the freedom to provide services, the protection of workers and legal certainty to justify the practice of a prior check.

The Court holds that the German authorities' practice exceeds what is necessary to prevent abuse and circumvention of the freedom to provide services. A requirement that the service provider furnish a simple prior declaration certifying that the situation of the workers concerned is lawful, particularly in the light of the requirements of residence, work visas and social security cover in the Member State where that provider employs them, would give the national authorities a guarantee that those workers' situation is lawful and that they are carrying on their main activity in the Member State where the service provider is established.

994. As regards the protection of workers, the Court points out that a prior declaration would enable the authorities to monitor compliance with German social welfare legislation during the deployment while taking account of the obligations by which that undertaking is already bound under the social welfare legislation applicable in the Member State of origin. It would be a more proportionate means because it is less restrictive than the requirement in question.

Finally, the check in advance cannot be justified by the necessity of ensuring that such posting is effected lawfully. It is for undertakings which do not comply with that legislation to bear the responsibility for a posting effected unlawfully.

The Requirement of at Least a Year's Prior Employment by the Undertaking Effecting the Posting.

995. The Court finds that such a requirement, which is a restriction on the freedom to provide services, is disproportionate in the light of the objective of the social welfare protection of workers who are nationals of non-member States and of the objective of seeking to ensure that the workers return to the Member State of origin at the ending of the posting.

As regards the defence based on the prevention of social dumping, the Court notes that the Member States may extend their legislation or collective agreements relating to minimum wages to any person who is employed, even temporarily, within their territory. In that regard, a prior declaration supplemented by the relevant information in respect of wages and employment conditions would constitute a measure less restrictive of the freedom to provide services.

Consequently, the Court concludes that Germany has infringed the provisions on the freedom to provide services.

H. The European Commssion v. Spain[375]

996. In this case the Court of Justice declared that, by maintaining in force provisions of Law on private security services which impose a series of requirements on foreign private security undertakings for the pursuit of their activities in Spain, namely the obligation:

– to be constituted as legal persons;
– to have a specific minimum share capital;
– to pay a security to a Spanish body;
– to employ a minimum number of workers, insofar as the undertaking in question carries out its activities in fields other than the transport and distribution of explosives; – generally, for members of their staff, to hold a special administrative authorisation issued by the Spanish authorities, and

by failing to adopt the provisions necessary to ensure recognition of attestations of professional competence for the pursuit of the activity of private detective, the Kingdom of Spain has failed to fulfil its obligations under Article 56 TFEU.

I. The European Commission v. Austria[376]

997. In a similar case the European Court of Justice declared that by making the posting of workers who are nationals of non-member states by an undertaking established in another Member State subject to obtaining the 'EU Posting Confirmation' provided for in the Austrian Law on the employment of foreign workers Austria has failed to fulfil its obligations under Article 49 EC (now Article 56 TFEU).

The issue of this EU Confirmation requires, first, that the workers concerned must have been employed for at least one year by that undertaking or must have concluded an employment contract of indefinite duration with it and, secondly, evidence that the Austrian employment and wage conditions are complied with.

By laying down a ground for the automatic refusal of an entry and residence permit, without exception, which does not allow the situation of workers from a non-Member State, lawfully posted by an undertaking established in another Member State, to be regularised when those workers have entered the national territory without a visa, the Republic of Austria has failed to fulfil its obligations under Article 56 TFEU.

---

375. C.O.J., 26 January 2006, *Commission of the European Communities* v. *Kingdom of Spain*, C514/03, ECR, 2006, 963.
376. C.O.J., 21 September 2006, *Commission of the European Communities* v. *Republic of Austria*, C-168/04, ECR, 2006, 9041.

J. The Viking[377] and the Laval Cases:[378] Freedom of Establishment and Services and Industrial Action

998. In both cases the fundamental question arrises whether trade unions can engage in collective action in order to enforce a provider of services or in case of freedom of establishment to live up to the local labour conditions which prevail.

1. The Viking Case

999. The International Transport Workers' Federation (ITF) is a federation of 600 transport workers' unions in 140 countries, based in London. One of its principal policies is the 'flag of convenience' (FOC) policy. According to this policy, so as to eliminate flags of convenience, unions in the country where beneficial ownership of the vessel is to be found, regardless of the flag of the vessel, have the right to conclude agreements covering that vessel.

1000. Viking Line, a Finnish ferry company, owns the Rosella, a Finnish-flagged ferry operating between Tallinn and Helsinki. It is crewed by members of the Finnish Seamen's Union (FSU) which is affiliated to the ITF.

In October 2003 Viking Line sought to reflag the loss-making Rosella, registering it in Estonia so as to allow Viking Line to employ an Estonian crew on the lower Estonian wages and therefore be able to compete with other ferries on the same route. This proposal was made known to the crew and the FSU, who opposed the reflagging. In November 2003, following a request from the FSU, the ITF sent a circular to all its members stating that the Rosella was beneficially owned in Finland and that therefore the FSU retained the negotiating rights. Affiliated unions were called upon not to enter into negotiations with Viking. Non-compliance with this circular could lead to sanctions and, potentially, exclusion from the ITF. This effectively prevented Viking Line from dealing with an Estonian union.

In December 2003, following threats of strike action by the FSU, Viking agreed to increase the crew numbers on the Rosella and not to commence reflagging before 28 February 2005. The ITF never withdrew its circular and therefore, as it still planned to reflag the loss-making Rosella at a later date, Viking Line brought the matter before the courts in England, where the ITF is based. Viking Line requested that the ITF be ordered to withdraw the circular and FSU be ordered not to interfere with Viking Line's rights to freedom of movement in relation to the reflagging of the Rosella.

---

377. 23 May 2007, *The International Transport Workers' Federation & The Finnish Seamen's Union v. Viking Line ABP & Ou Viking Line Eesti*, Advocate General's Opinion, C-438/05.
378. 23 May 2007, *Laval un Partneri Ltd v. Svenska Byggnadsarbetareförbundet and Others*, Advocate General's Opinion in Case C-341/05.

Part I, Ch. 2, Freedom of Services

1001. The Court of Appeal, before whom the case was brought on appeal by the FSU and ITF, has referred a number of questions to the Court of Justice for a preliminary ruling concerning the application of the Treaty rules on freedom of establishment to the case and whether the actions of the FSU and ITF constitute a restriction on freedom of movement.

1002. First, Advocate General Miguel Poiares Maduro states that, in his view, the Treaty rules on freedom of movement do apply to the situation in question. Public interests relating to social policy and fundamental rights may justify certain restrictions on freedom of movement, as long as they do not go beyond what is necessary. However, the fact that social policy is one of the aims of the TFEU does not mean that measures taken in this field are automatically excluded from the scope of the rules on freedom of movement.

Furthermore, Mr Poiares Maduro concludes that the provisions on freedom of movement should apply to situations involving two private parties where the action in question is capable of effectively restricting others from exercising their right to freedom of movement by raising an obstacle that they cannot reasonably circumvent. This is the case here, where the practical effect of the coordinated actions of the FSU and ITF is to render Viking Line's right to freedom of establishment subject to the FSU's consent.

1003. As to whether the actions in question strike a fair balance between the right to take collective action and the freedom of establishment, the Advocate General notes that a coordinated policy of collective action among unions normally constitutes a legitimate means to protect the wages and working conditions of seafarers. However, collective action that has the effect of partitioning the labour market and that impedes the hiring of seafarers from certain Member States in order to protect the jobs of seafarers in other Member States would strike at the heart of the principle of non-discrimination on which the common market is founded.

So far as concerns collective action to alleviate the adverse consequences of reflagging the *Rosella*, Mr Poiares Maduro points out that it is first for the national court to determine whether the action in question goes beyond what domestic law considers lawful, taking into account Union law. In this respect Union law does not preclude trade unions from taking collective action which has the effect of restricting the right of establishment of a company that intends to relocate to another Member State, in order to protect the workers of that company. However, collective action taken to prevent a company established in one Member State from lawfully providing its services in another Member State after relocation would be incompatible with Union law.

1004. Finally, the Advocate General recognises that the FSU, together with the ITF and its affiliated unions may use collective action as a means to improve the working conditions of seafarers throughout the Union. However, in the same way as there are limits to action at national level, there are limits to the right of collective action at European level. An obligation imposed on all national unions to support collective action by any of their fellow unions could easily be abused. Such a policy would be liable to protect the collective bargaining power of some national unions at the expense of the interests of others and to partition the labour market in breach of the rules on freedom of movement. By contrast, if the other unions were free to choose whether or not to participate in a given collective action then this danger would be prevented. It is for the national court to determine whether this is so in the present case.

1005. In a judgment of 11 December 2007 the Court decided that collective action seeking to induce a foreign undertaking to conclude a collective labour agreement with a trade union and liable to deter it from exercising its freedom of establishment was a restriction on that freedom.

Such a restriction may be justified on the basis of the protection of workers, provided that it is established that it is suitable for ensuring the achievement of the legitimate objective pursued and does not go beyond what is necessary to attain that objective.

The Court rules that collective action such as that envisaged by FSU has the effect of making less attractive, or pointless, Viking Line's exercise of its right to freedom of establishment, inasmuch as such action prevented both Viking Line and its Estonian subsidiary from enjoying the same treatment in the host Member State as other economic operators established in that state. Collective action taken in order to implement ITF's policy of combating the use of flags of convenience, which seeks, primarily, to prevent ship-owners from registering their vessels in a state other than that of which the beneficial owners of those vessels are nationals, must be considered to be at least liable to restrict Viking Line's exercise of its right of freedom of establishment.

It follows that such action constitutes a restriction on freedom of establishment. Such a restriction can be accepted only if it pursues a legitimate aim such as the protection of workers. It is for the national court to ascertain whether the objectives pursued by FSU and ITF by means of the collective action which they initiated concerned the protection of workers.

The Court states in this regard that, as regards the collective action taken by FSU, even if that action – aimed at protecting the jobs and conditions of employment of the members of that union liable to be adversely affected by the reflagging of the *Rosella* – could reasonably be considered to fall, at first sight, within the objective of protecting workers, such a view would no longer be tenable if it were established that the jobs or conditions of employment at issue were not jeopardised or under serious threat.

If it transpired that the jobs or conditions of employment at issue were in fact jeopardised or under serious threat, it would then have to be ascertained whether the collective action initiated by FSU is suitable for ensuring the achievement of the objective pursued and does not go beyond what is necessary to attain that objective.

In that regard, the Court points out that it is common ground that collective action, like collective negotiations and collective agreements, may, in the particular circumstances of the case, be one of the main ways in which trade unions protect the interests of their members. As regards the question of whether or not the collective action at issue in the main proceedings goes beyond what is necessary to achieve the objective pursued, it is for the national court to examine, in particular, first, whether, under the national rules and collective agreement law applicable to

Part I, Ch. 2, Freedom of Services

that action, FSU did not have other means at its disposal which were less restrictive of freedom of establishment in order to bring to a successful conclusion the collective negotiations entered into with Viking Line, and, secondly, whether that trade union had exhausted those means before initiating such action.

In relation to the collective action seeking to ensure the implementation of the policy in question pursued by ITF, the Court notes that, to the extent that that policy results in ship owners being prevented from registering their vessels in a state other than that of which the beneficial owners of those of vessels are nationals, the restrictions on freedom of establishment resulting from such action cannot be objectively justified. Nevertheless, the objective of that policy is also to protect and improve seafarers' conditions of employment.

The Court points out, however, that, in the context of its policy of combating the use of flags of convenience, ITF is required, when asked by one of its members, to initiate solidarity action against the beneficial owner of a vessel which is registered in a state other than that of which that owner is a national, irrespective of whether or not that owner's exercise of its right of freedom of establishment is liable to have a harmful effect on the work or conditions of employment of its employees. Therefore, the policy of reserving the right of collective negotiations to trade unions of the state of which the beneficial owner of a vessel is a national is also applicable where the vessel is registered in a state which guarantees workers a higher level of social protection than they would enjoy in the first state.

2. *The* Laval *Case*

1006. Directive 96/71 concerning the posting of workers provides that the guarantees given to posted workers are to be laid down by law, regulation or administrative action and/or, in the building sector, by collective agreements or arbitration awards that have been declared universally applicable.

1007. The Swedish Law on the posting of workers lays down the terms and conditions of employment applicable to posted workers, regardless of the law applicable to the contract of employment itself. In so doing, it refers to the terms and conditions of employment in relation to the matters listed in Directive 96/71, with the exception of that relating to the minimum rate of pay. The Law is silent regarding remuneration, which is traditionally governed in Sweden by collective agreements. On the other hand, Swedish law gives trade unions the right to take collective action, subject to certain conditions, with the aim of compelling an unaffiliated employer to sign a collective agreement.

1008. In May 2004, Laval un Partneri Ltd, a Latvian company, posted workers from Latvia to work on Swedish building sites. The works were undertaken by a subsidiary company named L&P Baltic Bygg AB. The works included the renovation and extension of school premises in the town of Vaxholm.

In June 2004, Laval and Baltic Bygg, on the one hand, and the Swedish building and public works trade union, *Svenska Byggnadsarbetareförbundet*, on the other, commenced negotiations with a view to concluding a tie-in to the collective agreement for the building sector. However, no agreement was reached.

On 2 November 2004, *Byggnadsarbetareförbundet* started collective action in the form of a blockade at all Laval building sites. The Swedish electricians' trade union joined the movement to express solidarity by stopping all electrical work being carried out on the Vaxholm work site. After the work on the site had been interrupted for some time, Baltic Bygg became the subject of liquidation proceedings. In the meantime, the Latvian workers posted by Laval to the Vaxholm site returned to Latvia.

The *Arbetsdomstolen*, before which Laval had brought proceedings relating *inter alia* to the legality of the collective action, asked the Court of Justice of the European Union whether Union law precluded such collective action.

1009. Mr Mengozzi first states that, in his opinion, the exercise by trade unions of a Member State of their right to take collective action in order to compel a foreign service provider to conclude a collective agreement in the Member State in which the service provider seeks to avail itself, in particular, of the freedom to provide services embodied in the Treaty, falls within the scope of Union law.

Next, he considers that the fact that Sweden leaves it to both sides of industry to determine terms and conditions of employment, in particular rules on pay, by means of collective agreements, cannot in itself constitute inadequate implementation of Directive 96/71, to such an extent that that Member State has waived the right to apply those terms and conditions to foreign service providers. In that regard, the Advocate General observes, in essence, that it is in particular by granting trade unions the right to take collective action to compel a service provider to subscribe to a rate of pay determined in accordance with a collective agreement which is applicable in practice to domestic undertakings in a similar situation, that the Kingdom of Sweden ensures that the objectives of the protection of workers and equal treatment between undertakings, to which Directive 96/71 refers, are achieved.

1010. Lastly, having examined collective actions and certain conditions which are specific to the collective agreement in the building sector in the light of the freedom to provide services, Mr. Mengozzi proposes that, where a Member State has no system for declaring collective agreements to be of universal application, Directive 96/71 and the freedom to provide services do not prevent trade unions from attempting, by means of collective action in the form of a blockade and solidarity action, to compel a service provider of another Member State to subscribe to a rate of pay determined in accordance with a collective agreement which is applicable in practice to domestic undertakings in the same sector that are in a similar situation and was concluded in the first Member State, to whose territory workers of the other Member State are posted. Collective action must, however, be motivated by publicinterest objectives, such as the protection of workers and the fight against social dumping, and must not be carried out in a manner that is disproportionate to the attainment of those objectives.

1011. When examining the proportionality of collective action, the Advocate General proposes that the national court should, in particular, verify whether the terms and conditions of employment laid down in the collective agreement for the building sector involve a real advantage significantly contributing to the social protection of posted workers and do not duplicate any identical or essentially comparable protection available to those workers under the legislation and/or collective agreement applicable to the service provider in the Member State in which it is established.

1012. In a judgment of 18 December 2007, the Court recalled that Sweden does not have a system for declaring collective agreements universally applicable, and, in order to avoid the creation of discriminatory situations, Swedish law does not require foreign undertakings to apply Swedish collective agreements, since not all Swedish employers are bound by a collective agreement. Nor does Swedish legislation not provide, however, for minimum rates of pay as referred to in the Article 3(1), first subparagraph, (c). Directive 96/71 provides the possibility to impose minimum wages in order to exclude social dumping between the country of origin and the host country. Sweden did not implement this possibility. Swedish trade unions cannot remedy this by imposing their local collective agreements by way of industrial action. Consequently, Sweden has to adopt either a legal minimum wage or the possibility of extending collective agreements.

1013. The Court ruled as follows. It first stated that the national court's *question* must be understood as asking, in essence, whether Article 56 TFEU, and Directive 96/71, do not allow a trade union, in a Member State in which the terms and conditions of employment, save for minimum rates of pay, are contained in legislative provisions, from attempting, by means of collective action in the form of blockaging sites to force a provider of services established in another Member State to enter into negotiations with it on the rates of pay for posted workers, and to sign a collective agreement, the terms of which lay down, as regards some of those matters, more favourable conditions than those resulting from the relevant legislative provisions, while other terms relate to matters not referred to in Article 3 of the directive.

1014. The Court answered that question as follows:

The Union legislature adopted Directive 96/71, with a view to laying down, in the interests of the employers and their personnel, the terms and conditions governing the employment relationship where an undertaking established in one Member State posts workers on a temporary basis to the territory of another Member State for the purposes of providing service.

It follows from recital 13 to Directive 96/71 that the laws of the Member States must be coordinated in order to lay down a nucleus of mandatory rules for minimum protection to be observed in the host country by employers who post workers there.

Nevertheless, Directive 96/71 did not harmonise the material content of those mandatory rules for minimum protection. That content may accordingly be freely defined by the Member States, in compliance with the Treaty and the general principles of Union law.

The first question must be examined with regard to the provisions of that directive interpreted in the light of Article 56 TFEU and, where appropriate, with regard to the latter provision itself.

The Possibilities Available to the Member States for Determining the Terms and Conditions of Employment Applicable to Posted Workers, Including Minimum Rates of Pay

1015. The Court noted, first, the fact that minimum rates of pay constitute the only term of employment which, in Sweden, is not laid down in accordance with one of the means provided for in Directive 96/71 and, second, the requirement imposed on Laval to negotiate with trade unions in order to ascertain the wages to be paid to its workers and to sign the collective agreement for the building sector.

It is clear from the file that the national authorities in Sweden have entrusted management and labour with the task of setting, by way of collective negotiations, the wage rates which national undertakings are to pay their workers and that, as regards undertakings in the construction sector, such a system requires negotiation on a case-by-case basis, at the place of work, having regard to the qualifications and tasks of the employees concerned.

As regards the requirements as to pay which can be imposed on foreign service providers, it should be recalled that the first subparagraph of Article 3(1) of Directive 96/71 relates only to minimum rates of pay. Therefore, that provision cannot be relied on to justify an obligation on such service providers to comply with rates of pay such as those which the trade unions seek in this case to impose in the framework of the Swedish system, which do not constitute minimum wages and are not, moreover, laid down in accordance with the means set out in that regard in Article 3(1) and (8) of the directive.

It must therefore be concluded that a Member State in which the minimum rates of pay are not determined in accordance with one of the means provided for in

Article 3(1) and (8) of Directive 96/71 is not entitled, pursuant to that directive, to impose on undertakings established in other Member States, in the framework of the transnational provision of services, negotiation at the place of work, on a case-by-case basis, having regard to the qualifications and tasks of the employees, so that the undertakings concerned may ascertain the wages which they are to pay their posted workers.

Assessment of the Collective Action at Issue in the Case in the Main Proceedings from the Point of View of Article 56 TFEU

1016. Although the right to take collective action must therefore be recognised as a fundamental right which forms an integral part of the general principles of Union law the observance of which the Court ensures, the exercise of that right may none the less be subject to certain restrictions. As is reaffirmed by Article 28 of the Charter of Fundamental Rights of the European Union, it is to be protected in accordance with Union law and national law and practices.

It follows that the fundamental nature of the right to take collective action is not such as to render Union law inapplicable to such action, taken against an undertaking established in another Member State which posts workers in the framework of the transnational provision of services.

It must therefore be examined whether the fact that a Member State's trade unions may take collective action in the circumstances described above constitutes a restriction on the freedom to provide services, and, if so, whether it can be justified.

It must be pointed out that the right of trade unions of a Member State to take collective action by which undertakings established in other Member States may be forced to sign the collective agreement for the building sector – certain terms of which depart from the legislative provisions and establish more favourable terms and conditions of employment as regards the matters referred to in Article 3(1), first subparagraph (a) to (g) of Directive 96/71 and others relate to matters not referred to in that provision – is liable to make it less attractive, or more difficult, for such undertakings to carry out construction work in Sweden, and therefore constitutes a restriction on the freedom to provide services within the meaning of Article 56 TFEU.

The same is all the more true of the fact that, in order to ascertain the minimum wage rates to be paid to their posted workers, those undertakings may be forced, by way of collective action, into negotiations with the trade unions of unspecified duration at the place at which the services in question are to be provided.

It is clear from the case-law of the Court that, since the freedom to provide services is one of the fundamental principles of the Union a restriction on that freedom is warranted only if it pursues a legitimate objective compatible with the Treaty and is justified by overriding reasons of public interest; if that is the case, it must be suitable for securing the attainment of the objective which it pursues and not go beyond what is necessary in order to attain it.

1017. In that regard, it must be pointed out that the right to take collective action for the protection of the workers of the host State against possible social dumping may constitute an overriding reason of public interest within the meaning of the case-law of the Court which, in principle, justifies a restriction of one of the fundamental freedoms guaranteed by the Treaty.

It should be added that the activities of the Union are to include not only an internal market characterised by the abolition, as between Member States, of obstacles to the free movement of goods, persons, services and capital, but also a policy in the social sphere. The Union is to have as its task, *inter alia*, the promotion of 'a harmonious, balanced and sustainable development of economic activities' and 'a high level of employment and of social protection'.

Since the Union has thus not only an economic but also a social purpose, the rights under the provisions of the TFEU on the free movement of goods, persons, services and capital must be balanced against the objectives pursued by social policy, which include, as is clear from the first paragraph of Article

151 TFEU, *inter alia*, improved living and working conditions, so as to make possible their harmonisation while improvement is being maintained, proper social protection and dialogue between management and labour.

It must be observed that, in principle, blockading action by a trade union of the host Member State which is aimed at ensuring that workers posted in the framework of a transnational provision of services have their terms and conditions of employment fixed at a certain level, falls within the objective of protecting workers.

However, as regards the specific obligations, linked to signature of the collective agreement for the building sector, which the trade unions seek to impose on undertakings established in other Member States by way of collective action such as that at issue in the case in the main proceedings, the obstacle which that collective action forms cannot be justified with regard to such an objective. With regard to workers posted in the framework of a transnational provision of services, their employer is required, as a result of the coordination achieved by Directive 96/71, to observe a nucleus of mandatory rules for minimum protection in the host Member State.

1018. Finally, as regards the negotiations on pay which the trade unions seek to impose, by way of collective action such as that at issue in the main proceedings, on undertakings, established in another Member State which post workers temporarily to their territory, it must be emphasised that Union law certainly does not prohibit Member States from requiring such undertakings to comply with their rules on minimum pay by appropriate means.

However, collective action cannot be justified in the light of the public interest objective where the negotiations on pay, which that action seeks to require an undertaking established in another Member State to enter into, form part of a national context characterised by a lack of provisions, of any kind, which are sufficiently precise and accessible that they do not render it impossible or excessively difficult in practice for such an undertaking to determine the obligations with which it is required to comply as regards minimum pay.

In the light of the foregoing, the answer to the first question must be that Article 56 TFEU and Directive 96/71 are to be interpreted as precluding a trade union, in a Member State in which the terms and conditions of employment covering the matters referred to in Article 3(1), first subparagraph, (a) to (g) of that directive are contained in legislative provisions, save for minimum rates of pay, from attempting, by means of collective action in the form of a blockade (*blockad*) of sites to force a provider of services established in another Member State to enter into negotiations with it on the rates of pay for posted workers and to sign a collective agreement the terms of which lay down, as regards some of those matters, more favourable conditions than those resulting from the relevant legislative provisions, while other terms relate to matters not referred to in Article 3 of the directive.

Part I, Ch. 2, Freedom of Services

3. *Laval* and *Viking*: Who Pays the Price?

a. Fundamental Rights

1019. Who cares about the workers of Laval? They came from the East, from Latvia, a new EU Member State. They were engaged by a Latvian company to build a school, near Stockholm in Sweden. Their Latvian trade union had concluded a collective agreement with their employer. They were going to make more money than by staying at home. How many they were we do not know.

Due to a boycott by a trade union of Swedish brother and sisters-workers their company became bankrupt and they lost their jobs. Whether they received any compensation from their bankrupt employer, we do not know either. Indeed, no one seems to care.

Most, if not all the attention, as well at national as at European level, went to the action of the Swedish trade union, which wanted to impose its own tariff agreement, which was considerably more expensive than the Latvian collective agreement. In fact, Swedish unions were defending their own interests and those of their members, even though Latvian workers would suffer and lose their jobs.

The issues at stake before the courts were social dumping by a cheaper labour force coming from an Eastern country and equal treatment – the right of workers to equal wages and conditions – the untouchability of the right to strike – a national prerogative – and the right for Sweden to impose its own industrial relations system.

And indeed, why would Latvian workers not be entitled to the same or similar wages and conditions as their Swedish brothers and sisters? Why would Swedish trade unions not be allowed to engage in the same industrial action regarding employers, regardless of the nationality of the workers they employ: equal treatment, why not? Why set up a double labour system in the same country? Why should the EU meddle in all this, especially since the EU Treaty clearly indicates that the EU is not competent to regulate remuneration, as well as freedom of association and strikes and lock-outs?

No wonder that quite a number of (older) EU Member States and especially all the trade unions were strongly pleading in this case for:

– equal treatment;
– the untouchability of the right to strike, as a fundamental human right;
– the right for a Member State to impose its own system of industrial relations.

b. Social Justice

1020. How strong these points may sound, they are wrong, not only for legal reasons, but also for societal reasons, namely for reasons of social justice.

Indeed, there has been, for more than fifty years now, a European common market, which provides for the right of EU citizens and employees to move freely in other Member States; start a business there, work permanently as well as the right to provide a service in another Member State. This common market has brought all of us of freedom, peace, more well-being and welfare. Although there are already 27 Member States, still many want to join the European Union.

The freedom of services has not only economic but also social advantages. It creates jobs. Today some 70 per cent of the jobs are service jobs. In order to create even more jobs we have to open the doors of the Member States, even more, so that workers have work, a more decent life and can contribute to the social security system in particular and overall welfare in general.

Freedom of services in the EU dates since 1957. One would think that this freedom – after more than fifty years – would function to perfection. However, nothing less is true. We needed the *Bolkestein* initiative and discussion and the related directive (2006) to try to do away with protective measures, prohibiting or limiting the freedom to provide services in other member states. Indeed, employers as well as employees and national social partners want to keep markets and jobs for themselves. Remember the conservative stand of most Western trade unions regarding the free movement of workers of the new Eastern Member States.

c. A Compromise

1021. One of the toughest problems over all those years related to which wages and working conditions and the industrial relations to apply to employers and employees coming from other Member States, within the framework of freedom of services. A lot of case law was developed, also by the European Court of Justice, trying to provide answers to these pressing queries. But these answers were insufficient and not comprehensive enough to answer the basic question which kind of working conditions would have to be mandatorily applied to employers and workers from other Member States, providing services.

The problem was and is not easy. Let us take a simple example. If the city of Brussels wants to build a new hospital, it has to publish a public tender and all construction companies from the EU Member States can submit a proposal and indicate for how much money they will build the hospital.

If a Portuguese construction firm submits a proposal, bringing with it Portuguese workers at Portuguese wages, the labour cost would be about 40 per cent of that of the Belgian workers. In that case Belgian construction companies, having to pay Belgian wages, would be unable to compete. If we asked the Portuguese construction firm to pay Belgian wages and conditions, that employer would be unable to compete, since on top of those wages, the Portuguese employer would have to pay travel expenses as well as housing for his Portuguese workers and he would not be able to compete, as costs would be exorbitant. So, what to do?

Consequently, the EU Member States looked for a compromise to solve this problem. It took them many years to agree on a solution. The agreement was reached in 1996, with the Directive of 16 December 1996, this is 12 years before Eastern European countries joined the Common market.

1022. The essence of Directive 96/71 is well known. It imposes a hard core of wages and conditions to be guaranteed to posted workers, such as minimum wages

Part I, Ch. 2, Freedom of Services

imposed by governmental rules or collective agreements, generally binding concerning building work. Workers can enjoy better conditions, which are provided by their home system. Receiving Member States can impose working conditions relating to (international) public order as well the core obligations, contained in generally binding collective agreements in sectors, other than the construction industry.

These are at the same time and minimum and maximum conditions. Some countries do not respect the directive and impose upon employers and their posted workers the same wages and almost all working conditions which prevail in the Member State. Thus Belgium, where an Act of 2002 imposes on all employees and workers, active in Belgium, all wages and conditions which are penally mandatory. The Belgian legislature pretends that all measures, penally sanctioned, belong to the public order. This is the case with all collective agreements, which are extended. They are penally sanctioned by fines and/or prison.

Thus also other working conditions, which exceed the core of the 1996 directive, are obligatory. Again, these measures in Belgium have been taken in order to protect the jobs for the locals. To this has to be added the fact that Belgium has prohibited the free movement of workers from Eastern Member States until 2011, although there is in Belgium a shortage of labour, especially for difficult to fill in jobs. Also for these jobs work permits have to been obtained. This all with the support of the Belgian trade unions. Belgium is a socially conservative country.

d. The Rule of Law: Limit on the Right to Strike

1023. This is the general framework in which the European Court had to deal with the *Laval* case, as well as the *Viking* and the *Rüffert* cases. There is freedom of services and posted workers are only guaranteed the minimum wages, which are generally binding. Fact is that this is not the case in Sweden. Sweden does not know a system of extending collective agreements to all enterprises of a given sector. In Sweden, the strong trade unions rely on their strength to impose the conditions they consider to be just and fair: this means practically the same as for Swedish workers.

1024. Was the industrial action, namely the boycott of Laval by the Swedish unions, compatible with the freedom of services? The Court said no, and rightly so. The boycott was contrary to the Directive 96/71, trying to impose conditions beyond the 'core' foreseen in Article 3, 7. Moreover, if the Court had judged otherwise, freedom of services from Eastern European countries would have virtually come to an end, as too expensive.

In doing so, the Court put certain limits to the right to strike: the right to strike has to respect the freedom of Latvian workers to work at the conditions, they negotiated at home and in line with the 96/71 Directive. If Sweden wants to make its minimum wages binding for posted workers, it has to extend its collective agreements or provide for a minimum legal wage.

e. *Viking*

1025. In the *Viking* case, the company was running at a loss due to the higher wages applicable under a collective bargaining agreement, governed by Finnish law, Therefore Viking Line ABP sought to reflag its vessel by registering it in Estonia.

f. Jobs and Solidarity

1026. In both cases, *Laval* and *Viking*, jobs were at a loss. In the Laval case the Latvian workers lost their job and in the Viking case Finnish workers risked losing their job as possibly workers from Estonia might have gained some.

The EU is still too much a region of nation states, without a lot of solidarity between them, neither between employers or between workers. Everyone is fighting for his own job. Pushing the European market, also the EU market of services would create more jobs for everyone. It is time to work for more European solidarity across borders, because in most cases workers pay the price of this lack of solidarity, usually the weakest ones, as the *Laval* case showed. The European Court took the right decision.

K. The Rueffert Case

1027. The *Dirk Rueffert* case[379] has important consequences for employment conditions. It focuses on the right of public authorities, when awarding contracts for work, to demand that tendering companies commit themselves to pay wages that are in line with rates already agreed through collective bargaining in the place where the work is done, or whether this could be outlawed as a restriction on the freedom to provide services under Article 56 TFEU.

Circumstances in the case: the company Objekt und Bauregie GmbH & Co secured a contract for building work in Germany, which it subcontracted to a Polish firm, with an undertaking that it would ensure compliance with wage rates already in force on the site through collective agreement. The contract was withdrawn when it was discovered that the 53 posted workers were in fact earning 46.57 per cent of the applicable minimum wage for the construction sector, and the Niedersachsen authority demanded costs. The company took legal action as a result.

1028. The Court of Justice ruled as folows:

> Article 3(7) of Directive 96/71 concerning the posting of workers in the framework of the provision of services cannot be interpreted as allowing the host Member State to make the provision of services in its territory conditional on the observance of terms and conditions of employment which go beyond the mandatory rules for minimum protection.

---

379. COJ, 3 April 2008, *Dirk Rüffert* v. *Land Niedersachsen*, C-346/06, ECR, 2008, 1989.

A Member State is not entitled to impose, pursuant to Directive 96/71, on undertakings established in other Member States, a rate of pay provided for by a collective agreement in force at the place where the services concerned are performed and not declared to be of general application, by requiring, by a measure of a legislative nature, the contracting authority to designate as contractors for public works contracts only contractors which, when submitting their tenders, agree in writing to pay their employees, in return for performance of the services concerned, at least the wage provided for in the collective agreement.

By requiring undertakings performing public works contracts and, indirectly, their subcontractors to apply the minimum wage laid down by such a collective agreement, such legislation may impose on service providers established in another Member State where minimum rates of pay are lower an additional economic burden that may prohibit, impede or render less attractive the provision of their services in the host Member State. Therefore, such a measure is capable of constituting a restriction within the meaning of Article 56 TFEU.

Such a restriction cannot be considered to be justified by the objective of ensuring the protection of workers inasmuch as the rate of pay fixed by such a collective agreement is applicable, as a result of the legislation at issue, only to a part of the construction sector, since, first, that legislation applies solely to public contracts and not to private contracts and, second, that collective agreement has not been declared universally applicable, and inasmuch as there is no evidence to support the conclusion that the protection resulting from such a rate of pay is necessary for a construction sector worker only when he is employed in the context of a public works contract but not when he is employed in the context of a private contract.

For the same reasons, the restriction also cannot be considered to be justified by the objective of ensuring protection for independence in the organisation of working life by trade unions.[380]

L. Commission v. Germany: *Documents: Temporary Agencies*

1029. In this case[381] the questions related to national legislation whereby:

- foreign undertakings are obliged to pay contributions to the German paid-leave fund even if the employees benefit from a comparable protection under the law of the State in which their employer is established;
- foreign undertakings are obliged to have the employment contract or the documents required, pursuant to Council Directive 91/533/EC of 14 October 1991 on an employer's obligation to inform employees of the conditions applicable to the contract or employment relationship under the law of the State where the

---

380. C.O.J., 3 April 2008, *Dirk Rüffert* v. *Land Niedersachsen*, C-346/06, ECR, 2008, 1989.
381. C.O.J., 18 July 2007. *Commission of the European Communities* v. *Germany*, Case C-490/04, ECR, 2007, 6095.

employee is resident, pay slips, time sheets, proof of payment of wages, and all other documents required by the German authorities, translated into German;
– foreign employment agencies are obliged not only to give prior notification each time a worker is posted to a user of the worker's services in Germany, but also each time a worker starts a new job on a building site at the request of the user of his services.

1030. The Court ruled as follows:

> A Member State which requires foreign employers employing workers in the national territory to translate into the language of that Member State certain documents required to be kept at the place of work for the duration of the posted workers' stay does not thereby fail to fulfil its obligations under Article 56 TFEU.
>
> It is true that the obligation thereby imposed constitutes a restriction on the freedom to provide services in that it involves additional expenses and an additional administrative and financial burden for undertakings established in another Member State, so that those undertakings do not find themselves on an equal footing, from a competitive point of view, with employers established in the host Member State and may thus be dissuaded from offering services in that Member State.
>
> That obligation may however be justified by a general-interest objective linked to the social protection of workers, since it enables the competent authorities of the host Member State to carry out the monitoring necessary to ensure compliance with relevant national provisions. In so far as it requires the translation of only a few documents and does not involve a heavy financial or administrative burden for the employer, it does not go beyond what is necessary to achieve the objective sought, which is social protection.
>
> A Member State requiring foreign temporary employment agencies to declare not only the start and end dates of the placement of a worker with a user of his services in the Member State concerned, but also the place of employment of that worker and any changes in that place, while similar undertakings established in that Member State are not required to fulfil that supplementary obligation, fails to fulfil its obligations under Article 56 TFEU.

M. Palhota *Case: No Prior Declaration to Posting (Belgium)*[382]

Facts

1031. Termiso Limitada, a Portuguese company, posted regularly Portuguese welders and fitters to the shipyard belonging to Antwerp Ship Repair NV to perform work on ships. During an inspection of that shipyard the Belgian inspection services found that 53 Portuguese workers from Termiso Limitada were working there and that none of those workers had been the subject of a

---

382. C.O.J., 7 October 2010, *Vítor Manuel dos Santos Palhota a.o.*, C-515/08, www.curia.

prior declaration of posting. In addition, the Portuguese foreman was unable to provide evidence of any Portuguese salary documents.

National legislation

1032. Article 8 of the Law of 5 March 2002 transposing Directive 96/71 and establishing a simplified regime for the keeping of social documents by undertakings posting workers to Belgium provides that employers satisfying the conditions referred to in Article 6b(2) of Royal Decree No 5 of 23 October 1978 concerning the keeping of social documents are not required, during the period fixed on the basis of that paragraph, to draw up, *inter alia*, the pay slip referred to in Article 15 of the Law of 12 April 1965 on the protection of workers' remuneration ('the payslip').

Article 9 of the Law of 5 March 2002 inserts in Royal Decree No 5 Chapter IIa containing, inter alia, Article 6b referred to, which sets out the simplified regime introduced by that law ('the simplified regime'). For the purposes of that chapter, Article 6b(1) defines employers, within the meaning of Royal Decree No 5, as those who employ within Belgian territory workers who either normally work in one or more countries other than the Kingdom of Belgium or were recruited in a country other than the Kingdom of Belgium.

1033. Under Article 6b(2), employers are relieved, during a specified period, of the requirement to draw up and keep the social documents provided for in Chapter II of Royal Decree No 5, including the individual account referred to in Article 4(1) thereof ('the individual account'), provided that, first, before the employees in question start work, the employers send the Belgian authorities a declaration of posting ('the prior declaration of posting') and, second, the employers keep available to those authorities copies of the documents provided for in the legislation of the country where they are established provided that those documents are equivalent to the individual account or to the pay slip ('the equivalent documents').

Under Article 2 of the Royal Decree of 29 March 2002 laying down rules for implementing the simplified regime for the drawing up and keeping of social docu ments for undertakings posting workers to Belgium and defining the activities in the field of construction referred to in the second paragraph of Article 6 of the Law of 5 March 2002 the period referred to in Article 6b(2) of Royal Decree No 5 is set at six months from the date on which the first worker posted to Belgium starts work.

1034. Under Article 3 of the Royal Decree of 29 March 2002, employers who employ workers posted to Belgium must, before the workers posted start work, send to the Social Laws Inspectorate, by letter, email or fax, a declaration of posting in accordance with Article 4 of that decree. The inspectorate must certify receipt and approval of the declaration within five working days of the date on which it was received, sending, by the same channels, a registration number to the employer, who may begin to employ the workers only after the date on which the registration number has been notified, failing which the employer will not be entitled to the dispensation from drawing up and keeping social documents provided for under the simplified regime.

1035. Article 4 of the Royal Decree of 29 March 2002 provides that the declaration of posting, which must be in accordance with the model annexed to the decree, must include the following information:

(1) with regard to the employer posting workers in Belgium: surname, first name, place of establishment or name or headquarters of the undertaking, the nature of its activity, the address, telephone number, fax number, email address and identification or registration number of the employer with the competent social security body in the State of origin;
(2) with regard to the employer's servant or agent who is responsible for keeping available the equivalent documents in accordance with Article 5[(1)] of the present decree: the surname, first name, company name, address, telephone and fax numbers, and email address;
(3) with regard to each employee posted to Belgium: the surname, name, domicile, date of birth, civil status, sex, nationality, address, telephone number, number and type of identity document, the date on which the employment contract was concluded, the date on which the employee began employment in Belgium and the work performed;
(4) with regard to the terms and conditions of employment applicable to the employees posted: the length of the working week and the hours of work;
(5) with regard to the posting: the type of services provided within the context of the posting, the starting date of the posting and its envisaged duration, and the place where the work is to be performed;
(6) With regard to the equivalent documents: the place where they are kept and retained, in accordance with Article 5 of the present Decree.

1036. Article 5 of that decree concerns the detailed rules for the keeping available and retention of the equivalent documents during the period of employment of workers posted to Belgium. Article 5(1) provides that copies of the equivalent documents must be kept available to the designated inspection services for the period of six months referred to in Article 2. Those copies are to be kept either at the workplace to which the worker is assigned in Belgium or at the Belgian address of a natural person who retains them as an agent or servant of the employer. Should they fail to comply with that obligation, employers must draw up and complete the individual account and payslip. Article 5(2) provides that, after that period of six months has passed, employers must retain the copies for a period of five years and, in addition, draw up the social documents provided for under Chapter II of Royal Decree No. 5 and also the pay slip.

1037. Article 6 of the Royal Decree of 29 March 2002 concerns the detailed rules for the keeping available and retention of the equivalent documents after the period of employment of the workers posted to Belgium. It provides that, at the end of the period of employment, employers must send by

Part I, Ch. 2, Freedom of Services

registered letter or lodge, with an acknowledgement of receipt, copies of the equivalent documents together with an inventory thereof at the Social Laws Inspectorate.

Question

1038. By its question, the referring Belgian court asks, in essence, whether Articles 56 TFEU and 57 TFEU preclude national legislation requiring an employer established in another Member State who posts workers to the territory of the first Member State to send a prior declaration of posting and also to keep available to the national authorities, during the posting, copies of documents equivalent to social or labour documents, such as an individual account or a pay slip, required under the law of the first Member State.

Restriction on the freedom to provide services

1039. It is clear that the procedure in Belgium cannot be considered to be merely a declaratory procedure. The mere transmission of information to the authorities of the Member State of destination and the certification of receipt are potentially capable of becoming mechanisms for verification and authorisation prior to commencement of the work. Since the notification must be issued before the posting can be carried out by an employer and is made only after verification by the national authorities of the conformity of the prior declaration of posting, a procedure of that kind must be regarded as an administrative authorisation procedure.

It follows that the requirement to send a prior declaration of posting and for notification of the registration number for that declaration, as provided for under the simplified regime, constitutes a restriction on the freedom to provide services within the meaning of Article 56 TFEU.

Although sending a prior declaration of posting is a suitable means of communicating the information above to the Belgian authorities, a registration and notification procedure, by virtue of which the declaration in question assumes the nature of an administrative authorisation procedure, goes beyond what is necessary in order to ensure that posted workers are protected.

1040. It follows that since a prior declaration enables compliance with the social welfare and wages legislation of the host Member State to be monitored during the posting, it constitutes a more proportionate means of attaining that objective than such authorisation or a prior check. In that connection, the Belgian Government itself does not state that the simplified regime has any purpose other than monitoring effectively the wages and working conditions of posted workers during the posting.

1041. The Court has held that the obligation to send, at the end of the period of employment, originals or copies of the documents which an employer is required to draw up under the legislation of the Member State of establishment, to the national authorities of the host Member State which may check them and, if necessary, retain them, is a less restrictive measure for monitoring compliance with rules concerning the protection of workers than an obligation on the employer to keep those documents in the territory of the host Member State after that period.

In the light of the foregoing, it is clear that such measures are proportionate to the aim of protecting workers.

1042. The answer to the question referred is therefore that:

– Articles 56 TFEU and 57 TFEU preclude national legislation requiring an employer, established in another Member State and posting workers to the territory of the first Member State, to send a prior declaration of posting, in so far as the employer must be notified of a registration number for the declaration before the planned posting may take place and the national authorities of that first State have a period of five working days from receipt of the declaration to issue that notification.
– Articles 56 TFEU and 57 TFEU do not preclude national legislation requiring an employer, established in another Member State and posting workers to the territory of the first Member State, to keep available to the national authorities of the latter, during the posting, copies of documents equivalent to the social or labour documents required under the law of the first Member State and also to send those copies to the authorities at the end of that period.

Concluding

1043. The posting declaration, as provided for in Belgium by the 2002 Act is contrary to European law. The Act needs to be rewritten. Less restrictive measures are indicated.

1044. Belgium was condemned again by the European Court[383] for adopting Articles 137(8), 138, third indent, 153 and 157(3) of the loi-programme (Programme Law) (I) of 27 December 2006, in the version in force since 1 April 2007 ('the provisions at issue' and 'the Programme Law' respectively), namely by imposing a prior declaration requirement on self-employed service providers established in Member States other than the Kingdom of Belgium in respect of their activity in Belgium ('the Limosa declaration), the Kingdom of Belgium has failed to fulfil its obligations under Article 56 TFEU.

1045. The Court repeated that It is settled case-law that Article 56 TFEU requires not only the elimination of all discrimination against providers of services on grounds of nationality or the fact that they are established in a Member State other than that where the services are to be provided, but also the abolition of any restriction, even if it applies without distinction to national providers of services and to those of other Member States, which is liable to prohibit, impede or render less

---

383. C.O.J., 19 December 2012, *European Commission* v. *Kingdom of Belgium*, C-577/10, www.curia.eu.

Part I, Ch. 2, Freedom of Services

advantageous the activities of a provider of services established in another Member State where he lawfully provides similar services.

1046. The Court indicated that it must be noted that the declaration requirement at issue means, for the persons referred to in Articles 137(8) and 138, third indent, of the Programme Law who reside or are established in a Member State other than the Kingdom of Belgium to register by creating an account before, in principle and in accordance with Article 153 of the Programme Law, then providing the Belgian authorities, before each supply of services on Belgian territory, with a certain amount of information such as the date, duration and place of the service which will be supplied, its nature and the identity of the legal or natural person receiving it. That information must be provided on a form which must preferably be completed online or, if that is impossible, which must be sent to the competent service by post or by fax. Failure to comply with those formalities is subject to criminal penalties laid down in Article 157(3) of the Programme Law.

1047. The formalities implied by the declaration requirement at issue are thus such as to impede the supply of services on the territory of the kingdom of Belgium by self-employed service providers established in another Member State. That obligation thus constitutes an obstacle to the freedom to provide services.

The same applies in the situation where a 'simplified' declaration is required. The self-employed service provider concerned is also required, after having registered by creating an account, to inform the Belgian authorities inter alia of the date, duration of his posting to Belgium and the type of service which he will supply. In addition, failure to comply with those requirements is also subject to criminal penalties laid down in Article 157(3) of the Programme Law.

1048. In that regard, it is appropriate to note that the objectives relied on in the present case by the Kingdom of Belgium can be taken into consideration as overriding requirements in the public interest which are capable of justifying a restriction on the freedom to provide services. On that point, it is sufficient to state that the objective of combating fraud, particularly social security fraud, and preventing abuse, in particular detecting 'bogus self-employed persons' and combating undeclared work, can form part not only of the objective of the financial balance of social security systems, but also of the objectives of preventing unfair competition and social dumping and protecting workers, including self-employed service providers.

1049. The fact, however, that self-employed service providers established in Belgium are not subject to strictly equivalent requirements, in particular as regards the information to be provided, to those following from the declaration requirement at issue for self-employed service providers established in another Member State may thus be attributed to objective differences between those two categories of self-employed service providers.

In those circumstances, the provisions at issue must be regarded as disproportionate since they go beyond what is necessary to achieve the objectives of public interest relied upon by the Kingdom of Belgium. Consequently, the declaration requirement at issue cannot be regarded as compatible with Article 56 TFEU.

It follows that the Commission's action should be upheld and that it should be declared that, by adopting the provisions at issue, namely by imposing a prior declaration requirement on self-employed service providers established in Member States other than the Kingdom of Belgium in respect of their activity in Belgium, the Kingdom of Belgium has failed to fulfil its obligations under Article 56 TFEU.

§5. BOLKESTEIN: THE DRAFT DIRECTIVE ON SERVICES[384]

1050. On 13 January 2004, the European Commission issued, on the initiative of Commissioner Fritz Bolkestein, a draft Directive on services in the internal market. This proposal was aimed at providing a legal framework that will eliminate the obstacles to the freedom of establishment for service providers and the free movement of services between the EU Member States. It covers services provided both to consumers and to businesses.

This is an important draft directive, as 70 per cent of the jobs are in the service sector and job growth is related to services, especially in the area of the personalised jobs.

The draft Directive covers any business activity that constitutes a service except for those services where there are already specific initiatives to complete the EU internal market (notably financial services, telecommunications and transport). It covers a wide range of activities, including: management consultancy; certification and testing; maintenance; facilities management and security; advertising services; recruitment services (including the services of temporary employment agencies); services provided by commercial agents; legal or tax consultancy; property services, such as those provided by estate agencies; construction services; architectural services; distributive trades; organisation of trade fairs and exhibitions; car hire; security services; tourist services, including travel agencies and tourist guides; audiovisual services; sports centres and amusement parks; leisure services; health services; and personal domestic services, such as assistance for old people.

1051. According to the Commission, the proposal covers all services that correspond to an economic activity within the meaning of the case law of the European Court of Justice. The draft does not, therefore, cover 'non-economic' services of 'general interest', such as state schools and welfare provision. It does, however, cover services of general interest if they are of an economic nature, such as postal services, energy and telecommunications, but only in so far as they are not covered by other specific EU legislation.

In total, the services covered by the proposal account for around 50 per cent of all economic activity in the EU.

---

384. Andrea Broughton, IRS, Controversy over draft Directive on services, www.eiro.eurofound.ie, 2004; *See*: 'Freedom of services in the European Union. Labour and Social Security Law', (Ed. R. Blanpain), *Bulletin of Comparative Labour Relations*, no. 58, Kluwer Law International, Deventer.

Part I, Ch. 2, Freedom of Services

1052. The Commission states that the establishment of a genuine internal market in services is indispensable to the achievement of the economic and social objectives set out by the Lisbon European Council summit in 2000. Therefore, in order to eliminate the obstacles to the freedom of establishment, the proposed Directive provides for a range of administrative simplification measures and the lifting of restrictive legal requirements that may still be in force in some Member States.

1053. Most controversially, however, the proposal provides for a number of measures aimed at eliminating obstacles to the free movement of services, including:

– the application of the 'country of origin' principle, according to which a service provider is subject only to the law of the country in which it is established and Member States may not restrict services from a provider established in another Member State. This principle is accompanied by derogations which are either general, or temporary or which may be applied on a case-by-case basis;
– the right of recipients to use services from other Member States without being hindered by restrictive measures imposed by the recipient's country or by discriminatory behaviour on the part of public authorities or private operators; – a mechanism to provide assistance to recipients that use a service provided by an operator established in another Member State; and
– in the case of the posting of workers in the context of the provision of services, the allocation of tasks between the Member State of origin and the Member State of destination and specification of the supervision procedures applicable.

1054. The Union of Industrial and Employers' Confederations of Europe (UNICE), stated its belief 'that an efficient internal market for services is of crucial importance for Europe's competitiveness'. UNICE's view is that 'the proposal is an appropriate basis for tackling a number of diverse obstacles in the heterogeneous services sectors' and would contribute to simplifying administrative burdens. It notes that small and medium-sized enterprises (SMEs) in particular would benefit from increased comparability between service providers.

However, UNICE also states that tackling a number of problems within a single instrument is an ambitious goal and that there is a need for clarification on many issues.

The draft Directive is proving to be extremely controversial among trade unions throughout Europe, some of which have been staging protests. They fear that it will result in service employers locating themselves in countries with the lowest fiscal, social and environmental requirements and subsequently extending from this base their activities throughout the whole of the EU.

1055. The European Trade Union Confederation (ETUC) said that it is gravely concerned about some of the provisions in the Commission's draft Directive on services in the internal market. It warns that they could speed up deregulation, seriously erode workers' rights and protection, and damage the supply of essential services to European citizens.

ETUC states that it 'acknowledges the important potential for job creation in many service sectors across Europe. It recognises efforts in the Commission's draft Directive to improve the efficiency of the internal market through reducing administrative costs and setting up single contact points for service providers. However, the draft as it stands is seriously flawed, and threatens to undermine existing collective agreements, national labour codes, and the success of the whole European social model. For these reasons, ETUC cannot support it, and has called for an urgent meeting with the European Council working group on competitiveness and growth to discuss its concerns.'

In particular, ETUC states that the proposal fails to distinguish between services of different kinds and with different objectives, and fails to make clear exactly which services it would cover. It stresses that 'European trade unions have long been calling for a framework Directive on services of general interest (SGI), covering healthcare and other essential services where a simple supplier-consumer relationship does not apply. In ETUC's view, these cannot be subject to the same rules as commercial services like retailing and property development, as proposed in the current draft.'

According to ETUC, the proposal for providers to be subject only to regulations in their 'country of origin' would allow organisations to shift their operational base to Member States with the lowest social and environmental standards, potentially leading to a downward spiral of deregulation with Member States competing against one another. ETUC believes that this principle could seriously damage the social cohesion of the EU.

1056. The Commission has declared itself to be surprised by the vehemence of the opposition to the proposal. In order to clarify the position and explain the likely impact of the Directive, it has produced a checklist in which it sets out its view on what the proposal will and will not do. It states that the proposal will:

– help boost economic growth and sustainable jobs by laying the foundations for a real European internal market for services;
– make it easier for business, and particularly SMEs, to provide services throughout the EU, thus improving quality and choice for customers;
– improve cooperation between national authorities and thus help combat illegal working and rogue operators;
– ensure that a service company posting workers to another Member State fully complies with that Member State's employment laws, including minimum wages, in order to avoid 'social dumping';
– remove 'pointless red tape';
– help stop discrimination against companies and customers on grounds of nationality; and
– clarify under which conditions patients are reimbursed for medical care obtained in another Member State.

Part I, Ch. 2, Freedom of Services 1057–1057

The Commission states emphatically that the proposal will not:

- force Member States to liberalise or privatise public services or open them to competition;
- affect the freedom of Member States to define what they consider to be public services or how they should be organised and financed;
- change the way that Member States organise health and social security services;
  - impose extra costs on Member States' social security systems;
- allow social dumping by bringing in 'cheap' workers; – prevent Member States from checking and controlling companies and workers operating on their territory; and
- endanger national laws that genuinely protect health, safety and consumer rights.

1057. On 19 July 2005, the Committee on Employment and Social Affairs of the EP (draftswoman Anne Van Lancker) issued the following report.[385]

> Launched by the Commission in January 2004, the proposal for a Directive on Services in the Internal Market sets out a general legal framework to reduce barriers to cross-border provision of services within the European Union. The draftswoman shares the view that the elimination of obstacles to the provision of services between Member States is an important element in achieving the goal set by the Lisbon European Council of making the European Union the most competitive and dynamic knowledge-based economy in the world capable of sustainable economic growth with more and better jobs and greater social cohesion. However, at the same time, she shares the opinion of many experts and MEPs that many concerns need to be addressed before this Directive can enter into force.
>
> This draft opinion is based on the findings of the public hearing,[386] on the impact study[387] as well as on the contributions from various organisations and expert groups. In her working document,[388] the draftswoman set out the orientations for amendment and identified the following controversial issues: the legal basis and scope of the proposal, the implications of requirements relating to establishment, the introduction of the country of origin principle and the relationship with other Community instruments.
>
> As Commissioner Mc Creevy has made clear in his statement before the European Parliament, the Commission does not have the intention to withdraw

---

385. Opinion of the Committee on Employment and Social Affairs for the Committee on the Internal Market and Consumer Protection on the proposal for a directive of the European Parliament and of the Council on services in the internal market (COM(2004)0002 – C5-0069/2004 – 2004/0001(COD)).
386. Public Hearing on the Proposal for a Directive on Services in the Internal Market, organised by IMCO and EMPL, 11 November 2004. Directorate-General for Internal Policies, Notice to Members IV/2004 – PE 350.059.
387. Towards a European Directive on Services in the Internal Market: Analysing the Legal Repercussions of the Draft Services Directive and its Impact on National Services Regulations, Wouter Gekiere, Institute for European Law, Catholic University Leuven, 24 September 2004.
388. Working Document on the Draft Services Directive, 11 January 2005, Committee on Employment and Social Affairs, Rapporteur Anne Van Lancker, PE 353.364v02-00.

its proposal, but confirms its willingness to amend the proposal concerning sensitive issues on the basis of the first reading in European Parliament. The draftswoman is of the opinion that at least the following concerns need to be addressed in the report in first reading of the proposal.

(1) Scope of the proposal

1058. The proposal reflects a horizontal approach; it covers a wide variety of services ranging from purely commercial services to health care and social services. As many experts have pointed out, this proposal fails to take into account that the services covered have heterogeneous features and raise a wide variety of public policy considerations. Therefore, it is essential that professions and activities which are permanently or temporarily connected with the exercise of official authority in a Member State, services provided by temporary employment agencies and services provided by security agencies be excluded from the scope of the proposal. In order not to affect the freedom of Member States – on the basis of the principle of subsidiarity – to define what they consider to be services of general economic interest as referred to in Articles 14 and 106 TFEU and not to anticipate a framework Directive on services of general interest, the proposal should neither apply to services which the Member States and/or the Community subject to specific universal or public service obligations, by virtue of a general interest criterion.

For reasons of legal certainty and consistency with sectoral internal market directives, specific network services, transport services and audiovisual services should be excluded from the scope of this proposal. Finally, in order to avoid any misunderstanding about the subject-matter and the scope of the proposal, it is essential to state that this Directive should not deal with the field of labour law and social security law and should not interfere with the distribution of regional or local powers within each Member State.

(2) Establishment

1059. As regards requirements relating to establishment, the current proposal will narrow down Member States' national regulatory powers to translate their duties in the social sphere into national/regional authorisation schemes. Including a number of clarifications and amendments in this draft opinion is justified by reasons of subsidiarity, proportionality, legal certainty as well as consistency with TFEU rules and the case law of the European Court of Justice.

(3) Country of origin principle

1060. In the absence of a minimum level of harmonisation at EU level or, at least, of mutual recognition on the basis of comparable rules within the Member States, the country of origin principle cannot be the basic principle governing temporary cross-border provision of services. The coordinated field to which the scope of the country of origin principle is linked covers any requirement applicable to the access to and the exercise of a service activity. However the fields actually coordinated by this Directive only relate to information on service providers, provisions on professional insurance and information of recipients on the existence of after-sale guarantees and the settlement of disputes. Therefore, the scope of the country of origin principle should be limited to the fields actually coordinated by this Directive and other Community instruments.

The competent authorities of the Member State in which the service is provided are best placed to ensure the effectiveness and the continuity of supervision and to provide protection for recipients. Even though this supervision should be complemented by an effective system of administrative cooperation between Member States, it is unacceptable that the principle according to which the Member State of origin carries the responsibility for the supervision of the service replaces the supervision by the Member State where the service is provided.

(4) Coherence with other Community instruments

1061. There is a lack of consistency between the proposal and other Community initiatives. Many experts have raised concerns on the repercussions of this proposal on the labour law provisions of the posting Directive and the rules of conflict of laws included in Rome I and Rome II. For reasons of legal certainty and consistency, it is essential to clearly state that this proposal will respect other Community instruments as well as the adoption of any Community instrument amending or replacing these instruments. For the same reasons, any clarification in the field of the posting of workers should be dealt with under the existing legal framework of Directive 96/71/EC.

The Employment Committee of the European parliament voted 13 July 2005 with a large majority, in favour of nearly all the amendments of Ms. Van Lancker.

1062. A large majority deleted the provisions limiting the possibilities for Member States to monitor and enforce regulations with regard to cross border posting of workers, reversed the country of origin principle so that it would not apply unless a minimum level of harmonisation was achieved, and decided that the Directive should not apply to a range of sectors with universal or public service obligations.

Most importantly, labour law and collective agreements were excluded from the scope of the directive. The directive on posting of workers of 1996 retains complete preference over the service directive. Labour and working conditions of the workland need to be respected; it is also the workland, who will control whether labour and working conditions of posted are respected.

Under the EP's procedure the Employment Committee has the lead on employment related aspects of the Services Directive: Worker protection, Employment law, collective agreements and social security.

The report of Van Lancker was discussed by the Plenary of the European Parliament, end October 2005.

§6. THE DIRECTIVE ON SERVICES IN THE INTERNAL MARKET (2006)[389]

1063. The Directive Directive 2006/123/EC of the European Parliament and of the Council of 12 December 2006[390] on services in the internal market aims to facilitate the provision of cross-border services. The European Parliament adopted the services directive at second reading in November 2006. The vote put an end to a longstanding controversy, particularly with regard to the industrial relations impact of the directive. The key contentious issue – the 'country of origin principle' – was replaced and EU labour law is not affected by the directive. Furthermore, services of general interest and other sensitive services are excluded from the application of the directive.

The adoption of the services directive was preceded by almost three years of debate and revision between the European Parliament, the Council of the European Union and the European Commission The most contested issues of the Commission's proposal in March 2004 were: the 'country of origin principle' – whereby a service provider could market its services in other Member States without having to comply with their legislation; the role of labour law; the recognition of fundamental rights to collective bargaining; and the exclusion of services of general interest and sensitive sectors such as temporary agency work.

I. Terms of the Directive

1064. The adopted text, considerably amended by the European Parliament, seeks to balance the aims of facilitating the provision of cross-border services by removing obstacles to the free movement of services in the internal market, on the one hand, with social protection for workers, on the other. Thus, the 'freedom to provide services principle' has replaced the country of origin principle. The directive does not affect labour law, employment and working conditions, and explicitly does not impact on the right to negotiate, conclude and enforce collective agreements, nor on the right to strike and to take industrial action.

1065. Several sectors and activities, such as services of general interest, social and health services, and temporary agency work, are excluded from the directive. Moreover, the services directive does not affect the terms and conditions of employment of posted workers. Directive 96/71/EC concerning the posting of workers obliges service providers to comply with the terms and conditions of employment laid down by law or in collective agreements in the Member State where the service is provided.

1066. The services directive entered into force on 28 December 2006 and must be implemented by the Member States within three years.

---

389. Anni Weiler, AWWW GmbH ArbeitsWelt – Working World, 'European Parliament adopts services directive', *Eurofound*, 2007.
390. O.J., 27 December 2006, L 376.

1067. In December 2010, the Council reported that:

over the past years the large majority of Member States has dedicated considerable efforts to deliver the benefits of the Services Directive to businesses and consumers on the ground.

Overall, the results of implementation, even if still under completion in a number of Member States, are very significant in terms of the abolition of unjustified barriers and the modernisation of the regulatory framework applicable to services. More than 1000 implementing measures (new horizontal laws and 'omnibus' laws containing changes to different pieces of existing legislation) have so far been notified by Member States to the Commission. The Directive has led to the setting up of the Points of Single Contact (PSCs) – e-government portals for businesses, now operational in most Member States. It has also brought about the creation of a comprehensive network of administrative cooperation to facilitate the free movement of services, which now links up over 5000 authorities across the EU in the 'IMI' system. Furthermore, the Services Directive has created a 'Single Market effect' that is quite unprecedented. Thousands of authorities at national, regional and local level have assessed their rules and the effects they have on citizens and businesses from a Single Market perspective.

But work is not completed yet. Efforts will need to be stepped up in a number of Member States in order to finalise the required changes in legislation, to set up fully operational PSCs and to further consolidate the network of administrative cooperation.[391]

II. Reaction from European Social Partners

1068. The European Trade Union Confederation (ETUC) considered the outcome of the European Parliament's second reading as a success for the European trade union movement. Nevertheless, ETUC announced that it would continue its fight for improvement in the European regulation of public services and in sensitive sectors such as temporary agencies.

On the employer side, the European Centre of Enterprises with Public Participation and of Enterprises of General Economic Interest (CEEP) welcomed the exclusion of services of general interest and of health and social services from the scope of the directive. BUSINESSEUROPE said it looked forward to real benefits arising from the freedom of establishment, but regrets 'the reduced scope of the directive and the legal uncertainty of certain provisions on cross-border provision of services'.

Meanwhile, the European Association of Craft, Small and Medium-sized Enterprises (UEAPME) stated that, if the directive is properly applied at national level, it would be beneficial for European small and medium-sized enterprises (SMEs).

---

391. Meeting of the Competitiveness Council, 10 December 2010. State of implementation of the services directive. *Information note from the commission services,* Council of the European Union, Brussels, 6 December 2010, 17470/10, LIMITE COMPET 416 SOC 826 JUSTCIV 226 MI 528.

Chapter 3. International Private Labour Law

1069. International private labour law deals with the question: which judge has jurisdiction and which legal system is applicable in the case where a labour contract is based on various legal systems and consequently more than one judge and more than one legal system could be competent to solve a given legal conflict. In this case, two European instruments should be mentioned, namely: the Council Regulation (EC) No. 44/2001 of 22 December 2000 on jurisdiction and the recognition and enforcement of judgments in civil and commercial matters,[392] replaced by Regulation (EU) No 1215/2012 of 12 December 2012 [393] on the one hand, and the Convention on the Law applicable to Contractual Obligations of 19 June 1980, on the other.[394]

A directive of 16 December 1996 concerns the posting of workers.

§1. THE COMPETENT JUDGE

I. Regulation 44/2001 (2000)

1070. The Regulation (EC) No. 44/2001 of 22 December 2000 on jurisdiction and the recognition and enforcement of judgments in civil and commercial matters applies in civil and commercial matters[395] whatever the nature of the court or tribunal. It shall not extend, in particular, to revenue, customs or administrative matters.

The Regulation does not apply to:

(a) the status or legal capacity of natural persons, rights in property arising out of a matrimonial relationship, wills and succession;
(b) bankruptcy, proceedings relating to the winding-up of insolvent companies or other legal persons, judicial arrangements, compositions and analogous proceedings;
(c) social security;
(d) arbitration (Article 1).

---

392. O.J., 16 January 2001, entering into force 1 March 2002. '1. This Regulation shall, as between the Member States, supersede the Brussels Convention, except as regards the territories of the Member States which fall within the territorial scope of that Convention and which are excluded from this Regulation pursuant to Article 349 and 355 TFEU.
    In so far as this Regulation replaces the provisions of the Brussels Convention between Member States, any reference to the Convention shall be understood as a reference to this Regulation' (Article 68).
393. O.J., 20 December 2012, L 351/1, The regulation applies from 10 January 2015.
394. *See* the consolidated version and the protocol on the interpretation by the Court of Justice, O.J., 26 January 1998, C 27/1.
395. The scope of the regulation was extended to Denmark, Iceland, Norway and Switzerland by the Convention on Jurisdiction and Enforcement of Judgments in Civil and Commercial Matters, 13 October 2007, O.J. L 339/13, 21 December 2007.

Part I, Ch. 3, International Private Labour Law

Section 5 of the regulation deals with 'Jurisdiction over individual contracts of employment'.[396]

1071. The jurisdiction is regulated as follows.

> Where an employee enters into an individual contract of employment with an employer, who is not domiciled in a Member State but has a branch, agency or other establishment in one of the Member States, the employer shall, in disputes arising out of the operations of the branch, agency or establishment, be deemed to be domiciled in that Member State (Art. 18(2)).

1072. An employer domiciled in a Member State may be sued:

(1) in the courts of the Member State where he is domiciled; or
(2) in another Member State:
   (a) in the courts for the place where the employee habitually carries out his work or in the courts for the last place where he did so, or
   (b) if the employee does not or did not habitually carry out his work in any one country, in the courts for the place where the business which engaged the employee is or was situated (Article 19).
(3) An employer may bring proceedings only in the courts of the Member State in which the employee is domiciled.
(4) The provisions of this section shall not affect the right to bring a counter-claim in the court in which, in accordance with this Section, the original claim is pending (Article 20).

These provisions may be departed from only by an agreement on jurisdiction:

(1) which is entered into after the dispute has arisen; or
(2) which allows the employee to bring proceedings in courts other than those indicated in this section (Article 21).

1073. Difficulties may arise when an employee works in another Member State than the one in which he is domiciled, which means that the judge would be alien to the labour law system, which will normally apply to the employment relation. In order to avoid this, parties might lay down in there individual labour agreement that the judge of the place where the work is performed is also a competent judge or

---

396. 1. In matters relating to individual contracts of employment, jurisdiction shall be determined by this Section, without prejudice to Article 4 and point 5 of Article 5 (Article 18(1)).

  Article 4 and Article 5(5) read as follows: '1. If the defendant is not domiciled in a Member State, the jurisdiction of the courts of each Member State shall, subject to Articles 22 and 23, be determined by the law of that Member State.' As against such a defendant, any person domiciled in a Member State may, whatever his nationality, avail himself in that State of the rules of jurisdiction there in force, and in particular those specified in Annex I, in the same way as the nationals of that State (Article 4): 'A person domiciled in a Member State may, in another Member State, be sued: as regards a dispute arising out of the operations of a branch, agency or other establishment, in the courts for the place in which the branch, agency or other establishment is situated' (Article 5(5)).

make such an agreement once the dispute has arisen. It is indeed indicated that the judge rules which is familiar with the applicable law.

1074. Questions concerning to the competent judge arose in the course of litigation concerning the legality of industrial action[397] in relation to Article 5(3) of the regulation.

Under Article 5(3) of the Regulation:

> A person domiciled in a Contracting State may, in another Contracting State, be sued: ...
> (3) in matters relating to tort, delict or quasi-delict, in the courts for the place where the harmful event occurred.

Facts

1075. The dispute concerns the legality of a notice of industrial action given by SEKO against DFDS, with the object of securing a collective agreement for Polish crew of the cargo ship Tor Caledonia owned by DFDS, serving the route between Göteberg (Sweden) and Harwich (United Kingdom).

The Tor Caledonia is registered in the Danish international ship register and is subject to Danish law. At the time of the facts in the main proceedings, the Polish crew were employed on the basis of individual contracts, in accordance with a framework agreement between a number of Danish unions on the one hand, and three Danish associations of shipping companies on the other. Those contracts were governed by Danish law.

After DFDS rejected a request by SEKO on behalf of the Polish crew for a collective agreement, on 21 March 2001, SEKO served a notice of industrial action by fax, with effect from 28 March 2001, instructing its Swedish members not to accept employment on the Tor Caledonia. The fax also stated that SEKO was calling for sympathy action. Following that request, the *Svenska Transport-arbetareförbundet* (Swedish Transport Workers Union, 'STAF') gave notice, on 3 April 2001, of sympathy action with effect from 17 April 2001, refusing to engage in any work whatsoever relating to the Tor Caledonia, which would prevent the ship from being loaded or unloaded in Swedish ports.

On 4 April 2001, DFDS brought an action against SEKO and STAF, seeking an order that the two unions acknowledge that the principal and sympathy actions were unlawful and that they withdraw the notices of industrial action.

On 11 April 2001, the day of the first hearing before the *Arbejdsret*, SEKO decided to suspend the industrial action pending the court's final decision, while the STAF's notice of industrial action was withdrawn on 18 April 2001.

---

397. C.O.J., 5 February 2004, *Danmarks Rederiforening, acting on behalf of DFDS Torline A/S v. LO Landsorganisationen i Sverige, acting on behalf of SEKO Sjöfolk Facket för Service och Kommunikation*, C-18/02, ECR, 2004, 1417.

However, on 16 April 2001, the day before the first day of sympathy action called by STAF, DFDS decided to withdraw the Tor Caledonia from the GöteborgHarwich route, which was served from 30 May by another ship leased for that purpose.

DFDS brought an action for damages against SEKO before the *Sø-og Handelsret* (Denmark), claiming that the defendant was liable in tort for giving notice of unlawful industrial action and inciting another Swedish union to give notice of sympathy action, which was also unlawful. The damages sought are for the loss allegedly suffered by DFDS as a result of immobilising the Tor Caledonia and leasing a replacement ship. The court decided to stay its decision on the action for damages pending the decision of the *Arbejdsret*.

Following questions were referred to the Court for a preliminary ruling:

1076. (1) (a) Must Article 5(3) be construed as covering cases concerning the legality of industrial action for the purpose of securing an agreement in a case where any harm which may result from the illegality of such industrial action gives rise to liability to pay compensation under the rules on tort, delict or quasi-delict, such that a case concerning the legality of notified industrial action can be brought before the courts of the place where proceedings may be instituted for compensation in respect of any harm resulting from that industrial action?

Answer

1077. First, it is clear from settled case law that the object of the regulation is not to unify the procedural rules of the Contracting States, but to determine which court has jurisdiction in disputes concerning civil and commercial matters in intraCommunity relations and to facilitate the enforcement of judgments.

Second, the Court has already held that it is not possible to accept an interpretation of Article 5(3) according to which application of that provision is conditional on the actual occurrence of damage. Likewise it has held that the finding that the courts for the place where the harmful event occurred are usually the most appropriate for deciding the case, in particular on the grounds of proximity and ease of taking evidence, is equally relevant whether the dispute concerns compensation for damage which has already occurred or relates to an action seeking to prevent the occurrence of damage.

It follows from the foregoing, that the answer to Question 1(a) must be that Article 5(3) must be interpreted as meaning that a case concerning the legality of industrial action, in respect of which exclusive jurisdiction belongs, in accordance with the law of the Contracting State concerned, to a court other than the court which has jurisdiction to try the claims for compensation for the damage caused by that industrial action, falls within the definition of 'tort, delict or quasi-delict'.

1078. (b) Is it necessary, as the case may be, that any harm incurred must be a certain or probable consequence of the industrial action concerned in itself, or is it sufficient that that industrial action is a necessary condition governing, and may constitute the basis for, sympathy actions which will result in harm?

Answer

1079. According to the case law of the Court, liability in tort, delict or quasidelict can only arise provided that a causal connection can be established between the damage and the event in which that damage originates. It cannot but be noted that in a situation such as that at issue in the main proceedings, a causal link could be established between the harm allegedly suffered by DFDS and SEKO's notice of industrial action.

Accordingly, the answer to Question 1(b) must be that for the application of Article 5(3) to a situation such as that in the dispute in the main proceedings, it is sufficient that the industrial action is a necessary precondition of sympathy action which may result in harm.

1080. (c) Does it make any difference that implementation of notified industrial action was, after the proceedings had been brought, suspended by the notifying party until the court's ruling on the issue of its legality?

Answer

1081. In that regard, it must be observed that, according to settled case law, the strengthening of the legal protection of persons established in the Community by enabling the claimant to identify easily the court in which he may sue and the defendant reasonably to foresee in which court he may be sued, is one of the objectives of the regulation.

That objective would not be achieved if, after an action falling within Article 5(3) is brought before the court of a Contracting State having jurisdiction, the suspension by the defendant of the tortious conduct giving rise to that action could have the effect of depriving the court seised of its jurisdiction, and of jurisdiction being assigned to a court in another Contracting State.

It follows that the answer to Question 1(c) must be that the application of Article 5(3) is not affected by the fact that the implementation of industrial action was suspended by the party giving notice pending a ruling on its legality.

1082. (2) Must Article 5(3) be construed as meaning that damage resulting from industrial action taken by a trade union in a country to which a ship registered in another country (the flag State) sails for the purpose of securing an agreement covering the work of seamen on board that ship can be regarded by the ship's owners as having occurred in the flag State, with the result that the ship's owners can, pursuant to Article 5(3), bring an action for damages against the trade union in the flag State?

Answer

1083. According to settled case law, where the place in which the event which may give rise to liability in tort, delict or quasi-delict occurs and the place where that event results in damage are not identical, the expression 'place where the harmful event occurred' in Article 5(3) must be understood as being intended to cover both the place where the damage occurred and the place of the event giving rise to it, so that the defendant may be sued, at the option of the plaintiff, in the courts for either of those places.

In the light of the foregoing, the answer to Question 2 must be that, in circumstances such as those in the main proceedings, Article 5(3) must be interpreted as meaning that the damage resulting from industrial action taken by a trade union in a Contracting State to which a ship registered in another Contracting State sails can be regarded as having occurred in the flag State, with the result that the shipowner can bring an action for damages against that trade union in the flag State.

II. Regulation (EU) No. 1215/2012 (2012)

1084. Regulation (EU) No. 1215/2012 of the European Parliament and of the Council of 12 December 2012 on jurisdiction and the recognition and enforcement of judgments in civil and commercial matters[398] repeals Regulation (EC) No. 44/2001 of 22 December 2000, applying from 10 January 2015.

1085. This Regulation shall apply in civil and commercial matters whatever the nature of the court or tribunal. It shall not extend, in particular, to revenue, customs or administrative matters or to the liability of the State for acts and omissions in the exercise of State authority (acta iure imperii).

The Regulation shall not apply to:

(a) the status or legal capacity of natural persons, rights in property arising out of a matrimonial relationship or out of a relationship deemed by the law applicable to such relationship to have comparable effects to marriage;
(b) bankruptcy, proceedings relating to the winding-up of insolvent companies or other legal persons, judicial arrangements, compositions and analogous proceedings;
(c) social security;
(d) arbitration;
(e) maintenance obligations arising from a family relationship, parentage, marriage or affinity;
(f) wills and succession, including maintenance obligations arising by reason of death.

---

398. *O.J.*, 20 December 2012, L 351.

Section 5 of the Regulation deals with 'Jurisdiction over individual contracts of employment'.[399]

1086. The jurisdiction is regulated as follows:

Where an employee enters into an individual contract of employment with an employer who is not domiciled in a Member State but has a branch, agency or other establishment in one of the Member States, the employer shall, in disputes arising out of the operations of the branch, agency or establishment, be deemed to be domiciled in that Member State (Art. 20(2).

1. An employer domiciled in a Member State may be sued:
    (a) in the courts of the Member State in which he is domiciled; or
    (b) in another Member State:
        (i) in the courts for the place where or from where the employee habitually carries out his work or in the courts for the last place where he did so; or
        (ii) if the employee does not or did not habitually carry out his work in any one country, in the courts for the place where the business which engaged the employee is or was situated.
2. An employer not domiciled in a Member State may be sued in a court of a Member State in accordance with point (b) of paragraph 1 (Article 21).

1087. 1. An employer may bring proceedings only in the courts of the Member State in which the employee is domiciled.

2. The provisions of this Section shall not affect the right to bring a counter-claim in the court in which, in accordance with this Section, the original claim is pending (Article 22).

The provisions of this Section may be departed from only by an agreement:

(1) which is entered into after the dispute has arisen; or
(2) which allows the employee to bring proceedings in courts other than those indicated in this Section (Article 23).

§2. The Law Applicable to Contractual Obligations

1088. The rule of special jurisdiction provided for in Article 6, point 1, of Council Regulation (EC) No. 44/2001 of 22 December 2000 cannot be applied to a dispute falling under Section 5 of Chapter II of that regulation concerning the jurisdiction rules applicable to individual contracts of employment.

---

399. In matters relating to individual contracts of employment, jurisdiction shall be determined by this Section, without prejudice to Article 6, point 5 of Article 7 and, in the case of proceedings brought against an employer, point 1 of Article 8 (Art. 20, 1).

Part I, Ch. 3, International Private Labour Law

Indeed, it is settled case-law that the rules of special jurisdiction must be interpreted strictly and cannot be given an interpretation going beyond the cases expressly envisaged by the Regulation. The wording of the provisions of Section 5 of Chapter II of the Regulation precludes the application of Article 6, point 1, in disputes concerning matters relating to contracts of employment.[400]

I. Convention on Contractual Obligations (1980)

1089. The Convention on the Law applicable to Contractual Obligations of 19 June 1980 applies to contractual obligations, and therefore also to individual employment contracts, in any situation involving a choice between the laws of different countries.[401] Jurisdiction to interpret the Convention rests with the Court of Justice.

1090. Pursuant to Article 3 of the Convention, a contract is governed by the law chosen by the parties. The choice must be expressed or demonstrated with reasonable certainty by the terms of the contract or the circumstances of the case. By their choice, the parties can select the law applicable to the whole or to a part only of the contract (§1). The fact that the parties have chosen a foreign law does not, where all the other elements relevant to the situation at the time of the choice are connected with one country only, prejudice the application of the rules of the law of that country which cannot be derogated from by contract (mandatory rules) (Article 3(1)). To the extent that the law applicable to the contract has not been chosen, the contract is governed by the law of the country with which it is most closely connected (Article 4(1)).

1091. The choice for the parties of an individual employment contract is not completely free. Indeed, Article 6 of the Convention provides that: 'notwithstanding the provisions of Article 3, in a contract of employment a choice of law made by the parties shall not have the result of depriving the employee of the protection afforded to him by the mandatory rules of the law which would be applicable in the absence of a choice' (§1). Where there is an absence of choice, a contract of employment is governed:

(a) by the law of the country in which the employee habitually carries out his work in performance of the contract, even if he is temporarily employed in another country; or

---

400. C.O.J., 22 May 2008, *Glaxosmithkline, Laboratoires Glaxosmithkline* v. *Jean-Pierre Rouard*, C-462/06, ECR, 2009, 3965.
401. C. Salaert, 'Krachtlijnen van het internationaal privaat arbeidsrecht', *Tijdschrift voor Sociaal Recht*, 1990, 101–127. The Convention of 19 June 1980 entered into force on 1 April 1991.

(b) if the employee does not habitually carry out his work in any country, by the law of the country in which the place of business through which he was engaged is situated;

unless it appears from the circumstances as a whole that the contract is more closely connected with another country, in which case the contract will be governed by the law of that country (§2).

1092. This does not mean that the law chosen must yield in its totality; only the least favourable conditions must be let go. Mandatory rules from which the parties cannot deviate concern, for instance, those relating to the health and safety of workers, which can be looked upon as of public order, and those relating to collective labour agreements, which are binding for the employer. The choice of laws regarding the individual employment contract by the Convention clearly indicates the will of the Contracting Parties to limit the freedom of choice of the employer and the employee and to make the law with which the contract is most closely connected applicable in most cases.

1093. In the absence of a choice made by the parties, Article 6(2) of the Rome Convention must be interpreted as meaning that the national court seised of the case must first establish whether the employee, in the performance of his contract, habitually carries out his work in the same country, which is the country in which or from which, in the light of all the factors which characterise that activity, the employee performs the main part of his obligations towards his employer.

In the case where the national court takes the view that it cannot rule on the dispute before it under Article 6(2)(a) of that convention, Article 6(2)(b) of the Rome Convention must be interpreted as follows:

- the concept of 'the place of business through which the employee was engaged' must be understood as referring exclusively to the place of business which engaged the employee and not to that with which the employee is connected by his actual employment;
- the possession of legal personality does not constitute a requirement which must be fulfilled by the place of business of the employer within the meaning of that provision;
- the place of business of an undertaking other than that which is formally referred to as the employer, with which that undertaking has connections, may be classified as a 'place of business' if there are objective factors enabling an actual situation to be established which differs from that which appears from the terms of the contract, and even though the authority of the employer has not been formally transferred to that other undertaking[402].

---

402. C.O.J., 15 December 201, *Jan Voogsgeerd* v. *Navimer SA*, C-384/10, www. curia.eu.

II. Regulation No. 593/2008 of 17 June 2008 on the Law Applicable to Contractual Obligations (Rome I)[403]

A. Scope

1094. This regulation shall apply, in situations involving a conflict of laws, to contractual obligations in civil and commercial matters.

It shall not apply, in particular, to revenue, customs or administrative matters.

B. Freedom of Choice

1095.

(1) A contract shall be governed by the law chosen by the parties. The choice shall be made expressly or clearly demonstrated by the terms of the contract or the circumstances of the case. By their choice the parties can select the law applicable to the whole or to part only of the contract (Article 3, 1).

C. Individual Employment Contracts

1096.

(1) An individual employment contract shall be governed by the law chosen by the parties. Such a choice of law may not, however, have the result of depriving the employee of the protection afforded to him by provisions that cannot be derogated from by agreement under the law that, in the absence of choice, would have been applicable pursuant to paragraphs 2, 3 and 4 of this Article.
(2) To the extent that the law applicable to the individual employment contract has not been chosen by the parties, the contract shall be governed by the law of the country in which or, failing that, from which the employee habitually carries out his work in performance of the contract. The country where the work is habitually carried out shall not be deemed to have changed if he is temporarily employed in another country.
(3) Where the law applicable cannot be determined pursuant to paragraph 2, the contract shall be governed by the law of the country where the place of business through which the employee was engaged is situated.
(4) Where it appears from the circumstances as a whole that the contract is more closely connected with a country other than that indicated in paragraphs 2 or 3, the law of that other country shall apply (Article 8).

---

403. O.J., 4 July 2008, L 177.

D. *Overriding Mandatory Provisions*

1097.

(1) Overriding mandatory provisions are provisions the respect for which is regarded as crucial by a country for safeguarding its public interests, such as its political, social or economic organisation, to such an extent that they are applicable to any situation falling within their scope, irrespective of the law otherwise applicable to the contract under this Regulation.
(2) Nothing in this Regulation shall restrict the application of the overriding mandatory provisions of the law of the forum.
(3) Effect may be given to the overriding mandatory provisions of the law of the country where the obligations arising out of the contract have to be or have been performed, in so far as those overriding mandatory provisions render the performance of the contract unlawful. In considering whether to give effect to those provisions, regard shall be had to their nature and purpose and to the consequences of their application or non-application (Article 9).

E. *Public Policy of the Forum*

1098. The application of a provision of the law of any country specified by this Regulation may be refused only if such application is manifestly incompatible with the public policy (*ordre public*) of the forum (Article 21).

In the recitals to the Regulation we read:

> The rule on individual employment contracts should not prejudice the application of the overriding mandatory provisions of the country to which a worker is posted in accordance with Directive 96/71/EC of the European Parliament and of the Council of 16 December 1996 concerning the posting of workers in the framework of the provision of services.
>
> Employees should not be deprived of the protection afforded to them by provisions which cannot be derogated from by agreement or which can only be derogated from to their benefit.
>
> As regards individual employment contracts, work carried out in another country should be regarded as temporary if the employee is expected to resume working in the country of origin after carrying out his tasks abroad. The conclusion of a new contract of employment with the original employer or an employer belonging to the same group of companies as the original employer should not preclude the employee from being regarded as carrying out his work in another country temporarily.
>
> Considerations of public interest justify giving the courts of the Member States the possibility, in exceptional circumstances, of applying exceptions based on public policy and overriding mandatory provisions. The concept of 'overriding mandatory provisions' should be distinguished from the expression 'provisions which cannot be derogated from by agreement' and should be construed more restrictively (34–37).

Part I, Ch. 3, International Private Labour Law

§3. THE LAW APPLICABLE TO NON-CONTRACTUAL OBLIGATIONS: INDUSTRIAL ACTION

1099. Regulation (EC) No. 864/2007 of 11 July 2007 applies, in situations involving a conflict of laws, to non-contractual obligations in civil and commercial matters (Rome II).[404]

The Regulation deals specifically with industrial action and states that 'the law applicable to a non-contractual obligation in respect of the liability of a person in the capacity of a worker or an employer or the organisations representing their professional interests for damages caused by an industrial action, pending or carried out, shall be the law of the country where the action is to be, or has been, taken' (Article 9).

As the exact concept of industrial action, such as strike action or lock-out, varies from one Member State to another and is governed by each Member State's internal rules this Regulation assumes as a general principle that the law of the country where the industrial action was taken should apply, with the aim of protecting the rights and obligations of workers and employers.[405]

The special rule on industrial action is without prejudice to the conditions relating to the exercise of such action in accordance with national law and without prejudice to the legal status of trade unions or of the representative organisations of workers as provided for in the law of the Member States.[406]

The regulations covers also torts and delicts (Article 4) and the rules of safety (Article 17).

This regulation shall apply from 11 January 2009 and is binding in its entirety and directly applicable in the Member States.

§4. POSTING OF WORKERS: DIRECTIVE 96/71 OF 16 DECEMBER 1996[407]

1100. Although the Directive (96/71) merits applause, it should be clearly stated that this measure combats social dumping only to a certain extent, as not all working conditions are covered; nor does it contribute to greater convergence of working conditions in the Common Market, or make things simpler.[408]

---

404. O.J., L 1999, 31 July 2007.
405. Considerans 27.
406. Considerans 28.
407. O.J. C 018, 21 January 1997, 1.
408. 'National legislation which requires an employer, as a person providing a service within the meaning of the Treaty, to pay employer's contributions to the social security fund of the host Member State in addition to the contributions already paid by him to the social security fund of the State where he is established places an additional financial burden on him, so that he is not, so far as competition is concerned, on an equal footing with employers established in the host State.

The public interest relating to the social protection of workers in the construction industry may, however, because of conditions specific to that sector, constitute an overriding requirement justifying such a restriction on the freedom to provide services. However, that is not the case where the workers in question enjoy the same protection, or essentially similar protection, by virtue of employer's contributions already paid by the employer in the Member State of establishment', and

There is no convergence, since the variety of systems remains as it is; which does not make matters easier, since one will have to be well informed not only about governmental rules and their interpretation, but also about collective agreements. In practical terms this means that these agreements should be available in official languages of the Member States. Whether this is really feasible is another matter.

Regulation No. 593/2008 of 17 June 2008 on the law applicable to contractual obligations (Rome I)[409] indicates in its Recital 34 that 'The rule on individual employment contracts should not prejudice the application of the overriding mandatory provisions of the country to which a worker is posted in accordance with Directive 96/71/EC of the European Parliament and of the Council of 16 December 1996 concerning the posting of workers in the framework of the provision of services'.

This means that the Directive 96/71 prevails over Regulation Rome I. It is thus only for those provision which are not covered by Directive 91/76 that Convention Rome I applies.

I. Legal Base

1101. The legal base of this directive is Article 56(2) TFEU, relating to the freedom of services, which allows for a majority vote.

II. Scope of Application

1102. The directive applies to undertakings, established in a Member State, which post workers for a limited period (Article 2(1)) in the framework of transnational services to the territory of a Member State (Article 1(1)) other than the Member State in which the worker works normally (Art. 2(1)) in the framework of either:

– subcontracting;[410]
– a group;[411]
– temporary work for a user (Art. 1(3)).[412]

---

is contrary to Articles 47 and 55 of the EC Treaty (C.O.J., 28 March 1996, *Michel Guiot and Climatec SA*, Case C-272/94, ECR, 1996, 1905).
409. O.J., 4 July 2008, L 177. This Regulation shall apply to contracts concluded after 17 December 2009. A similar clause was contained in the Rome Convention on the Law applicable to Contractual Obligations of 1980.
410. ' ... post workers to the territory of a Member State on their account and under their direction under a contract concluded between the undertaking making the posting and the party for whom the services are intended, operating in that Member State, provided there is an employment relationship between the undertaking of origin and the worker during the period of posting' (Article 1(3)(a)).
411. ' ... post workers to an establishment or to an undertaking owned by the group in the territory of a Member State, provided there is an employment relationship between the undertaking of origin and the worker during the period of posting' (Article 1(3)(b)).
412. ' ... being a temporary employment undertaking or placement agency, hire out a worker to a user undertaking established or operating in the territory of a Member State, provided there is an

Part I, Ch. 3, International Private Labour Law

The notion of worker is that which applies in the law of the Member State to whose territory the worker is posted (Art. 2(2)).

The merchant navy undertakings are excluded as regards seagoing personnel (Article 1(2)).

1103. The hiring-out of workers, within the meaning of Article 1(3)(c) of Directive 96/71, is a service provided for remuneration in respect of which the worker who has been hired out remains in the employment of the undertaking providing the service, no contract of employment being entered into with the user undertaking. It is characterised by the fact that the movement of the worker to the host Member State constitutes the very purpose of the provision of services effected by the undertaking providing the services and that that worker carries out his tasks under the control and direction of the user undertaking.[413]

III. Terms and Conditions of Employment

A. Minimum Conditions

1104. Working conditions which apply and have to be guaranteed to posted workers are those laid down by:

– governmental rules;
– collective agreements or arbitration awards, generally binding,[414] concerning building work,[415] and

---

employment relationship between the temporary employment undertaking or placement agency and the worker during the period of posting' (Article 1(3)(c)).

Member States can provide that temporary workers get equal treatment compared to temporary workers active on their territory (Article 3(9)).

413. C.O.J., 10 February 2011, Cases C-307/09 to C-309/09, *Vicoplus SC PUH a.o. v. Minister van Sociale Zaken en Werkgelegenheid*, www.curia.eu.
414. These are agreements or awards which must be observed by all undertakings in the geographical area and in the profession or industry concerned. In the absence of a system for declaring collective agreements or arbitration awards to be of universal application, Member States may, if they so decide, base themselves on:
   – collective agreements or arbitration awards which are generally applicable to all similar undertakings in the geographical area and in the profession or industry concerned, and/or
   – collective agreements which have been concluded by the most representative employers' and labour organisations at national level and which are applied throughout the national territory, provided that their application to the undertakings referred to in Article 1(1) ensures equality of treatment on matters listed in the first subparagraph of paragraph 1 of this article between those undertakings and the other undertakings referred to in this subparagraph which are in a similar position.
   Equality of treatment, within the meaning of this article, shall be deemed to exist where national undertakings in a similar position: – are subject, in the place in question or in the sector concerned, to the same obligations as posting undertakings as regards the matters listed in the first subparagraph of paragraph 1, and
   – are required to fulfil such obligations with the same effects (Article 3(8)).
415. All building work relating to the construction, repair, upkeep, alteration or demolition of buildings, and in particular the following work: (1) excavation, (2) earthmoving, (3) actual building work, (4)

– other collective agreements or arbitration awards, generally binding, for other activities indicated by the Member State (Article 3(10)) concerning:
(a) working time (maximum work and minimum rest periods);
(b) minimum paid annual vacation;
(c) minimum wage (including overtime);[416]
(d) rules concerning temporary work;
(e) safety, health and hygiene at work;
(f) protection of motherhood, children and youngsters;
(g) equal treatment for men and women and other matters relating to nondiscrimination (Art. 3(1)).

There are minimum conditions. They can obviously be improved upon (Art. 3(7)(1)).

1105. Under Norwegian law, workers within the maritime construction industry who are posted to its territory from another EEA State, are secured certain terms and conditions of employment, by way of nationwide collective agreements that have been declared universally applicable. Among these are maximum working hours, additional remuneration to the basic hourly wage for work assignments requiring overnight stays away from home and compensation for travel, board and lodging expenses in the case of work assignments that require overnight stays away from home. Borgarting lagmannsrett has asked the EFTA Court if the Directive precludes such terms and conditions of employment.

In its judgment the Court pointed out, first, that the Directive does not allow the host EEA State to make the provision of services in its territory conditional on the observance of terms and conditions of employment which go beyond the mandatory rules for minimum protection under the Directive.

1106. The Court found that terms and conditions regarding maximum normal working hours, such as those in question, are covered by the Directive's mandatory rules for minimum protection. Furthermore, the Court held that provisions concerning remuneration paid in compensation for working outside normal working hours are compatible with the Directive, provided these fall within the notion of 'minimum rates of pay'. However, as regards entitlement to additional remuneration for work assignments requiring overnight stays away from home, the Court found that it is liable to make it less attractive, or more difficult, for undertakings established

---

assembly and dismantling of prefabricated elements, (5) fitting out or installation, (6) alterations, (7) renovation, (8) repairs, (9) dismantling, (10) demolition, (11) maintenance, (12) upkeep, painting and cleaning work, (13) improvements.

416. This does not apply to complementary pension schemes (Article 3(1)(iii)). The notion of minimum wage is the wage as defined by law or practice of the posted Member State (Article 3(1) last para.). Allocations which go along with the posting are considered to be pay, except when they concern the payment of expenses made, such as for travel, housing and catering (Article 3(7), para. 2). Bonuses and allocations like a thirteenth and a fourteenth month, as well as vacation pay, quality bonuses and bonuses for dirty, heavy and dangerous work have to be treated as constituent elements of the minimum wage (C.O.J., 14 April 2005, *Commission v. Germany*, C-341/02,). One talks about gross pay.

in other EEA States to perform their services in Norway, and therefore constitutes a restriction on the freedom to provide services.

The Court held, further, that such a restriction may be justified only if it pursues a legitimate objective and is justified by overriding reasons of public interest. If so, the restriction must be suitable and not go beyond what is necessary in order to attain its objective. This is for the national court to determine on an objective basis.

1107. On the point concerning compensation for travel, board and lodging expenses the Court stated that such payments cannot fall within the notion of pay within the meaning of Article 3(1). An EEA State is therefore not permitted to impose such terms and conditions, unless this can be justified on the basis of public policy provisions[417].

1108. Mention should be made of the provisions concerning transnational situations relating to the protection of employees in the event of the insolvency of their employer.[418]

B. *Other Conditions*

1109. Member States can impose:

- working conditions relating to public order;[419]
- working conditions contained in generally binding collective agreements, other than construction, as indicated above (Article 3(10)).

These relate to the hard core of minimum conditions as indicated by Article 3, 1. The same for the application of the conditions of employment, which are more favourable to workers, according to Article 3, 7; they concern the hard core and not other conditions.

Undertakings of the Member States should be treated equally (Article 3(10)). Undertakings from non-Member States cannot have a more favourable treatment than enterprises located in Member States (Article 1(4)).

1110. Under the first indent of Article 3(10) of Directive 96/71 it is open to Member States, in compliance with the EC Treaty, to apply, in a non-discriminatory manner, to undertakings which post workers to their territory terms and conditions of employment on matters other than those referred to the first subparagraph of Article 3(1), in the case of public policy provisions.

---

417. C.O.J., 23 January 2012, *STX Norway Offshore AS and Others*, E-2/11, www.eftacourt.int.
418. Article 3(1) sets out an exhaustive list of the matters in respect of which the Member States may give priority to the rules in force in the host Member State; see Part I, Chatper X, §3, III.
    See Directive 2008/94/EC of 22 October 2008 on the protection of employees in the event of the insolvency of their employer (Codified version) O.J., 28 October 2008, L 283. C.O.J., 19 June 2008, *Commission v. Grand Duchy of Luxembourg*, C-319/06, ECR, 2008, 4323.
419. E.g. forced labour or labour inspection.

In that connection, it must be recalled that the classification of national provisions by a Member State as public-order legislation applies to national provisions compliance with which has been deemed to be so crucial for the protection of the political, social or economic order in the Member State concerned as to require compliance therewith by all persons present on the national territory of that Member State and all legal relationships within that State.

Therefore the public policy exception is a derogation from the fundamental principle of freedom to provide services which must be interpreted strictly, the scope of which cannot be determined unilaterally by the Member States (see, regarding freedom of movement for persons).

In the context of Directive 96/71, the first indent of Article 3(10), constitutes a derogation from the principle that the matters with respect to which the host Member State may apply its legislation to undertakings which post workers to its territory are set out in an exhaustive list in the first subparagraph of Article 3(1) thereof. The first indent of Article 3(10) must therefore be interpreted strictly.

The expression 'public policy provisions' is to be construed as covering those mandatory rules from which there can be no derogation and which, by their nature and objective, meet the imperative requirements of the public interest.

1111. Not falling as mandatory provisions falling under national public policy:

- the requirement of a written contract or document established pursuant to Directive 91/533;[420]
- the requirement relating to the automatic adjustment of rates of remuneration to the cost of living;
- the requirement of equal treatment relating to the rules on part-time and fixed-term work;
- the requirement relating to imperative provisions of national law in respect of collective agreements.[421]

---

420. The Court has consistently held that, although Community law does not preclude Member States from applying their legislation or collective labour agreements entered into by both sides of industry to any person who is employed, even temporarily, no matter in which Member State the employer is established, nevertheless such a possibility is subject to the condition that the workers concerned, who are temporarily working in the host Member State, do not already enjoy the same protection, or essentially comparable protection by virtue of obligations to which their employer is already subject in the Member State in which it is established.
421. C.O.J., 19 June 2008, *Commission v. Grand Duchy of Luxembourg*, C-319/06, ECR, 2008, 4323. Measures resulting, in particular, from collective agreements which have been declared universally applicable cannot, however, constitute a public policy exception within the meaning of the first indent of Article 3(10) of Directive 96/71. First, there is no reason why provisions concerning collective agreements, namely provisions which encompass their drawing up and implementation, should *per se* and without more fall under the definition of public policy. Second, such a finding must be made as regards the actual provisions of such collective agreements themselves, which in their entirety and for the simple reason that they derive from that type of measure, cannot fall under that definition either.

C. Exceptions[422]

1112. Possible exceptions are foreseen as follows.

(a) In the case of initial assembly and/or first installation of goods where this is an integral part of a contract for the supply of goods necessary for taking the goods supplied into use and carried out by the skilled and/or specialist workers of the supplying undertaking, the first subparagraph of paragraph 1(b) (annual holidays) and (c) (minimum pay) shall not apply, if the period of posting does not exceed eight days.
This exception does not apply to activities in the field of building work.
(b) Member States may, after consulting employers and labour, in accordance with the traditions and practices of each Member State, decide not to apply the first subparagraph of paragraph 1(c) (minimum pay) in the cases referred to in Article 1(3)(a) (subcontracting) and (b) (group) when the length of the posting does not exceed one month.
(c) Member States may, in accordance with national laws and/or practices, provide that exemptions may be made from the first subparagraph of paragraph 1(c) (minimum pay) in the cases referred to in Article 1(3)(a) (subcontracting) and
(b) (temporary work) and from a decision by a Member State regarding b. above, by means of generally binding collective agreements concerning one or more sectors of activity, where the length of the posting does not exceed one month.
(d) Member States may provide for exemptions to be granted from the first subparagraph of paragraph 1(b) (annual holidays) and (c) (minimum pay) in the cases referred to in Article 1(3)(a) (subcontracting) and (b) (group) on the grounds that the amount of work to be done is not significant.

IV. Cooperation and Transparency (Article 4)

1113. This covers the following points:

– Member States indicate one or more liaison offices and inform the other Member States and the Commission;
– Member States provide for cooperation between the administrations competent for the surveillance of the working conditions stated in Article 3, especially regarding information on the transnational supply of workers including manifest abuses or possible cases of unlawful transnational activities;
– Member States and the Commission look closely at the equal treatment of enterprises;
– Member States must see to it that the information concerning working conditions is 'generally available'.

---

422. The duration of the posting is done over a period of one year after its commencement. The duration of the posting effectuated by a replaced worker is taken into consideration (Article 3(6)).

V. Enforcement (Article 5)

1114. Member States take appropriate measures in the event of failure to comply with this directive.

They shall in particular ensure that adequate procedures are available to workers and/or their representatives for the enforcement of obligations under this directive.

A. Guarantee

1115. A possible measure is the obligation on an undertaking to act as guarantor in respect of the minimum remuneration of workers employed by a subcontractor. Such an obligation is not contrary to the freedom of services, the Court of Justice ruled in the *Wolff and Müller* case.[423]

The facts of this case were as follows. Mr. Pereira Félix is a Portuguese national who, from 21 February to 15 May 2000, was employed in Berlin (Germany) as a bricklayer on a building site by a construction undertaking established in Portugal. The latter carried out concreting and reinforced-concrete work on that building site for Wolff and Müller.

Mr. Pereira Félix sought payment jointly and severally from his employer and from Wolff and Müller of unpaid remuneration amounting to DEM 4,019.23. He claimed that Wolff and Müller, as guarantor, was liable, under German law, for sums in respect of wages not received by him.

Wolff and Müller opposed the claims by Mr. Pereira Félix, arguing in particular that it was not liable on the ground that the German legislation constituted an unlawful infringement of the constitutional right to carry on an occupation under Article 12 of the *Grundgesetz* (Basic Law) and of the freedom to provide services enshrined by the EC Treaty.

1116. The following question was referred to the Court for a preliminary ruling:

> Does Article 56 TFEU preclude a national system whereby, when subcontracting the conduct of building work to another undertaking, a building contractor becomes liable, in the same way as a guarantor who has waived benefit of execution, for the obligation on that undertaking or that undertaking's subcontractors to pay the minimum wage to a worker or to pay contributions to a joint scheme for parties to a collective agreement where the minimum wage means the sum payable to the worker after deduction of tax, social security contributions, payments towards the promotion of employment or other such social insurance payments (net pay), if the safeguarding of workers' pay is not the primary objective of the legislation or is merely a subsidiary objective?

---

[423]. C.O.J., 12 October 2004, *Wolff and Müller GmbH & Co. KG* v. *José Filipe Pereira Félix*, C60/03, ECR, 2004, 9553.

1117. The Court answered as follows:

'The provisions of the Directive 96/71 are to be taken into consideration for the purposes of the examination of the question referred for a preliminary ruling.'

Directive 96/71

1118. Under Article 5 of Directive 96/71, the Member States are to take appropriate measures in the event of non-compliance with its terms. In particular they are to ensure that the workers and/or their representatives have available to them adequate procedures for the enforcement of obligations under this Directive. Included in those obligations, as is apparent from Article 3(1)(c) of the directive, is the obligation to ensure that undertakings guarantee to workers posted in their territory the payment of minimum rates of pay.

It follows that the Member States must ensure, in particular, that workers posted have available to them adequate procedures in order actually to obtain minimum rates of pay.

Wide Margin of Appreciation

1119. It is apparent from the wording of Article 5 of Directive 96/71 that the Member States have a wide margin of appreciation in determining the form and detailed rules governing the adequate procedures under the second paragraph of Article 5. In applying that wide margin of appreciation they must however at all times observe the fundamental freedoms guaranteed by the Treaty and, thus, in regard to the main proceedings, freedom to provide services.

Elimination of all Discrimination

1120. In that regard it should first be recalled that, under settled case law, Article 56 TFEU requires not only the elimination of all discrimination on grounds of nationality against providers of services who are established in another Member State, but also the abolition of any restriction, even if it applies without distinction to national providers of services and to those of other Member States, which is liable to prohibit, impede or render less attractive the activities of a provider of services established in another Member State in which he lawfully provides similar services.

As the Court held, the application of the host Member State's domestic legislation to service providers is liable to prohibit, impede or render less attractive the provision of services by persons or undertakings established in other Member States to the extent that it involves expenses and additional administrative and economic burdens.

It is for the referring court to determine whether that is the case in the main proceedings concerning liability as guarantor. In that connection it is important to take account of the effect of that measure on the provision of services not only by subcontractors established in another Member State but also by any general undertakings from that State.

Overriding Requirements Relating to the Public Interest

1121. It is further clear from settled case law that, where legislation such as Paragraph 1a of the AEntG, on the supposition that it constitutes a restriction on freedom to provide services, is applicable to all persons and undertakings operating in the territory of the Member State in which the service is provided, it may be justified where it meets overriding requirements relating to the public interest in so far as that interest is not safeguarded by the rules to which the provider of such a service is subject in the Member State in which he is established and in so far as it is appropriate for securing the attainment of the objective which it pursues and does not go beyond what is necessary in order to attain it.

Overriding Reasons Relating to the Public Interest which have been Recognised by the Court Include the Protection of Workers

1122. However, although it may be acknowledged that, in principle, the application by the host Member State of its minimum-wage legislation to providers of services established in another Member State pursues an objective of public interest, namely the protection of employees, the same is true in principle of measures adopted by the host Member State and intended to reinforce the procedural arrangements enabling a posted worker usefully to assert his right to a minimum rate of pay.

Minimum Rates of Pay

1123. In fact, if entitlement to minimum rates of pay constitutes a feature of worker protection, the procedural arrangements ensuring observance of that right, such as the liability of the guarantor in the main proceedings, must likewise be regarded as being such as to ensure that protection.

In regard to the national court's observation that the priority purpose pursued by the German legislature is to protect the national job market rather than remuneration of the worker, it should be pointed out that it is for that court to verify whether, on an objective view, the legislation at issue in the main proceedings secures the protection of posted workers. It is necessary to determine whether those rules confer a genuine benefit on the workers concerned, which significantly augments their social protection. In this context, the stated intention of the legislature may lead to a more careful assessment of the alleged benefits conferred on workers by the measures which it has adopted.

Guarantee

1124. It is the case that such a provision benefits posted workers on the ground that, to the advantage of the latter, it adds to the first debtor of the minimum rate of pay, who is the employer, a second debtor who is jointly liable with the first debtor and is generally more solvent. On an objective view a rule of that kind is therefore such as to ensure the protection of posted workers. Moreover, the dispute in the main proceedings itself appears to confirm that the provision is of protective intent.

Inasmuch as one of the objectives pursued by the national legislature is to prevent unfair competition on the part of undertakings paying their workers at a rate less than the minimum rate of pay, a matter which it is for the referring court to determine, such an objective may be taken into consideration as an overriding requirement capable of justifying a restriction on freedom to provide services.

Moreover, there is not necessarily any contradiction between the objective of upholding fair competition on the one hand and ensuring worker protection, on the other. The fifth recital in the preamble to Directive 96/71 demonstrates that those two objectives can be pursued concomitantly.

Proportionality

1125. Finally, as regards the observations of Wolff and Müller according to which liability as guarantor is disproportionate in relation to the objective pursued, it is in fact clear from the case law cited hereof that, in order to be justified, a measure must be apt to ensure attainment of the objective pursued by it and must not go beyond what is necessary in that connection.

It is for the national court to determine that those conditions are met in regard to the objective sought, which is to ensure protection of the worker concerned.

Conclusion: not Contrary

1126. Article 5 of Directive 96/71/EC of the European Parliament and of the Council of 16 December 1996 concerning the posting of workers in the framework of the provision of services, interpreted in the light of Article 56 TFEU, does not preclude, in a case such as that in the main proceedings, a national system whereby, when subcontracting the conduct of building work to another undertaking, a building contractor becomes liable, in the same way as a guarantor who has waived benefit of execution, for the obligation on that undertaking or that undertaking's subcontractors to pay the minimum wage to a worker or to pay contributions to a joint scheme for parties to a collective agreement where the minimum wage means the sum payable to the worker after deduction of tax, social security contributions, payments towards the promotion of employment or other such social insurance payments (net pay), if the safeguarding of workers' pay is not the primary objective of the legislation or is merely a subsidiary objective.

The question is, as follows from the next case, whether the control and sanctions are necessary and appropriate.

B. Translation and Notification

1127. An action against the Federal Republic of Germany was brought by the European Commission before the Court of Justice on 29 November 2004[424] in order to

(1) declare that, by providing that the Federal Republic of Germany has failed to fulfil its obligations under Article 56 TFEU as …
  - (b) foreign undertakings are obliged to have the employment contract (or the documents required, pursuant to Directive 91/533/EEC, under the law of the State where the employee is resident), pay slips, time sheets, proof of payment of wages, and all other documents required by the German authorities, translated into German;
  - (c) foreign employment agencies are obliged not only to give prior notification each time a worker is posted to a user of the worker's services in Germany, but also each time a worker starts a new job on a building site at the request of the user of his services …

1128. The Court declared that in enacting a provision, such as paragraph 3(2) of the law on posting workers (*Arbeitsnehmerentsendegesetz*) of 26 February 1996, under which foreign temporary employment agencies are required to declare, not only the placement of a worker with a user of his services in Germany, but also any change relating to the place of employment of that worker, the Federal Republic of Germany had failed to fulfil its obligations under Article 49 EC.[425]

1129. The Commission contends that furthermore certain provisions of the *Arbeitnehmerentsendegesetz* (Law on the Posting of Workers) ('the AEntG'); which transposed Directive 96/71/EC on the posting of workers into national law do not comply with certain provisions of that directive.

Rules relating to the obligation of employers established in a Member State other than Germany to translate documents.

In the Commission's view, the requirement for documents to be translated is appropriate to meeting Germany's monitoring needs. However, having regard to the cooperation on information provided for by Article 4 of the Directive on the posting of workers, the obligation to translate all documents is no longer necessary and is therefore too far-reaching.

Rules relating to the obligation of employment agencies established in a Member State other than Germany to notify the competent authorities of the change before each transfer of a posted worker from one building site to another one are equally unacceptable.

Even if the obligation of employment agencies established outside Germany to notify each change has been slightly amended, the Commission is of the view that

---

424. Notice, O.J., Case C-490/04.
425. C.O.J., 18 July 2007, *Commission of the European Communities v. Federal Republic of Germany*, C-490/04, www.curia.eu.

there is still unequal treatment, as, in the case of employment agencies established in Germany, the obligation to notify each change falls on the user of the worker's services, while in the case of employment agencies established outside Germany that obligation falls in principle on the supplier of labour and can be transferred to the user of the worker's services only by means of a contractual agreement. This unequal treatment constitutes an inadmissible restriction on the freedom to provide services within the meaning of Article 56 TFEU.

C. EU Posting of Workers Certificate and Visa and Notification Procedure

1130. An action against the Republic of Austria was brought before the Court of Justice of the European Communities on 5 April 2004 by the Commission with the claim that the providers of services resident in another Member State are adversely affected by three different supervisory procedures with three different Austrian authorities in regard to the posting of workers who are third-country nationals to Austria:[426]

– an 'EU Posting of Workers Certificate' to be obtained at the regional branch of the employment service in addition to
– the 'visa' issued by the competent consulates, and
– a notification procedure to check pay and working conditions.

1131. The requirement of an EU Posting of Workers Certificate has a restrictive effect on freedom to provide services in the Union.

The requirement of an EU Posting of Workers Certificate in addition to the visa and the notification procedure is disproportionate to the objectives pursued by the Republic of Austria of combating abusive practices and protecting workers.

1. Prevention of Abusive Practices

1132. The Austrian government is infringing the principle of proportionality, as effective control of the conditions governing the posting of workers in connection with the provision of services can be ensured through less far-reaching measures.

The legitimate interest of a Member State in checking compliance with the conditions governing the posting of workers who are third-country nationals by companies providing services can be adequately served by the requirement of a visa. Any additional control, as here by way of an EU Posting of Workers Certificate, which is issued by another authority, is unjustified.

---

426. Action brought on 5 April 2004 by the Commission against the Republic of Austria, (Case C168/04), C.O.J., 21 September 2006.

2. Compliance with Pay and Working Conditions

1133. The substantive condition under which the EU Posting of Workers Certificate is issued only if the Austrian wage and working conditions laid down in the AVRAG are complied with likewise results in disproportionate duplicated checks.

The requirement of an EU Posting of Workers Certificate and the procedure associated with it are disproportionate to the objective sought of ensuring worker protection, since the Republic of Austria already has available to it less far-reaching means.

The Republic of Austria transposed the posting of workers directive by means of the AVRAG which provides for the possibility of *ex post* controls in order to check that the requisite salaries are actually being paid.

3. Regular Workers

1134. The requirement as a condition for the EU Posting of Workers Certificate of at least one-year's employment or an indefinite employment contract with the provider of services constitutes an unjustified restriction on freedom to provide services. The objective of combating abusive practices can also be attained through far less restrictive measures.

4. Refusal of Residence Permits

1135. A residence permit must be refused when the worker has already entered the country without a visa. That provision prohibits a posting, even if the providers of the services can establish lawfulness, namely that an application has already been made on the basis of which a Member State can carry out the required checks.

The automatic refusal of a residence permit is disproportionate to the objective of control of the conditions governing the right of residence and should therefore be declared unlawful.

The automatic refusal of a visa in cases of merely formal illegal entry considerably restricts freedom to provide services and renders that freedom illusory in some service sectors. In the current state of Union law the Austrian Republic has, by virtue of the checks on issue of entry visas, means available to it which are just as effective but less far-reaching of reviewing whether third-country nationals are entering the country for the purpose of providing services.

D. *Designate an ad hoc Agent*

1136. There is an infringement of Article 56 TFEU by reason of the requirement that the undertakings designate an *ad hoc* agent residing in the host country to retain the documents necessary for monitoring by the competent national authorities.

In that connection, the Court has held that the effective protection of workers may require that certain documents are kept at the place where the service is provided, or at least in an accessible and clearly identified place in the territory of the host Member State, so that they are available to the authorities of that State responsible for carrying out checks.

However, the Court added, that where there is an obligation to keep available and retain certain documents at the address of a natural person residing in the host Member State who holds them as the agent or representative of the employer by whom he has been designated, even after the employer has ceased to employ workers in that State, it is not sufficient, for the purposes of justifying such a restriction on the freedom to provide services, that the presence of such documents within the territory of the host Member State may make it generally easier for the authorities of that State to perform their supervisory task. It must also be shown that those authorities cannot carry out their supervisory task effectively unless the undertaking has, in that Member State, an agent or representative designated to retain the documents in question. In that connection, the Court has held that a requirement that a natural person domiciled in the territory of a host Member State should retain documents cannot be justified.

In any event, a worker present in the place where the services were provided could be designated to ensure that documents necessary for monitoring purposes were made available to the competent national authorities, which would be a measure less restrictive of freedom to provide services and just as effective as the contested obligation.

For the rest, the organised system for cooperation and exchanges of information between Member States provided for in Article 4 of Directive 96/71 renders superfluous the retention of the documents in the host Member State after the employer has ceased to employ workers there.

Consequently, a Member State cannot require undertakings which post workers to do what is necessary to retain such documents on its territory when the provision of services comes to an end.

Nor can such documents be required to be retained by an agent residing in Luxembourg in so far as, since the undertaking concerned is physically present on the territory when the services are provided, the documents in question may be held by a posted worker.[427]

VI. Jurisdiction (Article 6)

1137. In order to enforce the right to the terms and conditions of employment guaranteed in Article 3, judicial proceedings may be instituted in the Member State in whose territory the worker is or was posted, without prejudice, where applicable, to the right, under existing international conventions on jurisdiction, to institute proceedings in another state.

---

427. C.O.J., 19 June 2008, *Commission v. Grand Duchy of Luxembourg*, C-319/06, ECR, 2008, 4323.

VII. Implementation (Article 7) – Review (Article 8)

1138. Member States shall bring into force the laws, regulations and administrative provisions necessary to comply with this directive within a period of three years. They shall forthwith inform the Commission thereof.

When Member States adopt these provisions, they shall contain a reference to this directive or shall be accompanied by such reference on the occasion of their official publication. The methods of making such reference shall be laid down by Member States.

The Commission will review the operation of the directive with a view to propose the necessary amendments to the Council where appropriate five years after adoption.

VIII. Commission Guidance on the Posting of Workers in the Framework of the Provision of Services[428]

A. Guidance: Control Measures

1. General Application Measures

1139. Of the measures implemented by certain Member States, the following urgently require clarification on the basis of the case law of the Court of Justice based on Article 56 TFEU:

– the requirement to have a representative on the territory of the host Member State;
– the requirement to obtain authorisation from the competent authorities of the host Member State or to be registered with them, or any other equivalent obligation;
– the requirement to make a declaration;
– the requirement to keep and maintain social documents on the territory of the host country and/or under the conditions which apply in its territory.

a. The Requirement to have a Representative Established on the Territory of the Host Member State

1140. The Court described the requirement to have a subsidiary on the national territory as constituting 'the very negation of the free provision of services'. An obligation on the service provider to appoint a representative domiciled in a particular Member State in order to offer services there would appear to be incompat-

---

[428]. Brussels, 4 April 2006, Communication from the Commission COM(2006) 159 final SEC(2006) 439. *See* Commission's services report on the implementation of Directive 96/71/EC concerning the posting of workers in the framework of the provision of services, 4 April 2006 (COM(2006) 159 final); Posting of workers in the framework of the promotion of services: maximising its benefits and potential while guaranteeing the protection of workers, 13 June 2007 (SEC(2007) 747); Posting of workers in the framework of the promotion of services: archieving the full benefits and potential, 13 June 2007 (SEC(2007)747).

ible with Article 56 TFEU, being similar to the requirement to elect domicile with an approved agent, which has already been declared unlawful by the Court.

1141. In the judgment *Arblade et al.*, the Court ruled that the obligation to have available and keep certain documents at the domicile of a natural person resident in the host Member State, who would hold them as the employer's appointed agent or proxy, even after the employer has stopped employing workers in that state, could only be admissible if the national authorities were not able to effectively perform their control duties effectively in the absence of such an obligation. This case law must be interpreted on a case-by-case basis, but it can be considered that, to fulfil this role, the appointment of a person from among the posted workers, for example a foreman, to act as the link between the foreign company and the labour inspectorate, should be sufficient.

Conclusion: Pursuant to current case law, it must be concluded that the requirement made by a Member State that companies posting workers on its territory must have a representative domiciled in that host Member State is disproportionate for monitoring the working conditions of these workers. The appointment of a person from among the posted workers, for example a foreman, to act as the link between the foreign company and the labour inspectorate, should suffice.

b. The Requirement to Obtain Authorisation from the Competent Authorities of the Host Member State or to be Registered with Them, or any Other Equivalent Obligation

1142. According to the established case law of the Court of Justice, national rules which stipulate that the provision of services on national territory by a company established in another Member State is subject, as a general rule and for all activities, to obtaining an administrative authorisation, constitute a restriction of the free provision of services within the meaning of Article 56 TFEU.

There are certain activities whose exercise is regulated in the Member States by legal or regulatory provisions including a specific authorisation system for each activity. For example, many Member States insist that temporary employment agents must be properly authorised, so as to ensure that they have sufficient guarantees to perform this work.

The host Member State is entitled to require prior authorisation only for the performance of certain activities, whatever the posting situation, on condition that this can be justified by overriding reasons based on the general interest, is proportionate and is compatible with the relevant provisions of the Treaty concerning the free provision of services. This requirement must take into account the controls and monitoring already carried out in the Member State of origin.

Conclusion: Pursuant to current case law, it must be concluded that any rules which make the posting of workers subject to systematic prior control, including by way of compulsory and systematic prior authorisation or registration, would be disproportionate.

c. Requirement to Make a Declaration

1143. Almost half the Member States require service providers which post workers to their territory to submit a prior declaration to their authorities. The purpose of such declarations would appear to be, on the one hand, to enable the national authorities to verify the information on the posting of workers obtained during *in situ* checks and, on the other, to help the labour inspectorates to conduct risk assessments in order to target their checks at situations or companies which are at high risk.

At this stage, the Court has not delivered any judgments relating specifically to the admissibility of an obligation to make a declaration concerning the posting of workers. In the case *Commission* v. *Luxembourg* in which a posted worker who was a national of a third country was required to have a work permit in order to provide services, the Court declared that 'a measure which would be just as effective whilst being less restrictive than the measures at issue here would be an obligation imposed on a service-providing undertaking to report beforehand to the local authorities on the presence of one or more deployed workers, the anticipated duration of their presence and the provision or provisions of services justifying the deployment. It would enable those authorities to monitor compliance with Luxembourg social welfare legislation during the deployment while at the same time taking account of the obligations by which the undertaking is already bound under the social welfare legislation applicable in the Member State of origin.'

As regards the posting of workers who are nationals of a third country by a Community service provider, the Court concluded in its judgment in the case *Commission* v. *Federal Republic of Germany*, that 'as the Advocate General observed a requirement that the service provider furnishes a simple prior declaration certifying that the situation of the workers concerned is lawful … in the Member State where that provider employs them, would give the national authorities, in a less restrictive but as effective a manner as checks in advance of posting, a guarantee that those workers' situation is lawful and that they are carrying on their main activity in the Member State where the service provider is established. Such a requirement would enable the national authorities to check that information subsequently and to take the necessary measures if those workers' situation was not regular'.

Under this case law of the Court, a declaration is deemed to be a measure which is just as effective as and less restrictive than a prior authorisation when it comes to ensuring that Member States are informed at all times about the presence of posted workers from third countries on their territory.

The Member States must refrain from using declarations for purposes other than for providing information, such as for checking or registering companies which provide services, which would amount to a system of authorisation.

Conclusion: On the basis of existing case law, the Commission considers that the host Member State, in order to be able to monitor compliance with the conditions of employment laid down in the Directive, should be able to demand, in accordance with the principle of proportionality, that the service provider submit a declaration, by the time the work starts, at the latest, which contains information on the workers who have been posted, the type of service they will provide, where, and how long the work will take. The declaration could mention that posted workers from third countries are in a lawful situation in the country in which the service provider is established, including with regard to the visa requirements, and legally employed in that country.

d. The Requirement to Keep and Maintain Social Documents on the Territory of the Host Country and/or under the Conditions which Apply in its Territory

1144. The Court of Justice has expressed its opinion on the obligation to keep and store social security documents on posted workers in the host Member State.

In its judgment in the case concerning *Arblade et al.*, the Court pointed out that the effective protection of workers, particularly as regards health and safety matters and working hours, could require that certain documents be kept in an accessible and clearly identified place in the territory of the host Member State, so that they were available to the authorities of that State responsible for carrying out checks, 'particularly where there exists no organised system for cooperation or exchanges of information between Member States as provided for in Article 4 of Directive 96/71/EC'.

However, in the same judgment, the Court explained that, before imposing an obligation of this kind on a service provider, the competent authorities in the host country would have to verify that the social protection of the workers concerned was not sufficiently safeguarded by the production, within a reasonable time, of the documents kept in the Member State of establishment. In the *Finalarte* cases, the Court accepted that businesses established outside the host Member State could be required to provide more information than businesses established in that State, to the extent that this difference in treatment could be attributed to objective differences between those businesses and businesses established in the host Member State.

However, the Court also said that it was necessary to check whether the information provided in the documents required under the legislation of the Member State of establishment were sufficient as a whole to enable the checks needed in the host Member State to be carried out.

Since the period for transposing the Directive came to an end in 1999, and since a system of cooperation on information pursuant to Article 4 has been gradually put in place, the Member States have had less scope to demand that certain social documents be kept in the State to which workers have been posted. However, the Commission takes the view that the host Member State could still demand that certain documents which have to be generated and held *in situ* are kept in the workplace, such as records on actual hours worked or documents on conditions of health and safety in the workplace. In order that the authorities in the host Member State can monitor conditions of employment in accordance with the Directive, they are allowed to require the service provider to produce documents which are considered necessary for carrying out these checks within a reasonable period of time.

However, it is not acceptable for the host Member State to demand that a second set of documents which comply with its own legislation be provided simply because the documents which comply with the legislation of the Member State of establishment exhibit certain differences in terms of form and content. Nor is it acceptable for the host Member State to require that social security documents be provided as they are the subject of a specific procedure in the country of origin, pursuant to Regulation (EEC) No. 1408/71.

However, the Court of Justice recognised in the cases concerning *Arblade et al.* that 'the items of information respectively required by the rules of the Member State of establishment and by those of the host Member State ... may differ to such an extent that the monitoring required under the rules of the host Member State cannot be carried out on the basis of documents kept in accordance with the rules of the Member State of establishment.'

Conclusion: On the basis of the aforementioned case law, it must be concluded that, in order to be able to monitor compliance with the conditions of employment laid down in the Directive, the host Member State must be able to demand, in accordance with the principle of proportionality, that documents be kept in the workplace which are, by their nature, created there, such as time sheets or documents on conditions of health and safety in the workplace. The host Member State cannot demand a second set of documents if the documents required under the legislation of the Member State of establishment, taken as a whole, already provide sufficient information, to allow the host Member State to carry out the checks required.

2. Measures which Apply to Posted Workers who are Nationals of Third Countries

1145. In the existing case law on the freedom to provide services in accordance with Article 56 TFEU, the Court took the view that workers who were regularly and habitually employed by a service provider established in a Member State (country of origin) could be posted to another Member State (host country) without being subject in the latter State to administrative formalities, such as the obligation to obtain a work permit.

1146. The Court also held that a number of additional conditions which certain Member States imposed with regard to the posting of workers from third countries were excessive. In the case *Commission* v. *Germany*, the Court held that German legislation ran counter to Article 54 TFEU by requiring nationals of third countries posted to Germany by a company established in another Member State to have been employed by that company for at least a year in order to be eligible for a residence visa. In this case, the Court confirmed its judgment in the case *Commission* v. *Luxembourg*, in which it concluded that legislation requiring posted workers to have been employed for at least six months before being posted went beyond what was required for the objective of the social welfare protection of workers who were nationals of a third country and therefore was not justified. In the latter judgment, the Court also censured the requirement concerning contracts of employment of indefinite duration.

Conclusion: On the basis of existing case law, it must be concluded that the host Member State may not impose administrative formalities or additional conditions on posted workers from third countries when they are lawfully employed by a service provider established in another Member State, without prejudice to the right of the host Member State to check that these conditions are complied with in the Member State where the service provider is established.

B. Cooperation on Information

1. Access to Information

1147. Article 4(3) of the Directive sets out a clear obligation for Member States to take the appropriate measures to make the information on the terms and conditions of employment generally available to foreign service providers and to workers.

There is major scope for improvement as regards the use of tools to provide information on the terms and conditions of employment during posting, and on the obligations to fulfil.

Supplementary efforts are needed in order to bring about visible improvements on the following aspects:

– while the number of national internet sites dedicated specifically to posting has grown substantially, there is still a need for Member States to make better use of internet possibilities and to improve the accessibility and clarity of the information provided on the national websites;
– Member States need to make it clear which part of their national legislation has to be applied by foreign service providers, and avoid having only information on labour law in general, without specifying which terms and conditions have to be applied to posted workers;
– information should be made available in other languages than the national language(s) of the host country;
– liaison offices need to be equipped with appropriate staff and other resources to fulfil their information duties;
– Member States should indicate a contact person in charge of dealing with requests for information, as this works better than a large, anonymous structure;
– liaison offices also need to have at their disposal an efficiently organised structure.

They need to be able to function as an intermediary between the person requesting information and other competent national bodies.

1148. In order to fulfil their obligations, Member States are asked to redouble their efforts to enhance, and improve access to, the information on the terms and conditions of employment that must be applied by service providers, and to ensure that their liaison offices are in a position to carry out their tasks effectively. The Commission will continue to support the Member States in this area, especially through the expert group, and will monitor their efforts in order to make sure that they contribute to progress towards best practices.

2. Cooperation between Member States

1149. Article 4(1) and (2) of the Directive imposes clear obligations as regards cooperation between national administrations, and makes it the responsibility of Member States to create the necessary conditions for such cooperation. This obligation includes the creation of a monitoring authority that can reply to a reasoned request on, for instance, whether the company providing transnational services is truly established in the Member State of origin or to a request for documentary evidence to establish whether the worker is considered a worker according to the legislation of the host Member State.

The information request can also be needed in the reverse direction. For instance, when the posting is over and the posted worker wants to know whether he received what he was entitled to over the period of posting.

1150. In order to comply with Article 4 of the Directive, Member States have to ensure that liaison offices and monitoring authorities are organised and equipped in such a way as to function effectively and to be able to reply promptly to requests. This may require liaison offices and/or monitoring authorities to undertake investigations or to obtain information from other sources or bodies (such as social security institutions), and they will have to do so in the same way as in domestic cases and in accordance with national legislation.

Transnational cooperation can be improved by building on the initiatives taken by the Commission through the expert group, in particular the drafting of a code of conduct on good cooperation and the adoption of a multilingual form for the exchange of information between authorities. In order to facilitate the exchange of information, use can be made in due time of the electronic system which will be set up by the Commission in support of the Services Directive.

In order to fulfil their obligations, Member States are asked to take the necessary measures to ensure that their liaison offices and/or monitoring authorities have the necessary equipment and resources to respond effectively to requests for information and cross-border cooperation from the competent authorities of the other Member States. The Commission will continue to support the Member States in this area, especially by making more appropriate electronic systems available, and will monitor their progress closely.

C. *Monitoring of Compliance with the Directive and Measures in the Event of Failure to Comply*

1151. Member States have an obligation to guarantee certain terms and conditions to workers posted to their territory under Article 3 of the Directive, and to take measures to prevent and combat any unlawful behaviour by service providers, such as refusing to offer such terms and conditions. This is a fundamental condition for establishing fair competition, which improves public perception of the posting of workers in the context of the cross-border movement of services. Member States must, accordingly, ensure that mechanisms are in place to guarantee compliance with the implementing legislation on the posting of workers.

Part I, Ch. 3, International Private Labour Law

Posted workers and/or organisations representing them should have the possibility to complain directly to the relevant authority of the host Member State, and enforcement should be able to be prompted by complaints by workers or competing undertakings. While this can contribute to better monitoring and enforcement, it also means that the monitoring authority must have the necessary resources and powers to follow up on such complaints.

1152. Member States need to evaluate constantly the effectiveness of labour inspectorates and other monitoring systems and examine ways to improve them, in keeping with their obligations under the Directive. These efforts may be supported by strengthening the cooperation between the national authorities responsible for monitoring (including labour inspectorates) on matters covered by the Directive. At least once a year representatives of the labour inspectorates or other bodies responsible for the monitoring the application of the Directive should meet in the expert group on posting of workers.

In case of failure to comply with the obligations under the Directive, the Member States are obliged under Article 5 of the Directive to take appropriate measures. While it is left to the Member States to choose the appropriate instruments to introduce, these have to be capable of guaranteeing due protection of rights for the persons concerned and be similar to those applicable in case of violations of national law in purely domestic situations.

1153. Where irregularities are detected, Member States must provide for measures, including sanctions and penalties, which are genuine, proportionate and dissuasive in nature. They may also introduce appropriate procedures for workers and/or their representatives to enforce their rights. Easy access to courts and tribunals for posted workers, including arbitration or mediation procedures, on the same footing as national workers, is a precondition in this context.

In a preliminary ruling, the European Court of Justice expressed an opinion on a system of joint and several liability for general or principal contractors. The Court held that Article 5 of the Directive, interpreted in the light of Article 56 TFEU, did not preclude the use of such a system as an appropriate measure in the event of failure to comply with the Directive. The Court also laid down that such a measure must not go beyond what is necessary to attain the objective pursued, and referred to the national court for application of this judgment in the case in question.

Member States are invited to assess the impact of introducing a proportionate and non-discriminatory measure of this kind in national legislation. The Member States that already have such a system in place are invited to assess its effectiveness as a proportionate and non-discriminatory measure, in the event of failure to comply with the Directive.

In order to fulfil their obligations, Member States are asked to re-examine their systems for monitoring and implementing the Directive. They are asked, in particular, to ensure that there is a mechanism in place to remedy any deficiencies; that appropriate and proportionate monitoring measures are in place; and that service providers who do not comply can be effectively sanctioned. The Commission undertakes to work with the Member States in order to improve transnational cooperation of labour inspectorates in the subject areas covered by the Directive on the posting of workers.

D. Conclusions

1154. There is an urgent need to clarify the control measures which Member States can use, in the light of Article 56 TFEU as interpreted by the Court's judgments, and to improve access to information and administrative cooperation. Member States should act to ensure that the guidance provided in this Communication gives rise to concrete results as soon as possible. In order to assess progress, the Commission will adopt within 12 months a report which will examine the situation in all Member States with regard to all aspects covered by this Communication. In order to monitor developments in the Member States and to be able to undertake an objective assessment, on the basis of the guidance set out above, the Commission will:

– address a detailed questionnaire, as soon as possible, to national authorities and social partners, inviting them to comment not only on their own measures but also on how they perceive and assess measures or actions undertaken by other authorities or social partners;
– make a form available through the Commission's website, allowing users to set out their positive or negative experience with obtaining information, with international cooperation and with monitoring and enforcement;
– closely monitor and assess, on an ongoing basis, efforts made by the Member States to facilitate access to information and implement the code of conduct and the standard form for exchange of information. If, as a result of this monitoring exercise, the Commission comes to the conclusion that compliance with the relevant provisions of Union law and/or co-operation between Member States under Articles 4 and 5 of the Directive have not substantially improved, it will take the necessary steps to rectify this situation.

1155. The Commission proposed measures to boost protection for posted workers (21 March 2012).[429]

---

429. For more information Website of DG EMPL on the posting of workers: http://ec.europa.eu/social/posted-workers. Proposal for Directive concerning the enforcement of the provisions applicable to the posting of workers in the framework of the provision of services:http://ec.europa.eu/social/BlobServlet?docId=7479&langId=en Proposal for Regulation on the exercise of the right to take collective action within the context of the economic freedoms of the single market:http://ec.europa.eu/social/BlobServlet?docId=7480&langId=en Commission Staff Document, Impact Assessment, Revision of the legislative framework concerning the posting of workers in the context of the provision of services, SWD(2012) 63:http://ec.europa.eu/social/BlobServlet?docId=7481&langId=en.

Part I, Ch. 3, International Private Labour Law

1156. To make the EU single market work better for workers and for business, the Commission has proposed new rules to increase the protection of workers temporarily posted abroad. Worker protection and fair competition are the two sides of the EU single market's coin, yet findings suggest that minimum employment and working conditions are often not respected for the one million or so posted workers in the EU. To address the specific issues of abuse where workers do not enjoy their full rights in terms of for example, pay or holidays, especially in the construction sector, the Commission has put forward concrete, practical proposals as part of an enforcement Directive to increase monitoring and compliance and to improve the way existing rules on posted workers are applied in practice. This will ensure a level playing field between the businesses involved, excluding companies that don't follow the rules.

To send a strong message that workers' rights and their freedom to strike are on an equal footing with the freedom to provide services the Commission has also put forward a new regulation that takes on board existing case law. This is especially relevant in the context of cross-border services provision like the posting of workers. The overall aim of both proposals is to boost quality jobs and increase competitiveness in the EU by updating and improving the way the single market works, while safeguarding workers' rights.

1157. The proposed Enforcement Directive aims to improve the way the 1996 Directive on the posting of workers is applied in practice, without changing its provisions. In particular, the Enforcement Directive would:

– set more ambitious standards to inform workers and companies about their rights and obligations;
– establish clear rules for cooperation between national authorities in charge of posting;
– provide elements to improve the implementation and monitoring of the notion of posting to avoid the multiplication of "letter-box" companies that use posting as a way to circumvent employment rules;
– define the supervisory scope and responsibilities of relevant national authorities;
– improve the enforcement of workers' rights, including the introduction of joint and several liability for the construction sector for the wages of posted workers as well as the handling of complaints.

1158. The proposed Monti II Regulation addresses concerns that, in the single market, economic freedoms would prevail over the right to strike, stressing that there is no primacy between the right to take collective action and the freedom to provide services. It also sets out a new alert mechanism for industrial conflicts in cross-border situations with severe implications. In no way does the Regulation affect national legislation on the right to strike, nor would it create obstacles to the right to strike.

Each year, around one million workers are posted by their employers across EU borders to provide services (0.4 per cent of the EU workforce). The biggest 'sending' countries are Poland, Denmark, France, Lithuania, Belgium and Portugal.

These workers play an important role in filling labour and skill shortages in various sectors and regions like construction, agriculture and transport. Posting also plays an important role in providing specialised, high-skilled services, such as information technology.

The EU's single market gives companies the freedom to provide services in other Member States, including the possibility to post temporarily post workers to other Member States to carry out specific projects. This enables companies to offer their specialised services throughout the EU Single Market, contributing to greater efficiency and economic growth.

Posted workers do not enter the host country's labour market, as they remain employed by their company in the sending Member State.

1159. To facilitate the posting of workers and to ensure fair competition as well as guaranteeing an appropriate level of protection of posted workers, the 1996 Directive defines a core set of employment conditions which the service provider has to comply with during the posting in the host Member State. This includes the applicable minimum rates of pay, holidays, maximum working hours and minimum rest periods, as well as health and safety at work.

In practice, these core employment conditions are often incorrectly applied or not enforced in the host Member State. Posting can be abused by companies artificially establishing themselves abroad, just to benefit from a lower level of labour protection or lower social security contributions. Posted workers are often more vulnerable given their situation abroad. The new proposal would introduce more effective provisions to ensure the 1996 posting of workers Directive is applied effectively on the ground.

1160. The European Court of Justice *Viking Line* and *Laval* judgments triggered an intense debate about the extent to which trade unions are able to defend workers' rights in cross-border situations, involving posting or relocation of companies. The judgements have been interpreted by some stakeholders as meaning that economic freedoms would prevail over social rights and in particular the right to strike. The new enforcement Directive and Monti II Regulation confirm that this is not the case. Whether these will be accepted within the near future remains an open question, as *inter alia* the Monti II Regulation was heavily contested.

Chapter 4. Individual Employment Contracts

1161. Earlier proposals of the Commission concerning certain aspects of individual employment contracts, like the amended proposal for a directive on voluntary part-time work (5 January 1983), on the one hand, and on the supply of workers by temporary employment businesses and fixed-duration contracts of employment (6 April 1984), on the other, have been lost in the trenches of the EU labyrinths as they were countered by a veto from one or another Member State. The proposals of the Commission were taken in order to implement the Community Charter of the Fundamental Social Rights of Workers, adopted in Strasbourg in December 1989. Whether those proposals will have more success than their predecessors is doubtful. Three proposals for directives concern the approximation of the law of the Member States of 29 June 1990 relating to certain employment relationships (1) with regard to working conditions;[430] (2) with regard to distortions of competition;[431] and (3) supplementing the introduction of measures to encourage improvements in the safety and health at work of temporary workers.[432] A fourth proposal concerns 'a form of proof of an employment relationship'.

Of these proposals only two have up to now been adopted, be it in an amended form, namely concerning the safety and health of workers with a fixed-duration employment relationship or a temporary employment relationship (25 June 1991) and concerning the employer's obligation to inform employees of the conditions applicable to the contract or employment relationship (14 October 1991).

To this has to be added the framework agreement of 6 June 1997 concluded between the social partners and implemented by a Council Directive of 15 December 1997, the agreement on fixed term contracts of 18 March 1999, implemented by the Directive of 28 June 1999[433] and the Framework Agreement on Telework (2002).

§1. TEMPORARY WORK – PART-TIME – FIXED-TERM CONTRACTS – TELEWORK

I. Directive: Health and Safety

1162. On 25 June 1991 the Council adopted a directive (91/383) supplementing the measures to encourage improvements in the safety and health at work of workers with a fixed-duration employment relationship or a temporary employment relationship.[434] The directive is based on Article 153 TFEU. The motivation of the directive reads that 'recourse to forms of employment such as fixed-duration employment and temporary employment has increased enormously' and 'that

---

430. O.J. C 224/4, 8 September 1990.
431. O.J. C 224/6, 8 September 1990.
432. O.J. C 224/8, 8 September 1990.
433. O.J. L 175, 10 July 1999.
434. O.J. L 206/19, 29 July 1991. Amended by Directive 2007/30/EC of 20 June 2007 amending Council Directive 89/391/EEC, its individual Directives and Council Directives 83/477/EEC, 91/383/EEC, 92/29/EEC and 94/33/EC with a view to simplifying and rationalising the reports on practical implementation, OJ., 27 June 2007, L 165.

research has shown that in general workers with a fixed-duration employment relationship or temporary employment relationship are, in certain sectors, more exposed to the risk of accidents at work and occupational diseases than other workers'. These additional risks are linked to certain peculiar modes of integrating new workers into the undertaking and can be reduced through adequate provision of information and training from the beginning of the employment. The specific situation of these workers and the risks they face call for special rules, supplementing the directives on health and safety, notably Directive 89/391 of 12 June 1989, particularly as regards the provision of information, the training and the medical surveillance of the workers concerned.

A. Scope

1163. The directive applies to:

(1) fixed-duration contracts of employment: 'concluded directly between the employer and the worker, where the end of the contract is established by objective conditions such as: reaching a specific date, completing a specific task or the occurrence of a specific event' (Article 1(1));
(2) temporary employment: 'relationships between a temporary employment business which is the employer and the worker, where the latter is assigned to work for and under the control of an undertaking and/or establishment making use of his services' (Article 1(2)).

These definitions are rather broad. In certain legal systems fixed duration contracts exclusively relate to contracts which specify their duration, and thus are e.g. distinguished from seasonal contracts or contracts for a specific task to be performed. Also the definition of temporary work may differ from what is prevalent in some Member States as certain definitions relate only to certain types of work, e.g. of a limited temporary nature and the like. This means that the implementation of the directive into national law may be broader than the topics covered suggest.

B. Object: Equal Treatment

1164. The purpose of the directive is to ensure that the concerned workers are afforded, as regards safety and health at work, the same level of protection as that of other workers in the user undertaking and/or establishment (Article 2(1)), namely workers engaged for an indefinite period.

Article 2(2) affirms this abundantly: 'the existence of an employment relationship as referred to in Article 1 shall not justify different treatment with respect to working conditions inasmuch as the protection of safety and health at work are involved, especially as regards access to personal protective equipment'. Selfevidently, Directive 89/391 of 12 June 1989 and the individual directives concerning health and safety apply in full without prejudice to more binding and/or more specific provisions set out in this directive (Article 2(3)).

Part I, Ch. 4, Individual Employment Contracts

C. Provision of Information to Workers

1165. Before a worker takes up any activity he is informed by the undertaking (and/or establishment) making use of his services of the risks he faces.
Such information covers:

(1) any special occupational qualifications or skills or special medical surveillance required, as defined in national legislation;
(2) clear indications of increased specific risks, as defined in national legislation, that the job may entail (Article 3).

Regarding *temporary employment* Member States shall take the necessary steps to ensure that before workers are supplied, a user undertaking shall specify to the temporary employment business, *inter alia*, the occupational qualifications required and the specific features of the job to be filled; the temporary employment business shall bring all these facts to the attention of the workers concerned. The Member States may provide that the details of the information shall appear in a contract of assignment (Article 7).

D. Workers' Training

1166. Member States shall take the necessary measures to ensure that each worker receives sufficient training appropriate to the particular characteristics of the job, account being taken of his qualifications and experience (Article 4).

E. Use of Workers' Services and Medical Surveillance of Workers

1167. Member States have the option of prohibiting workers from being used for certain work which would be particularly dangerous to their safety and health, and to ensure that they are provided with appropriate special medical surveillance, also beyond the end of the employment relationship of the worker concerned (Article 5).

F. Protection and Prevention Services

1168. Member States shall take the necessary measures to ensure that protection and prevention agencies[435] are informed of the assignment of concerned workers to the extent necessary to be able to carry out adequately their activities for all the workers of the undertaking (Article 6).

---

435. *See* Article 7 of Directive 89/391 EC.

G. Temporary Employment: Responsibility

1169. Member States shall take the necessary measures to ensure that, without prejudice to the responsibility to the temporary employment business as laid down in national legislation, the user undertaking and/or establishment is/are responsible, for the duration of the assignment, for the conditions governing performance of the work. These conditions are limited to those connected with 'safety, hygiene and health at work' (Article 8).

H. Reporting

1170. Member States shall report to the Commission every five years on the practical implementation of the directive, setting out the points of view of workers and employers. The Commission shall bring the report to the attention of the EP, the Council, the ESC, the Advisory Committee on Safety, Hygiene and Health Protection at Work. The Commission shall submit to the EP, the Council and the ESC a regular report on the implementation of this directive (Article 10).

Every five years, the Member States shall submit to the Commission a report on the practical implementation of this Directive in the form of a specific chapter of the single report referred to in Article 17a(1), (2) and (3) of Directive 89/391/EEC, which serves as a basis for the Commission's evaluation, in accordance with Article 17a(4) of that Directive (Art. 10a).

II. Part-time Work: the Collective Agreement of 6 June 1997[436]

A. Developments

1171. The Commission made unsuccessful preliminary proposals, which tried to regulate and restrict the use of 'atypical work'. It later changed its attitude, as these forms of employment were increasingly perceived as opportunities for the creation of employment. At the same time they were seen as responding to both the need of employers for greater flexibility and the desire of employees to reconcile work and family life while retaining employment security.

In 1995, the Commission started consultations on 'flexibility in working time and security for workers', within the framework of the Maastricht Agreement on Social Policy. After these consultations, some social partners decided to try to negotiate an agreement on these issues, which was reached in June 1996.

The negotiation process was not easy. The ETUC wanted to have a deal on all forms of atypical work, while UNICE said that there were different forms of work at stake, which deserved appropriate consideration. After difficult negotiations an agreement was reached and finally signed on 6 June 1997.

---

436. The agreement was implemented by Council Directive 97/81 EC of 15 December 1997 concerning the Framework Agreement on part-time work concluded by UNICE, CEEP and the ETUC, O.J. L 14/9, 20 January 1998.

It is the intention of the parties to consider the need for similar agreements relating to other forms of flexible work.

The agreement will be rendered binding by a Council directive.

B. Purpose

1172. The purpose of the agreement is:

(a) The removal of discrimination against part-time workers and the improvement of the quality of part-time work; and
(b) to facilitate the development of part-time work on a voluntary basis and to contribute to the flexible organisation of working time in a manner which takes into account the needs of employers and workers (clause 1).

C. Scope

1173. This agreement applies to part-time workers, who have an employment contract or employment relationship as defined by the law, collective agreements or practice, in force in each Member State.

Member States may,[437] for objective reasons, exclude wholly or partly from the terms of this agreement part-time workers, who work on a casual basis[438] (clause 2).

D. Definitions

1174. Part-time worker refers to an employee, whose normal hours of work, calculated on a weekly basis or on average over a period of employment of up to one year, are less than the normal hours of work of a comparable full-time worker.

Comparable full-time worker means a full-time employee in the same establishment having the same type of employment contract or relationship, who is engaged in the same or similar work/occupation, due regard being given to other considerations which may include seniority, qualifications/skills.

Where there is no comparable full-time worker in the same establishment, the comparison shall be made by reference to the applicable collective agreement or, where there is no applicable collective agreement, in accordance with national law, collective agreements or practice (clause 3).

---

437. 'After consultation with the social partners in accordance with national law, collective agreements or practice, and/or the social partners at the appropriate level in conformity with national industrial relations practice'.
438. 'Such exclusions should be reviewed periodically to establish if the objective reasons for making them remain valid.'

1175. It is for the Member States to define the concept of 'workers who have an employment contract or an employment relationship' and, in particular, to determine whether judges fall within that concept, subject to the condition that that does not lead to the arbitrary exclusion of that category of persons from the protection offered by Directive 97/81, as amended by Directive 98/23, and that agreement. An exclusion from that protection may be allowed only if the relationship between judges and the Ministry of Justice is, by its nature, substantially different from that between employers and their employees falling, according to national law, under the category of workers[439].

E. *Principle of Non-discrimination*

1176. In respect of employment and conditions, part-time workers shall not be treated in a less favourable manner than comparable full-time workers solely because they work part time, unless different treatment is justified on objective grounds.

Where appropriate, the principle of *pro rata temporis* shall apply. The modalities of application of this clause shall be defined by the Member States and/or the social partners, having regard to European legislation, national law, collective agreements and practice.

When justified by objective reasons, Member States, after consultation of the social partners in accordance with national law or practice, and/or social partners may, where appropriate, make access to particular conditions of employment subject to conditions such as a period of service, time worked or earnings qualification. Qualifications relating to access by part-time workers to particular conditions of employment should be reviewed periodically having regard to the principle of non-discrimination (clause 4).

1. *Wippel* Case

1177. In the *Nicole Wippel* case[440] the question was raised whether clause 4 of the Framework Agreement precludes a contract for part-time employment under which weekly working time and the organisation of working time are not fixed but are dependent on quantitative requirements in terms of the *work* to be performed, which are to be determined on a case-by-case basis, with the workers concerned having the choice to accept or refuse such work.

Ms. Wippel's contract of employment ought in her view to have contained a clause stipulating a fixed weekly working time with a predetermined salary, whether the person concerned had or had not worked for the whole of that working time.

---

439. C.O.J., 1 March 2012, *Dermod Patrick O'Brien v. Ministry of Justice*, C-393/10, www.curia. eu.
440. C.O.J., 12 October 2004, *Nicole Wippel v. Peek & Cloppenburg GmbH & Co. KG.*, C-313/02, ECR, 2004, 9483.

In that regard, first, Clause 4 precludes part-time workers from being treated less favourably than comparable full-time workers on the sole ground that they work part-time unless different treatment is warranted on objective grounds.

1178. Secondly, in accordance with the settled case law national provisions discriminate indirectly against women where, although worded in neutral terms, they operate to the disadvantage of a much higher percentage of women than men, unless that difference in treatment is justified by objective factors unrelated to any discrimination on grounds of sex.

The prohibition on discrimination is merely a particular expression of a fundamental principle of Union law, namely the general principle of equality under which comparable situations may not be treated differently unless the difference is objectively justified.

Accordingly, it must first be examined whether a contract of part-time employment according to need, such as that at issue in the main proceedings, results in less favourable treatment of a worker such as Ms. Wippel than of fulltime workers in a situation comparable to hers within the meaning of Clause 4 of the Framework Agreement annexed to Directive 97/81.

1179. In that regard, clause 3 of the Framework Agreement provides guidelines for determining what is a comparable full-time worker'. Such a person is defined as a full-time worker in the same establishment having the same type of employment contract or relationship, who is engaged in the same or a similar work/occupation, due regard being given to other considerations which may include seniority and qualification/skills'. Under the same clause, where there is no comparable full-time worker in the same establishment, the comparison is to be made by reference to the applicable collective agreement or, where there is no applicable collective agreement, in accordance with national law, collective agreements or practice.

A part-time employee working according to need, such as Ms. Wippel, works under a contract which stipulates neither the weekly hours of work nor the manner in which working time is to be organised, but it leaves her the choice of whether to accept or refuse the work offered by P&C. The work is remunerated by the hour only for hours actually worked.

A full-time worker works under a contract which fixes a working week of 38.5 hours, fixing the organisation of the working week and salary, and which requires him to work for the whole working time thus determined without the possibility of refusing that work even if the worker cannot or does not wish to do it.

1180. Under those circumstances, the employment relationship differs, as to subject-matter and basis, from that of a worker such as Ms. Wippel. It follows that no full-time worker in the same establishment has the same type of contract or employment relationship as Ms. Wippel. It is apparent from the file that in the circumstances of the main proceedings, the same is true of all the full-time workers, in respect of whom the applicable collective agreement provides for a working week of 38.5 hours.

There is therefore no full-time worker comparable to Ms. Wippel within the meaning of the Framework Agreement annexed to Directive 97/81. It follows that a contract of part-time employment according to need which makes provision for neither the length of weekly working time nor the organisation of working time does not result in less favourable treatment within the meaning of Clause 4 of the Framework Agreement.

1181. Accordingly, in circumstances in which the two categories of workers are not comparable, a contract of part-time employment according to need which makes provision for neither the length of weekly working time nor the organisation of working time does not constitute an indirectly discriminatory measure within the meaning of Articles 2(1) and 5(1) of Directive 76/207.

Consequently, Clause 4 must be interpreted as meaning that, in circumstances where all the contracts of employment of the other employees of an undertaking make provision for the length of weekly working time and for the organisation of working time, they do not preclude a contract of part-time employment of workers of the same undertaking, such as that in the main proceedings, under which the length of weekly working time and the organisation of working time are not fixed but are dependent on quantitative needs in terms of work to be performed determined on a case-by-case basis, such workers being entitled to accept or refuse that work.

2. *Bruno* Case

1182. In the *Bruno* case[441] many important questions were raised:

- the scope of the Framework Agreement;
- the interpretation of the principle of non-discrimination;
- the meaning of employment conditions;
- the exception of pay, according to Article 153 TFEU.

a. Facts

1183. The defendants in the main proceedings are cabin crew members employed by the airline Alitalia. They work part-time in accordance with what are known as 'vertical-cyclical part-time' arrangements. That system consists in a method of organisation under which the employee works only during certain weeks or certain months of the year, on full or reduced hours. They submit that, due to the nature of work as a cabin crew member, vertical-cyclical part-time arrangements are the only arrangements for part-time work provided for in their collective agreement.

1184. Those workers criticise the INPS for taking into account, as qualifying periods of contributions for the purpose of acquiring pension rights, only

---

441. C.O.J., 10 June 2010, *Istituto nazionale della previdenza sociale (INPS)* v. *Tiziana Bruno a.o.*, C-395/08 and C-396/08, www. curia

the periods worked, to the exclusion of periods not worked, corresponding to the reduction in their working hours by reference to the hours worked by comparable full-time workers. They therefore brought proceedings before the *Tribunale di Roma* challenging the individual statements of the qualifying periods of contributions which the INPS had provided to them. In those actions, the respondents in the main proceedings argued, in essence, that, by disregarding periods not worked, a difference in treatment between 'vertical' part-time workers and workers who had chosen 'horizontal' part-time working arrangements had effectively been established, since the latter group was in a more advantageous position for an equal period of time worked. The INPS submitted, in essence, that the relevant contributions periods for calculating pensions are those during which the respondents in the main proceedings actually worked and for which remuneration and contributions were payable, calculated *pro rata temporis*.

b. Questions

1185. It is on that basis that the *Corte d'appello di Roma* decided to stay proceedings and to refer the following questions to the Court of Justice:

1. Is the Italian State legislation which results in periods not worked under 'vertical' part-time arrangements not being taken into account as periods of qualifying contributions for the purpose of acquiring pension rights compatible with Directive 97/81, in particular Clause 4 concerning the principle of non-discrimination?
2. Are those national provisions compatible with Directive 97/81 and, in particular, Clause 1, which provides that national legislation must facilitate the development of part-time work, and Clauses 4 and 5, which provide that the Member States are to eliminate obstacles of a legal or administrative nature which may limit the opportunities for part-time work, since it is unquestionable that the failure to take into account for pension purposes the weeks not worked constitutes a significant disincentive to choosing 'vertical' part-time working arrangements?
3. Can Clause 4 on the principle of non-discrimination also be extended to various kinds of part-time contracts, in view of the fact that, in the case of 'horizontal' part-time work, for an equal number of hours worked and for which remuneration is paid in the calendar year, all the weeks of the calendar year are taken into account under national legislation, whereas they are not in the case of 'vertical' part-time work?

c. Substance

1186. By its three questions, the Roman Court asked, in essence, whether Clauses 1, 4 and 5 of the Framework Agreement preclude legislation, such as that at issue in the main proceedings, in so far as it effectively disregards, in respect of vertical-cyclical part-time workers, periods not worked in calculating the period of service required to qualify for retirement pension rights, whereas horizontal part-time workers and those working full time are not subject to such a rule.

It is necessary, the Court indicated, to determine at the outset whether and, if so, to what extent, situations such as those in the main proceedings fall within the scope of Directive 97/81 and the Framework Agreement from substantive viewpoint.

The Court ruled as follows.

d. The Substantive Scope of the Framework Agreement

1187. The objective of Directive 97/81 and the Framework Agreement is, first, to promote part-time work and, second, to eliminate discrimination between part-time workers and full-time.

In accordance with the objective of eliminating discrimination between part-time workers and full-time workers, Clause 4 of the Framework Agreement provides that, in respect of employment conditions, part-time workers are not to be treated in a less favourable manner than comparable full-time workers solely because they work part-time, unless different treatment is justified on objective grounds.

It is therefore necessary to ascertain whether the provisions governing the pension rights of Alitalia cabin crew constitute employment conditions within the meaning of Clause 4 of the Framework Agreement.

1188. In adopting Directive 97/81 the Council of the European Union based its decision on the Agreement on social policy concluded between the Member States of the European Union which provides that agreements concluded at European Union level are to be implemented in matters covered by the Treaty..

1189. The matters thus covered include, 'working conditions', a provision which is reproduced in Article 153 TFEU. Clearly, it is not possible on the basis of the wording of that provision of the agreement on social policy or that of Clause 4 of the Framework Agreement alone to determine whether the working conditions or employment conditions encompass conditions relating to factors such as the remuneration and pensions at issue in the main proceedings. In order to interpret those provisions, it is therefore necessary, in accordance with settled case-law, to take into consideration the context and the objectives pursued by the rules of which that clause is part.

1190. It is apparent from the wording of Clause 1(a) of the Framework Agreement that one of the objectives of the agreement is 'to provide for the removal of discrimination against part-time workers and to improve the quality of part-time work'. Similarly, the second paragraph of the preamble to the Framework Agreement states that the agreement 'illustrates the willingness of the social partners to establish a general framework for the elimination of discrimination against part-time workers and to assist the development of opportunities for part-time working on a basis acceptable to employers and workers'. That objective is also stated in recital 11 in the preamble to Directive 97/81.

The Framework Agreement, in particular Clause 4, thus pursues an aim which is in line with fundamental objectives enshrined in Article 1 of the agreement on social policy, which are set out in the first paragraph of Article 151 TFEU, the third recital in the preamble to the TFEU and paragraph 7 and the first subparagraph of paragraph 10 of the Community Charter of the Fundamental Social Rights of Workers. Those fundamental objectives are associated with the improvement in living and working conditions and with the existence of proper social protection for workers. In particular, they are directed at improving working conditions for part-time workers and ensuring that they are protected from discrimination, as evidenced by recitals 3 and 23 in the preamble to Directive 97/81.

1191. The European Social Charter signed in Turin on 18 October 1961, includes at point 4 of Part I the right for all workers to a 'fair remuneration sufficient for a decent standard of living for themselves and their families' among the objectives which the contracting parties have undertaken to achieve, in accordance with Article 20 in Part III of the Charter.

In the light of those objectives, Clause 4 of the Framework Agreement must be interpreted as articulating a principle of European Union social law which cannot be interpreted restrictively.

To interpret Clause 4 of the Framework Agreement as excluding from the term 'employment conditions', within the meaning of that clause, financial conditions, such as those relating to remuneration and pensions, would effectively reduce – contrary to the objective attributed to that clause – the scope of the protection against discrimination for the workers concerned by introducing a distinction based on the nature of their employment conditions, which is not in any way implicit in the wording of that clause.

Moreover, such an interpretation would deprive the reference in Clause 4(2) of the framework agreement to the principle of pro rata temporis of all useful effect, that principle being intended by definition only to apply to divisible performance, such as that deriving from financial employment conditions linked, for example, to remuneration and pensions.

1192. According to Article 2(6) of the agreement on social policy, which is reproduced in Article 153(5) TFEU, the provisions of that article 'shall not apply to pay, the right of association, the right to strike or the right to impose lock-outs'. However, as the Court has already held in relation to Article 153(5), since that provision derogates from paragraphs 1 to 4 of that article, the matters reserved by paragraph 5 must be interpreted strictly so as not to affect unduly the scope of paragraphs 1 to 4, nor to call into question the aims pursued by Article 151 TFEU.

More particularly, it has already been held that the exception relating to 'pay' set out in Article 153(5) TFEU is explained by the fact that fixing the level of pay falls within the contractual freedom of the social partners at a national level and within the relevant competence of Member States. In those circumstances, as European Union law stood, it was decided to exclude determination of the level of wages from harmonisation under Article 151 TFEU *et seq.*

1193. That exception must therefore be interpreted as covering measures – such as the equivalence of all or some of the constituent parts of pay and/or the level of pay in the Member States, or the setting of a minimum guaranteed wage – which amount to direct interference by European Union law in the determination of pay within the Union. It cannot, however, be extended to any question involving any sort of link with pay; otherwise some of the areas referred to in Article 153(1) TFEU would be deprived of much of their substance.

It follows that the derogation in Article 2(6) of the agreement on social policy, which is reproduced in Article 153(5) TFEU, does not preclude an interpretation of Clause 4 of the Framework Agreement to the effect that the Member States are under an obligation to ensure that the principle of non-discrimination is applied to part-time workers also in relation to pay, while at the same time taking account, where appropriate, of the principle of *pro rata temporis*.

1194. While it is true that the establishment of the level of the various constituent parts of the pay of a worker falls outside the competence of the European Union legislature and is unquestionably still a matter for the competent bodies in the various Member States, those bodies must nevertheless exercise their competence consistently with European Union law – particularly Clause 4 of the framework agreement – in the areas in which the European Union does not have competence.

It follows that, in establishing both the constituent parts of pay and the level of those constituent parts, the competent national bodies must apply to part-time workers the principle of non-discrimination as laid down in Clause 4 of the Framework Agreement.

1195. With regard to pensions, it must be noted that, according to the settled case-law of the Court in relation to Article 157 TFEU, which concern the principle of equal treatment of men and women in relation to pay, the term 'pay' covers pensions which depend on the employment relationship between worker and employer, excluding those deriving from a statutory scheme, to the financing of which workers, employers and possibly the public authorities contribute in a measure determined less by the employment relationship than by considerations of social policy.

Taking that case-law into account, it must be held that the term 'employment conditions' within the meaning of Clause 4(1) of the framework agreement covers pensions which depend on an employment relationship between worker and employer, excluding statutory social security pensions, which are determined less by that relationship than by considerations of social policy.

1196. That interpretation is supported by the information in the third paragraph of the preamble to the Framework Agreement, according to which the parties to the agreement 'recognis[e] that matters relating to statutory social security are for decision by the Member States' and consider that effect should be given to the Employment Declaration adopted by the European Council in Dublin in December 1996,

Part I, Ch. 4, Individual Employment Contracts

which emphasised, inter alia, the need to adapt social security systems to new patterns of work in order to provide appropriate social protection to those engaged in such work.

That interpretation is also supported by the fact that, as it was concluded by management and labour represented by joint trade bodies, the Framework Agreement is not intended to regulate social security matters or impose obligations on national social security organisations, since they were not party to that agreement.

1197. Since Clause 4(1) of the Framework Agreement is applicable to pensions which depend on an employment relationship between worker and employer, excluding statutory social security pensions, it remains to be ascertained whether the pension scheme at issue in the main proceedings falls within one of those categories or the other. In order to do so, it is necessary to apply, by analogy, the criteria identified by caselaw so as to determine whether a retirement pension falls within the scope of Article 157 TFEU.

It is appropriate to bear in mind that the only possible decisive criterion is whether the retirement pension is paid to the worker by reason of the employment relationship between him and his former employer, that is to say, the criterion of employment, which is based on the wording of Article 157 TFEU itself. However, that criterion cannot be regarded as exclusive, since pensions paid under statutory social security schemes may reflect, wholly or in part, pay in respect of work. Such pensions do not constitute 'pay' for the purposes of Article 157 TFEU.

1198. However, considerations of social policy, of State organisation, of ethics, or even the budgetary concerns which influenced or may have influenced the establishment by the national legislature of a scheme cannot prevail if the pension concerns only a particular category of workers, if it is directly related to the period of service completed or if its amount is calculated by reference to the last salary.

In order to determine whether a retirement pension paid under a scheme such as that which is applicable to Alitalia cabin crew falls within the scope of the Framework Agreement, it is therefore necessary to consider whether such a pension satisfies the three above mentioned conditions. It is for the national court, which alone has jurisdiction to assess the facts in the cases before it and to interpret the national legislation applicable, to determine whether those conditions are met.

1199. However, when giving a preliminary ruling, the Court may, where appropriate, provide clarification designed to give the national court guidance in its interpretation.

The fact that the pension scheme for Alitalia cabin crew is administered by a public body such as the INPS, which, moreover, under provisions laid down by law, manages the Italian social security system, is not decisive for the purpose of determining whether that pension scheme forms part of the statutory social security scheme or, on the contrary, is covered by conditions of pay.

Similarly, whether the shareholding in Alitalia is public or private is not a decisive factor, since it has already been recognised by caselaw that, if the three conditions set out above are met, the pension paid by a public employer to an official is in that case entirely comparable to that paid by a private employer to his former employees.

e. The Temporal Scope of the Framework Agreement

1200. The INPS submits, in essence, that the Framework Agreement may be applied only to periods of employment after the entry into force of the national measure implementing Directive 97/81, the calculation of the period of service required to qualify for a retirement pension relates, wholly or in part, to periods before the expiry of the deadline for transposing Directive 97/81, which do not therefore fall within the scope of the Framework Agreement.

According to settled case-law, new rules apply, unless otherwise specifically provided, immediately to the future effects of a situation which arose under the old rule.

As the Advocate General pointed out neither Directive 97/81 nor the Framework Agreement derogates from the general principle referred to in the preceding paragraph.

1201. Accordingly, the calculation of the period of service required to qualify for a retirement pension such as the pensions at issue in the main proceedings is governed by Directive 97/81, including periods of employment before the directive entered into force.

f. Question 1: Vertical-cyclical Part-time Working Arrangements

1202. By its first question, the Roman Court asks, in essence, whether Clause 4 of the Framework Agreement concerning the principle of non-discrimination is to be interpreted as precluding the legislation of a Member State, such as that at issue in the main proceedings, where the effect of that legislation, as regards vertical-cyclical part-time working arrangements, is to disregard periods not worked in calculating the period of service required to qualify for a retirement pension.

Clause 4(1) of the Framework Agreement provides, with regard to employment conditions, that part-time workers are not to be treated in a less favourable manner than comparable full-time workers solely because they work part time, unless different treatment is justified on objective grounds.

The prohibition on discrimination laid down in that provision is simply a specific expression of one of the fundamental principles of European Union law, namely the general principle of equality.

1203. It is therefore necessary to consider whether the fact that periods not worked by vertical-cyclical part-time workers are disregarded in calculating the period of service required to qualify for a retirement pension solely because they work part time results in them being treated in a less favourable manner than full-time workers in a comparable position.

In that connection, Clause 3 of the Framework Agreement provides guidelines for determining what is a 'comparable full-time worker'. Such a person is defined in the first paragraph of Clause 3(2) as 'a full-time worker in the same establishment

Part I, Ch. 4, Individual Employment Contracts 1204–1206

having the same type of employment contract or relationship, who is engaged in the same or a similar work/occupation, due regard being given to other considerations which may include seniority and qualification/skills'. The second paragraph of Clause 3(2) provides that, where there is no comparable full-time worker in the same establishment, 'the comparison shall be made by reference to the applicable collective agreement or, where there is no applicable collective agreement, in accordance with national law, collective agreements or practice'.

1204. For a full-time worker, the period taken into account in calculating the qualifying period of service is the same as that of the employment relationship. By contrast, for vertical-cyclical part-time workers, the period of service is not calculated on the same basis, since it is calculated only by reference to the duration of the periods actually worked, taking account of the reduction in working hours.

Accordingly, for a period of employment covering 12 consecutive months, a full-time worker will be credited with one year's service for the purpose of determining the date on which he will be entitled to a pension. By contrast, a worker in a comparable situation who has opted, in accordance with vertical-cyclical parttime working arrangements, for a 25 per cent reduction in working hours will be credited, for the same period, with a period of service amounting to only 75% of that credited to his colleague who works full time, solely because he works part time. It follows that, even though their employment contracts are in effect of equivalent duration, the part-time worker will be credited with qualifying periods of service for a pension at a slower rate than the full-time worker. That therefore amounts to a difference in treatment based solely on the fact of part-time work.

1205. Both the INPS and the Italian Government submit, essentially, that that difference in treatment does not constitute unequal treatment, since full-time workers and vertical-cyclical part-time workers are not in comparable situations. They thus argue that the workers in each of those categories are simply credited with notional periods of service corresponding to the periods actually worked. Accordingly, they point out that employers pay social contributions only in respect of periods worked and that, as regards periods not worked, under Italian law all part-time workers have the right to purchase pension credits on a voluntary basis.

However, the principle of non-discrimination as between part-time and full-time workers applies to employment conditions, which cover remuneration, a concept which, as was pointed out also includes pensions, excluding those forming part of the social security scheme. Consequently, the remuneration of part-time workers must be equivalent to that of full-time workers, subject to the application of the principle of *pro rata temporis*, as provided for in Clause 4(2) of the Framework Agreement.

1206. Accordingly, the calculation of the amount of the pension is directly dependent on the amount of time worked by the employee and the corresponding amount of contributions, in accordance with the principle of pro rata temporis. It must be borne in mind, in that regard, that the Court has already held that European Union law does not preclude a retirement pension being calculated *pro rata temporis* in the case of part-time employment. Taking into account the amount of time actually worked by a part-time worker during his career, as compared with the amount of time actually worked by a person who has worked on a full-time basis throughout his career, is an objective criterion, allowing his pension entitlement to be reduced proportionately.

1207. On the other hand, the principle of *pro rata temporis* is not applicable for the purpose of determining the date required to acquire pensions rights, since that depends solely on the worker's length of service. The length of service is, in fact, the actual duration of the employment relationship and not the amount of time worked during that period. In accordance with the principle of non-discrimination as between full-time and part-time workers, therefore, the length of the period of service taken into account for the purpose of determining the date on which a worker becomes entitled to a pension should be calculated for a part-time worker as if he had held a full-time post, periods not worked being taken into account in their entirety.

The difference in treatment is further accentuated by the fact that it is apparent that vertical-cyclical part-time work is the sole form of part-time work available to Alitalia cabin crew under the collective agreement applicable to them.

1208. It follows that legislation such as that at issue in the main proceedings treats vertical-cyclical part-time workers in a less favourable manner than comparable full-time workers solely because they work part time.

However, Clause 4(1) of the Framework Agreement provides that such a difference in treatment may be regarded as consistent with the principle of non-discrimination if it is justified on objective grounds.

Invited to explain the reasons which might justify such a difference in treatment, the INPS and the Italian Government stated at the hearing that, under Italian law, a vertical-cyclical part-time contract is deemed to be suspended during periods not worked, and no remuneration or contributions are paid during such periods.

1209. It should be pointed out, first, that that justification is, prima facie, difficult to reconcile with the fact that the documents submitted to the Court and the proceedings before the Court have shown that, as regards public sector workers, Italian legislation expressly provides that 'in order to qualify for a pension from the administration concerned ... the total number of years of service spent working reduced hours must be taken into account'. That difference in the applicable rules leaves open to doubt the validity of the justification put forward by the INPS and the Italian Government.

Second, under Clause 3 of the Framework Agreement, a part-time worker is characterised by the simple fact that his normal hours of work are less than the normal hours of work of a comparable full-time worker. Accordingly, part-time work constitutes a particular mode of performing the employment contract, characterised by the simple fact that the normal hours of work are reduced. However, that characteristic cannot be treated in the same manner as it is in situations in which the performance of an employment contract, be it full or part-time, is suspended on account

Part I, Ch. 4, Individual Employment Contracts

of an impediment or temporary interruption attributable to the worker, the undertaking or some external cause. Periods not worked, which correspond to the reduction in working hours stipulated in a part-time contract, are the outcome of the normal performance of the contract and not its suspension. Part-time work does not involve a break in service.

1210. Consequently, even though the arguments put forward by the INPS and the Italian Government may be understood to mean that the difference in treatment at issue in the main proceedings is justified by the fact that periods corresponding to the reduction in working hours under a part-time employment contract have the effect of suspending performance of the contract, such an argument is at variance with the definition of part-time in Clause 3 of the Framework Agreement and effectively deprives of any effectiveness the principle set out in Clause 4(1) of the Framework Agreement that, as regards employment conditions, part-time workers must not be treated in a less favourable manner than comparable full-time workers solely because they work part time.

Even if those arguments were to be understood as intended to demonstrate that the difference in treatment between vertical-cyclical part-time workers and full-time workers is justified on grounds deriving from national law, it should be borne in mind that it is for the referring court, to the full extent of its discretion under national law, to interpret and apply national law in conformity with the requirements of European Union law and, where such an interpretation is not possible, to disapply any provision of domestic law that would be contrary to those requirements.

It follows from all the above considerations that the answer to the first question is that, with regard to retirement pensions, Clause 4 of the Framework Agreement must be interpreted as precluding national legislation which, for vertical-cyclical part-time workers, disregards periods not worked in calculating the period of service required to qualify for such a pension, unless such a difference in treatment is justified on objective grounds.

g. Question 2: Significant Disincentive

1211. By its second question, the Roman Court asks, in essence, whether Clauses 1 and 5(1) of the Framework Agreement must be interpreted as precluding national legislation such as that at issue in the main proceedings in so far as it constitutes for workers a significant disincentive to choosing vertical-cyclical part-time working arrangements.

It is apparent from Clause 1 of the Framework Agreement in particular that the agreement pursues a twofold objective, namely, first, to promote part-time work by improving the quality of such work and, second, to eliminate discrimination between part-time workers and full-time workers.

In accordance with that twofold purpose, Clause 5(1)(a) of the Framework Agreement imposes an obligation on Member States to 'identify and review obstacles of a legal or administrative nature which may limit the opportunities for part-time work and, where appropriate, eliminate them'.

1212. By disregarding periods not worked in calculating the period of service required to qualify for a pension, the legislation at issue in the main proceedings, in so far as it concerns retirement pensions which depend on the employment relationship, excluding those deriving from a statutory social security scheme, introduces a difference in treatment as between vertical-cyclical part-time workers and full-time workers and thus infringes the principle of non-discrimination laid down in Clause 4 of the Framework Agreement. Moreover, as was pointed out above, that difference in treatment is accentuated by the fact that vertical-cyclical part-time work is the sole form of part-time work offered to Alitalia cabin crew.

Those factors, taken together, tend to make part-time work less attractive for that category of workers; in other words, they are discouraged from pursuing their occupational activity on such a basis, since the effect of such a choice is to postpone the date on which they acquire the right to a pension by a proportion that is equal to the proportion by which their working hours are reduced by comparison with those of comparable full-time workers. Such effects clearly run counter to the objective of the Framework Agreement, which is to facilitate the development of part-time work.

The answer to the second question is, therefore, that if the referring court reached the conclusion that the national legislation at issue in the main proceedings is incompatible with Clause 4 of the Framework Agreement, Clauses 1 and 5(1) of the agreement would have to be interpreted as also precluding such legislation.

h. Question 3: Discrimination between Different Forms of Part-time work

1213. By its third question, the *Corte d'appello di Roma* asks, in essence, whether Clause 4 of the Framework Agreement on the principle of non-discrimination must be interpreted as prohibiting, in addition to discrimination between part-time workers and comparable full-time workers, discrimination between different forms of parttime work, such as vertical-cyclical part-time work and horizontal part-time work.

In view of the answers given to the two preceding questions, the Court concluded, there is no need to answer this question.

1214. On those grounds, the Court ruled:

(1) With regard to retirement pensions, Clause 4 of the Framework Agreement on part-time work must be interpreted as precluding national legislation which, for vertical-cyclical part-time workers, disregards periods not worked in calculating the period of service required to qualify for such a pension, unless such a difference in treatment is justified on objective grounds.
(2) If the referring court reached the conclusion that the national legislation at issue in the main proceedings is incompatible with Clause 4 of the Framework Agreement, Clauses 1 and 5(1) of the agreement would have to be interpreted as also precluding such legislation.

Part I, Ch. 4, Individual Employment Contracts

1215. The Framework Agreement on part-time work must be interpreted as meaning that it precludes, for the purpose of access to the retirement pension scheme, national law from establishing a distinction between full-time judges and part-time judges remunerated on a daily fee-paid basis, unless such a difference in treatment is justified by objective reasons, which is a matter for the referring court to determine[442].

F. Opportunities for Part-time Work

1216. Member States[443] and the social partners[444] should identify and review obstacles of a legal or administrative nature which may limit the opportunities for part-time work and, where appropriate, eliminate them.

A worker's refusal to transfer from full-time to part-time work or *vice versa* should not in itself constitute a valid reason for termination of employment, without prejudice to termination in accordance with national law, collective agreements and practice, for other reasons such as may arise from the operational requirements of the establishment concerned.

As far as possible, employers should give consideration to:

(a) requests by workers to transfer from full-time to part-time work that becomes available in the establishment;
(b) requests by workers to transfer from part-time to full-time work or to increase their working time should the opportunity arise;
(c) the provision of timely information on the availability of part-time and full-time positions in the establishment in order to facilitate transfers from full-time to part-time or *vice versa*;
(d) measures to facilitate access to part-time work at all levels of the enterprise, including skilled and managerial positions and, where appropriate, to facilitate access by part-time workers to vocational training to enhance career opportunities and occupational mobility;
(e) the provision of appropriate information to existing bodies representing workers about part-time working in the enterprise (clause 5).

1217. In the *Michaeler* case,[445] the question was raised whether

> national provisions (Articles 2 and 8 of Decree-Law No. 61/2000) which impose an obligation on employers to send a copy of part-time employment contracts within 30 days of their signature to the competent provincial office of

---

442. C.O.J., 1 March 2012, *Dermod Patrick O'Brien v. Ministry of Justice*, C-393/10, www. curia. eu.
443. 'Following consultations with the social partners in accordance with national law or practice'.
444. 'Acting within their sphere of competence and through the procedures set out in collective agreements'.
445. C.O.J., 24 April 2008, *Othmar Michaeler* (C-55/07 and C-56/07) *and others* v. *Amt für sozialen Arbeitsschutz*, ECR, 2008, 3135.

the Labour Inspectorate, which provide for imposition of a fine of EUR 15 in respect of each worker concerned and each day of delay in the event of failure to do so, and which do not set an upper limit for the administrative fine ... are contrary to Community law provisions and Directive 97/81 ... ?

The Italian government maintains that the objective pursued the protection and encouragement of part-time work. From that point of view, the obligation to give notice of part-time employment contracts is instrumental in ensuring the coordinated action of all of the bodies responsible for the monitoring of work in Italy. The measure is one which contributes to combating undeclared work and which ensures that the various bodies which monitor work have an up-to-date database of information on market practices.

Far from erecting a bureaucratic obstacle, the measure, it is argued, represents a guarantee to employers of transparency and is of use in combating unlawful work. Such a formality does not, moreover, create any inequality or any distortion of competition between enterprises.

The Commission considers that the obligation, on penalty of a fine, to notify the Labour Inspectorate of the contracts concerned fails to have regard to the objectives of Directive 97/81.

The purpose of that directive was, first, to remove any discrimination against part-time workers and, secondly, to facilitate the development of part-time work, *inter alia*, by the elimination of any obstacles which might discourage undertakings from making use of that form of work. Directive 97/81 required that part-time work be treated in the same way as full-time work, whether in relation to working conditions or to access to employment. Clause 5 of the framework agreement accordingly precludes the creation of obstacles which are not justified by objective reasons. In the recitals in its preamble, the directive refers to establishing a general framework for the elimination of any discrimination against part-time workers and the development of opportunities for part-time work. Paragraph 5 of the general considerations of the framework agreement sets out the duty to facilitate access for men and women to part-time work.

In accordance with the objective of promoting part-time work, Clause 5(1)(a) of the framework agreement provides that Member States are obliged to 'identify and review obstacles of a legal or administrative nature which may limit the opportunities for part-time work and, where appropriate, eliminate them'.

1218. The Court ruled:

> Requiring undertakings to send to the competent authorities a copy of every part-time employment contract, sets up an administrative obstacle likely to limit the opportunities for part-time work, within the meaning of clause 5(1)(a) of the framework agreement.
>
> In that connection, it must be observed that there is no indication in the documents submitted by the referring court to the Court of Justice that the signature of full-time employment contracts is subject to a comparable obligation to give notice.

The argument that the obligation to give notice is justified by the need to combat undeclared work and to keep the authorities informed of employers' practices is unconvincing. If the measure at issue in the main proceedings is to be justified by such concerns, that measure must be proportionate to the objective to be achieved. However, as the Advocate General stated in points 46 to 48 of his Opinion, there are other less restrictive measures to enable the Italian Government to achieve the pleaded objectives of combating fraud and undeclared work, areas in which the national authorities have at their disposal surveillance, monitoring and police resources.

Aside from the financial burden which that administrative formality of notification directly obliges undertakings to bear, a system of penalties which provides for imposition of a fine of EUR 15 in respect of each employment contract in question and in respect of each day of late notification of the contract, with no ceiling to limit the total amount of the fine.

The combination of that administrative formality and that system of penalties acts to discourage employers from making use of part-time work.

In addition, because of the cost and the associated penalties, the obligation to notify the authorities of part-time contracts risks particularly affecting small and medium-sized undertakings which, not having the same resources as larger undertakings, may consequently be inclined to avoid that form of organisation of work, namely part-time work, which it is the aim of Directive 97/81 to promote.

It is accordingly appropriate to reply that Clause 5(1)(a) of the framework agreement must be interpreted as precluding national legislation such as that at issue in the main proceedings which requires that copies of part-time employment contracts be sent to the authorities within 30 days of their signature.

G. *Provisions on Implementation*

1219. Member States and/or social partners can maintain or introduce more favourable provisions than set out in this agreement.

Implementation shall not constitute valid grounds for reducing the general level of protection. This does not prejudice the right of Member States and/or social partners to develop different provisions, in the light of changing circumstances.

The social partners retain the right to conclude, at the appropriate level, including European level, agreements adapting and/or complementing the provisions of this agreement.

The signatory parties will review this agreement, five years after the date of the Council decision, if requested by one of the parties to this agreement (clause 6).

III. The Agreement on Fixed-term Contracts of 18 March 1999

1220. Council Directive 1999/70/EC of 28 June 1999[446] puts the framework agreement on fixed-term contracts, concluded on 18 March 1999 between the general cross-industry organisations (ETUC, UNICE and CEEP), into effect. The directive entered into force on the day of its publication in the Official Journal.

The parties to this agreement recognise that contracts of an indefinite duration are, and will continue to be, the general form of employment relationship between employers and workers. They also recognise that fixed-term employment contracts respond, in certain circumstances, to the needs of both employers and workers.

This agreement sets out the general principles and minimum requirements relating to fixed-term work, recognising that their detailed application needs to take account of the realities of specific national, sectoral and seasonal situations. It illustrates the willingness of the social partners to establish a general framework for ensuring equal treatment for fixed-term workers by protecting them against discrimination and for using fixed-term employment contracts on a basis acceptable to employers and workers.

The agreement applies to fixed-term workers with the exception of those placed by a temporary work agency at the disposition of a user enterprise. It is the intention of the parties to consider the need for a similar agreement relating to temporary agency work.

The agreement relates to the employment conditions of fixed-term workers, recognising that matters relating to statutory social security are for decision by the Member States.

1221. It is, in this context, very important, to underline that employment contracts of an indefinite duration are and will remain the general form of employment relations between employers and workers. This fundamental principle is, as indicated, contained in and recognised by the framework agreement on fixed-term work.

With good reason, the Court of Justice has consequently judged that the contract of an indefinite duration is the general type and 'is a major element in the protection of workers, whilst the fixed-term contract may satisfy the needs of the employers as much as the workers in certain circumstances'.[447]

1222. If the contract of an indefinite duration is the general rule, then the fixed-term contract must be considered to be the exception. This exception must therefore be interpreted in a restrictive way and must be justified on the basis of objective reasons.

Consequently, a fixed-term contract can only be concluded if there are objective reasons.

---

446. O.J. L 175, 10 July 1999.
447. C.O.J., 22 November 2005, Mangold, C 144/04, ECR, 2005, 9981. *See also* Jaspers T., 'Bepaaldetijdcontracten I fasen', in *Een inspirerende Fase in het social recht*, Liber Amicorum voor Prof. Wil Fase, 10; Tribunal de la Fonction publique, 26 October 2006, *Landgren Pia* v. *Fondation Européenne pour la Formation (EFT)*, F-1/05.

1223. Objectivity must be interpreted in the framework of the aim and the result to be achieved as provided for in the framework agreement. This means that a reason set out in a general way is not suitable. The Court of Justice, again with good reason, requires that reasons be appreciated on the basis of precise and concrete circumstances which characterise the activity in question, in order to justify recourse to fixed-term contracts. Such specific justification is necessary, otherwise the beneficial effect of the framework agreement could be nullified.

In short, these are functional criteria, namely criteria, which are directly linked to the tasks and functions for which the employee has been engaged on a temporary basis.[448]

Striking examples are seasonal working, such as in agriculture, the theatre, holiday resorts, a summer school, an employment contract for a professional footballer to constitute a homogeneous team, a temporary increase in workload ... .

1224. To sum up, according to the Court's reasoning, the departure point of the said Directive, that employment stability is the general rule, demands justification for temporary employment. Using objective criteria, it seems these are criteria expressing a temporary need, given the direct link with the nature of the tasks or the activities.

A. *Purpose of the Framework Agreement*

1225. The purpose of the agreement is to:

(a) improve the quality of fixed-term work by ensuring the application of the principle of non-discrimination;
(b) establish a framework to prevent abuse arising from the use of successive fixed-term employment contracts or relationships (clause 1).

B. *Scope*

1226.

(1) The agreement applies to fixed-term workers who have an employment contract or employment relationship as defined in law, collective agreements or practice in each Member State.
(2) Member States, after consultation with the social partners and/or the social partners, may provide that this agreement does not apply to:
 (a) initial vocational training relationships and apprenticeship schemes;

---

448. *See* C.O.J., 4 July 2006, *Konstantinos Adeneler and others*, C-212/04, ECR, 2006, 6057. *See also* Jaspers, T. *op. cit.*

(b) employment contracts and relationships which have been concluded within the framework of a specific public or publicly-supported training, integration and vocational retraining programme (clause 2).

1227. According to the jurisprudence of the Court of Justice, all these rules are applicable equally in the public sector, this being a general principle of law. This comes clearly from the *Adelener* case,[449] mentioned above, and the *Vasallo* case.[450] In this latter case, the conversion of a fixed-term employment contract into one of an indeterminate period was accepted.

In the *Adelener* case, the Court of Justice clearly confirmed this:

> It should be made clear at the outset that Directive 1999/70 and the Framework Agreement can apply also to fixed-term employment contracts concluded with the public authorities and other public-sector bodies.
>
> The provisions of those two instruments contain nothing to permit the inference that their scope is limited to fixed-term contracts concluded by workers with employers in the private sector alone.
>
> On the contrary, first, as it is apparent from the very wording of clause 2(1) of the Framework Agreement, the scope of the Framework Agreement is conceived in broad terms, covering generally fixed-term workers who have an employment contract or employment relationship as defined in law, collective agreements or practice in each Member State. In addition, the definition of fixed-term workers for the purposes of the Framework Agreement, set out in clause 3(1), encompasses all workers without drawing a distinction according to whether their employer is in the public, or private, sector.
>
> Second, clause 2(2) of the Framework Agreement, far from providing for the exclusion of fixed-term employment contracts or relationships concluded with a public-sector employer, merely gives the Member States and/or the social partners the option of making the Framework Agreement inapplicable to initial vocational training relationships and apprentice schemes and employment contracts and relationships, which have been concluded within the framework of a specific public or publicly-supported training, integration and vocational retraining programme.

1228. A member of the interim staff (public service) falls within the scope *ratione personae* of Directive 1999/70 and that of the framework agreement[451]. Clause 4 of the framework agreement on fixed-term work must be interpreted as precluding account not being taken of periods of service completed as an interim civil servant in a public administration for the purposes of permitting such a person, who has subsequently become a career civil servant, to obtain an internal promotion available only to career civil servants, unless that exclusion is justified by objective grounds for the purposes of clause 4(1) of that agreement. The mere fact

---

449. C.O.J., 4 July 2006, C-212/04, ECR, 2006, 6057.
450. C.O.J., 7 September 2006, C-180/04, ECR, 2006, 7471.
451. C.O.J., 22 December 2010, *Rosa María Gavieiro Gavieiro v. Consellería de Educación e Ordenación Universitaria de la Xunta de Galicia,* (C444/09), www.curia.eu.

that the interim civil servant completed those periods of service under a fixed-term employment contract or relationship does not constitute such an objective ground.[452]

1229. The directive, must be interpreted as not applying either to the fixed-term employment relationship between a temporary worker and a temporary employment business or to the employment relationship between such a worker and a user undertaking.[453]

1230. It is amazing that the principles of the Agreement on Fixed Term Employment Contracts do not apply to the European Union,[454] which engages thousands of workers for (successive) fixed-term contracts in order to perform permanent tasks and pay them less than permanent civil servants. The directive does not apply, so it is argued, since directives are addressed to Member States and not to European institutions. Moreover, the principles contained in the agreement, like job security, the pre-eminence of an employment contract for an indefinite period, are not recognised as general principles of law.

The European institutions ask Member States to live up to standards, which they themselves do not respect. This is unacceptable. They should set the good example and simply 'walk their talk'.

C. *Definitions*

1231. For the purpose of this agreement the term:

– 'fixed-term worker' means a person having an employment contract or relationship entered into directly between an employer and a worker where the end of the employment contract or relationship is determined by objective conditions such as reaching a specific date, completing a specific task, or the occurrence of a specific event;
– 'comparable permanent worker' means a worker with an employment contract or relationship of indefinite duration, in the same establishment, engaged in the same or similar work/occupation, due regard being given to qualifications/skills.
– Where there is no comparable permanent worker in the same establishment, the comparison shall be made by reference to the applicable collective agreement, or where there is no applicable collective agreement, in accordance with national law, collective agreements or practice (clause 3).

---

452. C.O.J., 8 September 2011, *Francisco Javier Rosado Santana v. Consejería de Justicia y Administración Pública de la Junta de Andalucía*, C-177/10, www. curia.eu.
453. C.O.J., 11 April 2013, *Oreste Della Rocca v. Poste Italiane SpA.*, C-290/12, www.curia.eu.
454. *Tribunal de la Fonction Publique de L'union Européenne*, 4 June 2009, *Vahan Adjemian v. Commission*, F-8/08, www.curia.

D. *Principle of Non-discrimination*

1232. In respect of employment conditions, fixed-term workers may not be treated in a less favourable manner than comparable permanent workers solely because they have a fixed-term contract or relation unless different treatment is justified on objective grounds.

Where appropriate, the principle of *pro rata temporis* shall apply. The arrangements for the application of this clause shall be defined by the Member States after consultation with the social partners and/or the social partners, having regard to Union law and national law, collective agreements and practice.

Period-of-service qualifications relating to particular conditions of employment have to be the same for fixed-term workers as for permanent workers except where different length-of-service qualifications are justified on objective grounds (clause 4).

1233. The concept of 'employment conditions' referred to in clause 4(1) must be interpreted as meaning that it can act as a basis for a claim such as that at issue in the main proceedings, which seeks the grant to a fixed-term worker of a length-of-service allowance which is reserved under national law solely to permanent staff.

Clause 4(1) precludes the introduction of a difference in treatment between fixed-term workers and permanent workers, which is justified solely on the basis that it is provided for by a provision of statute or secondary legislation of a Member State or by a collective agreement concluded between the staff union representatives and the relevant employer.

1234. 'Employment conditions' include pay, ruled the Court of Justice in the *Impact* case:[455]

> It follows that Clause 4(1) of the framework agreement appears, so far as its subject-matter is concerned, to be unconditional and sufficiently precise for individuals to be able to rely upon it before a national court.
>
> In that regard, as the Court has already held, the Council, in adopting Directive 1999/70, in order to implement the framework agreement, relied on Article 155(2) TFEU, which provides that agreements concluded at a Community level are to be implemented for matters covered by Article 153 TFEU.
>
> Those matters include, in Article 153 TFEU, 'working conditions'. It cannot be determined from the wording of Article 153 TFEU alone, any more than from that of Clause 4 of the framework agreement, whether or not the working conditions or employment conditions respectively referred to in those two provisions include conditions relating to matters such as the remuneration and pensions at issue in the main proceedings.
>
> The framework agreement, in particular Clause 4, thus follows an aim which is akin to the fundamental objectives enshrined in the first paragraph of Article 151 TFEU and Article 7 and the first paragraph of Article 10 of the Community Charter of the Fundamental Social Rights of Workers to which Article 151

---

455. C.O.J., 15 April 2008, *Impact v. Minister for Agriculture and Food*, C-268/06, ECR, 2008, 2483.

TFEU refers, and which are associated with the improvement of living and working conditions and the existence of proper social protection for workers, in the present case, for fixed-term workers.

Moreover, the first paragraph of Article 151 TFEU, which defines the objectives with a view to which the Council may, in respect of the matters covered by Article 153 TFEU, implement in accordance with Article 155(2) TFEU agreements concluded between social partners at Community level, refers to the European Social Charter signed at Turin on 18 October 1961, which includes at point 4 of Part I the right for all workers to a 'fair remuneration sufficient for a decent standard of living for themselves and their families' among the objectives which the contracting parties have undertaken to achieve, in accordance with Article 20 in Part III of the Charter.

It follows that, in establishing both the constituent parts of pay and the level of those constituent parts, the national competent bodies must apply to fixed-term workers the principle of non-discrimination as laid down in Clause 4 of the framework agreement.

1235. Regarding 'pensions' the Court stated:

With regard to pensions, it must be noted that, according to the settled case-law of the Court in relation to Article 157 TFEU, which concern the principle of equal treatment of men and women in relation to pay, the term 'pay' within the meaning of the second subparagraph of Article 157(2) TFEU covers pensions which depend on the employment relationship between worker and employer, excluding those deriving from a statutory scheme, to the financing of which workers, employers and possibly the public authorities contribute in a measure determined less by the employment relationship than by considerations of social policy.

Taking that case-law into account, it must be held that the term 'employment conditions' within the meaning of Clause 4(1) of the framework agreement covers pensions which depend on an employment relationship between worker and employer, excluding statutory social-security pensions, which are determined less by that relationship than by considerations of social policy.

That interpretation is supported by the information in the fifth paragraph of the preamble to the framework agreement, according to which the parties to the agreement 'recognis[e] that matters relating to statutory social security are for decision by the Member States' and call on the Member States to give effect to the Employment Declaration of the Dublin European Council in 1996 which emphasised, inter alia, the need to adapt social-security systems to new patterns of work in order to provide appropriate social protection to those engaged in such work.

In the light of the foregoing, the answer to the fifth question must be that Clause 4 of the framework agreement must be interpreted as meaning that employment conditions within the meaning of that clause encompass conditions relating to pay and to pensions which depend on the employment relationship, to the exclusion of conditions relating to pensions arising under a statutory social-security scheme.

1236. As far as length-of-service increments are concerned, fixed-term workers must not be treated less favourably than permanent workers in a comparable situation, in the absence of any objective justification. As to the question whether the temporary nature of the employment of certain public servants may, in itself, amount to an objective ground within the meaning of clause 4 of the framework agreement, the Court has already held that the concept of objective grounds in point 1 of that clause must be understood as not permitting a difference in treatment between fixed-term workers and permanent workers to be justified on the basis that the difference is provided for by a general, abstract national norm, such as a law or collective agreement[456].

1237. EU law precludes 'stabilisation' of the employment relationship of public sector workers employed on a fixed-term basis which does not take account of the length of service accrued. The fixed-term nature of the contract does not constitute an 'objective ground' capable of justifying the refusal to take account of previous service. So the Court ruled in an Italian case.[457]

1238. A number of employees, including Ms Valenza, recruited by the Italian National Competition Authority (Autorità Garante della Concorrenza e del Mercato) ('the AGCM') under successive fixed-term employment contracts, obtained permanent contracts from that authority and were placed on its permanent staff.

That 'stabilisation' procedure in respect of public sector employees, provided for by a specific Italian law, confers upon the worker – who meets certain requirements concerning the length of his employment relationship and the selection procedure followed for his recruitment – the status of civil servant. His initial salary is fixed without any regard for the length of service accrued in employment under fixed-term contracts.

The AGCM thus refused to take into account the periods of service previously completed by those employees for that same public authority under fixed-term contracts. The employees consequently contested that refusal.

The *Consiglio di Stato* (Italy) asks the Court of Justice whether the European 'framework agreement' on fixed-term work precludes that Italian legislation.

1239. In its judgment the Court first of all points out that the principle of non-discrimination set out in the framework agreement provides that fixed-term workers must not be treated in a less favourable manner than comparable permanent workers solely because they work on a fixed-term basis, unless different treatment is justified on objective grounds. The fact that they have acquired the status of permanent workers does not exclude the possibility of relying on that principle, which is, accordingly, applicable in the present case.

The Court next compares the situations of fixed-term workers and permanent workers. It notes in that regard that – according to the explanations provided by the

---

456. C.O.J., 22 December 2010, *Rosa María Gavieiro Gavieiro* v. *Consellería de Educación e Ordenación Universitaria de la Xunta de Galicia*, (C-444/09), www.curia.eu.
457. C.O.J., 18 October 2012, *Rosanna Valenza* v. *Autorità Garante della Concorrenza e del Mercato*, C-302/11 to C-305/11, www.curia.eu.

Italian Government itself – the purpose of the national legislation is precisely to promote the experience accrued with the employer.

1240. The Court states that it is for the referring court to determine whether the employees, when they were working under fixed-term contracts, were in a situation comparable to that of career civil servants employed on a permanent basis. The nature of the duties performed by those employees under fixed-term employment contracts and the quality of the experience which they thereby acquired constitute criteria which make it possible to determine whether they are in a situation comparable to that of career civil servants. In any event, the fact that – unlike career civil servants – they have not passed the general competition for obtaining a post in the public sector does not mean that they are in a different situation, given that the conditions for stabilisation set by the national legislature are specifically intended to enable the stabilisation of only those fixed-term workers whose situation may be viewed in the same way as that of career civil servants.

In the event that the duties performed for the AGCM under fixed-term contracts correspond to those performed by a career civil servant in the corresponding category, it has to be ascertained whether there is an objective ground justifying the complete failure to take account of the length of service accrued under the fixed-term contracts.

1241. Thus, the Court points out that there may be an objective ground justifying a difference in treatment, in a particular context and accompanied by precise and specific factors, resulting from the specific nature of the tasks. The unequal treatment must be based on objective and transparent criteria enabling it to be ascertained whether that unequal treatment meets a genuine need and is appropriate and necessary for achieving the objective pursued. In any event, the mere fact that the fixed-term worker completed periods of service on the basis of a fixed-term contract does not constitute such an objective ground. To allow that the mere temporary nature of an employment relationship is sufficient to justify a difference in treatment as between fixed-term workers and permanent workers would render the objectives of EU law meaningless and would be tantamount to perpetuating a situation that is disadvantageous to fixed-term workers.

The Court acknowledges the discretion enjoyed by the Member States as regards the organisation of their own public administrations and the conditions for obtaining a post in the public sector. However, the criteria which the Member States lay down must be applied in a transparent manner and must be open to review in order to prevent any unfavourable treatment of fixed-term workers solely on the basis of the duration of the employment contracts which attest to their length of service and professional experience. Thus, some of the differences relating to the manner in which fixed-term workers are recruited under 'stabilisation' procedures with respect to career civil servants recruited following a general competition, the qualifications required and the nature of the duties which they must undertake could, in principle, justify a difference in treatment as regards their conditions of employment. Thus a difference in treatment could be justified if it takes account of objective requirements relating to the post which the recruitment procedure is intended to fill and which are unrelated to the fixed-term nature of the employment relationship.

1242. The objective – as claimed by the Italian Government – of preventing reverse discrimination against career civil servants recruited after passing a general competition, may constitute an 'objective ground'. However, the Court takes the view that the Italian legislation is disproportionate in that it completely prohibits all periods of service completed under fixed-term contracts being taken into account in order to determine the length of service upon recruitment on a permanent basis and, thus, the remuneration. Such a complete and absolute prohibition is based on the mistaken idea that the permanent nature of the employment relationship of certain public officials in itself justifies a difference in treatment with respect to public officials employed on a fixed-term basis, thereby rendering the objectives of the directive and of the framework agreement meaningless.

It is for the referring court to ascertain whether there are 'objective grounds' justifying that difference in treatment.

E. Measures to Prevent Abuse

1243. To prevent abuse arising from the use of successive fixed-term employment contracts or relationships, Member States, after consultation with social partners in accordance with national law, collective agreements or practice, and/or the social partners, shall, where there are no equivalent legal measures to prevent abuse, introduce, in a manner which takes account of the needs of specific sectors and/or categories of workers, one or more of the following measures:

(a) objective reasons justifying the renewal of such contracts or relationships;
(b) the maximum total duration of successive fixed-term employment contracts or relationships;
(c) the number of renewals of such contracts or relationships.

Member States, after consultation with the social partners and/or the social partners, shall, where appropriate, determine under what conditions fixed-term employment contracts or relationships:

(a) shall be regarded as 'successive';
(b) shall be deemed to be contracts or relationships of indefinite duration (clause 5).

1244. Against this background of ideas, the Advocate-General J. Kokot, in his conclusions of 27 October 2005 in the *Adelener* case, cited above, stated with good reason:

> The concept of succession is one of the main legal concepts in the Framework Agreement. Of course, the Framework Agreement and, by extension, Directive 1999/70 are not intended primarily to obstruct the conclusion of individual fixed-term employment relationships; on the contrary, they are focused above all on the possibilities for pursuing abusive practices by concluding such contracts in succession (successive employment relationships), as well as on

Part I, Ch. 4, Individual Employment Contracts

improving the quality of such fixed-term employment relationships. In particular where a number of fixed-term employment relationships have been concluded in succession, there is a danger that the employment relationship of indefinite duration, the employment relationship model defined by management and labour, will be circumvented, thus giving rise to the problem of abuse. That is why clause 5(1) of the Framework Agreement expressly requires that measures be introduced to prevent abuse arising from the use of successive fixed-term employment relationships.

1245. In the *Adelener* case, the Court of Justice stated with good reason:

Clause 5(1)(a) of the framework agreement on fixed-term work, is to be interpreted as precluding the use of successive fixed-term employment contracts where the justification advanced for their use is solely that it is provided for by a general provision of statute or secondary legislation of a Member State. On the contrary, the concept of objective reasons within the meaning of that clause requires recourse to this particular type of employment relationship, as provided for by national legislation, to be justified by the presence of specific factors relating in particular to the activity in question and the conditions under which it is carried out.

Those circumstances may result, in particular, from the specific nature of the tasks for the performance of which such contracts have been concluded and from the inherent characteristics of those tasks or, as the case may be, from pursuit of a legitimate social-policy objective of a Member State.

1246. On the other hand, a national provision which merely authorises recourse to successive fixed-term employment contracts in a general and abstract manner by a rule of statute or secondary legislation carries a real risk that it will result in misuse of that type of contract and, accordingly, is not compatible with the objective of the Framework Agreement and the requirement that it should have practical effect.

Thus, to admit that a national provision may, automatically and without further provision, justify successive fixed-term employment contracts would effectively have no regard to the aim of the Framework Agreement, which is to protect workers against instability of employment, and render meaningless the principle that contracts of indefinite duration are the general form of employment relationship.

More specifically, recourse to fixed-term employment contracts solely on the basis of a general provision of statute or secondary legislation, unlinked to what the activity in question specifically comprises, does not permit objective and transparent criteria to be identified in order to verify whether the renewal of such contracts actually responds to a genuine need, is appropriate for achieving the objective pursued and is necessary for that purpose.

Consequently, this means that a system in which permanent jobs are done by individual temporary agents, who are replaced by other individual temporary agents, contravenes the framework agreement, in the letter of the law and in the spirit of the law. Employers can not take the easy route of employing successive temporary personnel for permanent jobs. Besides, such a system is contrary to the principle that employment should be on the basis of an indeterminate period and that it is only possible to offer temporary contracts if there are objective reasons.

1247. In the *Mangold* case,[458] the Court decided that the objective of encouraging the integration into working life of unemployed older workers does not justify national legislation which authorises, without restrictions, the conclusion of fixed-term employment contracts for all workers over the age of 52.

> The principle of non-discrimination on grounds of age is a general principle of Union law. In this regard, the purpose of Directive 2000/78[459] is to lay down a general framework for combating certain forms of discrimination, including in particular discrimination on grounds of age, as regards employment and occupation. A difference of treatment on grounds directly of age as a rule constitutes discrimination prohibited by Union law. However, the directive allows the Member States to provide for such differences of treatment and to consider them non-discriminatory if, within the context of national law, they are justified objectively and reasonably by a legitimate aim, in particular by legitimate employment policy and labour market objectives. Furthermore, the means to achieving such objectives must be appropriate and necessary.

1248. The Labour Court, Munich (Germany) has referred to the Court of Justice of the European Union several questions for a preliminary ruling on the interpretation of Directive 2000/78 in a dispute concerning the German Law on part-time working and fixed-term contracts. That law authorises, without restriction, except in specific cases of a continuous employment relationship, the conclusion of fixed-term contracts of employment once the worker has reached the age of 52.

1249. The Court of Justice recognises that the purpose of this legislation is plainly to promote the integration into working life of unemployed older workers, in so far as they encounter considerable difficulties in finding work. An objective of that kind justifies, as a rule, "objectively and reasonably", a difference of treatment on grounds of age.

However, a provision of national law such as that contained in the German law goes beyond what is appropriate and necessary to attain the legitimate objective pursued.

Admittedly, the Member States enjoy broad discretion in their choice of the measures capable of attaining their objectives in the field of social and employment policy. However, according to the Court, application of the national legislation at issue leads to a situation in which all workers who have reached the age of 52, without distinction, whether or not they were unemployed before the contract was concluded and whatever the duration of any period of unemployment, may lawfully, until their retirement, be offered fixed-term contracts of employment which may be

---

458. C.O.J., 22 November 2005, *Werner Mangold* v. *Rüdiger Helm*, C-144/04, ECR, 2005, 9981.
459. Council Directive 2000/78/EC of 27 November 2000 establishing a general framework for equal treatment in employment and occupation, O.J., 2 December 2000 L 303.

renewed an indefinite number of times. This significant body of workers, determined solely on the basis of age, is thus in danger, during a substantial part of its members' working life, of being excluded from *the benefit of stable employment which, however, constitutes a major element in the protection of workers. In this case, it has not been shown that fixing an age threshold*, as such, regardless of any other consideration linked to the structure of the labour market in question or the personal situation of the person concerned, is objectively necessary to the attainment of the objective which is the integration into working life of unemployed older workers.

1250. The applicants in the *Marossu* case[460] were employed as technical kitchen staff by the hospital under a series of successive fixed-term contracts, the most recent of which were concluded during the month of January 2002 for a period of six months.

They were recruited from a list of suitable candidates drawn up following a public competition organised in 1998 by the hospital with a view to employing, on a temporary basis, 'technical kitchen staff', in which the applicants in the main proceedings were successful.

The last of the fixed-term contracts, which expired in July 2002, were not renewed by the hospital, which formally dismissed the applicants in the main proceedings when they arrived at their workplace on the date of expiry of their respective contracts.

The following question was referred to the Court for a preliminary ruling:

> Are Article 1 of Directive 1999/70/EC and clauses 1(b) and 5 of the [framework agreement] ... to be interpreted as precluding provisions of national law (in force before the directive was implemented) which differentiate between employment contracts signed with the public authorities and contracts with employers in the private sector by excluding the former from the protection afforded by establishing an employment relationship of indefinite duration in the event of an infringement of binding rules on successive fixed-term contracts?

The Court answered as follows.

1251. By its question, the national court asks essentially whether the framework agreement is to be interpreted as precluding national legislation which – where abuse arises from a public sector employer's use of successive fixed-term contracts or working relationships – prevents the latter from being converted into indefinite contracts or working relationships, even where such conversion applies to contracts and working relationships concluded with a private-sector employer.

With a view to giving an answer to the question submitted, it should be made clear at the outset that, contrary to the submissions of the Italian Government at the

---

460. C.O.J., *Cristiano Marrosu, Gianluca Sardino* v. *Azienda Ospedaliera Ospedale San Martino di Genova e Cliniche Universitarie Convenzionate*, C-53/04, 7 September 2006, ECR, 2006, 7213.

hearing, Directive 1999/70 and the framework agreement can apply also to fixed-term employment contracts and relationships concluded with the public authorities and other public-sector bodies.

The provisions of those two instruments contain nothing to permit the inference that their scope is limited to fixed-term contracts concluded by workers with employers in the private sector.

On the contrary, firstly, as is apparent from the very wording of clause 2(1) of the framework agreement, the scope of the framework agreement is conceived in broad terms, covering generally 'fixed-term workers who have an employment contract or employment relationship as defined in law, collective agreements or practice in each Member State'. In addition, the definition of 'fixed-term workers' for the purposes of the framework agreement, set out in clause 3(1), encompasses all workers without drawing a distinction according to whether their employer is in the public or private sector.

1252. Secondly, clause 2(2) of the framework agreement, far from providing for the exclusion of fixed-term employment contracts or relationships concluded with a public-sector employer, merely gives the Member States and/or the social partners the option of making the framework agreement inapplicable to 'initial vocational training relationships and apprentice schemes' and employment contracts and relationships 'which have been concluded within the framework of a specific public or publicly-supported training, integration and vocational retraining programme'.

It should also be recalled, as is apparent from clause 1(b) of the framework agreement, that its purpose is to 'establish a framework to prevent abuse arising from the use of successive fixed-term employment contracts or relationships'.

To this end, clause 5(1) imposes on Member States the obligation to introduce into domestic law one or more of the measures listed in clause 5(1)(a) to (c) where equivalent legal provisions intended to prevent effectively the misuse of successive fixed-term employment contracts do not already exist in the Member State concerned.

1253. However, it is important to note that, as is clear from its wording, that provision makes it possible for Member States to take account of the needs of specific sectors and/or categories of workers involved, provided it is justified on objective grounds.

It is true that clause 5(2) of the framework agreement does not give Member States the same ability with regard to laying down under what conditions successive fixed-term employment contracts or relationships are to be regarded as being of indefinite duration.

However, since the framework agreement neither lays down a general obligation on the Member States to provide for the conversion of fixed-term employment contracts into contracts of indefinite duration nor prescribes the precise conditions under which fixed-term employment contracts may be used, it gives Member States a margin of discretion in the matter.

Part I, Ch. 4, Individual Employment Contracts 1254–1256

It follows that clause 5 of the framework agreement does not preclude, as such, a Member State from treating misuse of successive fixed-term employment contracts or relationships differently according to whether those contracts or relationships were entered into with a private-sector or public-sector employer.

1254. However, in order for national legislation, such as that at issue here – which, in the public sector only, prohibits a succession of fixed-term contracts from being converted into an indefinite employment contract – to be regarded as compatible with the framework agreement, the domestic law of the Member State concerned must include, in that sector, another effective measure to prevent and, where relevant, punish the abuse of successive fixed-term contracts.

With regard to the latter condition, it should be noted that clause 5(1) of the framework agreement places on Member States the mandatory requirement of effective adoption of at least one of the measures listed in that provision intended to prevent the abusive use of successive fixed-term employment contracts or relationships, where domestic law does not already include equivalent measures.

1255. Furthermore, where, as in the present case, Union law does not lay down any specific sanctions should instances of abuse nevertheless be established, it is incumbent on the national authorities to adopt appropriate measures to deal with such a situation which must be not only proportionate, but also sufficiently effective and a sufficient deterrent to ensure that the provisions adopted pursuant to the framework agreement are fully effective.

While the detailed rules for implementing such provisions fall within the internal legal order of the Member States by virtue of the principle of procedural autonomy of the Member States, they must, however, not be less favourable than those governing similar domestic situations (principle of equivalence) or render impossible in practice or excessively difficult the exercise of rights conferred by Union law (principle of effectiveness).

1256. Therefore, where abuse of successive fixed-term contracts has taken place, a measure offering effective and equivalent guarantees for the protection of workers must be capable of being applied in order duly to punish that abuse and nullify the consequences of the breach of Union law. According to the very wording of the first paragraph of Article 2 of Directive 1999/70, the Member States must 'take any necessary measures to enable them at any time to be in a position to guarantee the results imposed by [the] directive'.

It is not for the Court to rule on the interpretation of national law, that being exclusively for the national court which must, in the present case, determine whether the requirements set out in the preceding three paragraphs are met by the provisions of the relevant national legislation. However, the Court, when giving a preliminary ruling, may, where appropriate, provide clarification designed to give the national court guidance in its interpretation.

In that regard, it should be noted that national legislation such as that at issue in the main proceedings which lays down mandatory rules governing the duration and renewal of fixed-term contracts and the right to compensation for damage suffered by a worker as a result of the abusive use by public authorities of successive fixed-term employment contracts or relationships appears, at first sight, to satisfy the requirements set out the present judgment.

1257. However, it is for the national court to determine to what extent the conditions for application and effective implementation of the national law constitute a measure adequate for the prevention and, where relevant, the punishment of the abusive use by the public authorities of successive fixed-term employment contracts or relationships.

In the light of the foregoing considerations, the answer to the question referred must be that the framework agreement must be interpreted as not in principle precluding national legislation which, where there is abuse arising from the use of successive fixed-term employment contracts or relationships by a public sector employer, precludes their being converted into contracts of indeterminate duration, even though such conversion is provided for in respect of employment contracts and relationships with a private-sector employer, where that legislation includes another effective measure to prevent and, where relevant, punish the abuse of successive fixed-term contracts by a public-sector employer.

1258. In the *Angelidaki case*[461] the Court ruled as follows:

(1) Clause 5(1) provides with regard to the implementation of the measures to prevent the misuse of successive fixed-term employment contracts or relationships for an 'equivalent legal measure' within the meaning of that clause already exists under national law provided, however, so that that legislation (i) does not affect the effectiveness of the prevention of the misuse of fixed-term employment contracts or relationships resulting from that equivalent legal measure, and (ii) complies with Union law and, in particular, with clause 8(3) of the Framework Agreement.

(2) 'Objective reasons' allow for renewal of fixed term contracts in order to meet certain temporary needs but not when those needs are fixed and permanent. By contrast, clause 5(1)(a) does not apply to the first or single use of a fixedterm employment contract or relationship.

(3) Clause 8(3) (reducing the general level of protection) must be interpreted as meaning that the 'reduction' with which that clause is concerned must be considered in relation to the general level of protection applicable in the Member State concerned both to workers who have entered into successive fixed-term employment contracts and to workers who have entered into a first or single fixed-term employment contract.

(4) Clause 8(3) work must be interpreted as not precluding national legislation, which (i) no longer provides for fixed-term employment contracts to be recognised as contracts of indefinite duration where abuse arises from the use of such contracts in the public sector, or which makes such recognition subject to certain cumulative and restrictive conditions, and (ii)

---

461. C.O.J., 23 April 2009, *Kiriaki Angelidaki v. Organismos Nomarkhiaki Aftodiikisi Rethimnis* (C378/07), www.curia.

excludes from the benefit of the protection measures provided workers who have entered into a first or single fixed-term employment contract.

1259. The renewal of fixed-term employment contracts may be justified by replacement needs, even when that need is recurring or even permanent, as the following case shows. Ms Bianca Kücük was employed by the Land Nordrhein-Westfalen (North Rhine-Westphalia, Germany) as a clerk in the court office of the civil procedural division of the Amtsgericht Köln (District Court, Cologne) for a period of 11 years, on the basis of a total of 13 fixed-term employment contracts. Those contracts were always concluded in order to replace court clerks employed for an indefinite duration who were on leave for an indeterminate period because of temporary leave (such as parental leave).

Before the Arbeitsgericht Köln (Labour Court, Cologne, Germany), Ms Kücük argued that her last employment contract had become a contract of indefinite duration in the absence of any objective reason justifying its being limited in time. A total of 13 fixed-term employment contracts concluded successively and without interruption over a period of 11 years cannot, in any event, be deemed to be a response to a temporary need for replacement staff. The Bundesarbeitsgericht (Federal Labour Court), which ultimately has to rule on the case, made a reference to the Court of Justice concerning the interpretation of the relevant provisions of EU law.

1260. In its judgment[462] the Court holds that that a temporary need for replacement staff – as provided for under German law – may, in principle, constitute an objective reason under EU law justifying both fixed-term contracts being concluded with replacement staff and the renewal of those contracts.

The mere fact that an employer may have to employ temporary replacements on a recurring, or even permanent, basis and that those replacements may also be covered by the hiring of employees under employment contracts of indefinite duration does not mean that there is no objective reason or that there is abuse. To require automatically the conclusion of contracts of indefinite duration when the size of the undertaking or entity concerned and the composition of its personnel mean that the employer is faced with a recurring or permanent need for replacement staff would go beyond the objectives pursued by the framework agreement of the European social partners implemented by European Union law and would disregard the discretion those instruments leave the Member States and the social partners.

1261. Clause 5 of the framework agreement on fixed-term work must be interpreted as meaning that a Member State, which provides in its national legislation for conversion of fixed-term employment contracts into an employment contract of indefinite duration when the fixed-term employment contracts have reached a certain duration, is not obliged to require that the employment contract of indefinite duration reproduces in identical terms the principal clauses set out in the previous

---

462. C.O.J., 26 January 2012, *Bianca Kücük* v. *Land Nordrhein-Westfalen*, C-586/10, www.curia.eu.

contract. However, in order not to undermine the practical effect of, or the objectives pursued by, Directive 1999/70, that Member State must ensure that the conversion of fixed-term employment contracts into an employment contract of indefinite duration is not accompanied by material amendments to the clauses of the previous contract in a way that is, overall, unfavourable to the person concerned when the subject-matter of that person's tasks and the nature of his functions remain unchanged.[463]

1262. By contrast, since clause 5(1) is not applicable to workers who have entered into a first or single fixed-term employment contract, that provision does not require the Member States to adopt penalties where such a contract does in fact cover fixed and permanent needs of the employer.

This last point allows for 'chain contracts', where successive workers for a fixed term contract succeed each other and perform permanent tasks. This can not have been the intention. Here the Court should review its position. There should be objective reasons for each fixed term contract, also for the first one. This follows clearly from the intention of the European legislator.[464]

F. Information and Employment Opportunities

1263. Employers shall inform fixed-term workers about vacancies which become available in the undertaking or establishment to ensure that they have the same opportunity to secure permanent positions as other workers. Such information may be provided by way of a general announcement at a suitable place in the undertaking or establishment.

As far as possible, employers should facilitate access by fixed-term workers to appropriate training opportunities to enhance their skills, career development and occupational mobility (clause 6).

G. Information and Consultation

1264. Fixed-term workers shall be taken into consideration in calculating the threshold above which workers' representative bodies provided for in national and Community law may be constituted in the undertaking as required by national provisions.

The arrangements for the application of this clause shall be defined by Member States after consultation with the social partners and/or the social partners in accordance with national law, collective agreements or practice. As far as possible, employers should give consideration to the provision of appropriate information to

---

463. C.O.J., 8 March 2012, Martial Huet v. Université de Bretagne occidentale, C-251/11, www.curia.eu.
464. R. Blanpain and C. Grant (ed.), *Fixed-Term Employment Contracts: A Comparative Study*, Bruges, Vanden Broele, 2009, 443 pp.

Part I, Ch. 4, Individual Employment Contracts

existing workers' representative bodies about fixed-term work in the undertaking (clause 7).

H. Provisions on Implementation

1265. Member States and/or the social partners can maintain or introduce more favourable provisions for workers than set out in this agreement.

The agreement shall be without prejudice to any more specific Union provisions, and in particular Union provisions concerning equal treatment or opportunities for men and women. Implementation of this agreement shall not constitute valid grounds for reducing the general level of protection afforded to workers in the field of the agreement.

1266. Clause 5(1) of the Framework Agreement on fixed-term work must be interpreted as meaning that the concept of 'a close objective connection with a previous employment contract of indefinite duration concluded with the same employer', provided for in Paragraph 14(3) of the German Law on parttime employment and fixed-term employment contracts of 21 December 2000, must be applied to situations in which a fixed-term contract has not been immediately preceded by a contract of indefinite duration concluded with the same employer and an interval of several years separates those contracts, where, for that entire period, the initial employment relationship continued for the same activity, with the same employer, by means of an uninterrupted succession of fixed-term contracts.

It is for the national court, to the fullest extent possible, to interpret the relevant provisions of national law in such a way as to comply with Clause 5(1) of the Framework Agreement.[465]

1267. The present agreement does not prejudice the right of the social partners to conclude at the appropriate level, including European level, agreements adapting and/or complementing the provisions of this agreement in a manner which will take note of the specific needs of the social partners concerned.

The prevention and settlement of disputes and grievances arising from the application of this agreement shall be dealt with in accordance with national law, collective agreements and practice.

The signatory parties shall review the application of this agreement five years after the date of the Council decision if requested by one of the parties to this agreement (clause 8).[466]

---

465. C.O.J., 10 March 2011, *Deutsche Lufthansa AG* v. *Gertraud Kumpan*, www.curia.eu.
466. Clause 8(3) of the framework agreement must be interpreted as meaning that the 'reduction' to which it refers must be considered in relation to the general level of protection applicable, in the Member State concerned, both to workers having entered into successive fixed-term employment contracts and to workers having concluded a first or single fixed-term employment contract (C.O.J., 24 June 2010, *Francesca Sorge* v. *Poste Italiane SpA*, C-98/09, www.curia).

IV. Temporary Agency Work

1268. On 19 November 2008, finally, the long time overdue Directive on temporary agency work saw the day light. That it took more than 20 years before the directive was adopted had first of all to do with the ideological differences relating to the role of the private sector on the labour market. Employers associations and trade unions did not succeed to conclude a collective agreement on this matter. Today temporary agency work is accepted. Employees are put at the disposal of employers-users by temporary work agencies, in a triangular relationship.

Last minute difficulties related to the pay of temporary workers and the principle of equal treatment. Also on these point an agreement was reached and finally, temporary work has a full fledged place on the labour market.

A. General Provisions

1. Aim

1269. The purpose of this directive is:

– to ensure the protection of temporary agency workers; and – to improve the quality of temporary agency work by ensuring that the principle of equal treatment is applied to temporary agency workers; and
– by recognising temporary-work agencies as employers, while taking into account
– the need to establish a suitable framework for the use of temporary agency work with a view
– to contributing effectively to the creation of jobs and to
– the development of flexible forms of working (Article 2).

2. Scope

1270. The directive applies:

– to workers with a contract of employment or employment relationship with a temporary-work agency who are assigned to user undertakings to work temporarily under their supervision and direction;
– to public and private undertakings which are temporary-work agencies or user undertakings engaged in economic activities whether or not they are operating for gain (Article 1).

Member States may, after consulting the social partners, provide that the Directive does not apply to employment contracts or relationships concluded under a specific public or publicly supported vocational training, integration or retraining programme (Article 1).

Part I, Ch. 4, Individual Employment Contracts 1271–1272

Member States shall not exclude from the scope of this Directive workers, contracts of employment or employment relationships solely because they relate to part-time workers, fixed-term contract workers or persons with a contract of employment or employment relationship with a temporary-work agency (Art. 3, 2).

3. Definitions

1271. For the purposes of this directive:

(a) 'worker' means any person who, in the Member State concerned, is protected as a worker under national employment law;
(b) 'temporary-work agency' means any natural or legal person who, in compliance with national law, concludes contracts of employment or employment relationships with temporary agency workers in order to assign them to user undertakings to work there temporarily under their supervision and direction;
(c) 'temporary agency worker' means a worker with a contract of employment or an employment relationship with a temporary-work agency with a view to being assigned to a user undertaking to work temporarily under its supervision and direction;
(d) 'user undertaking' means any natural or legal person for whom and under the supervision and direction of whom a temporary agency worker works temporarily;
(e) 'assignment' means the period during which the temporary agency worker is placed at the user undertaking to work temporarily under its supervision and direction;
(f) 'basic working and employment conditions' means working and employment conditions laid down by legislation, regulations, administrative provisions, collective agreements and/or other binding general provisions in force in the user undertaking relating to:
   (i) the duration of working time, overtime, breaks, rest periods, night work, holidays and public holidays;
   (ii) pay (Art. 3, 1).

4. Review of Restrictions or Prohibitions

1272. The door for temporary work is wide open. Member States and social partners are requested to reconsider prohibitions or restrictions. Prohibitions or restrictions on the use of temporary agency work shall be justified only on grounds of general interest relating in particular to the protection of temporary agency workers, the requirements of health and safety at work or the need to ensure that the labour market functions properly and abuses are prevented (Article 4, 1).[467] This is without prejudice to national requirements with regard to registration, licensing, certification, financial guarantees or monitoring of temporary-work agencies (Art. 4, 4).

B. Employment and Working Conditions (Article 5)

1. The Principle of Equal Treatment

1273. The basic working and employment conditions[468] of temporary agency workers shall be, for the duration of their assignment at a user undertaking, at least those that would apply if they had been recruited directly by that undertaking to occupy the same job.

Must also be complied with the rules in force in the user undertaking on:

(a) protection of pregnant women and nursing mothers and protection of children and young people; and
(b) equal treatment for men and women and any action to combat any discrimination based on sex, race or ethnic origin, religion, beliefs, disabilities, age or sexual orientation.

1274. An exemption can be made to the principle:

– where temporary agency workers have a permanent contract of employment with a temporary-work agency continue to be paid in the time between assignments.
– provided that an adequate level of protection is provided for temporary agency workers, Member States in which there is either no system in law for declaring collective agreements universally applicable or no such system in law or practice for extending their provisions to all similar undertakings in a certain sector or geographical area, may, after consulting the social partners at national level and on the basis of an agreement concluded by them, establish arrangements concerning the basic working and employment conditions which derogate from the

---

467. 2. By 5 December 2011, Member States shall, after consulting the social partners in accordance with national legislation, collective agreements and practices, review any restrictions or prohibitions on the use of temporary agency work in order to verify whether they are justified (Art. 4, 2). The Member States shall inform the Commission of the results of the review by 5 December 2011 (Art. 4, 5).
468. (f) 'Basic working and employment conditions' means working and employment conditions laid down by legislation, regulations, administrative provisions, collective agreements and/or other binding general provisions in force in the user undertaking relating to:
(i) the duration of working time, overtime, breaks, rest periods, night work, holidays and public holidays;
(ii) pay (Art. 3, 1).

principle of equal treatment. Such arrangements may include a qualifying period for equal treatment.[469]

1275. Member States shall take appropriate measures, in accordance with national law and/or practice, with a view to preventing misuse in the application of this Article and, in particular, to preventing successive assignments designed to circumvent the provisions of this Directive (Art. 5, 5).

2. Access to Employment, Collective Facilities and Vocational Training (Article 6)

a. Vacant Posts

1276. Temporary agency workers shall be informed of any vacant posts in the user undertaking to give them the same opportunity as other workers in that undertaking to find permanent employment. Such information may be provided by a general announcement in a suitable place in the undertaking for which, and under whose supervision, temporary agency workers are engaged.

b. Freedom of Labour

1277. Member States shall take any action required to ensure that any clauses prohibiting or having the effect of preventing the conclusion of a contract of employment or an employment relationship between the user undertaking and the temporary agency worker after his assignment are null and void or may be declared null and void.

Provisions under which temporary agencies receive a reasonable level of recompense for services rendered to user undertakings for the assignment, recruitment and training of temporary agency workers are allowed.

c. Free of Charge

1278. Temporary-work agencies shall not charge workers any fees in exchange for arranging for them to be recruited by a user undertaking, or for concluding a contract of employment or an employment relationship with a user undertaking after carrying out an assignment in that undertaking.

---

469. 'The arrangements referred to in this paragraph shall be in conformity with Community legislation and shall be sufficiently precise and accessible to allow the sectors and firms concerned to identify and comply with their obligations. In particular, Member States shall specify, in application of Article 3(2), whether occupational social security schemes, including pension, sick pay or financial participation schemes are included in the basic working and employment conditions. Such arrangements shall also be without prejudice to agreements at national, regional, local or sectoral level that are no less favourable to workers (Article 5, 4, second indent).

d. Access to the Amenities or Collective Facilities

1279. Temporary agency workers shall be given access to the amenities or collective facilities in the user undertaking, in particular any canteen, child-care facilities and transport services, under the same conditions as workers employed directly by the undertaking, unless the difference in treatment is justified by objective reasons.

Member States shall take suitable measures or shall promote dialogue between the social partners, in accordance with their national traditions and practices, in order to:

(a) improve temporary agency workers' access to training and to child-care facilities in the temporary-work agencies, even in the periods between their assignments, in order to enhance their career development and employability;
(b) improve temporary agency workers' access to training for user undertakings' workers.

3. Representation of Temporary Agency Workers

1280. Temporary agency workers shall count, under conditions established by the Member States, for the purposes of calculating the threshold above which bodies representing workers provided for under Community and national law and collective agreements are to be formed at the temporary-work agency. The same may be provided for the user undertaking (Art. 7).

4. Information of Workers' Representatives

1281. The user undertaking must provide suitable information on the use of temporary agency workers when providing information on the employment situation in that undertaking to bodies representing workers set up in accordance with national and Community legislation (Art. 8).

C. *Implementation*

1282. Member States shall adopt and publish the laws, regulations and administrative provisions necessary to comply with this Directive by 5 December 2011, or shall ensure that the social partners introduce the necessary provisions by way of an agreement, whereby the Member States must make all the necessary arrangements to enable them to guarantee at any time that the objectives of this Directive are being attained. They shall forthwith inform the Commission thereof (Article 11).

Part I, Ch. 4, Individual Employment Contracts

V. Framework Agreement on Telework

1283. On 16 July 2002, the central EU-level social partner organisations formally signed a new EU-level framework agreement on telework.[470] The agreement concludes consultation and debate on this topic since 2000.

The European Commission estimates that there are currently 4.5 million employed teleworkers (and 10 million teleworkers in total) in the EU.[471]

At the initiative of UNICE a so-called 'voluntary', meaning non-legally binding agreement was concluded. The text of the agreement can be summarised as follows.

A. *General Considerations*

1284. In the context of the European employment strategy, the European Council invited the social partners to negotiate agreements modernising the organisation of work, including flexible working arrangements, with the aim of making undertakings productive and competitive and achieving the necessary balance between flexibility and security.

The European Commission, in its second stage consultation of social partners on modernising and improving employment relations, invited the social partners to start negotiations on telework. On 20 September 2001, ETUC (and the liaison committee EUROCADRES/CEC), UNICE/UEAPME and CEEP announced their intention to start negotiations aimed at an agreement to be implemented by the members of the signatory parties in the Member States and in the countries of the European Economic Area. Through them, they wished to contribute to preparing the transition to a knowledge-based economy and society as agreed by the European Council in Lisbon.

Telework covers a wide and fast evolving spectrum of circumstances and practices. For that reason, social partners have chosen a definition of telework that permits various forms of regular telework to be covered.

The social partners see telework both as a way for companies and public service organisations to modernise work organisation, and as a way for workers to reconcile work and social life and giving them greater autonomy in the accomplishment of their tasks. If Europe wants to make the most out of the information society, it must encourage this new form of work organisation in such a way that flexibility and security go together and the quality of jobs is enhanced, and that the chances of disabled people on the labour market are increased.

---

470. A. Broughton, IRS, 'Social partners sign teleworking accord', <www.eiro.eurofound.ie>. The signatories were the European Trade Union Confederation (ETUC); the Council of European Professional and Managerial Staff (EUROCADRES)/European Confederation of Executives and Managerial Staff (CEC) liaison committee; the Union of Industrial and Employers' Confederations of Europe (UNICE)/the European Association of Craft, Small and Medium-Sized Enterprises (UEAPME); and the European Centre of Enterprises with Public Participation and of Enterprises of General Economic Interest (CEEP).
471. Agreements were concluded earlier in the telecommunications sector (2001) and in the commerce sector (2001).

1285. This voluntary agreement aims at establishing a general framework at the European level to be implemented by the members of the signatory parties in accordance with the national procedures and practices specific to management and labour. The signatory parties also invite their member organisations in candidate countries to implement this agreement.

Implementation of this agreement does not constitute valid grounds to reduce the general level of protection afforded to workers in the field of this agreement. When implementing this agreement, the members of the signatory parties avoid unnecessary burdens on SMEs.

This agreement does not prejudice the right of social partners to conclude, at the appropriate level, including the European level, agreements adapting and/or complementing this agreement in a manner which will take note of the specific needs of the social partners concerned.

B. *Definition and Scope*

1286. Telework is a form of organising and/or performing work, using information technology, in the context of an employment contract/relationship, where work, which could also be performed at the employers premises, is carried out away from those premises on a regular basis.

This agreement covers teleworkers. A teleworker is any person carrying out telework as defined above.

C. *Voluntary Character*

1287. Telework is voluntary for the worker and the employer concerned. Teleworking may be required as part of a worker's initial job description or it may be engaged in as a voluntary arrangement subsequently.

In both cases, the employer provides the teleworker with relevant written information in accordance with Directive 91/533/EEC, including information on applicable collective agreements, description of the work to be performed, etc.[472]

The specificities of telework normally require additional written information on matters such as the department of the undertaking to which the teleworker is attached, his/her immediate superior or other persons to whom she or he can address questions of professional or personal nature, reporting arrangements, etc.

1288. If telework is not part of the initial job description, and the employer makes an offer of telework, the worker may accept or refuse this offer. If a worker expresses the wish to opt for telework, the employer may accept or refuse this request.

The change to telework as such, because it only modifies the way in which work is performed, does not affect the teleworker's employment status. A worker's refusal

---

472. *See* Part I, Chapter 3, §2.

to opt for telework is not, as such, a reason for terminating the employment relationship or changing the terms and conditions of employment of that worker.

If telework is not part of the initial job description, the decision to change to telework is reversible by individual and/or collective agreement. The reversibility could imply returning to work at the employer's premises at the worker's or at the employer's request. The modalities of this reversibility are established by individual and/or collective agreement.

D. Employment Conditions

1289. Regarding employment conditions, teleworkers benefit from the same rights, guaranteed by applicable legislation and collective agreements, as comparable workers at the employers premises. However, in order to take into account the particularities of telework, specific complementary collective and/or individual agreements may be necessary.

E. Data Protection

1290. The employer is responsible for taking the appropriate measures, notably with regard to software, to ensure the protection of data used and processed by the teleworker for professional purposes.

The employer informs the teleworker of all relevant legislation and company rules concerning data protection. It is the teleworker's responsibility to comply with these rules.

The employer informs the teleworker in particular of any restrictions on the use of IT equipment or tools such as the internet, sanctions in the case of non-compliance.

F. Privacy

1291. The employer respects the privacy of the teleworker. If any kind of monitoring system is put in place, it needs to be proportionate to the objective and introduced in accordance with Directive 90/270 on visual display units.[473]

G. Equipment

1292. All questions concerning work equipment, liability and costs are clearly defined before starting telework.

---

473. Council Directive of 29 May 1990 on the minimum safety and health requirements for work with display screening equipment within the meaning of Article 16(1) of Directive 89/391/EEC.

As a general rule, the employer is responsible for providing, installing and maintaining the equipment necessary for regular telework unless the teleworker uses his/her own equipment.

If telework is performed on a regular basis, the employer compensates or covers the costs directly caused by the work, in particular those relating to communication.

The employer provides the teleworker with an appropriate technical support facility. The employer has the liability, in accordance with national legislation and collective agreements, regarding costs for loss and damage to the equipment and data used by the teleworker.

The teleworker takes good care of the equipment provided to him/her and does not collect or distribute illegal material via the internet.

H. Health and Safety

1293. The employer is responsible for the protection of the occupational health and safety of the teleworker in accordance with Directive 89/391[474] and relevant daughter directives, national legislation and collective agreements.

The employer informs the teleworker of the company's policy on occupational health and safety, in particular requirements on visual display units. The teleworker applies these safety policies correctly.

In order to verify that the applicable health and safety provisions are correctly applied, the employer, workers' representatives and/or relevant authorities have access to the telework place, within the limits of national legislation and collective agreements. If the teleworker is working at home, such access is subject to prior notification and his/her agreement.

The teleworker is entitled to request inspection visits.

I. Organisation of Work

1294. Within the framework of applicable legislation, collective agreements and company rules, the teleworker manages the organisation of his/her working time.

The workload and performance standards of the teleworker are equivalent to those of comparable workers at the employer's premises.

1295. The employer ensures that measures are taken preventing the teleworker from being isolated from the rest of the working community in the company, such as giving him/her the opportunity to meet with colleagues on a regular basis and access to company information.

---

474. Directive of 12 June 1989 on the introduction of measures to encourage improvements in the safety and health of workers at work. *See* Part I, Chapter 8, §2.II.A.

J. Training

1296. Teleworkers have the same access to training and career development opportunities as comparable workers at the employer's premises and are subject to the same appraisal policies as these other workers.

Teleworkers receive appropriate training targeted at the technical equipment at their disposal and at the characteristics of this form of work organisation. The teleworker's supervisor and his/her direct colleagues may also need training for this form of work and its management.

K. Collective Rights Issues

1297. Teleworkers have the same collective rights as workers at the employers premises. No obstacles are put to communicating with workers' representatives.

The same conditions for participating in and standing for elections to bodies representing workers or providing worker representation apply to them.

Teleworkers are included in calculations for determining thresholds for bodies with worker representation in accordance with European and national law, collective agreements or practices. The establishment to which the teleworker will be attached for the purpose of exercising his/her collective rights is specified from the outset.

Worker representatives are informed and consulted on the introduction of telework in accordance with European and national legislations, collective agreements and practices.

L. Implementation and Follow-up

1298. In the context of Article 155 TFEU, this European framework agreement shall be implemented by the members of BUSINESSEUROPE/UEAPME, CEEP and ETUC (and the liaison committee EUROCADRES/CEC) in accordance with the procedures and practices specific to management and labour in the Member States.

This implementation will be carried out within three years after the date of signature of this agreement.

Member organisations will report on the implementation of this agreement to an *ad hoc* group set up by the signatory parties, under the responsibility of the social dialogue committee. This *ad hoc* group will prepare a joint report on the actions of implementation taken. This report will be prepared within four years after the date of signature of this agreement.

In the case of questions on the content of this agreement, member organisations involved can separately or jointly refer to the signatory parties. The signatory parties shall review the agreement five years after the date of signature if requested by one of the signatory parties.

The non-binding agreement rightly insists on equal treatment of the teleworker regarding wages and working conditions, training, organisation of work and collective rights issues. They should benefit from the same advantages as comparable workers at the employer's premises. This, however, means that the teleworkers perform in the same country as where the employer is located, which may not be the case for teleworkers who operate from another country. In implementing the agreement, this aspect should be taken care of.

1299. The implementation report of the European Framework Agreement on Telework by the European Social Partners (28 June 2006) follows that the implementation differ enormously from Member State to Member State.

Indeed, in some countries the legislator plays a role; in other countries inter-industry wide collective agreements have been concluded, some of which have been extended by governmental decree and are enforced by way of penal sanctions. In still others there are sectoral agreement or even mere recommendations.

This means that we are heading for a social Europe with two speeds. Moreover, this looks more to liquid law than to soft law.

The concluding of voluntary agreements seems to be a new way of developing European labour law, where the social partners are acting on the basis of Article 154 TFEU. As a consequence, we may have to deal with a new category of a source of European labour law, a new kind of European Act, open to interpretation by the Court of Justice.[475]

§2. CONDITIONS APPLICABLE TO THE CONTRACT OF EMPLOYMENT: INFORMATION

1300. The Council adopted on 14 October 1991 Directive 91/553 EEC on an employer's obligation to inform employees of the conditions applicable to the contract of employment relationship.[476] This directive was adopted pursuant to point 9 of the Community Charter of Fundamental Social Rights for Workers, which states: 'the conditions of employment of every worker of the European Community shall be stipulated in laws, a collective agreement or a contract of employment, according to arrangements applying in each country'. 'The development in the Member States', the consideration reads, 'of new forms of work has led to an increase in the number of types of employment' and led certain Member States to consider it necessary to subject employment relationships to formal requirements, designed to provide employees with improved protection against possible infringements of their rights and to create greater transparency in the labour market. This legislation of the Member States differs considerably on such fundamental points as the requirement

---

475. Blanpain, R. (ed.) 'European Framework Agreements and Telework. Law and Practice: A European and Comparative Study', *Bulletin of Comparative Labour Relations*, No. 62, 2007, Kluwer Law International, Alphen aan den Rijn, 283 p.
476. O.J. L 288/32, 18 October 1991.

to inform employees in writing of the main terms of the contract or employment relationship, which may have a direct effect on the operation of the Common Market.

It is therefore necessary to establish at Community level the general requirement that every employee must be provided with a document containing information on the essential elements of his contract or employment relationship. This directive is without prejudice to national law and practice concerning: 'the form of the contract or employment relationship, proof as regards the existence and content of a contract or employment relationship, and the relevant procedural rules' (Article 6).

1301. The notification by an employer in so far as it informs an employee of the essential aspects of the contract of employment enjoys the same presumption as to its correctness as would attach, in domestic law, to any similar document drawn up by the employer and communicated to the employee. The employer must none the less be allowed to bring any evidence to the contrary, by showing that the information in the notification is either inherently incorrect or has been shown to be so in fact.

Individuals may rely on the directive directly before the national courts as against the State and any organisations or bodies which are subject to the authority or control of the State or have special powers beyond those which result from the normal rules applicable to relations between individuals, either where the state has failed to transpose the directive into national law within the prescribed period or where it has not done so correctly.[477]

I. Scope

1302. The directive applies to every paid employee having a contract or employment relationship defined by the law in force in a Member State and/or governed by the law in force in a Member State (Article 1(1)). In view of the need to maintain a certain degree of flexibility in employment relationships, Member States should be able to exclude certain limited cases of employment relationships from the scope of application, namely: 'with a total duration not exceeding one month and/or with a working week not exceeding eight hours or of a casual and/or specific nature provided, in these cases, that its non-application is justified by objective considerations' (Article 1(2)).

II. Obligation to Provide Information

A. *In General*

1303. An employer is obliged to notify the employee of the essential aspects of the contract or employment relationship.

---

477. C.O.J., 4 December 1997, *Helmut Kampelmann e.a.* v. *Stadtwerke Altena GmbH e.a.*, C-253/96 and C-258/96, ECR, 1997, 6907.

This information covers at least the following:

(a) the identities of the parties;
(b) the place of work; where there is no fixed or main place of work, the principle that the employee is employed at various places and the registered place of business or, where appropriate, the domicile of the employer;
    (i) the title, grade, nature or category of the worker for which the employee is employed; or
    (ii) a brief specification or description of the work;
(d) the date of commencement of the contract or employment relationship;
(e) in the case of a temporary contract or employment relationship, the expected duration thereof;
(f) the amount of a temporary contract or employment relationship, the expected duration thereof;
(g) the amount of paid leave to which the employee is entitled or, where this cannot be indicated when the information is given, the procedures for allocating and determining such leave;
(h) the length of the periods of notice to be observed by the employer and the employee should their contract or employment relationship be terminated or, where this cannot be indicated when the information is given, the method for determining such periods of notice;
(i) the initial basic amount, the other component elements and the frequency of payment of the remuneration to which the employee is entitled;
(j) the length of the employee's normal working day or week;
(k) where appropriate:
    (i) the collective agreements governing the employee's conditions of work; or (c)
    (ii) in the case of collective agreements concluded outside the business by special joint bodies or institutions, the name of the competent body or joint institution within which the agreements were concluded (Article 2(2)).

Information concerning paid leave, periods of notice, remuneration and working time may, where appropriate, be given in a form of reference to the laws, regulations and administrative or statutory provisions or collective agreements governing those particular points (Article 2(3)).

1304. The Court ruled that employers must inform employees of their obligation to work overtime. It said that an employee's obligation to work overtime whenever requested by his employer is an essential element of the contract or employment relationship which must be notified to the employee in writing.

The case went as follows. Mr. Lange was employed as from 1 June 1998 as a lathe operator by Georg Schünemann GmbH. The contract of employment, dating from 23 April 1998, gave no details concerning overtime.

Mr. Lange refused to work overtime at the request of his employer in order to fulfil orders within time-limits agreed with a customer, for which reason his employer, by letter of 15 December 1998, terminated his contract with effect from 15 January 1999.

Mr. Lange brought an action against his dismissal before the *Arbeitsgericht* (Labour Court) Bremen. He is at odds with his employer as to what was agreed between them, when Mr. Lange was recruited, with regard to overtime.

The German court sought a ruling from the Court of Justice of the European Union on the application of Union law in relation to the obligation of employers to inform employees of the conditions applicable to the contract or employment relationship. Must the employer bring to the employee's notice a term by virtue of which the employee is required to work overtime whenever requested to do so by his employer?

The Court ruled that the relevant directive laid down a general obligation on the employer to inform employees of all the essential elements of the contract or employment relationship. The list of such elements contained in the directive was not exhaustive. Therefore, a term under which an employee is required to work overtime whenever requested to do so by his employer is one of the matters which must be brought to the employee's notice in writing.

The Court made it clear that such information may, where appropriate, in the same way as information concerning normal working hours, take the form of a reference to the relevant laws, regulations and administrative or statutory provisions or collective agreements.

The Court stated that no provision of the directive requires an essential element of the contract or employment relationship (in this case, the obligation to work overtime) that has not been brought to the notice of the employee to be regarded as inapplicable. Non-application of that element is not automatic, and the Member States retain the power to define the appropriate penalties in the event of failure to provide an employee with information regarding an essential element of the contract or employment relationship.[478]

B. Expatriate Employees

1305. Where an employee is required to work in a country other than the Member State whose law and/or practice governs the contract, the duration of which is more than one month, the documents must be in his possession before departure and must include at least the following additional information:

(a) the duration of employment abroad;
(b) the currency to be used for the payment of remuneration;
(c) where appropriate, the benefits in cash or kind attendant on the employment abroad;
(d) where appropriate, the conditions governing the employee's repatriation.

---

478. C.O.J., 8 February 2001, *Wolfgang Lange v. Georg Schünemann GmbH*, C-350/99, ECR, 2001, 1061.

The information concerning currency and remuneration may 'where appropriate, be given in the form of a reference to the laws, regulations and administrative or statutory provisions or collective agreements governing those particular points' (Article 4).

C. Modifications

1306. Any change in the conditions must be the subject of a written document to be given by the employer to the employee at the earliest opportunity and not later than one month after the date of entry into effect of the change in question. This is not compulsory in the event of a change in the laws, regulations, etc. (Article 5).

D. Term and Form of Information

1307. The (general) information may be given to the employee, not later than two months after the commencement of the employment, in the form of:

(a) a written contract of employment; and/or
(b) a letter of engagement; and/or
(c) one or more other written documents, where one of these documents contains at least all the information referred to in Article 2(2)(a), (b), (c), (d), (h) and (i).

Where no or only partial information has been given, the employer is obliged to give to the employee, not later than two months after the commencement of the employment, a written declaration signed by the employer and containing at least the (general) information.

When the contract or the employment relationship comes to an end before expiry of a period of two months from the date of the start of work, the information must be made available to the employee by the end of this period at the latest (Article 3).

In case of employment relationships in existence upon entry into force of the directive (30 June 1993), the employer must give the employee, on request, the necessary documents within two months of receiving that request (Article 9(2)).

III. Defence of Rights

1308. The employees who consider themselves wronged by failure to comply with the obligations arising from this directive have the right to pursue their claims by judicial process after possible recourse to other competent authorities (Article 8(1)).

Article 8(1) must be interpreted as meaning that it does not prohibit national rules which provide that a collective agreement which is intended to transpose the provisions of the directive into national law are to apply to an employee even though he is not a member of an organisation which is a party to that agreement.[479]

Member States may, however, provide that access to the means of redress are subject to the notification of the employer by the employee and the failure by the employer to reply within 15 days of notification. The formality of prior notification may in no case be required in the cases of expatriates, referred to in Article 4 of the directive, nor for workers with a temporary contract or employment relationship, nor for employees not covered by a collective agreement or by collective agreements relating to the employment relationship (Article 8(2)).

The second subparagraph of Article 8(2) must be interpreted as meaning that it does not prevent an employee who is not a member of a union which is a party to a collective agreement governing his employment relationship being regarded as 'covered by' that agreement within the meaning of the abovementioned provision.

1309. The words 'a temporary contract or employment relationship' in the second subparagraph of Article 8(2) must be interpreted as referring to contracts and employment relationships entered into for a short period. If no norm has been laid down for that purpose in a Member State's rules, it is for the national courts to determine the duration in each case in the light of the specific characteristics of certain sectors or certain occupations or activities. That duration must, however, be fixed so as to provide effective protection of the rights conferred on workers by the directive.[480]

IV. Implementation

1310. The directive had to be transposed into national law, not later than 30 June 1993. Member States could also entrust employers' and workers' representatives with the task of introducing the required provisions into national law by way of agreements, being, however, obliged to take the necessary steps enabling them at all times to guarantee the results imposed by the directive (Article 9(2)).

§3. Recruitment and Placement: Monopoly of the Public Employment Office?

1311. In a landmark decision the Court challenged the monopoly of public employment offices in the activity of finding work for persons seeking employment.[481] The case concerned the putting in contact with employers of persons seeking work, which in Germany is, on the basis of the *Arbeitsförderungsgesetz* (Law

---

479. C.O.J., 18 December 2008, *Ruben Andersen* v. *Kommunernes Landsforening*, C-306/07, www.curia.
480. *Ibid.*
481. C.O.J., 23 April 1991, *K. Höfner and F. Elser* v. *Macroton GmbH*, No. C-41/90, ECR, 1991, 1979.

on the Promotion of Employment – 'the AFG'), the exclusive right of the *Bundesanstalt für Arbeit* (Federal Employment Office – 'the BA'). Notwithstanding that exclusive right, a specific recruitment and placement business has developed for business executives. It is carried on by recruitment consultants which are to some extent tolerated by the BA. The fact nevertheless remains that any legal measure which contravenes a legal prohibition is void by virtue of Article 134 of the German Civil Code and that, according to decisions of the German courts, that prohibition applies to recruitment activities carried on in breach of the AFG. In the case under review the recruitment consultants presented a candidate to a client, who the client decided not to recruit while refusing at the same time to pay the consultants' fees, on the basis that his contract with them was void. In the case which was ultimately submitted to the Court of Justice, the Court was asked whether the provisions of the Treaty on the freedom to provide services precluded a legal provision prohibiting private recruitment consultants from finding placements for business executives and whether the monopoly on the placement of executives vested in a public employment office constituted an abuse of a dominant position.

1312. The Court ruled as follows:

> A public employment office engaged in the activity of finding work for persons seeking employment is subject to the prohibition in Article 82 of the Treaty, provided the application of that provision does not defeat the specific task entrusted to it. A Member State which has conferred an exclusive right to carry on that activity upon that public employment office is in breach of Article 106 TFEU where it creates a situation in which that office is obliged to infringe the terms of Article 102 TFEU. That is the case, in particular, where the following conditions are met: – the exclusive right extends to finding employment for business executives; – the public employment office is manifestly incapable of satisfying demand on the market for such activity;
>
> – the actual pursuit of that activity by private personnel consultants is rendered impossible by the maintenance in force of a statutory provision prohibiting it, with the annulment of the corresponding contracts as a penalty for contravention;
> – the activity in question may extend to nationals or to the territory of other Member States.

1313. A second case (1997)[482] concerns the Italian Law of 23 October 1960 which lays down a prohibition on acting as an intermediary in employment relationships, whether as an employment agency or as an employment business. Failure to comply with the statute gives rise to penal sanctions.

The question which was asked is essentially whether the provisions of the Treaty preclude national legislation under which any activity as an intermediary between

---

482. C.O.J., 11 December 1997, *Job Centre Coop. arl*, Case No. C-55/96, ECR, 1997, 7119.

Part I, Ch. 4, Individual Employment Contracts

supply and demand in employment relationships is prohibited unless carried on by public employment agencies.

The Court decided in a landmark decision that:

(1) placement of employees is an economic activity, even if entrusted to public offices;
(2) a body such as a public placement office may therefore be classed as an undertaking for the purposes of the Union competition rules;
(3) public placement offices remain subject to competition rules unless and to the extent to which it is shown that their application is incompatible with discharge of their duties;
(4) the application of Article 86 of the Treaty (now Artikel 106 TFEU) cannot obstruct the performance of the particular task assigned to those offices if they are manifestly not in a position to satisfy demand in that area of the market;
(5) pursuant to Article 86(b) of the Treaty (now Artikel 106 TFEU), such abuse may in particular consist in limiting the provision of a service, to the prejudice of those seeking to avail themselves of it;
(6) as the Commission has rightly pointed out, the market in the provision of services relating to the placement of employees is both very extensive and extremely diverse. Supply and demand on that market covers all sectors of production and relates to a range of jobs requiring anything from unskilled labour to the scarcest and most specialised professional qualifications;
(7) on such an extensive and differentiated market, which is, moreover, subject to enormous changes as a result of economic and social developments, public placement offices may well be unable to satisfy a significant portion of all requests for services;
(8) by prohibiting, on pain of penal and administrative sanctions, any activity as an intermediary between supply and demand on the employment market unless carried on by public placement offices, a Member State creates a situation in which the provision of a service is limited, contrary to Article 106 TFEU, if those offices are manifestly unable to satisfy demand on the employment market for all types of activity;
(9) a potential effect of abusive conduct on trade between Member States is sufficient and arises in particular where the placement of employees by private companies may extend to the nationals or to the territory of other Member States.

1314. The conclusion of the Court is straightforward and clear. A monopoly on the labour market violates European competition law:

– as public placement offices are manifestly unable to satisfy demand on the market of all types of activity;
– the actual placement of employees by private companies is rendered impossible by the maintenance in force of statutory provisions under which such activities are prohibited and non-observance of that prohibition gives rise to penal and administrative sanctions; and

– the placement activities in question could extend to the nationals or to the territory of other Member States.

1315. In many countries placement of workers was still by and large a monopoly of the Public Employment Offices. The general rules, with some exceptions, were still that:

(1) placement by fee-charging private employment agencies; and
(2) that the putting of a worker at the disposal of a user-enterprise is forbidden, except e.g. in the case of temporary work.

It is clear that this situation is both illegal and obsolete.

1316. First of all, the monopoly of the Public Employment Office is contrary to the letter and the spirit of Convention No. 181 of the ILO (1997) and to European competition law. It is evident that the Official Employment Offices can no longer satisfy the demand on the market for all types of activity in a *de facto* manner. The national Public Employment Offices cannot cope with the diversity of the modern labour markets at European level.

In conclusion one can say that:

(1) the monopoly of the Public Employment Offices has to be abolished;
(2) enterprises must be able to propose a total package of services on the labour market, vocational training included;
(3) the scope of possibilities to put workers at the disposal of user-enterprises must be widened.

1317. Other issues, such as serving the needs of job seekers, also have to be addressed.

First, in general the present set of rules governing private employment agencies responds to the needs and the leverage of the employers. It is completely supply oriented. The employee has no input. He can mostly only react, not pro-act, as a full-fledged actor on the labour market. He undergoes developments. Indeed, search, selection and outplacement activities can in many countries only be undertaken on the initiative and at the expense of the employer.

All the individual job seeker can do is pass on his name and CV to advertisement agencies, temporary work agencies and job placement agencies, hoping they may do something. He cannot, however, ask them to provide him with a service of e.g. looking for a job, in accordance with his talents and experience, since these agencies cannot ask him for any fee.

The individual job seeker is left with the services of the Official Employment Office, which despite all its good will, cannot fulfil the requests it might be confronted with. This is certainly the case if someone is looking for work abroad. For practical purposes, the job seeker will have to continue to rely on informal amateurism, all job seekers writing the same letters to the same well-known companies, asking friends of friends, reading newspapers etc. Professional help seems to be excluded.

Part I, Ch. 4, Individual Employment Contracts

We all want, rightly, to protect the job seekers and the unemployed by preventing their exploitation, but we should do more to see to it that they effectively get professional services of the same quality as employers.

We should be more creative than to say that job seekers are not entitled to professional help outside the Public Employment Office as no fees can be asked. Maybe a kind of insurance system should be set up, like in the case of health services, when one can go to the doctor and get the fee refunded, totally or partially.

1318. We should also address the issue of contract labour as more and more agencies are becoming talent banks where the self-employed plug in their names and talents and the agencies provide them with self-employed job offers. The agencies match the demand and the supply of self-employed services. They are in a sense placement agencies for the self-employed. There is obviously plenty of room for this labour market service, which is growing in importance as the distinction between employee and self-employed in this outsourced and information society becomes in itself more and more obsolete. The only question is, how to organise this. Certainly, in a more relaxed and flexible way. Moreover, there is a bridge to be built between the employee and the self-employed world. The only (organised) service on the labour market for which the official regulation spells out that the service can lead to self-employment is outplacement.

1319. A last point concerns vocational training, of which all agree that there should be more training, permanent and open to all; also focusing on the 'social skills' needed to operate in this world of increasing teamwork.

In conclusion, it is obvious that we need a new and fresh look at the modern labour markets, at the way to really match demand and supply for both sides, employment seekers and those who employ, in a fair way, where the idea of co-investment could be retained. Permanent and adequate vocational training remains an essential feature of any labour market policy.

1320. Obviously, more and more, do social media, like Facebook, Twitter, Linkedin and others play a role as employers employ those media to try to recruit employees or as employees present their curriculum vitae, looking for employment. Carefull uses of these media is indicated, as the digital chatting, especially by employees, may play against themselves as the message spread or are made available by friends are inappropriate.

Employees have been dismissed for language used against e.g. their employer; pleading that the social media are private and belong to the privacy of the employee does not respond to reality. These are *de facto* public media and are judged as such by the Courts.

Chapter 5. Child Care and the Protection of Young People at Work

1321. Children should be at the forefront of social consideration and precaution, as they are particularly vulnerable. Some of the problems this involves are addressed in a recommendation and in a directive.

§1. CHILD CARE

1322. In each of the Union's Member States, without exception, the demand for reasonably priced child care services exceeds the supply. The lack of adequate child care services and initiatives to reconcile family responsibilities with employment or work-related training constitutes a major barrier to women's access to, and more widespread participation in, the labour market. This situation is, of course, at odds with the principle of equal opportunities for men and women. This problem was addressed in point 16 of the Community Charter of the Fundamental Social Rights of Workers under the heading of equal treatment for men and women: measures should also be developed enabling men and women to reconcile their occupational and family obligations.

The Recommendation on Child Care which was adopted on 31 March 1992[483] outlines various courses of action designed to remedy this situation. In practical terms, the Member States are invited to take and/or progressively encourage initiatives in four areas, so as to enable women and men to reconcile more effectively their occupational, family and upbringing responsibilities.

The first area concerns child care services as such. It is recommended that all the competent authorities should enable parents to have as much access as possible to these services, with particular endeavours being made to ensure, for example, through adequate financial contributions, that the services are offered at affordable prices and are available in all areas and regions, both urban and rural. Such services should, moreover, be flexible and diverse, so as to be fully responsive to the needs of the children and their parents. The recommendation also points to the need for child care workers to be given training, both initial and continuing, which is commensurate with the importance and the social and educative value of their work.

The other three areas are more general in nature, the intention being to shape certain aspects of society in such a way that having children will no longer constitute an insurmountable obstacle to pursuing a career.

Firstly, the recommendation calls on the Member States to take and/or encourage initiatives so that arrangements for special leave enabling employed parents, both men and women, to properly discharge their occupational, family and upbringing responsibilities take realistic account of women's increased participation in the labour force. Priority should be given to ensuring that leave arrangements are flexibly organised.

Secondly, it is recommended that the Member States should support action to create an environment, structure and organisation at work which take into account the

---

483. 92/24, O.J. L 123, 8 May 1992.

needs of working parents with responsibility for the care and upbringing of children.

Finally, Member States are asked to promote and encourage, with due freedom of the individual, a more equal sharing of parental responsibilities between men and women since the latter still tend to assume the full burden of the 'housewife', with the result that their career prospects are less secure.

§2. Protection of Young People at Work (Directive 94/33 EC of 22 June 1994)

I. Introductory Remarks

1323. The Directive of 22 June 1994 on the protection of young people at work[484] was adopted pursuant to points 20 and 22 of the Community Charter of the Fundamental Social Rights of Workers (1989) which state that:

> Without prejudice to such rules as may be more favourable to young people, in particular those ensuring their preparation for work through vocational training, and subject to derogations limited to certain light work, the minimum employment age must not be lower than the minimum school-leaving age and, in any case, not lower than 15 years (point 20).
>
> Appropriate measures must be taken to adjust labour regulations applicable to young workers so that their specific development and vocational training and access to employment needs are met (point 22).
>
> The duration of work must, in particular, be limited – without it being possible to circumvent this limitation through recourse to overtime – and night work prohibited in the case of workers of under eighteen years of age, save in the case of certain jobs laid down in national legislation or regulations.

In its Resolution on Child Labour of 1987, the EP summarised the various aspects of work by young people and stressed its effects on their health, safety and physical and intellectual development, and pointed to the need to adopt a directive harmonising national legislation in the field.

The directive rightly stresses that children and adolescents must be considered specific risk groups, and measures must be taken with regard to their safety and health; and that the vulnerability of children calls for Member States to prohibit their employment and ensure that the minimum working or employment age is not lower than the minimum age at which compulsory schooling as imposed by national law ends or 15 years in any event. Derogations from the prohibition on child labour may be admitted only in special cases and under specific conditions but, under no circumstances, may such derogations be detrimental to regular school attendance or prevent children from benefiting fully from their education. In view of the nature of the transition from childhood to adult life, work by adolescents should be strictly regulated and protected.

---

484. O.J. L 216/12, 20 August 1994.

It is consequently mandatory that every employer should guarantee young people working conditions appropriate to their age and that he should implement the measures necessary to protect the safety and health of young people on the basis of an assessment of work-related hazards to the young. Young people should in particular be protected against any specific risks arising from their lack of experience, absence of awareness of existing or potential risk, or from their immaturity.

Quite a number of specific measures are retained:

– the prohibition of the employment of young people for dangerous tasks; – the adoption of specific minimal requirements in respect of the organisation of working time;
– the maximum working time of young people should be strictly limited; – night work by young people should be prohibited, with the exception of certain jobs;
– young people should be granted minimum daily, weekly and annual periods of rest and adequate breaks.

1324. With respect to the weekly rest period, due account should be taken of the diversity of cultural, ethnic, religious and other factors prevailing in the Member States; it is ultimately for each Member State to decide whether Sunday should be included in the weekly rest period, and if so to what extent.

The directive was adopted pursuant to Article 153 TFEU which provides that the Council shall adopt, by means of directives, minimum requirements to encourage improvements, especially in the working environment, as regards the health and safety of workers, and in doing so avoid imposing administrative, financial and legal constraints in a way which would be detrimental to the creation and development of small- and medium-sized undertakings. This means that the directive has been adopted with a qualified majority. It is also important to note that account has been taken of the principles of the ILO regarding the protection of young people at work, including those relating to the minimum age for access to employment or work.

The UK had problems with this directive and was granted the right to refrain from implementing certain provisions for a given period of time.[485]

II. Purpose and Scope

A. *Purpose*

1325. The aim of the directive is to ensure that young people are protected against economic exploitation and against any work likely to harm their safety, health or physical, mental, moral or social development or to jeopardise their education.

Member States shall take the necessary measures:

– to prohibit work by children;
– to ensure that work by adolescents is strictly regulated; and

---

485. Article 17(1)(b).

– to see to it that employers guarantee that young people have working conditions which suit their age.

Regarding work of young people, the minimum working or employment age should not be lower than the minimum age at which compulsory full-time schooling as imposed by national law ends or 15 years in any event (Article 1).

B. Scope

1326. This directive applies to any person under 18 years of age having an employment contract or an employment relationship defined by the law in force in a Member State and/or governed by the law in force in a Member State.[486]

Member States may make legislative or regulatory provision for this directive not to apply to occasional work or short-term work involving:

(a) domestic service in a private household,[487] or
(b) work regarded as not being harmful, damaging or dangerous to young people in a family undertaking (Article 2).

III. Definitions

1327. For the purposes of this directive definitions are as follows:

(a) 'young person': any person under 18 years of age having an employment contract/ relationship;
(b) 'child': any young person of less than 15 years of age or who is still subject to compulsory full-time schooling under national law;
(c) 'adolescent': any young person of at least 15 years of age but less than 18 years of age who is no longer subject to compulsory full-time schooling;
(d) 'light work': all work which, on account of the inherent nature of the tasks which it involves and the particular conditions under which they are performed:
    (i) is not likely to be harmful to the safety, health or development of children, and
    (ii) is not such as to be harmful to their attendance at school, their participation in vocational guidance or training programmes approved by the competent authority or their capacity to benefit from the instruction received;
(e) 'working time': any period during which the young person is at work, at the employer's disposal and carrying out his activity or duties in accordance with national legislation and/or practice;
(f) 'rest period': any period which is not working time (Article 3).

---

486. 'Contracts for services are not covered' (statement of the Council and the Commission).
487. This includes activities such as babysitting (statement by the Council and the Commission).

IV. Prohibition of Work by Children

1328. Member States shall adopt the measures necessary to prohibit work by children.

They may make provision for the prohibition of work by children not to apply to:

(a) children pursuing cultural or similar activities;
(b) children of at least 14 years of age working under a combined work/training scheme or an in-plant work-experience scheme;
(c) children of at least 14 years of age performing light work other than cultural or similar; light work other than that may, however, be performed by children of 13 years of age for a limited number of hours per week in the case of categories of work determined by national legislation. In such a case, the working conditions relating to the light work in question must be determined (Article 4).

V. Cultural or Similar Activities

1329. The employment of children for the purposes of performance in cultural, artistic, sports or advertising activities shall be subject to prior authorisation to be given by the competent authority in individual cases.[488]

Member States shall lay down the working conditions for children and the details of the prior authorisation procedure, on condition that the activities:

(i) are not likely to be harmful to the safety, health or development of children, and
(ii) are not such as to be harmful to their attendance at school, their participation in vocational guidance or training programmes approved by the competent authority or their capacity to benefit from the instruction received.

In the case of children of at least 13 years of age, Member States may authorise the employment of children for the purposes of performance in cultural, artistic, sports or advertising activities.

The Member States which have a specific authorisation system for modelling agencies with regard to the activities of children may retain that system (Article 5).

VI. General Obligations on Employers

1330. The employer shall adopt the measures necessary to protect the safety and health of young people, taking particular account of the specific risks to their safety, health and development which are a consequence of their lack of experience, of

---

[488]. The phrase 'in individual cases' does not mean that, where the activities of a number of children are involved, prior authorisation is required for each individual child (statement by the Council and the Commission).

absence of awareness of existing or potential risks or of the fact that young people have not yet fully matured (Article 6(1)).

The employer shall implement these measures on the basis of an assessment of the hazards to young people in connection with their work. The assessment must be made before young people begin work and when there is any major change in working conditions and must pay particular attention to the following points:

(a) the fitting-out and layout of the workplace and the workstation;
(b) the nature, degree and duration of exposure to physical, biological and chemical agents;
(c) the form, range and use of work equipment, in particular agents, machines, apparatus and devices, and the way in which they are handled;
(d) the arrangement of work processes and operations and the way in which these are combined (organisation of work);
(e) the level of training and instruction given to young people.

When this assessment shows that there is a risk to the safety, the physical or mental health or development of young people, an appropriate free assessment and monitoring of their health shall be provided at regular intervals.[489] The free health assessment and monitoring may form part of a national health system (Article 6(2)).

Moreover, the employer shall inform young people of possible risks and of all measures adopted concerning their safety and health. Furthermore, he shall inform the legal representatives of children of possible risks and of all measures adopted concerning children's safety and health (Article 6(3)).

The employer shall involve the protective and preventive agencies[490] in the planning, implementation and monitoring of the safety and health conditions applicable to young people (Article 6(4)).

VII. Vulnerability of Young People – Prohibition of Work

1331. Member States must ensure that young people are protected from any specific risks to their safety, health and development which are a consequence of their lack of experience, of absence of awareness of existing or potential risks or of the fact that young people have not yet fully matured. To this end they must prohibit the employment of young people for:

(a) work which is objectively beyond their physical or psychological capacity;
(b) work involving harmful exposure to agents which are toxic, carcinogenic, cause heritable genetic damage or harm to the unborn child or which in any other way chronically affect human health;
(c) work involving harmful exposure to radiation;

---

489. Without prejudice to Directive 89/391/EC.
490. Referred to in Article 7 of Directive 89/391/EC.

(d) work involving the risk of accidents which it may be assumed cannot be recognised or avoided by young persons owing to their insufficient attention to safety or lack of experience or training; or
(e) work in which there is a risk to health from extreme cold or heat, or from noise or vibration.
(f) Work which is likely to entail specific risks for young people includes:
   – work involving harmful exposure to the physical, biological and chemical agents referred to in point I of the Annex, and
   – processes and work referred to in point II of the Annex to the directive.

Member States may authorise derogations in the case of adolescents where such derogations are indispensable for their vocational training, provided that protection of their safety and health is ensured by the fact that the work is performed under the supervision of a competent person[491] (Article 7).

VIII. Working Time

1332. In case of permitted child labour the working time of children must be limited to:

(a) 8 hours a day and 40 hours a week for work performed under a combined work/training scheme or an in-plant work-experience scheme;[492]
(b) 2 hours on a school day and 12 hours a week for work performed in term-time outside the hours fixed for school attendance, provided that this is not prohibited by national legislation and/or practice; in no circumstances may the daily working time exceed 7 hours; this limit may be raised to 8 hours in the case of children who have reached the age of 15;
(c) 7 hours a day and 35 hours a week for work performed during a period of at least a week when school is not operating; these limits may be raised to 8 hours a day and 40 hours a week in the case of children who have reached the age of 15;
(d) 7 hours a day and 35 hours a week for light work performed by children no longer subject to compulsory full-time schooling under national law.

Member States shall adopt the measures necessary to limit the working time of adolescents to 8 hours a day and 40 hours a week (Article 8(1)).

---

491. Within the meaning of Article 7 of Directive 89/391/EEC and provided that the protection afforded by that Directive is guaranteed. Member States may, by legislative or regulatory provision, authorise derogations from Article 8(2), Article 9(1)(b), Article 10(1)(b) and, in the case of adolescents, Article 12, for work in the circumstances referred to in Article 5(4) of Directive 89/391/EEC, provided that such work is of a temporary nature and must be performed immediately, that adult workers are not available and that the adolescents are allowed equivalent compensatory rest time within the following three weeks (work by adolescents in the event of *force majeure*).
492. The time spent on training by a young person working under a theoretical and/or practical combined work/training scheme or an in-plant work-experience scheme shall be counted as working time (Article 8(3)).

Part I, Ch. 5, Child Care and the Protection of Young People

Where a young person is employed by more than one employer, working days and working time shall be cumulative.

Member States may authorise derogations either by way of exception or where there are objective grounds for so doing and determine the conditions, limits and procedure for implementing such derogations (Article 8(5)).

Where daily working time is more than four and a half hours, young people are entitled to a break of at least 30 minutes, which shall be consecutive if possible[493] (Article 12).

IX. Night Work

1333. Permitted work by children cannot take place between 20.00 hours and 06.00 hours. Work by adolescents either between 22.00 hours and 06.00 hours or between 23.00 hours and 07.00 hours is prohibited (Article 9(1)).

Member States may authorise work by adolescents in specific areas of activity during the period in which night work is prohibited but in no case between 00.00 hours and 04.00 hours. In that event, Member States shall take appropriate measures to ensure that the adolescent is supervised by an adult where such supervision is necessary for the adolescent's protection.

However, Member States may authorise work by adolescents during the period in which night work is prohibited in the following cases, where there are objective grounds for so doing and provided that adolescents are allowed suitable compensatory rest time and that the objectives of the directive are not called into question:

- work performed in the shipping or fisheries sectors;
- work performed in the context of the armed forces or the police;
- work performed in hospitals or similar establishments;
- cultural, artistic, sports or advertising activities (Article 9(2)).

Prior to any assignment to night work and at regular intervals thereafter, adolescents shall be entitled to a free assessment of their health and capacities, unless the work they do during the period during which work is prohibited is of an exceptional nature (Article 9(3)).

X. Rest Period

1334. In case of permitted child work, for each 24-hour period, children are entitled to a minimum rest period of 14 consecutive hours; adolescents are entitled to a minimum rest period of 12 consecutive hours (Article 10(1)).

For each seven-day period, in case of permitted child labour, adolescents are entitled to a minimum rest period of two days, which shall be consecutive if possible. Where justified by technical or organisation reasons, the minimum rest period

---

493. Article 12 does not specify at what point during the daily working time a break must be allowed (statement by the Council and the Commission).

may be reduced, but may in no circumstances be less than 36 consecutive hours. The minimum rest period shall in principle include Sunday (Article 10(2)).

These minimum rest periods may be interrupted in the case of activities involving periods of work that are split up over the day or are of short duration (Article 10(3)).

Member States may make provision for derogations in respect of adolescents in the following cases, where there are objective grounds for so doing and provided that they are granted appropriate compensatory rest time:

(a) work performed in the shipping or fisheries sectors;
(b) work performed in the context of the armed forces or the police;
(c) work performed in hospitals or similar establishments;
(d) work performed in agriculture;
(e) work performed in the tourist industry or in the hotel, restaurant and café sector;
(f) activities involving periods of work split up over the day (Article 10).

In case of permitted child labour there must be a period free of any work including, as far as possible, the school holidays of children subject to compulsory full-time schooling under national law (Article 11).

XI. Measures; Non-reducing Clause; Final Provisions

1335. Each Member State shall lay down any necessary measures to be applied in the event of failure to comply with the provisions adopted in order to implement this directive; such measures must be effective and proportionate (Article 14).

Without prejudice to the right of Member States to develop, in the light of changing circumstances, different provisions on the protection of young people, as long as the minimum requirements provided for by this directive are complied with, the implementation of this directive shall not constitute valid grounds for reducing the general level of protection afforded to young people (Article 16).

The directive must enter in force not later than two years after its adoption. The directive can also be implemented by means of collective agreements.

Member States shall report to the Commission every five years on the practical implementation of the provisions of this directive, indicating the viewpoints of the two sides of industry. The Commission shall inform the European Parliament, the Council and the Economic and Social Committee thereof (Article 17).

Chapter 6. Equal Treatment

1336. Few principles received such an important and frequent backing in international legal instruments as the principle of equal treatment, also in the field of employment. All international organisations took initiatives in this area: the United Nations, the ILO especially, the Council of Europe and the EU.

The EU played an important role, first by adopting Article 157 TFEU, which contains the principle of equal pay for equal work, and consequently by adopting several directives:

- 1975: relating to the application of equal pay for men and women;[494]
- 1976: relating to the implementation of the principle of equal treatment for men and women as regards access to employment, vocational training and promotion, and working conditions;[495]
- 1978: concerning the progressive implementation of the principle of equal treatment for men and women in matters of social security;[496]
- 1986: on the implementation of the principle of equal treatment for men and women in occupational social security schemes;[497]
- 1997: on the burden of proof in cases of discrimination based on sex;[498]
- 2000: establishing a general framework for equal treatment in employment and occupation;[499]
- 2000: implementing the principle of equal treatment between persons irrespective of racial or ethnic origin;[500]
- 2006: on the implementation of the principle of equal opportunities and equal treatment of men and women in matters of employment and occupation.[501]

1337. Equal treatment was of course also retained as a fundamental social right in the Community Charter:

> Whereas, in order to ensure equal treatment, it is important to combat every form of discrimination, including discrimination on grounds of sex, colour, race, opinions and beliefs, and whereas, in a spirit of solidarity, it is important to combat social exclusion.

---

494. 10 February 1975, No. 75/117, O.J. L 45/19, 19 February 1975; repealed by Council Directive 5 July 2006, No. 2006/54/EC, O.J., 26 July 2006.
495. 9 February 1976, No. 76/207, O.J. L 39/40, 14 February 1976, amended by Directive 2002/73/ EC of 23 September 2002, O.J., 5 October 2002, L 269; repealed by Council Directive 5 July 2006, No. 2006/54/EC, O.J., 26 July 2006.
496. 19 December 1978, No. 79/7, O.J. L 6/24, 10 February 1979.
497. 24 July 1986, No. 86/378, O.J. L 45/40, 12 August 1986, amended by Directive 96/97 of 2 December 1996.
498. 15 December 1997, No. 97/80, O.J. L 14/6, 20 January 1998; repealed by Council Directive 5 July 2006, No. 2006/54/EC, O.J., 26 July 2006.
499. Council Directive 2000/78EC of 27 November 2000, O.J. L 303, 2 December 2000.
500. Council Directive 2000/43EC of 29 June 2000, O.J. L 180, 19 July 2000.
501. 5 July 2006, No. 2006/54/EC, O.J., 26 July 2006.

1338. Therefore principle 16 of the Charter was adopted, which reads as follows:

> Equal treatment for men and women must be assured. Equal opportunities for men and women must be developed. To this end, action should be intensified to ensure the implementation to the principle of equality between men and women as regards in particular access to employment, remuneration, working conditions, social protection, education, vocational training and career development. Measures should also be developed enabling men and women to reconcile their occupational and family obligations.

1339. The Treaty of Amsterdam (1997) and Article 157 strengthen the aims and objectives of the Union ina considerable way. First of all, equality of men and women becomes one of the main tasks of the Union (Article 3 TEU).

1340. Especially Article 19 TFEU has the greatest importance, given the wide range of grounds in combating discrimination. It allows the EU indeed to take 'appropriate action to combat discrimination based on sex, racial or ethnic origin, religion or belief, disability, age or sexual orientation'. On the basis of Article 19 two important directives have been adopted, namely one by Council Directive 2000/43EC of 29 June 2000 implementing the principle of equal treatment between persons irrespective of racial or ethnic origin[502] and Council Directive 2000/78EC of 27 November 2000 establishing a general framework for equal treatment in employment and occupation.[503] We will examine both directives in depth.

1341. Article 157 TFEU equally contains a number of important innovations. For the first time 'work of equal value' has been mentioned explicitly. Especially paragraph 3 is important. It provides for a new basis to adopt measures to ensure the application of the principle of equal opportunities and equal treatment of men and women in matters of employment and occupation. Moreover, the role of the EP is enhanced: decisions can be made with qualified majority in accordance with the co-decision procedure.

1342. Also the competence of the Union has been formulated in a broad manner, namely to implement, without any restriction, the principle of equal opportunity and treatment of men and women in matters of employment and occupation, including the principle of equal pay for equal work or work of equal value. Also positive discrimination gets a push in the back. On this last point, more later.

1343. Finally, we have to refer to Chapter III, which deals with equality, of the Charter of Fundamental Rights of the European Union (2007). Article 20 of the Charter proclaims that 'Everyone is equal before the law', while Article 21 states:

---

502. Council Directive 2000/43EC of 29 June 2000, O.J. L 180, 19 July 2000.
503. Council Directive 2000/78EC of 27 November 2000, O.J. L 303, 2 December 2000.

Part I, Ch. 6, Equal Treatment 1344–1345

(1) Any discrimination based on any ground such as sex, race, colour, ethnic or social origin, genetic features, language, religion or belief, political or any other opinion, membership of a national minority, property, birth, disability, age or sexual orientation shall be prohibited.
(2) Within the scope of application of the Treaty establishing the European Community and of the Treaty on European Union, and without prejudice to the special provisions of those Treaties, any discrimination on grounds of nationality shall be prohibited.

Article 23 of the Charter addresses equality between men and women and says:

> Equality between men and women must be ensured in all areas, including employment, work and pay. The principle of equality shall not prevent the maintenance or adoption of measures providing for specific advantages in favour of the under-represented sex.

Let us now have a detailed look at the various legal instruments by which the European Union tries to promote equality and combat discrimination.

1344. A specific point of attention: the directives of 1975, 1976 and 1997 relating to equal pay, to access to employment, vocational training and promotion and working conditions and burden of the proof were repealed by Council Directive 5 July 2006, No. 2006/54/EC, which is a recast of these directives and dealt with further. When referring to case law, which dates from before the recast, we left the articles of the repealed directives referred to as they were under the original version of those repealed directives directive.

§1. A GENERAL FRAMEWORK FOR EQUAL TREATMENT IN EMPLOYMENT AND OCCUPATION

1345. Council Directive 2000/78/EC of 27 November 2000[504] establishes a general framework for equal treatment in employment and occupation. It comprises four parts: general provisions, remedies and enforcement, particular provisions (relating to Northern Ireland) and final provisions.

I. General Provisions

A. *Purpose*

---

504. The prohibition under Community law of discrimination on the ground of age is not mandatory where the allegedly discriminatory treatment contains no link with Community law. No such link arises either from Article 13 EC, or, in circumstances such as those at issue in the main proceedings, from Council Directive 2000/78/EC of 27 November 2000, establishing a general framework for equal treatment in employment and occupation, before the time-limit allowed to the Member State concerned for its transposition has expired (C.O.J. 23 September 2008, *Birgit Bartsch* v. *Bosch und Siemens Hausgeräte* (BSH) *Altersfürsorge GmbH*, C-427/06, ECR, 2008, 7245.

1346. The purpose of this directive is to lay down a general framework for combating discrimination on the grounds of religion or belief, disability, age or sexual orientation as regards employment and occupation, with a view to putting into effect in the Member States the principle of equal treatment (Article 1).

The discriminatory grounds coincide with those laid down in Article 19 TFEU, with the exception of the ground of sex. With regard to sexual orientation a clear dividing line should be drawn between sexual orientation, which is covered by this directive, and sexual behaviour, which is not. Furthermore, it should be underlined that this directive does not affect marital status and therefore does not impinge upon entitlements to benefits for married couples.

1347. In 2001, Mr. Maruko entered into a registered life partnership with a designer of theatrical costumes. Since 1959 Mr. Maruko's partner had been a member of an institution responsible for managing old-age insurance for theatrical professionals from the German theatres and the related survivors' benefits. Following the death of his life partner in 2005, Mr. Maruko applied for a widower's pension. His application was rejected on the ground that there were no provision for such an entitlement in the case of surviving life partners.

Since, however, the directive does not cover social security and social protection schemes the benefits of which are not equivalent to pay within the meaning of Community law, the Court was asked to determine, first, whether the survivor's pension at issue can be classified as pay. On that point, the Court points out that the occupational pension scheme managed by the *Versorgungsanstalt* has its origin in a collective agreement on employment, the objective of which was to supplement the social security benefits payable under the national legislation of general scope. That scheme is funded exclusively by the workers and their employers, without any financial involvement on the part of the State.

Furthermore, the retirement pension by reference to which the survivor's pension is calculated concerns only a particular category of workers and, moreover, its amount is dependent on the period of the worker's membership and how much he has paid in contributions. The survivor's pension therefore derives from the employment relationship of the deceased partner and must therefore be classified as pay. That is why the directive applies.

As regards the question whether the refusal to pay the survivor's pension to the registered life partner constitutes discrimination on grounds of sexual orientation, the Court found in the light of the order for reference that Germany, while reserving marriage solely to persons of different sex, had none the less established the life partnership, the conditions of which have gradually been made equivalent to those applicable to marriage. The provisions of the *Versorgungsanstalt* Regulations restrict entitlement to survivor's pensions to surviving spouses. That being the case, and since life partners are denied the pension, the latter are thus treated less favourably than surviving spouses.

1348. Consequently, the Court ruled[505] that the refusal to grant the survivor's pension to life partners constitutes direct discrimination on grounds of sexual orientation, if surviving spouses and surviving life partners are in a comparable situation as regards that pension. It is for the national court to determine whether that condition is satisfied.

Stated the Court:

> The combined provisions of Articles 1 and 2 of Directive 2000/78 preclude legislation under which, after the death of his life partner, the surviving partner does not receive a survivor's benefit equivalent to that granted to a surviving spouse, even though, under national law, life partnership places persons of the same sex in a situation comparable to that of spouses so far as concerns that survivor's benefit. It is for the referring court to determine whether a surviving life partner is in a situation comparable to that of a spouse who is entitled to the survivor's benefit provided for under the occupational pension scheme.

B. Definitions and Concepts

1349. For the purposes of this directive, the 'principle of equal treatment' also covers direct as well as indirect discrimination on the grounds referred to in Article 1.

There is direct discrimination where one person is treated less favourably than another is, has been or would be treated in a comparable situation.

There is indirect discrimination where an apparently neutral provision, criterion or practice would put persons having a particular religion or belief,[506] a particular disability, a particular age, or a particular sexual orientation at a particular disadvantage compared with other persons unless:

(i) that provision, criterion or practice is objectively justified by a legitimate aim and the means of achieving that aim are appropriate and necessary, or
(ii) as regards persons with a particular disability, the employer or any person or organisation to whom this directive applies is obliged, under national legislation, to take appropriate measures in order to eliminate disadvantages entailed by such provision, criterion or practice.

1350. A social plan may provide for a reduction in redundancy compensation paid to workers approaching retirement age. However, taking account of possible early retirement due to disability in the calculation of that reduction constitutes discrimination prohibited by EU law and is contrary to article 2,2 of Directive 2000/78.[507]

---

505. C.O.J., 1 April 2008, *Tadao Maruko* v. *Versorgungsanstalt der deutschen Bühnen*, C-267/06, ECR, 2008, 1757.
506. C.O.J., 6 December 2012, *Johann Odar v. Baxter Deutschland GmbH*, C-152/11, www.curia. eu.
507. C.O.J., 6 December 2012, *Johann Odar v. Baxter Deutschland GmbH*, C-152/11, www.curia. eu.

1351. The social plan concluded by the German undertaking Baxter and its works council provides that the amount of compensation paid to workers made redundant on operational grounds is contingent, inter alia, on the length of service in the undertaking (standard formula compensation).

1352. However, the plan also provides that, for workers over 54 years of age, the amount of compensation is calculated according to the earliest possible beginning of pension (special formula compensation). The amount to be paid to those workers is lower than the amount obtained using the standard formula, although it must be equal to at least half of that amount.

Dr Odar, who was employed by Baxter for over 30 years, is recognised as being severely disabled. When his employment relationship with Baxter ended, he received compensation on termination under the social plan.

As he was over the age of 54, he received an amount lower than that to which he would have been entitled if he had not been older than 54. The calculation method provided for in the social plan in the event of termination of employment on operational grounds does, therefore, give rise to a difference in treatment on the basis of age.

The social plan further provides that when the worker has the possibility of receiving an early retirement pension on grounds of disability, that date is the one taken into account for the calculation under the special formula.

1353. By its judgment the Court holds that the prohibition, provided for by EU law, against any discrimination on grounds of age does not preclude rules under a social plan, which provide for differentiation in the calculation of the compensation according to age.

Such a difference in treatment may be justified by the objective of granting compensation for the future, protecting younger workers and facilitating their reintegration into employment, whilst taking account of the need to achieve a fair distribution of limited financial resources in a social plan. Moreover, the aim of preventing compensation on termination from being claimed by persons who are not seeking new employment but will receive a replacement income in the form of an occupational old-age pension must be considered to be legitimate.

1354. Rules such as those in the present case do not appear to be manifestly inappropriate and do not go beyond what is required to achieve the objective pursued. The Court observes that the social plan provides for a reduction in the amount of the compensation on termination but that plan provides for a reduction in the amount of the compensation on termination but that that amount varies according to age and must be at least equal to one half of the amount obtained using the standard formula. The Court further notes that the rules in question are the result of an agreement negotiated between employees' and employers' representatives exercising their right to bargain collectively which is recognised as a fundamental right. The fact that the task of striking a balance between their respective interests is entrusted to the social partners offers considerable flexibility, as each of the parties may, where appropriate, opt not to adopt the agreement.

However, the Court holds that the prohibition, provided for by EU law, against any discrimination on grounds of disability precludes the rules in question in so far as they take account, in the use of the special calculation formula, of the possibility of receiving an early retirement pension on grounds of disability.

1355. That difference in treatment of non-disabled and disabled workers disregards the risks faced by severely disabled people, who generally face greater difficulties in finding new employment, as well as the fact that those risks tend to become exacerbated as they approach retirement age. Severely disabled people have specific needs stemming both from the protection their condition requires and from the need to anticipate possible worsening of their condition. Regard must therefore be had to the risk that disabled workers may throughout their lives have financial requirements arising from their disability which cannot be adjusted and/or that, with advancing age, those financial requirements may increase

It follows that, in ultimately paying a severely disabled worker compensation on termination on operational grounds which is lower than the amount paid to a non-disabled worker, the rules in question have an excessive adverse effect on the legitimate interests of severely disabled workers and therefore go beyond what is necessary to achieve the social policy objectives they pursue.

1356. Harassment is a form of discrimination when unwanted conduct takes place with the purpose or effect of violating the dignity of a person and of creating an intimidating, hostile, degrading, humiliating or offensive environment. In this context, the concept of harassment may be defined in accordance with the national laws and practice of the Member States.

An instruction to discriminate against persons on any of the indicated grounds constitutes discrimination.

The directive is without prejudice to measures laid down by national law which, in a democratic society, are necessary for public security, for the maintenance of public order and the prevention of criminal offences, for the protection of health and for the protection of the rights and freedoms of others (Article 2)[508].

C. Scope

1357. The personal as well as the material scope of the directive are wide: it applies to all persons, as regards both the public and private sectors, including public bodies, in relation to:

(a) conditions for access to employment, to self-employment or to occupation, including selection criteria and recruitment conditions, whatever the branch of activity and at all levels of the professional hierarchy, including promotion;

---

508. The general prohibition of discrimination based on religion or belief applies also to atheists, agnostics and humanists (Parliamentary Question E. Lynne, 16 January 2001, given by the Commission).

(b) access to all types and to all levels of vocational guidance, vocational training, advanced vocational training and retraining, including practical work experience;
(c) employment and working conditions, including dismissals and pay;[509]
(d) membership of, and involvement in, an organisation of workers or employers, or any organisation whose members carry on a particular profession, including the benefits provided for by such organisations.

The directive does not cover differences of treatment based on nationality and is without prejudice to provisions and conditions relating to the entry into and residence of third-country nationals and stateless persons in the territory of Member States, and to any treatment which arises from the legal status of the third-country nationals and stateless persons concerned.

The directive does not apply to payments of any kind made by state schemes or similar, including state social security or social protection schemes.

Member States may provide that this directive, in so far as it relates to discrimination on the grounds of disability and age, shall not apply to the armed forces (Article 3).

1358. The prohibition of discrimination laid down by the directive on equal treatment in employment and occupation is not limited to disabled people alone. Ms. Coleman worked in a firm of solicitors in London as a legal secretary from January 2001. In 2002, she gave birth to a disabled child whose health condition requires specialised and particular care which is provided primarily by her.

On 4 March 2005, Ms. Coleman accepted voluntary redundancy, which brought the contract of employment between her and her former employer to an end. On 30 August 2005, she lodged a claim with the Employment Tribunal, London South, alleging that she had been subject to unfair constructive dismissal and had been treated less favourably than other employees because she was the primary carer of a disabled child. She claims that that treatment caused her to stop working for her former employer. In support of her claim, she put forward various facts amounting, in her view, to discrimination or harassment since, in similar circumstances, the parents of non-disabled children were treated differently. She cites, in particular, her employer's refusal to allow her to return to her previous job on her return from maternity leave, the refusal to allow flexibility as regards working hours and abusive and insulting comments made about both her and her child.

1359. In those circumstances, the Employment Tribunal referred the matter to the Court of Justice, asking whether the directive on equal treatment in employment and occupation must be interpreted as prohibiting direct discrimination on grounds of disability and harassment related to disability only in respect of an employee who is himself disabled, or whether the directive applies equally to an employee who is

---

509. A survivor's benefit granted under an occupational pension scheme falls within the scope of Council Directive 2000/78/EC of 27 November 2000 establishing a general framework for equal treatment in employment and occupation (C.O.J., 1 April 2008, *Tadao Maruko* v. *Versorgungsanstalt der deutschen Bühnen*, C-267/06, ECR, 2008, 1757).

treated less favourably by reason of the disability of his or her child, for whom he or she was the primary provider of the care required by virtue of the child's condition.

1360. The Court observed that the directive defines the principle of equal treatment as meaning that there is to be no direct or indirect discrimination whatsoever on the grounds, *inter alia*, of disability, and that it applies to all persons in relation to employment and working conditions, including dismissals and pay.

The Court notes that, while the directive includes certain provisions designed to accommodate specifically the needs of disabled people, that does not lead to the conclusion that the principle of equal treatment enshrined in that directive must be interpreted strictly, that is, as prohibiting only direct discrimination on grounds of disability and relating exclusively to disabled people. According to the Court, the directive, the purpose of which is to combat all forms of discrimination, applies not to a particular category of person but by reference to the nature of the discrimination. An interpretation limiting its application only to people who are themselves disabled is liable to deprive the directive of an important element of its effectiveness and to reduce the protection which it is intended to guarantee.

As regards the burden of proof, the Court observes that, in the event that Ms. Coleman established facts from which it might be presumed that there had been direct discrimination, the effective application of the principle of equal treatment then required that the burden of proof should fall on her employer, who must prove that there has been no breach of that principle.

1361. The Court concludes that the directive must be interpreted as meaning that the prohibition of direct discrimination laid down therein is not limited only to people who are disabled. Consequently, where an employer treats an employee who is not himself disabled less favourably than another employee in a comparable situation, and it is established that the less favourable treatment of that employee is based on the disability of his child, whose care is provided primarily by that employee, such treatment is contrary to the prohibition of direct discrimination laid down by the directive.

With regard to harassment, the Court adopts identical reasoning and concludes that the relevant provisions of the directive are not limited only to people who are themselves disabled. Where it is established that unwanted conduct amounting to harassment is suffered by an employee in the same situation as that of Ms. Coleman, such conduct is contrary to the prohibition of harassment laid down by the directive.[510]

D. *Occupational Requirements*

1362. Member States may provide that a difference of treatment which is based on a characteristic related to any of the indicated grounds does not constitute discrimination where, by reason of the nature of the particular occupational activities

---

510. C.O.J., 17 July 2008, *Coleman v. Attridge Law and Steve Law*, C-303/06, ECR, 2008, 5603.

concerned or of the context in which they are carried out, such a characteristic constitutes a genuine and determining occupational requirement, provided that the objective is legitimate and the requirement is proportionate.

1363. In the *Wolf* case the question was raised whether there is discrimination on grounds of age, when there is national provision setting a maximum age of 30 years for the recruitment of officials to posts in the fire service.[511] The Court ruled as follows.

The referring court raises the question of the discretion open to the national legislature to provide that differences of treatment on grounds of age do not constitute discrimination prohibited by Union law. It asks in particular whether aims such as the concern to ensure a long career for officials, to limit the amount of social benefits paid, to set up a balanced age structure within an occupation, or to ensure a minimum period of service before retirement are legitimate within the meaning of Article 6(1) of the Directive, and whether setting the maximum recruitment age for intermediate career posts in the fire service at 30 years is an appropriate and necessary means of achieving such aims.

1364. To answer those questions, it must be examined whether the legislation at issue in the main proceedings falls within the scope of the Directive, whether it contains a difference of treatment within the meaning of the Directive, and, if so, whether or not the difference in treatment is justified.

In the first place, as regards the question whether the legislation at issue in the main proceedings falls within the scope of the Directive, it must be noted that it follows from Article 3(1)(a) of the Directive that it applies, within the framework of the areas of competence conferred on the Union, 'to all persons, as regards both the public and private sectors, including public bodies, in relation to … conditions for access to employment, to self-employment or to occupation, including selection criteria and recruitment conditions, whatever the branch of activity and at all levels of the professional hierarchy'.

1365. Only persons not more than 30 years of age can be recruited to intermediate career posts in the professional fire service. That provision thus affects the conditions of recruitment to that career. Such legislation must therefore be regarded as laying down rules relating to recruitment conditions within the meaning of Article 3(1)(a) of the Directive.

In the second place, as regards the question whether the legislation at issue in the main proceedings contains a difference of treatment on grounds of age in relation to employment and occupation, it must be noted that, under Article 2(1) of the Directive, for the purposes of the Directive, the 'principle of equal treatment' is to mean that there must be no direct or indirect discrimination whatsoever on any of the grounds referred to in Article 1 of the Directive. Article 2(2)(a) states that, for the purposes of the application of Article 2(1), direct discrimination is to be taken to occur where one person is treated less favourably than another person in a comparable situation, on any of the grounds referred to in Article 1 of the.Directive.

---

511. C.O.J., 12 January 2010, *Colin Wolf* v. *Stadt Frankfurt am Main*, C-229/08, www. curia.

Part I, Ch. 6, Equal Treatment

Persons are treated less favourably than other persons in comparable situations on the ground that they have exceeded the age of 30 years. Such a provision introduces a difference of treatment on grounds of age for the purposes of Article 2(2)(a) of the Directive.

1366. In the third place, it must be examined whether, as the referring court asks, the difference of treatment is justified with reference to the Directive.

According to the German government's observations at the hearing, the aim of setting the age limit for recruitment to intermediate career posts in the fire service at 30 years is to ensure the operational capacity and proper functioning of the professional fire service.

According to the German Government, the intermediate career in the fire service makes exceptionally high physical demands in respect of certain operations, which can only be satisfied by younger officials. In view of the medically proven ageing process, officials past the age of 45 to 50 years no longer possess those greater physical abilities and those operations have to be carried out by younger officials. The maximum recruitment age is thus intended to ensure that officials in the intermediate career of the fire service can perform the tasks which present particularly high physical requirements for a comparatively long period of their career.

1367. It must be observed in this respect that, according to the very wording of Article 4(1) of the Directive, 'a difference of treatment which is based on a characteristic related to any of the grounds referred to in Article 1 [of the Directive] shall not constitute discrimination where, by reason of the nature of the particular occupational activities concerned or of the context in which they are carried out, such a characteristic constitutes a genuine and determining occupational requirement, provided that the objective is legitimate and the requirement is proportionate'. It follows that it is not the ground on which the difference of treatment is based but a characteristic related to that ground which must constitute a genuine and determining occupational requirement.

To examine whether the difference of treatment based on age in the national legislation at issue in the main proceedings is justified, it must be ascertained whether physical fitness is a characteristic related to age and whether it constitutes a genuine and determining occupational requirement for the occupational activities in question or for carrying them out, provided that the objective pursued by the legislation is legitimate and the requirement is proportionate.

This shows that the aim pursued is to guarantee the operational capacity and proper functioning of the professional fire service.

1368. In this respect, it must be pointed out that the professional fire service forms part of the emergency services. Recital 18 in the preamble to the Directive states that the Directive does not require those services to recruit persons who do not have the required capacity to carry out the range of functions that they may be called upon to perform with regard to the legitimate objective of preserving the operational capacity of those services.

1369. It is thus apparent that the concern to ensure the operational capacity and proper functioning of the professional fire service constitutes a legitimate objective within the meaning of Article 4(1) of the Directive.

1370. As regards, second, the genuine and determining occupational requirement for the activities of the fire service or for carrying them out, it follows from the uncontradicted information provided by the German Government that persons in the intermediate career of the fire service perform tasks of professional firefighters on the ground. In contrast to the management duties of persons in the higher careers of the fire service, the activities of persons in the intermediate career are characterised by their physical nature. Those persons take part in fighting fires, rescuing persons, environment protection tasks, helping animals and dealing with dangerous animals, as well as supporting tasks such as the maintenance and control of protective equipment and vehicles. It follows that the possession of especially high physical capacities may be regarded as a genuine and determining occupational requirement within the meaning of Article 4(1) of the Directive for carrying on the occupation of a person in the intermediate career of the fire service.

1371. As regards, third, the question whether the need to possess high physical capacities is related to age, it should be noted that the German Government submits, without being contradicted, that some of the tasks of persons in the intermediate career of the fire service, such as fighting fires or rescuing persons, require exceptionally high physical capacities and can be performed only by young officials. The German Government produces scientific data deriving from studies in the field of industrial and sports medicine which show that respiratory capacity, musculature and endurance diminish with age. Thus very few officials over 45 years of age have sufficient physical capacity to perform the fire-fighting part of their activities. As for rescuing persons, at the age of 50 the officials concerned no longer have that capacity. Officials who have passed those ages work in the other branches of activities mentioned above. It follows that the need to possess full physical capacity to carry on the occupation of a person in the intermediate career of the fire services is related to the age of the persons in that career.

The main proceedings, which sets at 30 years the maximum recruitment age for officials having the high physical capacity to carry on an occupation in the intermediate career in the fire service, is proportionate, it must be examined whether that limit is appropriate for achieving the objective pursued and does not go beyond what is necessary to achieve it.

1372. As has just been stated, the fire-fighting and rescue duties which are part of the intermediate career in the fire service can only be performed by younger officials. Officials older than 45 or 50 carry out other duties. To ensure the efficient functioning of the intermediate career in the fire service, it may be considered necessary for the majority of officials in that career to be able to perform physically demanding tasks, and hence for them to be younger than 45 or 50. Moreover, the assignment of officials older than 45 or 50 to duties which are less physically demanding requires them to be replaced by young officials. The age at which an official is recruited determines the time during which he will be able to perform physically demanding tasks. An official recruited before the age of 30, who will have to follow a training programme lasting two years, can be assigned to those duties for a minimum of 15 to 20 years. By contrast, if he is recruited at the age of 40, that period will be a maximum of 5 to 10 years only. Recruitment at an older age would have the consequence that too large a number of officials could not be assigned to the most physically demanding duties. Similarly, such recruitment would not allow the officials thus recruited to be assigned to those duties for a sufficiently long period. Finally, as the German Government submits, the rational organisation of the professional fire service requires, for the intermediate career, a correlation between the physically demanding posts not suitable for older officials and the less physically demanding posts suitable for those officials.

Consequently, it is apparent that national legislation such as that at issue in the main proceedings which sets the maximum age for recruitment to intermediate career posts in the fire service at 30 years may be regarded, first, as appropriate to the objective of ensuring the operational capacity and proper functioning of the professional fire service and, second, as not going beyond what is necessary to achieve that objective.

Since the difference of treatment on grounds of age is justified with regard to Article 4(1) of the Directive, there is no need to examine whether it could be justified under Article 6(1) of the Directive.

1373. It follows from all the foregoing that the answer is that Article 4(1) of the Directive must be interpreted as not precluding national legislation, such as that at issue in the main proceedings, which sets the maximum age for recruitment to intermediate career posts in the fire service at 30 years.

1374. On those grounds, the Court hereby rules:

> Article 4(1) of Council Directive 2000/78/EC must be interpreted as not precluding national legislation, such as that at issue in the main proceedings, which sets the maximum age for recruitment to intermediate career posts in the fire service at 30 years.

1375. Member States may maintain national legislation in force at the date of adoption of this directive or provide for future legislation incorporating national practices existing at the date of adoption of this directive pursuant to which, in the case of occupational activities within churches and other public or private organisations the ethos of which is based on religion or belief, a difference of treatment based on a person's religion or belief shall not constitute discrimination where, by reason of the nature of these activities or of the context in which they are carried out, a person's religion or belief constitutes a genuine, legitimate and justified occupational requirement, having regard to the organisation's ethos. This difference of treatment shall be implemented taking account of Member States' constitutional provisions and principles, as well as the general principles of Union law, and should not justify discrimination on another ground.

The directive shall not prejudice the right of churches and other public or private organisations, the ethos of which is based on religion or belief, acting in conformity with national constitutions and laws, to require individuals working for them to act in good faith and with loyalty to the organisation's ethos (Article 4).

E. Reasonable Accommodation for Disabled Persons

1376. In relation to persons with disabilities, reasonable accommodation shall be provided. This means that employers shall take appropriate measures, where needed in a particular case, to enable a person with a disability to have access to, participate in, or advance in employment, or to undergo training, unless such measures would impose a disproportionate burden on the employer (Article 5).

1377. Sickness cannot be regarded as discrimination. No provision of the TFEU prohibits discrimination on grounds of sickness as such.
Article 19 TFEU and Article 153 TFEU, read in conjunction with Article 151 TFEU, contain only the rules governing the competencies of the Union. Moreover, Article 19 TFEU does not refer to discrimination on grounds of sickness as such in addition to discrimination on grounds of disability, and cannot therefore even constitute a legal basis for Council measures to combat such discrimination.
There is no doubt that fundamental rights, which form an integral part of the general principles of Union law include the general principle of non-discrimination and that this principle is therefore binding on Member States where the national situation at issue falls within the scope of Union law. However, it does not follow from this that the scope of Directive 2000/78 should be extended by analogy beyond the discrimination based on the grounds listed exhaustively in Article 1 thereof.
Consequently, sickness cannot as such be regarded as a ground in addition to those in relation to which Directive 2000/78 prohibits discrimination.[512]

1378. In a Danish case, the European Court[513] ruled that a curable or incurable illness entailing a physical, mental or psychological limitation may be assimilated to a disability. And that a reduction in working hours may be regarded as an accommodation measure which the employer must take in order to enable a person with a disability to work

1379. The directive on equal treatment in employment and occupation creates a general framework for combating, in particular, discrimination on grounds of disability.
The directive was transposed by the Danish legislation on the prohibition of discrimination in the labour market. In addition, Danish employment law provides that an employer may terminate the employment contract with a 'shortened period of

---

512. C.O.J., 11 July 2006, *Sonia Chacón Navas v. Eurest Colectividades SA*, C-13/05, ECR, 2006, 6467.
513. C.O.J., 11 April 2013, HK Danmark, acting on behalf of Jette Ring v Dansk almennyttigt Boligselskab (C-335/11) and HK Danmark, acting on behalf of Lone Skouboe Werge v Dansk Arbejdsgiverforening acting on behalf of Pro Display A/S (C-337/11), www.curia eu.

notice' of one month if the employee concerned has been absent because of illness, with his salary being paid, for 120 days during the previous 12 months.

1380. HK Danmark, a Danish trade union, brought two actions for compensation on behalf of Ms Ring and Ms Skouboe Werge, because of their dismissal with a shortened notice period. HK Danmark claims that because those two employees were suffering from a disability, their respective employers were required to offer them a reduction in working hours. The trade union also argues that the national legislation on the shortened notice period cannot apply to those two workers, since their absences because of illness were caused by their disability.

1381. As disability is not defined in the directive, the Court gave a definition of that concept in its judgment in *Chacón Navas*. It held that the concept is distinct from illness and must be understood as referring to a long-term limitation which results in particular from physical, mental or psychological impairments and hinders the participation of the person concerned in professional life.

After that judgment was delivered, the EU ratified the United Nations Convention on the Rights of Persons with Disabilities3. It follows that the directive must be interpreted, as far as possible, in a manner consistent with that convention.

1382. By its judgment, the Court starts by explaining that the concept of 'disability' must be interpreted as including a condition caused by an illness medically diagnosed as curable or incurable, if that illness entails a limitation which results in particular from physical, mental or psychological impairments which in interaction with various barriers may hinder the full and effective participation of the person concerned in professional life on an equal basis with other workers, and the limitation is a long-term one. The Court observes that, contrary to the arguments of the employers in the two cases, the concept of 'disability' does not necessarily imply complete exclusion from work or professional life. In addition, a finding that there is a disability does not depend on the nature of the accommodation measures to be taken by the employer, such as the use of special equipment. It will be for the national court to assess whether, in the present cases, the workers were persons with a disability.

1383. The Court then recalls that the directive requires the employer to take appropriate and reasonable accommodation measures in particular to enable a person with a disability to have access to, participate in, or advance in employment. The Court observes that, even if it were not covered by the concept of 'pattern of working time' expressly mentioned in the directive, a reduction in working hours may be regarded as an appropriate accommodation measure in a case in which the reduction makes it possible for the worker to continue in his employment.

It is, however, for the national court to assess whether, in the present cases, a reduction in working hours, as an accommodation measure, represents a disproportionate burden on the employers.

1384. The Court then states that the directive precludes national legislation under which an employer can terminate the employment contract with a shortened period of notice if the disabled worker concerned has been absent because of illness, with his salary being paid, for 120 days during the previous 12 months, where those absences are the consequence of the employer's failure to take appropriate and reasonable accommodation measures in order to enable the disabled person to work.

1385. The Court, finally, rules on whether the national legislation concerning the shortened notice period is liable to produce discrimination against persons with a disability. Direct discrimination occurs where one person is treated less favourably than another, in a comparable situation, on grounds of disability. Indirect discrimination occurs where an apparently neutral provision, criterion or practice is liable to put disabled persons at a particular disadvantage compared with other persons, unless this is justifiable.

1386. The Court notes that the national legislation applies in the same way to disabled and non-disabled persons who have been absent for more than 120 days because of illness. That legislation cannot therefore be regarded as establishing a difference of treatment based directly on disability. But the Court finds that a worker with a disability is more exposed to the risk of application of the shortened notice period than a worker without a disability, since he has the additional risk of contracting an illness connected with his disability. It is therefore apparent that that legislation is liable to place disabled workers at a disadvantage and so to bring about a difference of treatment indirectly based on disability.

1387. In an Italian case,[514] the European Court ruled, that Member States must require all employers to adopt practical and effective measures for all persons with disabilities. The Court reasoned as follows.
The purpose of the United Nations Convention on the Rights of Persons with Disabilities – approved on behalf of the EU by a decision of the Council of the European Union – is to promote, protect and ensure the full and equal enjoyment of all human rights and fundamental freedoms by all persons with disabilities, and to promote respect for their inherent dignity.

1388. The European Directive on equal treatment in employment is based on the belief that discrimination based on disability may undermine the achievement of the objectives of the Treaty, in particular the attainment of a high level of employment and social protection, raising the quality of life, economic and social cohesion and solidarity, and the free movement of persons. Therefore, that directive lays down a general framework for combating that kind of discrimination as regards employment and occupation, with a view to putting into effect in the Member States the principle of equal treatment.

1389. In order to guarantee equal treatment of persons with disabilities, that directive requires, *inter alia*, employers to take appropriate measures, where needed in a particular case, to enable such persons to have access to, participate in, or advance in employment, and to undergo training, unless such measures would

---

514. C.O.J., 4 July 2013, *European Commission v. Italian Republic*, C-312/11, www. curia.eu.

impose a disproportionate burden on the employer. That burden will not be disproportionate when it is sufficiently remedied by State policy on persons with disabilities.

Italian law includes a number of legislative measures on the subject of assistance for, social integration of and the rights of persons with disabilities and their right to work.

1390. The Commission has brought an action for failure to fulfil obligations before the Court of Justice, claiming that Italy has transposed the directive into its national law without ensuring that the guarantees and adjustments provided for regarding the treatment of persons with disabilities in the workplace are to apply to all persons with disabilities, all employers, and all aspects of the employment relationship. Furthermore, application of the Italian legislation on that subject is dependent on the adoption of further measures by the local authorities or the conclusion of special agreements between those authorities and employers and thus does not confer upon persons with disabilities rights which could be directly relied on before a court.

1391. In its judgment, the Court indicates that, while it is true that the concept of a 'disability' is not directly defined in the directive, it should be understood, on the basis of the UN Convention, as referring to a limitation, resulting inter alia from a long-term physical, mental, or psychological impairment, which in interaction with various barriers may hinder a person's full and effective participation in the labour force on an equal basis with other workers.

The UN Convention then advocates a broad interpretation of the concept of 'reasonable accommodation', by which it means the adjustments to be made, where needed in a particular case, to ensure to a person with disabilities the enjoyment or exercise of all human rights and fundamental freedoms on an equal basis with other workers.

1392. Moreover, the Court has already held that that concept refers to the elimination of the barriers that hinder the full and effective participation of persons with disabilities in professional life on an equal basis with other workers.

Therefore, Member States must create an obligation for employers to adopt effective and practical measures (adapting premises, equipment, patterns of working time, the distribution of tasks), taking into account each individual situation, which will enable any person with a disability to have access to, participate in, or advance in employment, and to undergo training, without imposing a disproportionate burden on the employer.

The Court emphasises that that obligation covers all employers. It is not sufficient for Member States to provide support and incentives: they must require all employers to adopt effective and practical measures, where needed in particular cases.

F. Justification of Differences of Treatment on Grounds of Age

1393. Member States may provide that differences of treatment on grounds of age shall not constitute discrimination, if, within the context of national law, they are objectively and reasonably justified by a legitimate aim, including legitimate employment policy, labour market and vocational training objectives, and if the means of achieving that aim are appropriate and necessary.

Such differences of treatment may include, among others:

(a) the setting of special conditions on access to employment and vocational training, employment and occupation, including dismissal and remuneration conditions, for young people, older workers and persons with caring responsibilities in order to promote their vocational integration or ensure their protection;
(b) the fixing of minimum conditions of age, professional experience or seniority in service for access to employment or to certain advantages linked to employment;
(c) the fixing of a maximum age for recruitment which is based on the training requirements of the post in question or the need for a reasonable period of employment before retirement.

Member States may provide that the fixing for occupational social security schemes of ages for admission or entitlement to retirement or invalidity benefits, including the fixing under those schemes of different ages for employees or groups or categories of employees, and the use, in the context of such schemes, of age criteria in actuarial calculations, does not constitute discrimination on the grounds of age, provided this does not result in discrimination on the grounds of sex (Article 6).

1394. In a German case the European Court ruled[515] that failure to take into account professional experience acquired with another company in the same group does not constitute discrimination on grounds of age. The case went as follows.

1395. The airline Tyrolean Airways and its works council (Betriebsrat) disagree as to whether account should be taken, for the grading of that airline's cabin crew in employment categories and, consequently, for the determination of salaries, of periods of service completed by those staff members with two other subsidiaries in the Austrian Airlines group, namely Austrian Airlines and Lauda Air. The Tyrolean Airways collective agreement provides that advancement from category A to the higher category B is to occur on the completion of three years of service, that is, three years after the recruitment of the employee as a member of the cabin crew. The employment contracts normally stipulate that the date of commencement of employment, whenever relevant to the application of any rule or entitlement, is to mean the date of commencement of employment with Tyrolean Airways.

---

515. C.O.J., 7 June 2012, Tyrolean Airways Tiroler Luftfahrt Gesellschaft mbH v Betriebsrat Bord der Tyrolean Airways Tiroler Luftfahrt Gesellschaft mbH., C-132/11, www.curia.eu.

1396. In this context, the Higher Regional Court, Innsbruck, Austria wanted to know whether Directive 2000/78 precludes a clause of a collective agreement which takes into account, for the purposes of grading in employment categories and, therefore, determination of the level of pay, only the professional experience acquired as a cabin crew member of a specific airline belonging to a group of companies, while excluding identical experience acquired in the service of another airline belonging to the same group.

In its judgment the Court of Justice answered this question in the negative. A clause such as that contained in the Tyrolean Airways collective agreement does not establish a difference of treatment on grounds of age.

While such a clause is likely to entail a difference in treatment according to the date of recruitment by the employer concerned, such a difference is not, directly or indirectly, based on age or on an event linked to age. It is the experience which may have been acquired by a cabin crew member with another airline in the same group of companies which is not taken into account for grading, irrespective of the age of that staff member at the time of his or her recruitment. That clause is therefore based on a criterion which is neither inextricably nor indirectly linked to the age of employees, even if it is conceivable that, in some individual cases, a consequence of the application of the criterion at issue may be that the time of advancement of the cabin crew members concerned from employment category A to employment category B is at a later age than the time of advancement of staff members who have acquired equivalent experience with Tyrolean Airways.

1397. In the *Hennings* case,[516] the Court ruled that he principle of non-discrimination on grounds of age proclaimed in Article 21 of the Charter of Fundamental Rights of the European Union and given specific expression in Council Directive 2000/78/EC and more particularly Articles 2 and 6(1) of that directive, must be interpreted as precluding a measure laid down by a collective agreement which provides that, within each salary group, the basic pay step of a public sector contractual employee is determined on appointment by reference to the employee's age. The fact that European Union law precludes that measure and that it appears in a collective agreement does not interfere with the right to negotiate and conclude collective agreements recognised in Article 28 of the Charter of Fundamental Rights of the European Union.

Articles 2 and 6(1) of Directive 2000/78 and Article 28 of the Charter of Fundamental Rights of the European Union must be interpreted as not precluding a measure in a collective agreement, which replaces a system of pay leading to discrimination on grounds of age by a system of pay based on objective criteria[517] while maintaining, for a transitional period limited in time, some of the discriminatory effects of the earlier system in order to ensure that employees in post are transferred to the new system without suffering a loss of income.

---

516. C.O.J., *Sabine Hennings a.o.* v. *Alexander Mal*, 8 September 2011, www. curia.eu.
517. 'It must be noted that the referring court and the German Government state that the higher pay is justified by the employee's longer professional experience and rewards his loyalty to the undertaking. Moreover, according to some legal writers and some of the lower courts, the higher basic pay received by older employees on their appointment is compensation for their financial needs, which in most cases are greater because of their social environment'. *Idem*, no. 69.

1398. The European Court was also asked whether the objective of encouraging the integration into working life of unemployed older workers allows, without restrictions, the conclusion of fixed-term employment contracts for all workers over the age of 52.[518]

The principle of non-discrimination on grounds of age is a general principle of Union law. In this regard, the purpose of Directive 2000/78[519] is to lay down a general framework for combating certain forms of discrimination, including in particular discrimination on grounds of age, as regards employment and occupation. A difference of treatment on grounds directly of age as a rule constitutes discrimination prohibited by Union law. However, the directive allows the Member States to provide for such differences of treatment and to consider them non-discriminatory if, within the context of national law, they are justified objectively and reasonably by a legitimate aim, in particular by legitimate employment policy and labour market objectives. Furthermore, the means to achieving such objectives must be appropriate and necessary.

1399. The Labour Court, Munich (Germany) has referred to the Court of Justice several questions for a preliminary ruling on the interpretation of Directive 2000/78 in a dispute concerning the German Law on part-time working and fixed-term contracts. That law authorises, without restriction, except in specific cases of a continuous employment relationship, the conclusion of fixed-term contracts of employment once the worker has reached the age of 52.

The Court of Justice recognises that the purpose of this legislation is plainly to promote the integration into working life of unemployed older workers, in so far as they encounter considerable difficulties in finding work. An objective of that kind justifies, as a rule, 'objectively and reasonably', a difference of treatment on grounds of age.

However, a provision of national law such as that contained in the German law goes beyond what is appropriate and necessary to attain the legitimate objective pursued.

1400. Admittedly, the Member States enjoy broad discretion in their choice of the measures capable of attaining their objectives in the field of social and employment policy. However, according to the Court, application of the national legislation at issue leads to a situation in which all workers who have reached the age of 52, without distinction, whether or not they were unemployed before the contract was concluded and whatever the duration of any period of unemployment, may lawfully, until their retirement, be offered fixed-term contracts of employment which may be renewed an indefinite number of times. This significant body of workers, determined solely on the basis of age, is thus in danger, during a substantial part of its members' working life, of being excluded from the benefit of stable employment which, however, constitutes a major element in the protection of workers. In this case, it has not been shown that fixing an age threshold, as such, regardless of any

---

518. C.O.J., 22 November 2005, *Werner Mangold* v. *Rüdiger Helm*, C-144/04, ECR, 2005, 9981.
519. Council Directive 2000/78/EC of 27 November 2000 establishing a general framework for equal treatment in employment and occupation, O.J., 2 December 2000 L 303.

other consideration linked to the structure of the labour market in question or the personal situation of the person concerned, is objectively necessary to the attainment of the objective which is the integration into working life of unemployed older workers.

Discrimination on the basis of age is, given the greying of the population to be taken seriously. Workers have to work longer in order to finance the medical costs and the increased pension bill which go along with the greying. Those, who want to worker longer must have the possibility to do so. Mandatory measures, like the obligatory pension age at 60 or 65, are discriminatory and have to be banned; Pension is a right not a duty.

1401. The prohibition on any discrimination on grounds of age must be interpreted as not precluding national legislation such as that at issue in the main proceedings, pursuant to which compulsory retirement clauses contained in collective agreements are lawful where such clauses provide as sole requirements that workers must have reached retirement age, set at 65 by national law, and must have fulfilled the conditions set out in the social security legislation for entitlement to a retirement pension under their contribution regime, where

– the measure, although based on age, is objectively and reasonably justified in the context of national law by a legitimate aim relating to employment policy and the labour market, and
– the means put in place to achieve that aim of public interest do not appear to be inappropriate and unnecessary for the purpose.[520]

1402. In the case *Félix Palacios de la Villa*, the Court ruled that in the general context of national legislation the aim of promoting access to employment by means of better distribution of work between the generations may, in principle, be regarded as 'objectively and reasonably' justifying 'within the context of national law' a difference in treatment on grounds of age laid down by the Member States.

Spanish legislation, indeed, treats compulsory retirement clauses in collective agreements as lawful where those clauses provide as sole requirements that workers must have reached retirement age – set at 65 years – and must fulfil other social security conditions for entitlement to a contributory retirement pension.

1403. Felix Palacios de la Villa worked for Cortefiel from 1981 as organisational manager. In 2005, Cortefiel notified him of the termination of his contract of employment on the ground that he had reached the compulsory retirement age. At the date of notification, Mr Palacios de la Villa had completed the periods of employment necessary to draw a retirement pension under the social security scheme amounting to 100 per cent of his contribution base.

Taking the view that that notification amounted to dismissal, Mr Palacios de la Villa brought an action before the Spanish courts which referred a number of questions to the Court of Justice of the European Communities for a preliminary ruling

---

520. C.O.J., 16 October 2007, *Félix Palacios de la Villa v. Cortefiel Servicios SA*, C-411/05, ECR, 2007, 8531.

on the interpretation of Directive 2000/78 establishing a general framework for equal treatment in employment and occupation.

1404. First, the Court states that national legislation, according to which the fact that a worker has reached the age fixed for compulsory retirement leads automatically to the termination of his employment relationship, affects the duration of the employment relationship between the worker and his employer and, more generally, the engagement of the worker concerned in an occupation by preventing his future participation in the labour force. Such national legislation thus establishes rules relating to 'employment and working conditions, including dismissals and pay' within the meaning of Directive 2000/78 and, therefore falls within its scope.

The Court goes on to state that national legislation of that kind must be regarded as directly imposing less favourable treatment for workers who have reached that age as compared with all other persons in the labour force. Therefore, such legislation establishes a difference in treatment directly based on age.

Next, the Court examines possible justification for that difference in treatment. The Court states that the Spanish legislation was adopted at the instigation of the social partners as part of a national policy aiming to promote better access to employment by means of better distribution of work between the generations. The fact that the legislation does not formally refer to an aim of that kind does not automatically exclude the possibility that it may be justified.

The Court considers that other elements, taken from the general context of the measure concerned, may enable its underlying aim to be identified for the purposes of judicial review as regards its justification.

1405. The Court infers from the context in which the Spanish legislation was adopted that it was aimed at regulating the national labour market, in particular for the purposes of checking unemployment. The legitimacy of such an aim of public interest cannot reasonably be called into question with regard to Directive 2000/78 and the EU and TFEU Treaties, since the promotion of a high level of employment constitutes one of the ends pursued by the European Union.

Such an aim must therefore, in principle, be regarded as 'objectively and reasonably' justifying, 'within the context of national law', as provided for by Directive 2000/78, a difference in treatment on grounds of age laid down by the Member States.

1406. Finally, the Court recalls that, as Union law stands at present, the Member States and, where appropriate, the social partners at national level enjoy broad discretion in their choice, not only to pursue a particular aim in the field of social and employment policy, but also in the definition of measures capable of achieving it. However, the national measures laid down in that context may not go beyond what is 'appropriate and necessary' to achieve the aim pursued by the Member State concerned.

It does not appear unreasonable for the authorities of a Member State to take the view that compulsory retirement, because the worker has reached the age-limit provided for, may be appropriate and necessary in order to achieve a legitimate aim in the context of national employment policy consisting in promoting full employment by facilitating access to the labour market.

Furthermore, the measure cannot be regarded as unduly prejudicing legitimate claims of workers subject to compulsory retirement because they have reached the age limit provided for; the relevant national legislation is not based only on a specific age, but also takes account of the fact that the persons concerned are entitled to financial compensation by way of a retirement pension at the end of their working life, such as that provided for by the Spanish scheme, the level of which cannot be regarded as unreasonable.

1407. Accordingly, the Court considers that such legislation is not incompatible with the requirements of Directive 2000/78 establishing a general framework for equal treatment in employment and occupation.

1408. In another case on age,[521] the Court examined the United Kingdom regulations which transpose the directive and provide that employees who have reached their employer's normal retirement age or, if the employer does not have a normal retirement age, age 65, may be dismissed for reason of retirement without such treatment being regarded as discriminatory. The regulations set out a number of criteria designed to ascertain whether the reason for the dismissal is retirement and requires a set procedure to be followed. For employees under 65 years of age the regulations do not contain any particular provisions and merely lay down the principle that any discrimination on grounds of age is unlawful, unless the employer can show that it is 'a proportionate means of achieving a legitimate aim'.

The National Council on Ageing (Age Concern England), a charity which promotes the wellbeing of older people, challenged the legality of that legislation on the ground that it does not properly transpose the directive. It submits that the possibility to dismiss an employee aged 65 or more by reason of retirement is contrary to the directive.

1409. The High Court asked the Court of Justice whether the directive requires Member States to specify the kinds of differences of treatment which may be justified and whether it precludes legislation which merely provides in a general manner that a difference of treatment on grounds of age is not discrimination if it is a proportionate means of achieving a legitimate aim.

1410. The Court recalls that the transposition of a directive does not always require that its provisions be incorporated formally in express, specific legislation. In this case, the directive does not require Member States to draw up a specific list of the differences in treatment which may be justified by a legitimate aim.

In the absence of such precision, it is important, however, that other elements, taken from the general context of the measure concerned, enable the underlying aim

---

521. C.O.J., 5 March 2009, *The Incorporated Trustees of the National Council on Ageing (Age Concern England)* v. *Secretary of State for Business, Enterprise and Regulatory Reform*, C-388/07, www.curia.eu.

of that measure to be identified for the purposes of review by the courts of its legitimacy and whether the means put in place to achieve that aim are appropriate and necessary. The Court notes that the aims which may be considered 'legitimate' by the directive, and, consequently, appropriate for the purposes of justifying derogation from the principle prohibiting discrimination on grounds of age, are social policy objectives, such as those related to employment policy, the labour market or vocational training. By their public interest nature, those legitimate aims are distinguishable from purely individual reasons particular to the employer's situation, such as cost reduction or improving competitiveness.

It is for the national court to ascertain, first, whether the United Kingdom legislation reflects such a legitimate aim and, second, whether the means chosen were appropriate and necessary to achieve it.

Consequently, national legislation may provide, in a general manner, that this kind of difference of treatment on grounds of age is justified if it is a proportionate means to achieve a legitimate social policy objective related to employment policy, the labour market or vocational training.

1411. In a Greek case,[522] the Commission sought a declaration from the Court of Justice that the provisions of the Greek Civil and Military Pensions Code providing for differences between male and female workers with regard to pensionable age and minimum length of service required infringe the principle of equal treatment. It takes the view that that system lays down retirement conditions which are less favourable to men than to women.

Greece has not disputed the fact that there are differences in treatment, but submitted that the Greek pension system, as a statutory social security scheme, does not fall within the scope of the Treaty but under Directive 79/7. In any event, those differences correspond to the respective social roles of men and women and constitute measures which compensate for the disadvantages suffered by women because of the shorter duration of their working life.

1412. First of all, the Court notes that, according to the TFEU, each Member State is to ensure that the principle of equal pay for male and female workers for equal work is applied. 'Pay' means the wage or salary and any other consideration, whether in cash or in kind, which the worker receives directly or indirectly, in respect of his employment, from the employer. The concept of pay does not encompass social security schemes directly governed by legislation, but does include benefits paid under a pension scheme, which essentially relates to the employment of the person concerned.

It points out that among the criteria applied in its case-law in order to classify a pension scheme, only the criterion of employment (the fact that a pension is paid to the worker by reason of the employment relationship between him and his former employer) can be decisive, the means of financing and management of the scheme not constituting decisive factors.

---

522. C.O.J., 26 March 2009, *Commission v. Greece*, C-559/07, www.curia.eu.

Part I, Ch. 6, Equal Treatment

1413. The Court notes that the pension paid under the Greek Code complies with the three criteria defined by the Court's case-law enabling it to be classified as pay within the meaning of the Treaty:

– it is applied to a wide and varied group of workers which, although made up of disparate categories with tasks and employment relationships which are entirely dissimilar, can be distinguished by particular characteristics governing the employment relationship with the State or other public employers;
– it is calculated on the basis of the length of service completed; and, finally,
– it is calculated on the basis of the final salary.

1414. The Court then points out that it is contrary to the principle of equal treatment to impose for the grant of a retirement pension paid in relation to employment age conditions and rules on minimum periods of service required which differ according to sex for workers in identical or comparable situations.

That principle does not preclude a Member State from applying measures providing for specific advantages intended to facilitate the exercise of a professional activity by the under-represented sex or from preventing or compensating for disadvantages in professional careers. Furthermore, national measures covered by the principle of equal treatment must, in any event, contribute to helping women conduct their professional life on an equal footing with men.

The Court holds that the provisions of the Greek Civil and Military Pensions Code are not of a nature to offset the disadvantages to which the careers of female civil servants and military personnel are exposed by helping them in their professional life.

1415. Lately, the number of cases regarding discrimination based on age, especially relating to retirement, which were put to the European Court of Justice, have increased substantially. This will go on, until retirement becomes a right and not a duty. Some people resent mandatory retirement and want to continue to work. The Court is still hesitating. The *Rosenbladt* case concerned the automatic termination of an employment contract on reaching retirement age. The Court decided that such a clause in a collective agreement is not necessarily discriminatory.[523]

In Germany, the Law on equal treatment (*Allgemeines Gleichbehandlungsgesetz*) provides that clauses on automatic termination of employment contracts on the ground that an employee has reached retirement age may escape the prohibition on discrimination on grounds of age. Under the German legislation, the power to adopt such clauses may be entrusted to the social partners and implemented by a collective agreement.

1416. Gisela Rosenbladt worked as a cleaner for 39 years. Her employment contract, in accordance with the collective agreement for the commercial cleaning sector, ends at the end of the calendar month in which she may claim a retirement pension, or, at the latest, at the end of the month in which she reaches the age of 65.

---

523. C.O.J., 21 July 2011, *Gerhard Fuchs* v. *Land Hessen* (C-159/10), www.curia.

When she reached the age of 65, which was retirement age, her employer gave her notice of the termination of her employment contract. Ms Rosenbladt brought an action before the *Arbeitsgericht Hamburg* (Hamburg Labour Court), claiming that the termination of her employment contract constituted discrimination on grounds of age.

The referring court asked, essentially, whether the automatic termination of an employment contract at normal retirement age was consistent with the prohibition on discrimination on grounds of age laid down by Directive 2000/78/EC.

In its judgment the Court finds, first, that a clause on automatic termination of an employment contract on the ground that an employee is eligible to retire creates a difference of treatment based directly on age. The Court then considers whether there is any justification for that difference of treatment.

1417. In that regard, the Court considers that such a measure does not establish a regime of compulsory retirement but allows employers and employees to agree, by individual or collective agreements, on a means, other than resignation or dismissal, of ending employment relationships on the basis of the age of eligibility for a retirement pension.

As regards the aim of the legislation at issue, the Court observes that the mechanism is based on the balance to be struck between political, economic, social, demographic and/or budgetary considerations and the choice to be made between prolonging people's working lives or, conversely, providing for their early retirement.

1418. The Court notes that such clauses on automatic termination have been part of the employment law of many Member States for a long time and are in widespread use in employment relationships. By guaranteeing workers a certain stability of employment and, in the long term, the promise of foreseeable retirement, while offering employers a certain flexibility in the management of their staff, the clause on automatic termination of employment contracts is thus the reflection of a balance between diverging but legitimate interests, against a complex background of employment relationships closely linked to political choices in the area of retirement and employment. Those aims must, in principle, be considered to justify 'objectively and reasonably', 'within the context of national law', as provided in Directive 2000/78, a difference in treatment on the ground of age prescribed by Member States.

1419. Next, the Court holds that it does not appear unreasonable for the authorities or the social partners of a Member State to take the view that clauses on automatic termination of employment contracts may be appropriate and necessary in order to achieve those legitimate aims. In that regard the Court points out that the clause applicable to Ms Rosenbladt is not based solely on a specific age but also takes account of the fact that the persons concerned are entitled to financial compensation in the form of a retirement pension, and does not authorise employers to terminate an employment relationship unilaterally. Moreover, the fact that it is based on an agreement makes for considerable flexibility in the use of the mechanism, allowing the social partners to take account of the overall situation in the labour market concerned and of the specific features of the jobs in question. In addition, the German legislation contains a further limitation in that it requires employers to obtain or confirm the consent of workers to any clause on automatic termination of an employment contract on the ground that the employee has reached the age at which he is eligible for a pension, where that age is less than the normal retirement age. Finally, the Court observes that the German Law prevents a person who intends to continue to work beyond retirement age from being refused employment, either by his former employer or by a third party, on a ground related to his age.

1420. Consequently, the Court holds that Directive 2000/78 does not preclude clauses on automatic termination of employment contracts on the ground that the employee has reached the age of retirement such as that laid down in Germany by the collective agreement for employees in the commercial cleaning sector.

1421. Also professors and prosecutors went to court. In the Georgiev[524] case a professor took the floor. But the Court denied him. The Court ruled as follows:

> Council Directive 2000/78/EC, in particular Article 6(1), must be interpreted as meaning that it does not preclude national legislation, such as that at issue in the main proceedings, under which university professors are compulsorily retired when they reach the age of 68 and may continue working beyond the age of 65 only by means of fixed-term one-year contracts renewable at most twice, provided that that legislation pursues a legitimate aim linked inter alia to employment and labour market policy, such as the delivery of quality teaching and the best possible allocation of posts for professors between the generations, and that it makes it possible to achieve that aim by appropriate and necessary means. It is for the national court to determine whether those conditions are satisfied.
>
> Since this is a dispute between a public institution and an individual, if national legislation such as that at issue in the main proceedings does not satisfy the conditions set out in Article 6(1) of Directive 2000/78, the national court must decline to apply that legislation.

1422. The same was ruled in the case of mandatory retirement of a German prosecutor. So it was decided in the *Fuchs* case:[525]

(1) Council Directive 2000/78/EC does not preclude a law, which provides for the compulsory retirement of permanent civil servants – in this instance prosecutors – at the age of 65, while allowing them to continue to work, if it is in the interests of the service that they should do so, until the maximum age of 68, provided that that law has the aim of establishing a balanced age structure in order to encourage the recruitment and promotion of young people, to improve personnel management and thereby to prevent possible disputes concerning

---

524. C.O.J., 18 November 2010, *Vasil Ivanov Georgiev* v. *Tehnicheski universitet – Sofia, filial Plovdiv*, C-250/09, www.curia.
525. C.O.J., 21 July 2011, *Gerhard Fuchs* v. *Land Hessen* (C-159/10), www.curia.eu.

employees' fitness to work beyond a certain age, and that it allows that aim to be achieved by appropriate and necessary means.
(2) In order for it to be demonstrated that the measure concerned is appropriate and necessary, the measure must not appear unreasonable in the light of the aim pursued and must be supported by evidence the probative value of which it is for the national court to assess.
(3) A law such, which provides for the compulsory retirement of prosecutors when they reach the age of 65, does not lack coherence merely because it allows them to work until the age of 68 in certain cases or also contains provisions intended to restrict retirement before the age of 65, and other legislation of the Member State concerned provides for certain – particularly elected – civil servants to remain in post beyond that age and also the gradual raising of the retirement age from 65 to 67 years.

1423. The European Court[526] also ruled that the radical lowering of the retirement age for Hungarian judges, however,constitutes unjustified discrimination on grounds of age, as That measure is not proportionate to the objectives pursued by the Hungarian legislature seeking to standardise the retirement age for the public-service professions and to establish a more balanced age structure in the area of the administration of justice

1424. In Hungary, judges, prosecutors and notaries were permitted to remain in office until the age of 70. However, following the amendment of the relevant Hungarian legislation in 2011, with effect from 1 January 2012 judges and prosecutors who have reached the general retirement age, namely 62, are obliged to retire.

1425. The Court notes, first of all, that judges, prosecutors and notaries who have reached the age of 62 are in a comparable situation to that of younger individuals working in the same professions. However, the former, by reason of their age, are obliged to retire, with the result that they are subject to treatment which is less favourable than that accorded to those who continue to work. The Court notes therefore that that situation constitutes a difference of treatment directly based on age.

1426. The Court points out, however, that legitimate social policy objectives, such as those related to employment policy, the labour market or vocational training, may justify a derogation from the principle prohibiting discrimination on grounds of age. In that regard, the Court finds that the objectives invoked by Hungary, namely the need to standardise the age-limits for retirement for public sector professions and to establish a more balanced age structure facilitating access for young lawyers to the professions concerned, do indeed come within the scope of social policy.
However, as regards the objective of standardisation, the Court draws attention to the fact that, prior to 1 January 2012, the persons affected by the contested legislation had been able to remain in office until the age of 70, which gave rise, in their

---

526. C.O.J., 6 November 2012, *European Commission* v. *Hungary*, C-286/12, www.curia. eu.

regard, to a well-founded expectation that they would be able to remain in office until that age. However, the contested legislation abruptly and significantly lowered the age-limit for compulsory retirement, without providing for transitional measures such as to protect the legitimate expectations of those persons. Consequently, those persons are obliged to leave the labour market automatically and definitively, without having had the time to take the measures, in particular of an economic and financial nature, that such a situation calls for. The Court notes in that respect, firstly, that the retirement pension of those persons is at least 30% lower than their salary and, secondly, that the retirement does not take contribution periods into account and does not, therefore, guarantee the right to a pension at the full rate.

1427. The Court goes on to point out the existence of a contradiction between the immediate lowering of the retirement age for those professions by eight years, without providing for a gradual staggering of that change, and the increase of the age of retirement for the general pension scheme by three years (that is to say, from 62 to 65), which must be carried out with effect from 2014 over a period of eight years. That contradiction suggests that the interests of those who are affected by the lowering of the age-limit were not taken into account in the same way as those of other public sector employees for whom the age-limit has been increased.

In those circumstances, the Court concludes that the radical lowering of the retirement age for the professions concerned by eight years is not a measure which is necessary to achieve the objective of standardising the retirement age for public-sector professions.

1428. Finally, the Court examines the objective, invoked by Hungary, of establishing a more balanced age structure. In that regard, while recognising that the national legislation may facilitate, in the short term, the access of young lawyers to the professions concerned, the Court points out, however, that the immediate, apparently positive, effects are liable to cast doubt on the prospects of achieving a truly balanced 'age structure' in the medium and long term. While, in the course of 2012, the turnover of personnel in the professions concerned will be subject to a very significant acceleration, as eight age groups have been replaced by one single age group (that of 2012), that turnover rate will be subject to an equally radical slowing-down in 2013, when only one age group will have to be replaced. In addition, that rate of turnover will become slower and slower as the age-limit for compulsory retirement is raised progressively from 62 to 65, even leading to a deterioration in the prospects for young lawyers to enter the professions of the judicial system. It follows that the contested national legislation is not appropriate to achieve the pursued objective of establishing a more balanced 'age structure'.

1429. In the case of Ms Petersen,[527] where a national law setting a maximum age of 68 for practice as a panel dentist, the Court ruled, rightly that article 2(5) of Council Directive 2000/78/ precludes such a measure where the sole aim of that measure is to protect the health of patients against the decline in performance of

---

527. C.O.J., 12 January 2010, *Domnica Petersen* v. *Berufungsausschuss für Zahnärzte für den Bezirk Westfalen-Lippe,* C-341/08, www.curia.

those dentists after that age, since that age limit does not apply to non-panel dentists.

Article 6(1) of Directive 2000/78 must, however be interpreted as not precluding such a measure where its aim is to share out employment opportunities among the generations in the profession of panel dentist, if, taking into account the situation in the labour market concerned, the measure is appropriate and necessary for achieving that aim. It is for the national court to identify the aim pursued by the measure laying down that age limit, by ascertaining the reason for maintaining the measure.

1430. International and German legislation provide that, between the ages of 60 and 64, an airline pilot may not continue to act as a pilot unless he is a member of a multi-pilot crew and the other pilots are under 60. However, that legislation prohibits pilots from acting as pilots beyond 65.

The collective agreement applicable to the crew of the German airline Deutsche Lufthansa – which is recognised by German law – prohibits pilots from acting as pilots after the age of 60.

Reinhard Prigge, Michael Fromm and Volker Lambach were employed for many years by Deutsche Lufthansa as pilots then flight captains. When they reached 60 years of age their employment contracts terminated automatically, in accordance with the collective agreement. Considering themselves to be victims of discrimination on grounds of age, which is prohibited by the directive, they brought an action before the German courts for a declaration that their employment relationships with Deutsche Lufthansa had not terminated at age 60 and an order that their employment contracts should be continued.

The *Bundesarbeitsgericht* (Federal Labour Court, Germany) asked the Court of Justice whether a collective agreement which provides for an age-limit of 60 for airline pilots for the purposes of air safety is compatible with EU law.

The Court recalls, firstly, that the collective agreements entered into with the social partners must, as with the national laws of the Member States, respect the principle of non-discrimination on grounds of age, which is recognised as a general principle of EU law and given specific expression by the directive in the domain of employment and occupation.

Next, the Court states that the limitation of the possibility for pilots to act as pilots to age 60 pursues the objective of guaranteeing the safety of passengers, persons in areas over which aircraft fly and the safety and health of pilots themselves, which may justify a difference in treatment, and that that limitation may be provided for in a collective agreement. However, the Court notes that international and German legislation considered that it was not necessary to prohibit pilots from acting as pilots after the age of 60 but that it sufficed merely to restrict those activities. The Court therefore holds that the prohibition on piloting after that age, provided for by the collective agreement, is not a necessary measure for the protection of public health and security.

The Court moreover states that possessing particular physical capabilities may be considered as a genuine and determining occupational requirement for acting as an airline pilot and that the possession of such capabilities is related to age. As that requirement is aimed at guaranteeing air traffic safety, it pursues a legitimate objective which may justify a difference in treatment on grounds of age.

However, it is only in very limited circumstances that such a difference in treatment may be justified. In that regard, the Court notes that the international and German authorities consider that, until the age of 65, pilots have the physical capabilities to act as a pilot, even if, between 60 and 65, they may do so only as a member of a crew in which the other pilots are younger than 60. On the other hand, the Lufthansa social partners fixed at 60 the age-limit from which airline pilots are considered as no longer possessing the physical capabilities to carry out their occupational activity.

In those circumstances, the Court states that the age-limit of 60, imposed by the social partners, to be able to pilot an airplane, constitutes a disproportionate requirement in light of international and German legislation that fixed that age-limit at 65.[528]

1431. In a Swedish case, the court ruled that Directive 2000/78/EC does not preclude a national measure, which allows an employer to terminate an employee's employment contract on the sole ground that the employee has reached the age of 67 and which does not take account of the level of the retirement pension which the person concerned will receive, as that measure is objectively and reasonably justified by a legitimate aim relating to employment policy and labour-market policy and constitutes an appropriate and necessary means by which to achieve that aim.[529]

1432. In the *Hütter* case,[530] the Court rules that Articles 1, 2 and 6 of Council Directive 2000/78/EC of 27 November 2000 establishing a general framework for equal treatment in employment and occupation must be interpreted as precluding national legislation which, in order not to treat general education less favourably than vocational education and to promote the integration of young apprentices into the labour market, excludes periods of employment completed before the age of 18 from being taken into account for the purpose of determining the incremental step at which contractual public servants of a Member State are graded.

1433. Age discrimination is a fairly new concept under EU law and it has been at issue in only a small number of cases. However, as labour markets become tighter, it is possible that more employers will begin to argue that the dismissal of older workers is justifiable on the grounds of opening up opportunities for the employment of younger workers. This therefore makes the principle of non-discrimination on the grounds of age weaker. Similarly, the refusal of the ECJ to allow positive measures in relation to retirement and the retirement pension, where a disadvantage was not seen to have been offset, is disappointing, given that women unquestionably do have shorter service as a result of their specific social role.[531]

---

528. C.O.J., 13 September 2011, *Reinhard Prigge and others* v. *Deutsche Lufthansa AG*, C-447/09, www.curia. eu.
529. C.O.J., 5 July 2012, *Torsten Hörnfeldt* v. *Posten Meddelande AB*, 141/11, www.curia.eu.
530. C.O.J., 18 June 2009, *David Hütter* v. *Technische Universität Graz*, C-88/08, www.curia.eu..
531. Sonia McKay, 'ECJ rulings on retirement age and discrimination law', www.eurofound EIRonline, 2009.

1434. German legislation under which periods of employment completed before the age of 25 are not taken into account for calculating the notice period is contrary to the principle of non-discrimination on grounds of age, as expressed by Directive 2000/78, and must be disapplied if need be by the national court, even in proceedings between individuals. So it was judged in the *Ms Kücükdeveci* case.[532]

Under German employment law, the notice periods which an employer must comply with in the case of dismissal increase progressively according to the length of the employment relationship. However, periods of employment completed by an employee before reaching the age of 25 are not taken into account for calculating the period.

1435. Ms Kücükdeveci had been employed by Swedex since the age of 18. At the age of 28, she was dismissed by that company, with one month's notice. The company calculated the notice period as if she had three years' length of service, although she had worked for it for ten years: in accordance with the German legislation, no account was taken of the periods of employment completed before Ms Kücükdeveci was 25. She brought proceedings to challenge her dismissal, claiming that the legislation constituted discrimination on grounds of age, prohibited by European Union law. In her view, the notice period should have been four months, corresponding to ten years' service.

The Higher Labour Court, Düsseldorf, hearing the case on appeal, put questions to the Court of Justice on the compatibility of such a rule on dismissal with European Union law, and the consequences of any incompatibility.

1436. The Court of Justice examined those questions on the basis of the general principle of European Union law prohibiting all discrimination on grounds of age, as given expression by Directive 2000/78. As the dismissal of Ms Kücükdeveci took place after the date on which Germany had to transpose the directive into national law, the directive had the effect of bringing the German rule on dismissal within the scope of European Union law.

1437. The Court finds that the rule on dismissal contains a difference of treatment based on age. The rule gives less favourable treatment to employees who have entered the employer's service before the age of 25. It thus introduces a difference of treatment between persons with the same length of service, depending on the age at which they joined the undertaking.

While the aims of the rule clearly belong to employment and labour market policy, and are therefore legitimate objectives, the rule is not appropriate or necessary for achieving them.

In particular, as regards the objective mentioned by the national court of giving employers greater flexibility of personnel management by alleviating the burden on them in respect of the dismissal of young workers, from whom it is reasonable to expect a greater degree of personal or occupational mobility, the Court states that the rule in question is not appropriate for achieving that aim, because it applies to

---

532. C.O.J., 19 January 2010, *Seda Kücükdeveci* v. *Swedex GmbH & Co. KG*, C-555/07, www.curia.

all employees who joined the undertaking before the age of 25, whatever their age at the time of dismissal.

1438. The Court therefore concluded that European Union law, more particularly the principle of non-discrimination on grounds of age as given expression by Directive 2000/78, precludes national legislation such as the German rule which provides that periods of employment completed by an employee before reaching the age of 25 are not taken into account in calculating the notice period for dismissal.

The Court then points out that a directive cannot of itself impose obligations on an individual, and cannot therefore be relied on as such against an individual. However, Directive 2000/78 merely gives expression to the principle of equal treatment in employment and occupation. Moreover, the principle of non-discrimination on grounds of age is a general principle of European Union law. It is therefore for the national court, hearing a dispute involving the principle of non-discrimination on grounds of age as given expression in Directive 2000/78 to provide, within the limits of its jurisdiction, the legal protection which individuals derive from European Union law and to ensure the full effectiveness of that law, disapplying if need be any provision of national legislation contrary to that principle.

1439. Finally, after referring to the national court's entitlement to make a reference to the Court for a preliminary ruling on the interpretation of European Union law, the Court states that the national court, hearing proceedings between individuals, must ensure that the principle of non-discrimination on grounds of age as given expression in Directive 2000/78 is complied with, disapplying if need be any contrary provision of national legislation, independently of whether it makes use of its entitlement to ask the Court for a preliminary ruling on the interpretation of that principle.

1440. In a Danish case,[533] the Court ruled that:

> Articles 2 and 6(1) of Council Directive 2000/78 must be interpreted as precluding national legislation pursuant to which workers who are eligible for an old-age pension from their employer under a pension scheme which they have joined before attaining the age of 50 years cannot, on that ground alone, claim a severance allowance aimed at assisting workers with more than 12 years of service in the undertaking in finding new employment.

1441. That measure makes it more difficult for workers who are eligible for an old-age pension subsequently to exercise their right to work because, unlike other workers with the same years of service, they are not entitled to the severance allowance when in the process of seeking new employment.

In addition, the measure at issue in the main proceedings prohibits an entire category of workers defined on the basis of their age from temporarily waiving their

---

533. C.O.J., 12 October 2010, *Ingeniørforeningen i Danmark, acting on behalf of Ole Andersen* v. *Region Syddanmark,* C-499/08, www.curia.

right to an old-age pension from their employer in exchange for payment of the severance allowance, which, after all, is aimed at assisting them in finding new employment. That measure may thus force workers to accept an old-age pension which is lower than the pension which they would be entitled to if they were to remain in employment for more years, leading to a significant reduction in their income in the long term.

1442. Consequently, by not permitting payment of the severance allowance to workers who, although eligible for an old-age pension from their employer, none the less wish to waive their right to such a pension temporarily in order to continue with their career, Article 2a(3) of the Law on salaried employees unduly prejudices the legitimate interests of workers in such a situation and thus goes beyond what is necessary to attain the social policy aims pursued by that provision.

Therefore, the difference of treatment resulting from 2a(3) of the Law on salaried employees cannot be justified under Article 6(1) of Directive 2000/78.

G. Positive Action

1443. With a view to ensuring full equality in practice, the principle of equal treatment shall not prevent any Member State from maintaining or adopting specific measures to prevent or compensate for disadvantages linked to any of the grounds referred to.

With regard to disabled persons, the principle of equal treatment shall be without prejudice to the right of Member States to maintain or adopt provisions on the protection of health and safety at work or to measures aimed at creating or maintaining provisions or facilities for safeguarding or promoting their integration into the working environment (Art. 7).

H. Minimum Requirements

1444. Member States may introduce or maintain provisions which are more favourable to the protection of the principle of equal treatment than those laid down in this directive.

The implementation of this directive shall under no circumstances constitute grounds for a reduction in the level of protection against discrimination already afforded by Member States in the fields covered by this directive (Art. 8).

1445. Article 8 of the Directive provides that the implementation of the Directive is under no circumstances to constitute grounds for a reduction in the level of protection against discrimination already afforded by Member States in the fields covered by the Directive.

The Court had to answer the question[534], whether a national provision which provides that a victim of discrimination in recruitment on grounds of age must make a claim against the perpetrator of that discrimination within two months of receipt of the rejection of the job application or, by way of another interpretation of that provision, within two months of acquiring knowledge of the discrimination, constitutes a correct implementation of Articles 8 and 9 of the Directive.

1446. The Court ruled as follows:

> With regard to Council Directive 1999/70/EC of 28 June 1999 concerning the framework agreement on fixed-term work and, in particular, clause 8(3) of that Framework Agreement, under which implementation of the agreement cannot provide the Member States with valid grounds for reducing the general level of protection for workers previously guaranteed in the domestic legal order in the sphere covered by that agreement, the Court has held that reduction of the protection which workers are guaranteed in the sphere of fixed-term employment contracts is not prohibited as such by the Framework Agreement but, in order for that reduction to be caught by the prohibition laid down by clause 8(3) of the agreement, it must, first, be connected to the 'implementation' of the Framework Agreement and, second, relate to the 'general level of protection' afforded to fixed-term workers.
>
> In any event, since Article 1 of the Directive 2000/78 does not refer to sex as a ground for discrimination, any reduction in the level of protection against discrimination based on that ground cannot be regarded as falling within the fields covered by the Directive.

1447. Consequently, the length of a time-limit for claiming compensation for discrimination on grounds of sex in the version prior to the entry into force of the Equal Treatment legislation, is not covered by the notion of 'level of protection against discrimination' in Article 8(2) of the Directive.

In the light of those considerations, the answer is that Article 8 of the Directive must be interpreted as not precluding a national procedural rule, adopted in order to implement the Directive, which has the effect of amending earlier legislation which provided for a time-limit for claiming compensation for discrimination on grounds of sex.

II. Remedies and Enforcement

A. *Defence of Rights*

1448. Member States must ensure that judicial and/or administrative procedures, including, where they deem it, appropriate conciliation procedures, are available to all persons who consider themselves wronged by failure to apply the

---

534. C.O.J., 8 July 2010, *Susanne Bulicke* v. *Deutsche Büro Service GmbH*, C-246/09, www.curia.

principle of equal treatment to them, even after the relationship in which the discrimination is alleged to have occurred has ended.

They must also ensure that associations, organisations or other legal entities which have a legitimate interest in ensuring that the provisions of this directive are complied with may engage, either on behalf or in support of the complainant, with his or her approval, in any judicial and/or administrative procedure provided for the enforcement of the obligations.

Both are without prejudice to national rules relating to time limits for bringing actions as regards the principle of equality of treatment (Art. 9).

1449. The primary law of the EU and Article 9 of Council Directive 2000/78/EC must be interpreted as not precluding a national procedural rule under which a victim of discrimination in recruitment on grounds of age must make a claim against the perpetrator of that discrimination within two months in order to obtain compensation for pecuniary or non-pecuniary damage, provided:

– firstly, that that time-limit is not less favourable than that applicable to similar domestic actions in employment law,
– secondly, that the fixing of the point from which that time-limit starts to run does not render practically impossible or excessively difficult the exercise of rights conferred by the Directive.
– It is for the national court to ascertain whether those two conditions are met.[535]

B. Burden of Proof

1450. Member States must take such measures as are necessary to ensure that when persons who consider themselves wronged because the principle of equal treatment has not been applied to them establish, before a court or other competent authority, facts from which it may be presumed that there has been direct or indirect discrimination, it shall be for the respondent to prove that there has been no breach of the principle of equal treatment.

This does not prevent Member States from introducing rules of evidence which are more favourable to plaintiffs and does not apply to criminal procedures (Article 10).

1451. European legislation does not entitle a worker who has a plausible claim that he meets the requirements listed in a job advertisement and whose application was rejected to have access to information indicating whether the employer engaged another applicant at the end of the recruitment process. However, the refusal to grant any access to information may be one of the factors to take into account when establishing facts from which it may be presumed that there has been discrimination.

EU law prohibits discrimination on the grounds of sex, age and ethnic origin *inter alia* in recruitment procedures. Where a person considers himself wronged because the principle of equal treatment has not been applied to him, he must

---

535. C.O.J., 8 July 2010, *Susanne Bulicke v. Deutsche Büro Service GmbH*, C-246/09, www.curia.

establish, before a court or other competent authority, facts from which it may be presumed that there has been discrimination. It is then for the opposing party to prove that there has been no infringement of that principle. Member States must take such measures as are necessary, in accordance with their national judicial systems, to ensure the application of that principle.

1452. Ms Meister, a Russian national, was born in 1961. She holds a Russian degree in 'systems' engineering, which has been recognised in German as equivalent to a German degree awarded by a university of applied science.

The company Speech Design published two advertisements successively, with a similar content, to recruit an 'experienced software developer'. Ms Meister responded to those two advertisements by applying for the post. Her successive applications were rejected, without her being invited to interview and without the company telling her on what grounds her applications were unsuccessful. Being of the view that she fulfilled the requirements of the post, she considered that she suffered less favourable treatment than another person in a comparable situation on the grounds of her sex, age and ethnic origin. She brought an action before the German courts seeking, first, compensation from that company for employment discrimination and, secondly, the production of the file for the person who was engaged, which would enable her to prove that she was more qualified than that person.

1453. The *Bundesarbeitsgericht* (Federal Labour Court), to which the case was referred, asks the Court of Justice, in essence, whether EU law entitles a worker – who has a plausible claim that he meets the requirements listed in a job advertisement, but whose application was rejected – to have access to information indicating whether the employer engaged another candidate and if so, on the basis of what criteria. Moreover, the Court asks whether the fact that the employer does not disclose the requested information gives rise to a presumption that the discrimination alleged by the worker exists.

1454. The Court recalls, first, that it is the person who considers himself to have been wronged because the principle of equal treatment has not been applied who must initially establish the facts from which it may be presumed that there has been discrimination. It is only where that person has established those facts that the defendant must then prove that there has been no breach of the principle of non-discrimination. As the Court has already held, the assessment of the facts from which it may be presumed that there has been discrimination is a matter for national judicial bodies, in accordance with national law or practice.

The Court then confirms its case-law according to which EU law does not specifically entitle persons who consider themselves to be the victim of discrimination to information in order that they may establish facts from which it may be presumed that there has been discrimination. It is not, however, inconceivable that a refusal of disclosure by the defendant, in the context of establishing such facts, is liable to compromise the achievements of the objective pursued by that directive and, in particular to deprive that provision of its effectiveness.

1455. The Court considers that that case-law applies to the present case since, despite legislative developments, the EU legislator did not intend to amend the rules on the burden of proof. Therefore, it is for the German court to ensure that the refusal of disclosure by Speech Design is not liable to compromise the achievement of the objectives pursued by EU law. It must in particular take account of all the circumstances of the dispute in order to determine whether there is sufficient evidence for a finding that the facts from which it may be presumed that there has been such discrimination have been established. In that regard, the Court recalls that national law or the national practices of the Member States may provide that discrimination may be established by any means, including on the basis of statistical evidence.

Among the facts which may be taken into account is, in particular, the fact that Speech Design seems to have refused Ms Meister any access to the information which she seeks to have disclosed. Moreover, account can also be taken of the fact that the employer does not dispute that Ms Meister's level of expertise matches that referred to in the job advertisement and that, notwithstanding this, Speech Design did not invite her to a job interview after the publication of the two vacancy notices.

1456. The Court concludes that EU law must be interpreted as not entitling a worker who as a plausible claim that he meets the requirements listed in a job advertisement and whose application was rejected to have access to information indicating whether the employer engaged another candidate at the end of the recruitment process.

However, it cannot be ruled out that a refusal to grant any access to information may be one of the factors to take into account in the context of establishing facts from which it may be presumed that there has been direct or indirect discrimination. It is for the referring court to determine whether that is the case in the proceedings in question, taking into account all the circumstances of the case before it.[536]

1457. In a case on sexual orientation the European Court[537] ruled that homophobic statements by a patron of a professional football club may shift the burden of proof on to the club to prove that it does not have a discriminatory recruitment policy and that the appearance of discrimination on ground of sexual orientation may be refuted by a body of consistent evidence.

The directive on equal treatment in employment and occupation lays down a general framework for combating discrimination. Pursuant to that directive, where facts from which it may be presumed that there has been discrimination are established before a court or another competent authority, the burden of proof shifts to the defendants concerned who must prove that, notwithstanding the appearance of discrimination, there has been no breach of the principle of equal treatment.

---

536. C.O.J., 19 April 2012, *Galina Meister v. Speech Design Carrier Systems GmbH*, C-415/10, www.curia.eu.
537. C.O.J., 25 April 2013, *Asociaţia ACCEPT v. Consiliul Naţional pentru Combaterea Discriminării*, C-81/12, www.curia.eu.

Part I, Ch. 6, Equal Treatment

1458. On 3 March 2010, Accept, a non-governmental organisation whose aim is to promote and protect lesbian, gay, bisexual and transsexual rights in Romania, lodged a complaint before the National Council for Combatting Discrimination (CNCD) against SC Fotbal Club Steaua Bucureşti SA ('FC Steaua') and Mr Becali, who presents himself as being the 'patron' of that club. Accept claims that the principle of equal treatment was breached in recruitment matters. In an interview concerning the possible transfer of a professional footballer, Mr Becali had stated essentially that he would never hire a homosexual player. As regards the other defendant before the CNCD, FC Steaua, Accept maintains that the club has at no time distanced itself from Mr Becali's statements. The CNCD held, in particular, that since Mr Becali's statements could not be regarded as emanating from an employer or a person responsible for recruitment, those circumstances did not fall within the sphere of employment. However, the CNCD took the view that those statements constituted discrimination in the form of harassment and gave Mr Becali a warning.

1459. In its judgment, the Court observes that the directive applies to situations such as those on which the dispute which involve statements concerning the conditions for access to employment, including recruitment conditions. The Court states that the specificities of the recruitment of professional footballers are irrelevant in that regard because sport constitutes an economic activity which is covered by EU law.

As regards the position of FC Steaua in the case in the main proceedings, the Court points out that the mere fact that statements such as Mr Becali's do not come directly from a given defendant is not necessarily a bar to establishing, with respect to that defendant, the existence of 'facts from which it may be presumed that there has been ... discrimination' within the meaning of the directive. Consequently, a defendant employer cannot deny the existence of facts from which it may be presumed that it has a discriminatory recruitment policy by asserting that the statements indicative of a homophobic recruitment policy come from a person who, while claiming to play an important role in the management of that employer and appearing to do so, is not legally capable of binding it in recruitment matters. According to the Court, the fact that that employer might not have clearly distanced itself from those statements may be taken into account in the appraisal of its recruitment policy.

1460. Furthermore, the Court states that the burden of proof, as modified by the directive, does not require evidence which is impossible to adduce without interfering with the right to privacy. The appearance of discrimination on grounds of sexual orientation may be refuted with a body of consistent evidence, without the defendant having to prove that persons with a specific sexual orientation have been recruited in the past. That evidence may include, in particular, distancing itself from discriminatory public statements and the existence of express provisions in its recruitment policy aimed at ensuring compliance with the principle of equal treatment.

1461. Finally, the Court observes that the directive precludes national rules by virtue of which, where there is a finding of discrimination on grounds of sexual orientation, it is only possible to give a 'warning' after the expiry of six months from the date on which the facts occurred, if that penalty is not effective, proportionate and dissuasive. However, it is for the Romanian court to determine if that is the situation in the present case.

C. *Victimisation*

1462. Member States must introduce such measures as are necessary to protect employees against dismissal or other adverse treatment by the employer as a reaction to a complaint within the undertaking or to any legal proceedings aimed at enforcing compliance with the principle of equal treatment (Art. 11).

D. *Dissemination of Information*

1463. Member States must take care that the provisions adopted pursuant to this directive, together with the relevant provisions already in force in this field, are brought to the attention of the persons concerned by all appropriate means, for example at the workplace, throughout their territory (Art. 2).

E. *Social Dialogue*

1464. Member States must take adequate measures to promote dialogue between the social partners with a view to fostering equal treatment, including through the monitoring of workplace practices, collective agreements, codes of conduct and through research or exchange of experiences and good practices.

They have also to encourage the social partners, without prejudice to their autonomy, to conclude at the appropriate level agreements laying down antidiscrimination rules in the employment field which fall within the scope of collective bargaining. These agreements shall respect the minimum requirements laid down by this directive and by the relevant national implementing measures.

F. *Dialogue with Non-governmental Organisations*

1465. Member States shall encourage dialogue with appropriate nongovernmental organisations which have a legitimate interest in contributing to the fight against discrimination with a view to promoting the principle of equal treatment (Art. 14).

III. Final Provisions

A. *Compliance*

1466. Member States have to take the necessary measures to ensure that:

(a) any laws, regulations and administrative provisions contrary to the principle of equal treatment are abolished;
(b) any provisions contrary to the principle of equal treatment which are included in contracts or collective agreements, internal rules of undertakings or rules governing the independent occupations and professions and workers' and employers' organisations are, or may be, declared null and void or are amended (Art. 16).

B. *Sanctions*

1467. Member States have to lay down the rules on sanctions applicable to infringements of the national provisions adopted pursuant to this directive and shall take all measures necessary to ensure that they are applied. The sanctions, which may comprise the payment of compensation to the victim, must be effective, proportionate and dissuasive. Member States shall notify those provisions to the Commission by 2 December 2003 at the latest and have to notify it without delay of any subsequent amendment affecting them (Art. 17).

C. *Implementation*

1468. Member States have to implement the directive by 2 December 2003 at the latest or may entrust the social partners, at their joint request, with the implementation of this directive as regards provisions concerning collective agreements. In such cases, in order to take account of particular conditions, Member States may, if necessary, have an additional period of three years from 2 December 2003, that is to say a total of six years, to implement the provisions of this directive on age and disability discrimination. In that event they have to inform the Commission forthwith.

When Member States adopt these measures, they shall contain a reference to this Directive or be accompanied by such reference on the occasion of their official publication. The methods of making such reference shall be laid down by Member States (Art. 18).

D. *Report*

1469. Member States have to communicate to the Commission, by 2 December 2005 at the latest and every five years thereafter, all the information necessary for the Commission to draw up a report to the European Parliament and the Council on the application of this directive.

The Commission's report shall take into account, as appropriate, the viewpoints of the social partners and relevant non-governmental organisations. In accordance with the principle of gender mainstreaming, this report shall, *inter alia*, provide an assessment of the impact of the measures taken on women and men. In the light of the information received, this report shall include, if necessary, proposals to revise and update this directive (Art. 19).

§2. EQUAL TREATMENT BETWEEN PERSONS IRRESPECTIVE OF RACIAL OR ETHNIC ORIGIN

1470. Council Directive 2000/43/EC of 29 June 2000 implements the principle of equal treatment between persons irrespective of racial or ethnic origin. The directive comprises four chapters: general provisions, remedies and enforcement, bodies for the promotion of equal treatment and final provisions.

I. General Provisions

A. Purpose

1471. The purpose of the directive is to lay down a framework for combating discrimination on the grounds of racial or ethnic origin, with a view to putting into effect in the Member States the principle of equal treatment.

B. Definitions and Concepts of Discrimination

1472. The principle of equal treatment means that there is no direct or indirect discrimination based on racial or ethnic origin.

Direct discrimination occurs where one person is treated less favourably than another is, has been or would be treated in a comparable situation on grounds of racial or ethnic origin.

Indirect discrimination occurs where an apparently neutral provision, criterion or practice would put persons of a racial or ethnic origin at a particular disadvantage compared with other persons, unless that provision, criterion or practice is objectively justified by a legitimate aim and the means of achieving that aim are appropriate and necessary.

Harassment is discrimination when an unwanted conduct related to racial or ethnic origin takes place with the purpose or effect of violating the dignity of a person and of creating an intimidating, hostile, degrading, humiliating or offensive environment. In this context, the concept of harassment may be defined in accordance with the national laws and practice of the Member States.

An instruction to discriminate constitutes discrimination (Art. 2).

1473. Belgian legislation allows the Centre for equal opportunities and combating racism, a body charged with the task of promoting equal treatment in Belgium, to bring legal proceedings where discrimination exists or could exist, even in the absence of an identifiable complainant.

Feryn is a company specialising in the installation of garage doors. The Centre brought an action before the Belgian labour courts seeking a declaration that Feryn had applied a discriminatory recruitment policy. It relies on the public statements made by a director of that company in which he stated, in essence, that his company was seeking to recruit installers but it could not take on employees of a particular ethnic origin ('immigrants') owing to the reluctance of its customers to give such persons access to their homes during the installation work.

In essence the question before the Court of Justice is whether such statements made by an employer in the context of a recruitment process constitute discrimination if there is no identifiable complainant who considers himself to be the victim of it.

The Court, pointing to the objective of the Directive, considers that the absence of an identifiable complainant does not permit the conclusion that there is no direct discrimination within the meaning of the Directive. The promotion of a labour market that is favourable to social inclusion would be difficult to achieve if it were limited solely to cases in which an unsuccessful candidate for a post brought legal proceedings against an employer on the basis of discrimination. Furthermore, such statements are likely to strongly dissuade some applicants from applying for the post. They thus constitute direct discrimination in respect of recruitment within the meaning of the directive.[538]

C. Scope

1474. The directive applies to all persons, as regards both the public and private sectors, including public bodies, in relation to:

(a) conditions for access to employment, to self-employment and to occupation, including selection criteria and recruitment conditions, whatever the branch of activity and at all levels of the professional hierarchy, including promotion;
(b) access to all types and to all levels of vocational guidance, vocational training, advanced vocational training and retraining, including practical work experience;
(c) employment and working conditions, including dismissals and pay;
(d) membership of and involvement in an organisation of workers or employers, or any organisation whose members carry on a particular profession, including the benefits provided for by such organisations;
(e) social protection, including social security and healthcare;
(f) social advantages;
(g) education;

---

538. C.O.J., 10 July 2008, *Centrum voor gelijkheid van kansen en voor racismebestrijding* v. *Firma Feryn NV*, C-54/07, ECR, 2008, 5187.

(h) access to and supply of goods and services which are available to the public, including housing.

The directive does not cover difference of treatment based on nationality and is without prejudice to provisions and conditions relating to the entry into and residence of third-country nationals and stateless persons on the territory of Member States, and to any treatment which arises from the legal status of the third-country nationals and stateless persons concerned (Art. 3).

D. Genuine and Determining Occupational Requirements

1475. Member States may provide that a difference of treatment which is based on a characteristic related to racial or ethnic origin shall not constitute discrimination where, by reason of the nature of the particular occupational activities concerned or of the context in which they are carried out, such a characteristic constitutes a genuine and determining occupational requirement, provided that the objective is legitimate and the requirement is proportionate (Art. 4).

E. Positive Action

1476. Member States are allowed to maintain or adopt specific measures to prevent or compensate for disadvantages linked to racial or ethnic origin (Art. 5).

F. Minimum Requirements

1477. Member States may introduce or maintain provisions which are more favourable to the protection of the principle of equal treatment than those laid down in the directive.

The implementation of this directive can under no circumstances constitute grounds for a reduction in the level of protection against discrimination already afforded by Member States (Article 6).

II. Remedies and Enforcement

A. Defence of Rights

1478. Member States have to ensure that judicial and/or administrative procedures are available to all persons who consider themselves wronged by failure to apply the principle of equal treatment to them, even after the relationship in which the discrimination is alleged to have occurred has ended.

They have to ensure that associations, organisations or other legal entities which have a legitimate interest in ensuring that these provisions are complied with may engage, either on behalf or in support of the complainant, with his or her approval, in any judicial and/or administrative procedure.

This is without prejudice to national rules relating to time limits for bringing actions as regards the principle of equality of treatment (Art. 7).

B. *Burden of Proof and Victimisation and Dissemination of Information and Social Dialogue and Dialogue with Non-governmental Organisations*

1479. The directive (Articles 8–12) provides similar protection as under Directive 2000/78 (*see above*).

The Court ruled on the question of the reversal of the burden of proof in a situation in which the existence of a discriminatory recruitment policy is alleged by reference to statements made publicly by an employer with regard to its recruitment policy. The Court states that it is for the employer to prove that he has not infringed the principle of equal treatment. It is then for the national court to ascertain whether the facts alleged are established and to assess the sufficiency of the evidence put forward to support the employer's claims that it has not infringed the principle of equal treatment. The Court goes on to state that public statements by which an employer lets it be known that under its recruitment policy he will not recruit any employees of a certain ethnic or racial origin are sufficient for the purposes of the directive to give rise to a presumption of the existence of a recruitment policy which is directly discriminatory.[539]

III. Bodies for the Promotion of Equal Treatment

1480. Member States have to designate a body or bodies for the promotion of equal treatment of all persons without discrimination on the grounds of racial or ethnic origin. These bodies may form part of agencies charged at national level with the defence of human rights or the safeguard of individuals' rights.

They must ensure that the competences of these bodies include:

- without prejudice to the right of victims and of associations, organisations or other legal entities, providing independent assistance to victims of discrimination in pursuing their complaints about discrimination;
- conducting independent surveys concerning discrimination;
- publishing independent reports and making recommendations on any issue relating to such discrimination (Art. 13).

---

539. C.O.J., 10 July 2008, *Centrum voor gelijkheid van kansen en voor racismebestrijding* v. *Firma Feryn NV*, C-54/07, ECR, 2008, 5187.

IV. Final Provisions: Compliance and Sanctions and Implementation and Report

1481. The directive (Articles 14–18) provides similar protection as under Directive 2000/78 (*see above*).

The Court ruled on the question of what sanctions are appropriate for recruitment discrimination of the kind at issue. The directive requires that the Member States provide effective, proportionate and dissuasive sanctions, even where there is no identifiable victim. The Court states that they may consist, in particular, in a finding of discrimination by the national court in conjunction with an adequate level of publicity, in an order that the employer ceases the discriminatory practice, or in an award of damages to the body bringing the proceedings.[540]

§3. EQUAL PAY FOR MEN AND WOMEN

I. In General

1482. Contrary to Articles 151, 152 and 153 TFEU, which are limited to fixing in social matters the general objectives for an approximation of the laws and cooperation between Member States, Article 157 TFEU creates an obligation for the Member States to realise equal pay for men and women for work of equal value.[541]

Article 157, which was the outcome of a French initiative, has a double objective:

– a social objective: to lay down the principle of equal treatment, which was already embodied in Convention No. 100 of the ILO, into Union law;
– an economic objective: 'for in creating an obstacle to any attempt at "social dumping" by means of the use of female labour less well paid than male labour, it helped to achieve one of the fundamental objectives of the common market, the establishment of a system of ensuring that competition is not distorted'.[542]

1483. Article 157 is part of the social objectives of the Union aimed at social progress, as laid down in the preamble preceding the Treaty. The Court has repeatedly stated that the respect for fundamental personal human rights is one of the general principles of Union law, the observance of which it has a duty to ensure. There can be no doubt that the elimination of discrimination based on sex forms part of those fundamental rights.[543] It is part of the foundation of the Union. In particular, since Article 157 appears in the context of the harmonisation of working conditions while improvement is being maintained, the objection that the terms of this article

---

540. C.O.J., 10 July 2008, *Centrum voor gelijkheid van kansen en voor racismebestrijding* v. *Firma Feryn NV*, C-54/07, ECR, 2008, 5187.
541. Adv. Gen. Dutheillet de Lamothe, C.O.J., 25 May 1971, *G. Defrenne* v. *Belgium*, No. 80/70, ECR, 1981, 229.
542. C.O.J., 15 May 1986, *M. Johnston* v. *Chief Constable of the Royal Ulster Constabulary*, No. 222/84, ECR, 1986, 1651.
543. 15 June 1978, *G. Defrenne* v. *Sabena*, No. 149/77, ECR, 1978, 1365.

may be observed in no other way than by raising the lowest salaries must be set aside.[544] It is clear that Article 157 and the directives, form one body of rules that are complementary to each other and fortify each other.

1484. Article 157 and the directives have a general scope of application, which follows from the nature of the principle of equal treatment, and thus apply to the private sector as well as to the public sector,[545] and to the self-employed.[546]

II. Man and Woman; Sexual Orientation

1485. Article 157 TFEU prohibits discrimination between man and woman. This is not so clear as it seems at first sight.

The principle of equal treatment applies to transsexuals, in case of a worker's gender reassignment.[547] The Court of Justice considered that such discrimination was in fact based, essentially if not exclusively, on the sex of the person concerned. That reasoning, which leads to the conclusion that such discrimination is to be prohibited just as is discrimination based on the fact that a person belongs to a particular sex, is limited to the case of a worker's gender reassignment and does not therefore apply to differences of treatment based on a person's sexual orientation.

In *Grant* v. *South West Trains Ltd*,[548] the essential point raised was whether an employer's refusal to grant travel concessions to the person of the same sex with whom an employee has a stable relationship is prohibited by Article 157 TFEU and Directive 75/117, where such concessions are granted to an employee's spouse or the person of the opposite sex with whom an employee has a stable relationship outside marriage.

The refusal to allow Ms. Grant the concessions was based on the fact that she does not satisfy the conditions prescribed in those regulations, more particularly on the fact that she does not live with a 'spouse' or a person of the opposite sex with whom she has had a 'meaningful' relationship for at least two years. Thus the travel concessions were refused to a female worker as she was living with a person of the same sex.

The Court ruled that since the condition imposed by the undertaking's regulations applies in the same way to female as male workers, it cannot be regarded as constituting discrimination directly based on sex.

The Court had also to consider whether persons who have a stable relationship with a partner of the same sex are in the same situation as those who are married or have a stable relationship with a partner of the opposite sex. It was of the opinion that it is the case that the Community has not yet adopted rules providing for such equivalence.

---

544. C.O.J., *G. Defrenne* v. *Sabena*, 8 April 1976, No. 43/75, ECR, 1976, 455.
545. C.O.J., *G. Defrenne* v. *Sabena*, 8 April 1976, No. 43/75, IELL, *Case Law*, No. 22. ECJ, *Hellen Gester* v. *Freistaat Bayern*, 2 October 1997, C-1/95, ECR, 1997, 5253.
546. C.O.J., 8 November 1983, *Commission* v. *U.K. of Great Britain and Northern Ireland*, No. 165/82, ECR, 1983, 3431.
547. C.O.J., 30 April 1996, *P. and S. and Cornwall County Council*, C-13/94, ECR, 1996, 2143.
548. C.O.J., 17 February 1998, *L.J. Grant/South West Trains Ltd*, C-249/96, ECR, 1998, 621.

It follows that in the then state of the law within the Community, stable relationships between two persons of the same sex are not regarded as equivalent to marriages or stable relationships outside marriage between persons of the opposite sex. Consequently, an employer is not required by Community law to treat the situation of a person who has a stable relationship with a partner of the same sex as equivalent to that of a person who is married to or has a stable relationship outside marriage with a partner of the opposite sex.

It should, however, be considered that Article 19 TFEU allows the Council to take appropriate action to eliminate various forms of discrimination, including discrimination based on sexual orientation.

1486. The European Court of Justice ruled (2004)[549] that national legislation which denies transsexuals the right to marry is contrary to Union law if the effect of this is to deprive them of any entitlement to a survivor's pension.

In this case the Court heard that 'KB' had worked for the UK National Health Service (NHS) as a nurse for 20 years. During that time, she had contributed to the NHS pension scheme, which provides for a survivor's pension to be payable to the surviving spouse (taken to mean the person to whom the scheme member is married).

KB has shared a relationship for many years with 'R', who had undergone female-to-male gender reassignment surgery. KB wished R to have the right to the widower's pension under the NHS scheme. However, UK legislation prevents transsexuals from marrying in their acquired sex and deems void any marriage to which the parties are not male and female. Therefore, contrary to their wishes, KB and R have not been able to marry and R is thus prevented from receiving a survivor's pension.

1487. KB took a case to the UK courts, claiming that she was a victim of discrimination on grounds of sex in relation to pay. She argued that the term 'widower' must be interpreted as also encompassing the surviving member of a couple, who would have acquired the status of a widower, had his gender not resulted from surgical gender reassignment. The UK court of appeal referred the case to the Court.

The Court found that a survivor's pension paid under an occupational scheme falls within the scope of the TFEU's provisions prohibiting all discrimination on grounds of sex in relation to pay. It also found that the decision to restrict certain benefits to married couples cannot, of itself, be regarded as prohibited by Union law as discriminatory on grounds of sex as, for the purpose of awarding the survivor's pension, it is irrelevant whether the claimant is a man or a woman.

However, the Court found that there is inequality of treatment which, although it does not directly undermine a right enshrined in Union law, affects one of the conditions for the granting of that right. Here, the inequality of treatment relates to the capacity to marry, where marriage is a necessary precondition for the award of a widower's pension. The fact that the couple in this case are not able to marry arises from UK law on marriage and birth certificates.

---

549. C.O.J., 7 January 2004, *K.B.* v. *National Health Service Pensions Agency and Secretary of State for Health*, C-117/01, ECR, 2004, 541.

Part I, Ch. 6, Equal Treatment

1488. Thus, the Court ruled that the UK legislation in question must be regarded as being, in principle, incompatible with Union law. However, as it is for the Member States to determine the conditions under which legal recognition is given to changes of gender, the Court referred the case back to the national courts to determine whether a person in this situation can rely on Union law to nominate their partner as the beneficiary of a survivor's pension.[550]

In this the Court ruled that:

> Article 157 TFEU, in principle, precludes legislation, such as that at issue before the national court, which, in breach of the European Convention for the Protection of Human Rights and Fundamental Freedoms, signed in Rome on 4 November 1950, prevents a couple such as K.B. and R. from fulfilling the marriage requirement which must be met for one of them to be able to benefit from part of the pay of the other. It is for the national court to determine whether in a case such as that in the main proceedings a person in K.B.'s situation can rely on Article 157 TFEU in order to gain recognition of her right to nominate her partner as the beneficiary of a survivor's pension.

1489. The Court decided that the refusal to grant a pension to a male-to-female transsexual at the same age as a women is contrary to Union law. Such a refusal constitutes discrimination contrary to a Union directive on equal treatment in the field of social security.[551]

Under UK law prior to April 2005, the sex of a person under the rules applicable to social security is that stated on his or her birth certificate. A birth certificate can be changed only to rectify clerical or factual errors. As a result, transsexuals who have undergone gender reassignment surgery cannot change the sex on their birth certificate.

The Gender Recognition Act 2004, which came into force on 4 April 2005, allows for the issue of gender recognition certificates to transsexuals under certain conditions. The issue of a gender recognition certificate changes the sex of the person concerned for most official purposes but has no retroactive effect.

In the UK men are entitled to a retirement pension at the age of 65 and women at the age of 60.

1490. Sarah Margaret Richards was registered as male at the time of her birth in 1942. Having been diagnosed with gender dysphoria, she underwent gender reassignment surgery in May 2001. In February 2002 she applied for a retirement pension to be paid from her 60th birthday.

Her application was refused by the Secretary of State for Work and Pensions on the ground that it had been made more than four months before the applicant's 65th birthday. Ms Richards appealed against that decision and the Social Security Commissioner, hearing the case on appeal from the Social Security Appeal Tribunal, has

---

550. 'ECJ rules on occupational pensions for transsexuals', www.eiro.eurofound.ie, 2004.
551. C.O.J., 27 April 2006, *Sarah Margaret Richards v. Secretary of State for Work and Pensions*, C-423/04, ECR, 2006, 3585.

asked the Court of Justice whether such a refusal is contrary to the Union directive on equal treatment in the field of social security.

1491. First of all, the Court observes that the right not to be discriminated against on grounds of sex is one of the fundamental human rights the observance of which the Court has a duty to ensure. The scope of Directive 79/7 cannot thus be confined simply to discrimination based on the fact that a person is of one or other sex. The directive is also intended to apply to discrimination arising from the gender reassignment of the person concerned.

Secondly, the Court finds that the unequal treatment in this case is based on Ms Richards' inability to have the new gender which she acquired following surgery recognised. Unlike women whose gender is not the result of such surgery and who may receive a retirement pension at the age of 60, Ms Richards is not able to fulfil one of the conditions of eligibility for that pension, in this case that relating to retirement age. As it arises from her gender reassignment, that unequal treatment must thus be regarded as discrimination which is prohibited by Directive 79/7.

The Court rejects the United Kingdom's argument that those circumstances are covered by a derogation from the Directive permitting a Member State to prescribe different pensionable ages for men and women. It finds that that derogation, which must be interpreted strictly, does not cover the matter at issue in this case.

1492. In those circumstances, the Court finds that Directive 79/7 precludes legislation which denies a person who has undergone male-to-female gender reassignment entitlement to a pension on the ground that she has not reached the age of 65, when she would have been entitled to such a pension at the age of 60 had she been held to be a woman as a matter of national law.

1493. A supplementary retirement pension paid to a partner in a civil partnership, which is lower than that granted in a marriage, may, the European Court ruled,[552] constitute discrimination on grounds of *sexual orientation.*

This is the case if the partnership is reserved to persons of the same gender and if it is in a legal and factual situation comparable to that of marriage

1494. Jürgen Römer worked for the City of Hamburg, Germany as an administrative employee from 1950 until he became incapacitated for work on 31 May 1990. From 1969, he lived continuously with his companion, Mr U, with whom he entered into a civil partnership in accordance with the German Law of 16 February 2001 on registered life partnerships. Mr Römer informed his former employer of this by letter of 16 October 2001.

He subsequently requested a recalculation of the amount of his supplementary retirement pension on the basis of the more favourable tax category applicable to married pensioners. The City of Hamburg refused to apply the more favourable tax category in order to calculate the amount of his supplementary retirement pension,

---

552. C.O.J., 10 May 2011, *Jürgen Römer v. Freie und Hansestadt Hamburg*, C-147/08, www.curia.

Part I, Ch. 6, Equal Treatment 1495–1497

on the ground that only married, not permanently separated, pensioners and pensioners entitled to claim child benefit or an equivalent benefit are entitled to that advantage.

1495. Since Mr Römer took the view that he is entitled to be treated as a married, not permanently separated, pensioner for the calculation of his pension and that that right results from Directive 2000/78/EC establishing a general framework for equal treatment in employment and occupation, he brought a case before the Labour Court of Hamburg, Germany. That Court has referred questions to the Court of Justice concerning the interpretation of the general principles and provisions of European Union law on discrimination on grounds of sexual orientation in employment and occupation.

In its judgment the Court of Justice first notes that supplementary retirement pensions – such at that at issue in this case – fall within the scope of Directive 2000/78.

1496. Next, the Court recalls, first, that a finding of discrimination on the grounds of sexual orientation requires that the situations in question be comparable in a specific and concrete manner in the light of the benefit concerned.

The Court points out in that regard that the German Law on registered life partnerships established, for persons of the same gender, life partnership, having chosen not to permit those persons to enter into marriage, which remains solely open to persons of different gender. According to the referring court, following the gradual harmonisation of the regime of registered life partnership with that of marriage, there is no longer, in the German legal system, any significant legal difference between those two types of status of persons. The main remaining difference is the fact that marriage presupposes that the spouses are of different gender, whereas registered life partnership presupposes that the partners are of the same gender.

1497. In the case, entitlement to the supplementary retirement pension presupposes not only that the partner is married, but also that he is not permanently separated from his spouse, since that pension aims to provide a replacement income to benefit the recipient and, indirectly, the persons who live with him. In that regard, the Court emphasises that the German law on registered life partnerships provides that life partners have duties towards each other to support and care for one another and to contribute adequately to the common needs of the partnership by their work and from their property, as is the case between spouses during their life together. Therefore, according to the Court, the same obligations are incumbent on both registered life partners and married spouses. It follows that the two situations are thus comparable.

Second, the Court observes that as regards the criterion of less favourable treatment on the grounds of sexual orientation, it is apparent that Mr Römer's pension would have been increased if he had married instead of entering into a registered life partnership with a man. In addition, the increased benefit is not linked to the income of the parties to the union, to the existence of children or to other factors such as those relating to the spouse's financial needs. In addition, the Court notes that the contributions payable by Mr Römer in relation to his pension were wholly unaffected by his marital status, since he was required to contribute to the pension costs by paying a contribution equal to that of his married colleagues.

1498. Finally, as regards the effects of discrimination on the ground of sexual orientation, the Court indicates, first, that by reason of the primacy of European Union law, the right to equal treatment can be claimed by an individual against a local authority and it is not necessary to wait for that provision to be made consistent with that law by the national legislature. Second, the Court indicates that the right to equal treatment can be claimed by an individual only after the time-limit for transposing the Directive, namely from 3 December 2003.

§4. DEFINITION

1499. The notion 'equal treatment' is defined differently in the various Union instruments. In the 1975 directive, equal treatment is defined as 'the elimination of all discrimination on grounds of sex' (Article 1). The 1976 directive provides the following definitions:

- direct discrimination: where one person is treated less favourably on grounds of sex than another is, has been or would be treated in a comparable situation;
- indirect discrimination: where an apparently neutral provision, criterion or practice would put persons of one sex at a particular disadvantage compared with persons of the other sex, unless that provision, criterion or practice is objectively justified by a legitimate aim, and the means of achieving that aim are appropriate and necessary;
- –harassment: where unwanted conduct related to the sex of a person occurs with the purpose or effect of violating the dignity of a person, and of creating an intimidating, hostile, degrading, humiliating or offensive environment (Article 2(2));
- sexual harassment: where any form of unwanted verbal, non-verbal or physical conduct of a sexual nature occurs, with the purpose or effect of violating the dignity of a person, in particular when creating an intimidating, hostile, degrading, humiliating or offensive environment.

1500. Harassment and sexual harassment within the meaning of the directive are deemed to be discrimination on the grounds of sex and therefore prohibited (Article 2(3)).

A person's rejection of, or submission to, such conduct may not be used as a basis for a decision affecting that person (Article 2(3)).

An instruction to discriminate against persons on grounds of sex shall be deemed to be discrimination within the meaning of the directive (Article 2(4)).

The directive covers all forms of distinction or unequal treatment. What is meant is 'objective' discrimination: the existence of discrimination does not require a specific intention to discriminate.

'The directive precludes provisions of domestic law, which make reparation of damage suffered as a result of discrimination on grounds of sex in the making of an appointment subject to the requirement of fault.'[553]

1501. The principle of equal pay for men and women must be interpreted as follows.[554]

- employees perform the same work or work to which equal value can be attributed if, taking account of a number of factors such as the nature of the work, the training requirements and the working conditions, those persons can be considered to be in a comparable situation, which it is a matter for the national court to ascertain;
- in relation to indirect pay discrimination, it is for the employer to establish objective justification for the difference in pay between the workers who consider that they have been discriminated against and the comparators;
- the employer's justification for the difference in pay, which is evidence of a *prima facie* case of gender discrimination, must relate to the comparators who, on account of the fact that their situation is described by valid statistics which cover enough individuals, do not illustrate purely fortuitous or short-term phenomena, and which, in general, appear to be significant, have been taken into account by the referring court in establishing that difference, and
- the interests of good industrial relations may be taken into consideration by the national court as one factor among others in its assessment of whether differences between the pay of two groups of workers are due to objective factors unrelated to any discrimination on grounds of sex and are compatible with the principle of proportionality.

I. Equality of Opportunity or of Outcome

1502. The question arises whether Union law aims at equality of opportunity (at the start) or at equality of outcome (at the finish). In the case of equal pay, equality of outcome is what is really meant. This is, however, not so for all provisions of the directive of 1976. It provides for 'equal opportunity' regarding access to employment,[555] including promotion; no actual job is thus guaranteed. In the case, however, of working conditions, including dismissal, equality of outcome is meant.

---

553. C.O.J., 22 April 1997, *Nils Draehmpaehl* v. *Urania Immobilienreserve OHG*, C-180/95, ECR, 1997, 2195.
554. C.O.J., 28 February 2013, *Margaret Kenny a.o.* v. *Minister for Justice, Equality and Law Reform*, C-427/11, www.curia.eu.
555. C.O.J., 10 April 1983, *Colson and Kamann*, No. 14/83, ECR, 1983, 1891.

II. Direct and Indirect Discrimination

1503. Union law prohibits direct and indirect discrimination: direct on grounds of sex, indirect when other criteria are used, which are *prima facie* objective and acceptable, but *de facto* lead to a discriminatory treatment of one sex. This we find expressed in Article 2(2) of the amended 1976 directive regarding equal treatment: '... indirect discrimination: where an apparently neutral provision, criterion or practice would put persons of one sex at a particular disadvantage compared with persons of the other sex, unless that provision, criterion or practice is objectively justified by a legitimate aim, and the means of achieving that aim are appropriate and necessary.'

1504. A similar definition can be found in the directive of 15 December 1997 'indirect discrimination shall exist where an apparently neutral provision, criterion or practice disadvantages a substantially higher proportion of the members of one sex unless that provision, criterion or practice is appropriate and necessary and can be justified by objective factors unrelated to sex' (Article 2(2)). This applies in the case of Article 157 as well as for the 1975 directive on equal pay. In *Jeanette Jenkins* v. *Kingsgate* the Court ruled in that sense in relation of part-time work. Ms. Jenkins was a female part-time employee who received an hourly rate that was 10 per cent lower than the hourly rate of pay for full-time work. The Court ruled that a difference in pay between full-time and part-time workers does not amount to discrimination as prohibited by Article 157 of the Treaty unless it is in reality merely an indirect way of reducing the pay of part-time workers on the ground that the group of workers is composed exclusively or predominantly of women.[556] The same problem was dealt with in *Karin von Weber Hartz* v. *Bilka-Kaufhaus* since part-time employees working for Bilka could obtain a pension under the company scheme only if they had worked full-time for at least 15 years over a total period of 20 years.[557] Again the Court ruled that Article 157 is infringed when part-time employees are excluded from its occupational pension scheme, where that exclusion affects a far greater number of women than men, unless the undertaking shows that the exclusion is based on objectively justified factors unrelated to any discrimination on grounds of sex.[558]

1505. This ruling was confirmed in *Helga Nimz* v. *Hamburg* which involved a dispute between Mrs. Nimz and her employer Hamburg Stadt over the latter's refusal, based on the provisions of a collective wage agreement entered into with

---

556. 31 March 1981, No. 96/80, ECR, 1981, 911. In this case, the employer explained that he paid part-time workers less in order to encourage them to become full-time. *See also* C.O.J., 13 July 1989, *Ingrid Rinner-Kühn* v. *FWW Spezial-Gebäude-reinigung GmbH & Co. KG*, No. 171/88, ECR, 1989, 2743.
557. C.O.J., 13 May 1986, No. 170/84, IELL, *Case Law*, No. 93; *see also* C.O.J., 27 June 1990, *M. Kowalska* v. *Freie und Hansestadt Hamburg*, No. C-33/89, temporary severance grant provided for by collective agreement only for part-time workers, ECR, 1990, 2591.
558. For a difference in pay in case of job-sharing, *see* C.O.J., 17 June 1998, *Kathleen Hill and Ann Stapleton* v. *the Revenue Commissioners and the Department of Finance*, C-243/95, ECR, 1998, 3739.

the national public service, to grant her passage to a higher salary bracket on the ground that Mrs. Nimz worked less than three-quarters of the normal working hours. The Court indicated that this constitutes discrimination unless the employer can prove that there are factors which depend for their objectivity in particular on the relationship between the nature of the duties performed and the experience afforded by the performance of those duties after a certain number of working hours have been worked.

In case of indirect discrimination in a provision of a collective agreement, the national court is required to disapply that provision, without requesting or awaiting its prior removal by collective negotiations or any other procedure and to apply the same arrangements as are applied to other employees.[559]

It is also unlawful for national legislation applicable to many more women than men to limit, on the basis of their individual timetables, the compensation that members of staff committees employed on a part-time basis are to receive from their employer – in the form of paid holidays or overtime pay – in respect of their participation in training courses relating to the activities of staff committees. The training courses concerned were organised within the full-time work timetable in force in an undertaking. They therefore exceeded the individual work timetables of the part-time employees. Nevertheless compensation for the part-time employees was restricted to overtime pay or paid holidays, in accordance only with their part-time timetable, while full-time employees were compensated for their participation in the same training courses on the basis of their full-time work timetable. Only objective factors unrelated to any discrimination on the basis of sex can justify such difference in treatment.[560]

1506. In *Stadt Lengerich* v. *Angelika Helmig*,[561] the Court ruled on overtime pay for part-time employees. The questions were raised in the course of proceedings between women working part-time and their employers. The women claimed that they were entitled to overtime supplements for hours worked in addition to their individual working hours at the same rate as that applicable for overtime worked by full-time employees in addition to normal working hours. Under the relevant collective agreements, full-time or part-time employees were entitled to overtime supplements only for time worked in addition to the ordinary working hours laid down by those agreements, but part-time employees were not entitled to the supplements for hours they worked over and above their individual working hours.

The applicants considered that the relevant provisions of the collective agreements discriminated against them in breach of Article 157 TFEU and the 1975 directive by restricting overtime supplements to overtime worked in excess of the normal working hours.

---

559. 7 February 1991, *Helga Nimz* v. *Freie und Hansestadt Hamburg*, C-184/89, ECR, 1991, 297.
560. C.O.J., 4 June 1992, *Arbeitswohlfart des Stadt Berlin e. V (AWSB)* v. *M. Bötel*, No. C-360/90, ECR, 1992, 3589.
561. 15 December 1994, Cases C-399/92, C-409/92, C-425/92, C-34/93, C-50/93 and C-78/93, ECR, 1994, 5727.

The Court raised the question

whether these provisions may constitute indirect discrimination incompatible with Article 157 of the Treaty. To that end it must be determined whether they establish different treatment for full-time and part-time employees and whether that difference affects considerably more women than men.

There is unequal treatment wherever the overall pay of full-time employees is higher than that of part-time employees for the same number of hours worked on the basis of an employment relationship.

In the circumstances considered, part-time employees do receive the same overall pay as full-time employees for the same number of hours worked. Part-time employees also receive the same overall pay as full-time employees if they work more than the normal working hours fixed by the collective agreements because on doing so they become entitled to overtime supplements.

Consequently, the provisions at issue do not give rise to different treatment as between part-time and full-time employees and there is therefore no discrimination incompatible with Article 157 of the Treaty and Article 1 of the Directive.

1507. In Germany, certain categories of civil servants can receive remuneration for overtime instead of extra leave. However, the hourly rate of pay for overtime is lower than the hourly rate of pay for hours worked in the course of normal working hours.

Ms. Voß[562] is a civil servant employed as a teacher by Land Berlin. Although she worked part-time, she gave additional classes between January and May 2000. The remuneration which she received for that period was lower than that received by a full-time teacher for the same number of hours worked. Ms. Voß unsuccessfully claimed remuneration equal to that received by full-time teachers.

The Court points out that the principle of equal pay precludes not only direct discrimination but also any unequal treatment through the application of criteria unrelated to sex where such unequal treatment affects considerably more women than men and cannot be justified by objective factors wholly unrelated to discrimination based on sex.

The Court finds that the lower hourly rate for overtime gives rise to a difference in treatment to the detriment of teachers working part-time because a lower hourly rate is applied to them for those teaching hours which are worked over and above their normal working hours, but which are not sufficient to bring the number of hours worked overall above the level of normal working hours for full-time teachers.

That difference in treatment could affect a considerably higher number of women than men. Accordingly, the Court points out that the national court must take into account all the teachers subject to the national legislation in question in order to determine whether that is so.

---

562. C.O.J., 6 December 2007, *Ursula Voß* v. *Land Berlin*, C-300/06, ECR, 2007, 10573.

Since the order for reference did not refer to objectively justified criteria wholly unrelated to sex discrimination, the Court calls on the national court to check that point.

The Court holds that the principle of equal pay for male and female workers is infringed if a part-time civil servant is paid less for hours which are worked over and above his normal working hours, but which are not sufficient to bring the number of hours worked overall above the level of normal working hours for full-time civil servants, where the resulting difference in treatment affects a considerably higher number of women than men and cannot be justified by objective factors wholly unrelated to discrimination based on sex.

Consequently, national legislation which leads part-time workers to be paid less than full-time workers for the same number of hours worked breaches the principle of equal pay where it affects a considerably higher percentage of women than men and is not objectively justified.

1508. Jennifer Meyers[563] and an Adjudication Officer (UK) had a disagreement concerning her right to deduct child-care costs from her gross income in order to obtain family credit. Family credit is an income-related benefit which is awarded in order to supplement the income of low-paid workers who have the care of a child.

Meyers, being a single parent, made an application for family credit in respect of herself and her daughter, then aged three. The application was rejected by the Adjudication Officer on the ground that her income, as calculated for the purposes of that benefit, was greater than the level conferring entitlement.

In her appeal to the Social Security Appeal Tribunal, Meyers submitted that the non-deduction of child-care costs for the purposes of calculating her net income discriminated against single parents, since it is much easier for couples to arrange their working hours so that any children can be looked after by one of them. As most single parents are women, it also constitutes indirect discrimination against women.

One of the conditions for the award of family credit is that the claimant should be engaged in remunerative work. The aim of the benefit is to ensure that families do not find themselves worse off in work than they would be if they were not working. It is therefore intended to keep poorly paid workers in employment. That being so, family credit is concerned with access to employment, as referred to in Article 3 of the directive.

Furthermore, it is not only the conditions obtaining before an employment relationship comes into being which are involved in the concept of access to employment. The prospect of receiving family credit if he accepts low-paid work encourages an unemployed worker to accept such work, with the result that the benefit is related to considerations governing access to employment.

That finding was not invalidated by the UK's arguments which sought to show that there was no link with an employment relationship. It is precisely the existence of an employment relationship which confers entitlement to the benefit, even though the worker is not the direct recipient of that benefit, as in the case of a woman who is married or cohabiting and is unemployed, but who receives the benefit by virtue of her husband's or partner's work.

---

563. C.O.J., 13 July 1995, Case C-116/94, ECR, 1995, 2131.

Furthermore, compliance with the fundamental principle of equal treatment presupposes that a benefit such as family credit, which is necessarily linked to an employment relationship, constitutes a working condition within the meaning of Article 5 of the directive. To confine the latter concept solely to those working conditions which are set out in the contract of employment or applied by the employer in respect of a worker's employment would remove situations directly covered by an employment relationship from the scope of the directive.

1509. Another interesting case related to compensation for attendance at training courses providing staff council members with the necessary knowledge for performing their functions.[564]

That question was raised in proceedings between Johanna Lewark, the plaintiff, and the Kuratorium, the defendant, concerning the latter's failure to compensate the plaintiff for the time spent on a training course which was necessary for the performance of her staff council functions but which took place outside her individual working hours.

The plaintiff was employed for 30.8 hours a week in the care unit. She was also on the local staff council, which consisted of three members.

The dialysis centre employed twenty-one employees in the care unit, seven men and fourteen women. Of the men, six worked full-time and one part-time. Of the women, four worked full-time and ten part-time. The plaintiff was the only member of the staff council to work part-time.

From 12 to 16 November 1990, the plaintiff, on the basis of a decision of the staff council and with the defendant's consent, attended a full-time training course in order to obtain the knowledge that was necessary for performing her staff council functions. The training course on 13 November 1990 lasted for 7.5 hours. If she had not been on the course, the plaintiff would not have worked on that day, because of her being employed part-time. However, the defendant paid her on the basis of her contractual working hours of 30.8 hours a week, without compensation for the time she had spent on that course.

According to the Industrial Relations Law, the staff council members attending such courses are to be released by their employer from the obligations arising from their employment, without loss of pay.

The plaintiff sought compensation for the 7.5 hours she spent on the course. In her opinion, staff council members who work part-time could not be required to make special sacrifices compared with those who work full-time. She considered that the defendant's refusal constituted discrimination incompatible with both Article 157 of the Treaty and the directive (1975).

It followed that compensation received for losses of earnings due to attendance at training courses imparting the information necessary for performing staff council functions must be regarded as pay within the meaning of Article 157, since it constituted a benefit paid indirectly by the employer by reason of the existence of an employment relationship.

---

564. C.O.J., 6 February 1996, *Kuratorium für Dialyse und-Nierentransplantation eV* v. *Johanna Lewark*, Case C-457/93, ECR, 1996, 243. See also C.O.J., 7 March 1996, *Edith Freers, Hannelore Speckman* v. *Deutsche Bundespost*, Case C-278/93, ECR, 1996, 1165.

It is indisputable, the Court said, that where training courses, necessary for performing staff council functions, are organised during the full-time working hours in force in the undertaking but outside the individual working hours of part-time workers serving on those councils, the overall pay received by the latter is, for the same number of hours worked, lower than that received by the full-time workers serving on the same staff councils.

Since a difference in treatment was found to exist, it followed from settled case law that, if it were the case that a much lower proportion of women than men worked full-time, the exclusion of part-time workers from certain benefits would be contrary to Article 157 where, taking into account the difficulties encountered by women workers working full-time, that measure could not be explained by factors excluding any discrimination on grounds of sex.

According to the order for reference, the official employment and social statistics showed that at the end of June 1991, 93.4 per cent of all part-time workers were women and 6.6 per cent were men.

As those figures were not disputed, it was considered that the application of legislative provisions such as those at issue in the main proceedings in principle caused indirect discrimination against women workers. It would be otherwise only if the different treatment found to exist was justified by objective factors unrelated to any discrimination based on sex.

If a Member State is able to show that measures chosen reflect a legitimate aim of its social policy, are appropriate to achieve that and are necessary in order to do so, the mere fact that the legislative provision affects far more women workers than men cannot be regarded as a breach of Article 157.

1510. However, it was noted that legislation such as that at issue is likely to deter workers in the part-time category, in which the proportion of women is undeniably preponderant, from performing staff council functions or acquiring the knowledge necessary for performing them, thus making it more difficult for that category of workers to be represented by qualified staff council members.

In the light of all those considerations and taking into account the possibility of achieving the social policy aim in question by other means, the difference in treatment could be justified from the point of view of Article 157 and of the directive only if it appeared to be suitable and necessary for achieving that aim.

This reasoning brought the Court to the conclusion that:

> Where the category of part-time workers includes a much higher number of women than men, the prohibition of indirect discrimination in the matter of pay precludes national legislation which, not being suitable and necessary for achieving a legitimate social policy aim, has the effect of limiting to their individual working hours the compensation which staff council members employed on a part-time basis are to receive from their employer for attending training courses which impart the knowledge necessary for serving on staff councils and are held during the full-time working hours applicable in the undertaking but which exceed their individual part-time working hours, when staff council members employed on a full-time basis receive compensation for attendance at the same courses on the basis of their full-time working hours.

1511. It must also be added that Council Directive 76/207/EEC of 9 February 1976 precludes national legislation which requires that, for the purposes of calculating the length of service of public servants, periods of employment during which the hours worked are between one-half and two-thirds of normal working hours are counted only as two-thirds of normal working hours, save where such legislation is justified by objective criteria unrelated to any discrimination on grounds of sex.[565]

1512. Indirect discrimination was also discussed in *Luisia Sabbatini* v. *European Parliament*. Sabbatini, an EU official, had lost her expatriation allowance following her marriage. Under the EU staff regulations, an official

> who marries a person who at the date of the marriage does not qualify for the allowance shall forfeit the right to expatriation allowance unless that official thereby becomes a head of household.

Head of household refers normally to a married male official, whereas a married female official is considered to be head of household only in particular circumstances, for instance in cases of invalidity or serious illness of the husband. The Court ruled that the withdrawal of the expatriation allowance following the marriage of the recipient might be justified in cases in which this change in the family situation is such as to bring an end to the state of expatriation, which is the justification for the benefit in question. In this respect, however, officials cannot be treated differently according to whether they are male or female, since the termination of the status of expatriate must be dependent for both male and female officials on uniform criteria, irrespective of sex. Consequently, by rendering the retention of the allowance subject to the status of head of the household, an arbitrary difference of treatment was created between officials.[566] A similar problem was raised in *Jeanne Airola* v. *Commission*. Jeanne, working for Euratom in Italy, married an Italian and became Italian with the consequent loss of her expatriation allowance. The Court ruled that the concept of the term 'nationals' contained in the Staff Regulation must be interpreted in such a way as to avoid any unwarranted difference of treatment between male and female officials who are, in fact, placed in comparable situations. Such an unwarranted difference of treatment results from an interpretation of concepts of nationals as also embracing the nationality which was imposed by law on an official of the female sex by virtue of her marriage, and which she was unable to renounce.[567]

1513. Another case, involving part-time work, concerned Ms. Kachelmann, who was employed by Bankhaus as a qualified banker with certified German/ English bilingual drafting skills. She was responsible for managing cases in the 'recovery' department of the documentary transactions section of the Hamburg branch. She

---

565. C.O.J., 2 October 1997, *Hellen Gerster* v. *Freistaat Bayern*, C-1/195, ECR, 1997, 5253; C.O.J., 2 October 1997, *Brigitte Kording* v. *Senator für Finanzen*, ECR, 1997, 5289.
566. 7 June 1972, No. 20/71, ECR, 1972, 363.
567. 20 February 1975, No. 21/74, ECR, 1975, 235.

was employed on a part-time basis for 30 hours a week; the number of working hours fixed by the collective agreement for full-time work was 38 hours per week.

Owing to a reduction in the volume of its international activities, Bankhaus decided to merge its 'recovery' department, which until then had been separate, with the rest of the documentary transactions section. That involved a partial reallocation of duties. Taking the view that it had excess staff, Bankhaus gave Ms. Kachelmann notice of dismissal on economic grounds.

Ms Kachelmann contested her dismissal before the Labour Court (Hamburg). She claims that, during the process leading to her being given notice of dismissal on economic grounds, Bankhaus did not make a selection on the basis of social criteria from amongst all workers performing the same duties. It did not compare Ms. Kachelmann, who was working 30 hours a week, with full-time workers working 38 hours a week, even though she had stated, before she was given notice of dismissal, that she would be willing to work on a full-time basis.

The German Labour Court dismissed Ms. Kachelmann's claim. It found that she could not be transferred to a full-time post without amendment of her employment contract, so that her job and those of the full-time workers were not comparable. Nor was Bankhaus under a duty to increase Ms. Kachelmann's hours of work by amending her employment contract so that they could employ her on a full-time basis for the sole purpose of avoiding her dismissal. The applicant took the view that it was indirectly discriminatory and therefore contrary to the directive to exclude part-time workers from the category of workers from whom the employer must make a selection on the basis of social criteria when making redundancies on economic grounds.

1514. The Court rules as follows. It is common ground that in Germany part-time workers are far more likely to be women than men. It is therefore necessary to assess whether application of a national rule such as that at issue in the main proceedings results in full-time workers being treated differently from part-time workers. If this proves to be the case, the next question to be examined is whether that difference in treatment is justified by objective factors unrelated to any discrimination on grounds of sex.

It is important to note, first of all, that lack of comparability between full-time and part-time workers in the selection process based on social criteria does not entail any direct disadvantage for the latter category.

Both full-time and part-time workers receive the same advantageous or disadvantageous treatment according to whether in each particular case it is a fulltime post or a part-time post which is being abolished.

However, the number of workers employed full-time in Germany, and probably throughout the Union, is significantly higher in all sectors than the number of part-time workers. It follows that, where jobs are being cut, part-time workers are in general put at a greater disadvantage because they have less chance of finding another comparable job.

Consequently, lack of comparability between full-time and part-time workers in the selection process based on social criteria may give rise to a difference in treatment to the detriment of part-time workers and entail an indirect disadvantage for them.

That being so, it is necessary to determine whether such a difference in treatment is justified by objective factors unrelated to any discrimination on grounds of sex.

As Union law stands at present, social policy is a matter for the Member States, which enjoy a reasonable margin of discretion as regards the nature of social protection measures and the detailed arrangements for their implementation. If such measures meet a legitimate aim of social policy, are suitable and requisite for attaining that end and are therefore justified by reasons unrelated to discrimination on grounds of sex, they cannot be regarded as being contrary to the principle of equal treatment.

It appears from the case-file that the purpose of the German legislation in question is to protect workers facing dismissal whilst at the same time taking account of the undertaking's operational and economic needs.

In that regard, it is clear that job comparability is determined according to the actual content of the respective employment contracts, by assessing whether the worker whose job is being abolished for reasons peculiar to the undertaking would be capable, having regard to his professional qualifications and the activities he has hitherto been carrying out within the undertaking, of carrying out the different but equivalent work done by other workers.

Application of those criteria may well create an indirect disadvantage for part-time workers because their jobs cannot be compared with those of fulltime workers. However, if job comparability between full-time and part-time workers were to be introduced in the selection process on the basis of social criteria that would have the effect of placing part-time workers at an advantage, while putting full-time workers at a disadvantage. In the event of their jobs being abolished, part-time workers would have to be offered a full-time job, even if their employment contract did not entitle them to one.

The question whether part-time workers should enjoy such an advantage is a matter for the national legislature, which alone must find a fair balance in employment law between the various interests concerned. In this case, that assessment has been based on considerations unrelated to the sex of the workers.

In those circumstances, the answer must be that Articles 2(1) and 3(1) of the Directive are to be interpreted as not precluding an interpretation of a national rule, which proceeds on the general basis that part-time workers are not to be compared with full-time workers when an employer has to proceed to selection on the basis of social criteria when abolishing a part-time job on economic grounds.[568]

1515. In *Shirley Preston and Others* v. *Wolverhampton Healthcare NHS Trust and Others* and *Dorothy Fletcher and Others* v. *Midland Bank plc*,[569] the Court ruled that the United Kingdom procedural rules governing actions to secure the right to retroactive membership of an occupational pension scheme are contrary to Community law.

---

568. C.O.J., 26 September 2000, *Bärbel Kachelmann* v. *Bankhaus Hermann Lampe KG*, C-322/98, ECR, 2000, 7505.
569. 16 May 2000, Case C-78/98, ECR, 2000, 3201.

Part I, Ch. 6, Equal Treatment

In 1994[570] the Court of Justice confirmed already that entitlement to membership of an occupational pension scheme fell within the scope of the TFEU provisions which guarantee equal pay for men and women, particularly as regards part-time workers. The Court held that workers may rely on those provisions in order retroactively to claim equal treatment in relation to the right to join an occupational pension scheme as from 8 April 1976, the date of the Court's first judgment recognising the direct effect of those provisions.

In the United Kingdom, several occupational pension schemes excluded part-time workers from joining them. Between 1986 and 1995, changes were made to those pension schemes to enable part-time workers to become members on the same terms as full-time workers.

Nevertheless, a number of workers instituted proceedings in United Kingdom courts to secure recognition of their right to retroactive membership of those pension schemes for the periods of part-time work completed by them before those changes were made.

Thus, 60,000 actions were brought before United Kingdom courts. Of these, 22 were treated as test cases with a view to disposing of certain preliminary issues of law.

The Equal Pay Act 1970 requires workers to bring actions within a period of six months following cessation of their employment. Another provision of the Act limits to the two years prior to the date on which they instituted proceedings the period for which workers may secure entitlement to retroactive membership of the pension schemes from which they were excluded.

According to the United Kingdom courts those two procedural provisions are in conformity with Union law. The House of Lords sought a ruling from the Court of Justice of the European Union as to the compatibility with Union law of the procedural rules laid down by the United Kingdom legislation.

1516. The Court held, firstly, that Union law does not preclude a national procedural rule which requires that a claim for membership of an occupational pension scheme (from which the right to pension benefits flows) must, if it is not to be time-barred, be brought within six months of the end of the employment to which the claim relates. However, that limitation period must not be less favourable for actions based on Union law than for those based on domestic law.

> The Court held, on the other hand, that Union law precludes a national procedural rule which provides that a claimant's pensionable service is to be calculated only by reference to service after a date falling no earlier than two years prior to the date of her claim.

The Court made it clear that the workers concerned will be able to secure retroactive membership of the relevant schemes and payment of the resultant benefits only

---

570. 28 September 1994 in Case C-57/93 *Vroege* v. *NCIV Instituut voor Volkshuisvesting and Stichting Pensioenfonds*, ECR, 1994, 4541 and Case C-128/93 *Fisscher* v. *Voorhuis Hengelo and Stichting Bedrijfspensionenfonds voor de Detailhandel*, ECR, 1994, 4583.

if they first pay contributions to cover all the periods of part-time employment of which they seek recognition.

1517. In order to establish whether a measure adopted by a Member State has disparate effect as between men and women to such a degree as to amount to indirect discrimination for the purposes of Article 157, the national court must verify whether the statistics available indicate that a considerably smaller percentage of women than men is able to fulfil the requirement imposed by that measure. If that is the case, there is indirect sex discrimination, unless that measure is justified by objective factors unrelated to any discrimination based on sex.

If a considerably smaller percentage of women than men is capable of fulfilling the requirement of two years' employment, it is for the Member State, as the author of the allegedly discriminatory rule, to show that the said rule reflects a legitimate aim of its social policy, that that aim is unrelated to any discrimination based on sex, and that it could reasonably consider that the means chosen were suitable for attaining that aim.[571]

III. Exceptions

1518. One finds exceptions to the rule of equal treatment in Article 2(6) and (7) of the 1976 (amended) directive. As derogations from the fundamental principle of equal treatment they must be interpreted restrictively.[572]

A. Nature of the Activity

1519. According to Article 2(6) of the amended 1976 directive:

> Member States may provide, as regards access to employment including the training leading thereto, that a difference of treatment which is based on a characteristic related to sex shall not constitute discrimination where, by reason of the nature of the particular occupational activities concerned or of the context in which they are carried out, such a characteristic constitutes a genuine and determining occupational requirement, provided that the objective is legitimate and the requirement is proportionate.

1520. It should be pointed out that Article 2(6) (amended) constitutes a possibility and not an obligation. It does not have as its object or as its effect to require the Member States to exercise that power of derogation in a particular manner.

---

571. C.O.J., 9 February 1999, *Regina v. Secretary of State for Employment, ex parte Nicole Seymour-Smith and Laura Perez*, Case C-167/97, ECR, 1999, 623.
572. C.O.J., 15 May 1986, *M. Johnston v. Chief Constable of the Royal Ulster Constabulary*, No. 222/84, ECR, 1986, 1651.

However, Article 9(2) requires the Member States to compile a complete and verifiable list, in whatever form, of the occupations and activities excluded from the application of the principle of equal treatment and to notify the Commission of the results. The Commission must then verify the application of that provision.[573] In *Commission v. UK of Great Britain and Northern Ireland*, the Commission claimed that the prohibition of discrimination applied to employment in a private household or where the number of persons employed did not exceed five persons or in the case of midwives, all three cases being retained as exceptions to the equality principle. The UK was of the opinion that these exceptions were justified:

> because they involve close personal relationships between employees and employers, so that it would not be legally possible to prevent the latter from employing persons of a particular sex.[574]

As far as households are concerned, the Court ruled that it is undeniable that this consideration might be decisive for certain kinds of employment, but certainly not for all kinds of employment in question. With regard to small undertakings, the Court found that the United Kingdom had not put forward any argument to show that in any undertaking of that size the sex of the worker would be a determining factor by reason of the nature of his activities or the context in which they are carried out. The midwife exception was, however, an acceptable one. The Court recognised that at the present time personal sensitivities may play an important role in relations between midwife and patient.

1521. In the case *Johnston v. Chief Constable of Ulster, Northern Ireland*[575] the problem was that Ms. Johnston did not receive a contract as a full-time officer since the decision had been made that general police duties, frequently involving operations requiring the carrying of fire-arms, should no longer be assigned to women. She consequently had to accept a job as a part-time communications assistant with lower pay. The Court was of the opinion that a Member State may take into consideration requirements of public safety in order to restrict general policing duties, in an internal situation characterised by frequent assassinations, to men equipped with fire-arms.

1522. As indicated above, the Member States are obliged to examine the exceptions of Article 2(6) (amended) at regular intervals to see whether, in the light of social developments, they are still justified and should be retained. They are to inform the Commission of the results of their inquiry.

---

573. C.O.J., 21 May 1985, *Commission v. Germany*, No. 248/83, ECR, 1985, 1459.
574. *Ibid.*
575. *See* C.O.J., 26 October 1999, *Angela Maria Sirdar v. The Army Board and Secretary of State for Defence*, Case C-273/97, ECR, 1999, 7403. C.O.J., 11 January 2000, *Tanja Kreil v. Bundesrepublik Deutschland*, Case C-285/98, ECR, 2000, 69.

B. *Protection of Women – Parental Leave*

1523. Article 2(7) (amended) of the 1976 directive on equal treatment provides that it is 'without prejudice to provisions concerning the protection of women, particularly as regards pregnancy and maternity'. Moreover, this exception is, according to the Commission, to be interpreted restrictively.[576] The Court, however, ruled that the directive leaves the Member States with the discretion as to the social measures they adopt in order to guarantee the protection of women in connection with pregnancy and maternity in regard both to the nature of the protective measures and to the detailed arrangements for their implementation. In *Johnston* v. *Chief Constable*, the Court held that:

> it is clear from the express reference to pregnancy and maternity that the directive is intended to protect a woman's biological condition and the special relationship which exists between a woman and her child.

1524. In *Ulrich Hofmann*, the question concerned a father who obtained unpaid leave from his employer for the period between the expiry of the statutory protective period of eight weeks which was available to the mother and the day on which the child reached the age of six months; during that time he took care of the child while the mother continued her employment. Ulrich claimed the pay for maternity leave, arguing that the maternity leave introduced by the *Mutterschutzgesetz* was in fact not designed to give social protection to the mother on biological and medical grounds but rather to protect the child, which follows from the fact that the leave is withdrawn in the event of the child's death, which demonstrates that the leave was created in the interests of the child and not of the mother. The Court did not follow these arguments. It ruled that the directive is not designed to settle questions concerned with the organisation of the family, or alter the division of the responsibility between parents. The directive recognises the legitimacy, in terms of the principle of equal treatment, of protecting a woman's needs in two respects. First, it is legitimate to ensure the protection of a woman's biological condition during pregnancy and thereafter until such time as her physiological and mental functions have returned to normal after childbirth; secondly, it is legitimate to protect the special relationship between a woman and her child over the period which follows pregnancy and childbirth, by preventing that relationship from being disturbed by the multiple burdens which would result from the simultaneous pursuit of employment. In principle, therefore, a measure such as maternity leave granted to a woman on the expiry of the statutory protective period falls within the scope of Article 2(6) (amended) of Directive 76/207, inasmuch as it seeks to protect a woman in connection with the effects of pregnancy and motherhood. That being so, such leave may legitimately be reserved to the mother to the exclusion of any other person, in view of the fact that it is only the mother who may find herself subject to undesirable pressures to return to work prematurely. The directive does not impose on Member

---

576. C.O.J., 12 July 1984, *Ulrich Hofmann* v. *Barmer Ersatszkasse*, No. 184/83, ECR, 1984, 3047.

Part I, Ch. 6, Equal Treatment

States a requirement that they shall, as an alternative, allow such leave to be granted to fathers, even where the parents so decide.[577]

The 1976 directive is without prejudice to provisions concerning the protection of women, particularly as regards pregnancy and maternity.

A woman on maternity leave is entitled, after the end of her period of maternity leave, to return to her job or to an equivalent post on terms and conditions which are no less favourable to her and to benefit from any improvement in working conditions to which she would be entitled during her absence.

Less favourable treatment of a woman related to pregnancy or maternity leave within the meaning of Directive 92/85/EEC shall constitute discrimination within the meaning of the directive (Article 2(7) amended).

1525. The issue at the crux of the *Mckenna* case[578] is whether incapacity for work caused by a pregnancy-related illness and occurring during the period of pregnancy may, in accordance with Union law, be treated in the same way as incapacity for work caused by any other illness and be set against the number of days during which, under the sick-leave scheme applicable in the case, employees are entitled to have their pay maintained in full, and then in part.

1526. The Court rules as follows:

> A sick-leave scheme which treats identically female workers suffering from a pregnancy-related illness and other workers suffering from an illness that is unrelated to pregnancy comes within the scope of Article 157 TFEU and Council Directive 75/117/EEC of 10 February 1975.

1527. Article 157 TFEU and Directive 75/117 must be construed as meaning that the following do not constitute discrimination on grounds of sex:

- a rule of a sick-leave scheme which provides, in regard to female workers absent prior to maternity leave by reason of an illness related to their pregnancy, as also in regard to male workers absent by reason of any other illness, for a reduction in pay in the case where the absence exceeds a certain duration, provided that the female worker is treated in the same way as a male worker who is absent on grounds of illness and provided that the amount of payment made is not so low as to undermine the objective of protecting pregnant workers;
- a rule of a sick-leave scheme which provides for absences on grounds of illness to be offset against a maximum total number of days of paid sick-leave to which a worker is entitled over a specified period, whether or not the illness is pregnancy-related, provided that the offsetting of the absences on grounds of a pregnancy-related illness does not have the effect that, during the absence affected by that offsetting after the maternity leave, the female worker receives pay that is lower than the minimum amount to which she was entitled during the illness which arose while she was pregnant.

---

577. *Idem.*
578. C.O.J., 8 September 2005, *North Western Health Board* v. *Margaret McKenna*, C-191/03, ECR, 2005, 7631.

1528. The 1976 directive is also without prejudice to the provisions of Council Directive 96/34/EC of 3 June 1996 on the framework agreement on parental leave concluded by UNICE, CEEP and the ETUC and of Council Directive 92/85/EEC of 19 October 1992 on the introduction of measures to encourage improvements in the safety and health at work of pregnant workers and workers who have recently given birth or are breastfeeding (tenth individual directive within the meaning of Article 16(1) of Directive 89/391/EEC). It is also without prejudice to the right of Member States to recognise distinct rights to paternity and/or adoption leave.

Those Member States which recognise such rights shall take the necessary measures to protect working men and women against dismissal due to exercising those rights and ensure that, at the end of such leave, they shall be entitled to return to their jobs or to equivalent posts on terms and conditions which are no less favourable to them, and to benefit from any improvement in working conditions to which they would have been entitled during their absence (Article 2(7) amended).

C. Positive Discrimination

1529. This is accepted in Article 2(7) (amended) of the 1976 directive: Member States may maintain or adopt measures within the meaning of Article 141(4) of the Treaty with a view to ensuring full equality in practice between men and women (Article 2(8) amended).

1530. Article 157(4) TFEU reads as follows:

> with a view to ensuring full equality in practice between men and women in working life, the principle of equal treatment shall not prevent any Member State from maintaining or adopting measures providing for specific advantages in order to make it easier for the underrepresented sex to pursue a vocational activity or to prevent or compensate for disadvantages in professional careers.

A Declaration attached to the Treaty of Amsterdam clarifies that the Member States in adopting such measures have to aim in the first place at the improvement of the situation of women in employment and occupation.

1531. In this area, a very controversial decision was earlier taken by the Court of Justice in the case between Kalanke and *Freie Hansestadt Bremen* (City of Bremen)[579] in which the Court rejected the automatic nature of quotas. The case was as follows.

At the final stage of recruitment to a post of Section Manager in the Bremen Parks Department, two candidates were shortlisted: Mr. Eckhard Kalanke, the plaintiff in the main proceedings, holder of a diploma in horticulture and landscape gardening, who had worked since 1973 as a horticultural employee in the Parks Department and acted as permanent assistant to the Section Manager; and Ms. Glißmann, holder of a diploma in landscape gardening since 1983 and also employed, since 1975, as

---

579. 17 October 1995, Case C-450/93, ECR, 1995, 3051.

Part I, Ch. 6, Equal Treatment

a horticultural employee in the Parks Department. The Staff Committee refused to give its consent to Kalanke's promotion.

Reference to arbitration resulted in a recommendation in favour of Kalanke. The Staff Committee then stated that the arbitration had failed and appealed to the conciliation board which, in a decision binding on the employer, considered that the two candidates were equally qualified and that priority should therefore be given, in accordance with the Bremen law on equal treatment, hereinafter 'LGG', to the woman.

Before the Labour Court, Kalanke claimed that he was better qualified than Glißmann, a fact which the conciliation board had failed to recognise. He argued that, by reason of its quota system, the LGG was incompatible among others with the Bremen Constitution and with the German Basic Law. His application was dismissed at first instance, however, and again, on appeal, by the Regional Labour Court.

The Federal Labour Court asked, essentially, whether Article 2(1) and (4) of the directive of 1976 precludes national rules such as those in the present case which, where candidates of different sexes, shortlisted for promotion, are equally qualified, automatically give priority to women in sectors where they are under-represented, under-representation being deemed to exist when women do not make up at least half of the staff in the individual pay brackets in the relevant personnel group or in the function levels provided for in the organisation chart.

1532. The Court of Justice reasoned as follows:

> The purpose of the Directive is, as stated in Article 1(1), to put into effect in the Member States the principle of equal treatment for men and women as regards, *inter alia*, access to employment, including promotion. Article 2(1) states that the principle of equal treatment means that "there shall be no discrimination whatsoever on grounds of sex either directly or indirectly".
>
> A national rule that, where men and women who are candidates for the same promotion are equally qualified, women are automatically to be given priority in sectors where they are underrepresented, involves discrimination on grounds of sex.
>
> It must, however, be considered whether such a national rule is permissible under Article 2(4), which provides that the Directive "shall be without prejudice to measures to promote equal opportunity for men and women, in particular by removing existing inequalities which affect women's opportunities".
>
> That provision is specifically and exclusively designed to allow measures which, although discriminatory in appearance, are in fact intended to eliminate or reduce actual instances of inequality which may exist in the reality of social life.
>
> It thus permits national measures relating to access to employment, including promotion, which give a specific advantage to women with a view to improving their ability to compete on the labour market and to pursue a career on an equal footing with men.
>
> Nevertheless, as a derogation from an individual right laid down in the Directive, Article 2(4) must be interpreted strictly.

National rules which guarantee women absolute and unconditional priority for appointment or promotion go beyond promoting equal opportunities and overstep the limits of the exception in Article 2(4) of the Directive.

Furthermore, in so far as it seeks equal representation of men and women in all grades and levels within a department, such a system substitutes for equality of opportunity envisaged in Article 2(4) the result which is to be arrived at by providing such opportunity.

1533. Therefore the Court concluded that:

Article 2(1) and (4) of the Directive of 1976 precludes national rules whereby candidates of different sexes shortlisted for promotion are equally qualified, automatically give priority to women in sectors where they are under-represented, under-representation being deemed to exist when women do not make up at least half of the staff in the individual pay brackets in the relevant personnel group or in the function levels provided for in the organisation chart.

1534. In *Hellmut Marschall* v. *Land Nordrhein Westfalen*,[580] the Court qualified its position. It stated as follows:

A national rule which, in a case where there are fewer women than men at the level of the relevant post in a sector of the public service, and both female and male candidates for the post are equally qualified in terms of their suitability, competence and professional performance requires that priority be given to the promotion of female candidates unless reasons specific to an individual male candidate tilt the balance in his favour is not precluded by Article 2(1) and (4) of the Directive, provided that:

– in each individual case the rule provides male candidates who are as equally qualified as the female candidates with a guarantee that the candidatures will be the subject of an objective assessment which will take account of all criteria specific to the individual candidates and will override the priority accorded to female candidates where one or more of those criteria tilts the balance in favour of the male candidate, and
– such criteria are not such as to discriminate.

1535. In adopting the new Article 157 TFEU, especially paragraph 4, the European legislator refuted the Court's case law, laid down in *Kalanke*, and adopted a more progressive approach regarding positive discrimination in the line of the proposal of the Commission.

---

580. C.O.J., 11 November 1997, C-409/95, ECR, 1997, 6363.

§5. OBJECT

I. Equal Pay for Equal Work or Work of Equal Value

A. Equal Work or Work of Equal Value

1536. Article 157 TFEU concerns equal work or work of equal value.

1537. The Court was asked to compare, in a case involving equal value, female factory workers with male stores labourers. The first were engaged in such tasks as dismantling, cleaning, oiling and reassembling telephones and other equipment. The second group was engaged in cleaning, collecting and delivering equipment and components and in lending general assistance as required. In comparison to their male colleagues, the female workers not only performed work of higher value but also they were paid less. The question then was whether the Union law principle of equal work for equal pay extends to a claim for equal pay on the basis of work of equal value in circumstances where the work of the claimant has been assessed to be of higher value than that of the person with whom the claimant sought comparison. The answer, based on Article 157, was *a fortiori* positive. To adopt a contrary interpretation would be tantamount to rendering the principle of equal pay ineffective and nugatory. In this case, the employer would indeed easily be able to circumvent the principle by assigning additional or more onerous duties to workers of a particular sex who would then be paid a lower wage.[581]

1538. Another case[582] concerned the pay of two midwives, which was lower than that received by a clinical technician even though those midwives performed work of equal value. Questions were raised in respect of the differential between their pay and the higher amount received by a clinical technician, on the ground that their work was of equal value.
The Court ruled that:

> If a difference in pay between the two groups compared is found to exist, and if the available statistical data indicate that there is a substantially higher proportion of women than men in the advantaged group, Article 157 TFEU requires the employer to justify the difference by objective factors which are unrelated to any discrimination on grounds of sex.

---

581. 4 February 1988, *Mary Murphy and others v. Bord Telecom Eirann*, No. 157/86, ECR, 1989, 673.
582. C.O.J., 30 March 2000, *Jämställdhetsombudsmannen v. Orebro läns landsting*, C-236/98, ECR, 2000, 2189.

The Court also said:

> Neither the reduction in working time, by reference to the standard normal working time for day-work, awarded in respect of work performed according to a three-shift roster, nor the value of such a reduction, are to be taken into consideration for the purpose of calculating the salary used as the basis for a pay comparison for the purposes of Article 157 TFEU and Directive 75/117. However, such a reduction may constitute an objective reason unrelated to any discrimination on grounds of sex such as to justify a difference in pay. It is for the employer to show that such is in fact the case.

1539. Article 157 and the directive apply to piece-work pay schemes in which pay depends entirely or in large measure on the individual output of each worker.[583]

The principle of equal pay means that the mere finding that in a piece-work pay scheme the average pay of a group of workers, consisting predominantly of women carrying out one type of work, is appreciably lower than the average pay of a group of workers consisting predominantly of men, carrying out another type of work, to which equal value is attributed does not suffice to establish that there is discrimination with regard to pay. However, where, in a piece-work pay scheme in which individual pay consists of a variable element depending on each worker's output and a fixed element depending on the group of workers concerned, it is not possible to identify the factor which determined the rates or units of measurement used to calculate the variable element in the pay, the employer may have to bear the burden of proving that the differences found are not due to sex discrimination.

For the purposes of the comparison to be made between the average pay of two groups of piece-workers, the national court must satisfy itself that the two groups each encompass all the workers who, taking account of a set of factors such as the nature of the work, the training requirements and the working conditions, can be considered to be in a comparable situation and that they cover a relatively large number of workers ensuring that the differences are not due to purely fortuitous or short-term factors or to differences in the individual output of the workers concerned.

When ascertaining whether the principle of equal pay has been observed, it is for the national court to decide whether, in the light of circumstances such as, first, the factor that the work done by one of the groups of workers in question involves machinery and requires in particular muscular strength whereas that done by the other group is manual work requiring in particular dexterity and, secondly, the fact that there are differences between the work of the two groups with regard to paid breaks, freedom to organise one's own work and work-related inconveniences, the two types of work are of equal value or whether those circumstances may be considered to be objective factors unrelated to any discrimination on grounds of sex which can justify any pay differentials.

The principle of equal pay for men and women also applies where the elements of the pay are determined by collective bargaining or by negotiation at local level.

---

583. C.O.J., 31 May 1995, *Specialarbejderforbundet i Danmark* v. *Dansk Industri, originally Industriens Arbejdsgivere, acting for Royal Copenhagen A/S*, Case C-400/93, ECR, 1995, 1275.

However, the national court may take that fact into account in its assessment of whether differences between the average pay of two groups of workers are due to objective factors unrelated to any discrimination on grounds of sex.

1540. Article 1(2) of the 1975 directive provides that where a job classification system is used for determining pay, it must be based on the same criteria for both men and women and thus be drawn up so as to exclude any discrimination on grounds of sex.

Job classification was discussed in the case *Gisela Rummler* v. *Dato-Druck*. Beside elements like the degree of knowledge, concentration and responsibility, the factors muscle demand and muscular efforts were involved. The Court ruled that the directive did not prohibit the use, in a job classification system for the purpose of determining rates of pay, of the criteria of muscle demand or muscular effort or that of the heaviness of the work if, in view of the nature of the tasks involved, the work to be performed does require a certain degree of physical strength, as long as the system as a whole, by taking other criteria into account, precludes any discrimination on the grounds of sex. The Court further declared that the use of values reflecting the average performance of workers of one sex as a basis for determining the extent to which work makes demands or requires effort or whether it is heavy constitutes a form of discrimination on grounds of sex, contrary to the directive. A job classification system must take into account criteria for which workers of each sex may show particular aptitude.[584]

1541. Where seemingly identical tasks (for example graduate psychologists employed as psychotherapists) are performed by different groups of persons who do not have the same training or professional qualifications for the practice of their profession, it is necessary to ascertain whether, taking into account the nature of the tasks that may be assigned to each group respectively, the training requirements for performance of those tasks and the working conditions under which they are performed, the different groups in fact do the same work within the meaning of Article 157.

Professional training is not merely one of the factors that may be an objective justification for giving different pay for doing the same work; it is also one of the possible criteria for determining whether or not the same work is being performed.

In those circumstances, two groups of persons who have received different professional training and who, because of the different scope of the qualifications resulting from that training, on the basis of which they were recruited, are called on to perform different tasks or duties, cannot be regarded as being in a comparable situation.

Therefore be that the term 'the same work' does not apply, for the purposes of Article 157 TFEU or of the directive, where the same activities are performed over a considerable length of time by persons the basis of whose qualification to exercise their profession is different.[585]

---

584. 1 July 1986, No. 237/85, ECR, 1986, 2101.
585. C.O.J., 11 May 1999, *Angestelltenbetriebsrat der Wiener Gebietskrankenkasse* v. *Wiener Gebietskrankenkasse*, Case C-309/97, ECR, 1999, 2865.

The question arose whether the principle of equal pay for the same work is to be interpreted in relation only to a 'single workplace'. The question was not decided upon by the Court.[586] However, in the *Defrenne II* case, the Court stated that:

> it is impossible not to recognise that the complete implementation of the aim pursued in Article 157, by means of the elimination of all discrimination, direct and indirect, between men and women workers, not only as regards individual undertakings but also entire branches of industry and even of the economic system as a whole, may in certain cases involve the elaboration of criteria whose implementation necessitates the taking of appropriate measures at Union and at national level.[587]

1542. In the same judgment, moreover, the Court limited the direct effect of Article 157 to work that is carried out in the same establishment or service, whether private or public. Advocate-General VerLoren van Themaat was nevertheless of the opinion that the Danish Government, in the above-mentioned Danish case, by limiting the comparison of work to the same establishment, was adding a condition which did not appear either in Article 157 or in the directive. As appears from the second sentence of Article 1 of the directive, a comparison of duties within the same fixed establishment of an undertaking or even within a single undertaking will not always be sufficient. In certain circumstances, comparison of work of equal value in other undertakings covered by the same collective agreement will be necessary. As the Commission, however, did not formally raise that objection, there was no reason for the Court to decide the question.[588]

1543. In the case *Macarthys Ltd. v. Wendy Smith*, the question was raised whether the principle of equal pay for equal work is confined to situations in which men and women are contemporaneously doing equal work for their employer. Wendy Smith was a warehouse manageress with a weekly salary of £50. She complained of discrimination in pay because her predecessor, a man, whose post she took up after an interval of four months, received a salary of £60 per week. The Court had to acknowledge that, as the Employment Appeal Tribunal properly recognised, it cannot be ruled out that a difference in pay between two workers occupying the same post but at different periods in time may be explained by the operation of factors which are unconnected with any discrimination on grounds of sex, like the period of time between the periods of employment, a change in the general economic conditions or the adoption of a more restrictive income policy. In the absence of such justification unequal payment is contrary to Article 157. The principle enshrined in Article 157 that men and women should receive equal pay for equal work is thus not confined to situations in which men and women are contemporaneously doing equal work for the same employer. Submission was also made of the question whether a woman could claim not only the salary received by a man who previously did the same work for her employer, but also, more generally, the

---

586. *Commission v. Denmark*, 30 January 1985, No. 143/83, ECR, 1985, 427.
587. 8 April 1976, No. 43/75, ECR, 1976, 455.
588. *See also Macarthys Ltd. v. Wendy Smith, op. cit.*

Part I, Ch. 6, Equal Treatment 1544–1545

salary to which she would be entitled were she a man, even in the absence of any man who was concurrently performing, or had previously performed, similar work, of thus 'a hypothetical male worker'. The answer was that such a proposition requires comparative studies of entire branches of industry and therefore the elaboration by the Community and national legislative bodies of criteria of assessment. It follows from this that, in cases of actual discrimination falling within the scope of direct application of Article 157, comparisons are confined to parallels which may be drawn on the basis of concrete appraisals of the work actually performed by employees of different sex within the same establishment or service.

Finally, consecutive jobs are equal jobs in accordance to Article 157. The Court did not need the notion 'work of equal value' contained in the directive to arrive at that conclusion.

B. Equal Pay

1544. Article 157 contains the notion 'equal pay'. The 1975 directive simply refers to Article 157, while the 1976 directive only talks of working conditions, without mentioning the word 'pay'. One could indeed say that pay is a condition of work and thus is covered by the 1976 directive regarding equal treatment. In fact the question boils down to the interpretation of Article 157, which contains the following definition:

For the purpose of this article "pay" means the ordinary basic or minimum wage or salary and any other consideration, whether in cash or in kind, which the worker receives, directly or indirectly, in respect of his employment for his employer.

Equal pay without discrimination based on sex means:

(a) that pay for the same work at piece rates shall be calculated on the basis of the same unit of measurement;
(b) that pay for work at time rates shall be the same for the same job.

1545. An end-of-year bonus, which the employer pays to the worker under a law or a collective agreement, is received in respect of the worker's employment, so that it constitutes pay within the meaning of Article 157.

In that regard, it should be noted that Article 157 lays down the principle that men and women should receive equal pay for equal work, but it does not concern cases in which a group of workers is treated less favourably than another group of workers of the same sex.

On the other hand, that principle precludes not only the application of provisions leading to direct sex discrimination, but also the application of provisions which maintain different treatment between men and women at work as a result of the application of criteria not based on sex where those differences of treatment are not attributable to objective factors unrelated to sex discrimination. It should next be pointed out that since Article 157 is mandatory in nature, the prohibition of discrimination between male and female workers not only applies to the action of public authorities, but also extends to all collective agreements designed to regulate employment relationships and to contracts between individuals.

679

The exclusion by a collective agreement from entitlement to a special annual bonus of persons in employment, which involves a normal working week of less than 15 hours and normal pay not exceeding a fraction of the monthly baseline and who are, on that basis, exempt from compulsory social insurance, constitutes indirect discrimination based on sex, where that exclusion applies independently of the sex of the worker but actually affects a considerably higher percentage of women than men.[589]

1546. Article 157 does not preclude the making of a lump-sum payment exclusively to female workers who take maternity leave where that payment is designed to offset the occupational disadvantages which arise for those workers as a result of their being away from work.[590]

The notion 'pay' has given rise to quite a number of interpretation controversies.[591]

1547. A Christmas bonus constitutes pay, even if it is paid voluntarily by the employer and even if it is paid mainly or exclusively as an incentive for future work or loyalty to the undertaking or both.

Article 157 precludes an employer from excluding female workers on parenting leave entirely from the benefit of a bonus paid voluntarily as an exceptional allowance at Christmas without taking account of the work done in the year in which the bonus is paid or of the periods for the protection of mothers (in which they were prohibited from working) where that bonus is awarded retroactively as pay for work performed in the course of that year.

However, neither Article 157 nor Article 11(2) of Directive 92/85 nor clause 2(6) of the framework agreement on parental leave concluded by UNICE, CEEP and the ETUC (1996) precludes a refusal to pay such a bonus to a woman on parenting leave where the award of that allowance is subject to the sole condition that the worker must be in active employment when it is awarded.

Article 157, Article 11(2)(b) of Directive 92/85 and clause 2(6) of the mentioned agreement do not preclude an employer, when granting a Christmas bonus to a female worker, who is on parenting leave, from taking periods of parental leave into account, so as to reduce the benefit pro rata.

However, Article 157 precludes an employer, when granting a Christmas bonus, from taking periods for the protection of mothers (in which they were prohibited from working) into account, so as to reduce the benefit pro rata.[592]

---

589. C.O.J., 9 September 1999, *Andrea Krüger v. Kreiskrankenhaus Ebersberg*, Case C-281/97, ECR, 1999, 5127.
590. C.O.J., 16 September 1999, *Oumar Dabo Abdoulaye and Others v. Régie nationale des usines Renault SA*, Case C-218/98, ECR, 1999, 5723.
591. A maternity benefit is pay in the meaning of Article 141. To the extent that it is calculated on the basis of pay received by a woman before the commencement of the maternity leave, the amount of benefit must include pay rises awarded between the beginning of the period and the end of the maternity leave (C.O.J., 13 February 1996, *Joan Gillespie and Others v. Northern Health and Social Services Board and Others*, Case C-342/93, ECR, 1996, 475). 15 June 1978, *G. Defrenne v. Sabena*, No. 149/77, ECR, 1978, 1365.
592. C.O.J., 21 October 1999, *Susanne Lewen v. Lothar Denda*, Case C-333/97, ECR, 1999, 7243.

In particular, the distinction between direct and indirect wages remains a difficult one. The problem was first tackled in the case of *Gabrielle Defrenne (I)*. Defrenne was employed by Sabena as an air hostess. A Royal Decree of 3 November 1969 laid down the retirement pension scheme in respect of air crews of aviation companies. That decree, however, excluded air hostesses. Ms. Defrenne was covered by the overall general pension scheme. However, within that scheme she could not receive full benefits since her contract of employment, adopted under the terms of the collective agreement, provided that she could not continue to perform her duties beyond the age of 40 years. So there were no possibilities for her to have a full career and moreover she could not claim any retirement pension before the age laid down by the general scheme, that is to say 60 years for women. The question consequently put to the Court was whether the retirement pension granted under the terms of the social security financed by contributions from workers, employers and by state subsidy constitutes a consideration which the worker receives indirectly in respect of his employment from his employer.

1548. The Court based its reasoning in 1971 (thus before the 1976 directive) in line with the opinion of the Advocate General, ascertaining that the interpretation difficulties concentrate on the sentence 'any other consideration, whether in cash or in kind, which the worker receives directly or indirectly, in respect of his employment from the employer'.

According to the Court, the following elements must be retained:

(1) direct or indirect payment from the employer to the worker;
(2) payment in respect of his employment.

The question then was whether 'pensions' carry both elements. Here a distinction was made between different kinds of pensions: general schemes, which benefit all workers, and special schemes, which only benefit particular groups of workers.

1549. The Court ruled that, although consideration in the nature of social security benefits is not in principle alien to the concept of pay, there cannot be brought within this concept, as defined in Article 157, social security schemes or benefits, in particular retirement pensions directly governed by legislation without any element of agreement within the undertaking or the occupational branch concerned, which are obligatorily applicable to general categories of workers.[593] These schemes assure the workers the benefit of a legal scheme, to the financing of which workers, employers and possibly authorities contribute in a measure determined less by the employment relationship between the employer and the worker than by considerations of social policy. Accordingly, the part due from the employers in the financing

---

593. The Court observed that the Community legislature intended to authorise the determination of a different pensionable age according to sex for the purpose of granting old-age and retirement pensions, and also for forms of discrimination which are directly linked to that difference (C.O.J., 7 July 1992, *The Queen v. Secretary of State for Social Security Ex parte: The Equal Opportunities Commission (EOC)*, No. C-9/91, ECR, 1992, 4297; *see also: Ten Oever G.C. v. Stichting Bedrijfspensioenfonds voor het Glazenwassers-en Schoonmaakbedrijf*, 6 October 1993, No. C-109/91, ECR, 1993, 4287).

of such schemes does not constitute a direct or an indirect payment to the worker. Moreover, the worker will normally receive the benefits legally prescribed, not by reason of the employer's contribution but solely because the worker fulfils the legal conditions for the granting of benefits. These are likewise characteristics of special schemes, which, within the framework of the general system of social security established by legislation, relate in particular to certain categories of workers. It follows that a retirement pension established within the framework of a social security scheme laid down by legislation does not constitute consideration which the employee receives indirectly in respect of his employment from his employer within the meaning of Article 157.

1550. In the case of special retirement schemes, different hypotheses must be considered. Pensions that are directly paid by the employer constitute direct pay in the sense of Article 157. The reason is that they are a payment in respect of employment, while in most cases wage deductions take place. Additional retirement schemes, independent from the overall general legal schemes with employer's contributions and established for a specific group of workers employed in different occupational or inter-occupational enterprises, also constitute 'pay', although payment is made by a fund and one is thus confronted in a certain sense with a form of indirect pay. Indeed, the employer makes a contribution and there is a specific link with the employment relation. Such systems show close links with the employer.

1551. Special systems of social security, which are characterised by the fact that they are, from the administrative and organisational points of view, part of the general State system and which provide for higher amounts than the general system (thus specific systems for mine workers, seamen, for the sectors of gas and electricity and so on), cannot be separated from those general systems. Here the link with the employer is too weak. There is no real relationship between the contribution and the amount of the pension; the employer does not pay either directly or indirectly.

1552. In conclusion, one can say that general and specific retirement schemes – established within the framework of a more general social policy – are not 'pay' in the meaning of Article 157 TFEU Pensions paid by the employer, or through employers' funds established for that purpose, on the contrary do constitute 'pay'. This means that Ms. Defrenne lost her case. I repeat the criteria: there should be a consideration:

– paid directly or indirectly by the employer;
– in respect of employment: on the grounds of a (specific) employment relation in a (specific) undertaking.
– On this point, it should be recalled that the Court has stated on several occasions that the only possible decisive criterion is whether the pension is paid to the worker by reason of the employment relationship between him and his former employer, that is to say, the criterion of employment based on the wording of Article 157 itself.

- Admittedly, the Court has recognised that the employment criterion cannot be regarded as exclusive, since pensions paid under statutory social security schemes may reflect, wholly or in part, pay in respect of work.
- On the other hand, considerations of social policy, of State organisation, of ethics, or even budgetary concerns which influenced, or may have influenced, the establishment by the national legislature of a particular scheme cannot prevail if the pension concerns only a particular category of workers, if it is directly related to length of service and if its amount is calculated by reference to the last salary.
- Furthermore, a survivor's pension provided for by an occupational pension scheme is an advantage deriving from the survivor's spouse's membership of the scheme and accordingly falls within the scope of Article 157.
- It follows from the foregoing that a survivor's pension paid under an occupational pension scheme of the kind in issue,[594] which essentially arises from the employment of the beneficiary's spouse, is linked to the latter's pay and falls within the scope of Article 157 of the Treaty.[595]

1553. In *Liefting and others* v. *Direction of the Academic Hospital of Amsterdam*, pensions were again at the centre of attention. The case concerned a social security system under which:

(1) the contributions are calculated on the basis of the employee's salary but may not exceed a certain limit;
(2) husband and wife are treated as one person, the contributions being calculated on the basis of their combined salaries, subject once again to the upper limit;
(3) the State is bound to pay, on behalf of its employee, the contributions owned by him; and
(4) where both husband and wife are civil servants, the authority employing the husband is primarily responsible for paying the contributions and the authority employing the wife is required to pay the contributions only insofar as the upper limit is not reached by the contributions paid on behalf of the husband.

The contribution paid on behalf of the wife was thus smaller than the contribution on behalf of the husband. Both enjoyed the same disposable salary, but the husband's gross salary was higher than the wife's because the contribution was added to that salary. This is important since the gross salary is taken into account directly to determine the calculation of other advantages linked to the salary such as redundancy payments, unemployment benefits, family allowances and credit facilities. The Court rightly decided that such an arrangement is incompatible with the principle laid down in Article 157 TFEU insofar as the resultant differences between the gross salary of a female civil servant whose husband is also a civil servant and the gross salary of a male civil servant directly affect the calculation of other benefits

---

594. Insurance scheme of a state electricity company.
595. C.O.J., 17 April 1997, *Dimossia Epicheirissi Ilektrismou (DEI)* v. *Efthimios Evrenenopoulos*, C-147/95, ECR, 1997, 2057.

dependent on the salary, such as severance pay, unemployment benefit, family allowances and loan facilities.[596]

1554. In *D. Neath* v. *Hugh Steeper Ltd*[597] three questions were raised on the interpretation of Article 157 and on the effects in time of the *Barber* judgment.

The three questions were raised in the context of proceedings concerning the rules for granting a company pension and the transfer of pension rights. The point at stake was the use of actuarial factors differing according to sex in the sphere of private occupational pension schemes.

The Court stated that, in the context of a defined-benefit occupational pension scheme such as that in question in the main proceedings, the employer's commitment to his employees concerned the payment, at a given moment in time, of a periodic pension for which the determining criteria were already known at the time when the commitment was made and which constituted pay within the meaning of Article 157. However, that commitment did not necessarily have to do with the funding arrangements chosen to secure the periodic payment of the pension, which thus remained outside the scope of application of Article 157.

In contributory schemes, funding was provided through the contributions made by the employees and those made by the employers. The contributions made by the employees were an element of their pay since they were deducted directly from an employee's salary, which by definition was pay. The amount of those contributions had therefore to be the same for all employees, male and female, which was indeed so in the case before the Court. This was not so in the case of the employer's contributions which ensured the adequacy of the funds necessary to cover the cost of the pensions promised, thus securing payment in the future, that being the substance of the employer's commitment.

It followed that, unlike periodic payment of pensions, inequality of employers' contributions paid under funded defined-benefit schemes, which was due to the use of actuarial factors differing according to sex, was not struck at by Article 157.

1555. A similar case was dealt with in *Worringham and Humphreys* v. *Lloyd's Bank Limited*. In Lloyd's all permanent staff of the Bank are, on entering employment, required to become members of a retirement benefits scheme; each member, with the exception of women under 25, is required to contribute 5 per cent of his or her salary to the fund. Contributions are deducted from a member's salary at source and paid by the Bank directly to the trustees. Here also the gross salary of the male members was higher, which led to different rules regarding other aspects not related to that pension, such as that the above-mentioned 5 per cent contribution is included to determine the amount of certain benefits and social advantages such as redundancy payments, unemployment benefits and family allowances, as well as mortgage and credit facilities. Logically, the Court concluded that a contribution to a retirement benefits scheme that is paid by an employer in the name of employees by means of an addition to the gross salary and which therefore helps to determine the

---

596. 18 September 1984, No. 23/83, ECR, 1984, 3225.
597. 22 December 1993, No. Case C-152/91, ECR, 1993, 6935.

amount of that salary constitutes 'pay' within the meaning of the second paragraph of Article 157 TFEU.[598]

1556. In *Garland* v. *British Rail*, the dispute concerned discrimination alleged to be suffered by female employees who on retirement no longer continued to enjoy travel facilities for their spouses and dependent children although male employees continued to do so. The question was whether such facilities constitute pay within the meaning of Article 157, especially since the employer grants them although he is not contractually bound to do so. The Court first retained the point that the special rail travel facilities granted after retirement must be considered to be an extension of the facilities granted during the period of employment. As they are granted in kind by the employer to the retired male employee or his dependants directly or indirectly in respect of his employment, they fulfil the criteria enabling them to be treated as pay within the meaning of Article 157. The Court ruled that the argument that the facilities are not related to a contractual obligation is immaterial. The legal nature of the facilities is not important for the purposes of the application of Article 157 provided they are granted in respect of employment.[599]

Another case concerned an expatriation allowance for Union officials. The purpose of such an allowance is to compensate civil servants for the special expenses and disadvantages resulting from the entry into the service of the Union and the resulting obligation to change place of residence. Staff regulations provided that an official 'who marries a person who at the date of marriage does not qualify for the allowance shall forfeit the right to the expatriate allowance unless that official thereby becomes a head of household'. The head of a household, however, normally refers to a married male official, whereas a married female official is considered to be head of household only in exceptional circumstances, in particular in cases of invalidity or serious illness of the husband. This indicates that the allowance is paid to married officials not only in consideration of the personal situation of the recipient, but also of the family situation created by the marriage. Since the Staff regulations cannot treat officials differently according to whether they are male or female, and since termination of the status of expatriate must depend for both male and female officials on uniform criteria, irrespective of sex, the Court annulled the decisions by which the applicant's expatriate allowance was withdrawn.[600] Article 157 also applies to the conditions of access to voluntary redundancy benefits paid by an employer to a worker wishing to leave his employment.[601]

By retaining legislation which excludes female workers over the age of 60 from the benefit of additional redundancy payments, a Member State equally fails to fulfil its obligations under Article 157.[602]

Finally, conditions of age, such as the age of 40 years at which the employment contract of G. Defrenne had to come to an end, have indirectly to do with remuneration, but of course do not constitute 'pay' in the sense of Article 157.

---

598. 11 March 1981, No. 69/80, ECR, 1981, 767.
599. 2 February 1982, No. 12/81, ECR, 1982, 359.
600. C.O.J., 7 June 1972, *Sabbatini* v. *European Parliament*, No. 20/71, ECR, 1972, 363.
601. C.O.J., 16 February 1982, *Arthur Burton* v. *British Railways Board*, No. 19/81, ECR, 1982, 554.
602. C.O.J., 17 February 1993, *Commission of the European Communities* v. *Kingdom of Belgium*, No. C-173/91, ECR, 1993, 673.

1557. In *Newstead* v. *Department of Transport*, the following case was discussed: the occupational pension scheme to which Newstead belonged made a provision for a widow's pension fund. That fund was financed in part by the contributions of civil servants. However, although male civil servants, whatever their marital status, were obliged to contribute 1.5 per cent of their gross salary to the fund, female civil servants were never obliged to contribute to the fund but could in certain circumstances be permitted to do so. In the case of a civil servant who was at no time married while he was covered by the occupational scheme, it was provided that his contributions to the widow's pension fund should be returned to him, with compound interest at the rate of 4 per cent per annum, when he would leave the Civil Service. Should he die before then, that amount would be paid to his estate. Mr. Newstead, who was unmarried, argued that the obligation to contribute to the widow's pension fund had the effect of discrimination against him in comparison with a female civil servant in an equivalent post, since she was not obliged to give up 1.5 per cent of her gross salary. The Court, in judging the case, brought to mind its earlier judgments, whereby it simply observed that Article 157 was applicable in particular where the gross pay of men was higher than that of women in order to make up for the fact that only men were required to contribute to a social security scheme. The Court emphasised that although the extra pay was subsequently deducted by the employer and paid into a pension fund on behalf of the employee, it determined the calculation of other salary-related benefits (redundancy payments, unemployment benefits, family allowances, credit facilities) and was therefore a component of the worker's pay for the purposes of the second paragraph of Article 157. For Newstead, the Court ruled, those circumstances were not present. The deduction in question resulted in a reduction in net pay because of a contribution paid to a social security scheme and in no way affected gross pay, on the basis of which the other salary-related benefits mentioned above were normally calculated. It followed, rather surprisingly, that Article 157 was not applicable. Directive No. 76/207 of 9 February 1976 was not applicable either, as it is not intended to apply in social security matters, nor was Directive No. 79/7 of 19 December 1978, as Article 3(2) of that directive states that it 'shall not apply to the provisions concerning survivors' benefits'. It should be added that Article 9 of Directive No. 86/372 of 24 July 1986 on the implementation of the principle of equal treatment for men and women in occupational social security schemes provides that:

> Member States may defer compulsory application of the principle of equal treatment with regard to ... (b) survivors' pensions until a directive requires the principle of equal treatment in statutory social schemes in that regard.

1558. George Noel Newstead lost his case although *prima facie* he must have been sure that this was one he could not lose. It becomes immediately clear that the notion 'pay' in the meaning of Article 157 and the equal treatment directives belongs to advanced legal technology.

1559. This was confirmed in *Douglas Harvey Barber* v. *Guardian Royal Exchange Group*, which related to Barber's right to an early retirement pension on his being made compulsorily redundant. Barber's conditions provided that, in the event of redundancy, members of the pension fund established by the Guardian were entitled to an immediate pension subject to having attained the age of 55 for men and 50 for women. Staff who did not fulfil those conditions received certain cash benefits calculated on the basis of their years of service and a deferred pension payable at the normal pensionable age, which was fixed at 62 for men and 57 for women. Barber was made redundant when he was aged 52. The Guardian paid him the cash benefits provided for in the severance terms, the statutory redundancy payment and the *ex-gratia* payment. He would have been entitled to a retirement pension as from the date of his 62nd birthday. It was undisputed that a woman in the same position as Mr. Barber would have received an immediate retirement pension as well as the statutory redundancy payment and that the total value of those benefits would have been greater than the amount paid to Mr. Barber. Therefore, Mr. Barber contended that he was discriminated against.

1560. In deciding this case the Court took a number of important decisions on principle, while confirming some others:

(1) the fact that certain benefits are paid after the termination of the employment relationship does not prevent them from being in the nature of pay, within the meaning of Article 157 TFEU;[603]
(2) compensation in connection with redundancy constitutes a form of pay to which the worker is entitled in respect of his employment and which is paid to him upon the termination of his employment relationship, whether it is paid under a contract of employment, by virtue of legislative provisions or on a voluntary basis;
(3) unlike the benefits awarded by national statutory social security schemes, a pension paid under a contracted-out scheme constitutes consideration paid by the employer to the worker in respect of his employment and therefore falls within the scope of Article 157;
(4) it is contrary to Article 157 to impose an age condition which differs according to sex in respect of pensions paid under a contracted-out scheme, even if the difference between the pensionable age for men and that for women is based on the one provided for by the national statutory scheme;[604]
(5) the Court emphasised the fundamental importance of transparency and, in particular, of the possibility of a review by the national courts, in order to prevent and, if necessary, eliminate any discrimination based on sex;
(6) if the national courts are under the obligation to make an assessment and a comparison of all the various types of consideration granted, according to the circumstances, to men and women, juridical review would be difficult and the

---

603. This was confirmed in *Commission* v. *Belgium*, 17 February 1993, No. C-173/91, IELL, *Case Law*, No. 201. 'By maintaining in force legislation which renders female workers who have attained the age of 60 ineligible for a supplementary allowance payable upon redundancy, provided for by Collective Labour Agreement No. 17, which was given the force of law by Royal Decree of 16 January 1975, the Kingdom of Belgium has failed to fulfil its obligations under Article 141 of the Treaty.'
604. *See also* C.O.J., 14 December 1993, *M. Moroni* v. *Finma Collo GmbH*, No. C-110/91, ECR, 1993, 6591.

effectiveness of Article 157 would be diminished as a result. It follows that genuine transparency permitting an effective review is assured only if the principle of equal pay applies to each of the elements of remuneration granted to men or women;
(7) the Court held that, according to its established case law, Article 157 applies directly to all forms of discrimination which can be identified solely with the aid of the criteria of equal work and equal pay referred to by the article in question, without national or Union measures being required to define them with greater precision in order to permit their application;
(8) the direct effect of Article 157 may not be relied upon to claim entitlement to a pension, with effect from a date prior to that of this judgment, except in the case of workers or those claiming for them who have before that date initiated legal proceedings or raised an equivalent claim under the then applicable law. The Court recalled indeed that it could, by way of exception, taking account of the serious difficulties which its judgment might create in regard to past events, be moved to restrict the possibility for all persons concerned to rely on the interpretation which the Court, in proceedings with reference to a preliminary ruling, gave to a provision.[605]

1561. The pension saga continues. In the *Birds Eye Walls Limited* v. *F.M. Robert* case,[606] the question was raised whether when judging equal treatment regarding bridging pensions reference should be made to State pensions which the woman concerned actually receives. In this case the Court held that:

(1) It is not contrary to Article 141 TFEU, when calculating the amount of a bridging pension which is paid by an employer to male and female employees who have taken early retirement on grounds of ill health and which is intended to compensate, in particular, for loss of income resulting from the fact that they have not yet reached the age required for payment of the State pension, to take account of the amount of the State pension which they will subsequently receive and to reduce the amount of the bridging pension accordingly, even though, in the case of men and women aged between 60 and 65, the result is that a female ex-employee receives a smaller bridging pension than that paid to her male counterpart, the difference being equal to the amount of the State pension to which she is entitled as from the age of 60 in respect of the periods of service completed with that employer.
(2) It is not contrary to Article 157 TFEU, when calculating the bridging pension, to take account of the full State pension which a married woman would have received if she had not opted in favour of paying contributions at a reduced rate, entitling her to a reduced pension only, or not entitling her to a pension, or of

---

605. 17 May 1990, No. 262/88, IELL, *Case Law*, No. 146. *See also* C.O.J., 6 September 1993, *G.C. Ten Oever* v. *Stichting, op. cit.*; 14 December 1993, *M. Moroni, op. cit.*, and 22 December 1993, *D. Neath* v. *Hugh Steeper Ltd.*, No. C-152/91, ECR, 1993, 6935.
606. C.O.J., *Birds Eye Walls Limited* v. *F.M. Robert*, 9 November 1993, No. C-132/92, ECR, 1993, 5579.

Part I, Ch. 6, Equal Treatment

the widow's pension which may be drawn by the woman concerned and which is equivalent to a full State pension.

1562. On 28 September 1994, the Court of Justice decided in no fewer than six cases relating to the implications of the *Barber* case.[607] The harvest of these judgments can be summarised as follows:

(1) By virtue of the *Barber* judgment, the direct effect of Article 157 of the Treaty may be relied upon, for the purpose of claiming equal treatment in the matter of occupational pensions, only in relation to benefits payable in respect of periods of service subsequent to 17 May 1990, subject to the exception in favour of workers or those claiming under them who have, before that date, initiated legal proceedings or raised an equivalent claim under the applicable national law.
(2) The limitation of the effects in time of the *Barber* judgment applies to survivors' pensions and consequently equal treatment in this matter may be claimed only in relation to periods of service subsequent to 17 May 1990.
(3) The limitation of the effects in time of the *Barber* judgment is applicable to benefits not linked to the length of actual service only where the operative events occurred before 17 May 1990.
(4) The principles laid down in the *Barber* judgment, and more particularly the limitation of its effects in time, concern not only contracted-out but also non-contracted-out occupational schemes.
(5) The use of actuarial factors varying according to sex in funded defined-benefit occupational pension schemes does not fall within the scope of Article 157 of the Treaty. Consequently, inequalities in the amounts of capital benefits or substitute benefits, whose value can be determined only on the basis of the arrangements chosen for funding the scheme, are likewise not struck at by Article 157.
(6) The principle of equal treatment, laid down in Article 157, applies to all pension benefits paid by occupational schemes, without any need to distinguish according to the kind of contributions to which these benefits are attributed, namely employers' contributions or employees' contributions. However, in so far as an occupational pension scheme does no more than provide the membership with the necessary arrangements for management, additional benefits stemming from contributions paid by employees on a purely voluntary basis are not covered by Article 157.
(7) In the event of the transfer of pension rights from one occupational scheme to another owing to a worker's change of job, the second scheme is obliged, on the worker's reaching retirement age, to increase the benefits it undertook to pay him when accepting the transfer so as to eliminate the effects, contrary to

---

607. C.O.J., 28 September 1994, *Coloroll Pension Trustees Ltd.* v. *James Richard Russel and Others*, C-200/91, ECR, 1994, 4389; *Constance Christina Ellen Smith and Others* v. *Avdel Systems Ltd.*, Case C-408/92, ECR, 1994, 4435; *Maria Nelleke Gerda van den Akker and Others* v. *Stichting Shell Pensioenfonds*, Case C-28/93, ECR, 1994, 4527; *Bestuur van het Algemeen burgerlijk pensioenfonds* v. *G.A. Beune*, Case C-7/93, ECR, 1994, 4471; *Anna Adriaantje Vroege* v. *NCIV Instituut voor Volkshuisvesting BV and Stichting Pensioenfonds NCIV*, Case C-57/93, ECR, 1994, 4541; *Geertruida Catharina Fisscher* v. *Voorhuis Hengelo BV and Stichting Bedrijfs-pensioenfonds voor de Detailhandel*, Case C-128/93, ECR, 1994, 4583.

Article 157, suffered by the worker in consequence of the inadequacy of the capital transferred, this being due in turn to the discriminatory treatment suffered under the first scheme, and it must do so in relation to benefits payable in respect of periods of service subsequent to 17 May 1990.
(8) Article 157 is not applicable to schemes which have at all times had members of only one sex.
(9) Article 157 precludes an occupational scheme from retrospectively raising the retirement age for women in relation to periods of service completed between 17 May 1990 and the date of entry into force of the measures by which equality is achieved in the scheme in question.
(10) Article 157 does not allow a situation of equality to be achieved otherwise than by applying to male employees the same arrangements as those enjoyed by female employees.
(11) Benefits paid under a pension scheme for public servants must be regarded as pay within the meaning of Article 157.
(12) Married men placed at disadvantage by discrimination must be treated in the same way and have the same rules applied to them as married women.

1563. The right to join an occupational pension scheme falls within the scope of Article 157 and is therefore covered by the prohibition of discrimination. The limitation of the effects in time of the *Barber* judgment does not apply to the right to join an occupational pension scheme or to the right of the payment of a retirement pension. The fact that a worker can claim retroactive membership of an occupational pension scheme does not enable him to avoid paying contributions for the period of membership concerned.[608]

1564. It should be noted that Directive 86/378 of 24 July 1986 on the implementation of the principle of equal treatment for men and women in occupational social security schemes was amended by Directive 96/97 adopted on 2 December 1996.[609] This directive brings the 1986 Directive into line with the judgments of the Court of Justice in *Barber* and subsequent cases.

1565. A judicial award of compensation for breach of the right not to be unfairly dismissed constitutes pay within the meaning of Article 157, as well as the conditions determining whether an employee is entitled, where he has been unfairly dismissed, to obtain compensation. However, the conditions determining whether an employee is entitled, where he has been unfairly dismissed, to obtain reinstatement or re-engagement fall within the scope of Directive 76/207/EEC of 9 February 1976.

It is for the national court, taking into account all the material legal and factual circumstances, to determine the point in time at which the legality of a rule to the effect that protection against unfair dismissal applies only to employees who have

---

608. C.O.J., 24 October 1996, *Francina Johanna Maria Dietz* v. *Stichting Thuiszorg Rotterdam*, Case C-435/93, ECR, 1996, 5224. *See also* C.O.J., 25 May 2000, *Jean-Marie Podesta* v. *Caisse de retraite par répartition des ingénieurs cadres & assimilés (CRICA) and Others*, Case C-50/99, ECR, 2000, 39.
609. O.J. L 46, 17 February 1997.

Part I, Ch. 6, Equal Treatment

been continuously employed for a minimum period of two years is to be assessed.[610]

1566. Swedish legislation which automatically favours access for women to public posts, even where their qualifications are not equal to those of the male candidates, is contrary to Community law. The Court pointed out that priority for women where their qualifications are equal – as a way of restoring balance – is not contrary to Community law provided that an objective assessment of each candidature is guaranteed.

The case was as follows. The University of Göteborg announced a vacancy for the chair of Professor. The vacancy notice indicated that the appointment to that post should contribute to promotion of equality of the sexes in professional life and that positive discrimination might be applied in accordance with the Swedish legislation.

The selection board responsible ranked the candidates taking account both of the candidates' scientific merits and of the Swedish legislation on positive discrimination.

Under that legislation, appointments to posts of professor are to take account of the need to accord priority to the under-represented sex where it proves necessary to do so in order for the candidate belonging to that sex to be appointed and provided that the difference between the candidates' qualifications is not so great as to give rise to a breach of the requirement of objectivity in the making of appointments.

The decision of Rector of the University was the subject of an appeal by Mr. Anderson and Ms. Abrahamsson, who had not been appointed.

The Universities' Appeals Board sought a preliminary ruling from the Court of Justice as to whether the Swedish legislation conformed to Community law on equal treatment for men and women.

The Court referred first to its case law according to which a measure intended to give priority in promotion to women in sectors of the public service where they are under-represented must be regarded as compatible with the Community law:

– where it does not automatically and unconditionally give priority to women when women and men are equally qualified, and
– where the candidatures are the subject of an objective assessment which takes account of the specific personal situations of all candidates.

1567. The Court stated that the Swedish legislation enabled preference to be accorded to a candidate belonging to the under-represented sex who, although sufficiently qualified, did not possess the same qualifications as the other candidates of the opposite sex.

The Court observed that the assessment of the candidates' qualifications in the selection procedure at issue was not based on clear and certain criteria (for example, seniority, age, date of last promotion, family status or income of the partner). The

---

610. C.O.J., 9 February 1999, *Regina* v. *Secretary of State for Employment, ex parte Nicole Seymour-Smith and Laura Perez*, Case C-167/97, ECR, 1999, 623.

risk of arbitrary assessment of candidates' qualifications was not eliminated by the application of transparent criteria.

The Swedish legislation automatically accorded priority to candidates belonging to the under-represented sex who were adequately qualified, subject only to the proviso that the difference between the merits of the candidates of each sex was not so great as to give rise to a breach of the requirement of objectivity in the making of appointments.

The Court concluded that the selection method under the Swedish legislation did not conform to Union law: the selection was ultimately based merely on the fact of belonging to the under-represented sex, and candidatures were not subjected to an objective assessment taking account of the specific personal situations of all the candidates. The selection method was also disproportionate having regard to the aim pursued.[611]

1568. In the case *Helga Kutz-Bauer*,[612] the Court ruled on a scheme of part-time work for older employees, which is intended to reduce the normal working time, either by reducing the working hours at a uniform rate throughout the entire period concerned, or by allowing the person concerned to cease work at an earlier date. In each case the scheme affects the exercise of the occupation of the workers concerned by adjusting their working time.

The Court found that the scheme established rules relating to working conditions for the purposes of Article 5(1) of Directive 76/207.

The class of persons entitled to receive a full retirement pension at the age of 60 under the statutory old-age insurance scheme consists almost exclusively of women while the class of persons eligible for such a pension only from the age of 65 consists almost exclusively of men.

It follows from the documents in the file that while both female and male workers may benefit from the scheme of part-time working from the age of 55 with the employer's consent, the great majority of workers entitled to benefit from the scheme for a period of five years from the age of 60 are male.

In those circumstances, provisions of the kind at issue in the main proceedings result in discrimination against female workers by comparison with male workers and must in principle be treated as contrary to Articles 2(1) and 5(1) of Directive 76/207. It would be otherwise only if the difference of treatment found to exist between the two categories of worker were justified by objective factors unrelated to any discrimination based on sex.

1569. Two other cases related to part-time teachers. The first case[613] concerned the (non)remuneration for additional hours for as well to part-time as full-time teachers. The employer submitted that part-time teachers are treated in exactly the

---

611. C.O.J., 6 July 2000, *Katarina Abrahamsson and Leif Anderson v. Elisabet Fogelqvist*, Case C-407/98, ECR, 2000, 5539.
612. C.O.J., 20 March 2003, *Helga Kutz-Bauer and Freie und Hansestadt Hamburg*, C-187/00, ECR, 2003, 2741; *see also*: Case C.O.J., 11 September 2003, *Erika Steinicke v. Bundesanstalt für Arbeit*, C-77/02, ECR, 2003, 9027.
613. C.O.J., Case C-285/02, 27 May 2004, *Edeltraud Elsner-Lakeberg v. Land Nordrhein-Westfalen*, www.curia.eu.

same manner as full-time teachers. All teachers are en-titled to remuneration if more than three additional hours are worked. In that case the additional hours are remunerated in exactly the same manner. Equality of remuneration is ensured for both regular working hours and additional hours.

The Court has held, with respect to part-time workers, that the members of the class of persons placed at a disadvantage, be they men or women, are entitled to have the same scheme applied to them as that applied to the other workers, on a basis proportional to their working time.

Although that pay may appear to be equal inasmuch as the entitlement to remuneration for additional hours is triggered only after three additional hours have been worked by part-time and full-time teachers, three additional hours is in fact a greater burden for part-time teachers than it is for full-time teachers. A full-time teacher must work an additional three hours over his regular monthly schedule of 98 hours, which is approximately 3 per cent extra, in order to be paid for his additional hours, whilst a part-time teacher must work three hours more than his monthly 60 hours, which is five per cent extra. Since the number of additional teaching hours giving entitlement to pay is not reduced for part-time teachers in a manner proportionate to their working hours, they receive different treatment compared with full-time teachers as regards pay for additional teaching hours.

In case that different treatment affected considerably more women than men and there seemed no objective unrelated to sex which justified that different treatment or it is not necessary to achieve the objective pursued.

Therefore the Court ruled:

> In those circumstances, the question referred for a preliminary ruling should be answered as follows: Article 157 TFEU and Article 1 of Directive 75/117 must be interpreted as precluding national legislation which provides that teachers, part-time as well as full-time, do not receive any remuneration for additional hours worked when the additional work does not exceed three hours per calendar month, if that different treatment affects considerably more women than men and if there is no objective unrelated to sex which justifies that different treatment or it is not necessary to achieve the objective pursued.

1570. The second case relates to the calculation of the length of service.

Where the total exclusion of part-time employment when calculating length of service affects a much higher percentage of female workers than male workers, it constitutes indirect discrimination on grounds of sex contrary to Directive 76/207, unless that exclusion is attributable to factors which are objectively justified and are unrelated to any discrimination on grounds of sex. It is for the national court to determine whether that is the case. The proportional counting of part-time employment when making that calculation is also contrary to Directive 76/207, unless the employer establishes that it is justified by factors whose objectivity depends in particular on the aim pursued by taking length of service into account and, should it be a question of recognition of experience acquired, on the relationship between the nature of the duties carried out and the experience which performance of those duties brings after a certain number of hours of work have been completed.[614]

1571. Council Directive 76/207/EEC of 9 February 1976 must be interpreted as precluding a provision such as that at issue in the main proceedings, which grants to workers who have passed the age of 50 years in the case of women and 55 years in the case of men, as a *voluntary redundancy incentive*, an advantage consisting in taxation at a rate reduced by half, of sums paid on cessation of the employment relationship.[615]

II. Access to Employment, Promotion, Vocational Training

1572. Directive No. 76/207 of 9 February 1976 aims at the application of the principle of equal treatment, which means that there shall be no direct or indirect discrimination on the grounds of sex in the public or private sectors, including public bodies, in relation to:

(a) conditions for access to employment, to self-employment or to occupation, including selection criteria and recruitment conditions, whatever the branch of activity and at all levels of the professional hierarchy, including promotion;
(b) access to all types and to all levels of vocational guidance, vocational training, advanced vocational training and retraining, including practical work experience (Art. 3(1)).

To that end, Member States shall take the necessary measures to ensure that:

(a) any laws, regulations and administrative provisions contrary to the principle of equal treatment are abolished;
(b) any provisions contrary to the principle of equal treatment which are included in contracts or collective agreements, internal rules of undertakings or rules governing the independent occupations and professions and workers' and employers' organisations shall be, or may be declared, null and void or are amended (Art. 3(2) amended).
(c) Member States shall encourage, in accordance with national law, collective agreements or practice, employers and those responsible for access to vocational training to take measures to prevent all forms of discrimination on grounds of sex, in particular harassment and sexual harassment at the workplace (Art. 2(5) (amended)).

---

614. C.O.J., 10 March 2005, *Vasiliki Nikoloudi v. Organismos Tilepikinonion Ellados AE*, C-196/02, ECR, 2005, 1789.
615. C.O.J., 21 July 2005, *Paolo Vergani v. Agenzia delle Entrate, Ufficio di Arona*, C-207/04, ECR, 2005, 7453.

Part I, Ch. 6, Equal Treatment

It is interesting to note that offers of employment do not fall within the scope of the directive.[616]

1573. In October 1997 Ms. Schnorbus (Germany) passed the First State Examination in law. Under federal and *Land* Hesse legislation, in order to obtain a post in the judicial service or in the higher civil service, a person must have undergone practical legal training and then have passed the Second State Examination. Her application was, however, rejected, informing her that, since too many applications had been received, it had been necessary to make a selection.

She then lodged an objection to the refusal of admission to practical legal training, arguing, in particular, that the selection procedure discriminated against women because of the preference accorded to applicants who had completed compulsory military or civilian service, which can be done only by men. That objection was dismissed on the ground that the rule in question, which was designed to counterbalance the disadvantage suffered by applicants who were obliged to complete military or civilian service, was based on an objective distinguishing factor.

1574. The Court[617] ruled as follows:

> National provisions governing the date of admission to the practical legal training which is a necessary prerequisite of access to employment in the civil service fall within the scope of Council Directive 76/207/EEC of 9 February 1976.
>
> National provisions such as those at issue in the main proceedings do not constitute discrimination directly based on sex, but do constitute indirect discrimination based on sex.
>
> Directive 76/207 does not preclude national provisions such as those at issue in the main proceedings, in so far as such provisions are justified by objective reasons and prompted solely by a desire to counterbalance to some extent the delay resulting from the completion of compulsory military or civilian service.

1575. The Court of Justice ruled in a Dutch case that an employer is in direct contravention of the principle of equal treatment if he refuses to enter into a contract of employment with a candidate whom he had decided was suitable for the post in question where such refusal is based on the possible adverse consequences for him of employing a pregnant woman as a result of rules adopted by the public authorities on unfitness for work which treat inability to work because of pregnancy and confinement in the same way as inability to work because of illness.[618]

1576. In the *Badeck* case, the Court analyses whether the law of the *Land* of Hesse on equal rights for women and men and the removal of discrimination against women in the public service is compatible with Directive 76/207/EEC.

---

616. C.O.J., 21 May 1985, *Commission* v. *Germany*, No. 248/83, ECR, 1985, 1459.
617. C.O.J., 7 December 2000, *Julia Schnorbus* v. *Land Hessen*, C-79/99, ECR, 2000, 10997.
618. 8 November 1990, *E.J.P. Dekker* v. *Stichting Vormingscentrum voor Jong Volwassenen (VIV-Centrum) Plus*, No. C-177/88, ECR, 1990, 3941.

Under that law, administrative departments of the *Land* of Hesse are required to contribute to equal treatment of men and women in the public service, and in particular to eliminate under-representation of women, by means of advancement plans for women. Each plan must provide that more than half the posts to be filled (by appointment or promotion) in a sector in which women are under-represented must be given to women. The law lays down the details, selection criteria and exceptions.

The Court of Justice pointed out that, in accordance with its earlier judgments in *Kalanke* (17 October 1995) and *Marshall* (11 November 1997), a measure which is intended to give priority in promotion to women in sectors of the public service where women are under-represented must be regarded as compatible with Community law if

- it does not automatically and unconditionally give priority to women when women and men are equally qualified, and
- the candidatures are the subject of an objective assessment which takes account of the specific personal situations of all candidates.

1577. The Hesse law, which provides for a 'flexible result quota', does not determine quotas uniformly for all the sectors and departments concerned, but states that the characteristics of those sectors and departments are to be decisive for fixing the binding targets. Second, the law does not necessarily determine from the outset – automatically – that the outcome of each selection procedure must, in a 'stalemate' situation (candidates have equal qualifications), necessarily favour the woman.

1578. The Court of Justice found that the selection procedure for candidates under the law must start with an assessment of their suitability, capability and professional performance with respect to the requirements of the post to be filled or the office to be conferred.

According to the Court, the assessment criteria laid down by the law, although formulated in terms which are neutral as regards sex and thus capable of benefiting men too, in general favour women. They are manifestly intended to lead to an equality which is substantive rather than formal by reducing the inequalities which may occur in practice in social life.

In the Court's view, the priority rule introduced by the law is not absolute and unconditional in the sense of the *Kalanke* judgment, however; reasons of greater legal weight (for example, the priority to be given to seriously disabled persons, or to end a long period of unemployment) allow the rule of priority for women to be overridden. It is for the national court to assess whether the rule ensures that candidatures are the subject of an objective assessment which takes account of the specific personal situations of all candidates.

In those circumstances, the Court held that the Community directive does not preclude the law in question. The Court also stated that since the special system for temporary posts in the academic sector and for academic assistants does not fix an absolute ceiling but refers to the percentage of women with degrees in that sector, it is compatible with Union law.

Part I, Ch. 6, Equal Treatment

The law prescribes that at least half the training places in occupations for which the State does not have a monopoly of training are to be reserved for women, in order to enable access by them to trained occupations in which they are underrepresented. The Court found that that rule, which does not prevent men from receiving similar training organised by the private sector, is compatible with Union law.

The Court held, finally, that the Union directive does not preclude a national rule on the composition of representative bodies of workers and administrative and supervisory bodies which recommends that the legislative provisions adopted for its implementation take into account the objective that at least half the members of those bodies should be women.[619]

1579. However, Directive 76/207 is to be interpreted as not applying to a social security scheme, such as a supplementary allowance or income support, simply because the conditions of entitlement for receipt of the benefits may be such as to affect the ability of a single parent to take up access to vocational training or part-time employment.[620]

1580. The Union directive on equal treatment for men and women as regards access to employment precludes a refusal to appoint a pregnant woman to a post for an indefinite period on the basis of national legislation which seeks to ensure the protection of pregnant women. The case goes as follows.

Ms. Mahlburg was employed as an operating-theatre nurse by the Rostock University Heart Surgery Clinic of the *Land* Mecklenburg-Vorpommern under a fixed-term contract. When she applied, for one of two posts available for an indefinite period in the clinic, she was pregnant. Ms. Mahlburg gave written notice of the pregnancy to her employer. In order to comply with German legislation protecting pregnant women her employer immediately transferred her to another internal post.

Finally, however, the employer decided not to appoint Ms. Mahlburg, in accordance with the German legislation (*Mutterschutzgesetz*) which expressly prohibits employers from employing pregnant women in areas in which they would be exposed to the harmful effects of dangerous substances. The post concerned was in the operating-theatre.

Ms. Mahlburg appealed against her rejection. She claimed that the refusal to give her an employment contract for an indefinite period and the grounds for that refusal constituted unlawful dismissal.

1581. The Court of Justice ruled that the directive precludes a refusal to appoint a pregnant woman to a post for an indefinite period on the ground that a statutory prohibition on employment attaching to the condition of pregnancy prevents her from being employed in that post from the outset.

The Court cited its case law: only women can be refused employment on grounds of pregnancy and such a refusal therefore constitutes direct discrimination on

---

619. C.O.J., 28 March 2000, and *Others, interveners: Hessische Ministerpräsident and Landesanwalt beim Staatsgerichtshof des Landes Hessen*, Case C-158/97, ECR, 2000, 1875.
620. C.O.J., 16 July 1992, *S. Jackson and P. Cresswell v. Chief Adjudication Officer*, Joined Cases Nos. C-63/91 and C-64/91, ECR, 1992, 4737.

grounds of sex. It pointed out, however, that in this case the unequal treatment was not based directly on the woman's pregnancy but on a statutory prohibition on employment attaching to that condition. The question to be considered, therefore, was whether the directive allowed an employer not to conclude an employment contract for an indefinite period on account of the fact that compliance with the prohibition on pregnant women's employment would prevent the woman carrying out, from the outset, the work in the post to be filled.

According to the Court, it follows from its case law, in particular the cases concerning the dismissal of pregnant women, that the application of provisions concerning the protection of pregnant women cannot result in unfavourable treatment regarding their access to employment, so that it is not permissible for an employer to refuse to take on a pregnant woman on the ground that a prohibition on employment arising on account of the pregnancy would prevent her being employed from the outset and for the duration of the pregnancy in the post of unlimited duration to be filled.

As for the possible financial consequences of an obligation to take on pregnant women, in particular for small and mediumsized undertakings, the Court cited its case law to the effect that a refusal to employ a woman on account of her pregnancy cannot be justified on grounds relating to the financial loss which an employer who appointed a pregnant woman would suffer for the duration of her maternity leave.[621]

1582. In the cases *Sidar*[622] (*Royal Marines*) and *Kreil* (the *Bundeswehr*),[623] the Court of Justice addressed the question of female employment in the army, coming to a different result as to the exclusion of women from the army in general and from special combat units in particular.

The Court observes first of all that it is for the Member States, which have to adopt appropriate measures to ensure their internal and external security, to take decisions on the organisation of their armed forces. It does not follow, however, that such decisions are bound to fall entirely outside the scope of Union law.

As the Court has already held, the only articles in which the Treaty provides for derogations applicable in situations which may affect public security are Articles 36, 45, 52, 346 and Article 347, which deal with exceptional and clearly defined cases. It is not possible to infer from those articles that there is a general exception excluding from the scope of Union law all measures taken for reasons of public security. To recognise the existence of such an exception, regardless of the specific requirements laid down by the Treaty, might impair the binding nature of Union law and its uniform application.

The concept of public security covers both a Member State's internal security and its external security. Furthermore, some of the derogations provided for by the Treaty concern only the rules relating to the free movement of goods, persons and

---

621. C.O.J., 3 February 2000, *Silke-Karin Mahlburg* v. *Land Mecklenburg-Vorpommern*, Case C-207/98, ECR, 2000, 549.
622. C.O.J., 26 October 1999, *Angela Maria Sirdar* v. *The Army Board and Secretary of State for Defence*, Case C-273/97, ECR, 1999, 7403.
623. C.O.J., 11 January 2000, *Tanja Kreil* v. *Bundesrepublik Deutschland*, Case C-285/98, ECR, 2000, 69.

Part I, Ch. 6, Equal Treatment

services, and not the social provisions of the Treaty, of which the principle of equal treatment for men and women is one.

Under Article 2(2) of the directive, Member States may exclude from the scope of the directive occupational activities for which, by reason of their nature or the context in which they are carried out, sex constitutes a determining factor; it must be noted, however, that, as a derogation from an individual right laid down in the directive, that provision must be interpreted strictly.

The Court has thus recognised, for example, that sex may be a determining factor for posts such as those of prison warders and head prison warders for certain activities such as policing activities performed in situations where there are serious internal disturbances or for service in certain special combat units.

1583. A Member State may restrict such activities and the relevant professional training to men or to women, as appropriate. In such a case, as is clear from Article 9(2) of the directive, Member States have a duty to assess periodically the activities concerned in order to decide whether, in the light of social developments, the derogation from the general scheme of the directive may still be maintained.

In determining the scope of any derogation from an individual right such as the equal treatment of men and women, the principle of proportionality, one of the general principles of Union law, must also be observed. That principle requires that derogations remain within the limits of what is appropriate and necessary in order to achieve the aim in view and requires the principle of equal treatment to be reconciled as far as possible with the requirements of public security which determine the context in which the activities in question are to be performed.

However, depending on the circumstances, national authorities have a certain degree of discretion when adopting measures which they consider to be necessary in order to guarantee public security in a Member State.

The question is therefore whether the measures taken by the national authorities, in the exercise of the discretion which they are recognised to enjoy, do in fact have the purpose of guaranteeing public security and whether they are appropriate and necessary to achieve that aim.

The refusal to engage the applicant in the main proceedings in the service of the *Bundeswehr* in which she wished to be employed was based on provisions of German law which bar women outright from military posts involving the use of arms and which allow women access only to the medical and military-music services.

1584. In view of its scope, such an exclusion, which applies to almost all military posts in the *Bundeswehr*, cannot be regarded as a derogating measure justified by the specific nature of the posts in question or by the particular context in which the activities in question are carried out. However, the derogations provided for in Article 2(2) of the directive can apply only to specific activities.

Moreover, having regard to the very nature of armed forces, the fact that persons serving in those forces may be called on to use arms cannot in itself justify the exclusion of women from access to military posts. Even taking account of the discretion which they have as regards the possibility of maintaining the exclusion in question, the national authorities cannot, without contravening the principle of proportionality, adopt the general position that the composition of all armed units in the

Bundeswehr had to remain exclusively male.

It follows that the total exclusion of women from all military posts involving the use of arms is not one of the differences of treatment allowed by Article 2(3) of the directive out of concern to protect women.

The directive precludes the application of national provisions, such as those of German law, which impose a general exclusion of women from military posts involving the use of arms and which allow them access only to the medical and military-music services.

1585. The exclusion of women from service in special combat units, however, such as the Royal Marines (UK), may be justified under Article 2(2) of Council Directive 76/207/EEC by reason of the nature of the activities in question and the context in which they are carried out.[624] The organisation of the Royal Marines differs fundamentally from that of other units in the armed forces, of which they are 'the point of the arrow head'. They are a small force and are intended as the first line of attack.

1586. In *Alexander Dory and Federal Republic of Germany*,[625] the Court was asked whether Community law on equal treatment applies to the *compulsory military service*. The answer was negative.

Mr. Dory indeed requested to be exempted from call-up by the army and compulsory military service. In support of that request, he submitted that the German Federal Law on military service was contrary to Union law, according to which women were not to be excluded from access to all posts in the German armed forces.

1587. The Court ruled as follows: To determine whether or not limitation of compulsory military service to men is compatible with the principle of equal treatment of men and women in Union law, the conditions for applying that law to activities relating to the organisation of the armed forces must first be determined.

Measures taken by the Member States in this domain are not excluded in their entirety from the application of Community law solely because they are taken in the interests of public security or national defence.

As the Court has already held, the only articles in which the Treaty provides for derogations applicable in situations which may affect public security are Articles 36, 45, 52, 346 and 347 TFEU which deal with exceptional and clearly defined cases. It cannot be inferred from those articles that the Treaty contains an inherent general exception excluding all measures taken for reasons of public security from the scope of Union law. To recognise the existence of such an exception, regardless of the specific requirements laid down by the Treaty, might impair the binding nature of Union law and its uniform application.

---

624. C.O.J., 26 October 1999, *Angela Maria Sirdar v. The Army Board and Secretary of State for Defence*, Case C-273/97, ECR, 1999, 7403.
625. C.O.J., 11 March 2003, *Alexander Dory and Federal Republic of Germany*, C-186/01, ECR, 2003, 2479.

Part I, Ch. 6, Equal Treatment 1588–1590

The concept of public security, within the meaning of the Treaty articles cited in the preceding paragraph, covers both a Member State's internal security and its external security.

Furthermore, some of the derogations provided for by the Treaty concern only the rules relating to free movement of persons, goods, capital and services, and not the social provisions of the Treaty, of which the principle of equal treatment for men and women forms part. In accordance with settled case law, that principle is of general application and Directive 76/207 applies to employment in the public.

1588. Thus the Court held that Directive 76/207 was applicable to access to posts in the armed forces and that it was for the Court to verify whether the measures taken by the national authorities, in the exercise of their recognised discretion, did in fact have the purpose of guaranteeing public security and whether they were appropriate and necessary to achieve that aim.

Certainly, decisions of the Member States concerning the organisation of their armed forces cannot be completely excluded from the application of Union law, particularly where observance of the principle of equal treatment of men and women in connection with employment, including access to military posts, is concerned. But it does not follow that Union law governs the Member States' choices of military organisation for the defence of their territory or of their essential interests.

It is for the Member States, which have to adopt appropriate measures to ensure their internal and external security, to take decisions on the organisation of their armed forces.

The decision of the Federal Republic of Germany to ensure its defence in part by compulsory military service is the expression of such a choice of military organisation to which Union law is consequently not applicable.

It is true that limitation of compulsory military service to men will generally entail a delay in the progress of the careers of those concerned, even if military service allows some of them to acquire further vocational training or subsequently to take up a military career.

1589. Nevertheless, the delay in the careers of persons called up for military service is an inevitable consequence of the choice made by the Member State regarding military organisation and does not mean that that choice comes within the scope of Community law. The existence of adverse consequences for access to employment cannot, without encroaching on the competences of the Member States, have the effect of compelling the Member State in question either to extend the obligation of military service to women, thus imposing on them the same disadvantages with regard to access to employment, or to abolish compulsory military service.

In the light of all the foregoing, the answer must be that Community law does not preclude compulsory military service being reserved to men.

1590. A national law which does not afford a woman who is on maternity leave the same rights as other successful applicants from the same recruitment competition as regards conditions for access to the career of an official by deferring the start of her career to the end of that leave, without taking account of the duration of the leave, for the purpose of calculating her seniority of service is contrary to the Council Directive of 9 February 1976.[626]

1591. In the *Alvarez* case,[627] the Court, however, ruled that employed fathers are entitled to 'breastfeeding' leave irrespective of the professional status of their child's mother: Spanish legislation according to which an employed father is only entitled to make use of the leave in place of the mother of his child if she is an employee establishes an unjustified discrimination on grounds of sex.

1592. In Spain, the Workers' Statute provides that mothers whose status is that of employee are entitled, during the first nine months following the birth of their child, to 'breastfeeding' leave. That leave allows an absence from the workplace for an hour – which may be divided into two parts – or a half-hour reduction in the working day. It is expressly stated that the leave may be taken by the mother or the father without distinction provided that they are both employees.

1593. Pedro Manuel Roca Álvarez was an employee at the company Sesa Start España ETT SA. His request to be granted breastfeeding leave was refused on the ground that the mother of his child was not employed but self-employed. He therefore challenged his employer's decision before the national courts.

The High Court of Justice of Galicia, Spain, hearing the case on appeal, found that developments in national legislation and case-law have caused the leave to be detached from the biological fact of breastfeeding. Whilst it was instituted in 1900 to facilitate breastfeeding by the mother, for many years it has been granted in cases of bottle feeding. It should now be considered as time purely devoted to the child and as a measure which reconciles family life and work following maternity leave. However, the position remains that the father will be entitled to leave in place of the mother only if the mother is an employee, and so on that basis has herself a right to breastfeeding leave.

In that context, the Court of Justice was asked whether the right to breastfeeding leave should not be accorded to men in the same way as women and whether the fact of restricting it to employed women and the fathers of their children is not a discriminatory measure contrary to the principle of equal treatment of men and women afforded by the directives implementing this principle in the field of work and employment.

1594. In its judgment, the Court stated that those directives preclude a national measure which provides that employed mothers are entitled to breastfeeding leave whereas employed fathers are not entitled to the same leave unless the child's mother is also an employed person.

---

626. C.O.J., 16 February 2006, *Carmen Sarkatzis Herrero* v. *Instituto Madrileño de la Salud (Imsalud)*, C-294/04, ECR, 2006, 1513.
627. C.O.J., 30 September 2010, Pedro Manuel Roca Álvarez v. Sesa Start España ETT SA, Case C-104/09, www.curia.

Part I, Ch. 6, Equal Treatment

The Court observes, first, that this leave, which has the effect of changing working hours, affects the working conditions governed by directives which prohibit all forms of discrimination on grounds of sex.

Second, the Court hold that the positions of a male and a female worker, father and mother of a young child, are comparable with regard to their possible need to reduce their daily working time in order to look after their child. However, under the Spanish Workers' Statute, for men whose status is that of an employed person the fact of being a parent is not sufficient to gain entitlement to leave, whereas it is for women with an identical status. Thus, the Spanish legislation establishes a difference in treatment on grounds of sex between mothers and fathers who both have the status of an employed person.

1595. Lastly, the Court considered that this discrimination is not justified by the objective of the protection of women nor by the promotion of equal opportunities for men and women.

The leave does not seek to ensure the protection of the biological condition of the woman following pregnancy or the protection of the special relationship between a mother and her child. The fact that the leave might be taken by the father or the mother without distinction means that feeding and devoting time to the child can be carried out just as well by the father as by the mother, so that this leave is accorded to workers in their capacity as parents of the child.

Such legislation does not have the effect of eliminating or reducing existing inequalities for women in society. Nor does it seek to prevent or compensate for disadvantages in their professional careers.

1596. It is true that this measure could have the effect of putting women at an advantage by allowing employed mothers to keep their job and to be able to devote time to their child. That effect is even reinforced by the fact that, if the father is entitled to take this leave in the place of the mother, she would not suffer adverse consequences for her job as a result of care and attention devoted to the child.

However, the fact that only the employed mother is the holder of the right to qualify for the leave, whereas a father with the same status is not directly entitled to it, is liable to perpetuate a traditional distribution of the roles of men and women by keeping men in a role subsidiary to that of women in relation to the exercise of their parental duties. Furthermore, that could have as its effect that a self-employed woman such as the mother of Mr Roca Álvarez's child – the father not being entitled to the leave – would have to limit her self-employed activity and bear the burden resulting from the birth of her child alone, without the child's father being able to ease that burden.

1597. On those grounds, the Court ruled:

> that article 2(1), (3) and (4) and article 5 of Directive 76/207/EEC of 9 February 1976 must be interpreted as precluding a national measure such as the one at issue in the main proceedings, which provides that female workers who are mothers and whose status is that of an employed person are entitled, in various ways, to take leave during the first nine months following the child's birth,

whereas male workers who are fathers with that same status are not entitled to the same leave unless the child's mother is also an employed person.

III. Employment and Working Conditions

1598. Equal treatment concerning working conditions, including pay and dismissals, is provided for in Article 1 of the 1976 directive on equal treatment, while conditions governing dismissals, as well as pay are also retained in Article 3(1)(c).[628] The term 'working conditions' is not defined.

In Italy a law of 1977 provides that women who have adopted children or who have obtained custody thereof prior to adoption may claim maternity leave following the entry of the child into the adoptive family and the financial benefits relating thereto. The adoptive father does not have that right. That distinction, the Court ruled, is justified by the legitimate concern to assimilate as far as possible the conditions of entry of the child into the adoptive family to those of the arrival of a newborn child into the family during the very delicate initial period.[629]

1599. Mrs Kleist,[630] who was born in February 1948, was employed as chief physician by the pension insurance institution. The pension insurance institution took the decision to terminate the employment of all its employees, whether male or female, who satisfied the legal conditions for retiring. Mrs Kleist informed her employer that she did not intend to retire at the age of 60 but wished to work until she was 65. Her employer informed her, however, by letter of 6 December 2007, of its decision to retire her from 1 July 2008.

Mrs Kleist challenged her dismissal.

The Court's reply

1600. A preliminary point to note is that the conditions for payment of a retirement pension and the conditions governing termination of employment are separate issues.

In the case of the latter, Article 3(1)(c) of Directive 76/207 provides that application of the principle of equal treatment in relation to dismissals means that there is to be no direct or indirect discrimination on the grounds of sex in the public or private sectors, including public bodies.

The term 'dismissal' contained in that provision, a term which must be given a wide meaning, covers an age limit set for the compulsory dismissal of workers pursuant to an employer's general policy concerning retirement, even if the dismissal involves the grant of a retirement pension.

It follows that, since Mrs Kleist was retired by her employer, in accordance with the decision taken by it to dismiss all its employees who acquired the right

---

628. *See* concerning night work Part I, Chapter 7, §3.
629. 26 October 1983, *Commission* v. *Italy*, No. 163/82, ECR, 1983, 3273.
630. C.O.J, 18 November 2010, *Pensionsversicherungsanstalt* v. *Christine Kleist*, C-356/09, www.curia.eu.

to draw a retirement pension, the main proceedings concern dismissal within the meaning of Article 3(1)(c) of Directive 76/207.

It should be observed at the outset that the Court has held that a general policy concerning dismissal involving the dismissal of a female employee solely because she has attained or passed the qualifying age for a retirement pension, which age is different under national legislation for men and for women, constitutes discrimination on grounds of sex, contrary to Directive 76/207/EEC.

1601. In this connection, it should be noted, first, that under the first indent of Article 2(2) of Directive 76/207 direct discrimination occurs where one person is treated less favourably on grounds of sex than another is, has been or would be treated in a comparable situation.

In the present instance, it is apparent that doctors with protection from dismissal can nevertheless be dismissed when they acquire the right to draw a retirement pension. Men acquire that right when they have attained 65 years of age and women when they have attained 60 years of age. The effect of this is that female workers can be dismissed when they have attained 60 years of age whilst male workers cannot be dismissed until they have attained 65 years of age.

Since the criterion used by such provisions is inseparable from the worker's sex, there is, contrary to the assertions of the pension insurance institution, a difference in treatment that is directly based on sex.

1602. Second, it must be examined whether, in a context such as that governed by those provisions, female workers of 60 to 65 years of age are in a comparable situation, within the meaning of the first indent of Article 2(2) of Directive 76/207, to that of male workers in the same age bracket.

The national court inquires, in essence, whether the circumstance that female workers of 60 to 65 years of age have social cover by virtue of the statutory retirement pension is such as to make their situation specific *vis-à-vis* the situation of male workers in the same age bracket, who do not have such cover.

The comparability of such situations must be examined having regard inter alia to the object of the rules establishing the difference in treatment.

In the case in the main proceedings, the rules establishing the difference in treatment at issue are designed to govern the circumstances in which employees can lose their job.

1603. In the context of that case, contrary to the position in the cases which gave rise to the judgments in Case C-132/92 *Roberts* [1993] ECR I-5579 (paragraph 20) and in *Hlozek* (paragraph 48), the advantage accorded to female workers of being able to claim a retirement pension from an age five years younger than that set for male workers is not directly connected with the object of the rules establishing a difference in treatment.

That advantage cannot place female workers in a specific situation vis-à-vis male workers, as men and women are in identical situations so far as concerns the conditions governing termination of employment.

Furthermore, as is apparent from the order for reference, that the Republic of Austria wished to establish, in accordance with the exception laid down in Article 7(1)(a) of Directive 79/7 to the principle of equal treatment, a regime prescribing a different statutory pensionable age for men and women in order to compensate for the disadvantage suffered by women socially, in relation to the family and economically.

The Court has repeatedly held that, given the fundamental importance of the principle of equal treatment, the exception to the prohibition of discrimination on grounds of sex, provided for in that provision, must be interpreted strictly, so as to be applicable only to the determination of pensionable age for the purposes of granting old-age and retirement pensions and to the possible consequences thereof for other social security benefits.

Since, as is apparent the rules at issue in the main proceedings concern the subject of dismissal within the meaning of Article 3(1)(c) of Directive 76/207, and not the consequences referred to in Article 7(1)(a) of Directive 79/7, the exception is not applicable to those rules.

1604. Third, Directive 76/207 draws a distinction between discrimination directly on grounds of sex and 'indirect' discrimination inasmuch as only provisions, criteria or practices liable to constitute indirect discrimination can, by virtue of the second indent of Article 2(2) of that directive, avoid being classified as discriminatory if they are 'objectively justified by a legitimate aim, and the means of achieving that aim are appropriate and necessary'. Such a possibility is not, by contrast, provided for in respect of differences in treatment liable to constitute direct discrimination within the meaning of the first indent of Article 2(2) of the directive.

In those circumstances, given that (i) the difference in treatment established by rules such as those at issue in the main proceedings is directly on grounds of sex, whilst, as is apparent from paragraph 37 of the present judgment, the situations of men and women are identical in the present instance, and (ii) Directive 76/207 contains no exception, applicable in the present case, to the principle of equal treatment, it must be concluded that that difference in treatment constitutes direct discrimination on grounds of sex (see, to this effect, *Vergani*, paragraph 34).

That difference in treatment cannot therefore be justified by the objective, relied upon by the pension insurance institution, of promoting employment of younger persons.

Since the national court has not asked the Court to interpret that directive and the order for reference does not even reveal that such discrimination has been pleaded in the main proceedings, examination of this issue does not appear to be of use for disposing of those proceedings.

1605. The answer to the questions referred therefore is that Article 3(1)(c) of Directive 76/207 must be interpreted as meaning that national rules which, in order to promote access of younger persons to employment, permit an employer to dismiss employees who have acquired the right to draw their retirement pension, when that right is acquired by women at an age five years younger than the age at which it is acquired by men, constitute direct discrimination on the grounds of sex prohibited by that directive.

1606. Promotions also fall within the scope of the prohibition of discrimination. A question concerning promotions was raised in the case of Évelyne Thibault against a French insurance company.[631] According to the standard service regulations of that company, any employee who has been present at work for at least six months of the year must be the subject of an assessment of performance by his superiors. The company refused to carry out an assessment because Mrs. Thibault was not present at work for a period of six months, since she had been absent for reasons of maternity leave. She claimed that the failure to assess her performance, because of her absence on maternity leave, constituted discrimination and that she had as a result lost an opportunity for promotion.

1607. The Court ruled that:
the principle of non-discrimination requires that a woman who continues to be bound by her employer by her contract of employment during maternity leave should not be deprived of the benefit of working conditions which apply to both men and women and are the result of that employment relationship. In circumstances such as those in the case, to deny a female employee the right to have her performance assessed annually would discriminate against her merely in her capacity as a worker because, if she had not been pregnant and had not taken the maternity leave to which she was entitled, she would have been assessed for the year in question and could therefore have qualified for promotion.

1608. Subsidised nursery places made available by the employer to his staff are also a working condition.[632] That question has been raised in proceedings between Mr. Lommers and the Minister heading the Netherlands Ministry which employs concerning the latter's refusal to give Mr. Lommers' child access to the subsidised nursery scheme on the ground that access is in principle reserved only for female officials of that Ministry.

On 15 November 1993, the Minister for Agriculture adopted a circular advising Ministry staff that he was making available a certain number of nursery places to female staff. Officials who have obtained a nursery place for their child must make a parental contribution the amount of which is fixed in accordance with their income and is degressive for children in the same family. That contribution is deducted from the official's salary.

The Circular states in particular: 'In principle, nursery places are available only to female employees of the Ministry save in the case of an emergency, to be determined by the Director.' Mr. Lommers asked the Minister for Agriculture to reserve

---

631. C.O.J., 30 April 1998, *Caisse Nationale d'Assurance Vieillesse des Travailleurs Salariés (CNAVTS)* v. *Évelyne Thibault*, C-136/95, ECR, 1998, 2011.
632. C.O.J., 19 March 2002, Case C-476/99, *H. Lommers and Minister van Landbouw, Natuurbeheer en Visserij*, ECR, 2002, 2891.

a nursery place. His request was rejected on the ground that children of male officials could be given places in the nursery facilities in question only in cases of emergency.

1609. The question addressed to the European Court read as follows:

> Does Article 2(1) and (4) of Council Directive 76/207/EEC of 9 February 1976 preclude rules of an employer under which subsidised nursery places are made available only to female employees save where, in the case of a male employee, an emergency situation, to be determined by the employer, arises?

The Court rules as follows: First, the making available to employees, by their employer, of nursery places at their place of work, or outside it, is indeed to be regarded as a 'working condition' within the meaning of the directive.

That categorisation cannot be rejected in favour of a categorisation as 'pay simply' because the cost of the nursery places is partly borne by the employer, as in the present case. In that connection, it should be noted that the Court has previously held that the fact that the fixing of certain working conditions may have pecuniary consequences is not sufficient to bring such conditions within the scope of Article 157 TFEU which is a provision based on the close connection existing between the nature of the work done and the amount of pay.

1610. Furthermore, a measure such as that at issue in the main proceedings is essentially a practical one. Making nursery places available saves the employee from the uncertainties and difficulties involved in endeavouring to find for his or her child a nursery which is both suitable and affordable. The primary object and effect of such a measure, therefore, especially where the supply of nursery places is insufficient, is to facilitate the exercise of the occupational activity of the employees concerned.

1611. Secondly, a scheme under which nursery places made available by an employer to his staff are reserved only for female employees does in fact create a difference of treatment on grounds of sex, within the meaning of Articles 2(1) and 5(1) of the Directive. The situations of a male employee and a female employee, respectively father and mother of young children, are comparable as regards the possible need for them to use nursery facilities because they are in employment, and, by analogy, as regards the situation of female employees and male Employees assuming the upbringing of their children.

Consequently, the question to be examined in the third place is whether such a measure is nevertheless permissible under Article 2(4) of the Directive.

As far as that question is concerned, it is settled case law that Article 2(4) is specifically and exclusively designed to authorise measures which, although discriminatory in appearance, are in fact intended to eliminate or reduce actual instances of inequality which may exist in the reality of social life. It authorises national measures relating to access to employment, including promotion, which give a specific advantage to women with a view to improving their ability to compete on the labour market and to pursue a career on an equal footing with men.

Part I, Ch. 6, Equal Treatment   1612–1613

Second, a proven insufficiency of suitable and affordable nursery facilities is likely to induce more particularly female employees to give up their jobs.

A measure, like nursery places, which forms part of the restricted concept of equality of opportunity in so far as it is not places of employment which are reserved for women but enjoyment of certain working conditions designed to facilitate their pursuit of, and progression in, their career, falls in principle into the category of measures designed to eliminate the causes of women's reduced opportunities for access to employment and careers and are intended to improve their ability to compete on the labour market and to pursue a career on an equal footing with men.

Next, it must also be remembered that the measure at issue does not totally exclude male officials from its scope but allows the employer to grant requests from male officials in cases of emergency, to be determined by the employer.

1612. Consequently, the Court ruled, that:

> In view of all the foregoing considerations, the answer to be given to the question referred for a preliminary ruling must be that Article 2(1) and (4) of the Directive does not preclude a scheme set up by a Ministry to tackle extensive under-representation of women within it under which, in a context characterised by a proven insufficiency of proper, affordable care facilities, a limited number of subsidised nursery places made available by the Ministry to its staff is reserved for female officials alone whilst male officials may have access to them only in cases of emergency, to be determined by the employer. That is so, however, only in so far, in particular, as the said exception in favour of male officials is construed as allowing those of them who take care of their children by themselves to have access to that nursery places scheme on the same conditions as female officials.

1613. According to amended directive of 1976 harassment and sexual harassment within the meaning of the directive are deemed to be discrimination on the grounds of sex and therefore prohibited (Article 2(2) amended). The definitions are as follows:

– harassment: where an unwanted conduct related to the sex of a person occurs with the purpose or effect of violating the dignity of a person, and of creating an intimidating, hostile, degrading, humiliating or offensive environment;
– sexual harassment: where any form of unwanted verbal, non-verbal or physical conduct of a sexual nature occurs, with the purpose or effect of violating the dignity of a person, in particular when creating an intimidating, hostile, degrading, humiliating or offensive environment;
– A person's rejection of, or submission to, such conduct may not be used as a basis for a decision affecting that person (Article 2(3) amended).
– An instruction to discriminate against persons on grounds of sex shall be deemed to be discrimination within the meaning of this Directive (Article 2(4) amended).

1614. Also important for its practical implications is the ruling in the case of *Marshall v. Southampton Health Authority.*[633] Ms. Marshall was dismissed when she was aged 62. Had she been a man, she could have worked until 65 years of age. Following the Court, the term 'dismissal' contained in Article 5(1) of Directive No. 76/207 must be given a wide meaning: an age limit for the compulsory dismissal of workers pursuant to an employer's general policy concerning retirement falls within the term 'dismissal' construed in that manner, even if the dismissal involves the grant of a retirement pension. Article 5(1) must be interpreted as meaning that a general policy concerning dismissal involving the dismissal of a woman solely because she has attained the age limit for a state pension, which age is different for men and women, constitutes discrimination on grounds of sex. Article 5(1) may be relied upon as against a state authority acting in its capacity as employer, in order to avoid the application of any national provision which does not conform to Article 5(1). In doing so, the directive has a direct binding effect against public (state) authorities.

1615. The *Defrenne* case concerned questions on the interpretation of Protocol No. 2 to Article 157 TFEU ('the Protocol'), and Article 5 of Council Directive 76/207/EEC of 9 February 1976.

The Protocol provides:

> For the purposes of Article 157 of this Treaty, benefits under occupational social security schemes shall not be considered as remuneration if and in so far as they are attributable to periods of employment prior to 17 May 1990, except in the case of workers or those claiming under them who have before that date initiated legal proceedings or introduced an equivalent claim under the applicable national law.

The case concerned Collective Labour Agreement No. 17, concluded within the National Labour Council on 19 December 1974, which establishes a system of additional redundancy payments for workers aged at least 60 years, provided that they are in receipt of unemployment benefits. The additional payments are to be paid by the worker's last employer and are equal to half of the difference between the net reference wage and the unemployment benefit.

Under Article 144 of the Royal Decree of 28 December 1963 on Employment and Unemployment unemployed persons cease to be entitled to unemployment benefit from the first day of the calendar month following that in which they reach 65 years of age, in the case of men, and 60 years of age, in the case of women. That rule was not brought into line with the Law of 20 July 1990 establishing a flexible retirement age between 60 and 65 for both men and women.

Collective Agreement No. 17 provides for the possibility of concluding collective labour agreements at branch level, extending the scheme to female workers aged 55 and over. On 23 May 1984, such a collective agreement was concluded within Joint Sub-Committee No. 315(1) (Sabena) to deal with redundancy arising

---

633. C.O.J., 26 February 1986, No. 152/84, IELL, *Case Law*, No. 86, ECR, 1986, 6723. *See also Burton* (1982), *op. cit.*

inter alia from the development of automated work practices specific to commercial aviation and to protect jobs for younger workers.

That agreement extended the scheme for supplementing unemployment benefits to workers aged 55 and over who had taken voluntary redundancy. Payments continue until the worker reaches the age of 65 in the case of a man or the age of 60 in the case of a woman. Pursuant to the above-mentioned agreement, Sabena granted to staff with 25 years' service an additional payment amounting to 82 per cent of the net salary which they received in the last month before they were made redundant.

Following the judgment in Case C-173/91 *Commission* v. *Belgium* [1993] ECR I-673, in which the Court censured the exclusion of female workers over the age of 60 from eligibility for the additional redundancy payments provided for by Collective Agreement No. 17, the *Conseil National du Travail* adapted Article 4 of that Agreement on 17 December 1997 (Collective Agreement No. 17 vicies).

After that provision was adapted, all workers became entitled to the additional payment payable by the employer until the last day of the calendar month in which they reach 65 years of age, irrespective of the fact that their age is greater than the maximum age for grant of unemployment benefit.

Ms. Defrenne became an employee of Sabena on 27 June 1960. On 14 November 1984, she requested the application of the Collective Labour Agreement of 23 May 1984. On 29 November 1984, she was granted a pre-retirement payment with two years' notice (commencing on 1 December 1984 and expiring on 31 December 1986). Sabena therefore undertook to pay the supplement provided for by the collective agreement from 1 January 1987 until the end of the month in which she reached 60 years of age (30 November 1991). The unemployment benefit supplement was actually paid to Ms. Defrenne until the end of that month. At that date she began to receive a pension.

1616. On 17 February 1993, the Court delivered its judgment in Case C-173/91 *Commission* v. *Belgium*, cited above, in which it declared that by retaining legislation which excluded female workers over the age of 60 from eligibility for the additional redundancy payments provided for by Collective Agreement No. 17, rendered compulsory by the Royal Decree of 16 January 1975, the Kingdom of Belgium had failed to fulfil its obligations under Article 157 of the Treaty.

Following that judgment, Ms. Defrenne, by letter of 10 June 1993, asked Sabena to pay her the supplement to which she claimed to be entitled until her 65th birthday, that is to say until 30 November 1996.

When Sabena refused, Ms. Defrenne brought an action in the Labour Court Brussels, on 21 December 1993, seeking an order requiring Sabena to pay her the unemployment benefit supplement for the period from 1 December 1991 to 30 November 1996. By judgment of 28 June 1995, the *Tribunal du Travail* dismissed her claim.

The *Tribunal du Travail* took the view that the payments at issue were covered by the Protocol, which limited the temporal scope of Article 157. There was no dispute that Ms. Defrenne's claims related to a period of employment prior to 17 May 1990 or that she had initiated proceedings only after that date.

1617. The following questions were referred to the Court:

(1) Can the additional pre-retirement payment provided for by Collective Agreement No. 17, rendered compulsory by the Royal Decree of 16 January 1975 and provided for in the Collective Labour Agreement of 23 May 1984 concluded within Joint Sub-Committee No. 315(1), be treated as a benefit payable under an occupational social security scheme to which Article 157 TFEU applies.
(2) Are the provisions of Collective Labour Agreement No. 17 and the Collective Labour Agreement of 23 May 1984 concluded within Joint Sub-Committee No. 315(1) compatible with Article 5 of Directive 76/207/EC in that they exclude female workers over the age of 60 from the benefit of pre-retirement payments which constitute additional redundancy payments, granted in addition to unemployment benefit, whereas such payments are guaranteed for male workers until the age of 65?
(3) If the two questions above are answered in the affirmative, does the application of the Protocol on Article 157 of the Treaty preclude the action brought by Ms. Defrenne from succeeding, inasmuch as it is founded on breach of Article 5 of Directive 76/207?

In order to give a proper answer to the national court, it must first be determined whether the payment at issue in the main proceedings constitutes a benefit under an occupational social security scheme within the meaning of the Protocol.

It is not disputed that the benefit at issue in the main proceedings is a payment, provided under an agreement, supplementing one of the statutory social security schemes, namely that providing unemployment benefits.

However, contrary to the contentions of Ms. Defrenne and the Commission, the fact that the Court determined that the payment at issue in the main proceedings constituted 'pay' within the meaning of Article 157 of the Treaty cannot foreclose the answer to the question whether such pay constitutes a benefit under an occupational social security scheme for the purposes of the Protocol.

Before the entry into force of the Treaty on European Union and, therefore, of the Protocol, the question could not arise, so that the Court did not have to rule on the point.

Next, an occupational scheme such as the one at issue in the main proceedings, which provides protection against the risk of unemployment by providing workers employed by an undertaking, in this case Sabena, with benefits intended to supplement the unemployment benefit provided under a statutory social security scheme, must be classified as an occupational social security scheme within the meaning of Articles 2 and 4 of Council Directive 86/378/EEC of 24 July 1986 on the implementation of the principle of equal treatment for men and women in occupational social security schemes.

It follows that the additional payment at issue in the main proceedings constitutes a benefit under an occupational social security scheme within the meaning of the Protocol. The Protocol may therefore apply if the conditions it lays down are fulfilled.

The Protocol excludes application of Article 157 of the Treaty to benefits under occupational social security schemes attributable to periods of employment prior to

17 May 1990, except in the case of workers who initiated legal proceedings or introduced an equivalent claim before that date.

In those circumstances, the answer to the first question must be that the Protocol applies to a payment such as the additional pre-retirement payment provided for by Collective Agreement No. 17, rendered compulsory by the Royal Decree of 16 January 1975 and provided for in the Collective Labour Agreement of 23 May 1984 concluded within Joint Sub-Committee No. 315(1).

The essence of the second and third questions, which should be taken together, is whether Article 5 of the directive applies in the main proceedings. A benefit which, as in this case, constitutes 'pay' within the meaning of Article 141 of the Treaty cannot also be covered by Directive 76/207.

The answer must therefore be that an additional payment which, as in the present case, constitutes 'pay' within the meaning of Article 157 of the Treaty is not covered by Article 5 of the directive.

1618. The Court concluded as follows:

(1) 157 TFEU applies to a payment such as the additional pre-retirement payment provided for by Collective Agreement No. 17, rendered compulsory by the Royal Decree of 16 January 1975 and provided for in the collective Labour Agreement of 23 May 1984 concluded within Joint Sub-Committee No. 315(1).
(2) An additional payment which, as in the present case, constitutes 'pay' within the meaning of Article 157 TFEU is not covered by Article 5 of Council Directive 76/207/EEC of 9 February 1976.[634]

1619. Pay is, however, now covered by Article 3(c) of the 1976 amended directive, which reads as follows: 'employment and working conditions, including dismissals, as well as pay as provided for in Directive 75/117/EEC'.

1620. In the case between Mrs. Hertz and her former employer, Aldi Market, the question was raised whether equal treatment allows dismissal because of repeated absences due to illness, which originated in her pregnancy and confinement. The Court stated that the 1976 directive did not provide for the case in which an illness originated in pregnancy or confinement. It permitted, however, national provisions guaranteeing women specific rights on the ground of pregnancy and confinement, such as maternity leave. In the case of an illness which developed after maternity leave, it was unnecessary to distinguish an illness which originated in pregnancy or confinement from any other illness. A pathological condition of that kind was therefore covered by the general rules applicable to illness. The Court stated that women and men were both liable to be ill. Although certain problems were peculiar to one or other sex, the only question was therefore whether a woman was dismissed on the grounds of absence due to illness under the same condition as a man; if so, there was no direct discrimination on grounds of sex. The Court consequently concluded

---

634. C.O.J., 13 July 2000, *Marthe Defrenne v. Sabena SA*, Case C-166/99, ECR, 2000, 6155.

that the directive does not preclude dismissals resulting from absences due to an illness which originated in pregnancy or confinement.[635]

The Court ruled that the termination of a contract without a fixed term on account of a woman's pregnancy, whether by annulment or avoidance, cannot be justified on the ground that statutory prohibition, imposed because of pregnancy, temporarily prevents an employee from performing night-time work.[636]

1621. In *Mary Brown* v. *Rentokil Ltd.* the Court had to judge on the validity of a clause in an employment contract, which stipulated that, if an employee was absent because of sickness for more than 26 weeks continuously, he or she would be dismissed. Ms. Brown was absent due to incapacity for work caused by an illness resulting from a pregnancy. In such a case, the Court decided, the principle of equal treatment precludes the dismissal of a female worker at any time during her pregnancy for absences due to illness caused by the pregnancy.[637]

1622. It is contrary to Article 157 and Directive 75/117 for national legislation to provide that a pregnant woman who, before the beginning of her maternity leave, is unfit for work by reason of a pathological condition connected with her pregnancy, as attested by a medical certificate, is not entitled to receive full pay from her employer but is entitled to benefits paid by a local authority, when in the event of incapacity for work on grounds of illness, as attested by a medical certificate, a worker is in principle entitled to receive full pay from his or her employer. The fact that a woman in such a situation is deprived of her full pay must be regarded as treatment based essentially on the pregnancy and thus as discriminatory.

It is not contrary to Article 157 or Directive 75/117 to provide that a pregnant woman is not entitled to receive her pay from her employer where, before the beginning of her maternity leave, she is absent from work by reason either of routine pregnancy-related minor complaints, when there is in fact no incapacity for work, or of medical recommendation intended to protect the unborn child but not based on an actual pathological condition or on any special risks for the unborn child, while any worker who is unfit for work on the grounds of illness is in principle entitled thereto.

The fact that the employee forfeits some, or even all, of her salary by reason of such absences which are not based on an incapacity for work cannot be regarded as treatment based essentially on the pregnancy but rather as based on the choice made by the employee not to work.

It is contrary to Directive 76/207 and to Directive 92/85 on the introduction of measures to encourage improvements in the safety and health at work of pregnant workers and workers who have recently given birth or are breastfeeding for national legislation to provide that an employer may send home a woman who is pregnant,

---

635. 8 November 1990, *Handels-og Kontorfunktionaerernes Forbund i Danmark* v. *Dansk Arbejdsgiverforening*, No. C-179/88, ECR, 1990, I-3979.
636. C.O.J., 5 May 1994, *G. Habermann-Beltermann* v. *Arbeiterwohlfart, Bezirkverband Ndb./Opf. eV.*, No. C-421/92, ECR, 1994, 1657.
637. C.O.J., 30 June 1998, *Mary Brown* v. *Rentokil Ltd.*, C-394/96, ECR, 1998, I-4185.

Part I, Ch. 6, Equal Treatment

although not unfit for work, without paying her salary in full when he considers that he cannot provide work for her.[638]

Article 5(1) of Directive 76/207/EEC is to be interpreted as meaning that a worker must be able to take her annual leave during a period other than the period of her maternity leave, including in a case in which the period of maternity leave coincides with the general period of annual leave fixed, by a collective agreement, for the entire workforce.[639]

1623. In another case[640] the Court was asked to decide whether the Equal Treatment Directive prohibits the dismissal of a transsexual because of his/her decision to undergo gender reassignment.

P., who had been born with the physical attributes of a man, used to work as a manager in an educational establishment operated by Cornwall County Council. In April 1992 P.'s employer was informed that P. had decided to undergo gender reassignment which meant that, following a period of time during which P. would dress and behave as a woman, P. would have surgery to be given the physical attributes of a woman. P. was subsequently dismissed with effect from December 1992 and, although the Council maintained that the reason for the dismissal was redundancy, the Industrial Tribunal (UK) found that the real reason for the dismissal was P.'s proposal to undergo gender reassignment.

The Court referred first to jurisprudence of the European Court of Human Rights which states that 'Transsexuals who have been operated upon ... form a fairly well-defined and identifiable group.' It then observed that the stated aim of the directive is to ensure that there is 'no discrimination whatsoever on grounds of sex' and pointed out that the right not to be discriminated against on grounds of sex is one of the fundamental human rights whose observance the Court has a duty to ensure.

The Court continued:

> Accordingly, the scope of the directive cannot be confined simply to discrimination based on the fact that a person is of one or other sex. In view of its purpose and the nature of the rights which it seeks to safeguard, the scope of the directive is also such as to apply to discrimination arising, as in this case, from the gender reassignment of the person concerned.
>
> Such discrimination is based, essentially if not exclusively, on the sex of the person concerned. Where a person is dismissed on the ground that he or she intends to undergo, or has undergone, gender reassignment, he or she is treated unfavourably by comparison with persons of the sex to which he or she was deemed to belong before undergoing gender reassignment.

---

638. C.O.J., 19 November 1998, *Handels-og Kontorfunktionærernes Forbund i Danmark*, acting on behalf of *Berit Høj Pedersen* v. *Fællesforeningen for Danmarks Brugsforeninger* and *Dansk Tandlægeforening and Kristelig Funktionær-Organisation* v. *Dansk Handel & Service*, Case C-66/96, ECR, 1998, 7327.
639. C.O.J., 18 March 2004, *María Paz Merino Gómez* v. *Continental Industrias del Caucho SA.*, C-342/01, ECR, 2004, 2605.
640. C.O.J., 30 April 1996, *P.* v. *S. and Cornwall County Council*, Case C-13/94, ECR, 1996, 2143.

To tolerate such discrimination would be tantamount, as regards such a person, to a failure to respect the dignity and freedom to which he or she is entitled, and which the Court has a duty to safeguard.

The Court concluded that the dismissal of such a person was contrary to Article 5(1) of the directive, unless the dismissal could be justified under Article 2(2). There was, however, no material before the Court to suggest that there was a defence for the dismissal in this case.

1624. The *Bush* case concerns[641] the interruption of parental leave in order to return to paid work for the clinic.

Ms. Busch has worked as a nurse for the clinic since April 1998. After the birth of her first child in June 2000, she took parental leave which was supposed to be for three years. In October 2000, she became pregnant again.

By letter of 30 January 2001, Ms. Busch made a request for permission to terminate her parental leave early and return to full-time work as a nurse, which was accepted by her employer after there was a job vacancy in a ward in March 2001. Ms. Busch was to resume working in a ward with 39 beds looked after by three nurses per shift and in which there was an urgent need of staff. Her employer did not ask if she was pregnant.

Ms. Busch thus returned to work on 9 April 2001. The next day, she informed her employer for the first time that she was seven months pregnant.

Her maternity leave was to start on 23 May 2001, six weeks prior to the expected date of birth. The clinic released her from her obligation to work with effect from 11 April 2001 and, by letter of 19 April 2001, rescinded its consent to her returning to work, on grounds of fraudulent misrepresentation and mistake as to an essential characteristic.

In support of its position, the clinic submits that, having regard to the prohibitions on working under the German legislation, Ms. Busch would not have been able to carry out her duties effectively.

The documents before the court show that Ms. Busch wished to end her parental leave so that she would receive a maternity allowance, which is higher than the allowance paid during parental leave, and also the supplements to the maternity allowance.

Ms. Busch argued that she was not required to declare that she was pregnant and that she would have been able to carry out her duties as a nurse, with some restrictions, until the start of her maternity leave, as she had done during her first pregnancy.

1625. The Court ruled as follows: Article 5(1) of Directive 76/207 prohibits discrimination on grounds of sex as regards conditions of employment, which includes the conditions applicable to employees' returning to work following parental leave.

---

641. C.O.J., 27 February 2003, *Wiebke Busch* v. *Klinikum Neustadt GmbH & Co.*, Betriebs-KG, C-320/01, ECR, 2003, 2041.

Part I, Ch. 6, Equal Treatment 1626–1628

When an employer takes an employee's pregnancy into consideration in the refusal to allow her to return to work before the end of her parental leave, that constitutes direct discrimination on grounds of sex.

Since the employer may not take the employee's pregnancy into consideration for the purpose of applying her working conditions, she is not obliged to inform the employer that she is pregnant.

It also follows from the case law of the Court that discrimination on grounds of sex cannot be justified by the fact that she is temporarily prevented, by a legislative prohibition imposed because of pregnancy, from performing all of her duties.

1626. To be sure, Article 2(3) of Directive 76/207 reserves to Member States the right to retain or introduce provisions which are intended to protect women in connection with 'pregnancy and maternity', by recognising the legitimacy, in terms of the principle of equal treatment, first, of protecting a woman's biological condition during and after pregnancy and, second, of protecting the special relationship between a woman and her child over the period which follows pregnancy and childbirth. Articles 4(1) and 5 of Directive 92/85 also guarantee special protection for pregnant women and women who have recently given birth or are breastfeeding in respect of any activity liable to involve a specific risk to their safety or health or negative effects on the pregnancy or breastfeeding.

However, to accept that a pregnant employee may be refused the right the return to work before the end of parental leave due to temporary prohibitions on performing certain work duties for which she was hired would be contrary to the objective of protection pursued by Article 2(3) of Directive 76/207 and Articles 4(1) and 5 of Directive 92/85 and would rob them of any practical effect.

As regards the financial consequences which might ensue for the employer from the obligation to reinstate a pregnant employee unable for the duration of the pregnancy, to carry out all her duties, the Court has already held that discrimination on grounds of sex cannot be justified on grounds relating to the financial loss for an employer.

1627. Article 5 of Directive 92/85 allows the employer, where there is a risk to the safety or health of a worker, or a negative effect on her pregnancy or breastfeeding, temporarily to adjust the working conditions or hours or, if that is not possible, move the worker to another job or, as a last resort, grant the worker leave.

The fact that, in asking to return to work, Ms. Busch intended to receive a maternity allowance higher than the parental leave allowance, as well as the supplementary allowance paid by the employer, cannot legally justify sex discrimination over working conditions.

1628. Article 2(1) of Directive 76/207 is to be interpreted as precluding a requirement that an employee who, with the consent of her employer, wishes to return to work before the end of her parental leave must inform her employer that she is pregnant in the event that, because of certain legislative prohibitions, she will be unable to carry out all of her duties.

Article 2(1) of Directive 76/207 is to be interpreted as precluding an employer from contesting under national law the consent it gave to the reinstatement of an employee to return before the end of her parental leave on the grounds that it was in error as to her being pregnant.

1629. Another case related to the prohibition of the employment of women in underground work in mining or in a high-pressure atmosphere or in diving work.[642] In the Austrian Government's opinion, the restrictions on employment are justified on medical grounds relating specifically to women's activity.

That Government argues that in most cases work to be carried out in a high-pressure atmosphere and diving work involve significant physical stress, for example, in the construction of underground railways in a high-pressure atmosphere or in the carrying out of under-water repairs to bridges. Prohibiting the employment of women in physically very demanding work in a high-pressure atmosphere and their employment in diving work is justified because their respiratory capacity is less than men's and because they have a lower red blood cell count.

1630.

Findings of the Court
An absolute prohibition of the employment of women in diving work does not constitute a difference in treatment permitted under Article 2(3) of Directive 76/207.

The range of diving work is wide and includes, for instance, activity in the fields of biology, archaeology, tourism and police work.

The absolute prohibition excludes women even from work that does not involve significant physical stress and thus clearly goes beyond what is necessary to ensure that women are protected.

With regard to employment in a high-pressure atmosphere, the regulation of 1973 excludes women from work that places excessive strain on their bodies.

In so far as the Austrian Government claims that women have lesser respiratory capacity and a lower red blood cell count in order to justify such exclusion, it relies on an argument based on measured average values for women to compare them with those for men. However, as that Government itself acknowledged during the pre-litigation procedure, as regards those variables there are significant areas of overlap of individual values for women and individual values for men.

In those circumstances legislation that precludes any individual assessment and prohibits women from entering the employment in question, when that employment is not forbidden to men whose vital capacity and red blood cell count are equal to or lower than the average values of those variables measured for women, is not authorised by virtue of Article 2(3) of Directive 76/207 and constitutes discrimination on grounds of sex.

In light of the foregoing considerations, it must be declared that, by maintaining a general prohibition of the employment of women in work in a high-pressure atmosphere and in diving work, providing a limited number of

---

642. C.O.J., 1 February 2005, *Commission v. Republic of Austria*, C-203/03, ECR, 2005, 935.

exceptions in the former case, the Republic of Austria has failed to fulfil its obligations under Articles 2 and 3 of Directive 76/207.

1631. In the *Cadman* case the issue related to the criterion of length of service as a measure to determine the amount of pay.[643]

Mrs. Cadman was employed by the Health and Safety Executive (HSE). Since she has been working for that body the pay system has been altered several times. Before 1992 the system was incremental, that is to say that each employee received an annual increase until he reached the top of the pay scale for his grade. In 1992, the HSE introduced a performance-related element so that the amount of the annual increment was adjusted to reflect the employee's individual performance. Under this system high performing employees could reach the top of the scale more quickly. Following the introduction in 1995 of a Long Term Pay Agreement, annual pay increases were set in accordance with the award of points called 'equity shares' linked to the employee's performance. That change had the effect of decreasing the rate at which pay differentials narrowed between longer-serving and shorter-serving employees on the same grade. Finally, in 2000, the system was altered again to enable employees lower down the pay bands to be paid larger annual increases and, therefore, to progress more quickly through the pay band.

1632. In June 2001, Mrs. Cadman lodged an application before the Employment Tribunal based on the Equal Pay Act. At the date of her claim, she had been engaged as a band 2 inspector, a managerial post, for nearly five years. She took as comparators four male colleagues who were also band 2 inspectors.

Although they were in the same band as Mrs. Cadman, those four persons were paid substantially more than her.

It is common ground that at the date of the claim lodged at the Employment Tribunal the four male comparators had longer service than Mrs. Cadman, acquired in part in more junior posts.

1633. The following questions were referred to the Court for a preliminary ruling:

(a) Where the use by an employer of the criterion of length of service as a determinant of pay has a disparate impact as between relevant male and female employees, does Article 157 TFEU require the employer to provide special justification for recourse to that criterion? If the answer depends on the circumstances, what are those circumstances?
(b) Would the answer to the preceding question be different if the employer applies the criterion of length of service on an individual basis to employees so that an assessment is made as to the extent to which greater length of service justifies a greater level of pay?

---

643. C.O.J., 3 October 2006, *B. F. Cadman* v. *Health & Safety Executive*, Case C-17/05, ECR, 2006, 9583.

1634. The Court stated that:

it is not to be excluded that recourse to the criterion of length of service may involve less advantageous treatment of women than of men, held that the employer does not have to provide special justification for recourse to that criterion.

By adopting that position, the Court acknowledged that rewarding, in particular, experience acquired which enables the worker to perform his duties better constitutes a legitimate objective of pay policy.

As a general rule, recourse to the criterion of length of service is appropriate to attain that objective. Length of service goes hand in hand with experience, and experience generally enables the worker to perform his duties better.

The employer is therefore free to reward length of service without having to establish the importance it has in the performance of specific tasks entrusted to the employee.

1635. In the same judgment, the Court did not, however, exclude the possibility that there may be situations in which recourse to the criterion of length of service must be justified by the employer in detail.

That is so, in particular, where the worker provides evidence capable of giving rise to serious doubts as to whether recourse to the criterion of length of service is, in the circumstances, appropriate to attain the abovementioned objective. It is in such circumstances for the employer to prove that that which is true as a general rule, namely that length of service goes hand in hand with experience and that experience enables the worker to perform his duties better, is also true as regards the job in question.

It should be added that where a job classification system based on an evaluation of the work to be carried out is used in determining pay, it is not necessary for the justification for recourse to a certain criterion to relate on an individual basis to the situation of the workers concerned. Therefore, if the objective pursued by recourse to the criterion of length of service is to recognise experience acquired, there is no need to show in the context of such a system that an individual worker has acquired experience during the relevant period which has enabled him to perform his duties better. By contrast, the nature of the work to be carried out must be considered objectively.

1636. It follows from all of the foregoing considerations, that the answer to the first and second questions referred must be that Article 157 TFEU is to be interpreted as meaning that, where recourse to the criterion of length of service as a determinant of pay leads to disparities in pay, in respect of equal work or work of equal value, between the men and women to be included in the comparison:

– since, as a general rule, recourse to the criterion of length of service is appropriate to attain the legitimate objective of rewarding experience acquired which enables the worker to perform his duties better, the employer does not have to establish specifically that recourse to that criterion is appropriate to attain that

Part I, Ch. 6, Equal Treatment 1637–1638

objective as regards a particular job, unless the worker provides evidence capable of raising serious doubts in that regard;
– where a job classification system based on an evaluation of the work to be carried out is used in determining pay, there is no need to show that an individual worker has acquired experience during the relevant period which has enabled him to perform his duties better.

IV. Social Security, Pensions

1637. The directive of 1976 does not apply to matters of social security. Article 1(2) provides that the Council would act on this later and this was done through Directive No. 79/7 of 19 December 1978 on the progressive implementation of the principle of equal treatment for men and women in matters of social security. This directive concerns, for example, schemes which provide protection for old age. Article 7(1A) of the directive provides, however, that the directive shall be without prejudice to the rights of Member States to exclude 'the determination of pensionable age for the purposes of granting old-age and retirement benefits and the possible consequences thereof for other benefits'. The exception must be interpreted restrictively and must be distinguished from the qualifying age as a condition for dismissal, which, as indicated earlier, must be equal for men and women. It follows that the exception contained in Article 7(1A) applies only to the determination of pensionable age for the purposes of granting old-age and retirement pensions and the possible consequences thereof for other benefits.[644]

In one case the European Court of Justice furthermore held that once a Member State decides to introduce the same pensionable age for men and women and thus to abolish the different age requirement, both men and women have to be treated equally with regard to the calculation of pension benefits. A difference in calculation cannot be justified by an in the meantime abolished difference in age requirements.[645]

If, however, national legislation has maintained a different pensionable age for male and female workers, the Member State concerned is entitled to calculate the amount of pension differently depending on the worker's sex.[646]

V. Freedom of Association

1638. The 1976 directive aims at the application of the principle of equal treatment, which means that there shall be no direct or indirect discrimination on the grounds of sex in the public or private sectors, including public bodies, in relation to:

---

644. C.O.J., 26 February 1986, *Joan Roberts* v. *Tate & Lyle Industries Ltd.*, Case No. 151/84, ECR, 1986, 703, 26 February 1986, *Vera Mia Beets-Proper* v. *F. van Lanschot Bankiers NV*, No. 262/ 84, ECR, 1986, 773.
645. C.O.J., 1 July 1993, *R. Van Cant* v. *Rijksdienst voor Pensioenen*, No. C-154/92, ECR, 1993, 3811.
646. C.O.J., 22 October 1998, *Louis Wolfs* v. *Office national des pensions* (ONP), Case C-154/96, ECR, 1998, 6173.

membership of, and involvement in, an organisation of workers or employers, or any organisation whose members carry on a particular profession, including the benefits provided for by such organisations. (Article 3(1)(d) amended)

VI. Follow-up of the 1976 Directive; Promotion and Social Dialogue

A. Enforcement

1639. According to Article 6 of the directive, Member States must ensure that judicial and/or administrative procedures, including where they deem it appropriate conciliation procedures, for the enforcement of obligations under this directive are available to all persons who consider themselves wronged by failure to apply the principle of equal treatment to them, even after the relationship in which the discrimination is alleged to have occurred has ended (para. 1).

Member States must introduce into their national legal systems such measures as are necessary to ensure real and effective compensation or reparation as the Member States so determine for the loss and damage sustained by a person injured as a result of discrimination in a way which is dissuasive and proportionate to the damage suffered; such compensation or reparation may not be restricted by the fixing of a prior upper limit, except in cases where the employer can prove that the only damage suffered by an applicant as a result of discrimination within the meaning of the directive is the refusal to take his/her job application into consideration (para. 2).

Member States must ensure that associations, organisations or other legal entities which have, in accordance with the criteria laid down by their national law, a legitimate interest in ensuring that the provisions of the directive are complied with, may engage, either on behalf or in support of the complainants, with his or her approval, in any judicial and/or administrative procedure provided for the enforcement of obligations under the directive (para. 3).

Paragraphs 1 and 3 are without prejudice to national rules relating to time limits for bringing actions as regards the principle of equal treatment (para. 4).

In the case of a breach of Directive 76/207 by legislative provisions or by provisions of collective agreements introducing discrimination contrary to that directive, the national courts are required to set aside that discrimination, using all the means at their disposal, and in particular by applying those provisions for the benefit of the class placed at a disadvantage, and are not required to request or await the setting aside of the provisions by the legislature, by collective negotiation or otherwise.[647]

---

647. C.O.J., 20 March 2003, Helga Kutz-Bauer and Freie und Hansestadt Hamburg, C-187/00, ECR, 2003, 2741.

B. Protection of Employees, including Representatives

1640. Article 7 of the directive obliges Member States to introduce into their national legal systems such measures as are necessary to protect employees, including those who are employees' representatives provided for by national laws and/or practices, against dismissal or other adverse treatment by the employer as a reaction to a complaint within the undertaking or to any legal proceedings aimed at enforcing compliance with the principle of equal treatment.

C. Promotion

1641. Furthermore, Member States have to designate and make the necessary arrangements for a body or bodies for the promotion, analysis, monitoring and support of equal treatment of all persons without discrimination on the grounds of sex. These bodies may form part of agencies charged at national level with the defence of human rights or the safeguard of individuals' rights.

Member States shall ensure that the competences of these bodies include:

(a) without prejudice to the right of victims and of associations, organisations or other legal entities referred to in Article 6(3), providing independent assistance to victims of discrimination in pursuing their complaints about discrimination;
(b) conducting independent surveys concerning discrimination;
(c) publishing independent reports and making recommendations on any issue relating to such discrimination. (Article 8(a) amended)

D. Social Dialogue

1642. Member States have to take adequate measures to promote social dialogue between the social partners with a view to fostering equal treatment, including through the monitoring of workplace practices, collective agreements, codes of conduct, research or exchange of experiences and good practices.

Member States must encourage the social partners, without prejudice to their autonomy, to promote equality between women and men and to conclude, at the appropriate level, agreements laying down anti-discrimination rules in the fields referred to in Article 1 which fall within the scope of collective bargaining.

These agreements shall respect the minimum requirements laid down by the Directive and the relevant national implementing measures.

Member States must encourage employers to promote equal treatment for men and women in the workplace in a planned and systematic way. To this end, employers should be encouraged to provide at appropriate regular intervals employees and/or their representatives with appropriate information on equal treatment for men and women in the undertaking.

Such information may include statistics on proportions of men and women at different levels of the organisation and possible measures to improve the situation in cooperation with employees' representatives (Article 8(b) amended).

Member States shall encourage dialogue with appropriate non-governmental organisations which have, in accordance with their national law and practice, a legitimate interest in contributing to the fight against discrimination on grounds of sex with a view to promoting the principle of equal treatment (Article 8(c)).

E. Sanctions

1643. Member States must lay down the rules on sanctions applicable to infringements of the national provisions adopted pursuant to the directive, and shall take all measures necessary to ensure that they are applied.

The sanctions, which may comprise the payment of compensation to the victim, must be effective, proportionate and dissuasive. Member States must notify those provisions to the Commission and will notify it without delay of any subsequent amendment affecting them (Article 8(d)).

§6. PROOF

1644. Council Directive 97/80 of 15 December 1997 deals with the burden of proof in cases of discrimination based on sex.[648] The directive reverses the proof provided the plaintiff establishes the fact from which it may be presumed that there has been direct or indirect discrimination.

I. Aim

1645. The aim of the directive is to ensure that all persons who consider themselves wronged because the principle of equal treatment has not been applied to them have their rights asserted by judicial process after possible recourse to other competent bodies (Art. 1).

II. Definitions

1646. The following definitions prevail (Article 2):

– principle of equal treatment: the absence of discrimination whatsoever based on sex, either directly or indirectly;
– indirect discrimination: 'where an apparently neutral provision, criterion or practice disadvantages a substantially higher proportion of the members of one sex

---

648. O.J. L 14/6, 20 January 1998.

Part I, Ch. 6, Equal Treatment

unless that provision, criterion or practice is appropriate and necessary and can be justified by objective factors unrelated to sex'.

III. Scope

1647. The directive applies to:

- the situations covered by Article 157 TFEU and by the directives of 1975, 1976 and in so far as discrimination is concerned, 92/85[649] and 96/34;[650]
- any civil or administrative procedure concerning the public or private sector which provides for means of redress under national law with the exception of out-ofcourt procedures of a voluntary nature[651] or provided for in national law.

1648. The directive does not apply to criminal procedures, unless otherwise provided by the Member State (Art. 3).

IV. Burden of Proof

1649. Member States shall take such measures as are necessary to ensure that, when persons who consider themselves wronged because the principle of equal treatment has not been applied to them establish, before a court or a competent authority, facts from which it may be presumed that there has been direct or indirect discrimination, it shall be for the respondent to prove that there has been no breach of the principle of equal treatment (Article 4(1)). It is for the Member States to introduce, at any appropriate stage of the proceedings, rules of evidence which are more favourable to the plaintiff (*considerans* 14).

1650. In the *Kelly* case,[652] a reference has been made in the course of legal proceedings brought by Mr. Kelly against the National University of Ireland (University College Dublin) ('UCD'), following the latter's refusal to disclose unredacted documents relating to the selection procedure for a vocational training course.

1651. The Court hereby ruled:

(1) Article 4(1) of Council Directive 97/80/EC must be interpreted as meaning that it does not entitle an applicant for vocational training, who believes that his application was not accepted because of an infringement of the principle of

---

649. Directive of 19 October 1992 on the introduction of measures to encourage improvements in the safety and health at work of pregnant workers and workers who have recently given birth or are breastfeeding.
650. Directive of 3 June 1996 on the framework agreement on parental leave.
651. In particular procedures such as conciliation and mediation.
652. C.O.J, 21 July 2011, National Patrick Kelly v. University of Ireland (University College, Dublin), C-104/10, www.curia.

equal treatment, to information held by the course provider on the qualifications of the other applicants for the course in question, in order that he may establish 'facts from which it may be presumed that there has been direct or indirect discrimination' in accordance with that provision.
(1) Nevertheless, it cannot be ruled out that a refusal of disclosure by the defendant, in the context of establishing such facts, could risk compromising the achievement of the objective pursued by that directive and thus depriving Article 4(1) thereof in particular of its effectiveness. It is for the national court to ascertain whether that is the case in the main proceedings.
(2) Article 4 of Council Directive 76/207/EEC of 9 February 1976 must be interpreted as meaning that they do not entitle an applicant for vocational training to information held by the course provider on the qualifications of the other applicants for the course in question, either because he believes that he has been denied access to vocational training on the basis of the same criteria as the other candidates and discriminated against on grounds of sex, referred to in Article 4 of Directive 76/207, or because that applicant complains that he was discriminated against on the grounds of sex, referred to in Article 1(3) of Directive 2002/73, in terms of accessing that vocational training.
(3) Where an applicant for vocational training can rely on Directive 97/80 in order to obtain access to information held by the course provider on the qualifications of the other applicants for the course in question, that entitlement to access can be affected by rules of European Union law relating to confidentiality.
(4) The obligation contained in the third paragraph of Article 267 TFEU does not differ according to whether a Member State has an adversarial or an inquisitorial legal system.

1652. Member States are allowed to introduce rules of evidence which are more favourable to plaintiffs (Article 4(2)).[653]

1653. The 97/80 directive thus codified and expressly extended to the principle of equal treatment within the meaning of Directive 76/207 previous case law according to which the burden of proof, which in principle lies with the worker, may shift when this is necessary to avoid depriving workers who appear to be the victims of discrimination of any effective means of enforcing the principle of equal pay. Accordingly, when a measure distinguishing between employees on the basis of their hours of work has in practice an adverse impact on a substantially greater percentage of members of one or other sex, it is for the employer to show that there are objective reasons which justify the difference in pay that has been found.

In any event and in accordance with settled case law, when a situation falls within the scope of a directive, the national court is bound, when applying national law, to interpret it, so far as possible, in the light of the wording and the purpose of the directive concerned in order to achieve the result sought by the directive.

---

653. Member States need not apply paragraph 1 of Article 4 to proceedings in which it is for the court or competent body to investigate the facts of the case. The procedures thus referred to are those in which the plaintiff is not required to prove the facts, which it is for the court or competent body to investigate (*considerans* 16).

In light of the 17th and 18th recitals in the preamble to Directive 97/80, the result sought by that directive is, in particular, to ensure that the principle of equal treatment is applied more effectively inasmuch as, if there is a *prima facie* case of discrimination, it is for the employer to prove that that principle has not been infringed.[654]

V. Information

1654. Member States shall ensure that measures taken pursuant to this directive, together with the provisions already in force, are brought to the attention of all persons concerned by all appropriate means (Art. 5).

VI. Non-regression

1655. Implementation of the directive shall under no circumstance be sufficient ground for a reduction in the general level of protection of workers in the areas in which it applies (Art. 6).

VII. Implementation

1656. Member States have to implement the directive by 1 January 2001. Within two years of the entry into force of the directive, they shall communicate to the Commission all the information necessary for the Commission to draw up a report to the EP and the Council on the application of the directive (Art. 7).

§7. DIRECT EFFECT

1657. Article 157 TFEU is directly applicable and may thus give rise to individual rights which the courts must protect.[655] Indeed, the article is clear and sufficiently precise in its content, does not contain any reservation and is complete in itself in the sense that its application by national courts does not require the adoption of any subsequent measure of implementation either by the States or by the Union.

---

654. C.O.J., 10 March 2005, *Vasiliki Nikoloudi v. Organismos Tilepikinonion Ellados AE*, C-196/02, ECR, 2005, 1789.
655. C.O.J., *Defrenne II*.

§8. AGE DIVERSITY GUIDELINES AGREED IN COMMERCE SECTOR [656]

1658. On 11 March 2002 voluntary guidelines in the commerce sector regarding age diversity at work were agreed upon between the social partners.

The parties acknowledge that the workforce in Europe is ageing, due to demographic trends, and that employment policies and practices need to be adapted accordingly.

The document lists six points:

(1) 'ageing' or 'mature' workers are those defined as such in legislation, agreements or codes of practice at European or national level;
(2) ageing workers shall not be subject to discrimination at the workplace; an age-neutral approach should be adopted in employment relations, including in the areas of recruitment, vocational training and the distribution of positions within the company. The social partners in particular should work at abolishing age stereotypes at the workplace;
(3) older workers and their employers should jointly consider any mutually beneficial options allowing them to remain in active working life or to retire earlier. This could be achieved though flexible retirement schemes;
(4) age should be taken into account when designing jobs, bearing in mind that modern technology and ergonomics can increase productivity and enhance the quality of work;
(5) the social partners have a special role to play in facilitating the integration of ageing workers. There should be incentives for workers of all ages to embark upon learning and training. In particular, it is important for older workers to have equal access to training opportunities; and
(6) mutually-agreed schemes should, where relevant, pay attention to the specific requirements of older workers. For example, working time arrangements could be adjusted to ensure that the changing needs and capacities of workers are met. Further, voluntary part-time and flexible working time could be scheduled to allow ageing worker to remain in the workforce until retirement. The parties stress that the potential negative effects of such arrangements on the future pension entitlement of workers should, however, also be considered.

The social partners state that they will continue to examine ways in which to allow ageing workers the possibility of remaining in active life.

§9. FRAMEWORK AGREEMENT OF ACTIONS ON GENDER EQUALITY[657]

1659. On 22 March 2005, a joint text entitled Framework of actions on gender equality was concluded by the European social partners: BUSINESSEUROPE, CEEP, UEAPME and the ETUC. The framework highlights four priorities on which

---

656. 'Age diversity guidelines agreed In commerce sector', <www.eiro.eurofound.ie>.
657. See also: Frédéric Turlan, 'Social partners in audiovisual sector promote gender equality', Euronline, 2012.

Part I, Ch. 6, Equal Treatment

the signatory parties want the national social partners to focus over the coming five years. These are:

- addressing gender roles;
- promoting women in decision-making;
- supporting work–life balance; and
- tackling the gender pay gap.

The framework of actions states that these priorities are 'interconnected and of equal importance' and that any action taken at national, sectoral and/or company level will be most effective if these priorities are tackled in an 'integrated approach'.

I. Addressing Gender Roles

1660. The agreement states that traditional gender roles and stereotypes have a strong influence on the division of labour between men and women at home, in the workplace and more widely in society, which tends to 'continue a vicious circle of obstacles for achieving gender equality'. Although the rate of employment for women has increased significantly over the past three decades, the increase has not been equal in all sectors and occupations. The signatory parties believe that it is crucial to desegregate labour markets if occupational gender equality is to be achieved.

The parties acknowledge that some EU companies already check their internal practices and policies to encourage particular groups of people to enter and remain in employment. Further, there have been a range of initiatives in this area, undertaken by the social partners at company, sectoral and national levels.

The framework of actions singles out the following elements as key in the fight against stereotyped gender roles on the labour market:

- promoting non-gender biased education in schools and universities and providing efficient and non-stereotyped careers advice services. It is also important to encourage pupils, students and parents to consider all available career options for girls and boys at an early stage;
- making a special effort to attract girls and young women into technical and scientific professions;
- promoting the recruitment and retention of women and men with adequate skills at enterprise level in sectors and occupations where they are underrepresented. Further, the skills content of female occupations should be acknowledged and, where possible, enriched, so as to offer better career paths and opportunities for women in female-dominated sectors;
- raising awareness of middle managers in companies on ways to promote equal opportunities for all employees;
- promoting entrepreneurship as a career option for both women and men at sector and/or national level; and
- encouraging competence development for adults so that men and women can develop in their careers throughout their life.

II. Promoting Women in Decision-making

1661. The parties state that the number of women who are in decision-making positions is growing. However, only 30 per cent of managers are women, only 10 per cent of members of boards of directors are women and only 3 per cent of chief executive or equivalent positions are held by women. Therefore, they believe that the social partners have a responsibility to ensure that the overall working environment supports a more balanced participation of women and men in decision-making.

The text highlights the following areas as key to improving female participation at all levels within companies:

- promoting competence-based gender-neutral recruitment in enterprises;
- retaining women in enterprise, to avoid loss of competence;
- encouraging career development for both men and women;
- promoting female entrepreneurship as a complementary way of increasing the number of women in decision-making and increasing women's participation in the labour market; and
- promoting women's role in the social dialogue at all levels and on both the employer and the trade union side. In particular, special attention should be paid to enabling women to take up responsibilities in the area of worker representation, by addressing the scheduling of meetings and the availability of facilities.

III. Supporting Work–Life Balance

1662. The parties maintain that work-life balance can enhance employee satisfaction, promote 'workplace quality', contribute to an organisation's reputation as an employer of choice and benefit both employers and workers. They note that successful policies must take account of the needs of both the employer and the worker, with the best results being achieved by means of dialogue. The text highlights the following areas as key in supporting a good work-life balance:

- flexible working arrangements that can be taken up on a voluntary basis by both men and women. They should be designed in a way that does not undermine workers' long-term participation and position on the labour market;
- promoting a more balanced take-up of options designed to ease work-life balance. This could include encouraging take-up by men and encouraging parents to share leave periods more equally; and
- jointly approaching public authorities to develop instruments that help increase the availability of accessible and affordable child care facilities.

IV. Tackling the Gender Pay Gap

1663. The framework underlines that there is a strong EU legal framework supporting equal pay for equal work and work of equal value. However, there is a

Part I, Ch. 6, Equal Treatment

persistent gender pay gap across Europe, which the signatory parties believe may signal labour market dysfunction. They also feel that the reasons for the gender pay gap are not always well understood. However, they acknowledge that important work has been done in areas such as equal pay reviews, equality plans and benchmarking, following recognition of the link between labour market segregation and the gender pay gap. They identify key areas of action as follows:

– giving information on existing legislation on equal pay and guidance on how to help close the gender pay gap at different levels;
– developing clear and up-to-date statistics and sector and/or national level to enable the social partners to analyse and understand the complex causes of pay differentials; and
– ensuring that pay systems, including job-evaluation schemes, are transparent and gender-neutral. Attention should also be paid to the possible discriminatory effects of secondary elements of pay.

V. Annexed Case Studies

1664. The framework of actions has an annex containing 20 case studies of social partner agreements and practices from around the EU at national, sectoral and/or company level, presented at seminars held between January and September 2004. Together, they outline a range of good practice in various areas of equality actions and are drawn from a variety of public and private sector organisations, and sectoral and national agreements.

VI. Actions and Follow-up

1665. The signatory parties state that their member organisations will promote the joint text at all appropriate levels. It will also be transmitted to all relevant bodies at European and national levels. At national level, the social partner will draw up an annual report on the actions carried out in Member States in each of the four priority areas identified above. After four annual reports, the European social partners will evaluate the impact on companies and workers. This may then lead to an update of the text's priorities and/or an assessment of whether additional action is needed in one or more of the priority areas. The framework of actions on gender equality will also be taken into account when the next EU social dialogue work programme is prepared.

The impact of the text will be monitored over the coming four years and it will then be reviewed if deemed necessary. It is hoped that this will ensure that all actions taken in this area are relevant to the goal of improving gender equality and can make a positive contribution to achieving this aim.

§10. DIRECTIVE 2006/54/EC ON THE IMPLEMENTATION OF THE PRINCIPLE OF EQUAL OPPORTUNITIES AND EQUAL TREATMENT OF MEN AND WOMEN[658]

1666. Directive 2006/54/EC of 5 July 2006 on the implementation of the principle of equal opportunities and equal treatment of men and women in matters of employment and occupation recast previous Directives on equal treatment.[659] It was desirable, for reasons of clarity, that the provisions in question should be recast by bringing together in a single text the main provisions existing in this field as well as certain developments arising out of the case-law of the Court of Justice. Member States shall bring into force the laws, regulations and administrative provisions necessary to comply with this Directive by 15 August 2008 at the latest or shall ensure, by that date, that management and labour introduce the requisite provisions by way of agreement. Member States may, if necessary to take account of particular difficulties, have up to one additional year to comply with this Directive.

I. Purpose and Definitions

A. Purpose

1667. The purpose of this Directive is to ensure the implementation of the principle of equal opportunities and equal treatment of men and women in matters of employment and occupation.

To that end, it contains provisions to implement the principle of equal treatment in relation to:

(a) access to employment, including promotion, and to vocational training;
(b) working conditions, including pay;
(c) occupational social security schemes.

It also contains provisions to ensure that such implementation is made more effective by the establishment of appropriate procedures (Article 1).

B. Definitions

1668. For the purposes of this Directive, the following definitions shall apply:

(a) 'direct discrimination': where one person is treated less favourably on grounds of sex than another is, has been or would be treated in a comparable situation;

---

658. O.J., 26 July 2006, L 204.
659. Namely: (1) Council Directive 76/207/EEC of 9 February 1976 on the implementation of the principle of equal treatment for men and women as regards access to employment, vocational training and promotion, and working conditions [2] and Council Directive 86/378/EEC of 24 July 1986 on the implementation of the principle of equal treatment for men and women in occupational social security schemes [3] have been significantly amended [4]. Council Directive 75/117/EEC of 10 February 1975 on the approximation of the laws of the Member States relating to the application of the principle of equal pay for men and women [5] and Council Directive 97/80/EC of 15 December 1997 on the burden of proof in cases of discrimination based on sex [6].

(b) 'indirect discrimination': where an apparently neutral provision, criterion or practice would put persons of one sex at a particular disadvantage compared with persons of the other sex, unless that provision, criterion or practice is objectively justified by a legitimate aim, and the means of achieving that aim are appropriate and necessary;
(c) 'harassment': where unwanted conduct related to the sex of a person occurs with the purpose or effect of violating the dignity of a person, and of creating an intimidating, hostile, degrading, humiliating or offensive environment;
(d) 'sexual harassment': where any form of unwanted verbal, non-verbal or physical conduct of a sexual nature occurs, with the purpose or effect of violating the dignity of a person, in particular when creating an intimidating, hostile, degrading, humiliating or offensive environment;
(e) 'pay': the ordinary basic or minimum wage or salary and any other consideration, whether in cash or in kind, which the worker receives directly or indirectly, in respect of his/her employment from his/her employer.

1669. For the purposes of this Directive, discrimination includes:

(a) harassment and sexual harassment, as well as any less favourable treatment based on a person's rejection of or submission to such conduct;
(b) instruction to discriminate against persons on grounds of sex;
(c) any less favourable treatment of a woman related to pregnancy or maternity leave (Article 2).

II. Equal Pay: Prohibition of Discrimination

1670. For the same work or for work to which equal value is attributed, direct and indirect discrimination on grounds of sex with regard to all aspects and conditions of remuneration shall be eliminated.

In particular, where a job classification system is used for determining pay, it shall be based on the same criteria for both men and women and so drawn up as to exclude any discrimination on grounds of sex (Article 4).

III. Equal Treatment as Regards Access to Employment, Vocational Training and Promotion and Working Conditions

A. Prohibition of Discrimination

1671. There shall be no direct or indirect discrimination on grounds of sex in the public or private sectors, including public bodies, in relation to:

(a) conditions for access to employment, to self-employment or to occupation, including selection criteria and recruitment conditions, whatever the branch of activity and at all levels of the professional hierarchy, including promotion;

(b) access to all types and to all levels of vocational guidance, vocational training, advanced vocational training and retraining, including practical work experience;
(c) employment and working conditions, including dismissals, as well as pay as provided for in Article 157 TFEU.
(d) membership of, and involvement in, an organisation of workers or employers, or any organisation whose members carry on a particular profession, including the benefits provided for by such organisations.

Member States may provide, as regards access to employment including the training leading thereto, that a difference of treatment which is based on a characteristic related to sex shall not constitute discrimination where, by reason of the nature of the particular occupational activities concerned or of the context in which they are carried out, such a characteristic constitutes a genuine and determining occupational requirement, provided that its objective is legitimate and the requirement is proportionate (Article 14).

B. Return from Maternity Leave

1672. A woman on maternity leave shall be entitled, after the end of her period of maternity leave, to return to her job or to an equivalent post on terms and conditions which are no less favourable to her and to benefit from any improvement in working conditions to which she would have been entitled during her absence (Article 15).

C. Paternity and Adoption Leave

1673. This Directive is without prejudice to the right of Member States to recognise distinct rights to paternity and/or adoption leave. Those Member States which recognise such rights shall take the necessary measures to protect working men and women against dismissal due to exercising those rights and ensure that, at the end of such leave, they are entitled to return to their jobs or to equivalent posts on terms and conditions which are no less favourable to them, and to benefit from any improvement in working conditions to which they would have been entitled during their absence (Article 15).

IV. Remedies and Enforcement

A. Defence of Rights

1674. Member States shall ensure that, after possible recourse to other competent authorities including where they deem it appropriate conciliation procedures, judicial procedures for the enforcement of obligations under this Directive are available to all persons who consider themselves wronged by failure to apply the principle of equal treatment to them, even after the relationship in which the discrimination is alleged to have occurred has ended.

Member States shall ensure that associations, organisations or other legal entities which have, in accordance with the criteria laid down by their national law, a legitimate interest in ensuring that the provisions of this Directive are complied with, may engage, either on behalf or in support of the complainant, with his/her approval, in any judicial and/or administrative procedure provided for the enforcement of obligations under this Directive.

B. Compensation or Reparation

1675. Member States shall introduce into their national legal systems such measures as are necessary to ensure real and effective compensation or reparation as the Member States so determine for the loss and damage sustained by a person injured as a result of discrimination on grounds of sex, in a way which is dissuasive and proportionate to the damage suffered. Such compensation or reparation may not be restricted by the fixing of a prior upper limit, except in cases where the employer can prove that the only damage suffered by an applicant as a result of discrimination within the meaning of this Directive is the refusal to take his/her job application into consideration (Article 18).

C. Burden of Proof

1676. Member States shall take such measures as are necessary, in accordance with their national judicial systems, to ensure that, when persons who consider themselves wronged because the principle of equal treatment has not been applied to them establish, before a court or other competent authority, facts from which it may be presumed that there has been direct or indirect discrimination, it shall be for the respondent to prove that there has been no breach of the principle of equal treatment (Article 19).

V. Promotion of Equal Treatment – Dialogue

A. Equality Bodies

1677. Member States shall designate and make the necessary arrangements for a body or bodies for the promotion, analysis, monitoring and support of equal treatment of all persons without discrimination on grounds of sex. These bodies may form part of agencies with responsibility at national level for the defence of human rights or the safeguard of individuals' rights.

Member States shall ensure that the competences of these bodies include:

(a) without prejudice to the right of victims and of associations, organisations or other legal entities referred to in Article 17(2), providing independent assistance to victims of discrimination in pursuing their complaints about discrimination;

(b) conducting independent surveys concerning discrimination;
(c) publishing independent reports and making recommendations on any issue relating to such discrimination;
(d) at the appropriate level exchanging available information with corresponding European bodies such as any future European Institute for Gender Equality (Article 20).

B. Social Dialogue

1678. Member States shall, in accordance with national traditions and practice, take adequate measures to promote social dialogue between the social partners with a view to fostering equal treatment, including, for example, through the monitoring of practices in the workplace, in access to employment, vocational training and promotion, as well as through the monitoring of collective agreements, codes of conduct, research or exchange of experience and good practice.

Where consistent with national traditions and practice, Member States shall encourage the social partners, without prejudice to their autonomy, to promote equality between men and women, and flexible working arrangements, with the aim of facilitating the reconciliation of work and private life, and to conclude, at the appropriate level, agreements laying down antidiscrimination rules in the fields referred to in Article 1 which fall within the scope of collective bargaining. These agreements shall respect the provisions of this Directive and the relevant national implementing measures.

Member States shall, in accordance with national law, collective agreements or practice, encourage employers to promote equal treatment for men and women in a planned and systematic way in the workplace, in access to employment, vocational training and promotion.

To this end, employers shall be encouraged to provide at appropriate regular intervals employees and/or their representatives with appropriate information on equal treatment for men and women in the undertaking.

Such information may include an overview of the proportions of men and women at different levels of the organisation; their pay and pay differentials; and possible measures to improve the situation in cooperation with employees' representatives (Article 21).

C. Dialogue with Non-governmental Organisations

1679. Member States shall encourage dialogue with appropriate nongovernmental organisations which have, in accordance with their national law and practice, a legitimate interest in contributing to the fight against discrimination on grounds of sex with a view to promoting the principle of equal treatment (Article 22).

VI. Compliance

1680. Member States shall take all necessary measures to ensure that:

(a) any laws, regulations and administrative provisions contrary to the principle of equal treatment are abolished;
(b) provisions contrary to the principle of equal treatment in individual or collective contracts or agreements, internal rules of undertakings or rules governing the independent occupations and professions and workers' and employers' organisations or any other arrangements shall be, or may be, declared null and void or are amended;
(c) occupational social security schemes containing such provisions may not be approved or extended by administrative measures (Article 23).

VII. Victimisation

1681. Member States shall introduce into their national legal systems such measures as are necessary to protect employees, including those who are employees' representatives provided for by national laws and/or practices, against dismissal or other adverse treatment by the employer as a reaction to a complaint within the undertaking or to any legal proceedings aimed at enforcing compliance with the principle of equal treatment (Article 24).

VIII. Penalties

1682. Member States shall lay down the rules on penalties applicable to infringements of the national provisions adopted pursuant to this Directive, and shall take all measures necessary to ensure that they are applied. The penalties, which may comprise the payment of compensation to the victim, must be effective, proportionate and dissuasive. The Member States shall notify those provisions to the Commission by 5 October 2005 at the latest and shall notify it without delay of any subsequent amendment affecting them.

Chapter 7. Protection of Motherhood

1683. In its Action Programme implementing the Community Charter, the Commission has included among its aims the adoption by the Council of a directive on the protection of pregnant women at work. The Directive of 19 October 1992 (No. 92/85) is based on Article 153 TFEU, and constitutes the tenth individual directive within the meaning of Article 16(1) of Directive 89/391 of 12 June 1989 on the introduction of measures to encourage improvements in safety and health of workers at work.[660] It follows that the articles of the aforementioned framework directive are applicable, in particular Articles 10 (worker information), 11 (consultation and participation of workers) and 12 (training of workers). It should be recalled that in the definition of the framework directive, the meaning of worker is 'any person employed by an employer, including trainees and apprentices' and the meaning of employer is 'any natural or legal person who has an employment relationship with the worker and has responsibility for the undertaking and/or establishment'.

1684. A member of a capital company's Board of Directors who provides services to that company and is an integral part of it must be regarded as having the status of worker for the purposes of Council Directive 92/85/EEC if that activity is carried out, for some time, under the direction or supervision of another body of that company and if, in return for those activities, the Board Member receives remuneration. It is for the national court to undertake the assessments of fact necessary to determine whether that is so in the case pending before it.[661]

1685. The purpose of the directive is to implement measures to encourage improvements in the safety and health at work of pregnant workers and workers who have recently given birth or who are breast feeding.[662]

The directive provides the following protective measures:

(1) For all activities liable to involve a specific risk of exposure to the agents, processes or working conditions involving risks to safety or health and any possible effect on the pregnancies or breast feeding, the employer shall assess the nature, degree and duration of exposure in order to decide what measures should be taken. The employer shall take the necessary measures to ensure that, by temporarily *adjusting the working conditions* of the worker concerned, the exposure of that worker to such risks is avoided. If this is not possible, the employer shall take the necessary measures to move the worker to another job. If moving to another job is not technically and/or objectively feasible or cannot

---

660. Article 15 of the latter directive provides that particularly sensitive groups must be protected against dangers which specifically affect them (O.J. L 183/1, 29 June 1989).
661. C.O.J., *Dita Danosa* v. *LKB Lözings SIA*, 11 November 2010, C-232/09, www.curia.eu.
662. Council Directive 92/85/EC of 19 October 1992 on the introduction of measures to encourage improvements in the safety and health at work of pregnant workers and workers who have recently given birth or are breastfeeding (tenth individual directive within the meaning of Article 16(1) of Directive 89/391/EC), O.J. L 348/1, 28 November 1992.

Part I, Ch. 7, Protection of Motherhood 1686–1686

reasonably be required on duly substantiated grounds, the worker concerned shall be granted leave in accordance with national legislation and/or national practice (Article 5). This includes the maintenance of a payment to and/or entitlement to an adequate allowance (Article 11(1)). Article 11(3) indicates what an adequate allowance should look like.

(2) An alternative to night work. This may simply mean a transfer to daytime work, leave from work or extension of maternity leave (Article 7).
(3) A continuous period of maternity leave of at least 14 weeks allocated before and/or after confinement (Article 8(1)). This maternity leave must include a compulsory leave of at least two weeks, allocated before and/or after confinement (Article 8(2)).
(4) The prohibition of dismissal of the workers concerned during the period from the beginning of their pregnancy to the end of the maternity leave. If a worker is dismissed during this period, the employer must cite duly substantiated grounds for her dismissal in writing (Art. 10(1) and 10(2)).

Article 10 must be interpreted as prohibiting not only the notification of a decision to dismiss on the grounds of pregnancy and/or of the birth of a child during the period of protection but also the taking of preparatory steps for such a decision before the end of that period.[663]

The directive explicitly mentions 'that it may not have the effect of reducing the level of protection afforded to pregnant workers, workers who have recently given birth or who are breastfeeding as compared with the situation which exists in each Member State on the date on which this Directive is adopted' (Art. 1(3)).

1686. Article 2, in conjunction with Article 3, of Council Directive 76/207/EEC of 9 February 1976[664] (now Article 6 of Directive 2006/54, must be interpreted as precluding legislation of a Member State, which is specific to the protection provided for in Article 10 of Directive 92/85 in the event of the dismissal of a pregnant worker, or of a worker who has recently given birth or is breastfeeding, and which denies a pregnant employee who has been dismissed during her pregnancy the option to bring an action for damages whereas such an action is available to any other employee who has been dismissed, where such a limitation on remedies constitutes less favourable treatment of a woman related to pregnancy. That would be the case in particular if the procedural rules relating to the only action available in the case of dismissal of such workers do not comply with the principle of effective judicial protection of an individual's rights under Union law, a matter which it is for the referring court to determine.[665]

---

663. C.O.J., 11 October 2007, *Nadine Paquay* v. *Société d'architectes Hoet + Minne SPRL*, C-460/ 06, ECR, 2007, 8511.
664. On the implementation of the principle of equal treatment for men and women as regards access to employment, vocational training and promotion, and working conditions, as amended by Directive 2002/73/EC of the European Parliament and of the Council of 23 September 2002. Now Article 14(1), 23(a) and 23(b) of Directive 2006/54 of 5 July 2006 on the implementation of the principle of equal opportunities and equal treatment of men and women in matters of employment and occupation (recast), which repealed Directive 76/207 EC).
665. COJ, 29 October 2009, *Virginie Pontin* v. *T-Comalux SA*, C-63/08, www.curia.eu.

The social partners are allowed by way of collective bargaining agreement to take the necessary measures for the implementation of the directive at national level (Art. 14).

1687. Article 10 of Directive 92/85 is to be interpreted as precluding national legislation, which permits a member of a capital company's Board of Directors to be removed from that post without restriction, where the person concerned is a 'pregnant worker' within the meaning of that directive and the decision to remove her was taken essentially on account of her pregnancy. Even if the Board Member concerned is not a 'pregnant worker' within the meaning of Directive 92/85, the fact remains that the removal, on account of pregnancy or essentially on account of pregnancy, of a member of a Board of Directors who performs duties such as those described in the main proceedings can affect only women and therefore constitutes direct discrimination on grounds of sex, contrary to Article 2(1) and (7) and Article 3(1)(c) of Council Directive 76/207/EEC as amended by Directive 2002/ 73/EC.[666]

1688. Article 10 of Council Directive 92/85/EEC has direct effect and is to be interpreted to the effect that, in the absence of transposition measures taken by a Member State within the period prescribed by that directive, it confers on individuals rights on which they may rely before a national court against the authorities of that state.

In allowing derogations from the prohibition of dismissal of pregnant workers, workers who have recently given birth or workers who are breastfeeding in cases 'not connected with their condition which are permitted under national legislation and/or practice', Article 10(1) of Directive 92/85 does not require the Member States to specify the particular grounds on which such workers may be dismissed.

Whilst the prohibition of discrimination laid down in Article 10 of Directive 92/85 applies to both employment contracts for an indefinite period and fixed-term contracts, non-renewal of such a contract, when it comes to an end as stipulated, cannot be regarded as a dismissal prohibited by that provision. However, where non-renewal of a fixed-term contract is motivated by the worker's state of pregnancy, it constitutes direct discrimination on grounds of sex, contrary to Article 2(1) and 3(1) of Council Directive 76/207/EEC of 9 February 1976.[667]

In providing that the dismissal of a pregnant worker, of a worker who has recently given birth or of a worker who is breastfeeding may take place, in exceptional cases 'and, where applicable, provided that the competent authority has given its consent, Article 10(1) of Directive 92/85 is not to be interpreted as imposing on Member States any obligation to have a national authority, having found that there is an

---

666. C.O.J., 11 November 2010, *Dita Danosa v. LKB L zings SIA*, C-232/09, www.curia.eu. Now Articles 14(1) and 2(2) of Directive 2006/54 of 5 July 2006 on the implementation of the principle of equal opportunities and equal treatment of men and women in matters of employment and occupation (recast), which repealed Directive 76/207 EC.
667. Now Article 14(1) of Directive 2006/54 of 5 July 2006 on the implementation of the principle of equal opportunities and equal treatment of men and women in matters of employment and occupation (recast), which repealed Directive 76/207 EC.

Part I, Ch. 7, Protection of Motherhood 1689–1693

exceptional case justifying the dismissal of a pregnant worker, give its consent prior to the employer's decision to dismiss the worker'.[668]

1689. According to the European Court of Justice,[669] dismissed pregnant workers must enjoy effective judicial protection of their rights under Union law. Where the only remedy available under national legislation to a worker dismissed during pregnancy does not provide adequate time-limits within which to bring proceedings, that legislation introduces less favourable treatment linked to pregnancy and constitutes discrimination against female employees.

1690. The Luxembourg Labour Code, which transposes the Pregnant Workers Directive, prohibits the dismissal of an employee where she has been medically certified as being pregnant or within twelve weeks of her giving birth. It makes legal action by an employee dismissed during pregnancy, who wishes to bring an action for nullity of the dismissal and for reinstatement within the undertaking concerned, subject to a time-limit of 15 days from the date on which her contract is terminated.

1691. Ms Virginie Pontin worked for the Luxembourg company T-Comalux. She was notified of her dismissal with immediate effect 'on grounds of serious misconduct' consisting of 'unauthorised absence for more than three days'. The next day Ms Pontin informed T-Comalux that she was pregnant and that her dismissal was null and void by virtue of the legal protection enjoyed by pregnant workers. As she had not received a reply from the company and considered that she was the victim of wrongful dismissal, she referred the matter to the Employment Tribunal seeking a declaration that her dismissal was null and void.

1692. The Employment Tribunal asked the Court of Justice in essence whether Union law precludes national legislation which, on the one hand, makes legal action brought by a pregnant employee who has been dismissed during her pregnancy subject to short time-limits likely to deny her the opportunity to take legal proceedings to safeguard her rights and, on the other hand, denies her the possibility of bringing an action for damages against her employer, which is available to other employees who have been dismissed.

1693. The Court observed that Member States are required to take such measures as are necessary to enable persons who consider themselves wronged to pursue their claims by judicial process in accordance with the principle of judicial protection of an individual's rights under Union law. Thus, pregnant workers or those who have recently given birth or are breastfeeding must be protected from the consequences of dismissal which would be unlawful. National measures must be such as to ensure effective and efficient legal protection, must have a genuine dissuasive effect with regard to the employer and must in any event be commensurate

---

668. C.O.J., 4 October 2001, Case C-438/99, *Maria Luisa Jiménez Melgar and Ayuntamiento de Los Barrios*, ECR, 2001, 6915.
669. C.O.J., 29 October 2009, *Pontin Virginie v. T-Comalux SA*, C-63/08, www.curia.

with the injury suffered. It is for the national court, which alone has direct knowledge of the procedural rules governing actions in the field of domestic law, to determine whether those principles are complied with.

Although the Court recognised that Member States may lay down reasonable time-limits for bringing proceedings, such time-limits must not render impossible or excessively difficult the exercise of rights conferred by Union law. In that regard, the procedural rules relating to an action for nullity and reinstatement of a dismissed employee appear to give rise to problems likely to make exercise of the rights that pregnant women derive from Union law excessively difficult.

1694. The Court considers that the 15-day time-limit is particularly short for obtaining proper advice and, if appropriate, bringing an action for nullity and reinstatement within the undertaking. Furthermore, some of the days included in that period may expire before the pregnant woman receives the letter notifying her of the dismissal, since it would seem that period begins to run, according to the case-law of the Luxembourg courts, from the time the letter of dismissal is posted and not from the time it is received. If the referring court were, after conducting the necessary legal and factual verifications, to hold that the 15-day limitation period does not comply with the requirement of effective judicial protection of an individual's rights under Union law, such a time-limit would infringe the Pregnant Workers Directive.

According to the referring court, the only remedy open to a pregnant woman dismissed during pregnancy is an action for nullity and reinstatement within the undertaking, to the exclusion of all other remedies under employment law, such as an action for damages.

1695. Therefore, if it emerges, after verification by the referring court, that the procedural rules relating to the only action available in the event of the dismissal of pregnant workers do not comply with the principle of effective judicial protection of an individual's rights under Union law, such limitation of available remedies introduces less favourable treatment of a woman related to pregnancy and thus constitutes discrimination within the meaning of the Equal Treatment Directive.

If that referring court were to find there had been such an infringement of the principle of equal treatment, within the meaning of the Equal Treatment Directive, it would have to interpret the domestic jurisdictional rules in such a way that, wherever possible, they contribute to the attainment of the objective of ensuring effective judicial protection of a pregnant woman's rights under Union law.

1696. Article 10 of Council Directive 92/85/EEC is to be interpreted as precluding a worker from being dismissed on the ground of pregnancy:

– where she was recruited for a fixed period, she failed to inform the employer that she was pregnant even though she was aware of this when the contract of employment was concluded,
– and because of her pregnancy she was unable to work during a substantial part of the term of that contract.

Part I, Ch. 7, Protection of Motherhood 1697–1698

The fact that the worker has been recruited by a very large undertaking which employs temporary workers frequently is of no relevance to the interpretation of 10 of Directive 92/85.[670]

1697. A decision to dismiss on the grounds of pregnancy and/or child birth is also contrary to Articles 2(1)[671] and 5(1) of Council Directive 76/207/EEC, of 9 February 1976, irrespective of the moment when that decision to dismiss is notified and even if it is notified after the end of the period of protection set down in Article 10 of Directive 92/85. Since such a decision to dismiss is contrary to both Article 10 of Directive 92/85 and Article 2(1) of Directive 76/207[672], the measure chosen by a Member State under Article 6 of that latter directive to sanction the infringement of those provisions must be at least equivalent to the sanction set down in national law implementing Articles 10 and 12 of Directive 92/85.[673]

1698. In *Margaret Boyle and others* v. *Equal Opportunities Commission*,[674] the Court decided that:

(1) Article 157, Article 1 of Directive 75/117[675] and Article 11 of Council Directive 92/85 do not preclude a clause in an employment contract which makes the payment, during the period of maternity leave referred to by Article 8 of Directive 92/85, of pay higher than the statutory payments in respect of maternity leave conditional on the worker's undertaking to return to work after the birth of the child for at least one month, failing which she is required to repay the difference between the amount of the pay she will have received during the period of maternity leave, on the one hand, and the amount of those payments, on the other.
(2) Article 8 of Directive 92/85 and Article 5(1) of Council Directive 76/207[676] do not preclude a clause in an employment contract from requiring an employee who has expressed her intention to commence her maternity leave during the six weeks preceding the expected week of childbirth, and is on sick leave with a pregnancy-related illness immediately before that date and gives birth during

---

670. C.O.J., 4 October 2001, *Tele Danmark A/S and Handels-og Kontorfunktionærernes Forbund i Danmark (HK), acting on behalf of Marianne Brandt-Nielsen*, Case C-109/00, ECR, 2001, 6993.
671. Now Article 14(1) of Directive 2006/54 of 5 July 2006 on the implementation of the principle of equal opportunities and equal treatment of men and women in matters of employment and occupation (recast), which repealed Directive 76/207 EC.
672. Now Article 14(1) of Directive 2006/54 of 5 July 2006 on the implementation of the principle of equal opportunities and equal treatment of men and women in matters of employment and occupation (recast), which repealed Directive 76/207 EC.
673. C.O.J., 11 October 2007, *Nadine Paquay* v. *Société d'architectes Hoet+Minne SPRL*, C-460/ 06, ECR, 2007, 8511.
674. C.O.J., 27 October 1998, Case C-411/96, ECR, 1998, 6401.
675. Now Article 4 of Directive 2006/54 of 5 July 2006 on the implementation of the principle of equal opportunities and equal treatment of men and women in matters of employment and occupation (recast), which repealed Directive 75/117 EC.
676. Repealed by Directive 2006/54 of 5 July 2006 on the implementation of the principle of equal opportunities and equal treatment of men and women in matters of employment and occupation (recast).

the period of sick leave, to bring forward the date on which her paid maternity leave commences either to the beginning of the sixth week preceding the expected week of childbirth or to the beginning of the period of sick leave, whichever is the later.
(3) A clause in an employment contract which prohibits a woman from taking sick leave during the minimum period of 14 weeks' maternity leave to which a female worker is entitled pursuant to Article 8(1) of Directive 92/85, unless she elects to return to work and thus terminate her maternity leave, is not compatible with Directive 92/85. By contrast, a clause in an employment contract which prohibits a woman from taking sick leave during a period of supplementary maternity leave granted to her by the employer, unless she elects to return to work and thus terminate her maternity leave, is compatible with Directives 76/207[677] and 92/85.
(4) Directives 92/85 and 76/207[678] do not preclude a clause in an employment contract from limiting the period during which annual leave accrues to the minimum period of 14 weeks' maternity leave to which female workers are entitled under Article 8 of Directive 92/85 and from providing that annual leave ceases to accrue during any period of supplementary maternity leave granted to them by their employer.
(5) Directive 92/85 precludes a clause in an employment contract from limiting, in the context of an occupational scheme wholly financed by the employer, the accrual of pension rights during the period of maternity leave referred to by Article 8 of that directive to the period during which the woman receives the pay provided for by that contract or national legislation.

1699. A dismissal essentially based on the fact that a woman is at an advanced stage of *in vitro* fertilisation treatment is contrary to the principle of equal treatment for men and women. This was ruled in the *Mayr* case.[679]

Ms. Mayr was employed as a waitress. In the course of attempted *in vitro* fertilisation, and after hormone treatment lasting for about one and a half months, a follicular puncture was carried out on Ms. Mayr. Her general practitioner certified her sick. On the date when Ms. Mayr was given notice of her dismissal, her ova had already been fertilised with her partner's sperm cells and, therefore, *in vitro* fertilised ova already existed.

Three days after Ms. Mayr had been informed of her dismissal, two fertilised ova were transferred into her uterus.

Ms. Mayr then claimed payment of her salary and pro rata annual remuneration, maintaining that, from the date on which *in vitro* fertilisation of her ova took place, she was entitled to the protection against dismissal.

---

677. *Idem.*
678. Repealed by Directive 2006/54 of 5 July 2006 on the implementation of the principle of equal opportunities and equal treatment of men and women in matters of employment and occupation (recast).
679. C.O.J., 26 February 2008, *Sabine Mayr v. Bäckerei und Konditorei Gerhard Flöckner OHG*, C-506/06, ECR, 2008, 1017.

As the dispute concerns, in essence, the issue of whether Ms. Mayr benefited, at the date she was given notice of her dismissal, from the protection against dismissal granted to pregnant workers, at work of pregnant workers, a woman is pregnant before her fertilised ova have been transferred into her uterus.

In its judgment, the Court holds that, for reasons connected with the principle of legal certainty, the protection against dismissal established by the Directive on the safety and health at work of pregnant workers cannot be extended to a pregnant worker where, on the date she is given notice of her dismissal, the *in vitro* fertilised ova have not yet been transferred into her uterus. If such a premiss were allowed, the benefit of the protection could be granted even where the transfer of the fertilised ova into the uterus is postponed, for whatever reason, for a number of years, or even where such a transfer is definitively abandoned.

However, a worker who is undergoing *in vitro* fertilisation treatment can rely on the protection against discrimination on grounds of sex granted by the Directive on equal treatment for men and women.

On that basis, the Court points out that treatment such as that which Ms. Mayr has undergone directly affects only women. The dismissal of a worker essentially because she is undergoing a follicular puncture and a transfer of fertilised ova into her uterus therefore constitutes direct discrimination on grounds of sex. The dismissal of a worker, in a situation such as that of Ms Mayr, would, moreover, be contrary to the objective of protection pursued by the Directive on equal treatment for men and women.

1700. In the *Gassmayr* and *Parvianen* cases,[680] the Court ruled that workers given leave from work or transferred to another job because of pregnancy are entitled to their basic monthly pay and the supplementary allowances attached to their occupational status. They cannot, on the other hand, claim the allowances and supplements which are intended to compensate for the disadvantages related to the performance of specific tasks in particular circumstances, where they do not actually perform those tasks.

In these two cases concerning references from Austria and Finland for preliminary rulings, the Court of Justice was called on to rule on questions relating to the calculation of the remuneration to be paid to workers during pregnancy or maternity leave, where they are temporarily transferred to another job or granted leave from work.

1701. Susanne Gassmayr worked before her pregnancy as a junior hospital doctor at the University Anaesthesia Clinic of the University of Graz. In addition to her basic pay, she received an allowance for on-call duty at the workplace for extra hours that she worked. She stopped working during her pregnancy, on the basis of a medical certificate stating that continuing to work was likely to endanger her life or health or that of her child, and then took maternity leave.

---

680. C.O.J., 1 July 2010, *Susanne Gassmayr v. Bundesminister für Wissenschaft und Forschung*, C-194/08, www.curia; *Sanna Maria Parvainen v. Finnair Oyj*, C-471/08, www.curia.

Since Austrian law excludes the payment of the on-call duty allowance to persons who are not actually performing on-call duty, Ms Gassmayr was refused that allowance during the period when she was not working.

1702. In the other case, Sanna Maria Parviainen worked before her pregnancy as a purser for the airline Finnair. A substantial part of her pay was made up of supplementary allowances attached to her seniority or intended to compensate for the specific disadvantages connected with the organisation of working time in the air transport sector.

On becoming pregnant, she was temporarily transferred to a ground job corresponding to office work, and she occupied that position until her maternity leave began. Following that transfer, her monthly pay was reduced, in particular because she no longer received the allowances for being a purser.

1703. Both women brought judicial proceedings against their employers on the ground that their remuneration had been reduced during their pregnancy or maternity leave. The Administrative Court, Austria and the Helsinki District Court, Finland asked the Court of Justice whether the Pregnant Workers Directive allows employers to refuse to pay those workers certain allowances which they had received before their pregnancies.

1704. The Court finds that, during the temporary transfer to another job or the leave from work during their pregnancy and maternity leave, both Ms Gassmayr and Ms Parviainen were no longer able to perform the duties which had been entrusted to them before their pregnancies. The Court finds that the on-call duty allowance paid to Ms Gassmayr and certain supplementary allowances received by Ms Parviainen constitute components of their remuneration which are dependent on the performance of specific functions in particular circumstances and are intended to compensate for the disadvantages related to those functions. The payment of that allowance and those supplementary allowances may therefore be conditional on the pregnant worker actually performing specific duties in return.

1705. The Court none the less stated that a pregnant worker who is granted leave from work or temporarily transferred to another job because of her pregnancy must be entitled to remuneration consisting of her basic monthly pay and the pay components and supplementary allowances relating to her occupational status, such as those relating to her seniority, length of service and professional qualifications.

Moreover, the remuneration which must be maintained for a pregnant worker temporarily transferred to another job cannot in any event be less than that paid to workers occupying that job. For the duration of the temporary transfer, the pregnant worker is also entitled in principle to the pay components and supplementary allowances relating to that job.

1706. As regards workers on maternity leave, the Court noted that their position is not comparable to that of a worker actually at work. They are not therefore entitled to continue to receive their full pay or to be paid an on-call duty allowance. Moreover, the directive itself provides that the minimum remuneration payable to them is equivalent to that which the worker concerned would receive in the event of a break in her activities on grounds connected with her state of health.

1707. Finally, the Court recalled the need to respect the effectiveness of the directive and the aims it pursues, namely the protection of the safety and health of pregnant workers, workers who have recently given birth and those who are breast-feeding, and notes that the Member States are free to maintain, for workers granted leave from work or temporarily transferred to another job during their pregnancy or on maternity leave, their entire remuneration, at a higher level than that guaranteed by the directive.

1708. (1) Article 11(2)(a) of Directive 92/85/EEC is to be interpreted as meaning that a worker must be able to take her annual leave during a period other than the period of her maternity leave, including in a case in which the period of maternity leave coincides with the general period of annual leave fixed, by a collective agreement, for the entire workforce.
(2) Article 11(2)(a) of Directive 92/85 is to be interpreted as also applying to the entitlement of a worker in circumstances such as those of the case before the referring court to a longer period of annual leave, provided for by national law, than the minimum laid down by Directive 93/104.[681]

1709. Articles 8 and 11 of Council Directive 92/85/EEC preclude provisions of national law concerning child-care leave which, in so far as they fail to take into account changes affecting the worker concerned as a result of pregnancy during the period of at least 14 weeks preceding and after childbirth, do not allow the person concerned to obtain at her request an alteration of the period of her child-care leave at the time when she claims her rights to maternity leave and thus deprive her of the rights attaching to that maternity leave.[682]

1710. A Christmas bonus constitutes pay, even if it is paid voluntarily by the employer and even if it is paid mainly or exclusively as an incentive for future work or loyalty to the undertaking or both. However, it does not fall within the concept of payment within the meaning of Article 11(2)(b) of Directive 92/85/EEC.[683]

1711. Article 157 TFEU must be interpreted as requiring that, in so far as the pay received by the worker during her maternity leave is determined at least in part on the basis of the pay she earned before her maternity leave began, any pay rise awarded between the beginning of the period covered by the reference pay and the end of the maternity leave must be included in the elements of pay taken into account in calculating the amount of such pay. This requirement is not limited to cases where the pay rise is back-dated to the period covered by the reference pay.

---

681. C.O.J., 18 March 2004, *María Paz Merino Gómez* v. *Continental Industrias del Caucho SA.*, C-342/01, ECR, 2004, 2605. Directive 93/100 has been repealed and replaced by Directive 2003/88/EC of the European Parliament and of the Council of 4 November 2003 concerning certain aspects of the organisation of working time.
682. C.O.J., 20 September 2007, *Sari Kiiski* v. *Tampereen kaupunki*, C-116/06, ECR, 2007, 7643.
683. C.O.J., 21 October 1999, *Susanne Lewen* v. *Lothar Denda*, Case C-333/97, ECR, 1999, 7243.

Absent any Union legislation in this sphere, it is for the competent national authorities to determine how, in compliance with all the provisions of Union law, and in particular Directive 92/85/EEC any pay rise awarded before or during maternity leave must be included in the elements of pay used to calculate the pay due to a worker during maternity leave.[684]

Let us finally add that Article 33 of the Charter of Fundamental Rights (2007), states under the heading 'Family and professional life' that:

(1) The family shall enjoy legal, economic and social protection.
(2) To reconcile family and professional life, everyone shall have the right to protection from dismissal for a reason connected with maternity and the right to paid maternity leave and to parental leave following the birth or adoption of a child.

---

684. C.O.J., 30 March 2004, *Michelle K. Alabaster v. Woolwich plc and Secretary of State for Social Security*, C-147/02, ECR, 2004, 3101.

Chapter 8. Working Time, Sunday Rest, Night Work and Parental Leave

§1. WORKING TIME

I. In General

1712. Regarding working time, two recommendations must be mentioned. The first dates from 22 July 1975 and concerns the principle of the 40-hour work week and the principle of four weeks' annual paid holidays;[685] these principles were to be applied throughout the Union in all sectors by 31 December 1978 at the latest and as far as possible before that date. Needless to say, this recommendation has at present only a historical, symbolic value and has been overtaken by events.

A second recommendation, namely of 10 December 1982, relates to retirement age.[686] With this recommendation the Council invites the Member States to acknowledge flexible retirement, i.e. the right to choose when employed people will take their retirement pension, as one of the aims of social policy. Employed workers receiving a retirement pension cannot be excluded from any form of paid employment. The recommendation states further that retirement preparation programmes should be started during the years preceding the end of the working life with the participation of organisations representing employers and employed persons and other interested bodies.

1713. On 3 August 1990, a proposal for a directive concerning certain aspects of the organisation of working time was made by the Commission with the aim of implementing points 7 and 8 of the Community Charter for fundamental social rights. The proposal is made on the basis of Article 153 TFEU, which allows for a decision in the Council with a qualified majority, and concerns basic rules providing for:

– daily, weekly and yearly rest;
– night work, shift work;
– the protection of the health and safety of employees in the event of changes in working patterns resulting from adjustments to working time.

1714. The Commission departs from the fact that in recent years the disassociation of individual working time and plant operation hours has been becoming increasingly important in most of the Member States: individual hours are becoming shorter and operation hours longer. Exceptionally, individual working time may become longer such as in the case of weekend work, during which the employee works, for example, 2 × 12 hours. This tendency has helped enterprises to become

---

685. O.J. L 199, 30 July 1975.
686. O.J. L 357, 18 December 1982.

more flexible, to increase their capacity utilisation, to adapt smoothly to new circumstances, to achieve productivity gains and to enhance competitiveness. Furthermore, the increase in plant operating hours is often conducive to investment in modernisation and, in any case, enables undertakings to make savings in relation to the fixed productive capital for a given output. These tendencies also seem to match more closely with the aspiration of employees to combine occupational and family responsibilities more successfully. In addition, the increased flexibility of working time arrangements helps to integrate more people into the labour market and to enhance employment opportunities.

In this context, however, the Commission indicates that one must consider the extent to which workers can rely on minimum rules concerning certain rest periods to protect themselves against excessively long hours, which may be detrimental to the health and the safety of the workers at their workplace. There is no doubt that work fatigue (depending of course on the type of work and the conditions under which it is exercised) is increased by the duration of working hours. The physical and mental effort in work exceeding eight hours becomes increasingly strenuous as fatigue sets in, even in the case of light work. These effects are exacerbated considerably by jobs requiring static or strained postures, or involving repetitive movements or heavy complicated tasks. In the context of application of modern technologies in particular, long hours tend to increase the numbers of errors and mistakes. Greater probability of accidents at work – especially serious accidents – and increased stress often occurs in the final hours of work. The same is true for weekly working time: a weekly working time of more than 50 hours can, in the long run, be harmful to the health and the safety of workers (fatigue, disturbed sleep, problems revealed during medicals). The same considerations can be made in the case of night work and shift work. Hence the proposals of the Commission.

1715. Let us finally mention that Article 31(2) of the Charter of Fundamental Rights (2007) declares that: 'Every worker has the right to limitation of maximum working hours, to daily and weekly rest periods and to an annual period of paid leave.' And that statement, as expressly declared by the Presidium of the Convention which drew up the Charter, is inspired by Article 2 of the European Social Charter and by paragraph 8 of the Community Charter of Workers' Rights, and also took due account of Directive 93/104/EC concerning certain aspects of the organisation of working time.

II. Directive 2003/88/EC of 4 November 2003

1716. Directive 2003/88/EC[687] significantly amended and replaced Directive 93/104/EC of 23 November 1993, concerning certain aspects of the organisation of working time, which layd down minimum safety and health requirements for the organisation of working time, in respect of periods of daily rest, breaks, weekly rest,

---

687. Directive 2003/88/EC of the European Parliament and of the Council of 4 November 2003 concerning certain aspects of the organisation of working time, O.J. L 299, 18 November 2003.

Part I, Ch. 8, Working Time and Leave

maximum weekly working time, annual leave and aspects of night work, shift work and patterns of work.

Thus a codification of the provisions in question was drawn up. Article 153 TFEU provides that the Union is to support and complement the activities of the Member States with a view to improving the working environment to protect workers' health and safety. Thus the directive could be adopted with a qualified majority.

1717. For the directive objectives are:

- the improvement of workers' safety, hygiene and health at work is an objective which should not be subordinated to purely economic considerations;
- all workers should have adequate rest periods. The concept of 'rest' must be expressed in units of time, i.e. in days, hours and/or fractions thereof. Union workers must be granted minimum daily, weekly and annual periods of rest and adequate breaks. It is also necessary in this context to place a maximum limit on weekly working hours;
- account should be taken of the principles of the International Labour Organisation with regard to the organisation of working time, including those relating to night work;
- research has shown that the human body is more sensitive at night to environmental disturbances and also to certain burdensome forms of work organisation and that long periods of night work can be detrimental to the health of workers and can endanger safety at the workplace;
- there is a need to limit the duration of periods of night work, including overtime, and to provide for employers who regularly use night workers to bring this information to the attention of the competent authorities if they so request;
- it is important that night workers should be entitled to a free health assessment prior to their assignment and thereafter at regular intervals and that whenever possible they should be transferred to day work for which they are suited if they suffer from health problems;
- the situation of night and shift workers requires that the level of safety and health protection should be adapted to the nature of their work and that the organisation and functioning of protection and prevention services and resources should be efficient;
- specific working conditions may have detrimental effects on the safety and health of workers. The organisation of work according to a certain pattern must take account of the general principle of adapting work to the worker.

A. Scope and Definitions

1. Purpose and Scope

1718. This directive lays down minimum safety and health requirements for the organisation of working time. It applies to:

(a) minimum periods of daily rest, weekly rest and annual leave, to breaks and maximum weekly working time; and
(b) certain aspects of night work, shift work and patterns of work.
(c) all sectors of activity, both public and private[688] (Article 1).

This directive does not apply to seafarers, as defined in Council Directive 1999/63/EC of 21 June 1999 concerning the Agreement on the organisation of working time of seafarers, concluded by the European Community Shipowners' Association (ECSA) and the Federation of Transport Workers' Unions in the European Union.[689]

All workers employed in the road transport sector, including office staff, are excluded from the scope of that directive.[690]

2. Definitions

1719. For the purposes of this directive, the following definitions shall apply:

(1) working time means any period during which the worker is working, at the employer's disposal and carrying out his activity or duties, in accordance with national laws and/or practice;
(2) rest period means any period which is not working time;
(3) night time means any period of not less than seven hours, as defined by national law, and which must include, in any case, the period between midnight and 5 a.m.;
(4) night worker means:
  (a) on the one hand, any worker, who, during night time, works at least three hours of his daily working time as a normal course; and
  (b) on the other hand, any worker who is likely during night time to work a certain proportion of his annual working time, as defined at the choice of the Member State concerned:
    (i) by national legislation, following consultation with the two sides of industry; or
    (ii) by collective agreements or agreements concluded between the two sides of industry at national or regional level;
(5) shift work means any method of organising work in shifts whereby workers succeed each other at the same work stations according to a certain pattern,

---

688. Within the meaning of Article 2 of Directive 89/391/EEC, without prejudice to Articles 14, 17, 18 and 19 of this Directive. The provisions of Directive 89/391/EEC are fully applicable to the matters referred to in a and b, without prejudice to more stringent and/or specific provisions contained in this Directive.
689. Amended by Council Directive 2009/13/EC of 16 February 2009 implementing the Agreement concluded by the European Community Shipowners' Associations (ECSA) and the European Transport Workers' Federation (ETF) on the Maritime Labour Convention, 2006, and amending Directive 1999/63/EC, O.J., 20 May 2009, L 124. Without prejudice to Article 2(8) of the directive.
690. C.O.J., 4 October 2001, Case C-133/00, *J.R. Bowden, J.L. Chapman, J.J. Doyle and Tuffnells Parcels Express Ltd.*, ECR, 2001, 7031.

Part I, Ch. 8, Working Time and Leave 1720–1720

including a rotating pattern, and which may be continuous or discontinuous, entailing the need for workers to work at different times over a given period of days or weeks;
(6) shift worker means any worker whose work schedule is part of shift work;
(7) mobile worker means any worker employed as a member of travelling or flying personnel by an undertaking which operates transport services for passengers or goods by road, air or inland waterway;
(8) offshore work means work performed mainly on or from offshore installations (including drilling rigs), directly or indirectly in connection with the exploration, extraction or exploitation of mineral resources, including hydrocarbons, and diving in connection with such activities, whether performed from an offshore installation or a vessel;
(9) adequate rest means that workers have regular rest periods, the duration of which is expressed in units of time and which are sufficiently long and continuous to ensure that, as a result of fatigue or other irregular working patterns, they do not cause injury to themselves, to fellow workers or to others and that they do not damage their health, either in the short term or in the longer term.

1720. The Court has given a ruling on the application to medical staff assigned to primary health care teams of certain aspects of the Union directives concerning improvements in the safety and health of workers at work.

SIMAP is the union representing public health workers in the Valencia region. In proceedings against the Health Administration in that region it sought the implementation of certain provisions concerning the length and organisation of working time for staff assigned to primary health care teams at health centres.

According to that union, the doctors concerned are required to work without the benefit of any time-limit and without the duration of their work being subject to any daily, weekly, monthly or annual limits.

The *Tribunal Superior de Justicia de la Comunidad Valenciana* asked the Court of Justice to rule on the interpretation of the Union legislation concerning the promotion of improvements in the safety and health of workers at work and certain aspects of the organisation of working time.

The Court found, firstly, that the Union rules on improvements in the safety and health of workers at work, and in particular the directive concerning certain aspects of the organisation of working time, apply to the activities of doctors in primary health care teams. They do not fall into any of the professional categories (specific public service activities intended to uphold public order and safety, for example) for which, because of their special features, the Union provisions grant an exemption from their scope.

The Court considered whether time spent by doctors on call should be regarded under Union law as working time, that is to say time forming part of the period during which a worker is at work, carrying out his activities or duties, regardless of whether the doctors are actually present at the health centres or are merely contactable.

The Court pointed out that the objective of the directive was to ensure the safety and health of workers by granting them minimum periods of rest and adequate breaks.

753

According to the Court, the characteristic features of working time are present when doctors are present at the health centre where they are physically on call. On the other hand, when they are simply contactable at any time, the Court considers that they are in a position to manage their time with fewer constraints: only time actually spent providing primary health care services will therefore be classifiable as working time.

The Court also considered that work performed by doctors on primary health care teams whilst on call constitutes shift work within the meaning of Union law: the workers concerned are assigned successively to the same work posts, on a rotational basis which makes it necessary for them to perform work at different hours over a given period of days or weeks.

Finally, the Court ruled that individuals affected by any derogations from certain aspects of the Union rules on working time must give their own consent and that a collective agreement cannot be substituted for such consent.[691]

1721. An activity such as that of the medical and nursing staff providing services for *Servicio Galego de Saúde* in the on-call service, in primary care teams and in other services which treat outside emergencies fall within the scope of Council Directive 93/104/EC of 23 November 1993.

This activity does not come within the scope of the exception or exclusions laid down in Article 2 of Council Directive 89/391/EEC of 12 June 1989 on the introduction of measures to encourage improvements in the safety and health of workers at work. However, such an activity may come under the derogations provided for in Article 17 of Directive 93/104, in so far as the conditions set out in that provision are fulfilled.

Time spent on call, when their physical presence is required, by the medical and nursing staff providing services in the on-call service, in primary care teams and in other services which treat outside emergencies must be regarded in its entirety as working time, and where appropriate as overtime, within the meaning of Directive 93/104.[692]

1722. In September 2003, the European Court[693] ruled that time spent by a doctor working in a hospital on an on-call basis constitutes working time in its entirety, even if the employer provides a place of rest for the employee to use when not actively engaged in their duties.

Mr. Jaeger has worked as a doctor in the surgical department of a hospital. He spends three quarters of his normal working hours on call (that is to say 28.875 hours). Under an ancillary arrangement, he is also required to carry out on-call duty.

Generally, Mr. Jaeger carries out six periods of on-call duty each month, offset in part by the grant of free time and in part by the payment of supplementary remuneration.

---

691. C.O.J., 3 October 2000, *Sindicato de Médicos de Asistencia Pública (SIMAP)* v. *Conselleria de Sanidad y Consumo de la Generalidad Valenciana*, Case C-303/98, ECR, 2000, 7963.
692. C.O.J., 3 July 2001, Case C-241/99, *Confederación Intersindical Galega (CIG) and Servicio Galego de Saúde (Sergas)*, ECR, 2001, 5139.
693. C.O.J., 9 September 2003, *Landeshauptstadt Kiel* v. *Norbert Jaeger*, ECR, 2003, 8389.

Part I, Ch. 8, Working Time and Leave

On-call duty begins at the end of a normal working day and the length of each period is 16 hours in the week, 25 hours on Saturdays (from 8.30 a.m. to 9.30 a.m. on Sunday morning), and 22 hours 45 minutes on Sundays (from 8.30 a.m. to 7.15 a.m. on Monday morning).

On-call duty is organised in the following manner. Mr. Jaeger stays at the clinic and is called upon to carry out his professional duties as the need arises. He is allocated a room with a bed in the hospital, where he may sleep when his services are not required. The appropriateness of that accommodation is in dispute. However, it is common ground that the average time during which Mr. Jaeger is called upon to carry out a professional task does not exceed 49 per cent of the time spent on call.

1723. Mr. Jaeger was of the view that the on-call duty performed by him as a junior or emergency doctor in the context of the emergency service must in its entirety be deemed to constitute working time, which the employer contested.

1724. The following questions were referred to the Court for a preliminary ruling:

(1) Does time spent on call by an employee in a hospital, in general, constitute working time within the meaning of Article 2(1) of Directive 93/104 ... even where the employee is permitted to sleep at times when he is not required to work?
(2) Is it in breach of Article 3 of Directive 93/104/EC for a rule of national law to classify time spent on call as a rest period unless work is actually carried out, where the employee stays in a room provided in a hospital and works as and when required to do so?
(3) Is it in breach of Directive 93/104/EC for a rule of national law to permit a reduction in the daily rest period of 11 hours in hospitals and other establishments for the treatment, care and supervision of persons, where the amount of time actually worked during time spent on call or stand-by, not exceeding one half of the rest period, is compensated for at other times?
(4) Is it in breach of Directive 93/104/EC for a rule of national law to permit a collective agreement or a works agreement based on a collective agreement to allow rest periods, where time is spent on call and stand-by, to be adapted to the special circumstances of such duties, including in particular reductions in rest periods as a result of work actually being carried out, with these periods of duty being compensated for at other times?

1725. The Court ruled as follows.

(1) Council Directive 93/104/EC of 23 November 1993 must be interpreted as meaning that on-call duty (*Bereitschaftsdienst*) performed by a doctor where he is required to be physically present in the hospital must be regarded as constituting in its totality working time for the purposes of that directive even where the person concerned is permitted to rest at his place of work during the periods when his services are not required with the result that that directive precludes legislation of a Member State which classifies as rest periods an employee's

periods of inactivity in the context of such on-call duty.
(2) Directive 93/104 must also be interpreted as meaning that:
- in circumstances such as those in the main proceedings, that directive precludes legislation of a Member State which, in the case of on-call duty where physical presence in the hospital is required, has the effect of enabling, in an appropriate case by means of a collective agreement or a works agreement based on a collective agreement, an offset only in respect of periods of on-call duty during which the worker has actually been engaged in professional activities;
- in order to come within the derogating provisions set out in Article 17(2), subparagraph 2.1(c)(i) of the directive, a reduction in the daily rest period of 11 consecutive hours by a period of on-call duty performed in addition to normal working time is subject to the condition that equivalent compensating rest periods be accorded to the workers concerned at times immediately following the corresponding periods worked;
- furthermore, in no circumstances may such a reduction in the daily rest period lead to the maximum weekly working time laid down in Article 6 of the directive being exceeded.

1726. In the *Abdelkader Dellas*[694] case the Court confirmed that night duty carried out by a teacher in an establishment for handicapped persons must be taken into account in its entirety for ascertaining whether the rules of Union law laid down to protect workers – in particular the maximum permitted weekly working time – have been complied with.

In France, a decree lays down, for periods of night duty by workers in certain social and medico-social establishments,[695] a weighting mechanism for the purpose of calculating pay and overtime which is intended to take account of the fact that there are periods of inactivity during on-call duty. The decree establishes a 3 to 1 ratio for the first nine hours followed by a 2 to 1 ratio for subsequent hours between the hours of presence and the working hours actually counted. Mr. Dellas, a special needs teacher in residential establishments for handicapped young persons, was dismissed by his employer as a result of disagreements relating in particular to the definition of actual work and the remuneration due for hours of night work on call in a room on the premises. Mr. Dellas and a number of trade unions brought proceedings before the Council of State for the annulment of the decree in question. The Council essentially asked the Court of Justice whether such a system is compatible with the directive.

---

694. C.O.J., 1 December 2005, *Abdelkader Dellas and Others* v. *Premier ministre and Others*, C-14/04, ECR, 2005, 10235.
695. Including teaching staff, nurses and nursing auxiliaries working full-time in residential establishments run by private persons on a non-profit-making basis.

1727. The Court of Justice finds, first, that the directive does not apply to the remuneration of workers. On the other hand, the hours of presence in question must be counted in their entirety as working time for ascertaining whether all the minimum requirements laid down by Directive 93/104 in order to provide effective protection of the safety and health of workers have been complied with. The flat-rate weighting mechanism in question takes the hours of presence of the workers concerned into account only in part. The total working time of a worker may thus amount to, or even exceed, 60 hours a week. Consequently, such a national system of calculating on-call time exceeds the maximum weekly working time fixed by the directive at 48 hours.

1728. In a French case,[696] the European Court was asked the question 'whether persons employed under contracts such as the educational commitment contracts at issue in the main proceedings, carrying out casual and seasonal activities in holiday and leisure centres, and completing a maximum of 80 working days per annum, fall within the scope of Directive 2003/88'.

The Court stated that it must also be borne in mind that, while the concept of a 'worker' is defined in Article 3(a) of Directive 89/391 to mean any person employed by an employer, including trainees and apprentices but excluding domestic servants, Directive 2003/88 made no reference to either that provision of Directive 89/391 or the definition of a 'worker' to be derived from national legislation and/or practices.

The consequence of that fact is that, for the purposes of applying Directive 2003/88, that concept may not be interpreted differently according to the law of Member States but has an autonomous meaning specific to European Union law. The concept must be defined in accordance with objective criteria which distinguish the employment relationship by reference to the rights and duties of the persons concerned. The essential feature of an employment relationship, however, is that for a certain period of time a person performs services for and under the direction of another person in return for which he receives remuneration.

1729. It is for the national court to apply that concept of a 'worker' in any classification, and the national court must base that classification on objective criteria and make an overall assessment of all the circumstances of the case brought before it, having regard both to the nature of the activities concerned and the relationship of the parties involved.

In the light thereof persons employed under contracts such as the educational commitment contracts at issue in the main proceedings, carrying out casual and seasonal activities in holiday and leisure centres, and completing a maximum of 80 working days per annum, are within the scope of Directive 2003/88.

---

696. C.O.J., 14 October 2010, Union syndicale Solidaires Isère v. Premier ministre,Ministère du Travail, des Relations sociales, de la Famille, de la Solidarité et de la Ville,C-428/09, www.curia.

B. *Minimum Rest Periods, Other Aspects of the Organisation of Working Time*

1. Daily Rest

1730. Every worker is entitled to a minimum daily rest period of 11 consecutive hours per 24-hour period (Article 3).

1731. The UK guidelines on working time are liable to render the right of workers to daily and weekly rest periods meaningless because they do not oblige employers to ensure that workers actually take the minimum rest periods.[697] The case was as follows.

The Directive was transposed in the United Kingdom by a statutory instrument (Working Time Regulations 1998 (WTR)). In order to help people understand the WTR, the Department of Trade and Industry published a set of guidelines. According to those guidelines, 'employers must make sure that workers can take their rest, but are not required to make sure they do take their rest'.

As it took the view that the guidelines endorse and encourage a practice of non-compliance with the requirements of the Directive, the Commission initiated proceedings before the Court of Justice.

1732. The Court points out, first of all, that the purpose of the Directive is to lay down minimum requirements to improve the living and working conditions of workers by ensuring that they are entitled to minimum rest periods. Those principles constitute particularly important rules of Union social law from which every worker must benefit as a minimum requirement necessary to ensure protection of his safety and health.

In order to ensure that the rights conferred on workers are fully effective, Member States are under an obligation to guarantee that the right to benefit from effective rest is observed. A Member State which indicates that an employer is nevertheless not required to ensure that workers actually exercise such rights does not guarantee compliance with either the Directive's minimum requirements or its essential objective.

By providing that employers must merely give workers the opportunity to take the minimum rest periods provided for, without obliging them to ensure that those periods are actually taken, the guidelines are clearly liable to render the rights enshrined in the Directive meaningless and are incompatible with its objective.

The Court therefore ruled that the United Kingdom has failed to fulfil its obligations under the Working Time Directive.

2. Breaks

1733. Where the working day is longer than six hours, every worker is entitled to a rest break, the details of which, including duration and the terms on which it is

---

697. C.O.J., 7 September 2006, *Commission v. United Kingdom*, C-484/04, ECR, 2006, 7471.

Part I, Ch. 8, Working Time and Leave

granted, shall be laid down in collective agreement or agreements between the two sides of industry or, failing that, by national legislation (Art.4).

3. Weekly Rest Period

1734. Per each seven-day period, every worker is entitled to a minimum uninterrupted rest period of 24 hours plus the 11 hours' daily rest referred to in Article 3.[698]

If objective, technical or work organisation conditions so justify, a minimum rest period of 24 hours may be applied (Art. 5).

4. Maximum Weekly Working Time

1735. The period of weekly working time is limited by means of laws, regulations or administrative provisions or by collective agreements or agreements between the two sides of industry.

The average working time for each seven-day period, including overtime, does not exceed 48 hours (Article 6).

1736. Article 6(b) of Directive 2003/88/EC must be interpreted as precluding national rules, which allow a public-sector employer to transfer compulsorily to another service a worker employed as a fire fighter in an operational service on the ground that that worker has requested compliance, within the latter service, with the maximum average weekly working time (48 hours).[699]

5. Annual Leave

1737. Every worker is entitled to paid annual leave of at least four weeks in accordance with the conditions for entitlement to, and granting of, such leave laid down by national legislation and/or practice.

The minimum period of paid annual leave may not be replaced by an allowance in lieu, except where the employment relationship is terminated (Art. 7).

1738. In the *Dominguez case*[700] the Court rules, first, that the directive must be interpreted as precluding a national provision which makes entitlement to paid

---

698. The European Court annulled the section stating that the minimum weekly rest should in principle include Sunday (second sentence of Article 5). The Court stated that 'the Council had failed to explain why Sunday, as a weekly rest day, is more closely connected with the health and safety of workers than any other day of the week', *UK* v. *Commission*, 12 November 1996.
699. C.O.J., 14 October 2010, Günter Fuß v. Stadt Halle, C-243/09, www.curia. See also: 25 November 2010, *Günter Fuß* v. *Stadt Halle*, C-429/09, www.curia.eu.
700. C.O.J., 24 January 2012, *Maribel Dominguez* v. *Centre informatique du Centre Ouest Atlantique and Préfet de la région Centre*, C-282/10, www.curia.eu.

annual leave conditional on a minimum period of 10 days' (or one month's) actual work during the reference period.

1739. The Court notes that entitlement to paid annual leave must be regarded as a particularly important principle of EU social law, from which there can be no derogations and whose implementation by the national authorities must be confined within the limits expressly laid down by the directive. Although Member States may lay down conditions for the exercise and implementation of the right to paid annual leave, they are not entitled to make it subject to any preconditions whatsoever or to exclude the very existence of that right, which is expressly granted to all workers. Moreover, the Court confirms that the directive does not make any distinction between workers who are absent from work on sick leave during the reference period and those who have in fact worked in the course of that period. It follows that, with regard to workers on sick leave which has been duly granted, the right to paid annual leave conferred by that directive on all workers cannot therefore be made subject by a Member State to a condition that the worker has actually worked during the reference period.

Secondly, the Court states that, when applying domestic law, national courts are bound to interpret it, so far as possible, in the light of the wording and the purpose of the directive. In order to ensure that the latter is fully effective, it is for the national court to determine whether it can interpret national law as allowing the absence of the worker due to an accident on the journey to or from work to be treated as being equivalent to a work-related accident. In that regard, the Court observes that, according to the directive, a worker, whether he is on sick leave during the reference period as a result of an accident at his place of work or elsewhere, or as the result of sickness of whatever nature or origin, cannot have his entitlement to paid annual leave affected.

In the event that it is not possible to interpret national law as complying with the directive, however, it is necessary for the national court to determine whether a worker such as Ms Dominguez may rely directly on the directive. In that regard, the Court holds first of all that the provisions of the directive appear, so far as their subject-matter is concerned, to be unconditional and sufficiently precise that individuals may rely upon them before the national courts against the Member State. Also, since individuals are not able to rely directly on a directive as against private parties, it is for the national court to determine, on the basis of the capacity in which the CICOA is acting (as a body governed by private or public law), whether the directive may be relied upon against it. If the directive could be relied upon against the CICOA the national court would have to disregard any conflicting national provision.

If not, Ms Dominguez would be able to bring an action for damages against the State in order to obtain, if appropriate, compensation for the loss sustained as a result of the failure to acknowledge her entitlement to paid annual leave under the directive.

Thirdly, the Court holds that the directive allows Member States to make provision for a different period of paid annual leave, depending on the reason for the sick leave, provided that such period is equal to or exceeds the minimum period of four weeks laid down in that directive.

Part I, Ch. 8, Working Time and Leave

1740. In the *Neidel* case,[701] the Court points out that the directive applies, in principle, to all sectors of activity, both public and private , in order to regulate certain aspects of the organisation of workers' working time. In addition, the Court states that although it is true that the directive provides for exceptions to its scope, they were adopted purely for the purpose of ensuring the proper operation of services essential for the protection of public health, safety and order in circumstances the gravity and scale of which are exceptional. Consequently, the Court's answer is that the Working Time Directive applies to a public servant carrying out the activities of a fireman in normal circumstances.

1741. Next, the Court points out that it is clear from the directive that every worker is entitled to paid annual leave of at least four weeks. However, on termination of an employment relationship, it is in fact no longer possible to take paid annual leave. It is precisely because of that impossibility that, in such a case, in order to prevent a situation in which the worker loses all enjoyment of that right, even in pecuniary form, the directive entitles the worker to an allowance in lieu. In the present case, the Court takes the view that the retirement of a civil or public servant terminates the employment relationship. Consequently, the Court holds that a public servant is entitled, on retirement, to an allowance in lieu of paid annual leave not taken because of the fact that he was prevented from working by sickness.

1742. In the *Robinson-Steele* case,[702] the Court ruled that payment for annual leave included in hourly or daily remuneration (rolled up holiday pay) is contrary to the working time directive. Such a system may lead to situations in which the minimum period of paid annual leave is replaced by an allowance in lieu.

Under the United Kingdom regulations which transposed the directive, any contractual remuneration paid to a worker in respect of a period of leave goes towards discharging any liability of the employer to make payments under the relevant regulation in respect of that period.

1743. Messrs Robinson-Steele, Clarke, J.C. Caulfield, C.F. Caulfield and Barnes, who work for various undertakings, received payment for annual leave in the form of remuneration included in the hourly remuneration, a system known as 'rolled-up holiday pay', instead of receiving such payment in respect of a specific period of leave.

Those workers applied to the Employment Tribunal claiming payment for annual leave. The Court of Justice was asked whether the system of 'rolled-up holiday pay' is compatible with the working time directive.

1744. The Court recalled that the entitlement of every worker to paid annual leave is an important principle of Union social law from which there can be no derogation. Holiday pay is intended to enable the worker actually to take the leave to which he is entitled. The Court finds that the term 'paid annual leave' means that

---

701. C.O.J., 3 May 2012, *Georg Neidel* v. *Stadt Frankfurt am Main*, C-337/10, www.curia.eu.
702. C.O.J., 16 March 2006, *C.D. Robinson-Steele* v. *R.D. Retail Services Ltd, and others*, C-131/04, ECR, 2006, 2531.

remuneration must be maintained for the duration of the leave within the meaning of the directive and that workers must receive their normal remuneration for that period of rest. In those circumstances, the Court considers that the directive precludes part of the remuneration from being attributed to payment for annual leave without the worker receiving, in that respect, a payment additional to that for work done. Also, there can be no derogation from that entitlement by contractual arrangement.

As regards the point at which the payment for annual leave must be made, the Court notes that there is no provision in the directive which lays it down expressly. None the less, the purpose of the requirement of payment for that leave is to put the worker, during such leave, in a position which is comparable to periods of work as regards remuneration. Accordingly, the point at which the payment for annual leave is made must, as a rule, be fixed in such a way that, during that leave, the worker is put in a position comparable to periods of work as regards remuneration.

1745. Furthermore, the Court holds that a regime of 'rolled-up holiday pay' may lead to situations in which the minimum period of paid annual leave is, in effect, replaced by an allowance in lieu, which the directive prohibits, except where the employment relationship is terminated, in order to ensure that a worker is normally entitled to actual rest.

Consequently, the Court holds that payment for minimum annual leave through a system of 'rolled-up holiday pay' rather than by means of a payment in respect of a specific period during which the worker actually takes leave, is contrary to the working time directive.

1746. As regards sums already paid to workers in respect of holiday through the system of 'rolled-up holiday pay', the Court holds that payments made, transparently and comprehensibly, may, as a rule, be set off against the payment for specific leave. On the other hand, such set-off is excluded where there is no transparency or comprehensibility. The burden of proof in that respect is on the employer. The Court points out that the Member States are required to take the measures appropriate to ensure that practices incompatible with the provisions of the directive relating to the entitlement to annual leave are not continued.

1747. In a *Dutch* case[703] the Court decided that Union law precludes the replacement of the minimum period of paid annual leave by an allowance in lieu, where leave is carried over to a subsequent year. Financial compensation for the minimum annual leave carried over would encourage employees not to take that leave. In that regard, it is immaterial whether such compensation is or is not based on a contractual arrangement.

In a brochure, the Netherlands Ministry of Social Affairs and Employment interpreted the Netherlands rules regarding leave as meaning that employers and employees can, during a contract of employment, agree in writing that financial compensation be paid in a following year to an employee who has not made use (in

---

703. C.O.J., 6 April 2006, *Federatie Nederlandse Vakbeweging v. Staat der Nederlanden*, C-124/05, ECR, 2006, 3423.

whole or in part) of the minimum leave entitlement. In the Ministry's view, leave days, statutory as well as non-statutory, saved up from previous years exceed the minimum leave entitlement and can therefore be eligible for redemption.

1748. The Dutch Unions (DU) brought an action in the Court of 's-Gravenhage by an application seeking a declaration that that interpretation is incompatible with the working time directive. The question was referred to the Court of Justice.

The Court reminded that the entitlement to paid annual leave is an important principle of Union social law. Workers must be entitled to actual rest, with a view to ensuring effective protection of their safety and health. It is only where the employment relationship is terminated that payment of an allowance in lieu of paid annual leave is permitted.[704]

1749. The Court considers that the positive effect which that leave has for the safety and health of the worker is deployed fully if it is taken in the prescribed year. But the significance of that rest period, for the protection of workers, remains if it is taken during a later period. In any event, the possibility of financial compensation in respect of the minimum period of annual leave carried over would create an incentive, incompatible with the objectives of the directive, not to take leave or to encourage employees not to do so.

Consequently, the directive precludes the replacement, by an allowance in lieu, of the minimum period of paid annual leave, where that leave is carried over to a subsequent year. In that regard, it is immaterial whether financial compensation for paid annual leave is or is not based on a contractual arrangement.

Article 7(1) of the Directive does not allow a Member State to adopt national rules under which a worker does not begin to accrue rights to paid annual leave until he has completed a minimum period of 13 weeks' uninterrupted employment with the same employer.[705]

Article 7(1) of Council Directive 93/104/EC of 23 November 1993 is to be interpreted as meaning that a worker must be able to take her annual leave during a period other than the period of her maternity leave, including in a case in which the period of maternity leave coincides with the general period of annual leave fixed, by a collective agreement, for the entire workforce.[706]

1750. In the *Schultz-Hoff* case,[707] the Court was asked whether a worker does not lose his right to paid annual leave which he has been unable to exercise because of sickness.

---

704. C.O.J., 6 April 2006, *Federatie Nederlandse Vakbeweging* v. *Staat der Nederlanden*, C-124/05, ECR, 2006, 3423.
705. C.O.J., 26 June 2001, *The Queen* v. *Secretary of State for Trade and Industry, ex parte Broadcasting, Entertainment, Cinematographic and Theatre Union (BECTU)*, Case C-173/99, ECR, 2001, 4881.
706. C.O.J., 18 March 2004, *María Paz Merino Gómez* v. *Continental Industrias del Caucho SA*, C-342/01, ECR, 2004, 2605.
707. C.O.J., 20 January 2009, *Schultz-Hoff* v. *Deutsche Rentenversicherung Bund Stringer* and *Others* v. *Her Majesty's Revenue and Customs*, Joined Cases C-350/06 and C-520/06, www.curia.eu.

In its judgment, the Court notes that the right to sick leave and the conditions for the exercise of that right are not governed by Union law. With regard to the right to paid annual leave, it is for the Member States to lay down conditions for its exercise and implementation, by prescribing the specific circumstances in which workers may exercise the right to annual leave, without making the very existence of that right subject to any preconditions whatsoever.

In those circumstances, the entitlement to paid annual leave enshrined by the working time directive does not, as a rule, preclude either the authorisation of paid annual leave during a period of sick leave, or the prohibition of such paid annual leave. However, any such prohibition must be subject to the condition that the worker in question has the opportunity to exercise his right to leave during another period.

While the conditions for application of the right to paid annual leave in the various Member States are governed by them, the conditions for carrying over leave not taken are nevertheless subject to certain limits.

In that regard, the Court points out that the entitlement to annual leave of a worker on sick leave duly granted cannot be made subject to the obligation actually to have worked in the course of the leave year laid down by a Member State. Consequently, a Member State may provide for the loss of the right to paid annual leave at the end of a leave year or of a carry-over period only if the worker concerned has actually had the opportunity to exercise his right to leave.

The Court finds that a worker who is on sick leave for the whole leave year and beyond a carry-over period laid down by national law is denied any opportunity to benefit from his paid annual leave. The same is also true of a worker who has worked for part of the leave year before being put on sick leave.

1751. In a German case, the Court also notes that, in specific circumstances a worker who is unfit for work for several consecutive reference periods would as a result be entitled to accumulate, without any limit, all the entitlements to paid annual leave that are acquired during his absence from work.

However, a right to such unlimited accumulation of entitlements to paid annual leave, acquired during a period of unfitness for work, would no longer reflect the actual purpose of the right to paid annual leave. That right has the dual purpose of enabling the worker both to rest from his work and to enjoy a period of relaxation and leisure.

While the positive effect of paid annual leave for the safety and health of the worker is deployed fully where that leave is taken in the year prescribed for that purpose, namely the current year, the significance of that rest period in that regard remains if it is taken during a later period. However, in so far as the carry-over exceeds a certain temporal limit, annual leave ceases to have its positive effect for the worker as a rest period and is merely a period of relaxation and leisure.

In consequence, in light of the actual purpose of the right to paid annual leave, a worker who is unfit for work for several consecutive years cannot have the right to accumulate, without any limit, entitlements to paid annual leave acquired during that period.

In that context, in order to uphold the right to paid annual leave, the objective of which is the protection of workers, the Court holds that any carry-over period must take into account the specific circumstances of a worker who is unfit for work for several consecutive reference periods. Thus, the carry-over period must inter alia ensure that the worker can have, if need be, rest periods that may be staggered, planned in advance and available in the longer term. In addition, any carry-over period must be substantially longer than the reference period in respect of which it is granted.

Moreover, that period must also protect the employer from the risk that a worker will accumulate periods of absence of too great a length, and from the difficulties for the organisation of work which such periods might entail.

Therefore, the Court considers that a carry-over period of 15 months, as in this case, may reasonably be envisaged as it is not contrary to the purpose of the right to paid annual leave, in that it ensures that that right retains its positive effect for the worker as a rest period.

Accordingly, the answer given by the Court is that, in the case of a worker who is unfit for work for several consecutive reference periods, European Union law does not preclude national provisions or practices, such as collective agreements, which limit, by a carry-over period of 15 months on the expiry of which the right to paid annual leave lapses, the accumulation of entitlement to such leave.[708]

Article 7(1) of Directive 2003/88/EC must be interpreted as precluding national provisions under which a worker who becomes unfit for work during a period of paid annual leave is not entitled subsequently to the paid annual leave which coincided with the period of unfitness for work.[709].

1752. The Court concludes that the right to paid annual leave is not to be extinguished at the end of the leave year and/or of a carry-over period laid down by national law where the worker has been on sick leave for the whole or part of the leave year and where his incapacity to work has persisted until the end of his employment relationship, this being the reason why he could not exercise his right to paid annual leave.

With regard to the right, on termination of the employment relationship, to an allowance in lieu of the paid annual leave which the worker has been unable to take, the Court rules that the allowance must be calculated so that the worker is put in a position comparable to that he would have been in had he exercised that right during his employment relationship. It follows that the worker's normal remuneration, which is that which must be maintained during the rest period corresponding to the paid annual leave, is also decisive as regards the calculation of the allowance in lieu of annual leave not taken by the end of the employment relationship.

Consequently, a worker must be compensated for his annual leave not taken.

1753. In another German case,[710] the Court rules that paid annual leave may be reduced proportionally to the reduction in working time agreed to in a social plan.

---

708. C.O.J., 22 November 2011, *KHS AG* v. *Winfried Schulte*, C-214/10, www.curia.eu.
709. C.O.J., 21 June 2012, *Asociación Nacional de Grandes Empresas de Distribución (ANGED)* v. *Federación de Asociaciones Sindicales (FASGA), a.o.*, C-78/11, www.curia.eu.
710. C.O.J., 8 November 2012, *Alexander Heimann, Konstantin Toltschin* v. *Kaiser GmbH*, C-229/11 and C-230/11, www.curia.eu.

Part I, Ch. 8, Working Time and Leave

It is not contrary to EU law for an undertaking and its works council to conclude a social plan providing for the proportional reduction of the paid annual leave of a worker on short-time working

1754. The *Arbeitsgericht Passau* (Passau Labour Court, Germany) asked the Court of Justice whether EU law precludes national legislation or practice – such as a social plan agreed between an undertaking and its works council – under which paid annual leave is reduced proportionally to workers' reduced working time during a period of financial difficulties for the undertaking.

1755. The disputes before that court – between Mr Heimann and Mr Toltschin, respectively, and their former employer, Kaiser GmbH, a subcontracting business in the motor industry – concern an allowance in lieu claimed on the basis of annual paid leave which those workers were not able to take in 2009 and 2010. Due to financial difficulties, Kaiser had dismissed Mr Heimann and Mr Toltschin with effect from the end of June and August 2009, respectively. However, by means of a social plan agreed between Kaiser and its works council, their contracts had been formally extended for one year. During that period Heimann and Toltschin were not required to work ('zero hours short-time working' ['Kurzarbeit Null']), and Kaiser did not have to pay them a salary. In return, Mr Heimann and Mr Toltschin received, via Kaiser, an allowance known as 'Kurzarbeitergeld' from the Federal Employment Agency. Kaiser claims that, during that period of 'zero hours short-time working', Mr Heimann and Mr Toltschin did not acquire any rights to paid annual leave.

1756. In its judgment the Court answers that EU law does not preclude national legislation or practice – such as a social plan agreed between an undertaking and its works council – under which the paid annual leave of a worker is reduced in proportion to the reduction in working time (the rule of pro rata temporis).

The Court points out that the situation of a worker on short-time working in the context of a social plan is fundamentally different from that of a worker who is unable to work as a result of an illness, the latter being entitled, in accordance with the Court's case-law, to paid annual leave in the same way as a worker in active employment.

1757. In the context of short-time working, the obligations of both the worker and the employer are, by staff agreement, suspended. Moreover, in contrast to a worker unable to work due to his state of health, who is subject to physical or psychological constraints caused by his illness, the worker on short-time working may use his free time to rest or to engage in recreational and leisure activities. Furthermore, if the employer was required to pay annual paid leave during the period of short-time working, it would be liable to bring about a reluctance on the part of the employer to agree to a social plan under which the contract of employment is extended for purely social reasons and therefore in the interests of the worker.

1758. However, the situation of an employee on short-time working is comparable to that of a part-time worker. Accordingly, in accordance with its case-law, the

Part I, Ch. 8, Working Time and Leave

Court points out that, for a period of part-time working, paid annual leave may be reduced proportionally to the reduction in working time.

1759. The relevant European Union law, in particular, Article 7(1) of Directive 2003/88/EC concerning certain aspects of the organisation of working time and Clause 4(2) of the Framework Agreement on part-time work, must be interpreted as meaning that they preclude national provisions or a national practice, under which the number of days of paid annual leave which a full-time worker was unable to exercise during the reference period is, due to the fact that that worker moved to a scheme of part-time work, subject to a reduction which is proportional to the difference between the number of days of work per week carried out by that worker before and after such a move to part-time work[711].

C. Night Work/Shift Work, Pattern of Work

1. Length of Night Work

1760. Normal hours of work for night workers do not exceed an average of eight hours in any 24-hour period.

Night workers whose work involves special hazards or heavy physical or mental strain do not work more than eight hours in any period of 24 hours during which they perform night work.

Work involving special hazards or heavy physical or mental strain shall be defined by national legislation and/or practice or by collective agreements concluded between the two sides of industry, taking account of specific effects and hazards of night work (Article 8).

2. Health Assessment and Transfer of Night Workers to Day Work

1761. Night workers:

(a) are entitled to a free health assessment before their assignment and thereafter at regular intervals;
(b) suffering from health problems recognised as being connected with the fact that they perform night work are transferred whenever possible to day work to which they are suited.

The free health assessment must comply with medical confidentiality and may be conducted within the national health system (Article 9).

---

711. C.O.J., 13 June 2013, *Bianca Brandes* v. *Land Niedersachsen*, C-415/12, www.curia.eu.

3. Guarantees for Night-Time Working

1762. The work of certain categories of night workers may be subject to certain guarantees, under conditions laid down by national legislation and/or practice, in the case of workers who incur risks to their safety or health linked to night-time working (Article 10).

4. Notification of Regular Use of Night Workers

1763. An employer who regularly uses night workers brings this information to the attention of the competent authorities if they so request (Article 11).

5. Safety and Health Protection

1764. Member States shall take the measures necessary to ensure that:

(1) night workers and shift workers have safety and health protection appropriate to the nature of their work;
(2) appropriate protection and prevention services or facilities with regard to the safety and health of night workers and shift workers are equivalent to those applicable to other workers and are available at all times (Article 12).

6. Pattern of Work

1765. An employer who intends to organise work according to a certain pattern takes account of the general principle of adapting work to the worker, with a view, in particular, to taking the necessary measures to alleviate monotonous work and work at a predetermined work-rate, depending on the type of activity, and of safety and health requirements, especially as regards breaks during working time (Article 13).

D. Miscellaneous Provisions

1. More Specific Community Provisions

1766. The provisions of this directive do not apply where other Community instruments contain more specific requirements relating to the organisation of working time concerning certain occupations or occupational activities (Article 14).

Part I, Ch. 8, Working Time and Leave

2. More Favourable Provisions

1767. This directive does not affect Member States' right to apply or introduce laws, regulations or administrative provisions more favourable to the protection of the safety and health of workers or to facilitate or permit the application of collective agreements or agreements concluded between the two sides of industry which are more favourable to the protection of the safety and health of workers (Article 15).

3. Reference Periods

1768. Member States may lay down:

(1) for the application of Article 5 (weekly rest period), a reference period not exceeding 14 days;
(2) for the application of Article 6 (maximum weekly working time), a reference period not exceeding four months. The periods of paid annual leave and the periods of sick leave shall not be included or shall be neutral in the calculation of the average;
(3) for the application of Article 8 (length of night work), a reference period defined after consultation of the two sides of industry or by collective agreements or agreements concluded between the two sides of industry at national or regional level. If the minimum weekly rest period of 24 hours required by Article 5 falls within that reference period, it shall not be included in the calculation of the average (Article 16).

E. Derogations and Exceptions

1. Derogations

1769. With due regard for the general principles of the protection of the safety and health of workers, Member States may derogate from Articles 3 to 6, 8 and 16 when, on account of the specific characteristics of the activity concerned, the duration of the working time is not measured and/or predetermined or can be determined by the workers themselves, and particularly in the case of:

(a) managing executives or other persons with autonomous decision-taking powers;
(b) family workers; or
(c) workers officiating at religious ceremonies in churches and religious communities.

Derogations provided for in paragraphs 3, 4 and 5 may be adopted by means of laws, regulations or administrative provisions or by means of collective agreements or agreements between the two sides of industry provided that the workers concerned are afforded equivalent periods of compensatory rest or that, in exceptional cases in which it is not possible, for objective reasons, to grant such equivalent periods of compensatory rest, the workers concerned are afforded appropriate protection.

1770. In accordance with paragraph 2 of this Article, derogations may be made from Articles 3, 4, 5, 8 and 16:

(a) in the case of activities where the worker's place of work and his place of residence are distant from one another, including offshore work, or where the worker's different places of work are distant from one another;
(b) in the case of security and surveillance activities requiring a permanent presence in order to protect property and persons, particularly security guards and caretakers or security firms;
(c) in the case of activities involving the need for continuity of service or production, particularly:
   (i) services relating to the reception, treatment and/or care provided by hospitals or similar establishments, including the activities of doctors in training, residential institutions and prisons;
   (ii) dock or airport workers;
   (iii) press, radio, television, cinematographic production, postal and telecommunications services, ambulance, fire and civil protection services;
   (iv) gas, water and electricity production, transmission and distribution, household refuse collection and incineration plants;
   (v) industries in which work cannot be interrupted on technical grounds;
   (vi) research and development activities;
   (vii) agriculture;
   (viii) workers concerned with the carriage of passengers on regular urban transport services;
(d) where there is a foreseeable surge of activity, particularly in:
   (i) agriculture;
   (ii) tourism;
   (iii) postal services;
(e) in the case of persons working in railway transport:
   (i) whose activities are intermittent;
   (ii) who spend their working time on board trains; or
   (iii) whose activities are linked to transport timetables and to ensuring the continuity and regularity of traffic;
(f) in the circumstances described in Article 5(4) of Directive 89/391/EEC;
(g) in cases of accident or imminent risk of accident.

1771. In accordance with paragraph 2 of this Article derogations may be made from Articles 3 and 5:

Part I, Ch. 8, Working Time and Leave

(a) in the case of shift work activities, each time the worker changes shift and cannot take daily and/or weekly rest periods between the end of one shift and the start of the next one;
(b) in the case of activities involving periods of work split up over the day, particularly those of cleaning staff.

In accordance with paragraph 2 of this Article, derogations may be made from Article 6 and Article 16(b), in the case of doctors in training, in accordance with the provisions set out in the second to the seventh subparagraphs of this paragraph.

1772. With respect to Article 6 derogations referred to in the first subparagraph shall be permitted for a transitional period of five years from 1 August 2004.

Member States may have up to two more years, if necessary, to take account of difficulties in meeting the working time provisions with respect to their responsibilities for the organisation and delivery of health services and medical care. At least six months before the end of the transitional period, the Member State concerned shall inform the Commission giving its reasons, so that the Commission can give an opinion, after appropriate consultations, within the three months following receipt of such information. If the Member State does not follow the opinion of the Commission, it will justify its decision. The notification and justification of the Member State and the opinion of the Commission shall be published in the Official Journal of the European Union and forwarded to the European Parliament.

Member States may have an additional period of up to one year, if necessary, to take account of special difficulties in meeting the responsibilities referred to in the third subparagraph. They shall follow the procedure set out in that subparagraph.

Member States shall ensure that in no case will the number of weekly working hours exceed an average of 58 during the first three years of the transitional period, an average of 56 for the following two years and an average of 52 for any remaining period.

1773. The employer shall consult the representatives of the employees in good time with a view to reaching an agreement, wherever possible, on the arrangements applying to the transitional period. Within the limits set out in the fifth subparagraph, such an agreement may cover:

(a) the average number of weekly hours of work during the transitional period; and
(b) the measures to be adopted to reduce weekly working hours to an average of 48 by the end of the transitional period.

With respect to Article 16(b) derogations referred to in the first subparagraph shall be permitted provided that the reference period does not exceed 12 months, during the first part of the transitional period specified in the fifth subparagraph, and six months thereafter (Article 17).

2. Derogations by Collective Agreements

1774. Derogations may be made from Articles 3, 4, 5, 8 and 16 by means of collective agreements or agreements concluded between the two sides of industry at national or regional level or, in conformity with the rules laid down by them, by means of collective agreements or agreements concluded between the two sides of industry at a lower level.

Member States in which there is no statutory system ensuring the conclusion of collective agreements or agreements concluded between the two sides of industry at national or regional level, on the matters covered by this Directive, or those Member States in which there is a specific legislative framework for this purpose and within the limits thereof, may, in accordance with national legislation and/or practice, allow derogations from Articles 3, 4, 5, 8 and 16 by way of collective agreements or agreements concluded between the two sides of industry at the appropriate collective level.

1775. The derogations provided for in the first and second subparagraphs shall be allowed on condition that equivalent compensating rest periods are granted to the workers concerned or, in exceptional cases where it is not possible for objective reasons to grant such periods, the workers concerned are afforded appropriate protection.

Member States may lay down rules:

(a) for the application of this Article by the two sides of industry; and
(b) for the extension of the provisions of collective agreements or agreements concluded in conformity with this Article to other workers in accordance with national legislation and/or practice (Article 18).

3. Limitations to Derogations from Reference Periods

1776. The option to derogate from Article 16(b), provided for in Article 17(3) and in Article 18, may not result in the establishment of a reference period exceeding six months.

However, Member States shall have the option, subject to compliance with the general principles relating to the protection of the safety and health of workers, of allowing, for objective or technical reasons or reasons concerning the organisation of work, collective agreements or agreements concluded between the two sides of industry to set reference periods in no event exceeding 12 months.

Before 23 November 2003, the Council shall, on the basis of a Commission proposal accompanied by an appraisal report, re-examine the provisions of this Article and decide what action to take (Article 19).

Part I, Ch. 8, Working Time and Leave

4. Mobile Workers and Offshore Work

1777.

(1) Articles 3, 4, 5 and 8 shall not apply to mobile workers.
(2) Member States shall, however, take the necessary measures to ensure that such mobile workers are entitled to adequate rest, except in the circumstances laid down in Article 17(3)(f) and (g).
(3) Subject to compliance with the general principles relating to the protection of the safety and health of workers, and provided that there is consultation of representatives of the employer and employees concerned and efforts to encourage all relevant forms of social dialogue, including negotiation if the parties so wish, Member States may, for objective or technical reasons or reasons concerning the organisation of work, extend the reference period referred to in Article 16(b) to 12 months in respect of workers who mainly perform offshore work.
(4) Not later than 1 August 2005 the Commission shall, after consulting the Member States and management and labour at European level, review the operation of the provisions with regard to offshore workers from a health and safety perspective with a view to presenting, if need be, the appropriate modifications (Article 20).

5. Workers on Board Seagoing Fishing Vessels

1778.

(1) Articles 3 to 6 and 8 shall not apply to any worker on board a sea-going fishing vessel flying the flag of a Member State.
(2) Member States shall, however, take the necessary measures to ensure that any worker on board a seagoing fishing vessel flying the flag of a Member State is entitled to adequate rest and to limit the number of hours of work to 48 hours a week on average calculated over a reference period not exceeding 12 months.
(3) Within the limits set out in paragraph 1, second subparagraph, and paragraphs 3 and 4 Member States shall take the necessary measures to ensure that, in keeping with the need to protect the safety and health of such workers:
  (a) the working hours are limited to a maximum number of hours which shall not be exceeded in a given period of time; or
  (b) a minimum number of hours of rest are provided within a given period of time.
(4) The maximum number of hours of work or minimum number of hours of rest shall be specified by law, regulations, administrative provisions or by collective agreements or agreements between the two sides of the industry.
(5) The limits on hours of work or rest shall be either:
  (a) maximum hours of work which shall not exceed:
    (i) 14 hours in any 24-hour period; and

(ii) 72 hours in any seven-day period; or
(b) minimum hours of rest which shall not be less than:
   (i) ten hours in any 24-hour period; and
   (ii) 77 hours in any seven-day period.
(6) Hours of rest may be divided into no more than two periods, one of which shall be at least six hours in length, and the interval between consecutive periods of rest shall not exceed 14 hours.
(7) In accordance with the general principles of the protection of the health and safety of workers, and for objective or technical reasons or reasons concerning the organisation of work, Member States may allow exceptions, including the establishment of reference periods, to the limits laid down in paragraph 1, second subparagraph, and paragraphs 3 and 4. Such exceptions shall, as far as possible, comply with the standards laid down but may take account of more frequent or longer leave periods or the granting of compensatory leave for the workers. These exceptions may be laid down by means of:
   (a) laws, regulations or administrative provisions provided there is consultation, where possible, of the representatives of the employers and workers concerned and efforts are made to encourage all relevant forms of social dialogue; or
   (b) collective agreements or agreements between the two sides of industry.
(8) The master of a seagoing fishing vessel shall have the right to require workers on board to perform any hours of work necessary for the immediate safety of the vessel, persons on board or cargo, or for the purpose of giving assistance to other vessels or persons in distress at sea.
(9) Member States may provide that workers on board seagoing fishing vessels for which national legislation or practice determines that these vessels are not allowed to operate in a specific period of the calendar year exceeding one month, shall take annual leave in accordance with Article 7 within that period.

6. Miscellaneous Provisions

1779.

(1) A Member State shall have the option not to apply Article 6, while respecting the general principles of the protection of the safety and health of workers, and provided it takes the necessary measures to ensure that:
   (a) no employer requires a worker to work more than 48 hours over a seven-day period, calculated as an average for the reference period referred to in Article 16(b), unless he has first obtained the worker's agreement to perform such work;
   (b) no worker is subjected to any detriment by his employer because he is not willing to give his agreement to perform such work;
   (c) the employer keeps up-to-date records of all workers who carry out such work;

(d) the records are placed at the disposal of the competent authorities, which may, for reasons connected with the safety and/or health of workers, prohibit or restrict the possibility of exceeding the maximum weekly working hours;
(e) the employer provides the competent authorities at their request with information on cases in which agreement has been given by workers to perform work exceeding 48 hours over a period of seven days, calculated as an average for the reference period referred to in Article 16(b).
(f) Before 23 November 2003, the Council shall, on the basis of a Commission proposal accompanied by an appraisal report, re-examine the provisions of this paragraph and decide on what action to take.
(2) Member States shall have the option, as regards the application of Article 7, of making use of a transitional period of not more than three years from 23 November 1996, provided that during that transitional period:
(a) every worker receives three weeks' paid annual leave in accordance with the conditions for the entitlement to, and granting of, such leave laid down by national legislation and/or practice; and
(b) the three-week period of paid annual leave may not be replaced by an allowance in lieu, except where the employment relationship is terminated.
(3) If Member States avail themselves of the options provided for in this Article, they shall forthwith inform the Commission thereof (Article 22).

F. Final Provisions

1. Level of Protection

1780. Without prejudice to the right of Member States to develop, in the light of changing circumstances, different legislative, regulatory or contractual provisions in the field of working time, as long as the minimum requirements provided for in this Directive are complied with, implementation of this Directive shall not constitute valid grounds for reducing the general level of protection afforded to workers (Article 23).

2. Reports

1781. Member States shall communicate to the Commission the texts of the provisions of national law already adopted or being adopted in the field governed by this Directive.

Member States shall report to the Commission every five years on the practical implementation of the provisions of this Directive, indicating the viewpoints of the two sides of industry.

The Commission shall inform the European Parliament, the Council, the European Economic and Social Committee and the Advisory Committee on Safety, Hygiene and Health Protection at Work thereof.

Every five years from 23 November 1996 the Commission shall submit to the European Parliament, the Council and the European Economic and Social Committee a report on the application of this Directive taking into account Articles 22 and 23 and paragraphs 1 and 2 of this Article (Article 24).

3. Review of the Operation of Provisions with Regard to Workers on Board Seagoing Fishing Vessels

1782. Not later than 1 August 2009 the Commission shall, after consulting the Member States and management and labour at European level, review the operation of the provisions with regard to workers on board seagoing fishing vessels, and, in particular examine whether these provisions remain appropriate, in particular, as far as health and safety are concerned with a view to proposing suitable amendments, if necessary (Article 25).

4. Review of the Operation of Provisions with Regard to Workers Concerned with the Carriage of Passengers

1783. Not later than 1 August 2005 the Commission shall, after consulting the Member States and management and labour at European level, review the operation of the provisions with regard to workers concerned with the carriage of passengers on regular urban transport services, with a view to presenting, if need be, the appropriate modifications to ensure a coherent and suitable approach in the sector (Article 26).

5. Entry into Force

1784. This Directive entered into force on 2 August 2004 (Article 28).

III. Working Time for Seafarers

1785. Council Directive 1999/63/EC of 21 June 1999[712] implements the Agreement of 30 September 1998 on the organisation of working time of seafarers concluded by the European Community Shipowners' Association (ECSA) and the Federation of Transport Workers' Unions in the European Union (FST). Amended by Council Directive 2009/13/EC of 16 February 2009 implementing the Agreement concluded by the European Community Shipowners' Associations (ECSA) and the European Transport Workers' Federation (ETF) on the Maritime Labour Convention, 2006.[713]

---

712. O.J. L 167, 2 July 1999.
713. O.J., 20 May 2009, L 124.

Part I, Ch. 8, Working Time and Leave

A. Scope

1786. The Agreement applies to seafarers on board of every seagoing ship, whether publicly or privately owned, which is registered in the territory of any Member State and is ordinarily engaged in commercial maritime operations. For the purpose of this agreement a ship that is on the register of two states is deemed to be registered in the territory of the state whose flag it flies.

B. Definitions

1787. For the purpose of the Agreement:

(a) the term 'hours of work' means time during which a seafarer is required to do work on account of the ship;
(b) the term 'hours of rest' means time outside hours of work; this term does not include short breaks;
(c) the term 'seafarer' means any person who is employed or engaged or works in any capacity on board a ship to which this agreement applies;
(d) the term 'shipowner' means the owner of the ship or another organisation or person, such as the manager, agent or bareboat charterer, who has assumed the responsibility for the operation of the ship from the owner and who, on assuming such responsibility, has agreed to take over the duties and responsibilities imposed on shipowners in accordance with this Agreement, regardless of whether any other organisation or persons fulfil certain of the duties or responsibilities on behalf of the shipowner.

C. Hours of Work

1788. There shall be fixed either a maximum number of hours of work which shall not be exceeded in a given period of time, or a minimum number of hours of rest which shall be provided in a given period of time.

The normal working hours' standard of seafarers is, in principle, based on an eight-hour day with one day of rest per week and rest on public holidays. Member States may have procedures to authorise or register a collective agreement which determines seafarers' normal working hours on a basis less favourable than this standard.

(1) The limits on hours of work or rest shall be either:
    (a) maximum hours of work which shall not exceed:
        (i) fourteen hours in any 24-hour period; and
        (ii) 72 hours in any seven-day period; or
    (b) minimum hours of rest which shall not be less than:
        (i) ten hours in any 24-hour period; and
        (ii) 72 hours in any seven-day period.

(c) Hours of rest may be divided into no more than two periods, one of which shall be at least six hours in length and the interval between consecutive periods of rest shall not exceed 14 hours.
(d) Musters, fire-fighting and lifeboat drills prescribed by national laws and regulations and by international instruments shall be conducted in a manner that minimises the disturbance of rest periods and does not induce fatigue.
(e) In respect of situations when a seafarer is on call, such as when a machinery space is unattended, the seafarer shall have an adequate compensatory rest period if the normal period of rest is disturbed by call-outs to work.

1789. Night work of seafarers under the age of 18 shall be prohibited. For the purposes of this Clause, 'night' shall be defined in accordance with national law and practice. It shall cover a period of at least nine hours starting no later than midnight and ending no earlier than 5 a.m.

An exception to strict compliance with the night work restriction may be made by the competent authority when:

(a) the effective training of the seafarers concerned, in accordance with established programmes and schedules, would be impaired; or
(b) the specific nature of the duty or a recognised training programme requires that the seafarers covered by the exception perform duties at night and the authority determines, after consultation with the shipowners' and seafarers' organisations concerned, that the work will not be detrimental to their health or well-being.

The employment, engagement or work of seafarers under the age of 18 shall be prohibited where the work is likely to jeopardise their health or safety. The types of such work shall be determined by national laws or regulations or by the competent authority, after consultation with the shipowners' and seafarers' organisations concerned, in accordance with relevant international standards.

D. Table

1790. A table shall be posted, in an easily accessible place, with the shipboard working arrangements, which shall contain for every position at least:

(a) the schedule of service at sea and service in port; and
(b) the maximum hours of work or the minimum hours of rest required by the laws, regulations or collective agreements in force in the Member States.

The table shall be established in a standardised format in the working language or languages of the ship and in English.

Part I, Ch. 8, Working Time and Leave

E. *Seafarers under 18 years*

1791. No seafarer under 18 years of age shall work at night. 'Night' means a period of at least nine consecutive hours, including the interval from midnight to 5 a.m. This provision needs not be applied when the effective training of young seafarers between the ages of 16 and 18 in accordance with established programmes and schedules would be impaired.

F. *Distress at Sea*

1792. The master of a ship shall have the right to require a seafarer to perform any hours of work necessary for the immediate safety of the ship, persons on board or cargo, or for the purpose of giving assistance to other ships or persons in distress at sea.

The master may suspend the schedule of hours of work or hours of rest and require a seafarer to perform any hours of work necessary until the normal situation has been restored.

As soon as practicable after the normal situation has been restored, the master shall ensure that any seafarers who have performed work in a scheduled rest period are provided with an adequate period of rest.

G. *Records*

1793. Records of seafarers' daily hours of work or of their daily hours of rest shall be maintained. The seafarer shall receive a copy of the records pertaining to him or her which shall be endorsed by the master, or a person authorised by the master, and by the seafarer.

Procedures shall be determined for keeping such records on board, including the intervals at which the information shall be recorded. The format of the records of the seafarers' hours of work or of their hours of rest shall be established taking into account any available international guidelines.

A copy of the relevant provisions of the national legislation pertaining to this Agreement and the relevant collective agreements shall be kept on board and be easily accessible to the crew.

H. *Manning Levels*

1794. When determining, approving or revising manning levels, it is necessary to take into account the need to avoid or minimise, as far as practicable, excessive hours of work, to ensure sufficient rest and to limit fatigue.

If the records or other evidence indicate infringement of provisions governing hours of work or hours of rest, measures, including if necessary the revision of the manning of the ship, shall be taken so as to avoid future infringements.

All ships to which this Agreement applies shall be sufficiently, safely and efficiently manned, in accordance with the minimum safe manning document or an equivalent issued by the competent authority.

I. Persons under 16 Years

1795. No person under 16 years of age shall work on a ship.

J. Necessary Resources

1796. The shipowner shall provide the master with the necessary resources for the purpose of compliance with obligations under this Agreement, including those relating to the appropriate manning of the ship. The master shall take all necessary steps to ensure that the requirements on seafarers' hours of work and rest arising from this Agreement are complied with.

K. Health Certificate

1797.

(1) Seafarers shall not work on a ship unless they are certified as medically fit to perform their duties.
(2) Exceptions can only be permitted as prescribed in this Agreement.
(3) The competent authority shall require that, prior to beginning work on a ship, seafarers hold a valid medical certificate attesting that they are medically fit to perform the duties they are to carry out at sea.
(4) In order to ensure that medical certificates genuinely reflect seafarers' state of health, in light of the duties they are to perform, the competent authority shall, after consultation with the shipowners' and seafarers' organisations concerned, and giving due consideration to applicable international guidelines, prescribe the nature of the medical examination and certificate.
(5) This Agreement is without prejudice to the International Convention on Standards of Training, Certification and Watchkeeping for Seafarers, 1978, as amended (STCW). A medical certificate issued in accordance with the requirements of STCW shall be accepted by the competent authority, for the purpose of points 1 and 2 of this Clause. A medical certificate meeting the substance of those requirements, in the case of seafarers not covered by STCW, shall similarly be accepted.
(6) The medical certificate shall be issued by a duly qualified medical practitioner or, in the case of a certificate solely concerning eyesight, by a person recognised by the competent authority as qualified to issue such a certificate. Practitioners must enjoy full professional independence in exercising their medical judgement in undertaking medical examination procedures.

Part I, Ch. 8, Working Time and Leave

(7) Seafarers that have been refused a certificate or have had a limitation imposed on their ability to work, in particular with respect to time, field of work or trading area, shall be given the opportunity to have a further examination by another independent medical practitioner or by an independent medical referee.

(8) Each medical certificate shall state in particular that:
   (a) the hearing and sight of the seafarer concerned, and the colour vision in the case of a seafarer to be employed in capacities where fitness for the work to be performed is liable to be affected by defective colour vision, are all satisfactory; and
   (b) the seafarer concerned is not suffering from any medical condition likely to be aggravated by service at sea or to render the seafarer unfit for such service or to endanger the health of other persons on board.

(9) Unless a shorter period is required by reason of the specific duties to be performed by the seafarer concerned or is required under STCW:
   (a) a medical certificate shall be valid for a maximum period of two years unless the seafarer is under the age of 18, in which case the maximum period of validity shall be one year;
   (b) a certification of colour vision shall be valid for a maximum period of six years.

(10) In urgent cases the competent authority may permit a seafarer to work without a valid medical certificate until the next port of call where the seafarer can obtain a medical certificate from a qualified medical practitioner, provided that:
   (a) the period of such permission does not exceed three months; and
   (b) the seafarer concerned is in possession of an expired medical certificate of recent date.

(11) If the period of validity of a certificate expires in the course of a voyage, the certificate shall continue in force until the next port of call where the seafarer can obtain a medical certificate from a qualified medical practitioner, provided that the period shall not exceed three months.

(12) The medical certificates for seafarers working on ships ordinarily engaged on international voyages must as a minimum be provided in English.

(13) The nature of the health assessment to be made and the particulars to be included in the medical certificate shall be established after consultation with the shipowners' and seafarers' organisations concerned.

(14) All seafarers shall have regular health assessments. Watchkeepers suffering from health problems certified by a medical practitioner as being due to the fact that they perform night work shall be transferred, wherever possible, to day work to which they are suited.

(15) The health assessment referred to in points 13 and 14 shall be free and comply with medical confidentiality. Such health assessments may be conducted within the national health system.

L. Watchkeepers and Night Work

1798. Shipowners shall provide information on watchkeepers and other night workers to the national competent authority if they so request.

M. Safety and Health

1799. Every seafarer shall be entitled to paid annual leave. The annual leave with pay entitlement shall be calculated on the basis of a minimum of 2,5 calendar days per month of employment and pro rata for incomplete months. The minimum period of paid annual leave may not be replaced by an allowance in lieu, except where the employment relationship is terminated.

N. Annual Leave

1800. Every seafarer shall be entitled to paid annual leave of at least four weeks, or a proportion thereof for periods of employment of less than one year, in accordance with the conditions for entitlement to, and granting of, such leave laid down by national legislation and/or practice.

The minimum period of paid annual leave may not be replaced by an allowance in lieu, except where the employment relationship is terminated.

IV. Working Time of Mobile Workers in Civil Aviation

1801. Council Directive 2000/79/EC of 27 November 2000 concerns the implementation of the European Agreement on the Organisation of Working Time of Mobile Workers in Civil Aviation concluded by the Association of European Airlines (AEA), the European Transport Workers' Federation (ETF), the European Cockpit Association (ECA), the European Regions Airline Association (ERA) and the International Air Carrier Association (IACA).[714]

This directive and the Agreement lay down more specific requirements within the meaning of Article 14 of Directive 93/104/EC as regards the organisation of working time of mobile staff in civil aviation.

A. Scope

1802. The Agreement applies to the working time of mobile staff in civil aviation (clause 1).

B. Definitions

1803.

---

714. O.J. L 302, 1 December 2000.

Part I, Ch. 8, Working Time and Leave

(1) Working time means any period during which the worker is working, at the employer's disposal and carrying out his activity or duties, in accordance with national laws and/or practice.
(2) Mobile staff in civil aviation means crew members on board a civil aircraft, employed by an undertaking established in a Member State.
(3) Block flying time means the time between an aircraft first moving from its parking place for the purpose of taking off until it comes to rest on the designated parking position and until all engines are stopped (clause 2).

C. *Paid Annual Leave*

1804.

(1) Mobile staff in civil aviation are entitled to paid annual leave of at least four weeks, in accordance with the conditions for entitlement to, and granting of, such leave laid down by national legislation and/or practice.
(2) The minimum period of paid annual leave may not be replaced by an allowance in lieu, except where the employment relationship is terminated (clause 3).

D. *Health Assessment*

1805.

(1)
  (a) Mobile staff in civil aviation are entitled to a free health assessment before their assignment and thereafter at regular intervals.
  (b) Mobile staff in civil aviation suffering from health problems recognised as being connected with the fact that they also work at night will be transferred whenever possible to mobile or non-mobile day work to which they are suited.
(2) The free health assessment referred to in paragraph 1(a) shall comply with medical confidentiality.
(3) The free health assessment referred to in paragraph 1(a) may be conducted within the national health system (clause 4).

E. *Safety and Health*

1806.

(1) Mobile staff in civil aviation will have safety and health protection appropriate to the nature of their work.

(2) Adequate protection and prevention services or facilities with regard to the safety and health of mobile staff in civil aviation will be available at all times (clause 5).

Necessary measures will be taken to ensure that an employer, who intends to organise work according to a certain pattern, takes account of the general principle of adapting work to the worker (clause 6).

Information concerning specific working patterns of mobile staff in civil aviation should be provided to the competent authorities, if they so request (clause 7).

F. Working Time

1807.

(1) Working time should be looked at without prejudice to any future Community legislation on flight and duty time limitations and rest requirements and in conjunction with national legislation on this subject which should be taken into consideration in all related matters.
(2) The maximum annual working time, including some elements of standby for duty assignment as determined by the applicable law, shall be 2,000 hours in which the block flying time shall be limited to 900 hours.
(3) The maximum annual working time shall be spread as evenly as practicable throughout the year (clause 8).

G. Days Free

1808. Without prejudice to clause 3, mobile staff in civil aviation shall be given days free of all duty and standby, which are notified in advance, as follows:

(a) at least seven local days in each calendar month, which may include any rest periods required by law; and
(b) at least 96 local days in each calendar year, which may include any rest periods required by law (clause 9).

H. Review

1809. The parties shall review the above provisions two years after the end of the implementation period laid down in the Council Decision putting this Agreement into effect (clause 10).

Part I, Ch. 8, Working Time and Leave

I. Implementation

1810.

(1) Member States may maintain or introduce more favourable provisions than those laid down in this directive.
(2) The implementation of this directive shall under no circumstances constitute sufficient grounds for justifying a reduction in the general level of protection of workers in the fields covered by this directive. This shall be without prejudice to the rights of Member States and/or management and labour to lay down, in the light of changing circumstances, different legislative, regulatory or contractual arrangements to those prevailing at the time of the adoption of this directive, provided always that the minimum requirements laid down in this directive are complied with (Article 2).

Member States shall bring into force the laws, regulations and administrative provisions necessary to comply with this directive not later than 1 December 2003 or shall ensure that, by that date at the latest, management and labour have introduced the necessary measures by agreement. The Member States shall take any necessary measure to enable them at any time to be in a position to guarantee the results imposed by this directive. They shall forthwith inform the Commission thereof.

When Member States adopt these measures, they shall contain a reference to this directive or be accompanied by such a reference on the occasion of their official publication. The methods of making such a reference shall be laid down by the Member States (Article 3).

This directive enters into force on the day of its publication in the Official Journal of the European Communities (Article 4).

V. Working Time of Mobile Road Transport Workers

1811. Directive 2002/15/EC of 11 March 2002 concerns the organisation of the working time of persons performing mobile road transport activities.[715]

Although Council Regulation (EEC) No. 3820/85 of 20 December 1985 on the harmonisation of certain social legislation relating to road transport laid down common rules on driving times and rest periods for drivers; that Regulation does not cover other aspects of working time for road transport.

Since then, despite intensive negotiations between the social partners, it has not been possible to reach agreement on the subject of mobile workers in road transport, a specific directive has been taken.

---

715. O.J., 23 March 2002.

A. Purpose

1812. The purpose of this directive is to establish minimum requirements in relation to the organisation of working time in order to improve the health and safety protection of persons performing mobile road transport activities and to improve road safety and align conditions of competition (Article 1).

B. Scope

1813. The directive applies to mobile workers employed by undertakings established in a Member State, participating in road transport activities.[716] Without prejudice to the provisions of following subparagraph, the directive shall apply to selfemployed drivers from 23 March 2009 (Article 2(1)).

The provisions of Directive 93/104/EC[717] shall apply to mobile workers excluded from the scope of this directive (Article 2(2)).

C. Definitions

1814. For the purposes of this directive:

(a) 'working time' shall mean:
   (1) in the case of mobile workers: the time from the beginning to the end of work, during which the mobile worker is at his workstation, at the disposal of the employer and exercising his functions or activities, that is to say:
   – the time devoted to all road transport activities. These activities are, in particular, the following:
      (i) driving;
      (ii) loading and unloading;
      (iii) assisting passengers boarding and disembarking from the vehicle;
      (iv) cleaning and technical maintenance;
      (v) all other work intended to ensure the safety of the vehicle, its cargo and passengers or to fulfil the legal or regulatory obligations directly linked to the specific transport operation under way, including monitoring of loading and unloading, administrative formalities with police, customs, immigration officers etc.,
   – the times during which he cannot dispose freely of his time and is required to be at his workstation, ready to take up normal work, with certain tasks associated with being on duty, in particular during periods awaiting loading or unloading where their foreseeable duration is not known in advance, that is to say either before departure or just before

---

716. Covered by Regulation (EEC) No. 3820/85 or, failing that, by the AETR Agreement.
717. *See* Part I, Chapter 7, §1, II.

the actual start of the period in question, or under the general conditions negotiated between the social partners and/or under the terms of the legislation of the Member States;
(2) in the case of self-employed drivers, the same definition shall apply to the time from the beginning to the end of work, during which the self employed driver is at his workstation, at the disposal of the client and exercising his functions or activities other than general administrative work that is not directly linked to the specific transport operation under way. The break times referred to in Article 5, the rest times referred to in Article 6 and, without prejudice to the legislation of Member States or agreements between the social partners providing that such periods should be compensated or limited, the periods of availability referred to in (b) of this Article, shall be excluded from working time;
(b) 'periods of availability' shall mean:
– periods other than those relating to break times and rest times during which the mobile worker is not required to remain at his workstation, but must be available to answer any calls to start or resume driving or to carry out other work. In particular such periods of availability shall include periods during which the mobile worker is accompanying a vehicle being transported by ferryboat or by train as well as periods of waiting at frontiers and those due to traffic prohibitions.
– These periods and their foreseeable duration shall be known in advance by the mobile worker, that is to say either before departure or just before the actual start of the period in question, or under the general conditions negotiated between the social partners and/or under the terms of the legislation of the Member States,
– for mobile workers driving in a team, the time spent sitting next to the driver or on the couchette while the vehicle is in motion;
(c) 'workstation' shall mean:
– the location of the main place of business of the undertaking for which the person performing mobile road transport activities carries out duties, together with its various subsidiary places of business, regardless of whether they are located in the same place as its head office or main place of business,
– the vehicle which the person performing mobile road transport activities uses when he carries out duties, and
– any other place in which activities connected with transportation are carried out;
(d) 'mobile worker' shall mean any worker forming part of the travelling staff, including trainees and apprentices, who is in the service of an undertaking which operates transport services for passengers or goods by road for hire or reward or on its own account;
(e) 'self-employed driver' shall mean anyone whose main occupation is to transport passengers or goods by road for hire or reward within the meaning of Community legislation under cover of a Community licence or any other professional authorisation to carry out the aforementioned transport, who is

entitled to work for himself and who is not tied to an employer by an employment contract or by any other type of working hierarchical relationship, who is free to organise the relevant working activities, whose income depends directly on the profits made and who has the freedom to, individually or through a cooperation between self-employed drivers, have commercial relations with several customers.For the purposes of this Directive, those drivers who do not satisfy these criteria shall be subject to the same obligations and benefit from the same rights as those provided for mobile workers by this Directive;
(f) 'person performing mobile road transport activities' shall mean any mobile worker or self-employed driver who performs such activities;
(g) 'week' shall mean the period between 00.00 hours on Monday and 24.00 hours on Sunday;
(h) 'night time' shall mean a period of at least four hours, as defined by national law, between 00.00 hours and 07.00 hours;
(i) 'night work' shall mean any work performed during night time (Article 3).

D. *Maximum Weekly Working Time*

1815. Member States must take the measures necessary to ensure that:

(a) the average weekly working time may not exceed 48 hours. The maximum weekly working time may be extended to 60 hours only if, over four months, an average of 48 hours a week is not exceeded;[718]
(b) working time for different employers is the sum of the working hours. The employer shall ask the mobile worker concerned in writing for an account of time worked for another employer. The mobile worker shall provide such information in writing (Article 4).

E. *Breaks*

1816.

(1) Member States must take the measures necessary to ensure that persons performing mobile road transport activities, in no circumstances work for more than six consecutive hours without a break. Working time shall be interrupted by a break of at least 30 minutes, if working hours total between six and nine hours, and of at least 45 minutes, if working hours total more than nine hours.
(2) Breaks may be subdivided into periods of at least 15 minutes each (Article 5).

---

718. The fourth and fifth subparagraphs of Article 6(1) of Regulation (EEC) No. 3820/85 or, where necessary, the fourth subparagraph of Article 6(1) of the AETR Agreement shall take precedence over this Directive, in so far as the drivers concerned do not exceed an average working time of 48 hours a week over four months.

Part I, Ch. 8, Working Time and Leave

F. Rest Periods

1817. Apprentices and trainees are covered by the same provisions on rest time as other mobile workers (Article 6).

G. Night Work

1818. Member States must take the measures necessary to ensure that:

- if night work is performed, the daily working time does not exceed ten hours in each 24 period,
- compensation for night work is given in accordance with national legislative measures, collective agreements, agreements between the two sides of industry and/or national practice, on condition that such compensation is not liable to endanger road safety (Article 7(1)).

H. Derogations

1819. Derogations may, for objective or technical reasons or reasons concerning the organisation of work, be adopted by means of collective agreements, agreements between the social partners, or if this is not possible, by laws, regulations or administrative provisions provided there is consultation of the representatives of the employers and workers concerned and efforts are made to encourage all relevant forms of social dialogue.

The option to derogate may not result in the establishment of a reference period exceeding six months, for calculation of the average maximum weekly working time of 48 hours (Article 8).

I. Information and Records

1820. Member States shall ensure that:

(a) mobile workers are informed of the relevant national requirements, the internal rules of the undertaking and agreements between the two sides of industry, in particular collective agreements and any company agreements, reached on the basis of this Directive, without prejudice to Council Directive 91/533/EEC of 14 October 1991 on an employer's obligation to inform employees of the conditions applicable to the contract or employment relationship;
(b) the working time of persons performing mobile road transport activities is recorded. Records shall be kept for at least two years after the end of the period covered. Employers shall be responsible for recording the working time of mobile workers. Employers shall upon request provide mobile workers with copies of the records of hours worked (Article 9).

J. Final Provisions

1821. Member States shall adopt the laws, regulations and administrative provisions necessary to comply with this Directive by 23 March 2005 or shall ensure by that date that the two sides of industry have established the necessary measures by agreement, the Member States being obliged to take any steps to allow them to be able at any time to guarantee the results required by this Directive (Article 14(1)).

VI. Certain Aspects of the Working Conditions of Mobile Workers Engaged in Interoperable Cross-border Services in the Railway Sector[719]

A. Scope

1822. This Agreement shall apply to mobile railway workers assigned to interoperable cross-border services carried out by railway undertakings.

The application of this Agreement is optional for local and regional cross-border passenger traffic, cross-border freight traffic travelling no further than 15 kilometres beyond the border, and for traffic between the official border stations listed in the Annex.

It is also optional for trains on cross-border routes which both start and stop on the infrastructure of the same Member State and use the infrastructure of another Member State without stopping there (and which can therefore be considered national transport operations).

As regards mobile workers engaged in interoperable cross-border services, Directive 93/104/EC shall not apply to those aspects for which this Agreement contains more specific provisions.

B. Definitions

1823. For the purposes of this Agreement, the following definitions apply:

(1) 'interoperable cross-border services': cross-border services for which at least two safety certificates as stipulated by Directive 2001/14/EC are required from the railway undertakings;
(2) 'mobile worker engaged in interoperable cross-border services': any worker who is a member of a train crew, who is assigned to interoperable cross-border services for more than one hour on a daily shift basis;
(3) 'working time': any period during which the worker is at work, at the employer's disposal and carrying out his or her activities or duties, in accordance with national laws and/or practice;

---

719. Council Directive 2005/47/EC of 18 July 2005 on the Agreement between the Community of European Railways (CER) and the European Transport Workers' Federation (ETF) on certain aspects of the working conditions of mobile workers engaged in interoperable cross-border services in the railway sector, O.J., 16 June 2006, L 164 M.

(4) 'rest period': any period which is not working time;
(5) 'night time': any period of not less than seven hours, as defined by national law, and which must include in any case the period between midnight and 5 a.m.;
(6) 'night shift': any shift of at least three hours' work during the night time;
(7) 'rest away from home': daily rest which cannot be taken at the normal place of residence of the mobile worker;
(8) 'driver': any worker in charge of operating a traction unit;
(9) 'driving time': the duration of the scheduled activity where the driver is in charge of the traction unit, excluding the scheduled time to prepare or shut down that traction unit, but including any scheduled interruptions when the driver remains in charge of the traction unit.

C. Daily Rest at Home

1824. Daily rest at home must be a minimum of 12 consecutive hours per 24-hour period.

However, it may be reduced to a minimum of nine hours once every seven-day period. In that case, the hours corresponding to the difference between the reduced rest and 12 hours will be added to the next daily rest at home.

A significantly reduced daily rest shall not be scheduled between two daily rests away from home.

D. Daily Rest Away from Home

1825. The minimum daily rest away from home shall be eight consecutive hours per 24-hour period.

A daily rest away from home must be followed by a daily rest at home.

It is recommended that attention should be paid to the level of comfort of the accommodation offered to staff resting away from home.

E. Breaks

1. Drivers

1826. If the working time of a driver is longer than eight hours, a break of at least 45 minutes shall be taken during the working day.

Or When the working time is between six and eight hours, this break shall be at least 30 minutes long and shall be taken during the working day.

The time of day and the duration of the break shall be sufficient to ensure an effective recuperation of the worker.

Breaks may be adapted during the working day in the event of train delays. A part of the break should be given between the third and the sixth working hour. Clause

5(a) shall not apply if there is a second driver. In that case, the conditions for granting the breaks shall be regulated at national level.

2. Other On-board Staff

1827. For other on-board staff, a break of at least 30 minutes shall be taken if the working time is longer than six hours.

F. Weekly Rest Period

1828. Any mobile worker engaged in interoperable cross-border services is entitled, per seven-day period, to a minimum uninterrupted weekly rest period of 24 hours plus the 12 hours' daily rest period referred above.
Each year, every mobile worker shall have 104 rest periods of 24 hours, including the 24-hour periods of the 52 weekly rest periods, including:

– 12 double rest periods (of 48 hours plus a daily rest of 12 hours) including Saturday and Sunday,
– and
– 12 double rest periods (of 48 hours plus a daily rest of 12 hours) without the guarantee that this will include a Saturday or Sunday.

G. Driving Time

1829. The driving time, as defined in clause 2, shall not exceed nine hours for a day shift and eight hours for a night shift between two daily rest periods. The maximum driving time over a two-week period is limited to 80 hours.

H. Checks

1830. A record of daily working hours and rest periods for the mobile workers shall be kept to allow monitoring of compliance with the provisions of this Agreement. Information on actual working hours must be available. This record shall be kept in the undertaking for at least one year.

I. Non-regression Clause

1831. The implementation of this Agreement shall not constitute in any case valid grounds for reducing the general level of protection afforded to mobile workers engaged in interoperable cross-border services.

Part I, Ch. 8, Working Time and Leave

J. Follow-up to the Agreement

1832. The signatories shall follow up the implementation and application of this Agreement in the framework of the Sectoral Dialogue Committee for the railways sector, established in accordance with Commission Decision 98/500/EC.

K. Evaluation

1833. The parties shall evaluate the provisions of this Agreement two years after its signing in the light of initial experience in the development of inter-operable cross-border transport.

L. Review

1834. The parties shall review the above provisions two years after the end of the implementation period laid down in the Council Decision putting this Agreement into effect.

§2. SUNDAY REST

1835. Sunday rest was dealt with by the Court on different occasions.[720] More specifically the question was raised whether rules prohibiting retailers from opening their premises on Sunday are compatible with Union law and more especially whether such a prohibition is a measure having equivalent effect to a quantitative restriction on imports. In the case against *Marchandise and Cie* criminal proceedings were launched against them because they repeatedly employed workers in retail shops on Sundays after 12.00 noon in contravention of the Belgian LabourAct of 16 March 1971.

The first point which must be made, the Court stated, is that national rules prohibiting retailers from opening their premises on Sunday apply to imported and domestic products alike. In principle, the marketing of products imported from other Member States is not therefore made more difficult than the marketing of domestic products. Next it must be recalled that such a prohibition is not compatible with the free movement of goods provided for in the Treaty unless any obstacle to Union trade thereby created did not exceed what was necessary in order to ensure the attainment of the objective in view and unless that objective was justified with

---

720. C.O.J., 23 November 1989, *Torfean Borough Council v. B & Q plc*, No. C-145/88, ECR, 1989, 3851; C.O.J., 28 February 1991, *Union Départementale des Syndicats CGT de l'Aisne v. Sidef Conforama and Others*, No. C-312/89, ECR, 1991, 997 and *Criminal proceedings against A. Marchandise and Others*, No. C-332/89, ECR, 1991, 1027. *See also*: C.O.J., 16 December 1992, *Reading Borough Council v. Payless Diy Limited and Others*, No. C-304/90, ECR-I-6493, 1992; C.O.J., 16 December 1992, *Council of the City of Stoke-on-Trent and Norwich City Councils v. B & Q plc*, No. C-169/91, ECR, 1992, 6635.

regard to Union law. In those circumstances, the Court continued, it is therefore necessary that rules such as those at issue pursue an aim which is justified with regard to Union law. As far as that question is concerned, the Court has already stated in its judgment of 14 July 1981[721] that national rules governing the hours of work, delivery and sale in the bread and confectionery industry constitute a legitimate part of economic and social policy, consistent with the objectives of public interest pursued by the Treaty. The same consideration must apply as regards national rules governing the opening hours of retail premises. Such rules reflect certain political and economic choices insofar as their purpose is to ensure that working and non-working hours are so arranged as to accord with national and regional socio-cultural characteristics, and that, in the present state of Union law, is a matter for the Member States. Furthermore, such rules are not designed to govern the patterns of trade between the Member States.

Therefore, Article 44 TFEU must be interpreted as meaning that the prohibition which is laid down does not apply to national rules prohibiting retailers from opening their premises on Sunday where the restrictive effects on Union trade which may result therefrom do not exceed the effects intrinsic to rules of that kind.

§3. NIGHT WORK AND EQUAL TREATMENT

1836. The Union has tackled the problem of night work for women indirectly from the angle of equal treatment, namely on the basis of Article 5 of the Directive (76/207) of 9 February 1976[722]. Indeed, by judgment of 4 October 1989, the *Tribunal de Police* (local criminal court), Illkirch (France) referred a question on the interpretation of Article 5 of the 1976 directive to the Court for a preliminary ruling. The question arose in the course of criminal proceedings brought against Mr. Stoeckel, the manager of SUMA SA, who was charged with having employed 77 women on night work contrary to Article L-23 of the French *Code du Travail*. This question was even more delicate due to the fact that French legislation on night work resulted from the ratification of ILO Convention No. 89, containing a prohibition of night work for women in industry.[723] The decision of the Court led France, as well as Belgium, to denounce Convention No. 89.

The resolution of the problem of conflicting international instruments, namely emanating from the ILO on the one hand and the supranational norms, emanating from the Community, on the other hand, concerning night work for women and equal treatment of men and women, lies in Article 351 TFEU. Pursuant to this article, the Member States concerned shall to the extent that international agreements are not compatible with the Treaty 'take all appropriate steps to eliminate the incompatibilities'.

In the case under review a restructuration of the concerned enterprise had been negotiated between the employer and the trade unions and an agreement had been

---

721. *Oebel* (1981), ECR, 1993, No. 155/80.
722. Repealed by Council Directive 5 July 2006, No. 2006/54/EC, O.J., 26 July 2006.
723. *See* M.A. Moreau, 'Travail de nuit des femmes, observations sur l'arrêt de la CJCE du 25 juillet 1991', *Droit Social*, 1992, 174–185.

Part I, Ch. 8, Working Time and Leave

concluded to introduce shift and night work, in order to prevent the redundancy of some 200 employees. The agreement concerning night work applied also to female workers.

In the proceedings before the *Tribunal de Police* Mr. Stoeckel had maintained that Article L-213 of the *Code du Travail* contravened Article 5 of the 1976 directive concerning equal treatment between men and women.

The French Government argued that the prohibition of night work for women, qualified by numerous derogations, was in keeping with the general aims of protecting female employees and with special considerations of a social nature, such as the risk of assault and the greater burden of household work borne by women.

1837. Turning to the aims of protecting female employees, the Court held that it was not evident that, except in cases of pregnancy and maternity, the risks incurred by women in such work were broadly different in kind from the risks incurred by men. As far as the risks of assault were concerned, the Court ruled that, on the assumption that they were greater at night than by day, suitable measures could be adopted to deal with them without jeopardising the fundamental principle of equal treatment of men and women.

With regard to family responsibilities, the Court reiterated that the directive did not seek to settle questions as to the organisation of the family or alter the allocation of the responsibilities between the partners. Turning to the numerous derogations from the prohibition of night work to which the French Government had referred, the Court held that they were inadequate to give effect to Directive 76/207, since that directive did not allow any general principle excluding women from night work; the derogations could, indeed, be a source of discrimination. Therefore, the Court ruled as follows: Article 5 of the 1976 directive is sufficiently precise to impose on the Member States the obligation not to lay down by legislation the principle that night work by women is prohibited, even if that obligation is subject to exceptions, where night work for men is not prohibited.[724]

1838. A question to the Court for a preliminary ruling on the interpretation of Articles 1 to 5 of Council Directive 76/207/EC was raised in criminal proceedings brought by the French *Ministère Public* and the *Direction du Travail et de l'Emploi* against Jean-Claude Levy, who was summoned for having employed 23 women on night work contrary to Article L213-1 of the French *Code du Travail*.

That provision was adopted to implement Convention No. 89 of the International Labour Organisation of 9 July 1948 on night work for women in industry.

In its judgment of 25 July 1991 in the *Stoeckel* case the Court held that Article 5 of the directive was sufficiently precise to impose on the Member States the obligation not to lay down by legislation the principle that night work by women was prohibited, even if that is subject to exceptions, where night work by men is not prohibited. It followed that in principle the national court had to ensure the full effect of that rule and not apply any contrary national provision.

---

724. C.O.J., 25 July 1991, *Ministère Public* v. *A. Stoeckel*, No. C-345/89, ECR, 1991, 4047. For some critical background information on night work *see* Singleton and Dirikx, *Ergonomics, Health and Safety*, Leuven, 1991.

In the present case the question for a preliminary ruling was basically whether the national court had the same obligation where the national provision which was incompatible with the Union rule was intended to implement a convention such as the ILO Convention which was concluded by the Member State concerned with other Member States and non-Member States prior to the entry into force of the EC Treaty.

In determining whether a Union rule could be frustrated by a prior inter-national convention it was necessary to consider whether the convention imposed on the Member State concerned obligations compliance with which might still be insisted on by non-Member States who were parties to the convention.

In that respect the Court held that although it was true that equality of treatment for men and women constituted a fundamental right recognised by the Union legal system, its implementation even at Union level had been progressive, requiring the intervention of the Council by means of directives and those directives recognised temporarily certain derogations from the principle of equality of treatment.

In those circumstances it was not sufficient to cite the principle of equality of treatment to prevent compliance with obligations of a Member State in that field under a prior international convention where observance of the obligations was protected by the first paragraph of Article 351 of the Treaty.

In the present case, if it appeared from the development of international law that the prohibition of night work for women provided for by the ILO Convention was repealed by subsequent conventions binding the same parties, the provisions of the first paragraph of Article 351 of the Treaty would not be applicable. There would then be nothing to prevent the national court from applying Article 5 of the directive and disregarding contrary national provisions.

However, it was not for the Court in proceedings for a preliminary ruling but for the national court to determine the obligations under a prior international convention of the Member State concerned and to define the limits in order to determine to what extent those obligations precluded the application of Article 5 of the directive.

The Court ruled as follows:

> The national court must ensure full respect of Article 5 of Council Directive 76/207/EEC of 9 February 1976 on the implementation of the principle of equal treatment for men and women as regards access to employment, vocational training and promotion, and working conditions and not apply any contrary provision of national law unless application of such a provision is necessary to ensure compliance by the Member State concerned with obligations resulting from a convention concluded prior to the entry into force of the EC Treaty with non-Member States.[725]

§4. PARENTAL LEAVE

1839. Parental leave was introduced by Directive 96/34/EC of 3 June 1996 on the framework agreement on parental leave concluded by UNICE, CEEP and the

---

725. C.O.J., *Ministère Public* v. *J.C. Levy*, 2 August 1993, No. C-158/91, ECR, 1993, 4287.

Part I, Ch. 8, Working Time and Leave 1840–1841

ETUC, 14 December 1995.[726] The agreement referred to was the first European collective labour agreement concluded by the recognised social partners under the Maastricht Agreement on Social Policy (1991).[727]

The cross-industry organisations indeed concluded, on 14 December 1995, a framework agreement on parental leave and forwarded to the Commission their joint request to implement this framework agreement by a Council Decision on a proposal from the Commission.

At the occasion of the Madrid summit, the members of the European Council (except for the UK) welcomed the conclusion of this framework agreement. The text, before being implemented by way of a directive, was forwarded to the EP and ESC.

1840. The framework agreement was extended to the United Kingdom by the Directive 97/75 of 15 December 1997.[728]

1841. The agreement was revised by the Framework Agreement on Parental Leave (Revised) 18 June 2009. [729] The revision significantly improves the rights of parents in relation to parental leave. It applies to all workers who have an employment contract or an employment relationship as defined by law, to include specifically fixed-term, part-time and temporary agency workers. It also establishes a right for workers to return to the same job or, if this is not possible, 'to an equivalent or similar job consistent with their employment contract or employment relationship'. The social partners suggest that the revised framework agreement increases protection, not just against dismissal but also against unfavourable treatment as a result of exercising the right to parental leave. Specifically, the revised agreement's provisions:

– increase the length of parental leave from the current three months to four months;
– make part of the leave non-transferable to encourage fathers to take advantage of parental leave;
– offer a right to request flexible working when returning from parental leave;
– call on Member States to establish notice periods that workers should give in exercising the right to parental leave.

---

726. O.J. L 145/4, 19 June 1996.
727. *See further* Part II, Chapter 1.
728. Clause 2.6 and 2.7 of the framework agreement on parental leave concluded on 14 December 1995 must be interpreted as precluding, where an employer unilaterally terminates a worker's full-time employment contract of indefinite duration, without urgent cause or without observing the statutory period of notice, whilst the worker is on part-time parental leave, the compensation to be paid to the worker from being determined on the basis of the reduced salary being received when the dismissal takes place (COJ, 22 October 2009, *Christel Meerts* v. *Proost NV*, C-116/08, www.curia).
729. The agreement was put in to effect by Council Directive 2010/18/EU of 8 March 2010 implementing the revised Framework Agreement on parental leave concluded by BUSINESSEUROPE, UEAPME, CEEP and ETUC and repealing Directive 96/34/EC Text with EEA relevance O.J., 18 March 2010.

1842. The revised framework agreement also covers adoptive parents. The fact that the agreement specifically reserves some leave as non-transferable between the mother and father represents an important step 'to encourage a more equal take-up of leave by both parents'. This is also a new initiative for the social partners to encourage fathers to play a more active role in the upbringing of their children. By making some leave non-transferable, the agreement provides incentives to fathers to take up a period of leave reserved for them.[730]

I. Purpose and Scope

A. Purpose

1843. The agreement lays down minimum requirements designed to facilitate the reconciliation of parental and professional responsibilities for working parents, taking into account the increasing diversity of family structures while respecting national law, collective agreements and/or practice.

B. Scope

1844. The agreement applies to all workers, men and women, who have an employment contract or employment relationship as defined by the law, collective agreements and/or practice in force in each Member State.

Member States and/or social partners shall not exclude from the scope and application of this agreement workers, contracts of employment or employment relationships solely because they relate to part-time workers, fixed-term contract workers or persons with a contract of employment or employment relationship with a temporary agency.

II. Parental Leave

1845. The agreement entitles men and women workers to an individual right to parental leave on the grounds of the birth or adoption of a child to take care of that child until a given age up to eight years to be defined by Member States and/or social partners.

The leave shall be granted for at least a period of four months and, to promote equal opportunities and equal treatment between men and women, should, in principle, be provided on a non-transferable basis. To encourage a more equal take-up of leave by both parents, at least one of the four months shall be provided on a non-transferable basis. The modalities of application of the non-transferable period shall be set down at national level through legislation and/or collective agreements taking into account existing leave arrangements in the Member States.

---

730. The agreement was put in to effect by Council Directive 2010/18/EU of 8 March 2010 implementing the revised Framework Agreement on parental leave concluded by BUSINESSEUROPE, UEAPME, CEEP and ETUC and repealing Directive 96/34/EC Text with EEA relevance. O.J., 18 March 2010.

1846. The European Court was confronted with the rights of parents in the event of the birth of twins.[731] The following questions were raised:

(1) Can clause 2.1 of the Framework Agreement, interpreted in conjunction with Article 24 of the Charter of Fundamental Rights ... relating to the rights of the child – and in light of the enhanced level of protection of those rights which has been brought about by the Charter of Fundamental Rights – be regarded as also creating in parallel a right to parental leave for the child, so that, if twins have been born, the grant of one period of parental leave constitutes an infringement of Article 21 of the Charter of Fundamental Rights on the grounds of discrimination on the basis of birth and a restriction on the right of twins that is not permitted by the principle of proportionality?
(2) If the answer to the preceding question is in the negative, does the term 'birth' in clause 2.1 mean that a double right to the grant of parental leave is created for working parents, that right being based on the fact that pregnancy with twins results in two successive births of children (twins), or does it mean that parental leave is granted for one birth, irrespective of how many children are thereby born, without any infringement in the latter case of equality before the law under Article 20 of the Charter of Fundamental Rights ... ?'

1847. The Court ruled negative on the first question as Clause 2.1 cannot be interpreted as conferring an individual right to parental leave on the child. Clause 2.1 is not to be interpreted as requiring the birth of twins to confer entitlement to a number of periods of parental leave equal to the number of children born. However, read in the light of the principle of equal treatment, this clause obliges the national legislature to establish a parental leave regime which, according to the situation obtaining in the Member State concerned, ensures that the parents of twins receive treatment that takes due account of their particular needs. It is incumbent upon national courts to determine whether the national rules meet that requirement and, if necessary, to interpret those national rules, so far as possible, in conformity with European Union law.

III. Modalities of Application

1848.

(1) The conditions of access and detailed rules for applying parental leave shall be defined by law and/or collective agreements in the Member States, as long as the minimum requirements of this agreement are respected. Member States and/or social partners may, in particular:
    (a) decide whether parental leave is granted on a full-time or part-time basis, in a piecemeal way or in the form of a time-credit system, taking into account the needs of both employers and workers;

---

731. C.O.J., 16 September 2010, *Zoi Chatzi* v. *Ipourgos Ikonomikon*, Case C-149/10, www.curia.eu.

- (b) make entitlement to parental leave subject to a period of work qualification and/or a length of service qualification which shall not exceed one year; Member States and/or social partners shall ensure, when making use of this provision, that in case of successive fixed term contracts, as defined in Council Directive 1999/70/EC on fixed-term work, with the same employer the sum of these contracts shall be taken into account for the purpose of calculating the qualifying period;
- (c) define the circumstances in which an employer, following consultation in accordance with national law, collective agreements and/or practice, is allowed to postpone the granting of parental leave for justifiable reasons related to the operation of the organisation. Any problem arising from the application of this provision should be dealt with in accordance with national law, collective agreements and/or practice;
- (d) in addition to (c), authorise special arrangements to meet the operational and organisational requirements of small undertakings.
(2) Member States and/or social partners shall establish notice periods to be given by the worker to the employer when exercising the right to parental leave, specifying the beginning and the end of the period of leave. Member States and/or social partners shall have regard to the interests of workers and of employers in specifying the length of such notice periods.
(3) Member States and/or social partners should assess the need to adjust the conditions for access and modalities of application of parental leave to the needs of parents of children with a disability or a long-term illness.

IV. Adoption

1849. Member States and/or social partners shall assess the need for additional measures to address the specific needs of adoptive parents.

V. Employment Rights and Non-discrimination

1850.

(1) At the end of parental leave, workers shall have the right to return to the same job or, if that is not possible, to an equivalent or similar job consistent with their employment contract or employment relationship.
(2) Rights acquired or in the process of being acquired by the worker on the date on which parental leave starts shall be maintained as they stand until the end of parental leave. At the end of parental leave, these rights, including any changes arising from national law, collective agreements and/or practice, shall apply.
(3) Member States and/or social partners shall define the status of the employment contract or employment relationship for the period of parental leave.
(4) In order to ensure that workers can exercise their right to parental leave, Member States and/or social partners shall take the necessary measures to protect workers against less favourable treatment or dismissal on the grounds of an

application for, or the taking of, parental leave in accordance with national law, collective agreements and/or practice.
(5) All matters regarding social security in relation to this agreement are for consideration and determination by Member States and/or social partners according to national law and/or collective agreements, taking into account the importance of the continuity of the entitlements to social security cover under the different schemes, in particular health care.

1851. All matters regarding income in relation to this agreement are for consideration and determination by Member States and/or social partners according to national law, collective agreements and/or practice, taking into account the role of income – among other factors – in the take-up of parental leave.

1852. In a Latvian case, the European Court ruled[732] that the Framework Agreement on Parental Leave, must be interpreted as precluding:

– a situation where, as part of an assessment of workers in the context of abolishment of officials' posts due to national economic difficulties, a worker who has taken parental leave is assessed in his or her absence on the basis of assessment principles and criteria which place him or her in a less favourable position as compared to workers who did not take parental leave; in order to ascertain whether or not that is the case, the national court must inter alia ensure that the assessment encompasses all workers liable to be concerned by the abolishment of the post, that it is based on criteria which are absolutely identical to those applying to workers in active service and that the implementation of those criteria does not involve the physical presence of workers on parental leave; and
– a situation where a female worker who has been transferred to another post at the end of her parental leave following that assessment is dismissed due to the abolishment of that new post, where it was not impossible for the employer to allow her to return to her former post or where the work assigned to her was not equivalent or similar and consistent with her employment contract or employment relationship, inter alia because, at the time of the transfer, the employer was informed that the new post was due to be abolished, which it is for the national court to verify.

VI. Return to Work

1853.

(1) In order to promote better reconciliation Member States and/or social partners shall take the necessary measures to ensure that workers, when returning from parental leave, may request changes to their working hours and/or patterns for

---

732. C.O.J., 20 June 2013, *Nadežda Riežniece* v *Zemkopības ministrija and Lauku atbalsta dienests*, C-7/12, www.curia.eu.

a set period of time. Employers shall consider and respond to such requests, taking into account both employers' and workers' needs.
(2) The modalities of this paragraph shall be determined in accordance with national law, collective agreements and/or practice.
(3) In order to facilitate the return to work following parental leave, workers and employers are encouraged to maintain contact during the period of leave and may make arrangements for any appropriate reintegration measures, to be decided between the parties concerned, taking into account national law, collective agreements and/or practice.

VII. Time off from Work on Grounds of *Force Majeure*

1854.

(1) Member States and/or social partners shall take the necessary measures to entitle workers to time off from work, in accordance with national legislation, collective agreements and/or practice, on grounds of force majeure for urgent family reasons in cases of sickness or accident making the immediate presence of the worker indispensable.
(2) Member States and/or social partners may specify the conditions of access and detailed rules for applying clause 3.1 and limit this entitlement to a certain amount of time per year and/or per case.

VIII. Final Provisions

1855.

(1) Member States may apply or introduce more favourable provisions than those set out in this agreement.
(2) Implementation of the provisions of this agreement shall not constitute valid grounds for reducing the general level of protection afforded to workers in the field covered by this agreement. This shall not prejudice the right of Member States and/or social partners to develop different legislative, regulatory or contractual provisions, in the light of changing circumstances (including the introduction of non-transferability), as long as the minimum requirements provided for in the present agreement are complied with.
(3) This agreement shall not prejudice the right of social partners to conclude, at the appropriate level including European level, agreements adapting and/or complementing the provisions of this agreement in order to take into account particular circumstances.
(4) Member States shall adopt the laws, regulations and administrative provisions necessary to comply with the Council decision within a period of two years from its adoption or shall ensure that social partners introduce the necessary measures by way of agreement by the end of this period. Member States may,

Part I, Ch. 8, Working Time and Leave

if necessary to take account of particular difficulties or implementation by collective agreements, have up to a maximum of one additional year to comply with this decision.
(5) The prevention and settlement of disputes and grievances arising from the application of this agreement shall be dealt with in accordance with national law, collective agreements and/or practice.
(6) Without prejudice to the respective role of the Commission, national courts and the European Court of Justice, any matter relating to the interpretation of this agreement at European level should, in the first instance, be referred by the Commission to the signatory parties who will give an opinion.
(7) The signatory parties shall review the application of this agreement five years after the date of the Council decision if requested by one of the parties to this agreement.[733],[734]

---

733. O.J. L 010/24, 16 January 1998.
734. Sonia McKay, 'Social partner revision to parental leave directive', www.eurofound. Eiro (2009).

Chapter 9. Safety and Health

§1. FIRST MEASURES

I. Euratom

1856. Initially, the Treaties did not bestow on the Communities important competences regarding health and safety. It was only the Euratom Treaty that contained some explicit provisions regarding this issue: Chapter III of Title II of the Euratom Treaty is indeed devoted to 'health and safety'. Articles 30 and 31 oblige the Union to lay down basic standards for the protection of the health of workers and the general public against the dangers arising from ionising radiations. The expression 'basic' standards means:

(a) maximum permissible doses compatible with adequate safety;
(b) the maximum permissible levels of exposure and contamination;
(c) the fundamental principles governing the health surveillance of workers (Article 30).

Each Member State had to lay down the appropriate provisions to ensure compliance with the basic standards established and were obliged to take the necessary measures with regard to teaching, education and vocational training (Article 33).[735]

II. EC: Transport

1857. The Commission was obliged, in order to justify action regarding safety matters in the EC, to give a rather extensive interpretation to the general competence conferred on the Union by Article 91 TFEU regarding transport, namely: to lay down 'any appropriate measures'. On the basis of this (very implicit) competence, quite a number of important regulations and directives were adopted, of which we retain:

– Regulation (EC) No. 561/2006 of the European Parliament and of the Council of 15 March 2006 on the harmonisation of certain social legislation relating to road transport and amending Council Regulations (EEC) No. 3821/85 and (EC) No. 2135/98 and repealing Council Regulation (EEC) No. 3820/85.[736]
– Council Regulation (EEC) No. 3821/85 of 20 December 1985 on recording equipment in road transport.[737]

---

735. See Directive No. 80/836 of 15 July 1980 amending the directives laying down the basic safety standards for the health protection of the general public and workers against the dangers of ionising radiation (O.J. L 246, 17 December 1980, amended by Directive No. 84/467, O.J. L 265, 5 October 1984). Council Directive 2003/122 Euratom of 22 December 2003 on the control of high-activity sealed radioactive sources and orphan sources, O.J., 31 December 2003, L 346.
736. O.J., 11 April 2006, L 102.
737. O.J., 31 December 1985, L 370.

Part I, Ch. 9, Safety and Health   1858–1861

III. Other Actions

1858. Notwithstanding the fact that Union institutions had only limited competence in the area of health and safety, quite a number of important initiatives were taken in the framework of Article 122 TFEU regarding the approximation of laws. In its resolution of 21 January 1974 concerning a social action programme, the Council confirmed the necessity to establish an action programme for workers aimed at the harmonisation of their living and working conditions with particular reference to improvement in safety and health conditions at work. It was pointed out that protective measures differed from country to country and that those national measures which have a direct influence on the functioning of the common market had to be harmonised and improved upon in view of a harmonious economic and social development in the Union.

§2. 1987: THE SINGLE EUROPEAN ACT AND ARTICLE 153 TFEU

1859. The Single Act of 1986 introduced Article 153 TFEU and thus clearly affirmed the competence of the Union in relation to health and safety for workers.

1860. This competence is now retained in Article 153 TFEU, according to which the Union shall support and complement the activities of the Member States in the field of the working environment to protect workers' health and safety (1). The Council may adopt, with qualified majority, directives providing for minimum requirements. Such directives should avoid imposing administrative, financial and legal constraints in a way which would hold back the creation and development of small and medium-sized enterprises (2). Finally, the provisions adopted pursuant to Article 153(4) will not prevent any Member State from maintaining or introducing more stringent measures for the protection of working conditions compatible with the Treaty. These are thus far the basic legal provisions.

1861. It follows from the drafting and wording of Article 153 that this text is the result of difficult and complex negotiations, which will undoubtedly lead to a number of interpretative difficulties, even more so as the directives involved can be adopted by a qualified majority in the Council and consequently no State enjoys a right of veto, as is the case concerning 'the rights and interests' of employed persons (Article 114(2) TFEU). A great deal must thus be said in order to start to clarify this text. First, we must point out that health and safety is a shared responsibility: both the Member States and the Union are competent for the improvement of health and safety. Secondly, the Union institutions lay down minimum requirements, upon which the Member States can improve, not derogate to the detriment of the workers. These requirements will gradually be implemented over a certain period of time. Furthermore, one should avoid imposing administrative, financial and legal constraints that would hinder the development of small and mediumsized enterprises. Thus, there should be no unnecessary 'red tape'. Whether this last requirement is legally enforceable remains to be seen. We are here, once again, confronted with a more programmatic policy obligation than with a legally enforceable text of the Treaty.

1862. The interpretation difficulties, in which the Court will obviously play a decisive role, relate especially to the words in paragraph 1 of Article 153, namely: 'the working environment', 'health and safety of workers'.

1863. The Court has had an occasion to do so in the *UK v. Council of the European Union*,[738] in which the UK tried to obtain the annulment of the directive on the organisation of working time (1993). The UK contended that the directive was illegal, because it was based on Article 153 of the Treaty, which allowed for qualified majority voting. Article 153, according to the UK, has to be strictly interpreted and could thus not constitute an appropriate legal basis for a directive on working time. That directive should have been based on articles of the Treaty, like 115 or 352/353, which, however, require unanimity in the Council of Ministers.

The Court of Justice, however, ruled in favour of a broad interpretation. It stated:

> Article 153 confers upon the Union internal legislative competence in the area of social policy. The existence of other provisions in the Treaty does not have the effect of restricting the scope of Article 153. Appearing as it does in the Title of the Treaty which deals with 'Social Policy', Article 153 relates only to measures concerning the protection of the health and safety of workers. It therefore constitutes a more specific rule than Articles 114 and 115. That interpretation is confirmed by the actual wording of Article 114 itself, which states that its provisions are to apply save where otherwise provided in this Treaty. The applicant's argument cannot therefore be accepted.
>
> There is nothing in the wording of Article 153 to indicate that the concepts of 'working environment', 'safety' and 'health' as used in that provision should, in the absence of other indications, be interpreted restrictively, and not as embracing all factors, physical or otherwise, capable of affecting the health and safety of the worker in his working environment, including in particular certain aspects of the organisation of working time. On the contrary, the words 'especially in the working environment' militate in favour of a broad interpretation of the powers which Article 153 confers upon the Council for the protection of the health and safety of workers. Moreover, such an interpretation of the words 'safety' and 'health' derives support in particular from the preamble to the Constitution of the World Health Organisation to which all the Member States belong. Health is there defined as a state of complete physical, mental and social well-being that does not consist only in the absence of illness or infirmity.
>
> In conferring on the Council power to lay down minimum requirements, Article 153 does not prejudge the extent of the action which that institution may consider necessary in order to carry out the task which the provision in question expressly assigns to it – namely, to work in favour of improved conditions, as regards the health and safety of workers, while maintaining the

---

738. C.O.J., 12 November 1996, Case C-84/94, ECR, 1996, 5755.

Part I, Ch. 9, Safety and Health 1864–1864

improvements made. The significance of the expression 'minimum requirements' in Article 153 is simply, as indeed Article 153(2) confirms, that the provision authorises Member States to adopt more stringent measures than those which form the subject-matter of Union action.

Furthermore, there is no support in the wording of Article 153 for the argument that Union action should be restricted to specific measures applicable to given groups of workers in particular situations, whilst measures for wider purposes should be adopted on the basis of Article 115 of the Treaty. Article 153 refers to 'workers' generally and states that the objective which it pursues is to be achieved by the harmonisation of 'conditions' in general existing in the area of the health and safety of those workers.

In addition, the delimitation of the respective fields of application of Articles 114 and 115, on the one hand, and Article 153, on the other, rests not upon a distinction between the possibility of adopting general measures in the former case and particular measures in the latter, but upon the principal aim of the measure envisaged.

It follows that, where the principal aim of the measure in question is the protection of the health and safety of workers, Article 153 must be used, albeit such a measure may have ancillary effects on the establishment and functioning of the internal market.

1864. In his opinion the Advocate-General found confirmation of the view favouring a broad interpretation in the proposal made by Denmark at the Inter-Governmental Conference on the Single Act. According to the Advocate General:

> the concept of 'working environment' in Danish law is a very broad one, covering the performance of work and conditions at the workplace, as well as technical equipment and the substances and materials used. Accordingly, the relevant Danish legislation is not limited to classic measures relating to safety and health at work in the strict sense, but also includes measures concerning working hours, psychological factors, the way work is performed, training in hygiene and safety, and the protection of young workers and worker representation with regard to security against dismissal or any other attempt to undermine their working conditions. The concept of 'working environment' is not immutable, but reflects the social and technical evolution of society ...
>
> Ultimately, the only limits on the definition of the concept of 'working environment' which I have proposed are to be found in the term *workers*, which it underlies. That rules out the possibility of using Article 153 as a basis for a measure whose subject-matter is the safety and health of the population *in general*, perhaps by reference to a risk which is not peculiar to workers.
>
> In my view, the terms 'safety and health' should in their turn be given a broad interpretation, having regard to that conception of the working environment.
>
> ... the origin of Article 153 militates against a strict interpretation of the terms 'safety and health'. It is far removed from an approach confined to the protection of workers against the influence of physical or chemical factors alone. Secondly, it seems to me that a restrictive approach would run counter

to the trend in our society. The Council and the interveners have referred in that regard, very pertinently, to the principle adopted by the World Health Organisation – to which, I would note in passing, all the Member States of the European Union belong – to the effect that 'health is a state of complete physical, mental and social well-being and does not consist only in the absence of illness or infirmity'.

… … there is nothing in the wording of Article 153 which suggests that any aspect of the well-being or safety – broadly speaking – of workers should be excluded; on the contrary, that provision expressly refers to 'improvements' and to harmonisation 'while maintaining the improvements made'.

In any event, such a wide interpretation of the concept of health in particular, which is consistent with that advocated by the WHO, has already been accepted by the Union institutions for the adoption of directives on the basis of Article 153. For instance, in Directive 92/85/EEC (concerning pregnant women), the maintenance of income during maternity leave (whether in the form of remuneration or of an 'adequate' allowance) is regarded as indissociable from a pregnant woman's health.

In conclusion, Article 153 gives a broad mandate to the EU to proceed in this area.

I. Health and Safety in the Working Environment

1865. The question remains what the terms employed in Article 153 mean. It is obvious that they need to be employed in their normal significance. Indeed, words mean what they mean. This is our second basic rule. With these two basic rules in mind we propose the following definitions.

1866. The term 'working environment' relates to the place where the work is to be done. This is not only the facilities in the undertaking to which the employee has access. The notion is broader than that. It concerns the undertaking as well as the home, in the case of homework; it also relates to the construction site in the case of a construction worker, to the classroom for the teacher, to mines in the case of a miner, the soccer stadium for a professional soccer player, the racing circuit for the professional cyclist and so on.

1867. The terms 'safety' and 'health' are complementary. Both aim at the promotion of human integrity: the physical and mental status of the employee. The purpose is indeed not only the prevention of damage (stress, work accidents, professional diseases) but also, in a positive way (agreeable, comforting, refreshing), the promotion of health and safety of the employees. Article 153 aims not only at the elimination of the risks that endanger the health and safety of workers, but also at the establishment of those measures which promote them in a positive way.

Part I, Ch. 9, Safety and Health

1868. Thus the terms health and safety relate to:

- machines and installations, and to the introduction of new technologies, products and materials;
- lighting, temperature, radiation, electricity, gas;
- the situation at the workplace, the construction site;
- the organisation of work and the work rhythm;
- transport to and from the enterprise and within the undertaking;
- the organisation of catering and the cafeteria;
- the use of alcohol and drugs, as well as smoking;
- sport and leisure activities.

This enumeration is certainly not exhaustive, but exemplary. In any case it indicates that, notwithstanding a restrictive interpretation, which we defend – for legal, not political reasons – we are dealing with an important and wide ranging issue.

1869. To this we should add that Article 153, to our mind, also concerns the policy organisations relating to health and safety in the undertaking. As such, this included the eventual organisation, mission and working of a service for safety in the undertaking, an eventual service for industrial medicine, as well as possible medical, nursing or pharmaceutical services. Under the scope of this organisation, the following can also be added: the information and training of workers regarding the prevention of work accidents and occupational diseases. One must see to it that information on safety instruction is given in a language that the workers can effectively understand. In Belgium, for example, we well remember the catastrophe in Marcinelle, more than 30 years ago, when several dozen Italian workers died because they were not fully familiar with the safety instructions, which were written in French. The drafting of a safety plan, the organisation of a fire-brigade, specific measures of protection for handicapped workers and other measures are also needed.

1870. It is also evident that workers' participation is a concern here. Information to and the consultation of workers, as well as their involvement in decisions relating to policies, are a few points that can be dealt with by Union law on the basis of Article 153. It is equally clear that, when decisions are made at the distant headquarters of, say, a multinational group, the necessary measures should be taken so that local management as well as workers at the subsidiaries receive enough information beforehand so that they are able to exert sufficient influence on the decision-making process. Finally, one must remark that health and safety belong to the nucleus of the unalienable rights of workers. These rights must in principle be equal whatever the size of the enterprise in which these workers are employed. There is no room for deregulation within this subject.

II. Application

1871. The Union seems to use its competence regarding health and safety in a very dynamic way. Pursuant to Article 153 TFEU, a framework Directive of 12 June 1989 has been adopted, as well as more individual directives, with the intention to cover all risks relating to health and safety at work, concerning *inter alia*: the workplace, work equipment, personal protective equipment, work with visual display units, the handling of heavy loads involving risks of back injury, temporary or mobile work sites, fisheries and agriculture (Article 16(1) of the framework Directive), prohibition of certain agents and activities, the improvement of health and safety at work of workers with a fixed duration or temporary employment relationship, and improved medical treatment on board vessels.

A. *The Framework Directive of 12 June 1989*

1872. This framework Directive No. 89/391 concerns the introduction of measures to encourage improvements in the safety and health of workers at work.[739] It embraces general principles concerning the prevention of occupational risks, the protection of safety and health, the elimination of risk and accident factors, information, consultation, balanced participation and training of workers and their representatives, as well as general guidelines for the implementation of said principles (Article 1(2)).

1. Scope and Definitions

1873. The directive applies to all sectors of activity, both public and private (industrial, agriculture, commercial, administrative, service, educational, cultural, leisure, etc.), with the exception of certain specific activities in the civil protection services, such as the armed forces and the police. In any event, the safety and health of workers must be ensured as far as possible in the light of the objectives of the directive.

1874. For the purposes of the directive, the following terms have the following meanings:

(a) worker: any person employed by an employer, including trainees and apprentices, but excluding domestic servants;
(b) employer: any natural or legal person who has an employment relationship with the worker and who has responsibility for the undertaking and/or establishment;

---

739. O.J. L 183, 29 June 1989. Amended by Regulation (EC) No 1882/2003 of 29 September 2003, L 284 1 31.10.2003; Directive 2007/30/EC of the Council of 20 June 2007, L 165 21 27.6.2007; Regulation (EC) No 1137/2008 of of 22 October 2008, L 311 1 21.11.2008.

Part I, Ch. 9, Safety and Health

(c) workers' representative with specific responsibility for the safety and health of workers: any person elected, chosen or designated in accordance with national laws and/or practices to represent workers where problems arise relating to the safety and health protection of workers at work;
(d) prevention: all the steps or measures taken or planned at all stages of work in the undertaking to reduce occupational risks (Article 3).

2. Employer's Obligations

1875. The employer has the duty to ensure the safety and the health of workers in every aspect related to the work. Member States can exclude or limit the employer's responsibility for reasons of *force majeure* (Article 5(1) and (4)).

The employer must take the necessary measures, including the prevention of occupational risks and the provision of information and training (Article 6(1)). The employer of course carries the full financial burden: measures related to safety, hygiene and health at work may in no circumstances involve the workers in the financial cost (Article 6(5)).

The employer must implement the measures on the basis of the following general principles of prevention:

(a) avoid risks;
(b) evaluate the risks that cannot be avoided;
(c) combat the risks at source;
(d) adapt the work to the individual, especially as regards the design of workplaces, the choice of work equipment and the choice of working and production methods, with a view, in particular, to alleviating monotonous work and work at a predetermined work-rate and to reducing their effect on health;
(e) adapt to technical progress;
(f) replace the dangerous by the non-dangerous or the less dangerous;
(g) develop a coherent overall prevention policy to cover technology, the organisation of work, working conditions, social relationships and the influence of factors relating to the working environment;
(h) give collective protective measures priority over individual protective measures;
(i) give appropriate instructions to the workers (Article 6(2)).

1876. The employer is furthermore obliged, taking into account the nature of the activities of the enterprise and/or establishment, to:

(a) evaluate the risks to the safety and health of workers, *inter alia* in the choice of work equipment, the chemical substances or preparations used, and the fitting-out of workplaces;
(b) where he entrusts tasks to a worker, take into consideration the worker's capabilities as regards health and safety;

(c) ensure that the planning and introduction of new technologies are the subject of consultation with the workers and/or their representatives, as regards the consequences and the choice of equipment, the working conditions and the working environment for the safety and the health of workers;
(d) take appropriate steps to ensure that only workers who have received adequate instructions have access to areas where there is serious and specific danger (Article 6(3)).

Where several employers share a workplace, the employers shall cooperate in implementing safety and health provisions (Article 6(4)).

The employer designates one or more qualified workers to carry out activities related to the protection and prevention of occupational risks; eventually the employer enlists competent external services or persons (Article 7). Measures must be taken regarding first aid, fire fighting and evacuation of workers, etc. (Article 8).

3. Information, Consultation and Participation of Workers

1877. Workers should receive all the necessary information concerning the safety and health risks, and the protective and preventive measures and activities in respect of both the undertaking and/or establishment in general and each type of workstation and/or job. The employees' representatives must have access, in order to carry out their functions, to the risk assessment and protective measures and the list and reports which have been established to that end, etc. (Article 10). *Consultation* and *participation* are provided for in Article 11. This presupposes:

– the consultation of workers;
– the rights of workers and/or their representative to make proposals;
– balanced participation in accordance with national laws or practices. This means that reference is made, regarding workers' participation, to national law and practice and that there are no Community rules relating to that matter.

Workers' representatives may not be placed at a disadvantage because of their activities. They should enjoy adequate time off work, without loss of pay, and provided with the necessary means to exercise their functions. When they have grievances, workers and their representatives are entitled to appeal to the responsible authorities; representatives must be given the opportunity to submit observations during inspection visits by the competent authority (Article 11).

4. Miscellaneous

1878. The framework directive finally contains stipulations relating to the adequate safety and health training of workers; worker's obligations (namely, to take care as far as possible of his own safety and health and that of other persons) as well as health surveillance: each worker, if he so wishes, should receive health surveillance at regular intervals (Articles 12–14).

Part I, Ch. 9, Safety and Health

B. The Individual Directives

1879. Pursuant to the framework directive, different individual directives were adopted.

In these different directives we find stipulations concerning the information, training, consultation and participation of workers, whereby reference is made to the relevant rules in the framework directive.

§3. FRAMEWORK AGREEMENT ON WORK-RELATED STRESS, 8 OCTOBER 2004

1880. 8 October 2004, the social partners signed a framework agreement on work-related stress establishing a framework within which employers and employee representatives can work together to prevent, identify and combat stress at work. The signatories were: for trade unions, the European Trade Union Confederation (ETUC) and the Council of European Professional and Managerial Staff (EUROCADRES)/European Confederation of Executives and Managerial Staff (CEC) liaison committee; and for employers the Union of Industrial and Employers' Confederations of Europe (UNICE), the European Association of Craft, Small and Medium-Sized Enterprises (UEAPME) and the European Centre of Enterprises with Public Participation and of Enterprises of General Economic Interest (CEEP).[740]

I. Aim

1881. The framework agreement notes that stress can potentially affect any workplace and any worker, regardless of the size of the company, field of activity or form of employment contract or relationship. If stress at work is tackled, efficiency and occupational health and safety can be improved, resulting in 'economic and social benefits for companies, workers and society as a whole'.

The aim of the accord is to increase awareness and understanding of work-related stress amongst employers, workers and their representatives and draw their attention to signals that could indicate that workers are suffering from stress. The agreement does not seek to attach blame, but aims to provide a framework to enable both employers and workers to identify, prevent and manage stress at work. The accord does not cover violence, harassment and post-traumatic stress, as these issues will be dealt with in separate negotiations.

II. Description of Work-related Stress

1882. The agreement defines work-related stress as 'a state which is accompanied by physical, psychological or social complaints or dysfunctions and which

---

740. Andrea Broughton, IRS, 'Social partners sign work-related stress agreement', <www.eiro.eurofound.ie>, 2004.

results from individuals feeling unable to bridge a gap with the requirements or expectations placed on them'. It can be caused by factors such as work content, work organisation, work environment and poor communication. The agreement states that individuals have varying tolerance levels for stress and may react differently at different times of their lives – for some, short-term exposure to pressure can be a positive thing. The social partners emphasise that stress is not a disease, but that prolonged exposure to it may reduce effectiveness and cause ill health.

III. Identifying Problems of Work-related Stress

1883. The agreement gives a non-exhaustive list of potential stress indicators, including high absence from work, high staff turnover, frequent interpersonal conflicts or complaints by workers. A number of factors should be analysed during the identification of stress. These include:

- work organisation, including working time arrangements, degree of autonomy, the match between a worker's skills and the requirements of their job, and workload;
- working conditions and environment, including exposure to abusive behaviour, noise, heat and dangerous substances;
- communication issues, such as whether there is uncertainty about what is expected from someone at work, a worker's employment prospects, or details of forthcoming changes; and
- subjective factors, such as emotional and social pressures, feelings of being unable to cope and perceived lack of support.

Once work-related stress has been identified, the employer must take action to prevent, eliminate or reduce it, with the participation and collaboration of workers and/ or their representatives.

IV. Responsibilities of Employers and Workers

1884. The agreement states that employers have an obligation under the 1989 framework health and safety Directive (89/391/EEC) to protect the occupational health and safety of their workers, and that this extends to stress at work if this entails a risk to health and safety. Workers have a general duty to comply with measures put into place by employers to protect their health and safety at work.

V. Preventing, Eliminating or Reducing Work-related Stress

1885. The agreement sets out a range of measures that employers could use to tackle the issue of work-related stress, either individual or collective, or both. Employers may want to use specific targeted measures, or they may want to put into place an integrated stress policy containing both preventative and responsive measures. It is suggested that, where necessary, external expertise should be called upon, in accordance with EU and national legislation, collective agreements and practices. The text sets out examples of measures to combat stress:

- management and communication measures, including clarification of company objectives and the role of individual workers, ensuring adequate management support for individuals and teams, matching responsibility and control over work, improving work organisation and processes and enhancing working conditions and the working environment;
- training managers and workers to raise awareness and understanding of stress, its possible causes and how to deal with it, or how to adapt to change; and
- the provision of information and consultation of workers and their representatives, in accordance with the range of EU Directives, national legislation, collective agreements and practices on this issue.

VI. Implementation and Follow-up

1886. Article 155 TFEU gives the signatory parties to an EU-level agreement two implementation options: in accordance with the procedures and practices specific to management and labour in individual countries; or by requesting a Council of Ministers decision. The signatory parties to the stress agreement want it to be implemented in accordance with procedures and practices in individual countries (the same route they chose for their 2002 agreement on telework, rather than by Council decision and give a deadline of three years for implementation (8 October 2007).

The member organisations of the signatory parties will be obliged to report to the EU-level Social Dialogue Committee on the implementation of the accord. The Social Dialogue Committee will, during the three years that follow the signature of the agreement, prepare an annual table summarising its implementation and prepare a full report during the fourth year following signature.

Any questions on the content of the agreement can be referred jointly or separately by member organisations to the signatory parties, which will reply either jointly or separately. Unnecessary burdens on small and medium-sized enterprises should be avoided when implementing the agreement. The accord also states that its implementation does not constitute valid grounds to reduce the general level of protection afforded to workers in the areas covered by the agreement.

Any time after five years from signature, the signatory parties will, if one of them requests this, evaluate and review the agreement. The accord does not prejudice the right of the social partners to conclude, at the appropriate level, agreements adapting or complementing this agreement.

1887. The social partners' cross-sector agreement on stress at work, initiated in 2004 at EU level, has had a positive effect, a report by the European Commission[741] of 24 February 2011 has shown.[742] Although the implementation of the agreement has been uneven across the EU, it has led to new policy developments in 12 Member States.

The agreement has been implemented in EU Member States by several means, including national collective agreements, agreements on recommendations, guidance, and the development of practical tools or surveys.

1888. The report shows how the agreement was implemented in different Member States.

- A bipartite or tripartite social dialogue on work-related stress was held in all countries.
- Social dialogue and policy development was triggered or accelerated in 11 Member States (Czech Republic, Cyprus, France, Italy, Latvia, Luxembourg, Poland, Portugal, Romania, Slovakia and Slovenia) and in Norway, where work-related stress had mostly been an issue for experts in the field until the framework agreement was created.
- Practical guidance on how to deal with work-related stress was disseminated in many Member States. The agreement boosted efforts to raise awareness and agree on guidance, even in countries where work-related stress was already accepted as a problem.
- The number of countries with a legal framework that explicitly addresses psychosocial risks and/or stress has now risen to 14, after seven Member States (Belgium, Hungary, Italy, Latvia, Lithuania, Portugal and Slovakia) amended their laws.
- Five countries, Denmark, France, Greece, Italy and Romania, have implemented the agreement with binding national collective agreements.

A set of principles and rules is now enshrined in most Member States, either through legislation or through binding collective agreements, and in others the social partners have concluded voluntary agreements, or joint guidelines with a substantial joint effort to promote awareness-raising and follow-up.

1889. Nevertheless, the Commission states that the implementation of the agreement is uneven across the EU and that there are some shortcomings. For example, the social partners in Cyprus, Malta, Poland and Slovenia have not reported any follow-up to their general declarations about the implementation of the agreement. In 12 Member States – Bulgaria, Estonia, France, Greece, Hungary, Italy, Lithuania, Malta, Poland, Romania, Slovakia and Slovenia – the social partners do not seem to have fully used the potential of the agreement for improving awareness and understanding of work-related stress or the proposed solutions. It also found that, in

---

741. Commission Staff Working Paper, *Report on the implementation of the European social partners' Framework Agreement on Work-related Stress*, SEC(2011) 241 final, Brussels, 24 February 2011.
742. Andrea Broughton, 'Success of stress agreement is "uneven"', EIROnline, 19 April 2011.

some Member States, not all provisions of the agreement have been implemented, and highlights the fact that the social partners in Bulgaria, Estonia, Greece, Italy, Lithuania, and Malta have not reported on the implementation of the agreement at all.

1890. The report sets out the main challenges arising from implementing this agreement. These include:

– implementation difficulties in the newer EU Member States, where the issue goes beyond the traditional competencies of the social partners;
– low trade union density, which can make implementation and coverage difficult;
– a lack of authority of EU-affiliated national bodies (which are often themselves not involved in bargaining) over the bargaining activities of their sectoral and organisational members;
– challenges related to the topic of work-related stress, including a definition of stress and the interaction of work-related and non-work-related stress;
– the sensitivity of the topic and a lack of public awareness;
– the importance of joint action between the social partners;
– the important role of the public authorities in areas such as enforcing legal obligations and advising and guiding companies.

Lessons learnt included the fact that the social partners in many countries were able to build partly on the experience of implementing the social partners' 2002 telework agreement. It notes that, with few exceptions, the implementation instruments for work-related stress and telework are similar, despite the different nature of the agreements. The agreement has been taken as a starting point for a related social dialogue in five sectors at EU level: education, central government administration, private security, construction and electricity.

The Commission believes that there is room for improvement, both at national and EU level, in areas such as extending protection, and developing adequate responses to the challenge of work-related stress. It concludes that implementation of the agreement has not yet ensured a minimum degree of effective protection for workers from work-related stress throughout the EU and therefore all stakeholders need to consider further initiatives to ensure that this goal is achieved[743].

§4. FRAMEWORK AGREEMENT ON HARASSMENT AND VIOLENCE AT WORK (2007)

1891. On 26 April 2007, a new Framework agreement on harassment and violence at work was signed by the social partners: BUSINESSEUROPE, CEEP, UEAPME and the ETUC. Negotiations on the agreement began in the wake of an official European Commission consultation of the social partners in January 2005, as required by the EC Treaty prior to presenting social legislation.[744] It was the task

---

743. *Ibid.*
744. Sonia McKay, 'Social partner sign agreement to combat harassment and violence at work', eurof.

of the national social partners in all EU Member States to adopt the agreement within a three-year period, according to their own procedures and practices.

The social partners unequivocally condemn harassment and violence in all their forms' and recognise that harassment and violence can potentially affect any workplace and any worker, 'even if in practice some groups and sectors can be more at risk.'

The objective is to increase awareness and understanding on the issues of harassment and violence at work, and to provide employers and employees with an action-oriented framework to identify and manage problems of this kind. The fundamental objective of the agreement is to prevent, identify and manage problems related to harassment and violence at the workplace.

I. Aims

1892. Under the terms of the agreement, the social partners are required to ensure the following objectives:

– enterprises should have a clear statement outlining that harassment and violence at the workplace will not be tolerated and specifying the procedure to be followed if problems arise;
– responsibility for determining, reviewing and monitoring the appropriate measures rests with the employer, in consultation with workers and/or their representatives;
– provisions are put in place to deal with cases of violence by third parties, where appropriate.

II. Content

1893. The agreement acknowledges that harassment and violence can take many different forms, such as:

– physical, psychological and/or sexual harassment;
– one-off incidents or more systematic patterns of behaviour;
– among colleagues, between superiors and subordinates or even by third parties such as clients, customers, patients or students;
– a range of actions, from minor cases of disrespect to more serious acts of harassment or violence, including criminal offences.

1894. Furthermore, the agreement suggests that suitable procedures should be put in place which include both informal and formal stages to be followed in dealing with cases of harassment and violence. Such procedures should provide for the following measures:

– proceeding in private to protect the dignity of all parties involved;
– limiting information to the parties to the proceedings only;

- ensuring that complaints are investigated without undue delay;
- guaranteeing all parties the right to an impartial hearing and fair treatment;
- confirming that complaints are backed up by detailed information;
- making it clear that false accusations will not be tolerated;
- offering external assistance if necessary.

III. Guidelines for Prevention of Third Party Violence and Harassment at Work (2010)[745]

1895. The European social partners from various sectors adopted guidelines to prevent third-party violence and harassment at work on 30 September 2010. The guidelines encourage employers to establish a clear framework for the prevention and management of violence by third parties in the context of the employment relationship. The social partners have jointly requested the European Commission to support a series of workshops over the next year aimed at disseminating the guidelines.

1896. The social partner organisations involved are: the Council of European Municipalities and Regions (CEMR), the Confederation of European Security Services (CoESS), the European Federation of Education Employers (EFEE), the European Federation of Public Service Unions (EPSU), the European Trade Union Committee for Education (ETUCE), EuroCommerce representing wholesale, retail and international trade in the EU, the Union Network International-Europa (UNI-Europa), and the European Hospital and Healthcare Employers' Association (HOSPEEM). These organisations represent the regional government, healthcare, commerce, private security and education sectors. The guidelines aim to ensure that every workplace has a policy to deal with third-party violence against staff, for example from the general public or from customers.

1897. The guidelines are based on best practices identified in the sectors represented, They contain a list of the many forms that third-party violence can take, from 'disrespect, to more serious threats and physical assault' to 'criminal offences' or even 'cyber-bullying/cyber-harassment'. Harassment and violence at work can be inflicted by clients, customers, patients, service users, pupils or parents, members of the public, or service providers. The guidelines state that violence not only 'undermines an individual's health and dignity' but also has 'real economic impact in terms of absences from the workplace, morale and staff turnover'.

1898. Third-party violence was merely referred to in the 2007 cross-sectoral framework agreement, and so it was felt that third-party violence deserves a special approach, as outlined in these guidelines, because it is 'sufficiently distinct from the question of violence and harassment (among colleagues) in the workplace' and 'sufficiently significant in terms of its impact on the health and safety of workers and

---

745. Frédéric Turlan, Guidelines for prevention of third party violence and harassment at work, EIROline,15 November, 2010.

its economic impact'. The guidelines aim to support actions by employers, employees and their representatives to prevent, reduce and mitigate third-party violence. Employers are encouraged to establish a 'clear policy framework for the prevention and management' of these phenomena. The guidelines also state that: 'The most successful initiatives involve both social partners from the very beginning and involve a "holistic"approach, covering all aspects from awareness-raising over prevention and training to methods of reporting, support for victims and evaluation and ongoing improvement.'

1899. The social partners propose, on this basis, a policy framework for employers that includes a range of elements, such as:

– information, such as a definition of third-party violence or a warning to third parties that harassment and violence against employees will not be tolerated;
– a policy based on risk assessment which can take into account the various occupations, locations and working practices of employees;
– appropriate training for management and employees on, among other things, 'techniques to avoid or manage conflicts';
– a clear policy on the support to be provided to employees;
– the establishment of procedures to monitor and investigate allegations of harassment and/or violence from third parties or to record facts and figures for monitoring and ensure follow-up of the policies put in place.

§5. FRAMEWORK AGREEMENT ON PREVENTION FROM SHARP INJURIES IN THE HOSPITAL AND HEALTHCARE SECTOR (17 JULY 2009)[746]

1900. This Framework Agreement was concluded between HOSPEEM (European Hospital and Healthcare Employers' Association) and EPSU (European Public Services Union), the recognized European Social partners in the hospital and healthcare sector, have agreed the following:

1901. Preamble:

(1) Health and safety at work is an issue, which should be important to everyone in the hospital and healthcare sector. Taking action to prevent and protect against unnecessary injuries if properly carried out, will have a positive effect on resources;
(2) Health and safety of workers is paramount and is closely linked to the health of patients. This underpins the quality of care;
(3) The process of policy making and implementation in relation to medical sharps should be the result of social dialogue.

---

746. Implemented by Directive 2010/32/EU of 10 May 2010 implementing the Framework Agreement on prevention from sharp injuries in the hospital and healthcare sector concluded by HOSPEEM and EPSU, O.J., 1 June 2010.

Part I, Ch. 9, Safety and Health

I. Purpose

1902. The purpose of this framework agreement is:

- To achieve the safest possible working environment;
- To prevent workers' injuries caused by all medical sharps (including needlesticks);
- To protect workers at risk;
- To set up an integrated approach establishing policies in risk assessment, risk prevention, training, information, awareness raising and monitoring;
- To put in place response and follow-up procedures.

II. Scope

1903. This agreement applies to all workers in the hospital and healthcare sector, and all who are under the managerial authority and supervision of the employers. Employers should deploy efforts to ensure that subcontractors follow the provisions laid down in this agreement.

III. Definitions

1904. Within the meaning of this agreement:

(1) Workers: any persons employed by an employer including trainees and apprentices in the hospital and healthcare sector-directly related services and activities. Workers who are employed by temporary employment business within the meaning of Council Directive 91/383/EC supplementing the measures to encourage improvements in the safety and health at work of workers with fixed-duration employment relationship or a temporary employment relationship6 fall within the scope of the agreement.
(2) Workplaces covered: healthcare organisations/services in public and private sectors, and every other place where health services/activities are undertaken and delivered, under the managerial authority and supervision of the employer.
(3) Employers: natural/legal persons/organisations having an employment relationship with workers. They are responsible for managing, organising and providing healthcare and directly related services/activities delivered by workers.
(4) Sharps: objects or instruments necessary for the exercise of specific healthcare activities, which are able to cut, prick, cause injury and/or infection. Sharps are considered as work equipment within the meaning of Directive 89/655/ EEC on work equipment.
(5) Hierarchy of measures: is defined in order of effectiveness to avoid, eliminate and reduce risks as defined in article 6 of Directive 89/391/EEC and articles 3, 5 and 6 of Directive 2000/54/EC.
(6) Specific preventative measures: measures taken to prevent injury and/or transmission of infection in the provision of hospital and healthcare directly related

services and activities, including the use of the safest equipment needed, based on the risk assessment and safe methods of handling the disposal of medical sharps.
(7) Workers' representatives: any person elected, chosen or designated in accordance with national law and/or practice to represent workers.
(8) Worker's health and safety representatives are defined in accordance with Article 3(c) of Directive 89/391/EEC as any person elected, chosen or designated in accordance with national law and/or practices to represent workers where problems arise relating to the safety and health protection of workers at work.
(9) Subcontractor: any person who takes action in hospital and healthcare directly related services and activities within the framework of working contractual relations established with the employer.

IV. Principles

1905.

(1) A well trained, adequately resourced and secure health service workforce is essential to prevent the risk of injuries and infections from medical sharps. Exposure prevention is the key strategy for eliminating and minimizing the risk of occupationally acquired injuries or infections.
(2) The role of health and safety representatives is key in risk prevention and protection.
(3) The employer has a duty to ensure the safety and health of workers in every aspect related to the work, including psycho-social factors and work organisation.
(4) It shall be the responsibility of each worker to take care – as far as possible – of their own safety and health and that of other persons affected by their actions at work, in accordance with their training and the instructions given by their employer.
(5) The employer shall develop an environment where workers and their representatives are participating in the development of health and safety policies and practices.
(6) The principle of the following specific preventative measures indicated in clauses 5 – 10 of the present agreement means never assuming that there is no risk. The hierarchy of general principles of prevention according to article 6 of Directive 89/391/EEC and articles 3, 5 and 6 of Directive 2000/54/EC is applicable.
(7) Employers and workers' representatives shall work together at the appropriate level to eliminate and prevent risks, protect workers' health and safety, and create a safe working environment, including consultation on the choice and use of safe equipment, identifying how best to carry out training, information and awareness-raising processes.
(8) Action needs to be taken through a process of information and consultation, in accordance with national laws and/or collective agreements.

Part I, Ch. 9, Safety and Health

(9) The effectiveness of awareness-raising measures entails shared obligations of the employers, the workers and their representatives.
(10) In achieving the safest possible workplace a combination of planning, awarenessraising, information, training, prevention and monitoring measures is essential.
(11) Promote a 'no blame' culture. Incident reporting procedure should focus on systemic factors rather than individual mistakes. Systematic reporting must be considered as accepted procedure.

V. Risk Assessment

1906.

(1) Risk assessment procedures shall be conducted in compliance with Articles 3 and 6 of Directive 2000/54/EC, and Articles 6 and 9 of Directive /89/391/EEC.
(2) Risk assessment shall include an exposure determination, understanding the importance of a well resourced and organised working environment and shall cover all situations where there is injury, blood or other potentially infectious material.
(3) Risk assessments shall take into account technology, organisation of work, working conditions, level of qualifications, work related psycho-social factors and the influence of factors related to the working environment. This will:
   – identify how exposure could be eliminated;
   – consider possible alternative systems.

VI. Elimination, Prevention and Protection

1907.

(1) Where the results of the risk assessment reveal a risk of injuries with a sharp and/or infection, workers' exposure must be eliminated by taking the following measures, without prejudice to their order:
   – specifying and implementing safe procedures for using and disposing of sharp medical instruments and contaminated waste. These procedures shall be regularly reassessed and shall form an integral part of the measures for the information and training of workers referred in VIII;
   – eliminating the unnecessary use of sharps by implementing changes in practice and on the basis of the results of the risk assessment, providing medical devices incorporating safety-engineered protection mechanisms;
   – the practice of recapping shall be banned with immediate effect.
(2) Having regard to the activity and the risk assessment, the risk of exposure must be reduced to as low a level as necessary in order to protect adequately the safety and health of the workers concerned. The following measures are to be applied in the light of the results of the risk assessment:

- place effective disposal procedures and clearly marked and technically safe containers for the handling of disposable sharps and injection equipment as close as possible to the assessed areas where sharps are being used or to be found;
- prevent the risk of infections by implementing safe systems of work, by:
  (a) developing a coherent overall prevention policy, which covers technology, organisation of work, working conditions, work related psychosocial factors and the influence of factors related to the working environment;
  (b) training;
  (c) conducting health surveillance procedures, in compliance with article 14 of Directive 2000/54/EC;
- use of personal protective equipment.

(3) If the assessment referred to in clause 5 reveals that there is a risk to the safety and health of workers due to their exposure to biological agents for which effective vaccines exist, workers shall be offered vaccination.

(4) Vaccination and, if necessary, revaccination shall be carried out in accordance with national law and/or practice, including the determination of the type of vaccines.
- workers shall be informed of the benefits and drawbacks of both vaccination and non-vaccination;
- vaccination must be offered free of charge to all workers and students delivering healthcare and related activities at the workplace.

VII. Information and Awareness-raising

1908. As sharps are considered as work equipment within the meaning of Directive 89/655/EC, in addition to information and written instructions to be provided to workers specified in article 6 of Directive 89/655/EC, the employer shall take the following appropriate measures:

- to highlight the different risks;
- to give guidance on existing legislation;
- to promote good practices regarding the prevention and recording of incidents/accidents;
- to raise awareness by developing activities and promotional materials in partnership with representative trade unions and/or workers' representatives;
- to provide information on support programmes available.

VIII. Training

1909. In addition to measures established by article 9 of Directive 2000/54/EC, appropriate training shall be made available on policies and procedures associated with sharps injuries, including:

Part I, Ch. 9, Safety and Health

- the correct use of medical devices incorporating sharps protection mechanisms;
- induction for all new and temporary staff;
- the risk associated with blood and body fluid exposures;
- preventive measures including standard precautions, safe systems of work, the correct use and disposal procedures, the importance of immunisation, according to the procedures at the workplace;
- the reporting, response and monitoring procedures and their importance;
- measures to be taken in case of injuries.

Employers must organise and provide training which is mandatory for workers. Employers must release workers who are required to attend training. This training shall be made available on a regular basis taking into account results of monitoring, modernisation and improvements.

IX. Reporting

1910.

(1) This includes the revision of the reporting procedures in place with health and safety representatives and/or appropriate employers/workers representatives. Reporting mechanisms should include local, national and European wide systems.
(2) Workers shall immediately report any accident or incident involving sharps to the employers and/or the person in charge, and/or to the person responsible for safety and health at work.

X. Response and Follow-up

1911. Policies and procedures shall be in place where a sharp injury occurs. All workers must be made aware of these policies and procedures. These should be in accordance with European, national/regional legislation and collective agreements, as appropriate.

In particular the following action shall be taken:

- The employer takes the immediate steps for the care of the injured worker, including the provision of post-exposure prophylaxis and the necessary medical tests where indicated for medical reasons, and appropriate health surveillance in accordance with clause 6 §2,c.
- The employer investigates the causes and circumstances and records the accident/incident, taking – where appropriate – the necessary action. The worker must provide the relevant information at the appropriate time to complete the details of the accident or incident;
- The employer shall, in cases of injury, consider the following steps including counselling of workers where appropriate and guaranteed medical treatment.

Rehabilitation, continued employment and access to compensation shall be in accordance with national and/or sectoral agreements or legislation.

Confidentiality of injury, diagnosis and treatment is paramount and must be respected.

XI. Implementation

1912. This agreement will be without prejudice to existing, future national and Community provisions which are more favourable to workers' protection from medical sharps' injuries.

The signatory parties request the Commission to submit this framework agreement to the Council for a decision in order to make this agreement binding in the member states of the European Union.

If implemented through Council decision, at European level and without prejudice to the respective role of the Commission, national courts and the European Court of Justice, the interpretation of this agreement, could be referred by the Commission to the signatory parties who will give their opinion.

The signatory parties shall review the application of this agreement five years after the date of the Council decision if requested by one of the parties to the agreement.

Chapter 10. Restructuring of Enterprises

1913. During the 1970s, called by some the golden years for European labour law, three directives were adopted which were intended to protect the workers against the functioning of the common market. I remember from the discussions we had in the group of experts on labour law from the different Member States that the reasoning underlying those directives was the following: there is a larger market with an increase in scale to which the undertakings will have to adapt themselves; this means: restructuring, mergers, takeovers, collective dismissals and bankruptcies. Indeed, it was said, the worker should not have to pay the price for the establishment of a common, bigger market; rather the worker should be protected against the social consequences of this restructuring. On the basis of this reasoning, three directives were proposed and, also due to the then political composition of the Council, adopted. These directives relate respectively to collective redundancies (1975), the transfer of undertakings or parts thereof (1977) and the insolvency of the employer (1980). One will notice, when analysing these directives, that the managerial prerogative concerning economic decisions remains intact. There were at some times proposals regarding collective redundancies to prohibit dismissals, in conformity with the then prevalent French legislation, but these proposals were not retained, as will be made clear later. In short, the directives only address the social consequences of restructuring.

§1. COLLECTIVE REDUNDANCIES

1914. Directive No. 75/129 of 17 February 1975 on the approximation of laws of the Member States relating to collective redundancies[747] finds its origin in the *AKZO* case. In 1973 AKZO, a Dutch-German multinational enterprise, was engaged in a process of restructuring and wanted to make some 5,000 workers redundant. As AKZO had a number of subsidiaries in different Member States, it could in a sense compare the costs of dismissal in those countries and choose to dismiss in that country where the cost was the lowest. When this strategy became apparent, there was somewhat of an outrage in some European quarters and a demand for a European rule to make such strategies impossible in the future and to lay down a European-wide minimum floor of protection in the case of collective dismissals. This led to a proviso in the Council Resolution of 21 January 1974 concerning a social action programme and consequently to a directive concerning collective redundancies.

Council Directive No. 92/56 of 24 June 1992 amended the Directive No. 75/129. Several reasons inspired the amendments: other forms of termination of employment contracts on the initiative of the employer should be equated to redundancies, and the provisions of the original directive should be clarified and supplemented as regards the employer's obligations regarding informing and consulting of workers' representatives.

---

747. O.J. L 48, 22 February 1975.

The amended directive explicitly stated that it can be left to the social partners to take the appropriate measures by way of collective bargaining agreement to implement the amendments (Article 2).[748]

Both directives were consolidated for reasons of clarity and rationality by Council Directive 98/59 EC of 20 July 1998 on the approximation of the laws of the Member States relating to collective redundancies.[749]

1915. Directive No. 98/59 is based on Article 115 TFEU which relates to the approximation of laws, regulations or administrative rules of the Member States that directly affect the establishment or the funding of the common market. In the 'whereas' to the directive we can read that:

> it is important that greater protection should be afforded to workers in the event of collective redundancies while taking into account the need for balanced economic and social development within the Community';
>
> 'that despite increasing convergence' (one wonders which convergence?) 'differences are still maintained between the provisions in force in the Member States of the Community concerning the practical arrangements and procedures for such redundancies and the measures designed to alleviate the consequences of redundancy for workers, that these differences can have a direct effect on the functioning of the market.

Consequently, this approximation must be promoted while improvement is being maintained within the meaning of Article 151 TFEU. The provisions of the directive are thus intended to serve to establish a common body of rules applicable in all Member States, whilst leaving it up to the Member States to apply or introduce provisions that are more favourable to workers.[750] The directive provides for the information and consultation of the workers in the case of collective redundancies, as well as for a notification of the competent public authority. At the same time, periods are introduced during which no notice of termination may be given.

I. Definitions and Scope

1916. Article 1 of the directive contains a definition of both 'collective redundancies' and 'workers' representatives'. The directive applies in the case of (1) a dismissal, which is (2) collective. The first requirement thus is that there is an employer who dismisses employees.

The termination by workers of their contract of employment following an announcement by the employer that he is suspending payment of his debts cannot be treated as dismissal by the employer for the purposes of the directive.[751]

---

748. Directive No. 92/56, O.J. L 245, 26 August 1992.
749. O.J. L 225/16, 12 August 1998.
750. C.O.J., 8 June 1982, *Commission v. Italy*, No. 91/81, ECR, 1982, 2455.
751. C.O.J., 12 February 1985, *Metalarbejderforbund and Specialarbejderforbund i Danmark v. H. Nielsen & Son, Maskinfabrik A/S, in liquidation*, No. 284/83, ECR, 1985, 553; C.O.J., 7 September

Part I, Ch. 10, Restructuring of Enterprises 1917–1918

The dismissal must be effected by an employer for one or more reasons not related to the individual workers concerned. The dismissals further need to be collective; this means that, according to the choice of the Member States, the number of redundancies is:

– either, over a period of 30 days:
  (1) at least 10 in establishments normally employing more than 20 and less than 100 workers;
  (2) at least 10 per cent of the number of workers in establishments normally employing at least 100 but less than 300 workers;
  (3) at least 30 in establishments normally employing 300 workers or more;
– or, over a period of 90 days, at least 20, whatever the number of workers normally employed in the establishments in question.

1917. Although the directive primarily deals with collective dismissal of workers it holds that 'for the purpose of calculating the number of redundancies ... termination of an employment contract which applies to the individual workers concerned shall be assimilated to redundancies, provided that there are at least five redundancies' (Article 1(b)).

The directive in principle also applies to collective redundancies where the establishment's activities are terminated as a result of a judicial decision.[752]

1918. The Directive applies to a termination of the activities of an employing establishment as a result of a judicial decision ordering its dissolution and winding up on grounds of insolvency, even though, in the event of such a termination, national legislation provides for the termination of employment contracts with immediate effect.

Until the legal personality of an establishment whose dissolution and winding up have been ordered has ceased to exist, the obligations under Articles 2 and 3 of Directive 98/59 must be fulfilled. The employer's obligations pursuant to those provisions must be carried out by the management of the establishment in question, where it is still in place, even with limited powers of management over that establishment, or by its liquidator, where that establishment's management has been taken over in its entirety by the liquidator[753].

2006, *Georgios Agorastoudis and Others, Ioannis Panou and Others v. Goodyear Hellas AVEE,* Joined Cases C-187/05 to C-190/05, ECR, 2006, 7775.
752. C.O.J., 12 February 1985, *Metalarbejderforbund and Specialarrbejdeforbund Denmark v. H. Nielsen & Son. Maskinfabrik A/S., in liquidance,* No. 284/83, ECR, 1985, 533; C.O.J., 7 September 2006, *Gearguans Agorastoudis and Others, Jominis PAnou and Other v. Godyear Hellas AVEE.* Joined Cases C-187/05 o C-190/05, ECR, 2006, 7775.
753. C.O.J., 3 March 2011, *David Claes (C-235/10)* a.o. v. *Landsbanki Luxembourg SA,* in liquidation, www.curia.eu.

1919. Article 1(1)(a) of the Directive 98/59/EC must be interpreted as precluding national legislation which excludes, even temporarily, a specific category of workers from the calculation of staff numbers set out in that provision.[754]

1920. Article 1(1) of Council Directive 98/59/EC must be interpreted as not precluding national legislation according to which the termination of contracts of employment of a number of workers, whose employer is a natural person, as a result of the death of that employer is not classified as collective redundancy. The Directive does neither preclude national legislation which provides for different compensation depending on whether the workers lost their jobs as a result of the death of the employer or as a result of a collective redundancy[755].

1921. 'The concept of collective redundancies can not be restricted to redundancies for structural, technological or cyclical reasons'[756] and has to comprise the dismissals for any reason not related to the individual workers concerned. The Court reasoned in this case as follows.

> Pursuant to Article 1(1)(a) of the Directive, 'collective redundancies' means dismissals effected by an employer for one or more reasons not related to the individual workers concerned provided that certain conditions concerning numbers and periods of time are satisfied.
>
> The Directive does not give an express definition of 'redundancy'. That concept must, however, be given a uniform interpretation for the purposes of the Directive.
>
> It follows both from the requirements of the uniform application of Community law and the principle of equality that the terms of a provision of Community law which make no express reference to the law of the Member States for the purpose of determining its meaning and scope must normally be given an autonomous and uniform interpretation throughout the Community; that interpretation must take into account the context of the provision and the purpose of the legislation in question.
>
> In this case, Article 1(1)(a) of the Directive, unlike Article 1(1)(b) thereof which expressly provides that 'workers' representatives' means the workers' representatives provided for by the laws or practices of the Member States, does not make any express reference to the law of the Member States so far as the definition of 'redundancy' is concerned.
>
> In addition, it follows from the title of, and from the third, fourth and seventh recitals in the preamble to, the Directive that the objective pursued by the latter is to further the approximation of the laws of the Member States relating to collective redundancies.

---

754. C.O.J., 18 January 2007, *Confédération générale du travail (CGT) and others* v. *Premier ministre*, C-385/05, ECR, 2007, 611.
755. C.O.J., 10 December 2009, *Ovidio Rodríguez Mayor and Others* v. *Herencia yacente de Rafael de las Heras Dávila and Others*, C-323/08, www.curia.eu.
756. C.O.J., 12 October 2004, *Commission* v. *Portuguese Republic*, C-55/02, ECR, 2004, 9387.

Part I, Ch. 10, Restructuring of Enterprises

1922. By harmonising the rules applicable to collective redundancies, the Union legislature intended both to ensure comparable protection for workers' rights in the different Member States and to harmonise the costs which such protective rules entail for Union undertakings.

Accordingly, the concept of 'redundancy', as mentioned in Article 1(1)(a) of the Directive, may not be defined by any reference to the laws of the Member States, but has instead meaning in Union law.

The concept has to be interpreted as including any termination of contract of employment not sought by the worker, and therefore without his consent. It is not necessary that the underlying reasons should reflect the will of the employer.

That interpretation of the concept of 'redundancy' for the purposes of the Directive follows from the aim pursued by the latter and from the background to the provision at issue.

1923. The second recital in the preamble to the Directive makes it clear that that act is designed to strengthen the protection of workers in the case of collective redundancies. According to the third and seventh recitals in the preamble to the Directive, it is chiefly the differences remaining between the provisions in force in the Member States concerning the measures apt to mitigate the consequences of collective redundancies which must form the subject-matter of a harmonisation of laws.

The objectives referred to in the Directive would be attained only in part if the termination of a contract of employment that was not contingent on the will of the employer were to be excluded from the body of rules laid down by the Directive.

As regards the background to the provision at issue, the ninth recital in the preamble to the Directive and the second paragraph of Article 3(1) thereof make it clear that the Directive applies, as a rule, also to collective redundancies caused by termination of the establishment's activities as a result of a judicial decision. In that situation, the termination of contracts of employment is the result of circumstances not willed by the employer.

1924. In accordance with the first paragraph of Article 2(2) of the Directive, the purpose of consulting the workers' representatives is not only to avoid collective redundancies or to reduce the number of workers affected, but also, *inter alia*, to mitigate the consequences of such redundancies by recourse to accompanying social measures aimed, in particular, at aid for redeploying or retraining workers made redundant. It would run counter to the spirit of the Directive to narrow the ambit of that provision by giving a restrictive interpretation of the concept of "redundancy".

Considerations of the same kind hold good so far as the obligations laid down in Article 3 of the Directive to notify the competent public authority are concerned. Those obligations, adapted where appropriate in accordance with the power granted to the Member States by the second paragraph of

> Article 3(1), could quite well be performed by an employer in cases where contracts of employment have to be terminated because of circumstances not contingent on his will. A contrary interpretation would deprive workers of the protection given by that provision and by Article 4 of the Directive.

It follows from all the foregoing considerations that termination of a contract of employment cannot escape the application of the Directive just because it depends on external circumstances not contingent on the employer's will. Articles 2 to 4 of Council Directive 98/59/EC must be construed as meaning that the event constituting redundancy consists in the declaration by an employer of his intention to terminate the contract of employment.[757]

1925. The term employer within the meaning of Article 1(1)(a) of Directive 98/59 also covers employers engaged in non-profit-making activities. It is clear from the actual wording of Article 1 of the directive that the provision applies to redundancies effected by an employer, without further distinction, so that it applies to all employers. An interpretation to the contrary would not be consistent with the aims of the directive.[758]

1926. The question of the meaning of the notion of establishment arose in proceedings between the company Rockfon A/S and the Specialarbejderforbundet i Danmark[759] (the Danish trade union for semi-skilled workers, hereinafter the 'SID') concerning the dismissal of a number of employees alleged to have been carried out without observance of the consultation and notification procedures laid down by the directive. Rockfon is part of the Rockwool multinational group.

Questions were, first, whether Article 1(1)(a) of the directive precludes two or more undertakings in a group from establishing a joint recruitment and dismissal department so that dismissals in one of the undertakings may take place only with the approval of that department; and, secondly, whether, in such circumstances, the term 'establishment' in Article 1(1)(a) is to be taken to mean all the undertakings using that recruitment and dismissal department, or whether each undertaking in which the employees made redundant normally work must be counted as an 'establishment'.

As regards the first part of the question, the Court stated that:

> it is sufficient to state that the sole purpose of the Directive is the partial harmonisation of collective redundancy procedures and that its aim is not to restrict the freedom of undertakings to organise their activities and arrange their personnel departments in the way which they think best suits their needs.

The term 'establishment' is not defined in the directive. Rockfon maintained that it was not an establishment since it had no management which could independently effect large-scale dismissals.

The Court observed that the term 'establishment' is a term of Community law and cannot be defined by reference to the laws of the Member States. The various language versions of the directive use somewhat different terms to convey the concept

---

757. C.O.J., 27 January 2005, *Irmtraud Junk* v. *Wolfgang Kühnel*, C-188/03, ECR, 2005, 885.
758. C.O.J., 16 October 2003, *Commission* v. *Italian Republic*, C-32/02, ECR, 2003, 12063.
759. C.O.J., 7 December 1995, Case C-449/93, ECR, 1995, 4291.

in question. A comparison of the terms used shows that they have different connotations signifying, according to the version in question, establishment, undertaking, work centre, local unit or place of work.

1927. As was held in *Bouchereau*,[760] the different language versions of a Community text must be given a uniform interpretation and in the case of divergence between the versions the provision in question must therefore be interpreted by reference to the purpose and general scheme of the rules of which it forms part.

The directive was adopted on the basis of Articles 94 and 136 of the Treaty, the latter provision concerning the need for the Member States to promote improved working conditions and an improved standard of living for workers, so as to make possible their harmonisation while the improvement is being maintained. It is apparent from the first recital in its preamble that the directive is indeed intended to afford greater protection to workers in the event of collective redundancies.

Two observations may be made in that respect. First, an interpretation of the term 'establishment', like that proposed by Rockfon, would allow companies belonging to the same group to try to make it more difficult for the directive to apply to them by conferring on a separate decision-making body the power to take decisions concerning redundancies. By this means, they would be able to escape the obligation to follow certain procedures for the protection of workers and large groups of workers could be denied the right to be informed and consulted which they have as a matter of course under the directive. Such an interpretation therefore appears to be incompatible with the aim of the directive.

Secondly, the Court has held that an employment relationship is essentially characterised by the link existing between the employee and the part of the undertaking or business to which he is assigned to carry out his duties.

Therefore the Court concluded:

> the term establishment, appearing in Article (1)(a) of the directive, must be understood as meaning, depending on the circumstances, the unit to which the workers made redundant are assigned to carry out their duties. It is not essential, in order for there to be an establishment, for the unit in question to be endowed with a management which can independently effect collective redundancies.

1928. The Court has interpreted the concept of 'establishment' in Directive 98/59, in particular in Article 1(1)(a), as designating, depending on the circumstances, the unit to which the workers made redundant are assigned to carry out their duties.

> In so doing, the Court has defined the term 'establishment' very broadly, in order to limit as far as possible cases of collective redundancies which are not subject to Directive 98/59 because of the legal definition of that term at national level. However, given the general nature of that definition, it cannot

---

760. C.O.J., 22 October 1977, Case C-30/77, ECR, 1977, 1999.

by itself be decisive for the appraisal of the specific circumstances of the case at issue in the main proceedings.

Thus, an 'establishment', in the context of an undertaking, may consist of a distinct entity, having a certain degree of permanence and stability, which is assigned to perform one or more given tasks and which has a workforce, technical means and a certain organisational structure allowing for the accomplishment of those tasks.

1929. Given that the objective pursued by Directive 98/59 concerns, in particular, the socio-economic effects which collective redundancies may have in a given local context and social environment, the entity in question need not have any legal autonomy, nor need it have economic, financial, administrative or technological autonomy, in order to be regarded as an 'establishment'.

It is, moreover, in this spirit that the Court has held that it is not essential, in order for there to be an 'establishment', for the unit in question to be endowed with a management which can independently effect collective redundancies. Nor must there be a geographical separation from the other units and facilities of the undertaking.[761]

1930. The adoption, within a group of undertakings, of strategic decisions or of changes in activities which compel the employer to contemplate or to plan for collective redundancies gives rise to an obligation on that employer to hold consultations with workers' representatives. Whether the obligation has arisen for the employer to start consultations on the collective redundancies contemplated does not depend on whether the employer is already able to supply to the workers' representatives all the information required in Article 2(3)(b) of Directive 98/59.

In the case of a group of undertakings consisting of a parent company and one or more subsidiaries, the obligation to hold consulations with the workers' representatives falls on the subsidiary which has the status of employer only once that subsidiary, within which collective redundancies may be made, has been identified. The consultation procedure must be concluded by the subsidiary affected by the collective redundancies before that subsidiary, on the direct instructions of its parent company or otherwise, terminates the contracts of employees who are to be affected by those redundancies.[762]

1931. The directive is not applicable to:

(a) collective redundancies effected under contracts of employment concluded for limited periods of time or for specific tasks except where such redundancies take place prior to the date of expiry or the completion of such contracts;

---

761. C.O.J., 15 February 2007, *Athinaiki Chartopoiia AE* v. *L. Panagiotidis and Others*, C-270/05, ECR, 2007, 1499.
762. C.O.J., 10 September 2009, *Akavan Erityisalojen Keskusliitto AEK ry and Others* v. *Fujitsu Siemens Computers Oy*, C-44/08, www.curia.eu.

Part I, Ch. 10, Restructuring of Enterprises

(b) workers employed by public administrative bodies or by establishments governed by public law (or, in Member States where this concept is unknown, by equivalent bodies);
(c) the crews of sea-going vessels.

II. Information and Consultation of Workers' Representatives

1932. Information concerning the collective redundancies must be given beforehand. This means before the decision is taken. The text of Article 2(1) is clear on this point: it concerns an employer who is *contemplating* collective redundancies. The directive explicitly mentions that the employer has to consult the workers' representatives in good time. The directive only applies when the employer projects collective redundancies. Such a project is necessary if the employer contemplates dismissals and wants to notify the competent authority (Article 3(1)).

> 'The directive applies only where the employer has in fact contemplated collective redundancies or has drawn up a plan for collective redundancies. It does not apply in the case where, because of the financial state of the undertaking, the employer ought to have contemplated collective redundancies but did not do so.'[763]

1933. The purpose of the information is to enable the workers' representatives to make constructive proposals. The employer shall at least notify them of: the reasons for the projected redundancies; the number or categories of workers to be made redundant; the number or categories or workers normally employed; the period over which the projected redundancies are to be effected; the criteria proposed for the selection of the workers and the method for calculating any redundancy payment (other than those arising out of national legislation and/or practice). The employer is obliged to forward to the competent authority a copy of the information given to the workers with the exception of the information on the method of calculating redundancy payments (Article 2(3)). The workers' representatives are also entitled to a copy of the information which the employer must forward to the authorities. The workers' representatives may send any comments they may have to the competent authority (Article 3(2)).

1934. The directive holds irrespective of whether the decision regarding collective redundancies is being taken by the employer or by an undertaking controlling the employer (Article 2(4)). In considering alleged breaches of the information and consultation duties account shall not be taken of any defence on the part of the employer that the necessary information has not been provided to him by the undertaking which took the decision leading to collective redundancies. The employer is obliged to consult the workers' representatives with a view to reaching an agreement (Article 2(1)). This is a very strong form of consultation, which is very close to collective bargaining. The consultations must cover ways and means of avoiding

---

763. C.O.J., 7 December 1995, Case C-449/93, ECR, 1995, 4291.

collective redundancies or reducing the number of workers affected, and of mitigating the consequences (Article 2(2)).

The amended Article 2(2) specifies that this concerns accompanying social measures aimed, *inter alia*, at aid for redeploying or retraining workers made redundant.

1935. Workers' representatives are those provided for by the laws or the practices of the Member States. Since the judgment of the Court of Justice of 8 June 1994[764] it is no longer possible that there are no workers' representatives in the case where a Member State would not have an overall system of workers' representation. According to the Court of Justice – condemning the UK – 'employers face a statutory obligation to inform and consult with employees when they are planning collective redundancies, or if they transfer employees from one business to another. This means that even non-unionised companies will have to establish machinery for consultation even if it does not already exist.'

Thus, the European Court of Justice ruled that UK rules on the protection of employees' rights in the event of companies changing hands or when collective redundancies take place breached EC law. The Court said the UK had failed to implement fully binding EC directives. The directives relate, as said, to the safeguarding of employees' rights in the event of the transfer of a business or collective redundancies. Both place a duty on employers to inform and consult representatives of workers affected by a transfer or redundancies.

The UK was taken to court by the Commission for failure to implement these directives properly by not providing for the designation of employees' representatives in firms where the employer refused to recognise trade unions.

The UK argued that employers who did not recognise trade unions were not covered by the obligations in the directives because union recognition in companies was traditionally based on voluntary recognition.

The Court did not accept that argument. It said the aim of the directives was to ensure comparable protection for employees' rights in all Member States and to harmonise the costs of such provisions for companies in the EC. To that end, the directives laid down compulsory obligations on employers regarding informing and consulting employees' representatives.

The Court found Member States had no opportunities under the directives to limit the rights of employees to those companies which under national laws were obliged to have union representation. Although one of the directives specifically provided for situations in which companies did not have employees' representatives, the Court said this provision should not be read in isolation and that its effect was to allow employees without such representation to be properly informed. The Court said it was not the intention of the Union legislature to allow the different legal systems within the EU to accept a situation in which no employees' representatives were designated since designation was necessary to ensure compliance with the obligations laid down in the directive.

---

764. *Commission v. UK*, C-382/92 and 383/92, ECR-I-2435, 1994.

The Court was not concerned either by the fact that the directives did not contain specific provisions requiring Member States to designate workers' representatives if there were none.

The directives required Member States to take all the measures necessary to ensure employees were informed and consulted through their representatives in the event of either a transfer or collective redundancies. That obligation did not require there to be specific provisions on the designation of employees' representatives.

Two further claims were made by the Commission. The first was that UK rules only required the employer to consult with the employees' representatives, to take into consideration what was said, to reply and give reasons if the representations were rejected. The obligation under the directives was to consult representatives with a view to seeking agreement. The UK conceded its rules did not provide for this.

The second claim was that the sanctions provided for in the national rules for failure to comply with the obligations to consult and inform were not a sufficient deterrent for employers.

The Court said that where a Union directive did not specifically provide any penalty for an infringement, or where it referred for that purpose to national laws, the obligations of the Member States under the Rome Treaty were to require them to ensure that infringements of EU law were penalised under conditions, both procedural and substantive, which were analogous to those applicable to infringements of national law of a similar nature and importance and which, in any event, made the penalty effective, proportionate and dissuasive.

1936. An employer is entitled to carry out collective redundancies after the conclusion of the consultation procedure provided for in Article 2 of Directive 98/59 and after notification of the projected collective redundancies as provided for in Articles 3 and 4 of that directive.[765]

III. The Role of the Government

1937. The role of the competent public authority is limited to information, the laying down of a period during which dismissals have no effect and to seeking solutions to the problems raised by the projected collective redundancies. Once the workers' representatives are duly informed and consulted, the authority is notified. The employer must notify the authority in writing of any projected collective redundancies. This notification must contain the reasons for the redundancies, the number of the workers to be made redundant, the number of the workers normally employed and the period over which the redundancies are to be effected. *De facto* this is the same information that has already been forwarded to the workers. However, the Member States may provide that in the case of planned collective redundancies arising from termination of the establishment's activities as a result of a judicial decision, the employer shall be obliged to notify the competent authority in writing only if the latter so requests.

---

765. C.O.J., 27 January 2005, *Irmtraud Junk v. Wolfgang Kühnel*, C-188/03, ECR, 2005, 885.

1938. The collective redundancies take effect not earlier than 30 days after the notification of the competent authority without prejudice to any provisions governing individual rights with regard to the notice of dismissal. This period must be used by the competent public authority to seek solutions to the problems raised by the projected collective redundancies (Article 4(1)(2)). Which solutions ought to be sought is not indicated in the directive, but one might think of placement of workers, retraining, outplacement and others. Once more we must deal with a stipulation of a programmatic nature.

1939. The Member States can grant the competent authority the power to reduce the period of 30 days or to extend it. Where the initial period provided for is shorter than 60 days, Member States can grant the power to extend the period to 60 days following notification, or even longer, where the problems raised by the projected collective redundancies are not likely to be solved within the initial period. The employer must be informed of the extension and the grounds for it before the expiry of the initial period of 30 days (Article 4(3)).

The directive allows Member States not to apply Article 4 to collective redundancies arising from termination of the establishment's activities where this is a result of a judicial decision (Article 4(4)).

1940. In this Belgian case,[766] Mono Car appealed to the court making the reference against a judgment in an action between the parties to the main proceedings delivered by the *Tribunal du travail de Liège* on 3 February 2006.

Mono Car, a subsidiary of Mono International, manufactured parts, decorative accessories and interior trim for various vehicle manufacturers. In 2004, following large losses, the board of directors of Mono Car decided to study the possibility of either a voluntary liquidation of the company or a substantial reduction in staff.

It informed the works council of the financial situation and of the possibility of collective redundancies. Later, it signed a draft written agreement concerning a social plan with all the union representatives, later ratified by a collective labour agreement, which fixed the detailed arrangements for restructuring the business and the conditions for collective redundancies, among which were the absence of notice and factors for calculating compensation for dismissal and for non-material damage. The collective agreement stated that the procedure for information and consultation in cases of collective dismissal had been observed by Mono Car.

1941. A general meeting of the staff of Mono Car adopted the social plan and the works council ratified the vote taken at that meeting.

On 14 June 2004, Mono Car sent to the competent public authority the list of the 30 workers made redundant and the criteria used to select them, and made those workers redundant with effect from 21 June 2004. The staff representatives on the works council raised no objection concerning observance of one or more of the conditions laid down in Article 66 of the 1998 Law.[767]

---

766. C.O.J., 16 July 2009, *Mono Car Styling SA, in liquidation* v. *Dervis Odemis and Others*, C-12/ 08, www.curia.eu.
767. The Belgian Law of 13 February 1998 on measures in favour of employment (*Moniteur belge* of

Part I, Ch. 10, Restructuring of Enterprises 1941–1941

On 15 June 2004, the competent public authority granted a reduction in the waiting period prior to dismissal to one day and stated that the information and consultation procedure had been complied with.

None the less, following a meeting between Mono Car and the redundant workers, 21 of them challenged the regularity of that procedure before the *Tribunal du travail de Liège* on the basis of the third paragraph of Article 67[768] of the 1998 Law and applied, first, for reinstatement in the company and payment of earnings lost

---

19 February 1998, p. 4643, 'the 1998 Law') includes Chapter VII entitled 'collective redundancies'. According to Article 66 of that law:

I   An employer who intends to proceed with collective redundancies shall observe the procedure for informing and consulting provided for in the event of collective redundancies, as laid down in a collective labour agreement concluded by the National Labour Council.

In that regard, the employer must fulfil the following conditions:

(1) He must present to the works council or, where no such council exists, to the union delegation or, where no such delegation exists, to the workers, a written report in which he announces his intention to proceed with collective redundancies;

(2) he must be able to provide evidence that, as regards his intention to proceed with collective redundancies, he has assembled the works council or, where no such council exists, that he has met with the union delegation or, where no such delegation exists, with the workers;

(3) he must allow staff representatives within the works council or, where no such council exists, members of the union delegation or, where no such delegation exists, the workers, to ask questions regarding the collective redundancies contemplated and to put forward arguments or make counter-proposals on that issue;

(4) he must have examined the questions, arguments and counter-proposals referred to in 3 and have replied to them.The employer must provide evidence that he has satisfied the conditions referred to in the previous subparagraph.

II   The employer must notify the official appointed by the King of the intention to proceed with collective redundancies. That notification must confirm that the conditions referred to in the second subparagraph of Article 66(1) have been fulfilled.

On the date when the notification is sent to the official referred to in the first subparagraph, a copy of that notification shall be sent to the works council or, where no such council exists, to the union delegation, and shall be displayed in the workplace. In addition, a copy shall be sent, by recorded delivery, on the day the notification is displayed, to those workers who are affected by the collective redundancies and whose employment contracts have already expired on the day the notice is displayed.'

768. Article 67 of the 1998 Law provides as follows: 'A redundant worker may challenge due observance of the procedure for informing and consulting only on the ground that the employer has not satisfied one of the four conditions set out in the second subparagraph of Article 66(1).

A redundant worker may no longer challenge due observance of the procedure for informing and consulting if the staff representatives within the works council or, where no such council exists, the members of the union delegation or, where no such delegation exists, the workers who were to be informed and consulted, have not notified the employer of any objections in respect of satisfaction of one or more of the conditions provided for in the second subparagraph of Article 66(1), within a period of 30 days from the display of the notice referred to in the second subparagraph of Article 66(2).

Within a period of 30 days from the date of being made redundant or from the date on which the redundancies became collective redundancies, a redundant worker must inform the employer, in a letter sent by recorded delivery, that he challenges the due observance of the procedure for informing and consulting.'

Where a redundant worker challenges observance of the procedure for informing and consulting, and if that challenge is justified, Articles 68 and 69 of the 1998 Law provide for the suspension of the notice period or the reinstatement of the worker.

839

from the date on which their contracts were terminated and, secondly, compensation for the material and non-material loss suffered.

1942. By judgment of 3 February 2006, the *Tribunal du travail de Liège* declared the action admissible and partly granted the relief applied for, ordering Mono Car to pay damages for material loss arising from its failure to comply with the information and consultation procedure. That court noted as failings the lack of a written report and discussion in the works council, the failure to observe the waiting period prior to dismissal and the carrying-on of the social consultation procedure outside of the works council.

Mono Car appealed against that judgment to the *Cour du travail de Liège*, seeking that the judgment be completely set aside. The respondent workers cross-appealed, seeking an increase in the amounts of damages for material loss and a declaration that they had suffered non-material loss.

It was in that context that the Cour du travail de Liège, after declaring the appeal and the cross-appeal admissible, decided to stay proceedings and refer the following questions to the Court for a preliminary ruling.

1943. The Court ruled:

> By these questions, which it is appropriate to consider together, the national court is asking, in essence, whether Article 6 of Directive 98/59, read in conjunction with Article 2(1) to (3) thereof, precludes a national provision such as Article 67 of the 1998 Law, which, where workers acting individually challenge compliance by the employer with the information and consultation procedure laid down in that directive, first, limits the complaints which may be raised to failure to comply with the obligations laid down in a provision such as the second subparagraph of Article 66(1) of that law and, secondly, makes the admissibility of such a challenge subject to the giving of prior notice to the employer, by the representatives of the staff in the works council, of objections concerning compliance with those obligations and subject to the worker concerned providing the employer with prior information of the fact that he challenges compliance with the information and consultation procedure.
>
> According to Article 6 of Directive 98/59, Member States are to ensure that judicial and/or administrative procedures for the enforcement of obligations under the directive are available to the workers' representatives and/or workers.
>
> It is clear therefore from the terms of that provision that the Member States are required to introduce procedures to ensure compliance with the obligations laid down in Directive 98/59. On the other hand, and in so far as the directive does not develop that obligation further, it is for the Member States to lay down detailed arrangements for those procedures.
>
> However, it should be pointed out that, although it is true that Directive 98/59 merely carries out a partial harmonisation of the rules for the protection of workers in the event of collective redundancies, it is also true that the limited character of such harmonisation cannot deprive the provisions of the directive of useful effect.

Part I, Ch. 10, Restructuring of Enterprises

1944. Consequently, although it is for the Member States to introduce procedures to ensure compliance with the obligations laid down in Directive 98/59, such procedures must not deprive the provisions of the directive of useful effect.

In this instance, it is common ground that the Belgian legislation gives workers' representatives a right of challenge which, first, is not limited in regard to the complaints which may be raised and, secondly, is not subject to specific conditions, other than those relating to the general conditions of admissibility of legal proceedings in domestic law. Similarly, it is common ground that Article 67 of the 1998 Law gives workers an individual right of challenge, although it is limited in regard to the complaints which may be raised and subject to the conditions that workers' representatives should first have raised objections and that the worker concerned has informed the employer in advance of his intention to challenge compliance with the information and consultation procedure. The question therefore arises whether such a limitation of workers' individual right of challenge or such a condition placed on the exercise of that right could deprive the provisions of Directive 98/59 of their effectiveness or, as Mr Odemis and his fellow applicants claim, limit the protection of workers provided for in that directive.

In that regard, it is clear, first of all, from the text and scheme of Directive 98/59 that the right to information and consultation which it lays down is intended for workers' representatives and not for workers individually.

Thus, recital 10 and the second subparagraph of Article 2(2) of Directive 98/59 refer to experts on whose services workers' representatives may call on grounds of the technical complexity of the matters which are likely to be the subject of the informing and consulting. Also, Article 1(1) of the directive, which contains definitions for the purposes thereof, defines the expression 'workers' representatives' but not 'workers'. Similarly, Article 2 of the directive sets out the employer's obligations and the right to information and consultation but refers only to workers' representatives. In the same manner, Article 3 of the directive requires that notice be given to the competent public authority of any projected collective redundancies with all relevant information concerning those redundancies and the consultations with workers' representatives, to whom the employer is to forward a copy of the notification and who may send any comments they may have to the public authority concerned, but such possibilities are not open to workers.

1945. Secondly, the collective nature of the right to information and consultation also flows from a teleological interpretation of Directive 98/59. In so far as the information and consultation provided for in the directive are intended, in particular, to permit, first, the formulation of constructive proposals covering, at least, ways and means of avoiding collective redundancies or reducing the number of workers affected, and of mitigating the consequences

> of such redundancies and, secondly, the possible submission of comments to the competent public authority, workers' representatives are best placed to achieve the objective which the directive seeks to attain.

1946. Finally, the Court has already had occasion to rule that the right to information and consultation, previously provided for in an identical manner by Directive 75/129, is exercised through workers' representatives.

It must therefore be held that the right to information and consultation provided for in Directive 98/59, in particular by Article 2 thereof, is intended to benefit workers as a collective group and is therefore collective in nature.

The level of protection of that collective right required by Article 6 of the directive is reached in a context such as that of the main proceedings, since the applicable national rules give workers' representatives a right to act which, as was pointed out in paragraph 37 of the present judgment, is not limited by specific conditions.

Consequently, and without prejudice to remedies in domestic law intended to ensure protection of the individual rights of workers in the case of improper dismissal, it cannot reasonably be argued that the protection of workers is restricted or that the useful effect of Directive 98/59 is affected by the fact that, in the framework of the procedures permitting workers to act individually in order to ensure compliance with the information and consultation obligations laid down in that directive, the complaints which may be raised by them are limited or that their right of action is subject to the conditions that workers' representatives should first have raised objections and that the worker concerned has informed the employer in advance of his intention to challenge compliance with the information and consultation procedure.

In the light of the foregoing, the answer must be that Article 6 of Directive 98/59, read in conjunction with Article 2 thereof, is to be interpreted as not precluding national rules which introduce procedures intended to permit both workers' representatives and the workers themselves as individuals to ensure compliance with the obligations laid down in that directive, but which limit the individual right of action of workers in regard to the complaints which may be raised and makes that right subject to the requirement that workers' representatives should first have raised objections with the employer and that the worker concerned has informed the employer in advance of his intention to query whether the information and consultation procedure has been complied with.

1947. The court added that the fact that national rules, establishing procedures which permit workers' representatives to ensure that the employer has complied with all the information and consultation obligations set out in Directive 98/59, impose limits and conditions on the individual right of action which it also grants to every worker affected by collective redundancy is not of such a nature as to infringe the principle of effective judicial protection.

Article 2 of Directive 98/59 must be interpreted as precluding national rules which reduce the obligations of an employer who intends to proceed with collective redundancies below those laid down in Article 2 of that directive. In applying domestic law, the national court is required, applying the principle of interpreting national law in conformity with Union law, to consider all the rules of national law and to interpret them, so far as possible, in the light of the wording and purpose of

Directive 98/59 in order to achieve an outcome consistent with the objective pursued by the directive. Consequently, it must ensure, within the limits of its jurisdiction, that the obligations binding such an employer are not reduced below those laid down in Article 2 of that directive.

§2. TRANSFER OF UNDERTAKINGS, MERGERS AND DIVISIONS OF PUBLIC LIMITED LIABILITY COMPANIES

I. Transfer of Undertakings

1948. Directive No. 77/187 relates to the safeguarding of employees' rights in the event of transfers of undertakings, businesses or parts of businesses.[769] The directive of 1977 was amended by Directive 98/50 EC of 29 June 1998[770] 'in the light of the impact of the internal market, the legislative tendencies of the Member States with regard to the rescue of undertakings in economic difficulties and the case law of the Court of Justice'.[771] The directive was 'in the interests of clarity and rationality codified' by Council Directive 2001/23/EC of 12 March 2001.[772] The new directive is also based on Article 115 TFEU concerning the approximation of laws. The objective of the directive is to ensure that the rights of employees are safeguarded in the event of a change of employer by enabling them to remain in employment with the new employer on the terms and conditions agreed at the transfer.[773] The purpose of the directive is therefore to ensure that the restructuring of undertakings within the common market does not adversely affect the workers in the undertakings concerned.[774]

A. Definitions and Scope

1949. Different actors operate within the framework of this directive: the transferor, the transferee, and the representative of the employees. The transferor is any natural or legal person who, by reason of a transfer of an undertaking, ceases to be the employer. The transferee is any natural or legal person who, by reason of the transfer of an undertaking, becomes the employer of the undertaking (Article 2(1)(a) and (b)). The term 'representatives of employees' and related expressions shall mean the representatives of employees provided for by the laws or practices of the Member States (Article 2(1)(c)).

---

769. O.J. L 61, 5 March 1977.
770. O.J. L 201/88, 17 July 1998.
771. Considerans 3.
772. O.J., 22 March 2001.
773. O.J., 15 June 1988, *P. Bork International A/S in liquidation and others* v. *Foreningen of Arbejdsledere i Danmark, acting on behalf of Birger E. Peterson, and Junckers Industries A/S*, No. 101/87, ECR, 1988, 3057.
774. C.O.J., 7 February 1985, *H.B.M. Abels* v. *The Administrative Board of the Bedrijfsvereniging voor de Metaal Industrie en de Electronische Industrie*, No. 135/83, ECR, 1985, 519.

1950. The directive contains an express definition of the term 'employee'. The 'employee' shall mean any person who, in the Member State concerned, is protected as an employee under national employment law (Article 2(1)(d)).

The directive is without prejudice to national law as regards the definition of contract of employment or employment relationship. However, Member States shall not exclude from the scope of the directive contracts of employment solely because:

(a) of the number of working hours performed or to be performed;
(b) they are employment relationships governed by a fixed-duration contract of employment;[775]
(c) they are temporary employment relationships and the undertaking transferred is the temporary employment business which is the employer.[776]

It is for the national court to establish whether that is the case.

1951. The directive applies to the transfer of an undertaking, business or part of a business – situated within the territorial scope of the Treaty – to another employer as a result of a legal transfer or a merger (Article 1(1)(a)). The directive applies to public and private undertakings engaged in economic activities whether or not they are operating for gain. An administrative reorganisation of public administrative authorities, or the transfer of administrative functions between public administrative authorities, is not a transfer within the meaning of the directive (Article 1(1)(c)).

The directive applies where and insofar as the undertaking, business or part of the undertaking or business to be transferred is situated within the territorial scope of the Treaty (Article 1(2)). The directive does not apply to sea-going vessels (Article 1(3)).

There is a transfer within the meaning of the directive where there is a transfer of an economic entity which retains its identity, meaning an organised grouping of resources, which has the objective of pursuing an economic activity, whether or not that activity is central or ancillary (Article 1(1)(b)).

This definition summarises the abundant case law of the European Court regarding the notion of transfer. This case law reads as follows. The key element of the definition lies in the fact whether the employees are, as a consequence of the transfer of the undertaking, confronted with a new legal employer; in other words, the selling of a number of shares with the consequence that there is a new economic owner is not relevant.

> The directive is applicable where, following a legal transfer or merger, there is a change in the legal or natural person who is responsible for carrying on the business and who, by virtue of that fact, incurs the obligations of an employer

---

775. Within the meaning of Council Directive 91/383/EEC of 25 June 1991. *See* Part I, Chapter 3, §1.
776. *Idem.*

Part I, Ch. 10, Restructuring of Enterprises 1952–1953

vis-à-vis the employees of the undertaking, regardless of whether or not ownership of the undertaking is transferred.[777]

Thus any agreement by which the capacity of employer is transferred is covered. This is the case where there is a transfer of an undertaking pursuant to a lease-purchase agreement of the kind available under Dutch law (a purchase and sale on deferred payment, by which the parties agree that the object sold shall not become the property of the purchaser by mere transfer) and to the retransfer of the undertaking upon the termination of the lease-purchase agreement by judicial decisions;[778] also in the case where the owner of a leased undertaking takes over its operation following a breach of the lease by the lessee;[779] the directive applies as well where, after notice is given to bring the lease to an end or upon termination thereof, the owner of an undertaking retakes the possession of the lease and thereafter sells it to a third party who shortly afterwards brings back into operation the undertaking, which has ceased upon termination of the lease, with just over half the staff that was employed in the undertaking by the former lessee, provided that the undertaking in question retains its identity.[780]

1952. On 19 May 1992, the European Court of Justice determined that the directive also applies in a 'situation in which a public body decides to terminate the subsidy paid to one legal person, as the result of which the activities of that legal person are fully and definitively terminated and to transfer it to another legal person with similar aims'.[781]

The directive 'is to be interpreted as covering a situation in which an undertaking entrusts by contract to another undertaking the responsibility for carrying out cleaning operations which it previously performed itself, even though, prior to the transfer, such work was carried out by a single employee'.[782]

The Court of Justice, however, ruled rightly that the reorganisation of structures of the public administration or the transfer of administrative functions between public administrative authorities does not constitute a transfer of an undertaking within the meaning of the directive.[783]

1953. The directive applies provided that the undertaking in question retains its identity, as it does if it is a going concern whose operation is actually continued or

---

777. C.O.J., 5 May 1988, *H. Berg and J.T.M. Busschers* v. *I.M. Besselen*, Joined Cases Nos. 144 and 145,87, ECR, 1988, 2559.
778. *Idem.*
779. C.O.J., 17 December 1987, *Landesorganisationen i Danmark for Tjenerforbunket i Danmark* v. *Molle Kro*, No. 276/86, ECR, 1987, 5465.
780. C.O.J., *Bork International A/S, op. cit.*
781. C.O.J., 19 May 1992, *S. Redmond Stichting* v. *H. Bartol and Others*, No. C-29/91, ECR, 1992, 3189.
782. C.O.J., 14 April 1994, *Schmidt C.* v. *Spar und Leihasse*, No. C-392/92, ECR, 1994, 1311.
783. C.O.J., 15 October 1996, *Annette Henke* v. *Gemeinde Schierke and Verwaltungsgemeinschaft Brocken* Case C-298/94, ECR, 1996, 4989.

resumed by the new employer, with the same or similar activities. In order to determine whether those conditions are met, it is necessary to consider all the circumstances surrounding the transaction in question, including, in particular, whether or not the undertaking's tangible and intangible assets and the majority of its employees are taken over, the degree of similarity between the activities carried on before and after the transfer or the period, if any, for which those activities ceased in connection with the transfer.[784]

It is therefore 'necessary to determine, having regard to all the circumstances of the facts surrounding the transaction in question, whether the functions performed are in fact carried out or resumed by the new legal person with the same activities or similar activities, it being understood that activities of a special nature which pursue independent aims may, if necessary, be treated as a business or part of a business within the meaning of the directive'.[785]

The directive may thus apply in a situation in which an undertaking entrusts another undertaking by contract with the responsibility for running a service for employees, previously managed directed, for a fee and various benefits the terms of which are determined by agreement between them.[786]

1954. The same problem was dealt with in the case *Spijkers*.[787] Mr. Spijkers was employed as an assistant-manager by Gebroeders Colaris Abattoir at Ulbach over Worm (Netherlands). On 27 December 1982, by which date the business activities of Colaris 'had entirely ceased and there was no longer any goodwill in the business', the entire slaughterhouse with various rooms and offices, the land and certain specific goods were purchased by Benedik Abattoir. Since that date, although in fact only since 3 February 1983, Benedik Abattoir operated a slaughterhouse under the joint account of Alfred Benedik and itself. All the employees of Colaris were taken over by Benedik Abattoir, apart from Mr. Spijkers and one other employee. The business activity which Benedik Abattoir carries on in the buildings is of the same kind as the activity previously carried on by Colaris; the transfer of the business assets enabled Benedik Abattoir to continue the activities of Colaris, although Benedik Abattoir did not take over Colaris' customers. On 3 March 1983, Colaris was declared insolvent. By a writ of 9 March 1983, Mr. Spijkers summoned Benedik Abattoir and Alfred Benedik to appear in proceedings for interim relief and sought an order that they should pay him his salary from 27 December 1982, or at least from such a date as the President thought fit, and should provide him with work within two days of the order. In support of his claims he contended that there had been a transfer of an undertaking in the meaning of the directive and that this entailed, by operation of law, a transfer to Benedik Abattoir of the rights and obligations arising from his contract of employment with Colaris. After being dismissed in first instance and on appeal, Mr. Spijkers appealed in Cassation to the *Hoge Raad der Nederlanden*, which stayed the proceedings and referred the

---

784. C.O.J., *Bork International A/S, op. cit.*
785. C.O.J., 19 May 1992, *S. Redmond Stichting* v. *H. Bartol and Others*, No. C-29/91, *op. cit.*
786. C.O.J., 12 November 1992, *A. Watson Rask and K. Christensen* v. *ISS Kantineservice A/S*, No. C-209/91, ECR, 1992, 5755.
787. C.O.J., 18 March 1986, *J.M.A. Spijkers* v. *Gebroeders Benedik Abattoir CV and Alfred Benedik en Zonen BV*, No. 24/85; ECR, 1986, 1119.

Part I, Ch. 10, Restructuring of Enterprises 1955–1957

question to the Court of Justice whether this case fell under the application of the directive, namely whether a transfer of an undertaking had taken place.

1955. In the course of the proceedings before the Court, the United Kingdom Government and the Commission suggested that the essential criterion is whether the transferee is put in possession of a going concern and is able to continue its activities or at least activities of the same kind. The Netherlands Government emphasised that, in regard to the social objective of the directive, it was clear that the term 'transfer' implied that the transferee actually carried on the activities of the transferor as part of the same business. The Court accepted that view. It is clear from the scheme of Directive No. 77/187 and from the terms of Article 1(1) thereof that the directive is intended to ensure the continuity of employment relationships existing within a business, irrespective of any change of ownership. It follows that the decisive criterion for establishing whether there is a transfer for the purpose of the directive is whether the business in question retains its identity. Consequently, a transfer of an undertaking does not occur merely because its assets are disposed of. Instead it is necessary to consider, in the case such as the present, whether the business was disposed of as a going concern, as would be indicated, *inter alia*, by the fact that its operation was actually continued or resumed by the new employer, with the same or similar activities.

1956. In order to determine whether these conditions were met, it is necessary to consider all the facts characterising the transaction in question, including the type of undertaking or business, whether or not the tangible assets of the business, such as buildings and movable property, were transferred, the value of its tangible assets at the time of the transfer, whether or not the majority of its employees were taken over by the new employer, whether or not its customers were transferred and the degree of similarity between the activities carried on before or after the transfer and the period, if any, for which those activities were suspended. It should be noted, however, that all these circumstances are merely single factors in the overall assessment to be made and cannot be considered in isolation. It is for the national court to make the necessary factual appraisal, in the light of the criteria for the interpretation set out above, in order to establish whether there was a transfer in the sense indicated above. In conclusion, it is necessary to consider whether, with regard to all the facts characterising the transaction, the business was disposed of as a going concern, as would be indicated, *inter alia*, by the fact that the operation was actually continued or resumed by the new employer, with the same or similar activities.

1957. The issue was again addressed in *Albert Merckx and Patrick Neuhuys* v. *Ford Motor Company Belgium SA*,[788] in proceedings brought by Merckx and Neuhuys against Ford concerning the effects on the contracts of employment concluded by Merckx and Neuhuys with Anfo Motors SA of the discontinuance of Anfo Motors' business and the assumption by Novarobel SA of the dealership held by Anfo Motors. The judgment underlines again that the notion of transfer has to be evaluated on a case by case basis and that the Court of Justice is giving a very broad

---

788. C.O.J., 7 March 1996, Joined Cases C-171/94 and C-172/94, ECR, 1996, 1253.

interpretation. This is extremely important because of the increase of outsourcing in our growing information and networking society.

At the time, Merckx and Neuhuys were salesmen with Anfo Motors. Anfo Motors sold motor vehicles as a Ford dealer in a number of municipalities in the Brussels conurbation, Ford also being its main shareholder.

On 8 October 1987 Anfo Motors informed Merckx and Neuhuys that it would discontinue all its activities on 31 December 1987 and that with effect from 1 November 1987 Ford would be working with an independent dealer, Novarobel, in the municipalities covered by the Anfo Motors dealership. It stated that Novarobel would take on 14 of the 64 employees of Anfo Motors, who would retain their duties, seniority and all other contractual rights.

Anfo Motors also sent a letter to its customers in order to inform them of the discontinuance of its activities and to recommend to them the services of the new dealer.

By letter of 27 October 1987, Merckx and Neuhuys refused to accept the proposed transfer, claiming that Anfo Motors could not require them to work for another company, in another place and under different working conditions, without any guarantee as to whether the client base would be retained or a particular turnover achieved.

The question was first, whether Article 1(1) of the directive must be interpreted as applying where an undertaking holding a motor vehicle dealership for a particular territory discontinues its business and the dealership is then transferred to another undertaking which takes on part of its staff and is recommended to customers, without any transfer of assets. Secondly, having regard to the facts in the main proceedings and in order to provide a helpful response to the national court, it is necessary to establish whether Article 3(1) of the directive precludes an employee of the transferor at the date of transfer of the undertaking from objecting to the transfer of his contract of employment or employment relationship to the transferee.

1958. The Court stated again that:

> it is settled case law that the decisive criterion for establishing whether there is a transfer for the purposes of the Directive is whether the entity in question retains its economic identity, as indicated *inter alia* by the fact that its operation is actually continued or resumed. In order to determine whether that condition is met, it is necessary to consider all the facts characterising the transaction in question, including the type of undertaking or business, whether or not the business's tangible assets, such as buildings and movable property, are transferred, the value of its intangible assets at the time of the transfer, whether or not the majority of its employees is taken over by the new employer, whether or not its customers are transferred and the degree of similarity between the activities carried on before and after the transfer and the period, if any, for which those activities were suspended.
>
> All those factors, taken as a whole, support the view that the transfer of the dealership in the circumstances of the main proceedings is capable of falling within the scope of the Directive. It must be ascertained, however, whether certain factors relied on by Merckx and Neuhuys may rebut that finding.

The purpose of an exclusive dealership for the sale of motor vehicles of a particular make in a certain sector remains the same even if it is carried on under a different name, from different premises and with different facilities. It is also irrelevant that the principal place of business is situated in a different area of the same conurbation, provided that the contract territory remains the same.

In that regard, if the Directive's aim of protecting workers is not to be undermined, its application cannot be excluded merely because the transferor discontinues its activities when the transfer is made and is then put into liquidation.

Article 4(1) of the Directive provides that the transfer of an undertaking, business or part of the business does not in itself constitute grounds for dismissal. However, that provision is not to stand in the way of dismissals that may take place for economic, technical or organisational reasons entailing changes in the workforce.

Accordingly, the fact that the majority of the staff was dismissed when the transfer took place is not sufficient to preclude the application of the Directive.

It is clear from the case law that, for the Directive to apply, it is not necessary for there to be a direct contractual relationship between the transferor and the transferee. Consequently, where a motor vehicle dealership concluded with one undertaking is terminated and a new dealership is awarded to another undertaking pursuing the same activities, the transfer of the undertaking is the result of a legal transfer for the purposes of the Directive, as interpreted by the Court.

1959. Thus, the Court ruled:

Article 1(1) of the Directive of 14 February 1977 must be interpreted as applying where an undertaking holding a motor vehicle dealership for a particular territory discontinues its activities and the dealership is then transferred to another undertaking which takes on part of the staff and is recommended to customers, without any transfer of assets.

1960. In *Süzen* v. *Zehnacker*[789] the question was raised whether the directive applies to a situation in which a person who had entrusted the cleaning of his premises to a first undertaking terminates his contract with the latter and, for the performance of similar work, enters into a new contract with a second undertaking without any concomitant transfer of tangible or intangible business assets from one undertaking to the other.

A cleaning lady, Mrs. Süzen, whose job it was to clean a school, had been dismissed with seven other persons after the school had terminated the contract that bound it to their employer (the cleaning company, Zehnacker). Out of the eight persons, seven were re-employed by the cleaning company Leforth, which had signed the new contract with the school. Mrs. Süzen, who had not been taken on again, felt

---

789. C.O.J., 11 March 1997, *Ayse Süzen* v. *Zehnacker Gebäudereinigung GmbH Krankenhausservice*, C-13/95, ECR, 1997, 1259.

she was part of the same economic entity which had been moved to the new cleaning company.

The Court stated as follows:

> The mere fact that the service provided by the old and the new awardees of a contract is similar does not support the conclusion that an economic entity has been transferred. An entity cannot be reduced to the activity entrusted to it. Its identity also emerges from other factors, such as its workforce, its management staff, the way in which its work is organised, its operating methods or indeed, where appropriate, the operational resources available to it.
>
> The mere loss of a service contract to a competitor cannot therefore by itself indicate the existence of a transfer within the meaning of the directive. In those circumstances, the service undertaking previously entrusted with the contract does not, on losing a customer, thereby cease fully to exist, and a business or part of a business belonging to it cannot be considered to have been transferred to the new awardee of the contract.
>
> It must also be noted that, although the transfer of assets is one of the criteria to be taken into account by the national court in deciding whether an undertaking has in fact been transferred, the absence of such assets does not necessarily preclude the existence of such a transfer.
>
> The national court, in assessing the facts characterizing the transaction in question, must take into account among other things the type of undertaking or business concerned. It follows that the degree of importance to be attached to each criterion for determining whether or not there has been a transfer within the meaning of the directive will necessarily vary according to the activity carried on, or indeed the production or operating methods employed in the relevant undertaking, business or part of a business. Where in particular an economic entity is able, in certain sectors, to function without any significant tangible or intangible assets, the maintenance of its identity following the transaction affecting it cannot, logically, depend on the transfer of such assets.
>
> Since in certain labour-intensive sectors a group of workers engaged in a joint activity on a permanent basis may constitute an economic entity, it must be recognised that such an entity is capable of maintaining its identity after it has been transferred where the new employer does not merely pursue the activity in question but also takes over a major part, in terms of their numbers and skills, of the employees specially assigned by his predecessor to that task. In those circumstances, the new employer takes over a body of assets enabling him to carry on the activities or certain activities of the transferor undertaking on a regular basis.
>
> It is for the national court to establish, in the light of the foregoing interpretative guidance, whether a transfer has occurred in this case.

One conclusion is certain. A mere change of subcontractors is in itself not a transfer of an enterprise. The transfer must relate to a stable economic activity. The term entity refers to an organised grouping of persons and assets facilitating the exercise of an economic activity which pursues a specific objective.

1961. The question was raised whether the directive also applies if the undertaking is temporarily closed and consequently has no employees. In this case a seasonal business, such as a hotel, was meant. The Court ruled that, in order to decide this case, account must be taken of all the factual circumstances surrounding the transaction in question, including, where appropriate, the temporary closure of the undertaking and the fact that there were no employees at the time of the transfer, although these facts alone do not preclude the applicability of the directive in the case of a seasonal business.[790]

1962. The directive, however, applies where a company in voluntary liquidation transfers all or part of its assets to another company from which the worker then takes his orders which the company in liquidation states are to be carried out.[791]

1963. In *Allen v. Amalgamated Construction Co. Ltd.* (1999), involving a situation in which a company belonging to a group decides to subcontract to another company in the same group contracts for driveage work in mines, the following questions were referred to the Court of Justice:

(1) Is the Acquired Rights Directive capable of applying to two companies in the same corporate group which have common ownership, management, premises and work, or are such companies a single undertaking for the purpose of the Directive? In particular, can there be a transfer of an undertaking for the purposes of the Directive when Company A transfers a substantial part of its labour force to Company B in the same corporate group?
(2) If the answer to question 1 is in the affirmative, what are the criteria for deciding whether there has been such a transfer? In particular, has there been a transfer of an undertaking in the following circumstances:
   (a) over a period of time the workers involved have been dismissed from Company A, purportedly for redundancy, and offered employment with associated Company B carrying out a geographically distinct undertaking or part of the undertaking of Company A, namely the driving of mine tunnels;
   (b) no transfer of premises, management, infrastructure, materials or assets occurred between Company A and B and the majority of significant assets used by both companies in the work of driving main tunnels is supplied by a third party, the mine operator;
   (c) Company A remains the sole contractor with the third party client which engaged it to work on construction projects which were undertaken on a 'rolling' basis;
   (d) there was little or no contemporaneity between the movement of the workers from Company A to Company B and the beginning and/or end of the contracts under which the work was performed;
   (e) Company A and Company B share the same management and premises;

---

790. C.O.J., 17 December 1987, *Landesorganisationen i Danmark v. Ny Molle Kro, op. cit.*
791. C.O.J., 12 November 1998, *Europièces SA v. Wilfried Sanders and Automotive Industries Holding Company SA*, Case C-399/96, ECR, 1998, 6965.

(f) after being employed by Company B the employees carry out work for both Companies A and B as needed by the local management who are responsible for both companies;

(g) the work undertaken was continuous, there was no suspension of activities at any time or any change in the manner in which they were conducted?

1964. The Court answered as follows:

> The Directive is applicable where, following a legal transfer or merger, there is a change in the natural or legal person responsible for carrying on the business who by virtue of that fact incurs the obligations of an employer *vis-à-vis* employees of the undertaking, regardless of whether or not ownership of the undertaking is transferred. It is thus clear that the Directive is intended to cover any legal change in the person of the employer if the other conditions it lays down are also met and that it can, therefore, apply to a transfer between two subsidiary companies in the same group, which are distinct legal persons each with specific employment relationships with their employees.
>
> The fact that the companies in question not only have the same ownership but also the same management and the same premises and that they are engaged in the same works makes no difference in this regard. Nothing justifies a parent company's and its subsidiaries' uniform conduct on the market having greater importance in the application of the Directive than the formal separation between those companies which have distinct legal personalities. That outcome, which would exclude transfers between companies in the same group from the scope of the Directive, would be precisely contrary to the Directive's aim, which is, according to the Court, to ensure, so far as possible, that the rights of employees are safeguarded in the event of a change of employer by allowing them to remain in employment with the new employer on the terms and conditions agreed with the transferor.
>
> The answer to be given to the first part of the first question must therefore be that the Directive can apply to a transfer between two companies in the same corporate group which have the same ownership, management and premises and which are engaged in the same works.

1965. By the second part of its first question and its second question, the referring court is essentially seeking to ascertain the criteria for determining the existence of a transfer and whether those criteria are satisfied in the present case.

The aim of the Directive is to ensure continuity of employment relationships within an economic entity, irrespective of any change of ownership. The decisive criterion for establishing the existence of a transfer within the meaning of the Directive is whether the entity in question retains its identity, as indicated *inter alia* by the fact that its operation is actually continued or resumed.

First of all, the transfer must relate to a stable economic entity whose activity is not limited to performing one specific works contract. The term "entity" thus refers to an organised grouping of persons and assets facilitating the exercise of an economic activity which pursues a specific objective. It is for the referring court to establish, in the light of the interpretative criteria set forth above, whether the

Part I, Ch. 10, Restructuring of Enterprises　　　　　　　　　　　　　　　　**1966–1966**

driveage work carried out was organised in the form of an economic entity before that undertaking subcontracted that work.

Second, in order to determine whether the conditions for the transfer of an economic entity are met, it is necessary to consider all the facts characterising the transaction in question, including in particular the type of undertaking or business, whether or not its tangible assets, such as buildings and movable property, are transferred, the value of its intangible assets at the time of the transfer, whether or not essential staff are taken over by the new employer, whether or not its customers are transferred, the degree of similarity between the activities carried on before and after the transfer, and the period, if any, for which those activities are suspended. However, all those circumstances are merely single factors in the overall assessment which must be made and cannot therefore be considered in isolation.

So, the mere fact that the service provided by the undertaking holding the contracts for driveage work and then by the undertaking to which the work was then subcontracted is similar does not warrant the conclusion that an economic entity has been transferred between the first and the second undertaking. Such an entity cannot be reduced to the activity entrusted to it. Its identity also emerges from other factors, such as its workforce, its management staff, the way in which its work is organised, its operating methods or indeed, where appropriate, the operational resources available to it.

The national court, in assessing the facts characterising the transaction in question, must take into account, among other factors, the type of undertaking or business concerned. It follows that the degree of importance to be attached to each criterion for determining whether or not there has been a transfer within the meaning of the Directive will necessarily vary according to the activity carried on, or indeed the production or operating methods employed in the relevant undertaking, business or part of a business. Where, in particular, an economic entity is able, in certain sectors, to function without any significant tangible or intangible assets, the maintenance of its identity following the transaction affecting it cannot, logically, depend on the transfer of such assets.

1966. The Court has thus held that, since in certain sectors in which the activity is based essentially on manpower, a group of workers engaged in a joint activity on a permanent basis may constitute an economic entity, such an entity is capable of maintaining its identity after it has been transferred where the new employer does not merely pursue the activity in question but also takes over a major part, in terms of their numbers and skills, of the employees specially assigned by his predecessor to that task. In those circumstances, the new employer takes over a body of assets enabling him to carry on the activities or certain activities of the transferor undertaking in a stable way.

Although the driving of underground tunnels cannot be considered to be an activity based essentially on manpower since it requires a significant amount of plant and equipment, it is clear that, in the mining sector, it is common for the essential assets required for driveage work to be provided by the mine owner himself. The fact that ownership of the assets required to run the undertaking did not pass to the new owner does not preclude a transfer. In the circumstances, the fact that there was no transfer of assets is not of decisive importance.

The transfer of customers between transferor and transferee is only one factor amongst others in the overall assessment to be made to ascertain whether a transfer has taken place. Moreover, the Directive is applicable wherever, in the context of contractual relations, there is a change in the natural or legal person responsible for carrying on the business who incurs the obligations of an employer towards employees of the undertaking.

1967. As regards the fact that the re-engagement of the transferor's employees did not coincide with the beginning or end of the contracts, it must be observed that a transfer of an undertaking is a complex legal and practical operation which may take some time to complete. Accordingly, no particular importance can be attached to the lack of contemporaneity between the start of the work subcontracted and its re-engagement of employees.

Moreover, even if a temporary suspension of the undertaking's activity does not of itself preclude the possibility that a transfer has taken place, the fact that the work was performed continuously, with no interruption or change in the manner of performance, is none the less a normal feature of transfers of undertakings.

The fact that transferor and transferee share the same management and the same premises and that there was no transfer of management staff between the two companies cannot preclude the existence of a transfer in so far as the transaction between the two subsidiaries actually involved an economic entity.

There is no transfer where one undertaking merely makes available to another certain workers and material for carrying out certain works. However, that situation differs from the present case in that complete works projects were subcontracted.

The answer to the second part of the first question and the second question must therefore be that the Directive applies to a situation in which a company belonging to a group decides to subcontract to another company in the same group contracts for driveage work in mines in so far as the transaction involves the transfer of an economic entity between the two companies. The term 'economic entity' refers to an organised grouping of persons and assets facilitating the exercise of an economic activity which pursues a specific objective.[792]

1968. Another case related to proceedings between Temco Service Industries SA (hereinafter Temco), a cleaning undertaking which held the contract for cleaning the production plants of Volkswagen Bruxelles SA (hereinafter Volkswagen), and four employees of General Maintenance Contractors SPRL (hereinafter GMC), the undertaking responsible immediately beforehand, as a subcontractor of Buyle-Medros-Vaes Associates SA (hereinafter BMV), for providing the same services under a previous contract which was terminated. Temco disputes the claim that the

---

792. C.O.J., 2 December 1999, *G.C. Allen and Others v. Amalgamated Construction Co. Ltd.*, Case C-234/98, ECR, 1999, 8643.

employment contracts of those four employees were automatically transferred to it pursuant to the directive.[793]

The case goes as follows. Volkswagen entrusted the cleaning of a number of its production plants to BMV from 2 May 1993 until December 1994, when it terminated the contract. BMV subcontracted the cleaning work to its subsidiary GMC.

By contract Volkswagen instructed Temco to provide the same services. GMC, whose only business at the time was at Volkswagen's plants, dismissed all its staff, apart from four protected employees whom it retained pursuant to Article 1 of the collective agreement of 5 May 1993. Following the loss of that contract GMC ceased to be active but did not cease to exist. Temco re-engaged part of the staff of GMC.

At the same time, GMC tried to dismiss the four protected employees under the procedure provided for by national law; it asked the relevant joint committee to acknowledge that there were economic or technical grounds entitling it to dismiss them. That request was rejected.

1969. The four employees were assigned to short-time working by GMC although that company had apparently already stated in correspondence that the contracts of those four persons had automatically been transferred to Temco at the time when that company took over the cleaning of the Volkswagen plants, that is to say on 9 January 1995, pursuant to Collective Agreement No. 32*bis* implementing the directive. From December 1995, as GMC had ceased to pay them, those four employees brought proceedings against GMC, BMV and Temco before the *Tribunal du travail de Bruxelles*.

1970. The following questions were referred to the Court of Justice for a preliminary ruling:

(1) Does Article 1(1) of Council Directive 77/187 of 14 February 1977 apply in a situation where undertaking A contracts with undertaking B for the cleaning of its industrial plants and undertaking B entrusts that work to undertaking C, which, following loss of the contract by undertaking B, dismisses all its staff, except for four persons, whereupon undertaking D is awarded that contract by undertaking A, employs a proportion of the staff of undertaking C under a collective labour agreement but takes over none of the assets of undertaking C, which latter undertaking continues to exist and to pursue the objects for which it was incorporated?
(2) In the event that undertaking C is held to be the transferor, even though it continues to exist, does the abovementioned directive preclude it from being able to retain certain workers in its service?

---

793. C.O.J., 24 January 2002, *Temco Service Industries SA and Samir Imzilyen, Mimoune Belfarh, Abdesselam Afia-Aroussi, Khalil Lakhdar, intervener: General Maintenance Contractors SPRL (GMC), Buyle-Medros-Vaes Associates SA (BMV), formerly Weisspunkt SA,* Case C-51/00, ECR, 2002, 969.

The Court answered as follows:

> It is clear from the wording of Article 1(1) of the directive that its applicability is subject to three conditions: the transfer must result in a change of employer; it must concern an undertaking, a business or part of a business; and it must be the result of a contract. The question asked does not concern the change of employer but calls for an analysis of the subject of the transfer and its contractual nature.

1971. *The Subject of the Transfer*

> It must be observed that the directive is intended to ensure continuity of employment relationships existing within an economic entity, irrespective of any change of ownership. It follows that the decisive criterion for establishing whether there is a transfer for the purposes of the directive is whether the business in question retains its identity (*see*, in particular),
>
> The transfer must therefore relate to a stable economic entity whose activity is not limited to performing one specific works contract. The term entity thus refers to an organised grouping of persons and assets facilitating the exercise of an economic activity which pursues a specific objective.
>
> In order to determine whether the conditions for the transfer of an economic entity are met, it is necessary to consider all the facts characterising the transaction in question, including in particular the type of undertaking or business, whether or not its tangible assets, such as buildings and movable property, have been transferred, the value of its intangible assets at the time of the transfer, whether or not the majority of employees have been taken over by the new employer, whether or not its customers are transferred, the degree of similarity between the activities carried on before and after the transfer, and the period, if any, for which those activities are suspended.
>
> However, all those circumstances are merely single factors in the overall assessment which must be made and cannot therefore be considered in isolation.

1972.

> The Court has already had to consider the question of the transfer of an economic entity in the cleaning sector. It took the view that the degree of importance to be attached to each criterion for determining whether or not there has been a transfer within the meaning of the directive will necessarily vary according to the activity carried on, or indeed the production or operating methods employed in the relevant undertaking, business or part of a business. Thus, where, in particular an economic entity is able, in certain sectors, to function without any significant tangible or intangible assets, the maintenance of its identity following the transaction affecting it cannot, logically, depend on the transfer of such assets.

Thus, in certain labour-intensive sectors, a group of workers engaged in a joint activity on a permanent basis may constitute an economic entity. Such an entity is, therefore, capable of maintaining its identity after it has been transferred where the new employer does not merely pursue the activity in question but also takes over a major part, in terms of their numbers and skills, of the employees specially assigned by his predecessor to that task. Thus, an organised grouping of wage earners who are specifically and permanently assigned to a common task may, in the absence of other factors of production, amount to an economic entity.

1973. The fact that the staff of the transferor were dismissed only a few days before the employees in question were taken on again by the transferee, indicating that the reason for the dismissal was the transfer of the business, cannot have the effect of depriving workers of their right to have their contract of employment maintained by the transferee. In those circumstances, such staff must be regarded as still in the employment of the undertaking on the date of the transfer. The Court held that in order to determine whether the employees were dismissed solely as a result of the transfer, it is necessary to take into consideration the objective circumstances in which the dismissal took place, for example, the fact that it took effect on a date close to that of the transfer and that the employees in question were taken on again by the transferee. The staff of GMC must, therefore, be considered to have been part of that company until they were taken on by Temco.

Moreover, Article 1(1) of the directive expressly provides that the transfer can concern merely part of a business. Thus, the fact that the transferor undertaking continues to exist after one of its activities is taken over by another undertaking and that it retains part of the staff engaged in that activity has no effect on the classification of the transfer under the directive, since the transferred activity is an economic entity in its own right. In any event, it is clear from the case-file that, although GMC continued to exist as a legal entity after the termination of the cleaning contract between Volkswagen and BMV, it had ceased its only activity, which was taken over by Temco.

1974. *The Contractual Nature of the Transfer*

Under Article 1, the directive is applicable to transfers which are the result of a legal transfer or merger. Temco submits that there is no legal transfer where, as in the case in the main proceedings, there is neither any contractual relationship between the transferor and transferee nor any contractual relationship between the transferor and the original contractor who is only linked to the undertaking which subcontracted the cleaning work to the transferor. According to Temco, the undertaking which entered the cleaning contract with the original contractor did not, perforce, transfer any staff because the cleaning staff belonged to the subcontracting undertaking.

However, as the Court has held, the absence of a contractual link between the transferor and transferee cannot preclude a transfer within the meaning of the directive. The transfer can be effected in two successive contracts concluded by the transferor and transferee with the same legal or natural person. That case law certainly also applies in a situation where, as in the case in the main proceedings, a contractor enters into two successive cleaning contracts, the second on termination of the first, with two different undertakings.

1975.

The fact that the transferor undertaking is not the one which concluded the first contract with the original contractor but only the subcontractor of the original co-contractor has no effect on the concept of legal transfer since it is sufficient for that transfer to be part of the web of contractual relations even if they are indirect. In the case in the main proceedings, GMC's relationship with Volkswagen appears to be of a contractual nature within the meaning of the directive, since BMV, having had the contract awarded to it by Volkswagen, by contract concluded by the undertaking, in turn entrusted the performance of the contract to GMC by subcontract. Moreover, such subcontracts create direct links between the contractor and the subcontractor, which may be legal, as in the case of direct payment, and which are in any event practical links, as in the case of the monitoring and daily supervision of the work done. Such links are particularly important in the dispute in the main proceedings because GMC was set up, as a subsidiary, by BMV solely for the performance of the cleaning contract concluded by that company for the benefit of Volkswagen.

1976.

The answer to the first question referred for a preliminary ruling should therefore be that Article 1(1) of the directive must be interpreted as applying to a situation in which a contractor which has entrusted the contract for cleaning its premises to a first undertaking, which has that contract performed by a subcontractor, terminates that contract and enters into a new contract for the performance of the same work with a second undertaking, where the transaction does not involve any transfer of tangible or intangible assets, between the first undertaking or the subcontractor and the second undertaking, but the second undertaking has taken on, under a collective labour agreement, part of the staff of the subcontractor, provided that the staff thus taken on are an essential part, in terms of their number and their skills, of the staff assigned by the subcontractor to the performance of the subcontract.

Article 3(1) of the directive lays down the principle of the automatic transfer to the transferee of the rights and obligations incumbent on the transferor under the contracts of employment existing on the date of the transfer of the undertaking. The rule resulting from those provisions, according to which the transfer takes place without the consent of the parties, is mandatory; it is not possible to derogate from it in a manner prejudicial to employees. Consequently, the implementation of the rights conferred on employees by the directive may not be made subject to the consent of either the transferor or the transferee nor the consent of the employees' representatives or the employees themselves.

However, although the transfer of the contract of employment is thus imposed on both employer and employee the Court has conceded that the employee has the option of refusing to have his contract of employment transferred to the transferee. In such a case, the position of the employee depends on the legislation of the individual Member State: the contract binding the employee to the transferring undertaking may be terminated either by the employee or by the employer or the contract may be maintained with that undertaking.

1977.

The answer to the second question referred for a preliminary ruling should therefore be that Article 3(1) of the directive must be interpreted as meaning that it does not preclude the contract or employment relationship of a worker employed by the transferor on the date of the transfer of the undertaking within the meaning of Article 1(1) of the directive from continuing with the transferor where that worker objects to the transfer of his employment contract or employment relationship to the transferee.

1978.

The directive does not, unless Member States provide otherwise, apply to any transfer where the transferor is the subject of bankruptcy proceedings or any analogous insolvency proceedings which have been instituted with a view to the liquidation of the assets of the transferor and are under the supervision of a competent public authority.[794]

Where the directive applies to a transfer during insolvency proceedings which have been opened in relation to a transferor,[795] and provided that such proceedings are under the supervision of a competent public authority[796] a Member State may provide that:

(a) the transferor's debts arising from any contracts of employment or employment relationships and payable before the transfer or before the opening of the insolvency proceedings shall not be transferred to the transferee, provided that such proceedings give rise to protection at least

---

794. Which may be an insolvency practitioner authorised by a competent public authority.
795. Whether or not those proceedings have been instituted with a view to the liquidation of the assets of the transferor.
796. Which may be an insolvency practitioner determined by national law.

equivalent to that provided for in the insolvency directive[797] (Article 5(2)(a));
and, or alternatively, that
(b) the transferee, the transferor, person or persons exercising the transferor's functions, on the one hand, and the representatives of the employees on the other hand may agree alterations, insofar as current law or practice permits, to the employees' terms and conditions of employment designed to safeguard employment opportunities by ensuring the survival of the undertaking (Article 5(2)(b)).[798]

Member States have to take appropriate measures with a view to preventing misuse of insolvency proceedings in such a way as to deprive employees of the rights provided for in this directive (Article 5(4)).

1979. In the *Mayeur* case,[799] the questions were whether, and under what conditions, Directive 77/187 applies in the case where a municipality, which is a legal person governed by public law acting within the framework of the specific rules of administrative law, takes over activities concerning publicity and information on the services which it offers to the public, where such activities were previously carried out, in the interests of that municipality, by a non-profit-making association which was a legal person established under private law. The Court answered as follows:

On a proper construction of Article 1(1) the directive applies where a municipality, a legal person governed by public law operating within the framework of specific rules of administrative law, takes over activities relating to publicity and information concerning the services which it offers to the public, where such activities were previously carried out, in the interests of that municipality, by a non-profit-making association which was a legal person governed by private law, provided always that the transferred entity retains its identity.

In the *Liikenne* case[800] the question was raised whether the taking over by an undertaking of non-maritime public transport activities – such as the operation of scheduled local bus routes – previously operated by another undertaking, following a procedure for the award of a public service contract under Directive 92/50, may fall

---

797. Council Directive 80/987/EEC of 20 October 1980 on the approximation of the laws of the Member States relating to the protection of employees in the event of the insolvency of their employer. *See* Part I, Chapter 10, §2.
798. 'A Member State may apply 2 (b) to any transfer where the transferor is in a situation of serious economic crisis, as defined by national law, provided that the situation is declared by a competent public authority and open to juridical supervision, on condition that such provisions already exist in national law by 17 July 1998. The Commission shall present a report on the effects of this provision before 17 July 2003 and shall submit any appropriate proposals to the Council' (Article 5(3)).
799. C.O.J., 26 September 2000, *Didier Mayeur v. Association Promotion de l'information messine* (APIM); C-175/99, ECR, 2000, 7455.
800. C.O.J., 25 January 2001, *Oy Liikenne Ab v. Pekka Liskojärvi and Pentti Juntunen*, C-172/99, ECR, 2001, 745.

Part I, Ch. 10, Restructuring of Enterprises 1980–1980

within the material scope of Directive 77/187, as set out in Article 1(1) of that directive. The facts were as follows:

> Following a tender procedure, the Greater Helsinki Joint Board (YTV) awarded the operation of seven local bus routes, previously operated by Hakunilan Liikenne Oy ('Hakunilan Liikenne'), to Liikenne for three years. Hakunilan Liikenne, which operated those routes with 26 buses, thereupon dismissed 45 drivers, 33 of whom – that is, all those who applied – were re-engaged by Liikenne. Liikenne also engaged 18 other drivers. The former Hakunilan Liikenne drivers were re-engaged on the conditions laid down by the national collective agreement in the sector, which are less favourable overall than those which applied in Hakunilan Liikenne.
>
> When Liikenne replaced Hakunilan Liikenne, no vehicles or other assets connected with the operation of the bus routes concerned were transferred. Liikenne merely leased two buses from Hakunilan Liikenne for two or three months while waiting for the 22 new buses it had ordered to be delivered, and bought from Hakunilan Liikenne the uniforms of some of the drivers who entered its service.

1980. Mr. Liskojärvi and Mr. Juntunen are among the 33 drivers dismissed by Hakunilan Liikenne and taken on by Liikenne. Since they considered that there had been a transfer of an economic entity between the two undertakings and they were therefore entitled to continue to enjoy the conditions of employment applied by their former employer, they brought an action against Liikenne. Liikenne denied that a transfer had taken place.

In its order for reference, the national court considers that the concept of a transfer of an undertaking remains unclear, especially in cases such as this one where the taking over of an activity is not based on a contract between the parties and no significant assets are transferred. It further observes that the context of the case before it is an award procedure conducted in accordance with Directive 92/50. Application of Directive 77/187 in such a context, while protecting the rights of employees, may obstruct competition between undertakings and prejudice the aim of effectiveness pursued by Directive 92/50. The national court is uncertain as to the interrelationship of the two directives in those circumstances.

It stayed the proceedings and referred the following question to the Court for a preliminary ruling:

> Is a situation in which the operation of bus routes passes from one bus undertaking to another as a consequence of a tender procedure under Directive 92/50/EEC on public service contracts to be regarded as a transfer of a business for the purposes of Article 1(1) of Directive 77/187/EEC?

It must be recalled that the aim of Directive 77/187 is to ensure continuity of employment relationships within an economic entity, irrespective of any change of ownership. The fact that the activity carried on by such an entity is awarded successively to different operators by a public body cannot exclude the application of

Directive 77/187, if passenger transport by bus does not involve the exercise of public authority.

The Court thus held that Directive 77/187 may apply to a situation in which a public body which has contracted out its home-help service for persons in need or awarded a contract for the surveillance of some of its premises to one undertaking decides, on expiry or after termination of its contract with that undertaking, to contract out that service or award that contract to another undertaking.

That conclusion cannot be challenged on the ground that the contract for bus transport in question was awarded following a public procurement procedure conducted in accordance with Directive 92/50. Directive 77/187 does not provide for any such exception to its scope, nor does Directive 92/50 contain any provision to that effect. So the circumstance that a transaction comes under Directive 92/50 does not of itself rule out the application of Directive 77/187.

The fact that the provisions of Directive 77/187 may in certain cases be applicable in the context of a transaction which comes under Directive 92/50 cannot be seen as calling into question the objectives of the latter directive.

1981. Directive 92/50 is not intended to exempt contracting authorities and service providers who offer their services for the contracts in question from all the laws and regulations applicable to the activities concerned, in particular in the social sphere or that of safety, so that offers can be made without any constraints. The aim of Directive 92/50 is that, in compliance with those laws and regulations and under the conditions it lays down, economic operators may have equal opportunities, in particular for putting into practice their rights of freedom of establishment and freedom to provide services.

In such a context, operators retain their room to manoeuvre and compete with one another and submit different bids. In the field of passenger transport by scheduled bus services they may, for instance, adjust the standard of facilities of the vehicles and their performance in terms of energy and ecology, the efficiency of the organisation and methods of contact with the public, and, as with any undertaking, the profit margin desired. An operator who makes a bid must also be able to assess whether, if his bid is accepted, it will be in his interests to acquire significant assets from the present contractor and take over some or all of his staff, or whether he will be obliged to do so, and, if so, whether he will be in a situation of a transfer of an undertaking within the meaning of Directive 77/187.

That assessment, and that of the costs involved in the various possible solutions, are also part of the workings of competition and, contrary to Liikenne's submissions, cannot be regarded as disclosing an infringement of the principle of legal certainty. Any action in the field of competition will be subject to some uncertainty in relation to a number of factors, and it is the responsibility of operators to make realistic analyses. Admittedly, unlike its competitors, the undertaking which formerly had the contract knows precisely the costs it incurs in order to provide the service which is the subject of the contract; but this is inherent in the system and cannot justify not applying the social legislation, and that advantage is probably offset in most cases by the greater difficulty for that undertaking of changing its operating conditions in order to adapt them to the new conditions of the call for tenders, compared with competitors who make a bid from scratch.

The first answer to be given to the national court must therefore be that the taking over by an undertaking of non-maritime public transport activities – such as the operation of scheduled local bus routes – previously operated by another undertaking, following a procedure for the award of a public service contract under Directive 92/50, may fall within the material scope of Directive 77/187, as set out in Article 1(1) of that directive.

In view of the possible application of Directive 77/187 to a situation such as that before the national court, that court should, second, be given the criteria necessary to enable it to assess whether there was a transfer within the meaning of Article 1(1) of that directive in the present case. The national court observed in this respect that the takeover of the bus routes was not based on a contract between the old and new contractors and no significant assets were transferred between them.

The test for establishing the existence of a transfer within the meaning of Directive 77/187 is whether the entity in question retains its identity, as indicated *inter alia* by the fact that its operation actually continued or resumed.

While the absence of any contractual link between the transferor and the transferee or, as in this case, between the two undertakings successively entrusted with the operation of bus routes may point to the absence of a transfer within the meaning of Directive 77/187, it is certainly not conclusive.

Directive 77/187 is applicable wherever, in the context of contractual relations, there is a change in the natural or legal person responsible for carrying on the business and entering into the obligations of an employer towards employees of the undertaking. Thus there is no need, in order for that directive to be applicable, for there to be any direct contractual relationship between the transferor and the transferee: the transfer may take place in two stages, through the intermediary of a third party such as the owner or the person putting up the capital.

> Directive 77/187 can therefore apply where there is no direct contractual link between two undertakings successively awarded a contract, following procedures for the award of public service contracts in accordance with Directive 92/50, for a non-maritime public transport service, such as the operation of scheduled local bus routes, by a legal person governed by public law.

1982. For Directive 77/187 to be applicable, however, the transfer must relate to a stable economic entity whose activity is not limited to performing one specific works contract. The term 'entity' thus refers to an organised grouping of persons and assets facilitating the exercise of an economic activity which pursues a specific objective.

It is for the national court to establish if necessary, in the light of the guiding factors set out above, whether the operation of the bus routes at issue in the main proceedings was organised as an economic entity within Hakunilan Liikenne before being entrusted to Liikenne.

However, to determine whether the conditions for the transfer of an economic entity are satisfied, it is also necessary to consider all the factual circumstances characterising the transaction in question, including in particular the type of undertaking or business involved, whether or not its tangible assets such as buildings and movable property are transferred, the value of its intangible assets at the time of the transfer, whether or not the core of its employees are taken over by the new employer, whether or not its customers are transferred, the degree of similarity between the activities carried on before and after the transfer, and the period, if any, for which those activities were suspended. These are, however, merely single factors in the overall assessment which must be made, and cannot therefore be considered in isolation.

So the mere fact that the service provided by the old and the new contractors is similar does not justify the conclusion that there has been a transfer of an economic entity between the two undertakings. Such an entity cannot be reduced to the activity entrusted to it. Its identity also emerges from other factors, such as its workforce, its management staff, the way in which its work is organised, its operating methods or indeed, where appropriate, the operational resources available to it.

As pointed out above, the national court, in assessing the facts characterising the transaction in question, must take into account among other things the type of undertaking or business concerned. It follows that the degree of importance to be attached to the various criteria for determining whether or not there has been a transfer within the meaning of the directive will necessarily vary according to the activity carried on, and indeed the production or operating methods employed in the relevant undertaking, business or part of a business.

On this point, the Commission submits, referring to *Süzen*, that the absence of a transfer of assets between the old and new holders of the contract for bus transport is of no importance, whereas the fact that the new contractor took on an essential part of the employees of the old contractor is decisive.

1983. The Court has indeed held that an economic entity may, in certain sectors, be able to function without any significant tangible or intangible assets, so that the maintenance of the identity of such an entity following the transaction affecting it cannot, logically, depend on the transfer of such assets.

The Court thus held that, since in certain sectors in which activities are based essentially on manpower a group of workers engaged in a joint activity on a permanent basis may constitute an economic entity, it must be recognised that such an entity is capable of maintaining its identity after it has been transferred where the new employer does not merely pursue the activity in question but also takes over a major part, in terms of their numbers and skills, of the employees specially assigned by his predecessor to that task. In those circumstances, the new employer takes over an organised body of assets enabling him to carry on the activities or certain activities of the transferor undertaking on a regular basis.

However, bus transport cannot be regarded as an activity based essentially on manpower, as it requires substantial plant and equipment (the same conclusion has been reached with respect to driving work in mines). The fact that the tangible assets used for operating the bus routes were not transferred from the old to the new contractor therefore constitutes a circumstance to be taken into account.

Consequently, in a situation such as that in the main proceedings, Directive 77/187 does not apply in the absence of a transfer of significant tangible assets from the old to the new contractor.

The second answer to be given to the national court must therefore be that Article 1(1) of Directive 77/187 is to be interpreted as meaning that:

- that directive may apply where there is no direct contractual link between two undertakings which are successively awarded, following procedures for the award of public service contracts conducted in accordance with Directive 92/50, a non-maritime public transport service – such as the operation of scheduled local bus routes – by a legal person governed by public law;
- in a situation such as that in the main proceedings, Directive 77/187 does not apply where there is no transfer of significant tangible assets between those two undertakings.

In proceedings between Mr. Collino and Ms. Chiappero and Telecom Italia SpA,[801] the following question was raised:

> does a transfer for value, authorised by law enacted by the State and implemented by ministerial decree, of an undertaking managed by a public body which is a direct emanation of the State to a private company formed by another public body which holds all its shares, where the activity transferred is assigned to the private company under an administrative concession, fall within the scope of Article 1 of Directive 77/187/EEC?

1984. The Court answered as follows:

> Article 1(1) of Council Directive 77/187/EEC of 14 February 1977 on the approximation of thes laws of the Member States relating to the safeguarding of employees' rights in the event of transfers of undertakings, businesses or parts of businesses must be interpreted as meaning that that directive may apply to a situation in which an entity operating telecommunications services for public use and managed by a public body within the State administration is, following decisions of the public authorities, the subject of a transfer for value, in the form of an administrative concession, to a private-law company established by another public body which holds its entire capital. The persons concerned by such a transfer must, however, originally have been protected as employees under national employment law.

1985. In the *Abler* case[802] the following question was raised: 'is there a transfer where a hospital authority, which has previously employed a catering undertaking to supply meals and beverages to patients and hospital staff at a price based on a day of catering per person, and to that end has made available to that undertaking water and energy as well as its service premises (hospital kitchen) together with the necessary equipment, transfers, after giving notice of termination of that contract,

---

801. C.O.J., 14 September 2000, *Renato Collino and Luisella Chiappero v. Telecom Italia SpA*, C-343/98, ECR, 2000, 6659.
802. C.O.J., 20 November 2003, *Carlito Abler and Others v. Sodexho MM Catering Gesellschaft mbH*, C-340/01, ECR, 2003, 14023.

those operations and the assets previously made available to that first catering undertaking to a second catering undertaking which does not take over the assets (staff, stock, accounting material and menu, diet, recipe or general records) brought in by the first catering undertaking itself?'

1986. The facts were as follows. On 2 November 1990 the management authority of the Wien-Speising orthopaedic hospital (the management authority) concluded an agreement with Sanrest under which the latter took over the management of catering services within the hospital, providing patients and staff with meals and drinks. Special services were to be paid for separately.

Meals were to be prepared on the hospital premises. The obligations of Sanrest included, in particular, drawing up menus, purchasing, storing, producing, portioning and transporting the portioned meals to the various departments of the hospital (but not serving them to the patients), serving meals in the staff dining room, washing the crockery and cleaning the premises used.

The premises themselves, as well as water, energy and the necessary small and large equipment were provided for Sanrest by the management authority. Sanrest bore the cost of wear and tear of that equipment.

In addition, Sanrest took over the running of the cafeteria, which was also located in the hospital.

Further, until the summer of 1998, Sanrest supplied outside customers, *inter alia*, the Kindergarten St. Josef, a day nursery located near the hospital, with meals prepared in the hospital kitchen.

In the middle of 1998, disagreements arose between the management authority and Sanrest leading Sanrest to refuse to provide the contracted services for two months. During that time, Sodexho provided the catering services in the hospital from its other business premises.

By letter, the management authority terminated its contract with Sanrest, giving the six months' notice required under the contract.

By letter, the management authority informed Sanrest, which had submitted a bid in response to a new call for tenders, that the contract would not be awarded to it and the contract was awarded to Sodexho from 16 November 1999.

Sanrest then contended that this constituted a transfer of the undertaking. However, as Sodexho had refused to take over Sanrest's materials, stock and employees, the latter reduced stocks so that there was nothing left after 15 November 1999. According to the order for reference, Sodexho received no accounting data, menu plans, diet plans, recipe collections or general records from Sanrest.

Of the other activities of Sanrest, in addition to the catering service for the hospital, Sodexho took over some six to ten menus for the Kindergarten St. Josef.

By letter Sanrest terminated the employment contracts of its employees, with effect from 19 November 1999.

Mr. Abler and Others then brought an action against Sodexho before the *Arbeits- und Sozialgericht Wien* seeking a declaration that their employment relationship continued with Sodexho on the basis of the provisions on transfers of undertakings.

Part I, Ch. 10, Restructuring of Enterprises 1987–1989

1987. Sodexho contended that there had been no transfer of an undertaking as it had refused to take over even one of Sanrest's employees. It also stated that there was no contractual relationship between the two companies.

The answer to the preliminary question was affirmative:

> Article 1 of Directive 77/187 must be interpreted as applying to a situation in which a contracting authority which had awarded the contract for the management of the catering services in a hospital to one contractor terminates that contract and concludes a contract for the supply of the same services with a second contractor, where the second contractor uses substantial parts of the tangible assets previously used by the first contractor and subsequently made available to it by the contracting authority, even where the second contractor has expressed the intention not to take on the employees of the first contractor.

1988. In the *Nurten* case, the referring court points out that, under the Court's case-law, a transfer of assets to the contractor is one of the criteria characterising a transfer of a business. The Court of Justice summarised the case as follows:

> The referring German court is uncertain whether the condition that a transfer of assets exists only if the assets are used on an independent commercial basis, a criterion inserted by the case-law of the Federal Employment Tribunal, is permitted by Community law.
>
> The referring court considers that a significant issue as far as the decision in the main proceedings is concerned is whether there was a transfer of the assets, composed of the aviation security equipment, such as walk-through metal detectors, a baggage conveyor belt with automatic X-ray screening (baggage checking system), hand-held metal detectors and explosives detectors, from Securicor to Kötter.
>
> The referring court takes the view that the equipment in question was not used in an independent commercial manner, in so far as its maintenance was the responsibility of the German State, the contracting authority, which also had to bear the cost. There was absolutely no scope for the relevant contractors to use the equipment for their own purposes. They could neither obtain any additional economic benefit from it, nor determine the manner and extent of its use. Furthermore, under the contractual specifications, the contractor was obliged to use that equipment.

1989. In those circumstances, the referring court decided to stay the proceedings and refer the following question to the Court for a preliminary ruling:

> In examining whether there is – irrespective of the question of ownership – a transfer of a business within the meaning of Article 1 of Directive 2001/23/EC in the context of a fresh award of a contract, does the transfer of the assets from the original contractor to the new contractor – having regard to all the facts – presuppose their transfer for independent commercial use by the transferee? By extension, is conferment on the contractor of a right to determine the manner in which the assets are to be used in its own commercial interest the essential

criterion for a transfer of assets? On that basis, is it necessary to determine the operational significance of the contracting authority's assets for the service provided by the contractor?

1990. The Court of Justice ruled as follows:

The national court, in assessing the facts characterising the transaction in question, must take into account the type of undertaking or business concerned. It follows that the degree of importance to be attached to each criterion indicating a transfer within the meaning of Directive 2001/23 will necessarily vary according to the activity carried on, or indeed the production or operating methods employed in the relevant undertaking, business or part of a business.

The aim of the questions referred by the referring court is to define the conditions under which it may be considered that one of the circumstances to be taken into consideration, namely, that relating to the transfer of assets, is met. The referring court asks whether a finding that there was transfer of assets presupposes their transfer for independent commercial use.

In this connection, it must be noted that it is clear from the wording of Article 1 of Directive 2001/23 that it is applicable whenever, in the context of contractual relations, there is a change in the legal or natural person who is responsible for carrying on the undertaking or business and who by virtue of that fact incurs the obligations of an employer *vis-à-vis* the employees of the undertaking or business, regardless of whether or not ownership of the tangible assets is transferred.

1991. Earlier, the Court held that the fact that the tangible assets taken over by the new contractor did not belong to its predecessor but were provided by the contracting authority cannot preclude the existence of a transfer of an undertaking or business within the meaning of Directive 77/187.

It does not appear that the fact that independent commercial use was made of the assets taken over by a contractor is decisive in establishing whether or not there has been a transfer of assets.

That criterion is derived neither from the wording of Directive 2001/23 nor from its objectives, which are to ensure the protection of workers where there is a change of undertaking or business and to allow the completion of the internal market.

Thus, the fact that the tangible assets are taken over by the new contractor without those assets having been transferred to him for independent commercial use does not preclude there being either a transfer of assets, or a transfer of an undertaking or business within the meaning of Directive 2001/23.

1992. The answer to the question asked by the referring court is thus that Article 1 of Directive 2001/23 must be interpreted as meaning that, in examining whether there is a transfer of an undertaking or business within the meaning of that article, in the context of a fresh award of a contract and having regard to all the facts, the transfer of the assets for independent commercial use is not an essential criterion for the transfer of those assets from the original contractor to the new contractor.[803]

1993. Article 1(1) of Council Directive 2001/23/EC of 12 March 2001 must be interpreted as applying to a situation where part of the administrative personnel and part of the temporary workers are transferred to another temporary employment business in order to carry out the same activities in that business for the same clients and – which is a matter for the referring court to establish – the assets affected by the transfer are sufficient in themselves to allow the services characterising the economic activity in question to be provided without recourse to other significant assets or to other parts of the business.[804]

1994. In the *Albron* case, involving the Dutch beer producer group Heineken International, the Court ruled that in the event of a transfer of an undertaking belonging to a group to an undertaking outside that group, it is also possible to regard as a 'transferor', within the meaning of Article 2(1)(a) the group company to which the employees were assigned on a permanent basis without however being linked to the latter by a contract of employment, even though there exists within that group an undertaking with which the employees concerned were linked by such a contract of employment.[805]

1995. The Directive does however not apply to a situation in which a municipal authority which has contracted out the cleaning of its premises to a private company decides to terminate its contract with that company and to undertake the cleaning of those premises itself by hiring new staff for that purpose.[806]

1996. Between 1980 and 1999, Ms Scattolon, employed by the municipality of Scorzè (Italy) as a cleaner in State schools, carried out that task as a member of the administrative, technical and auxiliary (ATA) staff of the local authority. As from 2000, she was transferred onto the list of State ATA employees and placed on a salary scale corresponding, on that list, to nine years of service. She had thus suffered a considerable reduction in her remuneration, Ms Scattolon brought an action before the Tribunale di Venezia (Italy) seeking recognition of the whole of that length of service.

According to EU legislation on maintaining the rights of workers in the event of the transfer of an undertaking, the transferor's rights and obligations arising from a contract of employment or from an employment relationship existing on the date of a transfer are transferred to the transferee. In addition, the transferee must continue to observe the terms and conditions agreed in any collective agreement on the same terms applicable to the transferor under that agreement, until the date of termination

---

803. C.O.J., 15 December 2005, *Nurten Güney-Görres, Gul Demir v. Securicor Aviation (Germany), Ltd., Kötter Aviation Security GmbH & Co. KG*, Joined Cases C-232/04 and C-233/04, ECR, 2005, 11237.
804. C.O.J., 13 September 2007, *Mohamed Jouini and others*, C-458/05, www.curia.eu.
805. C.O.J., 21 October 2010, *Albron Catering BV v. FNV Bondgenoten, John Roest*, C-242/09, www.curia.eu.
806. C.O.J., 20 January 2011, *CLECE SA v. María Socorro Martín Valor*, C-463/09, www.curia.eu.

or expiry of the collective agreement or the entry into force or application of another collective agreement.

The *Tribunale di Venezia* asks the Court of Justice whether EU legislation on the maintenance of workers' rights in the event of the transfer of an undertaking applies to the takeover, by a public authority of a Member State, of staff employed by another public authority. Should that question be answered in the affirmative, the Italian court also asks whether, in order to calculate the remuneration of transferred workers, the transferee must take those workers' length of service with the transferor into account.

The Court of Justice finds that the takeover by a public authority of a Member State of staff employed by another public authority and entrusted with the supply to schools of auxiliary services such as maintenance and administrative assistance constitutes a transfer of an undertaking where that staff consists in a structured group of employees who are protected as workers by virtue of the domestic law of that Member State.[807]

B. Acquired Rights

1. Individual Rights

1997. The rule of thumb is that the rights and obligations of the employee arising from his contract of employment in the case of a transfer are *automatically* transferred. In other words, the employees who are employed on the date of transfer are automatically transferred to the new employer with all their acquired rights. Therefore, the terms of the contract work or of the working relationship may not be altered with regard to the salary, in particular its day of payment and composition, notwithstanding that the total amount is unchanged. The directive does not preclude, however, an alteration of the working relationship with the new head of the undertaking in so far as the national law allows such an alteration independently of a transfer of the undertaking.[808]

As the Court has repeatedly held,

> the Directive is intended to safeguard the rights of workers in the event of a change of employer by making it possible for them to continue to work for the new employer under the same conditions as those agreed with the transferor.
>
> It is likewise settled case law that the rules of the Directive, in particular those concerning the protection of workers against dismissal by reason of the transfer, must be considered to be mandatory, so that it is not possible to derogate from them in a manner unfavourable to employees.
>
> It follows that in the event of the transfer of an undertaking the contract of employment or employment relationship between the staff employed by the

---

807. C.O.J., 6 September 2011, *Ivana Scattolon*, v. *Ministerio* ... , C-108/10, www.curia;eu.
808. C.O.J., 12 November 1992, *A. Watson Rask and K. Christensen* v. *ISS Kantineservice A/S*, No. C-209/91, *op. cit.*

undertaking transferred may not be maintained with the transferor and is automatically continued with the transferee.

It must, however, be stated that, according to the second subparagraph of Article 3(1), the automatic transfer of employment relationships to the transferee does not prevent the Member States from providing that, after the date of transfer, the transferor and the transferee shall be jointly and severally liable in respect of obligations which arose before the date of transfer from a contract of employment or an employment relationship existing on the date of the transfer.

By reason of the mandatory nature of the protection afforded by the Directive, and in order not to deprive workers of that protection in practice, the transfer of the contracts of employment may not be made subject to the intention of the transferor or the transferee, and more particularly, that the transferee may not obstruct the transfer by refusing to fulfil his obligations.[809]

1998. It is, for the safeguarding of the employees' rights, only of importance whether the part of the undertaking for which the employees were working is transferred or not. This is to say that the directive does not cover the transferor's rights and obligations arising from a contract of employment or an employment relationship with employees who, although not employed in the transferred part of the undertaking, performed certain duties which involved the use of assets assigned to the part transferred or who, whilst being employed in an administrative department of the undertaking, which has not itself been transferred, carried out certain duties for the benefit of the part transferred. An employment relationship, the Court argued, is essentially characterised by the link existing between the employee and the part of the undertaking or the business to which he is assigned to carry out his duties. In order to decide whether the rights and obligations under an employment relationship are transferred, it is therefore sufficient to establish to which part of the undertaking or business the employee was assigned.[810] Whether or not such a contract or a relationship exists at that time must be assessed on the basis of national law, subject, however, to compliance with the mandatory provisions of the directive concerning the protection of employees from dismissal as a result of the transfer.[811]

1999. In proceedings between Mr. Collino and Ms. Chiappero and Telecom Italia SpA,[812] the following questions were raised:

(a) Does Article 3(1) of Directive 77/187/EEC require it to be held that the continuation of the employment relationship with the transferee is mandatory, so that the worker's length of service continues as from the date on which he was

---

809. C.O.J., 14 November 1996, *Claude Rotsaett de Hertaing* v. *J. Benoidt SA, in liquidation and others*, C-305/94, ECR, 1996, 5927.
810. *Idem.*
811. Bork, *op. cit.*
812. C.O.J., 14 September 2000, *Renato Collino and Luisella Chiappero* v. *Telecom Italia SpA*, C-343/98, ECR, 2000, 6659.

engaged by the transferor and he continues to be entitled to receive a single termination payment which treats as a whole the period spent by him in the transferor and transferee's employment?

(b) Must Article 3(1) be interpreted in any event as meaning that the worker's 'rights' transferred to the transferee also include the advantages acquired by him while employed by the transferor, such as length of service, if rights of a financial nature are attached thereto under the collective agreements applicable to the transferee?

The Court answered as follows. The first paragraph of Article 3(1) of Directive 77/187 must be interpreted as meaning that, in calculating the rights of a financial nature attached, in the transferee's business, to employees' length of service, such as a termination payment or salary increases, the transferee must take into account the entire length of service, in both his employment and that of the transferor, of the employees transferred, in so far as his obligation to do so derives from the employment relationship between those employees and the transferor, and in accordance with the terms agreed in that relationship. Directive 77/187 does not, however, preclude the transferee from altering the terms of the employment relationship where national law allows such an alteration in situations other than the transfer of an undertaking.

2000. The *Boor* case[813] relates to a transfer, which resulted in a reduction of the amount of remuneration.

Mrs. Boor was an employee of Foprogest. There was no collective agreement governing her remuneration.

Foprogest's objects consisted in particular of promoting and implementing training activities intended to improve the social and occupational position of persons seeking work and unemployed persons in order to enable them to be integrated or reintegrated into the workforce. Its resources consisted essentially of grants, donations and legacies.

Foprogest's activity was transferred to the Luxembourg State, namely the Minister for National Education, Vocational Training and Sport. The activity thus taken over is now carried on in the form of an administrative public service.

With effect from 1 January 2000, Mrs. Boor was taken on as an employee of the Luxembourg State. Other workers who had previously been employed by Foprogest were also taken on by the State. That operation gave rise to the conclusion of new contracts of employment between the State and the employees concerned. It was in those circumstances that Mrs. Boor on 22 December 1999 concluded a contract for an indefinite period with the minister concerned.

By virtue of the Grand-Ducal regulation on the remuneration of State employees, Mrs. Boor was then allocated a lower remuneration than that she had received under the contract originally concluded with Foprogest.

---

813. C.O.J., 11 November 2004, *Johanna Maria Boor* v. *Ministre de la Fonction publique et de la Réforme administrative*, C-425/02, ECR, 2004, 823.

She submitted at the hearing, without being contradicted by the Luxembourg Government, that she had been classified by the Luxembourg State, with no allowance for length of service, in the first grade, last step, of the salary scale, which meant that she lost 37 per cent of her monthly salary.

The parties to the main proceedings disagreed essentially on whether the State is obliged, after the transfer in question, to maintain all the rights of the employees, including in particular the right to remuneration, deriving from the contract of employment concluded between them and the transferor association.

2001. The Court ruled as follows. It should be recalled that, according to the Court's case law, the transfer of an economic activity from a legal person governed by private law to a legal person governed by public law is in principle within the scope of Directive 77/187. Only the reorganisation of structures of the public administration or the transfer of administrative functions between public administrative authorities is excluded from that scope.

Under Article 3(1) of Directive 77/187, the transferor's rights and obligations under the contract of employment or employment relationship are transferred to the transferee by reason of that transfer.

Since Directive 77/187 is intended to achieve only partial harmonisation of the field in question, it does not preclude, in the event of a transfer of an activity to a legal person governed by public law, the application of national law which prescribes the termination of contracts of employment governed by private law. However, such a termination constitutes, in accordance with Article 4(2) of Directive 77/187, a substantial change in working conditions to the detriment of the employee resulting directly from the transfer, so that the termination of those contracts of employment must, in such circumstances, be regarded as resulting from the action of the employer.

The same must apply where, as in the case at issue in the main proceedings, application of the national rules governing the position of State employees entails a reduction in the remuneration of the employees concerned by the transfer. Such a reduction must, if it is substantial, be regarded as a substantial change in working conditions to the detriment of the employees in question, within the meaning of Article 4(2) of the directive.

2002. Moreover, the competent authorities responsible for applying and interpreting the national law relating to public employees are obliged to do so as far as possible in the light of the purpose of Directive 77/187. It would be contrary to the spirit of that directive to treat an employee taken over from the transferor without taking length of service into account, in so far as the national rules governing the position of State employees take a State employee's length of service into consideration for calculating his remuneration.

2003. Consequently, the answer to the national court's question must be that Directive 77/187 must be interpreted as not precluding in principle, in the event of a transfer of an undertaking from a legal person governed by private law to the State, the latter, as new employer, from reducing the amount of the remuneration of the employees concerned for the purpose of complying with the national rules in force for public employees. However, the competent authorities responsible for applying and interpreting those rules are obliged to do so as far as possible in the light of the purpose of that directive, taking into account in particular the employee's length of service, in so far as the national rules governing the position of State employees take a State employee's length of service into consideration for calculating his remuneration. If such a calculation leads to a substantial reduction in the employee's remuneration, such a reduction constitutes a substantial change in working conditions to the detriment of the employees concerned by the transfer, so that the termination of their contracts of employment for that reason must be regarded as resulting from the action of the employer, in accordance with Article 4(2) of Directive 77/187.

2004. In the above mentioned *Scattolon* case[814] concerning the calculation of the remuneration of transferred workers, the Court considers that, whilst it is permissible for the transferee to apply, from the date of transfer, the working conditions laid down by the collective agreement in force with the transferee, including those concerning remuneration, the arrangements chosen for salary integration of the transferred workers must be in conformity with the aim of EU legislation on protection of the rights of transferred workers, which consists, in essence, of preventing those workers from being placed in a less favourable position than before solely as a result of the transfer.

The Court emphasises that, in this case, rather than recognising that length of service as such and in its entirety, the *Ministero* calculated a 'notional' length of service for each transferred worker, which played a decisive role in fixing the conditions of remuneration henceforth applicable to the staff transferred. Since the tasks carried out before the transfer in State schools by local authority ATA staff were similar, or even identical, to those carried out by the ATA staff employed by the Ministero, the length of service completed with the transferor by a transferred staff member could have been classified as equivalent to that completed by an ATA staff member having the same profile and employed, before the transfer, by the *Ministero*.

The Court of Justice therefore concludes that, where a transfer leads to the immediate application to the transferred workers of the collective agreement in force with the transferee, and where the conditions for remuneration are linked in particular to length of service, EU law precludes the transferred workers from suffering, in comparison with their situation immediately before the transfer, a substantial loss of salary by reason of the fact that their length of service with the transferor, equivalent to that completed by workers in the service of the transferee, is not taken into account when determining their starting salary position with the latter. It is for the national court to examine whether, at the time of the transfer at issue, there was such a loss of salary.

2005. The acquired rights are not only those that exist on the date of the transfer (Article 3(1)), but also those arising before the date of the transfer.[815] This means

---

814. C.O.J., 6 September 2011, *Ivana Scattolon*, v. *Ministerio* ... , , C-108/10, www.curia.eu.
815. Abels, *op. cit.*

that the transferor, after the date of the transfer and by virtue of the transfer alone, is discharged from all obligations arising under the contract of employment or the employment relationship, even if the workers employed in the undertaking do not consent or if they object.[816] Article 3(1), 2nd subparagraph stipulates, indeed, that the Member States may provide for joint responsibility of the transferor and the transferee following the transfer. It follows that, unless the Member States avail themselves of this possibility, the transferor is released from his obligations as an employer solely by the reason of the transfer and that this legal consequence is not conditional on the consent of the employees concerned. Similarly, the argument based on the principle of the law of obligations which, it is claimed, is generally recognised in the legal systems of the Member States, namely that a debt may be transferred only with the creditor's consent, cannot be accepted in the light of the clear language of the directive which provides for the automatic transfer of obligations arising from employment contracts to the transferee.[817] It should be added that an employee cannot waive the rights conferred upon him by mandatory provisions of Directive No. 2001/23 even if the disadvantages resulting from his waiver are offset by such benefits that, taking the matter as a whole, he is not placed in a worse position.[818] The directive refers only to the rights and obligations of workers whose contract of employment or employment relationship is in force at the date of the transfer and not to those who have ceased to be employed by the undertaking in question at the time of the transfer. The transferee of an undertaking is not liable in respect of obligations concerning holiday pay and compensation to employees who were not employed in the undertaking on the date of the transfer.[819] We must also add that Directive No. 2001/23 does not cover the transfer of the rights and obligations of persons who were employed by the transferor at the date of the transfer, but who, by their own decision, do not continue to work as employees of the transferee.[820]

The question arises whether the transfer of the contracts of employment and employment relationships pursuant to Article 3(1) of the directive necessarily takes place on the date of the transfer of the undertaking, or whether it may be postponed to another date at the will of the transferor or the transferee.

From the actual wording of the directive it follows that the transfer of the contracts of employment and employment relationships takes place on the date of the transfer of the undertaking.

Article 3(1) is to be interpreted as meaning that after the date of transfer the transferor is in principle discharged, by virtue of the transfer alone, from all obligations arising under the contract of employment or in the employment relationship. Given the Directive's objective of protecting workers, that can only be done if the obligations in question are transferred to the transferee as from the date of transfer.

---

816. *Berg, op. cit.*
817. *Idem.*
818. C.O.J., 10 February 1988, *Foreningen af Arbejdsledere I Danmark* v. *Daddy's Dance Hall AS No. 324/86*, ECR, 1988, 739.
819. C.O.J., 7 February 1985, *Knud Wendelboe and others* v. *L.J. Musie A/S, in liquidation*, No. 19/ 83, ECR, 1985, 457.
820. *Foreningen*, No. 105/84, *op. cit.*

To allow the transferor or transferee the possibility of choosing the date from which the contract of employment or employment relationship is transferred would amount to allowing employers to derogate, at least temporarily, from the provisions of the directive. However, those provisions are mandatory.[821]

The directive does not, in view of the fundamental freedom of labour the employee enjoys, require Member States to provide that the contract of employment or the employment relationship should be maintained with the transferor, in the event of the employee freely deciding not to continue the contract of employment or the employment relationship with the transferee. Neither does the Directive preclude it. In such a case, it is for the Member States to determine the fate of the contract of employment or the employment relationship with the transferor.[822] This means that, in cases where national law does not provide otherwise, the employee deciding not to continue the employment relationship with the transferee may still be bound by an employment contract with the transferor. This reasoning of the European Court may lead to bizarre consequences and calls for great caution in case of transfer of an enterprise.

Member States may adopt appropriate measures to ensure that the transferor notifies the transferee of all the rights and obligations which will be transferred to the transferee, so far as those rights and obligations are or ought to have been known to the transferor at the time of the transfer. A failure by the transferor to notify the transferee of any such right or obligation shall not affect the transfer of that right or obligation and the rights of any employees against the transferee and/or transferor in respect of that right or obligation (Article 3(2)).

2006. The date of a transfer is the date on which responsibility as employer for carrying on the business of the unit transferred moves from the transferor to the transferee. That date is a particular point in time which cannot be postponed to another date at the will of the transferor or transferee.

For the purposes of applying that provision, contracts of employment or employment relationships existing on the date of the transfer between the transferor and the workers assigned to the undertaking transferred are deemed to be handed over, on that date, from the transferor to the transferee, regardless of what has been agreed between the parties in that respect.[823]

2. Collective Agreements

2007. Pursuant to Article 3(3) of the directive the transferee shall, following the transfer, continue to observe the terms and conditions agreed in any collective agreement on the same terms applicable to the transferor under that agreement, until the date of termination or expiry of the collective agreement or the entry into force

---

821. *Idem.*
822. C.O.J., 16 December 1992, *G. Katsikas and Others* v. *A Konstantinidis and Others*, Joined Cases Nos. C-132/91, C-138/91, ECR, 1992, 6577.
823. C.O.J., 26 May 2005, *Celtec Ltd.* v. *John Astley and Others*, C-478/03, ECR, 2005, 4389.

or application of another collective agreement.[824] The directive does not oblige the transferee to continue to observe the terms and conditions agreed in any collective agreement in respect of workers who are not employed by the undertaking at the time of the transfer.[825] Member States may limit the period of observing such terms and conditions, with the proviso that it shall not be less than one year (Article 3(3), 2nd subparagraph).

2008. In a situation where the contract of employment refers to a collective agreement binding the transferor, it follows that the transferee, who is not party to such an agreement, is not bound by collective agreements subsequent to the one which was in force at the time of the transfer of the business.[826]

3. Social Security

2009. The provisions regarding acquired rights do not, unless Member States provide otherwise, cover employees' rights to old age, invalidity or survivors' benefits under supplementary company or intercompany pension schemes outside the statutory social security schemes in Member States. Member States have, however, to adopt the measures necessary to protect the interests of employees and of persons no longer employed in the transferor's business at the time of the transfer in respect of the rights conferring on them immediate or prospective entitlements to old-age benefits, including survivors' benefits, under the supplementary schemes (Article 3(4)).

2010. Early retirement benefits and benefits intended to enhance the conditions of such retirement, paid in the event of dismissal to employees who have reached a certain age, such as the benefits at issue in the main proceedings, are not old-age, invalidity or survivors' benefits under supplementary company or inter-company pension schemes within the meaning of Article 3(3) of Council Directive 77/187/EEC.

On a proper construction of Article 3 of Directive 77/187, the obligations applicable in the event of the dismissal of an employee, arising from a contract of employment, an employment relationship or a collective agreement binding the transferor as regards that employee, are transferred to the transferee subject to the conditions and limitations laid down by that article, regardless of the fact that those obligations derive from statutory instruments or are implemented by such instruments and regardless of the practical arrangements adopted for such implementation.[827]

---

824. *See also* C.O.J., 12 November 1992, *A. Watson Rask and K. Christensen v. ISS Kantineservice A/S*, No. C-209/91, ECR, 1997, 5753.
825. *Landesorganisationen v. Ny Molle Kro*, 17 December 1978, No. 287/86, ECR, 1987, 5465.
826. C.O.J., 9 March 2006, *Hans Werhof v. Freeway Traffic Systems GmbH & Co. KG*, C-499/04, ECR, 2006, 2397.
827. *Beckmann Katia v. Dynamco Whichloe Macfarlane Ltd.*, 4 June 2002, Case C-164/00, ECR, 2002, 4893.

2011. The European Court,[828] stated that early retirement benefits should be paid for by a new employer after a transfer of undertakings.

The case was as follows. Prior to 1 November 1994, Serene Martin, Rohit Daby and Brian Willis were employed as nursing lecturers at a college which formed part of the UK National Health Service (NHS). However, this college subsequently became part of South Bank University (SBU). Shortly before this transfer, the college staff were informed by SBU that they would be offered a new employment contract and, although they were not obliged to accept the new terms and conditions, they would in any case not be able to continue their membership of the NHS retirement scheme. They could either: leave the NHS scheme as it was and join a new scheme; transfer pension rights from the NHS scheme to one of the SBU's retirement schemes; or leave the NHS pension scheme as it was and not join a new scheme. The applicants did not accept the new SBU terms and conditions, but joined the teachers' superannuation scheme and applied to transfer their existing NHS pension rights into that scheme. However, only Mr. Daby and Mr. Willis were able to do so – Ms. Martin could not as she was over 60 at the time of the transfer.

In January 1997, SBU wrote to all university staff aged over 50 stating that it would not be able to offer early retirement after 31 March 1997 and offered them a last change of taking early retirement before that date. Ms. Martin and Mr. Daby accepted the offer. Mr. Willis remained in SBUs' employment. At this point, a dispute arose, as the applicants claimed to be entitled to the NHS terms of early retirement instead of SBU's terms, which were less favourable.

The Employment Tribunal, UK, decided to refer a total of nine questions to the Court relating to the application of the Directive on the transfer of undertakings with regard to early retirement benefits. In essence, the rule contained in the Directive protecting employees' terms of employment in the event of a transfer of undertakings does not apply to old-age, invalidity or survivors' benefits. The Court therefore had to decide whether conditional benefits paid before normal retirement age at the discretion of an employer would fall within this exclusion. If they did, then the protection offered by the Directive could not be applied.

2012. The Court held that only benefits paid for the time when employees reach the end of their normal working life, under the rules of the pension scheme in question, and not benefits paid in other circumstances, could be classified as old-age benefits, even if calculated by reference to the rules for calculating normal pension benefits. The Court therefore ruled that there was no reason to treat the early retirement benefits in question any differently from benefits payable on redundancy and that therefore they came within the scope of the Directive's protection.

The Court also looked at the issue of whether, if rights were transferred, they could be waived or varied by the employee's acceptance of new terms of employment offered by the new employer. It held that legislation on this issue is in place in order to safeguard employees' rights and it should therefore not be possible to derogate from those rights in a manner unfavourable to employees, unless altering the rights was unconnected with a transfer of undertaking. However, in this case,

---

828. C.O.J., 6 November 2003, Serene Martin, Rohit Daby, *Brian Willis* v. *South Bank University*, C-4/01, ECR, 2003, 12895; 'ECJ ruling on early retirement benefits', www.eiro.eurofound.ie, 2003

the new terms were designed to bring the applicants' early retirement benefits into line with those offered to existing SBU employees and were therefore connected with the transfer.

'This means that employers have to factor the cost of early retirement benefits into transfers of undertakings. Further, there is no specific time limit for bringing claims relating to the transfer of rights and therefore there is a possibility that claims could be backdated to 1977, when the Directive came into force.'

2013. In the *Klarenberg case*,[829] the transferee apart from the products which were the subject-matter of that contract, develops, manufacturers and distributes other products in the field of the metallurgical measurement techniques, and former employees of the transferor were integrated into the structure established by the transferee. In addition, those employees also carried out duties in relation to products other than those acquired by the transferee from the transferor.

In the case before it, the transferee did not retain the organisational autonomy of the relevant part of the business, in so far as the re-engaged employees were integrated into different units, and the functions taken over are now carried out in the framework of a different organisational structure.

The Court was asked, in essence, whether Article 1(1)(a) and (b) of Directive 2001/23 must be interpreted as meaning that that Directive may also apply in a situation where the new employer does not preserve the organisational autonomy of the part of the undertaking or business transferred.

2014. The Court ruled as follows:

> At the outset, it should be borne in mind that, according to settled case-law, in interpreting a provision of Community law it is necessary to consider not only its wording but also the context in which it occurs and the objectives pursued by the rules of which it is.
>
> It is clear from the very wording of Article 1(1)(a) that any transfer, to another employer, involving an undertaking, a business, or part of an undertaking or business and brought about by a legal transfer or merger falls within the scope of that directive.
>
> Subject to those conditions, the transfer must nevertheless also satisfy the conditions laid down in Article 1(1)(b) if that directive is to apply: that is to say, it must concern an economic entity – understood by 'an organised grouping of resources which has the objective of pursuing an economic activity, whether or not that activity is central or ancillary' – which, following the transfer, retains its 'identity'.
>
> It should at the outset be recalled that, as is clear from recital 8 in the preamble to Directive 2001/23, the above provision was adopted to clarify the concept of transfer in the light of the case-law of the Court. According to that case-law, Directive 2001/23 is intended to ensure the continuity of employment relationships existing within an economic entity, irrespective of any

---

829. C.O.J., 12 February 2009, *Dietmar Klarenberg v. Ferrotron Technologies GmbH*, C-466/07, www.curia.eu.

change of ownership and, thus, to protect employees in the event that such a change occurs.

It is clear from the provisions of Article 1(1)(a), read in conjunction with those of Article 1(1)(b) thereof, that, in the event that the economic entity transferred does not retain its identity, the application of point (b) of Article 1(1) forestalls the operation of point (a) of that provision. It follows that Article 1(1)(b) is capable of restricting the scope of Article 1(1)(a) of that directive, hence the scope of the protection afforded by that directive. Such a provision must therefore be construed narrowly.

As regards, specifically, the factor relating to organisation, although the Court has previously held that that factor contributes to defining an economic entity, it has also held that an alteration in the organisational structure of the entity transferred is not such as to prevent the application of Directive 2001/23.

Moreover, of itself, Article 1(1)(b) defines the identity of an economic entity by referring to an 'organised grouping of resources which has the objective of pursuing an economic activity, whether or not that activity is central or ancillary', thus emphasising not only the organisational element of the entity transferred but also the element of pursuing an economic activity.

Having regard to the foregoing, in order to interpret the condition relating to the preservation of the identity of an economic entity, within the meaning of Directive 2001/23, account should be taken of the two elements – as laid down in Article 1(1)(b) – which, taken together, constitute that identity, and of the objective pursued by that directive, namely the protection of employees.

The reply to the question is therefore that Article 1(1)(a) and (b) must be interpreted as meaning that that directive may also apply in a situation where the part of the undertaking or business transferred does not retain its organisational autonomy, provided that the functional link between the various elements of production transferred is preserved, and that that link enables the transferee to use those elements to pursue an identical or analogous economic activity, a matter which it is for the national court to determine.

2015. Article 3(1) does not require, in the event of transfer of an undertaking, the preservation of the lease of commercial premises entered into by the transferor of the undertaking with a third party even though the termination of that lease is likely to entail the termination of contracts of employment transferred to the transferee.[830]

4. Protection against Dismissal

2016. Article 4(1) of the directive protects the concerned employees in the case of a transfer against dismissal by the transferor or the transferee on the grounds of the transfer, except for economic, technical or organisational reasons entailing

---

830. C.O.J., 16 October 2008 Kirtruna SL, *Elisa Vigano* v. *Red Elite de Electrodomésticos SA*, in Case C-313/07, www.curia.eu.

changes in the workforce. In order to ascertain whether the employees were dismissed solely as a result of the transfer, it is necessary to take into consideration the objective circumstances in which the dismissal took place such as, in particular, the fact that it took effect on a date close to that of the transfer and that the employees in question were taken on again by the transferee. Accordingly, the employees whose contract of employment or employment relationship was terminated with effect from a date prior to that of the transfer, contrary to Article 4(1), must be regarded as still in the employment of the transferor, with the result, in particular, that the employer's obligations toward them are automatically transferred from the transferor to the transferee.[831]

2017. This case law has been confirmed in the *Dethier* case. Both the transferor and the transferee may dismiss employees for economic, technical or organisational reasons. Employees unlawfully dismissed by the transferor shortly before the undertaking is transferred and not taken on by the transferee may claim, as against the transferee, that their dismissal was unlawful.[832] In *Merckx and Neuhuys* v. *Ford Motor Company Belgium SA*[833] the issue of the employee's power to prevent the transfer of his contract or the employment relationship was raised. Here, the Court held, as in *Foreningen af Arbejdsledere i Danmark* v. *Danmols Inventar*,[834] that the protection which the directive is intended to guarantee is redundant where the person concerned decides of his own accord not to continue the employment relationship with the new employer after the transfer.

It also follows, the Court said, from the judgment in *Katsikas and Others* v. *Konstandinidis*,[835] that, whilst the directive allows the employee to remain in the employ of his new employer on the same conditions as were agreed with the transferor, it cannot be interpreted as obliging the employee to continue his employment relationship with the transferee. Such an obligation would jeopardise the fundamental rights of the employee, who must be free to choose his employer and cannot be obliged to work for an employer whom he has not freely chosen.

It follows that, in the event of the employee deciding of his own accord not to continue with the contract of employment or employment relationship with the transferee, it is for the Member States to determine what the fate of the contract of employment or employment relationship should be. In the light of that submission, it should be noted that Article 4(2) provides that if the contract of employment or the employment relationship is terminated because the transfer within the meaning of Article 1(1) involves a substantial change in working conditions to the detriment of the employee, the employer is to be regarded as having been responsible for termination. Consequently, if, as Merckx and Neuhuys pretend, Novarobel (the transferee) refused to guarantee to maintain their former level of remuneration, it must be regarded as responsible for the termination of the employment relationship.

---

831. P. Bork, *op. cit.*
832. C.O.J., 12 March 1998, *Jules Dethier Equipement SA/J. Dassy en Sovam SPRL, in liquidation*, C-319/94, ECR, 1998, 1061.
833. *Op. cit.*
834. *Op. cit.*
835. *Op. cit.*

2018. Article 3(1) of the directive does, however, not preclude a worker employed by the transferor at the date of the transfer of an undertaking from objecting to the transfer of his contract of employment or employment relationship to the transferee, provided he decides to do so of his own accord. It is for the national court to determine whether the contract of employment proposed by the transferee involves a substantial change in working conditions to the detriment of the worker. If it does, Article 4(2) of the directive requires Member States to provide that the employer is to be considered responsible for the termination.[836]

2019. This was confirmed by the Court, which ruled that 'A state entity which transfers its operations cannot rely on Articles 3(1) and 1(1)(c) of Directive 2001/23 against its employees in order to force them to continue their employment relationships with a transferee'.[837]

2020. Pursuant to the second sub-paragraph of Article 4, the Member States may provide that this protection against dismissal does not apply to certain specific categories of employees who are not covered by the laws or practices of the Member States in respect of protection against dismissal. This exception must be interpreted restrictively.

It is clear from the wording of Article 4(1) and from the scheme of the directive that the provision in question is designed to ensure that employees' rights are maintained by extending the protection against dismissal by the employer afforded by national law to cover the case in which a change in employer occurs upon the transfer of an undertaking.

Consequently, that provision applies to any situation in which employees affected by the transfer enjoy some, albeit limited – in the case of the trial period – protection against dismissal under national law, with the result that, under the directive, that protection may not be taken away from them or curtailed solely because of the transfer.[838]

2021. If the contract of employment or the employment relationship is terminated because the transfer involves a substantial change in working conditions to the detriment of the employee, the employer shall be regarded as having been responsible for termination of the contract of employment or the employment relationship (Article 4(2)).

2022. In the *Juuri case*[839] the question was asked whether Article 4(2) of Directive 2001/23 must be interpreted as requiring Member States, in cases where a contract of employment or an employment relationship falling within the scope of that

---

836. C.O.J., 12 November 1998, *Europièces SA* v. *Wilfried Sanders and Automotive Industries Holding Company SA*, Case C-399/96, ECR, 1998, 6965.
837. C.O.J., 26 May 2005, *Sozialhilfeverband Rohrbach* v. *Arbeiterkammer Oberösterreich, Österreichischer Gewerkschaftsbund*, C-297/03, ECR, 2005, 4305.
838. C.O.J., 15 April 1986, *Commission* v. *Belgium*, No. 237/84, 89.
839. C.O.J., 27 November 2008, *Mirja Juuri* v. *Fazer Amica Oy*, C-396/07, www.curia..

provision is terminated, to guarantee employees the right to financial compensation, for which the transferee employer is liable, in accordance with conditions identical to the right on which the employee can rely where an employer unlawfully terminates the employment contract or the employment relationship, or, at least, on which he can rely by virtue of the notice period to be observed by an employer under the applicable national law where the employment contract is terminated on material and serious grounds.

2023. The Court answered:

> Article 4(2) of Directive 2001/23 must be interpreted as meaning that, in cases where the termination of a contract of employment or an employment relationship is brought about because the conditions for the applicability of that provision have been met, independently of any failure on the part of the transferee employer to fulfil its obligations under that directive, the Member States are not required to guarantee the employee a right to financial compensation, for which the transferee employer is liable, in accordance with the same conditions as the right upon which an employee can rely where the contract of employment or the employment relationship is unlawfully terminated by his employer. However, the national court is required, in a case within its jurisdiction, to ensure that, at the very least, the transferee employer in such a case bears the consequences that the applicable national law attaches to termination by an employer of the contract of employment or the employment relationship, such as the payment of the salary and other benefits relating, under that law, to the notice period with which an employer must comply.

5. Workers' Representation

2024. If the business preserved its autonomy, the status and function of the representatives or of the representations of the employees affected by the transfer shall be preserved, unless the conditions necessary for the reappointment of the representatives of the employees or for the reconstituting of the representation of the employees are fulfilled.[840] If the undertaking, business or part of an undertaking or business does not preserve its autonomy, the Member States shall take the necessary measures to ensure that the employees transferred who were represented before the transfer continue to be properly represented during the period necessary for the reconstitution or reappointment of the representation of employees in accordance with national law or practice (Article 6(1), 4th indent).

Where the transferor is the subject of bankruptcy proceedings or any analogous insolvency proceedings which have been instituted with a view to the liquidation of the assets of the transferor and are under the supervision of a competent public

---

840. This does not apply if, under the laws, regulations, administrative provisions or practice in the Member States, or by agreement with the representatives of the employees, the conditions necessary for the reappointment of the representatives of the employees or for the reconstitution of the representation of the employees are fulfilled (Article 6(1), 2nd indent).

authority (which may be an insolvency practitioner authorised by a competent public authority), Member States may take the necessary measures to ensure that the transferred employees are properly represented until the new election or designation of representatives of the employees (Article 6(1), 3rd indent).

If the term of office of the representatives of those employees affected by the transfer expires as a result of the transfer, the representatives shall continue to enjoy the protection provided by national law or practice (Article 6(2)).

2025. A transferred economic entity preserves its autonomy, within the meaning of Article 6(1) provided that the powers granted to those in charge of that entity, within the organisational structures of the transferor, namely the power to organise, relatively freely and independently, the work within that entity in the pursuit of its specific economic activity and, more particularly, the powers to give orders and instructions, to allocate tasks to employees of the entity concerned and to determine the use of assets available to the entity, all without direct intervention from other organisational structures of the employer, remain, within the organisational structures of the transferee, essentially unchanged. The mere change of those ultimately in charge cannot in itself be detrimental to the autonomy of the entity transferred, except where those who have become ultimately in charge have available to them powers which enable them to organise directly the activities of the employees of that entity and therefore to substitute their decision-making within that entity for that of those immediately in charge of the employees.[841]

C. Information and Consultation

2026. The directive provides that the transferor and the transferee shall be required to inform the representatives of their respective employees affected by the transfer of the following information:

– the date or proposed date of the transfer;
– the reasons for the transfer;
– the legal, economic and social implications of the transfer for the employees;
– the measures envisaged in relation to the employees.

The transferor must give such information in good time before the transfer is carried out. The transferee must give such information in good time, and in any event before his employees are directly affected by the transfer as regards their conditions of work and employment (Article 7(1)). If the transferor or the transferee envisages measures in relation to his employees, he shall consult his workers' representatives in good time on such measures with a view to seeking agreement (Article 7(2)).

2027. If national rules provide that workers' representatives may have recourse to an arbitration board to obtain a decision on the measures to be taken in relation

---

841. C.O.J., 29 July 2010, *Federación de Servicios Públicos de la UGT (UGT-FSP)* v. *Ayuntamiento de La Línea de la Concepción*, C-151/09, www.curia.

to employees, the Member States may limit the information and consultation to cases where the transfer carried out gives rise to a change in the business likely to entail serious disadvantages for a considerable number of the employees. The information and consultations shall at least cover the measures envisaged in relation to the employees and take place in good time before the change in the business (Article 7(3)). Member States may limit the obligations to undertakings or businesses which, in respect of the number of employees, fulfil the conditions for the election or designation of a collegiate body representing the employees (Article 7(5)). They may also provide that where there are no workers' representatives in an undertaking or a business, the employees must be informed in advance when a transfer is about to take place (Article 7(6)).

The employees concerned must be informed in advance of:

– the date or proposed date of the transfer,
– the reason for the transfer,
– the legal, economic and social implications of the transfer for the employees,
– any measures envisaged in relation to the employees (Article 7(6)).

The obligations laid down in Article 7 are binding irrespective of whether the decision resulting in the transfer is taken by the employer or an undertaking controlling the employer.

In considering alleged breaches of the information and consultation requirements, the argument that such a breach occurred because the information was not provided by an undertaking controlling the employer shall not be accepted as an excuse (Article 7(4)).

II. Mergers and Divisions of Public Limited Liability Companies

2028. The (third and sixth) directives concerning the mergers and divisions of public limited liability companies of 9 October 1978 and 17 December 1982[842], as amended respectively provide that Directive No. 2001/23 concerning acquired rights regulates the protection rights of the employees of each of the merging companies (Article 12) or of the companies involved in a decision (Article 11). These directives were taken in view of the coordination of national legislation regarding public limited liability companies, provided for in Article 50(2g) TFEU.

2029. For the purpose of these directives, *merger* (by acquisition or by the formation of a new company) means the operation whereby one or more companies are wound up without going into liquidation and transfer to another all their assets and liabilities in exchange for the issue to the shareholders of the company or companies being acquired of shares in the acquiring company and cash payments, if any, not exceeding 10 per cent of the nominal value of the shares so issued or, where they have no nominal value, of their accounting par value (Articles 3(1) and 4(1)).

---

842. Based on Article 54(3G) of the EC Treaty, No. 78/855 (O.J. L 295, 20 October 1978) and No. 82/891, O.J. L 287, 31 December 1982.

2030. For the purpose of the directive, *division* (by acquisition or by formation of new companies) means the operation whereby, after being wound up without going into liquidation, a company transfers to more than one company all its assets and liabilities in exchange for the allocation to the shareholders of the company being divided of shares in the companies receiving contributions as a result of the division (hereinafter referred to as 'recipient companies') and possibly a cash payment not exceeding 10 per cent of the nominal value of the shares allocated or, where they have no nominal value, of their accounting par value (Articles 2(1) and 21(1)).

§3. INSOLVENCY OF THE EMPLOYER

2031. The protection of employees in the event of the insolvency of their employer is regulated by Directive 2008/94/EC of 22 October 2008 (Codified version).[843] The recital to the directive indicates that:

> It is necessary to provide for the protection of employees in the event of the insolvency of their employer and to ensure a minimum degree of protection, in particular in order to guarantee payment of their outstanding claims, while taking account of the need for balanced economic and social development in the Community. To this end, the Member States should establish a body which guarantees payment of the outstanding claims of the employees concerned.
>
> In order to ensure equitable protection for the employees concerned, the state of insolvency should be defined in the light of the legislative trends in the Member States and that concept should also include insolvency proceedings other than liquidation. In this context, Member States should, in order to determine the liability of the guarantee institution, be able to lay down that where an insolvency situation results in several insolvency proceedings, the situation is to be treated as a single insolvency procedure.

2032. In a very important case the Court ruled that interested parties may not assert the rights laid down in the directive against the state in proceedings before the national courts in the absence of implementing measures adopted within the prescribed period.[844] The Court accepted, however, the principle of liability of the state. Indeed the full effectiveness of Union law would be undermined and the rights deriving from it would be less safeguarded if individuals were unable to obtain reparation when their rights were undermined by the infringement of Community law imputable to a Member State. It follows that Union law lays down the principle according to which the Member States are obliged to compensate individuals for

---

843. O.J., 28 October 2008, L 283.
844. 19 November 1991, *A. Francovich and Others* v. *Italian Republic*, Joined Cases Nos. C-6/90 and C-9/90, ECR, 1995, 3843. *See also* C.O.J., 3 December 1992, *M. Suffritti and Others* v. *Instituto Nazionale Della Previdenze Sociale (INPS)*, Joined Cases Nos. C-140/01, 141/91, 278/ 91 and 279/ 91, ECR, 1992, 6337.

damage caused to them by infringements of Union law imputable to the Member State.

The Court expanded at length on the principle of state liability. First, the Court said, it was important to bear in mind that the Treaty created the Union's own legal order, which was integrated into the legal systems of the Member States, was binding on their courts and covered not only the Member States but also their nationals, and, just as it imposed burdens on individuals, Union law also gave rise to rights forming part of their legal heritage; such rights arose not only where they were expressly provided for by the Treaty but also by virtue of obligations which the Treaty imposed in clear terms both on individuals and Member States and on Union institutions.

Furthermore, as the Court had consistently held, it was incumbent on the national courts responsible for applying Union law in the areas within their purview to ensure that those provisions took full effect and to safeguard the rights which they conferred on individuals.

The full effectiveness of Union law would be undermined and the rights deriving from it would be less safeguarded if individuals were unable to obtain reparation when their rights were undermined by an infringement of Union law imputable to a Member State.

The possibility of obtaining reparation from Member States was particularly necessary where, as in the present case, the full effectiveness of Union provisions was conditional upon action being taken by a Member State and where, consequently, individuals were unable, in the absence of such action, to enforce before the national courts the rights granted to them by Union law.

It followed that the principle whereby a state was liable for damage caused to individuals as a result of infringements of Union law attributable to it was inherent in the system of the Treaty. The Member States' obligation to make reparation for such damage was also based on Article 13 TEU, pursuant to which the Member States were required to take all appropriate measures, whether general or particular, to ensure fulfilment of the obligations incumbent on them under Union law. Those obligations included the duty of neutralising the unlawful consequences of infringements of Union law.

It followed from the foregoing considerations that Union law laid down the principle according to which the Member States were obliged to compensate individuals for damage caused to them by infringements of Union law imputable to the Member States. Where, as in the present case, a Member State failed to fulfil the obligation incumbent on it under the third paragraph of Article 14 TFEU to take all necessary measures to achieve the result pursued by a directive, the full effectiveness of that provision of Union law created a right to compensation provided that three conditions were fulfilled. The first such condition was that the result to be achieved by the directive involved the attribution of rights attaching to individuals. The second condition was that the subject-matter of those rights could be identified by reference to provisions of the directive. Finally, the third condition was the existence of a causal link between the infringement of the obligation incumbent upon the Member State and the damage suffered by the persons aggrieved.

Those conditions were sufficient to confer on individuals entitlement to obtain compensation, based directly on Union law. Subject to that reservation, it was on the basis of national law concerning liability that the Member State concerned was required to compensate for the damage caused. In the absence of Union rules, it was for the legal system of each Member State to designate the competent courts and lay down the procedures for legal proceedings intended fully to safeguard the rights of individuals under Union law.

The Court also stated that the substantive and formal conditions laid down by the legislation of the Member States concerning compensation for damage could not be less favourable than those applicable to similar claims of an internal nature and could not be so arranged as to make it virtually impossible or excessively difficult to obtain compensation.

In those circumstances, it was the responsibility of the national court to give effect, in the context of national law on liability, to the right of workers to obtain compensation for damage suffered by them as a result of failure to transpose the directive.

2033. In *Federica Maso and others*,[845] the Court decided that:

> In making good the loss or damage sustained by employees as a result of the belated transposition of the Directive on the insolvency of their employer, a Member State is entitled to apply retroactively to such employees belatedly adapted implementing measures, including rules against aggregation or other limitations on the liability of the guarantee institution, provided that the Directive has been properly transposed. However, it is for the national court to ensure that reparation of the loss or damage sustained by the beneficiaries is adequate. Retroactive and proper application in full of the measures implementing the Directive will suffice for that purpose unless the beneficiaries establish the existence of complementary loss sustained on account of the fact that they were unable to benefit at the appropriate time from the financial advantages guaranteed by the Directive with the result that loss must also be made good.

2034. In another case relating to the liability of a Member State for damage caused to individuals by infringements of Union law for which it is responsible the Court ruled:

> The principle that Member States are obliged to make good damage caused to individuals by infringements of Union law for which they are responsible is also applicable where the alleged infringement stems from a decision of a court adjudicating at last instance where the rule of Union law infringed is intended to confer rights on individuals, the breach is sufficiently serious and there is a direct causal link between that breach and the loss or damage sustained by the injured parties. In order to determine whether the infringement is sufficiently serious when the infringement at issue stems from such a decision, the competent national court, taking into account the specific nature of the judicial function, must determine whether that infringement is manifest. It is for the

---

845. C.O.J., 10 July 1997, C-373/95, ECR, 1997, 4051.

legal system of each Member State to designate the court competent to determine disputes relating to that reparation.[846]

2035. In the *Robins* cases,[847] the question was raised whether the Directive (Article 8) is to be interpreted as requiring Member States to ensure, by whatever means necessary, that employees' accrued rights under supplementary company or inter-company final salary pension schemes are fully funded by Member States in the event that the employees' private employer becomes insolvent and the assets of their schemes are insufficient to fund those benefits?

2036. The Court's answered as follows:

> The wording of Article 8 of the Directive, inasmuch as it states in a general manner that the Member States 'shall ensure that the necessary measures are taken', does not oblige those States themselves to fund the rights to benefits that must be protected by virtue of the Directive.
> The words used leave the Member States some latitude as to the means to be adopted for the purposes of that protection.
> A Member State may therefore impose, for example, an obligation on employers to insure or provide for the setting up of a guarantee institution in respect of which it will lay down the detailed rules for funding, rather than provide for funding by the public authorities.
> With regard to the degree of protection required by the Directive, it is to be borne in mind that, by virtue of the first recital in the preamble thereto, the measures necessary to protect employees in the event of their employer's insolvency are to be adopted 'while taking account of the need for balanced economic and social development in the Community'.
> The Directive is thus designed to reconcile the interests of employees with the need for balanced economic and social development.

2037. Directive 2008/94 is intended to guarantee employees a minimum level of protection under Union law in the event of the insolvency of their employer without prejudice, in accordance with its Article 11, to more favourable provisions which the Member States may apply or introduce.

> The level of protection required by the Directive for each of the specific guarantees that it establishes must be determined having regard to the words used in the corresponding provision, interpreted, if need be, in the light of those considerations.
> So far as the guaranteeing of rights to old-age benefits under supplementary pension schemes is concerned, Article 8 of the Directive cannot be interpreted as demanding a full guarantee of the rights in question.

---

846. C.O.J., 30 September 2003, *Gerhard Köbler* v. *Republik Österreich*, C-224/01, ECR, 2003, 10239
847. C.O.J., 25 January 2007, *Carol Marilyn Robins and Others* v. *Secretary of State for Work and Pensions*, C-278/05, ECR, 2007, 1053.

Admittedly, Article 8, like Article 7 of the Directive on national statutory social security schemes, but unlike Articles 3 and 4 of the Directive on outstanding claims relating to pay, does not provide any express option for Member States to limit the degree of protection.

However, the absence of any explicit indication to that effect does not in itself imply, irrespective of the wording of the provision concerned, that the Union legislature intended to require an obligation to guarantee rights to benefits in their entirety.

2038. In this regard, in so far as it does no more than prescribe in general terms the adoption of the measures necessary to "protect the interests"of the persons concerned, Article 8 of the Directive gives the Member States, for the purposes of determining the level of protection, considerable latitude which excludes an obligation to guarantee in full.

The answer to be given to the first question must therefore be that, on a proper construction of Article 8 of the Directive, where the employer is insolvent and the assets of the supplementary company or inter-company pension schemes are insufficient, accrued pension rights need not necessarily be funded by the Member States themselves or be funded in full.

2039. In summary, one can say that the purpose of the directive is to approximate the laws of the Member States relating to the protection of the employees in the event of the insolvency of their employer and for that purpose it provides specific safeguards to ensure the payment of their outstanding claims. The directive provides in particular:

- for the insurance of the payment of employees' outstanding claims resulting from contracts of employment by guarantee institutions, the assets of which are independent from the employer's operating capital and inaccessible to proceedings for insolvency;
- that the non-payment of compulsory contributions due from the employer within the framework of national statutory social security schemes does not adversely affect the employee's benefit entitlements;
- that the employees' entitlement to old-age and survivors' benefit under supplementary company or inter-company pension schemes outside the statutory social security schemes is protected.

I. Definitions and Scope

2040. The directive applies to employees' claims arising from contracts of employment or employment relationships and existing against employers who are in a state of insolvency (Article 1(1)). For the definition of the terms 'employee',

Part I, Ch. 10, Restructuring of Enterprises

'employer', 'pay', 'right conferring immediate entitlement' and 'right conferring prospective entitlement', the directive refers to national law (Article 2(2)).[848]

In *Wagner Miret* v. *Fondo de garantia salarial*[849] the national court (Spain) asked whether members of higher management staff cold be excluded from the scope of the directive on insolvency of employers. The Court observed that the directive on insolvency of employers was intended to apply to all classes of employees defined as such by the national law of a Member State, thus also to higher management.

2041. Member States may, by way of exception, exclude claims by certain categories of employee from the scope of this Directive, by virtue of the existence of other forms of guarantee if it is established that these offer the persons concerned a degree of protection equivalent to that resulting from this Directive.

Where such provision already applies in their national legislation, Member States may continue to exclude from the scope of this Directive:

(a) domestic servants employed by a natural person;
(b) share-fishermen (Article 1, 3).

However, the Member States may not exclude from the scope of this Directive:

(a) part-time employees within the meaning of Directive 97/81/EC;
(b) workers with a fixed-term contract within the meaning of Directive 1999/70/EC;
(c) workers with a temporary employment relationship within the meaning of Article 1(2) of Directive 91/383/EEC (Article 2, 2).

Member States may not set a minimum duration for the contract of employment or the employment relationship in order for workers to qualify for claims under this Directive (Article 2, 3).

2042. Articles 3 and 4 must be interpreted as precluding a national rule which obliges employees to register as job-seekers in the event of the insolvency of their employer, in order to fully assert their right to payment of outstanding wage claims.[850]

---

848. See also C.O.J., 3 December 1992, *M. Suffritti and Others* v. *Instituto Nazionale della Previdenza Sociale (INPS)*, Joined Cases Nos. C-140/91, 141/91, 278/91 and 279/91, ECR, 1992, 6337: 'Employees may not rely on the provisions of the Council Directive 80/987/EEC of 20 October 1980, ... in proceedings before the national courts in order to obtain payment from the guarantee fund established under Italian Law No. 297/82 of the severance grant provided for by that Law without taking into account the temporal requirement which it lays down, namely that the benefits provided for by the fund are to be granted only if the employment relationship ceased and the insolvency or implementation procedure took place after the entry into force of that Law.'
849. C.O.J., 16 December 1993, *T. Wagner Miret* v. *Fondo de garantia salarial*, No. C-334/92, ECR, 1993, 6911.
850. C.O.J., 17 November 2011, *J. C. van Ardennen* v. *Raad van bestuur van het Uitvoeringsinstituut werknemersverzekeringen*, C-435/10, www.curia. eu.

2043. An employer is deemed to be in a state of insolvency where a request has been made for the opening of collective proceedings based on insolvency of the employer, as provided for under the laws, regulations and administrative provisions of a Member State, and involving the partial or total divestment of the employer's assets and the appointment of a liquidator or a person performing a similar task, and the authority which is competent pursuant to the said provisions has:

(a) either decided to open the proceedings, or
(b) established that the employer's undertaking or business has been definitively closed down and that the available assets are insufficient to warrant the opening of the proceedings (Article 2, 2).[851]

II. Guaranteed Pay

2044. Member States shall take the measures necessary to ensure that guarantee institutions guarantee payment of employees' outstanding claims resulting from contracts of employment or employment relationships, including, where provided for by national law, severance pay on termination of employment relationships.[852]

The claims taken over by the guarantee institution shall be the outstanding pay claims relating to a period prior to and/or, as applicable, after a given date determined by the Member States (Article 3).[853]

Member States shall have the option to limit the liability of the guarantee institutions.

When Member States exercise this option, they shall specify the length of the period for which outstanding claims are to be met by the guarantee institution. However, this may not be shorter than a period covering the remuneration of the last three months of the employment relationship prior to and/or after the date referred to in Article 3. Member States may include this minimum period of three months in a reference period with a duration of not less than six months.

---

851. The Directive does not prevent Member States from extending workers' protection to other situations of insolvency, for example where payments have been de facto stopped on a permanent basis, established by proceedings different from those mentioned in paragraph 1 as provided for under national law (Article 2, 4).
852. Article 3(1) and the first subparagraph of Article 4(3) of Council Directive 80/987/EEC of 20 October 1980 on the approximation of the laws of the Member States relating to the protection of employees in the event of the insolvency of their employer are to be interpreted as meaning that they do not allow a Member State to limit the liability of the guarantee institutions to a sum which covers the basic needs of the employees concerned and from which are to be deducted payments made by the employer during the period covered by the guarantee (C.O.J., 4 March 2004, *Istituto nazionale della previdenza sociale (INPS)* v. *Alberto Barsotti and Others* (C-19/ 01), *Milena Castellani* v. *Istituto nazionale della previdenza sociale (INPS)* (C-50/01) and *Istituto nazionale della previdenza sociale (INPS)* v. *Anna Maria Venturi* (C-84/01), ECR, 2004, 2005).
853. The first paragraph of Article 3 is to be interpreted as meaning that a Member State has the power to exclude compensation granted for unfair dismissal from the payment guarantee of the guarantee institutions pursuant to that provision where they have been recognised by an extra-judicial conciliation settlement and such exclusion, objectively justified, constitutes a measure necessary to avoid abuses within the meaning of Article 13 of that directive (C.O.J., 21 February 2008, *Maira María Robledillo Núñez* v. *Fondo de Garantía Salarial (Fogasa)*, ECR, 2008, 921).

Member States, having a reference period of not less than 18 months, may limit the period for which outstanding claims are met by the guarantee institution to eight weeks. In this case, those periods which are most favourable to the employee are used for the calculation of the minimum period.

Furthermore, Member States may set ceilings on the payments made by the guarantee institution. These ceilings must not fall below a level which is socially compatible with the social objective of this Directive (Article 4).

2045.

> Directive 2008/94/ must be interpreted as not requiring the Member States to provide guarantees for employees' claims at every stage of the insolvency proceedings of their employer. In particular, it does not preclude Member States from providing a guarantee only for employees' claims arising before the entry of the decision to open insolvency proceedings in the register of companies, even though that decision does not order the termination of the employer's activities[854].

2046. Articles 3 and 4 of the directive do not preclude national legislation which allows employees' outstanding claims to be classified as 'social security benefits' where they are paid by a guarantee institution.[855]

2047. National law may provide a time-limit laid down for the lodging of an application by an employee seeking to obtain, in accordance with the detailed rules laid down in that directive, a compensation payment in respect of outstanding salary claims resulting from his employer's insolvency, provided that the time-limit is no less favourable than those governing similar domestic applications (principle of equivalence) and is not framed in such a way as to render impossible in practice the exercise of rights conferred by Union law (principle of effectiveness).[856]

2048. In the context of an application by an employee for payment by a guarantee fund of outstanding claims relating to pay, the directive does not preclude the application of a limitation period of one year (principle of equivalence). However, it is for the national court to examine whether it is framed in such a way as to render impossible in practice or excessively difficult the exercise of the rights recognised by Community law (principle of effectiveness).[857]

2049. In the *Rodríguez Caballero* case the question was raised whether an agreement on compensation for unfair dismissal is pay in the sense of the Directive 80/987/EEC.

---

854. C.O.J., 18 April 2013, *Meliha Veli Mustafa* v. *Direktor na fond 'Garantirani vzemania na rabotnitsite i sluzhitelite' kam Natsionalnia osiguritelen institut*, C-247/12, www.curia.eu.
855. C.O.J., 16 July 2009, *Raffaello Visciano* v. *Istituto nazionale della previdenza sociale (INPS)*, C-69/08, ECR, 2009, 6741.
856. C.O.J., 18 September 2003, *Peter Pflücke* v. *Bundesanstalt für Arbeit*, C-125/01, ECR, 2003, 9375.
857. C.O.J., 16 July 2009, *Raffaello Visciano* v. *Istituto nazionale della previdenza sociale (INPS)*, C-69/08, ECR, 2009, 6741.

Mr. Rodríguez Caballero was dismissed by his employer on 30 March 1997. The judicial procedure prescribed led to an agreement under which that undertaking acknowledged that the dismissal was unfair and accepted that the *salarios de tramitación* which it owed would be paid with effect from the date of dismissal up to the date of the conciliation agreement.

Those *salarios de tramitacíon* were not paid by the undertaking. The failure to pay led to the commencement of the enforcement procedure against the insolvency fund (Fogosa).

The Court ruled as follows.

> Claims in respect of *salarios de tramitación* must be regarded as employees' claims arising from contracts of employment or employment relationships and relating to pay, within the meaning of Articles 1(1) and 3(1) of Directive 80/987/EEC irrespective of the procedure under which they are determined, if, according to the national legislation concerned, such claims, when recognised by judicial decision, give rise to liability on the part of the guarantee institution and if a difference in treatment of identical claims acknowledged in a conciliation procedure is not objectively justified.
>
> The national court must set aside national legislation which, in breach of the principle of equality, excludes from the concept of 'pay' within the meaning of Article 2(2) of Directive 80/987 claims in respect of *salarios de tramitación* agreed in a conciliation procedure supervised and approved by a court; it must apply to members of the group disadvantaged by that discrimination the arrangements in force in respect of employees whose claims of the same type come, according to the national definition of 'pay', within the scope of that directive.[858]

2050. Mr. Cordero Alonso worked in an undertaking employing less than 25 employees. He was dismissed on grounds connected with the undertaking's economic situation. The action before the courts brought by Mr. Cordero Alonso against that dismissal led to a conciliation settlement concluded with the defendant – his employer –, supervised by and with the participation of the district judge, who subsequently approved it, which led to that settlement being accorded the same force as a judgment for the purposes of its enforcement in the event of non-compliance. Under that settlement, the parties agreed to accept the termination of the employment relationship on the grounds put forward by the employer and set, *inter alia*, compensation for the employee at €5,540.06, which was to be paid by the employer.

Since the employer did not voluntarily discharge the amounts awarded in the conciliation settlement, Mr. Cordero Alonso applied for the judicial enforcement of that settlement, following which the employer was declared insolvent on the ground that no assets had been found which could be seized and realised to cover payment of the sums owed to the employee.

---

858. C.O.J., 12 December 2002, *Ángel Rodríguez Caballero* v. *Fondo de Garantía Salarial (Fogasa)*, C-442/00, ECR, 2002, 11915; *see also*: C.O.J., 16 December 2004, *José Vicente Olaso Valero* v. *Fondo de Garantía Salarial (Fogasa)*, C-520/03, ECR, 2004, 12065.

Part I, Ch. 10, Restructuring of Enterprises

2051. Mr. Cordero Alonso then applied to the Wage Guarantee Fund for payment of the amounts at issue. The Fund awarded him 40 per cent of the compensation for dismissal, in accordance with Article 33(8) of the Worker's Statute, but refused to pay the remaining 60 per cent on the ground that the compensation had been awarded in a conciliation agreement rather than in a judgment or administrative decision.

So, the question was raised whether the fundamental right of equality before the law deriving from Community law imposes an obligation to treat equally cases where the right of an employee to be compensated for the termination of his contract has been laid down in a court judgment and cases where that right is the result of an agreement between the employee and the employer, entered into under the supervision and with the approval of a court?

2052. The Court of Justice answered as follows:

> It is apparent from the decision of the referring court that, so far as compensation for termination of an employment contract is concerned, in the event of the employer's insolvency the Fund must pay only compensation fixed by a judgment or an administrative decision.
>
> Since the general principle of equality and non-discrimination is a principle of Union law, Member States are bound by the Court's interpretation of that principle. That applies even when the national rules at issue are, according to the constitutional case-law of the Member State concerned, consistent with an equivalent fundamental right recognised by the national legal system.
>
> Therefore, the answer to the question must be that, within the scope of Directive 80/987, as amended, the general principle of equality, as recognised in the Union legal order, requires that when, under national rules such as those at issue in the main proceedings, statutory compensation payable on termination of an employment contract and fixed in a judgment is payable by a guarantee institution in the event of an employer's insolvency, compensation of the same nature, fixed in an agreement between the employee and the employer which was entered into under the supervision and with the approval of a court, must be treated in the same way.[859]

2053. Member States lay down detailed rules for the organisation, financing and operation of guarantee institutions, complying with the following principles in particular:

(a) the assets of the institutions shall be independent of the employers' operating capital and inaccessible to proceedings for insolvency;
(b) employers shall contribute to financing, unless it is fully recovered by the public authorities;
(c) the institutions' liabilities shall not depend on whether or not obligations to contribute to financing have been fulfilled (Article 5).

---

[859]. C.O.J., 7 September 2006, *Anacleto Cordero Alonso v. Fondo de Garantía Salarial (Fogasa)*, C-81/05, ECR, 2006, 7569.

The directive on the insolvency of employers does not require Member States to create a single guarantee institution for all classes of employees and consequently to make management staff dependent on the guarantee institution set up for other classes of employees. From the discretion given to Member States it has to be concluded that management staff could not rely on the directive to claim payment of arrears of salary from the guarantee institution set up for classes of employees.

When it interprets and applies national law every national court must assume that 'the State intended fully to implement the obligations under the directive in question'.

The Member State concerned is required to make good the damage suffered by the management staff by reason of the failure to comply with the directive in relation thereto.[860]

2054. Where the employer is established in a Member State other than that in which the employee resides and was employed, the guarantee institution responsible, in the event of the insolvency of their employer, for the payment of that employee's claims in the event of the employer's insolvency is the institution of the state in which either it is decided to open the proceedings for the collective satisfaction of creditors' claims or it has been established that the employer's undertaking or business has been closed down.[861]

2055. Article 3 is to be interpreted as meaning that, for the payment of the outstanding claims of workers having been habitually employed in a Member State other than that where their employer is established and not in that other Member State and fulfils its obligation to contribute to the financing of the guarantee institution in the Member State where it is established, it is that institution which is liable for the obligations defined by that article.

Directive 80/987 does not preclude a Member State's legislation from providing that employees may avail themselves of the salary guarantee from that Member State's institution in accordance with its law, either in addition to or instead of the guarantee offered by the institution designated as competent under that directive, provided however that that guarantee results in a greater level of worker protection[862].

III. Provisions Concerning Transnational Situations

2056. When an undertaking with activities in the territories of at least two Member States is in a state of insolvency, the institution responsible for meeting employees' outstanding claims shall be that in the Member State in whose territory they work or habitually work.

---

860. C.O.J., 16 December 1993, *T. Wagner Miret* v. *Fondo de garantia salarial*, No. C-334/92, ECR, 1993, 6911.
861. C.O.J., 17 September 1997, *Carina Mosbaeck* v. *Lonmodtagernes Garantifond*, C-117/96, ECR, 1997, 5017.
862. C.O.J., 10 March 2011, Charles Defossez v. Christian Wiart, in his capacity as liquidator of Sotimon Sarl, C-477/09, www.curia.eu.

The extent of employees' rights shall be determined by the law governing the competent guarantee institution.

Member States shall take the measures necessary to ensure that decisions taken in the context of insolvency proceedings, which have been requested in another Member State, are taken into account when determining the employer's state of insolvency (Article 9).

For the purposes of implementing Article 9, Member States shall make provision for the sharing of relevant information between their competent administrative authorities and/or the guarantee institutions making it possible in particular to inform the guarantee institution responsible for meeting the employees' outstanding claims.

Article 9 must be interpreted as meaning that, in order for an undertaking established in a Member State to be regarded as having activities in the territory of another Member State, that undertaking does not need to have a branch or fixed establishment in that other State. The undertaking must, however, have a stable economic presence in the latter State, featuring human resources which enable it to perform activities there.

In the case of a transport undertaking established in a Member State, the mere fact that a worker employed by it in that State delivers goods between that State and another Member State cannot demonstrate that the undertaking has a stable economic presence in another Member State.[863]

Member States shall notify the Commission and the other Member States of the contact details of their competent administrative authorities and/or guarantee institutions. The Commission shall make these communications publicly accessible (Article 10).

IV. Social Security

2057. Member States may stipulate that the guarantee funds are not obliged to pay contributions due under national statutory schemes or under supplementary company or inter-company schemes outside the national statutory social security schemes (Article 6). An interpretation of Article 6, which would in effect allow the Member States unilaterally to limit the scope of obligations deriving from the directive, cannot be upheld. It is apparent from the mere wording of Article 6 that it merely authorises the Member States not to impose upon the guarantee institutions responsibility for the contributions not paid by the insolvent employer, by allowing them to choose for that purpose another system for guaranteeing employees' entitlement to social security benefits.[864]

Member States must take the necessary measures to ensure that non-payment of compulsory contributions due from the employer under national statutory social security does not adversely affect the employees' benefit entitlement in respect of those insurance institutions inasmuch as the employees' contributions were deducted at source from the remuneration paid (Article 7). Member States shall

---

863. C.O.J., 16 October 2008, *Svenska staten* v. *Anders Holmqvist*, C-310/07, ECR, 2008, 7871.
864. C.O.J., 2 February 1989, *Commission* v. *Italy*, No. 22/87, ECR, 1989, 143.

equally ensure that the necessary measures are taken to protect the interests of employees and of persons having already left the employer's undertaking or business at the date of the onset of the insolvency in respect of rights conferring on them immediate or prospective entitlements to old-age benefits, including survivors' benefits, under supplementary company or inter-company pension schemes outside the national statutory social security schemes (Article 8).

2058. In an Irish case the Court ruled[865] that Directive 2008/94/EC must be interpreted as meaning that it applies to the entitlement of former employees to old-age benefits under a supplementary pension scheme set up by their employer.

It further indicated that Article 8 of Directive 2008/94 must be interpreted as meaning that State pension benefits may not be taken into account in assessing whether a Member State has complied with the obligation laid down in that article; and must be interpreted as meaning that, in order for that article to apply, it is sufficient that the pension scheme is underfunded as of the date of the employer's insolvency and that, on account of his insolvency, the employer does not have the resources to contribute sufficient money to the pension scheme to enable the pension benefits owned to the beneficiaries of that scheme to be satisfied in full. It is not necessary for those beneficiaries to prove that there are other factors giving rise to the loss of their entitlement to old-age benefits.

Finally it said that Directive 2008/94 must be interpreted as meaning that that the economic situation of the Member State concerned does not constitute an exceptional situation capable of justifying a lower level of protection of the interests of employees as regards their entitlement to old-age benefits under a supplementary occupational pension scheme.

V. Options for Member States

2059. This Directive does not affect the option of Member States:

(a) to take the measures necessary to avoid abuses;
(b) to refuse or reduce the liability referred to in the first paragraph of Article 3 or the guarantee obligation referred to in Article 7 if it appears that fulfilment of the obligation is unjustifiable because of the existence of special links between the employee and the employer and of common interests resulting in collusion between them;
(c) to refuse or reduce the liability referred to in the first paragraph of Article 3 or the guarantee obligation referred to in Article 7 in cases where the employee, on his or her own or together with his or her close relatives, was the owner of an essential part of the employer's undertaking or business and had a considerable influence on its activities (Art. 12).

---

865. C.O.J., 25 April 2013, *Thomas Hogan and Others* v. *Minister for Social and Family Affairs, Ireland and Attorney General*, C-398/11, www.curia.eu.

2060. Thus the Court ruled that Article 12(c) of Directive 2008/94/EC must be interpreted as not precluding a provision of national law which excludes an employee from entitlement under the guarantee of payment of employees' outstanding claims on the ground that the employee, alone or together with close relatives, within the six months preceding the application for a declaration of insolvency, was the owner of an essential part of the undertaking or business concerned and had a considerable influence on its activities.[866]

---

866. C.O.J., 10 February 2011, *Lotta Andersson* v. *Staten genom Kronofogdemyndigheten i Jönköping, Tillsynsmyndigheten*, C-30/10, www.curia.eu.

Part II. Collective Labour Law

2061. Traditionally, collective labour law embraces the body of rules that govern the relations between the collectivity of employees and the employer or a group of employers. The following rights come to mind: the right to trade union freedom, the right of employers and employees to set up organisations at their own choosing in view of the promotion of their professional interests, the right to workers' participation in the company in decisions that affect their interests, including the right to free and autonomous collective bargaining and the right to conclude collective agreements. The rules concerning economic warfare, namely regarding strikes and lockouts as well as the set of measures aimed at the prevention of the settlement of collective labour conflicts, belong equally to collective labour law. One can say without any hesitation that these issues have remained within the national jurisdiction and that the collective measures that are proposed at European level are mostly so controversial that a consensus between both sides of industry and among the Member States seems to be impossible; this state of affairs will remain so in the near future.

2062. There is no doubt that the Community Charter on the Fundamental Social Rights of Workers (December 1989) contains quite a number of points that belong to the field of collective labour law. Thus the right of association for employers and employees, including positive and negative trade union freedom (point 11), the right to negotiate and conclude collective agreements, eventually, if the parties deem it desirable, at European level (point 12). The right to resort to collective action, including the right to strike, is explicitly recognised, while recourse to conciliation, mediation and arbitration in order to facilitate the settlement of industrial disputes is encouraged (point 13). Information, consultation and participation of workers shall especially be developed in companies or groups of companies having subsidiaries in various Member States. These must be implemented in due time, particularly in the following cases: technological change, restructuring and mergers of undertakings, collective redundancy procedures, and when transfrontier workers in particular are affected by employment policies pursued by the undertaking where they are employed (points 17–18).

2063. One cannot but underline again that the Charter refers for most of the collective labour law rights to existing national legislation or practice, which suggests a very definite division of competence between the Member States and the Union in terms of the subsidiarity principle. The wording of the Charter is not accidental, but rather very deliberate. I must add that when one analyses the information and consultation rights that workers' representatives have under the directives concerning collective redundancies (1975), transfer of undertakings (1977) and the different health and safety directives, one must ascertain time and again that the notion of 'workers' representatives' must be seen in the national context. Also the Charter of Fundamental Rights of the European Rights (2007) contains collective rights and namely:

– freedom of assembly and of association (Article 12);
– workers' right to information and consultation within the undertaking (Article 27);
– right of collective bargaining and action (Article 28).

In Part II of this monograph on European Labour Law and Industrial Relations, we will first examine the likelihood of European collective bargaining (Chapter 1); secondly, we deal with the proposals concerning workers' participation (Chapter 2), namely: information and consultation (§1) the European SE (§2), the Directive on European Works Councils (§3) which opens new perspectives since the adoption of a directive on EWCs and/or a procedure for the purpose of informing and consulting the employees in the European Community. (§4). Finally we discuss the SCE (§5), the Directive on take over bids and cross-border mergers of limited liability companies (§6) and the Directive concerning mergers of public limited liability companies (§7).

Chapter 1. Collective Bargaining

§1. The Social Dialogue

2064. The promotion of a social dialogue constitutes one of the key elements of European social policies. This follows clearly from Article 154(1) TFEU, which reads as follows: 'The Commission shall have the task of promoting the consultation of management and labour at Union level and shall take any relevant measure to facilitate their dialogue by ensuring balanced support for the parties.' The notion of social dialogue self-evidently also includes collective bargaining, the conclusion of agreements between the social partners. Consequently, Article 155(1) TFEU says: 'should management and labour so desire, the dialogue between them at Union level may lead to contractual relations, including agreements'.

2065. Collective bargaining, however, is a delicate flower. Indeed, quite a number of questions pop up over which opinions, especially between the social partners, are diverse. First of all, what is the division of tasks between European and national levels? That the answer to that question leads to controversies follows clearly from the rather heated discussions concerning the appropriateness of the conclusion of a European agreement on information and consultation rights of employees at national level. For the employers, this is an issue to be dealt with exclusively at national level and no business whatsoever for the Union, while the trade unions defend fiercely that this is a matter to be dealt with at European level and that European minimum requirements are necessary.

Secondly, there is the reality of the *power relationship* between the European social partners, or better the lack of power of European trade unions in pushing the employers to the European bargaining table. That lack of power was, however, efficiently compensated by political pressures from the European institutions, especially from the European Commission. There was indeed a kind of situation which one could call 'Damocles bargaining'. This went as follows. The European Commission invites the European social partners to have a dialogue and negotiate an agreement on a given issue, let's say on information and consultation rights at national level. The parties and especially the employers know that the Commission, if no agreement is reached, will push for European legislation. So employers are put under pressure and have to consider to join or not to join and eventually to negotiate a given deal in order to prevent legislation, the outcome that would escape them almost completely anyway. So there was a sword hanging above their heads.

2066. There is, on top of that, the problem of credibility. The European social partners exist. They want to prove that they are more than mere lobbyists and are able and willing to play a constructive role. Concluding agreements is one way of indicating that they are doing more than merely talking to each other.

2067. The Damocles tactic was widely used at European level. This was not only so for inter-industry-wide agreements, like the ones we discussed concerning parental leave and part-time work, but also for the level of the European enterprise. Let us take the example of the EWCs. Here also, enterprises were put under pressure of either negotiating an agreement, allowing for some flexibility or undergoing mandatory rules, which come into force when no agreement is reached.

2068. Lately, important developments have taken place. It seems that the Commission wants the social partners to take complete responsibility for collective bargaining, by leaving it to them to make their own arrangements and not by 'Damoclising' them into an agreement if no agreement is reached, unless Union rules are urgently needed, like in the case of temporary work. In the latter case, when bargaining broke down, the Commission made a proposal for a directive.[867]

At the same time parties are also engaging in voluntary agreements, like the agreement on telework,[868] the framework agreement on work-related stress[869],on harassment and violence at work[870] and youth unemployment[871] where the 'accord' is not only legally not binding, but the parties themselves leave it up to their members, to integrate the agreement in their own national system, as they see fit.

So more 'autonomy' and more 'voluntary' type of guidelines, codes of conduct and the like.

§2. EUROPEAN COLLECTIVE AGREEMENTS

2069. In this section we want to raise some problems which accompany the possibility to conclude European collective agreements, pursuant to Articles 154 and 155 TFEU. In order to do so a number of introductory remarks are called for since collective bargaining constitutes a complex and delicate set of relationships, which are not self-explanatory. Collective bargaining within national boundaries already is not an easy subject, neither politically, sociologically, nor legally; *a fortiori* it is even more complex if undertaken at European or at a wider international level. We also put the first European Collective Agreement on Parental Leave (14 December 1995) into perspective.[872]

I. Introductory Remarks

A. *Broad and Narrow*

---

867. *See* Part I, Chapter 3, §1.
868. *See* General Introduction.
869. *Idem.*
870. *Idem.*
871. *Idem.*
872. *See* Part I, Chapter 7, §4. *See*: Thomas Blanke & Edgar Rose (eds), 'Collective bargaining and Wages in Comparative Perspective. Germany, France, The Netherlands, Sweden and the United Kingdom', *Bulletin of Comparative Labour Relations*, No. 56, 2005, 176 p.

Part II, Ch. 1, Collective Bargaining

2070. There are at least two meanings of the term 'collective bargaining':[873] a broad one and a narrow one. In a broad sense collective bargaining embraces 'all sorts of bipartite or tripartite discussions concerning labour problems' involving both sides of industry and governmental authorities aimed at wider understanding, resolutions, preparing or implementing policies, trying eventually to reach compromises, without necessarily resulting in a binding agreement. Self-evidently this broad meaning of bargaining comprises all forms of consultation, co-operation and concertation.

A narrower meaning of collective bargaining focuses on discussions leading to binding agreements, either *de facto*, moral or legal and usually confined to both sides of industry. Collective bargaining in this sense involves a process of negotiations between employers and representatives of the employees as well as an agreement containing binding rules. It is in this latter and thus narrower sense which we use the term throughout this chapter.

B. A Multifaceted Role

2071. Collective bargaining serves various functions, namely: determining wages and working conditions, settlement of disputes and the regulation of relations between the collective parties, and it is *de facto* also a form of employee participation.

C. Agreement with a Double Content

2072. Given its complex nature the collective agreement is like a double-yolked egg: it has a double content.

1. The Normative Part

2073. On the one hand the collective agreement contains stipulations about wages and working conditions which regulate the labour relations between the employer(s) and the employees. These wages and working conditions have a normative nature; they are the norms which regulate the working conditions of those which fall within the territorial, personal and occupational scope of the collective agreement.

2074. The normative part of the collective agreement contains individual normative stipulations, comprising the conditions of the individual employees (wages, benefits, cost of living clauses, job classification, working time, holidays, vacations and so on). They also comprise collective normative stipulations in the enterprise or the branch of activity. They are norms which generate obligations neither for the

---

873. S.G. Bamber, and P. Sheldon, 'Collective Bargaining' in: *Comparative Labour Law and Industrial Relations in Industrialised Market Economies* (ed. R. Blanpain), 10th edn., Kluwer, 2010.

contracting parties nor for the employer in relation to individual employees. They are a sort of in-between rules (between individual normative and obligatory), which regulate 'collective' labour relations. Examples of collective normative rules are the provisions in e.g. sectoral collective agreements covering: (1) the establishment, competence and functioning of the works council in the enterprise; (2) procedures for the settlement of industrial disputes; (3) establishment of certain funds and the like.

2. The Obligatory Part

2075. The collective agreement, like any other agreement, generates obligations between the contracting parties which have to be clearly distinguished from the normative rules. These obligations can be explicit (e.g. concerning the interpretation of the agreement) or implicit. To the implicit obligations, in certain EU countries, belong among others the peace obligation (abstention from industrial action as long as the agreement is in force), which can be relative or absolute. Some also accept that there is an implicit duty for the contracting parties to implement the collective agreement (exercise influence on their members to live up to the agreement). A peace obligation can, self-evidently, also be dealt with *explicit verbis*.

D. Free Collective Bargaining: Pluralist Democracy

2076. It is not superfluous to recall in this context that free collective bargaining and the autonomy of the parties have always been regarded as fundamental aspects of the freedom of association.[874] Indeed, freedom of association, collective bargaining and the right to strike go, like we said earlier, hand in hand. Employees, and eventually employers, associate in order to bargain collectively and bargaining without the right to strike amounts to collective begging. Autonomous collective bargaining constitutes a prerequisite for a pluralist democratic society; 'pluralist' means more institutions and persons than one group, e.g. a given political party, participate in social decision and rule making. Needless to say, collective bargaining (point 12) as well as the right to strike (point 13) belong to the fundamental social rights of workers as expressed in the Community Charter of 1989.

E. Subsidiarity

2077. The subsidiarity rule, pointing out that problems must be settled at the most suitable level, addresses not only the relation between the European and national or regional levels, as far as European or national governmental authorities are concerned, but also whether problems can be dealt with either by governmental intervention or by agreements between the parties concerned, which in the social

---

874. B. Creighton, 'Freedom of Association' in: *Comparative Labour Law and Industrial Relations in Industrialised Market Economies* (ed. R. Blanpain), 10th edn., 2010.

Part II, Ch. 1, Collective Bargaining

arena means the social partners. So the subsidiarity rule also points out that there is room for collective bargaining at European level when this is the best way of doing things.

F. Abstention from an International (Legal) Framework

2078. There is no doubt that international legal instruments have always been almost mute as far as collective bargaining at international or European level between management and labour is concerned, as bargaining at that level is bedevilled by strategic considerations by the parties involved. Even the Guidelines for Multinational Enterprises, like those promulgated by the OECD Member States (1976, as amended) or the ILO Tripartite Declaration on Social Policy of Multinational Enterprises (1977), neither explicitly nor implicitly refer to transnational bargaining, given the conflicting views of the governments and the social partners involved. Thus, Articles 153 and 154 TFEU are a break-through in this area, but they self-evidently do not contain precisely formulated rules, legally organising and monitoring the different juridical questions which accompany European collective agreements.

G. Specific Legislation

2079. In the absence of specific European legal rules, the question arises as to which legal rules should apply in case a collective agreement is concluded at European level. There is no doubt that there are insufficient European general principles of law to deal satisfactorily with the legal problems which accompany a European collective agreement. In order to do so one will have to look to national law for a solution. Here one must distinguish between two possibilities: either the parties choose the national law which will apply to their agreement or they do not. In the latter case the national legal system with which the agreement is most closely connected may apply. Reference in this framework could be made to the Convention on the Law applicable to Contractual Obligations of 19 June 1980 or the Regulation No. 593/2008 (Rome I), although the drafters of that Convention certainly did not have collective European agreements in their minds when they elaborated the Convention. In any case, unless European law ultimately would prevail, national law will be applied by the local courts in case of a dispute concerning the application of the terms and conditions, laid down by a European collective agreement, of e.g. an individual employment contract.

2080. It follows from the judgment by the Court of First Instance of 17 June 1998 in the UEAPME case, concerning the notion social partner under European law, that the European judge intervenes in the legality of European collective agreements and more especially in the decision by the Council to implement the framework agreement on parental leave by way of a directive.

It is, however, not excluded that the Court of Justice would have to answer questions regarding the 1994 directive on EWCs and eventually concerning the agreements parties establishing an EWC have concluded, including the legal status of the agreements, the legal capacity of the parties, content and the like.

2081. In the present legal state of affairs, the European Court does not seem to be competent to handle any preliminary question regarding the validity or the interpretation of a European agreement, giving the wording of Article 267 TFEU, whereby preliminary questions are limited to actions of the Union institutions.

II. Parties to the Agreement

2082. A collective agreement is an agreement between one or more employers or employers' association(s) and one or more trade unions, including other *bona fide* representatives of employees, concerning the terms and conditions of employment and the rights and the obligations of the contracting parties.

Agreements at European level can be either a:

(1) European company agreement;
(2) European industry agreement;
(3) European multi-industry-wide agreement;
(4) European multi-regional agreement.

A. The European Company Agreement

2083. In the case of a European company agreement the employers' side is composed of either a European company having non-incorporated subsidiaries in various EU Member States or the representatives of various legally incorporated subsidiaries located in Member States which are part of a European or a multinational group. It is clearly not necessary that there are subsidiaries in all EU countries. One could, moreover, envisage that some subsidiaries are not situated in the EU and yet nevertheless are involved in the bargaining and the consequent agreement; equally that agreements are only concluded with some of the subsidiaries.

2084. The labour side could be composed of representatives of the trade unions, which represent employees working in the different subsidiaries, or (theoretically at least) of a European company trade union, which may have been established and which has competence and thus a mandate to bargain over and conclude an agreement concerning wages and conditions in the company.

One can also envisage that an EWC could be party to a European collective company agreement, depending on the composition and the competences of the council. The EWC could be composed of representatives of employees who are directly elected to that end, e.g. at national level, or who are delegates of national councils or similar bodies, such as shop stewards, committees of hygiene and others. These (direct and indirect) representatives should have a mandate to bargain and to agree at a European level. There should be at best an explicit mandate in both cases. In the case of direct representation, this is self-evident; in the case of indirect representation, there should be an explicit mandate certainly for those representatives who do not enjoy that competence at home, which is the case for many works councils, since in a number of countries the (legal) right to bargain is reserved to the trade unions. The problems which ensue are discussed in the light of the structure of EWCs, below.[875]

2085. The possibility of multi-company agreements cannot be excluded *a priori*.

B. The European Industry Agreement

2086. Parties to the European industry agreement are self-evidently employers' associations and trade unions.

The (national) trade unions, representative of the employees in that branch of industry and competent to bargain, could either form one or more European sectoral trade unions, which have a mandate to negotiate and conclude agreements or be represented as such around the negotiation table and become parties to the collective agreement, or could mandate a negotiating committee.

The same goes *ceteris paribus* for the employers' side. We refer in this context to the sectoral dialogue committees.[876]

C. The European Multi-industry Agreement

2087. The European multi-industry agreement could either cover the European private sector (profit – socio-profit)[877] as a whole or more than one branch of industry. Again one can conceive that one or more European confederal trade unions, grouping national confederations, could be party to a collective agreement provided that they have a mandate to that end. There may be a difficulty, resulting from the fact that some national confederations may not themselves have the competence to conclude collective agreements and therefore could not delegate that competence to a European body. One could also imagine that national confederations would be party to the agreement.

2088. In the case of an inter-industry-wide agreement, covering only some sectors of industry, one might imagine that national unions, representing those sectors, could be party to the collective agreement.

---

875. *See* Chapter 2, §4, IV.
876. *See* General Introduction.
877. Public companies, affecting the functioning of the common market, included.

2089. On the part of the employers one or more European confederations of employers' associations may be a party, may be the national confederations themselves. The same thing can be said regarding competence and agreement covering only some sectors, as is the case with the unions.

D. The European Multi-regional Agreement

2090. An agreement could also be concluded covering different regions of the European Union, situated in different Member States. These agreements could be industry or multi-industry agreements.

Here European regional employers' association(s) could be a party to the agreement as well as the (national) regional employers' organisations or national employers' organisations.

From the trade union side, there could be European regional trade unions, (national) regional trade unions or national trade unions at the negotiation table.

III. The Competence to Conclude Collective Agreements

2091. In order to be able to conclude collective agreements the parties must have the necessary competence. Here we have to distinguish between the power to negotiate, the power to conclude and the power to ratify the agreement.

In the case of organisations; there must be a mandate to this end, given by employer or employee members to their organisation or conferred by law. In the case of a European organisation, the composing organisations must have the competence to give such a mandate to their European organisation.

Such a mandate can be explicit or implicit. Of course there is the possibility for e.g. national organisations to constitute a bargaining team, which would conduct negotiations on behalf of the organisations and conclude the agreement while retaining the power of ratification.

IV. Articles 154 and 155 TFEU; Specific Legal Problems

2092. As has already been indicated, very intricate problems arise regarding European collective agreements under the TFEU, both for those which will be implemented by a decision of the Council as well as for those agreements which will have to stand on their own (legal) feet.

A. Implementation in Accordance with National Practice

1. Contracting Parties

2093. The first question which arises is: who can be a party to a European collective agreement? A party may be an employer, let us say a European company, or a European employers' organisation, or a European trade union of employees organised at either regional, sectoral, or confederal level. As indicated earlier, parties must have the necessary competence to conclude a collective agreement. In order to do so they should have a (explicit) mandate from their members. Members of BUSINESSEUROPE, who do not have the practice of bargaining at a national level like e.g. the *Deutsche Arbeitgebersbund* or the Confederation of British Industries, may be in a difficult position to give such a mandate, unless the constituent members of the latter organisations would agree to do so. This may eventually involve an amendment of the by-laws of those organisations.

Contracting parties in the Agreement on Parental Leave are the 'cross-industry organisations', BUSINESSEUROPE, CEEP for the employers' side and ETUC for the employees' side. In the *considerans* (13) to the directive it is noted that the Commission has 'taken into account the representative status of the signatory parties ... '. *See*, however, regarding this point our earlier remarks on the representativity of the European social partners.[878]

2. Content of the Agreement

2094. Parties can conclude agreements on wages and working conditions, in the broadest sense of the word. The parties are autonomous and are not bound by the areas which are excluded in Article 153(5) TFEU, although one must recognise that agreements on issues like the right to strike or the right to impose lock-outs at a European level are hardly likely, although theoretically possible.

The Collective Agreement of 18 June 2009 deals with parental leave, which is a working condition in the sense of Article 153 TFEU.

3. Form and Language

2095. The European collective agreement will probably have to be drafted in writing in the various official languages of the Member States in which the agreement is intended to have an effect, although it does not seem that this would condition its validity, except when national legislation, applicable to the agreement, would contain certain linguistic requirements, as is the case in Belgium.

4. Scope

2096. The territorial scope of the agreement will not necessarily be limited to the 28 Member States and the EEA Members as some of the possible contracting parties, e.g. BUSINESSEUROPE and the ETUC, have membership outside the Community (of the Member States and the EEA Members). The personal scope of application of the agreement will depend on the content of the agreement itself,

---

878. *See* General Introduction.

namely the kind of employers and employees which are meant to be covered: in principle all employers and employees who fall within the territorial and professional scope of the collective agreement. The professional scope is determined by the sectors of activity for which the contracting social partners are competent. The agreement can apply to all undertakings which operate in the common market. It is in this context not relevant whether they are private or public (owned by the Government or other public authorities or operating under their control). The only important factor is whether they affect the functioning of the common market. The agreement can, however, not apply to the public sector *sensu stricto*, i.e. those institutions which involve direct or indirect participation in the exercise of powers conferred by public law in the discharge of functions whose purpose is to safeguard the general interests of the State or of other public authorities.[879]

5. Binding Effect

2097. As far as the binding effect of the agreement is concerned we must distinguish between the obligatory and the normative part of the agreement. The binding effect of the obligatory part will depend on the law applicable to the contract. If this is Belgian, as e.g. the agreement was concluded in Brussels and parties did not choose another legal system, the relations between the contracting parties might be governed by the Belgian Act of 5 December 1968 on joint committees and collective agreements, with all the problems this involves.

2098. The binding effect of the agreement on the members of the contracting parties, e.g. on the national confederations of employers as far as BUSINESSEUROPE is concerned, will depend on the by-laws of BUSINESSEUROPE. The obligations resulting from those by-laws may eventually be sanctioned by disciplinary measures in case of non-compliance. At any rate, there is no legal obligation whatsoever for any national association to put a European collective agreement on the national negotiation table, nor is there an obligation of result, namely that there should be a collective agreement at national level. Mandatory bargaining does indeed not belong to a widespread European tradition.[880]

2099. The only obligation which exists for members of contracting parties, like employers' associations or trade unions, may follow, as indicated earlier, from the by-laws of their respective European organisations and may oblige them to engage in collective bargaining at national or lower levels. It is questionable, however, whether e.g. an individual employee could sue either a national employers' organisation or a trade union which does not start to bargain on the issues laid down in the European agreement. Much will depend here on the status of national law and the rights of third parties relating to contractual or other obligations others may have.

---

879. *Cf. Lawrie-Blum* v. *Land Baden-Würtemberg*, 3 July 1986, No. 66/85, ECR, 1986, 2121.
880. A legal obligation for some forms of mandatory bargaining does, however, exist in France, Luxemburg, Portugal and Spain and for some issues in Denmark and the Netherlands.

Part II, Ch. 1, Collective Bargaining

2100. Implementation of the normative part of the European collective agreement will consist in developing collective bargaining according to the rules of each Member State. Here problems arise as certain Member States do not have procedures to provide for an *erga omnes* effect of collective agreements, while at the same time, the binding effect of the collective agreements, as far as the hierarchy of legal sources (legislation, work rules, individual agreements, custom ...) is concerned, differs considerably from country to country. Some Member States have procedures of extension of agreements to the private sector as a whole, others do not. In certain countries, the non-compliance with a collective agreement, thus extended, is penally sanctioned, while in other countries no penal sanctions apply.

Thus, there are no real guarantees that the agreements will be fully and *erga omnes* implemented through normal (national) collective bargaining structures or mechanisms. In order to obtain an *erga omnes* effect with a comparable legal outcome, consequently one is, in attendance of further legislative Union developments in this area, *de facto* bound to turn to the Council for a decision.

6. Interpretation

2101. As has already been indicated, the European Court does not seem to be competent to handle any preliminary question regarding the interpretation of a European collective agreement, given the wording of Article 267 TFEU, whereby preliminary questions are limited to actions of the Union institutions. Interpretation mechanisms may, however, be provided for by the contracting parties themselves in the collective agreement, either by way of conciliation or even arbitration mechanisms. National courts could also be called upon to rule on the meaning of the language of European collective agreements. As a general rule, the party seeking interpretation will, in order to qualify as a litigating party, have to give evidence of a manifest interest.

The first Collective Agreement, namely on Parental Leave, provides, in its final provisions (6), that 'without prejudice to the respective role of the Commission, national courts and the Court of Justice, any matter relating to the interpretation of this agreement at European level should, in the first instance, be referred by the Commission to the signatory parties who will give an opinion'. That opinion, obviously, has only an indicative nature and is not binding. Final binding decisions on the interpretation of the agreement will be made by the Court of Justice.

Parties could obviously conclude an interpretative agreement that could be rendered binding by a Council decision, but that is another matter.

7. Duration

2102. Parties will have to lay down in their agreements rules concerning the duration and termination of the agreement: as a general rule, agreements are either for an indefinite or a fixed duration. In case of an indefinite duration a period of notice and certain formalities might be provided for. The national law applying to the agreement will then have to be followed.

The Agreement on Parental Leave is for an indefinite period. It does not contain provisions to denounce the agreement partly or totally. It has, however, a clause that parties will review the application of the agreement after the date of the Council decision if requested by one of the parties. This does not take away that either party has the right to denounce the agreement at any time. In that case, the directive might become an empty shell.

B. Implementation by Council Decision

2103. Much of what has been said about the implementation by national procedures is also relevant to the implementation of a European collective agreement by way of a Council decision. We limit ourselves to a number of specific points.

As indicated earlier, the first inter-industry-wide European Collective Agreement on Parental Leave was implemented by a directive of 4 June 1996.

1. Which Agreements?

2104. It is evident that the collective agreements which qualify the first to be implemented by a Council decision are the European multi-industry agreements, which cover all employers and all employees. It is indeed these agreements which are meant to replace Council directives, which apply in principle to all employers and employees of the Union. One can, however, not exclude *a priori* the possibility of implementing by way of a Council decision sectoral, regional or even European company agreements. First, the text of Article 155 TFEU is fairly general and not limited to exclusively inter-industry-wide collective agreements. Secondly, one has to respect and to promote, also in view of fully implementing the subsidiarity principle, the dynamism and the autonomy of collective bargaining. In other words, a decision by the Council implementing collective agreements other than inter-industry-wide is not only *de jure* but also *de facto* a viable possibility.

2. Content

2105. The content of the agreement has to be limited to matters covered by Article 153(1) and (3) TFEU, which were enumerated above. It seems to me that the Council has to accept or reject the text of the agreement as a whole and that it cannot change the content or retain only a part of the agreement, unless the contracting parties and the Commission agree. The Council decision will only implement the normative part of the agreement. Actually, it does not seem necessary that the decision should cover the contractual relations (obligatory part of the collective agreement) between the parties as well.

3. Scope

2106. The territorial scope of the agreement will, self-evidently, be limited to the territory of the 28 Member States. The decision will affect the EFTA countries in the framework of the EEA Agreement.

4. Binding Effect

2107. The binding effect of the decision will depend on the instrument which the Council decides to use: a regulation, a directive or a decision. Here the Council is the guardian of the *erga omnes* effect. This means that the European agreement, in case of a regulation or a directive, will supersede national legislation and national collective agreements, work rules, individual agreements and the like. Such a Council decision could also, it seems to me, amend or abolish previous regulations, directives or recommendations.

One may ask whether multi-industry Union agreements, implemented by a Council decision, would also supersede sectoral agreements or regional or company agreements, which are also implemented by a Council decision. The answer seems, in the present state of affairs, to be positive, in the sense that the higher collective agreement contains minimum standards which agreements at a lower level have to respect and can expand. As indicated earlier, the Council always has the last word and can at all times withdraw its decision implementing the agreement or adopt another instrument, which simply amends or abolishes the collective agreement completely or partially.

The CollectiveAgreement on Parental Leave was, as indicated earlier, implemented by way of a directive. This seems to be the logical path, since it is a framework agreement leaving much to be filled in at national level, either by the Member States or by the competent social partners. The directive is binding on the Member States as to the results to be achieved, but leaves them the choice of form and method.

5. Interpretation

2108. In case of a Council decision the agreement is self-evidently up for eventual interpretation by the European Court pursuant to the relevant Treaty provisions concerning preliminary questions.

Again, the contracting parties may elaborate their proper arrangements to settle interpretation problems, e.g. by way of conciliation or arbitration.

Regarding the Collective Agreement on Parental Leave, we refer to A.6 of this section.

6. Master or Slave

2109. The relation between the (European collective) agreement and the Council decision implementing the agreement is of the utmost importance. The question arises indeed whether the collective agreement will, through the implementation procedure, become incorporated in the Council decision and thus *de jure* disappear, as being absorbed by the Council decision, cease to exist or whether the agreement will continue to live its own life and the decision is thus only giving an *erga omnes* effect to an agreement which remains in a sense in the hands of the contracting parties. Much will depend on how the Council decision will be constructed: whether the decision will simply absorb the text of the agreement or whether the decision will state that the (following) agreement has become implemented by a Council decision. In the latter case, the agreement remains the property of the social partners, which can denounce the agreement at their will or follow the provisions of the agreement if they want to do so, which otherwise would not be possible. In that case the Council decision would become an empty shell. It is appropriate, in order to respect to a maximum the autonomy of the social partners, not to follow the road of incorporation of the agreement into the Council decision.

The Directive of 3 June 1996, implementing the Collective Agreement on Parental Leave, respected the autonomy of the social partners by giving binding force to the agreement, which was published as an annex to the Directive. The text of the agreement was thus not amended in any way. The European Parliament, however, complained that it was not really involved and could only come in after the text was agreed upon by the social partners and the Commission had taken the steps for implementation by a Council decision.

7. Collective Bargaining and Competition

2110. In three similar cases[881] of the same date, the Court of Justice had essentially to ascertain whether a decision taken by the organisations representing employers and workers in a given sector, in the context of a collective agreement, to set up in that sector a single pension fund responsible for managing a supplementary pension scheme and to request the public authorities to make affiliation to that fund compulsory for all workers in that sector is contrary to Article 105 TFEU. All three cases dealt with a single sectoral pension fund and a supplementary occupational scheme established by a sectoral collective agreement that had been declared binding *erga omnes*. This has a consequence that all employers and employees had

---

881. C.O.J., 21 September 1999, *Albany* v. *Stichting Bedrijfspensioenfonds Textielindustries*, Case C-67/96; *Brentjes' Handelsonderneming* v. *Stichting Bedrijfspensioensfonds voor de handel in bouwmaterialen*, Joined Cases 115–117/97 and *Drijvende Bokken* v. *Stichting Pensioenfonds voor de vervoer en havenbedrijven*, Case C-219/97, ECR, 1999, 5751. *See* N. Bruun and J. Hellsten (eds), *Collective Agreement and Competition in the EU: The Report of the COLCOM project*, Copenhagen, 2001, 226 pp.

Part II, Ch. 1, Collective Bargaining

to be affiliated to this fund. Some companies did not like this compulsion and contended that they could provide arrangements at a lower price and that the compulsory arrangement was contrary to free competition in the common market. The Court confirmed the validity of the collective agreements declared binding *erga omnes*.

The Court stated that Article 101(1) and Articles 151 to 159 TFEU are construed as an effective and consistent body of provisions; it follows that agreements concluded in the context of collective negotiations between management and labour, in pursuit of social policy objectives such as the improvement of conditions of work and employment, must, by virtue of their nature and purpose, be regarded as falling outside the scope of 101(1) of the Treaty. The Court continued:

> An understanding in the form of a collective agreement which sets up in a particular sector a supplementary pension scheme to be managed by a pension fund to which affiliation may be made compulsory by the public authorities does not, by virtue of its nature and purpose, fall within the scope of Article 101(1) of the Treaty. Such a scheme seeks generally to guarantee a certain level of pension for all workers in that sector and therefore contributes directly to improving one of their working conditions, namely their remuneration.
>
> A decision by the public authorities, at the request of the parties to the agreement, to make affiliation to such a fund compulsory cannot therefore be regarded as requiring or favouring the adoption of agreements, decisions or concerted practices contrary to Article 101 of the Treaty or as reinforcing their effects. Accordingly, the Treaty does not preclude a decision by the public authorities to make affiliation to a sectoral pension fund compulsory at the request of organisations representing employers and workers in a given sector.

Chapter 2. Workers' Participation

§1. INFORMATION AND CONSULTATION

2111. Under this heading we pay first special attention to the so-called Vredeling proposal,[882] named after the then social Commissioner H. Vredeling, which was adopted by the Commission on 24 October 1980 concerning the information and consultation of employees employed in undertakings with a complex structure, especially multinational enterprises.[883] The target of the proposal was both the national enterprise and the group as a whole, so that local management would be in a position to give the employees of the subsidiary a clear picture of the activities of the undertaking as a whole, when this undertaking operates in various countries. Secondly, the proposal intended to provide for the local workers' representatives to have access to top management when information at a local level would be insufficient. Finally its purpose was that local management would be able to provide the workers' representatives with adequate information at a local level and with consultation opportunities regarding important decisions affecting local conditions that would be taken at distant headquarters.

2112. According to the proposal, at least every six months the management of the parent company would forward to the local management information concerning the group as a whole and relating in particular to:

(a) structure and manning;
(b) the economic and financial situation;
(c) the situation and probable development of business and production and sales;
(d) the employment situation and probable trends;
(e) production and investment programmes;
(f) rationalisation plans;
(g) manufacturing and working methods, in particular the introduction of new work methods;
(h) all procedures and plans able to have a substantial effect on employees' interests.

The management of the subsidiary will forward this information to the workers' representatives. If the information is not available, then the representatives are

---

882. One should also mention the following proposals, which provide for a certain role to be played by workers (participation, or if not possible, at least information and consultation):
    – Proposal for a Council Directive supplementing the statute for a European association with regard to the involvement of employees, O.J. C-99, 21 April 1992;
    – Proposal for a Council Directive supplementing the statute for a European cooperative society with regard to the involvement of employees, O.J., 21 April 1992, No. C-99;
    – Proposal for a Council Directive supplementing the statute for a European mutual society with regard to the involvement of employees, O.J., 21 April 1992, No. C-99.
883. *See further* for a more detailed study: R. Blanpain, F. Blanquet and others, *The Vredeling Proposal, Information and Consultation of Employees in Multinational Enterprises*, Kluwer, 1983, 219 pp.

Part II, Ch. 2, Workers' Participation

allowed to request that information from top management (the famous by-pass of local management by the employees).

2113. Where the management of a dominant undertaking proposes to take a decision concerning the whole or a major part of the dominant undertaking or one of its subsidiaries which is liable to have substantial effects on the interests of its employees, it is required to forward precise information to the management of each of its subsidiaries within the Union not later than 40 days before the adoption of the decision, giving details of:

- the grounds for the proposed decision;
- the legal, economic and social consequences of such a decision for the employees concerned;
- the measures planned in respect to the employees.

This information must be given in the case of decisions relating to:

(a) the closure or transfer of an establishment or a major part thereof;
(b) restrictions, extensions or substantial modifications to the activities of the undertaking;
(c) major modifications with regard to organisation;
(d) the introduction of long-term cooperation with other undertakings or the cessation of such cooperation.

2114. The management of the subsidiary is required to communicate this information without delay to the workers' representatives and to ask for their opinion within a period of not less than 30 days. In the case of decisions likely to have a direct effect on the employees' terms of employment and conditions, the management of the subsidiary is required to hold consultations with the workers' representatives with a view to reaching agreement on the measures planned in respect of the employees. Where the information is not communicated or consultations do not take place as required, another access to top management is possible (another by-pass of local management).

2115. Few proposals have aroused such heated debate as the Vredeling proposal. Both camps entrenched themselves. Everybody proclaimed that employees were entitled to information and consultation. The way in which this had to be organised and the dimension involved were other matters. A consensus between the social partners seemed impossible and moreover the governments were deeply divided. An amended proposal for a directive on procedures for informing and consulting employees of 13 July 1983 was equally unsuccessful and the Vredeling proposal was buried. The problem was postponed and was to be discussed in 1989, but nothing happened and Vredeling belongs to history. As indicated above, the Commission would, within the framework of the social action programme of 1990, prepare an 'instrument concerning the information and consultation of employees'. This took the form of a proposal for a directive on the establishment of a European Works Council in Community-scale undertakings or groups of undertakings for the purpose of informing and consulting employees and of a directive on information and consultation.

§2. THE SOCIETAS EUROPAEA (SE)

I. More than 30 Years of Discussion

2116. The first proposal for a regulation on the statute for a European company (Societas Europaea, SE) dates from 1970; the proposal was amended in 1975. Later, the idea was revitalised with a proposal for a Council regulation on the statute for a European company, on the one hand, and a directive complementing the statute for a European company with regard to the involvement of employees in the European company, on the other, both of 25 August 1989.[884] In 1991, amended proposals were made.[885] The proposal remains, after more than 30 years, as controversial as it was in 1970.

2117. In the reformulation of its proposals, the Commission took account of the new dimension by the Single Act of 1986, on the one hand, and of the dynamics of the 1992 project, on the other. The completion of the internal market, and the improvement it must bring about in the economic and the social situation throughout the Union, mean not only that barriers to trade must be removed, but also that the structures of production must be adapted to the Union dimensions. For this purpose it is essential that companies whose business is not limited to satisfying purely local needs should be able to plan and carry out the reorganisation of their business on a Union-wide scale. In the actual state of affairs companies still have to choose a form of company governed by a particular national law. The legal framework within which business must still be carried on in Europe, as it is still based entirely on national laws, no longer applies to the creation of groups consisting of companies from different Member States. It is thus essential to ensure as far as possible that the economic unit and the legal unit of business in Europe coincide.

2118. The essential objective of the legal rules governing a European company is to make it possible for companies from different Member States to merge or to create a holding company, and to enable companies or other legal bodies carrying on economic activities and governed by the law of different Member States to form a joint subsidiary. Companies may be formed throughout the Union under the form of a European public limited company (SE). The capital of the SE shall be divided into shares. The liability of the shareholders for the debts and obligations of the company shall be limited to the amount subscribed by them. The SE is a commercial company whatever the object of its undertaking. It shall have legal personality (Article 1 regulation). The capital of the SE amounts to no less than ECU 1,000,000 (Article 4). It should be pointed out that the statute is not legally binding, but voluntary: companies are free to choose it or not.

---

884. O.J. C-263, 16 October 1989.
885. O.J. C-138, 29 May 1991 and C-178/1, 8 July 1991.

2119. The proposed statute is legally based upon Article 114 TFEU. This is of course important, since proposals based on Article 114 TFEU can be adopted by qualified majority. This is obviously a controversial point, certainly as regards taxes. It is also remarkable that workers' participation is the subject of a separate instrument, namely, a directive based upon Article 50 TFEU, within the framework of freedom of establishment in which different directives aiming at the approximating of national legislation regarding limited liability companies have been enacted. We should also point out that the proposed directive retains the one-tier system as well as the two-tier system, similar to the proposed fifth directive, to which we basically refer as far as organs of the company and their competences are concerned. In a nutshell: the fifth directive aims at the coordination of national legislation the SE has a uniform European system as its target. Both proposals are inspired by the same principles regarding workers' participation.

II. Models of Participation

2120. Workers' participation in the SE is regulated by the proposed directive of 25 August 1989, with the exception of Article 33 of the regulation of the same date, pursuant to which:

> the administration or management of each of the founder companies shall discuss with its workers' representatives the legal economic and employment implications of the formation of a SE holding company for the employees and any measures proposed to deal with them.

The 'whereas' to the proposed directive indicates that in order to promote the economic and social objectives of the Union, arrangements should be made for employees to participate in the supervision and strategic development of the SE. The great diversity of rules and practices existing in the Member States regarding the manner in which employees' representatives participate make it possible to lay down uniform rules on the involvement of employees in the SE. This means that account should be taken of the specific characteristics of the laws of the Member States by establishing for the SE a framework comprising several models of participation, and authorising first Member States to choose the model best corresponding to their national traditions, and secondly the management or administrative board, as the case may be, and the workers' representatives of the SE or of its founder companies to choose the model most suited to their social environment. The directive forms an indispensable complement to the provisions of the regulation and it is therefore necessary to ensure that the two sets of provisions are applied concomitantly. An SE may not be formed unless one of the systems of workers' participation has been chosen (Article 3(2)).

2121. The involvement of employees means the participation 'in the supervision and strategic development of the SE' (Article 2). A distinction must, however, be made between the registered office and the establishments of the SE. The status and duties of the workers' representatives in the establishment is determined by national law. Regarding the registered office, Member States can choose between four models, just as for the fifth directive. Each Member State determines the manner in which the participation models shall be applied for an SE having its registered office in its territory (Article 3(4)). Each Member State may retain all models or restrict its choice to one or more models (Article 3(5)).

2122. The models retained by the Commission are the following:

- the German model: the members of the supervisory board or the administrative board are at least by one-third and not more than one-half appointed by the employees or their representatives (model 1) (Article 4, 1st indent);
- the Dutch model: co-option by the board. However, the general meeting of shareholders or the workers' representatives may, on specific grounds, object to the appointment of a particular candidate. In such cases, the appointment may not be made until an independent body established under public law has declared the objection inadmissible (model 2) (Article 4, 2nd indent);
- a separate body shall represent the employees of the SE. The number of members of that body and the detailed rules governing their election or appointment shall be laid down in the statutes in consultation with the workers' representatives of the founder companies in accordance with the law or practices of the Member States (Article 5(1)). These representatives have rights to information and consultation comparable to those provided for in the proposed fifth directive (model 3);
- another model may be established by means of an agreement concluded between the management boards and the administrative boards of the founder companies and the employees or their representatives in those companies. The parties to the negotiation may be assisted by experts of their choice at the expense of the founder companies. The agreement may be concluded for a fixed period and renegotiated at the expiry of that period. However, the agreement concluded shall remain in force until the entry into force of the new agreement. Where the two parties to the agreement so decide, or where no such agreement can be reached, a standard model provided by the law of the State shall apply. This model shall ensure, for the employees, at least the rights of information and consultation as mentioned (Article 6) (model 4).

2123. The model to be applied shall be determined by an agreement concluded between the management boards and the administrative boards of the founder companies and the workers' representatives of those companies, as provided by the laws and practices of the Member States. Where no agreement can be reached, the management and the administrative boards shall choose the model applicable to the SE (Article 3(1)). A chosen model may always be replaced by another by means of an agreement. The workers' representatives of the SE shall be elected in accordance with systems which appropriately take into account the number of staff they represent. All the employees must be able to participate in the vote (Article 7). The first time, the workers' representatives of the SE shall be appointed by the workers' representatives of the founder companies in proportion to the number of employees they represent (Article 8). The workers' representatives receive such financial material resources as enable them to meet and perform their duties in an appropriate manner (Article 9).

Employee participation in the capital or in the profits or losses of the SE may be organised by means of a collective agreement (Article 11).

2124. In a Communication on worker information and consultation of 14 November 1995,[886] the Commission relaunched the debate on workers' participation and indicated possible directions for Union action:

2125. Various options are possible.

A. *Option 1: Maintain the Status quo*

2126. This option would mean continuing the discussions in the Council on the basis of the existing proposals and maintaining the fragmented approach to Union action on employee information, consultation and involvement. The main disadvantage of this option is that as things stand, it seems to offer little hope of progress.

B. *Option 2: Global Approach*

2127. This option involves a change in the way of looking at the whole question. Instead of attempting to establish, at Union level, sets of specific rules for each entity to be covered by Union rules on company law, attempts would be made to establish a general framework at European level on informing and consulting employees. This would make it possible to withdraw the proposals for directives annexed to the proposals for regulations on the statute for a European company, a European association, a European co-operative society and a European mutual society. The same would apply to the social provisions in the proposal for the 'fifth directive' and the 'Vredeling proposal'.

Given that the European Union already has a legal framework for employee information and consultation at transnational level, this global approach would mean quite simply that a Union instrument on information and consultation at national level would have to be adopted. Before taking this approach, a number of questions need to be answered: Would it be in keeping with the principles of subsidiarity and proportionality? What would be the nature of the proposal (approximation of legislation or establishment of minimum requirements)? and, lastly which legal basis should be used (Treaty or Maastricht Social Agreement)?

The main advantage of this option is that it is a step towards simplifying Union law and European social policy. It could also make it easier – and, in fact, might even be necessary – to achieve progress with the above-mentioned proposals, since the businesses concerned which are of purely national scale would then be covered by this general framework.

---

886. COM(95) 547 final.

C. *Option 3: Immediate Action on the Proposals concerning the Statute for a European Company, a European Association, a European Co-operative society and a European Mutual Society*

2128. If the global approach set out above is adopted, immediate steps could be taken to unlock these proposals, especially the proposal on the statute for a European company, the adoption of which is particularly urgent. This would be justified by the importance of this instrument for the organisation of companies at European level and by the urgent need to find a legal vehicle which meets the needs of major trans-European transport infrastructure projects (the Member States have indicated that they will need two years to introduce the implementing provisions for the statute, in spite of its immediate legal effect).

This could be done in two ways: The above-mentioned proposals for directives would be withdrawn on the same condition, *mutatis mutandis*, as that set out in Article 136 of the proposal for a regulation on the statute for a European company, which stipulates that no European company, European association, European co-operative society or European mutual society could be set up in a Member State which had not transposed the 'European Works Councils' Directive.

This solution would have the advantage of maintaining the compulsory link between the establishment of these organisations and their application of the procedures for employee information and consultation, which has always been a key element in these proposals. It would also prevent discrimination between these organisations depending on the Member State in which they decided to locate their registered office.

No conditions would be attached to the withdrawal of these proposals. In this case, only the Union provisions in force (the 'European Works Councils', 'collective redundancies' and 'business transfers' Directives) would be applicable to the organisations concerned, as appropriate.

The disadvantage of this sub-option is that one Member State is not covered by the 'European Works Councils' Directive. This would mean that the European companies, European associations, European co-operative societies and European mutual societies which are of multinational scale and have their registered offices in this Member State would not be subject to the same obligations in the area of transnational information and consultation of employees, as would be the case for organisations with their registered office in another Member State.

The arguments set out above are provided as a contribution to the discussion which the Commission would like to see developed among the Member States, in the EP and the ESC and between the social partners at Union level. The Commission reaffirms that it is open to any way of achieving the objectives at the heart of this debate. These are, first, to put an end to the unacceptable situation of never-ending institutional discussion of the above-mentioned proposals and, second, to supplement the Union legal framework in the area of employee information and consultation and to make it more coherent and effective.

The Commission would like to receive the comments and views of the Member States, the EP, the ESC and the social partners at European level on these matters. It is particularly interested in knowing their views on the options set out in this communication.

Part II, Ch. 2, Workers' Participation 2129–2129

2129. The discussion got a new lease of life, thanks to the expert group, presided over by Mr. E. Davignon, a leading industrialist and former vice-president of the European Commission. The group of experts on 'European systems of worker involvement' was set up in November 1996.

The group was given as its main task the following by the Commission: to examine the type of involvement rules to be applied to the European Company. It delivered its final report in May 1997.

The proposals of the Davignon group (1997)[887] can be summarised as follows. The group decided to limit its discussions to three of the four ways of setting up a European company set out in the draft ECS:

– the merger of existing companies;
– the creation of a joint holding company; and
– the creation of a joint subsidiary.

The conversion of existing national public limited liability companies was not retained, in order to avoid the possibility of becoming a European company in order to escape national systems.

All European companies, whatever their number of employees, would have a system of worker involvement.[888] It follows the route of the EWC since it recommends that negotiation should be the primary method of establishing the worker involvement system. Only if these negotiations fail would a set of statutory 'reference rules' apply.

The report provides for detailed recommendations on the negotiating procedure for the European company's worker involvement arrangements.

The employees would be represented by a negotiating body, made up of workers' representatives appointed 'in accordance with national practices and procedures'. Workers' representatives are entitled to the services of experts.

The content of the agreement would be flexible, but the report gives an indicative list of what the content of the agreement might be. Again, there is a parallel with the EWC.

If no agreement is reached, a set of reference rules will apply. There are two forms of involvement:

– information and consultation through a group of employee representatives;
– the representation of employees on the European company's board.

Workers' representatives would be members of the management board or supervisory board. Workers' representatives would make up one-fifth of the total members of the board in question, with a minimum of two members.

---

887. 'European Company Statute revisited, European Works Council Bulletin', 1997, 10, pp. 8–13.
888. 'All arrangements allowing workers' representatives to take part in company decision-making processes with a view to ensuring the collective expression and permanent consideration of their interests in the context of decisions concerning the management and economic and financial development of the company.'

The employee representatives on the board would be full members. The report was welcomed by the Council, by the EP, and the social partners.

III. Board-level Participation Agreed at Aventis[889]

2130. An agreement (7 March 2001) on European board-level employee participation was concluded between Aventis management, the German chemical workers' trade union, IG BCE, the French chemical workers' unions affiliated to CGT and CFDT and the European Mine, Chemical and Energy Workers' Federation (EMCEF). Aventis, which has its headquarters in Strasbourg, France, was created in 1999 following the merger of the German chemicals multinational, Hoechst AG and the French Rhône-Poulenc SA. The company employs some 95,000 people in more than 120 countries.

The agreement, hailed as the first of its kind, especially in the light of the European Company Statute, provides for a total of six worker representatives to sit on the supervisory board of Aventis. Four of these six representatives (two French and two German) are full members of the board, nominated by trade unions and voted onto the board by the company's shareholder assembly. The two remaining worker representatives are, in line with French law appointed by the works council. Under the terms of the agreement, EMCEF will nominate the candidate for one of these seats and, in return for the French works council agreeing to this, it will have the right to be represented on the Aventis European Works Council (or European Dialogue Committee). The four regular worker representatives will have the same rights as the 10 shareholder representatives on the board, whereas the works council representative will attend in a consultative capacity and the EMCEF representative will attend as a guest.

IV. Nice Summit (7–10 December 2000): the Break-through

2131. The European Council of Nice reached agreement on the European Company Statute.

According to the Nice summit conclusions, the agreement, in order to take into account different national employment relations systems, allows Member States the option of whether or not to transpose into their national law the fall-back reference provisions (which apply where no agreement can be reached between management and employee representatives) relating to board-level employee participation applicable to European companies constituted by merger. In order for a European company to be registered in a Member State which has not transposed these reference provisions, either: an agreement must have been concluded on the arrangements for worker involvement in that company, including board-level participation; or none of the companies involved in the merger must have been governed by board-level participation rules prior to the registration of the European company.[890]

---

889. <www.eiro.eurofound.ie>.
890. A. Broughton, <www.eiro.eurofound.ie>.

Part II, Ch. 2, Workers' Participation

In December 2000, the EU Council of Ministers on the worker involvement provisions relating to the European Company Statute reached political unanimous agreement.

The draft directive and the regulation on the company law aspects of the Statute are forwarded to the European Parliament for an opinion. The texts will subsequently be sent back to the Council of Ministers for adoption. The draft directive and regulation will come into force three years after adoption. The draft directive will require negotiations between management and employee representatives in each European company over the worker involvement arrangements to be applied, with statutory reference provisions applying where no agreement is reached.[891]

V. The Directive of 8 October 2001

2132. Two documents of the Council of the EU relate to the European company: a Council regulation on the Statute for a European Company (SE) and a Council directive supplementing the Statute for a European Company with regard to the involvement of employees.[892] Arrangements for the involvement of employees are to be established in every SE.

We summarise the provisions in both instruments relating to the involvement of employees.

A. *Definitions*

2133. The directive contains a number of definitions, amongst which, for the purposes of this directive:

- 'Employees' representatives' means the employees' representatives provided for by national law and/or practice;
- 'Representative Body (RB)' means the body representative of the employees set up by the agreements or in accordance with the provisions of the Annex, with the purpose of informing and consulting the employees of an SE and its subsidiaries and establishments situated in the Community and, where applicable, of exercising participation rights in relation to the SE;
- 'Special Negotiating Body (SNB)' means the body established to negotiate with the competent body of the participating companies regarding the establishment of arrangements for the involvement of employees within the SE;
- 'Involvement of employees' means any mechanism, including information, consultation and participation, through which employees' representatives may exercise an influence on decisions to be taken within the company;
- 'Information' means the informing of the body representative of the employees and/or employees' representatives by the competent organ of the SE on questions

---

891. 'Agreement on European Company Statute and working time in road transport industry', <www.eiro.eurofound.ie>.
892. O.J. L 294, 10 November 2001.

which concern the SE itself and any of its subsidiaries or establishments situated in another Member State or which exceed the powers of the decision-making organs in a single Member State at a time, in a manner and with a content which allows the employees' representatives to undertake an in-depth assessment of the possible impact and, where appropriate, prepare consultations with the competent organ of the SE;
– 'Consultation' means the establishment of dialogue and exchange of views between the body representative of the employees and/or the employees' representatives and the competent organ of the SE, at a time, in a manner and with a content which allows the employees' representatives, on the basis of information provided, to express an opinion on measures envisaged by the competent organ which may be taken into account in the decision-making process within the SE;
– 'Participation' means the influence of the body representative of the employees and/or the employees' representatives in the affairs of a company by way of:
– the right to elect or appoint some of the members of the company's supervisory or administrative organ; or
– the right to recommend and/or oppose the appointment of some or all of the members of the company's supervisory or administrative organ.

B. Formation of an SE

2134. The following formations are, according to the Regulation (Title II), possible:

– formation by means of a merger. In the case of a merger by acquisition, the acquiring company shall take the form of an SE when the merger takes place. In the case of a merger by the formation of a new company, the SE shall be the newly formed company;
– formation of a holding SE: public and private limited-liability companies may promote the formation of a holding SE provided that each of at least two of them:
– is governed by the law of a different Member State, or
– has for at least two years had a subsidiary company governed by the law of another Member State or an establishment situated in another Member State;
– formation of a subsidiary SE: companies and firms formed under the law of a Member State with registered offices and head offices within the Community may form a subsidiary SE by subscribing for its shares, provided that each of at least two of them:
– is governed by the law of a different Member State, or
– has for at least two years had a subsidiary company governed by the law of another Member State or an establishment situated in another Member State;
– conversion of an existing public limited liability company into an SE: a public limited-liability company, formed under the law of a Member State, which has its

registered office and head office within the Community may be transformed into an SE if for at least two years it has had a subsidiary company governed by the law of another Member State.

C. Structure of the SE

2135. An SE shall comprise:

(a) a general meeting of shareholders, and
(b) either a supervisory organ and a management organ (two-tier system) or an administrative organ (one-tier system) depending on the form adopted in the statutes.

1. The Two-tier System

2136. In a two-tier system, the management organ shall be responsible for managing the SE. The member or members of the management organ shall be appointed and removed by the supervisory organ.

The supervisory organ shall supervise the work of the management organ. It may not itself exercise the power to manage the SE. The members of the supervisory organ are appointed by the general meeting. The management organ shall report to the supervisory organ at least once every three months on the progress and foreseeable development of the SE's business. The supervisory organ elects a chairman from among its members. If employees appoint half of the members, only a member appointed by the general meeting of shareholders may be elected chairman.

2. The One-tier System

2137. The administrative organ shall manage the SE. The administrative organ will consist of at least three members where employee participation is regulated in accordance with the directive. The administrative organ shall elect a chairman from among its members. If half of the members are appointed by employees, only a member appointed by the general meeting of shareholders may be elected chairman.

D. Workers' Involvement

2138. According to the directive arrangements for the involvement of employees have to be established in every SE in accordance with either a negotiating procedure or in case of absence thereof by standard rules.

1. The Negotiating Procedure

a. Creation of an SNB

2139. When management draws up a plan for the establishment of an SE, it must as soon as possible after publishing the draft terms take the necessary steps[893] to start negotiations with the representatives of the companies' employees on arrangements for the involvement of employees in the SE.

(1) Composition

2140. For this purpose, an SNB representative of the employees of the participating companies and concerned subsidiaries or establishments is created in accordance with the following provisions:

(a) in electing or appointing members of the SNB, it must be ensured:
   (i) that these members are elected or appointed in proportion to the number of employees employed in each Member State by allocating in respect of a Member State one seat per each portion of employees employed in that Member State which equals 10 per cent, or a fraction thereof, of the number of employees employed in all the Member States taken together;
   (ii) that in the case of an SE formed by way of merger, there are such further additional members from each Member State as may be necessary in order to ensure that the SNB includes at least one member representing each participating company which is registered and has employees in that Member State and which it is proposed will cease to exist as a separate legal entity following the registration of the SE, insofar as:
      – the number of such additional members does not exceed 20 per cent of the number of members designated by virtue of point (i); and
      – the composition of the SNB does not entail a double representation of the employees concerned.
      – If the number of such companies is higher than the number of additional seats, these additional seats shall be allocated to companies in different Member States by decreasing order of the number of employees they employ.
(b) Member States shall determine the method to be used for the election or appointment of the members of the SNB who are to be elected or appointed in their territories. They shall take the necessary measures to ensure that, as far as possible, such members shall include at least one member representing each participating company which has employees in the Member State concerned. Such measures must not increase the overall number of members.

---

893. Including providing information about the identity of the participating companies, concerned subsidiaries or establishments, and the number of their employees.

Member States may provide that such members may include representatives of trade unions whether or not they are employees.

Without prejudice to national legislation and/or practice laying down thresholds for the establishing of a representative body (RB), Member States shall provide that employees in undertakings or establishments in which there are no employees' representatives through no fault of their own have the right to elect or appoint members of the SNB.

(2) *Arrangements for Involvement*

2141. The SNB and management determine, by written agreement, arrangements for the involvement of employees within the SE.

To this end the SNB will be informed of the plan and the actual process of establishing the SE, up to its registration.

(3) *Rules for Decision-making*

2142. The SNB shall take decisions by an absolute majority of its members, provided that such a majority also represents an absolute majority of the employees.[894]

(4) *Experts*

2143. For the purpose of the negotiations, the SNB may request experts of its choice, for example representatives of appropriate Union level trade union organisations, to assist it with its work. Such experts may be present at negotiation meetings in an advisory capacity at the request of the SNB, where appropriate to promote coherence and consistency at Union level. The SNB may decide to inform the representatives of appropriate external organisations, including trade unions, of the start of the negotiations.

894.
1. Each member shall have one vote. However, should the result of the negotiations lead to a reduction of participation rights, the majority required for a decision to approve such an agreement shall be the votes of two-thirds of the members of the SNB representing at least two-thirds of the employees, including the votes of members representing employees employed in at least two Member States,
    - in the case of an SE to be established by way of merger, if participation covers at least 25 per cent of the overall number of employees of the participating companies, or
    - in the case of an SE to be established by way of creating a holding company or forming a subsidiary, if participation covers at least 50 per cent of the overall number of employees of the participating companies.
2. Reduction of participation rights means a proportion of members of the organs of the SE within the meaning of Article 2(k), which is lower than the highest proportion existing within the participating companies.

(5) *Opt-out*

2144. The SNB may decide by majority vote[895] not to open negotiations or to terminate negotiations already opened, and to rely on the rules on information and consultation of employees in force in the Member States where the SE has employees. Such a decision shall stop the procedure to conclude an agreement. Where such a decision has been taken, none of the provisions of the standard rules will apply.

The SNB will be reconvened on the written request of at least 10 per cent of the employees of the SE, or their representatives, at the earliest two years after the above-mentioned decision, unless the parties agree to negotiations being reopened sooner. If the SNB decides to reopen negotiations with the management but no agreement is reached as a result of those negotiations, none of the provisions of the standard rules will apply.

(6) *Expenses*

2145. Any expenses relating to the functioning of the SNB and, in general, to negotiations are borne by the participating companies so as to enable the SNB to carry out its task in an appropriate manner.

In compliance with this principle, Member States may lay down budgetary rules regarding the operation of the SNB. They may in particular limit the funding to cover one expert only.

b. Content of the Agreement

2146. Without prejudice to the autonomy of the parties,[896] the agreement has to specify:

(a) the scope of the agreement;
(b) the composition, number of members and allocation of seats on the RB in connection with arrangements for the information and consultation of the employees of the SE and its subsidiaries and establishments;
(c) the functions and the procedure for the information and consultation of the RB;
(d) the frequency of meetings of the RB;
(e) the financial and material resources to be allocated to the RB;

---

895. The majority required to decide not to open or to terminate negotiations shall be the votes of two-thirds of the members representing at least two-thirds of the employees, including the votes of members representing employees employed in at least two Member States.
   In the case of an SE established by way of transformation, this paragraph shall not apply if there is participation in the company to be transformed.
896. Without prejudice to Article 13(3)(a), in the case of an SE established by means of transformation, the agreement shall provide for at least the same level of all elements of employee involvement as the ones existing within the company to be transformed into an SE.

Part II, Ch. 2, Workers' Participation

(f) if, during negotiations, the parties decide to establish one or more information and consultation procedures instead of an RB, the arrangements for implementing those procedures;
(g) if, during negotiations, the parties decide to establish arrangements for participation, the substance of those arrangements including (if applicable) the number of members in the SE's administrative or supervisory body which the employees will be entitled to elect, appoint, recommend or oppose, the procedures as to how these members may be elected, appointed, recommended or opposed by the employees, and their rights;
(h) the date of entry into force of the agreement and its duration, cases where the agreement should be renegotiated and the procedure for its renegotiation.

The agreement is not, unless provision is made otherwise therein, subject to the standard rules.

c. Duration of Negotiations

2147. Negotiations shall commence as soon as the SNB is established and may continue for six months thereafter. The parties may, however, decide, by joint agreement, to extend negotiations beyond that period up to a total of one year from the establishment of the SNB.

d. Spirit of Cooperation

2148. Management and the SNB have to negotiate in a spirit of cooperation with a view to reaching an agreement on arrangements for the involvement of the employees within the SE.

e. Legislation Applicable to the Negotiation Procedure

2149. As a general rule, the legislation applicable to the negotiation procedure is the legislation of the Member State in which the registered office of the SE is to be situated.

2. Standard Rules

2150. Member States have to lay down standard rules on employee involvement, which must satisfy the provisions set out in the Annex of the directive. These are as follows.

a. Composition of the Body of Representatives of the Employees

2151. A representative body (RB) is to be set up in accordance with the following rules:

(a) The RB is composed of employees of the SE and its subsidiaries and establishments elected or appointed from their number by the employees' representatives or, in the absence thereof, by the entire body of employees.
(b) The election or appointment of members of the RB is to be carried out in accordance with national legislation and/or practice. Member States have to lay down rules to ensure that the number of members of, and allocation of seats on, the RB will be adapted to take account of changes occurring within the SE and its subsidiaries and establishments.
(c) Where its size so warrants, the RB will elect a select committee from among its members, comprising at most three members.
(d) The RB shall adopt its rules of procedure.
(e) The members of the RB are elected or appointed in proportion to the number of employees employed in each Member State by the participating companies and concerned subsidiaries or establishments, by allocating in respect of a Member State one seat per each portion of employees employed in that Member State which equals 10 per cent, or a fraction thereof, of the number of employees employed by the participating companies and concerned subsidiaries or establishments in all the Member States taken together.
(f) The competent organ of the SE has to be informed of the composition of the RB.
(g) Four years after the RB is established, it has to examine whether to open negotiations for the conclusion of an agreement or to continue to apply the standard rules.

If a decision has been taken to negotiate an agreement the term 'SNB' is replaced by 'RB'. Where, by the deadline by which the negotiations come to an end, no agreement has been concluded, the arrangements initially adopted in accordance with the standard rules will continue to apply.

b. Standard Rules for Information and Consultation

2152. The competence and powers of the RB set up in an SE are governed by the following rules:

(a) The competence of the RB is limited to questions which concern the SE itself, and any of its subsidiaries or establishments situated in another Member State or which exceed the powers of the decision-making organs in a single Member State.

Part II, Ch. 2, Workers' Participation

(b) The RB has the right to be informed and consulted and, for that purpose, to meet with the management of the SE at least once a year, on the basis of regular reports on the progress of the business of the SE and its prospects. The local managements shall be informed accordingly.

Management has to provide the RB with the agenda for meetings of the administrative, or, where appropriate, the management and supervisory organ, and with copies of all documents submitted to the general meeting of its shareholders.

The meeting shall relate in particular to the structure, economic and financial situation, the probable development of the business and of production and sales, the situation and probable trend of employment, investments, and substantial changes concerning organisation, introduction of new working methods or production processes, transfers of production, mergers, cut-backs or closures of undertakings, establishments or important parts thereof, and collective redundancies.

(c) Where there are exceptional circumstances affecting the employees' interests to a considerable extent, particularly in the event of relocations, transfers, the closure of establishments or undertakings or collective redundancies, the RB has the right to be informed. The RB or, where it so decides, in particular for reasons of urgency, the select committee, has the right to meet at its request the competent organ of the SE or any more appropriate level of management within the SE having its own powers of decision, so as to be informed and consulted on measures significantly affecting employees' interests.

Where management decides not to act in accordance with the opinion expressed by the RB, this body shall have the right to a further meeting with the competent organ of the SE with a view to seeking agreement.

In the case of a meeting organised with the select committee, those members of the RB who represent employees who are directly concerned by the measures in question also have the right to participate.

The meeting referred to above does not affect the prerogatives of the competent organ.

(d) Member States may lay down rules on the chairing of information and consultation meetings. Before any meeting with management, the RB or the select committee are entitled to meet without the representatives of management being present.

(e) The members of the RB will inform the representatives of the employees of the content and outcome of the information and consultation procedures.

(f) The RB or the select committee may be assisted by experts of its choice.

(g) The members of the RB are entitled to time off for training without loss of wages.

(h) The costs of the RB are borne by the SE, which will provide the body's members with the financial and material resources needed to enable them to perform their duties in an appropriate manner.

In particular, the SE will, unless otherwise agreed, bear the cost of organising meetings and providing interpretation facilities and the accommodation and travelling expenses of members of the RB and the select committee.

In compliance with these principles, the Member States may lay down budgetary rules regarding the operation of the RB. They may in particular limit funding to cover one expert only.

c. Standard Rules for Participation

2153. Employee participation in an SE is governed by the following provisions:

(a) In the case of an SE established by transformation, if the rules of a Member State relating to employee participation in the administrative or supervisory body applied before registration, all aspects of employee participation shall continue to apply to the SE. Point (b) shall apply *mutatis mutandis* to that end.
(b) In other cases of the establishing of an SE, the employees have the right to elect, appoint, recommend or oppose the appointment of a number of members of the administrative or supervisory body of the SE equal to the highest proportion in force in the participating companies concerned before registration of the SE.

If none of the participating companies was governed by participation rules before registration of the SE, the latter is not required to establish provisions for employee participation.

2154. The RB shall decide on the allocation of seats within the administrative or supervisory body among the members representing the employees from the various Member States or on the way in which the SE's employees may recommend or oppose the appointment of the members of these bodies according to the proportion of the SE's employees in each Member State. If the employees of one or more Member States are not covered by this proportional criterion, the RB shall appoint a member from one of those Member States, in particular the Member State of the SE's registered office where that is appropriate. Each Member State may determine the allocation of the seats it is given within the administrative or supervisory body.

Every member of the administrative body or, where appropriate, the supervisory body of the SE who has been elected, appointed or recommended by the RB or, depending on the circumstances, by the employees is a full member with the same rights and obligations as the members representing the shareholders, including the right to vote.

d. The Application of Standard Rules

2155. The standard rules as laid down by the legislation of the Member State in which the registered office of the SE is to be situated shall apply from the date of the registration of the SE where either:

(a) the parties so agree; or
(b) by the deadline no agreement has been concluded, and:

Part II, Ch. 2, Workers' Participation

- the management of each of the participating companies decides to accept the application of the standard rules in relation to the SE and so to continue with its registration of the SE; and
- the SNB has not taken the decision not to open negotiations.

Moreover, the standard rules regarding participation, fixed by the national legislation of the Member State of registration, will apply only:

(a) in the case of an SE established by transformation, if the rules of a Member State relating to employee participation in the administrative or supervisory body applied to a company transformed into an SE;
(b) in the case of an SE established by merger:
   - if, before registration of the SE, one or more forms of participation applied in one or more of the participating companies covering at least 25 per cent of the total number of employees in all the participating companies; or
   - if, before registration of the SE, one or more forms of participation applied in one or more of the participating companies covering less than 25 per cent of the total number of employees in all the participating companies and if the SNB so decides;
(c) in the case of an SE established by setting up a holding company or establishing a subsidiary:
   - if, before registration of the SE, one or more forms of participation applied in one or more of the participating companies covering at least 50 per cent of the total number of employees in all the participating companies; or
   - if, before registration of the SE, one or more forms of participation applied in one or more of the participating companies covering less than 50 per cent of the total number of employees in all the participating companies and if the SNB so decides.

2156. If there was more than one form of participation within the various participating companies, the SNB shall decide which of those forms must be established in the SE. Member States may fix the rules, which are applicable in the absence of any decision on the matter for an SE registered in their territory. The SNB shall inform the competent organs of the participating companies of any decisions taken pursuant to this paragraph.

Member States may provide that the reference provisions concerning 'standard rules for participation' do not apply in the case provided for in case of merger.

3. Miscellaneous Provisions

a. Reservation and Confidentiality

2157. Member States have to provide that members of the SNB or the RB, and experts who assist them, are not authorised to reveal any information which has been given to them in confidence.

The same applies to employees' representatives in the context of an information and consultation procedure.

This obligation continues to apply, wherever the persons referred to may be, even after the expiry of their terms of office.

Each Member State will provide, in specific cases and under the conditions and limits laid down by national legislation, that an SE or a participating company established in its territory is not obliged to transmit information where its nature is such that, according to objective criteria, to do so would seriously harm the functioning of the SE (or, as the case may be, the participating company) or its subsidiaries and establishments or would be prejudicial to them.

A Member State may make such dispensation subject to prior administrative or judicial authorisation.

Each Member State may lay down particular provisions for SEs in its territory which pursue directly and essentially the aim of ideological guidance with respect to information and the expression of opinions, on condition that, on the date of adoption of this directive, such provisions already exist in the national legislation.

In doing so Member States will make provision for administrative or judicial appeal procedures which the employees' representatives may initiate when an SE or participating company demands confidentiality or does not give information.

Such procedures may include arrangements designed to protect the confidentiality of the information in question.

b. Operation of the RB and Procedure for the Information and Consultation of Employees

2158. The competent organ of the SE and the RB work together in a spirit of cooperation with due regard for their reciprocal rights and obligations.

The same applies to cooperation between the supervisory or administrative organ of the SE and the employees' representatives in conjunction with a procedure for the information and consultation of employees.

c. Protection of Employees' Representatives

2159. The members of the SNB, the members of the RB, any employees' representatives exercising functions under the information and consultation procedure and any employees' representatives in the supervisory or administrative organ of an SE, who are employees of the SE, its subsidiaries or establishments or of a participating company will, in the exercise of their functions, enjoy the same protection and guarantees provided for employees' representatives by the national legislation and/or practice in force in their country of employment.

This applies in particular to attendance at meetings of the SNB or RB, any other meeting in case of an information and conciliation procedure or any meeting of the administrative or supervisory organ, and to the payment of wages for members employed by a participating company or the SE or its subsidiaries or establishments during a period of absence necessary for the performance of their duties.

Part II, Ch. 2, Workers' Participation

d. Misuse of Procedures

2160. Member States have to take appropriate measures in conformity with Community law with a view to preventing the misuse of an SE for the purpose of depriving employees of rights to employee involvement or withholding such rights.

e. Compliance with this Directive

2161. Each Member State has to ensure that the management of establishments of an SE and the supervisory or administrative organs of subsidiaries and of participating companies which are situated within its territory and the employees' representatives or, as the case may be, the employees themselves abide by the obligations laid down by this Directive, regardless of whether or not the SE has its registered office within its territory.

Member States have to provide for appropriate measures in the event of failure to comply with this directive; in particular they shall ensure that administrative or legal procedures are available to enable the obligations deriving from this directive to be enforced.

f. Link between this Directive and Other Provisions

2162. Where an SE is a Union-scale undertaking or a controlling undertaking of a Union-scale group of undertakings within the meaning of directives on EWCs, the provisions of these directives and the provisions transposing them into national legislation shall not apply to them or to their subsidiaries.

However, where the SNB decides not to open negotiations or to terminate negotiations already opened, the EWC directives and the provisions transposing them into national legislation shall apply.

Provisions on the participation of employees in company bodies provided for by national legislation and/or practice, other than those implementing this directive, will not apply to companies covered by this directive.

This directive shall not prejudice:

(a) the existing rights to involvement of employees provided for by national legislation and/or practice in the Member States as enjoyed by employees of the SE and its subsidiaries and establishments, other than participation in the bodies of the SE;
(b) the provisions on participation in the bodies laid down by national legislation and/or practice applicable to the subsidiaries of the SE.

In order to preserve these rights Member States may take the necessary measures to guarantee that the structures of employee representation in participating companies, which will cease to exist as separate legal entities, are maintained after the registration of the SE.

(1) Some Preliminary Observations

2163.

(1) In gauging the meaning and importance of the establishment of an SE for the 'involvement of employees', one has first to keep in mind that such establishment remains a voluntary affair for the companies concerned and whether they see advantages in creating an SE. Much will depend on the possible tax incentives which will go along with the setting up of an SE: are companies allowed to deduct the debts incurred in one country from the profits made in another Member State?
(2) The directive foresees various forms of workers' involvement, namely:
 – information;
 – consultation; and
 – participation: sitting on the boards of companies.
(3) The way of introducing information and consultation and participation is very similar to the procedures laid down in the 2009 Directive on EWCs. Either parties involved conclude an agreement or standard rules are imposed.
(4) In case of an agreement procedure an SNB will negotiate to set up an RB or a procedure and/or a formula of employees' representatives sitting on the board(s) of companies.
(5) In case no agreement is reached standard rules will apply. These standard rules provide information and consultation to be exercised through an RB, which are similar to the rights of EWCs. Regarding employees sitting on boards, this will be the case, when such formulas already exist at national level in (the) companies concerned and when Member States do not opt out from the participation rights, as they can do in the case of the establishment of an SE by way of a merger.
(6) When the directive on involvement of employees applies, the rules concerning EWCs do not apply.
(7) It is also remarkable that, like for the EWCs, a spirit of cooperation between the parties concerned should prevail.
(8) Trade unions are expressly referred to for the composition of an SNB as possible experts.
(9) Also this directive remains more or less mute regarding the time when information has to be given concerning restructurings. Even expressions such as 'in good time' or 'in appropriate time' have been left out.

2164. On 19 November 2010, the European Commission presented a Report to the European Parliament and the Council on the application of the Regulation on the Statute for a European Company. Roughly 650 companies have been set up as SEs within the EU. The Statute has helped these companies to do business more easily in Europe, but there are issues that remain unaddressed.

Since the introduction of the European Company Statute in October 2004, the number of SEs has increased steadily year by year (at almost exponential growth rates). As of 1 April 2013 the ETUI's European Company Database (ECDB) provides information on a total of 1,766 SEs. However, this rather impressive total should not blind observers to the fact that many SEs are partly SEs without or with very few employees ('empty/micro SEs') and/or partly even without a specific business purpose.

(2) Geographical Distribution of European Companies

2165. SEs can currently be found in 25 of the 30 countries of the European Economic Area (EEA). An important observation when looking at the SE and its impact is the very unbalanced distribution of SEs between the different countries. The Czech Republic (68 per cent) and Germany (14 per cent) host by far the highest share of the overall number of SEs. Besides these two countries, significant SE home countries are the United Kingdom, Slovakia, the Netherlands, Luxemburg, France, Austria, Cyprus and Ireland. The TOP-10 SE countries together are home to approximately 95 per cent of all SEs.

By 1 April 2013, only 244 SEs (14 per cent) had been identified by the ECDB as 'normal SEs' in the sense that they are known to have both business activities and more than 5 employees. Germany is home to almost half of the identified normal SEs (121), followed by the Czech Republic (48) and the Netherlands (13). But especially in the Czech Republic, the number of normal SEs is likely now to be significantly higher as a result of the evolution of originally employee-free SEs. Most Czech SEs are set up as employee-free shelf companies by specialised providers. Later on, the shelf SEs are sold to customers that wish to establish businesses quickly. As often little is known about the further development of the workforce after sale they have to be classified in the database as so-called 'UFO SEs'[897].

§3. INFORMATION AND CONSULTATION: THE DIRECTIVE ON EUROPEAN WORKS COUNCILS OR PROCEDURES

I. Introduction

2166. The Directive 2009/28/EC of 6 May 2009 amends Council Directive 94/45/EC of 22 September 1994 on the establishment of a European Works Council (EWC) or a procedure in Community-scale undertakings and Community-scale groups of undertakings for the purposes of informing and consulting employees. This Directive was extended to the United Kingdom by Council Directive 97/74/EC of 15 December 1997 and adapted by Council Directive 2006/109/EC of 20 November 2006 because of the accession of Bulgaria and Romania.

Article 15 of Directive 94/45/EC provided that the Commission, in consultation with the Member States and with management and labour at the European level, was to review its operation and, in particular, examine whether the workforce-size thresholds are appropriate, with a view to proposing suitable amendments to the Council where necessary not later than 22 September 1999. In its Report (2000)

---

897. http://www.worker-participation.eu/European-Company-SE/Facts-Figures (7 July 2013).

from the Commission to the European Parliament and the Council on the application of Directive 94/45/EC, the Commission stated that it would take a decision on a possible review of the Directive based on the required further assessments and the evolution of the other legislative proposals on the involvement of employees.

Fifteen years from the adoption of Directive 94/45/EC, approximately 820 EWCs were active, representing 14.5 million employees with a view to providing them with information and consultation at the transnational level.

2167. However, there were some problems with the practical application of Directive 94/45/EC. The right to transnational information and consultation lacked effectiveness because the EWCs had been set up in only 36 per cent of undertakings that fell within the scope of the Directive. There were legal uncertainties, particularly with regard to the relationship between the national and transnational levels of consultation and in cases of mergers and acquisitions. Lastly, the consistency and linkage of the various Directives on the information and consultation of employees were insufficient.

2168. The objective of the 2009 Directive is, thus, to ensure that employees' transnational information and consultation rights are effective, to increase the proportion of EWCs established, legal certainty, and to ensure that the Directives on information and consultation of employees are better linked.

2169. The most important changes concern:

(1) a definition of information;
(2) change of the definition of consultation;
    (i) the notion transnational;
    (ii) links between various levels of employee information and consultation.
(3) passing on information to local representatives of employees:
    (i) training to EWC members;
    (ii) composition of the special negotiating body (SNB);
    (iii) facilities to the SNB: pre-and post-meetings, the presence of experts – including trade union members – in the negotiation meetings;
    (iv) informing the European social partners of upcoming negotiations;
    (v) rights for the employee representatives in the EWC to collectively represent the employees;
    (vi) Timing to adapt existing Articles 6 and 13 (pre-existing) agreements.

2170. In this study, we examine in the first chapter, the historical development and the genesis of the new 2009 Directive. In the following chapters, we mainly pay attention to the following aspects of the Directive:

– objective and scope;
– definitions and notions;
– establishment of an EWC or a procedure;
– prejudicial and confidential information – ideological guidance;
– role and protection of employees;

– subsidiary requirements;
– agreements in force.

2171. A first remark concerns the legislative quality of the preparatory documents, namely, the documents emanating from the European Commission as well as the Reports from the EP Committee on Employment and Social Affairs and from the EP itself. One would expect that those documents would contain detailed information on the legal meaning of the various notions and changes introduced. This is, however, not the case. For example, the members of the EWC 'have the means required to apply the rights arising from the Directive, to represent collectively the interests of all the employees of the group' (Article 10(1)).

Great! However, what rights are we talking about? One finds no guiding of any significance in the preparative documents or in the recitals. It is, thus, up to those who have to apply the Directive, either in practice or in court, to tell what this means. In the meantime, as commentators we do our best to analyse their meaning with common legal sense. Other examples could be given, such as this one: Article 6(1)(e) provides that 'Where necessary, a select committee will be set up.' What does the European legislator mean by 'Where necessary?' Again, no help for a meaningful explanation is found in the preparatory documents. For us, there is only one way. Go ahead and row with the oars at our disposal.

2172. No wonder the European Court of Justice has a very broad playing field when interpreting the meaning of the directives.

Second, one of the objectives of the new directive is to increase the number of EWCs. One wonders how this will come about. One of the main reasons that there are practically no EWCs in companies with less than 10,000 employees is the fact that the trade unions lack manpower to effectively assist workers in the setting up and running of EWCs. Will the fact that trade unions can act as experts and will be paid for doing so allow for more logistical support? This is a possibility.

2173. Lastly, a real breakthrough leading to 2009 came when the social partners finally could agree on common proposals in order to amend the Directive. This opened the door, also for the Parliament and the Council, to agree and enact the new Directive. It underlines again the importance of the social dialogue if the social partners succeed in finding common ways.

II. General Remarks

A. *Involvement of Employees*

2174. Involvement of employees remains an ongoing and vigorous concern of the European Union (EU).

> Involvement of employees' means, according to Council Directive 2001/86/EC of 8 October 2001, supplementing the Statute for a European company with

regard to the involvement of employees 'any mechanism, including information, consultation and participation, through which employees' representatives may exercise an influence on decisions to be taken within the company' (Article 2(h)).[898]

1. During the 1970s

2175. It started in the 1970s. During the 1970s, called by some the golden years for European labour law, three directives that were intended to protect workers against the functioning of the common market were adopted. I remember from the discussions we had in the group of experts on labour law from the different Member States that the reasoning underlying those directives was as follows. There is a larger market with an increase in scale to which the undertakings will have to adapt themselves; this means restructuring, mergers, takeovers, collective dismissals and bankruptcies.

2176. It was indeed said that the worker should not have to pay the price for the establishment of a common, bigger market; rather the worker should be protected against the social consequences of this restructuring. Based on this reasoning, three directives were proposed and, due to the then political composition of the Council, were adopted. These directives relate, respectively, to collective redundancies (1975), the transfer of undertakings or parts thereof (1977) and the insolvency of the employer (1980). It will be noticed, when analysing these directives, that the managerial prerogative concerning economic decisions remains intact. There were at times proposals regarding collective redundancies to prohibit dismissals in conformity with the then prevalent French legislation, but these proposals were not retained. In short, the directives only address the social consequences of restructuring.

2. During the 1980s

2177. Here we have to pay special attention to the so-called Vredeling proposal,[899] named after the then social Commissioner H. Vredeling, which the Commission adopted on 24 October 1980 concerning the information and consultation of employees employed in undertakings with a complex structure,

---

898. O.J. L 294, 10 November 2001.
899. One should also mention the following proposals, which provide for a certain role to be played by workers (participation, or if not possible, at least information and consultation):
  – proposal for a Council Directive supplementing the Statute for a European association with regard to the involvement of employees, O.J. C 99, 21 April 1992;
  – proposal for a Council Directive supplementing the Statute for a European cooperative society with regard to the involvement of employees, O.J. C 99, 21 April 1992;
  – proposal for a Council Directive supplementing the Statute for a European mutual society with regard to the involvement of employees, O.J. C 99, 21 April 1992.

Part II, Ch. 2, Workers' Participation

especially multinational enterprises.[900] The target of the proposal was both the national enterprise and the group as a whole, so that local management would be in a position to give the employees of the subsidiary a clear picture of the activities of the undertaking as a whole when this undertaking operates in various countries.

Second, the proposal intended to provide for the local workers' representatives to have access to top management when information at a local level would be insufficient. Finally, its purpose was that local management would be able to provide the workers' representatives with adequate information at a local level and with consultation opportunities regarding important decisions affecting local conditions that would be taken at distant headquarters.

2178. According to the proposal, the management of the parent company would forward to the local management, at least every six months, information concerning the group as a whole and relating in particular to:

(a) structure and manning;
(b) the economic and financial situation;
(c) the situation and probable development of business and production and sales;
(d) the employment situation and probable trends;
(e) production and investment programmes;
(f) rationalisation plans;
(g) manufacturing and working methods, in particular the introduction of new work methods;
(h) all procedures and plans able to have a substantial effect on employees' interests.

2179. The management of the subsidiary would forward this information to the workers' representatives. If the information was not available, then the representatives were allowed to request that information from top management (the famous bypass of local management by the employees).

Where the management of a dominant undertaking proposes to take a decision concerning the whole or a major part of the dominant undertaking or one of its subsidiaries that was liable to have substantial effects on the interests of its employees, it was required to forward precise information to the management of each of its subsidiaries within the Community. This information had to be forwarded not later than 40 days before the adoption of the decision, giving details of:

– the grounds for the proposed decision;
– the legal, economic and social consequences of such a decision for the employees concerned;
– the measures planned with respect to the employees.

---

900. See further for a more detailed study R. Blanpain *et al.*, *The Vredeling Proposal, Information and Consultation of Employees in Multinational Enterprises* (Kluwer, 1983), 219.

2180. This information had to be given in the case of decisions relating to:

(a) the closure or transfer of an establishment or a major part thereof;
(b) restrictions, extensions or substantial modifications to the activities of the undertaking;
(c) major modifications with regard to organisation;
(d) the introduction of long-term cooperation with other undertakings or the cessation of such cooperation.

The management of the subsidiary was required to communicate this information immediately to the workers' representatives and to ask for their opinion within a period of not less than 30 days. In the case of decisions likely to have a direct effect on the employees' terms of employment and conditions, the management of the subsidiary was required to hold consultations with the workers' representatives with a view to reaching agreement on the measures planned in respect of the employees. Where the information was not communicated or consultations did not take place as required, another access to top management was possible (another bypass of local management).

2181. Few proposals have aroused such heated debate as the Vredeling proposal. Both camps entrenched themselves. Everybody proclaimed that employees were entitled to information and consultation. The way in which this had to be organised and the dimension involved were other matters. A consensus between the social partners seemed impossible; moreover, the governments were deeply divided. An amended proposal for a directive on procedures for informing and consulting employees of 13 July 1983 was equally unsuccessful and the Vredeling proposal was buried. The problem was postponed and was to be discussed in 1989, but nothing happened and Vredeling belongs to history. As indicated previously, the Commission would prepare an 'instrument concerning the information and consultation of employees' within the framework of the social action programme of 1990.

2182. This took the form of a proposal for a Directive on the establishment of a European Works Council (EWC) in Community-scale undertakings or groups of undertakings for the purpose of informing and consulting employees and of a Directive on information and consultation.

3. In the 1990s

a. 1994: Information and Consultation in Community-scale Undertakings

2183. After so many years, the adoption of the European Directive of 22 September 1994 on the establishment of an EWC or a procedure in Community-scale undertakings and Community-scale groups of undertakings for the purposes of informing and consulting employees was a fact.[901]

Community-scale undertakings are legally obliged to have an EWC or an information and consultation procedure. The directive applies to enterprises that occupy at least 1,000 employees and have at least two subsidiaries in two Member States of the EU (excluding the UK) and/or of the EEA–EFTA countries each with at least 150 employees. It was estimated that some 1,800 companies would have to comply. From 15 December 1999, the directive also applied to the UK.[902] Council Directive 2006/109/EC of 20 November 2006 adapted Directive 94/45/EC on the establishment of an EWC or a procedure by reason of the accession of Bulgaria and Romania.[903] Croatia joined the EU on 1st July 2013.

b. 1997: the Treaty of Amsterdam

2184. The European Top of 16–17 June 1997 led to the Treaty of Amsterdam, which includes a new specific chapter on Social Policy. There is an extension of social competence, which will be confirmed in the Treaty of Lisbon. Article 153(1)(e) TFEU allows with qualified majority to support and complement the activities of the Member States in the following fields: the information and consultation of workers.

4. The Years 2000–2013

a. Charter of Fundamental Rights of the European Union (2007)[904]

2185. Under the Charter, information and consultation are proclaimed to be fundamental rights and well as follows:

CHAPTER IV. SOLIDARITY

Article 27

Workers' right to information and consultation within the undertaking 'Workers or their representatives must, at the appropriate levels, be guaranteed information and consultation *in good time* in the cases and under the conditions provided for by Community law and national laws and practices'.

---

901. (94/95 EC) O.J. L 254/65, 30 September 1994.
902. Council Directive 97/74 of 15 December 1997 extending to the UK Directive 94/45 (O.J. L 10/22, 16 January 1998).
903. O.J., 20 December 2006.
904. (2010/C 83/02) O.J. 83/389, 30 March 2010.

b. The Six Sisters

2186. In the meantime, six important directives were adopted, underlining the importance of the 'involvement of employees' in the EU:

(1) Council Directive 2001/86/EC of 8 October 2001 supplementing the Statute for a European company with regard to the involvement of employees;[905]
(2) Directive 2002/14/EC of the European Parliament and of the Council of 11 March 2002 establishing a general framework for informing and consulting employees in the European Community;[906]
(3) Council Directive 2003/72/EC of 22 July 2003 supplementing the Statute for a European Cooperative Society with regard to the involvement of employees;[907]
(4) Directive 2004/25/EC of the European Parliament and of the Council of 21 April 2004 on takeover bids (Text with European Economic Area (EEA) relevance);[908]
(5) Directive 2009/38/EC of the European Parliament and of the Council of 6 May 2009 on the establishment of a European Works Council or a procedure in Community-scale undertakings and Community-scale groups of undertakings for the purposes of informing and consulting employees (Recast) (Text with EEA relevance).[909]
(6) Directive 2011/35/EU of the European Parliament and of the Council of 5 April 2011 concerning mergers of public limited liability companies.[910]

B. *The Directive of 6 May 2009*

1. Review of the 1994 Directive

2187. Article 15 of Directive 94/45/EC provided that, not later than 22 September 1999, the Commission, in consultation with the Member States and with management and labour at the European level, was to review its operation and, in particular examine whether the workforce-size thresholds were appropriate with a view to proposing suitable amendments to the Council where necessary.

2. The 2000 Report of the Commission

2188. In its 2000 Report, the Commission to the European Parliament and the Council on the application of Directive 94/45/EC,[911] the Commission stated that it would take a decision on a possible review of the Directive based on the required

---

905. O.J. L 294, 10 November 2001.
906. O.J. L 80, 23 March 2002.
907. O.J. L 207, 18 August 2003.
908. O.J. L 142, 30 April 2004.
909. O.J. L 122, 16 May 2009.
910. O.J., L 110/1, 29 April 2011.
911. COM (2000) 188; Marhk Hall, 'Commission reports on implementation of European Works Councils Directive', eiro, eurfoundation/2000/05.

Part II, Ch. 2, Workers' Participation

further assessments and the evolution of the other legislative proposals on the involvement of employees.[912] These proposals were adopted in 2001, 2002 and 2003.

3. The European Parliament and the Economic and Social Committee (2001–2007)

2189. On 18 February 2000, the European Parliament called on the European Commission to evaluate the application of the collective redundancies Directive and to speed up its current review of the EWC Directive.

This call was contained in a parliamentary resolution criticizing US-based tyre manufacturer Goodyear-Dunlop for not following redundancy and information and consultation procedures when closing its plant in Latina, Italy, and electricity suppliers ABB and Alstom for not following European-level information and consultation procedures when restructuring.

The resolution called on the Commission to:

– undertake an evaluation of the application of the collective redundancies Directive and propose financial sanctions in the case of infringement;
– hasten its current review of the 1994 EWC Directive (94/45/EC) in order to improve measures on worker information and consultation; and
– authorize mergers or similar operations only if the companies involved respect

European social legislation, mainly on worker information and consultation rights.[913]

2190. The Parliament adopted on 4 September 2001 a Resolution[914] on the Commission's 2000 report, calling on the Commission to submit a proposal for the revision of Directive 94/45/EC at an early date and to include in that proposal 'precise definitions of information and consultation, an increased number of ordinary meetings, enhanced consultation in cases of restructuring, the role of trade unions, training and facilities, an adaptation clause in the event of changes, conditions for maintaining existing agreements, reduction of the negotiation period, lowering of the threshold to 500 workers, and sanctions in cases of non-compliance'.[915]

---

912. See Chs 1, §1, IV.
913. Neil Bentley, 'Parliament seeks review of Directives on collective redundancies and EWCs', <www.eurofound.europa.eu/eiro/2000/03/inbrief/eu0003233n.htm>.
914. A5-0282/2001 (Report W. Menrad).
915. Commission Staff Working Document accompanying the proposal for a Directive of the European Parliament and the Council on the Establishment of a European Works Council or a procedure in Community-scale undertakings and Community-scale groups of undertakings for the purposes of informing and consulting employees (recasting), Brussels, 2 Jul. 2008, SEC (2008) 2166). *Impact Assessment*, COM (2008) 419 final}, SEC (2008) 2167). See Annex.

2191. In 2002, the Commission requested the European Economic and Social Committee (EESC) to draw up an exploratory opinion on the practical application of the EWC Directive (94/45/EC) and on any aspects of the Directive that might need to be revised. In 2003, the EESC adopted an exploratory opinion on the EWC Directive,[916] presenting a joint assessment of the added value of EWCs and the challenges facing their operation as well as identifying a number of open questions for the future.

In its conclusions, the opinion states that 'a number of fundamental questions remain open'. Specifically, these concern:

- 'the concepts of "useful effect"and "timeliness"with regard to informing and consulting employees';
- the scope of the Directive in terms of the nature of the enterprises covered by the concept of 'undertaking' and the position of joint ventures, public enterprises etc;
- 'the question of representation and proportionality of representation on EWCs, which is not covered by transnational rules';
- the impact of EWCs on social dialogue in the company at national level;
- the possibility of EWC representatives visiting establishments to communicate with the workers they represent; and
- enhancing the role of EWCs and workers' representatives in the EU's merger control procedures.[917]

In 2006, the EESC delivered an own-initiative opinion[918] on EWCs, recommending a 'rapid updating' with respect to three points of the Directive: the definitions of information and consultation, the role of trade unions and the maximum number of members in the bodies.

2192. In 2006 and 2007, two resolutions referring to EWCs were adopted by the Parliament: (i) the Resolution on *Restructuring and employment*[919] reiterated its request for the Commission to submit a proposal to amend Directive 94/45/EC and called on the Commission to launch a specific second-stage consultation of the social partners on the revision of the Directive; (ii) the Resolution on Strengthening European legislation in the field of information and consultation of workers[920] called on the Commission to update this legislation in order to ensure a coherent and efficient framework of law, guarantee legal certainty, improve the linking of social dialogue at national and European levels, and present a timetable for the 'long-awaited revision of the Directive on European works councils'.

---

916. (CESE 1164/2003 Report J. Piette). See Annex.
917. Mark Hall, 'European Economic and Social Committee Adopts Opinion Non-revision of EWCs Directive', www.eurofound.europa.eu/eiro/2003/10/feature/eu0310204f.htm.
918. (CESE 1170/2006 Report E. Iozia).
919. (PA_TA (2006)0088 Report J.L. Cottigny).
920. (PA_TA (2007)0185 joint motion).

Part II, Ch. 2, Workers' Participation

4. The European Social Partners

a. The European Trade Union Confederation (ETUC) (1999)

2193. In 1999, the ETUC adopted a resolution on the review of the EWC Directive.[921] The ETUC demanded for the strengthening of the right to be informed and consulted: comprehensive, provided in good time and on an ongoing basis. The directive should also provide a right for EWCs to give an opinion within a reasonable time delay and to be consulted on this opinion by central management or the relevant management level.

The ETUC also asked to indicate clearly that management decisions that are reached in breach of the directive's information and consultation procedures would be null and void and suggests that any companies that contravene against the directive should be excluded from any European financial support.

One of the ETUC's substantive demands was for a lowering of the workforce-size threshold for inclusion within the scope of the directive from Community-scale companies with 1,000 employees in the EEA to those with 500 employees. With regard to meetings, the ETUC would like to give EWC members the right to hold preparatory and follow-up meetings, in addition to the right to training, time off and continuation of payment; the right to meet each other at least annually; and the right to communicate with each other. In addition, the directive should clarify the existing right for EWCs to be assisted by experts of their choice.

2194. Other ETUC demands included:

– the recognition of the role played by its affiliated European industry federations;
– making negotiations simpler and more efficient by, amongst other changes, reducing the special negotiating body (SNB) negotiating period from three years to one and allowing the SNB to hold preparatory and follow-up meetings after each negotiating round;
– clarification of the procedure for renegotiating EWC agreements in the event of mergers and takeovers; and
– allowing worker representatives from countries outside the EEA the opportunity to participate in both the SNB and the EWC.

b. Union of Industrial and Employers' Confederations of Europe (UNICE)

2195. On 19 April 2004, the European Commission launched a first-stage consultation of the European social partners on the review of the EWC Directive. The ETUC were in favour of a rapid revision, especially with regard to the definition and fundamental concepts of information.

---

921. Andrea Broughton, 'ETUC Adopts Resolution on Review of EWCs Directive', www.eurofound.europa.eu/eiro/2000/01/inbrief/eu0001221n.htm.

'UNICE', on the contrary, was 'strongly opposed to a revision of the EWC Directive. European employers are convinced that the best way to develop worker information and consultation in Community-scale undertakings is through dialogue at the level of the companies concerned. However, convinced of the value of exchanging and learning from experience at the EU level, UNICE wishes to discuss this issue in the European social dialogue'.[922]

UNICE launched an invitation to study the experience with EWCs in the framework of the Social Dialogue, which happened.

c. 'Lessons Learned'

2196. In 2004, the European social partners indeed examined company cases in order to assess the functioning of EWCs. In 2005, they produced a joint document on 'Lessons Learned on European Works Councils', which highlights the usefulness of EWCs, the benefits of clear procedures, training for members and assistance from experts, and the positive role that trade unions can play.

2197. In September and October 2004, the social partners held two seminars to discuss case studies of how EWCs are operating, with a view to identifying best practice. The social partners subsequently drew up a detailed report describing the experience of each of the EWCs concerned. Following is a summary of nine cases.

The EWC Case Studies

Company	Sector	Comments
Fortis Group	Banking and insurance	'The EWC played a useful role [in helping to integrate] the different entities in the Fortis group, in which 75% of the total workforce is based in Belgium and the Netherlands and in which diverse professional and industrial relations cultures coexist.'
Lafarge	Construction materials	'Lafarge is present in 75 countries, and employs 75,000 employees on more than 2,100 sites. In a context of very rapid internationalisation of the group's activities, the EWC proved useful to communicate on the group's strategy and to develop a group culture.'

---

922. June 2004, First-Stage Consultation of the European Social Partners on the Review of the European Works Councils Directive UNICE Answer.

The EWC Case Studies

Company	Sector	Comments
EDF	Energy	'EDF was originally a public company in a monopoly situation in France, which has rapidly grown in [recent] years and now functions as an international group. The EWC was established fairly recently and evolved positively, allowing for good communication between management and workers without a marked French hegemony, despite the weight of French operations in the group.'
Ericsson	Telecommunications	'Faced with a telecoms market which ran into severe problems, Ericsson embarked on a restructuring and cost-cutting programme to ensure its long-term future in 2001. The EWC was instrumental in this process.'
Carrefour	Retail/wholesale	'The good climate of cooperation in the European Committee on Information and Consultation helped the group [in] realising strategic business objectives and reinforcing its competitiveness.'
Unilever	Food, home care and personal care	'The establishment of an EWC has been a gradual process in Unilever. Through the EWC, management and workers have developed information and dialogue at European level, based on mutual trust.'
Henkel	Home care, personal care and adhesives, sealants and surface treatments	'The relationship and cooperation between the European Employee Council and Henkel's management is seen as a dynamic process involving learning and improving on a permanent basis. The European Employee Council agreement provides a broad basis as a framework to find practical solutions to deal with mutual problems.'

The EWC Case Studies

Company	Sector	Comments
GKN	Engineering	'GKN has very diversified portfolio of products and there is a big contrast between production and services divisions. The experience of their European Forum is positive but illustrates the complexity of running an EWC and ensuring a real sense of ownership of the EWC by the whole workforce.'
EDS	IT applications and business process services	'EDS has integrated the EWC at the heart of its business strategy and is developing a highly interactive way of operating in its EWC.'

2198. In their report 'Lessons Learned' the following main points were retained:

– EWCs 'can help management and workers to build a corporate culture and adapt to change in fast-evolving transnational companies';
– the establishment of 'a climate of mutual trust' between management and workers' representatives in the EWC is important for its effective functioning;
– investing in language as well as technical training helps to 'optimise' the functioning of the EWC;
– finding ways of reconciling different national industrial relations practices and addressing an increasingly diverse workforce is a 'constant challenge';
– all the case studies demonstrated that ensuring a real sense of ownership of the EWC by the whole workforce was a 'considerable challenge';
– some companies seeking to enlarge their EWC have encountered difficulties in identifying worker representatives in the new Member States;
– managing multiple layers of information and consultation can sometimes be very complex; and
– all the case studies underlined that the effective functioning of EWCs is a 'learning and evolving process' requiring 'fine tuning' over the years.[923]

d. No Negotiations

2199. In 2005, through its Communication *Restructuring and employment*,[924] the Commission consulted the European social partners simultaneously on the

---

923. Mark Hall, 'EU Social Partners Issue Joint Statement on EWCs', 31 May 2005, www.eurofound.europa.eu/ eiro/2005/05/feature/eu0505204f.htm.
924. COM (2005) 120.

restructuring of undertakings and on the 'best practice' aspect of EWCs, encouraging them to negotiate with a view to reaching agreement on the promotion of best practices. The European social partners reiterated their 2004 positions on the revision of the Directive, and in 2006 decided to include the promotion and evaluation of their joint 'Lessons Learned' in their 2006–2008 work programme.

On 20 February 2008, the Commission adopted the document,[925] launching the second-stage consultation of the European social on the content of a possible Community initiative to revise the EWC Directive and inviting them to negotiate.

2200. At the end of the consultation period, the ETUC and the European employer organisations, BUSINESSEUROPE, CEEP and UEAPME, declared their willingness to negotiate on the review of the EWC Directive. However, the ETUC concluded after a few days that it was 'not ready for negotiations within the framework of the social dialogue' considering 'the time constraints and the depth of differences with the employers' and counted on the Commission to present a revised Directive. The employers' organisations regretted this decision and asked the Commission not to start the legislative process by itself. On 30 April 2008, the Commission made a last call to the social partners, inviting them to make their best efforts to negotiate on EWCs. A few days later, it was confirmed that there would be no such negotiation.[926]

5. The Commission Takes the Legal Initiative (2008)

2201. Because the social partners were not in a position to negotiate a revision of the EWC Directive, it became the task of the European Commission to take an initiative.

a. Status Questions

(1) Insufficient Number of EWCs: Overview

2202. EWCs have been set up in only 36 per cent of undertakings that fall within the scope of the Directive. According to the available data, 2,257 companies employing 24 million workers fell within the scope of the directive in 2007. These companies are mostly headquartered in Germany (20 per cent), the USA (16 per cent), the UK (12 per cent) and France (10 per cent) and are active notably in the metal, services and chemicals sectors. In 2007, EWCs were operating in 816 companies with some 14.5 million employees. Nearly half of the EWCs were established by a pre-existing agreement (Article 13 of the directive); that is, before

---

925. COM (2008) 660.
926. Commission Staff Working Document accompanying the proposal for a Directive of the European Parliament and the Council on the Establishment of a European Works Council or a procedure in Community-scale undertakings and Community-scale groups of undertakings for the purposes of informing and consulting employees (recasting), Brussels, 2 July 2008, SEC (2008) 2166). *Impact Assessment*, COM (2008) 419 final, SEC (2008) 2167. See Annex.

the directive entered into force in 1996. Since then, the number of companies with an EWC, mostly large multinationals, has grown slowly over the years.

2203. The information and consultation process in EWCs mainly covers the economic and social topics set out in the directive and is of particular importance in cases of restructuring. However, some councils discuss topics related, for example, to health and safety, the environment, and equal opportunities.

Main characteristics of European Works Councils (EPEC 2008)[927]

Companies with EWC	Worldwide employees per company: up to 207,000, average 49,000 Employees in EEA countries per company: 1,039 to 182,200, average 29,000 Turnover: EUR 54 million to EUR 202 billion, average EUR 20 billion
	Transnational restructuring event in the last three years: 74%
Governing agreement	Under Directive ('Article 6'): 52%, pre-existing ('Article 13'): 48% Not modified since first signed: 53%, modified: 47%
Employee members	Number: from five to forty-seven, average of twenty-three Coming from two to twenty-four countries, average of nine Coming from host country: from 7% to 87%, average of 33%
	Trend over the last three years: increase 62%, no change 30%, decrease 8%
Company representatives	Involved in meetings: from two to thirteen, average of five
	Top management, general and HR managers
	Number/year: one 60%, two 33%, three 1%, four 6%
	Length: average of two days
Ordinary meetings	Preparatory meeting between employee delegates: 96%; increasing de-briefings
	Role: discussing economic and financial situation, strategic orientations, employment trends
Extraordinary meetings	Provision in the agreement: 88%
	Face-to-face meeting held in the last three years: 59%
	With all members: 78%; with select committee or part of the members: 22%

---

927. *Ibid.*

	Role: addressing specific restructuring decisions
Total plenary meetings	Average number: 2.0/year
	Present, with face-to-face meeting: 88% Employee members: from two to fifteen, average of five Managers in meetings: from zero to four, average of two Face-to-face meetings: from zero to twelve, average of three per year
Select committee	Length of meeting: one day
	Role: planning, coordination, regular information exchange, discussion of restructuring decisions
	Present: 29%
	Members: from three to twenty, average nine, mixed employee-management
Working groups	Face-to-face meetings: usually from one to four per year
	Role: working out specific issues (e.g. health and safety) or specific restructuring events

2204. Fourteen years after the adoption of the Directive, 57 per cent of managers feel that the benefits of having an EWC in their company outweigh the costs in terms of time and resources spent, because it allows them to communicate information regarding company strategies and the rationale for certain decisions to employees, particularly in times of change. On the other side, all employee representatives consider the existence of EWCs to be very beneficial. However, expectations regarding the role of EWCs have grown over the years, with the increasing internationalisation of corporate activities, and are far from being fulfilled, particularly as regards the role of EWCs in anticipating and managing change. This has led various stakeholders and EU institutions to ask the Commission to review the legal framework in which EWCs operate.[928]

(2) Challenges and Objectives

2205. The following shortcomings and challenges were noted:

(1) Lack of effectiveness:
 (i) Restructuring EWCs are not sufficiently informed and consulted in the case of restructuring.
 (ii) Legal uncertainties There are legal uncertainties in relationship between the national and transnational levels of consultation and in cases of mergers and acquisitions.
 (iii) Consistency

---

928. *Ibid.*

(iv) The consistency and linkage of the various Directives on the information and consultation of employees are insufficient.
(2) Consequently, the following objectives are pursued.
(3) Objectives:
  (i) Anticipating and managing change Building up a genuine transnational dialogue between management and labour. Ensure that the employees' transnational information and consultation rights are effective.
  (ii) Increasing the number of EWCs Increase the proportion of EWCs established.
  (iii) Legal certainty Increase legal certainty.
  (iv) Linkage Ensure that the Directives on information and consultation of employees are better linked.[929]

b. The Proposal for a Recast[930] Directive of 2 July 2008 by the European Commission[931]

2206. The proposal of the Commission made the following substantive changes to Articles 1, 2, 4, 5, 6, 10, 11, 12, 13 and 14 of Directive 94/45/EC and to its annex. Articles 3 and 9 of Directive 94/45/EC are slightly adapted, whereas Articles 7 and 8 are unchanged.

2207. General principles and concepts of information and consultation. Article 1 of Directive 94/45/EC stipulates that the arrangements for informing and consulting employees must follow the general principle of effectiveness. Article 2 adds a definition of information and brings the definition of consultation into line with that of more recent Directives, including the concepts of time, fashion and content appropriate to the information and consultation.

---

929. This proposal takes account of the fact that there are other directives in the area of the information and consultation of employees. Directive 2002/14/EC of the European Parliament and of the Council of 11 March 2002 establishing a general framework for informing and consulting employees in the European Community lays down the general principles to be applied at the national level. Directive 98/59/EC and Directive 2001/23/EC are applicable where redundancies or transfers are specifically envisaged. Directives 2001/86/EC and 2003/72/EC govern the involvement of employees in European Companies (SE) and the European Cooperative Societies (SCE).
930. This means that the proposal does not comprise any substantive amendments other than those identified as such. The Working Party was also able to establish, with regard to the codification of the unchanged provisions of the previous act with the substantive amendments, that the proposal was indeed a straightforward codification without substantive changes to the acts to which it related (European Parliament, Draft Report of 23 Sep. 2008 on the proposal for a directive of the European Parliament and of the Council on the establishment of a European Works Council or a procedure in Community-scale undertakings and Community-scale groups of undertakings for the purposes of informing and consulting employees (recast), (COM (2008) 0419 – C6-0258/2008 – 2008/0141 (COD)), Committee on Employment and Social Affairs, Rapporteur: Philip Bushill-Matthews). See Annex.
931. Proposal of 2 Jul. 2008 for a European Parliament and council Directive on the establishment of a European Works Council or a procedure in Community-scale undertakings and Communityscale groups of undertakings for the purposes of informing and consulting employees (recast), COM (2008) 419 final. See Annex.

Part II, Ch. 2, Workers' Participation

2208. Transnational competence of the EWC. Article 1 establishes the principle of the relevant level according to the subject under discussion. To achieve this, the competence of the EWC is limited to transnational issues, and the determination of whether an issue is transnational is transferred from the current subsidiary requirements to Article 1, so that it can be applied to the EWCs established by agreement. It is specified as relating in particular to the potential effects of an issue in at least two Member States.

2209. Links between the levels of information and consultation of employees. Article 12 introduces the principle of a link between the national and transnational levels of information and consultation of the employees with due regard for the competences and areas of action of the representative bodies. The arrangements for this link are defined by the agreement concluded pursuant to Article 6, which now covers this matter. Where there are no such arrangements and where decisions likely to lead to substantial changes in work organisation or contractual relations are envisaged, the process would have to start in parallel at the national and European levels. Because certain national legislation may have to be adapted to ensure that the EWC can, where applicable, receive information earlier or at the same time as the national bodies, a clause has been added to stipulate that there must be no reduction in the general level of protection of employees. The titles of the directives relating to collective redundancies and to transfers of undertakings have been updated, and a reference to the framework Directive 2002/14/EC has been incorporated.

2210. Role and capacity of employees' representatives. The obligation on the employees' representatives to report to the employees whom they represent has been moved from the subsidiary requirements of the directive to Article 10, which thus deals with the role of the employees' representatives and their protection. The competence of the members representing the employees on the EWC to represent the employees of the undertaking or group of undertakings is established. The possibility for employees' representatives to benefit from training without loss of salary is clarified.

2211. Opening and process of negotiations. Article 5 clarifies the responsibility of the local managements to provide the information allowing negotiations to be opened with a view to setting up new EWCs. In order to resolve legal uncertainty and simplify the composition of the SNB, it is modified to one representative per 10 per cent portion of the employees in a Member State in which at least fifty employees are employed. The right of employees' representatives to meet without the employer being present is clarified.

2212. Role of trade union and employers' organisations. Article 5 introduces the obligation to inform the trade union and employers' organisations of the start of negotiations on setting up an EWC and explicitly mentions the trade union organisations among the experts on whom employees' representatives may call for assistance in the negotiations.

2213. Content of the subsidiary requirements (which apply in the absence of an agreement). The annex draws a distinction between fields where information is required and those where consultation is required, and it introduces the possibility of obtaining a response, and the reasons for that response, to any opinions expressed. With a view to anticipating such eventualities, the exceptional circumstances requiring information and opening the possibility of a select committee meeting are extended to include circumstances in which decisions that are likely to affect the employees' interests to a considerable extent are envisaged. In order to enable the select committee to perform this more important function, its maximum number of members is set at five and a provision is added stipulating that the conditions enabling it to exercise its activities on a regular basis must be met.

2214. Adaptation clause and agreements in force. The agreements pursuant to Article 6 must include provisions for amendments and renegotiation. Where the structure of the undertaking or group of undertakings changes significantly, Article 13 provides for the agreements in force to be adapted in accordance with the provisions of the applicable agreement or, by default and where a request is made, in accordance with the negotiation procedure for a new agreement in which the members of the existing EWC(s) are to be associated. These EWCs will continue to operate, possibly with adaptations, until a new agreement is reached. They will then be dissolved and the agreements terminated. Except where this adaptation clause applies, the agreements in force that were concluded in anticipation will still not fall under the provisions of the directive and there will be no general obligation to renegotiate those concluded pursuant to Article 6.

2215. Other provisions. In Article 6, the establishment and the operation of a select committee are, where applicable, part of the content of the agreement. Article 15 provides for a review clause under which the review is due five years after the time limit for transposition. In the annex, the composition of the EWC setup in the absence of an agreement is aligned with the new composition of the SNB.

c. Advice of the European Social Partners

2216. To the surprise of many did the European Social Partners, ETUC and the European employers, BUSINESSEUROPE, CEEP, UEAPME, settle their differences and forwarded a joint advice on 28 August 2008[932] in which they accepted the Commission's proposal as a basis for the revision and proposed the following changes to the proposal.
Proposals on the issues considered in the joint advice to European Parliament and Council of Ministers
1941.

---

932. Stefan Lücking, 'Social Partners give advice on European Works Council "recast" Directive', 21 November 2008, www.eurofound.europa.eu/eiro/2008/10/articles/eu0810019i.htm. See Annex.

Part II, Ch. 2, Workers' Participation

(1) Article 2 (f): 'Information' means transmission of data by the employer to the employees' representatives in order to enable them to acquaint themselves with the subject matter and to examine it; information shall be given at such time, in such fashion and with such content as are appropriate to enable employees' representatives *to undertake an in-depth assessment of the possible impact and where appropriate prepare consultations with the competent organ of the Communityscale undertaking or Community-scale group of undertakings*;

(2) Article 2 (g): 'Consultation' means the establishment of dialogue and exchange of views between employees' representatives and central management or any more appropriate level of management, at such time, in such fashion and with such content *(as)* enables employees' representatives to express an opinion on the basis of the information provided *about the proposed measures to which the consultation is related, without prejudice to the responsibilities of the management*, and within a reasonable time, *which may be taken in to account within* the Community-scale undertaking or Community-scale group of undertakings.

(3) Article 5.4 §3: For the purpose of the negotiations, the special negotiating body may request assistance with its work from experts of its choice *which can include representatives of competent recognised Community-level trade union organisations*. Such experts *and such trade union representatives* may be present at negotiation meetings in an advisory capacity at the request of the special negotiating body.

(4) Article 10.1: Without prejudice to the competence of other bodies or organisations in this respect, the members of the European Works Council shall *have the means required to apply the rights stemming from this Directive, to collectively represent the interests of the employees of the Community-scale undertaking or Community-scale group of undertakings.*

(5) Article 10.4: In so far as this is necessary for the exercise of their representative duties in an international environment, the members of the special negotiating body and of the European Works Council shall *be provided with* training without loss of wages.

(6) Article 12.3: Where no such arrangements have been defined by agreement, the Member States shall ensure that the processes of informing and consulting *are conducted in the European Works Council as well as in the national bodies* in cases where decisions likely to lead to substantial changes in work organisation or contractual relations are envisaged.

(7) Article 13.1: Without prejudice to paragraph 3, the obligations arising from this Directive shall not apply to Community-scale undertakings or Community-scale groups of undertakings in which there was already an agreement on 22 September 1996, *or in which an agreement is signed or an existing agreement is revised during the two years following the adoption of the present text*, or in undertakings in which such agreements exist and which are due to negotiate under paragraph 3, covering the entire workforce providing for the transnational information and consultation of employees. When these agreements expire, the parties to those agreements may decide jointly to renew them. Where this is not the case, the provisions of the Directive shall apply.

(8) Article 13.3: Last paragraph to be deleted.

2217. A second letter followed on 2 October 2008[933] in which the social partners wrote:

> We appreciate the positive reception the joint advice has been given and would like to reiterate and confirm our support to the joint advice. We also support a clarification, as proposed by the Presidency, regarding the changes to article 13 suggested by the social partners. The text proposed by the Presidency however does not include all situations envisaged in the joint advice.
>
> In order to respect the proposal of European social partners, the Presidency compromise wording for a new article 13 bis should therefore be modified as follows:
>
> *Article 13bis §1 i): an agreement or agreements covering the entire workforce providing for the transnational information and consultation of employees have been concluded pursuant to article 13(1) of Directive 94/45/EC or article 3(1) of Directive 97/74/EC[..], or where such agreements are adjusted because of changes in the structure of the undertakings or groups of undertakings;*
>
> *Article 13bis §2: When the agreements referred to in paragraph 1 expire, the parties to those agreements may decide jointly to renew, or revise, them. Where this is not the case, the provisions of the Directive shall apply.*
>
> In addition, we would suggest a further point for clarification to be included in the text. The definition of 'information' which was agreed by European social partners in their joint advice stipulates that the information provided to employees' representatives should enable them to undertake 'an in-depth assessment'. In order to clarify the notion of 'in-depth assessment', which should not slow down decision-making in companies, recital 22 should read as follows:
>
> *(22) The definition of 'information' needs to take into account of the goal of allowing employees' representatives to undertake an in-depth assessment of the possible impact and where appropriate prepare consultations, which implies that the information be provided at such time, in such fashion and with such content as are appropriate without slowing down the decision-making process in companies.*

d. The European Parliament

(1) The Committee on Employment and Social Affairs

2218. The Committee on Employment and Social Affairs adopted on 17 November 2008 the report drafted by Philip Bushill-Matthews and made some amendments to the proposal for a Directive of the European Parliament and of the Council on the establishment of an EWC or a procedure in Community-scale undertakings and Community-scale groups of undertakings for the purposes of informing and consulting employees (recast).

---

933. See Annex.

The main amendments adopted in committee (in first reading of the codecision procedure) can be summarised as follows:

2219. Transnational issue. MEPs consider that matters that concern the entire undertaking or group or at least two Member States, or that exceed the powers of the decision-making bodies in a single Member State in which employees who will be affected are employed, are considered to be transnational.

2220. Definitions. MEPs clarify the terms information and consultation. 'Information' shall mean the transmission of data by the employer to the employees' representatives in order to enable them to acquaint themselves with the subject matter and to examine it. It shall be given at such time, in such fashion and with such content as are appropriate to enable employees' representatives to undertake an in-depth assessment of the possible impact and, where appropriate, prepare consultations with the competent body of the Community-scale undertaking or Community-scale group of undertakings in question. 'Consultation' shall mean the establishment of dialogue and exchange of views between employees' representatives and central management or any more appropriate level of management at such time, in such fashion and with such content as enables employees' representatives to express an opinion on the basis of the information provided about the proposed measures to which the consultation relates without prejudice to the responsibilities of the management.

2221. Special negotiating bodies: Deletion of the fifty-worker threshold for the setting up of an SNB. MEPs consider that the introduction by the Commission of the fifty-worker threshold in setting up SNBs is discriminatory against smaller Member States, which will find it difficult to reach this threshold. The number of fifty employees as a threshold is random, and according to the committee, it does not represent an indicator for the output of the particular undertaking. MEPs have deleted this measure.

2222. Dissolution of previously existing EWCs. MEPs do not consider it necessary to dissolve previously existing EWCs when the new EWC is established. They have deleted the paragraph concerning this issue.

2223. Revision of the Directive. MEPs consider that three years (and not five as suggested by the Commission) after the date of entry into force of this Directive, the Commission shall present a full revision of this Directive to the European Parliament and the Council.

2224. Penalties for non-compliance. A new recital is added, stipulating that Member States should ensure that measures taken in the event of a failure to comply with this Directive be adequate, proportionate, and dissuasive.

2225. Annex. Changes have been made to the annex to enable the EWCs to have a say in the economic and financial future of their company rather than just being passively informed about it.

(2) Plenary Session

2226. The Parliament adopted an agreement at first reading on the recast Directive on EWCs on 18 December 2008. The Committee on Employment and Social Affairs had proposed seventeen amendments to the draft last November. Council and the European Parliament reached an informal agreement on 4 December. The compromise text included proposals on the social partners taken up in the report by Philip Bushill-Matthews.

The directive defines the general principle and norms for information and consultation. The amendments state that information transmitted from employer to employees' representatives must be 'given at such a time, in such a fashion' to enable employees' representatives 'to undertake an in-depth assessment of the possible impact and, where appropriate, prepare consultations with the competent body of the Community-scale undertaking or Community-scale group of undertakings in question'.

The text stresses that members of the EWC must have the means required to apply the rights stemming from this directive and to collectively represent the interests of the employees of the Community-scale undertaking or Community-scale group of undertakings.

Moreover, the obligations arising from this directive do not apply to Community-scale undertakings or Community-scale groups of undertakings in which there was already an agreement, or in which an agreement is signed or an existing agreement is revised during the two years following the adoption of this directive, or in undertakings in which such agreements exist.

2227. The directive also states that matters that concern the entire undertaking or group or at least two Member States, or that exceed the powers of the decision-making bodies in a single Member State in which employees who will be affected are employed, are considered to be transnational. Following the court judgments in the *Vilvoorde*, *British Airways* and *Marks* and *Spencer* cases, MEPs also adopted amendments to clarify where a situation is 'transnational'. They decided that a decision of closure or restructuring taken in one Member State but affects the workers in another must be considered transnational.

They also abolished the threshold of 50 employees for setting up SNBs (as a first step to constituting EWCs) so as not to discriminate against small Member States that would have difficulty reaching this threshold.

For the purpose of the negotiations, the SNB may request assistance with its work from experts of its choice, who may include representatives of the competent recognized Community-level trade union organisations. Such experts and trade union representatives may be present at negotiation meetings in an advisory capacity at the request of the SNB.

Finally, Member States must ensure that measures taken in the event of a failure to comply with this Directive are 'adequate, proportionate and dissuasive'.

Part II, Ch. 2, Workers' Participation 2228–2230

C. *Summing up*

2228. Although EWCs have been successful in many areas, they could not fully play their role in the anticipation and proper management of change and in developing genuine cross-border social dialogue. Indeed, evidence suggested that they were not properly informed and consulted in many transnational restructuring cases and that the take-up of EWCs was lower than hoped for. Therefore, the 1994 legal framework needed to be adapted to recent legislative, economic and social changes whereby cross-border aspects have become more and more important and to ensure that, in practice, employees really do have a voice in important restructuring decisions.

1. Changes

2229. The changes in the legislation are aimed at:

(1) Improving the concepts of information and consultation:
    (i) defining the competences of EWCs more clearly and linking the national and European levels of information and consultation;
    (ii) improving the fallback rules that apply in the absence of agreement by strengthening the coordination of the EWC and improving its consultation in case of restructuring;
    (iii) providing for the training of employee representatives and introducing a duty for them to report back to workers;
    (iv) recognising the fundamental role of the social partners in supporting fruitful social dialogue in companies and providing tailored mechanisms to that aim;
    (v) adapting EWCs in the event of significant change in the structure of companies;
    (vi) simplifying the legislation by replacing three different Directives (94/45/EC 97/74/EC and 2006/109/EC) with a single recast and updated directive.

2. Decision-making

2230. EWCs should contribute to efficient decision-making and help companies to adapt as rapidly as possible to compete in the global economy. This need is fully taken into account by the new legislation. Provisions to ensure that EWCs are informed and consulted in a timely fashion without calling into question the company's capacity to adapt are included in the new directive, and a better interplay between national and European levels of consultation is provided under the new rules.

3. Genesis

2231. The Commission adopted a proposal to recast the directive in July 2008 after examining the implementation of the existing directive, consulting the social partners and carrying out an extensive impact assessment for the new proposal.

At the invitation of the Council Presidency, the European social partners adopted a common opinion in August 2008 accepting the Commission's proposal and suggesting a number of amendments. The Commission, which has always supported negotiations between the social partners, welcomed this initiative, which strengthened consensus on the measures needed.

With the cooperation of the Commission, the Council and the European Parliament adjusted the package comprising the Commission proposal and the social partners' joint opinion and reached an agreement on the new Directive at first reading in December 2008. Having made legal and linguistic checks, the Council has formally adopted the new Directive.

4. In Force?

2232. The new directive was published in the EU's Official Journal on 16 May 2009 and entered into force twenty days later. The Member States will then have two years to implement the new rules at the national level, this being 2011.

III. Objective and Scope

A. *Objective*

2233. The purpose of the directive is to improve the right to information and to consultation of employees in Community-scale undertakings and groups of undertakings. To this end, appropriate mechanisms for transnational information and consultation (i.e. one or more European Works Councils (EWCs) or one or more procedures with the purpose of informing and consulting employees) have to be established in every Community-scale undertaking and every Community-scale group of undertakings where this is requested (Article 1(1)).

2234. This objective is justified in the recital to the directive as follows:

> Whereas the functioning of the internal market involves a process of concentrations of undertakings, cross-border mergers, take-overs, joint ventures and, consequently, a transnationalisation of undertakings and groups of undertakings; whereas, if economic activities are to develop in a harmonious fashion, undertakings and groups of undertakings operating in two or more Member States must inform and consult the representatives of those of their employees that are affected by their decisions (10);

Whereas procedures for informing and consulting employees as embodied in legislation or practice in the Member States are often not geared to the transnational structure of the entity which takes the decisions affecting those employees; whereas this may lead to the unequal treatment of employees affected by decisions within one and the same undertaking or group of undertakings 11);

Whereas appropriate provisions must be adopted to ensure that the employees of Community-scale undertakings or Community-scale groups of undertakings are properly informed and consulted when decisions which affect them are taken in a Member State other than that in which they are employed (12);

Whereas, in order to guarantee that the employees of undertakings or groups of undertakings operating in two or more Member States are properly informed and consulted, it is necessary to set up EWCs or to create other suitable procedures for the transnational information and consultation of employees (13).

B. Scope

1. Territorial

a. The 28 EU Member States

2235. The directive applies to the twenty-eight Member States; thus, Austria, Belgium, Bulgaria, Croatia, Cyprus (Greek part), Czech Republic, Denmark, Estonia, Finland, France, Germany, Greece, Hungary, Ireland, Italy, Latvia, Lithuania, Luxembourg, Malta, Netherlands, Poland, Portugal, Romania, Slovakia, Slovenia, Spain, Sweden and United Kingdom of Great Britain and Northern Ireland.

b. The European Economic Area (28 + 3)

2236. The directive applies to such countries as Iceland, Liechtenstein and Norway.

The non-EU members of the European Economic Area (EEA) (Iceland, Liechtenstein and Norway) have indeed agreed to enact legislation similar to that passed in the EU in the areas of social policy, consumer protection, environment, company law and statistics. These are some of the areas covered by the European Community (the 'first pillar' of the European Union).

c. Companies with Headquarters outside the EEA

2237. The directive also covers cases where undertakings or groups of undertakings have their headquarters outside the territory of the Member States. Where this is the case, such businesses should be treated in a similar way as Community-scale undertakings based on a representative either of the undertaking or group of undertakings or the undertaking with the highest number of employees in the territory of one of the Member States.

Practically speaking, companies that have undertakings and a given number of employees, as indicated later, within the territories of the twenty-eight Member States and the European Economic Area-European Free Trade Association (EEA-EFTA) countries, wherever their headquarters are based, will have to comply with the Directive. In this way the Directive applies to American-and Japanese-based multinationals and the like with regard to their European-based operations.

In relation to this point, the recital to the directive, reads as follows:

> Whereas the mechanism for informing and consulting employees in such undertakings or groups must encompass all of the establishments or, as the case may be, the group's undertakings located within the Member States, regardless of whether the undertaking or the group's controlling undertaking has its central management inside or outside the territory of the Member States. (18).

2. Personal: Which Companies?

2238. The directive applies to private as well as to public undertakings, irrespective of whether they belong to the private or to the public (economic) sphere. The notion undertaking covers any legal form of undertaking. This undertaking, not explicitly defined in the directive, may be a parent company, a subsidiary, an establishment, a branch or any other form of economic entity. In addition, an 'undertaking' may consist of a group of subsidiaries, establishments and the like.

One retains the notion of 'undertaking' in the framework of social legislation, according to which any entity should be considered an undertaking if it performs an economic activity, even if it is a non-profit-making activity. Undertakings that belong to private individuals should, therefore, be considered to be 'undertakings' within the meaning of the Directive.

a. Numbers

2239. According to the directive, an EWC or a procedure for informing and consulting employees has to be established in every Community-scale undertaking and in every Community-scale group of undertaking (Article 1(2)).

(1) Community-scale Undertaking

2240. A 'Community-scale undertaking' means an undertaking with at least 1,000 employees within the Member States and at least 150 employees in each of at least two of the addressed Member States.

Unless the agreement provides for a broader scope, the powers and competence of EWC(s) and the scope of information and consultation procedures cover, in the case of a Community-scale undertaking, all the establishments located within the Member States (Article 1(6)).

The prescribed thresholds for the size of the workforce are based on the average number of employees, including part-time employees, employed during the previous two years, calculated (pro rata)[934] according to national legislation and/or practice (Article 2(2)).

2241. The directive does not contain an express definition of the term 'employee'. Considering that it intends to achieve only partial harmonisation of information and consultation processes in the EU, the term 'employee' should be interpreted as covering any person who, in the Member State concerned, is considered to be an employee under national employment law. The same goes for the notion of a part-time worker, as is clearly indicated in Article 2(2).

The employees concerned must be employed by a Community-scale undertaking/establishment. This means that temporary workers who are working for the benefit of a Community-scale undertaking-user and subcontracted or posted workers will not count as employees of that undertaking, unless national law and/or practice would indicate otherwise.

It seems that it is of no interest whether the employee is engaged as a blue-collar worker, a white-collar worker, a manager or an official (*fonctionnaire*), or even whether the terms on which he is employed come under public or private law.

2242. The directive applies equally to employees engaged for an indefinite period as for those engaged for a fixed-term contract, contracts for replacement and the like. The same normally goes for employees whose contract of employment is suspended for reason of sickness leave, military service and the like, again unless national law or practice would say otherwise.

The term of the previous two years will have to be calculated starting (back) from the date that the directive enters into force, or from the date of the implementation of the Directive in the Member Sate in question, when this is earlier than the above-mentioned date,[935] or from the date parties conclude a (pre-existing) agreement.

(2) Group of Undertakings

2243. A 'group of undertakings' comprises, according to Article 2(b), 1 of the Directive, a controlling undertaking and its controlled undertakings.

(a) Definition of 'controlling undertaking'[936]

---

934. Declaration by the Council and the European Commission
935. See Article 13, 1.
936. Notwithstanding paras 1 and 2, an undertaking shall not be deemed to be a 'controlling undertaking' with respect to another undertaking in which it has holdings where the former undertaking is a company referred to in Article 3(5)(a) or (c) of Council Regulation (EC) No. 139/2004 of 20 January 2004 on the control of concentrations between undertakings

2244. For the purposes of the Directive, a 'controlling undertaking' means an undertaking that can exercise a dominant influence over another undertaking ('the controlled undertaking') by virtue of, for example, ownership, financial participation or the rules that govern it (Article 3(1)).

Article 3(1) aims at covering all possible 'controlling undertakings'. All undertakings, which may exercise a dominant influence, can be deemed to fulfil the duties under the Directive (Article 4) and they will have to decide which of them will be the 'controlling undertaking'. This can equally occur if employee representatives would differ on which company should be looked upon as the 'controlling undertaking'.

2245. The ability to exercise a dominant influence shall be presumed, without prejudice to proof to the contrary, when, in relation to another undertaking, an undertaking directly or indirectly:

(a) holds a majority of the undertaking's subscribed capital; or
(b) controls a majority of the votes attached to that undertaking's issued share capital; or
(c) can appoint more than half the members of the undertaking's administrative, managerial or supervisory body (Article 3(2)).

2246. The controlling undertaking's rights as regards voting and appointment shall include the rights of any other controlled undertaking and those of any person or body acting in his or its own name but on behalf of the controlling undertaking or of any other controlled undertaking (Article 3(3)).

A dominant influence shall not be presumed to be exercised solely by virtue of the fact that an office holder is exercising his functions, according to the law of a Member State relating to liquidation, winding-up insolvency, cessation of payments, compositions or analogous proceedings (Article 3(5)).

The law applicable in order to determine whether an undertaking is a 'controlling undertaking' shall be the law of the Member State which governs that undertaking (Article 3(6), paragraph 1).

As the possibility of exercising a dominant influence can be indicated by the central management, who can equally reverse the presumption of Article 3(2) central management seems to have a certain flexibility to choose the applicable law. The same applies in case of conflict of laws.

2247. Where the law governing that undertaking is not that of a Member State, the law applicable shall be the law of the Member State within whose territory the representative of the undertaking is situated. In the absence of such a representative, the law applicable shall be that of the Member State within whose territory the central management of the group undertaking that employs the highest number of employees in any one Member State is situated (Article 3(6), paragraph 2).[937]

In this case, central management can freely, without possible intervention of the employees, indicate which undertaking or person shall act as 'representative', thereby choosing at the same time the law it wants to apply.

(b) Community-scale group of undertakings

2248. A 'Community-scale group of undertakings' means a group of undertakings with the following characteristics:

- at least 1,000 employees within the Member States;
- at least two group undertakings in different Member States; and
- at least one group undertaking having at least 150 employees in one Member State and at least one other group undertaking with at least 150 employees in another Member State (Article 2(1)(c)).

Where a Community-scale group of undertakings comprises one or more Community-scale undertakings, the EWC will be established at the level of the group, unless the agreement(s) provide(s) otherwise (Article 1(5)).

2249. Unless a wider scope is provided for by the agreements, the powers and competence of EWCs and the scope of information and consultation procedures cover, in the case of a Community-scale undertaking, all the establishments located within the Member State, and in the case of a Community-scale group of undertakings, all group undertakings located within the Member States (Article 1(6)).

b. Central Management

2250. 'Central management' means the central management of a Community-scale undertaking or, in the case of a Community-scale group of undertakings, of the controlling undertaking (Article 2(1)(e)).

c. Merchant Navy Crews

2251. 'Member States may provide that this Directive shall not apply to merchant navy crews' (Article 1(7)).

---

937. Where, in case of a conflict of laws in the application of para. 2, two or more undertakings from a group satisfy one or more of the criteria laid down in that paragraph, the undertaking that satisfies the criterion laid down in point c thereof shall be regarded as the controlling undertaking, without prejudice to proof that another undertaking is able to exercise a dominant influence (Article 3, 7).

One reason for the authorisation to exclude merchant navy crews is that, in general, these crews work at a great distance from one another and from the management, and that it is, therefore, very difficult to bring them together for consultation. Bearing this in mind it would seem adequate not to exclude crews of ferryboats covering only smaller distances.

IV. Definitions and Notions

A. *Information and Consultation*

1. Information

a. Notion

2252. One of the reasons to recast the 1994 directive on information and consultation was to improve the effectiveness of the information, taking into account the challenges of globalization of the economy and restructuring as regarding the impact of the information and consultation process. These points are addressed in the recital of the 2009 Directive and lead to a more comprehensive definition.

(1) Globalisation and Restructuring

2253. The functioning of the internal market involves a process of concentrations of undertakings, cross-border mergers, takeovers, joint ventures and, consequently, a transnationalisation of undertakings and groups of undertakings. If economic activities are to develop in a harmonious fashion, undertakings and groups of undertakings operating in two or more Member States must inform and consult the representatives of those of their employees who are affected by their decisions (Recital 10). This should happen in an effective way.

(2) Effectiveness

2254. The arrangements for informing and consulting employees need to be defined and implemented in such a way as to ensure their effectiveness. To that end, informing and consulting the European Works Council (EWC) should make it possible for it to give an opinion to the undertaking in a timely fashion without calling into question the ability of undertakings to adapt. Only dialogue at the level where directions are prepared and effective involvement of employees' representatives make it possible to anticipate and manage change (Recital 14).

Part II, Ch. 2, Workers' Participation

(3) Definition

2255. 'Information'means transmission of data by the employer to the employees' representatives in order to enable them to acquaint themselves with the subject matter and to examine it; information shall be given at such time, in such fashion and with such content as are appropriate to enable employees' representatives to undertake an in-depth assessment of the possible impact and, where appropriate, prepare for consultations with the competent organ of the Community-scale undertaking or Community-scale group of undertakings' (Article 2, f).

This means:

- information in writing;
- in principle, information before decisions are taken;
- allowing for an in-depth assessment of the possible impact;
- enabling meaningful consultations;
- with the competent management.

2256. The information and consultation provisions laid down in this directive must be implemented in the case of an undertaking or a group's controlling undertaking which has its central management outside the territory of the Member States by its representative agent, to be designated if necessary, in one of the Member States or, in the absence of such an agent, by the establishment or controlled undertaking employing the greatest number of employees in the Member States (Recital 24).

b. Scope: Transnational

2257. The scope of the information is limited to transnational issues (Article 1(3)). 'Matters are considered to be transnational where they concern the Community-scale undertaking or Community-scale group of undertakings as a whole, or at least two undertakings or establishments of the undertaking or group situated in two different Member States' (Article 1(4)):

The transnational character of a matter should be determined by taking account of both the scope of its potential effects, and the level of management and representation that it involves. For this purpose, matters which concern the entire undertaking or group or at least two Member States are considered to be transnational. These include matters which, regardless of the number of Member States involved, are of importance for the European workforce in terms of the scope of their potential effects or which involve transfers of activities between Member States (Recital 16).

2258. Practically speaking, this means that an issue is transnational:

- when it concerns at least two Member States; or

– a decision by (central) management, situated in one State, that affects employees in another Member State. This also can be the case when decisions are taken in headquarters in the USA and affect an establishment in one Member State.[938]

2. Consultation

a. Notion

2259. The arrangements for consulting employees need to ensure their effectiveness. It should make it possible to give an opinion in a timely fashion without calling into question the ability of undertakings to adapt. Only dialogue at the level where directions are prepared and effective involvement of employees' representatives make it possible to anticipate and manage change (Recital 14).

Consultation has been (re)defined by the 2009 Directive and means:

> the establishment of dialogue and exchange of views between employees' representatives and central management or any more appropriate level of management, at such time, in such fashion and with such content as enables employees' representatives to express an opinion on the basis of the information provided about the proposed measures to which the consultation is related, without prejudice to the responsibilities of the management, and within a reasonable time, which may be taken into account within the Community-scale undertaking or Community-scale group of undertakings (Article 2(1)(g)).

2260. Thus, various elements are being retained, namely:

– dialogue and exchange of views;
– between employees' representatives and central management or any more appropriate level of management;
– time;
– fashion;
– content;
– express an opinion about the proposed measures;
– which may be taken into account by management;
– within a reasonable time.

2261. Managerial prerogative remains in full: the ability of the undertakings to adapt to change. Undertakings remain free to take the decisions as they see them.

The definition remains vague, but it has to be a real consultation. Again, it undoubtedly means that consultation, in principle, has to take place before decisions are made. Representatives must have comprehensive and detailed information

---

938. Appropriate provisions must be adopted to ensure that the employees of Community-scale undertakings or Community-scale groups of undertakings are properly informed and consulted when decisions that affect them are taken in a Member State other than that in which they are employed (Recital 12).

about the decision, the reasons and the consequences for the employees. Representatives must be able to make proposals to amend decisions or mitigate their impact. Management 'may' consider the representatives' opinion but it is not necessary. Eventually, however, management would have to explain why they did not follow the advice of the representatives of the employees. This is explicitly indicated in the definition.

b. Scope: Transnational

2262. The level of the consultation has to be transnational.[939]

B. Representation of Employees

2263. According to Article 2(1)(d) of the Directive on EWCs or procedures, 'employees' representatives' means the representatives of the employees provided for by national law and/or practice of the Member States.

The directive contains the very important provision that Member States must provide that employees in undertakings and/or establishments in which there are no employees' representatives through no fault of their own have the right to elect or appoint members of the special negotiating body (SNB) (Article 5(2)(a), second paragraph); this without prejudice to national legislation and/or practice laying down thresholds for the establishment of employee representation bodies (Article 5(2)(a), paragraph 3).

Because the notion 'employees' representatives' refers to the laws or practice of the Member States, this implies that it might be possible for 'non-employees' (e.g. permanent trade union business agents) to be elected or appointed, provided that national law and/or practice would foresee this possibility.

V. Establishment of an EWC or a Procedure

2264. Chart/establishment of an EWC or a procedure

Timing	Steps to Be Taken
Prior to the date of entry into force of the Directive	Agreement in force (Article 13(1)). The obligations of the Directive do not apply
From the date of entry into force of the Directive	1. Initiation of the negotiation (Article 5(1)) a. Initiative by central management Or b. Request of at least 100 employees or representatives (two undertakings/establishments/two Member States)

---

939. See above: Ch. 3, Section I.A.2.

	2. Establishment of the SNB (Article 5(2)) a. Members are elected or appointed (Article 5(2)(a)) b. Central, local management and competent European workers' and employers' organizations are informed of the composition of the body (Article 5(2)(d))
The latest within six months after the request to initiate negotiations (Article 7(1))	3. Negotiation starts a. Central management convenes a meeting with the SNB b. and informs local management's accordingly (Article 5(4))
Six months after the request to initiate negotiations	4. No negotiations: subsidiary requirements apply (Article 7(1))
Three years after the request to negotiate	5. No agreement: subsidiary requirements apply (Article 7(1))
Agreement comes to an end – no new appropriate agreement concluded	6. Subsidiary requirements apply (Article 7(1))

2265. The establishment of a European Works Council (EWC) or procedure by way of agreement between the parties takes different steps that have to be accomplished within a given period. This is the latest within a period of three years after the initial request by the employees to initiate negotiations has been launched. Therefore, if neither party moves, nothing will happen; the process can also be terminated by the special negotiation body (SNB), who may decide not to open negotiations or to cancel negotiations already opened, by a two-thirds majority of the members of the SNB.

The management of every undertaking belonging to the group of undertakings and the central management or the deemed central management is responsible for obtaining and transmitting to the parties concerned by the application of this directive the information required for commencing the negotiations and, in particular, the information concerning the structure of the undertaking or the group and its workforce. This obligation shall relate in particular to the information on the number of employees (Article 4(4)).

2266. The steps are:

– the request to initiate negotiations, either on the initiative of the employees/ representatives or of the central management;
– the establishment of the SNB;
– the convening of a negotiating meeting;
– the conclusion of an agreement.

Part II, Ch. 2, Workers' Participation

All this has to be accomplished within a time span of three years after the request to initiate negotiations. If not, the subsidiary requirements will apply. One and another could be evaded if parties conclude an agreement before the date of entry into force of the directive.

The same applies ceteris paribus in case of re-negotiation of the agreement with this understanding that the existing EWC (or its members/employees) will constitute the negotiating body (see Annex-subsidiary requirements 1(f) 2nd paragraph).

In case the subsidiary agreements apply and an EWC has been established, that EWC shall examine, four years after its establishment, whether to open negotiations for the conclusion of the agreement referred to in Article 6 or to continue to apply the subsidiary requirements adopted in accordance with the annex (Annex 1(f), paragraph 1).

A. The Obligation to Negotiate in a Spirit of Cooperation

2267. The directive contains a mandatory duty for the parties to negotiate, namely, 'in a spirit of cooperation with a view to reaching an agreement on the detailed arrangements for implementing the information and consultation of employees' (Article 6(1)). This mandatory requirement is self-evidently important and has many implications.

First, it means that the elaboration of an EWC or an information and consultation procedure is not a unilateral management affair to be seen as a pure instrument of HRM strategies. It is more than that. It indicates that both parties, central management and representatives of employees, are full-fledged partners in this, regulating a subject of common concern on a foot of equality. Second, it indicates – in a spirit of well-conceived subsidiarity – that the parties themselves will regulate their own relations, not the government. This is consequently an expression of 'social autonomy' of the negotiation parties. Third, it allows for maximum flexibility, giving parties the possibility to take into account their proper needs and aspirations, thus, of both the management and the employees.

2268. The obligation to negotiate in a spirit of cooperation, and certainly not in a spirit of confrontation, is *de facto*, and not much more than a mere policy guideline, which is an expectation from the European authorities and less a legally enforceable rule unless applicable law states the contrary. Self-evidently, in case of rude refusal or obstructions to negotiate, measures and procedures should be available (Article 11(2)) and the subsidiary requirements (Article 7(1)) will apply. One cannot dictate love, however, especially to those who still believe in class war.

2269. The point is nevertheless important. It underlines the need for a spirit of trust and good faith that should carry employee relations. However, such a state of mind and soul is not necessarily the case and depends a lot on the ideology of those who are involved. The truth of the matter is that trust can be built even between parties who have eventually opposing interests. Building of trust and fostering a spirit of cooperation indeed do not fall out of the blue sky but supposes continuous and conscientious efforts from all sides and is a delicate plant to be cherished and nourished permanently.

B. Responsibility and Initiation of Negotiations

1. Responsibility of Central Management

2270. The central management of the Community-scale undertaking or group of undertakings is responsible for creating the conditions and the means necessary for setting up an EWC or procedure for transnational information and consultation upon the terms and in the manner laid down by this Directive (Article 4(1)).[940]

Where the central management is not situated in a Member State, a central management's representative in a Member State, to be designated if necessary, shall take on the responsibility for setting up an EWC or a procedure. In the absence of such a representative, the above-mentioned responsibility will lie with the management of the establishment or the central management of the group undertaking employing the highest number of employees in any one Member State (Article 4(2)).

2271. The term 'employee' should be interpreted as covering any person who, in the Member State concerned, is considered to be an employee and that the calculation will take place according to national legislation and/or practice. What we said earlier concerning the notion employee in relation to the Community-scale undertaking or group of undertakings applies accordingly.[941]

2272. For the purposes of this directive, the representative of management, as provided for in Article 4(2) shall be regarded as central management (Article 4, paragraph 3). This 'representative' can be either a physical person (e.g. a manager, a consultant, or any other person) or a legal entity (whether or not part of the undertaking, or group of undertakings), provided the representative has been specifically designated to that end and has the full powers to fulfil the duties of this responsibility and is thus authorised to take all necessary decisions.

2. Initiation of the Negotiation

2273. The procedure designed to establish the right to transnational information and consultation of employees shall be initiated either on the initiative of the central management or at the written request of at least 100 employees in total or their representatives in at least two undertakings or establishments in at least two different Member States (Article 5(1)). The request by the employee representatives will have to be addressed to central management in the language chosen by the employees and signed by them, taking into account the linguistic legal requirements that are prevalent in the establishment(s) where the employees are employed. It may thus

---

940. 'The responsibility of undertakings or groups of undertakings in the transmission of the information required to commence negotiations must be specified in a way that enables employees to determine whether the undertaking or group of undertakings where they work is a Community-scale undertaking or group of undertakings and to make the necessary contacts to draw up a request to commence negotiations' (Recital 25).
941. See Ch. 2, §2, B, 1(a).

well be that request(s) emanate from different countries and are formulated in various languages. The request(s) can be signed by individual employees or by their representatives; for example, president(s) of local works councils, members of a trade union committee, and so on, provided they have the legal powers to do so. One hundred employees in total are sufficient. There is no need to have 100 employees or their representatives in each of the two undertakings or establishments in the different Member States.

3. One or More EWCs: Procedures

2274. The Directive only provides for the obligation of setting up one (negotiated or standard) EWC or one alternative procedure, even if a Community-scale undertaking or group of undertakings is composed of Community-scale undertakings or groups that on their own would also qualify for the establishment of an EWC or an alternative procedure (Article 1, paragraphs 5 and 6). In this case, the directive obliges to establish an EWC or an alternative procedure at the 'highest' level only.

However, additional EWC/procedures may be set up, also at 'sub' level, if management and employees' representatives agree to that end (Articles 1, 5, 6, 2(a) and 6, 3), taking the specific features of the 'sub'-levels (e.g. diversity of activities, branches, etc.) into account. The problem remains that in a group of groups, a central EWC/procedure still has to be set up at the highest level, even if EWCs/ procedures have been set up in some of the subgroups only unless there is (a) preexisting agreement(s) in force.

C. *The Negotiation of the Agreement*

2275. The negotiation for the establishment of an EWC or a procedure will take place between central management and a SNB composed of representatives of the employees (Article 5(2)). With a view to the conclusion of such an agreement, the central management has to convene a meeting with the SNB. It has to inform the local management accordingly (Article 5(4)).

1. Parties to the Agreement and the SNB

2276. Parties to the agreement are, thus, the Community-scale undertaking or group of undertakings represented by the central management on the one hand and, on the other hand, the representatives of the employees (as defined in every Member State) who will constitute an SNB, according to Article 5 of the directive. The SNB has in a sense a restricted legal personality with the necessary competence to conclude and eventually to terminate an agreement, establishing an EWC or a procedure. For the same reason, the SNB should have the legal competence to introduce actions before the courts in case of dispute relating to the matters covered by the directive (Article 10(1)). For the purposes of concluding an agreement, the SNB acts by a majority of its members (Article 6(5)).

a. Composition of the SNB

2277. The SNB must represent employees from the various Member States in a balanced fashion. Employees' representatives must be able to cooperate to define their positions in relation to negotiations with the central management (Recital 26).

2278. The SNB shall be established in accordance with the following guidelines:

(a) The Member States shall determine the method to be used for the election or appointment of the members of the special negotiating body who are to be elected or appointed in their territories' (Article 5(2)(a), paragraph 1).

The election or appointment of the members within each Member State shall be organised according to the legislation of those Member States. The Member States will have to pay special attention to who can elect and be elected. It comes to mind that managers – at the local as well as at the central levels – although they may legally be considered employees, would not qualify, neither as possible candidates for election nor as electors. However, it seems reasonable to limit that group of managers to those, who really run the local or central undertaking (senior management) and thus to interpret this notion restrictively. This means that blue collars, white collars and 'cadres' (middle and higher management) would qualify as electors and as elected or appointed members of the SNB. To become a member, employees self-evidently need to agree to be a candidate to that end.

This also means that, for example, trade unions could represent the employees according to national law/practice. As indicated 'Member States provide that employees in undertakings and/or establishments in which there are no employees' representatives through no fault of their own, have the right to elect or appoint members of the special negotiating body' (Article 5(2)(a) paragraph 2). Member States have the right to lay down thresholds for the establishment of employee representation bodies (Article 5(2)(a) paragraph 3).

(b) The members of the SNB shall be elected or appointed in proportion to the number of employees employed in each Member State by allocating, with respect to each Member State, one seat per portion of employees employed in that Member State, amounting to 10 per cent, or a fraction thereof, of the number of employees employed in all the Member States taken together.

The central management and local management and the competent European workers' and employers' organisations shall be informed of the composition of the SNB and of the start of the negotiations (Article 5(2)(c)).[942]

---

942. 'Recognition must be given to the role that recognised trade union organisations can play in negotiating and renegotiating the constituent agreements of European Works Councils, providing support to employees' representatives who express a need for such support. In order to enable them to monitor the establishment of new European Works Councils and promote best practice, competent trade union and employers' organisations recognised as European social partners shall be informed

b. Legal Personality of the SNB

2279. There is no doubt that the SNB has an (limited) implicit legal personality, namely, the legal capacity to conclude an agreement with central management regarding the establishment of an EWC or a procedure for informing and consulting. The SNB is entitled to introduce, eventually a case in justice, in order to enforce its rights.

c. Task of the Negotiating Parties

2280. The SNB shall have the task of determining with the central management by written agreement the scope, composition, functions and term of office of the EWC(s) or the arrangements for implementing a procedure for the information and consultation of employees (Article 5, paragraph 3).
This is explained in more detail in Article 6(2).

2281. The SNB and the central management of the Community-scale undertaking or group of undertakings have the task, without prejudice to the autonomy of the parties, of determining by means of a written agreement on the detailed arrangements for implementing the transnational information and consultation of employees the following:

– the scope (undertakings or establishments);
– the composition of the EWC, the number of members, the allocation of seats[943] and the term of office;
– the functions and the procedure for information and consultation of the EWC;
– the arrangements for linking information and consultation of the EWC and national employee representation bodies;
– the venue, frequency and duration of meetings of the EWC;
– where necessary, the composition, the appointment procedure, the functions and the procedural rules of the select committee;[944]
– the financial and material resources to be allocated to the EWC;
– the date of entry into force of the agreement and its duration;
– the arrangements for amending or terminating the agreement and the cases in which the agreement shall be renegotiated and the procedure for its re-negotiation, including, where necessary, where the structure of the

---

of the commencement of negotiations. Recognised competent European trade union and employers' organisations are those social partner organisations that are consulted by the Commission under 154 TFEU. The list of those organisations is updated and published by the Commission' (Recital 27).
943. 'Taking into account where possible the need for balanced representation of employees with regard to their activities, category and gender.'
944. 'Those agreements must provide, where necessary, for the establishment and operation of a select committee in order to permit coordination and greater effectiveness of the regular activities of the European Works Council, together with information and consultation at the earliest opportunity where exceptional circumstances arise' (Recital 30).

Community-scale undertaking or Community-scale group of undertakings changes[945] (Article 6(2)).

2282. With a view to the conclusion of an agreement, the central management shall convene a meeting with the SNB. It shall inform the local managements accordingly.

Before and after any meeting with the central management, the SNB shall be entitled to meet without representatives of the central management being present, using any necessary means for communication (Article 5(4)).

The SNB may decide, by at least two-thirds of the votes, not to open negotiations or to terminate the negotiations already opened. Such a decision stops the procedure to conclude an agreement. Where such a decision has been taken, the provisions (subsidiary requirements) in the annex do not apply. A new request to convene the SNB may be made at the earliest two years after the above-mentioned decision, unless the parties concerned lay down a shorter period (Article 5(5)).

2. Experts and Costs

2283. For the purpose of the negotiations, the SNB may request assistance from experts of its choice, which can include representatives of competent recognized Community-level trade union organisations. Such experts and such trade union representatives may be present at negotiation meetings in an advisory capacity at the request of the SNB (Article 5(4), paragraph 3). These experts can be employees or non-employees and, as indicated, trade union representatives. There is no doubt that the trade unions consider this a role for them and want to assist the employees' representatives to that end.

Any expenses relating to the negotiations have to be borne by the central management to enable the SNB to carry out its task in an appropriate manner (Article 5(6) paragraph 1). In compliance with this principle, Member States may lay down budgetary rules regarding the operation of the SNB. In particular, they may limit funding to cover one expert only (Article 5(6) paragraph 2).

2284. Inspiration can be found in point 6 of the annex to the Directive on Subsidiary Requirements: 'The central management concerned shall provide the members of the EWC with such financial and material resources as to enable them to perform their duties in an appropriate manner.' Always subject to this fundamental rule, the annex gives some additional indications.

2285. It seems reasonable that the employer takes on the following expenses:

---

945. 'The agreements governing the establishment and operation of European Works Councils must include the methods for modifying, terminating, or renegotiating them when necessary, particularly where the make-up or structure of the undertaking or group of undertakings is modified' (Recital 28).

Part II, Ch. 2, Workers' Participation

- the costs of the election of the members of the SNB as provided for by national legislation;
- the costs of the meetings of the SNB, including translation, accommodation, travelling, and rent of the room;
- the costs of expert advisers chosen by the SNB.

The directive authorises the Member States to limit the funding to cover one expert only. The question then arises of what this limitation means: one expert per meeting, one expert per year, or one expert per subject? Although it is certainly the purpose of this limitation to reduce the costs for undertakings, it should be borne in mind that the EWC must have adequate resources to perform its duties in an appropriate manner. Thus, a limitation with reference to a fixed period seems to be inappropriate because the duties of the EWC may vary from one meeting to another. Furthermore, a limitation based on the subject alone is not appropriate.

The same subject may be dealt with in meetings over several years. Therefore, a limitation within the spirit of the directive should be one expert adviser per subject per meeting.

3. Role of the Trade Unions and of the Employers' Associations

2286. Thanks to the 2009 Directive, trade unions and employers' associations can be directly involved experts to the SNB and the EWC. As experts to the agreement to be concluded concerning information and consultation, they may play an active role in practice.

Undoubtedly, the European Trade Union Secretariats (European sectoral level) and the European Trade Union Confederation (ETUC) (European inter-industrywide level) are strongly behind the move for a European social dialogue, but the European Union's choice that the agreements be concluded by the representatives of the employees and not necessarily by the trade unions has been a deliberate one. In a sense, this leaves all options open.

Trade unions can also play a role, for example, in the training of members of the EWCs, next acting as experts and even as contracting parties and the like. The same goes for BUSINESSEUROPE as well as for the (national) employers' associations, which can help to monitor and guide undertakings/members.

National trade unions may play a role in the election or appointment of the (national) representatives in the SNB if national law or practice provides them with such a role as, for example, might be the case in Belgium or France.

D. *Nature, Binding Effect, Form, Language and Interpretation of the Agreement*

1. Nature and Binding Effect of the Agreement

2287. The agreement can be looked upon as a special kind of collective labour agreement concluded between representatives of European management on the one hand and the European representatives of the employees under the form of a negotiating body, establishing an EWC or an information or consultation procedure on the other hand.

One can qualify the agreement as, like the French say, a 'contract institution', namely, a contract that creates an institution, a framework for information and consultation between management and labour, which will lead its own life once it has been created. The agreement has, like any other collective labour agreement, an obligatory part and a normative part. The obligatory part relates to the rights and obligations of the contracting parties; the normative part being the information and consultation institution procedure that has been set up with its scope, composition, competence, and the like. The contracting parties not only create but also control the very existence of the EWC or the procedure because they will always have the right, taking agreed-upon formalities and/or terms of notice into account, to denounce the agreement.

2288. The binding effect of the agreement – of both (obligatory and normative) parts – thus will depend on the law applicable to the contract. For example, if this is Belgian because the agreement was concluded in Brussels, the venue of the meeting of the EWC or the framework of a procedure is there as well as central management's location, and the parties did not choose another legal system, the relations between the contracting parties might be governed by Belgian law.

This would then be the general principles of Belgian contractual law because the Belgian Act of 5 December 1968 on joint committees and collective labour agreements would not apply. In order to qualify for a binding legal collective agreement (in the sense of the 1968 Act) the parties need to be, from the employees' side, representative (Belgian) trade unions, which is not the case for the SNB operating in the framework of the directive.

2. Form and Language of the Agreement

2289. It makes sense that the agreement establishing an EWC or a procedure has to be drawn up in writing and that it has to be signed by the representatives of management and by the majority of the individual representatives of the employees assembled in the SNB. The negotiating body is, as said, a fully fledged legal party, and not only a forum, an instrument, or, if you will, more than a vehicle for communication between the involved actors. More formal aspects of the agreement for its legality, the number of copies to be signed and so on will be taken care of according to the requirements of the applicable law.

2290. The agreement could be drafted in various official languages of the Member States, depending on the (national) composition of the negotiating parties. One language is also possible, coupled to translations or without translations, provided the signing parties understand what they sign. Special attention will have to be paid to the national legislation applicable to the agreement, especially if this legislation might contain certain linguistic requirements, as is, for example, the case in Belgium and France.

Part II, Ch. 2, Workers' Participation

3. Interpretation of the Agreement

2291. This interpretation is, in the first place, the responsibility of the parties to the agreement themselves and to the EWC itself, or in the framework of the procedure in what one could call a form of permanent dialogue or negotiation about the content of the agreement and its application. In case of a (legal) dispute that the parties and/or actors cannot settle themselves, it would be up to the competent national judge to have the last word unless the parties provide for binding arbitration, which might be a (legal) venue in a number of European Union/European Economic Area (EU/EEA) Member States.

E. Content of the Agreement

2292. The content of the agreement is self-evidently the business of the contracting parties: They decide autonomously what they want to put in the agreement and what to exclude. Article 6 of the directive contains a list in case of the establishment of an EWC. That list is a mandatory list of subjects, but the parties are autonomous in deciding on the concrete content to be given to the listed points.

According to the directive, a distinction must be made between setting up an EWC and the elaboration of a procedure. It is not so easy to see the difference between an EWC and a procedure, especially because Article 6(3), second paragraph, provides in case of a procedure also for the right of the employees' representatives to meet to discuss the information conveyed to them. Indeed, 'the agreement must stipulate by what method the employees' representatives shall have the right to meet to discuss the information conveyed to them. This information shall in particular relate to the transnational questions which affect workers' interests'.

It would, therefore, seem logical that an EWC is a more institutionalized form of communication and dialogue, whereas the procedure is a much looser one. However, as said, it is not clear where the procedure ends and where the EWC begins and vice versa.

One might say that an agreement that does not lay out in detail all the points covered by Article 6(2) may preferably qualify for a procedure instead than for an EWC. The parties could, however, make their intentions clear and indicate in the agreement whether they opt for an EWC or for a procedure.

2293. For a procedure one could imagine *inter alia*: written reports forwarded by management, information and consultation at the local level by any means; within or outside existing proceedings at the national level, for example, the visit of a (European or national) human resources manager to the employees' representatives at a plant or national level, provided the information and consultation relates to transnational issues. This procedure must not necessarily be the same in all undertakings but may differ from one Member State to another, between different businesses of the group and the like.

In any case, parties are free to decide on these matters and can qualify their arrangement as they see fit, taking into account the right of the employees' representatives to discuss the information conveyed to them and engage in a dialogue.

The agreement is not, unless it provides otherwise, subject to the subsidiary requirements referred to in the annex (Article 6(4) paragraph 1).

1. Scope

2294. The agreement has to indicate 'the member undertakings of the Community-scale undertakings or the establishments of the Community-scale undertaking which are covered by the agreement' (Article 6(2a)).

The agreement will have to indicate the territorial and personal scope (establishments/undertakings) covered by the agreement, possibly addressed by various EWCs in case of a group. The scope may also contain undertakings outside the EU and the European Economic Area-European Free Trade Association (EEA-EFTA) countries.

2. The Setting-up of an EWC

2295. (Article 6(2)(b)): the composition of the EWC and the number of members, the allocation of seats, taking into account where possible the need for balanced representation of employees with regard to their activities, category and gender and the term of office.

The agreement can provide that the EWC may be composed of representatives of employees only or also of representatives of management, whereas parties could also agree that the EWC be (consecutively) chaired by a representative of either group (management – employees). Parties should reflect on an appropriate representation of the different groups of employees, like blue-white collars, managerial employees, female workers, and the like. Parties can also agree on other members, for example, trade union business agents, who may also participate either as fully fledged members or as pure observer members/advisers or as experts and the like. Complete freedom prevails for the parties to the agreement regarding these matters. Parties should also set up a select committee for the workers' group or of the EWC itself if the EWC is to be composed of employees only. If necessary, the directive says.

2296. Main problems could arise in the case of, for example, mergers or other restructuring of undertakings/establishments that might affect the composition of the EWC (especially, for example, in case of a merger of two groups that have their own EWCs). Article 6(2)(g) provides that the agreement should contain 'the arrangements for amending or terminating the agreement and the cases in which the agreement shall be renegotiated and the procedure for its renegotiation, including, where necessary, where the structure of the Community-scale undertaking or Community-scale group of undertakings changes'.

Allocation of seats in the EWC will usually take into account the numerical strength of the employees in the undertaking(s) and establishments. Regarding elections or appointments, the parties would be well advised to stick as closely as possible to national law and/or practice and follow, for example, the same way as for the election of the representatives to the SNB. Candidates should ideally have a given seniority (e.g. of one year) in the establishment or undertaking as an employee in order to be able to represent their colleagues with a certain degree of insight and competence. The term of office should cover a number of years, not too long and not too short. Two to three years seems a minimum; five years a maximum.

2297. (Article 6(2)(c)): the functions and the procedure for information and consultation of the EWC

The agreement might specify the competencies of the EWC more precisely as far as the nature of the consultation is concerned and *inter alia* indicate that the prerogatives of management will not be affected. The agreement should also clearly indicate the subject matter of the information and consultation exercise; for this, a source of inspiration may be the subjects enumerated in the subsidiary requirements.

In enumerating the subject matters, one should take into account that the employees are especially entitled to information and consultation regarding transnational questions that significantly affect their interests, such as jobs, working conditions in the broad sense of the word and so on. Employees are particularly interested in the mitigation of social consequences of some managerial decisions. Here information about future developments and prospects comes to mind especially; indeed, employees are more interested in the future of the business than in the social-economic history of the company.

2298. The agreement should also contain

> the arrangements for linking information and consultation of the European Works Council and national employee representation bodies, in accordance with the principles set out in Article 1(3)' (Article 6(2)(3)). Indeed, the agreements must lay down the arrangements for linking the national and transnational levels of information and consultation of employees appropriate for the particular conditions of the undertaking or group of undertakings. The arrangements must be defined in such a way that they respect the competences and areas of action of the employee representation bodies, in particular with regard to anticipating and managing change (Recital 29).

2299. The agreement should equally contain something on the 'when' (yearly and/or ad hoc?) of the information and consultation (before decisions are taken or as soon as possible in ad hoc cases?). It should also contain the organisation of the exchange of views or the dialogue, or both, and of possible feedback; and on confidential and/or prejudicial information, on the role of experts, on accountants to check the veracity of the information, and the like. Other points may concern voting majorities, the drafting of the agenda, the drafting of reports, the organisation of working parties, the training of the delegates, communication of information and consultation results to the rank and file and to the trade unions, contacts with the press and so forth.

Written and/or oral procedure and timing should also be considered. Regarding information, will documents be sent beforehand? How long before the meeting takes place? One might equally agree on the timing between information and consultation, on tabling of motions, on voting, on interpretation and translation (languages), on the role of experts and so on.

2300. (Article 6(2)(d)): the venue, frequency, and duration of meetings The agreement may say something about invitations to the meetings, about the place of the meetings, differentiate between general (e.g. yearly) information and ad hoc information meetings and when special important events should take place such as closures, collective dismissals and the like. The agreement may also provide for pre-meetings; meetings of working parties, the select committee, the workers' group and the like; the length of the meetings and so on.

2301. (Article 6(2)(e)): the select committee The agreement should also contain, when necessary, the composition, the appointment procedure, the functions and the procedural rules of the select committee set up within the EWC.

2302. (Article 6(2)(f)): the financial and material resources to be allocated to the EWC

Central management will have to provide the necessary financial resources to pay for the functioning of the EWC (secretariat, catering, housing and so on), whereas the agreement has to cover payment of expenses of travel, loss of wages of the employees' representatives and the like. Experts will normally be paid by the party they assist, or by the organisation they represent, which may be subsidised to this end by the EU. However, the agreement could provide otherwise and eventually indicate that the costs of the experts will be borne by central management.

2303. (Article 6(2)(g)): The date of entry into force of the agreement and its duration, the arrangements for amending or terminating the agreement and the cases in which the agreement shall be renegotiated and the procedure for its re-negotiation, including, where necessary, where the structure of the Community-scale undertaking or Community-scale group of undertakings changes:

The agreements governing the establishment and operation of European Works Councils must include the methods for modifying, terminating, or renegotiating them when necessary, particularly where the make-up or structure of the undertaking or group of undertakings is modified (Recital 28).

2304. Finally, the agreement should indicate its duration. The agreement may be open ended with a term of notice and contain certain forms (e.g. a registered letter) and proposals for re-negotiation to be respected in case of denouncement of the agreement and the like. Either central management or the (majority of) members of the negotiating body could denounce the agreement totally or partially. Both parties may also agree to terminate the agreement.

Part II, Ch. 2, Workers' Participation 2305–2306

The agreement can also be concluded for a fixed period, after which it ends automatically. Parties can also decide on a fixed period with a prolongation for a (similar) period unless one of the parties terminates the agreement before a certain date (e.g. one year before the term ends).

In any case, there must be a procedure for its re-negotiation. The re-negotiation would normally take place between central management and a negotiating body, especially when there are structural changes in the group, which can lead to one or more EWCs.

However, according to the annex (point 1(f), paragraph 2) this is the (employee representatives of) EWC. If no new agreement is reached before the old one expires, the subsidiary requirements will apply.

2305. Others. The agreement could also expand on the law applicable to the agreement, on the settlement of interpretation or application difficulties by way of either conciliation or arbitration, on the competent court, and the like.

For the purposes of concluding the agreement, the SNB shall act by majority of its members (Article 6(5)).

3. The Setting-up of a Procedure

2306. Article 6(3) of the directive states that:

> the central management and the special negotiating body may decide, in writing, to establish one or more information and consultation procedures instead of an EWC. The agreement must stipulate by what method the employees' representatives have the right to meet to discuss the information conveyed to them. This information shall relate in particular to transnational questions which significantly affect workers' interest.

Addressing this issue, the recital to the directive reads as follows: 'Employees' representatives may decide not to seek the setting-up of a European Works Council or the parties concerned may decide on other procedures for the transnational information and consultation of employees' (31).

Parties should among others focus, and *ceteris paribus*, on:

(a) the scope of the procedure;
(b) the mode of operation, including 'the right to meet to discuss the information';
(c) the matters subject to information and consultation;
(d) the financial and material resources to be allocated for the functioning of the procedure;
(e) the duration of the agreement and the procedure for its re-negotiation;
(f) the law applicable to the agreement.

VI. Prejudicial and Confidential Information: Ideological Guidance

2307. According to Article 8(2), paragraph 1, of the directive, Member States have to provide, in specific cases under the conditions and limits laid down by national legislation, that the central management situated in its territory is not obliged to transmit information that would seriously harm the functioning of the undertakings concerned or would be prejudicial to them.

A Member State may make such dispensation subject to prior administrative or judicial authorization (Article 8(2), paragraph 2).

Member States shall, according to Article 8(1) of the Directive, also provide that members of special negotiating bodies (SNBs) or of European Works Councils (EWCs) and any experts who assist them are not authorized to reveal any information that has expressly been provided to them in confidence.

The same applies to the employees' representatives in the framework of an information and consultation procedure. This obligation continues to apply wherever these persons are, even after the expiry of their terms of office.

The disclosure of certain key data on a business or on strategic sectors (e.g. on manufacturing processes) may indeed be detrimental to the business concerned.

Article 8 of the Directive sets out two ways of protecting this information:

- an obligation on members of SNBs or EWCs and experts involved in the procedure not to divulge certain information defined as confidential by the central management ('Member States shall provide that members of SNBs or of EWCs and any experts, who assist them, are not authorized to reveal any information which has expressly been provided to them in confidence');
- the right of the central management not to provide information in certain circumstances.

In their agreement, parties could define more precisely the kind of information that is either prejudicial or confidential. The (nature of the) confidential and/or the prejudicial information could also be identified at the moment that the information is given.

2308. It should be added that Article 8(3) of the directive contains the possibility for Member States to lay down particular provisions for the central management of undertakings and establishments in its territory that pursue directly and essentially the aim of ideological guidance with respect to information and the expression of opinions. In this regard, the Council and the Commission stated:[946]

this means undertakings and establishments which directly and essentially pursue:

- political, professional organisation, religious, charitable, educational, scientific or artistic aims,
- aims involving information and the expression of opinions.

---

946. Statements for entry in the Council Minutes.

Where Member States apply Article 8 of the directive concerning confidential (and prejudicial) information, they have to provide for administrative or judicial appeal procedures that the employees' representatives may initiate when the central management requires confidentiality or does not give information in accordance with Article 8 (Article 11(3)). 'Such procedures may include procedures designed to protect the confidentiality of the information in question' (Article 11(3), paragraph 2).

VII. Role and Protection of Employees' Representatives

A. *Role of Employees' Representatives*

1. Representation of the Interest of the Employees

2309. Directive 2009 explicitly states that 'the members of the European Works Council shall have the means required to apply the rights arising from this Directive, to represent collectively the interests of the employees' (Article 10(1)). This means *inter alia* members have the right to go to justice in order to obtain the information and consultation rights to which they are entitled based on the directive and/or the agreement they concluded with central management. The rights are limited to information and consultation, even if the agreement would go further and provide collective bargaining rights. Collective bargaining, indeed, is a matter that calls for a directive based on unanimity in the Council, according to Article 153(1)(f) TFEU.

2. Information of National Representatives or Workforce

2310. The members of the European Works Council (EWC) shall inform the representatives of the employees of the establishments or of the undertakings or, in the absence of representatives, the workforce as a whole, of the content and outcome of the information and consultation procedure carried out in accordance with this Directive (Article 10(2)). Self-evidently, taking the rules of confidentiality, according to Article 8, into account.

3. Training

2311. Insofar as this is necessary for the exercise of their representative duties in an international environment, the members of the special negotiating body (SNB) and of the EWC shall be provided with training without loss of wages (Article 10(4)). This is a possible point for negotiation, which may be taken up by the parties when they conclude their agreement.

B. *Protection of Employees' Representatives*

2312. The employees' representatives have similar protection to their national colleagues. Indeed, Article 10 of the directive provides that members of SNBs, members of EWCs and employees' representatives who are exercising their functions under an information and consultation procedure should enjoy similar protection and guarantees provided for employees' representatives by the national legislation and/or practice in force in the country of employment, especially the attendance at meetings of SNBs or EWCs or any other meetings within the framework of the agreement. In addition, this article establishes a procedure and the payment of wages for members who are on the staff of the Community-scale undertaking or group of Community-scale undertakings for the period of absence necessary for the performance of their duties.

2313. Rightly, the recital states that:

> Provision should be made for the employees' representatives acting within the framework of this directive to enjoy, when exercising their functions, the same protection and guarantees as those provided to employees' representatives by the legislation and/or practice of the country of employment. They must not be subject to any discrimination as a result of the lawful exercise of their activities and must enjoy adequate protection as regards dismissal and other sanctions (34).
>
> This protection includes *inter alia* promotion, dismissals and working conditions. Here one has to take into account that the different national systems regarding protection vary extremely from one Member State to another. It is also a fact that there may be different systems of protection within the same national system.

2314. So, in Belgium where there is a difference between the protection of, for example, Works Council members and members of the trade union committees. In such a case, one can presume, unless national legislation implementing the Directive should state otherwise, that the most favourable system of protection would apply.

One should also consider that in case of a dispute concerning, for example, the proposed dismissal of a (European) representative, national procedures have to be followed. In Belgium, for example, this means that national joint committees of employers and trade unions, operating at branch/industry level, might be involved as well as labour courts and that the (national) trade unions would have a role to play. This may lead to rather intricate legal complications.

2315. At the same time, it may also be the case that one has to have recourse to international private labour law rules in order to determine which national system is applicable in case an employee representative is employed, for example, in more than one country, such as in the capacity of commercial traveller.

Part II, Ch. 2, Workers' Participation   2316–2318

VIII. Compliance with the Directive – Links – Adaptation

A. Compliance with the Directive

2316. Each Member State has to ensure that the management of establishments and the management of a Community-scale undertaking or which form part of a Community-scale group of undertakings, which are situated within its territory and their employees' representatives or, as the case may be, employees abide by the obligations laid down by the Directive, regardless of whether or not the central management is situated in its territory (Article 11, 1).

Member States have to provide for appropriate measures in the event of failure to comply with this Directive. In particular, they shall ensure that administrative or judicial procedures are available to enable the obligations deriving from this directive to be enforced (Article 11, 2).

Member States must indeed take appropriate measures in the event of failure to comply with the obligations laid down in this directive (Recital 35).

2317. In accordance with the general principles of Community law, administrative or judicial procedures, as well as sanctions that are effective, dissuasive and proportionate in relation to the seriousness of the offence, should be applicable in cases of infringement of the obligations arising from this Directive (Recital 36).

As indicated before, Member States provide for administrative or judicial procedures which the employees' representatives may initiate when the management requires confidentiality or does not give information for reasons of confidentiality. Such procedures may include procedures designed to protect the confidentiality of the information in question (Article 11, 3).

B. Links

2318. Article 12 introduces the principle of a link between the national and transnational levels of information and consultation of the employees with due regard for the competences and areas of action of the representative bodies. The arrangements for this link are defined by the agreement concluded pursuant to Article 6, c, which covers this matter. Where there are no such arrangements and where decisions likely to lead to substantial changes in work organisation or contractual relations are envisaged, the process would have to start in parallel at national and European level. Because certain national legislation may have to be adapted to ensure that the EWC can, where applicable, receive information earlier or at the same time as the national bodies, a clause has been added to stipulate that there must be no reduction in the general level of protection of employees.[947]

---

947. For reasons of effectiveness, consistency and legal certainty, there is a need for linkage between the directives and the levels of informing and consulting employees established by Community and national law and/or practice. Priority must be given to negotiations on these procedures for linking information within each undertaking or group of undertakings. If there are no agreements on this subject and where decisions likely to lead to substantial changes in work organisation or contractual relations are envisaged, the process must be conducted at both national and European level in

2319. The directive is without prejudice to the information and consultation procedures referred to in Directive 2002/14/EC of 11 March 2002 establishing a general framework for informing and consulting employees in the European Community and to the specific procedures referred to in Article 2 of Council Directive 98/59/EC of 20 July 1998 on the approximation of the laws of the Member States relating to collective redundancies and Article 7 of Council Directive 2001/23/EC of 12 March 2001 on the approximation of the laws of the Member States relating to the safeguarding of employees' rights in the event of transfers of undertakings, businesses or parts of undertakings or businesses (Article 12, 4).

2320. Implementation of this directive shall not be sufficient grounds for any regression in relation to the situation which already prevails in each Member State and in relation to the general level of protection of workers in the areas to which it applies (Article 12, 5).

C. *Adaptation*

2321. When the structure of the undertaking or group of undertakings changes significantly, for example, due to a merger, acquisition or division, the existing EWC(s) must be adapted. This adaptation must be carried out as a priority pursuant to the clauses of the applicable agreement[948] if such clauses permit the required adaptation to be carried out. If this is not the case and a request establishing the need is made, negotiations, in which the members of the existing EWC(s) must be involved, will commence on a new agreement. In order to permit the information and consultation of employees during the often decisive period when the structure is changed, the existing EWC(s) must be able to continue to operate, possibly with adaptations, until a new agreement is concluded. Once a new agreement is signed, the previously established councils must be dissolved, and the agreements instituting them must be terminated, regardless of their provisions on validity or termination.[949]

The central management shall initiate the negotiations referred to in Article 5 on its own initiative or at the written request of at least 100 employees or their representatives in at least two undertakings or establishments in at least two different Member States.

At least three members of the existing EWC or of each of the existing EWCs shall be members of the special negotiating body, in addition to the members elected or appointed pursuant to Article 5(2).

---

such a way that it respects the competences and areas of action of the employee representation bodies. Opinions expressed by the EWC should be without prejudice to the competence of the central management to carry out the necessary consultations in accordance with the schedules provided for in national legislation and/or practice. National legislation and/or practice may have to be adapted to ensure that the EWC can, where applicable, receive information earlier or at the same time as the national employee representation bodies, but must not reduce the general level of protection of employees (Recital 37).

948. See Article 6 (g).
949. Recital 40.

During the negotiations, the existing ECW(s) shall continue to operate in accordance with any arrangements adapted by agreement between the members of the European Works Council(s) and the central management (Article 13).

IX. Subsidiary Requirements: a Mandatory EWC

2322. If the central management and the special negotiating body (SNB) so decide, or if the central management refuses to commence negotiations within six months of the request by the representatives of the employees to initiate negotiations, or if after three years from the date of this request, they are unable to conclude an agreement providing for a EWC or a procedure for informing and consulting employees, the subsidiary requirements, laid down by the legislation of the Member State in which the central management is situated, apply (Article 7(1)):

2323. The subsidiary requirements set out in the annex apply automatically in three situations (Article 7 of the directive):

- where the central management and the SNB so decide;
- where the central management refuses to commence negotiations within six months of the request made by the workers or their representatives for negotiations to be opened;
- where, after three years from the date of this request, they are unable to conclude an agreement.

The subsidiary requirements as adopted in the legislation of the Member State must satisfy the provisions set out in the annex to the directive (Article 7(2)).

The subsidiary requirements, thus, constitute in a sense the mandatory core regarding information and consultation rights, the European legislator wants European undertakings to live up to, if the parties do not follow the voluntary road by concluding an agreement, setting up an EWC or by establishing an information and consultation procedure. Indeed, the subsidiary requirements provide, as indicated, for a mandatory establishment of an EWC.

2324. Addressing these issues, Recitals 42 and 43 to the directive read as follows:

> Without prejudice to the possibility of the parties to decide otherwise, a European Works Council set up in the absence of agreement between the parties must, in order to fulfil the objective of this Directive, be kept informed and consulted on the activities of the undertaking or group of undertakings so that it may assess the possible impact on employees' interests in at least two different Member States. To that end, the undertaking or controlling undertaking must be required to communicate to the employees' appointed representatives general information concerning the interests of employees and information relating more specifically to those aspects of the activities of the undertaking

or group of undertakings which affect employees' interests. The European Works Council must be able to deliver an opinion at the end of the meeting.

Certain decisions having a significant effect on the interests of employees must be the subject of information and consultation of the employees' appointed representatives as soon as possible.

A. *Composition of the EWC*

2325. The EWC is to be composed of employees of the Community-scale undertaking or Community-scale group of undertakings, elected or appointed from their midst by the employees' representatives or, in the absence thereof, by the entire body of employees (Annex 1(b), paragraph 1).

The election or appointment of members of an EWC shall be carried out in accordance with national legislation and/or practice (Annex 1(b), paragraph 2).

The members of the EWC shall be elected or appointed in proportion to the number of employees employed in each Member State by the Community-scale undertaking or Community-scale group of undertakings. This is accomplished by allocating, with respect to each Member State, one seat per portion of employees employed in that Member State, amounting to 10 per cent, or a fraction thereof, of the number of employees employed in all the Member States taken together (Annex I(1)(c)).

2326. To ensure that it can coordinate its activities, the EWC shall elect a select committee from among its members, comprising at most five members, which must benefit from conditions enabling it to exercise its activities on a regular basis. It shall adopt its own rules of procedure (Annex I(1)(d)).

The central management and any other more appropriate level of management shall be informed of the composition of the EWC (Annex 1(e)).

B. *Competence*

2327. The competence of the EWC shall be determined in accordance with Article 1(3).

The information of the EWC shall relate in particular to the structure, economic and financial situation, probable development and production, and sales of the Community-scale undertaking or group of undertakings. The information and consultation of the EWC shall relate in particular to the situation and probable trend of employment, investments and substantial changes concerning organization, introduction of new working methods or production processes, transfers of production, mergers, cut-backs or closures of undertakings, establishments or important parts thereof, and collective redundancies.

The consultation shall be conducted in such a way that the employees' representatives can meet with the central management and obtain a response, and the reasons for that response, to any opinion they might express (Annex I(1)(a)).

Part II, Ch. 2, Workers' Participation

1. General Information (Annual)

2328. The EWC has the right to meet with the central management once a year, to be informed and consulted, on the basis of a report drawn up by the central management, on the progress of the business of the Community-scale undertaking or Community-scale group of undertakings and its prospects. The local management shall be informed accordingly (Annex I(2)).

2. *Ad Hoc* Information

2329. When there are exceptional circumstances or decisions affecting the employees' interests to a considerable extent, particularly in the event of relocations, the closure of establishments or undertakings or collective redundancies, the select committee or, where no such committee exists, the EWC shall have the right to be informed. It shall have the right to meet, at its request, the central management, or any other more appropriate level of management within the Community-scale undertaking or group of undertakings having its own powers of decision, to be informed and consulted.

Those members of the EWC who have been elected or appointed by the establishments and/or undertakings and who are directly concerned by the circumstances or decisions in question shall also have the right to participate where a meeting is organized with the select committee (Annex I(3)).

C. *Procedure*

2330. The EWC shall have the right to meet with the central management once a year and if there are exceptional circumstances, particularly affecting the interests considerably, as indicated above. The yearly meeting takes place on the basis of a written report (Annex I(2)).

The special ad hoc information and consultation meeting has to take place as soon as possible on the basis of a report drawn up by the central management or any other appropriate level of the management of the Community-scale group of undertakings, on which an opinion may be delivered at the end of the meeting or within a reasonable time. One may assume that this report should also be in writing, unless great urgency would prevent this and an oral report would have to be made.

This meeting shall not affect the prerogatives of the central management (Annex I(3), paragraph 4).

Member States may provide for rules concerning the chairing of the information and consultation meetings (Annex 4, paragraph 1). This means that the applicable law may, for example, provide for management to preside the meeting because this is a common practice in most Member States.

Before any meeting with the central management, the EWC or the select committee, where necessary enlarged in accordance with the second paragraph of point 3, shall be entitled to meet without the management concerned being present (Annex I(4), paragraph 2).

The EWC shall adopt its own rules of procedure (Annex I(d), paragraph 2).

D. Role of Experts – Trade Unions – Employers' Associations

2331. The EWC or the select committee may be assisted by experts of its choice insofar as this is necessary for it to carry out its tasks (Annex I(5)). These experts can be employees as well as non-employees and thus, for example, also trade union representatives. There is no doubt that the trade unions consider this a role for them and are eager to assist the representatives of the employees towards that end.

Whatever, the European Trade Union Secretariats and the European Trade Union Confederation (ETUC) are strongly behind the moves for a European social dialogue. Trade unions can also play a role in the training of members of the EWCs by acting as experts and the like.

Employers' associations can help to monitor and guide undertakings in similar ways.

E. Expenses

2332. The operating expenses of the EWC are, according to Annex I(67) to the directive, borne by central management. The central management concerned has to provide the members of the EWC with such financial and material resources as to enable them to meet and perform their duties in an appropriate manner.

In particular, the central management shall meet the cost of organizing meetings and arranging for interpretation facilities and the accommodation and travelling expenses of members of the EWC and its select committee unless otherwise agreed.

In compliance with these principles, the Member States may lay down budgetary rules regarding the operation of the EWC. They may, in particular, limit funding to cover one expert only (Annex, I(6), paragraph 4). One and another means that Member States (i.e., the applicable law) may provide for specific provisions on the matter.

They may, for example, reasonably limit certain expenses (travel or accommodation class, cost of translations, interpretation, etc.), or they could provide for a maximum global budget, provided employee-members of the EWC procedure are able to meet and perform their duties and exercise their rights in an adequate manner.

F. Enforcement of the Subsidiary Requirements

2333. Member States have to ensure that the subsidiary requirements are lived up to, whether the central management is situated in their territory or not.[950] Therefore, they have to enact measures to that effect. These should be effective. The Court of Justice is, as said earlier, of the opinion that where a Union Directive does not specifically provide any penalty for an infringement, or where it refers for that purpose to national laws, the obligations of the Member States under the Treaty are to require them to ensure that infringements of EC law are penalised under conditions,

---

950. See Article 11 of the directive.

both procedural and substantive, that are analogous to those applicable to infringements of national law of a similar nature and importance and that, in any event, make the penalty effective, proportionate and dissuasive.[951]

G. Future Developments

2334. Four years after the EWC is established, it shall examine whether to open negotiations for the conclusion of the agreement referred to in Article 6 or to continue to apply the subsidiary requirements adopted in accordance with this annex.

Articles 6 and 7 will apply, *mutatis mutandis*, if a decision has been taken to negotiate an agreement according to Article 6 and the 'SNB' shall be replaced by 'EWC' (Annex I(1)(f)).

X. Agreements in Force

A. Pre-existing Agreements

2335. A question raised when the 1994 Directive was negotiated read as follows. Does the EU want to favour voluntarism in the setting-up of a EWC or of an information and consultation procedure by encouraging the conclusion of agreements to that end even before the Directive entered into force?

With this objective in mind, Article 13 of the 1994 Directive declares as follows:

> The obligations arising from this Directive shall not apply to Community-scale undertakings and groups of undertakings in which, on the date of the implementation of this Directive according to Article 14, 1 or the date of its earlier transposition into the law of the Member State in question, there is already an agreement, providing for the transnational information and consultation, covering the entire workforce. When the agreements referred to expire, the parties to such agreements may jointly decide to renew them. Where this is not the case, the provisions of this Directive shall apply.

2336. These so-called agreements in force or pre-existing agreements thus escaped the obligations arising from the Directive. This was on the condition that there was 'an agreement providing for the transnational information and consultation of employees' (Article 13, 1/1994 Directive).

This has been confirmed in the new 2009 Directive. Article 14 of the 2009 Directive reads:

---

951. 8 June 1994, C-382/92 and 383/92, *Commission v. UK*.

The obligations arising from this Directive does not apply to Community-scale undertakings or Community-scale groups of undertakings in which, an agreement or agreements covering the entire workforce, providing for the transnational information and consultation of employees have been concluded pursuant to Article 13(1) of Directive 94/45/EC or Article 3(1) of Directive 97/74/EC, or where such agreements are adjusted because of changes in the structure of the undertakings or groups of undertakings.

Upon expiry of the agreements, the parties to those agreements may decide jointly to renew or revise them. Where this is not the case, the provisions of this Directive shall apply (Article 14).

1. Timing, Form, Language and Format of the Agreement: Applicable Law

a. Timing, Form and Language

2337. The agreement has to be concluded before the implementation of the Directive in national law; this is 22 September 1996 or the date of its transposition in the Member State in question where this is earlier than the above-mentioned date.

Although Article 13 of the 1994 Directive does not indicate that the agreement should be in writing, it seems absolutely indicated that it should. This is because the existing agreement will be up for examining whether it qualifies as an agreement in force, escaping the obligations under the Directive on the establishment of an EWC or a procedure for the purposes of informing and consulting employees.

The agreement could be drafted in various official languages, depending on the composition of the negotiating parties. One language is also possible, coupled to translations or without translations, provided the signing parties understand what they sign. Special attention will have to be paid to the national legislation that is applicable to the agreement, especially if this legislation might contain certain linguistic requirements, as is, for example, the case in Belgium and France.

b. Nature, Binding Effect and Applicable Law

2338. For these questions we can refer to Chapter 4, Section IV.

2. Scope and Parties to the Agreement

a. Scope

2339. Special attention has to be given to the (personal) scope of the agreement. Indeed, Article 13 stipulates that the agreement should cover the entire workforce. This condition leads to the following questions that parties have to consider carefully:

- Does the agreement cover all establishments/undertakings concerned by the definition of Community-scale undertaking or group of undertakings in Articles 2 and 3 of the 1994 Directive?
- Does the agreement cover all employees of all the establishments/undertakings concerned?

b. Parties

2340. The parties to the agreement are, self-evidently, the representatives of the Community-scale undertaking or groups of undertakings, for example, the central management on the one hand and the representatives of the employees on the other hand.

For management this can be the chief executive officer (CEO), a managing director, a European human resources manager and the like. Regarding the representatives of the employees, there are equally as many possibilities: members of existing works councils or shop stewards who operate at national level, or employees especially elected or appointed for the purpose of representation at the European level. The following would also qualify: representatives of national trade unions, representatives of European Industry Committees like the EMF, UNI-Europe and others. Some pre-negotiation will have to take place as to who qualifies as a party to the agreement. Indeed, as a general rule (international), management prefers to deal with the employees only, whereas trade unions want to have a foot in the door, preferably as a party to the agreement, in order to be able to monitor the EWC or the information and consultation procedure efficiently.

3. Content of the Agreement

a. An EWC, a Procedure or Another Mechanism

2341. The parties have to decide whether they want to establish in an EWC, a procedure or another mechanism for the purposes of information and consultation. They can call their creation whatever they like: a forum, a 'liaison committee' and so on. In the case of an EWC or similar committee, they have to decide on its composition: of employees only, or (alternatively?) chaired by a representative of central management or an employee representative, or they may decide to have a joint committee composed of representatives of both sides.

They will also have to agree on the number of members. Points to take into account are, for example:

- one member from each Member State, where the undertaking has an establishment;
- supplementary members according to the number of employees in the establishments/ undertakings;
- substitute members.

2342. There is also the possibility to create a select or executive committee, representing the employee members or the EWC as a whole, which could steer the EWC and/or be available for ad hoc interventions.

Decisions are also required on pre-meetings, the role of experts and so on. In case of a procedure instead of an EWC committee, similar questions arise: Who will be involved, informed and consulted? How will parties relate to each other? Again, maximum flexibility is allowed, but at a given point, employees' representatives and those of management should meet and engage in a dialogue. All this has to be laid down in writing.

b. Competence: Information and Consultation

2343. Reference points to determine the content of the information and consultation obligations between parties are self-evidently Article 1 of the Directive and the subsidiary requirements. Information and consultation relate to transnational issues in particular, involving undertakings/establishments of at least two Member States (Article 13, 1/1994 Directive). We refer to what has been said previously (Chapter 7, Section II.B).

c. Functioning

2344. Parties have to decide when the representatives of the (central) management and of the employees will meet: annually and/or ad hoc when important events are affecting the interests of the employees, on meeting(s) of the select executive committee, on possible pre-meetings before meeting with central management and the like. Other points concern the drafting of the agenda (e.g. every party has the right to put points on the agenda), documents to be submitted, meeting rules, ways of expressing opinions, exchange of views, dialogue, reporting (minutes of the meetings), feedback, and the like.

Employees' representatives may need the help of some form of secretariat; eventually the benefit of some facilities, like a room; access to modern information technology; telecommunications; and the like. This could also be a subject of the agreement.

The agreement might also contain wording concerning the languages and interpretation facilities to be used for the implementation of the information and consultation exercise. It is self-evident that languages that employees' and management's representatives understand effectively must be used. This will, thus, depend entirely on the composition of the EWC committee or of those involved in the procedure and their respective linguistic skills.

d. Role of Experts

2345. The role of experts is essential for the functioning of the EWC committee or the successful conduct of a procedure. Employees' representatives should be free to choose their experts. These may be other employees, trade union representatives or even outside independent persons. The agreement may lay down rules on who can be experts, their numbers, whether they have access to which documents, whether they can assist in pre-meetings or meetings of an EWC procedure and the like. It is normal that the undertaking pay the experts' expenses, unless, for example, trade unions could benefit from EU subsidies to that end.

e. Expenses

2346. Expenses for the functioning of the EWC procedure should be borne by the undertaking. As far as the expenses of the employees' representatives are concerned, this can be done by way of paying proven expenses or (partly?) by allocating a budget to the representatives of the employees. Part of the expenses may be paid by the central management and part by the local establishments, depending on the case.

Wages for activities during working time are self-evidently to be covered probably by local management of the undertakings/establishments where the employees' representatives are employed.

4. Prejudicial and Confidential Information

2347. These points could be addressed in the agreement along the lines of what the Directive contains:[952] which information will and can be given and which information is prejudicial/confidential and which information can be passed on to local management, to other employees, to trade unions(?), to governmental authorities and the public at large. The possibility of press conferences and/or statements should also be envisaged.

5. Status of the Employees' Representatives

2348. In addition, the status of employees' representatives may be addressed in the agreement. The parties could envisage whether they adopt language indicating that employees cannot be discriminated against for reasons of opinions defended and/or confer upon them the same protection as under national law. We, therefore, refer to what has been said in Chapter 6.[953]

In case of a dispute that the parties cannot solve by negotiations and no other voluntary mechanism for dispute settlement like, for example, mediation, conciliation or arbitration is foreseen, the parties will have to take action under the national law that governs the agreement. Because the Directive does not apply to pre-existing agreements, general principles of law and legal procedure will prevail. Depending

---

952. See Ch. 5.
953. See also ILO Convention No. 135 of 1971.

on the national law applicable, one will have to decide who qualifies to be a litigating party, which judge is competent, what remedies are available and the like. This may be a lawyer's paradise, but the normal course of action would be that the parties sort out their differences themselves in a spirit of cooperation instead of going to court. Again, to a large extent, this will be determined by the legal cultures involved.

6. Duration of the Agreement

2349. The agreement should indicate its duration. The agreement may be openended, with a term of notice and certain forms (e.g. a registered letter) and proposals for re-negotiation to be respected in case of denouncement of the agreement.

Either management or the representatives of the employees could denounce the agreement totally or partially, taking the requirements of the applicable legislation into account. Both parties may also agree to terminate the agreement.

The agreement can also be for a fixed period, after which it ends automatically. The parties can also foresee a fixed period with a prolongation for the same period unless one of the parties has terminated the agreement before a certain date (e.g. one year before the term ends).

The parties might also agree on a procedure for its re-negotiation. In case of renewal, the agreement will continue to escape the obligations that arise under the directive. If no new agreement is reached before the old one expires, the directive will apply.

B. Article 6 Agreements

2350. The same goes for Article 6 agreements. The obligations arising from the 2009 Directive do not apply to Community-scale undertakings or Community-scale groups of undertakings in which an agreement concluded pursuant to Article 6 of Directive 94/45/EC is signed or revised between 5 June 2009 and 5 June 2011.

The national law applicable when the agreement is signed or revised shall continue to apply to the undertakings or groups of undertakings.

Upon expiry of the agreements, the parties to those agreements may decide jointly to renew or revise them. Where this is not the case, the provisions of the 2009 Directive shall apply (Article 14).

XI. Report of the Directive by the Commission

2351. No later than 5 June 2016, the Commission shall report to the European Parliament, the Council and the European Economic and Social Committee (EESC) on the implementation of this Directive, making appropriate proposals where necessary (Article 15).

Part II, Ch. 2, Workers' Participation

XII. Transposition, Repeal, Entry into Force

A. Transposition

2352. Member States shall bring into force the laws, regulations and administrative provisions necessary to comply with Article 1(2), (3) and (4); Article 2(1), points (f) and (g); Article 3(4); Article 4(4); Article 5(2), points (b) and (c); Article 5(4); Article 6(2), points (b), (c), (e) and (g); and Articles 10, 12, 13 and 14, as well as Annex I, point 1(a), (c) and (d) and points 2 and 3, no later than 5 June 2011, or they shall ensure that management and labour introduce on that date the required provisions by way of agreement. Member States are being obliged to take all necessary steps enabling them at all times to guarantee the results imposed by this Directive.

When Member States adopt those provisions, they shall contain a reference to this Directive or be accompanied by such a reference on their official publication. They shall also include a statement that references in existing laws, regulations and administrative provisions to the Directive repealed by this Directive shall be construed as references to this Directive. Member States shall determine how such reference should be made and how that statement should be formulated.

Member States shall communicate to the Commission the text of the main provisions of national law that they adopt in the field covered by this Directive (Article 16).

B. Repeal

2353. Directive 94/45/EC, as amended by the Directives listed in Annex II, Part A, is repealed with effect from 6 June 2011 without prejudice to the obligations of the Member States relating to the time limit for transposition into national law of the Directives set out in Annex II, Part B.

Annex II

Part A

Repealed Directive with Its Successive Amendments (Referred to in Article 17)

Council Directive 94/45/EC	(O.J. L 254, 30 September 1994, p. 64)
Council Directive 97/74/EC	(O.J. L 10, 16 January 1998, p. 22)
Council Directive 2006/109/EC	(O.J. L 363, 20 December 2006, p. 416)

Part B

Time Limits for Transposition into National Law (Referred to in Article 17)

Directive	Time limit for transposition
94/45/EC	22 September 1996
97/74/EC	15 December 1999
2006/109/EC	1 January 2007

References to the repealed Directive shall be construed as references to this Directive and shall be read in accordance with the correlation table in Annex III (Article 17).

C. Entry into Force

2354. This Directive shall enter into force on the twentieth day following its publication in the Official Journal of the European Union.

Article 1(1), (5), (6) and (7); Article 2(1), points (a) to (e), (h) and (i); Article 2(2); Articles 3(1), (2), (3), (5), (6) and (7); Article 4(1), (2) and (3); Article 5(1), (3), (5) and (6); Article 5(2), point (a); Article 6(1); Article 6(2), points (a), (d) and (f); Article 6(3), (4) and (5); and Articles 7, 8, 9 and 11, as well as Annex I, point 1(b), (e) and (f), and points 4, 5 and 6, shall apply from 6 June 2011 (Article 18).

§4. A GENERAL FRAMEWORK FOR INFORMING AND CONSULTING RIGHTS OF EMPLOYEES IN THE EUROPEAN COMMUNITY

I. Genesis of the Directive

2355. On 11 November 1998[954] the European Commission issued a proposal for a directive 'establishing a general framework for informing and consulting employees in the European Community'. The move followed the refusal of UNICE to enter into negotiations over a European agreement on the subject. The draft directive provides for rules on the information and consultation of workers at national level – based on agreement or legislation – applying to undertakings with 50 or more employees. The ETUC welcomed the draft directive, but considers that it does not go far enough on a number of issues. UNICE rejects European legislation in this area as unnecessary.

The possibility of the introduction of an EU-level framework for employee in-formation and consultation was first raised in the European Commission's 1995 medium-term Social Action Programme. Calls for EU legislative action in this area

---

954. COM/98/0612 final – SYN 98/0315, O.J., 5 January 1999, C 002.

Part II, Ch. 2, Workers' Participation

became louder after the crisis sparked off by the closure of the Renault plant at Vilvoorde in Belgium, which was seen by many to have demonstrated the in-adequacies of current EU legislation in this area. In June 1997, the Commission initiated a first round of consultations of the European-level social partners on the advisability of legislation in this area.

In November 1997, the Commission opened a second round of consultations on the content of possible EU legislation on this issue. The social partners had an opportunity at this stage – within a six-week deadline – to decide to attempt to negotiate a framework agreement, thus forestalling a directive.

At the second stage of consultations, the Commission expressed a clear preference for a social partner initiative to reach a European agreement on this topic. However, while ETUC and CEEP indicated their willingness to negotiate on this basis, UNICE remained opposed and in March 1998 rejected joining such talks. UNICE said that member federations were virtually unanimous in their conviction that the European Union should not intervene in such a matter, which has no transnational implications.

ETUC maintained its position that the objective of a framework agreement in this area would not be to replace well-functioning systems for information and consultation at national level, but to set minimum standards for this basic right. National provisions that are more advantageous should take precedence over those laid down in a European agreement.

The draft directive offers a substantial degree of flexibility in relation to the exact shape and scope of information and consultation arrangements to be instituted.

2356. The draft was amended by the EP, the ESC and the Committee of the Regions.

The Commission justifies the proposal as follows:

> The existence of legal frameworks at national and Community level intended to ensure that workers are involved in the affairs of the undertaking employing them and in decisions which affect them has not always prevented serious decisions affecting workers from being taken and made public without adequate procedures having been put in place beforehand to inform and consult them;
>
> There is a need to strengthen dialogue and promote mutual trust within undertakings in order to improve risk anticipation, make work organisation more flexible and facilitate employee access to training within the undertaking while maintaining security, make employees aware of adaptation needs, increase employees' availability to undertake measures and activities to increase their employability, promote employee involvement in the operation and future of the undertaking and increase its competitiveness;
>
> In particular, there is a need to promote and strengthen information and consultation on the situation and probable development of employment within the undertaking and, where it ensues from the evaluation carried out by the employer that employment within the undertaking is likely to come under

threat, on any anticipatory measures envisaged, in particular in terms of training and enhancing employees' skills, with a view to offsetting negative developments or their consequences and improving the employability and adaptability of the employees likely to be affected;

Timely information and consultation is a prerequisite for the success of restructuring and adaptation of undertakings to the new conditions created by globalisation of the economy, particularly via the development of new forms of work organisation;

... The existing legal frameworks for employee information and consultation at Community and national level tend to adopt an excessively *a posteriori* approach to the process of change, neglect the economic aspects of decisions taken and do not contribute to genuine anticipation of employment developments within the undertaking or to risk prevention;

...

In accordance with the principles of subsidiarity and proportionality as set out in Article 5 of the Treaty, the objectives of the proposed action, as outlined above, cannot be adequately achieved by the Member States, in that the object is to establish a framework for employee information and consultation appropriate for the new European context described above; however, in view of the scale and impact of the proposed action, these objectives can be better achieved at Community level by the introduction of minimum regulations applicable to the entire European Community; the present Directive constitutes no more than the minimum necessary to achieve these objectives.

2357. The Directive 2002/14/EC of the European Parliament and of the Council establishing a general framework for informing and consulting employees in the European Community was adopted on 11 March 2002.[955]

II. Object and Principles

2358. The purpose of this directive is to establish a general framework setting out minimum requirements for the right to information and consultation of employees in undertakings or establishments within the Community.

The practical arrangements for information and consultation have to be defined and implemented in accordance with national law and industrial relations practices in individual Member States in such a way as to ensure their effectiveness.

When defining or implementing practical arrangements for information and consultation, the employer and the employees' representatives have to work in a spirit of cooperation and with due regard for their reciprocal rights and obligations, taking into account the interests both of the undertaking or establishment and of the employees (Article 1).

---

955. O.J., 23 March 2002.

Part II, Ch. 2, Workers' Participation 2359–2360

III. Definitions

2359. For the purposes of this directive:

(a) 'undertaking' means a public or private undertaking carrying out an economic activity, whether or not operating for gain, which is located within the territory of the Member States;
(b) 'establishment' means a unit of business defined in accordance with national law and practice, and located within the territory of a Member State, where an economic activity is carried out on an ongoing basis with human and material resources;
(c) 'employer' means the natural or legal person party to employment contracts or employment relationships with employees, in accordance with national law and practice;
(d) 'employee' means any person who, in the Member State concerned, is protected as an employee under national employment law and in accordance with national practice;
(e) 'employees' representatives' means the employees' representatives provided for by national laws and/or practices;[956]
(f) 'information' means transmission by the employer to the employees' representatives of data in order to enable them to acquaint themselves with the subject matter and to examine it;
(g) 'consultation' means the exchange of views and establishment of dialogue between the employees' representatives and the employer (Article 2).

IV. Scope

2360. This directive shall apply, according to the choice made by Member States, to:

(a) undertakings employing at least 50 employees in any one Member State, or
(b) establishments employing at least 20 employees in any one Member State. Member States shall determine the method for calculating the thresholds of employees employed.

In conformity with the principles and objectives of this directive, Member States may lay down particular provisions applicable to undertakings or establishments which pursue directly and essentially political, professional organisational, religious, charitable, educational, scientific or artistic aims, as well as aims involving information and the expression of opinions, on condition that, at the date of entry

---

956. Joint declaration of the European Parliament, the Council and the Commission on employee representation: 'With regard to employee representation, the European Parliament, the Council and the Commission recall the judgements of the European Court of Justice of 8 June 1994 in Cases C-382/92 (Safeguarding of employees rights in the event of transfers of undertakings) and C-383/92 (Collective redundancies).'

into force of this directive, provisions of that nature already exist in national legislation.

Member States may derogate from this directive through particular provisions applicable to the crews of vessels plying the high seas (Article 3).

Article 3(1) of Directive 2002/14/EC of the European Parliament and of the Council of 11 March 2002 establishing a general framework for informing and consulting employees in the European Community must be interpreted as precluding national legislation which excludes, even temporarily, a specific category of workers from the calculation of staff numbers within the meaning of that provision.[957]

V. Practical Arrangements for Information and Consultation

2361. The Member States shall determine the practical arrangements for exercising the right to information and consultation at the appropriate level. Information and consultation shall cover:

(a) information on the recent and probable development of the undertaking's or the establishment's activities and economic situation;
(b) information and consultation on the situation, structure and probable development of employment within the undertaking or establishment and on any anticipatory measures envisaged, in particular where there is a threat to employment;
(c) information and consultation on decisions likely to lead to substantial changes in work organisation or in contractual relations.[958]

Information shall be given at such time, in such fashion and with such content as are appropriate to enable, in particular, employees' representatives to conduct an adequate study and, where necessary, prepare for consultation.

Consultation shall take place:

(a) while ensuring that the timing, method and content thereof are appropriate;
(b) at the relevant level of management and representation, depending on the subject under discussion;
(c) on the basis of information supplied by the employer and of the opinion which the employees' representatives are entitled to formulate;
(d) in such a way as to enable employees' representatives to meet the employer and obtain a response, and the reasons for that response, to any opinion they might formulate;
(e) with a view to reaching an agreement on decisions within the scope of the employer's powers (Article 4).

---

957. C.O.J., 18 January 2007, *Confédération générale du travail (CGT) and others* v. *Premier ministre*, C-385/05, www.curia.eu.
958. Including those covered by the Community provisions referred to in Article 9(1) of this directive.

VI. Information and Consultation Deriving from an Agreement

2362. Member States may entrust management and labour at the appropriate level, including at undertaking or establishment level, with defining freely and at any time through negotiated agreement the practical arrangements for informing and consulting employees. These agreements, and agreements existing on the date of implementation of the directive, as well as any subsequent renewals of such agreements, may establish provisions which are different from those referred to in Article 4 (Article 5).

2363. The Directive can be transposed by way of a collective agreement which results in a group of employees being covered by the agreement in question, even though the employees in that group are not members of the union which is a party to that agreement and their field of activity is not represented by that union, provided that the collective agreement is such as to guarantee to the employees coming within its scope effective protection of the rights conferred on them by the Directive.[959]

VII. Confidential Information

2364. The employees' representatives, and any experts, who assist them, are not authorised to reveal to employees or to third parties, any information which, in the legitimate interest of the undertaking or establishment, has expressly been provided to them in confidence. This obligation shall continue to apply, wherever the said representatives or experts are, even after expiry of their terms of office. However, a Member State may authorise the employees' representatives and anyone assisting them to pass on confidential information to employees and to third parties bound by an obligation of confidentiality.

Member States shall provide, in specific cases and within the conditions and limits laid down by national legislation, that the employer is not obliged to communicate information or undertake consultation when the nature of that information or consultation is such that, according to objective criteria, it would seriously harm the functioning of the undertaking or establishment or would be prejudicial to it.

Without prejudice to existing national procedures, Member States shall provide for administrative or judicial review procedures for the case where the employer requires confidentiality or does not provide the information. They may also provide for procedures intended to safeguard the confidentiality of the information in question (Article 6).

---

[959]. C.O.J., 11 February 2010, *Ingeniørforeningen i Danmark, acting on behalf of Bertram Holst*, C-405/08, www.curia.

VIII. Protection of Employees' Representatives

2365. Employees' representatives, when carrying out their functions, enjoy adequate protection and guarantees to enable them to perform properly the duties which have been assigned to them (Article 7).

2366. Article 7 of Directive 2002/14 must be interpreted as not requiring that more extensive protection against dismissal be granted to employees' representatives. However, any measure adopted to transpose that directive, whether provided for by legislation or by collective agreement, must comply with the minimum protection threshold laid down in Article 7.[960]

IX. Protection of Rights

2367. Member States shall provide:

- for appropriate measures in the event of non-compliance with this directive by the employer or the employees' representatives. In particular, they shall ensure that adequate administrative or judicial procedures are available to enable the obligations deriving from this directive to be enforced.
- for adequate sanctions to be applicable in the event of infringement of this directive by the employer or the employees' representatives. These sanctions must be effective, proportionate and dissuasive.

X. Link between this Directive and Other Community and National Provisions

2368. This directive is without prejudice

- to the specific information and consultation procedures set out in Article 2 of Directive 98/59/EC[961] and Article 7 of Directive 2001/23/EC;[962]
- to provisions adopted in accordance with Directives 94/45/EC and 97/74/EC.[963]
- to other rights to information, consultation and participation under national law.

Implementation of this directive shall not be sufficient grounds for any regression in relation to the situation which already prevails in each Member State and in relation to the general level of protection of workers in the areas to which it applies (Article 9).

---

961. On Collective Redundancies (*see* Part I, Chapter 10, §1).
962. Transfer of Undertakings (*see* Part I, Chapter 10, §2).
963. European Works Councils (*see* Part II, Chapter 2, §3).

XI. Transitional Provisions

2369. A Member State in which there is, at the date of entry into force of this Directive, no general, permanent and statutory system of information and consultation of employees, nor a general, permanent and statutory system of employee representation at the workplace allowing employees to be represented for that purpose, may limit the application of the national provisions implementing this directive to:

(a) undertakings employing at least 150 employees or establishments employing at least 100 employees until 23 March 2007, and
(b) undertakings employing at least 100 employees or establishments employing at least 50 employees during the year following the date in point (a) (Article 10).

XII. Transposition

2370. Member States shall adopt the laws, regulations and administrative provisions necessary to comply with this directive not later than 23 March 2005 or shall ensure that management and labour introduce by that date the required provisions by way of agreement, the Member States being obliged to take all necessary steps enabling them to guarantee the results imposed by this directive at all times. They shall forthwith inform the Commission thereof.

Where Member States adopt these measures, they shall contain a reference to this directive or shall be accompanied by such reference on the occasion of their official publication. The methods of making such reference shall be laid down by the Member States (Article 11).

XIII. Review by the Commission

2371. Not later than 23 March 2007, the Commission shall, in consultation with the Member States and the social partners at Community level, review the application of this directive with a view to proposing any necessary amendments.

XIV. Entry into Force

2372. This Directive shall enter into force on the day of its publication in the Official Journal of the European Communities (Article 13).

XV. Some Concluding Remarks

A. Renewed Interest

2373. Lately, there is a renewed and vigorous interest in the involvement of employees in the European Union.

'Involvement of employees' means, according to the Council Directive supplementing the Statute for a European Company, approved by the Employment and

Social Affairs Council of 8 October 2001, 'any mechanism, including information, consultation and participation, through which employees' representatives may exercise an influence on decisions to be taken within the company' (Article 2(h)).

The reasons for this renewed interest are self-evident. Indeed, economic globalisation and the speedy advance of the market economy world wide evolved in many countries in a retreat by governments from the running of the economy and more freedom for management as well as the enhancement of managerial prerogative. Moreover, the practice of shareholder's value is on the move, also in continental Europe and Japan. Short-term financial forecasts and benefits prevail. Stakeholder's value becomes part of a lost European dream.

2374. At the same time and as a consequence, traditional, especially national collective bargaining structures, slowly erode in many countries, while overall trade unions are loosing members and their grip on the labour markets. In our information driven societies, characterised by outsourcing and more smaller enterprises than before, employees tend to unionise less.

Increased and often worldwide competition leads to ongoing restructurations, mergers, outsourcing, downsizing and to the atomisation of individual employment relationships. Enterprises need to be competitive. So the best product or service at the lowest cost is imperative. Do more with less is the compelling objective.

B. Employee Involvement

2375. So, and the question arises naturally, where are the employees in all this? Where do they stand? How should they be involved? What input should they have on the decision-making in the enterprises for which they work? What should the European Union do in this regard? In short, what about the employees' voice?

C. Influence on Decision-making?

2376. According to the aforementioned definition of 'involvement' of employees, its purpose is to 'exercise an influence on decisions to be taken within the company'. That influence is, however, as a rule limited to information and consultation, leaving the prerogative of management intact, as is clearly indicated in the directives concerning the European Works Council and the European Company Statute. Moreover, management decisions are – self-evidently – increasingly dictated by market conditions, and are often made at headquarters, situated in other countries, even in other continents, outside the EU. Experience, also with the European Works Councils, shows that strategic economic management decisions are, as a general rule, not fundamentally changed due to involvement of employees.

Consequently, the objective, which goes along with 'involvement of employees', has, to my mind, less to do with power, in the sense that employees get a chance to influence management's decision-making regarding important issues, like e.g. restructurings.

Involvement of employees has, in the first place, to do with the fact that enterprises need the support of their employees-collaborators in a competitive environment in which creativity and information-in-action are the basic ingredients for economic success. Information and consultation are a must in the information society and an essential factor for companies to be competitive and for employees to have good wages and working conditions.

D. Employability

2377. Moreover, employees want to know where they are heading in this rapidly changing world. What is happening and will happen to them? How will this affect their employability? Whether they will find a new job tomorrow will not only depend on the status of the economy, but especially on their skills and competences.

Information and consultation, as well as the dialogue in the enterprise, undoubtedly create a climate of mutual understanding and better working together. For sure, the representatives of the employees have a role to play (indirect participation), but self-evidently management, will, beyond the legally imposed involvement structures, see to it that a well-conceived HRM strategy directly embraces all employees (direct participation) and will organise an ongoing dialogue with them.

E. The Three Sisters

2378. In the last 10 years, various European initiatives have seen the daylight, aiming to provide more involvement of the employees as well at the European level as at the national level.

There was first of all the Directive on European Works Councils, promulgated in 1994 and operative since 1996. This directive was quite successful, as no fewer than 1260 works councils have already been established and more are in the making. 1031 councils are active. 957 multinationals are involved. In total, there should be some 1,800 European Works Councils. Moreover, the European Works Council was the subject of an in-depth review by the European Commission and a thorough discussion by the European Parliament.

Secondly, and at last, there was a break through for the European Company Statute at the Nice Top (December 2000), which was successfully carried through by the Employment and Social Affairs Council meeting of 8 October 2001. The Employment and Social Affairs Council adopted the proposals (regulation and directive) as they laid on the table since 1 February 2000 without taking onboard any of the amendments put forward by the European Parliament, which was not a big surprise. These new legal instruments will be published in the Official Journal in due course and the transition period of 3 years will then begin.

Thirdly, there is the directive establishing 'a general framework for improving information and consultation rights of employees in the European Community'.

F. Coherence

2379. Undoubtedly, there is great need for coherence between those various European legal instruments.

First, regarding the notions used. Here, the directive concerning the SE is the most detailed. It contains definitions of 'involvement of employees', as indicated above, as well as of:

'Information' 'means the informing of the body representative of the employees and/or employees' representatives by the competent organ of the SE on questions which concern the SE itself and any of its subsidiaries or establishments situated in another Member State or which exceed the powers of the decision-making organs in a single Member State at a time, in a manner and with a content which allows the employees' representatives to undertake an in-depth assessment of the possible impact and, where appropriate, prepare consultations with the competent organ of the SE';

'Consultation' 'means the establishment of dialogue and exchange of views between the body representative of the employees and/or the employees' representatives and the competent organ of the SE, at a time, in a manner and with a content which allows the employees' representatives, on the basis of information provided, to express an opinion on measures envisaged by the competent organ which may be taken into account in the decision-making process within the SE';

'Participation' means the influence of the body representative of the employees and/or the employees' representatives in the affairs of a company by way of:

– the right to elect or appoint some of the members of the company's supervisory or administrative organ; or
– the right to recommend and/or oppose the appointment of some or all of the members of the company's supervisory or administrative organ.

2380. The EWC directive and the general information and consultation directive contain both the notions of information and consultation, which read as follows:

Information means 'transmission of details by the employer to the employees' representatives of data in order to enable them to acquaint themselves with the subject matter and to examine it while

Consultation means 'the exchange of views and establishing of a dialogue between the employees' representatives and the employer' (general directive) and 'and central management or any other more appropriate level of management' (EWC directive).

Part II, Ch. 2, Workers' Participation   2381–2382

The notion 'employees' representatives' means in the various instruments, the employees' representatives provided for by national law and/or practice; the same goes for the notion employees.

The special negotiating body is an institution, which operates both within the framework of the SE and the EWC.

By and large, the various notions used are more or less 'coherent', in the sense that they have the same meaning or point in the same direction, namely that the 'involvement' exercise by the employees does not affect managerial prerogative. It is however indicated that exactly identical notions should be used in the various European instruments regarding the involvement of employees.

Similarly, the various European instruments provide for rules concerning confidential information, protection of employee representatives, protection of rights and links with other directives, which provide information and consultation rights for employees, like the directives on collective dismissals and the acquired rights in case of transfer of an enterprise do. It should however be noted that the collective redundancy's directive provides for 'consultations ... with a view of reaching agreement' (Article 2(1)), notion, which is also retained in the amended proposal for a general information and consultation directive (Article 4(4)).

G. Spirit of Cooperation

2381. At the same the three aforementioned EU directives leave enough flexible room for Member States, when implementing the directives, to take account of the requisites and characteristics of their own systems. In doing so, the directives rightfully respect the proper fabric of each national industrial relations system of the various EU Member States.

It is, however, remarkable that the three European involvement instruments retain the spirit of cooperation, which should animate the relations between the involved parties – employers and employees. Indeed, quite a number of national systems do not endorse that notion, e.g. the French and the Italian ones. One wonders what meaning and significance 'the spirit of cooperation' has within those national systems.

H. When?

2382. One point where the various European involvement instruments lack clarity is regarding the timing of the information and consultation exercises. When should information be given and consultation be held? The different directives are extremely vague on this point. We read 'at an appropriate time' in the general information and consultation directive (Article 4(4)); and 'as soon as possible' in the EWC directive (Annex 3), while there is no answer to the question of timing in the SE directive. This vagueness undoubtedly reflects the complexity of management decision-making, especially when decision are taken at higher levels, e.g. in a multinational enterprise. But at the same time it gives an indication that the real purpose of the 'involvement' of the employees is not so much to have an impact on strategic management decisions but a.o. to help alleviate the social consequences of managerial decisions, and, as said above get the support of employees, also in view of their employability.

I. Summarising

2383. Summarising, one can say that there is a great degree of coherence in the various European instruments, which, however, still could be improved upon, especially as the identical meaning of the various notions is concerned.

Moreover, the various expressions concerning the timing of the information and consultation are unsatisfactory. It would be preferable to use the language of the OECD in its *Guidelines for Multinational Enterprises* (2011). The OECD in its employment and industrial relations guideline 6 provides that 'reasonable notice of such changes should be given ... In the light of the specific circumstances of each case, it would be appropriate if management were to give such notice prior to the final decision to be taken.' Put otherwise, this means that if management cannot provide prior information it should explain the employees why this is the case.

A last question relates to the SE. It has taken more than 30 years for the statute of SE to be adopted for reason of divergences between the various Member States concerning the way and degree of involvement of workers. The SE directive, however, resembles in great lines the provisions foreseen in the EWC directive. Would it not have been easier to say that all SEs which employ 1,000 employees in the EU, should have a European works council? But may be this was too easy.

§5. THE EUROPEAN COOPERATIVE SOCIETY

I. In General

A. Background and Purpose

2384. The completion of the internal market and the improvement it brings about in the economic and social situation throughout the Union mean not only that barriers to trade should be removed, but also that the structures of production should be adapted to the Union dimension. For that purpose it is essential that companies of all types, the business of which is not limited to satisfying purely local needs, should be able to plan and carry out the reorganisation of their business on a Union scale. However, the legal framework within which business is carried on in the Union is still based largely on national laws. This situation forms a considerable obstacle to the creation of groups of companies from different Member States, which is why the Council adopted Regulation (EEC) No. 2137/85 on the European Economic Interest Grouping and Regulation (EC) No. 2157/2001 establishing the legal form of the European Company. These two instruments are not, however, suited to the specific features of cooperatives (independent associations of individuals voluntarily associated to satisfy their common economic, social and cultural aspirations and needs by means of a collectively-owned enterprise in which power

Part II, Ch. 2, Workers' Participation

is exerted democratically by the members). Anxious to ensure equal terms of competition and to contribute to its economic development, the Union therefore decided to provide cooperatives, which are a form of organisation generally recognised in all Member States, with adequate legal instruments capable of facilitating the development of their cross-border activities, through collaboration, cooperation or mergers between existing cooperatives in the different Member States, or through the creation of new cooperative enterprises at European level.

2385. With the adoption of Council Regulation on the Statute for a European Cooperative Society (SCE),[964] a genuine single SCE entity has been established. These new texts do in effect permit the creation of a cooperative by persons residing in different Member States or by legal entities established in different Member States. With a minimum capital requirement of 30,000 euros, these new SCEs can operate throughout the internal market with a single legal identity, set of rules and structure. They can expand and restructure their cross-border operations without the costly and time-consuming exercise of setting up of a network of subsidiaries. Cooperatives from several different countries can also now merge as SCEs. Finally, a national cooperative operating in a different Member State from the one in which it has its registered office can be converted into a European cooperative without first having to be wound up.

In order to promote the social objectives of the Union, special provisions have also been adopted by means of a Directive, particularly as regards employee involvement in the SCE, aimed at ensuring that the establishment of an SCE does not entail the disappearance or reduction of practices of employee involvement existing within the entities participating in its establishment.

B. *Form of the SCE*

2386. The SCE is defined as a body with legal personality for which the capital subscribed by its members is divided into shares. Its registered office, which is to be specified in its rules, must be within the Union and must be in the same place as its central administration. The SCE is to have legal personality from the day of its registration in the State in which it has its registered office.

An SCE shall have as its principal object the satisfaction of its members' needs and/or the development of their economic and social activities, in particular through the conclusion of agreements with them to supply goods or services or to execute work of the kind that the SCE carries out or commissions.

C. *Formation of the SCE*

2387. Subject to this Regulation, the formation of an SCE is governed by the law applicable to cooperatives in the State in which it has its registered office. An SCE may be formed as follows:

---

964. Council Regulation (EC) No. 1435/2003 of 22 July 2003 on the Statute for a European Cooperative Society (SCE); Council Directive 2003/72/EC of 22 July 2003 supplementing the Statute for a European Cooperative Society with regard to the involvement of employees (O.J., 18 August 2003).

- by five or more natural persons resident in at least two Member States,
- by five or more natural persons and companies and firms within the meaning of the second paragraph of Article 54 TFEU and other legal bodies governed by public or private law, formed under the law of a Member State, resident in, or governed by the law of, at least two different Member States,
- by companies and firms within the meaning of the second paragraph of Article 54 TFEU and other legal bodies governed by public or private law formed under the law of a Member State which are resident in, or governed by the law of, at least two different Member States,
- by a merger between cooperatives formed under the law of a Member State with registered offices and head offices within the Union, provided that at least two of them are governed by the law of different Member States,
- by conversion of a cooperative formed under the law of a Member State, which has its registered office and head office within the Union if for at least two years it has had an establishment or subsidiary governed by the law of another Member State.

A Member State may provide that a legal body the head office of which is not in the Union may participate in the formation of an SCE provided that legal body is formed under the law of a Member State, has its registered office in that Member State and has a real and continuous link with a Member State's economy.

D. Structure of the SCE

2388. The Regulation provides for the SCE structure to be made up of a general meeting on the one hand, and for either a management board with a supervisory board monitoring its activities (the two-tier system), or for an administrative board (the one-tier system), depending on which option is chosen in the SCE statutes.

The general meeting must be held at least once a year, not later than six months after the end of the financial year.

In the two-tier system, a management board is to manage the SCE. The member or members of the management board have power to represent the SCE in dealings with third parties and in legal proceedings. They are to be appointed and removed by the supervisory board. The same person may not serve on both boards of the same SCE at the same time. The supervisory board may, however, nominate one of its members to occupy a vacancy through holiday absence on the management board. During this period, the member concerned then ceases to exercise his/her functions on the supervisory board.

In the one-tier system, a single administrative board is to manage the SCE. The member or members of the administrative board have power to represent the SCE in dealings with third parties and in legal proceedings. The administrative board may delegate powers of management, but not other powers, to one or more of its members.

The statutes of the SCE shall list the categories of transactions requiring:

- under the two-tier system, authorisation from the supervisory organ or the general meeting to the management organ,

Part II, Ch. 2, Workers' Participation

– under the one-tier system, an express decision adopted by the administrative organ or authorisation from the general meeting.

II. The Involvement of Employees

A. *In General*

2389. The directive governs the involvement of employees in the affairs of SCEs. It aligns the laws, regulations and administrative provisions in force in the Member States so as to cater for the involvement of employees in the running of the SCE. The arrangements for the involvement of employees shall be established in every SCE in accordance with the negotiating procedure or in accordance with the standard rules on the involvement of employees set by this directive.

B. *Negotiating Procedure Applicable to SCEs Established by at Least Two Legal Entities or by Transformation*

1. The Special Negotiating Body

2390. Where the management or administrative organs of participating legal entities draw up a plan for the establishment of an SCE, they shall as soon as possible take the necessary steps to start negotiations with the representatives of the legal entities' employees on arrangements for the involvement of employees in the SCE. For this purpose, a special negotiating body representative of the employees of the participating legal entities and concerned subsidiaries or establishments shall be created in accordance with the following provisions:

– members are elected or appointed in proportion to the number of employees employed in each Member State by the participating legal entities and concerned subsidiaries or establishments, by allocating in respect of a Member State one seat per each portion of employees employed in that Member State which equals ten per cent, or a fraction thereof, of the number of employees employed in all the Member States taken together;
– in the case of an SCE formed by way of merger, there are such further additional members from each Member State as may be necessary in order to ensure that the special negotiating body includes at least one member representing each participating cooperative which is registered and has employees in that Member State and which it is proposed will cease to exist as a separate legal entity following the registration of the SCE;
– Member States shall determine the method to be used for the election and appointment of the members of the special negotiating body.

2391. The special negotiating body and the competent organs of the participating legal entities shall determine, by written agreement, arrangements for the involvement of employees within the SCE. To this end, the competent organs of the participating legal entities shall inform the special negotiating body of the plan and the actual process of establishing the SCE, up to its registration.

The special negotiating body shall take decisions by an absolute majority of its members, provided that such a majority also represents an absolute majority of the employees. Each member shall have one vote. However, should the result of the negotiations lead to a reduction of participation rights, the majority required for a decision to approve such an agreement shall be the votes of two thirds of the members of the special negotiating body representing at least two thirds of the employees, including the votes of members representing employees employed in at least two Member States:

– in the case of an SCE to be established by way of merger, if participation covers at least 25 per cent of the overall number of employees of the participating cooperatives, or
– in the case of an SCE to be established by any other way, if participation covers at least 50 per cent of the overall number of employees of the participating legal entities.

2392. With the exception of an SCE established by way of transformation, the special negotiating body may decide by a majority of the votes of two thirds of the members representing at least two thirds of the employees not to open negotiations or to terminate them. In this case, these votes should represent employees employed in at least two Member States.

The special negotiating body shall be reconvened at the written request of at least ten per cent of the employees of the SCE, its subsidiaries and establishments, or their representatives, at the earliest two years after the above-mentioned decision, unless the parties agree to negotiations being reopened sooner.

2. The Agreement on Arrangements for the Involvement of Employees

2393. This agreement shall be negotiated in a spirit of cooperation between the competent organs of the participating legal entities and the special negotiating body, in accordance with the legislation of the Member State in which the registered office of the SCE is to be situated. Negotiations shall commence as soon as the special negotiating body is established and may continue for six months thereafter. The parties may decide, by joint agreement, to extend these negotiations up to a total of one year from the establishment of the special negotiating body.

This agreement specifies:

– the scope of the agreement itself;
– the composition, number of members and allocation of seats on the representative body which will be the discussion partner of the competent organ of the SCE in connection with arrangements for the information and consultation of the employees of the SCE and its subsidiaries and establishments;

Part II, Ch. 2, Workers' Participation

- the functions and the procedure for the information and consultation of the representative body;
- the frequency of meetings of the representative body;
- the financial and material resources to be allocated to the representative body;
- the arrangements for implementing information and consultation procedures if, during negotiations, the parties decide to establish one or more of those procedures instead of establishing a representative body;
- the procedures to be followed so that employees can elect, appoint, recommend or oppose their members and their rights if, during negotiations, the parties decide to establish arrangements for participation, the substance of those arrangements including the number of members in the SCE's administrative or supervisory body which the employees will be entitled to elect, appoint, recommend or oppose;
- the date of entry into force of the agreement and its duration, cases where the agreement should be renegotiated and the procedure for its renegotiation, including, where appropriate, in the event of structural changes in the SCE and its subsidiaries and establishments which occur after the creation of the SCE.

3. Standard Rules

2394. The Member States shall lay down standard rules on employee involvement which must satisfy the provisions set out in the Annex to the Directive. As laid down by the legislation of the Member State in which the SCE has its registered office, these standard rules shall apply from the date of the registration of the SCE where either:

- the parties so agree, or
- no agreement has been concluded between the competent organs of the participating legal entities and the special negotiating body within the deadline given and
- the competent organ of each of the participating legal entities decides to accept the application of the standard rules in relation to the SCE and so to continue with its registration of the SCE, and
- the special negotiating body has not taken the decision not to open negotiations or to terminate negotiations already opened with the competent organs of the participating legal entities.

2395. Moreover, it should be stressed that the standard rules set by the national legislation of the Member State of registration shall only apply in the specific cases listed by the Directive which differ depending on the way in which the SCE was formed (conversion, merger, etc.).

§6. TAKE-OVER BIDS AND CROSS-BORDER MERGERS

I. Take-over Bids

2396. The Directive 2004/25/EC on takeover bids[965] contains also provisions on involvement of employees, namely information and consultation. Reference is made to other directives providing for involvement of employees, in particular by way of information and consultation.

2397.

II. Definitions

(1) For the purposes of this Directive:
 (a) 'takeover bid' or 'bid' shall mean a public offer (other than by the offeree company itself) made to the holders of the securities of a company to acquire all or some of those securities, whether mandatory or voluntary, which follows or has as its objective the acquisition of control of the offeree company in accordance with national law;
 (b) 'offeree company' shall mean a company, the securities of which are the subject of a bid;
 (c) 'offeror' shall mean any natural or legal person governed by public or private law making a bid;
 (d) 'persons acting in concert' shall mean natural or legal persons who cooperate with the offeror or the offeree company on the basis of an agreement, either express or tacit, either oral or written, aimed either at acquiring control of the offeree company or at frustrating the successful outcome of a bid;
 (e) 'securities' shall mean transferable securities carrying voting rights in a company;
 (f) 'parties to the bid' shall mean the offeror, the members of the offeror's board if the offeror is a company, the offeree company, holders of securities of the offeree company and the members of the board of the offeree company, and persons acting in concert with such parties;
 (g) 'multiple-vote securities' shall mean securities included in a distinct and separate class and carrying more than one vote each (Article 2).

2398. The disclosure of information to and the consultation of representatives of the employees of the offeror and the offeree company should be governed by the relevant national provisions, in particular those adopted pursuant to

– Council Directive 94/45/EC of 22 September 1994 on the establishment of a European Works Council or a procedure in Community-scale undertakings and

---

965. The Directive 2004/25/EC of the European Parliament and of the Council of 21 April 2004 on takeover bids, O.J. L 142, 30 April 2004.

Part II, Ch. 2, Workers' Participation   2399–2400

Community-scale groups of undertakings for the purposes of informing and consulting employees (now Directive 2009/28 EC of 6May2009),
- Council Directive 98/59/EC of 20 July 1998 on the approximation of the laws of the Member States relating to collective redundancies,
- Council Directive 2001/86/EC of 8 October 2001 supplementing the statute for a European Company with regard to the involvement of employees and,
- Directive 2002/14/EC of 11 March 2002 establishing a general framework for informing and consulting employees in the European Community. The employees of the companies concerned, or their representatives, should nevertheless be given an opportunity to state their views on the foreseeable effects of the bid on employment. Without prejudice to the rules of Directive 2003/6/EC of 28 January 2003 on insider dealing and market manipulation (market abuse).

Member States may always apply or introduce national provisions concerning the disclosure of information to and the consultation of representatives of the employees of the offer or before an offer is launched.

2399. Article 14 on Information for and consultation of employees' representatives consequently provides:

> This Directive shall be without prejudice to the rules relating to information and to consultation of representatives of and, if Member States so provide, co-determination with the employees of the offeror and the offeree company governed by the relevant national provisions, and in particular those adopted pursuant to Directives 94/45/EC (now Directive 2009/28 EC), 98/59/EC, 2001/86/EC and 2002/14/EC.

III. Cross-border Mergers

2400. Directive 2005/56/EC of the European Parliament and of the Council on cross-border mergers of limited liability companies[966] also contains the right for involvement of employees. The directive was adopted on 26 October 2006.[967]
States the considerans:

> Employees' rights other than rights of participation should remain subject to the national provisions referred to in:
>
> - Council Directive 98/59/EC of 20 July 1998 on collective redundancies,
> - Council Directive 2001/23/EC of 12 March 2001 on the safeguarding of employees' rights in the event of transfers of undertakings, businesses or parts of undertakings or businesses,

---

966. 27 July 2005, EP & the Council, *PE-CONS 3632/05 GV/MO/lu.*
967. O.J., 25 November 2005, L 310.

- Directive 2002/14/EC of the European Parliament and of the Council of 11 March 2002 establishing a general framework for informing and consulting employees in the European Community, and
- Council Directive 94/45/EC of 22 September 1994 on the establishment of a European Works Council or a procedure in Community-scale undertakings and Community-scale groups of undertakings for the purposes of informing and consulting employees.

If employees have participation rights in one of the merging companies under the circumstances set out in this Directive and if the national law of the Member State in which the company resulting from the cross-border merger has its registered office does not provide for the same level of participation as operated in the relevant merging companies, including in committees of the supervisory board that have decision-making powers, or does not provide for the same entitlement to exercise rights for employees of establishments resulting from the cross-border merger, the participation of employees in the company resulting from the cross-border merger and their involvement in the definition of such rights are to be regulated.

2401. Definitions For the purposes of this Directive:

(1) 'limited liability company', hereinafter referred to as 'company', means:

(a) a company as referred to in Article 1 of Directive 68/151/EEC, or
(b) a company with share capital and having legal personality, possessing separate assets which alone serve to cover its debts and subject under the national law governing it to conditions concerning guarantees such as are provided for by Directive 68/151/EEC for the protection of the interests of members and others; (First Council Directive 68/ 151/EEC of 9 March 1968 on coordination of safeguards which, for the protection of the interests of members and others, are required by Member States of companies within the meaning of the second paragraph of Article 58 of the Treaty, with a view to making such safeguards equivalent throughout the Community (O.J. L 65, 14 March 1968). Directive as last amended by the 2003 Act of Accession (Article 2).

2402. To that end, the principles and procedures provided for in

- Council Regulation (EC) No. 2157/2001 of 8 October 2001 on the Statute for a European company (SE) and in
- Council Directive 2001/86/EC of 8 October 2001 supplementing the Statute for a European company with regard to the involvement of employees

are to be taken as a basis, subject, however, to modifications that are deemed necessary because the resulting company will be subject to the national laws of the Member State where it has its registered office. A prompt start to negotiations under Article 16 of this Directive with a view to not unnecessarily delaying mergers may be ensured by Member States in accordance with Article 3(2)(b) of Directive 2001/86/EC.

For the purpose of determining the level of employee participation operated in the relevant merging companies, account should also be taken of the proportion of employee representatives amongst the members of the management group, which covers the profit units of the companies, subject to employee participation'.

2403. Article 16 provides consequently as follows:

Employee Participation

(1) ... the company resulting from the cross-border merger shall be subject to the rules in force concerning employee participation, if any, in the Member State where it has its registered office.

(2) However, the rules in force concerning employee participation, if any, in the Member State where the company resulting from the cross-border merger has its registered office shall not apply, where at least one of the merging companies has, in the six months before the publication of the draft terms of the cross-border merger as referred to in Article 6, an average number of employees that exceeds 500 and is operating under an employee participation system within the meaning of Article 2(k) of Directive 2001/86/EC,[968] or where the national law applicable to the company resulting from the cross-border merger does not

   (a) provide for at least the same level of employee participation as operated in the relevant merging companies, measured by reference to the proportion of employee representatives amongst the members of the administrative or supervisory organ or their committees or of the management group which covers the profit units of the company, subject to employee representation, or

   (b) provide for employees of establishments of the company resulting from the cross-border merger that are situated in other Member States the same entitlement to exercise participation rights as is enjoyed by those employees employed in the Member State where the company resulting from the cross-border merger has its registered office.

(3) In the cases referred to in paragraph 2, the participation of employees in the company resulting from the cross-border merger and their involvement in the definition of such rights shall be regulated by the Member States, *mutatis mutandis* and subject to paragraphs 4 to 7 below, in accordance with the principles and procedures laid down in Article 12(2), (3) and (4) of Regulation (EC) No. 2157/2001 and the following provisions of Directive 2001/86/EC:

   (a) Article 3(1), (2) and (3), (4) first subparagraph, first indent, and second subparagraph, (5) and (7);

   (b) Article 4(1), (2), points (a), (g) and (h), and (3);

---

968. Of 8 October 2001 supplementing the statute for a European Company with regard to the involvement of employees.

(c) Article 5;
(d) Article 6;
(e) Article 7(1), (2) first subparagraph, point (b), and second subparagraph, and (3).
(e) However, for the purposes of this Directive, the percentages required by Article 7(2), first subparagraph, point (b) of Directive 2001/86/EC for the application of the standard rules contained in Part 3 of the Annex to that Directive shall be raised from 25 per cent to 33G;
(f) Articles 8, 10 and 12;
(g) Article 13(4);
(h) Part 3 of the Annex, point (b).
(4) When regulating the principles and procedures referred to in paragraph 3, Member States:
  (a) shall confer on the relevant organs of the merging companies the right to choose without any prior negotiation to be directly subject to the standard rules for participation referred to in paragraph 3(h), as laid down by the legislation of the Member State in which the company resulting from the cross-border merger is to have its registered office, and to abide by those rules from the date of registration;
  (b) shall confer on the special negotiating body the right to decide, by a majority of two thirds of its members representing at least two thirds of the employees, including the votes of members representing employees in at least two different Member States, not to open negotiations or to terminate negotiations already opened and to rely on the rules on participation in force in the Member State where the registered office of the company resulting from the cross-border merger will be situated;
  (c) may, in the case where, following prior negotiations, standard rules for participation apply and notwithstanding these rules, determine to limit the proportion of employee representatives in the administrative organ of the company resulting from the cross-border merger. However, if in one of the merging companies employee representatives constituted at least one third of the administrative or supervisory board, the limitation may never result in a lower proportion of employee representatives in the administrative organ than one third.
(5) The extension of participation rights to employees of the company resulting from the cross-border merger employed in other Member States, referred to in paragraph 2(b), shall not entail any obligation for Member States which choose to do so to take those employees into account when calculating the size of workforce thresholds giving rise to participation rights under national law.
(6) When at least one of the merging companies is operating under an employee participation system and the company resulting from the cross-border merger is to be governed by such a system in accordance with the rules referred to in paragraph 2, that company shall be obliged to take a legal form allowing for the exercise of participation rights.

(7) When the company resulting from the cross-border merger is operating under an employee participation system, that company shall be obliged to take measures to ensure that employees' participation rights are protected in the event of subsequent domestic mergers for a period of three years after the cross-border merger has taken effect, by applying mutatis mutandis the rules laid down in this Article.

§7. Mergers of Public Limited Liability Companies

2404. Directive 2011/35/EU[969] of 5 April 2011 concerning mergers of public limited liability companies sets rules for merger by acquisition, merger by formation of a new company, and other operations treated as mergers. The main objective of the directive is that the shareholders of merging companies be kept adequately informed.

According to Article 12 of the Directive, 'protection of the rights of the employees of each of the merging companies shall be regulated in accordance with Directive 2001/23/EC'.

2405. The protection of employees' rights in the event of transfers of undertakings, businesses or parts of undertakings or businesses is at present regulated by Council Directive 2001/23/EC of 12 March 2001 on the approximation of the laws of the Member States relating to the safeguarding of employees' rights in the event of transfers of undertakings, businesses or parts of undertakings or businesses.[970]

---

969. O.J., L 110/6, 29 April 2011.
970. See Part I, Chapter 10, § 2.

Epilogue: In Search of a European Social Model (ESM): a Dream?

The Modernisation of European Labour Law

2406. Europeans boast about a European social model (ESM), which would be superior to e.g. the US social model. According to the European Parliament,[971]

> the European social model is first and foremost a question of values. Whatever European social system we examine we find the common values of equality and solidarity and redistribution as fundamentals, with universal, free or cheap access to education and health care, and a variety of other public services as the right of a citizen and as essential to creating the basis for a successful modern economy and a fair society. It is in this respect that our European model differs from the US model for instance.
>
> Social policies (including social protection, health, education and care services) are highly developed in the EU, reflecting a strong attachment to social cohesion.
>
> Academics distinguish four different models (Nordic, Anglo-Saxon, continental, Mediterranean) with differences (in level of protection, space for individual initiatives) but also having common features.
>
> All 28 Member States share the same values and the same objective of combining economic performance, competitiveness with social justice. They have different instruments to reach the same goals. These national models are the result of long and complex historical processes.

Individualism and profit-seeking seemingly dominate the US model. An ESM seems to be taken for granted. What do we mean when we claim the existence of an ESM? What is 'the' ESM? Is there one model or are there more models? Is the ESM a dream, a wish or a reality or both?

An ESM presupposes three elements:

– a model;
– social;
– European.

---

971. Committee on Employment and Social Affairs, Rapporteur JoséAlbino Silva Peneda, 'Report on a European Social Model for the future', (2005/2248(INI), 13 July 2006).

Let us have a look at these three elements and see whether Europe qualifies to claim an ESM.

Model

2407. A model is a way of doing things, of organising, of solving a given problem. In order to have a model, you need:

- a vision: about what you want, the values, goals and objectives you want to realise;
- competence: the power to make the necessary decisions, so you can organise, solve problems, lay down rules, legislation, create institutions, control the outcome, judge it and the like. You need material power (*ratione materiae*) as well as formal power (the ability to reach decisions);
- actors: those that will implement the vision, implementing the power which is available.

Social

2408. What do we mean by 'social'? Do we give 'social' a broad or a narrow interpretation? Personally, I favour a rather broad interpretation. In a material sense, social would include the relations involving work, employment and thus embrace employers, employees, and civil servants, voluntary work included. Social means self-evidently also social security in the broadest sense, also for those who do not work; housing, education ... as laid down by the formulation of fundamental social rights as were adopted in Nice (December 2000) by the European Top.

Social implies, self-evidently, also a democratic Europe. Social in the formal sense refers to the actors, the state, but especially to the social partners and possibly NGOs, as well as employers, employees, works councils, shop stewards, hygiene committees and the like.
Europe

2409. Europe, as an element, relates to its geographical dimension and as a level of decision-making in relation to other levels. Do we mean the EU, the EEA, the Council of Europe or an even wider Europe? Do we also mean an ESM that would be common to various Member States or common to the regions in e.g. the EU?

Personally, I would prefer the EU, a European level in the first place and, secondly, the level of the Member States.

Summarising, the question is whether the EU has a vision, competence and power as well as involvement of social actors of such a nature that one can speak of a – or the – or more European social models?

Vision

2410. There are certainly clear European social visions, ambitions and goals. They are *inter alia* laid down in Article 153 TFEU, where they read as follows:

Epilogue

- promotion of employment;
- improved living and working conditions;
- harmonisation while improvement is being maintained;
- proper social protection;
- dialogue between management and labour;
- the development of human resources;
- with a view to lasting employment and the combating of social exclusion.

This sounds great: the social sky seems the limit.

There are also fundamental social rights formulated in the Treaty like equality and free movement of labour. These rights are also promulgated in the Community Charter of Fundamental Social Rights of Workers (1989) and in the Charter of Fundamental Rights of the European Union (2007).

These Charters are, however, only political declarations, although some of the rights they contain may be legally binding, according to Article 6 of the TEU, be it only vertical (to be respected by the European institutions and the Member States, when drafting or implementing legislation) and not horizontal between e.g. employers and employees.

Moreover, the 'social vision' comes only second as far as objectives of the EU are concerned. Legally and politically, the EMU with its goal of non-inflationary growth comes first. First comes also, *de facto*, in the framework of the global economy, the practice of shareholders' value, according to which the interests of shareholders are the only ones companies have to pursue. Shareholders' value means that companies constantly have to rationalise, right size, get labour costs down ... because if not, the shares will go down or companies will be taken over. Here 'huge pension funds', which invest worldwide, shopping for the best deal, play a very important role.

So, the social vision of Europe is at best second rate, as it is in the grip of the EMU and shareholders' value.

Competence

2411. Does the EU have sufficient competence to develop a fully-fledged European social policy? In answering this question, one needs to recall that the EU only has the competences which are transferred by the Member States to the EU and that these competences have to be exercised in the way indicated by the Treaty.

On this point, the ESM is extremely weak. Indeed, social 'core' issues are excluded from the EU competence, namely:

- pay, the right of association, the right to strike and the right to impose lock-outs (Article 153(5) TFEU).
- For other important matters, unanimity in the Council is needed, namely:
- social security and social protection of workers;
- job security;
- representation and collective defence of interests, including co-determination (Article 153(2) TFEU).

2412. Unanimity between 28 Member States, is almost impossible. Moreover, requirements for unanimity have been fortified in Nice at the request of the British Prime Minister in a move to quieten down criticism from the Eurosceptics in the UK.

Even more, qualified majority voting has also been made more difficult to achieve. There is no doubt that 'the absurdly complex voting system enshrined in the Treaty of Nice threatens democracy, efficiency and enlargement'.[972] On top of weighted votes, two more requirements were added in Nice for a positive decision: a simple majority of Member States and at least 62 per cent of the EU population. The weighted votes are the worst cause of eventual decision-making paralysis. Nice gives the bigger Member States more votes to compensate for the accession of many small states. The qualified threshold rises to 74 per cent of the votes. The 12 new states can form a blocking minority and so can three bigger states. After joining the European Union, Croatia will have 7 votes in the Council, out of a total of 352. At least 260 votes will be required for legislation to be adopted by qualified majority.

2413. Needless to say that the ESM, as far as competence is concerned, is almost non-existent. The catastrophe is that this will be a permanent feature as the Treaty can only be changed by way of unanimity, which will, as far as social policies are concerned, prove to be impossible.

Obviously, there are other ways of convergence in the social field, like the so-called 'enhanced co-ordination strategy', as shown in the case of the employment guidelines, which lead to national action plans and to peer pressure for Member States to conform to the guidelines. This strategy, which is important, could be used in other fields.

But this does not avoid the EU being incompetent to enact binding measures on core issues such as a European minimum wage, to declare a collective wage agreement at EU level binding; on core issues such as social security, job security, collective bargaining and others, for which unanimity is required, binding European measures are absolutely unlikely.

The conclusion is clear: the EU lacks the essential competences which are needed to organise and establish a full-fledged ESM. Even worse is that the political will is lacking to socially integrate further and that the more countries become members of the EU, the more difficult it will be to muster such a political will.

The Actors

2414. The main actors engaged in elaborating social policies are self-evidently the institutions of the EU and the EU social partners. At EU level there is increased reliance on the advice and on the consultation with the social partners in various tripartite dealings. The social partners are also *de facto* involved.

Central in this stands the European social dialogue, at intersectoral and sectoral levels, which leads to agreements, eventually rendered binding by way of European directive, or to (voluntary) guidelines, codes of conduct and the like.

---

972. Q. Peel, 'Europe's guaranteed gridlock', *Financial Times*, 9 July 2001.

Epilogue

This social dialogue constitutes an essential feature in the establishment of an ESM.

But again, there are fundamental flaws.

2415. First, here also 'European competence' is lacking. The social partners can, self-evidently, have a dialogue and conclude agreements at whatever level and on whatever issue they want. But one has to say that there is a lot of 'contact' between the social partners, but not so much 'contract'. A fact is that there are few agreements at European level. Moreover, agreements can only get an official sanction and be made legally binding according to the competence rules of the EU, where qualified majority or unanimity in the Council is required. Agreements on pay cannot be rendered legally binding, as already indicated above.

As important is the fact that there are marked weaknesses in the social dialogue process. First, the power relationship between the social partners at European level is almost non-existent. Indeed, the trade unions have no 'market power' at EU level. They only have political clout in the sense that, if no agreement is reached, the European Commission may initiate legislation. So, one talks about Damocles bargaining. But even this power seems to be a thing of the past as the European Commission has indicated that if the partners cannot agree, that may be the end.

2416. Moreover, the trade unions, as well as the EU employers' associations, are becoming more and more internally divided about the merits of bargaining at European level. Scandinavian, German and other unions, to give one example, which are rather strong at national level, are less and less willing to pass power and means to the ETUC and do their own bargaining at national level. BUSINESSEUROPE wants to conclude voluntary agreements, as in the case of telework and work-related stress.

The fact is that the social partners have no grip on the globalised economy: they flail in empty air.

These factors, especially the new information economy, globalisation and the changing nature of the workforce, have as a consequence that the social partners lose members, representativeness and in that manner a mandate at European level.[973] The fact is that the majority of workers are not represented at EU level.

To this has to be added that many trade unions show a consistent democratic deficit. Except for the UK, rank and file members do not vote for the leadership of the trade unions. Self-appointed minorities control the trade union organisations, which first think about their own power and only in the second place of the interests of the members. Trade unions should become more democratic institutions.

There is no doubt that the role of the EP has to be fortified, especially in the areas covered by the social dialogue, where agreements are extended by way of a directive.

2417. To this should be added that there remains a problem with the notion of social partners, as the UEAPME case demonstrates. At present only the ETUC, BUSINESSEUROPE and CEEP are considered to be 'the' social partners, which constitute the club of negotiators. This has to be corrected. It is evident that all the national organisations, which are recognised as representative at national level, should be fully involved.

There is also the fact that the collective agreements concluded at European level testify to a doubtful craftsmanship, while there is, as the directives regarding EWCs, the SE and information and consultation amply demonstrate, no real impact on managerial decision-making. In particular, the question of when employees have to be informed in the case of restructuring remains open.

Here again a lot needs to be improved in order to strengthen the social dialogue at EU level. But, as said, the political will is lacking and market forces are not moving in the direction of more employee input. Social partners are involved, but have less and less impact on 'real decision-making'.

2418. Summarising, there is no doubt that the EU has made a major contribution on a number of important social issues like equal treatment, free movement of labour, health and safety, restructuring ... but by and large one cannot say that there is an ESM. The greatest flaws are:
– the lack of competence and the fact that there is – no political will to increase the EU social competences.

The consequence of the lack of an ESM is that there is no European labour law system, but that there are various national systems. Labour law in Europe remains mainly a national affair and this is going to stay so.

These national systems diverge considerably. Of course, there are some common fundamental principles between the Member States like trade union freedom, the right to collective bargaining, equal treatment, no child labour, nor forced labour, but these are universal values, embodied in the ILO standards.

Various national systems can be discerned, corporatist systems vs. shareholders' value systems and the like. It is evident that the British and the German systems, to give one example, are oceans away from each other. Divergence between Member States is even growing.

The overall conclusion is that there is no ESM, either at European or at national level.

For those who believe in and hope for an ESM, the answer is clear: continue to push for more European competence and for more social democracy, involvement of the EP and more binding fundamental social rights.

The road seems long, the path steep and narrow. Miracles are called for. Sometimes dreams come true.

Appendix 1. Community Charter on the Fundamental Social Rights of Workers (1989)

THE HEADS OF STATE OR THE GOVERNMENT OF MEMBER STATES OF THE EUROOPEAN COMMUNITY MEETING AT STRASBOURG ON 9 DECEMBER 1989[974]

WHEREAS under the terms of Article 117 of the EEC Treaty, the Member States have agreed on the need to promote improved living and working conditions for workers so as to make possible their harmonisation while the improvement is being maintained;

WHEREAS following on from the conclusions of the European Councils of Hanover and Rhodes the European Council of Madrid considered that, in the context of the establishment of the single European market, the same importance must be attached to the social aspects as to the economic aspects and whereas, therefore, they must be developed in a balanced manner;

HAVING REGARD to the Resolutions of the European Parliament of 1 March 1989, 14 September 1989 and 22 November 1989, and to the Opinion of the Economic and Social Committee of 22 February 1989;

WHEREAS the completion of the internal market is the most effective means of creating employment and ensuring maximum well-being in the Community; whereas employment development and creation must be given first priority in the completion of the internal market; whereas it is for the Community to take up the challenges of the future with regard to economic competitiveness, taking into account, in particular, regional imbalances;

WHEREAS the social consensus contributes to the strengthening of the competitiveness of undertakings, of the economy as a whole and to the creation of employment; whereas in this respect it is an essential condition for ensuring sustained economic development;

WHEREAS the completion of the internal market must favour the approximation of improvements in living and working conditions, as well as economic and social cohesion within the European Community while avoiding distortions of competition;

WHEREAS the completion of the internal market must offer improvements in the social field for workers of the European Community, especially in terms of freedom of movement, living and working conditions, health and safety at work, social protection, education and training;

WHEREAS in order to ensure equal treatment, it is important to combat every form of discrimination, including discrimination on grounds of sex, colour, race, opinions and beliefs, and whereas, in a spirit of solidarity, it is important to combat social exclusion;

WHEREAS it is for Member States to guarantee that workers from non-member countries and members of their families who are legally resident in a Member State of the European Community are able to enjoy, as regards their living and working conditions, treatment comparable to that enjoyed by workers who are nationals of the Member State concerned;

Appendix 1

WHEREAS inspiration should be drawn from the Conventions of the International Labour Organisation and from the European Social Charter of the Council of Europe;

WHEREAS the Treaty, as amended by the Single European Act, contains provisions laying down the powers of the Community relating *inter alia* to the freedom of movement of workers (Articles 7, 48 to 51), the right of establishment (Articles 52 to 58), the social field under the conditions laid down in Articles 117 to 122 in particular as regards the improvement of health and safety in the working environment (Article 118(a)), the development of the dialogue between management and labour at European level (Article 118(b)), equal pay for men and women for equal work (Article 119) the general principles for implementing a common vocational training policy (Article 128), economic and social cohesion (Article 130(a) to 130(e)) and, more generally, the approximation of legislation (Articles 100, 100(a) and 235); whereas the implementation of the Charter must not entail an extension of the Community's powers as defined by the Treaties;

WHEREAS the aim of the present Charter is on the one hand to consolidate the progress made in the social field, through action by the Member States, the two sides of industry and the Community;

WHEREAS its aim is on the other hand to declare solemnly that the implementation of the Single European Act must take full account of the social dimension of the Community and that it is necessary in this context to ensure at appropriate levels the development of the social rights of workers of the European Community, especially employed workers and self-employed persons;

WHEREAS, in accordance with the conclusions of the Madrid European Council, the respective Community rules, national legislation and collective agreements must be clearly established;

WHEREAS, by virtue of the principle of subsidiarity, responsibility for the initiatives to be taken with regard to the implementation of these social rights lies with the Member States or their constituent parts and, within the limits of its powers, with the European Community; whereas such implementation may take the form of laws, collective agreements or existing practises at the various appropriate levels and whereas it requires in many spheres the active involvement of the two sides of industry;

WHEREAS the solemn proclamation of fundamental social rights at European Community level may not, when implemented, provide grounds for any retrogression compared with the situation currently existing in each Member State,

HAVE ADOPTED THE FOLLOWING DECLARATION CONSTITUTING THE 'COMMUNITY CHARTER OF THE FUNDAMENTAL SOCIAL RIGHTS OF WORKERS':

Appendix 1

Title I. Fundamental Social Rights of Workers

Freedom of movement

1. Every worker of the European Community shall have the right to freedom of movement throughout the territory of the Community, subject to restrictions justified on grounds of public order, public safety or public health.

2. The right to freedom of movement shall enable any worker to engage in any occupation or profession in the Community in accordance with the principles of equal treatment as regards access to employment, working conditions and social protection in the host country.

3. The right of freedom of movement shall also imply:

(i) harmonisation of conditions of residence in all Member States, particularly those concerning family reunification;
(ii) elimination of obstacles arising from the non-recognition of diplomas or equivalent occupational qualifications;
(iii) improvement of the living and working conditions of frontier workers.

Employment and remuneration

4. Every individual shall be free to choose and engage in a occupation according to the regulations governing each occupation.

5. All employment shall be fairly remunerated. To this end, in accordance with arrangements applying in each country:

(i) workers shall be assured of an equitable wage, i.e. a wage sufficient to enable them to have a decent standard of living;
(ii) workers subject to terms of employment other than an open-ended full-time contract shall benefit from an equitable reference wage;
(iii) wages may be withheld, seized or transferred only in accordance with national law; such provisions should entail measures enabling the worker concerned to continue to enjoy the necessary means of subsistence for him or herself and his or her family.

6. Every individual must be able to have access to public placement services free of charge.

Improvement of living and working conditions

7. The completion of the internal market must lead to an improvement in the living and working conditions of workers in the European Community. This pro cess must result from an approximation of these conditions while the improvement is

Appendix 1

being maintained, as regards in particular duration and organisation of working time and forms of employment other than open-ended contracts, such as fixed-term contracts, part-time working, temporary work and seasonal work.

The improvement must cover, where necessary, the development of certain aspects of employment regulations such as procedures for collective redundancies and those regarding bankruptcies.

8. Every worker of the European Community shall have a right to a weekly rest period and to annual paid leave, the duration of which must be progressively harmonised in accordance with national practises.

9. The conditions of employment of every worker of the European Community shall be stipulated in laws, a collective agreement or a contract of employment, according to arrangements applying in each country.

Social protection

According to the arrangements applying in each country:

10. Every worker of the European Community shall have a right to adequate social protection and shall, whatever his status and whatever the size of the under taking in which he is employed, enjoy an adequate level of social security benefits.

Persons who have been unable either to enter or re-enter the labour market and have no means of subsistence must be able to receive sufficient resources and social assistance in keeping with their particular situation.

Freedom of association and collective bargaining

11. Employers and workers of the European Community shall have the right of association in order to constitute professional organisations or trade unions of their choice for the defence of their economic and social interests.

Every employer and every worker shall have the freedom to join or not to join such organisations without any personal or occupational damage being thereby suffered by him.

12. Employers or employers' organisations, on the one hand, and workers' organisations, on the other, shall have the right to negotiate and conclude collective agreements under the conditions laid down by national legislation and practice.

The dialogue between the two sides of industry at European level which must be developed, may, if the parties deem it desirable, result in contractual relations in particular at inter-occupational and sectoral level.

13. The right to resort to collective action in the event of a conflict of interests shall include the right to strike, subject to the obligations arising under national regulations and collective agreements.

Appendix 1

In order to facilitate the settlement of industrial disputes the establishment and utilisation at the appropriate levels of conciliation, mediation and arbitration procedures should be encouraged in accordance with national practice.

14. The internal legal order of the Member States shall determine under which conditions and to what extent the rights provided for in Articles 11 to 13 apply to the armed forces, the police and the civil service.

Vocational training

15. Every worker of the European Community must be able to have access to vocational training and to benefit therefrom throughout his working life. In the conditions governing access to such training there may be no discrimination on grounds of nationality.

The competent public authorities, undertakings or the two sides of industry, each within their own sphere of competence, should set up continuing and permanent training systems enabling every person to undergo retraining more especially through leave for training purposes, to improve his skills or to acquire new skills, particularly in the light of technical developments.

Equal treatment for men and women

16. Equal treatment for men and women must be assured. Equal opportunities for men and women must be developed.

To this end, action should be intensified to ensure the implementation of the principle of equality between men and women as regards in particular access to employment, remuneration, working conditions, social protection, education, vocational training and career development.

Measures should also be developed enabling men and women to reconcile their occupational and family obligations.

Information, consultation and participation for workers

17. Information, consultation and participation for workers must be developed along appropriate lines, taking account of the practises in force in the various Member States.

This shall apply especially in companies or groups of companies having establishments or companies in two or more Member States of the European Community.

18. Such information, consultation and participation must be implemented in due time, particularly in the following cases:

(i) when technological changes which, from the point of view of working conditions and work organisation, have major implications for the workforce, are introduced into undertakings;
(ii) in connection with restructuring operations in undertakings or in cases of mergers having an impact on the employment of workers;

Appendix 1

(iii) in cases of collective redundancy procedures;
(iv) when transfrontier workers in particular are affected by employment policies pursued by the undertaking where they are employed.

Health protection and safety at the workplace

19. Every worker must enjoy satisfactory health and safety conditions in his working environment. Appropriate measures must be taken in order to achieve further harmonisation of conditions in this area while maintaining the improvements made.

These measures shall take account, in particular, of the need for training, information, consultation and balanced participation of workers as regards the risks incurred and the steps taken to eliminate or reduce them.

The provisions regarding implementation of the internal market shall help to ensure such protection.

Protection of children and adolescents

20. Without prejudice to such rules as may be more favourable to young people, in particular those ensuring their preparation for work through vocational training, and subject to derogations limited to certain light work, the minimum employment age must not be lower than the minimum school-leaving age and, in any case, not lower than 15 years.

21. Young people who are in gainful employment must receive equitable remuneration in accordance with national practice.

22. Appropriate measures must be taken to adjust labour regulations applicable to young workers so that their specific development and vocational training and access to employment needs are met.

The duration of work must, in particular, be limited without it being possible to circumvent this limitation through recourse to overtime and night work prohibited in the case of workers of under 18 years of age, save in the case of certain job laid down in national legislation or regulations.

23. Following the end of compulsory education, young people must be entitled to receive initial vocational training of a sufficient duration to enable them to adapt to the requirements of their working life; for young workers, such training should take place during working hours.

Elderly persons

According to the arrangements applying in each country:

24. Every worker of the European Community must, at the time of retirement, be able to enjoy resources affording him or her a decent standard of living.

25. Any person who has reached retirement age but who is not entitled to a pension or who does not have other means of subsistence, must be entitled to sufficient resources and to medical and social assistance specifically suited to his needs.
Disabled persons

26. All disabled persons, whatever the origin and nature of their disablement, must be entitled to additional concrete measures aimed at improving their social and professional integration.

These measures must concern, in particular, according to the capacities of the beneficiaries, vocational training, ergonomics, accessibility, mobility, means of transport and housing.

TITLE II. IMPLEMENTATION OF THE CHARTER

27. It is more particularly the responsibility of the Member States, in accordance with national practices, notably through legislative measures or collective agreements, to guarantee the fundamental social rights in this Charter and to implement the social measures indispensable to the smooth operation of the internal market as part of a strategy of economic and social cohesion.

28. The European Council invites the Commission to submit as soon as possible initiatives which fall within its powers, as provided for in the Treaties, with a view to the adoption of legal instruments for the effective implementation, as and when the internal market is completed, of those rights which come within the Community's area of competence.

29. The Commission shall establish each year, during the last three months, a report on the application of the Charter by the Member States and by the European Community.

30. The report of the Commission shall be forwarded to the European Council, the European Parliament and the Economic and Social Committee.

Appendix 2

Appendix 2. Cooperation Agreement between UNICE and UEAPME of 12 November 1998

Pending legal proceedings introduced by UEAPME concerning the directives implementing framework agreements have however been put to an end according to a Co-operation agreement concluded between UNICE and UEAPME of 12 November 1998. The agreement reads as follows:

1. Purpose

'The purpose of the present Cupertino agreement is to achieve a mutually supportive, constructive relationship between UNICE and UEAPME, characterised by close Cupertino and full respect for the autonomy of the signatory parties, define the modalities of co-operation between UNICE and UEAPME in social dialogue meetings, including negotiations.

2. Mutual recognition

2.1. UEAPME recognises that UNICE is the only European level horizontal organisation representing companies of all sizes, active in all sectors of the economy, and acknowledges that the vast majority of the companies UNICE represents are SMEs.

2.2. UNICE recognises that UEAPME is the principal cross sectoral organisation representing the specific interests of SMEs at EU-1evel that UEAPME has therefore a role to play in the Social Dialogue and can usefully contribute to defending employers interests in negotiations with ETUC by co-operating with UNICE.

3. Principles to ensure good co-operation in the social dialogue and in negotiations

3.1. As leader and spokesbody from the employers side in the social dialogue, UNICE undertakes to consult UEAPME prior to taking public positions on behalf of the employers group in social dialogue and negotiating meetings.

3.2. UEAPME representatives fully participate in preparatory meetings of the employers group and in plenary meetings with ETUC. UNICE takes the fullest possible account of the views expressed by UEAPME during the employers' preparatory meetings.

3.3. The parties to this agreement undertake to act in good faith, use their best endeavours to reach consensus among employers, and to move forward together without delaying the decision making process. If the views of UEAPME and UNICE remain different from each other, they agree to disagree in a way which will

Appendix 2

not block progress in negotiations. All employers' representatives retain their autonomy in the preparatory meetings of the employers and no one has a veto.

3.4. Both parties will fully respect the confidentiality of negotiations and will abstain from any public comments or criticism on differences that may occur in their respective views during the course of a negotiation or on the result of a negotiation.

3.5. In case of breach of the principle of confidentiality as expressed in Articles 3(4) above, the present co-operation agreement can be suspended or terminated after discussions at the level of the Presidents of both organisations.

4. Practical modalities

4.1. Two representatives of UEAPME will participate in meetings of the social dialogue committee and in preparatory meetings of the employers group.

4.2. Two representatives of UTEAPME will be invited to participate in negotiating meetings. These representatives must be nominated in writing and have the full authority to negotiate on behalf of UEAPME. They should be present at all negotiating meetings as well as all preparatory meetings of the employer's team and can be substituted only in case of force majeur.

4.3. One representative of UEAPME will participate in restricted high level meetings of the social dialogue.

5. Final provisions

The present co-operation agreement will enter into force on the date of its signature provided that an and has been put to all pending legal proceedings introduced by UEAPME concerning the directives implementing framework agreements on parental leave and on part-time work concluded by UNICE, CEEP and ETUC. However, the provisions concerning participation in negotiations will not apply to negotiations, which started before entry into force of the present co-operation agreement.

The signatory parties will review this co-operation agreement five years after its entry into force if requested by one of the parties'.

Appendix 3

Appendix 3. Charter of Fundamental Rights of the European Union (12 December 2007)[975] (2007/C 303/01)

The European Parliament, the Council and the Commission solemnly proclaim the following text as the Charter of Fundamental Rights of the European Union.

Preamble

The peoples of Europe, in creating an ever closer union among them, are resolved to share a peaceful future based on common values.

Conscious of its spiritual and moral heritage, the Union is founded on the indivisible, universal values of human dignity, freedom, equality and solidarity; it is based on the principles of democracy and the rule of law. It places the individual at the heart of its activities, by establishing the citizenship of the Union and by creating an area of freedom, security and justice.

The Union contributes to the preservation and to the development of these common values while respecting the diversity of the cultures and traditions of the peoples of Europe as well as the national identities of the Member States and the organisation of their public authorities at national, regional and local levels; it seeks to promote balanced and sustainable development and ensures free movement of persons, services, goods and capital, and the freedom of establishment.

To this end, it is necessary to strengthen the protection of fundamental rights in the light of changes in society, social progress and scientific and technological developments by making those rights more visible in a Charter.

This Charter reaffirms, with due regard for the powers and tasks of the Union and for the principle of subsidiarity, the rights as they result, in particular, from the constitutional traditions and international obligations common to the Member States, the European Convention for the Protection of Human Rights and Fundamental Freedoms, the Social Charters adopted by the Union and by the Council of Europe and the case-law of the Court of Justice of the European Union and of the European Court of Human Rights. In this context the Charter will be interpreted by the courts of the Union and the Member States with due regard to the explanations prepared under the authority of the Praesidium of the Convention which drafted the Charter and updated under the responsibility of the Praesidium of the European Convention.

Enjoyment of these rights entails responsibilities and duties with regard to other persons, to the human community and to future generations.

The Union therefore recognises the rights, freedoms and principles set out hereafter.

Appendix 3

TITLE I. DIGNITY

Article 1. Human dignity

Human dignity is inviolable. It must be respected and protected.

Article 2. Right to life

1. Everyone has the right to life.

2. No one shall be condemned to the death penalty, or executed.

Article 3. Right to the integrity of the person

1. Everyone has the right to respect for his or her physical and mental integrity.

2. In the fields of medicine and biology, the following must be respected in particular:

(a) the free and informed consent of the person concerned, according to the procedures laid down by law;
(b) the prohibition of eugenic practices, in particular those aiming at the selection of persons;
(c) the prohibition on making the human body and its parts as such a source of financial gain;
(d) the prohibition of the reproductive cloning of human beings.

Article 4. Prohibition of torture and inhuman or degrading treatment or punishment

No one shall be subjected to torture or to inhuman or degrading treatment or punishment.

Article 5. Prohibition of slavery and forced labour

1. No one shall be held in slavery or servitude.

2. No one shall be required to perform forced or compulsory labour.

3. Trafficking in human beings is prohibited.

Appendix 3

TITLE II. FREEDOMS

Article 6. Right to liberty and security

Everyone has the right to liberty and security of person.

Article 7. Respect for private and family life

Everyone has the right to respect for his or her private and family life, home and communications.

Article 8. Protection of personal data

1. Everyone has the right to the protection of personal data concerning him or her.

2. Such data must be processed fairly for specified purposes and on the basis of the consent of the person concerned or some other legitimate basis laid down by law. Everyone has the right of access to data which has been collected concerning him or her, and the right to have it rectified.

3. Compliance with these rules shall be subject to control by an independent authority.

Article 9. Right to marry and right to found a family

The right to marry and the right to found a family shall be guaranteed in accordance with the national laws governing the exercise of these rights.

Article 10. Freedom of thought, conscience and religion

1. Everyone has the right to freedom of thought, conscience and religion. This right includes freedom to change religion or belief and freedom, either alone or in community with others and in public or in private, to manifest religion or belief, in worship, teaching, practice and observance.

2. The right to conscientious objection is recognised, in accordance with the national laws governing the exercise of this right.

Article 11. Freedom of expression and information

1. Everyone has the right to freedom of expression. This right shall include freedom to hold opinions and to receive and impart information and ideas without interference by public authority and regardless of frontiers.

2. The freedom and pluralism of the media shall be respected.

Appendix 3

Article 12. Freedom of assembly and of association

1. Everyone has the right to freedom of peaceful assembly and to freedom of association at all levels, in particular in political, trade union and civic matters, which implies the right of everyone to form and to join trade unions for the protection of his or her interests.

2. Political parties at Union level contribute to expressing the political will of the citizens of the Union.

Article 13. Freedom of the arts and sciences

The arts and scientific research shall be free of constraint. Academic freedom shall be respected.

Article 14. Right to education

1. Everyone has the right to education and to have access to vocational and continuing training.

2. This right includes the possibility to receive free compulsory education.

3. The freedom to found educational establishments with due respect for democratic principles and the right of parents to ensure the education and teaching of their children in conformity with their religious, philosophical and pedagogical convictions shall be respected, in accordance with the national laws governing the exercise of such freedom and right.

Article 15. Freedom to choose an occupation and right to engage in work

1. Everyone has the right to engage in work and to pursue a freely chosen or accepted occupation.

2. Every citizen of the Union has the freedom to seek employment, to work, to exercise the right of establishment and to provide services in any Member State.

3. Nationals of third countries who are authorised to work in the territories of the Member States are entitled to working conditions equivalent to those of citizens of the Union.

Article 16. Freedom to conduct a business

The freedom to conduct a business in accordance with Union law and national laws and practices is recognised.

Appendix 3

Article 17. Right to property

1. Everyone has the right to own, use, dispose of and bequeath his or her lawfully acquired possessions. No one may be deprived of his or her possessions, except in the public interest and in the cases and under the conditions provided for by law, subject to fair compensation being paid in good time for their loss. The use of property may be regulated by law in so far as is necessary for the general interest.

2. Intellectual property shall be protected.

Article 18. Right to asylum

The right to asylum shall be guaranteed with due respect for the rules of the Geneva Convention of 28 July 1951 and the Protocol of 31 January 1967 relating to the status of refugees and in accordance with the Treaty on European Union and the Treaty on the Functioning of the European Union (hereinafter referred to as 'the Treaties').

Article 19. Protection in the event of removal, expulsion or extradition

Collective expulsions are prohibited.

No one may be removed, expelled or extradited to a State where there is a serious risk that he or she would be subjected to the death penalty, torture or other inhuman or degrading treatment or punishment.

Title III. Equality

Article 20.   Equality before the law

Everyone is equal before the law.

Article 21. Non-discrimination

1. Any discrimination based on any ground such as sex, race, colour, ethnic or social origin, genetic features, language, religion or belief, political or any other opinion, membership of a national minority, property, birth, disability, age or sexual orientation shall be prohibited.

2. Within the scope of application of the Treaties and without prejudice to any of their specific provisions, any discrimination on grounds of nationality shall be prohibited.

Article 22. Cultural, religious and linguistic diversity

The Union shall respect cultural, religious and linguistic diversity.

Article 23. Equality between women and men

Equality between women and men must be ensured in all areas, including employment, work and pay.

The principle of equality shall not prevent the maintenance or adoption of measures providing for specific advantages in favour of the under-represented sex.

Article 24. The rights of the child

1. Children shall have the right to such protection and care as is necessary for their well-being. They may express their views freely. Such views shall be taken into consideration on matters which concern them in accordance with their age and maturity.

2. In all actions relating to children, whether taken by public authorities or private institutions, the child's best interests must be a primary consideration.

3. Every child shall have the right to maintain on a regular basis a personal relationship and direct contact with both his or her parents, unless that is contrary to his or her interests.

Article 25. The rights of the elderly

The Union recognises and respects the rights of the elderly to lead a life of dignity and independence and to participate in social and cultural life.

Article 26. Integration of persons with disabilities

The Union recognises and respects the right of persons with disabilities to benefit from measures designed to ensure their independence, social and occupational integration and participation in the life of the community.

TITLE IV. SOLIDARITY

Article 27. Workers' right to information and consultation within the undertaking

Workers or their representatives must, at the appropriate levels, be guaranteed information and consultation in good time in the cases and under the conditions provided for by Union law and national laws and practices.

Appendix 3

Article 28. Right of collective bargaining and action

Workers and employers, or their respective organisations, have, in accordance with Union law and national laws and practices, the right to negotiate and conclude collective agreements at the appropriate levels and, in cases of conflicts of interest, to take collective action to defend their interests, including strike action.

Article 29. Right of access to placement services

Everyone has the right of access to a free placement service.

Article 30. Protection in the event of unjustified dismissal

Every worker has the right to protection against unjustified dismissal, in accordance with Union law and national laws and practices.

Article 31. Fair and just working conditions

(1) Every worker has the right to working conditions which respect his or her health, safety and dignity.
(2) Every worker has the right to limitation of maximum working hours, to daily and weekly rest periods and to an annual period of paid leave.

Article 32. Prohibition of child labour and protection of young people at work

The employment of children is prohibited. The minimum age of admission to employment may not be lower than the minimum school-leaving age, without prejudice to such rules as may be more favourable to young people and except for limited derogations.
Young people admitted to work must have working conditions appropriate to their age and be protected against economic exploitation and any work likely to harm their safety, health or physical, mental, moral or social development or to interfere with their education.

Article 33. Family and professional life

1. The family shall enjoy legal, economic and social protection.

2. To reconcile family and professional life, everyone shall have the right to protection from dismissal for a reason connected with maternity and the right to paid maternity leave and to parental leave following the birth or adoption of a child.

Article 34. Social security and social assistance

The Union recognises and respects the entitlement to social security benefits and social services providing protection in cases such as maternity, illness, industrial accidents, dependency or old age, and in the case of loss of employment, in accordance with the rules laid down by Union law and national laws and practices.

Everyone residing and moving legally within the European Union is entitled to social security benefits and social advantages in accordance with Union law and national laws and practices.

In order to combat social exclusion and poverty, the Union recognises and respects the right to social and housing assistance so as to ensure a decent existence for all those who lack sufficient resources, in accordance with the rules laid down by Union law and national laws and practices.

Article 35. Health care

Everyone has the right of access to preventive health care and the right to benefit from medical treatment under the conditions established by national laws and practices. A high level of human health protection shall be ensured in the definition and implementation of all the Union's policies and activities.

Article 36. Access to services of general economic interest

The Union recognises and respects access to services of general economic interest as provided for in national laws and practices, in accordance with the Treaties, in order to promote the social and territorial cohesion of the Union.

Article 37. Environmental protection

A high level of environmental protection and the improvement of the quality of the environment must be integrated into the policies of the Union and ensured in accordance with the principle of sustainable development.

Article 38. Consumer protection

Union policies shall ensure a high level of consumer protection.

TITLE V. CITIZENS' RIGHTS

Article 39. Right to vote and to stand as a candidate at elections to the European Parliament

1. Every citizen of the Union has the right to vote and to stand as a candidate at elections to the European Parliament in the Member State in which he or she resides, under the same conditions as nationals of that State.

2. Members of the European Parliament shall be elected by direct universal suffrage in a free and secret ballot.

Appendix 3

Article 40. Right to vote and to stand as a candidate at municipal elections

Every citizen of the Union has the right to vote and to stand as a candidate at municipal elections in the Member State in which he or she resides under the same conditions as nationals of that State.

Article 41. Right to good administration

 1. Every person has the right to have his or her affairs handled impartially, fairly and within a reasonable time by the institutions, bodies, offices and agencies of the Union.

 2. This right includes:

(a) the right of every person to be heard, before any individual measure which would affect him or her adversely is taken;
(b) the right of every person to have access to his or her file, while respecting the legitimate interests of confidentiality and of professional and business secrecy;
(c) the obligation of the administration to give reasons for its decisions.

3. Every person has the right to have the Union make good any damage caused by its institutions or by its servants in the performance of their duties, in accordance with the general principles common to the laws of the Member States.

 4. Every person may write to the institutions of the Union in one of the languages of the Treaties and must have an answer in the same language.

Article 42. Right of access to documents

Any citizen of the Union, and any natural or legal person residing or having its registered office in a Member State, has a right of access to documents of the institutions, bodies, offices and agencies of the Union, whatever their medium.

Article 43. European Ombudsman

Any citizen of the Union and any natural or legal person residing or having its registered office in a Member State has the right to refer to the European Ombudsman cases of maladministration in the activities of the institutions, bodies, offices or agencies of the Union, with the exception of the Court of Justice of the European Union acting in its judicial role.

Article 44. Right to petition

Any citizen of the Union and any natural or legal person residing or having its registered office in a Member State has the right to petition the European Parliament.

Appendix 3

Article 45. Freedom of movement and of residence

1. Every citizen of the Union has the right to move and reside freely within the territory of the Member States.

2. Freedom of movement and residence may be granted, in accordance with the Treaties, to nationals of third countries legally resident in the territory of a Member State.

Article 46. Diplomatic and consular protection

Every citizen of the Union shall, in the territory of a third country in which the Member State of which he or she is a national is not represented, be entitled to protection by the diplomatic or consular authorities of any Member State, on the same conditions as the nationals of that Member State.

TITLE VI. JUSTICE

Article 47. Right to an effective remedy and to a fair trial

Everyone whose rights and freedoms guaranteed by the law of the Union are violated has the right to an effective remedy before a tribunal in compliance with the conditions laid down in this Article.

Everyone is entitled to a fair and public hearing within a reasonable time by an independent and impartial tribunal previously established by law. Everyone shall have the possibility of being advised, defended and represented.

Legal aid shall be made available to those who lack sufficient resources in so far as such aid is necessary to ensure effective access to justice.

Article 48. Presumption of innocence and right of defence

1. Everyone who has been charged shall be presumed innocent until proved guilty according to law.

2. Respect for the rights of the defence of anyone who has been charged shall be guaranteed.

Article 49. Principles of legality and proportionality of criminal offences and penalties

1. No one shall be held guilty of any criminal offence on account of any act or omission which did not constitute a criminal offence under national law or international law at the time when it was committed. Nor shall a heavier penalty be

Appendix 3

imposed than the one that was applicable at the time the criminal offence was committed. If, subsequent to the commission of a criminal offence, the law provides for a lighter penalty, that penalty shall be applicable.

2. This Article shall not prejudice the trial and punishment of any person for any act or omission which, at the time when it was committed, was criminal according to the general principles recognised by the community of nations.

3. The severity of penalties must not be disproportionate to the criminal offence.

Article 50. Right not to be tried or punished twice in criminal proceedings for the same criminal offence

No one shall be liable to be tried or punished again in criminal proceedings for an offence for which he or she has already been finally acquitted or convicted within the Union in accordance with the law.

TITLE VII. GENERAL PROVISIONS GOVERNING THE INTERPRETATION AND APPLICATION OF THE CHARTER

Article 51. Field of application

1. The provisions of this Charter are addressed to the institutions, bodies, offices and agencies of the Union with due regard for the principle of subsidiarity and to the Member States only when they are implementing Union law. They shall therefore respect the rights, observe the principles and promote the application thereof in accordance with their respective powers and respecting the limits of the powers of the Union as conferred on it in the Treaties.

2. The Charter does not extend the field of application of Union law beyond the powers of the Union or establish any new power or task for the Union, or modify powers and tasks as defined in the Treaties.

Article 52. Scope and interpretation of rights and principles

1. Any limitation on the exercise of the rights and freedoms recognised by this Charter must be provided for by law and respect the essence of those rights and freedoms. Subject to the principle of proportionality, limitations may be made only if they are necessary and genuinely meet objectives of general interest recognised by the Union or the need to protect the rights and freedoms of others.

2. Rights recognised by this Charter for which provision is made in the Treaties shall be exercised under the conditions and within the limits defined by those Treaties.

3. In so far as this Charter contains rights which correspond to rights guaranteed by the Convention for the Protection of Human Rights and Fundamental Freedoms, the meaning and scope of those rights shall be the same as those laid down by the said Convention. This provision shall not prevent Union law providing more extensive protection.

4. In so far as this Charter recognises fundamental rights as they result from the constitutional traditions common to the Member States, those rights shall be interpreted in harmony with those traditions.

5. The provisions of this Charter which contain principles may be implemented by legislative and executive acts taken by institutions, bodies, offices and agencies of the Union, and by acts of Member States when they are implementing Union law, in the exercise of their respective powers. They shall be judicially cognisable only in the interpretation of such acts and in the ruling on their legality.

6. Full account shall be taken of national laws and practices as specified in this Charter.

7. The explanations drawn up as a way of providing guidance in the interpretation of this Charter shall be given due regard by the courts of the Union and of the Member States.

Article 53. Level of protection

Nothing in this Charter shall be interpreted as restricting or adversely affecting human rights and fundamental freedoms as recognised, in their respective fields of application, by Union law and international law and by international agreements to which the Union or all the Member States are party, including the European Convention for the Protection of Human Rights and Fundamental Freedoms, and by the Member States' constitutions.

Article 54. Prohibition of abuse of rights

Nothing in this Charter shall be interpreted as implying any right to engage in any activity or to perform any act aimed at the destruction of any of the rights and freedoms recognised in this Charter or at their limitation to a greater extent than is provided for herein.

The above text adapts the wording of the Charter proclaimed on 7 December 2000, and will replace it as from the date of entry into force of the Treaty of Lisbon.

Appendix 3

Selected Bibliography

Adinolfi, A., 'Free movement and access to work of citizens of the new Member States: the transitional measures', *Common Market Law Review*, 2005, vol. 42, no. 2, April, 469–498.

Addison, John T. 'Do Works Councils Inhibit Investment?'. *Industrial and Labor Relations Review*, vol. 60, no. 2 (January 2007): 187–203.

Ahlberg, Kerstin, *Transnational Labour Regulation: a Case Study of Temporary Agency Work*, Brussels: P. Lang, 2008, 376 pp. Ales, Edoardo, 'Transnational collective bargaining in Europe: need for legislative action at EU level', *International Labour Review*, Geneva, ILO, vol. 148, no. 1, 2009.

Ales Edoardo, Tonia Novitz, *Collective action and fundamental freedoms in Europe: striking the balance*, Antwerp: Intersentia, 2010, xii, 273 p.

Aliprantis Nikitas, Ioannis Papageorgiou, *Social Rights: challenges at European, regional and international level*, Brussels, Bruylant, 2010, 408 p.

Alston, P., 'Core labour standards' and the transformation of international labour rights regime', *European Journal of International Law*, 2004, vol. 15, no. 3, June, 457–521.

Banyuls, Josep, Thomas Haipeter and Lázló Neumann, 'European Works Council at General Motors Europe: Bargaining Efficiency in Regime Competition?', *Industrial Relations Journal*, vol. 39, no. 6 (November 2008): 532–547.

Barnard, C., S. Deakin and G. Morris, *The Future of Labour Law: Liber Amicorum Bob Hepple*, Oxford, Hart, 2004.

Barnard, C., *EC employment law*, 2nd ed., Chichester Wiley, 2000.

Barnard, C., 'Flexibility and Social Policy', in *Constitutional Change in the EU*, 2000, 197–217.

Barnard, C., *EC Employment law*, Oxford University Press, Oxford, 2006.

Bedrac, J., *What Makes a Good Company? Employee Interest Representation in European Company Law: Reflections and Legal Provisions*, European Trade Union Institute for Research, Education, Health and Safety, Brussels, 2006, 76.

Bercusson, B., *European Labour Law*, Butterworths, London, 1996.

Bercusson, B., 'Trade Union Rights in EU Law', *The Europeanisation of Law*, 2000, 195–209.

Bercusson, B. 'Regulatory Competition in the EU System: Labour', *Regulatory Competition and Economic Integration*, 2001, 241–262.

Bercusson, B. et al., *European Labour Law and the EU Charter of Fundamental Rights*, Baden-Baden, Nomos, 2006.

Selected Bibliography

Bercusson, Brian, *Labour law and social Europe: selected writings of Brian Bercusson*/introduced by the ETUI Transnational Trade Union Rights Experts Group, Brussels: European Trade Union Institute (ETUI), 2009, 701 p.
Bermann, G.A. and K. Pistor (eds), *Law and governance in an Enlarged Europe*, Oxford, Hart, 2004.
Betten, L., *International Labour Law, Selected Issues*, Kluwer, Deventer, 1993.
Betten, L. (ed.), *The Future of European Social Policy*, Kluwer, Deventer, 1989.
Biagi, M., 'Forms of Employee Representational Participation', in Blanpain, R. and Engels, C. (eds), *Comparative Labour Law and Industrial Relations in Industrialised Market Economies*, Kluwer, The Hague, 2001, 483–524.
Biagi, M., 'The European Monetary Union and Industrial Relations' *International Journal of Comparative Labour Law and Industrial Relations*, no. 1 (2000), 39–45.
Biagi, M., 'The Impact of European Employment Strategy on the Role of Labour Law and Industrial Relations', *International Journal of Comparative Labour Law and Industrial Relations*, vol. 16, no. 2 (2000), 155–173.
Biagi, M., 'Quality in Community Industrial Relations: an Institutional Viewpoint', *International Journal of Comparative Labour Law and Industrial Relations*, vol. 17, (2001) no. 3, 385–394.
Biagi, M., 'Social Europe and Labour Law: the Role of the European Social Charter', in *The Council of Europe and the social challenges of the XXIst century*, 2001, 71–85.
Bicknell, Helen and Herman Knudsen. 'Comparing German and Danish Employee Representatives on European Works Councils'. *Journal of Industrial Relations*, vol. 48, no. 4 (September 2006), 435–451.
Bigo, D. and E. Guild (eds), *Controlling frontiers: free movement into and within Europe*, Ashgate, 2005.
Birk, R., 'The European Social Charter and the European Union', in *The Council of Europe and the social challenges of the XXIst century*, 2001, 41–48.
Blanke, T. and E. Rose (eds), 'Collective bargaining and Wages in Comparative Perspective. Germany, France, The Netherlands, Sweden and the United Kingdom', *Bulletin of Comparative Labour Relations*, no. 56, 2005, 176 p.
Blanpain, R. (ed.), 'Confronting Globalisation. The Quest for a Social Agenda', *Bulletin for Comparative Labour Relations*, no. 55, 2005, 218.
Blanpain, R. (ed.), 'Freedom of services in the European Union. Labour and Social Security Law', *Bulletin of Comparative Labour Relations*, no. 58, Kluwer Law International, Deventer, (forthcoming).
Blanpain, R. and R. Graham, 'Temporary Agency work and the Information Society', *Bulletin of Comparative Labour Relations* (eds), Kluwer Law International, Deventer, 2004.
Blanpain, R., *Will I still have a Job Tomorrow? Reflections on a new Strategy: From Routine Jobs to Creativity*, Peeters, Leuven, 1994.
Blanpain, R., *The Bosman Case: The End of the Transfer System?*, Peeters, Leuven, 1996.
Blanpain, R., *International Changes and European Social Policies after the Treaty of Amsterdam*, Kluwer, The Hague, 1998.
Blanpain, R., *Arbeidsrecht*, Die Keure, Leuven, 1999.

Selected Bibliography

Blanpain, R. (ed.), *Temporary Work and Labour Law in the European Community and Member States*, Kluwer, Deventer, 1993.

Blanpain, R. (ed.), *Europa na het Verdrag van Amsterdam. Institutioneel en Sociaal*, Reeks Europees Recht, Peeters, Leuven, 1998.

Blanpain, R. and F. Blanquet, *The Vredeling Proposal; Information and Consultation of Employees in Multinational Enterprises*, Deventer, 1983.

Blanpain, R. and C. Engels (eds), *Comparative Labour Law and Industrial Relations in Industrialised Market Economies*, 6 ed., Kluwer Law International, The Hague, 1997.

Blanpain, R. and T. Hanami (eds), *European Works Council. The Implementation of the European Directive, Views from Overseas: Japan and UK*, Peeters, Leuven, 1995.

Blanpain, R. and M. Weiss (eds), *The Changing Face of Labour Law and Industrial Relations, Liber Amicorum for Clyde W. Summers*, Nomos Verlagsgesellschaft, Baden-Baden, 1993.

Blanpain, R. and P. Windey, *The European Directive on European Works Councils: Information and Consultation of Employees in Multinational Enterprises in Europe*, second revised ed., Peeters, Leuven, 1996.

Blanpain, R., M. Colucci and C. Engels, *Codex European Labour Law*, IELL, Kluwer Law International.

Blanpain, R., C. Engels and C. Pellegrini (eds), *Contractual Policies Concerning Continued Vocational Training in the European Community Member States*, Peeters, Leuven, 1994.

Blanpain, R., B. Hepple, S. Sciarra and M. Weiss, *Fundamental Social Rights: Proposals for the European Union*, Peeters, Leuven, 1996.

Blanpain, R., E. Köhler and J. Rojot (eds), *Legal and Contractual Limitations to Working Time*, Peeters, Leuven, 1997.

Blanpain, R. and M. Colucci, *Il diritto communitario del lavoro ed il suo impatto sull'ordinamento guiridico litaliano*, Padova, 2000.

Blanpain, R. (ed.), 'The Council of Europe and the Social Challenges of the XXIst Century', *Bulletin of Comparative Labour Relations*, no. 39, Kluwer, Deventer, 2001.

Blanpain, R., *Europees arbeidsrecht*, Seventh and revised edn, Brugge, 2001.

Blanpain, R., 'The European Union and Employment Law', in Blanpain, R. and Engels, C. (eds), *Comparative Labour Law and Industrial Relations in Industrialised Market Economies*, Kluwer, The Hague, 2001, 157-83.

Blanpain, R. and C. Engels (eds), *The ILO and the Social Challenges of the 21st Century*, Kluwer, Deventer, 2001.

Blanpain, R. and F. Hendrickx (eds), *Codex European Labour Law and Social Security*, Kluwer, The Hague, 2001.

Blanpain, R., 'Equal Treatment and the Prohibition of Discrimination in Employment and Occupation: Implementation in the European Union and Belgium', in *The Council of Europe and the social challenges of the XXIst century*, 2001, 121–155.

Blanpain, R., 'Social Rights in the European Union: Challenges and Opportunities: Looking for a New Balance in the Information Society', in *Soziale Grundrechte in der Europäischen Union*, 2001, 199–225.

Selected Bibliography

Blanpain, R., 'Involvement of the Employees in the European Union', *Bulletin of Comparative Labour Relations*, Kluwer, 2002.

Blanpain, R., 'The Future of Sports in Europe. Specificity of Sports. A Legal Perspective', *Liber Amicorum Axel Adelcreutz*, Stockholm, 2007, 47–55.

Blanpain, R., *The Status of Sportsmen and Sportswomen under International, European and Belgian National and Regional law*, Brussels, Larcier, 2002.

Blanpain, R. (ed.), Freedom of Services in the European Union. Labour and Social Security law: The Bolkestein initiative, *Bulletin of Comparative Labour Relations*; 58, The Hague, Kluwer Law International, 2006.

Blanpain, R., Colucci, M. and Sica, S. (eds), *The European Social Model*, Intersentia, Antwerp, 2006.

Blanpain, R. (ed.), 'Decentralizing Industrial Relations and the Role of Labour unions and Employee Representatives', *Bulletin of Comparative Labour Relations*, no. 61, Kluwer Law International, The Hague, 2007.

Blanpain, R. et al., *The Global Work Place: International and Comparative Employment Law: Cases and Materials*, Cambridge University Press, Cambridge, 2007.

Blanpain, Roger; Editor, *Diversity, Equality and Integration: Beyond the law: a Comparative Study*, Brugge: Vanden Broele, 2008, 427 pp.

Blanpain, R., *European Labour Law*, Deventer, Kluwer Law International, 2008, 858 pp.

Blanpain, Roger, Colucci, Michele, Hendrickx, Frank, 'The future of sports law in the European Union: beyond the EU reform treaty and the white paper', *Bulletin of Comparative Labour Relations*, no. 66, 2008.

Blanpain, Roger, Grant Claire, (ed.), *Fixed-Term Employment Contracts. A comparative study*, Brugge, Vanden Broele, 2009, 443 pp.

Blanpain, Roger, & Andrzej M. Światkowski, *The Laval and Viking Cases : freedom of services and establishment v. industrial conflict in the European Economic Area and Russia*, Alphen aan den Rijn : Kluwer Law International, 2009.

Blanpain, Roger, European Works Councils : *the European directive 2009/38/EC of 6 May 2009*, Alphen aan den Rijn:Kluwer Law International, 2009., xi, 286 p.

Blanpain, Roger (ed.) *Comparative labour law and industrial relations in industrialized market economies,*Alphen aan den Rijn:Kluwer Law International, 2010, xxxvi, 806 p.

Blanpain, Roger, Frank Hendrickx, Labour law between change and tradition : Liber Amicorum Antoine Jacobs, *Bulletin for Comparative Labour Relations*, No 78, Alphen aan den Rijn:Kluwer Law International, 2011, xvii, 198 p.

Blanpain, Roger, *European labour law*, Kluwer Law International, 2012, 1006 p.

Blanpain, Roger and others, *The global workplace: international and comparative employment law: cases and materials*, Wolters Kluwer law & business, 2012, 991 p.

Boswell, Christina, *Migration and mobility in the European Union*, Basingstoke: Palgrave Macmillan, 2011, xiv, 272 p.

Blanquet, F., *L'Europe. Vers l'Harmonisation des législations sociales*, Dalloz, Paris, 1987.

Brewster, C. and P. Teague, *European Community Social Policy*, Institute of Personnel Management, London, 1989.

Selected Bibliography

Bruun, N. and J. Hellsten (eds), *Collective Agreement and Competition in the EU. The Report of the COLCOM project*, Copenhagen, 2001.

Bruun, N., 'The European Employment Strategy and the *acquis communautaire* of labour law', *International Journal of Comparative Labour Law and Industrial Relations*, vol. 17 (2001), 3, 309–324.

Byre, A., *Leading Cases and Materials on the Social Policy of the EEC*, Kluwer, Deventer, 1989.

Campbell, J. (ed.), *European Labour Unions*, Greenwood Press, London, 1992.

Cantillon, Bea, Verschueren, Herwig en Ploscar, Paula, *Social inclusion and social protection in the EU : interactions between law and policy*, Intersentia, 2012, 231 p.

Carley, M. and Hall, M., 'The Implementation of the European Works Councils Directive', *Industrial Law Journal*. vol. 29, no. 2 (2000), 103–124.

Casale, Giuseppe, *The employment relationship: a comparative overview*, International Labour Office, 2011, 322 p.

Casey, B. and M. Gold, *'Peer review of labour market programmes in the European Union: what can countries really learn from one another?'*, *Journal of European Public Policy*, 2005, vol. 12, no. 1, February, 23–43.

CES, *Creating the European Social Dimension in the Internal Market*, Brussels, 11 February 1998.

Clauwaert, S. and Harger, S., *Analysis of the Implementation of the Parental Leave Directive in the EU Member States*, Brussels, European Trade Union Institute, 2000.

Colucci, M., 'The European Social Charter and the Right to Information and Consultation of Workers: its Implementation in the European Union and in Italy', in *The Council of Europe and the social challenges of the XXIst century*, 2001, 87–120.

Colucci, M., 'The Impact of the Internet and New Technologies on the Workplace: A legal Analysis from a Comparative Point of View', *Bulletin of Comparative Labour Relations*, no. 43, 2002, 186 p.

Conchon, Aline, *Board-level employee representation rights in Europe: facts and trends*, ETUI 2011, 72 p.

Cremers, J. and P. Donders, *The free movement of workers in the European Union: Directive 96/71/EC on the posting of workers within the framework of the provision of services: its implementation, practical application and operation*, Reed Business Information, Bruxelles, CLR, 2004.

Da Costa, Isabel and Udo Rehfeldt. 'European Works Councils and Transnational Bargaining about Restructuring in the Auto Industry', *Transfer. European Review of Labour and Research*, vol. 13, no. 2 (2007).

Da Costa, Hermes Augusto and Pedro Araújo. 'European Companies without European Works Councils, Evidence from Portugal'. *European Journal of Industrial Relations*, vol. 14, no. 3 (September 2008): 309–325.

Davies, P.L. and Freedland, M., 'Employees, Workers, and the Autonomy of Labour Law', in *Zur Autonomie des Individuums: Liber Amicorum Spiros Simitis*, 2000, 31–46.

Davies, A.C.L., *EU labour law*, Edward Elgar, 2012, 271 p.

Selected Bibliography

De Búrca, G., L. Ogertschnig and B. Witte, *Social rights in Europe*, Oxford, University Press, 2005.

De Vos Marc (ed.), *European Union Internal Market and Labour Law: Friends or Foes?*, Social Europe Series, vol. 19, June 2009, Interscentia, xiii + 149 pp.

De Waele, H., 'Vrij verkeer van personen en het recht op sociale uitkeringen: de Europese burger als paard van Troje', *Nederlands tijdschrift voor Europees recht*, 2004, jaarg. 10, no. 12, 321–325.

Dolvik, J., *The ETUC and the Developments of Social Dialogue and European Negotiations after Maastricht*, Working Paper 2/97, ARENA, Oslo, 1997.

Dorssemont, F., and others, *Cross-Border Collective Actions in Europe: A legal Challenge. A study of the Legal Aspects of Transnational Collective Actions from a Labour Law and Private International Law Perspective*, Intersentia, Antwerp, 2007, 481 p.

Dufresne, A., Degryse, C. and Pochet, P. (eds), *The European Sectoral Social Dialogue: Actors, Developments and Challenges*, Brussels: P.I.E. – Peter Lang, 2006.

Engels, C., and L. Salas, 'Transnational Information and Consultation: the European Works Council Directive', in Blanpain, R. and Engels, C. (eds), *Comparative Labour Law and Industrial Relations in Industrialised Market Economies*, Kluwer, The Hague, 2001, 525–48.

Engels, C. and Salas, L., *European Works Councils in Belgium*, Kluwer, The Hague, 1999.

European Commission, *Industrial Relations in Europe*, Luxembourg, 2000.

European Foundation for Living and Working Conditions, *Negotiating European Works Councils. A Comparative Study of Article 6 and Article 13 Agreements*, Dublin, 2000.

European Commission, *A Social Europe*, 4th ed., Brussels, 1990.

European Commission, *Green Paper on European Social Policy*, Brussels, 1993.

European Commission, *Interim Report on Trans-European Networks. White Paper follow-up*, in Bulletin of the European Union, Supplement 2/94, Brussels, 1994.

European Commission, *White Paper on Growth, Competitiveness, Employment*, Brussels, Luxembourg, 1994.

European Commission, *Action for Employment: A Confidence Pact*, Bulletin of the European Union, Supplement 4/96, Brussels, 1996.

European Commission, *Green Paper: Modernising Labour Law to Meet the Challenges of the 21st Century*, COM Documents, 2006/0708 final, Luxembourg, 2006.

European Commission, *EU Social Policy*, Brussels, 1996.

European Commission, *Employee Representatives in an Enlarged Europe*, Luxembourg, 2008, 110 pp.

European Trade Union Institute, *The Social Dimension of the Internal Market*, part IV, Brussels, 1991.

European Trade Union Institute, *The European Industry Committees and the Social Dialogue: Experiences at Sectoral Level and in Multinational Companies*, Brussels, 1993.

Fareed Zakaria, *The Future of Freedom. Illiberal Democracy at Home and Abroad*, 2004, New York, Norton. Ferner, A. and R. Hyman (eds), *Industrial Relations in the New Europe*, Blackwell, Oxford, 1992.

Selected Bibliography

Fenwick, Colin F. en Novitz, Tonia, *Human rights at work : perspectives on law and regulation*, Hart Publishing, 2010, 638 p.

Fetzer, Thomas. 'European Works Councils as Risk Communities: The Case of General Motors'. *European Journal of Industrial Relations*, vol. 14, no. 3 (September 2008): 289–308.

Flanagan, R.J., *Globalisation and Labor Conditions: Working Conditions and Worker Rights in a Global Economy*, Oxford University Press, Oxford, 2006.

Foglia, R., 'I diritti di informazione e partecipazione dei lavoratori dopo la società europea', *Diritto del lavoro*, 2003, anno 77, n. 4, July–August, 345–353.

Follesdal, Andreas, Wessel, Ramses A., Wouters, Jan, *Multilevel Regulation and the EU: the Interplay between Global, European, and National Normative Processes*, Leiden. Boston, Martinus Nijhoff Publishers, 2008, xxi, 420 pp.

France, D., 'International Employers' Associations', in Blanpain, R. and Engels, C. (eds), *Comparative Labour Law and Industrial Relations in Industrialised Market Economies*, Kluwer, The Hague, 2001, 55–72.

Fredman, S., 'Transformation or Dilution: Fundamental Rights in the EU Social Space', *European Law Journal*, 2006, vol. 12, no. 1, January, 41–60.

Gilson, Clive and Anni Weiler, 'Transnational company industrial relations: the role of European Works Councils and the implications for international human resource management', *Journal of industrial relations*, no. 5, 2008, 697–717.

Giubboni, S., *Social Rights and Market Freedom in the European Constitution: a Labour Law Perspective*, Cambridge University Press, Cambridge, 2006.

Gobin, C., *L'Europe syndicale. Entre désire et réalité. Essai sur le syndicalisme et la construction Européenne à l'abule du XXIe siècle*, Bruxelles, Labor, 1997.

Gold, M. (ed.), *The Social Dimension: Employment Policy in the European Community*, Mackays of chatham plc, london, 1993.

Grandi, Barbara, 'Would Europe benefit from the adoption of a comprehensive definition of the term "employee"applicable in all relevant legislative modes?', *International Journal of Comparative Labour Law and Industrial Relations*, vol. 24, no. 4, 2008, 495–510.

Grieve Smith, J., *Full Employment: A Pledge Betrayed*, Butterworths, London, 1997.

Guild, Elspeth en Carrera, Sergio, *Labour migration and unemployment: what can we learn from EU rules on the free movement of workers?*, CEPS, 2012, 14 p.

Gündüz, A., 'Enlargement of the European Union: A View from the East, with special Reference to Turkey', *Exeter Paper in European Law*, no. 5, 2001, 36 p.

Hendrickx, Frank, *Labour law for the United States of Europe*, Tilburg University, 2011, 63 p.

Hendrickx, Frank and others., *Active ageing and labour law : contributions in honour of professor Roger Blanpain*, Intersentia, 2012, 320 p.

Hardy, Stephen, *European employment laws: a comparative guide*, London: Spiramus, 2011, xxi, 293 p.

Hepple, B.A., *European Social Dialogue: Alibi or Opportunity?* The Institute of Employment Rights, London, 1993.

Hermes, Agusto Costa and Pedro Araújo, 'European companies without European works councils: evidence from Portugal', *European Journal of Industrial Relations*, vol. 14, no. 3, 2008, 309–325.

Selected Bibliography

ILO, *A fair Globalisation. Creating Opportunities for All*, Geneva, 2004.

Jacobs, A., *The European Constitution. How it was created. What it will change*, Wolf Legal Publishers, Nijmegen, 2005.

Jacobs, A. and H. Zeijen, *European Labour Law and Social Policy*, Tilburg, 1993.

Jacobs, A., T.J.M. and Ojeda, A., 'The European Social Dialogue: Some Legal Issues', in *A Legal Framework for European Industrial Relations*, 1999, 57–75.

Jacobs, A., T.J.M., 'De Europese sociale dialoog', in *De onderneming en het arbeidsrecht in de 21e eeuw*, 2000, 207–221.

Jagodziński, Romuald. 'Involving European Works Councils in Transnational Negotiations: A Positive Functional Advance in Their Operation or Trespassing?'. *Industrielle Beziehungen. Zeitschrift für Arbeit, Organisation und Management*, vol. 14, no. 4, 2007, 316–333.

Jagodziński, Romuald, 'Progress on the Revision of the EWC Directive'. *Transfer. European Review of Labour and Research*, vol. 14, no. 4, 2007, 700–701.

Jagodziński, Romuald, 'New Thread in the Revision Process of Directive 94/95 on EWCs'. *Transfer: European Review of Labour and Research*, vol. 13, no. 3, 2007, 504–505.

Jaspers, T., 'The EWC as a Real Partner in the "European company"', *Comités d'entreprise européens*, 1999, 341–353.

John, D.R., Craig, J.D.R. and Lynk, S.M. (eds), *Globalisation and the Future of Labour Law*, Cambridge University Press, Cambridge, 2006.

Kapteyn, P.G.J. and P. Verloren van Themaat, *Introduction to the Law of the European Communities*, 2nd ed., Deventer, Kluwer, 1989.

Kaufman, B.E., The Global Evolution of Industrial Relations, Geneva, 2004.

Kaufmann, C., *Globalisation and Labour Rights: the Conflict between Core Labour Rights and International Economic Law*, Hart, Oxford, 2007.

Kenner, J., *EU employment law: from Rome to Amsterdam*, Oxford, Hart, 2003.

Kerkhofs, J., *De Europeanen en hun waarden. Wat wij denken en voelen*. Davidsfonds, Leuven, 1997.

Kerstin, A. et al., 'Mobility of Services and Posting of Workers in the Enlarged Europe', *Transfer*, vol. 12, no. 2, Summer, 2006.

Kessler, F. and J-P. Lhernould, *Droit social et politiques sociales communautaires*, Rueil-Malmaison, Éd. Liaisons, 2003.

Kjaergaard, C. and Sven-Äge Westphalen, *From Collective Bargaining to Social Partnerships: New Roles of the Social Partners in Europe*, The Copenhagen Center, 2001.

Kovar, R., *Observations sur l'Intensité Normative des Directives*, Dalloz, Paris, 1987.

Krebber Sebastian, 'Status and Potential of the Regulation of Labor and Employment Law at the European Level', *Comparative Labor Law and Policy Journal*, vol. 30, no. 4, 2009, 875–903.

Ladó, M., 'EU Enlargement: Reshaping European and National Industrial Relations?', *International Journal of Comparative Labour Law and Industrial Relations*, vol. 18 (2002), 1, 101–124.

Lansbury, R.D. and Park, Y.B. (eds), 'The Impact of Globalisation on Employment Relations', *Bulletin of Comparative Labour Relations*, no. 45, 2002, 151 p.

Selected Bibliography

Leary, V., and Warner, A.D. (eds), *Social Issues, Globalisation and International Institutions: Labour Rights and the EU, ILO, OECD and WTO*, Leiden, M. Nijhoff, 2006.

Lenaerts, K. and Desomer Marlies, *Recente Ontwikkelingen van Europees Recht. Het Verdrag van Nice. Het Handvest van de grondrechten van de Europese Unie, Verslagboek*, VRG. Alumni, Leuven Faculty of Laws, 2001, 163-80.

Lenaerts, K. and Foubert, P., 'Social Rights in the Case law of the European Court of Justice: the Impact of the Charter of Fundamental Rights of the European Union on Standing Case law', *Legal Issues of European Integration*, vol. 28, no. 3, 2001, 267–296.

Lenaerts, K. and Van Nuffel, P., *Europees recht in hoofdlijnen*, third ed., Maklu, Antwerpen, 2003.

Lewis, P., 'Pregnant workers and sex discrimination: the limits of purposive non comparative methodology', *International Journal of Comparative Labour Law and Industrial Relations*, no. 1, 2000, 55–69.

Lourte, P., *Solving Europe's Unemployment Problem: The Demystification of Flexibility*, European Interuniversity, Press and College of Europe, Bruges, 1995.

Maillet, P. and W. Kösters, *Une Europe plus favorable à l'emploi. Un Programme volontariste*, L'Harmattan, Paris, 1996.

Margison, P., *EWC Agreements under Article 13 reviewed, European Works Councils: An Analysis of Agreements under Article 13*, European Foundation of Living and Working Conditions, Dublin, 1998.

Marginson, P. and K. Sisson, *European integration and industrial relations: multi-level governance in the making*, Palgrave Macmillan, 2004.

Mestre, B., 'Some Preliminary Comments on the Opinion of Advocate-General Mengozzi in the Laval case (AG Mengozzi, opinion of 23 May 2007, Laval un Partneri Ltd, C-341/05', *European Law Reporter*, 2007, no. 5, May, 174–185.

Mikkola, M., 'Social Human Rights in Europe: Regulated by the European Convention on Human Rights and the European Social Charter', in *Soziale Grundrechte in der Europäischen Union*, 2001, 95–103.

Moreau, Marie-Ange, *Before and after the economic crisis : what implications for the "European social model"?*, Edward Elgar, 2011, 321 p.

Moreira de Sousa, S. and W. Heusel (ed.), *Enforcing Community Law from Francovich to Köler: Twelfe Years of the State Liability Principle*, ERA, Köln, 2004.

Moussis Nicholas, *Access to European Union: Law, Economics, Policies*, Rixensart: European Study Service, 2008, xi, 557 p.

Moussis, Nicholas, *Guide to European policies*, Rixensart, European Study Service, 2009, 14th rev. ed., xii, 473 pp.

Muir, Elise, *EU regulation of access to labour markets : a case study of EU constraints on member state competences*, Kluwer Law International, 2012, 282 p.

Murray, J., *Transnational Labour Regulation: the ILO and EC Compared*, The Hague, Kluwer 2001.

Neal, A., *European Labour Law and Social Policy: Cases and Materials*, The Hague, Kluwer, 1999.

Neal, A., 'We Love You Social Dialogue: but Who exactly Are You?', *La contrattazione collettiva europea*, 2001, 113–127.

Selected Bibliography

Neal, A., *European Social Policy and the Nordic Countries*, Ashgate, Aldershot, 2000.

Neal, A.C. (ed.), *The changing face of European labour law and social policy*, Kluwer Law International, 2004.

Nielsen, R., *Employer's Prerogatives in a European and Nordic Perspective*, Munksgaard, Copenhagen, 1996.

Nielsen, R., *European Labour Law*, Djof Publishing, Copenhagen, 2000.

Nielsen, R., 'The Concept of Sex Discrimination: Recent Developments and Future Perspectives in EU law', *Perspectives of Equality*, 2000, 208–233.

Outram, S., *European Social Policy*, Blackwell, Oxford, 1996.

Pierre, R., 'Les droits sociaux fondamentaux à l'épreuve de la Constitution européenne', *La semaine juridique*, Edition générale 2005, no. 20, 887–893.

Quesada Segura, R. (ed.), *La Constitución europea y las relaciones laborales: XXII Jornadas Universitarias Andaluzas de Derecho del Trabajo y Relaciones Laborales*, Mergablum. Edición y Comunicación, 2004.

Quesada, Rosa, Bortone, Roberta en Peran, Salvador, *Gender equalty in the European Union. Comparative study of Spain and Italy*, Thomsom Reuters, 2012, 380 p.

Riesenhuber, Karl, *European employment law : a systematic exposition*, Intersentia, 2012, 803 p.

Rodríguez, P.R., 'Flexibility and European Law: a Labour Lawyer's view', in *Constitutional Change in the EU*, 2000, 219–235.

Rojot, Jacques et al., 'European Collective Bargaining, New Prospects or Much Ado about Little?' *International Journal of Comparative Labour Law and Industrial Relations*, vol. 17 (2001), 3, 345–370.

Rönnmar, Mia, *Labour law, fundamental rights and social Europe*, CPI, 2011, 280 p.

Rourke, Marilyn, *Legal Prohibitions against Employment Discrimination Available to Migrant Workers Employed in Europe: a Review of International Instruments and National Law in Four Selected Countries*, ILO, Geneva, 2008, 78 pp.

Pennings, Frans, Veldman, Albertine and Konijn, Yvonne, *Social Responsibility in Labour Relations: European and Comparative Perspectives*, Wolters Kluwer Law & Business, Alphen aan den Rijn, 2008, xlii, 532 pp.

Phinnemore, David and McGowan, Lee, *A Dictionary of the European Union*, London, Routledge, 2008, xi, 474 pp.

Pulignano, Valeria and Norbert Kluge. 'Employee involvement in restructuring: are we able to determine the price?', *Transfer. European Review of Labour and Research*, vol. 13, no. 2, 2007.

Ramos Marti´n and Nuria E., *Gender Equality in the Netherlands: an Example of Europeanisation of Social Law and Policy*, Amsterdam, AIAS, 2008, 58 pp.

Rigaux Marc, *Labour Law or Social Competition Law? On Labour in Its Relation with Capital Through Law*, Social Europe Series, vol. 21, July 2009, Interscientia, xvi + 158 pp.

Rogowski, Ralf, 'Governance of the European social model: the case of flexicurity. Flexicurity – a European approach to labour market policy', *Intereconomics*, vol. 43, no. 2, 2008, 82–91.

Selected Bibliography

Sadowski, D. and O. Jacobi, *Employers Association in Europe: Policy and Organisation*, Baden-Baden, 1991.
Salesse, Y., *Proposition pour une autre Europe. Construire Babel*, Paris, Félin, 1997.
Sallesse, Y., *L'Europe que nous voulons*, Paris, Fayard, 1999.
Sciarra, S., 'The Employment Title in the Amsterdam Treaty: a Multi-language Legal Discourse', *Legal Issues of the Amsterdam Treaty*, 1999, 157–170.
Sciarra, S., 'Global or Re-nationalised? Past and Future of European Labour Law', *The Europeanisation of Law*, 2000, 269–291.
Sciarra, S., 'Integration through Coordination: the Employment Title in the Amsterdam Treaty', *The Columbia Journal of European Law*, vol. 6, (2000), 209–229.
Sciarra, S., *Labour Law in the Courts: National Judges and the European Court of Justice*, Oxford, Hart, 2001.
Sciarra, S., *The evolution of labour law in the European Union: 1992–2002. Report on Italy*, Brussels: EC, DG Employment and Social Affairs, 2003.
Sciarra, S., P. Davies and M. Freedland (eds), *Employment Policy and the Regulation of Part-time Work in the European Union*, Cambridge, 2004.
Seifert, Hartmut, 'Regulated flexibility: flexible working time patterns in Germany and the role of works councils', *International Journal of Comparative Labour Law and Industrial Relations*, vol. 24, no. 2 (June 2008): 229–242.
Servais, J.M., 'The Impact of Globalization on Employment and Social Inclusion Policies: Experiences and Proposals in Individual European Countries', *Bulletin of Comparative Labour Relations* (ed. R. Blanpain), 2009, Nr.71, 3–32.
Semmelmann, C., 'The transfer of undertaking: a going concern of the European Courts?', *European Law Reporter*, 2005, no. 3, März, 120–126.
Simitis, S., 'Reconsidering the Premises of Labour Law: Prolegomena to an EU Regulation on the Protection of Employees' Personal Data', *Scritti in onore di Gino Giugni*, 1999, tomo II, 1581–1601.
Smismans, S., 'The European Social Dialogue between Constitutional and Labour Law', *European Law Review*, 2007, vol. 32, no. 3, June, 341–364.
Spyropoulos, G., 'L'avenir incertain du modèle social européen dans une Europe élargie', *Droit social* 2005, no. 6, juin, 603–605.
Terry, M. and L. Dickens, *European Employment and Industrial Relations Glossary*, London, 1991.
Teyssié, B., *Droit européen du travail*, Paris, Litec, 2003.
Timming, Andrew and R. Croydon, 'European Works Councils and the Dark Side of Managing Worker Voice', *Human Resource Management Journal*, vol. 17, no. 3 (2007): 248–264.
Tobler, Christa, *Limits and Potential of the Concept of Indirect Discrimination*; European Commmission, Luxembourg, 2008, 90 pp.
Traversa, E., 'The consequences of European Monetary Union on collective bargaining and the national social security systems', *International Journal of Comparative Labour Law and Industrial Relations*, no. 1 (2000), 47–54.
Treu, T., 'A New Phase of European Social Policy: the EMU and Beyond', *International Journal of Comparative Labour Law and Industrial Relations*, vol. 17 (2001), 4, 461–472.

Selected Bibliography

Vanderbruggen, P., *De Europese leugen. De onzin van de Europese Muntunie*, Kritak, Leuven, 1996.
Van Doorne-Huiskes, A., *Women and the European Labour Markets*, Chapman, London, 1995.
Van Gerven, W., *Tort Law: Scope of Protection*, Hart Publishing, Oxford, 1998.
Veneziani, B. (ed.), *Law, Collective Bargaining and Labour Flexibility in EC Countries*, Asap, Rome, 1992.
Verschueren, H., *Grensoverschrijdende arbeid*, Brugge, Die Keure, 2000.
Vogel-Polsky, E. and J. Vogel, *L'Europe Sociale 1993: Illusion, Alibi, ou Réalité?*, Brussels, 1991.
Waaldijk, K. and Bonini-Baraldi, M., *Sexual Orientation Discrimination in the European Union: National Llaws and the Employment Equality Directive*, The Hague: T.M.C. Asser Press, 2006.
Waddington, Jeremy, *European Works Councils and industrial relations:a transnational industrial relations institution in the making*, Abingdon, Routledge, 2011. xxi, 277 p.
Watson, P., *EU social and employment law*, Richmond Law and Tax, 2005.
Watson, Philippa, *EU Social and Employment Law: Policy and Practice in an Enlarged Europe*, New York, Oxford University Press, 2009, 538 pp.
Weatherill, S. and P. Beaumont, *EC Law: The Essential Guide to the Legal Working of the European Community*, Penguin Books, London, 1993.
Weiss, M., 'Collective Bargaining in Germany from a European Perspective', *La contrattazione collettiva europea*, 2001, 69–95.
Welz, Christian, *The European Social Dialogue under Articles 138 and 139 of the EC Treaty: Actors, Processes, Outcomes*, Alphen aan den Rijn, Kluwer Law International, 2008, xxiii, 659 pp.
Wilkinson, Adrian, Tony Dundon and Irena Grugulis. 'Information but not consultation: exploring employee involvement in SMEs', *International Journal of Human Resource Management*, vol. 18, no. 7, 2007, 302–331.
Whittal, Michael, Herman Knudsen and Fred Huijgen, *Towards a European Labour Identity: The Case of the European Work Council*, London, Routledge, 2007, xix, 233 pp.
Whittall, Michael, Stefan Lücking and Rainer Trinczek. 'Understanding the European Works Council deficit in German multinationals', *Transfer: European Review of Labour and Research*, vol. 14, no. 3, 2008, 453–467.
Windmuller, J. and S. Pursey, 'The International Trade Union Movement', in Blanpain, R. and Engels, C. (eds), *Comparative Labour Law and Industrial Relations in Industrialised Market Economies*, Kluwer, The Hague, 2001, 73–100.
Wolf, M., *Why Globalisation Works*, Yale University Press, New Haven, 2005.
Woolfson, C. and Sommers, J., 'Labour Mobility in Construction: European Implications of the Laval un Partneri dispute', *European Journal of Industrial Relations*, 2006, vol. 12, no. 1, March, 49–68.
Wyatt, D. and A. Dashwood, *European Community Law*, Sweet and Maxwell, London.
Web Sites: The Institutions of the European Union

Selected Bibliography

Committee of the Regions
website: <www.cor.eu.int>

Council of the European Union
website: <www.ue.eu.int/en/summ.htm>

Court of Auditors
website: <www.eca.eu.int>

Court of Justice
website: <www.curia.eu.int/en/index.htm>

Economic and Social Committee
website: <www.ces.eu.int>

European Agency for Safety and Health at Work
website: <www.europe.osha.eu.int>

European Central Bank (ECB)
website: <www.ecb.int>

European Commission
website: <www.europa.eu.int/comm/indexen.htm>
Directorate-General competent for employment and social policy:
<www.europa.eu.int/comm/dg05/index en.htm>

European Parliament
website: <www.europarl.eu.int>

European Council
website: <www.ue.eu.int/en/info/eurocouncil>

European Foundation for the Improvement of Living and Working Conditions
website: <www.eiro.eurofound.ie>

European Investment Bank
website: <www.eib.eu.int>

European Training Foundation
website: <www.etf.eu.int>

The European Centre for the Development of Vocational Training (CEDEFOP)
website: <www.cedefop.gr>

Selected Bibliography

Ombudsman
website: <www.euro-ombudsman.eu.int>

European Social Partners

Etuc (European Trade Union Confederation)
website: <www.etuc.org>

Ceep (European Centre of Enterprises with Public Participation and of Enterprises of General Economic Interest)
website: <www.ceep.org/ceep.htm>

Unice (Union of Industrial and Employers' Confederations of Europe)
website: <www.unice.org/unice>

European Official Documents European Parliament
website: <www.europarl.eu.int/r/dors/oeil/en/default.htm>

European Commission
website: <www.europa.eu.int/comm/off/indexen.htm>

European Council
website: <www.europa.eu.int/council/off/conclu/index.htm>

Databases

EurLex (European Union law)
website: <www.europa.eu.int/eur-lex/en/index.html>

Celex (European Community law) – use is not free!
website: <www.europa.eu.int/celex>

Eudor (Office for Official Publications of the European Communities)
website: <www.eudor.com:8444/EUDOR/PROC/ orientation?LANGUAGE=english>

Bibliographic Databases

Eclas (European Commission Library Automated System)
website: <www.europa.eu.int/eclas/abouten.htm>

Scad Database (documentary references)
website: <www.europa.eu.int/scadplus/scaden.htm>

Alphabetical List of Cited Cases of the European Court of Justice

Abdoulaye O.P. and Others v. *Régie nationale des usines Renault SA*, 16 September 1999, C-218/98, ECR, 1999, 5723.
Abels H.B.M. v. *The Administrative Board of the Bedrijfsvereniging voor de Metaalindustrie en de Electrotechnische Industrie*, 7 February 1985, C-135/83, ECR, 1985, 519–529.
Abler Carlito and Others v. *Sodexho MM Catering GmbH*, 20 November 2003, C-340/01, ECR, 2003, 14023.
Abrahamsson Katarina and Leif Anderson v. *Elisabet Fogelqvist*, 6 July 2000, C-407/98, ECR, 2000, 5539.
Adoui Rezguia v. *Belgian State and City of Liège; Dominique Cornuaille* v. *Belgian State*, 18 May 1982, C-115 and 116/81, ECR, 1985, 1665–1713.
AGR Regeling v. *Bestuur van de Bedrijfsvereniging voor de Metaalnijverheid*, 14 July 1998, C-125/97, ECR, 1998, 4493.
AGS Assedic Oas-de-Calais and François Dumon v. *Maître Froment, liquidator and representative of Establishments Pierre Gilson*, 16 July 1998, C-235/95, ECR, 1998, 4531.
Airola Jeanne v. *Commission of the European Communities*, 20 February 1975, C-21/74, ECR, 1975, 221–227.
Akavan Erityisalojen Kesku sliitto AEK ry and others v. *Fujitsu Siemens Computers Oy*, 10 September 2009, C-44/08, www.curia.
Alabaster Michelle K. v. *Woolwich plc and Secretary of State for Social Security*, 30 March 2004, C-147/02, ECR, 2004, 3101.
Alaimo Angelo v. *Préfet du Rhône*, 29 January 1975, C-68/74, ECR, 1975, 109–115.
Albany v. *Stichting Bedrijfspensioenfonds Textielindustries*, 21 September 1999, C-67/96, ECR, 1999, 5751.
Albron Catering BV v. *FNV Bondgenoten*, John Roest, 21 October 2010, C242/09, www.curia.eu.
Alexander Heimann, Konstantin Toltschin v. Kaiser GmbH, 8 November 2012, C-229/11 and C-230/11, www. curia.eu.
Allen, G.C. and Others v. *Amalgamated Construction Co. Ltd.*, 2 December 1999, C-234/98, ECR, 1999, 8643.
Allué P. and Mary C. Coonan v. *Università degli Studi di Venezia*, 30 May 1989, C-33/88, ECR, 1989, 1591.
Allué P. and others v. *Università degli Studi di Venezia and others*, 2 August 1993, C-259/91, C-331/91 and C-332/91, ECR, 1993, 4309.

List of Cases of the ECJ

Andersen Ruben v. *Kommunernes Landsforening*, 18 December 2008, C-306/07, www.curia.eu.
Angelo Rubino v. *Ministero dell'Università e della Ricerca*, 17 December 2009, C-586/08, www.curia.eu.
Angestelltenbetriebrat der Wiener Gebietskrankenkasse v. *Wiener Gebietskrankenkasse*, 11 May 1999, C-309/97, ECR, 1999, 2865.
Anton Las v PSA Antwerp NV, 16 April 2013, C-202/11, www. curia. eu.
Aranitis Georgios v. *Land Berlin*, C-164/94, ECR, 1996, 139. *Arbeitswohlfart des Stadt Berlin e.V. (ASWB)* v. *M. Böttel*, 4 June 1992, C-360/90, ECR, 1992, 3589.
Arben Kaba v. *Secretary of State for the Home Department*, 11 April 2000, C-356/98, ECR, 2000, 2623.
Aslanidou Maria v. *Ypourgos Ygeias & Pronoias*, C-142/04, 14 July 2005, ECR, 2005, 7181.
Asociación Nacional de Grandes Empresas de Distribución (ANGED) v. Federación de Asociaciones Sindicales (FASGA), a.o., 21 June 2012, C-78/11, www. curia.eu
Asociaţia ACCEPT v Consiliul Naţional pentru Combaterea Discriminării, 25 April 2013, C-81/12, www. curia.eu
Association de soutien aux travailleurs immigrés (ASTI) v. *Chambre des Employés Privés*, 4 July 1991, C-213/90, ECR, 1991, 3507.
Badeck and Others, 28 March 2000, C-158/97, ECR, 2000, 1875.
Barber Douglas Harvey v. *Guardian Royal Exchange Assurance Group*, 17 May 1990, C-262/88, ECR, 1990, 1889.
Barra Bruno v. *Belgian State and City of Liège*, 2 February 1988, C-309/85, ECR, 1988, 355.
Bartsch Birgit v. *Bosch und Siemens Hausgeräte (BSH) Altersfürsorge GmbH*, 23 September 2008, C-427/06, ECR, 2008, 7245.
Beckmann Katia v. *Dynamco Whichloe Macfarlane Ltd.*, 4 June 2002, C-164/00, ECR, 2002, 4843.
Beets-Proper Vera Mia v. *F. van Lanschot Bankiers N.V.*, 26 February 1986, C-262/84, ECR, 1986, 773.
Belgian State v. *René Humbel and Marie-Thérèse Humbel née Edel*, 27 September 1988, C-263/86, ECR, 1988, 5365.
Berg Harry and Johannes Theodorus Maria Busschers v. *Ivo Martens Busselsen*, 5 May 1988, C-144 and 145/87, ECR, 1988, 2559.
Bernini M.J.E. v. *Netherlands Ministry of Education and Science*, 26 February 1992, C-3/90, ECR, 1992, 1071.
Bestuur van het Algemeen Burgerlijk Pensioenfonds v. *G.A. Beune*, 28 September 1994, C-7/93, ECR, 1994, 4471.
Betriebsrat der Bofrost Josef H. Boquoi Deutschland West GmbH & Co. KG and Bofrost Josef H. Boquoi Deutschland West GmbH & Co. KG, 29 March 2001, C-62/99, ECR, 2001, 2579.
Betriebsrat der Firma ADS Anker GmbH v. *ADS Anker GmbH*, 15 July 2004, C-349/01, ECR, 2004, 6803.
Bettray I. v. *Staatssecretaris van Justitie*, 31 May 1989, C-344/87, ECR, 1989, 1621.

List of Cases of the ECJ

Bianca Brandes v Land Niedersachsen, 13 June 2013, C-415/12, www. curia.eu.

Bianca Kücük v Land Nordrhein-Westfalen, 26 January 2012, C-586/10, www.curia.eu

Bilka-Kaufhaus GmbH v. *K. Weber von Hartz*, 13 May 1986, C-170/84, ECR, 1986, 1607.

Birds Eye Walls Limited v. *F.M. Robert*, 9 November 1991, C-132/92, ECR, 1993, 5579.

Blaizot Vincent v. *University of Liège and others*, 2 February 1988, C-24/86, ECR, 1988, 379.

Bleis A. v. *Ministère de l'Education Nationale*, 27 November 1991, C-4/91, ECR, 1991, 5627.

Bonino Anna v. *Commission of the European Communities*, 12 February 1987, C-233/85, ECR, 1987, 739.

Bonsignore C.A. v. *Oberstadtdirektor der Stadt Köln*, 26 February 1975, C-67/74, ECR, 1975, 297.

Boor Johanna Maria v. *Ministre de la Fonction publique et de la Réforme administrative*, 11 November 2004, C-425/02, ECR, 2004, 823.

Botzen Arie and others v. *Rotterdamsche Droogdok Maatschappij BV*, 7 February 1985, C-186/83, ECR, 1985, 519.

J.R. Bowden, J.L. Chapman, J.J. Doyle and Tuffnells Parcels Express Ltd., 4 October 2001, Case C-133/00, ECR, 2001, 7031.

Brentjes' Handelsonderneming v. *Stichting Bedrijfspensioensfonds voor de handel in bouwmaterialen*, Joined Cases 115–117/97 and *Drijvende Bokken* v. *Stichting Pensioenfonds voor de vervoer en havenbedrijven*, 21 September 1999, C-219/97, ECR, 1999, 5751.

Brown Malcolm Steven v. *Secretary of State for Scotland*, 21 June 1988, C-197/86, ECR, 1988, 3205.

Brown Mary v. *Rentokil Ltd.*, 30 June 1998, C-394/96, ECR, 1998, 4185.

Burbaud Isabel v. *Ministère de l'Emploi et de la Solidarité*, 9 September 2003, C-285/01, ECR, 2003, 8219.

Burton Arthur v. *British Railway Board*, 16 February 1982, C-19/81, ECR, 1982, 555.

Busch Wiebke v. *Klinikum Neustadt GmbH & Co. Betriebs-KG*, 27 February 2003, C-320/01, ECR, 2003, 2041.

Cadman, B.F. v. *Health & Safety Executive*, 3 October 2006, C-17/05, ECR, 2006, 9583.

Caisse d'Allocations Familiales de la Région Parisienne v. *Mr. and Mrs. Richard Meade*, 5 July 1984, C-238/83, ECR, 1984, 2631.

Caisse Nationale d'Assurance Vieillesse des Travailleurs Salariés (CNAVTS) v. *Evelyne Thibault*, 30 April 1998, C-136/95, ECR, 1998, 2011.

Campana Angelo v. *Bundesanstalt für Arbeit*, 4 June 1987, C-375/85, ECR, 1987, 2387.

Castelli Carmela v. *Office National des Pensions pour Travailleurs Salariés (ONTPS)*, 12 July 1984, C-261/83, ECR, 1984, 3199.

Celtec Ltd. v. *John Astley and Others*, 26 May 2005, C-478/03, ECR, 2005, 4389.

Centre public d'aide sociale de Courcelles v. *Marie-Christine Lebon*, 18 June 1987, C-316/85, ECR, 1987, 2811.

List of Cases of the ECJ

Centrum voor gelijkheid van kansen en voor racismebestrijding v. *Firma Feryn NV*, 10 July 2008, C-54/07, ECR, 2008, 5187.
Chacón Navas Sonia v. *Eurest Colectividades SA*, 11 July 2006, C-13/05, ECR, 2006, 6467.
Charles Defossez v. *Christian Wiart, in his capacity as liquidator of Sotimon Sarl*, 10 March 2011, C-477/09, www.curia.eu. *Chartopoiia Athinaiki AE* v. *L. Panagiotidis and Others*, 15 February 2007, C-270/05, ECR, 2007, 1499.
Chollet Monique (née Bauduin) v. *Commission of the European Communities*, 7 June 1972, C-32/71, ECR, 1972, 363.
Christina Ioanni Toki v. *Ipourgos Ethnikis Pedias kai Thriskevmaton*, 5 April 2011, C-424/09, www.curia.eu. *Clean Car Autoservice GesmbH* v. *Landeshauptmann von Wien*, 7 May 1998, C-350/96, ECR, 1998, 2512.
CLECE SA v. *María Socorro Martín Valor*, 20 January 2011, C-463/09, www.curia.eu.
Colegio de Oficiales de la Marina Mercante Española v. *Administración del Estado*, 30 September 2003, C-405/01, ECR, 2003, 10391.
Colegio de Ingenieros de Caminos, Canales y Puertos v. *Administración del Estado*, C-330/03, 19 January 2006, ECR, 2006, 807.
Coleman v. *Attridge Law and Steve Law*, 17 July 2008, C-303/06, ECR, 2008, 5603.
Colin Wolf v. *Stadt Frankfurt am Main*, 12 January 2010, C-229/08, www.curia.eu.
Coloroll Pension Trustees Ltd. v. *James Richard Russel and others*, 28 September 1994, C-200/91, ECR, 1994, 4389.
Commission v. *Belgium*, 2 July 1996 (distribution of water, gas and electricity), C-173/94, ECR, 1996, 3265.
Commission v. *Belgium*, 12 September 1996, C-278/98, ECR, 1989, 987.
Commission of the European Communities v. *Council of the European Communities*, 30 May 1989, C-242/87, ECR, 1989, 1425.
Commission of the European Communities v. *Council of the European Communities*, 30 May 1989, C-355/87, ECR, 1989, 1517.
Commission of the European Communities v. *Federal Republic of Germany*, 21 May 1985, C-248/83, ECR, 1985, 1459.
Commission of the European Communities v. *Federal Republic of Germany*, 23 May 1985, C-29/84, ECR, 1985, 1661.
Commission of the European Communities v. *Federal Republic of Germany*, 18 May 1989, C-249/86, ECR, 1989, 1263.
Commission of the European Communities v. *French Republic*, 4 April 1974, C-167/73, ECR, 1974, 359.
Commission of the European Communities v. *French Republic*, 30 April 1986, C-96/85, ECR, 1986, 1475–1488.
Commission of the European Communities v. *French Republic*, 3 June 1986, C-312/86, ECR, 1988, 6315.
Commission of the European Communities v. *French Republic*, 25 October 1988, C-307/84, ECR, 1986, 1725–1740.
Commission of the European Communities v. *French Republic*, 30 June 1988, C-318/86, ECR, 1988, 3559.
Commission v. *French Republic*, 24 September 1998, C-35/97, ECR, 5325.

List of Cases of the ECJ

Commission of the European Communities v. *Grand Duchy of Luxembourg*, 9 June 1982, C-58/81, ECR, 1982, 2175–2182.
Commission of the European Communities v. *Grand Duchy of Luxembourg*, 19 March 1993, C-111/91, ECR, 1993, 817.
Commission v. *Hellenic Republic*, 2 July 1996, C-290/94, ECR, 1996, 3285.
Commission v. *Hellenic Republic*, 12 March 1998, C-187/96, ECR, 1998, 1095.
Commission of the European Communities v. *Hellenic Republic*, 15 March 1988, C-147/86, ECR, 1988, 1637.
Commission of the European Communities v. *Hellenic Republic*, 30 May 1989, C-305/87, ECR, 1989, 1461.
Commission of the European Communities v. *Hellenic Republic*, 8 November 1990, C-53/88, ECR, 1990, 3971.
Commission of the European Communities v. *Italian Republic*, 8 June 1982, C-91/81, ECR, 1982, 2133–2141.
Commission of the European Communities v. *Italian Republic*, 6 November 1985, C-131/84, ECR, 1985, 3531–3537.
Commission of the European Communities v. *Italian Republic*, 10 July 1986, C-235/84, ECR, 1986, 2291–2304.
Commission of the European Communities v. *Italian Republic*, 15 October 1986, C-168/85, ECR, 1986, 2945–2963.
Commission of the European Communities v. *Italian Republic*, 15 November 1986, C-160/85, ECR, 1986, 3245–3254.
Commission of the European Communities v. *Italian Republic*, 16 June 1986, C-225/85, ECR, 1987, 2625.
Commission of the European Communities v. *Italian Republic*, 2 February 1989, C-22/87, ECR, 1989, 143.
Commission of the European Communities v. *Italian Republic*, 30 May 1989, C-340/87, ECR, 1989, 1483.
Commission of the European Communities v. *Italian Republic*, 26 October 1983, C-163/82, ECR, 1983, 3273–3290.
Commission of the European Communities v. *Italian Republic*, C-283/99, 31 May 2001, ECR, 2001, 4363.
Commission of the European Communities v. *Jean-Louis Tourdeur and others*, 3 October 1985, C-232/84, ECR, 1985, 3223–3236.
Commission v. *Luxembourg*, 2 July 1996, C-473/93, ECR, 1996, 3207.
Commission of the European Communities v. *Kingdom of Belgium*, 28 March 1985, C-215/83, ECR, 1985, 1039–1055.
Commission of the European Communities v. *Kingdom of Belgium*, 17 December 1980, C-149/79, ECR, 1982, 3881–3905.
Commission of the European Communities v. *Kingdom of Belgium*, 26 May 1982, C-149/9, ECR, 1982, 1845.
Commission of the European Communities v. *Kingdom of Belgium*, 24 October 1985, C-293/85R, ECR, 1985, 3521–3529.
Commission of the European Communities v. *Kingdom of Belgium*, 15 April 1986, C-237/84, ECR, 1986, 1247–1257.
Commission of the European Communities v. *Kingdom of Belgium*, 2 February 1988, C-293/85, ECR, 1988, 305.

List of Cases of the ECJ

Commission of the European Communities v. *Kingdom of Belgium*, 27 September 1988, C-42/87, ECR, 1988, 5445.

Commission of the European Communities v. *Kingdom of Belgium*, 27 April 1989, C-321/87, ECR, 1989, 997.

Commission of the European Communities v. *Kingdom of Belgium*, 17 February 1993, C-173/91, ECR, 1993, 673.

Commission of the European Communities v. *Kingdom of Belgium*, 3 March 1994, C-47/93, ECR, 1994, 1593.

Commission v. *Belgium*, 20 February 1997, C-344/95, ECR, 1997, 1035.

Commission of the European Communities v. *Kingdom of Denmark*, 30 January 1985, C-143/83, ECR, 1985, 427–437.

Commission of the European Communities v. *Kingdom of the Netherlands*, C-68/89, 30 May 1991, ECR, 1991, 2637.

Commission of the European Communities v. *Kingdom of Spain*, 22 March 1994, C-375/92, ECR, 1994, 923.

Commission of the European Communities v. *United Kingdom of Great Britain and Northern Ireland*, 6 July 1982, C-61/81, ECR, 1982, 2601–2618.

Commission of the European Communities v. *United Kingdom of Great Britain and Northern Ireland*, 8 November 1983, C-165/82, ECR, 1983, 3431–3451.

Commission of the European Communities v. *United Kingdom of Great Britain and Northern Ireland*, 8 June 1994, C-382/93 and C-383/92, ECR, 1994, 2479.

Commission v. *Republic of Austria*, 7 July 2005, C-147/03, ECR, 2005, 5969.

Commission v. *Kingdom of Belgium*, 1 July 2004, C-65/03, ECR, 2004, 6427.

Commission of the European Communities v. *Grand Duchy of Luxemburg*, 21 October 2004, C-445/03, ECR, 2004, 3067.

Commission v. *Portuguese Republic*, 12 October 2004, C-55/02, ECR, 2004, 9387.

Commission v. *Italian Republic*, 16 October 2003, C-32/02, 12063.

Commission v. *Federal Republic of Germany*, 25 October 2001, C-493/99, ECR, 2001, 8163.

Commission v. *Republic of Austria*, 1 February 2005, C-203/03, ECR, 2005, 935.

Commission v. *Republic of Austria*, 5 April 2004, C-168/04, ECR, 2006, 9041.

Commission of the European Communities v. *Federal Republic of Germany*, 18 July 2007, C-490/04, ECR, 2007, 6095.

Commission of the European Communities v. *Grand Duchy of Luxembourg*, 14 April 2005, C-519/03, ECR, 2005, 3067.

Commission of the European Communities v. *The Italian Republic*, 12 May 2005, C-278/03, ECR, 2005, 3747.

Commission of the European Communities v. *Germany*, 19 January 2006, C-244/04, ECR, 2006, 885.

Commission of the European Communities v. *Kingdom of Spain*, 26 January 2006, C-514/03, ECR, 2006, 963.

Commission v. *United Kingdom*, 7 September 2006, C-484/04, ECR, 2006, 7471.

Commission of the European Communities v. *Republic of Austria*, 21 September 2006, C-168/04, ECR, 2006, 9041.

Commission of the European Communities v. *Italian Republic*, C-371/04, 26 October 2006, ECR, 2006, 10257.

List of Cases of the ECJ

Commission v. Germany, 18 July 2007, Case C-490/04, ECR, 2007, 6095. *Commission v. Grand Duchy of Luxembourg*, 19 June 2008, C-319/06, ECR, 2008, 4323.
Commission v. Greece, 26 March 2009, C-559/07, www.curia.eu.
Commission v Kingdom of the Netherlands, 14 June 2012, C-542/09, www.curia.eu.
Commission v. Hungary, 6 November 2012, C-286/12, www. curia. eu.
Commission v. Kingdom of Belgium, 19 December 2012, C-557/10, www. curia.eu
Commission v Italian Republic, 4 July 2013, C-312/11, www. curia.eu.
Collino Renato and Luisella Chiappero v. Telecom Italia SpA, 14 September 2000, C-343/98, ECR, 2000, 6659.
Confederación Intersindical Galega (CIG) and Servicio Galego de Saúde (Sergas), 3 July 2001, C-241/99, ECR, 2001, 5139.
Confédération générale du travail (CGT) and others v. Premier ministre, 18 January 2007, C-385/05, ECR, 2007, 611.
Coote, Belinda Jane v. Granada Hospitality Ltd., 22 September 1998, C-185/97, ECR, 1998, 5199.
Anacleto Cordero Alonso v. Fondo de Garantía Salarial (Fogasa), 7 September 2006, C-81/05, ECR, 2006, 7569.
Council of the City of Stoke-on-Trent and Norwich City Councils v. B&Q plc., C-169/91, 16 December 1992, ECR, 1992, 6635.
Criminal proceedings against A. Marchandise and others, 28 February 1991, C-332/89, ECR, 1991, 1027.
Criminal proceedings v. Florus Ariël Wijsenbeek, 21 September 1999, C-378/97, ECR, 1999, 6207.
Criminal proceedings against Lothar Messner, 12 December 1989, C-265/88, ECR, 1989, 4209.
Criminal proceedings against Michel Choquet, 28 November 1978, C-16/78, ECR, 1978, 2293–2304.
Criminal proceedings against Jean-Claude Arblade and Arblade & Fils SARL (C-369/96) and *Bernard Leloup, Serge Leloup and Sofrage SARL* (C-376/96), 23 November 1999, ECR, 1999, 8453.
Criminal proceedings against André Mazzoleni and Inter Surveillance Assistance SARL, 15 March 2001, C-165/98, ECR, 2001, 2189.
Criminal proceedings against André Mazzoleni and Inter Surveillance Assistance SARL, 15 March 2001, C-165/98, ECR, 2001, 2189.
Cristini Anita v. Société nationale des chemins de fer français, 30 September 1975, C-32/75, ECR, 1975, 1085.
d'Urso G. and others v. Ercole Marelli Elettromeccanica (EMG), Nuova EMG and others, 25 July 1991, C-362/89, ECR, 1991, 4105.
Dansk Metalarbejderforbund and Specialarbejderforbundet i Danmark v. H. Nielsen & Son, Maskinfabrik A/S, in liquidation, 12 February 1985, C-284/83, ECR, 1985, 553.
Danmark Aktive Handelrejsende acting for Carina Mosbaeck v. Lonmodtagernes Garantifond, 17 September 1997, C-117/96, ECR, 1997, 5017.
Danmarks Rederiforening, acting on behalf of DFDS Torline A/S v. LO Landsorganisationen i Sverige, acting on behalf of SEKO Sjöfolk Facket för Service och Kommunikation, 5 February 2004, C-18/02, ECR, 2004, 1417.

List of Cases of the ECJ

David Claes a.o. v. *Landsbanki Luxembourg SA, in liquidation*, 3 March 2011, C-235/10, www.curia.eu.
Defrenne Gabrielle v. *Belgian State*, 25 May 1971, C-80/70, ECR, 1971, 445–454.
Defrenne Gabrielle v. *Société Anonyme Belge de Navigation Aérienne Sabena*, 8 April 1976, C-43/75, ECR, 1976, 455–483.
Defrenne Gabrielle v. *Société Anonyme Belge de Navigation Aérienne Sabena*, 15 June 1978, C-149/77, ECR, 1978, 1365–1380.
Defreyn Marthe v. *Sabena SA*, 13 July 2000, C-166/99, ECR, 2000, 6155.
Dekker E.J.P. v. *Stichting Vormingscentrum voor Jong Volwassenen (VJV-centrum) Plus*, 8 November 1990, C-177/88, ECR, 1990, 3941.
Delay Nancy v. *Università degli studi di Firenze*, 15 May 2008, C-276/07, ECR, 2008, 3635.
Del Cerro Alonso Yolanda v. *Osakidetza-Servicio Vasco de Salud*, 13 September 2007, C-307/05, ECR, 2007, 7109.
Deliège Christelle v. *Ligue Francophone de Judo et Disciplines ASBL and Others*, 11 April 2000, Joined Cases C-51/96 and C-191/97, ECR, 2000, 2549.
Abdelkader Dellas and Others v. *Premier ministre and Others*, 1 December 2005, C-14/04, ECR, 2005, 10235.
Demirel Meryem v. *Stadt Schwäbisch Gmünd*, 30 September 1987, C-12/86, ECR, 1987, 3719.
Dermod Patrick O'Brien v. Ministry of Justice, 1 March 2012, C-393/10, www.curia. eu.
Deutsche Lufthansa AG v. *Gertraud Kumpan*, 10 March 2011, C-109/09, www.curia.eu.
Deutscher Handballbund eV v. *Maros Kolpak*, 8 May 2003, C-438/00, ECR, 2003, 4135.
Jules Dethier Equipement SA/J. Dassy en Sovam SPRL, 12 March 1998, C-319/94, ECR, 1998, 1061.
De Vos Peter v. *Stadt Bielefeld*, 14 March 1996, C-315/94, ECR, 1996, 1447.
Diatta Aissatou v. *Land Berlin*, 13 February 1985, C-267/83, ECR, 1985, 567.
Dietrich Margrit v. *Westdeutscher Rundfunk*, 6 July 2000, C-11/99, ECR, 2000, 5589.
Dietz Francina Johanna Maria v. *Stichting Thuiszorg Rotterdam*, 24 October 1996, C-435/93, ECR, 1996, 5224.
Di Leo C. v. *Land Berlin*, 13 November 1990, No. C-308/89, ECR, 1990, 4185.
Dimossia Epicheirissi Ilektrismou (DEI) v. *Efthimios Evrenenopoulos*, 17 April 1997, C-147/95, ECR, 1997, 2057.
Directeur régional de la sécurité sociale de Nancy v. *Auguste Hirardin and Caisse régionale d'assurance maladie du Nord-Est*, 8 April 1976, C-112/75, ECR, 1976, 553–562.
Dita Danosa v. *LKB L zings SIA*, 11 November 2010, C-232/09, www.curia.eu.
Domnica Petersen v. *Berufungsausschuss für Zahnärzte für den Bezirk Westfalen-Lippe*, 12 January 2010, C-341/08, www.curia.eu.
Dona Gaetano v. *Mario Mantero*, 14 July 1976, C-13/76, ECR, 1976, 1333–1342.
Donato Casagrande v. *Landeshauptstadt München*, 3 July 1974, C-9/74, ECR, 1974, 773–780.

List of Cases of the ECJ

Dory Alexander v. *Federal Republic of Germany*, 11 March 2003, C-186/01, ECR, 2003, 2479.

Draehmpaehl Nils v. *Urania Immobilienreserve OHG*, 22 April 1997, C-180/95, ECR, 1997, 1317.

Dzodzi M. v. *Belgian State*, 18 October 1990, Joined Cases C-297/88 and 197/89, ECR, 1990, 3763.

Echternach G.B.C. and A. Moritz v. *the Netherlands Minister for Education and Science*, 15 March 1989, Joined Cases C-389 and 390/87, ECR, 1989, 723.

Elefanten Schuh GmbH v. *Pierre Jacqmain*, 24 June 1981, C-150/80, ECR, 1981, 1671–1690.

Elodie Giersch and Others v État du Grand-Duché de Luxembourg, 20 June 2013, C-20/12, www. curia.eu.

Elsner-Lakeberg Edeltraud v. *Land Nordrhein-Westfalen*, 27 May 2004, C-285/02, ECR, 2004, 5861.

Europièces SA v. *Wilfried Sanders and Automotive Industries Holding Company SA*, 12 November 1998, C-399/96, ECR, 1998, 6965.

Everson G. and Barrass T.J. v. *Secretary of State for Trade and Industry, Bell Lines Ltd.*, 16 December 1999, C-198/98, ECR, 1999, 8903.

F. (Mr. and Mrs.) v. *Belgian State, 17 June 1975, C-7/75, ECR, 1975, 679–691.*

Federación de Servicios Públicos de la UGT (UGT-FSP) v. *Ayuntamiento de La Línea de la Concepción*, 29 July 2010, C-151/09, www.curia.eu.

Federal Republic of Germany and others v. *Commission of the European Communities*, 9 July 1987, Joined Cases C-281, 283 and 287/85, ECR, 1987, 3203.

Federatie Nederlandse Vakbeweging v. *Staat der Nederlanden*, 6 April 2006, C-124/05, ECR, 2006, 3423.

Fisscher Geertruida Catharina v. *Voorhuis Hengelo BV and Stichting Bedrijfspensioenfonds voor de Detailhandel*, 28 September 1994, C-128/93, ECR, 1994, 4583.

John O'Flynn v. *Adjudication Officer*, 23 May 1996, C-237/94, ECR, 1996, 2617.

Foreningen af Arbejdsledere i Danmark v. *A/S Danmols Inventar, in liquidation*, 11 July 1985, C-105/84, ECR, 1985, 2639–2654.

Foreningen af Arbejdsledere i Danmark v. *Daddy's Dance Hall A/S*, 10 February 1988, C-324/86, ECR, 1988, 739.

Foster A. and others v. *British Gas plc*, 12 July 1990, C-188/89, ECR, 1990, 3313.

Francesca Sorge v. *Poste Italiane SpA*, 24 June 2010, C-98/09, www.curia.eu.

Franchovich A. and others v. *Italian Republic*, 19 November 1991, C-6/90 and C-9/90,
ECR, 1991, 5357.

Francovich Andrea v. *Italian Republic*, 9 November 1995, C-479/93, ECR, 1995, 3843.

Francisco Javier Rosado Santana v Consejería de Justicia y Administración Pública de la Junta de Andalucía, 8 September 2011, C-177/10, www. curia.eu

Frascogna Maria v. *Caisse des dépôts et consignations*, 9 July 1987, C-256/86, ECR, 1987, 3431.

Freers Edith, Hannelore Speckman v. *Deutsche Bundespost*, 7 March 1996, C-278/93, ECR, 1996, 1165.

List of Cases of the ECJ

Garland Eileen v. *British Rail Engineering Limited*, 9 February 1982, C-12/81, ECR, 1982, 359.
Galina Meister v. Speech Design Carrier Systems GmbH., 19 April 2012, Case C-415/10, www. curia.eu
Gebhard Reinhard v. *Consiglio dell'Ordine degli Avvocati e Procuratori di Milano*, 30 November 1995, C-55/94, ECR, 1995, 4165.
Georg Neidel v Stadt Frankfurt am Main, 3 May 2012, C-337/10, www. curia.eu
Gerhard Fuchs v. *Land Hessen*, 21 July 2011 (C159/10), www.curia.eu.
Gerster Hellen v. *Freistaat Bayern*, 2 October 1997, C-1/95, ECR, 1997, 5253.
Gesamtbetriebsrat der Kühne & Nagel AG & Co. KG v. *Kühne & Nagel AG & Co. KG*, 13 January 2004, C-440/00, ECR, 2004, 787.
Wendy Geven v. *Land Nordrhein-Westfalen*, 18 July 2007, C-213/05, ECR, 2007, 6347.
Giagounidis P. v. *Stadt Reutlingen*, 5 March 1991, C-376/89, ECR, 1991, 1069.
Gillespie Joan and others v. *Northern Health and Social Services Board and others*, 13 February 1996, C-342/93, ECR, 1996, 475.
Giménez Zaera Fernando Roberto v. *Instituto Nacional de la Seguridad Social y Tesoreria General de la Seguridad Social*, 29 September 1987, C-126/86, ECR, 1987, 3697.
Giovanni Maria Sotgiu v. *Deutsche Bundespost*, 12 February 1974, C-172/73, ECR, 1974, 153.
Gisela Rosenbladt v. *Oellerking Gebäudereinigungsges mbH*, 12 October 2010, C-45/09, www.curia.eu.
Glaxosmithkline, Laboratoires Glaxosmithkline v. *Jean-Pierre Rouard*, 22 May 2008, C-462/06, ECR, 2009, 3965.
Graf, Volker v. *Filzmoser Maschinenbau GmbH*, 27 January 2000, C-190/98, ECR, 2000, 493.
Grant L.J. v. *South West Trains Ltd.*, 17 February 1998, C-249/96, ECR, 1998, 671.
Gravier Françoise v. *City of Liège*, 13 February 1985, C-293/83, ECR, 1985, 593.
Grimaldi S. v. *Fonds des Maladies Professionnelles*, 13 December 1989, C-332/88, ECR, 1989, 4407.
Groener A. v. *Minister for Education and the City of Dublin Vocational Education Committee (CDVEC)*, 28 November 1989, C-379/87, ECR, 1989, 3967.
Guiot Michel v. *Climatec SA*, C-272/94, ECR, 1996, 1905.
Gül E. v. *Regierungspräsident Dusseldorf*, 7 May 1986, C-131/85, ECR, 1986, 1573.
Günter Fuß v. *Stadt Halle*, 14 October 2010, C-243/09, www.curia.eu.
Günter Fuß v. *Stadt Halle*, 25 November 2010, C-429/09, www.curia.eu.
Nurten Güney-Görres, Gul Demir v. *Securicor Aviation (Germany), Ltd, Kötter Aviation Security GmbH & Co. KG*, 15 December 2005, Joined Cases C-232/04 and C-233/04, ECR, 2005, 11237.
Habermann-Beltermann G. v. *Arbeiterwohlfarht, Bezirksverband Ndb./Opf. e.V.*, 5 May 1994, C-421/92, ECR, 1994, 1657.
Haim S. v. *Kassenzahnärztliche Vereinigung Nordrhein (KVN)*, 9 February 1994, C-319/92, ECR, 1994, 425.
Handels-og Kontorfunktionaeremes Forbund i Danmark v. *Dansk Arbejdsgiverforening (for Danfoss)*, 17 October 1989, C-109/88, ECR, 1989, 3979.

List of Cases of the ECJ

Handels-og Kontorfunktionaeremes Forbund i Danmark v. *Dansk Arbejdsgiverforening*, 8 November 1990, C-179/88, ECR, 1990, 3979.

Handels-og Kontorfunktionærernes Forbund i Danmark, acting on behalf of Berit Høj Pedersen v. *Fællesforeningen for Danmarks Brugsforeninger and Dansk Tandlægeforening and Kristelig Funktionær-Organisation* v. *Dansk Handel & Service*, 19 November 1998, C-66/96, ECR, 1998, 7327.

Gertraud Hartmann v. *Freistaat Bayern*, 18 July 2007, C-212/05, ECR, 2007, 6303.

Harz Dorit v. *Deutsche Tradax GmbH*, 10 April 1984, C-79/83, ECR, 1984, 1921.

Henke Annette v. *Gemeinde Schierke and Verwaltungsgemeinschaft 'Brocken'*, 15 October 1996, C-298/94, ECR, 1996, 4989.

Hill Kathleen and Ann Stapleton v. *the Revenue Commissioners and the Department of Finance*, 17 June 1998, C-243/95, ECR, 1998, 3739.

HK Danmark, acting on behalf of Jette Ring v Dansk almennyttigt Boligselskab (C-335/11) and HK Danmark, acting on behalf of Lone Skouboe Werge v Dansk Arbejdsgiverforening acting on behalf of Pro Display A/S (C-337/11), 11 April 2013, www. curia eu.

Hoekstra M.K.M. (née Unger) v. *Bestuur der Bedrijfsvereniging voor Detailhandel en Ambachten (Administration of the Industrial Board for Retail Trades and Businesses)*, 19 March 1964, C-75/63, ECR, 1964, 369.

Höfner K. and F. Elser v. *Macrotron GmbH*, 23 April 1991, C-41/90, ECR, 1991, 1979.

Hofmann Ulrich v. *Barmer Ersatzkasse*, 12 July 1984, C-184/83, ECR, 1984, 3047.

Hütter David v. *Technische Universität Graz*, 18 June 2009, C-88/08, not yet published.

Impact v. *Minister for Agriculture and Food*, 15 April 2008, C-268/06, ECR, 2008, 2483.

Industriebond FNV and Federatie Nederlandse Vakbeweging (FNV) v. *The Netherlands State*, 7 February 1985, C-179/83, ECR, 1985, 511.

Ingeniørforeningen i Danmark, acting on behalf of Bertram Holst, 11 February 2010, C-405/08, www.curia.eu.

Ingeniørforeningen i Danmark, acting on behalf of Ole Andersen v. *Region Syddanmark*, 12 October 2010, C-499/08, www.curia.eu.

Institut national d'assurances sociales pour travailleurs independents v. *Nicola Cantisani*, 11 July 1985, C-111/84, ECR, 1985, 2671.

Istituto nazionale della previdenza sociale (INPS) v. *Alberto Barsotti and Others*, 4 March 2004, (C-19/01), *Milena Castellani* v. *Istituto nazionale della previdenza sociale (INPS)* (C-50/01) and *Istituto nazionale della previdenza sociale (INPS)* v. *Anna Maria Venturi* (C-84/01), 4 March 2004, Joined Cases C-19/01, C-50/01 and C-84/01, ECR, 2004, 2005.

Istituto nazionale della previdenza sociale (INPS) v. *Tiziana Bruno a.o.*, 10 June 2010, C-395/08 and C-396/08, www.curia.eu.

International Transport Workers' Federation, Finnish Seamen's Union v. *Viking Line ABP, OÜ Viking Line Eesti*, 11 December 2007, C-438/05, ECR, 2007, 779.

Inzirillo Vito v. *Caisse d'Allocations Familiales de l'Arrondissement de Lyon*, 16 December 1976, C-63/76, ECR, 1976, 2057.

Iorio Paolo v. *Azienda autonoma delle Ferrovie dello Stato*, 23 January 1986, C-298/84, ECR, 1986, 247.

List of Cases of the ECJ

Ivana Scattolon, v. Ministerio ... , 6 September 2011, Case C-108/10, www. curia;eu.
Ivenel Roger v. *Helmut Schwab*, 8 June 1982, C-133/81, ECR, 1982, 1891.
Jackson S. and P. Cresswell v. *Chief Adjudication Officer*, 16 July 1992, C-63/91 and C-64/91, ECR, 1992, 4737.
Jämställdhetsombudsmannen v. *Orebro läns landsting*, 30 March 2000, C-236/98, ECR, 2000, 2189.
Jan Voogsgeerd v. Navimer SA, 15 December 2011, C-384/10, www. curia.eu
J. C. van Ardennen v. Raad van bestuur van het Uitvoeringsinstituut werknemersverzekeringen, 17 November 2011, C-435/10,www. curia. eu
Jenkins J.P. v. *Kingsgate (Clothing Productions) Ltd.*, 31 March 1981, C-96/80, ECR, 1981, 911. *Job Centre coop.arl*, 11 December 1997, C-55/96, ECR, 1997, 7119.
Johann Odar v Baxter Deutschland GmbH., 6 December 2012, C-152/11, www.curia. eu.
John O'Flynn v. *Adjudication Officer*, 23 May 1996, C-237/94, ECR, 1996, 2617.
Johnston M. v. *Chief Constable of the Royal Ulster Constabulary*, 15 May 1986, C-222/84, ECR, 1986, 1651.
Jouini Mohamed and others, 13 September 2007, C-458/05, OJ., 10 November 2007.
Junk Irmtraud v. *Wolfgang Kühnel*, 27 January 2005, C-188/03, ECR, 2005, 885.
Jürgen Römer v. *Freie und Hansestadt Hamburg*, 10 May 2011, C-147/08, www.curia.eu.
Juuri Mirja v. *Fazer Amica Oy*, 27 November 2008, C-396/07, www.curia.eu.
Kachelmann Bärbel v. *Bankhaus Hermann Lampe KG*, 26 September 2000, C-322/98, ECR, 2000, 7505.
Kalanke v. *Freie Hansestadt Bremen (City of Bremen)*, 17 October 1995, C-450/93, ECR, 1995, 3051.
Kampelmann Helmut and others v. *Stadtwerke Altena GmbH e.a.*, 4 December 1997, C-53/96 and C-258/96, ECR, 1997, 6907.
Kapasakalis A., Skiathitis D., Kougiankas A., Joined Cases, 2 July 1998, C-225/95, C-226/95 and C-227/95, ECR, 1998, 4239.
Katsikas G. and others v. *A. Konstantinidis and others*, 16 December 1992, C-132/91, C-138/91 and C-139/91, ECR, 1992, 6577.
K.B. v. *National Health Service Pensions Agency and Secretary of State for Health*, 7 January 2004, C-117/01, ECR, 2004, 541.
*Kempf R.H.*v. *Staatssecretaris van Justitie*, 3 June 1986, C-139/85, ECR, 1986, 1741.
KHS AG v. Winfried Schulte, 22 November 2011, C-214/10, www. curia. eu
Kiiski Sari v. *Tampereen kaupunki*, 20 September 2007, C-116/06, www.curia.eu.
Kiriaki Angelidaki v. *Organismos Nomarkhiaki Aftodiikisi Rethimnis*, 23 April 2009, (C-378/07), www.curia.eu.
Kirshammer P., Hack v. *Nurham Sidal*, 30 November 1993, C-189/91, ECR, 1993, 6185.
Kirtruna SL, Elisa Vigano v. *Red Elite de Electrodomésticos SA*, 16 October 2008, C-313/07, www.curia.eu.

List of Cases of the ECJ

Klarenberg Dietmar v. *Ferrotron Technologies GmbH*, 12 February 2009, C-466/07, www.curia.eu.
Klein Steffen v. *Commission of the European Communities*, 20 June 1985, C-29/84, ECR, 1985, 1907.
Knud Wendelboe and others v. *K.J. Music ApS in liquidation*, 7 February 1985, C-19/83, ECR, 1985, 457.
Köbler Gerhard v. *Republik Österreich*, 30 September 2003, C-224/01, ECR, 2003, 10239.
Koks G.F. v. *Raad van Arbeid*, 23 September 1982, C-275/81, ECR, 1982, 3013.
Adeneler Konstantinos and others, 4 July 2006, C-212/04, ECR, 2006, 6057.
Kording Brigitte v. *Senator für Finanzen*, 2 October 1997, C-100/95, ECR, 1997, 5289.
Kowalska Maria v. *Freie und Hansestadt Hamburg*, 27 June 1990, C-33/89, ECR, 1990, 2591.
Kranemann Karl Robert v. *Land Nordrhein-Westfalen*, 17 March 2005, C-109/04, ECR, 2005, 2421.
Kraus Dieter v. *Land Baden-Württemberg*, 31 March 1993, C-19/92, ECR, 1993, 1663.
Kreil, Tanja v. *Bundesrepublik Deutschland*, 11 January 2000, C-285/98, ECR, 2000, 69.
Krüger, Andrea v. *Kreiskrankenhaus Ebersberg*, 9 September 1999, C-281/97, ECR, 1999, 5127.
Kuratorium für Dialyse und Nierentransplantation v. *Johanna Lewark*, 6 February 1996, C-457/93, ECR, 1996, 243.
Kutz-Bauer Helga v. *Freie und Hansestadt Hamburg*, 20 March 2003, C-187/00, ECR, 2003, 2741.
Lair Sylvie v. *Universität Hannover*, 21 June 1988, C-39/86, ECR, 1988, 3161.
Landesambt für Ausbildungsförderung Nordrhein-Westfalen v. *Lubor Gaal*, C-7/94, ECR, 1995, 1031.
Landeshauptstadt Kiel v. *Norbert Jaeger*, 9 September 2003, C-151/02, ECR, 2003, 8389.
Landgren Pia v. *Fondation Européenne pour la Formation (EFT)*, 26 October 2006, F-1/05, Tribunal de la Fonction publique, www.curia.eu.
Land Nordrhein Westfalen v. *Uecker Kari; Jacquet Vera* v. *Land Nordrhein Westfalen*, 5 June 1997, C-64/96 and C-65/96, ECR, 1997, 3171.
Landsorganisationen i Danmark for tjenerforbundet i Danmark v. *Ny Molle Kro*, 17 December 1987, C-287/86, ECR, 1987, 5465.
Lange Wolfgang v. *Georg Schünemann GmbH*, 8 February 2001, C-350/99, ECR, 2001, 1061.
Laval un Partneri Ltd v. *Svenska Byggnadsarbetareförbundet, Svenska Byggnadsarbetareförbundets avdelning 1, Byggettan, Svenska Elektrikerförbundet*, 18 December 2007, C-341/05, ECR, 2007, 11767.
Lawrie-Blum Deborah v. *Land Baden-Württemberg*, 3 July 1986, C-66/85, ECR, 1986, 2121.
Lehtonen Jyri, Castors Canada Dry Namur-Braine ASBL and Fédération Royale Belge des Sociétés de Basket-ball ASBL (FRBSB), C-176/96, 13 April 2000, ECR, 2000, 26814.

List of Cases of the ECJ

Levez B.S. v. Jennings T.H. (Harlow Pools Ltd.), 1 December 1998, C-326/96, ECR, 1998, 7835.

Levin D.M. v. *Staatssecretaris van Justitie*, 23 March 1982, C-53/81, ECR, 1982, 1035.

Lommers H., and Minister van Landbouw, Natuurbeheer en Visserij, 19 March 2002, C-476/99, ECR, 2001, 2891.

Lewen, Susanne v. *Lothar Denda*, 21 October 1999, C-333/97, ECR, 1999, 7243.

Liefting W.G.M. and others v. *Directie van het Academisch Ziekenhuis Amsterdam*, 18 September 1984, C-23/83, ECR, 1984, 3225.

2Lotta Andersson v. *Staten genom Kronofogdemyndigheten i Jönköping, Tillsyns myndigheten*, 10 February 2011, C-30/10, www.curia.eu.

Maag H. v. *Commission of the European Communities*, 11 July 1985, C-43/84, ECR, 1985, 2581.

Macarthys Ltd. v. *Wendy Smith*, 27 March 1980, C-129/79, ECR, 1980, 1275.

Mahlburg Silke-Karin v. *Land Mecklenburg-Vorpommern*, 3 February 2000, C-207/98, ECR, 2000, 549.

Maira María Robledillo Núñez v. *Fondo de Garantía Salarial (Fogasa)*, 21 February 2008, C-498/06, ECR, 2008, 921.

Werner Mangold v. *Rüdiger Helm*, 22 November 2005, C-144/04, ECR, 2005, 9981.

Margaret Kenny a.o. v. Minister for Justice, Equality and Law Reform, 28 February 2013, C-427/11, www. curia.eu.

Maribel Dominguez v Centre informatique du Centre Ouest Atlantique and Préfet de la région Centre, 24 January 2012, C-282/10, www.curia.eu.

Marschall Hellmut v. *Land Nordrhein-Westfalen*, 11 November 1997, C-409/959, ECR, 1997, 6363.

Marshall M.H. v. *Southampton and South-West Hampshire Area Health Authority (Teaching)*, 26 February 1986, C-152/84, ECR, 1986, 723.

Marshall M.H. v. *Southampton and South West Area Health Authority*, 2 August 1993, C-271/91, ECR, 1993, 4367.

Marsman Pieter v. *M. Roskamp*, 13 December 1972, C-44/72, ECR, 1972, 1243.

Martial Huet v. Université de Bretagne occidentale, 8 March 2012, C-251/11, www. curia. eu.

Martin Serene, Daby Rohit, Willis Brian v. *South Bank University*, 6 November 2003, C-4/01, ECR, 2003, 12895.

Cristiano Marrosu, Gianluca Sardino v. *Azienda Ospedaliera Ospedale San Martino di Genova e Cliniche Universitarie Convenzionate*, 7 September 2006, C-53/04, ECR, 2006, 7213.

Maruko Tadao v. *Versorgungsanstalt der deutschen Bühnen*, 1 April 2008, C-267/06, ECR, 2008, 1757.

Maso Frederico and others v. *Italian Republic*, 10 July 1997, C-373/95, ECR, 1997, 4051.

Cynthia Mattern and Hajrudin Cikotic v. *Ministre du Travail et de l'Emploi*, 30 March 2006, C-10/05, ECR, 2006, 3145.

Matteuci Annunziata v. *Communauté française of Belgium and Commissariat général aux relations internationales of the Communauté française of Belgium*, 27 September 1988, C-235/87, ECR, 1988, 5589.

List of Cases of the ECJ

Maxwell Middleburgh D. v. *Chief Adjudication Officer*, 4 October 1991, C-151/90, ECR, 1991, 4655.
Mayeur Didier v. *Association Promotion de l'information messine (APIM)*, 26 September 2000, C-175/99, ECR, 2000, 7755.
Mayr Sabine v. *Bäckerei und Konditorei Gerhard Flöckner OHG*, C-506/06, 26 February 2008, ECR, 2008, 1017.
David Meca-Medina & Igor Majcen v. *Commission of the European Communities*, 18 July 2006, C-519/04, ECR 2006, 6991.
Meerts Christel v. *Proost NV*, 22 October 2009, C-116/08, not yet published.
Meeusen C.P.M., and Hoofddirectie van de Informatie Beheer Groep, 8 June 1999, C-337/97, ECR, 1999, 3289.
Melgar Maria Luisa Jiménez and Ayuntamiento de Los Barrios, 4 October 2001, Case C-438/99, ECR, 2001, 6915.
Merci Convenzionali porto di Genova v. *Siderurgica Gabrielli SpA*, 10 December 1991, C-179/90, ECR, 1991, 5889.
Merckx Albert and Patrick Neuhuys v. *Ford Motor Company Belgium*, 7 March 1996, C-171/94 and C-172/94, ECR, 1996, 1253.
Meyers Jennifer v. *UK*, 13 July 1995, C-116/94, ECR, 1995, 2131.
Michaeler Othmar (C-55/07 and C-56/07) *and others* v. *Amt für sozialen Arbeitsschutz*, 24 April 2008, ECR, 2008, 3135.
Meliha Veli Mustafa v Direktor na fond "Garantirani vzemania na rabotnitsite i sluzhitelite" kam Natsionalnia osiguritelen institut, 18 April 2013, C-247/12, www. curia.eu
Ministre de l'Intérieur v. *Aitor Oteiza Olazabal*, 26 November 2002, C-100/01, ECR, 2002, 10981.
Ministère Public v. *Gilbert Even and Office National des Pensions pour Travailleurs Salariés*, 31 May 1979, C-207/78, ECR, 1979, 2019.
Ministère Public v. *J.C. Levy*, 2 August 1993, C-158/91, ECR, 1993, 4287.
Ministère Public v. *Robert Heinrich Maria Mutsch*, 11 July 1985, C-137/84, ECR, 1985, 2781.
Ministère Public v. *A Stoeckel*, 25 July 1991, C-345/89, ECR, 1991, 4047.
Mono Car Styling SA, in liquidation, v. *Dervis Odemis and Others*, 16 July 2009, C-12/08, www.curia.
Moroni M. v. *Firma Collo GmbH*, 14 December 1993, C-110/91, ECR, 1995, 6591.
Morson Elestina Esselina Christina v. *State of the Netherlands and Head of the Plaatselijke Politie within the meaning of the Vreemdelingenwet; Sewradjie Jhanjan* v. *State of the Netherlands*, 27 October 1982, C-35 and 36/82, ECR, 1982, 3723.
Mosbaeck Carina v. *Lonmodtagerness Garantifond*, C-117/96, ECR, 1997, 5017.
Moser Hans v. *Land Baden-Württemberg*, 28 June 1984, C-180/83, ECR, 1984, 2539.
Mulox IBC Limited v. *H. Geels*, 13 July 1993, C-125/92, ECR, 1994, 4075.
Murphy Mary and others v. *Board Telecom Eireann*, 4 February 1988, C-157/86, ECR, 1988, 673.
Mutu Adrian v. *Chelsea Football Club Limited*, CAS 2008/A/1644 Arbitral Award, 31 July 2009.

List of Cases of the ECJ

Nadežda Riežniece v Zemkopības ministrija and Lauku atbalsta dienests, 20 June 2013, Case C-7/12, www. curia. eu.
National Patrick Kelly v. *University of Ireland (University College, Dublin)*, 21 July 2011, C-104/10, www.curia.eu.
Neath D. v. *Hugh Steeper Ltd.*, 22 December 1993, C-152/91, ECR, 1993, 6935.
Newstead George Noel v. *Department of Transport of Her Majesty's Treasury*, 3 December 1987, C-192/85, ECR, 1987, 4753.
Nikoloudi Vasiliki v. *Organismos Tilepikinonion Ellados AE*, 10 March 2005, C-196/02, ECR, 2005, 1789.
Nimz H. v. *Freie Hansestadt Hamburg*, 7 February 1991, C-184/89, ECR, 1991, 297.
Nonnenmacher, widow of H.E. Moebs v. *Bestuur der Sociale Verzekeringsbank*, 9 June 1964, C-92/63, ECR, 1964, 583.
North Western Health Board v. *Margaret McKenna*, 8 September 2005, C-191/03, ECR, 2005, 7631.
Olaso Valero José Vicente v. *Fondo de Garantía Salarial (Fogasa)*, 16 December 2004, C-520/03, ECR, 2004, 12065.
Olympique Lyonnais v. *Olivier Bernard and Newcastle United FC*, 16 March 2010, C-325/08, www.curia.eu.
Oreste Della Rocca v Poste Italiane SpA., 11 April 2013, C-290/12,www. curia.eu.
Österreisschicher Gewerkschaftsbund, Gewerkschaft öffentlicher Dienst v. *Republik österreich*, 30 November 2000, C-195/98, ECR, 2000, 10497.
Ovidio Rodríguez Mayor and Others v. *Herencia yacente de Rafael de las Heras Dávila and Others*, 10 December 2009, C-323/08, www.curia.eu.
Oy Liikenne Ab v. *Pekka Liskojärvi and Pentti Juntunen*, 25 January 2001, C-172/99, ECR, 2001, 745.
Palacios de la Villa Felix v. *Cortefiel Servicios SA*, 16 October 2007, C-411/05, OJ., 8 December 2007, 6.
Paquay Nadine v. *Société d'architectes Hoet + Minne SPRL*, 11 October 2007, C-460/06, OJ., 8 December 2007, 12.
P. v. *S. and Cornwall County Council*, 30 April 1996, C-13/94, ECR, 1996, 2143.
P. Bork International A/S, in liquidation, and others v. *Foreningen of Arbejdsledere i Danmark, acting on behalf of Birger E. Petersen and Junckers Industrier A/S*, 15 June 1988, C-101/87, ECR, 1988, 3057.
Paz Merino Gómez María v. *Continental Industrias del Caucho SA.*, 18 March 2004, C-342/01, ECR, 2004, 2605.
Pecastaing Josette v. *Belgian State*, 5 March 1980, C-98/79, ECR, 1980, 691.
Pedro Manuel Roca Álvarez v. *Sesa Start España ETT SA*, 30 September 2010, Case C-104/09, www.curia.eu.
Pensionsversicherungsanstalt v. *Christine Kleist*, 18 November 2010, C-356/09, www.curia.eu.
Pesca Valencia Limited v. *Minister for Fisheries and Forestry, Ireland and the Attorney General*, 19 January 1988, C-233/86, ECR, 1988, 83.
Peskeloglou Anstasia v. *Bundesanstalt für Arbeit*, 23 March 1983, C-77/82, ECR, 1983, 1085.
Petit C. v. *Office National des pensions (ONP)*, 22 July 1992, C-153/91, ECR, 1992, 4973.

List of Cases of the ECJ

Petrie David and others v. *Università degli studi di Verona and Camilla Bettoni*, 20 November 1997, C-90/96, ECR, 1997, 6527.
Pflücke Peter v. *Bundesanstalt für Arbeit*, 18 September 2003, C-125/01, ECR, 2003, 9375.
Laurent Piau v. *European Commission*, 26 January 2005, T-193/02, ECR, 2005, 209.
Podesta Jean-Marie v. *Caisse de retraite par répartition des ingénieurs cadres & assimilés (CRICA) and Others*, 25 May 2000, C-50/99, ECR, 2000, 39.
Pontin Virginie v. *T-Comalux SA*, 29 October 2009, C-63/08, www.curia.eu.
Portugaia Construções Lda, 24 January 2002, C-164/99, ECR, 2002, 787.
Preston e.a. and Fletcher and Others, 16 May 2000, C-78/98, ECR, 2000, 3201.
Harold Price v. *Conseil des ventes volontaires de meubles aux enchères publiques*, 7 September 2006, C-149/05, ECR, 2006, 7691.
Prodest Sarl v. *Caisse Primaire d'Assurance Maladie de Paris*, 12 July 1984, C-237/83, ECR, 1984, 3153.
Raccanelli Andrea v. *Max-Planck-Gesellschaft zur Förderung der Wissenschaften eV*, 17 July 2008, C-94/07, www.curia.eu.
Raulin V.J.M. v. *Netherlands Ministry of Education and Science*, 26 February 1992, C-357/89, ECR, 1992, 1027.
Razzouk C. and A. Beydoun v. *Commission of the European Communities*, 20 March 1984, C-75 and 117/82, ECR, 1984, 1509.
Reading Borough Council v. *Payless DIY Limited and others*, 16 December 1992, C-304/90, ECR, 1992, 6493.
Redmond Stichting v. *H. Bartol and others*, 19 May 1992, C-29/91, ECR, 1992, 4189.
Regina v. *Pierre Bouchereau*, 27 October 1977, C-30/77, ECR, 1977, 1999.
Regina v. *Secretary of State for Employment, ex parte Nicole Seymour-Smith and Laura Perez*, 9 February 1999, C-167/97, ECR, 1999, 623.
Regina v. *Secretary of State for Home Affairs ex parte Mario Santillo*, 22 May 1980, C-131/79, ECR, 1980, 1585.
Regina v. *Stanislaus Pieck*, 3 July 1980, C-157/79, ECR, 1980, 2171.
Regina v. *Vera Ann Saunders*, 28 March 1979, C-175/78, ECR, 1979, 1129.
Reina Francesco and Letizia Reina v. *Landeskreditbank Baden-Württemberg*, 14 January 1982, C-65/81, ECR, 1982, 33.
Reinhard Prigge and others v. Deutsche Lufthansa AG, 13 September 2011, C-447/09, www. curia. eu.
Sarah Margaret Richards v. *Secretary of State for Work and Pensions*, 27 April 2006, C-423/04, ECR, 2006, 3585.
Rinner-Kühn Ingrid v. *FWW Spezial-Gebäudereinigung GmbH & Co. KG*, 13 July 1989, C-171/88, ECR, 1989, 2743.
Roberts Joan v. *Tate & Lyle Industries Limited*, 26 February 1986, C-151/84, ECR, 1986, 703.
Carol Marilyn Robins and Others v. *Secretary of State for Work and Pensions*, 25 January 2007, C-278/05, ECR, 2007, 1053.
C.D. Robinson-Steele v. *R.D. Retail Services Ltd, and others*, 16 March 2006, C-131/04, ECR, 2006, 2531.

List of Cases of the ECJ

Rockfon A/S v. *Specialarbejderforbundet i Danmark*, 7 December 1995, C-449/93, ECR, 1995, 4291.
Rodríguez Caballero Ángel v. *Fondo de Garantía Salarial (Fogasa)*, 12 December 2002, C-442/00, ECR, 2002, 11915.
Roman Angonese v. *Cassa di Risparmio di Bolzano SpA*, 6 June 2000, C-281/98, ECR, 2000, 4139.
Rosa María Gavieiro Gavieiro v. *Consellería de Educación e Ordenación Universitaria de la Xunta de Galicia*, 22 December 2010 (C-444/09), www.curia.eu.
Rosanna Valenza v Autorità Garante della Concorrenza e del Mercato, 18 October 2012, C-302/11 to C-305/11, curia.eu.
Claude Rotsaert de Hertaing v. *J. Benoidt SA, in liquidation and others*, 14 November 1996, C-305/94, ECR, 1996, 5927.
Roux D. v. *Belgian State*, 5 February 1991, C-363/89, ECR, 1991, 273.
Royer Jean Noel, 8 April 1976, C-48/75, ECR, 1976, 497.
Rüffert Dirk v. *Land Niedersachsen*, 3 April 2008, C-346/06, ECR, 2008, 1989.
Rummler Gisela v. *Dato-Druck GmbH*, 1 July 1986, C-237/85, ECR, 1986, 2101.
Rush Portuguesa Lda v. *Office National d'Immigration*, 27 March 1990, C-113/89, ECR, 1990, 1417.
Rutili Roland v. *Minister for the Interior*, 22 October 1975, C-36/75, ECR, 1975, 1219.
Wilhelmus Rutten Petrus v. *Cross Medical Ltd.*, 9 January 1997, C-383/95, ECR, 1977, 57.
S. Michel v. *Fonds national de reclassement social des handicapés*, 11 April 1973, C-76/72, ECR, 1973, 457.
Sabbatini Luisa (née Bertoni) v. *European Parliament*, 7 June 1972, C-20/71, ECR, 1972, 345.
Sabine Hennings a;o. v. Alexander Mal, 8 September 2011, www. curia.eu.
Säger Manfred v. *Dennemeyer & Co. Ltd.*, 25 July 1991, C-76/90, ECR, 1991, 4221.
Sagulo Concetta, Gennaro Brenca and Addelmadjid Bakhouche, 14 July 1977, C-8/77, ECR, 1977, 1495.
Sanna Maria Parvainen v. *Finnair Oyj*, 1 July 2010, C-471/08, www.curia.
Sanicentral GmbH v. *René Collin*, 13 November 1979, C-25/79, ECR, 1979, 3423.
Carmen Sarkatzis Herrero v. *Instituto Madrileño de la Salud (Imsalud)*, 16 February 2006, C-294/04, ECR, 2006, 1513.
Schmid Hugo v. *Belgian State*, 27 May 1993, C-310/91, ECR, 1993, 3011.
Schmidt C. v. *Spar-und Leihkasse der früheren Amter Bordeesholm, Kiel und Cronshagen*, 14 April 1994, C-392/92, ECR, 1994, 1311.
Schnorbus Julia v. *Land Hessen*, 7 December 2000, C-79/99, ECR, 2000, 10997.
Scholz Ingetraut v. *Opera Universitaria di Cagliari and others*, 23 February 1994, C-419/92, ECR, 1994, 505.
Schöning Kalliope-Kougebetopoulo v. *Freie und Hansestad Hamburg*, 15 January 1998, C-15/96, ECR, 1998, 47.
Schultz-Hoff v. *Deutsche Rentenversicherung Bund Stringer* and *Others* v. *Her Majesty's Revenue and Customs*, 20 January 2009, Joined Cases C-350/06 and C-520/06, www.curia.eu.

List of Cases of the ECJ

Seda Kücükdeveci v. *Swedex GmbH & Co. KG*, 19 January 2010, C-555/07, www.curia.eu.

Sindicato de Médicos de Asistencia Pública (Simap) v. *Conselleria de Sanidad y Consumo de la Generalidad Valenciana*, 3 October 2000, C-303/98, ECR, 2000, 7963.

Sirdar A.M. v. *The Army Board and Secretary of State for Defence*, 26 October 1999, C-273/97, ECR, 1999, 7403.

Six Constructions Ltd. v. *Paul Humbert*, 15 February 1989, C-32/88, ECR, 1989, 341.

Sloman Neptun Schiffarts AG v. *Seebetriebsrat Bodo Ziesemer der Sloman Neptun Schiffarts AG*, 17 March 1993, Joined Cases Nos. C-72/91 and C-73/91, ECR, 1993, 887.

Smith Constance Christina Ellen and Others v. *Avdel Systems Ltd.*, 28 September 1994, C-408/92, ECR, 1994, 4435.

Somafer SA v. *Saar-Ferngas AG*, 22 November 1978, C-33/78, ECR, 1978, 2183.

Specialarbjderforbundet i Danmark v. *Dansk Industri, originally Industriens Arbejdsgivere, acting for Royal Copenhagen A/S*, 31 May 1995, C-400/93, ECR, 1995, 1275.

Spijkers J.M.A. v. *Gebroeders Benedik Abattoir CV and Alfred Benedik en Zonen BV*, 18 March 1986, C-24/85, ECR, 1986, 1119.

Spotti M.C. v. *Freistaat Bayern*, 20 October 1993, C-272/92, ECR, 1993, 5185.

Spruyt L.A. v. *Bestuur van de Sociale Verzekeringsbank*, 25 February 1986, C-284/84, ECR, 1986, 685.

Stadt Lengerich v. *Angelika Helmig*, 15 December 1994, C-399/92, C-409/92, C-425/92, C-34/93, C-50/93 and C-78/93, ECR, 1994, 5727.

State of the Netherlands v. *Ann Florence Reed*, 17 April 1986, C-59/85, ECR, 1986, 1283.

Steen V. v. *Deutsche Bundespost*, 20 January 1992, C-332/90, ECR, 1992, 341.

Steinicke Erika v. *Bundesanstalt für Arbeit*, 11 September 2003, C-77/02, ECR, 2003, 9027.

STX Norway Offshore AS and Others, 23 January 2012, E-2/11, www.eftacourt.int.

Suffritti M. and others v. *Instituto Natzionale della Previdenza Sociale (INPS)*, 3 December 1992, C-140/91, C-141/91, C-278/91 and C-279/91, ECR, 1992, 6337.

Susanne Bulicke v. *Deutsche Büro Service GmbH*, 8 July 2010, C-246/09, www.curia.eu.

Susanne Gassmayr v. *Bundesminister für Wissenschaft und Forschung*, 1 July 2010, C-194/08, www.curia.eu.

Ayse Süzen v. *Zehnacker Gebäudereinigung GmbH Krankenhausservice*, 11 March 1997, C-13/95, ECR, 1997, 1259.

Svenska staten v. *Anders Holmqvist*, 16 October 2008, C-310/07, not yet published.

Swedish Government, *Action in Response to the Laval Judgement, Summary*, Stockholm, 2008, 45 p.

Tele Danmark A/S and Handels-og Kontorfunktionærernes Forbund i Danmark (HK), acting on behalf of Marianne Brandt-Nielsen, 4 October 2001, C-109/00, ECR, 2001, 6993.

List of Cases of the ECJ

Temco Service Industries SA and Samir Imzilyen, Mimoune Belfarh, Abdesselam Afia-Aroussi, Khalil Lakhdar, intervener: General Maintenance Contractors SPRL (GMC), Buyle-Medros-Vaes Associates SA (BMV), formerly Weisspunkt SA, 4 January 2002, C-51/00, ECR, 2002, 21.

Ten Oever G.C. v. *Stichting Bedrijfspensioenfonds voor het Glazenwassers-en Schoonmaakbedrijf*, 6 October 1993, C-109/91, ECR, 1993, 4879.

The Incorporated Trustees of the National Council on Ageing (Age Concern England) v. *Secretary of State for Business, Enterprise and Regulatory Reform*, 5 March 2009, C-388/07, www.curia.eu.

The Queen v. *Immigration Appeal Tribunal, ex parte Gustaff Desiderius Antonissen*, 26 February 1991, C-292/89, ECR, 1991, 745.

The Queen v. *Ministry for Agriculture, Fisheries and Food, ex parte Agegate Limited*, 14 December 1989, C-3/87, ECR, 1989, 4459.

The Queen v. *Secretary of State for Social Security ex parte The Equal Opportunities Commission (EOC)*, 7 July 1992, C-9/91, ECR, 1992, 4297.

The Queen v. *Secretary of State for Trade and Industry, ex parte Broadcasting, Entertainment, Cinematographic and Theatre Union (BECTU)*, 26 June 2001, Case C-173/99, ECR, 2001, 4881.

The Queen (on the application of Dany Bidar) v. *London Borough of Ealing, Secretary of State for Education and Skills*, 15 March 2005, C-209/03, ECR, 2005, 2119.

Thomas Hogan and Others v Minister for Social and Family Affairs, Ireland and Attorney General, 25 April 2013, C-398/11, www. curia.eu

Torfean Borough Coucil v. *B & Q plc*, 23 November 1989, C-145/88, ECR, 1989, 3851.

Torsten Hörnfeldt v Posten Meddelande AB, 5 July 2012, C- 141/11, www. curia.eu.

Tribunal de Police de Metz v. *J.-C. Levy*, 2 Augustus 1993, C-158/91, ECR, 1993, I, 4287.

Tsiotras D. v. *Landeshauptstadt Stuttgart*, 26 May 1993, C-171/91, ECR, 1993, 2925.

Tyrolean Airways Tiroler Luftfahrt Gesellschaft mbH v Betriebsrat Bord der Tyrolean Airways Tiroler Luftfahrt Gesellschaft mbH., 7 June 2012, C-132/11, www. curia.eu.

UEAPME v. *Council*, 17 June 1998, T-135/96, ECR, 1998, 2235.

Una Coonan v. *Insurance Officer*, 24 April 1980, C-110/79, ECR, 1980, 1445.

Union Départementale des Syndicats CGT de l'Aisne v. *Sidef Conforma and others*, 28 February 1991, C-312/89, ECR, 1991, 997.

Union nationale des entraîneurs et Cadres techniques professionels du football (Unectef) v. *Georges Heylens and others*, 15 October 1987, C-222/86, ECR, 1987, 4097.

Union Royale Belge des Sociétés de Football Association ASBL and others v. *Jean Marc Bosman and others*, C-415/93, ECR, 1995, 4921.

Union syndicale Solidaires Isère v. *Premier ministre, Ministère du Travail, des Relations sociales, de la Famille, de la Solidarité et de la Ville*, 14 October 2010, C-428/09, www.curia.eu.

List of Cases of the ECJ

United Kingdom of Great Britain and Northern Ireland v. *Council of European Communities*, 30 May 1989, C-56/88, ECR, 1989, 1615.
United Kingdom v. *Commission of the European Communities*, 1 October 1987, C-84/85, ECR, 1987, 3765.
United Kingdom of Great Britain and Northern Ireland v. *Council of the European Union*, 12 November 1996, C-84/94, ECR, 1996, 5755.
Vahan Adjemian c. Com, Tribunal de la Fonction Publiqye de L'union Européenne, 4 June 2009, mission, F-8/08, www.curia.eu.
Van Cant R. v. *Rijksdienst voor Pensioenen*, 1 July 1993, C-154/92, ECR, 1993, 3811.
Van den Akker Maria Nelleke Gerda and others v. *Stichting Shell Pensioenfonds*, 28 September 1994, C-57/93, ECR, 1994, 4527.
Van den Broeck Chantal v. *Commission of European Communities*, 20 February 1975, C-37/74, ECR, 1975, 235.
Vander Elst R. v. *Office des Migrations Internationales*, C-43/93, ECR, 1994, 3803.
Van Duyn Yvonne v. *Home Office*, 4 December 1974, C-41/74, ECR, 1974, 1337.
Vasallo, 7 September 2006, C-180/04, ECR, 2006, 7471.
Vasil Ivanov Georgiev v. *Tehnicheski universitet – Sofia, filial Plovdiv*, 18 November 2010, C-250/09, www.curia.eu.
Vassiliki Stylianou Vandorou v. *Ipourgos Ethnikis Pedias kai Thriskevmaton*, 2 December 2010, C-422/09, www.curia.eu.
Vergani Paolo v. *Agenzia delle Entrate, Ufficio di Arona*, 21 July 2005, C-207/04, ECR, 2005, 7453.
Vicoplus SC PUH a.o., v. *Minister van Sociale Zaken en Werkgelegenheid*, 10 February 2011, Cases C-307/09 to C-309/09, www.curia.eu.
Visciano Raffaello v. *Istituto nazionale della previdenza sociale (INPS)*, 16 July 2009, C-69/08, www.curia.eu.
Vítor Manuel dos Santos Palhota a.o., 7 October 2010, C-515/08, www.curia.eu.
Von Colson Sabine and Elisabeth Kamann v. *Land Nordrhein-Westfalen*, 10 April 1984, C-14/83, ECR, 1984, 1891.
Voß Ursula v. *Land Berlin*, 6 December 2007, C-300/06, ECR, 2007, 10573.
Vroege Anna Adriaantje v. *NCIV Instituut voor Volkshuisvesting BV and Stichting Pensioenfonds NCIV*, 28 September 1994, C-57/93, ECR, 1994, 4541.
Wagner Miret T. v. *Fondo de garantia salarial*, 16 December 1993, C-334/92, ECR, 1993, 6911.
Walrave B.N.O. and L.J.N. Koch v. *Association Union Cycliste Internationale, Koninklijke Nederlandsche Wielren Unie and Federación Española Ciclismo*, 12 December 1974, C-36/74, ECR, 1974, 1405.
Watson A. Rask and K. Christensen v. *ISS Kantineservice A/S*, 12 November 1992, C-209/91, ECR, 1992, 5755.
Watson Lynne and Allessandro Belmann, 7 July 1976, C-118/75, ECR, 1976, 2057.
Hans Werhof v. *Freeway Traffic Systems GmbH & Co. KG*, 9 March 2006, C-499/04, ECR, 2006, 2397.
Wolff & Müller GmbH & Co. KG v. *José Filipe Pereira Félix*, 12 October 2004, C-60/03, ECR, 2004, 9553.
Wolfs L. v. *Office national des pensions (ONP)*, 22 October 1998, C-154/96, ECR, 1998, 6173.

List of Cases of the ECJ

Worringham Susan Jane and Margaret Humphreys v. *Lloyd's Bank Limited*, 11 March 1981, C-69/80, ECR, 1981, 767.
Wörsdorfer Marianne (née Koschniske) v. *Raad van Arbeid*, 12 July 1979, C-9/79, ECR, 1979, 2717.
Württembergische Milchverwertung-Südmilch-AG v. *Salvatore Ugliola*, 15 October 1969, C-15/69, ECR, 1969, 363.
Zaoui Saada v. *Caisse régionale d'assurance maladie de l'île de France*, 17 December 1987, C-147/87, ECR, 1987, 5511.
Zoi Chatzi v. *Ipourgos Ikonomikon*, 16 September 2010, Case C-149/10, www.curia.eu.

Index

The numbers given refer to paragraphs.

AB Inbev: 13
Access to employment: 1276–1279, 1572–1597, 1671–1673
Accident: 196, 341, 352, 476, 489, 630, 637, 1162, 1331, 1714, 1739, 1770, 1854, 1867, 1869, 1872, 1908, 1910, 1911, 2062
Acquis communautaire: 41, 98, 144, 356, 434, 590
Act of God: 352
Actions on gender equality: 1659–1665
Active employment policies: 508
Administrative law: 1979
Administrative licence: 916
Adoption leave: 1528, 1673
Adoption: 247, 257, 263, 436, 439, 471, 472, 502, 711, 747, 833, 1061, 1063, 1138, 1150, 1254, 1323, 1335, 1343, 1375, 1528, 1543, 1598, 1657, 1673, 1683, 1711, 1810, 1845, 1849, 1855, 1864, 1930, 2038, 2063, 2110, 2113, 2126, 2131, 2157, 2166, 2179, 2183, 2204, 2216, 2226, 2385
Advice: 48, 175, 180, 199, 256, 353, 405, 458, 633, 798, 863, 890, 1660, 1694, 2216, 2217, 2261, 2414
Age discrimination: 1433
AKZO: 1914
Alcohol and drug abuse: 1868
Amsterdam Treaty: 87, 88, 94, 99, 133, 136, 152, 238, 331, 374, 492, 507, 509, 517, 727, 1339, 1530, 2255
Annual bonus: 1545
Annual leave: 527, 528, 950, 1622, 1698, 1708, 1716, 1718, 1737–1752, 1768, 1778, 1779, 1799–1800, 1804
Annual vacation: 352, 1104
Applicable law: 844, 877, 1073, 1560, 1807, 2246, 2268, 2289, 2330, 2332, 2337, 2338

Apprentices: 36
Arbitration: 81, 363, 488, 750, 761, 774, 784, 1006, 1070, 1085, 1104, 1153, 1531, 2027, 2062, 2101, 2108, 2291, 2305, 2348
Armed forces: 488, 1333, 1334, 1357, 1582, 1584–1588, 1873
Artistic works: 1329, 1333, 2308, 2360
Attribution of powers, principle of: 146
Authors: 781
Autonomous agreements: 393–397
Autonomy: 107, 143, 202, 298, 309, 318, 393, 413, 419, 434, 636, 747, 758, 760, 773, 1255, 1284, 1464, 1642, 1678, 1883, 1929, 2013, 2014, 2024, 2025, 2068, 2076, 2104, 2109, 2146, 2267, 2281

Bankruptcy: 1070, 1085, 1978, 2024
Belgian s Liaison Office: 1113, 1147, 1148, 1150
Benchmarking: 317, 1663
Bernard Case: 762–771
Bibliography: 127
Blockades: 715, 1008, 1010, 1018
Blue Card: 840–849
Blue-collar worker: 791, 2241
Bolkestein: 1050
Bonus: 13, 14, 310, 682, 1545, 1547, 1710
Bosman case: 711–746
Breastfeeding: 1528, 1591–1594, 1622, 1626, 1627, 1685, 1688, 1693, 1707

Cadres: 2278
Canteen: 1279
Career breaks: 515
CAS: 763, 774–777
Cause: 759, 1209, 1331, 1719, 1882, 1904, 2412

1095

Index

Centre for the Development of Vocational Training (CEDEFOP): 189, 799
Certificate: 651, 652, 1130–1134, 1489, 1622, 1701, 1797
Charter of Fundamental Rights of the European Union binding effect: 525
  content: 521
  equal treatment: 1164
  level of protection: 523
  list of rights: 521
  preamble: 519
  prohibition of abuse of rights: 524
  scope: 522
Charter of Fundamental Rights: 102, 103, 105, 108, 116, 119, 125, 138, 226, 263, 335, 338, 518, 519, 520, 525–528, 753, 1016, 1343, 1397, 1715, 1846, 2063, 2185, 2410
Cheap workers: 1056
Child care: 640, 1279, 1321, 1322, 1508, 1662, 1709
Child labour: 81, 108, 205, 263, 269, 521, 1323, 1332, 1334, 2418
Christian trade unions (ACV–CSC): 302
Christmas bonus: 1547, 1710
Civil servants: 343, 1230, 1414, 1422, 1507, 1553, 1556, 1557, 2408
Code of conduct: 445, 750, 1150, 1154
Collective agreements
  binding effect: 2097–2100, 2107
  competence to conclude: 2091
  contracting parties: 2093
  European Company Agreement: 2083–2085
  European Industry Agreement: 2086
  European Multi-Industry Agreement: 2087–2089
  European Multi-Regional Agreement: 2090
  Germany: 959
  implementation: 2103 et seq.
  normative part: 2073–2074
  obligatory part: 2075
  parties to: 2082
Collective agreements, accession: 805
  beginning: 2096–2110
  binding effect: 2097–2100, 2107
  content: 2094, 2105
  duration: 2102
  duty of implementation: 2093
  end: 2091

European: 2082–2090
  extension: 2100
  interindustry-wide level: 2014
  normative part: 2073–204
  obligatory part: 2075
  parties: 2082–2090
  peace obligation: 2075
  scope of application: 2096
Collective bargaining abstention from an international framework: 1294
  competition, and: 2110
  meaning: 2070
  social dialogue: 2064
  subsidiarity rule: 2077
Collective dismissals: 360, 372, 1913, 1914, 1917, 1940, 2175, 2300, 2380
Collective labour law: 127, 130, 2061–2063
Collective redundancies: 1914 et seq.
Commerce: 1658, 1896
Commercial travellers: 352, 2315
Commission of the European Communities: 262
Committee of Experts (ILO): 191, 223–224
Committee of Experts on Posting of Workers: 223–225
Committee of the Regions: 150, 178, 197, 358, 379, 2353
Community Charter of Basic Social Rights
  collective bargaining: 485
  content: 484
  employment and remuneration: 485
  equal treatment: 481
  foundation: 480
  freedom of association: 485
  implementation: 490
  information and consultation: 489
  living and working conditions: 480
  objectives: 481
  scope: 482–483
  social protection: 485
  twelve commandments: 485–489
Comparable obligation: 986, 1218
Compensation: 726–771, 1675
Compensatory rest: 1333, 1334, 1769, 1788
Competence development: 457, 1660
Competitiveness: 497–500, 576
Conciliators (government): 242–244
Confidence Pact for Employment (1996): 127, 506

Index

Consent: 360, 657, 742, 781, 783,1002, 1419, 1509, 1531, 1568, 1624, 1628, 1688, 1720, 1922, 1976, 2005
Constitution for Europe: 104–105, 116
Constitution: 104–115, 121
Consultation: 353–355, 387–416, 434, 1264, 1877, 1932–1936, 2026–2027, 2111–2115, 2152, 2158, 2166–2354, 2361–2363
Consultation of management and labour at Community level: 384, 387, 415, 423, 2064
Consumer rights: 1056
Contract for an indefinite period: 1230, 1580, 1581, 2000
Contract of employment: 1300–1310
Contractual obligations: 683, 1064, 1088, 1089, 1094, 1099, 1100, 1556, 2079
Control: 127
Control measures: 1139–1146
Convention: 336
Coreper: 245
Corporate governance: 2, 310
Corporate social responsibility: 266, 536
Cost of living: 1111, 2074
Council of State: 1726
Council of the European Communities: 156–167
Country of origin: 908, 921, 927
  principle: 1053
Cour de Cassation: 726, 766
Court of Arbitration Sports: 777, *see also* CAS
Court of First Instance: 462
Court of Justice: 171–174, 902–906
Covenant of non-competition: 352
Creativity: 49, 631, 2376
Crisis: 6, 22, 23, 41, 45, 46, 271, 273, 287, 289, 311, 314, 570–571, 620
Cross-border mergers: 2396–2403
Currency: 136, 137, 140, 312, 330, 373, 1305

Daily hours: 1793
Data protection: 1290
Death: 865, 1085, 1347, 1348, 1524, 1920
Decent working conditions: 598
Declarations: 404
Decree: 229, 419, 653, 654, 656–659, 928–932, 1032, 1033
Demographic changes: 1658

Department of Employment and Labour: 931, 932
Direct democracy: 121
Directives: 229–231, 417–422, 1810
Disability: 101, 110, 1382, 1386
Discrimination: 339, 540, 895–898, 969, 1120, 1213–1215, 1472–1473, 1503–1517, 1529–1535, 1670, 1671
  direct: 899, 1496–1517
  generally: 1472
  harassment: 898
  indirect: 899, 1496–1517
  positive: 1529–1535
Dismissal: 360, 372, 465, 361, 521, 525, 604, 607, 609, 610, 615, 616, 619, 649, 667, 676, 679, 730, 848, 1304, 1357–1360, 1393, 1403, 1404, 1408, 1417, 1433–1438, 1462, 1474, 1502, 1513, 1514, 1528, 1565, 1580, 1581, 1598–1603, 1614, 1619–1623, 1637, 1640, 1671, 1673, 1681, 1685, 1686, 1688, 1690–1695, 1699, 1711, 1841, 1850, 1864, 1913, 1914, 1916, 1917, 1921, 1926, 1932, 1937, 1938–1942, 1946, 1958, 1973, 1997, 1998, 2010, 2016–2023, 2049–2051, 2175, 2176, 2300, 2313, 2314, 2366, 2380
Disproportionate administrative burden: 942
Dispute Resolution Chamber: 761, 774
Dissolution: 360, 1918, 2222
Divisions of public limited liability companies: 2028–2030
Doctors: 824, 1601, 1720, 1770
Draft directive on services: 1050–1061
DRC: 774–776
Dues: 54, 99, 1618, 1620, 1621, 1941, 2057, 2215
Dutch: 51, 89, 131, 132, 136, 201, 333, 362, 653, 654–657, 687, 804, 1575, 1747, 1748, 1914, 1951, 1994, 2122

Early retirement: 308, 538, 551, 562, 1350, 1352, 1354, 1417, 1559, 1561, 2010–2012
EC Treaty: 135, 249, 329, 406, 414, 434, 448, 480, 486, 491, 644, 1110, 1115, 1838, 1891, 2028
Economic aims: 329, 858, 976
Economic and Monetary Union (EMU): 59, 85, 88, 136, 137, 140, 330, 331, 376, 463, 2410

1097

Index

Economic and Social Committee (ESC): 127, 153, 175, 174, 175, 178, 236, 295, 358, 379, 383, 412, 433, 438, 490, 491, 530, 1170, 1335, 1781, 1839, 2126, 2189, 2191, 2351, 2356

Economic Free Trade Association (EFTA): 225, 274, 434, 2106, 2183, 2237, 2294

Education: 313, 556–557, 567–568

Elections: 124, 309, 700, 1297, 2296

Employee participation in profits and enterprise results: 2123

Employees' representative: 2159, 2309–2315, 2348, 2365–2366, 2399

Employer's agent: 931–932

Employers' associations: 2286, 2331

Employers' organisations: 276–298

Employment agencies: 1029, 1030, 1058, 1127–1129, 1313, 1315, 1317,

Employment Committee: 194

Employment policy: 375–377

Employment status: 1288

End-of-year bonus: 1545

Enhanced cooperation: 120

Enlargement: 57–59

Entrepreneurship, promotion of: 180

Equal opportunities: 515, 560, 1322, 1338, 1532, 1666–1682

Equal pay: 309, 310, 368, 378, 475, 575, 604, 1336, 1342, 1412, 1482–1498, 1502, 1504, 1507, 1515, 1536–1571, 1632, 1653, 1663, 1670

Equal treatment: 356, 647–703, 818, 823, 847, 848, 895, 897, 898, 906, 915, 951, 1009, 1019, 1104, 1111, 1113, 1164, 1195, 1220, 1195, 1265, 1268, 1269, 1273, 1298, 1322, 1336–1338, 1340–1341, 1345, 1346, 1349, 1358–1361, 1365, 1403, 1407, 1411, 1414, 1415, 1432, 1438, 1443, 1444, 1447, 1448, 1450, 1462, 1464–1466, 1470–1473, 1477–1480, 1482, 1484, 1485, 1489, 1490, 1495, 1498, 1499, 1503, 1508, 1514, 1515, 1518, 1520, 1523, 1524, 1530–1532, 1544, 1557, 1558, 1561, 1562, 1564, 1566, 1572, 1575, 1576, 1580, 1582, 1583, 1586–1588, 1593, 1598, 1600, 1603, 1604, 1617, 1620, 1621, 1623, 1626, 1637–1642, 1645, 1646, 1649, 1651, 1653, 1666, 1667, 1671, 1674, 1676–1681, 1695, 1699, 1836–1838, 1845, 1847, 2418

Equality of outcome: 1502

Equivalent position: 941, 1661

Ethnic origin: 110, 339, 1273, 1336, 1338, 1340, 1451, 1452, 1470–1481

European Agency for Safety and Health at Work: 195–196

European Association of Craft, Small and Medium-sized Enterprises (UEAPME): 447–448, 454, 1068, 1880

European Atomic Energy Community (Euratom): 135

European Centre for the Development of Vocational Training: 189, 799

European Coal and Steel Community (ECSC): 135

European Company Statute: 637, 2130–2131, 2376, 2378

European Convention for the Protection of Human Rights and Fundamental freedoms: 137, 226, 335, 336, 519, 523, 528, 717, 1488

European Convention on Human Rights: 336

European Council in Essen (1994): 504

European Economic Area (EEA): 274, 277, 442, 451, 731, 736, 746, 1284, 2186, 2236, 2237, 2291, 2294

European Economic Community (EEC): 135, 139

European Employment Guidelines: 511

European Foundation for the Improvement of Living and Working Conditions: 190, 453

European Globalisation Adjustment Fund: 207–211

European Institute for Gender Equality: 212–215, 1677

European Jobs Summit 1997: 511–516

European Parliament: 123, 145, 147, 150, 151–155, 206, 219, 222, 242–244, 295, 309, 338, 390, 393, 433, 437, 438, 446, 518, 525, 528, 835, 949, 968, 1057, 1061–1064, 1068, 1098, 1100, 1126, 1335, 1469, 1512, 1772

European Social Charter: 94, 101, 334, 481, 1191, 1715

European social dialogue: 288, 296, 298, 301, 310, 390, 394, 448, 449, 2195, 2286, 2331, 2414

European Social Fund: 55, 127, 164, 174, 176–178, 197, 318, 377, 382, 388, 472, 502, 549, 560

Index

European social model: 2406 *et seq.*
European Trade Union Confederation (ETUC): 193, 305, 411, 447, 448, 454, 1055, 1068, 1880, 2193, 2286, 2331
European Union: 25–37, 38–50, 73, 139–147, 216–222, 519–529
European Union Agency for Fundamental Rights: 216–219
European Works Council: 2166–2354
Expatriation allowance: 1512, 1556
Expert: 223–225, 2331, 2345
Experts on posting of workers: 223–225

Failure: 492, 1151–1153
Family life: 313, 315, 438, 515, 521, 551, 595, 648, 1171, 1593
Federalism: 136
Federation of Belgian Enterprises (VBO–FEB): 284
Female employees: 1556, 1561, 1562, 1607, 1608, 1611, 1633, 1837
FIFPro: 411, 749, 759, 760, 761, 777
Fixed-term contracts: 1162–1170
Fixed-term work: 398, 440, 1111, 1220, 1221, 1225–1236, 1245, 1251, 1263, 1264, 1266, 1446, 1848
Flexibility: 41, 287, 465–466, 600–619
Flexicurity: 289, 315, 559, 565, 589, 600–619
Football trainers: 715, 826
Force majeure: 1854
Forced labour: 68, 263, 521, 755
Ford Motor Cie: 10, 635
Foreign workers: 911, 997
Frameworks of action: 399
Free collective bargaining: 2076
Free enterprise: 465
Free movement of labour: 653, 700
Free movement of workers: 641–888
Freedom of association: 11–14, 61, 62, 1638
Freedom of association: 1638
Freedom of labour: 753, 1277
Freedom of services: 888–1068
Frontier workers: 593, 2062
Full employment: 179, 310, 533, 549, 1406
Functioning of the EU: 139, 772
Fundamental social rights: 1–30, 93–103, 337, 338
Future social policy: 428

Generation Pact: 407
Genuine benefit: 959, 961, 978, 1123
Global Jobs Pact: 21–22, 270
Global plan: 5–7, 8
Globalization: 5, 16–50, 208–211, 2252
Good governance: 544, 549, 560
Good practices: 195, 206, 219, 223, 398, 401, 405, 508, 1464, 1642, 1664, 1678, 1908
Group insurance: 683
Guaranteed daily wage: 2044–2055
Guaranteed monthly wage: 13, 81, 90, 2044–2055
Guaranteed weekly wage: 2044–2055

Handicapped workers: 92, 352, 1726
Harassment: 310, 397, 448–450, 453, 1349–1359, 1361, 1472, 1499–1500, 1573, 1613, 1668–1669, 1881, 1891–1895, 1897–1899, 2068
Health and safety: 351–352, 1162–1170, 1293, 1856, 1858–1870, 1871, 1876, 1881, 1884, 1898, 1901, 1904, 1905, 1910, 2063, 2203, 2418
Health and social security services: 1056
Health care sector: 1900
Hierarchy: 330–333
Highly qualified employment: 840–847
Hiring: 512, 628, 1103
Holidays: 528, 1112, 1159
Hospital: 1900–1912
Hospitality sector: 200
Housing: 701
Human dignity: 106, 501
Human resources management (HRM): 71, 2377
Human rights: 336

Immigration: 137, 287, 871
Imperative character: 672, 902, 1111
In vitro fertilisation: 1699
Incapacity, definitive: 352
Inclusive labour market: 454, 456
Individual account: 930–934
Individual disputes: 695, 770, 1267
Individual labour contracts: 352
Individual labour law: 640
Individual record: 928–929, 934–935
Industrial conflict: 1158
Industrial internationals: 64–68
Industrial peace: 137, 140, 330, 2075

Index

Industrial unions: 61, 62, 301, 302
Inflation: 463–464
Informing and consulting, general framework: 2335–2383
Injuries: 1900–1902, 1905, 1907, 1909, 1912
Inland waterways: 1668
Innovation: 325, 613, 1341
Insolvency of employer: 2040, 2053
Insolvency: 2031–2060
Interindustry-wide agreement: 1299
International Labour Organization: 23, 247–271
International private labour law: 1069–1160
Internationalization: 2204
Internet: 63, 1147
Inventions: 12
Isolation: 1935, 1982
ITUC: 64, 301, 302

Jail: 14
Job classification: 1540
Job creation: 47, 534, 535, 545, 555
Job security: 70, 72, 360
Jobs-Pact
Joint committee: 199–205, 1968
Joint opinions: 402
Jurisdictional disputes: 1695
Just cause: 750
Justified leave of absence: 742, 1141

Knowledge society: 51

Labour costs: 39, 308, 315, 368, 465, 466
Labour Courts: 1473, 2314
Labour law, hierarchy: 330–333
Labour market participation: 538, 539, 574, 575
Labour standards: 24, 48, 255, 257, 263, 266
Labour Tribunal: 1070, 1085, 1184
Language: 2095, 2289, 2290, 2337, 2338
Leave of absence: 742, 1141
Legal capacity: 1070, 1085, 2279
Legislation: 927–933, 2079–2081
Legislative competence: 348–374
Length of service: 1207, 1232, 1233, 1236, 1411, 1413, 1435, 1437, 1511, 1552, 1570, 1631, 1633–1636, 1705, 1848, 1999–2003
Level of protection: 523, 961, 1780
Liability: 882, 2404, 2405

Liberal trade unions: 302
Lifelong learning: 39, 51, 180, 211, 313, 314, 508, 537, 545, 551, 554–557, 562, 565–568, 600, 605, 607, 609–610, 612, 616, 619
LIMOSA notification: 1044
Lisbon European Council 2000: 1052, 1057
Lisbon strategy: 51
Living and working conditions: 190
Local employment agencies (LEAs): 179
Lock-outs: 111, 348, 366, 370
Lock-outs, right to impose: 370

Maastricht Agreement: 480–496
Maintenance of membership: 59, 224, 225
Managerial employees: 2295
Managerial prerogative: 3, 142, 353, 2261
Maritime Labour Standards: 200
Market economy: 2, 5, 59, 91, 137, 140, 316, 330, 375, 466, 467, 632, 2373
Marriage: 136, 170, 1085, 1347, 1485
Married women: 1562
Maternity: 1672
Maternity leave: 1358, 1524, 1527, 1546, 1581, 1590, 1593, 1598, 1606, 1620–1624, 1669, 1672, 1685, 1698, 1701–1711, 1749, 1864
Matuzalem Case: 777
Meal voucher: 1986
Medical examination: 1797
Medical staff: 1720
Medical surveillance of workers: 1167
Merger Treaty: 156
Mergers and divisions of public limited liability companies: 2028–2030
Mergers of public limited companies: 2028–2030
Migrant workers: 113, 114, 806–808
Military service: 352, 679, 683, 1588
Minimum service: 751, 1156
Minimum wage: 373, 465, 467, 877, 908, 922, 937, 939, 940, 942–944, 967, 974, 976, 978, 979, 995, 1012, 1015, 1016, 1022–1024, 1027, 1028, 1056, 1104, 1116, 1122, 1126, 1544, 1668, 2413
Minors: 748
Mobile workers: 1777, 1801, 1811–1821
Mobility: 211, 840–870
Modernization of labour law: 588–599
Most representative organization: 251
Motherhood, protection of: 1683–1711

Index

Multinational Enterprises: 9–17
Mutu case: 775

National Labour Council: 229, 1615
Negotiation: 2144, 2147, 2199
New technologies: 49, 61, 310, 514, 554, 565
Nice Treaty: 81
Night work: 1333, 1760–1765
Night workers: 1760–1765
  guarantees: 1762
  health assessment: 1761
  health and safety: 1764
  notification of regular use: 1763
  transfer to day work: 1761
Non-accelerating inflation role of employment (NAIRU): 467
Non-profit sector: 296, 306, 1979
Notice: 74, 360, 649, 1075

Object: 1536–1643
Occupational disease: 1162, 1869
Occupational medicine: 306
Occupations: 547, 825, 1466, 1578
Offshore work: 1777
Old-age benefits: 2009, 2012, 2058
Older workers: 47, 51, 579, 1399, 1658
On-line communication: 1046
Organisation for Economic Co-operation and Development (OECD): 22, 82, 2383
Outplacement: 74, 180
Overtime: 1304

Paid educational leave: 1800
Paid leave: 528, 945, 961
Paid public holidays: 1788
Parental leave: 438, 1523–1528, 1839–1855
Part-time work: 439, 1171–1219, 1216–1218, 1504, 1513, 1515, 1568, 2067
Paternity leave: 1673
Peace obligation: 631, 2075
Penal sanctions: 1299, 1313, 2100
Pension funds: 604, 2410
Pensions: 1637
Personal services: 204
Personalized service: 17, 210, 211
Personnel costs: 890
Personnel management: 1422, 1437
Personnel register: 930
Placement of employees: 1311–1320

Pluralistic society: 142, 636
Police: 795, 1218, 1521
Policy orientations: 401
Political leave: 638, 1868, 2413
Political system: 61, 923, 2418
Population: 60
Posting declaration: 1043
Posting of Workers Directive: 1100–1160
Posting of workers: 946, 1100–1160
Poverty: 18–20, 22, 315, 331, 574
Practical effectiveness: 896, 952
Pregnancy: 1523–1527, 1575, 1620–1627, 1685–1705
Privacy: 1291
Private security sector: 1890, 1896
Private security: 205, 206, 792, 996
Procedural texts: 406
Process-oriented texts: 398
Productivity: 17, 179, 308, 549, 566
Project supervisor: 1296
Proof: 1644–1656
Property: 369, 1085, 1497, 1983
Proportionality, principle of: 146
Prospects: 30, 289, 292, 513, 1883
Protection of domestic businesses: 976
Provinces: 651
Public employment offices: 1311
Public interest: 902, 903, 938, 939, 953, 972–976, 984, 993, 1002, 1016–1018, 1097, 1098, 1110, 1121, 1122, 1401, 1405, 1410, 1835
Public limited liability companies: 1948–1950
Public order: 753, 934, 1109
Purely administrative nature: 985

Qualification passport: 824
Qualifications: 824–839
Qualified majority voting: 118, 350–357
  equal treatment: 356
  health and safety: 351
  information and consultation: 353
  integration of excluded persons: 357
  procedure: 350
  working conditions: 352

Racism: 220, 1473
Railway: 205, 396, 398, 411, 679, 792, 905, 1629
Railway sector: 1822–1834
Recovery plan: 52–54
Recruitment: 1311–1320

Index

Re-engineering: 16
Referenda: 121
Reform Treaty: 122–126, 772–773
Regulations: 228
Reimbursement: 963
Reinstatement: 676, 1565, 1690
Religious communities: 785, 1769
Remuneration: 892
Renault: 2355
Result oriented bonus: 13, 1547
Retirement: 290, 1200–1210
Right of dismissal: 1620, 1699
Right to be heard: 123, 636, 1486
Right to work: 644, 2061
Risk assessment: 1906
Rolled-up holiday pay: 1743–1746
Rule of reason: 899, 902
Rules of work: 663, 664

Sabena: 1547
Scientific research: 12, 219
SE (European company): 2402
Seafarers: 1518–1533
Sectoral dialogue committees: 199–205
Self-employment: 512
Seniority: 661, 666, 1567, 2296
Settlement of disputes: 95, 407, 1267, 2348
Sex discrimination: 1507, 1517, 1539, 1545, 1627
Sexual harassment: 1499, 1500, 1613, 1668, 1893
Sexual orientation: 1485–1498
Shareholders' value: 2410
Shift work: 1760–1765
Shortage of labour: 1022
Short-stay visas: 920
Sick leave: 1698
Sick-leave scheme: 1526–1528
Sickness: 815, 1377
Single European Act 1986: 1859–1864
Single Permit: 850–887
Small and Medium-sized Enterprises (SMEs): 281, 296, 1054
Smoking: 1868
Soccer players: 715, 716, 717
Soccer trainers: 715, 826
Social Action Programme 1998–2000: 480–496
Social Council: 156
Social dialogue structures: 2064–2068
Social dumping: 463–467

Social elections: 124, 309, 700, 1297, 2296
Social inspection: 875, 885
Social Legislation Inspectorate: 180, 615, 656, 1037
Social partners: 276–328
Social programming: 168, 182
Social Protection Committee: 206
Social Protection: 18–20, 77–92
Social report: 1469
Social rights: 93–103
Social secretariat: 932
Social security: 341, 1579, 1603, 1617, 1673, 1850, 2009–2015, 2057
Social services: 104, 553, 564
Socialist trade unions (ABVV–FGTB): 302
Societas Europaea (SE): 2120–2132
Solidarity: 66, 777, 1026, 2185
Specificity of sports: 772–777
Sportsman: 725, 731
Sportsmen and sportswomen: 758
Staff register: 926–930
Standing Committee on Employment: 192–193
Start-jobs: 39, 513, 534
State Employment Agency: 1313, 1755
Statute of limitations: 109, 522, 668
Strategy 2020: 56, 570
Stress at work: 130, 447, 1880, 1881, 1884, 1887
Strike: 374
   definition: 1023
   economic: 867
   essential services: 545, 762, 876
   law: 2094
   occupation: 370
   peace obligation: 2061
   political: 310, 314
   regular: 62, 310, 631
   sit-in: 1003
   sorts: 2094
   sporadic: 892
   unofficial: 374
   wild-cat: 631
Structural change: 207, 208, 496
Sub-contracting: 879
Subordination: 96–97, 674, 706, 710, 788
Subsidiarity: 141–146, 2077
Sugar: 205, 411, 926
Sunday rest: 1712, 1835
Supercapitalism: 8–10

Index

Surveillance: 1167, 1218, 1856, 1981
Sustainable development: 47, 137, 140, 178, 179, 265

Take over bids: 2396–2399
Taxation: 39, 310, 512, 941, 1571
Technical disturbance: 427
Technical reasons: 1776–1778, 1819
Technical unity: 1292
Telework: 441–446, 1283–1299
Teleworker: 1283–1297
Temporary work: 1162–1299
Termination of the labour contract: 210, 1920, 1923, 1939
Theatre: 466, 527, 1223, 1347
Third-country nationals: 842
Time credit: 1848
Tools: 402
Trade union committee: 304, 411, 1896, 2273, 2314
Trade union freedom: 700
Trade unions: 301–310, 2286
 administration: 61
 benefits: 62
 democracy: 64
 freedom: 61, 62
 legal status: 67
 migrant workers: 63
 most representative: 68
 state: 1017
 structure: 74, 301
 unified: 66, 74, 302
 white-collar: 791, 2241
Training clause: 115
Training compensation: 755, 762–771
Trans border: 894
Transfer of a business: 1935, 1988, 1989
Transfer of an undertaking: 1949, 1951–1959
Transfer of the employment relationship: 360, 592
Transnational: 2357, 2358
Transnational Company Agreements: 67, 68
Transport: 1811–1821
Treaty of Amsterdam: 507–517
Trial clause: 352
Tribunals: 830, 1153

Undeclared work: 542
Unemployment benefits: 613, 617, 1157
Unemployment: 11, 22, 29, 42, 56, 287–293, 504–506
Unfair competition: 957
Union security: 17, 111, 125, 1589
Unofficial strikes: 374, 631, 637, 1003

Victimization: 1462, 1479, 1675
Violence: 448, 1891–1899
Violence at work: 448, 1891, 1897, 2068
Vocational training: 115–134, 189, 379, 405, 799–823, 1572, 1651
Volkswagen: 1968–1969, 1973, 1975
Vredeling proposal: 2111, 2115

Wage costs: 10, 90, 466
Wage level: 566
Wage restraint: 47, 79, 308, 315
Waiting day: 1941, 1942
Wal Mart Stores: 9
Weather: 928
Weekly hours: 1179, 1773
Welfare at work: 941
White-collar worker: 791, 2241
White Paper on European Social Policy (1994): 501–503
White Paper on Growth, Competitiveness and Employment (1993): 497–500
Widowers' pension: 1347, 1486
Wildcat strikes: 631
Women: 1482–1498, 1504–1515
Work accident: 1867, 1869
Work card: 842, 849
Work land: 927–935
Work organization: 66, 2327
Work permits: 907–909, 912, 913, 921
Work rules: 659, 930, 934, 2107
Workers: 593–601, 848–873, 946, 1100–1160
Workers, posted: 949, 962
Workers' participation: 2111–2405
Working abroad: 1305, 1317
Working conditions: 190, 191, 305, 352, 1133, 1598, 1607–1609, 1671–1673, 1822
Working time: 1322, 1712–1821
Works council: 2166–2354

Xenophobia: 220, 310

Young People: 35, 1321–1335
Young workers: 625, 1323

Index

CPSIA information can be obtained
at www.ICGtesting.com
Printed in the USA
LVOW13s0423230518
578094LV00014B/68/P